KT-199-516

INTRODUCTION TO Operations Research Techniques

Second Edition

Hans G. Daellenbach • John A. George • Donald C. McNickle

University of Canterbury, Christchurch, New Zealand

ALLYN AND BACON, INC.

Boston London Sydney Toronto

Copyright © 1983, 1978 by Allyn and Bacon, Inc.,
7 Wells Avenue, Newton, Massachusetts 02159.
All rights reserved.

No part of the material protected by this copyright notice may be reproduced or utilized in any form or by any means, electronic or mechanical, including photocopying, recording, or by any information storage and retrieval system, without written permission from the copyright owner.

Library of Congress Cataloging in Publication Data

Daellenbach, Hans G.
Introduction to operations research techniques.

Includes bibliographical references and index.
1. Operations research. I. George, John A.
II. McNickle, D. C. III. Title.
T57.6.D3 1983 658.4'034 82-16303
ISBN 0-205-07718-8
0-205-07974-1 (International)

Printed in the United States of America.

10 9 8 7 6 5 4 3 2 1 88 87 86 85 84 83

84 010447

CONTENTS

5 SENSITIVITY AND POSTOPTIMAL ANALYSIS OF LINEAR PROGRAMMING 128

6 TRANSPORTATION AND ASSIGNMENT PROBLEMS 152

7 NETWORK FLOW PROBLEMS 186

8 PROJECT PLANNING AND SCHEDULING TECHNIQUES 201

9 DETERMINISTIC DYNAMIC PROGRAMMING 232

Part Two STOCHASTIC MODELS

10 ELEMENTS OF PROBABILITY AND STOCHASTIC PROCESSES 272

13 MARKOV CHAINS 365

14 STOCHASTIC DYNAMIC PROGRAMMING AND MARKOVIAN DECISION PROCESSES 391

15 INTRODUCTION TO WAITING LINES 426

18 INTEGER PROGRAMMING 519

19 CLASSICAL OPTIMIZATION METHODS WITH APPLICATIONS TO INVENTORY CONTROL 549

20 UNCONSTRAINED NONLINEAR PROGRAMMING METHODS 571

21 CONSTRAINED NONLINEAR PROGRAMMING 590

22 MULTIPLE-OBJECTIVE DECISION MAKING 615

23 HEURISTIC PROBLEM SOLVING 647

PREFACE

This text is a survey of the most important quantitative tools and techniques used by operations researchers in addition to the indispensible bag of statistical tools of data analysis. We make no pretense of providing a complete treatment of any of them. However, our objectives go beyond giving simply a broad appreciation. We hope that intensive study of this text will give the reader a sufficiently solid working knowledge of what we consider the core tools (those covered in Parts One and Two) to use them with some degree of confidence. We also see our text as a springboard to the study of more advanced specialized texts, either practical or theoretical. For each model or technique four questions were foremost in our minds: What are its assumptions? How is a real-life problem translated to fit into it? What are the basic ideas underlying its solution method? What are its strengths and weaknesses?

The text is divided into three parts, preceded by what may well be the most important chapter of the text—a fairly detailed and practical review of the basics of the operations research methodology. Part One studies deterministic models and techniques, mainly linear programming, some of its variations, and various types of networks, including dynamic programming. Part Two covers predominantly stochastic models and techniques. Part Three is devoted to some of the more advanced extensions of tools covered in Parts One and Two (particularly mathematical programming), as well as a brief incursion into some of the newer areas of operations research—multiple-objective decision making and heuristic methods.

We have attempted to keep the mathematical prerequisites to a minimum. Parts One and Two require no calculus, but assume that the reader has been exposed to the material taught in elementary college algebra and introductory probability and statistics courses, courses commonly required of students in business administration, economics, engineering, and computer science. Chapters 3–7, 13, 14, 17, 18, 20, 21, and 22 use some linear algebra—the ideas underlying manipulation of systems of linear equations. The only matrix algebra—some matrix and vector multiplication in Chapter 13 (Markov Chains) and Chapter 17 (Extensions to Linear Programming) is covered in Appendix A on linear algebra. Chapters 19–21 and 23 use elementary concepts of differential calculus, such as first- and second-order derivatives, partial derivatives, and gradients. Part Two is introduced by a brief review of probability and stochastic processes. Starred sections either require a higher level of mathematical maturity or make cross reference to chapters that are normally not considered a prerequisite for the material covered in that chapter. The starred sections cover optional material and can be skipped without loss of continuity. Part Three, except for Chapters 22 and 23, is at a more advanced level than the first two parts by virtue of the very nature of the subject treated.

The text is suited for introductory and intermediate courses in operations research at a junior, senior, or first-year-graduate level in almost any field, but especially business, economics, computer science, engineering, and forestry, as well as mathematics, where its stress on practical modeling will be particularly useful.

Whenever possible, the various chapters or sets of chapters have been made self-contained in the sense that they do not rely on any material covered earlier (except for some starred sections). Naturally, the basic philosophy and methodology of operations research expounded in Chapter 1 forms the framework within which all modeling is done. The precedence relations among chapters are shown in the table following.

Chapter precedence and prerequisites

Chapter	Precedence and prerequisites												
	2	3	4	9	10	11	12	13	19	20	A*	M*	C*
2 Linear programming											x		
3 The simplex method	x										x		
4 Duality	x	x									x		
5 Sensitivity analysis	x	x	x								x		
6 Transportation and assignment problems	x	x	x								x		
7 Networks	x										x		
8 Project planning													
9 Deterministic dynamic programming											x		
10 Probability													
11 Bayesian decision analysis					x								
12 Inventory control					x								
13 Markov chains					x						x	x	
14 Stochastic dynamic programming				x	x			x					
15 Waiting lines					x						x		
16 Simulation					x								
17 Extensions to linear programming	x	x									x	x	
18 Integer programming	x	x									x		
19 Classical optimization							x						x
20 Unconstrained nonlinear programming									x		x	x	x
21 Constrained nonlinear programming									x	x	x	x	x
22 Multi-objective decision making	x	x			x	x							
23 Heuristic problem solving													x

*A = basic linear algebra; M = vectors, matrices, matrix inverse; C = differential calculus.

The instructor has considerable scope in choosing the collection and sequence of topics. Following are some suggested sequences:

- Deterministic models: Part I
- Stochastic models: Part II
- Introduction to linear programming and networks: Chapters 2–7
- Introduction to mathematical programming: Chapters 3–5, 17, 18, 21, 22
- Introduction to operations research: Chapters 1–3, 7–9, 11–13, 15, 16, 22, 23

The text contains more material than can be covered adequately in a sequence of courses covering a full academic year, except at a graduate level.

ACKNOWLEDGMENTS

Thanks to all the undergraduate and graduate students and instructors who used the first edition, as well as the reviewers who have contributed to this new edition by suggesting improvements in coverage and presentation of the material. Chapter 23 on Heuristic Problem Solving has been adapted from Chapter 16 of the first edition, written by John Rodgers.

INTRODUCTION TO

Operations Research Techniques

CHAPTER ONE

Methodology of Operations Research

What is operations research? The name, which reflects its first applications, is of little help in explaining what the field is all about. There is not even total agreement on the name. The British use *operational research*, while large sections in the business community refer to it as *management science*. A product of World War II, operations research was first used for the analysis of and research into the conduct of military operations. The term "research" itself is somewhat misleading. It is not scientific research, with its connotation of advancing fundamental knowledge in some science. In fact, there is no generally accepted definition for operations research. The view taken in this text is that it is a scientific approach to the analysis of many kinds of complex decision-making problems—economic, engineering, or environmental—as encountered by individuals and organizations of all types, be they profit making or nonprofit, private or governmental. Often the problem studied involves the design and/or the operation of systems or parts of systems. The aim is the evaluation of probable consequences of decision choices, usually under conditions requiring the allocation of scarce resources—funds, manpower, time, or raw materials. The objective is to improve the effectiveness of the system as a whole, with emphasis on the last three words. We shall return to this point.

The concept of a system—an interrelated set of parts making up a coherent whole that is more than just the sum of its parts—is central to operations research. The system concept applies to most organized human activities: the business activities of an individual; the running of a company, a hospital, or a law enforcement agency; or the operation of man–machine systems, such as all or part of a manufacturing plant, a network of power stations, or a port. Implicit in this view of operations research is the notion that systems may be operated in many different ways and that the "best" way may not be obvious or necessarily unique. The process of finding a best way is called *optimization*. Thus most operations research projects involve the optimization of some operation of a system, such as minimizing production costs, maximizing profits, maximizing the capacity of a flow (of goods or information) through a network, or minimizing the cost of achieving certain technical properties for some engineering entity or operation. In contrast to mathematics, physical sciences, or economics, operations research is thus a prescriptive discipline.

In this chapter we will explore how operations research projects are dealt with. We will demonstrate some of the philosophy underlying operations research. As you read through these pages, you will become increasingly aware of the fact that the complexities of reality call for great flexibility in how operations research projects are tackled. There exists no one correct approach. The "best" approaches to be followed depend not only on the nature of the problem and the amount of time and funds available, but also on the training and personality of the operations researcher. Therefore, all we can do is to highlight the most important aspects of the methodology, give some illustrations, and point out the various pitfalls that will invariably crop up along the crooked way to the successful completion of a project.

While writing this chapter we found that it is not really possible to discuss the methodology of operations research without assuming at least some familiarity with operations research techniques. Thus, should we expose you to the most basic operations research techniques first? On the other hand, it does not make much sense to study individual techniques without a framework of methodology and the philosophy of operations research. Discussing techniques in a "vacuum" tends to convey a completely wrong picture of the true nature of operations research. We chose to consider methodology first, accepting the risk that some concepts will remain fuzzy on first reading. In fact, Chapter 1 should be studied again when you have become familiar with some of the techniques in the following chapters.

1-1 THE PHASES OF AN OPERATIONS RESEARCH PROJECT

Any operations research project that has a happy ending goes through five major steps or phases:

1. formulating the problem;
2. constructing a mathematical model to represent the operation studied;
3. deriving a solution to the model;
4. testing the model and evaluating the solution;
5. implementing and maintaining the solution.

No single phase can be labeled as the most crucial element in the success or failure of an operations research project. But what distinguishes operations research from related disciplines is the formal construction of mathematical models, consisting of functions, equations and inequalities, and the techniques available to find optimal solutions to such models. Furthermore, while it is possible to give some general guidelines and advice on how to tackle the other three phases, actual practice is the only truly effective teacher. This is the main reason why the remaining chapters of this text are devoted almost exclusively to phases two and three.

Although the phases are normally initiated in sequential order, they do not necessarily terminate in the same order. In fact, each phase usually continues until the project is successfully implemented. All phases overlap subsequent as well as preceding phases. For example, the successful formulation of the problem depends on having at least tentatively considered each of the other four phases. Why? Interrelationships between various aspects of the operation may suggest a form of model, which in turn may dictate what data are needed for problem formulation, testing, and implementation. The complexity of the solution to a model may call for additional simplifications to be introduced into the model. The form of the solution used must be suitable for implementation. Testing the model and consideration of the implementation may reveal obstacles that lead to a reformulation of the original problem. So, even if we must discuss each phase separately, it should be borne in mind that they overlap.

As pointed out earlier, the objective of an operations research project is to improve the effectiveness of the system as a whole. This improvement can, however, only be secured if the solution to the problem is fully implemented. Securing the implementation of the solution is thus the prime concern underlying the first four phases. All measures that enhance the chances of implementation have to be initiated and planned for from the very outset of the project.

During all phases, it is crucial to record for future reference all assumptions made (e.g., the basis for all simplifications introduced into the model) and all data used, including their sources. This point cannot be stressed enough. As a project progresses through its various phases, it invariably will undergo minor and major revisions and corrections. Assumptions, simplifications, and shortcuts introduced earlier are easily forgotten unless they have been documented. It is also a prerequisite to establish effective maintenance procedures for the solution.

Most operations research projects are the fruit of a team effort where team members complement each other with specialized knowledge. The composition of the team may change as the project progresses. However, the team should include at least one person intimately involved with the operation being studied, to provide the necessary physical and technical know-how about the operation. This person will serve not only as the liaison between the operations research team and the sponsor of the project, but also as a sounding board for the other members of the team. His or her participation throughout the project will improve the chances of successful implementation.

Although there are numerous possibilities for using operations research techniques for small projects that can be completed within a few days, many projects may require a few months or even several years to reach a successful conclusion. The total manpower invested may easily be a multiple of the total elapsed time. The sponsor of a project should be made aware from the outset of these realities. He or she should be warned that unforeseen factors (such as incomplete or incorrect data, or unexpectedly complex relationships) can result in deadlines being overshot.

1-2 FORMULATION OF THE PROBLEM

The formulation of the problem is a sequential process—the initial and often tentative formulation goes through a series of progressive reformulations and refinements as the project proceeds and as deeper insight into the problem is obtained. It is in this phase that the ultimate success or failure of a project usually has its roots!

What is a problem? For a problem to exist:

1. There must be an individual or a group of individuals—referred to as the *decision maker(s)*—who has a felt-needs to be satisfied or objectives and goals to be achieved.
2. The decision maker must have at least two alternative courses of action available that achieve the objectives or have a significant probability of achieving them.
3. There must be some doubt as to which course of action is best in terms of achieving the decision maker's objectives.
4. There is an environment within which the problem to be solved is relevant.

In short, a decision maker is said to have a problem if he or she wants something within a real context, has alternative ways of obtaining it, and is in doubt as to which alternative is best in terms of the objectives. The components of a problem are thus: (1) the decision maker, (2) the objectives, (3) the alternative courses of action, and (4) the environment. To formulate the problem, we first have to identify these components.

1-3 THE COMPONENTS OF A DECISION PROBLEM

The decision maker is the individual or group who has control over the choice of actions to be taken. In many instances, there are several levels of decision makers: those who actually make the day-to-day decisions for the operation studied, those who have the power to initiate and change policies governing how decisions are to be made, and those who have delegated the power of decision making. The operations researcher should have a thorough understanding of the span of control vested in each level. This is important in order to define the scope of a project—those aspects of the decision problem that can be changed and those that are "off limits." Organization charts help to provide part of the information, but a complete picture can be obtained only by interviewing and questioning the people within an organization.

A decision maker may have several often conflicting objectives. Some objectives are acquisitive—there is something to be achieved, e.g., maximizing some desirable attribute, such as profits or output, or minimizing an undesirable consequence, such as high costs or environmental deterioration. Others are retentive, such as keeping a given share of the market or maintaining a certain degree of customer goodwill. Retentive objectives may be hidden or implicit in the policies currently pursued.

The alternative courses of action or decision choices are given by those aspects of the system that are controllable by the decision maker. In contrast, the environment consists of the uncontrollable aspects, such as the available financial resources, manpower, and machine capacity; costs and returns associated with decision choices; and those aspects that are external to the system, e.g., demand and supply patterns, legal constraints, and possible countermeasures that can be taken by competitors.

The distinction between controllable and uncontrollable aspects may not be clear-cut or may even be somewhat arbitrary. For instance, the decision maker may consider the demand for a product or service as uncontrollable (as part of the environment) in spite of the fact that if the firm chooses, it can affect the volume and pattern of demand in various ways, such as by granting quantity discounts and engaging in promotional activities. C. W. Churchman, in *The Systems Approach* (Dell, 1968), asks the following two questions: "Can I [the decision maker] do anything about it?" and "Does it matter relative to my objectives?" If the answer to both questions is yes, this particular aspect is part of the decision choice relevant to the problem. If the answer to the first is no but to the second is yes, then this aspect is part of the environment. If the answer to both questions is no, then this aspect is not relevant to the problem.

Analysis of the environment will reveal whether the data base, such as detailed records for sales or demand and cost factors, is adequate for proceeding with the project. If it is not, then procedures for collecting the required data must be initiated without further delay so that later, when solutions are to be computed and tested, the project is not jeopardized by missing or bad data.

1-4 STATE OF ENVIRONMENT

Most decision problems involve some element of uncertainty. Not all aspects of the current or the future environment in which the decision has to be made may be known exactly. In many problems, the effects of uncertainty may be so small that they can be ignored for purposes of analysis. We then talk about *decision making under certainty*. Each action leads to one and only one known outcome, as depicted in Figure 1-1. This does not necessarily mean that such problems are easy to solve. Consider the problem of the traveling salesperson who has to visit a number of cities and would like to find an itinerary that minimizes the total distance traveled. Theoretically, problems of this sort can be solved by enumerating all possible itineraries (actions). From a practical point of view, such enumeration may not be economically feasible. If there are only ten cities, the number of possible itineraries is 3,628,800. For twenty cities, it is 2,432,902,008,176,640,000—clearly an impossible task. More powerful methods of evaluation are needed.

If a given action may lead to one of a number of possible outcomes, as shown in Figure 1-1, depending on which future *event* occurs or which state of the environment is true, and if the outcome is only known after the action has been taken, then we are dealing with *decision making under uncertainty*. Decision problems under uncertainty may be graduated further according to the degree of uncertainty. If it is possible to specify a probability distribution over the outcomes for each action, the problem is classified as a *decision problem under risk*, whereas the label *decision making under uncertainty* is then reserved for those problems for which no objective information about the likelihood of the various outcomes is available. For example, from past experience, a newspaper vendor may have a fair idea of the chances of selling more than 50, 60, or 70 copies of the Saturday edition of the local paper. Thus, she faces a decision problem under risk. On the other hand, a firm contemplating whether or not to finance a given research project, which, if successful, may lead to development

Figure 1-1. *Decision making under certainty and uncertainty.*

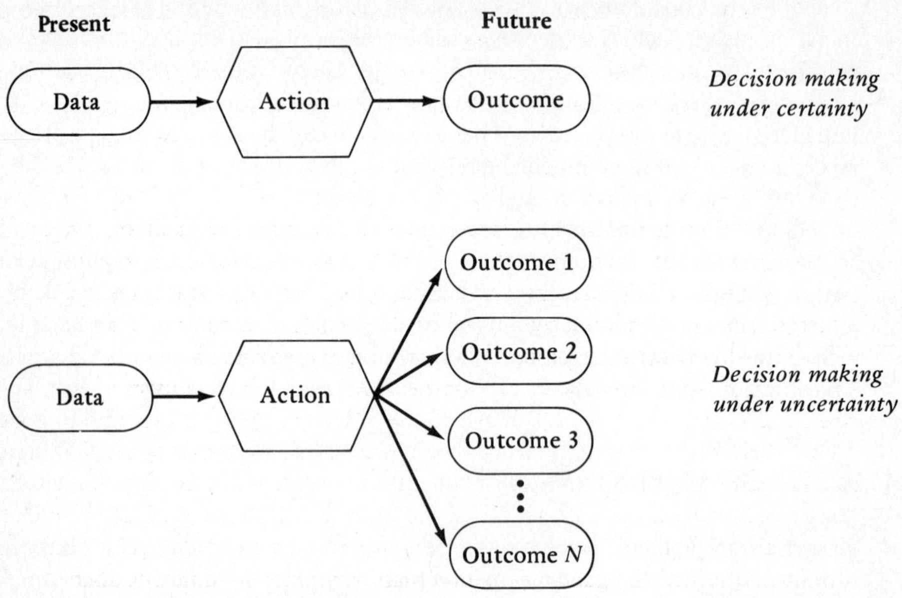

of a new product, usually will have no hard information about the chances of success, but only the subjective judgment of the possibly biased researchers. Chapter 11 will introduce you to some elementary approaches to analyzing problems of this nature.

Similarly, in situations where two or more competitors try to outguess the opponents, little or nothing may be known about the likelihood or the various strategies that the competitors may take. *Game theory*, a subject not covered in this text, is an attempt to deal with such problems. (See J. D. Williams, *The Compleat Strategyst*, McGraw-Hill, 1965.)

Although interesting in theory, in practice these fine distinctions are not really helpful. The boundary between objective and subjective judgments is rather fuzzy. The method finally chosen by the operations researcher will depend on many other elements, including the time and amount of funds available to complete the project or the accuracy required, rather than on the classification of the problem.

1-5 ON SYSTEMS

For the actual identification of the components of a problem, a systems approach is used. But first, what is a system? A system is a set of interrelated parts or subsystems, each one of which is in charge of some *mission* or *task*, with the following properties:

1. Each part contributes toward the objectives of the system. These contributions are measurable in terms of the objectives of the system as a whole.

2. Each part's effectiveness depends on the contributions of at least one other part; i.e., no part has an independent effect on the system.
3. Every possible subgroup of parts has properties 1 and 2. Hence, the parts cannot be organized into independent subsystems.
4. The system has an outside—an environment—which gives inputs into the system and receives outputs from the system. What is considered part of the system and what lies outside of it (the *boundary* of the system) depends on the analyst's purpose for studying the system.

Consider a manufacturing firm organized along functional lines: procurement of raw materials, production, marketing, finance, and personnel. In response to competitive pressures, the marketing department proposes to increase the length of the guarantee period offered on one of the products sold. The operations research group is asked to investigate this proposal. What is an appropriate choice for the system to be studied, its boundary, and its environment? Marketing itself consists of distribution, sales, and customer service. A change in the guarantee period is expected to increase sales. It will also increase guarantee costs incurred by customer service. Therefore, as a first choice, the system studied could be confined to sales and customer service (System 1), with all other operations of the firm, the customer population, and competitive firms in the industry forming the system's environment. The objective of System 1 is to find the guarantee period that maximizes the difference between sales revenues and guarantee costs.

System 1 views product quality as part of the environment. Product quality will affect both sales and guarantee costs. Hence, the system studied could be enlarged to include production. The objective of this larger system—System 2—is to find the optimal combination of product quality and guarantee period so as to maximize profits. Product quality is affected by the quality of the raw materials used, which are part of the environment of System 2. The system studied could thus be enlarged further to also include procurement, yielding System 3. System 3 could be extended to include other products of the firm if sales of these products are affected by changes in the guarantee period of the first product, yielding System 4. And so on it goes, with the universe as the ultimate system.

We thus see a *hierarchy* of systems. Each system is embedded in some larger system, as depicted in Figure 1-2. Viewed in this framework, the distinction between *optimization* (dealing with the system as a whole) and *suboptimization* (dealing with only part of a system) becomes academic. All optimization is in fact suboptimization.

1-6 THE SYSTEMS APPROACH OF OPERATIONS RESEARCH

Most projects start with an *orientation period* which involves visits to the facilities, interviews with the personnel involved, and, very early in the project, establishing lines of communication and procedural rules for obtaining the various bits and pieces

Figure 1-2. *Hierarchy of systems.*

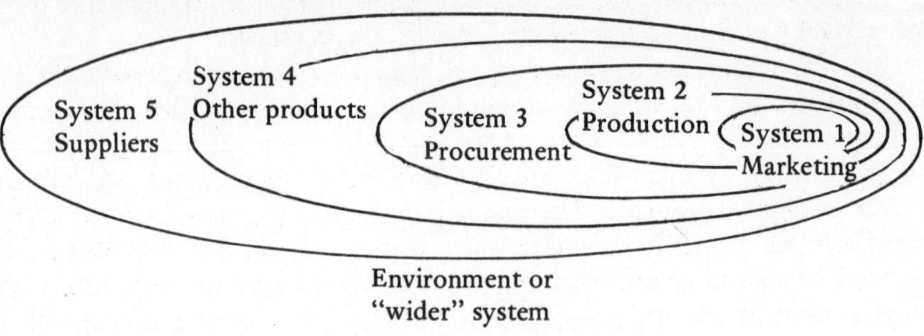

of information and data needed during the formulation of the problem. At this stage the operations researcher would seek answers to the following questions:

1. How does the sponsor or client of the project see the nature of the problem? How did the problem arise? Is it generally agreed to be important and why? Is it the "real" problem? Will the probable benefits justify the probable costs of undertaking the project?
2. What resources in terms of manpower, funds, and computer facilities are available to tackle the problem? How much time is available for completion of the project?
3. What is the system for which the sponsor has direct responsibility? What subsystems and parts exist, and what are their missions? What interactions take place between them? Who are the decision makers? This information is best presented on charts depicting the flow of documents and materials. These charts will show where decisions are being made and where they could be made.
4. What is the wider system that encompasses the system under study? What are the links between the system and the wider system? This will define the environment.
5. What are the objectives of the wider system? What are the objectives of the system being reviewed? Are they compatible?
6. What actions are available to control the system? What constraints restrict the choice of actions? How do the actions available affect the wider system? The aim is to identify effects that may impair the performance of other subsystems of the wider system, thus avoiding unnecessary suboptimization. Should new actions be developed?
7. How can the contribution of each action be measured in terms of the objectives of the system? What data and information must be collected to measure these contributions? Where are they available? Who should collect them? How reliable are the data?

The answers to some questions may invalidate answers to earlier questions and therefore necessitate their restatement. The whole process is an iterative one, requiring several partial or complete passes through the questions.

The boundary of the system and the components of the problem are delineated in steps 3 through 6. Given the complexity of systems behavior, the description of the system appropriate for a project will never be complete, and we should not aim to make it so. We stop when we have discovered enough about the system to be able to predict all significant consequences of the actions available to control the system. The difficulty lies in judging at which point an effect can be regarded as insignificant and hence can be safely ignored in the analysis. In general, the larger the portion of the wider system explicitly included in the analysis, the more expensive the project will be in terms of manpower and funds. But also the benefits that can be gained from the implementation of the findings will usually be greater. Thus, there exists a strategic problem of balancing the additional costs of enlarging the system with the additional benefits derived from it. The determination of the scope of a project therefore becomes an integral part of the project itself. Finding this proper balance is largely a matter of educated guess and experience, rather than of science.

1-7 SOME FURTHER IMPLICATIONS OF THE SYSTEMS APPROACH

Analysis of the environment of a decision problem is usually done on the basis of past records. Take for instance the problem of identifying and determining the relevant cost factors and demand characteristics for a production and inventory control problem. Most of the relevant cost factors are obtained either from cost accounting data or by actual observation on the production floor. Similarly, the demand for the various products is extracted from past sales records. These records and the observations made on the production floor reflect the present organizational structure and the present mode of operation.

The parameters extracted from these data are then used to derive new "optimal" policies for the system. These new policies may involve changes in the mode of operation. But any parameters extracted from data prior to these changes may become out of date and may not be valid for the new mode of operation. For instance, under the current mode of operation, stock runouts may occur quite regularly. Suppose the proposed mode of operation promises to reduce such shortages to a small fraction of the present rate. As a result, total sales will increase. Parameters derived from past sales records, without appropriate adjustments for lost sales, therefore, underestimate demand. Thus, it is clear that **the values of all environmental parameters relevant for the derivation of "optimal" policies are those that reflect the proposed mode of operation once the project has been implemented and not the current mode of operation.**

There is a ı ther trap for novice operations researchers who look to the accounting system for readily available cost data. It often comes as a surprise to them that the costs as recorded by accountants are rarely in the form required for an operations research project. The purpose of financial accounting is to provide evaluations of the financial standing and performance of an organization, such as are needed for a financial report to the stockholders. Similarly, cost accounting records are geared to monitor the average cost performance of a particular operation. These costs are usually based on a total concept, including overhead costs that are often arbitrarily allocated to the various operations, e.g., on the basis of direct labor costs. Furthermore, some costs relevant for decision making are never recorded. All costs related to lost opportunities (aptly named *opportunity costs*), such as profits lost because of stock shortages, never appear in accounting records.

1-8 SHOULD THE PROJECT CONTINUE?

As the formulation of the problem progresses, the operations researcher will have fairly definite ideas about the form of the mathematical model contemplated for the problem. Before plunging fully into the next phase, he or she should pause and attempt to evaluate the economic feasibility of the project. The operations researcher should estimate the total manpower and funds required to complete the project, including the costs of implementation. Approximate potential benefits should be evaluated as well. Then, all the information should be submitted to the sponsor of the project, who, on the basis of such information, will decide whether the project should be continued or abandoned. More ambitious and innovative projects have to be treated like research and development projects. Before a decision can be made as to whether such a project is worthwhile, some expenditures have to be made, similar to the initial research expenditures in new product development. Final judgment may have to be postponed until the project has gone well into the actual mathematical modeling phase.

1-9 AN ABBREVIATED CASE STUDY

The manager of the lubricating oil division of a large oil company approaches the supervisor of the company's operations research section with a request for a preliminary study of the division's inventory control system. As a first step, the operations researcher assigned to the project arranges for a guided tour of the offices, plant, and warehouse of the lubricating oil division. A talk with the division manager reveals some of the reasons why the study was requested. The main reason is a statement in the company auditors' report that inventories seem excessively high—a remark passed on by the company comptroller to the vice-president of manufacturing, the immediate boss of the division manager and the person in charge of the whole refinery complex where the division facilities are located.

Physically, the division consists of five parts:

1. A lubricating oil mixing plant, where various base oils stocked in tanks outside the plant are mixed in large vats of different sizes.
2. A filling plant, where the finished lubricating oils are packed into containers of various sizes.

3. The finished goods warehouse, where the filled containers for over 800 products are stored until they are shipped by rail or truck to customers.
4. A reconditioning plant, where drums returned from customers are cleaned and made ready for reuse.
5. An office, where customer orders are processed.

The tour is followed up over the next two weeks by a more thorough analysis of the various tasks performed in the division, including a detailed study of the current inventory replenishment procedures. Leaving out most technological aspects (which in practice are important), the following picture emerges. The customers of the division consist of about 500 company-owned regional wholesale distributors, who sell to company-owned service stations and other retailers, and a small number of large industrial firms and governmental institutions that purchase on a wholesale basis. The warehouse also serves as the wholesale distribution center for the region in which it is located.

Wholesale orders are always executed in a four-day cycle. Wholesale orders received on day n are processed in the offices on the same day. Each order usually covers an assortment of different products in various containers. The entire order is assembled for shipment during day $n + 3$ and is shipped early on day $n + 4$. Retail orders are executed on the same day that they are received. They amount to only about 10 percent of total sales.

Inventory records, kept on magnetic discs, are updated whenever an inventory transaction occurs. The computer system automatically flags any product for which the current inventory position (current inventory equals stock on hand plus outstanding replenishments less goods sold but not yet shipped) falls below a specified critical level called the *reorder point*. A clerk reviews the current inventory positions daily and issues a replenishment request for each product flagged. On the average, about 30 replenishment requests are issued every working day. The reorder points and order quantities are reviewed annually. They are set to an equivalent of one and of six weeks' average sales, respectively, resulting in an average inventory turnover of about $8\frac{2}{3}$ times per year (52 weeks/6 weeks).

The replenishment request is forwarded on the same day to the foreman of the mixing plant, who prepares a batch specification sheet, listing the exact quantities of base oils and additives to be mixed. The batch is scheduled for mixing by day $n + 2$. Prior to releasing a batch for filling, a laboratory technician tests it. If it fails the test, it is upgraded appropriately. When a batch has passed the test, it is released for filling.

A second copy of the inventory replenishment request is forwarded to the foreman of the filling plant, who orders the required number of empty containers to be delivered to the plant on day $n + 2$. Drums come from the reconditioning plant, other containers from the stock of empty containers. Once the release notice from the operator of the mixing plant is received, the foreman schedules a filling run for day $n + 2$ or day $n + 3$. Therefore, the replenishment is added to the stock no later than day $n + 3$. The *replenishment lead time*, i.e., the time between placement of a replenishment request and receipt of the goods, is thus less than the 4 days available to execute a wholesale customer order.

According to the foreman of the warehouse, floor space is presently at a premium. In fact, the foreman estimates that the division needs an additional 4000 square feet of space.

The description of the problem has already answered some of the questions listed in Section 1-6, particularly those in step 1 concerning the nature of the problem, how it arose, and its importance. The rigidity of the current replenishment rules is a good indicator that more flexible rules could generate substantial savings.

The answers to steps 3 and 4 are best tackled jointly. Essentially the lubricating oil division forms the first part of a complex inventory system whereby inventories are kept at several different levels and in different forms: base oils in storage tanks; oil additives in small bulk quantities; empty containers and packaged finished goods in the warehouse; finished goods by a large number of company-owned wholesale distributors; and finally, finished goods by an even larger number of company-owned retail outlets. See Figure 1-3.

Figure 1-3. *Multi-stage inventory system.*

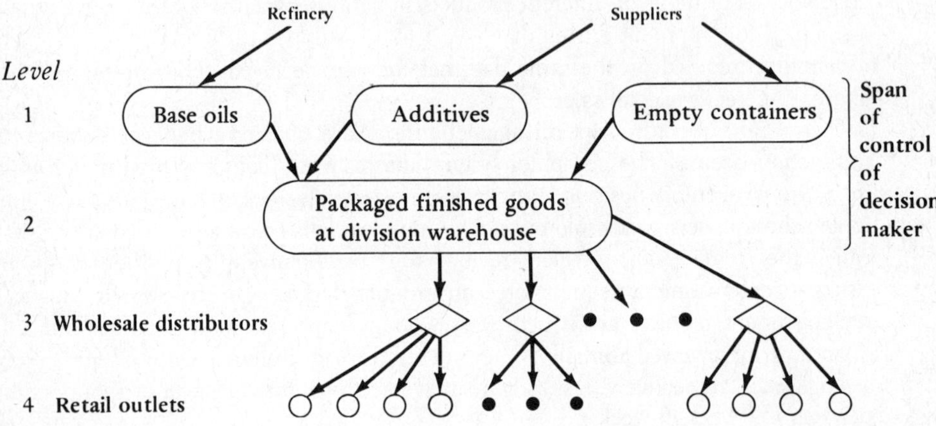

The span of control of the decision maker covers levels 1 and 2, whereas levels 3 and 4 are controlled by the marketing department. After some discussions, it is agreed that this first project should not go beyond the division manager's span of control. In order to assure that the project can be completed within a reasonable length of time (one to two years), it is further restricted to packaged finished goods only. The decision on extending the project to include inventories at level 1 is postponed for the present time. The packaged goods operation of level 2 becomes the system, whereas levels 1, 3, and 4 are part of the wider system or the environment. The analyst is aware that this choice ignores significant interactions. For instance, shortages of base oils, additives, or empty containers could seriously disrupt the replenishment of packaged goods, which in turn could affect levels 3 and 4.

There are three levels of decision makers involved: the vice-president of manufacturing, whose approval is required for any nonroutine expenditures and who has delegated the day-to-day management of the division to the division manager; the division manager, who is in charge of introducing any operational changes subject to the approval of the vice-president of manufacturing; and the inventory clerk, who actually makes the decisions on inventory control according to the policy laid down by the division manager. Clearly, the inventory clerk has little say in any policy matters. The crucial person and prime decision maker is the division manager.

What are the manager's objectives? They include the acquisitive objective of (1) minimizing operation costs, and the retentive objectives of (2) maintaining the smooth operation of the division, (3) maintaining prompt service to the marketing department, (4) avoiding shortages, and (5) keeping the levels of inventory within the available space limits. None of these objectives seems to be in conflict with the principal objective of the wider system—profit maximization. Further probing for hidden objectives reveals that the division manager will not implement any recommendation to shorten or lengthen the present 4-day cycle to execute wholesale customer orders. This time period was established as a result of a recent lengthy study by the company's department of methods and procedures and has been very satisfactory.

With these restrictions, the controllable aspects of the problem are reduced to (1) the time of placing an inventory replenishment, and (2) the amount of inventory replenishments for each product. Analysis of the production process and the nature of the products points to additional aspects that are controllable within the scope of the project, and that opens up the possibility of developing new alternative courses of action. Most lubricating oils are packaged in 3 or 4 different size containers. Should some or all sizes be replenished jointly whenever the inventory of one size has to be replenished, or should they all be replenished individually? A second set of possibilities is given by the fact that the replenishment lead time is shorter than the 4-day cycle for executing wholesale orders. This means that there actually exists the possibility of mixing and filling a product and then shipping it directly to wholesale customers, bypassing the inventory stage. Finished goods are then handled only once rather than twice. (Why?) Under what conditions is this course of action advantageous? (The answer to this second question is left as exercise 19.11 in Chapter 19.)

Finally, the data needed to evaluate the effectiveness of each action in terms of the objectives of the system consists of: (1) the technological aspects of the mixing, filling, and warehousing operations; (2) the costs associated with each operation as a function of changes in the controllable aspects; (3) the technological constraints on the controllable aspects, such as the minimum and maximum feasible batch sizes for mixing oils; and (4) the demand pattern for the products. Some information, particularly the cost factors, has to be obtained from cost accounting data. Other inputs, such as the time needed for mixing or filling, may be obtained only by actual observation of the operations. Annual sales summaries, by product, are compiled periodically. More detailed demand data can be extracted from sales records or taken directly from the original customer orders. Although the latter source is more representative of the demand pattern than past sales records, the effort of collecting information for more than 800 products would be staggering. Individual sales records, on the other hand, are stored in readily accessible form on magnetic tapes.

This analysis largely completes the formulation of the problem. We shall pick up the thread later on as we proceed through the remaining phases of operations research.

1-10 CONSTRUCTION OF A MATHEMATICAL MODEL

Mathematical models are the essence of the operations research approach to problem solving. As is true for any model, a mathematical model is a partial representation of some entity of reality, such as a process, an operation, or a system. The kinds of models of interest to operations researchers are those that allow manipulation of the entity modeled. The manipulation is aimed at answering certain questions about this entity, e.g., "What is the effect of a change in some aspect or some property of this entity in terms of its effectiveness toward achieving some set of objectives?" The purpose of a model is to explain, predict, or control the behavior of the entity modeled.

There are certain qualities a "good" model should have. According to J. C. D. Little ("Models and Managers: Concepts of a Decision Calculus," *Management Science*, April, 1970, pp. B466–85), a model should be

- **Simple.** Simple models are more easily understood by the decision maker, who is often mathematically untrained. Hence, only those aspects that have a significant effect on the performance of the system should be included.
- **Robust.** It should be difficult for the model to give bad answers, particularly answers that are outside the previous range of experience.
- **Easy to manipulate.**
- **Adaptive.** It should be easy to update the solution to a model in response to changes in the values of the input parameters. Given that we live in a rapidly evolving world, even the structure of the model itself should be easily adaptable.
- **Complete.** All important aspects should be included in the model.
- **Easy to communicate with.** The user should be able to change inputs easily and to obtain answers quickly.

In a mathematical model, the controllable properties of the entity modeled usually take the form of *decision variables* whose values can be chosen by the decision maker from a specified set of values. The uncontrollable aspects are represented by uncontrollable variables, such as *random variables*, or by *parameters* and *constants*, such as the parameters of a probability distribution or technological and cost constants. The contribution of each decision variable toward the decision maker's objectives is expressed by a functional relationship called the *measure of effectiveness*. Other technological and behavioral relationships between the variables give rise to *constraints*, which may also be in the form of functions, equations, or inequalities.

A mathematical model is called *deterministic* if it represents a problem of decision making under certainty. It is termed *probabilistic* or *stochastic* if it deals with a problem of decision making under uncertainty (or risk) and the probabilities of the alternative states of nature are known.

A mathematical model is a *general purpose model* if any problem that satisfies certain assumptions as to the form of the decision variables and the nature of the functional relationships between them can be cast into the structure of this model. It is a *special purpose model* if its structure is peculiar to a given problem. Most models and the associated solution methods discussed in this text are general purpose models.

With most general purpose models we associate one or several specialized techniques to find the optimal solution. For this reason, general purpose models are often referred to simply as *techniques*. Many problems can be solved by several techniques, each offering certain advantages. Familiarity with all essential features of the various techniques is a must, therefore, in order to choose the technique that best fits the special aspects of the problem studied.

Consider the inventory control problem in the preceding section. The time of placing an inventory replenishment—one of the controllable aspects—is equivalent to specifying a critical number of the inventory level which, whenever the inventory falls below this number, triggers the initiation of an inventory replenishment. This is simply the reorder point. Let r_i denote this number for product i. Similarly, the second controllable aspect is the inventory replenishment quantity Q_i. These are our decision variables.

The demand for each product is one of the uncontrollable variables. It fluctuates randomly and is expressed in the form of a random variable. Let X_i denote the random variable for the daily demand. Its probability distribution may be approximated by a theoretical probability distribution, such as the normal distribution defined by its two parameters—the mean daily demand and the variance of the daily demand. Or we may approximate it by using the empirical frequency distribution derived directly from past sales data. Other uncontrollable aspects give rise to: cost factors c_{ik} (the cost factor of type k for product i), such as the product value for product i; or technological coefficients w_{ik}, such as the amount of warehouse space required for product i.

1-11 THE MEASURE OF EFFECTIVENESS

With each alternative course of action or value of the decision variables we associate an outcome, described by one or several attributes. The attributes of interest to the analyst are those which can be used to express the response or performance of the system in terms of the decision maker's objectives, or those which are needed to verify if constraints imposed on the decision choices are satisfied. The objectives and constraints thus determine which attributes are relevant for evaluating alternative courses of action. In the case study, three of the attributes associated with each alternative inventory replenishment policy are the average inventory level, the maximum inventory level, and the average number of replenishments per year.

There is often a one-to-one correspondence between objectives and attributes. For instance, the problem may be to get by car from point A to point B in a city. If the objective is to get from A to B in minimum time, then "time from A to B" completely measures the achievement of this objective. On the other hand, the objective in the case study to "minimize total annual operating costs" requires that several attributes be measured for each inventory replenishment policy. There are also instances where no suitable set of attributes can be defined to evaluate the performance. A case in point is the objective of an emergency ambulance system to "deliver patients to the treatment center in the best possible condition under the circumstances." In such cases, we may have to substitute *proxy attributes*. "Response time," defined as the time between receipt of a call for an ambulance and the arrival of the ambulance at the scene, has been used as a suitable proxy attribute for studies of emergency ambulance systems.

The attributes are used as input into measures of effectiveness that evaluate the response of the system in terms of each of the decision maker's objectives to an alternative course of action. For a single objective the measure of effectiveness to be optimized is usually referred to as the *objective function*. As the name indicates, the objective function may be expressed in numerical form as a function. It is not essential, though, that the function be numerical. A better–worse or nonnumerical ranking of each alternative action may often suffice to identify the best decision. Unless the problem is a one-shot deal, the measure of effectiveness is defined for some specific interval of time or a specific *planning horizon*, e.g., one year.

If the number of alternative actions is sufficiently small, the measure of effectiveness may be expressed in the form of a *payoff table* or *payoff matrix*. The entries in the table represent the numerical value of the outcomes (payoffs) for each combination of event s_j, $j = 1, \ldots, J$, and action a_i, $i = 1, \ldots, I$. Thus, the table has one row for each action and one column for each event.

$$
\begin{array}{cc}
 & \text{Events, } s_j \\
 & \begin{array}{cccccc} 1 & 2 & 3 & \ldots & J \end{array} \\
\text{Actions, } a_i \begin{array}{c} 1 \\ 2 \\ 3 \\ \cdot \\ \cdot \\ \cdot \\ I \end{array} &
\begin{bmatrix}
r_{11} & r_{12} & r_{13} & \ldots & r_{1J} \\
r_{21} & r_{22} & r_{23} & \ldots & r_{2J} \\
r_{31} & r_{32} & r_{33} & \ldots & r_{3J} \\
\cdot & \cdot & \cdot & & \cdot \\
\cdot & \cdot & \cdot & & \cdot \\
\cdot & \cdot & \cdot & & \cdot \\
r_{I1} & r_{I2} & r_{I3} & \ldots & r_{IJ}
\end{bmatrix}
\end{array}
$$

A decision problem under certainty has only one column, since there is only one possible event or outcome for each action. For a decision problem under uncertainty, there will be two or more alternative events. With each event s_j we may associate a probability p_j, where $\sum_{j=1}^{J} p_j = p_1 + p_2 + \ldots + p_J = 1$. Under certain conditions, the worth of each action a_i (remember that this may be a strategy) can then be expressed as the expected value of the payoffs over all possible events:

$$\begin{bmatrix} \text{Expected outcome} \\ \text{of action } a_i \end{bmatrix} = E_i\,(\text{payoff}) = \sum_{j=1}^{J} r_{ij}\, p_j$$

If the decision maker wants to achieve several objectives simultaneously as well as possible—the multiple objective case—the measure of effectiveness may need to be expressed not simply as a single number for each action, but as a set of numbers (or a vector), one number for each objective measured. For instance, if the objectives are to minimize costs of production ($k = 1$) and to minimize down-time of the production facilities ($k = 2$), then the performance of alternative action i (perhaps determined by a particular size of a production run) in terms of the two objectives is expressed as the two-tuple (r_{i1}, r_{i2}) for a decision problem under certainty.

If the number of alternative courses of action is large or even infinite—such as for continuous decision variables—the measure of effectiveness is more conveniently expressed in analytical form as a functional relationship of the decision variables.

Say that the objective of the division manager in our inventory problem is to minimize operating costs and that we use one year as the base period. The measure of effectiveness has to cover only those costs that change if the values of the decision variables change. All those costs that remain constant regardless of what values the decision variables assume are irrelevant for the problem.

What types of costs are incurred in an inventory operation? There are material costs, labor costs, machine costs, financial charges, and overhead. To determine which of these costs are relevant, we have to study how each is affected by changes in the decision variables. To simplify the discussion let us consider changes in the order quantity only. A change in the order quantity of product i will affect its average inventory level and the number of replenishments that have to be made per year to satisfy a given annual demand of, say, R_i units.

To determine the average inventory level, assume that a replenishment is issued for product i whenever its inventory has been reduced to zero. Such a policy is feasible if replenishments are *instantaneous* (i.e., the replenishment lead time is zero) or if the time available to execute a customer order is longer than the replenishment lead time. In either case, no shortages can occur. If we ignore retail sales, the second condition is satisfied for our example. Just prior to a replenishment, the inventory level is therefore zero, and just after a replenishment it is Q_i. Assuming that demand occurs at a constant rate (which is not true here), inventories will reduce as the straight line shown in Figure 1-4. The time between replenishments will be a fraction of Q_i/R_i of a year. (Explain why!) From Figure 1-4 it follows immediately that the average inventory is $Q_i/2$.

Figure 1-4. *Inventory level over time for batch replenishments.*

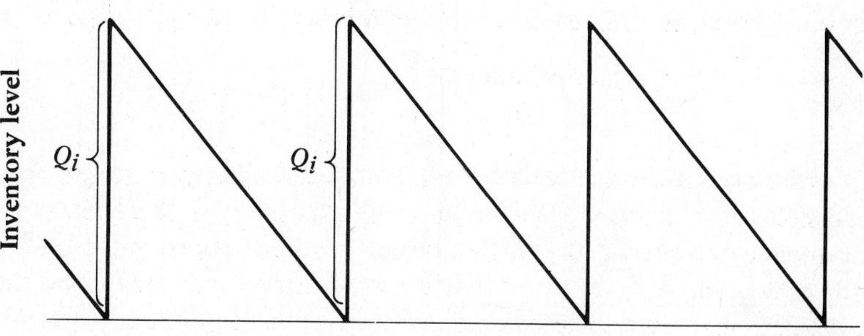

Inventories tie up funds, a scarce resource. The cost of investing funds in inventories is the *opportunity cost* equal to the return that the company could earn on an investment of equal risk. Let c_1 stand for this cost, expressed as a fraction per dollar invested per year. Let V_i be the value per unit (a drum, a carton of cans) of product i once it is on the warehouse floor. V_i is assumed to be constant regardless of the size of Q_i. Then $V_iQ_i/2$ is the average inventory investment for product i, and

$$(1\text{-}1) \qquad c_1V_iQ_i/2$$

is the annual cost of holding this product in inventory. There might be other costs of similar nature associated with holding goods in inventory, such as insurance, warehouse space rental, and pilferage. If so, c_1 would be adjusted appropriately.

The number of inventory replenishments per year required to satisfy a demand of size R_i if each replenishment is of size Q_i is equal to the ratio R_i/Q_i. Every time a replenishment is made, two types of costs are incurred: a fixed cost independent of the replenishment size Q_i which covers clerical costs and equipment set-up costs (on mixers and filling machines, including cleaning costs); and variable costs, such as the cost of raw materials, additives, and containers used, variable equipment operating costs, and handling costs of storing the goods in inventory. The variable costs are usually proportional to the replenishment size. Let V_i denote the total variable cost per unit. (This is obviously the same as the value per unit of the goods on the warehouse floor.) Let c_{2i} be the fixed cost per replenishment. Then for each replenishment for product i, a cost of $c_{2i} + V_iQ_i$ is incurred. For a total of R_i/Q_i replenishments per year, the annual fixed and variable replenishment costs are

$$(1\text{-}2) \qquad (c_{2i} + V_iQ_i)\,R_i/Q_i = (c_{2i}R_i/Q_i) + V_iR_i$$

As expected, the annual product cost V_iR_i is a constant. It is not affected by changes in the decision variable Q_i, and therefore can be considered irrelevant.

The relevant total annual cost for product i, denoted by $T_i(Q_i)$ (a function of Q_i), is equal to the sum of expressions (1-1) and (1-2), excluding V_iR_i:

$$(1\text{-}3) \qquad T_i(Q_i) = c_1V_iQ_i/2 + (c_{2i}R_i/Q_i)$$

The relevant total annual cost for all products (say there are N of them) is given by expression (1-3) summed over all N products.

$$(1\text{-}4) \qquad T(Q_1, Q_2, \ldots, Q_N) = \sum_{i=1}^{N} T_i(Q_i)$$

Ignoring any costs associated with the reorder points r_i, expression (1-4) is the measure of effectiveness for this simplified version of our inventory control problem. The decision maker's objective is to find those values of $Q_1, Q_2, \ldots, Q_N$ that minimize expression (1-4).

1-12 MULTIPLE OBJECTIVES

A decision maker may wish to achieve several objectives by the action chosen. Expression (1-4) represents the measure of effectiveness of one objective associated with the problem, namely minimizing operating costs. How can we deal with several objectives, such as maximizing profits and maximizing sales, which may be in partial conflict with each other? Maximizing profits may imply sacrificing some sales, while maximizing sales may imply reduced profits.

A commonly used approach to modeling such conflicts is to determine the most important objective and set minimal performance targets on all other objectives. For instance, we could decide that maximizing profits is the most important objective and substitute for the objective a "maximize sales" constraint specifying that sales cannot drop below a certain level or minimum share of the market.

If the objectives can be measured in comparable units, then we may be able to construct *trade-off functions* that translate all objectives into some common measure, such as costs and returns, or into units of the most important objective. A trade-off function shows how much successive changes in one objective are worth in terms of another objective. For instance, how much each successive 1-percent decrease in sales is worth in terms of successive increments in profits. (For a more detailed analysis of this approach, the reader is referred to Churchman et al., *Introduction to Operations Research.*)

Retentive objectives naturally lend themselves to being expressed in the form of surrogate constraints on the decision variables. For instance, the retentive objective of keeping inventory levels within the available warehouse space would be expressed as a constraint on the Q_i values as follows: if each unit of product i requires an area of w_i square feet of warehouse space and warehouse space is allocated proportionately to the maximum inventory level (Q_i in our case), then each product requires an area of w_iQ_i square feet. The total area required for all N products cannot exceed the presently available space of W square feet, or

$$\sum_{i=1}^{i=N} w_iQ_i \leq W \tag{1-5}$$

Although surrogate constraints are derived by policy decisions and are thus not absolute but relative constraints, they are treated from a mathematical point of view in exactly the same way as those representing physical conditions. However, in the analysis of the optimal solution, the operations researcher has to examine carefully how changes in these constraints, reflecting alternative policy decisions, affect the solution.

Sometimes the various objectives can be expressed in the form of target levels to be achieved as closely as possible. If the objectives are highly conflicting, it may not be possible to reach each target level exactly. In such instances, the decision maker may wish to choose an objective function that minimizes an appropriately weighted sum of the deviations from the target levels. In other instances, the objectives may be ranked in order of priority. The solution procedure would then attempt to satisfy the objectives in that order. No attempt to satisfy any lower order objective would be made until all higher order objectives had been reached. Such approaches have been formalized in what has become known as *goal programming*. Section 2-14 of Chapter 2 gives a simple example of goal programming where all relationships are linear.

The need to deal effectively with multiple objectives in a complex environment, particularly with noncommensurable objectives, has given rise to a new branch of operations research—*multiple-objective decision making.* This is the topic of Chapter 22.

1-13 DISCOUNTING OF FUTURE COSTS AND BENEFITS

As pointed out in Section 1-11, the measure of effectiveness may represent net benefits accrued over some specific time interval or planning horizon. Two alternative courses of action, then, may differ not only in terms of the total net benefits but also in terms of the pattern over time of these benefits. Which action is preferred? To deal with such aspects, we use the same approach as in the *appraisal of investment projects* or *capital budgeting.* For simplicity, assume that the benefits are measured in monetary terms. Funds received today can be put to productive use and therefore will be worth more than the same amount of funds received some time in the future. The difference in total monetary value is equal to the return that can be earned on these funds over this time interval. To render costs incurred and benefits received in different time periods comparable, all costs and benefits are expressed in terms of their value at a common point in time, usually the present. In other words, they are *discounted* to the present. The measure of effectiveness then expresses the *present value* of the stream of costs and benefits over time.

Let us briefly review some of the principles of discounting. If \$1 invested now has a value of \$$(1 + r)$ one period from now, where r is the rate of return (e.g., interest), then \$1 received in one period's time has a present value now of:

$$\alpha = 1/(1 + r) \tag{1-6}$$

α is called the *discount factor* and r the *discount rate.* From expression (1-6) and the fact that $r > 0$, it follows that $0 < \alpha \leqslant 1$. If $r = 0$, then $\alpha = 1$, i.e., future funds are not discounted.

R dollars received one period from now have a present value of αR. R dollars received two periods from now have to be discounted for two periods. Discounting for one period reduces their value to αR, and discounting this amount for a second period gives a present value of $\alpha^2 R$. In general, R dollars received k periods from now have a present value of $\alpha^k R$.

Consider now the stream of funds $R_0, R_1, R_2, \ldots, R_n$, where R_i represents the costs incurred or benefits received at the end of the ith period. The present value of this stream of funds, discounted at the factor α, is

$$S_n = R_0 + \alpha R_1 + \alpha^2 R_2 + \ldots + \alpha^{n-1} R_{n-1} + \alpha^n R_n = \sum_{i=0}^{n} \alpha^i R_i \tag{1-7}$$

If $R_i = R$ over all future periods, that is, if the planning horizon is *unbounded,* the present value of this infinite stream of funds becomes

$$S = \sum_{i=0}^{\infty} \alpha^i R = R/(1 - \alpha) \tag{1-8}$$

for $0 < \alpha < 1$.

1-14 UTILITY MEASURES

The worth of an action in terms of the decision maker's objectives can often adequately be expressed in dollars and cents. Hence, profits or costs become the natural choice for the measure of effectiveness. For many decision problems in business and industry, particularly those of a day-to-day nature with outcomes within the normal range of experience of the decision maker, a decision based on maximizing profits (or minimizing costs) will properly reflect the preference ordering. For strategic and nonrecurrent decisions or decisions with highly uncertain and extreme outcomes (say large profits or losses), other factors, such as the decision maker's financial ability to overcome large losses or the personal likes or dislikes of engaging in risky situations, may influence what decision is considered "best."

Decisions to carry insurance or to buy lottery tickets are clearly not based on a criterion of maximizing monetary returns. Otherwise, insurance companies and lottery organizers could not cover their operating costs and make profits at the same time. Should we infer that such decisions are not made on a rational basis? Far from it! It simply means that there are situations where monetary values do not measure the true worth of a given outcome. The true worth reflects personal, social, and financial elements. What kind of risks is the decision maker willing to assume in general and for the particular situation in question? How does society view certain risk decisions? What is the size of the monetary outcome in relation to the decision maker's total wealth? A loss of $20,000 may spell financial ruin for a small, one-person firm, while it may have few or no serious consequences for a giant corporation.

Furthermore, for many decision problems, especially in the public sector, the outcomes cannot be measured in monetary terms without introducing questionable value judgments. For instance, what is the monetary value of safety, recreation, scenic beauty, or equity? To measure the worth of actions with qualitative outcomes, we need some method of quantification of personal value judgments.

In 1944, Von Neumann and Morgenstern, a mathematician and an economist, proposed an index designed to quantify the true but personal worth of an outcome to a decision maker, valid for a particular decision situation. They called it *utility*—not to be confused with the concept of the same name used by nineteenth-century economists. In Chapter 11 we will see how to go about constructing utility functions that reflect a decision maker's evaluation of the personal worth of an outcome and will demonstrate the use of such functions for decision making.

1-15 MODELS AS APPROXIMATIONS

An operations researcher is confronted with conflicting modeling goals. On the one hand, the model should be sufficiently simple to remain tractable, and on the other hand, it should be elaborate enough to be a close representation of reality. Simplicity in a model can be achieved only by making suitable approximations. Striking a proper balance between detail and simplicity is a delicate matter of weighing the cost of constructing the model, collecting the required data, and implementing and operating the model against the expected benefits that can be gained from its implementation. These are all increasing functions of the sophistication and complexity of the model, though rarely quantifiable in practice.

What type of approximations can be made?

- **Omitting variables:** Often variables that have relatively small effects or that tend to behave like other variables can be omitted. For instance, inventories for goods-in-process are often ignored if production lead times are short. To determine whether a variable has a significant effect on the measure of effectiveness, the operations researcher will have recourse to various statistical techniques and tests, such as *correlation* and *regression analysis*, *analysis of variance* and *covariance*, and *tests of significance*. Knowledge of these techniques, their capabilities and limitations, is part of the required bag of tools of any operations researcher. We refer the reader to a statistics text, such as G. W. Snedecor and W. G. Cochran, *Statistical Methods* (Iowa State University Press, 1967).
- **Aggregating variables:** In inventory models covering thousands of different products, low usage items are dealt with completely or partially in groups, using an average group cost for some of the cost factors. Similarly, in large corporate models depicting an entire organization, activities are grouped and expressed as a common standard activity.
- **Changing the nature of variables:** Variables may be treated as constants. For instance, an average is substituted for a random variable. Discrete variables are treated as continuous and vice versa to simplify the solution procedure.
- **Approximating the relationship between variables:** The true functional relationship between variables is approximated by a form that is simpler to manipulate, such as in substituting *linear* or *quadratic* functions for *nonlinear* functions.
- **Omitting constraints:** Constraints may be ignored initially and only those violated by the solution introduced subsequently.
- **Disaggregating the entity modeled:** One single model that covers the entire system may be highly complex and difficult to solve. Such a problem may be broken into smaller and partially self-contained submodels. For example, each level in a multilevel inventory system may be modeled separately.

Let us briefly hint at the various approximations made in the inventory problem that led to expression (1-4). The products are sold in discrete units. We treated them as continuous and would simply round the solution to the nearest integer. The daily demand is a random variable—we treated the demand rate as a constant. This is justified since individual sales are in small lots of a few packages per customer and tend to occur at a fairly even trickle. We assumed that mixing and filling set-up costs are independent of the sequence in which products are produced, which in fact is not true, although the cost differences due to sequence are small. If we build separate models to determine the replenishment quantities and reorder points, then we use a multiple-model approach. Again, this may be justified since a positive reorder point is only required to allow retail sales to be executed immediately during the replenishment lead time. However, retail sales are a small portion of total sales.

1-16 DERIVING A SOLUTION TO THE MODEL

Once the problem has been formulated mathematically, a solution has to be derived. The solution may be found by the basic economic principles of marginal analysis for the case of increasing marginal costs and decreasing marginal returns. The value of the decision variable is increased until marginal costs are equal to marginal returns. This principle is easily extended to discrete decision variables. The decision variable is increased until the incremental cost is not covered any more by the incremental return achieved. The mathematical basis for marginal analysis is part of classical calculus (see Chapter 19). For instance, disregarding the constraint (1-5), the optimal values of $Q_1, Q_2, \ldots, Q_N$ that minimize the measure of effectiveness (1-4) can be obtained by the use of differential calculus. We set the derivative of (1-4) equal to zero and solve for each Q_i. This yields the well-known *economic order quantity* (EOQ) formula

(1-9)
$$Q_i^* = \sqrt{2R_i c_{2i}/c_1 V_i}, \qquad i = 1, 2, \ldots, N$$

More often than not, the optimal solution to a model has to be computed by numeric methods. The most powerful numeric methods are based on an *algorithm*—a set of logical and mathematical operations performed in a specific sequence. The algorithm is applied to a given initial solution to the problem, to derive a new and ideally better solution. The sequence of operations that lead to the new solution is called an *iteration*. The new solution is now substituted as the starting point, and the process is repeated until certain conditions—referred to as *stopping rules*—are satisfied, indicating that an optimal solution has been reached with the desired degree of accuracy, or that no feasible or bounded solution exists to the problem.

For an algorithm to be a practical solution method, the algorithm has to have certain properties: (1) each successive solution has to be an improvement over the preceding one; (2) successive solutions have to converge to the optimal solution; (3) convergence arbitrarily close to the optimal solution has to occur in a finite number of iterations; and (4) the computational requirements at each iteration have to be sufficiently small to remain economically feasible.

Numeric methods invariably require access to high-speed electronic computers. In fact, it was the availability of more and more sophisticated computers that made the development and use of algorithmic methods possible. A major portion of any operations research text is usually devoted to a detailed study of algorithmic techniques. This book is no exception.

Many models are solved using *heuristically* derived decision rules to find "good" policies rather than the "best" policy (see Chapter 23). At other times the performance of specific decision rules is evaluated by *simulation* (Chapter 16). Finally, many decision problems simply involve the comparison of a relatively small number of possible courses of action. Complete *enumeration* may then be the most efficient solution method. Sequential decision problems under uncertainty, where each action represents a strategy, are often solved by *decision trees*—a simple but effective evaluation method (Chapter 11).

1-17 SENSITIVITY ANALYSIS

The systematic evaluation of the response of the optimal solution to changes in input data is referred to as *sensitivity analysis*. It is a highly valuable and important part of evaluating the optimal solution and should always be performed on all crucial input data. The three main uses of sensitivity analysis are

1. To determine the accuracy required for input data for the model.
2. To establish control ranges for changes in input parameters and constants over which the present optimal solution remains near-optimal.
3. To evaluate the marginal value of scarce resources.

For example, it would be very valuable to find out how sensitive the EOQ developed for our case study is to errors or deviations in the various input parameters. (We will perform this analysis in Chapter 12, Section 12-7.) This would indicate how much effort should be spent on developing accurate forecasts for the demand or accurate set-up costs for production runs.

Some operations research techniques, especially linear programming (Chapter 2), provide a certain amount of sensitivity analysis either as a by-product of the algorithmic computations or with little additional effort. For other problems, sensitivity analysis requires solving the model from scratch for various combinations of input parameters.

1-18 TESTING THE SOLUTION FOR PERFORMANCE

The purpose of an operations research project is to improve the performance of the system. Before deciding whether to implement the proposed solution or shelve it, usually the decision maker will want convincing proof that the proposed solution performs better than the present rules. Demonstrating such superiority may help more in having the solution accepted than in gaining full understanding of how the model works in all its complexities.

When testing the solution, the operations researcher wants to ascertain (1) that the decision rules derived from the optimal solution perform as expected and (2) what the expected net benefits of implementing the solution will be.

A solution may be tested retrospectively (against past observed behavior) or prospectively (against future behavior). In either case the test has to entail a detailed comparison of the "actual" performance of the optimal solution derived from the model, as if it were implemented, with the actual performance of present decision rules based on the same set of data. For instance, the test could consist of running both sets of rules in parallel over a length of time, such as a year. The actual operations would be based on the present decision rules; the new decision rules would be simulated (see Chapter 16) on paper alongside the old ones. This would permit a very realistic evaluation, but would also result in an unreasonably long delay before any conclusions could be drawn. For this reason, testing is usually done by simulation alone and is performed separately for each set of decision rules on the same data. Testing may be restricted to a random sample of observations.

Here are some rules for valid testing:

1. The evaluation of the proposed solution has to be based on observations of actual (simulated) performance. It is invalid to simply substitute the optimal values of the decision variables associated with the data used into the measure of effectiveness, such as expression (1-3) with the Q obtained from (1-9) for actual data. The latter would be a meaningless test since it reflects an idealized and simplified reality.
2. The test should be independent of how the optimal solution was derived. For instance, a test against past demand data, that also served to estimate the various input parameters of the model used to derive the optimal solution will not yield an independent test. Since the model supposedly optimizes the performance, it should perform better than the present decision rules for these demand data. Either some data have to be set aside specifically for the test and not used to derive the optimal solution, or new data have to be generated artificially on the basis of projected behavior of the system, such as the projected demand distribution.
3. The data used should be "representative" of future behavior, i.e., they should cover the entire range of behavior likely to be observed in the future.
4. Tests should cover a sufficiently long time interval to allow for evaluation of not only a *point estimate* but also the *variability* of the outcome.

The difference in average benefits for the present and proposed sets of rules derived from the tests is adjusted for any difference in the cost of applying and maintaining the two sets of rules. This yields an average net benefit. The present value of this average net benefit over the projected lifetime of the project is finally compared with any further costs projected for the project, such as costs of initial data collection, further model refinements, and implementation—a process similar to the evaluation of investment proposals. Note that at this point only future costs are relevant. All costs incurred so far are *sunk costs* and no longer relevant to whether or not the project should be completed.

Operations research projects are usually high risk investments. Even if testing turns out to be favorable, unforeseen snags during implementation or further refinements of the model tend to cause cost overruns, whereas benefits may be highly variable. This calls for relatively high discount rates on the order of 20 to 100 percent. Furthermore, full benefits will not be realized from the very beginning, but only after a transition period that may easily extend over several months. It is essential that the decision maker be made aware of this fact or else he or she might decide to scrap implementation long before the project has reached its full potential.

1-19 IMPLEMENTATION OF THE SOLUTION

Implementation of an operations research project is putting the tested solution to work. This means translating the mathematical solution into a set of easily understood operating procedures or decision rules for each of the persons involved in using and applying the solution; training these people in the proper use of the rules; planning and executing the transition from the present to the desired mode of operations; instituting controls to maintain and update the solution; and, finally, checking the initial performance periodically until the new mode of operation has become routine.

Full implementation of all the recommendations of an operations research project is rare. It is more useful to talk about the degree of implementation achieved. The objective of the operations researcher is to achieve a sufficiently high degree of implementation to capture the major portion of the potential benefits that can be derived from the solution.

Problems of implementation can be reduced to three basic factors:

1. Those relating to the task of implementation, such as the complexity of the solution, the sensitivity of the solution to implementation, the degree of deviation of the solution from current practice. The greater any of these are, the greater the problems that have to be overcome.
2. Those relating to the individuals using the solution, such as the personalities of the users, their motivation and pride in the job (does the proposed solution restrict their freedom of action, reduce their importance, transform a challenging job that requires years of experience to one of merely feeding data into a computer program?); their ages (routine becomes more entrenched with age, and change is more difficult to accept); the users' backgrounds, levels of education, and the importance of the activities related to the solution in the framework of their total jobs (the less important the solution activities are, the less attention they receive).
3. Those relating to the environment, such as the support given to the solution by higher echelons in the hierarchy and organizational implications of the solution (does one department become more dependent on another?); or potentially threatening implications to employees (labor-replacement through automation) or customers.

Generally, the operations researcher pays full attention to the first factor, which is a question of technology. The tendency is to neglect the human factors (2 and 3), which are qualitative in nature and evade the formal treatment that can be given to the technological factors of implementation. It should come as no surprise that neglecting the human constraints in a system can easily lead to a "solution" that in fact is a solution on paper only, and is not workable in practice. From this point of view, implementation can be viewed as a problem of relaxing the human constraints versus adjusting the technical solution. The human constraints may be relaxed in a number of ways. Individuals that could become obstacles to proper implementation may be replaced or transferred to other equally attractive jobs. Proper training or soliciting active participation in the project may increase their understanding of the solution. The technical solution can be adjusted by simplifying the solution policy (for instance, by the use of close quick-and-dirty rules).

The literature on implementation is unanimous on one point—that implementation and continued use of a solution is almost guaranteed if the sponsor and the ultimate user(s) "own" the research results. The users will develop a feeling of ownership if they can contribute to the project in a meaningful way with their experience and detailed knowledge of the operations.

Planning for implementation has to start with the formulation of the problem and the groundwork laid throughout all other phases. It is not sufficient to start planning this phase once the model has been completed and tested. Planning includes technical aspects, such as preparing the proper data base and data collection procedures needed for implementation and continued maintenance, deciding what to do with bad data, preparing detailed instruction manuals, and preparing any special forms and tools needed for use of the solution. The actual process of changing from the present mode of operation to the new solution requires a detailed timetable of the various activities to be undertaken, their sequence and precedence relationships, and their assignment to the people or department best equipped to execute them.

For large projects or projects that cover a large number of identical activities (such as an inventory control project), the solution may have to be implemented in stages rather than as a whole in order to avoid straining the resources and facilities available. For instance, although an inventory control project may promise to reduce the average inventory investment by a substantial percentage, implementing the model for all products simultaneously will often result in an initial increase in the total inventory (why?), straining limited warehouse capacity. Gradual introduction of the new rules may avoid such a situation.

1-20 CONTROLLING AND MAINTAINING THE SOLUTION

The environment in which most organizations operate is constantly undergoing change. Such change may be quantitative (environmental parameters or relationships change in magnitude only) or structural (the form or nature of environmental parameters or relationships changes). In the first case, the form of the operations research solution usually remains valid. Only the values of the decision variables may have to be adjusted to reflect quantitative changes in the environment. For example, the value of the products stored in inventory may change, calling for a corresponding adjustment in the economic order quantities. In the second case, the form of the solution may not be valid any longer, necessitating a reformulation of the model. For instance (in terms of the example in Section 1-9), introduction of new mixing and filling equipment may result in substantial savings in production set-up costs if all container sizes of the same oil are replenished jointly, whereas the present solution may be based on separate replenishments for each container size.

Procedures have to be set up to monitor such quantitative and qualitative changes in the environment, and corrective action must be undertaken when such changes become significant. A change is considered significant if the improvement in the benefits that can be gained by adjusting the solution exceeds the cost of making the adjustment.

Establishing controls over the solution consists of:

1. Listing for each variable, parameter, constraint or relationship—for those that are explicitly included in the model as well as for those that have been excluded

as insignificant—the range of values for which the present solution remains optimal or near-optimal and the type of qualitative change which invalidates the current form of the solution.

2. Specifying in detail how each variable and parameter has to be measured, which relationships have to be checked, and the occasion and frequency of such controls and checks.
3. Determining who is responsible for each item to be controlled and who has to be notified if significant changes are detected.
4. Specifying in detail how the solution has to be adjusted for significant quantitative changes and what action has to be taken to deal with qualitative changes in the environment.

The job of the operations researcher is not finished once the solution has been implemented. In order to assure that the implementation does not deteriorate after a while, the actual performance of the solution (including control procedures) must be carefully checked and the actual benefits achieved compared to those projected initially. Significant deviations have to be examined and adjustments made. Training of all people involved may have to be followed up. Only then can the success of the project be judged.

EXERCISES

1.1 The marketing department of a firm proposes to introduce a new item to its product line. The product would be made by the firm's own facilities. Analyze how such a decision might affect the performance of each of the other departments (parts) of the firm (system)? Do the same type of analysis for a decision to adjust the price of a product in response to a general price increase by the competition.

1.2 Identify the components of both the system and the wider system for the following decision problems:
(a) Assigning the course grade to each student in a quantitative methods class,
(b) Buying a second-hand car,
(c) Designing a new advertising campaign.

1.3 The production department of a firm is considering changing from a batch method of replenishing inventories to a continuous production process whereby stocks are replenished at a constant rate equal to the average sales rate. Define the system and the wider system, and trace all significant effects of that change on other parts of the wider system, including procurement of raw materials, warehousing, and marketing.

1.4 Trace the effects of each of the following proposed changes on the remaining parts of the system (shown in parentheses):
(a) Conversion of a number of downtown streets into one-way streets (public transport, fire department, traffic police, municipal refuse collection, street cleaning, and business community).
(b) Toughening of university entrance standards (university system, high school system, state finances, and public employment agencies).
(c) Introduction of laws on compulsory wearing of seat belts for all car occupants aged

6 or over under penalty of stiff fines and loss of insurance coverage (traffic police and court system; also consider transition problems of introducing laws).

1.5 A small bakery produces a whole meal bread, which it sells to local supermarkets at a contractually fixed price of 40 cents per loaf. Fixed costs associated with the operation amount to $2000 per month. Each baker hired has a salary of $600 per month and can produce 8000 loaves of bread in that time. The cost of the ingredients depends on the output; it is 20 cents a loaf for a monthly output of 12,000 loaves or less; 18 cents for a monthly output of more than 12,000, but at most 20,000; 16 cents for more than 20,000 and at most 40,000; and 15 cents for more than 40,000.

(a) Construct a mathematical model for the difference between total monthly revenue and total monthly cost as a function of output and number of bakers.

(b) Construct a mathematical model for the break-even point for 4 bakers.

(c) Contrast your models with the real-life operation of such a small bakery. What approximations did you make in these models?

1.6 A typical sequence of a New Zealand freezing works' daily output of boned meat appears as follows:

Day of week	M	Tu	W	Th	F	M	Tu	W	Th	F
Tons	50	54	49	47	49	52	51	46	49	53

No processing is done on the weekends. Boned meat is immediately packed for shipment and then frozen and stored in the company's cold storage warehouse. All sales are to overseas customers and are made in large shipments by refrigerator ships. Over the past several months, shipments of the company's entire stock in the warehouse have been made on the following dates: Jan. 13, Feb. 11, March 12, April 10, and May 10. Payments to farmers are due immediately after killing. Payments for shipments are received after loading. Build a mathematical model that approximates the company's investment in frozen meat. Show how you derived the model. Justify why your model is a suitable representation of the real system.

1.7 When a model is tested, the following deficiencies may be discovered:

(a) The model may include irrelevant factors.

(b) It may exclude relevant factors.

(c) Constants or parameters may be evaluated incorrectly.

(d) Functional relationships may be misrepresented.

Consider the case study discussed in Section 1-9 and the simplified model given in Section 1-11, and give examples for each of these deficiencies.

1.8 Discuss the apparent contradiction that if at the start of an operations research project all costs and potential benefits were known accurately, the project would not be undertaken at all, whereas if the total costs and potential benefits could only be ascertained after the model was tested for performance (but prior to implementation), the correct decision may have been to implement the model. What implications does this have for the evaluation of operations research projects?

1.9 From the working definition of operations research given at the beginning of this chapter it follows that the operations researcher should take a systems approach and incorporate into a model all aspects that are affected by changes in the values of the decision variables or that limit or affect in any other way the optimal values of the decision variables. On the other hand, in real life the approach often used by operations researchers to model a complex problem is to build a series of separate models that may be only very loosely connected with one another. (Effects are only considered in one direction, while any feedbacks are ignored.) Each subproblem is then solved separately or in a given sequence. Discuss this apparent contradiction.

1.10 The following argument between A and B was overhead at a meeting of a "University Committee to Save Energy."

A: Clearly, every light turned off means some electricity saved. Hence, the task of this committee is to educate all members of the university community and, in particular, all staff to turn off lights whenever they are the last to leave a room, a corridor, or a lecture hall.

B: Admittedly, a policy of turning off lights may generate immediate power savings. But the greater frequency of turning lights on and off will burn the bulbs out sooner and result in higher lamp replacement costs. Furthermore, dark corridors and lecture halls may increase the incidence of accidents, imposing higher costs on society as a whole. An optimal energy policy cannot restrict itself to considering only ways of reducing power consumption.

Discuss, appraise, and criticize the viewpoints taken by A and B.

1.11 Discuss the apparent contradiction between the sequence of the five phases of an operations research project [(1) formulation of problem, (2) construction of model, (3) derivation of solution, (4) testing of model, and (5) implementation of solution] and the following statement, attributed to C. W. Churchman: "Implementation is the first phase of an O.R. project."

1.12 Discuss the following humorous or sarcastic statements made by well-known operations researchers. Find a practical example from everyday life that demonstrates the truth or fallacy of each.

(a) "Building a better mousetrap is not enough." (Solve problems that are relevant.)
(b) "Don't go around looking for problems to fit a solution." (R. E. Machol, *Interfaces*, May 1974.)
(c) "Steer clear of sacred cow zones." (Don't suggest solutions that infringe on vested interests.) (P. Rivett, *Concepts of Operational Research*, Watts, 1968.)
(d) "Don't ever try to teach a sponsor or client something until you have learned something from him."
(e) "Never do a project for free." (R. L. Ackoff, *Operations Research*, March–April 1960.)
(f) "Don't let the Mathematics come in the way of Common Sense." (The Gozinto–Woolsey Principle.)
(g) "Models are for managers, not mathematicians." (Konczal's Theorem, *J. Systems Management*, No. 12, 1975.)
(h) "Look for hidden agendas." (Is the project ritualistic to confirm some preconceived strategy?) (H. N. Shycon, *Interfaces*, Nov. 1976.)
(i) "Don't undertake a management science project unless there is a clear and present need, one recognized by management." (Go for demand pull rather than technology push.) (H. N. Shycon, *Interfaces*, Nov. 1976.)
(j) "Use quick-and-dirtys." (G. Woolsey & H. S. Swanson, *A Quick and Dirty Manual*, Harper and Row, 1975.)

REFERENCES

General

Ackoff, R. L. "Science in the Systems Age: Beyond IE, OR, and MS," *Operations Research*, May–June 1973, pp. 661–71.

"The Future of Operational Research Is Past," *J. of the Operational Research Society*, Vol. 30, Feb. 1979, pp. 93–104.

"Resurrecting the Future of Operational Research," *J. of the Operational Research Society*, Vol. 30, March 1979, pp. 189–99.

In these three papers, Ackoff looks at the connection between operations research and systems, with a warning for operations researchers as to their possible fate. Controversial, but thought provoking.

Churchman, C. West. *The Systems Approach*. New York: Dell, 1968. A must on the reading list of any student in operations research and systems analysis. Lucid, challenging, inspiring, and critical review, in a climate of debate, of what the systems approach means, in less than 250 pages of easy reading.

Churchman, C. W. "Operations Research as a Profession," *Management Science*, Vol. 17, Oct. 1970. The paper defines operations research and discusses each component of the definition in detail in light of the preparation for the operations research profession.

Methodology

Ackoff, Russell L. "Optimization + Objectivity = Opt Out," *European Journal of Operational Research*, Vol. 1, 1977, pp. 1–7. It is argued that the preoccupation of operations researchers with optimization and objectivity leads to their withdrawal from reality. By clinging to optimality, they lose reality. Optimal solutions deteriorate because the system and the environment change. Therefore, operations research should engage in designing models that adapt well rather than optimize.

Ackoff, R. L. *The Art of Problem Solving*. Farnborough, England: Saxon House, 1979. Part I deals with the various aspects of problem solving, while Part II gives six applications in detail. Enjoyable reading.

Ackoff, Russell L., and Maurice W. Sasieni. *Fundamentals of Operations Research*. New York: Wiley, 1968. This text is in some sense an updated version of *Introduction to Operations Research* by Churchman, Ackoff, and Arnoff. Excellent treatment of methodology in Chapters 1 to 4, 15 to 17. Recommended as alternative reading on this subject to Churchman. The methods part is somewhat outdated now.

Churchman, C. West, Russell L. Ackoff, and E. L. Arnoff. *Introduction to Operations Research*. New York: Wiley, 1957. The first complete text published on operations research. It contains one of the best treatments of the methodology of operations research, from problem formulation to implementation (Chapters 1 to 7, 20 to 22). Chapter 2 discusses the complete case history of an operations research project. The methods part is somewhat outdated now.

Rivett, Patrick. *Principles of Model Building*. New York: Wiley, 1972. "Model construction is an amalgam of theory and practice . . . When theory is dominant, elegance of mathematical exposition may lead to consequences which are incapable of implementation. On the other hand, hurried problem solving which conceals within it a technical ineptitude may mean that insight into the structure is lost. . . . This book seeks to explore the middle ground." (Quote from the book.) Short, easy to read for an audience with some familiarity in operations research techniques.

Sensitivity Analysis

Blanning, Robert W. "The Sources and Uses of Sensitivity Information," *Interfaces*, Vol. 4, Aug. 1974. Briefly reviews the various approaches of sensitivity analysis.

Implementation

Churchman, C. W., and A. H. Schainblatt. "The Researcher and the Manager: A Dialectic of Implementation," *Management Science*, Vol. 11, Feb. 1965. Conceptual analysis of the activities and attitudes by the operations researcher and the manager which are most appropriate to bring about a climate conducive to proper implementation. See also *Management Science*, October 1965, for a follow-up discussion on this very provocative paper, particularly the commentary by W. Alderson.

Schultz, R. L., and D. P. Slevin, eds. *Implementation of Operations Research/Management Science*. New York: Elsevier, 1975. A collection of papers on various facets of implementation. Read "Strategies for implementing systems studies" by A. Reisman and C. A. de Kluyver for a pragmatic view of how to increase the chances of successful implementation.

Urban, Glen L. "Building Models for Decision Makers," *Interfaces*, Vol. 4, May 1974. The paper draws on the literature along with practical experience to propose a process of building models that may have a high chance of being implemented.

PART ONE

Deterministic Models

CHAPTER TWO

Linear Programming—Introduction and Applications

Linear programming, or LP as it is called for short, is one of the most important tools used in operations research. Linear programming is a mathematical structure, involving particular mathematical assumptions, that can be solved using a standard solution technique called the *simplex method*. Any problem that satisfies the assumptions of this structure can be formulated as a linear program and solved by the simplex method. It is thus a general purpose model.

2-1 THE PROBLEM

Consider the following example, simplified for expository purposes. The management of a coal-fired electric power generating plant is studying the plant's operational setup in order to comply with the latest emission standards under the air pollution control laws. For the plant in question, maximum emission rates are

- maximum sulfur oxide emission: 3000 parts per million (PPM),
- maximum particulate emission (smoke): 12 kilograms/hour (kg/hr).

Coal is brought to the plant by railroad and dumped onto stockpiles near the plant. From there it is carried by a conveyor belt to the pulverizer unit, where it is pulverized and fed directly into the combustion chamber at the desired rate. The heat produced in the combustion chamber is used to make steam to drive the turbines. Two types of coal are used: grade A, which is a hard and clean-burning coal with a low sulfur content—fairly expensive though; and grade B, which is a cheap, relatively soft and smoky coal with a high sulfur content, as shown in Table 2-1.

Table 2-1. *Emission of pollutants*

Coal	Sulfur Oxides in Flue Gases	Particulate (emission/ton)
A	1800 PPM	0.5 kg
B	3800 PPM	1.0 kg

The thermal value in terms of steam produced is higher for coal A than for coal B, namely 24,000 pounds per ton for A against 20,000 pounds per ton for B. Since coal A is a hard coal, the pulverizer unit can handle at most 16 tons of coal A per hour, whereas it can pulverize up to 24 tons of coal B per hour. The conveyor loading system has a capacity of 20 tons per hour regardless of which coal is loaded.

Here is one of several questions management wants to have answered: Given the limits on emission of pollutants and the grades of coal available, what is the maximum possible output of electricity of the plant? The answer will enable management to determine the margin of safety available to meet peak demands for power.

2-2 DECISION VARIABLES

In the short run, the plant facilities are fixed. The only aspect of the problem that is controllable and that can be used to affect the output of the plant is the amount of each type of coal to be burned. Thus the *decision variables* of the problem are

- the amount of coal A used per hour, denoted by x_1,
- the amount of coal B used per hour, denoted by x_2.

In linear programming we often refer to the controllable aspects of a decision problem as *activities*. Hence x_1 and x_2 represent the *activity levels* of burning coal A and coal B, respectively.

LP ASSUMPTION 1: DIVISIBILITY

All variables can assume any real value.

Some activities in the real world can be varied in an almost continuous manner, i.e., they are infinitely divisible. For instance, the amount of coal burned per hour can be adjusted to any value, integer, or fraction, within reasonable limits. However, many real activities can only occur in integer values, such as the number of truck trips needed to haul a certain cargo from one location to another.

If the real activity is not infinitely divisible but the normal activity level is a large number in terms of its units of measurement, then the assumption of divisibility may serve as a convenient approximation. This usually means that the solution value for the activity is in the tens or larger. Fractional values of the solution are simply rounded to the nearest integer. However, if the normal activity level is relatively small, say less than 10, a solution technique is needed that guarantees an integer solution. This is not the case for linear programming. The more advanced techniques, called *integer programming*, form the topic of Chapter 18.

LP ASSUMPTION 2: NONNEGATIVITY CONDITIONS

All variables are nonnegative.

This assumption reflects the nature of most activities in the real world, where it rarely makes sense within an economic or engineering context to talk about negative activity levels. In our example, negative activity levels would represent a reversal of the process of generating electricity, i.e., converting electricity back into coal. However, this assumption is not a loss of generality. Any number—positive, zero, or negative—can be expressed as the algebraic difference of two nonnegative numbers. If an activity can occur at negative as well as at positive levels, such as buying or selling marketable securities, we introduce two decision variables for this activity, x^+ for nonnegative levels, and x^- for nonpositive levels. Their difference $x = x^+ - x^-$ represents the actual level of the activity. By this trick both x^+ and x^- are restricted to be nonnegative.

2-3 OBJECTIVE FUNCTION

Management's objective is to maximize the output of electricity of the plant. Since electricity is produced through steam and there is a direct relationship between steam produced and output of electricity, maximizing electricity output is equivalent to maximizing steam output. Therefore, management's objective can be reformulated as "Find the combination of fuels that maximizes steam output."

How much steam is produced for any arbitrary amount of coal used? A simple and systematic way of determining this is shown in Table 2-2.

Table 2-2. *Construction of objective function*

Coal	Steam (in lb/ton of fuel used)	Fuel Used/Hour	Steam Produced (in lb/hour)
A	24,000	x_1	$24{,}000x_1$
B	20,000	x_2	$20{,}000x_2$
	Total amount of steam/hour	=	$24{,}000x_1 + 20{,}000x_2$

It is rather cumbersome to write numbers that are in the thousands. Let us therefore *scale* this sum by a factor of 1000; i.e., rather than quoting the steam produced in pounds, we express it in units of 1000 pounds. Hence coal A produces 24 units and coal B 20 units of steam per ton of fuel. In terms of these new units, the total amount of steam produced per hour is

$$24x_1 + 20x_2 = z \tag{2-1}$$

The left-hand side of expression (2-1) is called the *objective function*, and z is the value of the objective function. The coefficients of the decision variables are referred to as *objective function coefficients*. The problem calls for finding values of x_1 and x_2 that maximize the value of z. Figure 2-1 depicts the objective function for arbitrary values of z in the form of *contour lines* of equal output.

Notice that in two-dimensional Euclidean space any given value of z yields a straight line for the objective function. As the value of z changes, this straight line moves parallel to itself. The objective function is thus seen to be *linear*.

LP ASSUMPTION 3: LINEARITY

All relationships between variables are linear. In linear programming this implies:

1. Proportionality of contributions. The individual contribution of each variable is strictly proportional to its value, and the factor of proportionality is constant over the entire range of values that the variable can assume.
2. Additivity of contributions. The total contribution of all variables is equal to the sum of the individual contributions regardless of the values of the variables.

Figure 2-1. *Objective function.*

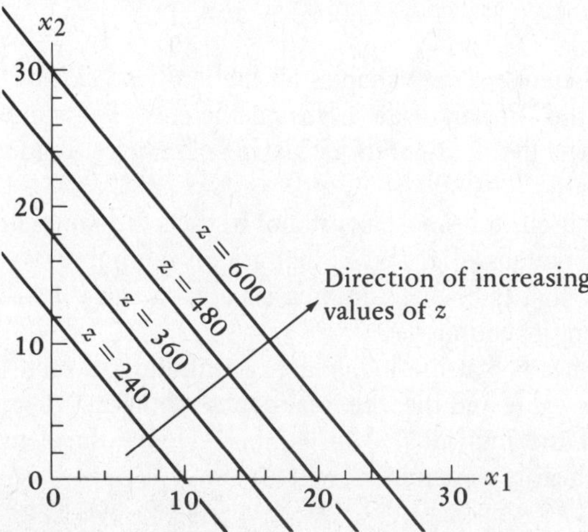

A relationship such as $z = (5x_1 + 3x_1^2 + 2x_2)$ or $z = (24x_1 + 20x_2$ for $x_1 \leq 5$ and $10 + 22x_1 + 20x_2$ for $x_1 > 5)$ would violate the condition of proportionality, whereas $z = (24x_1$ for $x_2 = 0$, $20x_2$ for $x_1 = 0$, and $22x_1 + 18x_2$ for $x_1 > 0$ and $x_2 > 0)$ would violate additivity.

Assumption 3 implies *constant returns to scale* and precludes *economies* or *diseconomies of scale*. In practice this assumption may not hold exactly, particularly for very small or very large values of the activity levels. However, if it holds approximately within the normal range of the solution values, we may use the linear programming model as a convenient and powerful approximation. This assumption also excludes *fixed charges* which are incurred for positive activity levels but not for zero levels. Note that it is sometimes possible to approximate diseconomies of scale by the use of several variables, as will be discussed in Section 17-4.

2-4 CONSTRAINTS

In addition to the nonnegativity conditions, the activity levels are restricted by various constraints which may be of physical, economic, or legal nature.

Constraint on particulate emission

The maximum amount of smoke that the plant is allowed to emit per hour is limited to 12 kg. According to Table 2-1, each ton of coal A produces 0.5 kg of smoke, and each ton of coal B produces 1 kg of smoke. If the plant burns x_1 tons of coal A and x_2 tons of coal B, the total amount of smoke emitted from both coals is equal to

$$0.5x_1 + x_2 \qquad \text{(kg/hr)}$$

This sum cannot exceed 12 kg/hr. We thus have the following *inequality constraint*:

$$0.5x_1 + x_2 \leq 12 \tag{2-2}$$

The coefficients of the variables on the left-hand side of the inequality sign are referred to as the *left-hand-side (LHS)* coefficients. The constant to the right of the inequality sign is the *right-hand-side (RHS) parameter*. Figure 2-2 depicts this constraint graphically.

Taken by itself, the smoke constraint restricts the values of the decision variables to those combinations of x_1 and x_2 that are on the line $0.5x_1 + x_2 = 12$ or to the left and below that line. Such an area is called a *closed half-space*—closed because it includes all of its boundaries.

We note again that the individual contribution of each variable is strictly proportional to its value and that the total contribution toward smoke emission is equal to the sum of the individual contributions. Hence the constraint satisfies the assumption of linearity as required by Assumption 3.

Figure 2-2. *Smoke constraint.*

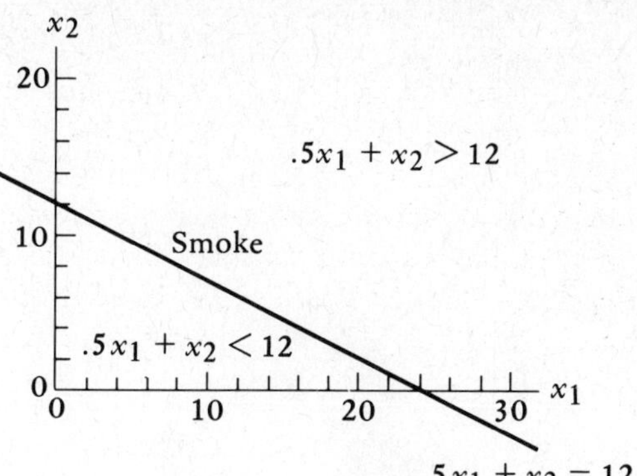

Constraint on loading facilities

The conveyor system transporting coal from the stockpiles to the pulverizer has an hourly capacity of 20 tons. The total number of tons loaded per hour is equal to the sum of the two decision variables. Therefore, the loading constraint reads

$$x_1 + x_2 \leqslant 20 \tag{2-3}$$

You should show this constraint graphically.

Constraint on pulverizer unit

The maximum pulverizer capacity is 16 tons per hour for coal A or 24 tons per hour for coal B. In other words, it takes $\frac{1}{16}$ of an hour to pulverize one ton of coal A and $\frac{1}{24}$ of an hour to pulverize one ton of coal B. If the solution calls for a combination of both coals, the amount of time taken to pulverize a mixture of x_1 tons of coal A and x_2 tons of coal B is $(\frac{1}{16})\ x_1 + (\frac{1}{24})\ x_2$. Only those combinations of x_1 and x_2 which require at most 1 hour of time are admissible. Hence, the pulverizer constraint reads

$$\tfrac{1}{16}x_1 + \tfrac{1}{24}x_2 \leqslant 1 \tag{2-4}$$

Note how we overcame the difficulty introduced by different maximum rates. We translated these rates into length of time needed per ton and expressed the constraint in terms of time rather than capacity.

Constraint on sulfur oxide emission

The maximum sulfur oxide emission is not to exceed 3000 PPM at any time. Given that the two coals are burned simultaneously, we assume that the combination of x_1 tons of coal A and x_2 tons of coal B per hour is fed into the combustion chamber as a homogeneous mixture. $x_1/(x_1 + x_2)$ of the mixture is coal A with a sulfur oxide

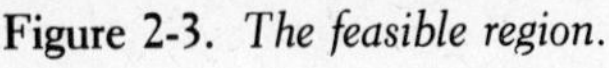

Figure 2-3. *The feasible region.*

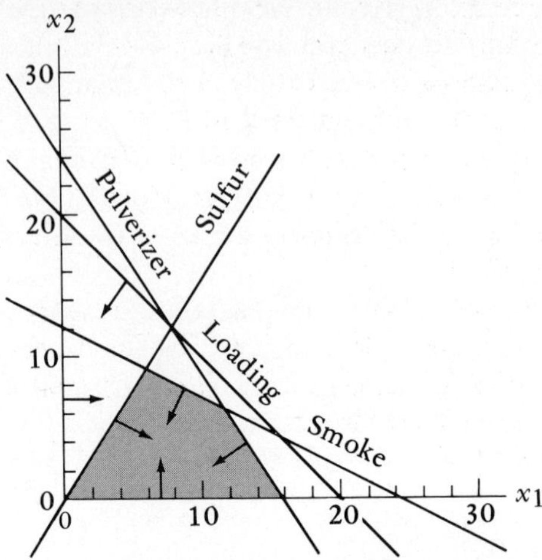

emission rate of 1800 PPM, and $x_2/(x_1 + x_2)$ of it is coal B with an emission rate of 3800 PPM. The emission rate of the mixture is equal to the weighted average of the individual emission rates, where the fractions of each coal used serve as weights. This weighted average cannot exceed 3000 PPM:

$$\text{weighted average emission rate} \leq 3000 \text{ PPM}$$

or

$$1800\left(\frac{x_1}{x_1 + x_2}\right) + 3800\left(\frac{x_2}{x_1 + x_2}\right) \leq 3000$$

Multiplying both sides of the inequality by $(x_1 + x_2)$ and rearranging terms, we get the sulfur constraint:

(2-5) $$1200x_1 - 800x_2 \geq 0$$

All four constraints are shown simultaneously in Figure 2-3.

2-5 THE FEASIBLE REGION

To be an admissible solution, a combination of activity levels must satisfy simultaneously all constraints, including the nonnegativity conditions. Such a solution is called a *feasible solution* to the problem. The set of all feasible solutions forms the *feasible region*. A solution that does not fall in this region is an *infeasible solution*. Figure 2-3 shows all four constraints and the nonnegativity conditions on the same graph. Inspection of the arrows shows that only those combinations of activity levels that are in the shaded area or its boundary satisfy all constraints simultaneously. This area therefore forms the feasible region.

Since each constraint and each nonnegativity condition represents a closed half-space, the feasible region is given by the *intersection* of these closed half-spaces. Note that the feasible region does not depend on the objective function. This is an interesting property of most operations research models and has important effects on the solution method and the properties of the optimal solution.

If the boundary of a constraint has no point in common with the feasible region, then this constraint is *redundant*. It can be dropped from further consideration. It will never be limiting on the values of the decision variables. Is there a redundant constraint in our problem?

In practice, where a problem may have hundreds of constraints and hundreds of variables, it is seldom possible to identify whether or not a constraint is redundant. Fortunately, the simplex method of solving linear programs works irrespective of whether the formulation contains redundant constraints.

2-6 GRAPHICAL SOLUTION

Let us now superimpose the objective function as shown in Figure 2-1 onto the graph of Figure 2-3. This gives us Figure 2-4. The contour lines for a steam output of $z = 240$ and $z = 360$ both have a segment that falls inside the feasible region, whereas the contour line for $z = 480$ has no point in common with the feasible region. Since our objective is to maximize the steam output of the plant, we want to find the highest contour line for z that contains at least one feasible solution. Consider the line given by $z = 408$ passing through point A. Note that if z is increased by an infinitesimal amount beyond 408, the resulting line has no point in common with the feasible region; whereas if z is decreased by an infinitesimal amount below 408, the number of feasible solutions with a value higher than z is infinite. Hence $z = 408$ is the maximal value of the objective function that yields a feasible solution.

The optimal values of the decision variables can be read as $x_1 = 12$ and $x_2 = 6$. A combination of 12 tons of coal A and 6 tons of coal B per hour maximizes the steam output of the plant within the physical and legal restrictions imposed on the decision variables. Verify that this solution corresponds to a value of $z = 408$.

It seems intuitively obvious that the optimal solution will always occur at the boundary of the feasible region, either at a *corner point* (*extreme point*) or all along one of the edges, and thus again at an extreme point. As we shall see in Section 2-9, it is the *slope* of the objective function that determines where on the boundary the optimal solution actually occurs.

If the problem called for the minimization of the objective function, how would you change the graphical procedure to find the optimal solution? Say we want to find the minimum-cost solution to produce a steam output of at least 216 units per hour, and the cost per ton is \$18 for coal A and \$15 for coal B. Reformulate the problem to include an output constraint and the new objective function and find the least-cost solution graphically.

Finally, let us point out that not all linear programming problems have happy endings. Two other types of solutions may occur occasionally. First, the constraints

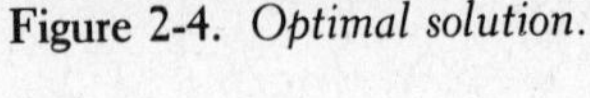

Figure 2-4. *Optimal solution.*

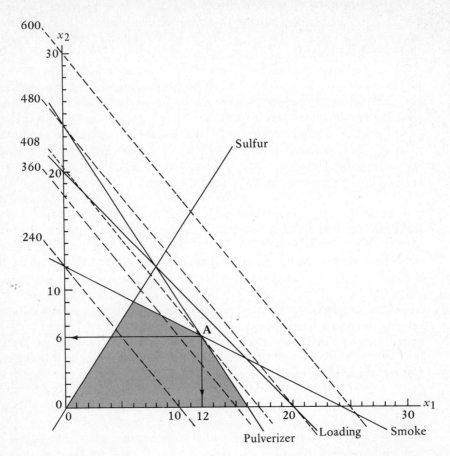

may be inconsistent in the sense that no feasible solution exists—the problem is *infeasible*. Second, the feasible region may be open in some direction such that the objective function can be increased indefinitely and no finite solution exists—the solution is *unbounded*. Note though that few real problems have infeasible or unbounded solutions. Often such solutions are the result of mistakes or misrepresentations in the mathematical formulation.

At this point we urge you to check your understanding by doing the formulation, parts (a) and (b), in exercises 2.1 to 2.4.

2-7 MATHEMATICAL SUMMARY

Let us now summarize the problem in mathematical form.

Objective function:

Determine values for x_1 and x_2 that

$$\text{maximize } z = 24x_1 + 20x_2$$

Constraints:

(2-6)

$$\begin{aligned}
\text{subject to} \quad 0.5x_1 + x_2 &\leq 12 && \text{(smoke)}\\
x_1 + x_2 &\leq 20 && \text{(loading)}\\
\tfrac{1}{16}x_1 + \tfrac{1}{24}x_2 &\leq 1 && \text{(pulverizer)}\\
1200x_1 - 800x_2 &\geq 0 && \text{(sulfur)}
\end{aligned}$$

Nonnegativity conditions:

$$x_1 \geq 0, \qquad x_2 \geq 0$$

In general, if we denote x_j as the value of the jth activity or variable, a_{ij} as the LHS coefficient of variable j in constraint i, b_i as the RHS parameter of the ith constraint, and c_j as the objective function coefficient of the jth variable, then the structure of a linear program is as follows:

Determine values for x_j, $j = 1, 2, \ldots, n$, that

(2-7)

$$\begin{aligned}
&\text{maximize } z = \sum_j c_j x_j\\
&\text{subject to} \quad \sum_j a_{ij} x_j [\leq \text{ or } = \text{ or } \geq] b_i, \qquad i = 1, 2, \ldots, m\\
&\text{and} \quad x_j \geq 0, \qquad j = 1, 2, \ldots, n
\end{aligned}$$

where n is the number of variables, m is the number of constraints, and the constraints may be equalities or inequalities of the type $\leq$ or $\geq$.

2-8 SLACK VARIABLES

For any given feasible solution, the difference between the LHS and the RHS of a constraint is called the amount of *slack* (for $\leq$ inequalities) or *surplus* (for $\geq$ inequalities). It is often convenient to show this difference explicitly by introducing an additional variable into each constraint. These variables are called *slack* or *surplus variables*. For convenience, we shall use the term *slack variables* for both. They are subject to the same assumptions of divisibility and nonnegativity as the decision variables. Each constraint is then converted to an equality.

Let x_{i+2} be the slack variable for the ith constraint in our example. Introducing them into our constraints, we get the following four equalities:

(2-2A) $$0.5x_1 + x_2 + x_3 = 12 \qquad \text{(smoke)}$$

(2-3A) $$x_1 + x_2 + x_4 = 20 \qquad \text{(loading)}$$

$$\text{(2-4A)} \qquad \tfrac{1}{16}x_1 + \tfrac{1}{24}x_2 \qquad + x_5 \qquad = 1 \qquad \text{(pulverizer)}$$

$$\text{(2-5A)} \qquad 1200x_1 - 800x_2 \qquad - x_6 = 0 \qquad \text{(sulfur)}$$

Why is the slack variable for the sulfur constraint (2-5A) subtracted from the LHS rather than added, as for the other three constraints?

The slack variables can often be interpreted as *unused resources* or *unused capacity* for a given solution. For instance, x_3 is the amount of unused smoke emission capacity and x_4 the amount of unused loading capacity. What is the interpretation for x_5? Because of the way the sulfur constraint was obtained, there is no simple interpretation for x_6. For resource constraints, each such equality says that the amount of resources or capacity used by the activities plus the unused amount of resources or capacity is equal to the total available amount of resources or capacity.

If a slack variable is equal to zero in a feasible solution, the corresponding constraint is *binding*. If a slack variable is positive, the corresponding constraint is *not binding*, or *slack*. By substituting the values of the decision variables into each constraint, verify that we have for the optimal solution:

Constraint	Smoke	Loading	Pulverizer	Sulfur
Amount of slack	0	2	0	9600
Status of constraint	binding	slack	binding	slack

2-9 SENSITIVITY ANALYSIS

Let us next consider some "what if" questions. We mentioned earlier that the slope of the objective function determines where the optimal solution occurs. The slope of the objective function is determined by the objective function coefficients. What happens if the value of one of the objective function coefficients changes?

Assume that the thermal value of coal A is equivalent to 32,000 pounds of steam rather than 24,000, with all other coefficients remaining at their previous values. The objective function changes to

$$\text{(2-8)} \qquad \text{maximize } 32x_1 + 20x_2$$

This new objective function is shown in Figure 2-5 as the broken line for the optimal value of z. The optimal original objective function (2-1) is shown as dotted. The maximal value of (2-8) occurs at point B.

A change in the value of an objective function coefficient—with all other objective function coefficients remaining unchanged—causes a change in the slope of the objective function. If the change in the slope is sufficiently large, the optimal solution shifts to another extreme point of the feasible region.

Let us study this effect more closely. What is the largest possible value of the original objective function coefficient of x_1, denoted by c_1, before the optimal solution

Figure 2-5. *Alternative objective function.*

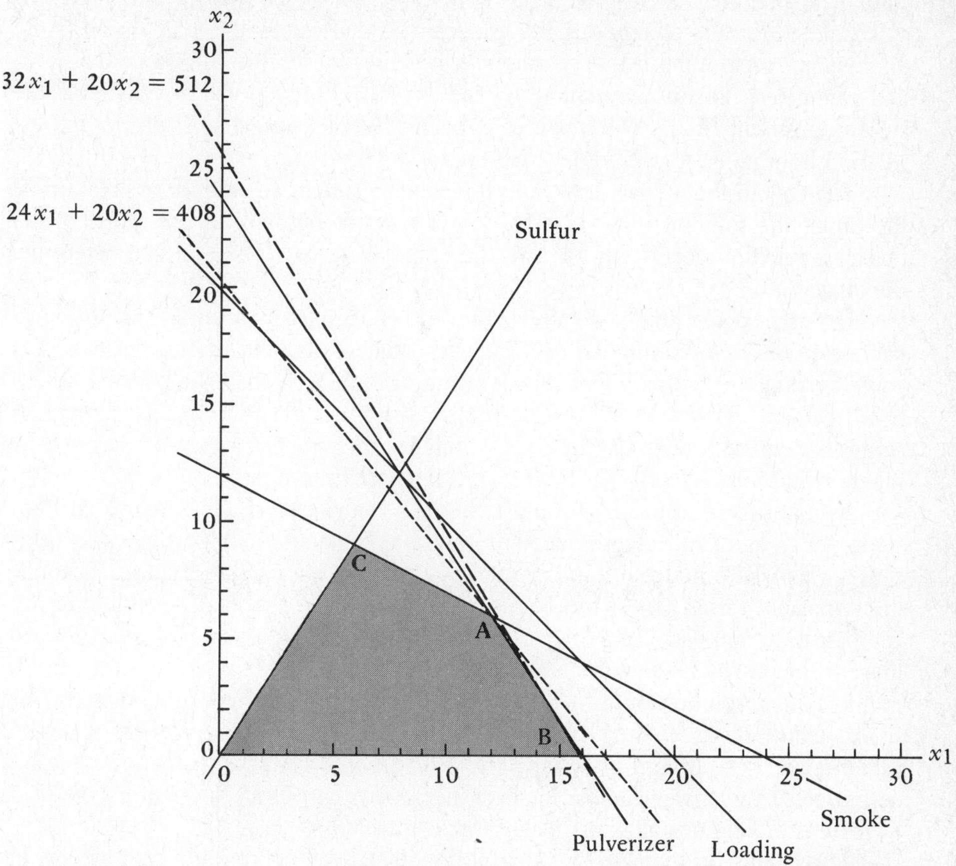

shifts from point A to point B? From Figure 2-5 we see that, as c_1 is increased, the slope of the maximal value of the objective function gets closer and closer to the slope of the boundary of the pulverizer constraint and will ultimately coincide with the pulverizer constraint. At that value of c_1, any point along the line from A to B is optimal; i.e., we obtain *alternative optimal solutions*, all with the same value of z. (Note that in many real-life problems alternative optimal solutions may occur naturally.) If c_1 is increased slightly more, the optimal solution will occur only at point B. Thus, provided c_1 is no greater than the value needed to make the objective function parallel to the pulverizer constraint, the optimal solution will remain at A. The objective function and pulverizer constraint are parallel when their slopes are the same. This implies that the ratio of the coefficients for the lines is the same. So we require that

$$\frac{c_1}{1/16} = \frac{20}{1/24} = 480$$

This yields $c_1 = 30$. For an increase in c_1 beyond 30, the optimal solution will shift from A to B. For $c_1 = 30$ the objective function $30x_1 + 20x_2$ assumes its maximal value of 480 for any point along the line from A to B, including both A and B. By an analogous reasoning it follows that if c_1 is decreased to 10—all other coefficients and parameters remaining unchanged—the objective function will be parallel to the smoke constraint (2-2). A decrease of c_1 below 10 will cause a shift of the optimal solution from point A to point C. (See Figure 2-5.)

The conclusion we can draw from this exercise is that, all other things remaining the same, the solution $x_1 = 12$ and $x_2 = 6$ remains optimal for any value of the objective function coefficient for x_1 in the range $10 \leq c_1 \leq 30$. Can you determine the range on c_2?

Let us next see how the optimal solution is affected by a change in the RHS parameter of a constraint. To motivate this analysis assume that management is contemplating the installation of emission control equipment that would reduce smoke by 20 percent. This would allow the legal emission standards to be met by an uncontrolled emission of smoke from the combustion chamber of up to 15 kg/hr. How much would this be worth per hour in increased steam output?

Assume first that the maximum permissible smoke emission is increased from 12 kg to 13 kg/hr, all other coefficients and parameters remaining the same. This causes a parallel upward shift in the smoke constraint, as shown in Figure 2-6. Since this constraint forms part of the boundary of the feasible region, the feasible region is enlarged by the dark shaded area. In this enlarged feasible region, $z = 408$ is no longer the optimal value of the objective function—the best value is now at point D. So the optimal solution shifts from A to D. This change occurs because originally the smoke constraint is binding at point A. The new optimal values of the decision variables are $x_1 = 11$ and $x_2 = 7.5$. The decrease in x_1 causes a reduction in steam output of 24 units, whereas the increase in x_2 increases output by 30 units. The net increase is 6. The new maximal value of z is thus $408 + 6 = 414$.

The change in the optimal value of the objective function for a unit change in the RHS parameter of a constraint is called the *shadow price* or *imputed value* of the constraint. The shadow price of the smoke constraint (2-2) is 6.

What happens if the maximum smoke emission is further relaxed to 14, 15, 16, and 17 kg/hr? The dotted lines in Figure 2-6 show how the smoke constraint shifts upward, adding an additional area to the feasible region for each such shift up to a maximum of 16. You should confirm that the resulting changes in the decision variables increase the maximal value of the objective function by 6 units for each unit increase in the RHS parameter.

For an increase of the RHS beyond 16, the smoke constraint becomes redundant. The optimal solution is now restricted by the pulverizer and sulfur constraints (as well as by the loading constraint). Hence, for values of the RHS parameter of the smoke constraint larger than 16, the shadow price of that constraint is zero.

Our original question asked for the increase in steam output for a change in the permissible smoke level from 12 to 15 kg/hr. This will be 3×6 or 18 units of steam/hr.

What is the shadow price of a constraint that not binding in the optimal

Figure 2-6. *Sensitivity analysis for RHS parameters.*

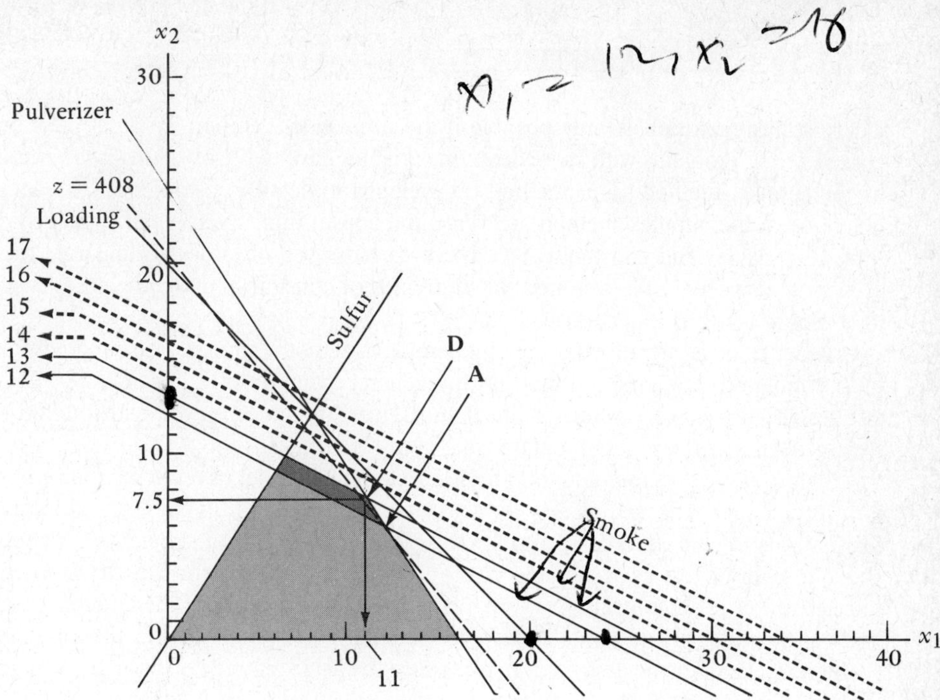

solution? Clearly, if a portion of a resource remains unused—the corresponding slack variable is positive—additional amounts of that resource have no value. They would only increase the amount of slack. Hence, the shadow price of such a constraint is zero. Find the shadow prices for the remaining constraints.

Observe the interesting complementarity between the value of the shadow price of a constraint and the slack variable associated with the same constraint:

Status of constraint	Value of shadow price	Value of slack variable
binding	(usually) positive	zero
not binding	zero	(usually) positive

We hedge somewhat by saying "usually positive." We shall see in Chapter 4 that a more accurate statement is "nonnegative."

Shadow prices provide management with valuable information about the benefits that can be gained by relaxing constraints. If these benefits exceed the costs incurred for relaxing a given constraint, then such changes are attractive.

You are now ready to do parts (c) through (e) of exercises 2.1 to 2.4.

2-10 SOLUTION BY COMPUTER

The graphical solution is only possible if the number of decision variables does not exceed 2 (3?). Problems with more decision variables have to be solved mathematically by the simplex method. This method is developed in detail in Chapter 3. The computations of the simplex method are very time-consuming. Even small problems of 5 to 10 variables and constraints take hours to be solved on a desk calculator. Real problems, however, have hundreds or thousands of constraints and variables. Access to computers is thus a necessity.

Because of its iterative nature, the simplex method can easily be programmed for a computer. Any problem that has the general structure of expressions (2-7) and satisfies the three assumptions of linear programming can be solved with the aid of such general purpose linear programming computer codes.

Before we discuss the input into these computer codes, let us represent the general form of a linear program, as it is shown by expressions (2-7), in the form of a table that has one row for each constraint plus an additional row for the objective function, and one column for each variable plus an additional column for the RHS. At the intersection of each constraint row and variable column, we insert the corresponding LHS coefficient. In the bottom row we insert the corresponding objective function coefficients, and in the last column we show the RHS parameters and the type of constraint ($\leq$ or $=$ or $\geq$). This table is commonly referred to as the *linear program in detached coefficient form*. Instead of indicating the type of relationship in the column for the RHS, it is often convenient to add additional columns for the slack variables. Each constraint is then implied as an equality. This has been done in Table 2-3 for the original power plant capacity problem.

Table 2-3. *Linear program in detached coefficient form*

	Variable						
Constraint	x_1	x_2	x_3	x_4	x_5	x_6	RHS
(2-2A)	0.5	1	1	0	0	0	12
(2-3A)	1	1	0	1	0	0	20
(2-4A)	$\frac{1}{16}$	$\frac{1}{24}$	0	0	1	0	1
(2-5A)	1200	-800	0	0	0	-1	0
Obj. function	24	20	0	0	0	0	maximize

This table contains all of the input data needed for most LP computer codes. Therefore, the computer has to be told the size of the table (i.e., the number of decision plus slack variables and the number of constraints); the value of each entry in the table, usually identified by its row name and column name; and whether the objective function is to be minimized or maximized.

Rows and columns are usually identified by *mnemonic* names, i.e., words or abbreviations that immediately suggest what activity or constraint is being referred to. This avoids a lengthy translation process if the numbers of variables and constraints are large. For our example we could use the following names.

Constraint (2-2A): SMOKE	Variable x_1: ACOAL
(2-3A): LOAD	x_2: BCOAL
(2-4A): PULVER	x_3: SMOKSL
(2-5A): SULFUR	x_4: LOADSL
	x_5: PULVSL
	x_6: SULFSL

We have solved this problem using the simple LP code "LPGOGO," described in Chapter 5 of Daellenbach and Bell, *User's Guide to Linear Programming* (see References). This code typically requires that each nonzero entry of Table 2-3 be specified on a separate card. Figure 2-7 shows the printout of the optimal solution. The code first reproduces the input data. This is a useful feature, since it allows us to check whether the problem actually solved was the one we intended to solve!

Small rounding errors may occur when the data are read into the computer as well as during the computations of the simplex method. As a consequence the optimal solution printed may contain small rounding errors, as is the case here.

In addition to the optimal values of the variables and the objective function, LPGOGO also provides a considerable amount of information useful for sensitivity analysis. In particular, the shadow price of each constraint is shown under the heading "IMPUTED VALUE." The range of the RHS parameter over which each shadow price is valid, all other inputs remaining unchanged, is shown under the headings "DECREASE" and "INCREASE." For instance, the shadow price of 6.0 of the SMOKE constraint is valid for a decrease of up to 4 kg and an increase of up to 4 kg from the original value of 12 kg/hr, confirming our earlier results obtained graphically. On the other hand, the shadow price of the PULVER constraint is only valid for a decrease of up to $\frac{1}{4}$ hour or an increase of up to $\frac{1}{6}$ hour. The effect of changes in RHS parameters on the variables, however, is not shown.

The printout also provides sensitivity analysis with respect to the objective function coefficients of variables that have a zero value in the optimal solution. The numbers listed under the heading "DELTAJ" represent the change in the value of the objective function if the corresponding variable—which at present has a zero value—were forced to a value of one. Alternatively, the negative of the DELTAJ value is the amount by which the objective function coefficient of the corresponding variable would have to increase to make this variable a candidate to enter alternative optimal solutions.

In our example only the slack variables have nonzero DELTAJ values. Therefore, let us look at an expanded version of the power generating capacity problem.

Figure 2-7. *Computer printout of optimal solution using LPGOGO.*

```
MAXIMUM POWER GENERATING CAPACITY PROBLEM
  4    6
SMOKE                12.000000
LOAD                 20.000000
PULVER                1.000000
SULFUR                0.0
          ACOAL      24.000000
          BCOAL      20.000000
          SMOKSL      0.0
          LOADSL      0.0
          PULVSL      0.0
          SULFSL      0.0
SMOKE     ACOAL       0.500000
SMOKE     BCOAL       1.000000
SMOKE     SMOKSL      1.000000
LOAD      ACOAL       1.000000
LOAD      BCOAL       1.000000
LOAD      LOADSL      1.000000
PULVER    ACOAL       0.062500
PULVER    BCOAL       0.041667
PULVER    PULVSL      1.000000
SULFUR    ACOAL    1200.000000
SULFUR    BCOAL    -800.000000
SULFUR    SULFSL     -1.000000
SOLVE

SOLUTION OPTIMAL AFTER          7 ITERATIONS
MAXIMAL OBJECTIVE =          407.999268
 VARIABLE   STATUS    OPTIMAL VALUE        DELTAJ
   ACOAL    BASIC          11.99996         -0.0
   BCOAL    BASIC           6.00002         -0.0
   SMOKSL                   0.0             -5.99994
   LOADSL   BASIC           2.00002         -0.0
   PULVSL                   0.0           -336.00000
   SULFSL   BASIC        9599.93750          0.0

CONSTRAINT STATUS    IMPUTED VALUE        DECREASE           INCREASE
   SMOKE    BINDNG          5.99994        4.00001            3.99995
   LOAD     SLACK           0.0            2.00002           OPEN
   PULVER   BINDNG        336.00000        0.25000            0.16667
   SULFUR   SLACK           0.00000       OPEN             9599.93750
```


2-11 AN EXPANDED VERSION OF THE POWER PLANT CAPACITY PROBLEM

The plant is offered a third type of fuel, grade C coal, that results in a sulfur oxide emission rate of 2000 PPM, a smoke emission rate of 0.8 kg/ton of fuel burnt, and requires $\frac{1}{20}$ hour each of pulverizer and loader capacity per ton. Its thermal value is the equivalent of 21,000 lb of steam per ton of fuel. Would it be advantageous for the plant to use this fuel?

Let us reformulate the problem with this third coal. Let x_3 be the number of tons per hour of coal C used. Then

$$
\begin{aligned}
&\text{maximize} && 24x_1 + 20x_2 + 21x_3 && \\
&\text{subject to} && 0.5x_1 + x_2 + 0.8x_3 \leq 12 && \text{(smoke)} \\
\text{(2-9)}\quad & && x_1 + x_2 + x_3 \leq 20 && \text{(loading)} \\
& && \tfrac{1}{16}x_1 + \tfrac{1}{24}x_2 + \tfrac{1}{20}x_3 \leq 1 && \text{(pulverizer)} \\
& && 1200x_1 - 800x_2 + 1000x_3 \geq 0 && \text{(sulfur)} \\
& && x_1 \geq 0,\ x_2 \geq 0,\ x_3 \geq 0 &&
\end{aligned}
$$

Figure 2-8 reproduces the computer printout of the optimal solution for this expanded version. Note that we have again converted all constraints to equalities by introducing slack variables. The listing of the input data has been omitted. The optimal solution is unchanged. Under the present conditions, it is not advantageous to use coal C. In fact, according to the DELTAJ value of variable CCOAL (x_3), the objective function would change by -0.6, a decrease from 408 to 407.4 units of steam, if $x_3 = 1$. Alternatively, the thermal value of coal C would need to be 600 lbs/ton greater or the objective function coefficient of x_3 would need to be 21.6 rather than 21 (larger by the negative of -0.6) before variable x_3 could assume positive values in alternative optimal solutions.

Figure 2-8. *Expanded version of power plant capacity problem.*

```
SOLUTION OPTIMAL AFTER          7 ITERATIONS
MAXIMAL OBJECTIVE =        407.999512
 VARIABLE   STATUS    OPTIMAL VALUE          DELTAJ
   ACOAL    BASIC          12.00000            -0.0
   BCOAL    BASIC           6.00000            -0.0
   CCOAL                    0.0                -0.60001
   SMOKSL                   0.0                -6.00000
   LOADSL   BASIC           2.00001            -0.0
   PULVSL                   0.0              -335.99976
   SULFSL   BASIC        9599.99609             0.0

CONSTRAINT STATUS     IMPUTED VALUE          DECREASE             INCREASE
   SMOKE    BINDNG          6.00000             4.00000              4.00000
   LOAD     SLACK           0.0                 2.00001             OPEN
   PULVER   BINDNG        335.99976             0.25000              0.16667
   SULFUR   SLACK           0.00000            OPEN               9599.99609
```

There was really no need to solve the expanded version of the problem to get this result. The shadow prices of the original problem give us all the required information. Let us arbitrarily decide to use one ton of coal C and determine its effect on the objective function. Setting $x_3 = 1$ is equivalent to reducing the RHS parameters of the four constraints of the original problem as follows:

$$0.5x_1 + x_2 \leq (12 - 0.8) \text{ or } 11.2 \qquad \text{(smoke)}$$

$$x_1 + x_2 \leq (20 - 1) \text{ or } 19 \qquad \text{(loading)}$$

$$\tfrac{1}{16}x_1 + \tfrac{1}{24}x_2 \leq (1.0 - 1/20) \text{ or } 19/20 \qquad \text{(pulverizer)}$$

$$1200x_1 - 800x_2 \geq (0 - 1000) \text{ or } -1000 \qquad \text{(sulfur)}$$

The loading constraint and the sulfur constraint are both slack, and their shadow prices are therefore zero. But 1/20 hour of pulverizer capacity reduction results in a decrease of 1/20 × 336, or 16.8, in the value of the objective function, and a reduction of 0.8 kg of the maximum smoke emission decreases the value of the objective function by 0.8 × 6, or 4.8. The total decrease of the objective function value is equal to the sum of 16.8 plus 4.8, or 21.6 units of steam. On the other hand, the additional steam output gained per hour by burning one ton of coal C is only 21 units. The net loss in steam output is thus 0.6 units, confirming our earlier finding.

Try your hand now with exercises 2.5 and 2.6.

2-12 A PRODUCTION SCHEDULING PROBLEM

A metal processing plant receives an order to produce 10,000 casings. The contract specifies a sale price of $4.85 per casing. The products design engineer proposes four alternative designs for the casings, resulting in different machine time usages and material costs. The material costs differ because of varying amounts of wastage.

Table 2-4. *Input data for casing production*

Production Design	Machine Time (in minutes)				Material Cost	Rejects Produced
	Cutting	Forming	Welding	Finishing		
1	0.40	0.70	1.00	0.50	$3,355	3%
2	0.80	1.00	0.40	0.30	$4.150	1%
3	0.35	0.60	1.20	0.75	$3.005	4%
4	0.70	0.80	0.60	0.55	$3.705	2%
Cost/minute	$0.20	$0.30	$0.15	$0.10		

The customer wants to receive delivery within one month of signing of the contract. On the basis of the present production commitments, the production manager forecasts that the plant has excess capacities of 90 hours of cutting machine time, 140 hours of forming machine time, 154 hours of welding time, and 120 hours of finishing time. The production engineer's problem is to determine which designs to use so as to guarantee delivery within the contractual arrangement.

What should we use as the firm's objective? The usual objective in problems of this sort is the maximization of profits. In this example the relevant measure of profit is given as the difference between gross revenues and all variable costs.

What aspects provide the decision variables? The production manager is given four designs that each yield exactly the same end product from the user's point of view. The choice thus boils down to which combination of designs to use—in particular, how many casings of each design to produce. Let x_j denote the number of casings of design j produced. This choice cannot be arbitrary. In order for the company to guarantee delivery on the due date, the machine usages have to be within the predicted excess capacities. Furthermore, the total number of good casings produced has to be equal to 10,000.

Total output constraint

From past experience, it is possible to predict the average fraction of defectives resulting from each product design. This is shown in the last column of Table 2-4. To satisfy the output requirement, only good casings can be counted. So if x_1 casings of design 1 are scheduled, and on the average 3 percent defectives are produced or 97 percent are expected to be good casings, then $0.97x_1$ is the number of good casings of design 1 obtained. Using the same reasoning for all four designs we require that

[expected total number of good casings produced] = [number of good casings required]

$$0.97x_1 + 0.99x_2 + 0.96x_3 + 0.98x_4 = 10{,}000 \qquad (2\text{-}10)$$

(Note that in practice it might be advisable to add some small safety margin.)

Machine time constraints

The machine time used for each operation cannot be more than the excess time available within the delivery period. For instance, each unit of design 1 requires 0.4 minutes of cutting time, so x_1 units require $0.4x_1$ minutes. For all four designs, the amount of cutting time needed is

$$0.4x_1 + 0.8x_2 + 0.35x_3 + 0.7x_4$$

The amount of cutting time available is 90 hours, or 5400 minutes. Thus, we get the following relation:

Cutting time constraint:

$$0.4x_1 + 0.8x_2 + 0.35x_3 + 0.74x_4 \leq 5400 \qquad (2\text{-}11)$$

Similarly, for the other three operations:

Forming time constraint:

$$0.7x_1 + 1.0x_2 + 0.6x_3 + 0.8x_4 \leq 8400 \qquad (2\text{-}12)$$

Welding time constraint:

(2-13) $$1.0x_1 + 0.4x_2 + 1.20x_3 + 0.6x_4 \leq 9240$$

Finishing time constraint:

(2-14) $$0.5x_1 + 0.3x_2 + 0.75x_3 + 0.55x_4 \leq 7200$$

To determine the profits we need the unit costs. These are made up of the variable machine cost for each operation and the material cost. Table 2-5 shows the detailed components for each design.

Table 2-5. *Unit profits rounded to $\frac{1}{2}$ cent*

Design	1	2	3	4
Costs: Materials	\$3.355	\$4.150	\$3.005	\$3.705
Cutting time	0.08	0.16	0.07	0.14
Forming time	0.21	0.30	0.18	0.24
Welding time	0.15	0.06	0.18	0.09
Finishing time	0.05	0.03	0.075	0.055
Total unit cost	3.845	4.700	3.510	4.230

Total profits are given by total revenues minus total costs:

$$4.85(10{,}000) - 3.845x_1 - 4.7x_2 - 3.51x_3 - 4.23x_4$$

Substituting the left-hand side of expression (2-10) for 10,000, we get

$$4.85(0.97x_1 + 0.99x_2 + 0.96x_3 + 0.98x_4) - 3.845x_1 - 4.7x_2 - 3.51x_3 - 4.23x_4$$

Collecting terms and rounding to the nearest $\frac{1}{2}$ cent, we finally obtain the

Objective function:

(2-15) $$\text{maximize } 0.86x_1 + 0.1x_2 + 1.145x_3 + 0.525x_4$$

Nonnegativity conditions:

$$x_j \geq 0, \qquad j = 1,2,3,4$$

We have solved this problem using the LP code LPGOGO. Figure 2-9 reproduces the computer printout of the optimal solution. Note that for the computer solution we introduced slack variables for the machine time constraints, which were all $\leq$ inequalities. With this change the problem has 8 variables and 5 equality constraints. Constraints and variables are given mnemonic names that are self-explanatory.

The optimal solution provides that approximately 476 units of design 1, 4776 units of design 3, 5054 units of design 4, and no units of design 2 are produced at

Figure 2-9. *Computer printout of optimal solution to production scheduling problem.*

```
SOLUTION OPTIMAL AFTER        7 ITERATIONS
MAXIMAL OBJECTIVE =      8531.603325
 VARIABLE   STATUS    OPTIMAL VALUE        DELTAJ
   DES1     BASIC          476.00950          0.00000
   DES2                      0.00000         -0.19559
   DES3     BASIC         4776.24703          0.00000
   DES4     BASIC         5054.15677          0.00000
   CUTSL                     0.00000         -1.11188
   FORMSL   BASIC         1157.71971          0.00000
   WELDSL                    0.00000         -1.63985
   FINSL    BASIC          600.02375          0.00000

CONSTRAINT STATUS     IMPUTED VALUE        DECREASE          INCREASE
   OUTPUT   BINDNG          -1.26247          31.80952        437.13043
   CUT      BINDNG           1.11188         505.22613         33.40000
   FORM     SLACK            0.00000        1157.71971         OPEN
   WELD     BINDNG           1.63985         700.62718         60.91185
   FINISH   SLACK            0.00000         600.02375         OPEN
```

a total profit of \$8531.60. All available cutting and welding machine time is used up, whereas there still remain about 1158 minutes of forming machine time and 600 minutes of finishing machine time.

From the imputed value (our shadow prices for the constraints), we can infer that, at the margin, additional cutting machine time has a value of \$1.11 per minute, and additional welding time is valued at \$1.64 per minute. These shadow prices are valid for increases of, respectively, 33 and 61 minutes only. For instance, if 60 more minutes of welding machine time were available, profits would increase by 60 × \$1.64, or \$98.40. Such information may be highly useful for deciding whether or not to schedule overtime and on which machines.

How are profits affected if the total output of good parts has to be increased by 100 units? The answer to this question is supplied by the shadow price of the total output constraint. For a unit increase in the RHS of constraint (2-10), profits change by \$ − 1.26. In other words, total profit decreases by \$1.26. For a 100-unit increase in output, this amounts to a decrease in profits of 100(\$1.26), or \$126. The reason for this rather unexpected result is that such an increase would force a proportionately larger shift from more profitable designs, such as design 3, to less profitable designs, such as 1 and 4.

Given the small number of units using design 1 required in the optimal solution, the production manager may not wish to use design 1 at all. The unit costs may only be valid if sufficiently large quantities of a design are produced. Under these circumstances, the manager would eliminate designs 1 and 2 and only use designs 3 and 4. Solving the problem again, he or she will discover that with the present excess machine times, no feasible solution exists. In fact, at least 33.4 minutes of overtime on the cutting machine is needed to produce 10,000 good units using designs 3 and 4 only. If this additional cutting time can be arranged, the optimal solution calls for 5092 units of design 3 and 5216 of design 4, at a total profit of \$8568.74 less the overtime cost of the additional cutting time. Ignoring the cost of overtime, this is \$37.14 higher than the original maximum profit. Note that this number is equal to 33.4 times the imputed value of CUT constraint = (33.4) (\$1.11188).

2-13 CORPORATE PLANNING MODEL

Forest Industries Corporation has just signed contracts for the clear-felling of two large forest tracts of second-growth radiata pines. The harvested trees will supply the firm's sawmill and chipboard plant. Some of the logging output is also available for export. Figure 2-10 depicts the materials flow schematically.

All trees harvested are cut on location into sections 20 feet long (about 6 meters), referred to as first cuts, second cuts, third cuts, etc. On the basis of a detailed survey of each forest, the firm's chief forester estimated the average composition of each forest's total output, as shown in Table 2-6.

Table 2-6. *Composition of logging output*

Log Cuts	Forest 1	Forest 2
first and second	42%	46%
third and fourth	40%	41%
fifth and over	18%	13%

Although a particular day's output may differ substantially from these proportions, the average daily output over one month is expected to be fairly close to these figures.

Figure 2-10. *Materials flow of Forest Industries.*

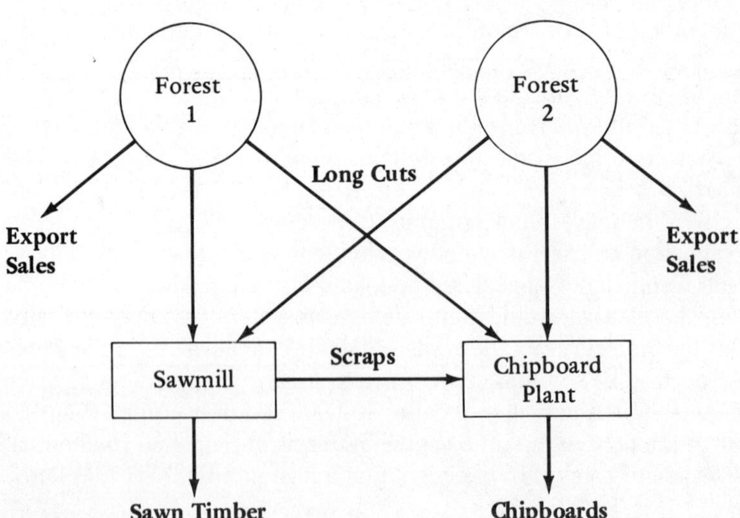

The average daily output is 128 HC for forest 1 and 192 HC for forest 2 (1 HC = 100 cubic feet ≅ 2.832 cubic meters).

The log cuts are sorted and loaded onto logging trucks for transportation to either the sawmill or the chipboard plant, the two facilities being at different locations. Transportation costs from forest 1 amount to $4 per HC to the sawmill and $7 per HC to the chipboard plant. From forest 2 the costs are $3 and $5, respectively. Handling costs at the two plants depend on the type of log cuts, as shown in Table 2-7.

Table 2-7. *Handling costs per HC at plants*

Log Cuts	Sawmill	Chipboard Plant
first and second	$2.50	$1.20
third and fourth	$3.50	$1.50
fifth and over	$5.00	$2.00

At the sawmill, logs are sawn into three grades of finished products: clear grade, dressing grade, and construction grade. A substantial fraction of the incoming volume of wood ends up as scraps and sawdust. Table 2-8 shows the average log conversion factors at the sawmill, as well as the average processing rates. Excluding breakdowns, the productive capacity at the mill averages 360 minutes per day.

Table 2-8. *Log conversion factors at sawmill*

Log Cuts	Sawn Timber (MBF/HC*)	Scraps (HC/HC)	Sawdust (HC/HC)	Processing Time per HC
first and second	0.72	0.26	0.14	1.8
third and fourth	0.66	0.30	0.15	2.6
fifth and over	0.54	0.39	0.16	3.9

* 1 MBF = 1000 board feet ≅ 2.36 cubic meters

From sample logs processed at the sawmill, average yields for each grade of sawn timber were determined. They are summarized in Table 2-9.

Table 2.9. *Sawn timber yields by grades*

	Clear		Dressing		Construction	
Log Cuts	Forest 1	Forest 2	Forest 1	Forest 2	Forest 1	Forest 2
first and second	35%	28%	48%	42%	17%	30%
third and fourth	10%	3%	18%	9%	72%	88%
fifth and over	0	0	5%	0	95%	100%

The ex-mill wholesale price per MBF is \$150 for clear grades, \$110 for dressing grades, and \$80 for construction grades. Scraps at the sawmill are transferred by truck to the chipboard plant for chipping. The transportation cost is \$4 per HC. Sawdust is used as fuel in the mill's drying kiln and saves \$12 in other fuel costs per HC.

At the chipboard plant, logs and scraps are chipped. The chips are then mixed with additives and glues, filled into 4′ by 8′ forms (about 1.2 by 2.4 meters) and then compressed into boards of various thicknesses. The whole process is highly automated. Each HC of wood yields 0.76 $M\frac{3}{4}$ of chipboard or an equivalent (1 $M\frac{3}{4}$ = 1000 square feet of $\frac{3}{4}$ inch thickness ≅ 1.77 cubic meters). The plant can produce up to 112 $M\frac{3}{4}$ of chipboard per day. Chipboard prices ex-factory are \$105 per $M\frac{3}{4}$.

In the light of predicted demand and desired stock levels, certain minimum daily output rates of finished products are set by Forest Industries' management for a given planning period. These are 36 MBF of clear grades, 40 MBF of dressing grades, 48 MBF of construction grades, and 96 $M\frac{3}{4}$ of chipboards. Export prices valid during the same planning period are \$95 per HC for first and second cuts and \$88 per HC for third and fourth cuts. Fifth or higher cuts are not exported.

What is the optimal daily operating policy during the planning period in question?

This problem deals with the operation of an entire firm. Admittedly, these operations are considered only in their most essential aspects, with most of the details ignored. For instance, the final products are lumped into a small number of sawn timber grades. Similarly, only the most important operation at the sawmill, namely the actual sawing of the logs, is represented. No doubt, for real applications considerably more detail would normally be included; but even then, some aggregation would still have to be made to keep the problem at a manageable size.

Our approach to formulating this problem as a linear program is to divide the operations into sequential phases whereby the outputs of one phase become inputs into subsequent phases. For each phase we construct a submodel, and then we tie these submodels together appropriately to form a single model. In this example, there are four logical phases: a log supply phase, the operation of the sawmill, the operations of the chipboard plant, and finally the finished product distribution phase which in our case boils down to a specification of minimum daily outputs.

Since we shall at the end solve this problem by computer, we will use mnemonic labels for the constraints and mnemonic names for the variables from the outset.

Supply phase

The output for each type of log cut at each forest can be allocated either to the sawmill, to the chipboard plant, to export orders, or to any combination of these uses. This is depicted schematically in Figure 2-11. Each allocation of a cut to a given use requires a separate decision variable. The decision variables will thus have the interpretation of "cut i from forest j allocated to use k." Let Lij SAW, LijCH, and LijEXP denote the number of HC per day of cut i from forest j allocated to the sawmill, to the chipboard plant, and to export, respectively; $i = 1$ refers to first and second cuts, $i = 2$ refers to third and fourth cuts, and $i = 3$ refers to fifth and higher cuts

Consider cuts $i = 1$ at forest 1. According to Table 2-6, the average daily output of first and second cuts is 42 percent of 128 HC, or 53.76. If L11SAW, L11CH, and

Figure 2-11. *Possible allocation of cuts.*

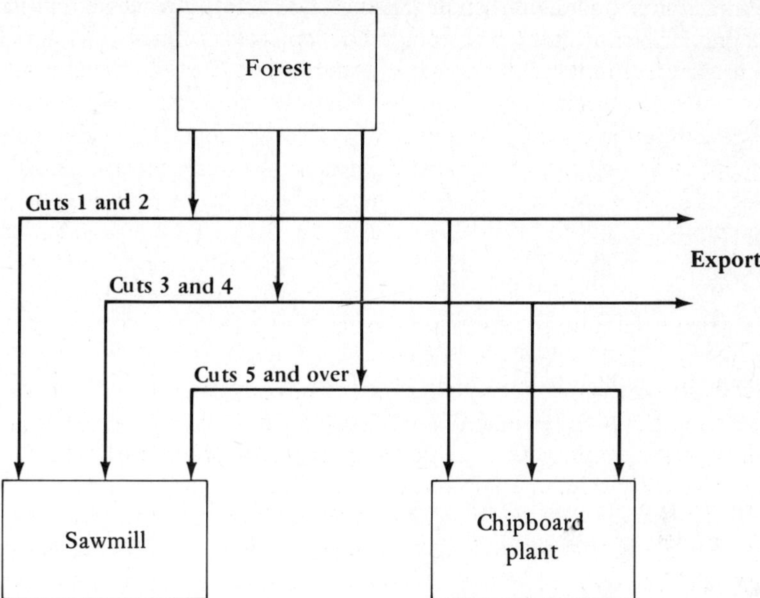

L11EXP are the amounts per day allocated to the three uses, then their total has to equal 53.76 HC, assuming that the firm does not wish to stockpile any output at the forests. This yields the following availability constraint:

(L1F1AV) L11SAW + L11CH + L11EXP = 53.76

If Forest Industries would consider stockpiling some logs at the forests for use in later planning periods, then (L1F1AV) would be expressed as a $\leq$ inequality. We get a similar constraint for each of the other types of cuts at each forest:

(L2F1AV) L21SAW + L21CH + L21EXP = 51.20

(L3F1AV) L31SAW + L31CH = 23.04

(L1F2AV) L12SAW + L12CH + L12EXP = 88.32

(L2F2AV) L22SAW + L22CH + L22EXP = 78.72

(L3F2AV) L32SAW + L32CH = 24.96

Note that log cuts $i = 3$ are not exported.

The L*ij*SAW variables now become the input into the next phase.

Sawmill phase

At the sawmill, log cuts are converted to three grades of timber, scraps, and sawdust. Consider first the production of sawn timber. According to Table 2-8, only a portion of each log cut ends up as sawn timber. For instance, one HC of log cuts $i = 1$ from forest 1 yields 0.72 MBF of sawn timber, of which, according to Table 2-9, 35 percent becomes clear grades, 48 percent dressing grades, and 17 percent construction grades. So one HC of log cuts $i = 1$ from forest 1 yields 0.72 times 0.35, or 0.252 MBF of clear grades. Similarly,

1 HC of	cuts $i = 2$ from forest 1	cuts $i = 1$ from forest 2	cuts $i = 2$ from forest 2
yields	0.66(0.10) = 0.066	0.72 (0.28) = 0.2016	0.66(0.3) = 0.0198

MBF of clear grades.

Multiplying these coefficients by the daily number of HC of each type of cut brought to the sawmill gives the average daily output of clear grades. Letting CLEAR denote the number of MBF of clear grades produced per day, we obtain

$$\begin{aligned} 0.252\,\text{L11SAW} + 0.066\,\text{L21SAW} + 0.2016\,\text{L12SAW} \\ + 0.0198\,\text{L22SAW} = \text{CLEAR} \end{aligned}$$

Expressed in the usual linear programming form, we have the following constraint, labeled (CLPROD):

$$\begin{aligned} \text{(CLPROD)}\quad 0.252\,\text{L11SAW} + 0.066\,\text{L21SAW} + 0.2016\,\text{L12SAW} \\ + 0.0198\,\text{L22SAW} - \text{CLEAR} = 0 \end{aligned}$$

Such a constraint is referred to as a *material balance equation* or an *input–output relation*. Verify the following input–output relations for the production of dressing and construction grades:

$$\begin{aligned} \text{(DRPROD)}\quad 0.3456\,\text{L11SAW} + 0.1188\,\text{L21SAW} + 0.027\,\text{L31SAW} \\ + 0.3024\,\text{L12SAW} + 0.0594\,\text{L22SAW} - \text{DRESS} = 0 \end{aligned}$$

$$\begin{aligned} \text{(COPROD)}\quad 0.1224\,\text{L11SAW} + 0.4752\,\text{L21SAW} + 0.513\,\text{L31SAW} \\ + 0.216\,\text{L12SAW} + 0.5808\,\text{L22SAW} + 0.54\,\text{L32SAW} - \text{CONST} = 0 \end{aligned}$$

Similar input–output relations are obtained for the production of scraps and sawdust (using the data in Table 2-8):

$$\begin{aligned} \text{(SCPROD)}\quad 0.26\,\text{L11SAW} + 0.3\,\text{L21SAW} + 0.39\,\text{L31SAW} + 0.26\,\text{L12SAW} \\ + 0.3\,\text{L22SAW} + 0.39\,\text{L32 SAW} - \text{SCRAP} = 0 \end{aligned}$$

$$\begin{aligned} \text{(SDPROD)}\quad 0.14\,\text{L11SAW} + 0.15\,\text{L21SAW} + 0.16\,\text{L31SAW} \\ + 0.14\,\text{L12SAW} + 0.15\,\text{L22SAW} \\ + 0.16\,\text{L32SAW} - \text{SDUST} = 0 \end{aligned}$$

Finally, the sawmill time required to process the amounts of the various log cuts must not exceed the average productive capacity of 360 minutes per day. Multiplying the processing times per HC for each type of cut by the log input into the sawmill and summing, we obtain

$$\begin{aligned} \text{(SAWCAP)}\quad 1.8\,\text{L11SAW} + 2.6\,\text{L21SAW} + 3.9\,\text{L31SAW} \\ + 1.8\,\text{L12SAW} + 2.6\,\text{L22SAW} + 3.9\,\text{L32SAW} \leqslant 360 \end{aligned}$$

This completes the submodel for the sawmill operation. The variable for SCRAP becomes an input into the chipboard plant phase. The variables for CLEAR, DRESS, and CONST become inputs into the finished products distribution phase.

Chipboard plant phase

The inputs into this phase consist of the various amounts of log cuts allocated from each forest and the scraps transferred from the sawmill. Each HC of input yields 0.76 M_4^3 of chipboard. We therefore obtain the following input–output relation:

$$\text{(CBPROD)} \quad 0.76\,(\text{L11CH} + \text{L21CH} + \text{L31CH} + \text{L12CH} + \text{L22CH} + \text{L32CH} + \text{SCRAP}) - \text{CBOARD} = 0$$

The output of chipboard is restricted to at most 112 M_4^3 per day. Thus,

$$\text{(CBCAP)} \quad \text{CBOARD} \leq 112$$

The variable CBOARD becomes another input into the last phase.

Finished products distribution phase

For this example, the finished products distribution phase takes the simplified form of lower bounds to the decision variables:

$$\text{(CLMIN)} \quad \text{CLEAR} \geq 31$$

$$\text{(DRMIN)} \quad \text{DRESS} \geq 36$$

$$\text{(COMIN)} \quad \text{CONST} \geq 48$$

$$\text{(CBMIN)} \quad \text{CBOARD} \geq 96$$

All that is left is to formulate the objective function. The objective is to maximize the difference between revenues and variable costs, loosely referred to as the gross profit. Revenues are generated from sales of sawn timber and chipboard. Costs are incurred from the transportation and handling of the log cuts and scraps; costs are reduced by burning sawdust. All other costs are assumed to be fixed and not affected by the allocation of logs to the various uses or by the mix in the final products. Such an assumption is clearly true for the logging operation and, in the short run, may be a good approximation for the costs of the sawmill and chipboard plants. The objective function is

$$\begin{aligned}\text{maximize } & 150\,\text{CLEAR} + 110\,\text{DRESS} + 80\,\text{CONST} + 105\,\text{CBOARD} \\ & + 95\,\text{L11EXP} + 88\,\text{L21EXP} + 95\,\text{L12EXP} + 88\,\text{L22EXP} \\ & + 12\,\text{SDUST} - 4\,\text{SCRAP} - 6.5\,\text{L11SAW} - 7.5\,\text{L21SAW} \\ & - 9\,\text{L31SAW} - 5.5\,\text{L12SAW} - 6.5\,\text{L22SAW} - 8\,\text{L32SAW} \\ & - 8.2\,\text{L11CH} - 8.5\,\text{L21CH} - 9\,\text{L31CH} - 6.2\,\text{L12CH} \\ & - 6.5\,\text{L22CH} - 7\,\text{L32CH}\end{aligned}$$

The coefficients for L*ij*SAW and L*ij*CH are obtained by adding the handling costs shown in Table 2-7 to the transportation costs.

Figure 2-12. *Computer printout of optimal solution for Forest Industries Corporation.*

SOLUTION OPTIMAL AFTER 26 ITERATIONS
MAXIMAL OBJECTIVE = 27865.577036

	VARIABLE	STATUS	OPTIMAL VALUE	DELTAJ
	L11SAW	BASIC	53.76000	0.00000
	L21SAW	BASIC	8.96336	0.00000
	L31SAW		0.00000	-12.52445
	L12SAW	BASIC	88.32000	0.00000
	L22SAW	BASIC	31.13510	0.00000
	L32SAW		0.00000	-13.30764
	L11CH		0.00000	-14.01491
	L21CH		0.00000	-2.00000
	L31CH	BASIC	23.04000	0.00000
	L12CH		0.00000	-11.75055
	L22CH	BASIC	29.34545	0.00000
	L32CH	BASIC	24.96000	0.00000
	L11EXP		0.00000	-5.31491
	L21EXP	BASIC	42.23664	0.00000
	L12EXP		0.00000	-5.05055
	L22EXP	BASIC	18.23944	0.00000
	CLEAR	BASIC	32.56089	0.00000
	DRESS	BASIC	48.20170	0.00000
	CONST	BASIC	48.00000	0.00000
	SCRAP	BASIC	48.97034	0.00000
	SDUST	BASIC	25.90597	0.00000
	CBOARD	BASIC	96.00000	0.00000
(SAWCAP)	SAWSL		0.00000	-4.81000
(CBCAP)	CBSL	BASIC	16.00000	0.00000
(CLMIN)	CLXS	BASIC	0.56089	0.00000
(DRMIN)	DRXS	BASIC	12.20170	0.00000
(COMIN)	COXS		0.00000	-38.03030
(CBMIN)	CBXS		0.00000	-19.34211

CONSTRAINT	STATUS	IMPUTED VALUE	DECREASE	INCREASE
L1F1AV	BINDNG	100.31491	4.83829	3.38418
L2F1AV	BINDNG	88.00000	42.23664	OPEN
L3F1AV	BINDNG	85.50000	18.23944	29.34545
L1F2AV	BINDNG	100.05055	5.26770	5.08635
L2F2AV	BINDNG	88.00000	18.23944	OPEN
L3F2AV	BINDNG	87.50000	18.23944	29.34545
CLPROD	BINDNG	-150.00000	OPEN	0.56089
DRPROD	BINDNG	-110.00000	OPEN	12.20170
COPROD	BINDNG	-118.03030	3.28787	0.94653
SCPROD	BINDNG	-90.50000	29.34545	18.23944
SDPROD	BINDNG	-12.00000	OPEN	25.90597
SAWCAP	BINDNG	4.81000	4.23722	17.98917
CBPROD	BINDNG	-124.34211	22.30254	13.86198
CBCAP	SLACK	-0.00000	16.00000	OPEN
CLMIN	SLACK	-0.00000	OPEN	0.56089
DRMIN	SLACK	-0.00000	OPEN	12.20170
COMIN	BINDNG	-38.03030	3.28787	0.94653
CBMIN	BINDNG	-19.34211	22.30254	13.86198

This completes the formulation of this problem. We have a total of 18 constraints and 22 decision variables. (A real corporate model may easily have several hundred constraints with several thousand variables.)

Figure 2-12 reproduces the computer printout for the optimal solution. All constraints have been converted to equalities by adding or subtracting slack variables. In the printout, we have flagged each slack variable with its corresponding constraint label.

The daily gross profit for the optimal solution amounts to $27,865.60. The optimal mode of operation provides for meeting the minimum requirements for construction grades and chipboard, with a small excess for clear grades and a substantial excess for dressing grades. The sawmill is used to full capacity, but the chipboard plant has some unused capacity left. Export sales amount to slightly more than 60HC per day, all of which come from third and fourth log cuts.

The output allows for some interesting sensitivity analysis. Under what conditions would it become profitable to have some of the first and second log cuts exported? From the DELTAJ values for the variables L11EXP and L12EXP we see that the export prices ex-forest for the first and second cuts would have to increase from $95 by at least $5.32 and $5.05 to reach $100.32 and $100.05. At that point, these variables could enter alternative optimal solutions.

The shadow prices (imputed values) for the log cuts availability constraints L*i*F*j*AV provide management with information as to the increase in gross profit for additional output. For instance, each additional HC per day of first and second cuts from forest 1 increases gross profit by $100.32 (= imputed value for L1F1AV). Additional sawmill capacity has a value of $4.81 per minute (= imputed value for SAWCAP). On the other hand, increases in the minimum daily requirements for construction grades and chipboard would have a detrimental effect on gross profit. Each additional M_4^3 of chipboard produces a loss of $19.34 (= imputed value for CBMIN). Hence, it would be a bad move to launch a sales promotion for chipboard now. In fact, lowering the minimum daily requirement from the present 96 M_4^3 to 73.7 (= 96 less the entry of 22.3 shown under DECREASE for the CBMIN constraint), and optimally allocating to other uses the log cuts thus freed, increases gross profits by 22.3 × $19.34 or $431.28. (Note that the imputed values for input–output relations do not lend themselves to an easy interpretation.)

2-14 ADVERTISING MEDIA SELECTION—AN EXAMPLE OF GOAL PROGRAMMING

A firm is the distributor of a seasonal, packaged product for a given region that covers a large metropolitan area. The product is especially appealing to persons with children. The manufacturer of the product has offered to participate in a preseason price discount promotion, and the firm is planning to launch an advertising campaign. Full-page color advertisements in the supplements to the Sunday editions of the two major daily newspapers are planned. The advertising message and copy have been prepared. The only point that remains to be settled is the media schedule, i.e., the number of consecutive insertions in each newspaper.

Ideally, one would like to relate this to the profit that can be generated by each insertion. However, it is extremely difficult to measure the profits of a media schedule. In practice, therefore, one uses surrogate measures that have been shown to positively correlate with profits. Examples of such measures include the *reach* of the media schedule (defined as the fraction of people in a given customer population exposed at least once to the advertisement) and the *frequency* of the schedule (defined as the average number of exposures among population members who have been reached at least once). One may also wish to appeal to different segments of the population to a different degree. Let us assume that, for our problem, reach is the most appropriate criterion and that we want to differentiate between a *primary* group of all persons with at least one child of elementary school age (goal 1), and a *secondary* group that covers all elementary families with an annual income of over $8000 (goal 2).

Data about the reach of the Sunday supplements for various population groups can be obtained from the newspapers. For instance, for newspaper X and the primary group, they indicate the following average fraction of the people in the group reached as a function of the number of insertions:

Number of insertions x	1	2	3	4	5	6
Cumulative fraction y	0.54	0.66	0.75	0.83	0.87	0.89

Unfortunately, this is a nonlinear relationship with a significant drop-off of increased reach after four insertions. The same picture holds true for the secondary group reach in newspaper X. Hence, it seems uneconomical to exceed four insertions in newspaper X. Over the first four insertions, we may approximate the above relationship fairly closely by the equation

$$y = 0.49 + 0.08x \qquad \text{for } 1 \leq x \leq 4$$

Applying this procedure to similar data (not shown) on reach for the other media group combinations, we obtain the following equations:

Newspaper	Group	Equation
X	primary	$0.49 + 0.08x$
Y	primary	$0.47 + 0.12x$
X	secondary	$0.44 + 0.12x$
Y	secondary	$0.37 + 0.09x$

For newspaper Y the drop-off occurs after five insertions.

Estimates indicate that the two newspapers share the primary group evenly, but newspaper X has 60 percent of the secondary group. Management would like to reach at least 80 percent of the primary group (goal 1) and 70 percent of the secondary group (goal 2). Furthermore, they want to keep the past tradition of having at least twice as many insertions in X as in Y (goal 3). Newspaper X charges $3000 per insertion;

newspaper Y, which uses a lower quality paper, charges only \$2000 per insertion. Management has allocated an advertising campaign budget of \$16,000 (budget constraint).

The problem as it stands now is ill-defined. We have several objectives or goals that management would like to achieve. Most of them are somewhat arbitrary policy decisions, such as the two acquisitive goals (1 and 2) and the retentive goal (3). Others, such as the allowable budget and the maximum number of insertions, are stated as upper limits but really do not have the character of firm physical constraints. We have seen in Section 1-12 that one way to deal with multiple goals is to select the most important one as the basis for the objective function and express the others as surrogate constraints. Suppose management considers reach as the most important objective to be maximized subject to achieving goal 3, the budget allocation, and the upper limits on the number of insertions.

Our decision variables are the number of insertions in newspaper X and newspaper Y, denoted by x_1 and x_2, respectively. Note that we now allow these variables to assume any real values within their range. This may be a more questionable approximation than the fitting of equations for reach. The reach achieved for each group is calculated as the weighted average of the reach for each newspaper. Using the four equations listed earlier, the weighted average reach is

$$0.5(0.49 + 0.08x_1) + 0.5(0.47 + 0.12x_2) = 0.48 + 0.04x_1 + 0.06x_2$$

for the primary group, and

$$0.6(0.44 + 0.12x_1) + 0.4(0.37 + 0.09x_2) = 0.412 + 0.072x_1 + 0.036x_2$$

for the secondary group. If management assigns equal importance to the reach for each group, then we could define the objective as maximizing the average total reach, given as the sum of the reach for both groups divided by 2:

$$\text{maximize}\ \tfrac{1}{2}[(0.48 + 0.04x_1 + 0.06x_2) + (0.412 + 0.072\,x_1 + 0.036x_2)]$$

Collecting terms and dropping the constant (as it does not affect the optimal values of the decision variables), we obtain

(2-16) $$\text{maximize}\ 0.056x_1 + 0.048x_2$$

Note that this implies that goals 1 and 2 are commensurable in the sense that it is possible to quantify a trade-off function between them, which in this instance has a simple linear form.

To ensure that at least twice as many insertions are made in newspaper X as in Y, we restrict the decision variables to

(2-17) $$x_1 \geq 2x_2 \quad \text{or} \quad x_1 - 2x_2 \geq 0 \qquad \text{(goal 3)}$$

while the budget allocation imposes that

(2-18) $$3000x_1 + 2000x_2 \leq 16{,}000 \qquad \text{(budget constraint)}$$

Figure 2-13. *Media selection problem.*

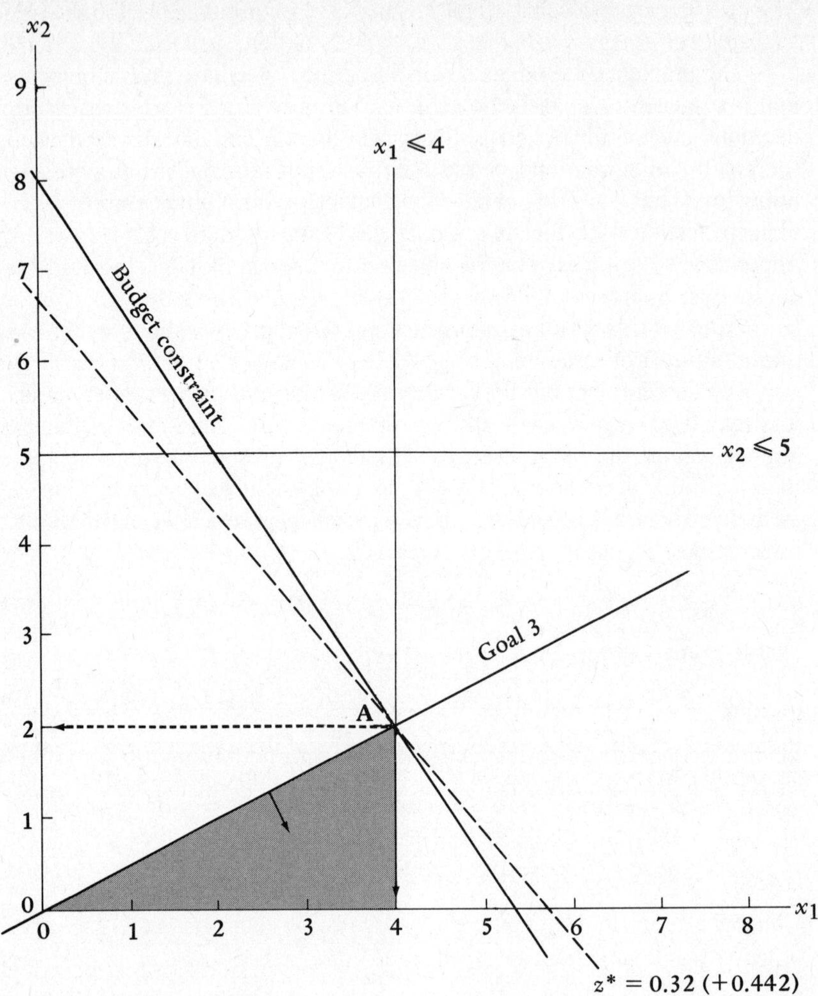

and x_1 and x_2 are restricted to

(2-19) $0 \leq x_1 \leq 4$ (limit on insertions)

(2-20) $0 \leq x_2 \leq 5$

Figure 2-13 shows the feasible region for this problem. The optimal solution occurs at point A and calls for 4 insertions in newspaper X and 2 in newspaper Y. All funds allocated are used up, and the desired relationship between the number of insertions in each newspaper is maintained. Verify that the total average reach is 0.766 or 76.6 percent.

A more detailed analysis shows that the reach for the primary group is 76 percent, or 4 percentage points below the desired level of 80 percent, while the reach for the secondary group is 77.2 percent, or 7.2 percentage points above the desired level. This does not correspond to the desired goals that management initially set out to achieve. The overachievement in the secondary group may not really compensate for the underachievement in the primary group. The acquisitive (and presumably more important) goals were not achieved completely, while the retentive (and presumably less important) goals were achieved completely, largely because they were expressed in the form of constraints. It would be useful to formulate the problem in such a manner that the character of objectives is explicitly retained for all goals. It is exactly this that a variation of linear programming, called *weighted-sum goal programming*, attempts to achieve.

In goal programming, each objective or goal is expressed in equality form by introducing slack variables that represent the deviations from the goal. Let s_i^- denote an underachievement of the goal i and let s_i^+ denote an overachievement. Retaining the budget constraint (2-18) in its present form, the three goals of our problem can then be expressed as follows:

$$0.04x_1 + 0.06x_2 + s_1^- - s_1^+ = 0.32 \qquad \text{(goal 1)} \tag{2-21}$$

$$0.072x_1 + 0.036x_2 + s_2^- - s_2^+ = 0.288 \qquad \text{(goal 2)} \tag{2-22}$$

$$x_1 - 2x_2 + s_3^- - s_3^+ = 0 \qquad \text{(goal 3)} \tag{2-23}$$

where all s_i^+ and s_i^- are restricted to nonnegative values.

Management would like to achieve each of the three objectives as closely as possible, subject to constraints (2-18) through (2-20). It is at this point that certain difficulties of interpretation arise. What is meant by "achieve each objective as closely as possible"? Does it mean to minimize the weighted sum of the deviations? What should be the proper weights? Taking this interpretation, let a_i^- and a_i^+ be the weights for goal i. Then our objective function is

$$\text{minimize } a_1^- s_1^- + a_1^+ s_1^+ + a_2^- s_2^- + a_2^+ s_2^+ + a_3^- s_3^- + a_3^+ s_3^+ \tag{2-24}$$

(Note that the simplex method will guarantee that of each pair (s_i^- and s_i^+) only one variable may be positive, since if both were positive the total value of the objective function could be decreased by reducing both variables by an amount equal to the smaller of the two.) Say we decide that we only want to penalize underachievement. Setting $a_i^+ = 0$ and $a_i^- = 1$, for each i, the objective function becomes

$$\text{minimize } 1(s_1^- + s_2^- + s_3^-) + 0(s_i^+ + s_2^+ + s_3^+) \tag{2-25}$$

Figure 2-14 shows the new feasible region for the two original variables x_1 and x_2 as the shaded area *CDFAB*. We also show one goal line for each objective, representing all solutions for which the corresponding objective is satisfied without any deviation. (Note that our problem now has more than two variables. In Figure 2-14 only the solution space for the original variables x_1 and x_2 is shown explicitly. The values of all other variables can be inferred implicitly from the deviation of solutions from the goal lines.) The optimal solution with a value of $z_2^* = 0.04$ occurs again at point A, for which only goal 3 is satisfied without deviation. We thus see that the first

Figure 2-14. *Media selection by goal programming.*

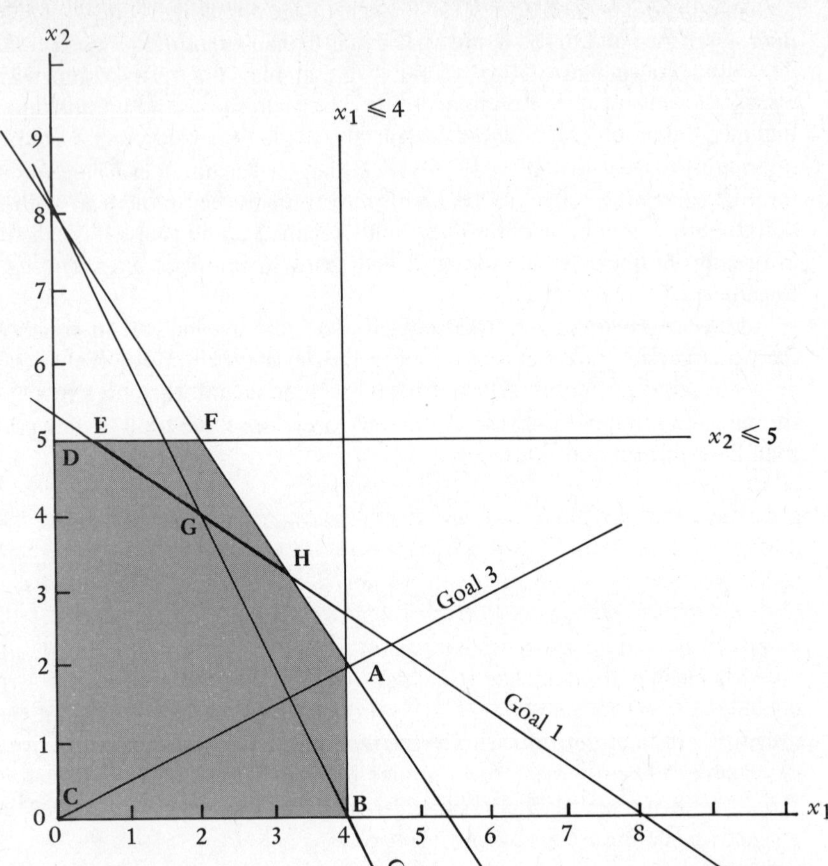

formulation corresponds to a goal programming formulation with equal penalties for underachievements of all three objectives. Had we assigned different penalties to deviations from the three goals, different solutions might become optimal. For instance, had we given a_1^- a value of $80a_3^-$, with $a_i^+ = 0$, all i, and any value for a_2^-, then any point along the line from H to A would be optimal.

No doubt, it is extremely difficult to derive an objective function such as expression (2-24), where the penalties attached to underachievement and overachievement of goals properly represent the preferences of the decision maker. In fact, it is only possible if the objectives are commensurable. In most applications, some of the objectives may lack any common basis for comparison or trade-offs among them. Clearly this is the case here. Although two of the goals may be commensurable as to reach, it would be rather hard to find a trade-off function between them and the third goal.

An alternative approach that avoids the necessity of constructing trade-off functions between objectives is to rank the objectives in *priority ordering*. The solution procedure would then attempt to first satisfy the objective with the highest priority as closely as possible, while completely ignoring all lower ranking objectives. If the highest ranking objective has been achieved, then the second highest ranking one is satisfied as closely as possible without, however, impairing the achievement level of the highest ranking one. The same steps are followed for each of the lower ranking objectives in descending order of priority. The procedure usually terminates as soon as one of the objectives cannot be satisfied completely. This approach is called *preemptive goal programming*.

For our example, say that management gives the highest priority to achieving the desired reach for the primary group (goal 1), the second ranking to achieving the desired reach for the secondary group (goal 2), and the lowest priority to the relationship between the number of insertions in X and Y (goal 3). Referring back to Figure 2-14, goal 1 is satisfied completely for any solution of x_1 and x_2 along the heavy line from point E to H. We can now proceed to satisfy the second ranking objective as closely as possible without impairing the achievement level for the first objective. Hence only solutions on the line from E to H may be considered. Goal 2 is completely satisfied at the intersection of the goal lines for goal 1 and goal 2, point G. Finally, we can turn to the third ranking objective. No improvements can be made on goal 3 without impairing the achievement level of the two higher ranking goals. Hence the optimal solution for this priority ranking is given at point G, which calls for 2 insertions in newspaper X and 4 in newspaper Y (with $s_3^- = 6$ and all other s_i^- and $s_i^+ = 0$) at a cost of \$14,000. This is \$2000 below the budget allocation. We shall pick up this discussion again in Chapter 22.

2-15 SOME FURTHER APPLICATIONS

The list of possible applications for linear programming is enormous. It ranges from allocation of scarce resources for various end uses to the determination of the optimal phasing pattern for traffic lights along city streets.

1. *Allocation of scarce resources*. The decision variables are given by the various activities that consume the resources, such as products to manufacture. Each scarce resource gives rise to a constraint. The objective consists of maximizing total output or of minimizing total costs subject to achieving some specified output.
2. *Smoothing problems*. This term refers to scheduling overtime of production or manpower to satisfy seasonal demands for products or services. The level of and changes in manpower in each period, the number of idle employees or the amount of overtime, the size of the production during regular time and overtime in each period, and the size of the inventory carried forward to each succeeding period give rise to decision variables. The material balance or input–output relations between levels of manpower of consecutive periods and

similar relations between production, inventories, and demand form constraints. The objective is usually to minimize total production costs, including costs for training manpower, severance pay, and inventory carrying costs.

3. *Distribution problems.* A firm may operate a number of plants supplying a number of different regional marketing centers. The decision variables are given by the amount produced by each plant to be shipped to each marketing center. The production capacities at the plants, the demand requirements at the marketing centers, and any possible limitations on shared transportation facilities give rise to constraints.
4. *Blending problems.* Various raw materials of different chemical or physical properties have to be blended for final products. The amounts of each raw material used for each final product constitute the decision variables. The amounts of the raw materials available, the amounts of the final products required, the limitations as to the composition of the final products, and their required properties all give rise to constraints. A possible objective is minimizing the cost of the raw materials used.
5. *Diet and feed-mix problems.* These are special forms of blending problems where the output usually consists of a single blend or mix. If some of the inputs are only available in limited quantities and are shared by a number of different mixes, the formulation may cover several mixes at the same time.
6. *Trim problems.* Given quantities of goods of different shapes to be cut from a material that comes in various sizes, a number of possible efficient patterns are considered. How much of each pattern should be cut? The numbers of each pattern cut represent the decision variables. The constraints are given by the required quantities and by the amount of material of each size available. The objective may be to minimize the cost of the material used or the amount of waste produced.
7. *Planning problems.* Planning the operation of a whole organization or firm is another application. The Forest Industries example discussed in Section 2-13 belongs in this category.

In the business world, few problems occur in one of these pure forms; rather, the problems exhibit characteristics of several different types of basic linear programming models.

EXERCISES

2.1 A furniture manufacturer produces two types of desks: Standard and Executive. These desks are sold to an office furniture wholesaler, and for all practical purposes there is an unlimited market for any mix of these desks, at least within the manufacturer's production capacity. Each desk has to go through four basic operations: cutting the lumber, joining the pieces, prefinishing, and final finishing. Each unit of the Standard desk produced takes 48 minutes of cutting time, 2 hours of joining, 40 minutes of prefinishing, and 5 hours and 20 minutes of final finishing time. Each unit of the Executive desk requires 72 minutes of cutting, 3 hours of joining, 2 hours of prefinishing, and 4 hours of final finishing time. The daily capacity for each operation amounts to 16 hours of cutting, 30 hours of joining, 16 hours of prefinishing, and 64 hours of final finishing time. The profit per unit produced is \$40 for the Standard desk and \$50 for the Executive desk. What product mix is optimal?

(a) Formulate this problem as a linear program maximizing daily profit, and show each constraint graphically. Show the objective function for z = \$400 and z = \$600. Are there any redundant constraints? Which ones?

(b) Find the optimal solution graphically. What is the amount of slack for each constraint?

(c) Find the shadow price for each constraint graphically and interpret its meaning.

(d) Determine individually for each objective function coefficient the range of values for which the present solution remains optimal.

(e) The firm receives a request to produce 1 unit per day of a third type of desk style called the Economy desk, which requires 30 minutes of cutting, 90 minutes of joining, 30 minutes of prefinishing, and 3 hours of finishing time. The profit would amount to \$20 per unit. Should the firm offer to make one unit of the Economy per day? Why or why not?

2.2 A chicken feed manufacturer wants to find the lowest-cost mix for a high-protein formula that contains 90 grams of nutrient A, 48 grams of nutrient B, 20 grams of nutrient C, and 1.5 grams of vitamin X for each kilogram of feed. He can mix the formula from two ingredients and a filler. Ingredient 1 contains 100 grams of nutrient A, 80 grams of nutrient B, 40 grams of nutrient C, and 10 grams of vitamin X, and costs 40 cents per kilogram. Ingredient 2 contains 200 grams of A, 150 grams of B, 20 grams of C, none of vitamin X, and costs 60 cents per kilogram.

(a) Formulate this problem as a linear program minimizing cost per kilogram of mix. Note that you do not need a variable for the filler. The amount of filler that has to be added can be determined once the optimal mix of ingredients 1 and 2 has been found. Show each constraint graphically, and show the objective function for z = 24 cents and z = 36 cents. Are there any redundant constraints? Which ones?

(b) Find the optimal solution that minimizes the cost of the mix. What is the amount of slack for each constraint? How much filler has to be added?

(c) Find the shadow price for each constraint graphically and interpret its meaning.

(d) Determine individually for each objective function coefficient the range of values for which the present solution remains optimal.

(e) The firm receives a call from a supplier offering a third ingredient that contains 120 grams of A, 100 grams of B, 20 grams of C, and no X per kilogram, at a cost of 50 cents per kilogram. Should they buy any of it for use in this formula? Why or why not?

2.3 A firm produces three types of refined chemicals: A, B, and C. At least 4 tons of A, 2 tons of B, and 1 ton of C have to be produced per day. The inputs used are compounds X and Y. Each ton of X yields $\frac{1}{4}$ ton of A, $\frac{1}{4}$ ton of B, and $\frac{1}{12}$ ton of C. Each ton of Y yields $\frac{1}{2}$ ton of A, $\frac{1}{10}$ ton of B, and $\frac{1}{12}$ ton of C. Compound X costs \$250 per ton, compound Y \$400 per ton. The cost of processing is \$250 per ton of X and \$200 per ton of Y. Amounts produced in excess of the daily requirements have no value, as the products undergo chemical changes if not used immediately. The problem is to find the mix with minimum cost input.

(a) Formulate this problem as a linear program with the objective of minimizing total daily costs. Show each constraint graphically and the objective function for z = \$6000 and z = \$12,000.

(b) Find the optimal solution graphically. What is the amount of excess produced for each chemical?

(c) The daily requirement for C is increased to 1.25 tons. By how much does the daily cost increase? The daily requirement for B is increased to 2.25 tons. By how much does the daily cost increase? The requirement for A is reduced by $\frac{1}{2}$ ton. By how much does the daily cost change?

(d) Determine for each individual compound the range of prices for which the present solution remains optimal.

(e) The firm receives an offer for a third compound that yields $\frac{1}{5}$ ton of A, $\frac{1}{2}$ ton of B, and $\frac{1}{10}$ ton of C at a price of $300 per ton and a processing cost of $300 per ton. Should the firm accept this offer? Why or why not?

2.4 The Playsafe Insurance Company of Knockville, ME, or PICKME for short, has idle funds of 20 million dollars available for short-term and long-term investments. Government regulations require that no more than 80 percent of all investments be long term, that no more than 40 percent be invested at short term, and that the ratio of long-term to short-term investments not exceed 3 to 1. Long-term investments currently yield 15 percent annually, while the annual rate for short-term investments is 10 percent.

(a) Formulate this problem as a linear program with the objective of maximizing the weighted return. Formulate it in terms of what fraction of the funds to invest in each investment, rather than in dollar amounts. Show all constraints graphically, shade in the feasible region, and show the objective function for three values (one for 9 percent, one for 15 percent, and the optimal one).

(b) Find the optimal solution graphically. Which constraints are slack? What is the amount of slack? Are any constraints redundant? What is the annual revenue from the funds available for investment?

(c) Find the shadow prices of all constraints and interpret their meaning.

(d) For each objective function coefficient, find the range for which the current solution remains optimal.

(e) How does the solution change if no more than 20 percent of total funds can be invested short-term?

2.5 A fiberglass boat manufacturer produces four different models that have to go through three different operations: molding, assembly, and finishing. The table given contains all pertinent information.

Model	Molding (hrs/unit)	Assembly hrs/unit)	Finishing (hrs/unit)	Molding Compound (gal/unit)	Profit ($/unit)
1	2.8	5	10	200	160
2	2.1	3	7.5	200	124
3	4	6	12	280	212
4	3	4	3	220	170
Capacity/wk	48 hr	96 hr	160 hr	4800 gal	

Sales forecasts project that on the average not more than 8 units of model 4 should be produced per week. Except for this restriction, demand would be sufficient to absorb any amount produced. The objective is to maximize profits. This problem was solved

```
FIBERGLASS BOAT MANUFACTURE PROBLEM
   5   9   1
MOLD                 48.000000
ASSEMB               96.000000
FINISH              160.000000
MCC                 480.000000
DEMM4                 8.000000
          M1        160.000000
          M2        120.000000
          M3        212.000000
          M4        170.000000
          MSLACK      0.000000
          ASLACK      0.000000
          FSLACK      0.000000
          CSLACK      0.000000
          M4SLK       0.000000
MOLD      M1          2.800000
MOLD      M2          2.100000
MOLD      M3          4.000000
MOLD      M4          3.000000
MOLD      MSLACK      1.000000
ASSEMB    M1          5.000000
ASSEMB    M2          3.000000
ASSEMB    M3          6.000000
ASSEMB    M4          4.000000
ASSEMB    ASLACK      1.000000
FINISH    M1         10.000000
FINISH    M2          7.500000
FINISH    M3         12.000000
FINISH    M4          3.000000
FINISH    FSLACK      1.000000
MCC       M1         20.000000
MCC       M2         20.000000
MCC       M3         28.000000
MCC       M4         22.000000
MCC       CSLACK      1.000000
DEMM4     M4          1.000000
DEMM4     M4SLK       1.000000
SOLVE

SOLUTION OPTIMAL AFTER         6 ITERATIONS
MAXIMAL OBJECTIVE =        2740.740741
 VARIABLE    STATUS     OPTIMAL VALUE       DELTAJ
   M1                         0.00000          0.00000
   M2        BASIC           20.74074          0.00000
   M3                         0.00000        -16.14815
   M4        BASIC            1.48148          0.00000
   MSLACK                     0.00000        -56.48148
   ASLACK    BASIC           27.85185          0.00000
   FSLACK                     0.00000         -0.18519
   CSLACK    BASIC           32.59259          0.00000
   M4SLK     BASIC            6.51852          0.00000

CONSTRAINT STATUS       IMPUTED VALUE       DECREASE          INCREASE
   MOLD                      56.48148          3.20000           5.02857
   ASSEMB                     0.00000         27.85185          OPEN
   FINISH                     0.18519         50.28571          11.42857
   MCC                        0.00000         32.59259          OPEN
   DEMM4                      0.00000          6.51852          OPEN
```

by LPGOGO. The printout is shown above. The status of the constraints has been left blank.

(a) What is the optimal production mix? Which resources are binding? How much slack is available for the other constraints?

(b) The firm receives a request to produce 1 unit of model 1 every 4 weeks ($= \frac{1}{4}$ unit per week). Should the firm accept this offer? Why or why not? If yes, by how much would profits increase? If no, by how much would profits decrease?

(c) One of the workers at the finishing operation has enrolled in a course and will only be able to work 40 hours/week rather than 48. No wages will be paid while he is off work. This means that the available capacity of the finishing operation is reduced accordingly. Should the firm try to make up the lost production time by overtime from other workers if the workers at the finishing operation earn $2/hour and overtime is paid at 2 times regular pay? (Note that the profit figures include labor cost at regular time. Assume regular pay per worker covers 48 hours/week.) Give details of your reasoning.

(d) The firm is approached about producing 1 unit of a new model per week. This model requires 2 hours of molding, 3 hours of assembly, 4 hours of finishing time, and 180 gallons of molding compound. What is the minimum price (exclusive of material) that the firm should quote if it wants to make a profit of $100 per unit produced?

2.6 A firm produces three products: A, B, and C. The three products share four machines, X, Y, S, and T, for their production process. Product A goes through three operations using machines X, S, and T. Product B goes through two operations using only either machines X and S or machines Y and T. Product C can be produced using either machines X and S or machines Y, S, and T. The time requirement in minutes per unit produced for each production option on each machine and the variable production cost per minute for each machine are summarized in the table below.

		Time (in minutes/unit on machine)				
Product	Process	X	Y	S	T	Mnemonic
A	1	10		6	3	A
B	1	8		10		B1
	2		6		9	B2
C	1	8		16		C1
	2		10	3	8	C2
Variable production cost/minute ($)		0.40	0.50	0.24	0.30	

Each machine has a daily production capacity of 480 minutes. The minimum daily requirements for the three products are 36 for A, 45 for B, and 10 for C. The objective is to determine a production setup that minimizes the total variable production cost. This problem was solved using LPGOGO. The printout follows. The status of constraints has been left blank.

(a) How many units of each product are produced by each process?

(b) Which machines have unused capacity and how much?

(c) It is possible to have $\frac{1}{2}$ hour of overtime per day on machine X. What effect would this have on the total cost of the output?

(d) If the daily requirement for product A decreased to 30 units, what effect would this have on the total cost of the output?

(e) What can you say about the effect on the total cost of an increase in the demand for C from 10 to 12 units per day?

```
PRODUCT SCHEDULING PROBLEM
   7    9    1
CAPX                   480.000000
CAPY                   480.000000
CAPS                   480.000000
CAPT                   480.000000
DEMA                    36.000000
DEMB                    45.000000
DEMC                    10.000000
          A             -6.340000
          B1            -5.600000
          B2            -5.700000
          C1            -7.040000
          C2            -8.120000
          XSLACK         0.000000
          YSLACK         0.000000
          SSLACK         0.000000
          TSLACK         0.000000
CAPX      A             10.000000
CAPX      B1             8.000000
CAPX      C1             8.000000
CAPX      XSLACK         1.000000
CAPY      B2             6.000000
CAPY      C2            10.000000
CAPY      YSLACK         1.000000
CAPS      A              6.000000
CAPS      B1            10.000000
CAPS      C1            16.000000
CAPS      C2             3.000000
CAPS      SSLACK         1.000000
CAPT      A              3.000000
CAPT      B2             9.000000
CAPT      C2             8.000000
CAPT      TSLACK         1.000000
DEMA      A              1.000000
DEMB      B1             1.000000
DEMB      B2             1.000000
DEMC      C1             1.000000
DEMC      C2             1.000000
SOLVE

SOLUTION OPTIMAL AFTER       8 ITERATIONS
MAXIMAL OBJECTIVE =      -554.640000
 VARIABLE    STATUS    OPTIMAL VALUE          DELTAJ
    A         BASIC        36.00000           0.00000
    B1        BASIC         5.00000           0.00000
    B2        BASIC        40.00000           0.00000
    C1        BASIC        10.00000           0.00000
    C2                      0.00000          -0.98000
    XSLACK                  0.00000          -0.01250
    YSLACK    BASIC       240.00000           0.00000
    SSLACK    BASIC        54.00000           0.00000
    TSLACK    BASIC        12.00000           0.00000

CONSTRAINT STATUS     IMPUTED VALUE          DECREASE           INCREASE
    CAPX                    0.01250          10.66667           43.20000
    CAPY                    0.00000         240.00000           OPEN
    CAPS                    0.00000          54.00000           OPEN
    CAPT                    0.00000          12.00000           OPEN
    DEMA                   -6.46500           8.30769            0.84211
    DEMB                   -5.70000          40.00000            1.33333
    DEMC                   -7.14000          10.00000            1.33333
```

(f) The firm has received a request to produce 5 units of product D per day. Each unit of D would require: 2 minutes on machine X, 12 minutes on machine Y, and 6 minutes on machine S. The net profit per unit of D is \$0.25. Should the firm make this product? Show why or why not!

2.7 You are organizing a party and have the following amounts of liquor available as brainkillers: 48 fl. oz. of bourbon, 72 fl. oz. of vodka, 64 fl. oz. of white vermouth, 72 fl. oz. of red vermouth, 24 fl. oz. of brandy, and 18 fl. oz. of coffee liqueur. You contemplate mixing the following drinks: Chauncies, Black Russians, Sweet Italians. Molotov Cocktails (Russian Martinis), and bourbon on the rocks. A Chauncy consists of $\frac{2}{3}$ bourbon and $\frac{1}{3}$ red vermouth. A Black Russian consists of $\frac{3}{4}$ vodka and $\frac{1}{4}$ coffee liqueur. A Sweet Italian contains $\frac{1}{4}$ brandy, $\frac{1}{2}$ red vermouth, and $\frac{1}{4}$ white vermouth. Molotov Cocktails are a mixture of $\frac{2}{3}$ vodka and $\frac{1}{3}$ white vermouth. Finally, bourbon on the rocks consists of just bourbon. Each drink contains 4 fl. oz. Your objective is to mix the ingredients in such a way that the largest number of drinks can be made. However, you feel that at least twice as many Molotov Cocktails as Black Russians have to be mixed to provide a balanced selection. Formulate as an LP.

2.8 The Western Paper Company operates a cardboard plant in Seattle. The plant has been operating at 75 percent capacity, producing 2700 tons per month at a total cost of $77.33 per ton. Included in the total cost per ton is the cost of wastepaper—the major raw material. For each 100 tons of product, 80 tons of wastepaper are required. Up to 1440 tons per month of wastepaper can be purchased locally for $18.75 per ton. Additional wastepaper may be purchased through brokers at $27.50 per ton delivered at the plant. Of the present total monthly costs at the plant, $59,400 is estimated to be fixed regardless of production level. The remainder, with the exception of the cost of wastepaper, varies in proportion to output. The company has another plant in Oregon that has been operating at 60 percent capacity, producing 3600 tons per month at a total cost per ton of $85. Local wastepaper costs $20 per ton and is limited to 4000 tons per month. Additional wastepaper can be obtained through brokers at $27.50 per ton delivered at the plant. Of the present operating costs, $108,000 per month is regarded as fixed cost. The total production is to continue at the present rate of 6300 tons per month. Formulate a linear program to minimize the total cost where the optimal solution may involve shifting part of the scheduled 6300 tons/month from one of the plants to the other.

2.9 Market Research Surveys wants to conduct home interviews in Nogoodtown, satisfying certain average quota requirements for each of three target populations. Calls can be made during the daytime at a cost of $2 per call or in the evening at a cost of $3 per call. Unfortunately only a fraction of the calls are successful, i.e., find someone at home and willing to cooperate. The table gives the relevant data. Because of employment conditions, the total number of evening calls cannot exceed 40 percent of the total number of day calls. The objective is to minimize the total cost of the calls. Formulate this problem as a linear program.

		Fraction of Successful Calls	
Population	Calls Quota	Daytime	Evening
Single persons	100	0.1	0.4
Married couples without children	100	0.4	0.5
Married couples with children	200	0.7	0.8

2.10 A farmer wishes to determine the best selection of stock for his farm, his objective being to maximize the profit after sale of the animals at the end of the period. The alternatives available are Merino sheep, Romney sheep, Southdown sheep, Hereford cattle, and Jersey cattle. The farmer has calculated that each Merino would require 1 acre of land and would cost \$1.50 in extra feed, treatment, etc. The purchase price is \$6, and the farmer estimates that the selling price at the end of the period will be \$10. For Romneys, the corresponding figures are 1 acre, \$1.75, \$4.25, \$9.00; for Southdowns: 1 acre, \$1, \$3, \$6; for Herefords: 4 acres, \$15, \$30, \$60; for Jerseys: 6 acres, \$12, \$28, \$58. The size of the farm is 400 acres, and the farmer has \$3800 with which to purchase and maintain the stock. Formulate this problem as a linear program maximizing profits.

2.11 A paper company has received the following order for stationery:

Type	A	B	C	D
No. of reams ordered	4000	8000	3000	5000

In order to facilitate cutting, it is customary that the actual amount supplied may exceed the order by up to 5 percent. Any excess beyond 5 percent becomes wastage. The stationery can be cut from paper rolls of 3 widths by one of two or three patterns, resulting in waste (or trim) as shown in the table.

	24″ Width (weight 1 ton)		30″ Width (weight 1.25 tons)		36″ Width (weight 1.5 tons)			Weight (per 1000 reams)
Type	#1	#2	#1	#2	#1	#2	#3	
A	36	—	—	6	—	16	24	25.5
B	—	24	40	12	—	12	—	28.1
C	—	6	—	—	27	16	32	16.8
D	—	6		24	30	14	10	29.1
Waste per roll	8.2%	5%	10%	5.6%	8.8%	5.2%	6.6%	

Formulate this problem as a linear program.

(a) Minimize total wastage.

(b) Minimize the total cost of the rolls used given that the 24″ width has a cost of \$30, the 30″ width costs \$34, and the 36″ width costs \$37 per roll.

2.12 A firm would like to find the least-cost production schedule for a seasonal product. The demand is 2000 units in May, 4000 in June, 6000 in July, 6000 in August, and 2000 in September. The product cannot be kept in storage for more than 2 months; e.g., if produced in April, it has to be sold by the end of June. The work force of seasonal workers has to be hired at the beginning of the season (early April) and kept until the close of the season (end of September). Initial training costs per worker amount to \$200. Each worker can produce 400 units a month on regular time and, if desired, up to an additional 100 units on overtime. Each worker costs \$800 per month for regular time work. Overtime is paid at 1.5 times the regular rate. Units produced are available for sale that same month. Each unit put into storage incurs a handling cost of \$0.50. The cost of holding one unit in storage amounts to \$0.40 per month carried forward. Formulate this problem as a linear program minimizing the sum of all costs.

2.13 A firm produces two products, S and T, which have to go through two manufacturing operations. The first operation is performed at either machine center 1 or 2, and the second at either machine center 3 or 4. Operation times for each machine center per unit produced, machine center capacities, and machine center costs per minute are shown in the table. Daily requirements are 600 units for product S and 300 units for product T. The objective is to find a production schedule that minimizes total machine center production costs. Formulate this problem as a linear program.

Machine Centers	1	2	3	4
Product S	10	6	16	12 minutes
Product T	20	8	12	10 minutes
Capacity	4800	3600	6000	6000 minutes
Cost/minute	30	50	30	50 cents

2.14 A sawmill can obtain three qualities of radiata pines that differ mainly in terms of diameter. Three products are made from these logs: grade A 1 × 4, grade A 2 × 4, and grade B 2 × 4. Any scraps produced are sold to a wood chipping mill. The table gives the yield conversion table, production rates, log supply, and lumber demand positions. Scraps are sold to the chipping mill at \$40 per HC. The sawmill works 10 hours per day at most. The hourly cost is \$20. Grade A 2 × 4 can be broken down to grade A 1 × 4 by an additional cutting operation performed on a special saw at a rate of 5 MBF per hour and at a cost of \$5.00 per hour. Under present market conditions any excess lumber produced has to be sold at a loss of \$5 per MBF. Formulate this problem as a linear program minimizing total daily costs.

Log Type	Price per HC	Sawmill Hours (in hours/MBF)	Yield in MBF/HC Grade A 1 × 4	Grade A 2 × 4	Grade B 2 × 4	Scraps in HC/HC	Maximum Daily Supply
1	\$120	0.04	0.15	0.50	0.30	0.10	100 HC
2	\$110	0.05	0.20	0.30	0.40	0.15	80 HC
3	\$ 90	0.06	0.20	0.10	0.60	0.20	50 HC
	Daily demand in MBF		60	50	75	0	

(MBF denotes units of 1000 board feet; HC denotes units of 100 cubic ft.)

2.15 During the construction of a reservoir dam, large quantities of aggregate suitable for concrete mixing have to be transported from some or all of four deposit sites to the concrete mixing plant at the dam. The table shows estimated quantities and costs to produce and transport aggregate from the deposit sites to the mixing plant. Three

Deposit Site	Quantity (m^3)	Cost/m^3
River-dredge material A	8000	\$3.20
River-dredge material B	16000	\$4.50
Island aggregate C	8000	\$2.80
River bar aggregate D	6000	\$4.00

aggregate blends with the following limits on the aggregate used, and costs of cement, fly ash, and additives, have to be produced in the quantities shown. The objective is to find the blends that minimize the total cost of transportation and mixing. Formulate as a linear program.

Blend	Specified Limits	Cost/m^3	Requirement (m^3)
1	$(A + B) \leqslant 50\%$, $C \geqslant 10\%$, D is limitless	\$4.80	6000
2	$(A + B) \leqslant 60\%$, $C \geqslant 10$, $(C + D) \leqslant (A + B)$	\$4.20	15,000
3	$A \geqslant 20\%$, $(C + D) \geqslant \frac{1}{2}(A + B)$	\$5.40	8000

2.16 The administrative planner of a large city hospital wants to determine the number of orderlies to be hired for the coming 2-month period based on the following estimates for requirements in terms of ward-hours.

Period	Jan/Feb	March/Apr	May/June	July/Aug	Sep/Oct	Nov/Dec
Hours	8000	7600	7200	7000	8000	9000

During the first 2 months, an orderly hired will receive training requiring 90 hours of the time of an experienced orderly, who will have that much less time available to do normal duties. Each trainee is able to do 160 hours of productive work during the first 2 months of service. Each experienced orderly can put in an average of 320 hours of work during a 2-month period. As of the beginning of January the hospital will have 28 experienced orderlies on staff. This includes those who have just completed their 2-month training period. At the end of each 2-month period, approximately 10 percent of the experienced orderlies quit their jobs. Only 80 percent of the trainees complete their training. The others quit during training, and on the average receive about 50 percent of the training and put in an equal traction of productive work. No orderlies are laid off. It is desired to have at least 30 experienced orderlies by the beginning of next January. An experienced orderly costs the hospital \$2200 and a trainee \$1800 for a 2-month period. Formulate a linear programming problem minimizing total costs.

Note that only the optimal decision for the first period will be implemented and that the problem must be solved again for a new interval of 6 periods prior to next period's decision. Can you explain why?

2.17 A firm has been contracted to manufacture two types of industrial components. The contract calls for certain quantities each year for the next 5 years. There is no prospect of production after that. The contracted quantities are

Year	1	2	3	4	5
Demand type A	4000	15,000	12,000	20,000	8000
Demand type B	6000	20,000	15,000	10,000	2000

A special machine is required to handle both kinds of components at a certain stage in manufacture. One machine will handle 3000 Type A components or 2000 Type B components a year, or any proportional combination of them. These machines can be either purchased or rented. The cost of buying the machine is \$120,000 in year 1 and will increase \$6000 each year thereafter. Each year of its life the machine loses \$12,000 of its value, except in the first year, when the loss is \$20,000. Machines purchased can be sold at their salvage value at the end of each year. Machines can be rented for either a 1-year, 2-year, or 5-year term at rental charges starting at \$28,000, \$25,000, or \$24,000 per year, respectively. Each year the rental charges will increase by \$2000, except that machines already on hire stay at their original charge until their rental period expires. All expenditures are assumed to occur at the beginning of each year, when machines can be rented or purchased. The firm wishes to minimize the net cost of acquiring or renting these machines. Assume the firm's discount factor is $\alpha = 0.9$ per annum. Formulate the problem as a linear program, and carefully note any assumptions you make. Can linear programming really solve this problem satisfactorily? (See Section 1-13 for a review of the principles of discounting.)

2.18 Consider the production scheduling example discussed in Section 2-12. Note that for an output of 10,000 casings the shadow price for the total output constraint (2-10) is negative. This indicates that it would be desirable to reduce the required total output somewhat.

(a) Indicate what will happen to the value of the shadow price as the total output requirement is gradually reduced.

(b) How would you reformulate the problem so as to find the optimal total output?

2.19 Pineapple Delight, Inc., uses fruit grown on its own plantations as input into its plants. For the coming year, the crop is estimated at 120,000 metric tons (one metric ton = 1000 kilograms) of skinned fruit. Pineapple products are differentiated by the various ways of cutting the fruit. The secret of successful marketing is to find imaginative ways of using the offcuts. Pineapple Delight, in addition to selling the conventional premium cuts, outsells its more conservative competitors by marketing such novel products as "Spears Delight" (C), "Wafers Delight" (D), "Passion Fruit–Pineapple Delight" (E), and "Crush Delight" (F). The table shows the skinned fruit weight required per can, the amount of offcuts produced, and the selling price. All offcuts have to be processed.

Note that "Passion Fruit–Pineapple Delight" (E) requires the addition of passion fruit at a cost of \$0.10 per can. The objective is to determine the product mix that maximizes sales revenue. Formulate as an LP.

	Premium Products		Offcut Products			
	A	B	C	D	E	F
Maximum demand (1000 cans)	50,000	20,000	30,000	40,000	10,000	unlimited
Selling price/can	\$0.80	\$0.92	\$0.72	\$0.52	\$0.62	\$0.30
Skinned fruit/can	1.2 kg	1.4 kg	0.9 kg	0.75 kg	0.6 kg	0.6 kg
Offcuts for use in C	0	0.4 kg	0	0	0	0
Offcuts for use in D, E, F	0.4 kg	0.2 kg	0.10 kg	0	0	0
Offcuts suitable for F only	0	0	0.05 kg	0.05 kg	0	0

2.20 The construction of an 11-mile stretch of interstate highway alignment requires cutting and filling as shown in the profile on page 82. Fill can also be obtained from three borrow pits. The hauling costs are a function of distance and grade and therefore vary with both location and direction of haul. The availabilities of earth and the requirements for fill are shown in units of thousand m^3. The hauling costs are shown in \$/m^3. Excess cut has to be discarded at a cost shown in the discard cost row in \$/m^3. The unit cost of transporting earth from an origin to a destination is obtained by adding the section hauling costs for all sections between the origin and the destination plus the smaller of the section costs at the origin and the destination. For instance, the cost of hauling earth from section 2 to section 6 is $[2.0 + 1.7 + 1.5 + \min(2.1, 2.8)] = 7.3$ \$/m^3. The objective is to find a fill hauling plan that minimizes the sum of hauling and discarding costs. Formulate as a linear program.

2.21 A coal mine has installed a briquetting plant to increase the revenue from low grade coals, particularly small material (so-called slack). At each pit, coal is brought to a screening plant where slack and coal between $\frac{1}{2}$ and 1 inch ("smalls") are separated from the more-than-1-inch material (+1″). All coals are then washed to extract stones, etc. Slack is sold to power plants. Washed smalls and +1″ material are sold to commercial and domestic markets. The coal mine operates two pits, with the characteristics shown in the table. The briquetting plant requires an annual input of 50,000 tons of washed coals: slack, smalls, or +1″. The cost of processing 1 ton of washed coal at the briquetting plant is \$1.2. The weighted average sulfur content cannot exceed 1.4 percent and the weighted average ash content has to be no more than 15 percent. Briquettes are sold mainly on the domestic market at a price of \$13/ton. The total market for smalls, +1″, and briquettes is limited and cannot absorb more than 120,000 tons annually. There is no limit on slack sales. The entire pit output has to be disposed of. The objective is to find the best allocation of coals to the briquetting plant so as to maximize total revenue. Formulate this problem as a linear program.

Distance in miles	0		1		2		3		4		5		6		7		8		9		10	
Borrow pit availability				300								500							400			
Excess earth	30	90	100	30			10	100	200	210	40						120	200	250	180	20	
Elevation profile Road Terrain	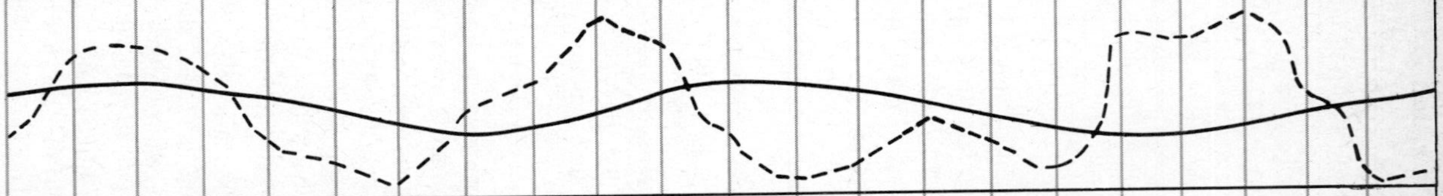																					
Fill requirements	30			20	120	180	150				30	200	280	180	50	110	80			.	90	270
Section no.	1	2	3	4	5	6	7	8	9	10	11	12	13	14	15	16	17	18	19	20	21	22
Hauling cost →	2.3	2.1	2.0	1.7	1.5	2.8	2.5	2.6	2.4	1.7	1.4	1.4	2.0	2.3	1.9	1.6	3.0	2.3	2.4	1.5	1.5	1.7
Hauling cost ←	1.7	1.8	2.0	2.3	2.5	2.0	1.3	1.4	1.6	2.3	2.6	2.6	2.0	1.7	2.1	2.9	1.0	1.7	1.6	2.5	2.5	2.3
Discarding cost	1.2	1.4	2.1	0.7			0.5	0.9	2.4	1.2	0.6						0.3	0.9	1.8	1.7	0.4	
Borrow pit to road cost				12								20							8			

	Pit A	Pit B
Output of unwashed coal	50,000 tons	80,000 tons
Percentage of slack	20%	30%
smalls	30%	40%
+1″	50%	30%
Weight loss by washing		
slack	10%	10%
smalls	20%	15%
+1″	15%	20%
Sulfur content of washed coal		
slack	1.0%	1.8%
smalls	0.9%	1.7%
+1″	0.7%	1.6%
Ash content of washed coal		
slack	9%	18%
smalls	8%	14%
+1″	6%	12%
Transportation cost to briquetting plant	$2.4/ton	$1.2/ton (washed)
Production cost at pit	$4/ton	$4.5/ton (unwashed)
Revenue (washed) slack	$7/ton	$6.5/ton
smalls	$10/ton	$9/ton
+1″	$12/ton	$10/ton

2.22 *(Goal programming problem—graphical)* The superintendent of a country hospital is reviewing the staffing needs of the wards for nursing care. Because the hospital is being financed by public funds, the superintendent feels the obligation to keep running costs low while providing a good but not extravagant service. The service quality depends largely on the number of nurses employed. Past experience indicates that for this hospital at least 100 trained nurses are needed to provide satisfactory service. As a public hospital, there is also the social obligation to provide training for student nurses, with the teaching role falling largely on the trained nursing staff. In terms of meeting the workload, two student nurses are equivalent to one trained nurse. Good practice also indicates that the ideal ratio of trained nurses to student nurses is about 4 to 3. The current budget allocates $124,000/month for nursing staff. Trained nurses get $1200/month, while student nurses cost the hospital $800/month in pay, food and lodging, and teaching expenses. The student nurses home has accommodations for 60 people.

(a) Formulate a mathematical expression for each of the four relationships mentioned in the problem, and represent them graphically. Which ones would you consider to be constraints, and which ones have more the character of goals? Verify that the lowest-cost solution in terms of providing a satisfactory service is to hire only trained nurses.

(b) Consider the restriction of places at the student nurses home as the only hard constraint, while all other relationships are goals (not necessarily the best interpretation for this problem). Introduce slack (and surplus) variables for each goal. Form a goal objective function giving equal weight to positive and negative deviations from the ideal trained nurses/student nurses ratio, to underachievements (only) in the satisfactory workload goal, and to overruns (only) of the budget goal. In terms of the graph in (a), shade in the feasible region. Find the optimal solution. (Hint: Evaluate all intersections of goal lines and select the best.)

(c) Assume now that the ideal ratio of trained nurses to student nurses has highest priority, the satisfactory service level second priority, and the budget goal third priority. What is the optimal solution now?

2.23 *(Goal programming formulation)* A publisher has 4500 spare man-machine hours available in the printing department and 4000 spare man-machine hours available in the binding department. Four books eligible for reprinting require the following time in each department per book produced.

Book	1	2	3	4
Printing dept. (hr)	0.1	0.3	0.8	0.4
Binding dept. (hr)	0.2	0.1	0.1	0.3

The profit on each book is $1 on Book 1; $1 on Book 2; $4 on Book 3; and $3 on Book 4. The publisher's primary aim is to reprint all of the books, if possible, in the following quantities: 6000 for Book 1, 2000 for Book 2, 2000 for Book 3, and 5000 for Book 4. The publisher would prefer not to deviate from any of these quantities by more than 10 percent. The second aim is to use as much binding capacity as possible, since other uses for it are difficult to find. The third aim is to maximize profits. Formulate this problem, and indicate carefully the procedure you would follow in solving it.

REFERENCES

Aronofsky, J. S., J. M. Dutton, and M. T. Tayyabkhan. *Managerial Planning with Linear Programming: In Process Industry Operations*. New York: Wiley, 1978. Book focuses on process industry with emphasis on the oil and petrochemical industry. Strong applications to both tactical and strategic planning.

Daellenbach, H. G., and E. J. Bell. *User's Guide to Linear Programming*. Englewood Cliffs, N.J.: Prentice-Hall, 1970. Introduction to linear programming at an elementary level. Stresses graphical interpretation of concepts and includes sensitivity analysis, with emphasis on problem formulations and solution by computer and detailed analysis of computer sensitivity analysis printout. Easy to read. Chapter 4 develops step by step a number of different types of problem formulations, and Chapter 8 gives the formulation of company-wide operations from supplying raw materials to distributing finished products.

Driebeek, Norman J. *Applied Linear Programming*. Reading, Mass.: Addison-Wesley, 1969. This text has a flavor of real-life applications at a fairly elementary level.

Eck, R. D. *Operations Research for Business*. Belmont, Ca.: Wadsworth, 1976. Chapter 5 has a number of interesting formulation problems.

Levin, R. I., and R. P. Lamone. *Linear Programming for Management Decisions*. Homewood, Ill.: Irwin, 1969. Chapter 9 shows a number of interesting and detailed applications of linear programming.

Smythe, William R., and Lynwood A. Johnson. *Introduction to Linear Programming with Applications*. Englewood Cliffs, N.J.: Prentice-Hall, 1966. Chapter 5 contains an excellent treatment of a number of formulations.

Swanson, L. W. *Linear Programming—Basic Theory and Applications*. New York: McGraw-Hill, 1980. Highly recommended, advanced text. Chapter 9 discusses modeling approaches for more effective interpretation of results.

See also the list of general operations research texts in the Bibliography. Most texts in operations research give a number of formulations, but usually with few or no intermediate steps.

CHAPTER THREE

The Simplex Method

In Chapter 2, we solved linear programming problems graphically with only two decision variables. Real-life problems may have hundreds or even thousands of variables and constraints. We therefore need an efficient solution technique that is easily programmed for electronic computers. In this chapter we will derive an algebraic solution technique, the *simplex method*, developed in 1947 by the U.S. mathematician George B. Dantzig.

The simplex method exploits the fact that an optimal solution has to occur at an extreme point of the feasible region. Thus, we need to show that with each extreme point we associate a particular form of an algebraic solution, called a *basic feasible solution*. The central idea of the simplex method is to move from one basic feasible solution to another, improving the objective function value at each move until the optimal solution has been found. We will first develop the steps of the simplex algorithm. Then we will show how to find a basic feasible solution (if one exists) to start the algorithm.

If you are not familiar with the concepts of *systems of linear equations*, you should study first the short introduction to linear algebra in Appendix A.

3-1 EXTREME POINTS

In the following sections we shall work with a simplified version of the power generating problem studied in Chapter 2. Only the two constraints that are binding at the optimal solution, namely the smoke and pulverizer constraints, will be retained. The optimal solution to both problems will thus be the same. The reduced problem in two decision variables x_1 and x_2 is then to find values for x_1 and x_2 which

$$\text{(3-1)} \qquad \begin{aligned} \text{maximize } & 24x_1 + 20x_2 \\ \text{subject to } & 0.5x_1 + x_2 \leq 12 && \text{(smoke)} \\ & \tfrac{1}{16}x_1 + \tfrac{1}{24}x_2 \leq 1 && \text{(pulverizer)} \\ & x_1 \geq 0, x_2 \geq 0 \end{aligned}$$

Figure 3-1 represents the constraints and nonnegativity conditions for this problem. In Section 2-6 we pointed out that if a linear program has a finite optimal solution, at least one extreme point of the feasible region will be optimal. What does this mean algebraically? Let us convert the two constraints of problem (3-1) to equalities by introducing the two slack variables x_3 and x_5 (we retain the subscripts used in Section 2-8), namely

$$
\begin{aligned}
0.5x_1 + x_2 + x_3 \qquad &= 12 \\
\tfrac{1}{16}x_1 + \tfrac{1}{24}x_2 \qquad + x_5 &= 1
\end{aligned}
\tag{3-2}
$$

Each extreme point of the feasible region can be generated by setting two appropriately chosen variables equal to zero and solving (3-2) for the remaining two.

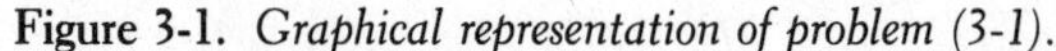

Figure 3-1. *Graphical representation of problem (3-1).*

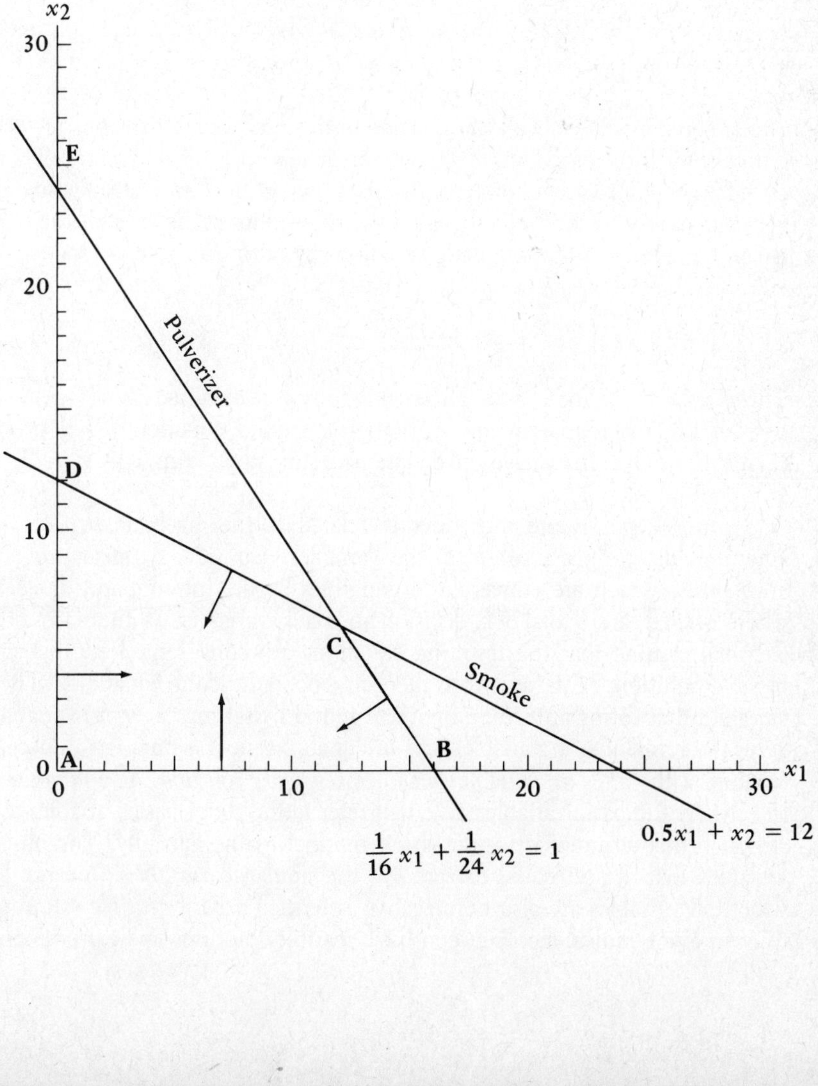

For example, the optimal extreme point ($x_1 = 12$, $x_2 = 6$), labeled C in Figure 3-1, is obtained by setting $x_3 = 0$, $x_5 = 0$ and solving in (3-2) for x_1 and x_2. The extreme point B in Figure 3-1 is obtained by setting $x_2 = 0$ and $x_5 = 0$ and solving for x_1 and x_3. Verify that the solution is $x_1 = 16$, $x_3 = 4$.

The choice of which variables to set equal to zero is not arbitrary. Not every such choice yields a feasible solution. For example, setting $x_1 = 0$ and $x_5 = 0$, we get the solution $x_2 = 24$, $x_3 = -12$, which corresponds to point E in Figure 3-1. This solution is not feasible since one of the variables is negative; hence it is not an extreme point of the feasible region. However, every solution obtained by this procedure that is a feasible solution is an extreme point and vice versa.

Finding the values of the variables associated with these extreme points is easier with some manipulation of the equations in (3-2). For extreme point C, we write the first equation in terms of x_1 but not x_2, and the second in terms of x_2 but not x_1. We leave it to you to verify that eliminating x_2 from the first equation and x_1 from the second gives

$$
\begin{aligned}
x_1 \qquad - x_3 + 24x_5 &= 12 \\
x_2 + \tfrac{3}{2}x_3 - 12x_5 &= 6
\end{aligned}
\tag{3-3}
$$

When equations have been transformed in this way, we say that they are in *canonical form*. From these equations we can immediately read off the values of the variables at extreme point C by simply setting $x_3 = x_5 = 0$. The first equation then yields $x_1 = 12$ and the second $x_2 = 6$. Similarly, the values of the variables at extreme point B can be read from the following equations by setting $x_2 = x_5 = 0$:

$$
\begin{aligned}
x_1 + \tfrac{2}{3}x_2 \qquad + 16x_5 &= 16 \\
\tfrac{2}{3}x_2 + x_3 - 8x_5 &= 4
\end{aligned}
$$

This gives $x_1 = 16$ and $x_3 = 4$. These equations were obtained from (3-2) by eliminating x_3 from the first equation and x_1 from the second equation. And, of course, the equations in (3-2) themselves give extreme point A by setting $x_1 = x_2 = 0$. This yields $x_3 = 12$ and $x_5 = 1$.

Extreme points are thus directly related to the algebraic structure of solving equations using only a subset of the variables. Consider a linear program with m constraints, which are converted to equalities by the introduction of slack variables where needed, and a total of n (decision and slack) variables. Without loss of generality, we shall assume that the resulting equations are consistent, i.e., that at least one feasible solution exists and that there are no redundant equations. The subset of variables that forms an extreme point is found by setting $(n - m)$ variables equal to zero; the remaining m variables and m equations yield a unique solution. We call a solution with $(n - m)$ variables set to zero a *basic solution*. The m variables not set to zero are the basic variables. We will refer to the set of basic variables as the *basis*, although this terminology is not strictly correct mathematically. The other $(n - m)$ variables that are set equal to zero are the *nonbasic variables*. A basic solution in which all variables are also nonnegative is termed a *basic feasible solution*. There is thus an exact equivalence between basic feasible solutions and extreme points.

ALGEBRAIC FORM OF OPTIMAL SOLUTION

The extreme points of the feasible region of a linear program correspond to the basic feasible solutions of the constraint equations. If a linear program has a finite optimal solution, then at least one optimal solution is a basic feasible solution.

The fact that the optimal solution is a basic (feasible) solution has some interesting practical consequences in regard to the form of the solution. Suppose we want to find the optimal activity levels for k activities (other than slack activities) subject to m resource constraints, and $k > m$. The optimal solution will never have more than m of the k activities at positive levels and may have fewer if any slack variables are positive. This property is not intuitively obvious and is sometimes viewed as a disadvantage by decision makers with little mathematical training.

3-2 GENERAL IDEAS OF THE SIMPLEX METHOD

The general idea of the simplex method is to search through the basic feasible solutions (or extreme points) by moving from one basic feasible solution to an adjacent one having a better objective function value. This process continues until no further improvement can be obtained. At that point, an optimal solution has been found. To achieve this change of basic feasible solutions, we need to know:

1. How to find a basic feasible solution adjacent to the previous one.
2. How to ensure that this new basic solution is feasible and hence is an extreme point.
3. How to make sure that the new solution is better than the previous one.

We will only discuss the simplex method for a maximization problem. This is not really a loss of generality, since any minimization problem can be converted readily into a maximization problem by reversing the signs of the coefficients in the objective function.

For example,

$$\text{minimize } z = 2x_1 + 3x_2$$

gives the same solution as

$$\text{maximize } (-z) = -2x_1 - 3x_2$$

So we can transform a minimizing problem to a maximizing problem using

$$\text{minimize } z = -\text{ maximize } (-z)$$

Hence, the same method can handle both maximization and minimization problems. In a two-dimensional representation, the reversing of signs leaves the slope of the objective function unchanged but reverses the direction of movement when the function increases in value. The value of the objective function now increases for movements toward the origin rather than away from the origin.

3-3 SIMULTANEOUS EQUATION APPROACH TO THE SIMPLEX METHOD

Consider again the equations in (3-2). They represent extreme point A with $x_1 = 0$, $x_2 = 0$, $x_3 = 12$, and $x_5 = 1$. The slack variables x_3 and x_5 are the basic variables, while the two decision variables (x_1 and x_2) are nonbasic variables at zero. This is a natural initial basic solution for our algorithm. It says "do nothing." It has an objective function value of $z = 0$. Also, the two constraint equations are already in canonical form.

Let us now also include the objective function in this set of equations. Treating z as a variable, we rewrite the objective functions by transferring all variables to the left-hand side. Its RHS value is set equal to the value of z at that basic feasible solution. In this manner, the three equations are in canonical form, and the values of the basic variables and z can be read off directly, as shown by equations (3-4):

$$
\begin{aligned}
0.5x_1 + x_2 + x_3 \quad &= 12 \\
\tfrac{1}{16}x_1 + \tfrac{1}{24}x_2 \quad + x_5 &= 1 \\
z - 24x_1 - 20x_2 \quad &= 0
\end{aligned}
\tag{3-4}
$$

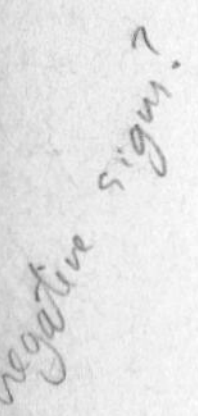

We now ask ourselves if this solution is optimal. To find the answer, we use the equivalent question, "Can the value of the objective function z be increased by increasing the value of any of the nonbasic variables?" Note that it is not possible to change the solution other than by increasing nonbasic variables, because the solution in terms of the basic variables is unique. If we set $x_1 = 1$, z increases by 24. If we set $x_2 = 1$, z increases by 20. By increasing the value of either x_1 or x_2, we can increase z, and the solution ($x_3 = 12$, $x_5 = 1$, and $x_1 = x_2 = 0$) is not optimal. Thus, there may exist extreme points with a higher value of z.

We cannot jump straight to the optimal extreme point—the one with the highest z value—because we do not know which point it is. Instead, the simplex method proceeds in small steps by moving to an extreme point adjacent to the current one but with a higher z value. Such an adjacent point can be found by replacing one of the basic variables (x_3 or x_5) with one of the nonbasic variables (x_1 or x_2); in other words, by changing the basis. We first choose the nonbasic variable to become the new basic variable, or to *enter the basis*. Then we find which of the old basic variables it replaces—or the variable to *leave the basis*. A logical choice for the variable to enter the basis is the one that gives the greatest per unit increase in z, i.e., the variable with the most negative coefficient in the objective function equation in canonical form. In our case, this is x_1 with a coefficient of -24.

Since each unit of x_1 increases z by 24, we should increase x_1 as much as possible. The largest value x_1 can assume depends on what happens to the values of the other variables. In fact, only variables currently in the basis will change as x_1 increases, since all other nonbasic variables will be kept at zero. Using equations (3-4), we can write x_1 in terms of x_3 and x_5:

$$x_1 = (12 - x_3)/0.5 \quad \text{or} \quad x_3 = 12 - 0.5x_1 \qquad (3\text{-}5)$$

$$x_1 = (1 - x_5)/\tfrac{1}{16} \quad \text{or} \quad x_5 = 1 - \tfrac{1}{16}x_1$$

Verify that as x_1 increases, both x_3 and x_5 decrease. Since neither x_3 or x_5 is permitted to become negative, x_1 must not increase beyond the value that first reduces one of them to zero. By equations (3-5), the largest value x_1 may assume is

$$x_1 = \text{minimum}\,(12/0.5,\ 1/\tfrac{1}{16}) = 16 \qquad (3\text{-}6)$$

At this point $x_5 = 0$, while $x_3 = 4$. So x_5 leaves the basis to become a nonbasic variable. The new solution is a basic solution because only m $(=2)$ variables are nonnegative. It is a basic feasible solution because all variables remain nonnegative. This solution corresponds to extreme point B in Figure 3-1, with $x_1 = 16$, $x_3 = 4$, and $x_2 = x_5 = 0$. Note that this point is indeed adjacent to point A. By increasing x_1 from 0 to 16, we move along the edge from point A to point B.

The next task is to find the set of equations in canonical form for this new solution, with x_1 and x_3 as the new basis and with x_2 and x_5 as the nonbasic variables. Starting with equations (3-4), we divide the second equation by $\frac{1}{16}$. We then eliminate x_1 from the first equation by subtracting 0.5 times the new second equation from the first equation. The new objective function is found by subtracting -24 times the new second equation from the old objective function equation. These operations result in the following set of equations:

$$\begin{aligned} \tfrac{2}{3}x_2 + x_3 - \quad 8x_5 &= 4 \\ x_1 + \tfrac{2}{3}x_2 \quad + \ 16x_5 &= 16 \qquad (3\text{-}7) \\ z \quad - 4x_2 \quad + 384x_5 &= 384 \end{aligned}$$

We can now read off the values of the basic variables as $x_1 = 16$ and $x_3 = 4$. The new value of $z = 384$ corresponds to the increase of x_1 to 16; i.e., an increase in z of 24 for each unit increase in x_1 gives $24(16) = 384$. This completes the first iteration of the simplex algorithm.

We are now in a position analogous to the beginning of iteration 1. We again have a basic feasible solution in canonical form (with a higher z value, though) and can repeat the whole process. So, we start a second iteration by asking again whether the z value can be further increased by increasing any of the nonbasic variables. Verify from equations (3-7) that a unit increase in x_2 increases z by 4, while a unit increase in x_5 reduces z by 384. Hence the extreme point corresponding to (3-7) is not optimal, since the z value may be further increased if x_2 enters the basis. Clearly we would not wish to increase x_5, because then the objective function would decrease in value.

Which of the currently basic variables, x_1 and x_3, is to leave the basis? Using the same logic as for the first iteration, we have

$$\begin{aligned} x_2 &= (4 - x_3)/\tfrac{2}{3} \quad \text{or} \quad x_3 = 4 - \tfrac{2}{3}x_2 \\ x_2 &= (16 - x_1)/\tfrac{2}{3} \quad \text{or} \quad x_1 = 16 - \tfrac{2}{3}x_2 \end{aligned} \tag{3-8}$$

The largest value x_2 may assume then is

$$x_2 = \text{minimum}(4/\tfrac{2}{3}, 16/\tfrac{2}{3}) = 6 \tag{3-9}$$

Thus, x_3 leaves the basis.

The final operations of iteration 2 involve finding the canonical form associated with the new basis so that we may determine the values of the new basic variables and of z. This is achieved by dividing the first equation of (3-7) by $\frac{2}{3}$, subtracting $\frac{2}{3}$ times this new equation from the second equation, and subtracting -4 times the new first equation from the objective function equation:

$$\begin{aligned} x_2 + \tfrac{3}{2}x_3 - 12x_5 &= 6 \\ x_1 \qquad - x_3 + 24x_5 &= 12 \\ z \qquad + 6x_3 + 336x_5 &= 408 \end{aligned} \tag{3-10}$$

Verify that by setting $x_3 = x_5 = 0$, we find $x_1 = 12$, $x_2 = 6$, and $z = 408$. z increases from 384 by 6(4).

We now start iteration 3. Checking first for a nonbasic variable that will increase z, we see that there is none. The objective function value cannot be improved any further, so we have reached the optimal extreme point. The simplex method thus terminates after two iterations. Let us now formalize the rules used at various points in the above operations.

3-4 THE VARIABLE ENTERING THE BASIS

To find the variable to enter the basis, we examine the coefficient of each nonbasic variable in the z row—the objective function expressed in canonical form corresponding to the current basis. These coefficients are often referred to as the *reduced objective function coefficients*, or the *reduced cost coefficients*. What is their meaning?

Each coefficient measures the difference between the contribution toward the z value of a unit of that nonbasic variable and the contribution from the same quantities of the resources used via the current basic variables. Let us explain this using an example from the equations in canonical form in (3-7). Recall that 1 unit of x_2 (burning 1 ton of coal B) produces $c_2 = 20$ units of steam while consuming 1 kilogram of smoke emission capacity and $\frac{1}{24}$ hour of pulverizer capacity. What proportion of the basic variables use the same amount of resources as 1 unit of x_2? To answer this we set $x_2 = 1$ in equations (3-7) with $x_5 = 0$. For the first equation to hold true, x_3 (smoke emission slack) is reduced by $\frac{2}{3}$ ($= \gamma_1$), and for the second equation to hold true, x_1 (burning of coal A) is reduced by $\frac{2}{3}$ ($= \gamma_2$). We see that burning 1 ton of coal B is equivalent, in terms of the resources used, to having $\gamma_1 = \frac{2}{3}$ of smoke emission slack plus burning $y_2 = \frac{2}{3}$ ton of coal A. We might think of this combination of the basic variables as 1 ton of "synthetic coal B." (Verify that this is also correct for the original problem in the form of (3-4) by setting $x_1 = (16 - y_2)$, $x_2 = 1$, $x_3 = (4 - y_1)$, and $x_5 = 0$.) Let z_2 denote the contribution toward steam output of 1 ton of "synthetic coal B" (in terms of the basic variables x_1 and x_3). It is

$$z_2 = c_3 y_1 + c_1 y_2 = (0)\tfrac{2}{3} + (24)\tfrac{2}{3} = 16 \tag{3-11}$$

By tradition, we subtract the original objective function coefficient from this "equivalent resource use" contribution; i.e., the reduced objective function coefficient is given as $z_2 - c_2 = 16 - 20 = -4$. This is the coefficient of x_2 in the transformed z row of equations (3-7). It is the decrease in value of the objective function for a unit increase in the variable.

The above reasoning is couched in terms of the use of scarce resources. However, it can be generalized to any type of activity variable and any type of constraint. The reduced objective function coefficient $(z_j - c_j)$ always represents the reduction in the objective function that results from one unit of the variable x_j replacing the equivalent amount of the constraints used by the basic variables. This even holds true for the reduced objective function coefficients of the basic variables. The equivalent resource use of a basic variable is the basic variable itself. Hence $z_j = c_j$, resulting in a reduced objective function coefficient of zero.

If the direct contribution c_j exceeds the indirect contribution z_j, i.e, if $(z_j - c_j) < 0$, then introducing x_j into the basis will increase the objective function value. If more than one nonbasic variable has $(z_j - c_j) < 0$, then a common criterion is to choose the one that yields the largest per unit improvement in the objective function. What if there is no $(z_j - c_j) < 0$? Then no further improvement is possible, and we have reached the optimal basic feasible solution. Thus the reduced objective function coefficients tell us whether the current solution can be further improved or whether it is optimal.

SIMPLEX CRITERION 1: VARIABLE ENTERING BASIS

The variable to enter the basis is the one that has the most negative $(z_j - c_j)$ value.

OPTIMALITY CRITERION

A basic feasible solution is optimal if all $(z_j - c_j) \geq 0$ for the nonbasic variables.

3-5 THE VARIABLE LEAVING THE BASIS

We will now examine what happens to the values of current basic variables when we introduce x_2 into the basis. In the preceding section, we observed that a unit increase in x_2 in expressions (3-7) resulted in a simultaneous decrease in x_3 of $\gamma_1 = \frac{2}{3}$, and in x_1 of $\gamma_2 = \frac{2}{3}$. Similarly, an increase of $x_2 = \theta$ in (3-7) will cause x_3 and x_1 to decrease proportionately, i.e.,

$$x_3 = 4 - \gamma_1\theta = 4 - \tfrac{2}{3}\theta$$
$$x_1 = 16 - \gamma_2\theta = 16 - \tfrac{2}{3}\theta$$

As θ increases, x_1 or x_3 will ultimately be driven to zero. Any further increase in θ will cause one or the other or both of these variables to become negative. Such a solution is not feasible. Hence, the largest value of θ that x_2 may assume (while still maintaining feasibility) is the smaller of the two ratios $4/\gamma_1$ and $16/\gamma_2$. In our case this is

$$\theta = \text{minimum } (4/\tfrac{2}{3},\ 16/\tfrac{2}{3}) = 6$$

If either γ_1 or γ_2 had been negative or zero, then that ratio could have been ignored. The corresponding basic variable would either increase in value or remain unchanged as x_2 increased. Generalizing these observations, we get the next important rule of the simplex method.

SIMPLEX CRITERION 2: VARIABLE LEAVING BASIS

Given the γ_i's for the nonbasic variable entering the basis, the variable leaving is the one that satisfies

$$\theta = \text{minimum } \frac{(\text{value of basis variable } x_i)}{(\text{corresponding } \gamma_i)} \quad \text{for all } \gamma_i > 0$$

θ is the value of the new basic variable x_j in the new solution.

If there are no positive γ_i's, θ can be increased without bound because none of the variables in the present basis will go to zero. As θ increases, so does the value of the objective function; and since θ can be increased without bound, the objective function also goes to infinity. This is called an *unbounded solution*.

CRITERION FOR UNBOUNDED SOLUTION

If, for some $(z_j - c_j) < 0$, all γ_i values are nonpositive, the linear programming problem has no finite optimal solution.

Given the interpretation of the reduced objective function coefficients $(z_j - c_j)$, it also follows that the new value of the objective function increases to $z - \theta\,(z_j - c_j)$. [Remember that $(z_j - c_j) < 0$.]

3-6 THE SIMPLEX TABLEAU

The computations of the simplex method are most conveniently performed in a tableau structure known as the *simplex tableau*. For the reduced version of the power generating problem (3-1), the simplex tableau for the initial basic solution of slack variables is shown in Table 3-1. This table does no more than set the coefficients of the equations (3-4) in a convenient form.

The first two rows are header rows for reference purposes only. The top row has the values of the objective function coefficients c_j for each variable x_j, and the second row indicates to which variable each column refers. The c_j column on the extreme left contains the objective function coefficients for the basic variables. These coefficients are required to find the z_j values. The variables that form the basis are listed in the second column. The columns under the variable names give the coefficients in the canonical form. The column labeled "Solution" contains the values of the basic variables. The $(z_j - c_j)$ row of the table corresponds to the z row of (3-4). Using logic similar to that used in equation (3-11), z_j can be calculated by multiplying each element in the x_j column by the corresponding element in the c_j column and summing over all rows, e.g., $z_1 = (0.5)(0) + (\frac{1}{16})(0)$. For all subsequent discussions, when we refer to the rows of the simplex tableau, the two header rows at the top will be ignored. For example, in Table 3-1, row 1 is the x_3 row.

Table 3-1. *Initial simplex tableau*

	c_j			24	20	0	0	Ratio
	c_j	Basis	Solution	x_1	x_2	x_3	x_5	x_i/γ_i
	0	x_3	12	0.5	1	1	0	$\frac{12}{0.5} = 24$
Variable out ←	0	x_5	1	$\textcircled{\frac{1}{16}}$	$\frac{1}{24}$	0	1	$\frac{1}{1/16} = 16$
		$z_j - c_j$	0	-24	-20	0	0	
				↑ Variable in				

3-7 ITERATIONS OF THE SIMPLEX METHOD

We are now ready for the first iteration of the simplex method. By simplex criterion 1, the nonbasic variable x_1 enters the basis because it has the most negative $(z_j - c_j)$ value, as shown by the arrow below $(z_1 - c_1)$ in Table 3-1.

The values of the basic variables are the corresponding elements in the solution column, and the γ_i coefficients of x_1 are the elements in column x_1. To find the variable leaving the basis, we compute the ratio of these two numbers for all $\gamma_i > 0$, as shown in the last column of Table 3-1. By simplex criterion 2, x_5 leaves the basis because it has the smallest value of this ratio. The new basis is (x_3, x_1).

Our next task is to transform this tableau into the canonical form corresponding to the new basis. We will define the *pivot row* as the row of the variable leaving the basis, which becomes the row of the new basic variable. This is row 2 in Table 3-1. We will define the *pivot column* as the column associated with the variable entering the basis—in our case column x_1 in Table 3-1. The *pivot element* is defined as the element that is in both the pivot row and the pivot column. In our case, it is the fraction $\frac{1}{16}$, shown circled in Table 3-1.

To get the tableau into the new canonical form, we must transform the pivot column so that the pivot element equals 1 and all other column elements are zero. This is achieved by the following rules.

TRANSFORMATION RULES

1. The pivot row is transformed by dividing it by the pivot element.
2. All other rows, including the $(z_j - c_j)$ row, are transformed as follows: if $\bar{\gamma}_i$ is the element in both the pivot column and row i, then row i is transformed by subtracting $\bar{\gamma}_i$ times the transformed pivot row from row i.

You should confirm that these rules are the same as the transformation operations used in Section 3-3.

Table 3-2 gives the second and third simplex tableaux, which correspond to equations (3-7) and (3-10). The application of the simplex criteria confirms the calculations shown in Section 3-3. You may wish to refer back to Sections 3-3 through 3-5 to strengthen your understanding of the data in Table 3-2 and the reasons for the simplex criteria.

From the solution column we can read off the basic feasible solution $x_2 = 6$, $x_1 = 12$, with the nonbasic variables x_3 and x_5 equal to zero and a value of $z = 408$.

Table 3-2. *Second and third simplex tableaux*

		c_j		24	20	0	0	Ratio
	c_j	Basis	Solution	x_1	x_2	x_3	x_5	x_i/γ_i
←	0	x_3	4	0	$\frac{2}{3}$ (circled)	1	−8	$\frac{4}{2/3} = 6$
	24	x_1	16	1	$\frac{2}{3}$	0	16	$\frac{16}{2/3} = 24$
		$z_j - c_j$	384	0	−4 ↑	0	384	
	20	x_2	6	0	1	$\frac{3}{2}$	−12	
	24	x_1	12	1	0	−1	24	
		$z_j - c_j$	408	0	0	6	336	

By the optimality criterion, we also have reached the optimal solution, since no $(z_j - c_j)$ values are negative.

3-8 INITIAL BASIC FEASIBLE SOLUTION AND ARTIFICIAL VARIABLES

How do we find an initial basic feasible solution to start the simplex method iterations? Most linear programming problems do not have an initial solution of nonnegative slack variables in canonical form. Some constraints may be equality constraints or "larger-than-or-equal-to" constraints. The original (or "do nothing") solution is no longer feasible. In such a case, there is no guarantee that a feasible solution even exists—the constraints may be inconsistent. What is needed is a systematic and efficient method to generate an initial basic feasible solution.

One of the outstanding features of the simplex method is that the method itself can be used to generate its own initial feasible basis (provided one exists) or else to indicate that the problem has no feasible solution.

To initiate the simplex method, we use the trick of artificially creating a set of equations in canonical form. We do this by introducing into each constraint not containing a slack variable with a +1 LHS coefficient a so-called *artificial variable* that does have such a property. The new problem thus created is called the *augmented problem*. Geometrically, we are expanding the feasible region to include the origin of the space. Therefore, we are sure that the augmented problem is feasible.

Let us illustrate this idea with the original power generating problem as summarized below:

$$\begin{array}{llr} & \text{maximize} & 24x_1 + 20x_2 \\ & \text{subject to} & 0.5x_1 + x_2 + x_3 = 12 \\ (3\text{-}12) & & x_1 + x_2 + x_4 = 20 \\ & & \tfrac{1}{16}x_1 + \tfrac{1}{24}x_2 + x_5 = 1 \\ & & 1200x_1 - 800x_2 - x_6 = 0 \\ & & x_1, x_2, x_3, x_4, x_5, x_6 \geqslant 0 \end{array}$$

There are four equations, so we need four basic variables. The slack variables x_3, x_4, and x_5 can be used as the basic variables for the first three equations. But since the sulfur constraint is a $\geqslant$ inequality, its slack variable has the wrong sign. (Note that in this example we could obtain an initial basis by multiplying this constraint by -1. However, for demonstration purposes, we will not do that here.)

We now augment the original problem by adding the artificial variable x_7 to the fourth constraint:

$$\begin{array}{lr} & 0.5x_1 + x_2 + x_3 = 12 \\ & x_1 + x_2 + x_4 = 20 \\ (3\text{-}13) & \tfrac{1}{16}x_1 + \tfrac{1}{24}x_2 + x_5 = 1 \\ & 1200x_1 - 800x_2 - x_6 + x_7 = 0 \\ & x_1, \ldots, x_7 \geqslant 0 \end{array}$$

The variables (x_3, x_4, x_5, x_7) form an initial basis to equations (3-13). The artificial variable x_7 has no meaning in terms of the original linear program (3-12). So, although we have an initial basic feasible solution to the augmented problem, the solution is not a basic feasible solution of the original problem, since x_7 is not a part of that problem. Our first task is to construct, from the initial solution to the augmented problem, a basic feasible solution to the original problem by removing all artificial variables from the basis. This then becomes our "initial basic feasible solution" from which we find an optimal solution to the original problem. We will consider two methods of doing this—the *big M method* and the *two-phase method*. The big M method is attractive because it is a simple extension of the simplex method developed so far. However, most large-scale computer programs use the two-phase method.

3-9 THE BIG *M* METHOD

The idea of the big M method is very simple. We give the augmented problem the same objective function as the original problem, except that we penalize each artificial variable heavily with a large negative objective function coefficient, say an amount $-M$ (hence the name of the method). So any basic feasible solution that includes artificial variables is most unattractive. In the process of reaching the optimal solution to the augmented problem, the simplex method will remove the artificial variables from the basis if at all possible. The big M method just uses the inherent logic of linear programming and the simplex method to provide an optimal solution to the augmented problem that is also optimal for the original problem.

What if the optimal solution to the augmented problem has artificial variables at a nonzero level? We must argue that the simplex method would have excluded these variables if it could. Since it cannot exclude them, there is no feasible solution to the augmented problem that is also feasible for the original problem. That simply means that there is no feasible solution to the original problem because its feasible region is completely contained in the feasible region of the augmented problem.

We have then the following two criteria.

BIG *M* METHOD CRITERION: OPTIMALITY

The optimal solution to the augmented problem is optimal to the original problem if there are no artificial variables with nonzero value in the optimal solution.

BIG *M* METHOD CRITERION: NO FEASIBLE SOLUTION

If any artificial variable is in the basis with nonzero value at the optimal solution of the augmented problem, then the original problem has no feasible solution.

Table 3-3 *The big M method for problem (3-14)*

			c_j	24	20	0	0	0	0	$-M$	Ratio
	c_j	Basis	Solution	x_1	x_2	x_3	x_4	x_5	x_6	x_7	x_i/Y_i
	0	x_3	12	$\frac{1}{2}$	1	1	0	0	0	0	24
	0	x_4	20	1	1	0	1	0	0	0	20
	0	x_5	1	$\frac{1}{16}$	$\frac{1}{24}$	0	0	1	0	0	16
←	$-M$	x_7	0	(1200)	-800	0	0	0	-1	1	0
		z_j-c_j	0	$(-1200M - 24)$ ↑	$(800M - 20)$	0	0	0	M	0	
←	0	x_3	12	0	($\frac{4}{3}$)	1	0	0	$\frac{1}{2400}$	$-\frac{1}{2400}$	9
	0	x_4	20	0	$\frac{5}{3}$	0	1	0	$\frac{1}{1200}$	$-\frac{1}{1200}$	12
	0	x_5	1	0	$\frac{1}{12}$	0	0	1	$\frac{1}{19200}$	$-\frac{1}{19200}$	12
	24	x_1	0	1	$-\frac{2}{3}$	0	0	0	$-\frac{1}{1200}$	$\frac{1}{1200}$	
		z_j-c_j	0	0	-36 ↑	0	0	0	$-\frac{1}{50}$	$\frac{1}{50}+M$	
	20	x_2	9	0	1	$\frac{3}{4}$	0	0	$\frac{1}{3200}$	$-\frac{1}{3200}$	28800
	0	x_4	5	0	0	$-\frac{5}{4}$	1	0	$\frac{1}{3200}$	$-\frac{1}{3200}$	16000
←	0	x_5	$\frac{1}{4}$	0	0	$-\frac{1}{16}$	0	1	($\frac{1}{38400}$)	$-\frac{1}{38400}$	9600
	24	x_1	6	1	0	$\frac{1}{2}$	0	0	$\frac{1}{1600}$	$\frac{1}{1600}$	
		z_j-c_j	324	0	0	27	0	0	$-\frac{7}{800}$ ↑	$\frac{7}{800}+M$	
	20	x_2	6	0	1	$\frac{3}{2}$	0	-12	0	0	
	0	x_4	2	0	0	$-\frac{1}{2}$	1	-12	0	0	
	0	x_6	9600	0	0	-2400	0	38400	1	-1	
	24	x_1	12	1	0	-1	0	24	0	0	
		z_j-c_j	408	0	0	6	0		0	M	

So to solve equations (3-13), we give an objective function coefficient of $-M$ to x_7, whereas all other variables have the original coefficients shown in (3-12). Thus we have the linear program

(3-14)
$$\text{maximize } 24x_1 + 20x_2 - Mx_7$$
$$\text{subject to the constraint set (3-13)}$$

Table 3-3 lists the sequence of tableaux for solving problem (3-14). The top row reflects the augmented objective function with $c_7 = -M$. Before we can begin the computations, we need to find the $(z_j - c_j)$ row using the method outline in Section 3-6. Since $c_7 = -M$ is the only nonzero objective function coefficient of the basic variables, we find the $(z_j - c_j)$ row by subtracting M times the row x_7 from the negative of the c_j row. We thus get the top tableau in canonical form.

At the first iteration, the choice of x_1 to enter the basis is determined by the $-1200M$ part of $(z_1 - c_1)$, since that completely dominates the term -24. By coincidence, x_7 is removed immediately—that need not have been the case because it is the ratio (x_i / γ_i) that determines the variable to leave the basis. The rest of the iterations are not affected by the penalty cost, except that the penalty prevents x_7 from entering the basis again. In fact, the x_7 column could be removed from the tableau after the first iteration without altering the outcome.

The big M method may lead to difficulties when used on a computer. The first difficulty is that if M is very large, the non-M part of each $(z_j - c_j)$ (i.e., the part that is not a multiple of M) may get lost because of the machine's finite precision. Naturally, $(z_j - c_j)$ could be computed from first principles at each iteration, but this would be extravagant in computing time. On the other hand, if M is too small, wrong answers may arise through the non-M part of $(z_j - c_j)$ negating the effect of the penalty cost. Unfortunately, the best value for M will vary from problem to problem.

3-10 THE TWO-PHASE METHOD

The two-phase method avoids the weakness of the big M method by distinguishing the two phases implicit in it. We saw that the big M method simultaneously seeks a feasible solution to the original problem and an optimal solution to the original problem. In the two-phase method, we first try to find an initial basic feasible solution to the original problem in phase 1. If no feasible solution exists, phase 1 indicates this right away. Phase 2 starts with this initial basic feasible solution and finds the optimal solution to the original problem. So we use the simplex method to find its own starting solution as well as to find an optimal solution.

In the two-phase method we remove the artificial variables from the basis in the following way. In phase 1 we introduce a separate objective function, often referred to as the *infeasibility form*, which gives each artificial variable an objective function coefficient of -1 and each true variable a coefficient of 0. By maximizing the infeasibility form, we endeavor to force the artificial variables to leave the basis. If a feasible solution exists for the original problem, the maximum value of the infeasibility form is zero. If phase 1 terminates with basic artificial variables at a positive value, no feasible solution exists for the original problem. (It is possible, though, to have basic artificial variables with a value of zero at the end of phase 1. These will not be permitted to assume positive values in the phase 2 optimization.)

**TWO-PHASE METHOD CRITERION:
NO FEASIBLE SOLUTION**

If phase 1 terminates with positive-valued basic artificial variables, then there is no feasible solution to the original linear programming problem.

For our example, the phase 1 problem consists of

$$\text{(3-15)}\qquad \begin{aligned}&\text{maximize } 0x_1 + 0x_2 + 0x_3 + 0x_4 + 0x_5 + 0x_6 - x_7\\ &\text{subject to the constraint set (3-13)}\end{aligned}$$

Table 3-4. *Phase 1 of two-phase method*

First Simplex Tableau

			c_j	24	20	0	0	0	0	0	Ratio
			$\bar{c}_j$	0	0	0	0	0	0	-1	
c_j	$\bar{c}_j$	Basis	Solution	x_1	x_2	x_3	x_4	x_5	x_6	x_7	x_i/γ_i
0	0	x_3	12	$\frac{1}{2}$	1	1	0	0	0	0	24
0	0	x_4	20	1	1	0	1	0	0	0	20
0	0	x_5	1	$\frac{1}{16}$	$\frac{1}{24}$	0	0	1	0	0	16
← 0	-1	x_7	0	(1200)	-800	0	0	0	-1	1	0
		$z_j - c_j$	0	-24	-20	0	0	0	0	0	
		$\bar{z}_j - \bar{c}_j$	0	-1200 ↑	800	0	0	0	1	0	

Second Simplex Tableau

c_j	$\bar{c}_j$	Basis	Solution	x_1	x_2	x_3	x_4	x_5	x_6	x_7
0	0	x_3	12	0	$\frac{4}{3}$	1	0	0	$\frac{1}{2400}$	$-\frac{1}{2400}$
0	0	x_4	20	0	$\frac{5}{3}$	0	1	0	$\frac{1}{1200}$	$\frac{1}{1200}$
0	0	x_5	1	0	$\frac{1}{12}$	0	0	1	$\frac{1}{19200}$	$-\frac{1}{19200}$
24	0	x_1	0	1	$-\frac{2}{3}$	0	0	0	$-\frac{1}{1200}$	$\frac{1}{1200}$
		$z_j - c_j$	0	0	-36	0	0	0	$-\frac{1}{50}$	$\frac{1}{50}$
		$\bar{z}_j - \bar{c}_j$	0	0	0	0	0	0	0	1

The simplex tableaux for phase 1 are shown in Table 3-4. Again, our first task is to transform the objective function of phase 1 into canonical form. We denote $(z_j - c_j)$ values of the infeasibility form by $(\bar{z}_j - \bar{c}_j)$. The value of $(\bar{z}_j - \bar{c}_j)$ is found by subtracting the x_7 row from the negative of the $\bar{c}_j$ row (show as the second row of the top tableau). During the phase 1 computations, we find it useful to carry the $(z_j - c_j)$ values of the original objective function along in the usual manner, except that these values are not used to decide which variables should enter the basis.

At the first iteration, variable x_1 enters the basis and drives out x_7. The canonical form for the new basis (x_3, x_4, x_5, x_1) is shown in the second tableau. The infeasibility form has a value of zero, and no negative $(\bar{z}_j - \bar{c}_j)$ values remain. Phase 1 has terminated in a basic feasible solution to the original problem in one iteration.

As an interesting footnote, let us point out that x_1 is a basic variable at a zero value. Such a solution is called a *degenerate solution*. We shall discuss this further in Section 3-12.

Once phase 1 has yielded a basic feasible solution to the original linear program, we reinstate the original objective function and ignore the artificial variables in all subsequent computations.

If we carry the original objective function along during the phase 1 computations, phase 2 can start immediately because the original linear program is in canonical form. Otherwise the $(z_j - c_j)$ row has to be computed in the manner described in Section 3-4. For reasons that will become clear in Chapter 5, it is also advantageous to carry the columns for the artificial variables along in the usual manner during the phase 2 computations, except that the artificial variables will never be allowed to become positive again.

The phase 2 tableaux are the same as the last three in Table 3-4 except for the $(z_7 - c_7)$ values. The optimality condition is satisfied at the third tableau with the optimal solution of $x_1 = 12$, $x_2 = 6$, $x_3 = 0$, $x_4 = 2$, $x_5 = 0$, $x_6 = 9600$, $z = 408$. The reader may find it instructive to trace the sequence of solutions of phase 1 and phase 2 on Figure 2-3 in Chapter 2.

3-11 ALTERNATIVE OPTIMAL SOLUTIONS

When the objective function is parallel to the edge of a constraint, the optimal solution is not unique. We illustrated this point in Section 2-9. This condition can be identified as follows.

> ALTERNATIVE OPTIMAL SOLUTIONS
>
> If at the optimal tableau one or more of the nonbasic variables has $(z_j - c_j) = 0$, then each one of them is a candidate to enter alternative optimal bases.

This is intuitively reasonable because a $(z_j - c_j)$ value of zero means that it is neither beneficial nor detrimental to have that variable in the basis—the value of the objective function will not change. The alternative optimal basic solutions can be found by evaluating each basis formed by all combinations of variables with $(z_j - c_j)$ values of zero at the optimal solution. Note that in the case of degenerate solutions, a different basic solution need not result in different values of the variables and a different extreme point. Furthermore, any convex combinations (linear combinations with proportions summing to 1) of the alternative optimal basic solutions will yield an optimal nonbasic solution. The set of all convex combinations is the edge of the feasible region along which the objective function lies. (Section A-4 of Appendix A discusses convex combinations.) Table 3-5 illustrates the example of Section 2-9 with

Table 3-5. *Alternative optimal solutions*

	c_j		30	20	0	0	0	0	—
c_j	Basis	Solution	x_1	x_2	x_3	x_4	x_5	x_6	x_7
← 20	x_2	6	0	1	($\frac{3}{2}$)	0	−12	0	0
0	x_4	2	0	0	$-\frac{1}{2}$	1	−12	0	0
0	x_6	9600	0	0	−2400	0	38400	1	−1
30	x_1	12	1	0	−1	0	24	0	0
	$z_j - c_j$	480	0	0	0 ↑	0	480	0	—
0	x_3	4	0	$\frac{2}{3}$	1	0	−8	0	0
0	x_4	4	0	$\frac{1}{3}$	0	1	−16	0	0
0	x_6	19200	0	1600	0	0	19200	1	−1
30	x_1	16	1	$\frac{2}{3}$	0	0	16	0	0
	$z_j - c_j$	480	0	0	0	0	480	0	—

the objective function

$$\text{maximize } 30x_1 + 20x_2$$

The simplex method arrives at an optimal basis of (x_2, x_4, x_6, x_1) with $(z_3 - c_3) = 0$. Introducing x_3 into the basis, we get the alternative optimal basis of (x_3, x_4, x_6, x_1).

Not only are these two basic solutions optimal, i.e.,

$$x_1 = 12, \quad x_2 = 6, \quad x_3 = 0, \quad x_4 = 2, \quad x_5 = 0, \quad x_6 = 9600$$

and

$$\bar{x}_1 = 16, \quad \bar{x}_2 = 0, \quad \bar{x}_3 = 4, \quad \bar{x}_4 = 4, \quad \bar{x}_5 = 0, \quad \bar{x}_6 = 19{,}200$$

but so are all the points on the line segment between these two solutions, i.e.,

$$\text{(3-16)} \qquad \hat{x}_j = (1 - \lambda)x_j + \lambda\bar{x}_j, \qquad 0 < \lambda < 1$$

These are optimal solutions (though not basic), all with the same value of the objective function of $z = 480$.

3-12 DEGENERACY

When one or more basic variables has a value of zero (as x_1 did at the end of phase 1 in Table 3-4), the basic solution is called a *degenerate solution*. Theoretically, this may spell trouble for the simplex method. To prove the convergence of the simplex method in a finite number of iterations, we must assume that the value of the objective function increases at each iteration. When this occurs, each basis in the sequence traced out by the simplex method has a unique value of z, and so no basis can appear more than once. Since there is only a finite number of basic feasible solutions, the simplex method converges to the optimal solution in a finite number of iterations.

However, when a variable enters a basic solution at a zero value, the value of the objective function does not change at that iteration. If this occurs a number of times in sequence, it is conceivable that a previous basis will reappear. If we then follow exactly the same sequence of computations and selection rules as we did when this basis was encountered for the first time, we are caught in a circle without exit. This is known as *cycling*.

Although degeneracy is fairly common, the danger of cycling seems to be negligible and is usually ignored. However, there are a number of ways to prevent cycling. The most satisfactory and sophisticated way is a special version of the simplex method called the *lexicographic form of the simplex method*. (See M. Simmonard, *Linear Programming*, pp. 63–66.) Another method used to prevent cycling is to remove the degeneracy. This can be done by *perturbing* the degenerate variable (i.e., by giving it a very small nonzero value). If the perturbation is very small, the effect on the optimal solution is also small, although it may rise substantially over many iterations. This is a danger. Computer codes by the very nature of their computational system accumulate rounding errors during the arithmetic operations from iteration to iteration and thus automatically introduce minute perturbations. Thus, in practice, cycling can usually be ignored. Most of the examples of cycling reported in the literature are mathematical fabrications designed to illustrate the problem.

The authors have encountered a practical problem in which degeneracy has created difficulties. The original problem had many zero RHS parameters. While it is not clear that cycling occurred, perturbing the variables greatly improved the convergence of the problem. In this situation, the computer will not do its own perturbing.

3-13 COMPUTER CODES AND THE SIMPLEX METHOD

Most commercial linear programming computer codes do not use the *full tableau simplex method* as described in this chapter. Instead they work with the *revised simplex method* in which less data are updated at each iteration. With this method, it is also possible to periodically (after a predetermined number of iterations) rid the current solution of many of the rounding errors accumulated during the updating operations. We will study the revised simplex method in Chapter 17.

The accuracy of the final solution depends also on the various *tolerances* built into the computer code or specified by the user at data input time. At various points in the computations of the simplex method, checks are made on certain entries in the tableau, such as the $(z_j - c_j)$ values and the pivot column, to determine if they are equal to zero. Errors may be introduced by the manner in which the computer stores and manipulates decimal numbers. Therefore, for all practical purposes, entries with small deviations from zero, such a plus or minus 10^{-6}, are taken to be equal to zero. These limits are referred to as tolerances.

Choosing the tolerances is not always easy. Tighter (smaller) tolerances are more difficult to satisfy and may let through computer errors, i.e., allow zero elements to be treated as nonzero. For example, the authors have experienced cases where too tight a tolerance for the optimality condition of the infeasibility form resulted in problems being diagnosed wrongly as having no feasible solution. By loosening this tolerance, we resolved the difficulty and produced a feasible solution. Alternatively, loose tolerances may treat genuinely nonzero data as zero.

The accuracy of the final answer can also be improved by proper *scaling* of the input data. Extremely large and extremely small numbers in the same problem should be avoided whenever possible, since their simultaneous presence increases the danger of large error accumulation. By suitable elementary row-and-column operations on the input data, we can eliminate some of these variations. This procedure, called scaling, was used on the objective function of the power generating problem. Rather than specify the objective function coefficients in pounds, we used units of 1000 pounds. This is equivalent to multiplying the objective function by $\frac{1}{1000}$. The combined effect of scaling is often confusing. Fortunately, the better computer codes have options for internal scaling and unscaling before the results are printed.

EXERCISES

3.1 Graph the constraint set in solution space:

$$2x_1 + 4x_2 \leq 8$$
$$x_1 - x_2 \leq 1$$
$$x_1, x_2 \geq 0$$

Find the basic solutions that correspond to each of the extreme points of the feasible region. Remember to add slack variables.

3.2 For the constraint set

$$2x_1 + 4x_2 + x_3 \leq 8$$
$$3x_1 + 2x_2 + 6x_3 \leq 6$$
$$x_1, x_2, x_3 \geq 0$$

find all the basic solutions. Which ones are basic feasible solutions?

3.3 For each of the equation sets below, graph the feasible region. Show that the corner points correspond to the basic feasible solutions.

(a) $x_1 + x_2 \leq 4$
$2x_1 + 3x_2 \leq 9$
$x_1, x_2 \geq 0$

(b)
$$\begin{aligned} x_1 + x_2 &\leq 4 \\ x_1 + 2x_2 &\geq 6 \\ x_1, x_2 &\geq 0 \end{aligned}$$

(c)
$$\begin{aligned} x_1 + x_2 &\leq 4 \\ x_1 - x_2 &\leq 0 \\ x_1, x_2 &\geq 0 \end{aligned}$$

3.4 Using the constraint set of exercise 3.2 and the objective function

$$\text{maximize } z = 5x_1 + 6x_2 + 4x_3 + 2x_4$$

construct the simplex tableau for the basis (x_1, x_2).

3.5 For the problem

$$\begin{aligned} \text{minimize } z = {} & 2x_1 + 9x_2 - 4x_3 \\ \text{subject to } \quad & 2x_1 + 3x_2 + 4x_3 \leq 12 \\ & x_1 + 6x_2 - 4x_3 \geq 4 \\ & x_1, x_2 \geq 0 \end{aligned}$$

set up the initial tableau and solve.

3.6 Solve the following problems by the simplex method:

(a)
$$\begin{aligned} \text{maximize } z = {} & 4x_1 + 5x_2 \\ \text{subject to } \quad & 2x_1 + 3x_2 \leq 6 \\ & 2x_1 + 2x_2 \leq 5 \\ & x_1, x_2 \geq 0 \end{aligned}$$

(b)
$$\begin{aligned} \text{minimize } z = {} & x_1 - 2x_2 \\ \text{subject to } \quad & 4x_1 + 2x_2 \leq 6 \\ & -x_1 + x_2 \leq 0 \\ & x_1, x_2 \geq 0 \end{aligned}$$

3.7 An insurance company has \$100,000 of idle funds to invest and a choice of two different investments of unequal risk—investment type X and investment type Y. X yields an annual return of 10 percent and Y yields an annual return of 15 percent. The investor's choice is limited because government restrictions require that at least 25 percent of the funds be invested in X. Company policy demands that the ratio of the funds invested in Y to the funds invested in X should be no more than 1.5:1. How should the company apportion its funds? Formulate this problem. Solve it by the simplex method.

3.8 Solve the problem in exercise 3.7 with the annual yield on X at 15 percent. Find an alternative optimal basic solution and two optimal nonbasic solutions.

3.9 (a) Solve this problem by the two-phase method:

$$\begin{aligned} \text{minimize } z = {} & 2x_1 + 9x_2 - 4x_3 \\ \text{subject to } \quad & 2x_1 + 3x_2 + 4x_3 \leq 8 \\ & x_1 + 6x_2 - 4x_3 \geq 24 \\ & x_1, x_2, x_3 \geq 0 \end{aligned}$$

(b) What is the maximum value of the RHS parameter of the second constraint that will yield a feasible solution? Explain how you reached this value.

3.10 Solve the following problems using either the big M or the two-phase method:

(a)
$$\begin{aligned} \text{maximize } z = \; & 4x_1 + 5x_2 \\ \text{subject to } \; & 2x_1 + 3x_2 \leqslant 6 \\ & 3x_1 + x_2 \geqslant 3 \\ & x_1, x_2 \geqslant 0 \end{aligned}$$

(b)
$$\begin{aligned} \text{minimize } z = \; & x_1 - 2x_2 \\ \text{subject to } \; & 4x_1 + 2x_2 \leqslant 6 \\ & -2x_1 + 3x_2 \leqslant -1 \\ & x_1, x_2 \geqslant 0 \end{aligned}$$

3.11 Using the optimal tableau of exercise 3.10 (a), replace the objective function with

$$\text{maximize } z = 6x_1 + 9x_2$$

Hint: You need only work out new $(z_j - c_j)$'s.

(a) Find the optimal solution.
(b) Find the alternative optimal basic feasible solution.
(c) Find two nonbasic optimal solutions.

3.12 Show by the two-phase method that the following problem has no feasible solution:

$$\begin{aligned} \text{maximize } z = \; & 4x_1 + 5x_2 \\ \text{subject to } \; & 2x_1 + 4x_2 \leqslant 8 \\ & x_1 + 3x_2 \geqslant 9 \\ & x_1, x_2 \geqslant 0 \end{aligned}$$

3.13 Show by the simplex method that the following problem has an unbounded solution:

$$\begin{aligned} \text{maximize } z = \; & 2x_1 + x_2 \\ \text{subject to } \; & x_1 - x_2 \leqslant 1 \\ & -x_1 + x_2 \leqslant 1 \\ & x_1, x_2 \geqslant 0 \end{aligned}$$

3.14 Consider the following linear programming problem:

$$\text{maximize } z = c_1x_1 + c_2x_2 + c_3x_3$$

subject to

$$\begin{bmatrix} a_{11} \\ a_{21} \end{bmatrix} x_1 + \begin{bmatrix} a_{12} \\ a_{22} \end{bmatrix} x_2 + \begin{bmatrix} a_{13} \\ a_{23} \end{bmatrix} x_3 + \begin{bmatrix} 1 \\ 0 \end{bmatrix} x_4 + \begin{bmatrix} 0 \\ 1 \end{bmatrix} x_5 = \begin{bmatrix} b_1 \\ b_2 \end{bmatrix}$$

$$x_1, \ldots, x_5 \geqslant 0$$

The optimal tableau follows:

	c_j		c_1	c_2	c_3	c_4	c_5
c_j	Basis	Solution	x_1	x_2	x_3	x_4	x_5
c_3	x_3	$\frac{3}{2}$	1	0	1	$\frac{1}{2}$	$-\frac{1}{2}$
c_2	x_2	2	$\frac{1}{2}$	1	0	-1	2
	$z_j - c_j$	20	3	0	0	0	4

(a) Find the values of

$$\begin{bmatrix} a_{11} \\ a_{21} \end{bmatrix}, \begin{bmatrix} a_{12} \\ a_{22} \end{bmatrix}, \begin{bmatrix} a_{13} \\ a_{23} \end{bmatrix}, \text{ and } \begin{bmatrix} b_1 \\ b_2 \end{bmatrix}$$

(b) Find the values of c_1, c_2, c_3, and c_5.

3.15 The following is a tableau of the simplex method for a linear programming problem. Find the second best basic feasible solution, that is, the basic solution that differs from the optimal one and also gives a value of z nearest to the optimal value. Write out the tableau in full.

	c_j		1	4	5	10	0	0	0
c_j	Basis	Solution	x_1	x_2	x_3	x_4	x_5	x_6	x_7
1	x_1	2	1	0	0	1	-3	1	3
4	x_2	3	0	1	0	2	1	1	-2
5	x_3	1	0	0	1	2	2	0	2
	$z_j - c_j$	19	0	0	0	9	11	5	5

3.16 Suppose $(x_1^*, x_2^*, \ldots, x_n^*)$ is an optimal basic solution to the linear program

$$\text{maximize } z = \sum_{j=1}^{n} c_j x_j$$

$$\text{subject to} \quad \sum_{j=1}^{n} a_{ij} x_j = b_i, \quad i = 1, \ldots, m$$

$$x_j \geq 0, \quad j = 1, \ldots, n$$

Will this solution still be optimal for the problems with the following objective functions? Give reasons. λ is a scalar.

(a) maximize $z = \lambda \sum_{j=1}^{n} c_j x_j$

(b) maximize $z = \sum_{j=1}^{n} (c_j + \lambda) x_j$

REFERENCES

Daellenbach, H. G., and E. J. Bell. *User's Guide to Linear Programming.* Englewood Cliffs, N.J.: Prentice-Hall 1970. Chapter 9 gives a cookbook treatment of the simplex method at an elementary level.

Garvin, W. W. *Introduction to Linear Programming.* New York: McGraw-Hill, 1960. In general, this book—though not a recent publication—provides a remarkably thorough treatment of all aspects of linear programming without requiring advanced mathematics.

Gass, Saul I. *Linear Programming,* 3rd ed. New York: McGraw-Hill, 1969. A readable, advanced text in linear programming, requiring expertise in matrix algebra.

Swanson, Leonard W. *Linear Programming: Basic Theory and Applications.* New York: McGraw-Hill, 1980. This text treats the main areas of linear programming using matrix algebra. It is an easy step up from this chapter.

CHAPTER FOUR

Duality of Linear Programming

One of the interesting features of linear programming is *duality*. For every linear programming problem, there is a twin linear programming problem that has a special and unique relationship to the first one. These two problems stand as pairs, or *duals* of each other.

Not only is duality a rather nice theoretical relationship; it has also proved to be of immense value in devising other operations research techniques. Furthermore, duality has a useful economic interpretation and is widely used in economic theory. Besides being of theoretical interest, duality is at the core of sensitivity analysis in linear programming. That, however, is the topic of Chapter 5. Chapter 4 assumes that you have a thorough grasp of Chapter 3.

4-1 THE DUAL PROBLEM

The power generating problem was viewed in Chapter 2 as a problem of allocating scarce resources. Let us now look at this problem from an entirely different angle. The county council, which is the largest customer of the power generating plant, is considering making an offer to purchase the plant. In order to make such an offer, the council needs to determine fair prices for the existing plant resources. For our purpose these resources can be viewed as the available loading capacity, the available pulverizer capacity, and the available capacity to emit smoke. (We shall neglect the "capacity" to emit sulfur for the moment and reintroduce it later on.)

Theoretically, the prices of resources are not necessarily related to their average or marginal costs, but rather to the revenues that they can produce. Economists tell us that as long as the price offered for a resource is less than the *marginal revenue product* of the resource, i.e., the revenue produced by the last unit of the resource employed, the firm has no incentive to sell any of this resource. The marginal revenue products can also be viewed as the prices the firm should be willing to pay for additional amounts of scarce resources. In linear programming, these prices or marginal revenue products are called *imputed values* or *shadow prices*—imputed because they are not actual costs or prices, but the prices or values that can be inferred from the particular productive system in question.

The problem of finding these prices turns out to be another linear program. In our example, the resources are used to produce steam. Hence, rather than express the prices in monetary units, we shall express them in terms of steam equivalents. Furthermore, since the original resource allocation problem is on a per-hour basis, the prices of the resources will be on the basis of per-hour use. Let

- w_1 be the steam that can be produced by using up 1 kg of smoke emission capacity,
- w_2 be the steam that can be produced by 1 ton of loading capacity,
- w_3 be the steam that can be produced by 1 hour of pulverizer capacity.

The objective of the problem is to find prices w_1, w_2, and w_3 that minimize the council's total cost of acquiring the resources presently owned by the firm. The cost of acquiring the smoke capacity is $12w_1$ (= quantity available × price); the cost of the loading capacity is $20w_2$; and the cost of the pulverizer capacity is $1w_3$. So the objective function is as follows:

(4-1) $$\text{minimize } 12w_1 + 20w_2 + w_3$$

The prices that the firm will accept depend on what the resources can do for the firm. The firm will insist on prices that give a return that is at least equal to the return produced by each of the two activities in which the resources are used, namely, burning coal A and burning coal B.

In burning 1 ton of coal A, the firm produces 24 units of steam. The resources required to burn 1 ton of coal A are 0.5 kg/hr of smoke emission capacity, 1 ton of loading capacity, and $\frac{1}{16}$ hr of pulverizer capacity. At the prices w_1, w_2, and w_3, the council will pay $0.5w_1 + w_2 + \frac{1}{16}w_3$ per hour for these resources. However, since the firm can already make 24 units of steam from 1 ton of coal A, the council must be willing to pay (per hour) at least 24 units of steam for these resources for the firm to find their offer acceptable, i.e.,

(4-2) $$0.5w_1 + w_2 + \tfrac{1}{16}w_3 \geqslant 24$$

Similarly, for coal B,

(4-3) $$w_1 + w_2 + \tfrac{1}{24}w_3 \geqslant 20$$

The prices must also be nonnegative:

(4-4) $$w_1, w_2, w_3 \geqslant 0$$

Let us write out this linear program again and compare it with problem (2-6) of Chapter 2 (without the sulfur constraint):

New problem (pricing of resources):

$$
\begin{array}{lrl}
\text{minimize } Z = & 12w_1 + 20w_2 + \ \ w_3 & \\
\text{subject to} & 0.5w_1 + \ \ w_2 + \frac{1}{16}w_3 & \geqslant 24 \\
\text{(4-5)} & w_1 + \ \ w_2 + \frac{1}{24}w_3 & \geqslant 20 \\
& w_1, w_2, w_3 & \geqslant 0
\end{array}
$$

Original problem (allocation of resources):

$$
\begin{array}{lrl}
\text{maximize} & z = 24x_1 + 20x_2 & \\
\text{subject to} & 0.5x_1 + \ \ x_2 & \leqslant 12 \\
\text{(4-6)} & x_1 + \ \ x_2 & \leqslant 20 \\
& \frac{1}{16}x_1 + \frac{1}{24}x_2 & \leqslant 1 \\
& x_1, x_2 & \geqslant 0
\end{array}
$$

How are the problems (4-5) and (4-6) related?

DUALITY RELATION 1 (DR1)

1. Each constraint in one problem is associated with a variable in the other and vice versa.
2. The LHS coefficients of each constraint of one problem are the same as the LHS coefficients of the corresponding variable of the other problem.
3. The RHS parameters of one problem are the objective function coefficients of the corresponding variables in the other problem and vice versa.
4. One problem is a minimizing problem with $\geqslant$ constraints and nonnegative variables, and the other is a maximizing problem with $\leqslant$ constraints and nonnegative variables.

Each problem is called the *dual* of the other problem. The relationship between them is two-way: what applies from problem (4-5) to problem (4-6) also applies from (4-6) to (4-5). Some algebraic manipulations are needed to show this for part 4 of DR1. In the terminology of linear programming, we call one problem the *primal* and the other the *dual*. It does not matter which problem is called the primal and which is called the dual. Normally, the problem we formulate first is referred to as the primal, the other becomes the dual. In this case, problem (4-6) is the primal, and problem (4-5) is the dual. (Note our convention of denoting the value of the dual objective function by a capital Z and the value of the primal objective function by a lowercase z.)

4-2 MORE ON DUALITY RELATIONS

Let us define *standard form problems* as follows:

1. A *standard form maximizing problem* is a linear program with all constraints as $\leqslant$ inequalities and nonnegative variables.

2. A *standard form minimizing problem* is a linear program with all constraints as $\geqslant$ inequalities and nonnegative variables.

The dual of a standard form maximizing problem is a standard form minimizing problem and vice versa. This is part 4 of DR1. If the primal is not in standard form, neither is the dual. Deviations from the standard form could mean that a problem has both $\geqslant$ and $\leqslant$ constraints or equality constraints and/or some nonpositive or unrestricted variables. Fortunately, any nonstandard problem can be converted to a standard form problem by some simple algebraic manipulations.

We will use the concept of the standard form to develop rules for finding the dual of a nonstandard primal. The fact that all linear programming problems have a standard form equivalent also means that statements about duality in terms of standard form problems are completely general. Let us demonstrate these ideas with the original problem (2-6) from Chapter 2.

Original primal:

$$
\begin{aligned}
\text{maximize } z = \quad & 24x_1 + 20x_2 \\
\text{subject to} \quad & 0.5x_1 + x_2 \leqslant 12 \\
& x_1 + x_2 \leqslant 20 \\
& \tfrac{1}{16}x_1 + \tfrac{1}{24}x_2 \leqslant 1 \\
& 1200x_1 - 800x_2 \geqslant 0 \\
& x_1, x_2 \geqslant 0
\end{aligned}
\tag{4-7}
$$

This problem is not in standard form. The sulfur constraint is a $\geqslant$ inequality. However, the problem can easily be converted to a standard form by multiplying the sulfur constraint through by -1.

Standardized primal:

$$
\begin{aligned}
\text{maximize } z = \quad & 24x_1 + 20x_2 \\
\text{subject to} \quad & 0.5x_1 + x_2 \leqslant 12 \quad (w_1) \\
& x_1 + x_2 \leqslant 20 \quad (w_2) \\
& \tfrac{1}{16}x_1 + \tfrac{1}{24}x_2 \leqslant 1 \quad (w_3) \\
& -1200x_1 + 800x_2 \leqslant -0 \quad (\hat{w}_4) \\
& x_1, x_2 \geqslant 0
\end{aligned}
\quad \Bigg\} \text{ associated dual variable}
$$

The dual associated with this standardized primal is as follows.

Standardized dual:

$$\begin{aligned} \text{minimize } Z = \quad & 12w_1 + 20w_2 + w_3 - 0\hat{w}_4 \\ \text{subject to} \quad & 0.5w_1 + w_2 + \tfrac{1}{16}w_3 - 1200\hat{w}_4 \geqslant 24 \\ & w_1 + w_2 + \tfrac{1}{24}w_3 + 800\hat{w}_4 \geqslant 20 \\ & w_1, w_2, w_3, \hat{w}_4 \geqslant 0 \end{aligned}$$

Compare now the original primal with the standardized dual. Properties 2 and 3 of DR1 are not satisfied for those coefficients associated with the sulfur constraint and $\hat{w}_4$. The standardized dual is thus not the proper dual of the original problem. The proper dual can, however, easily be obtained by reversing the standardization operation used to get the standardized primal. We multiply the coefficients of $\hat{w}_4$ through by -1 and define a new variable w_4 which is the negative of $\hat{w}_4$. This yields the following dual.

Dual of the original primal:

$$\begin{aligned} \text{minimize } Z = \quad & 12w_1 + 20w_2 + w_3 + 0w_4 \\ \text{subject to} \quad & 0.5w_1 + w_2 + \tfrac{1}{16}w_3 + 1200w_4 \geqslant 24 \\ & w_1 + w_2 + \tfrac{1}{24}w_3 - 800w_4 \geqslant 20 \\ & w_1, w_2, w_3 \geqslant 0 \\ & w_4 \leqslant 0 \end{aligned} \tag{4-8}$$

We now see that properties 2 and 3 of DR1 are satisfied. But we also note that the new dual variable w_4 is restricted to be nonpositive (since $\hat{w}_4$ was nonnegative). There is no need to go through the process of first standardizing, then finding the dual, and finally unscrambling the dual. Instead, we can go directly to the dual by using the following duality relationship.

DUALITY RELATION 2 (DR2)

If the direction of the inequality constraint in one problem deviates from the standard form, the corresponding variable in the other problem is restricted to be nonpositive and vice versa.

What is the nature of the dual if the primal has equality constraints? In order to find out, we resort to the following trick for each such constraint. We replace the equality by two inequalities of opposite direction, i.e., one is a $\leqslant$ inequality, the other a $\geqslant$ inequality. The LHS coefficients and the RHS parameter are the same as in the original constraint. Since both have to be satisfied simultaneously, the feasible region will be identical to the original constraint. We have just seen how to handle a problem with mixed inequality constraints. The dual will have two dual variables, say w_i^+ and w_i^-, one of which is restricted to be nonnegative and the other to be nonpositive. Both variables have, however, exactly the same coefficients in the dual. We now undo the trick of substituting two inequality constraints for the equality constraint. We define a new variable w_i that can assume both nonnegative and nonpositive values, i.e., one that is unrestricted in sign, where $w_i = (w_i^+ - w_i^-)$. So w_i replaces w_i^+ if w_i assumes a nonnegative value, and replaces w_i^- if w_i assumes a nonpositive value. Again, we can avoid actually using this trick by applying the next duality relation.

DUALITY RELATION 3 (DR3)

If a constraint in the one problem is a strict equality, then the corresponding variable in the other problem has no sign restriction and vice versa.

Table 4-1 demonstrates the duality relations DR1 through DR3 in general terms.

Table 4-1. *Primal and dual in general form*

Primal		Dual
maximize $z = \sum_{j=1}^{3} c_j x_j$		minimize $Z = \sum_{i=1}^{3} b_i w_i$
subject to		subject to
$\sum_{j=1}^{3} a_{1j} x_j \leq b_1$	implies DR1	$w_1 \geq 0$
$\sum_{j=1}^{3} a_{2j} x_j \geq b_2$	implies DR2	$w_2 \leq 0$
$\sum_{j=1}^{3} a_{3j} x_j = b_3$	implies DR3	w_3 unrestricted
x_1 unrestricted	implies DR3	$\sum_{i=1}^{3} a_{i1} w = c_1$
$x_2 \leq 0$	implies DR2	$\sum_{i=1}^{3} a_{i2} w \leq c_2$
$x_3 \geq 0$	implies DR1	$\sum_{i=1}^{3} a_{i3} w \geq c_3$

4-3 DUALITY THEOREMS

So far we have only considered relationships between the structures of the primal and the dual. There are also relationships between the solutions of the problems.

Consider solutions of the primal and the dual taken at random, e.g., $(x'_1, x'_2) = (10, 4)$ and $(w'_1, w'_2, w'_3, w'_4) = (6, 1, 640, -0.01)$. From expressions (4-7) and

(4-8), the objective function values are

$$z' = 24(10) + 20(4) = 320$$

and

$$Z' = 12(6) + 20(1) + 1(640) + 0(-0.01) = 732$$

We notice that $z' < Z'$. Does this relationship hold true in general? Is it still true in particular for the optimal objective function values of the primal and the dual? In Chapter 3 we found that the optimal solution to the primal is $(x_1^*, x_2^*) = (12, 6)$. The optimal solution to the dual is $(w_1^*, w_2^*, w_3^*, w_4^*) = (6,0,336,0)$. (You may wish to confirm this result using the simplex method on the dual; we will establish the answer by other methods shortly.) The objective function values of these optimal solutions are:

$$z^* = 24(12) + 20(6) = 408$$

and

$$Z^* = 12(6) + 20(0) + 1(336) + 0(0) = 408$$

We notice that $z^* = Z^*$. In addition, since z^* is the maximal value of the primal objective function, all feasible solutions to the primal yield $z' \leq z^*$. Similarly, since Z^* is the minimal value of the dual, all feasible solutions to the dual yield $Z' \geq Z^*$. Hence, $z' \leq z^* = Z^* \leq Z'$.

We have just illustrated two theorems of duality. In stating these theorems, we define the primal to be a standard form maximizing problem and the dual to be a standard form minimizing problem. Section 4-2 showed that there is no loss in generality with this assumption.

DUALITY RELATION 4 (DR4)

The objective function value of any feasible solution to the primal will be less than or equal to the objective function value of every feasible solution to the dual, i.e., $z \leq Z$.

DUALITY RELATION 5: DUALITY THEOREM (DR5)

If the primal and the dual both have feasible solutions, then both have finite optimal solutions, and the optimal values of the objective functions of the two problems are equal, i.e., $z^* = Z^*$.

The next theorem deals with the structure of the optimal solution rather than with the objective function values.

DUALITY RELATION 6: COMPLEMENTARY SLACKNESS THEOREM (DR6)

If a constraint of either problem is slack at any optimal solution to that problem, then in the other problem the variable associated with that constraint is zero at every optimal solution. If a variable of either problem at an optimal solution is nonzero, then in the other problem the constraint associated with that variable is binding at every optimal solution.

This theorem says that an abundant resource (slack constraint) has a zero price, and a resource with a nonzero price is scarce (binding constraint).

Let us now apply the complementary slackness theorem (DR6):

Optimal primal solution:		*Optimal dual solution:*
$x_1 = 12 > 0$	implies	constraint 1 binding
$x_2 = 6 > 0$	implies	constraint 2 binding
constraint 2 is slack	implies	$w_2 = 0$
constraint 4 is slack	implies	$w_4 = 0$

With this information, problem (4-8) is now reduced to

$$\begin{aligned} \text{minimize } Z = \; & 12w_1 + w_3 \\ \text{subject to } \; & 0.5w_1 + \tfrac{1}{16}w_3 = 24 \\ & w_1 + \tfrac{1}{24}w_3 = 20 \\ & w_1, w_3 \geqslant 0 \end{aligned}$$

The two constraints define a unique solution $w_1 = 6$, $w_3 = 336$, and $Z^* = 408$, as stated previously.

4-4 FURTHER INTERPRETATION OF THE DUAL PROBLEM

We have already noted in Section 4-2 that there is a close relationship between the primal constraints and the dual variables. In fact, we interpreted the dual variables in problem (4-5) as the imputed values (i.e., the marginal revenue product, where the constraint refers to a resource) of each of the primal constraints. This concept can be generalized and applied to other primal problems.

INTERPRETATION OF THE OPTIMAL VALUES OF DUAL VARIABLES

The optimal value of a dual variable associated with a particular primal constraint gives the marginal change (increase, if positive, or decrease, if negative) in the optimal value of the primal objective function for a marginal increase in the RHS parameter of that constraint.

Note that this does not mean that we can always find an intuitively appealing interpretation of the dual variable. The dual variable w_4 associated with the sulfur constraint is an example. The manner in which the constraint was constructed renders an appealing interpretation impossible.

4-5 THE DUAL VARIABLES, $(z_j - c_j)$ VALUES, AND THE SIMPLEX MULTIPLIERS

In Section 3-4 we saw that each z_j represents the contribution to the objective function of the equivalent resource use (in terms of the basic variables) of one unit of x_j. This is true for any basis. However, at the optimal basis, the value of z_j is the optimal valuation the system imputes to one unit of x_j.

In particular, let us consider variable x_3—the slack variable of constraint 1. In the optimal tableau, z_3 is the optimal contribution (or valuation) of a unit of x_3. But a unit of x_3 is simply a unit of smoke emission capacity. So z_3 is the valuation imputed to one unit of smoke emission capacity. However, in the dual problem, we have already defined the optimal value of a unit of smoke emission capacity as w_1. The optimal value of w_1 and the valuation of z_3 in the optimal simplex tableau are thus equivalent. The same reasoning applies to w_2 and z_4, w_3 and z_5, and w_4 and z_7. We choose z_7 rather than z_6 to determine the value of w_4 because x_6 represents the negative of a unit of the RHS constraint 4, and so z_6 is the negative of w_4.

Hence, we can find the optimal values of the dual variables from the final simplex tableau as follows.

z_j VALUES AND OPTIMAL DUAL VARIABLES

The z_j value of the slack and artificial variables of each constraint in the optimal simplex tableau of the primal gives the optimal value of the dual variable associated with that constraint.

Since the c_j values of the slack and artificial variables in the primal objective function are all zero, the z_j values are equal to the $(z_j - c_j)$ values. From the optimal simplex tableau for the primal problem in Table 3-4, we can read off the optimal values of the dual variables in problem (4-8) as $w_1 = z_3 = 6$, $w_2 = z_4 = 0$, $w_3 = z_5 = 336$, and $w_4 = z_7 = 0$. This analysis also indicates how the numbers shown under the heading IMPUTED VALUE of the computer printout (Figure 2-7) in Chapter 2 were derived.

Consider now the optimal z_j value of a variable other than a slack or an artificial variable. The optimal valuation of one unit of x_1 (= burning 1 ton of coal A) is the sum of the values of the individual resources involved in burning 1 ton of coal A (0.5 kg of smoke emission, 1 ton of loading capacity, $\frac{1}{16}$ hr of pulverizer capacity, and 1200 units of sulfur emission). This valuation is $z_1 = 24$ in the optimal tableau. We know that 1 kg of smoke emission is valued at w_1, 1 ton of loading capacity at w_2, 1 hour of pulverizer capacity at w_3, and 1 unit of sulfur emission at w_4. So the optimal valuation of the individual resources is $0.5w_1 + 1w_2 + \frac{1}{16}w_3 + 1200w_4 = 0.5(6) + 1(0) + \frac{1}{16}(336) + 1200(0) = 24$. Thus we have the relationship

$$z_1 = 0.5w_1 + 1w_2 + \tfrac{1}{16}w_3 + 1200w_4$$

Verify that $z_2 = 1w_1 + 1w_2 + \frac{1}{24}\ w_3 - 800w_4$.

Let us compare these results with the dual problem (4-8). Using the relationships we have just established, we see that the value of the LHS of the first constraint of (4-8) at the optimal solution is z_1. In general, z_j is the value of the left-hand side of the jth dual constraint. Since the RHS parameter of the jth dual constraint is c_j, the optimal values of the slack variables of the dual give us the optimal $(z_j - c_j)$ values. Furthermore, for all basic variables at the primal optimum, $(z_j - c_j) = 0$. Therefore, the slack variables of the dual constraints associated with the optimal basc primal variables are zero and these constraints are binding. But this is just one of the complementary slackness conditions.

Can the dual equations be used to provide the $(z_j - c_j)$ values for nonoptimal primal tableaux? Let us apply the complementary slackness conditions for the basis (x_3, x_4, x_5, x_1) shown in the second tableau of Table 3-4 in Chapter 3. We can conclude that the first dual constraint is binding because x_1 is basic. Normally, the complementary slackness conditions is that $x_j > 0$. However, in the case of a degenerate solution, it is sufficient that x_j is basic. Similarly, $w_1 = w_2 = w_3 = 0$ because the first three primal constraints are slack. The dual problem (4-8) thus reduces to $1200w_4 = 24$, or $w_4 = \frac{1}{50}$. In the second equation of (4-8), we obtain a value of the left-hand side of $-800(\frac{1}{50}) = -16$, which is also the value of z_2 in Table 3-4. The difference between the left-hand-side value and the RHS parameter of $(-16 - 20) = -36$ is the $(z_2 - c_2)$ value in Table 3-4. We again see that the value of the left-hand side of the dual constraint is the z_j value of the corresponding primal variable, and the RHS parameter is c_j. Thus, the difference between the value of the left-hand side and the RHS parameter is $(z_j - c_j)$. However, the w_i's are an infeasible solution to the dual. Rather than refer to the w_i's as dual variables in this context, we call them *simplex multipliers*. It is only at the optimal solution, with all $z_j \geqslant c_j$, that simplex multipliers become feasible and, at the same time, become the optimal values for the dual variables. The primal objective function value in Table 3-4 is $z = 0$. The simplex multiplier value $w_4 = \frac{1}{50}$ makes $Z = 0$ in problem (4-8). Thus the objective function value of the primal solution equals the value of the dual objective function for the corresponding simplex multipliers.

To summarize, for any basic feasible solution of the primal, the simplex multipliers are found by applying the complementary slackness conditions to the dual, i.e., by setting $z_j = c_j$ for all basic variables. All the other $(z_j - c_j)$ values can then be computed by substituting the simplex multipliers into the dual constraints.

4-6 DUAL SIMPLEX METHOD

In the simplex method, we start with a feasible basic solution in which all $x_j \geqslant 0$. Usually this solution will not be optimal; i.e., some $(z_j - c_j) < 0$. At each iteration, we proceed toward optimality while maintaining feasibility. When a basic feasible solution with all $(z_j - c_j) \geqslant 0$ is reached, we have an optimal solution. In terms of the primal-dual relationships of Section 4-5, the simplex method starts with a primal-feasible/dual-infeasible solution. It works toward a primal-feasible/dual-feasible solution. Such a solution is optimal.

At times, situations occur where the initial solution is primal-infeasible/dual-feasible; i.e., some $x_j < 0$, but all $(z_j - c_j) \geqslant 0$. The *dual simplex method* handles this situation by maintaining dual feasibility [i.e., all $(z_j - c_j) \geqslant 0$], while working toward primal feasibility (i.e., all $x_j \geqslant 0$). Let us immediately stress that this is a method to solve the primal problem. It is not merely the use of the simplex method to solve the dual problem—although that is how we will derive the principles of the dual simplex method. (Note that the two-phase method can also be used to solve a problem starting at any primal-infeasible solution. For the two-phase method, though, it does not matter whether the current tableau is dual-feasible or dual-infeasible. We leave it to you to verify this fact.)

Consider again problem (4-6). With slack variables added, the primal problem is

$$
\begin{aligned}
\text{maximize } z = \ & 24x_1 + 20x_2 \\
\text{subject to } \quad & 0.5x_1 + x_2 + x_3 = 12 \\
& x_1 + x_2 + x_4 = 20 \\
& \tfrac{1}{16}x_1 + \tfrac{1}{24}x_2 + x_5 = 1 \\
& x_j \geqslant 0, \quad j = 1, \ldots, 5
\end{aligned} \tag{4-9}
$$

The corresponding dual problem (with slack variables included) is

$$
\begin{aligned}
\text{minimize } Z = \ & 12w_1 + 20w_2 + w_3 \\
\text{subject to } \quad & 0.5w_1 + w_2 + \tfrac{1}{16}w_3 - w_4 = 24 \\
& w_1 + w_2 + \tfrac{1}{24}w_3 - w_5 = 20 \\
& w_i \geqslant 0, \quad i = 1, \ldots, 5
\end{aligned} \tag{4-10}
$$

Let (x_3, x_5, x_1) be the initial basis to the primal problem (4-9). Solving (4-9) for the basic variables, we get $x_1 = 20$, $x_3 = 2$, $x_5 = -\frac{1}{4}$, with $x_2 = x_4 = 0$. This solution is not feasible. The corresponding dual solution is given by the simplex multipliers derived from the complementary slackness conditions. If x_3 and x_5 are nonzero (constraints 1 and 3 of the primal are slack) it implies that $w_1 = w_3 = 0$, while $x_1 > 0$ implies that $w_4 = 0$ (constraint 1 of the dual is binding). Using these values, we find from problem (4-10) the solution $w_2 = 24$ and $w_5 = 4$. Since all $w_i \geq 0$, this is a feasible solution to the dual problem. Both problems have an objective function value of $z = Z = 480$.

Tables 4-2 and 4-3 give the first tableaux to the primal and dual problems, respectively. These were obtained from the canonical forms for the basic solutions (x_3, x_5, x_1) for the primal, and (w_5, w_2) for the dual.

Table 4-2. *Tableau for basis (x_3, x_5, x_1) to primal problem (4-9)*

		c_j		24	20	0	0	0
	c_j	Basis	Solution	x_1	x_2	x_3	x_4	x_5
	0	x_3	2	0	$\frac{1}{2}$	1	$-\frac{1}{2}$	0
←	0	x_5	$-\frac{1}{4}$	0	$\left(-\frac{1}{48}\right)$	0	$-\frac{1}{16}$	1
	24	x_1	20	1	1	0	1	0
		$z_j - c_j$	480	0	4↑	0	24	0
	Ratio:	$(z_j - c_j)/\alpha_j$			$4/(-\frac{1}{48})$		$24/(-\frac{1}{16})$	

Table 4-3 *Tableau for basis (w_5, w_2) to dual problem (4-10)*

		C_i		−12	−20	−1	0	0	Ratio
	C_i	Basis	Solution	w_1	w_2	w_3	w_4	w_5	w_i/γ_i
←	0	w_5	4	$-\frac{1}{2}$	0	$\left(\frac{1}{48}\right)$	−1	1	$4/(\frac{1}{48})$
	−20	w_2	24	$\frac{1}{2}$	1	$\frac{1}{16}$	−1	0	$24/(\frac{1}{16})$
		$Z_i - C_i$	−480		0	$-\frac{1}{4}$↑	20	0	

Note that since (4-10) is a minimizing problem, it has been converted to a maximizing problem by multiplying all objective function coefficients by −1. Hence, the objective function value is shown as $Z = -480$ rather than 480.

Let us now compare in detail the primal and dual tableaux in Tables 4-2 and

4-3. From our discussion in Section 4-5, we can establish the following relationships:

Primal to dual:			*Dual to primal:*		
$(z_j - c_j)$ for primal decision variables	$\left\{ \begin{array}{l} (z_1 - c_1) = w_4 \\ (z_2 - c_2) = w_5 \end{array} \right\}$	values of dual slack variables	Z_i values for dual slack variables	$\left\{ \begin{array}{l} Z_4 = x_1 \\ Z_5 = x_2 \end{array} \right\}$	values of primal decision variables
z_j values for primal slack variables	$\left\{ \begin{array}{l} z_3 = w_1 \\ z_4 = w_2 \\ z_5 = w_3 \end{array} \right\}$	values of dual decision variables	$(Z_i - C_i)$ for dual decision variables	$\left\{ \begin{array}{l} (Z_1 - C_1) = x_3 \\ (Z_2 - C_2) = x_4 \\ (Z_3 - C_3) = x_5 \end{array} \right\}$	values of primal slack variables

Verify these values in Tables 4-2 and 4-3. There is also a correspondence between the columns of coefficients in Table 4-2 and the rows in Table 4-3. Ignoring the columns of coefficents of basic variables, the relationships between primal and dual variables yield:

From Table 4-2			From Table 4-3	
column	$x_2 = (\frac{1}{2}, -\frac{1}{48}, 1)$	$\leftrightarrow$	row	$w_5 = (-\frac{1}{2}, \frac{1}{48}, -1)$
column	$x_4 = (-\frac{1}{2}, -\frac{1}{16}, 1)$	$\leftrightarrow$	row	$w_2 = (\frac{1}{2}, \frac{1}{16}, -1)$
row	$x_3 = (\frac{1}{2}, -\frac{1}{2})$	$\leftrightarrow$	column	$w_1 = (-\frac{1}{2}, \frac{1}{2})$
row	$x_5 = (-\frac{1}{48}, -\frac{1}{16})$	$\leftrightarrow$	column	$w_3 = (\frac{1}{48}, \frac{1}{16})$
row	$x_1 = (1, 1)$	$\leftrightarrow$	column	$w_4 = (-1, -1)$

We thus see that the relevant coefficients of the columns of one problem are the negatives of the corresponding rows of the other problem and vice versa.

The next step is to take advantage of these correspondences and find for the primal tableau a set of rules that is equivalent to the normal rules of the simplex method applied to the dual problem. The resulting algorithm is the dual simplex method. Let us solve the dual problem (4-10) by the normal simplex method. The result is shown in Table 4-4.

For the dual problem, simplex criterion 1 determines the dual variable to enter the basis. It selects the variable w_i that has the most negative $(Z_i - C_i)$ value. In Table 4-3, this is w_3 with a coefficient of $-\frac{1}{4}$. The equivalent rule for the dual simplex method applied to the primal problem determines the primal variable to leave the basis. By analogy to the above rule, it selects the variable x_j that has the most negative value. Applied to Table 4-2, this rule selects x_5 with a value of $-\frac{1}{4}$, i.e, the same number as above.

For the dual problem, simplex criterion 2 determines the variable leaving the basis as the one with the smallest ratio (w_i/γ_i) for all $\gamma_i > 0$, that ratio becoming the pivot element.

Table 4-4. *Second and third tableaux for dual problem (4-10)*

	C_i		-12	-20	-1	0	0
C_i	Basis	Solution	w_1	w_2	w_3	w_4	w_5
-1	w_3	192	-24	0	1	-48	48
← -20	w_2	12	(2)	1	0	2	-3
	$Z_i - C_i$	-432	-4 ↑	0	0	8	12
-1	w_3	336	0	12	1	-24	12
-12	w_1	6	1	$\frac{1}{2}$	0	1	$-\frac{3}{2}$
	$Z_i - C_i$	-408	0	2	0	12	6

In Table 4-3, this rule selects the smaller of $4/\frac{1}{48}$ and $24/\frac{1}{16}$. An equivalent rule for the dual simplex method determines the primal variable to enter the basis as the one with the largest ratio $(z_j - c_j)/\alpha_j$ for all $\alpha_j < 0$, where α_j is the coefficient of variable x_j in the row of the variable leaving the basis (pivot row). Applied to Table 4-2, this rule indicates variable x_2, and results in the same pivot element, $-\frac{1}{48}$. Thus at the first iteration the dual simplex criteria select x_5 as the variable to leave the primal basis and x_2 as the variable to enter it. The second tableau of the dual simplex method is derived from Table 4-2 by applying the usual simplex tableau transformation rules. The result is shown in the top tableau of Table 4-5.

Table 4-5. *Dual simplex tableaux for problem (4-9)*

	c_j		24	20	0	0	0
c_i	Basis	Solution	x_1	x_2	x_3	x_4	x_5
← 0	x_3	-4	0	0	1	(-2)	24
20	x_2	12	0	1	0	3	-48
24	x_1	8	1	0	0	-2	48
	$z_j - c_j$	432	0	0	0	12 ↑	192
0	x_4	2	0	0	$-\frac{1}{2}$	1	-12
20	x_2	6	0	1	$\frac{3}{2}$	0	-12
24	x_1	12	1	0	-1	0	24
	$z_j - c_j$	408	0	0	6	0	336

Let us now formally state the dual simplex criteria.

DUAL SIMPLEX CRITERION 1: VARIABLE TO LEAVE THE BASIS

The variable x_i leaving the basis is the basic variable that has the most negative value.

DUAL SIMPLEX OPTIMALITY CRITERION

The solution associated with a basis is optimal if all $x_i \geq 0$.

DUAL SIMPLEX CRITERION 2: VARIABLE TO ENTER THE BASIS

The variable entering the basis is the one with the maximum ratio $(z_j - c_j)/\alpha_j$ for all $\alpha_j < 0$, where α_j is the tableau coefficient of variable x_j in the pivot row.

What happens if we cannot find an $\alpha_j < 0$ when we apply simplex criterion 2? Clearly the algorithm cannot continue, and no further progress toward feasibility is possible. Thus we have discovered an infeasible primal problem.

DUAL SIMPLEX INFEASIBILITY CRITERION

The problem is infeasible if all $\alpha_j \geq 0$, where α_j is the tableau coefficient of variable x_j in the pivot row.

Let us apply these rules to the second dual simplex tableau—the top tableau of Table 4-5. By the dual simplex criterion 1, x_3 leaves the basis, and, by the dual simplex criterion 2, x_4 enters the basis. Applying the normal simplex transformation rules, we derive the third dual simplex tableau—the bottom tableau of Table 4-5. This tableau has all $x_i \geq 0$, so the solution is primal-feasible. Also all $(z_j - c_j) \geq 0$, so the solution is dual-feasible and primal-optimal.

Note that each dual simplex iteration reduces the objective function value and that all $(z_j - c_j)$ values remain nonnegative, implying dual feasibility throughout.

An example of infeasibility can be found in exercise 4.12.

EXERCISES

4.1 (a) Convert the following linear program into standard form:

$$\text{maximize } z = 3x_1 + 4x_2 + x_3$$

$$\begin{aligned} \text{subject to} \quad x_1 + 3x_2 + 2x_3 &\geq 10 \\ 6x_1 + 2x_2 + x_3 &\leq 30 \\ x_1 + x_2 + x_3 &= 5 \\ x_1, x_2, x_3 &\geq 0 \end{aligned}$$

(b) Write (i) the dual of the linear program in (a), and (ii) the dual of the standard form of the linear program in (a). Show that these two dual problems are equivalent.

4.2 (a) Find the dual of the following problem:

$$\begin{aligned} \text{maximize } z &= 4x_1 + 6x_2 + 10x_3 + 12x_4 \\ \text{subject to} \quad x_1 + 3x_2 + 2x_3 + 4x_4 &\leq 5 \\ x_1 + x_2 + 5x_3 + 3x_4 &\leq 15 \\ x_1, \ldots, x_4 &\geq 0 \end{aligned}$$

(b) Graph the dual, and, using DR6 (Complementary Slackness Theorem), find the solution of the primal. Check your answer using DR5 (Duality Theorem). Show that your solution to the primal is an extreme point to that problem.

4.3 For each of the following problems, write out the dual (*not* the standard form dual).

(a)
$$\begin{aligned} \text{maximize } z &= 4x_1 + 2x_2 + x_3 \\ \text{subject to} \quad x_1 + x_2 + x_3 &\leq 8 \\ 2x_1 - x_2 + 3x_3 &\leq 12 \\ x_1, x_2, x_3 &\geq 0 \end{aligned}$$

(b)
$$\begin{aligned} \text{maximize } z &= 4x_1 + 2x_2 + 3x_3 \\ \text{subject to} \quad x_1 + 2x_2 + 2x_3 &\leq 10 \\ -2x_1 - x_2 + x_3 &= -2 \\ x_1, x_2, x_3 &\geq 0 \end{aligned}$$

(c)
$$\begin{aligned} \text{minimize } Z &= 2x_1 + 9x_2 - 4x_3 \\ \text{subject to} \quad 2x_1 + 3x_2 + 4x_3 &\leq 12 \\ x_1 + 6x_2 - 4x_3 &\geq 4 \\ x_1, x_2 &\geq 0, \ x_3 \text{ unrestricted in sign.} \end{aligned}$$

(d)
$$\begin{aligned} \text{maximize } z &= 3x_1 - 2x_2 \\ \text{subject to} \quad x_1 + x_2 &\geq 5 \\ x_1 - x_2 &\leq 1 \\ x_2 &= 4 \\ x_1, x_2 &\geq 0 \end{aligned}$$

4.4 For each of the problems in exercise 4.3, find:
(a) The standard form primal.
(b) The standard form dual.

4.5 Reconcile the duals and standard form duals of exercises 4.3 and 4.4.

4.6 For the problem in exericse 4.3 (c), solve the dual graphically, and, using that solution, find the optimal primal solution. Use the quickest check you know to verify the optimality of the primal solution.

4.7 Give the interpretations of the optimal values of w_2 and w_3 of the power generating problem, summarized in Table 3-3.

4.8 For the problem in exercise 4.3(b), after making the changes necessary to solve it by the big M method, we have the following optimal tableau.

	c_j		4	2	3	0	$-M$
c_j	Basis	Solution	x_1	x_2	x_3	x_4	x_5
3	x_3	$\frac{18}{5}$	0	$\frac{3}{5}$	1	$\frac{2}{5}$	$-\frac{1}{5}$
4	x_1	$\frac{14}{5}$	1	$\frac{4}{5}$	0	$\frac{1}{5}$	$\frac{2}{5}$
	$z_j - c_j$	22	0	3	0	2	$1 + M$

(a) Using this tableau, write down (i) the optimal values of the variables and z, and (ii) the optimal values of the dual variables.
(b) Interpret w_1, the first dual variable.

4.9 Solve the following by the dual simplex method:

$$\begin{aligned} \text{minimize } z = \ & 3x_1 + 2x_2 \\ \text{subject to } \quad & x_1 + x_2 \geq 10 \\ & 2x_1 + x_2 \geq 14 \\ & x_1, \ x_2 \geq 0 \end{aligned}$$

4.10 Solve the following by the dual simplex method:

$$\begin{aligned} \text{minimize } z = \ & 2x_1 + x_2 \\ \text{subject to } \quad & x_1 + x_2 \geq 15 \\ & x_1 - x_2 \leq 1 \\ & x_1, \ x_2 \geq 0 \end{aligned}$$

4.11 Solve the following by the dual simplex method:

$$\begin{aligned} \text{maximize } z = \ & x_1 - x_2 - 2x_3 \\ \text{subject to } \quad & 2x_1 + x_2 - x_3 = 8 \\ & x_1 - 3x_2 \leq 3 \\ & x_1, x_2, x_3 \geq 0 \end{aligned}$$

4.12 For the problem in exercise 4.10, use the dual simplex method to show that there is no feasible solution if a third constraint, $2x_1 + x_2 \leq 7$, is added.

REFERENCES

Daellenbach, H. G., and E. J. Bell. *User's Guide to Linear Programming.* Englewood Cliffs, N.J.: Prentice-Hall, 1970.

Gale, D. *The Theory of Linear Economic Models.* New York: McGraw-Hill, 1960. Chapter 1 has an interesting set of linear programming applications and an interpretation of their duals.

Garvin, W. W. *Linear Programming.* New York: McGraw-Hill, 1960.

Hadley, G. *Linear Programming.* Reading, Mass.: Addison-Wesley, 1962.

Swanson, L. W. *Linear Programming: Basic Theory and Applications.* New York: McGraw-Hill, 1980.

CHAPTER FIVE

Sensitivity and Postoptimal Analysis of Linear Programming

One of the outstanding features of linear programming is the ease with which we can analyze the response of the optimal solution to changes in the input data. Since we assume that the input data to linear programming models can be specified with certainty and this may often not be true, there is a need for systematic exploration of the solution space around the optimum.

This chapter deals with the mechanical aspects of postoptimal analysis. This includes analyzing the sensitivity of the current optimal solution to changes in the input data, as well as finding the new optimal solution to changes in both the input data and the model itself. We will analyze how the optimal solution responds to changes in the objective function coefficients, the RHS parameters, the LHS coefficients, and the addition of new variables.

Before proceeding, you may wish to refer back to Chapter 2, Section 2-9, where the concepts of sensitivity analysis are introduced graphically. This chapter also assumes that you have a thorough grasp of the material in Chapters 3 and 4. The starred Section 5-5 should only be attempted with Section 4-6 as background.

5-1 POSTOPTIMAL ANALYSIS OF OBJECTIVE FUNCTION COEFFICIENTS

Most queries of postoptimal analysis can be answered readily on the basis of the information contained in the optimal simplex tableau. For this analysis, we shall again use the original power generating problem, whose initial and final simplex tableaux are summarized in Table 5-1.

Table 5-1. *Initial and final simplex tableaux*

	Objective Function (c_j)		24	20	0	0	0	0	0
c_j	Basis	Solution	x_1	x_2	x_3	x_4	x_5	x_6	x_7
Initial Tableau									
0	x_3	12	$\frac{1}{2}$	1	1	0	0	0	0
0	x_4	20	1	1	0	1	0	0	0
0	x_5	1	$\frac{1}{16}$	$\frac{1}{24}$	0	0	1	0	0
0	x_7	0	1200	−800	0	0	0	−1	1
	$z_j - c_j$	0	−24	−20	0	0	0	0	0
Final Tableau									
20	x_2	6	0	1	$\frac{3}{2}$	0	−12	0	0
0	x_4	2	0	0	$-\frac{1}{2}$	1	−12	0	0
0	x_6	9600	0	0	−2400	0	38400	1	−1
24	x_1	12	1	0	−1	0	24	0	0
	$z_j - c_j$	408	0	0	6	0	336	0	0

A change in the coefficients of the objective function is equivalent to a change in the slope of the objective function line (or hyperplane in more than two dimensions). If the slope is tilted sufficiently in one direction or another, the optimal solution may shift to another extreme point of the feasible region. Changes in the objective function coefficients may thus affect the optimality of the current solution. However, these changes can never affect the feasibility of this solution. In terms of the optimal simplex tableau, this means that only the $(z_j - c_j)$ values are affected.

The most common test of sensitivity of the objective function involves finding the range of values within which each objective function coefficient can lie without affecting the optimality of the solution. We perform this analysis for one objective function coefficient at a time, allowing only that particular coefficient to change; all other input coefficients and parameters must remain unchanged.

Consider c_3. A change is c_3 in the optimal tableau of Table 5-1 does not alter any of the c_j values associated with the basic variables because x_3 is nonbasic. So none of the z_j values are changed, nor are any of the $(z_j - c_j)$ values, except $(z_3 - c_3)$ through the change in c_3. Hence, provided the change in c_3 does not violate $(z_3 - c_3) \geqslant 0$, the present solution remains optimal. Since $z_3 = 6$, $(z_3 - c_3) \geqslant 0$ if $c_3 \leqslant 6$. The range for c_3 is thus $-\infty \leqslant c_3 \leqslant 6$.

Next consider c_1. This time the corresponding variable, x_1, is basic. A change in c_1 will potentially affect all the z_j and, hence, $(z_j - c_j)$ values, except those for basic variables. (These are always zero.) Let us find the range of c_1 that keeps $(z_j - c_j) \geqslant 0$ for all nonbasic variables [except $(z_7 - c_7)$, since x_7 is an artificial variable].

From Table 5-1 we see that as c_1 changes, z_3 changes also:

$$z_3 = 20(\tfrac{3}{2}) + 0(-\tfrac{1}{2}) + 0(-2400) + c_1(-1) = 30 - c_1$$

For $(z_3 - c_3) \geqslant 0$, we need

$$(30 - c_1) - 0 \geqslant 0$$

or

$$c_1 \leqslant 30$$

As c_1 changes, z_5 becomes

$$z_5 = 20(-12) + 0(-12) + 0(38400) + c_1(24) = -240 + 24c_1$$

For $(z_5 - c_5) \geqslant 0$, we need

$$(24c_1 - 240) - 0 \geqslant 0$$

or

$$c_1 \geqslant 10$$

For the current solution to remain optimal, c_1 has to satisfy both of these conditions, i.e., $(z_j - c_j)$ has to be nonnegative for all nonbasic variables. This will be so if c_1 lies in the range

$$10 \leqslant c_1 \leqslant 30 \tag{5-1}$$

This case was studied graphically in Section 2-9.

Here is the interpretation of expression (5-1): provided that the steam output of coal A falls within the range of 10,000 to 30,000 lb/ton, with all other coefficients or parameters unchanged, the solution in Table 5-1 remains optimal. This range is very large. It is unlikely that the steam output would ever go beyond it. Since there could have been measurement errors when this coefficient was determined (or slight variation from load to load), it is useful to know the range of acceptable variations.

You should verify that similar analysis yields the following ranges for the remaining objective function coefficients, each taken alone.

$$\begin{aligned} 16 &\leqslant c_2 \leqslant 48 \\ -\infty &\leqslant c_4 \leqslant 12 \\ -\infty &\leqslant c_5 \leqslant 336 \\ -\tfrac{7}{800} &\leqslant c_6 \leqslant \tfrac{1}{400} \end{aligned} \tag{5-2}$$

Looking at these ranges, we conclude that the optimal solution is very insensitive to realistic changes in any one of the c_j coefficients—a comforting thought!

Next let us look at simultaneous changes in more than one objective function coefficient. The engineers discovered a substantial error in the measurement of the steam produced by both coal A and coal B. The true coefficients are $c_1 = 28$ and $c_2 = 18$. Is the current solution in Table 5-1 still optimal?

It is not possible to use the ranges of values found for each coefficient individually.

We can, however, use similar reasoning. Since x_1 and x_2 are both basic variables, some of the $(z_j - c_j)$ values for nonbasic variables may change.

For the new values of c_1 and c_2, we obtain

$$z_3 = 18(\tfrac{3}{2}) + 0(-\tfrac{1}{2}) + 0(-2400) + 28(-1) = -1$$

and $$z_3 - c_3 = -1$$

$$z_5 = 18(-12) + 0(-12) + 0(38400) + 28(24) = 456$$

and $$z_5 - c_5 = 456$$

$$z = 18(6) + 0(2) + 0(9600) + 28(12) = 444$$

Since one of the new $(z_j - c_j)$ values is negative, namely $(z_3 - c_3) = -1$, the basis of Table 5-1 is no longer optimal. To find the new optimal solution, we insert the new c_j and $(z_j - c_j)$ values and then apply the simplex method. The resulting tableau, with x_3 replacing x_2 in the basis, is shown in Table 5-2. This is the new optimal solution: $x_1 = 16$, $x_2 = 0$, $x_3 = 4$, $x_4 = 4$, $x_5 = 0$, $x_6 = 19200$, and $z = 448$.

Table 5-2. *Solution of postoptimal change to objective function*

	New c_j		28	18	0	0	0	0	0
c_j	Basis	Solution	x_1	x_2	x_3	x_4	x_5	x_6	x_7
0	x_3	4	0	$\frac{2}{3}$	1	0	-8	0	0
0	x_4	4	0	$\frac{1}{3}$	0	1	-16	0	0
0	x_6	19200	0	1600	0	0	19200	1	-1
28	x_1	16	1	$\frac{2}{3}$	0	0	16	0	0
	$z_j - c_j$	448	0	$\frac{2}{3}$	0	0	448	0	0

5-2 PARAMETRIC PROGRAMMING OF OBJECTIVE FUNCTIONS

In *parametric programming* of the objective function we let some or all objective function coefficients change continuously over some range and trace the sequence of optimal solutions so obtained.

For example, if we consider the problem of independently varying c_1 from zero to ∞, we find that one form of the objective function involving the parameter θ is as follows:

(5-3) $$\text{maximize } z = (24 + 24\theta)x_1 + 20x_2, \qquad -1 \leq \theta \leq \infty$$

Had we varied c_1 and c_2 together, the objective function would have been

(5-4) maximize $z = (24 + 24\theta)x_1 + (20 + 20\theta)x_2, \qquad -1 \leqslant \theta \leqslant \infty$

The coefficients in front of θ can be varied to suit the particular needs of the analysis.

Let us perform some parametric programming using expression (5-3). Starting at the tableau in Table 5-1, we find the optimal basic solution for $\theta = -1$. Then we increase θ to infinity, noting the changes of basis and the values of θ at which they occur. The sequences of simplex tableaux are given in Table 5-3. (We omitted x_7 from the table because, being an artificial variable, it adds nothing to the analysis.)

We can trace these solutions on Figure 5-1. When $\theta = -1$ the objective function line is horizontal, so the optimal solution occurs at point A and remains there as long as $\theta \leqslant -\frac{7}{12}$. At $\theta \leqslant -\frac{7}{12}$, which implies $c_1 = 10$, the basis changes. The optimal solution occurs at point B for $-\frac{7}{12} \leqslant \theta \leqslant \frac{1}{4}$. Another change of basis occurs at $\theta = \frac{1}{4}$, or $c_1 = 30$. The optimal solution remains now at point C, because at that basis θ can then be increased indefinitely. Table 5-4 lists the set of optimal solutions. For example, if $c_1 = 45$, the optimal solution is $x_1 = 16$, $x_3 = 4$, $x_4 = 4$, $x_6 = 19200$.

Figure 5-1. *Parametric programming on c_1.*

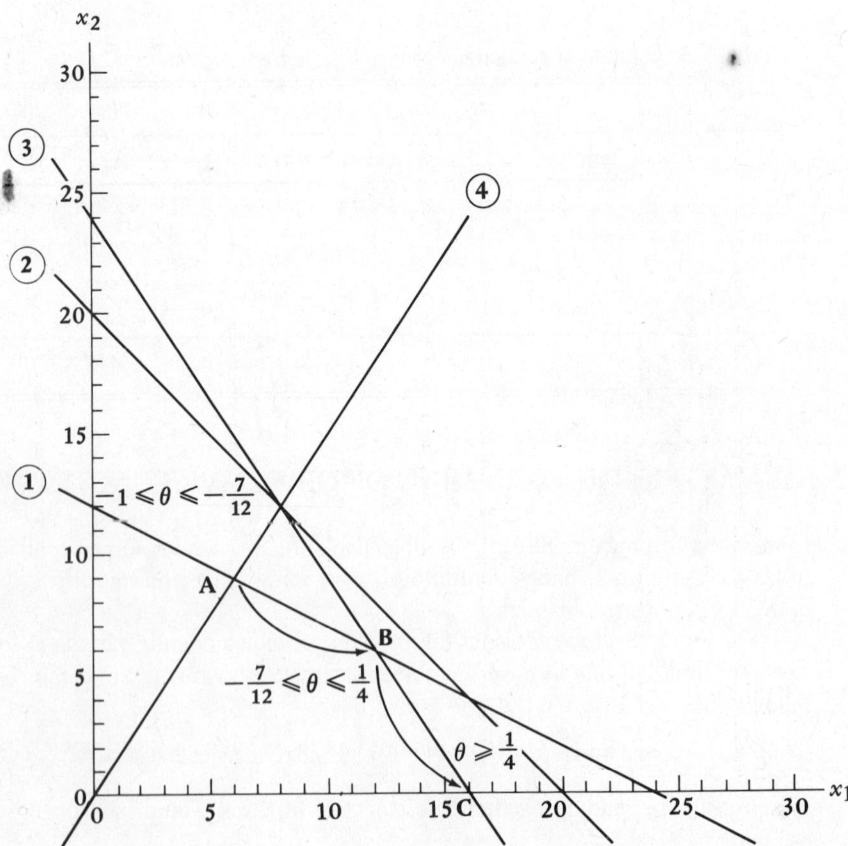

Table 5-3. *Parametric programming of c_1*

		c_j		$24(1+\theta)$	20	0	0	0	0
	c_j	Basis	Solution	x_1	x_2	x_3	x_4	x_5	x_6
	20	x_2	9	0	1	$\frac{3}{4}$	0	0	$\frac{1}{3200}$
$-1 \leqslant \theta \leqslant -\frac{7}{12}$	0	x_4	5	0	0	$-\frac{5}{4}$	1	0	$\frac{1}{3200}$
	0	x_5	$\frac{1}{4}$	0	0	$-\frac{1}{16}$	0	1	$\frac{1}{38400}$
	$24(1+\theta)$	x_1	6	1	0	$\frac{1}{2}$	0	0	$-\frac{1}{1600}$
		$z_j - c_j$	$(324 + 144\theta)$	0	0	$(27 + 12\theta)$	0	0	$(-\frac{7}{800} - \frac{3}{200}\theta)$
	20	x_2	6	0	1	$\frac{3}{2}$	0	-12	0
$-\frac{7}{12} \leqslant \theta \leqslant \frac{1}{4}$	0	x_4	2	0	0	$-\frac{1}{2}$	1	-12	0
	0	x_6	9600	0	0	-2400	0	38400	1
	$24(1+\theta)$	x_1	12	1	0	-1	0	24	0
		$z_j - c_j$	$(408 + 288\theta)$	0	0	$(6 - 24\theta)$	0	$(-336 + 576\theta)$	0
	0	x_3	4	0	$\frac{2}{3}$	1	0	-8	0
$\theta \geqslant \frac{1}{4}$	0	x_4	4	0	$\frac{1}{3}$	0	1	-16	0
	0	x_6	19200	0	1600	0	0	19200	1
	$24(1+\theta)$	x_1	16	1	$\frac{2}{3}$	0	0	16	0
		$z_j - c_j$	$(384 + 384\theta)$	0	$(-4 + 16\theta)$	0	0	$(384 + 384\theta)$	0

Table 5-4. *Results of the parametric programming on c_1*

Variable	$-1 \leqslant \theta \leqslant -\frac{7}{12}$ $0 \leqslant c_1 \leqslant 10$	$-\frac{7}{12} \leqslant \theta \leqslant \frac{1}{4}$ $10 \leqslant c_1 \leqslant 30$	$\frac{1}{4} \leqslant \theta \leqslant \infty$ $30 \leqslant c_1 \leqslant \infty$
x_1	6	12	16
x_2	9	6	0
x_3	0	0	4
x_4	5	2	4
x_5	$\frac{1}{4}$	0	0
x_6	0	9600	19200

5-3 POSTOPTIMAL ANALYSIS OF RHS PARAMETERS

Now let us study the response of the optimal solution to changes in an RHS parameter. Consider the pulverizer constraint

(5-5) $$\tfrac{1}{16}x_1 + \tfrac{1}{24}x_2 + x_5 = b_3$$

Currently $b_3 = 1$. Figure 5-2 shows that for this value the optimal basic solution is $x_1 = 12$, $x_2 = 6$, $x_4 = 2$, $x_6 = 9600$, with $x_3 = x_5 = 0$. As we increase b_3, the optimal solution changes—in fact it "slides down" the smoke constraint. As long as $b_3 \leqslant 1\frac{1}{6}$, the increase in b_3 does not affect which variables are in the basis. The same two constraints form the corner point. This condition indicates that, while the values of the basic variables have changed, the basis has not. Similarly, a decrease of b_3 below 1 does not alter the final basis as long as $b_3 \geqslant 0.75$. The values of the basic variables for different values of b_3 are given in Table 5-5. As b_3 increases, x_2 and x_4 decrease in value. At $b_3 = 1\frac{1}{6}$, x_4 becomes zero. Any further increase in b_3 causes x_4 to become negative, and the basis is no longer feasible. It does not represent an extreme point of the feasible region. Thus, for $b_3 > 1\frac{1}{6}$, the optimal basis changes. The same is true for $b_3 < 0.75$.

Let us now analyze these changes. First, we set $\hat{b}_3 = 1 + \Delta$. The pulverizer constraint now reads

(5-6) $$\tfrac{1}{16}x_1 + \tfrac{1}{24}x_2 + x_5 = 1 + \Delta$$

Table 5-5. *Values of basic variables for values of c_3*

Basic Solution	Value of Pulverizer Capacity (b_3)							
	.7	.75	.8	.9	1	1.1	$1\frac{1}{6}$	1.2
x_1	4.8	6	7.2	9.6	12	14.4	16	16.8
x_2	9.6	9	8.4	7.2	6	4.8	4	3.6
x_4	5.6	5	4.4	3.2	2	0.8	0	−0.4
x_6	−1920	0	1920	5760	9600	13440	16000	17280

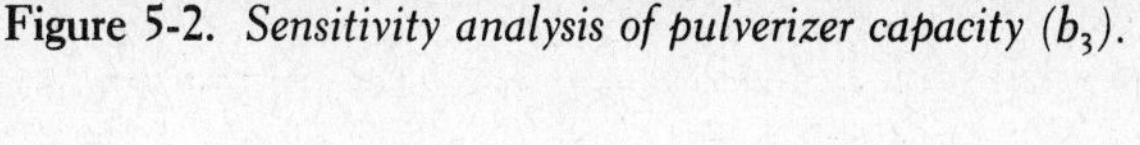

Figure 5-2. *Sensitivity analysis of pulverizer capacity (b_3).*

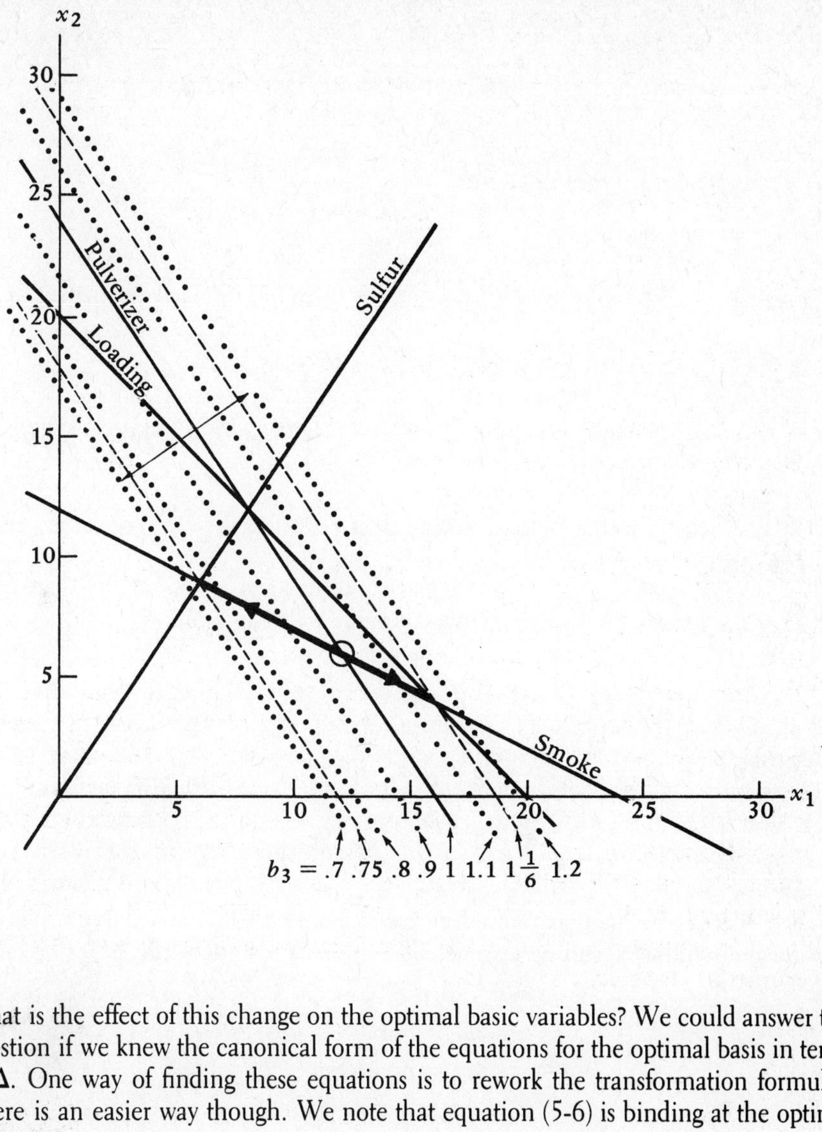

What is the effect of this change on the optimal basic variables? We could answer this question if we knew the canonical form of the equations for the optimal basis in terms of Δ. One way of finding these equations is to rework the transformation formulas. There is an easier way though. We note that equation (5-6) is binding at the optimal tableau, i.e.,

$$\frac{1}{16}x_1 + \frac{1}{24}x_2 = 1 + \Delta \tag{5-7}$$

However, equation (5-7) is the same as $\frac{1}{16}x_1 + \frac{1}{24}x_2 + x_5 = 1$, with $x_5 = -\Delta$. Thus we can analyze the change of the RHS parameter by analyzing a change of the corresponding slack variable. (If the equation has no positive slack variable, the artificial variable has the same effect.) This is done directly with the equations in canonical form for the optimal basis. We write them from the final tableau of Table 5-1 as

$$
\begin{aligned}
&x_2 + \tfrac{3}{2}x_3 \quad - \quad 12x_5 \quad = 6 \\
&-\tfrac{1}{2}x_3 + x_4 \quad - \quad 12x_5 \quad = 2 \\
&-2400x_3 \quad + 38400x_5 + x_6 - x_7 = 9600 \\
&x_1 \quad - \quad x_3 \quad + \quad 24x_5 \quad = 12 \\
&z \quad + \quad 6x_3 \quad + \quad 336x_5 \quad = 408
\end{aligned}
\tag{5-8}
$$

Setting $x_5 = -\Delta$ with $x_3 = 0$, we find the values of the basic variables are

$$
\begin{aligned}
&x_2 = 6 - 12\Delta \qquad x_4 = 2 - 12\Delta \\
&x_6 = 9600 + 38400\Delta \qquad x_1 = 12 + 24\Delta \qquad z = 408 + 336\Delta
\end{aligned}
\tag{5-9}
$$

Since a change in the RHS parameter does not affect the $(z_j - c_j)$ values, the present basis is optimal as long as it remains feasible.

What values of Δ will give a feasible solution to equations (5-9)? By definition, they must satisfy the nonegativity conditions on all variables—

$$
\begin{aligned}
&x_2 = 6 - 12\Delta \geqslant 0 \qquad \text{or} \qquad \Delta \leqslant \tfrac{6}{12} = \tfrac{1}{2} \\
&x_4 = 2 - 12\Delta \geqslant 0 \qquad \text{or} \qquad \Delta \leqslant \tfrac{2}{12} = \tfrac{1}{6} \\
&x_6 = 9600 + 38400\Delta \geqslant 0 \qquad \text{or} \qquad \Delta \geqslant -\frac{9600}{38400} = -\tfrac{1}{4} \\
&x_1 = 12 + 24\Delta \geqslant 0 \qquad \text{or} \qquad \Delta \geqslant -\tfrac{12}{24} = -\tfrac{1}{2}
\end{aligned}
\tag{5-10}
$$

Let Δ^- be the maximum decrease in b_3 and Δ^+ be the maximum increase in b_3 for the solution to still be feasible, i.e., $(\hat{b}_3 - \Delta^-) \leqslant \hat{b}_3 \leqslant (b_3 + \Delta^+)$. Then

$$
\begin{aligned}
\Delta^- &= \text{minimum}\left(\tfrac{1}{4}, \tfrac{1}{2}\right) = \tfrac{1}{4} \\
\Delta^+ &= \text{minimum}\left(\tfrac{1}{2}, \tfrac{1}{6}\right) = \tfrac{1}{6}
\end{aligned}
\tag{5-11}
$$

Since the existing value of the RHS parameter b_3 is 1, it can lie anywhere between $\frac{3}{4}$ and $\frac{7}{6}$ (all other parameters unchanged) and the corresponding solution will still be feasible and optimal.

Using the optimal tableau directly, we can formalize this procedure. We get the following rules for determining the range within which each RHS parameter can be varied individually without violating the feasibility of the current optimal basis, all other input data remaining unchanged.

RANGES FOR RHS PARAMETERS

In the optimal simplex tableau, let β_i denote the ith element in the "solution" column, and let γ_i be the ith element of the column corresponding to the slack or artificial variable for constraint k. Then

$$\text{(5-12)} \quad \left\{\begin{array}{l}\text{maximum increase in RHS} \\ \text{parameter of constraint } k\end{array}\right\} = \left\{\begin{array}{ll}\text{minimum } (-\beta_i/\gamma_i) & \text{for all } \gamma_i < 0 \\ +\infty \text{ if all } \gamma_i \geq 0 & \end{array}\right\}$$

$$\text{(5-13)} \quad \left\{\begin{array}{l}\text{maximum decrease in RHS} \\ \text{parameter of constraint } k\end{array}\right\} = \left\{\begin{array}{ll}\text{minimum } (\beta_i/\gamma_i) & \text{for all } \gamma_i > 0 \\ +\infty \text{ if all } \gamma_i \leq 0 & \end{array}\right\}$$

You should verify that if all $\gamma_i \geq 0$, then the range for the RHS parameter is open from above. Whereas if all $\gamma_i \leq 0$, then this range is open from below. Table 5-6 shows the ranges derived from the optimal simplex tableau in Table 5-1.

Table 5-6. *Ranges on RHS parameters at optimal solution*

Constraint	Original RHS	Maximum Decrease	Maximum Increase	Range
Smoke	12	4	4	8 to 16
Loading	20	2	$+\infty$	18 to $+\infty$
Pulverizer	1	$\frac{1}{4}$	$\frac{1}{6}$	$\frac{3}{4}$ to $\frac{7}{6}$
Sulfur	0	$+\infty$	9600	$-\infty$ to 9600

We can use equations (5-9) in a different way. They allow us to determine the new values of the basic variables for a change in the RHS parameter b_3 within its permissible range. For example, assume that the pulverizer capacity can be increased by 10 percent, i.e., the pulverizer rate for coal A increases to 17.6 tons per hour, and the rate for coal B increases to 26.4 tons per hour. The pulverizer constraint changes to

$$\frac{1}{17.6}x_1 + \frac{1}{26.4}x_2 \leq 1$$

or, in terms of the previous rates (multiplying through by 1.1), it is

$$\frac{1}{16}x_1 + \frac{1}{24}x_2 \leq 1.1$$

This change is within the permissible range. So with $\Delta = 0.1$, equations (5-9) give the new solution

$$\begin{array}{ll} x_2 = 6 - (12)(0.1) = 4.8 & x_4 = 2 - (12)(0.1) = 0.8 \\ x_6 = 9600 + (38400)(0.1) = 13440 & x_1 = 12 + (24)(0.1) = 14.4 \\ z = 408 + (336)(0.1) = 441.6 & x_3 = 0 \quad x_5 = 0 \end{array}$$

The ranges of values developed in Table 5-6 do not apply to changes of more than one RHS parameter at a time. In theory the required analysis is a direct extension of the one-by-one analysis, although in practice it becomes cumbersome without matrix algebra to make more than two changes at the same time.

Let us consider increases in the RHS parameters of all the constraints, i.e., $b_1 = 12 + \Delta_1$, $b_2 = 20 + \Delta_2$, $b_3 = 1 + \Delta_3$, and $b_4 = 0 + \Delta_4$. Using the slack and artificial variables of these constraints, with $x_3 = -\Delta_1$, $x_4 = -\Delta_2$, $x_5 = -\Delta_3$ and $x_7 = -\Delta_4$, we obtain the new solution from equations (5-8):

$$
\begin{aligned}
x_2 &= 6 + \tfrac{3}{2}\Delta_1 - 12\Delta_3 \\
x_4 &= 2 - \tfrac{1}{2}\Delta_1 + \Delta_2 - 12\Delta_3 \\
x_6 &= 9600 - 2400\Delta_1 + 38400\Delta_3 - \Delta_4 \\
x_1 &= 12 - \Delta_1 + 24\Delta_3 \\
z &= 408 + 6\Delta_1 + 336\Delta_3
\end{aligned}
\tag{5-14}
$$

So, for example, if the pulverizer capacity is increased by 10 percent and the smoke emission restriction is reduced to 11 kg/hr, we have $\Delta_1 = -1$, $\Delta_3 = 0.1$, and $\Delta_2 = \Delta_4 = 0$. From equations (5-14), the new solution is $x_2 = 3.3$, $x_4 = 1.3$, $x_6 = 15840$, $x_7 = 15.4$, and $z = 435.6$. You will notice that the coefficients of the Δ_1, Δ_2, Δ_3, and Δ_4 in (5-14) are the coefficients of the x_3, x_4, x_5, and x_7 columns in the optimal tableau. So the effect of changes in the RHS parameters on the values of the variables can be worked out directly from the tableau.

The previous analysis breaks down if we wish to consider changes in an RHS parameter beyond the permissible range over which the current basis remains feasible and, therefore, optimal. Section 5-5 deals with changes of this sort. However, only students who are familiar with the dual simplex method (Section 4-6) should attempt it.

5-4 PROFITABILITY OF CHANGING THE RHS

An analysis of the RHS is not complete without considering the profitability of changing the RHS. We have discussed how to find the new solution for a change in the RHS. But is the change worth making? In the final analysis, this is the fundamental question. Section 2-9 introduced this topic.

Let us return to the problem of increasing pulverizer capacity by 10 percent, as discussed in Section 5-3. Recall from Sections 4-4 and 4-5 that the dual variable associated with a constraint represents the change in the value of the objective function for a unit increase in the RHS of that constraint. This holds true, of course, only while the current basis remains feasible. From Table 5-1 we see that the dual variable associated with the pulverizer constraint ($= z_j$ of the corresponding slack variable) has a value of 336 units of steam per hour. Hence, a 10 percent increase in pulverizer capacity results in 0.1 (336), or an increase in the steam output of 33.6, units per hour.

Let us assume that the increased pulverizer capacity can be obtained at a capital cost of \$75,000 per annum. Also, we assume that a unit of steam (1000 lb) will return an average profit of \$1.5 (equal to the difference between the revenue and the variable cost of production of the extra steam produced). Assume that there are 2500 hours per annum when the additional steam can be used. Since the capital cost of the additional pulverizing capacity can only be recovered over 2500 hours, the capital cost per hour is \$75,000/2500, or \$30. Let us compare this with the profit per hour that this capacity will generate. Each hour the additional pulverizer capacity is used, it will generate 33.6 units of steam. A unit of steam returns \$1.5 profit, so 33.6 units return \$50.4 profit. Thus, the incremental hourly capital cost of \$30 is less than the incremental hourly profit of \$50.4. By installing the extra capacity, the company increases its annual profit by (50.4 − 30)(2500) = \$51,000.

*5-5 RHS CHANGES THAT CREATE INFEASIBILITY

When the change in the RHS parameters is too great for the existing basic solution to remain feasible, we need to find a new optimal feasible basis. Although the solution column of the optimal tableau changes under a change in the RHS parameters, the $(z_j - c_j)$ values do not change. They retain their nonnegative values. Where a change in the RHS parameters causes the optimal basic solution to become infeasible (yet with $(z_j - c_j) \geqslant 0$ for all j), the dual simplex method is required to find the new optimal basis.

Let us assume that the pulverizer capacity is increased by 20 percent. The pulverizer constraint becomes

$$\tfrac{1}{19.2}x_1 + \tfrac{1}{28.8}x_2 \leqslant 1$$

or

$$\tfrac{1}{16}x_1 + \tfrac{1}{24}x_2 \leqslant 1.2$$

Table 5-7. *Dual simplex tableaux for 20 percent increase in pulverizer capacity*

	c_j			24	20	0	0	0	0	—
	c_j	Basis	Solution	x_1	x_2	x_3	x_4	x_5	x_6	x_7
	20	x_2	3.6	0	1	$\frac{3}{2}$	0	−12	0	0
←	0	x_4	−0.4	0	0	($-\frac{1}{2}$)	1	−12	0	0
	0	x_6	17280	0	0	−2400	0	38400	1	−1
	24	x_1	16.8	1	0	−1	0	24	0	0
		$z_j - c_j$	475.2	0	0	6↑	0	336	0	—
	20	x_2	2.4	0	1	0	3	−48	0	0
	0	x_3	0.8	0	0	1	−2	4	0	0
	0	x_6	19200	0	0	0	−4800	96000	1	−1
	24	x_1	17.6	1	0	0	−2	48	0	0
		$z_j - c_j$	470.4	0	0	0	12	192	0	—

Setting $\Delta = 0.2$ in equations (5-9), we get $x_2 = 3.6$, $x_4 = -0.4$, $x_6 = 17280$, $x_1 = 16.8$, and $z = 475.2$. Since $x_4 < 0$, this solution is infeasible. In Table 5-7, we take this infeasible basic solution and use the dual simplex method to find the new optimal feasible basis. Dual simplex criterion 1 chooses x_4 to leave the basis, and criterion 2 selects x_3 to enter. The next dual simplex tableau is optimal. The new hourly steam output is 470.4 —an increase of 62.4 units over the solution in Table 5-1. We now use 17.6 tons of coal A and 2.4 tons of coal B per hour. Previously, the loading capacity was slack; now it is binding, while the smoke emission restriction has become slack. It should be noted that when we change the basis in Table 5-7, the values of the dual variables also change. For this reason, we must be careful in using the dual variables for interpreting the profitability of a change in the RHS when the change causes infeasibility.

5-6 PARAMETRIC PROGRAMMING OF THE RHS

In parametric programming of the RHS, we let some or all of the RHS parameters change continuously over a range from 0 to $+\infty$. The computations are done using the dual simplex method. However, the principles of the process involved can easily be grasped conceptually from a graphical demonstration. If we alter the RHS parameter of the pulverizer constraint by adding a parameter θ, varying continuously from -1 to $+\infty$, the problem to be solved, as a function of θ, is then

$$
\begin{aligned}
\text{maximize}\quad & 24x_1 + 20x_2 \\
\text{subject to}\quad & 0.5x_1 + x_2 \leqslant 12 \\
& x_1 + x_2 \leqslant 20 \\
& \tfrac{1}{16}x_1 + \tfrac{1}{24}x_2 \leqslant 1 + \theta \\
& 1200x_1 - 800x_2 \geqslant 0 \\
& x_1, x_2 \geqslant 0 \\
& -1 \leqslant \theta < +\infty
\end{aligned}
\tag{5-15}
$$

Figure 5-3 traces the optimal solution as θ increases. We note that the optimal basis changes at points A, B, C, and D. Unlike parametric programming of the objective function, parametric programming of the RHS causes the optimal solution to change continually along the path *ABCD* until the constraint becomes redundant at point *D*. Between each change of basis, the optimal solution changes linearly; but at a change of basis, the linear relationship (the slope of the line along the path of the optimal solution) itself changes.

Let us look at an example. What is the optimal solution for $\theta = 0$ (point *E*)? From the table in Figure 5-3, we see that the solution lies on a straight line between points *B* and *C*. If we denote by θ_B and θ_C the values of θ at *B* and *C*, then *E* is $[(1+\theta) - (1+\theta_B)]/[(1+\theta_C) - (1+\theta_B)] = (\theta - \theta_B)/(\theta_C - \theta_B)$ of the way from *B* to *C*. For $\theta = 0$, $\theta_B = -\frac{1}{4}$, $\theta_C = \frac{1}{6}$, we obtain $(\theta - \theta_B)/(\theta_C - \theta_B) = (\frac{1}{4})/(\frac{5}{12}) = \frac{3}{5}$. We find the solution at $\theta = 0$ by adding to the solution at point *B* $\frac{3}{5}$ of the difference between the solutions at B and C. This solution is

$$x_1 = 6 + \tfrac{3}{5}(16 - 6) = 12 \qquad x_2 = 9 + \tfrac{3}{5}(4 - 9) = 6$$
$$x_3 = 0 + \tfrac{3}{5}(0 - 0) = 0 \qquad x_4 = 5 + \tfrac{3}{5}(0 - 5) = 2$$
$$x_5 = 0 + \tfrac{3}{5}(0 - 0) = 0 \qquad x_6 = 0 + \tfrac{3}{5}(16{,}000 - 0) = 9600$$

and $$z = 324 + \tfrac{3}{5}(464 - 324) = 408$$

which is the optimal solution to the original problem.

If you are familiar with the dual simplex method, you should verify the table in Figure 5-3 by finding the sequence of dual simplex tableaux. (See exercise 5.9.)

Figure 5-3. *Sequence of solutions for equations (5-15).*

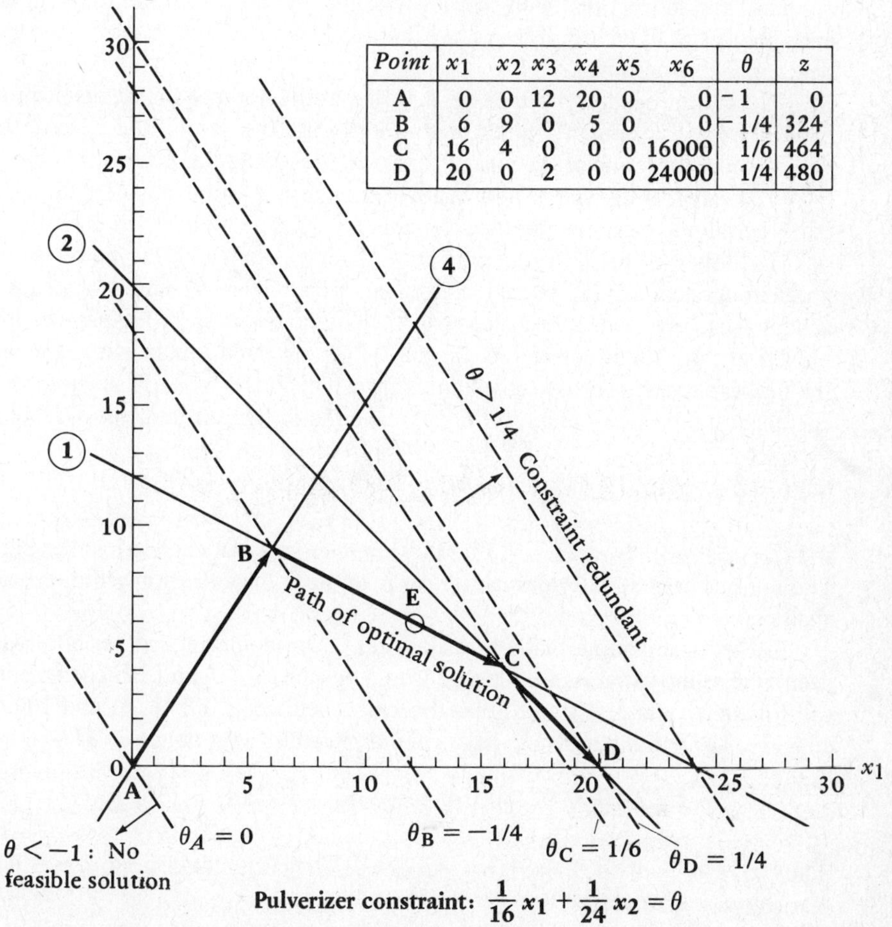

Point	x_1	x_2	x_3	x_4	x_5	x_6	θ	z
A	0	0	12	20	0	0	−1	0
B	6	9	0	5	0	0	−1/4	324
C	16	4	0	0	0	16000	1/6	464
D	20	0	2	0	0	24000	1/4	480

5-7 POSTOPTIMAL ANALYSIS OF LHS COEFFICIENTS AND ADDITION OF NEW VARIABLES

The computational difficulty associated with changes in LHS coefficients depends on whether the change is in a basic or a nonbasic variable. For a basic variable, a change means that potentially we have affected all the coefficients in the canonical form equations. This is because the arithmetic of the simplex transformations depends on the LHS coefficients of the basic variables. An analysis of this case is beyond the scope of this text.

When the changes in the LHS coefficients involve a nonbasic variable, the postoptimal analysis is somewhat simpler. It is convenient to view the variable as totally new, with new coefficients, and to eliminate the old variable from the problem. This is, of course, formally identical to the problem of adding a genuinely new variable (such as another type of coal in our example). Since both of these cases are of interest to us, we deal with them together.

As we consider the addition of a new variable, we ask the question: Is the old optimal basis still optimal with the new variable present, or should the new variable enter the basis? In technical terms, we are asking whether the $(z_j - c_j)$ value of the new variable is negative.

We saw in Section 4-5 that the z_j values at the optimal simplex tableau can be derived from the optimal values of the dual variables. Thus, the z_j value for the new variable (in terms of the current basis) can be computed in this manner. If the $(z_j - c_j)$ value so derived is nonnegative, the current basis remains optimal. If the $(z_j - c_j)$ value is negative, the new variable becomes a candidate to enter the basis.

To illustrate this idea, consider the expanded version of the power generating problem in Section 2-11, where management is offered the possibility of an additional activity—namely, the burning of coal C. The coefficients in the smoke, loading, pulverizer, and sulfur constraints are 0.8, 1, $\frac{1}{20}$, and 1000, respectively. We will call the new variable x_8. The objective function coefficient is $c_8 = 21$. Using the constraint coefficients and the w_i values in the optimal simplex tableau in Table 5-1, we obtain

$$z_8 = 0.8w_1 + 1w_2 + \tfrac{1}{20}w_3 + 1000w_4 = 0.8(6) + 1(0) + \tfrac{1}{20}(336) + 1000(0) = 21.6$$

and $(z_8 - c_8) = 21.6 - 21 = 0.6 > 0$. Therefore, x_8 is not eligible to enter the basis. The current basis is still optimal. There is no need to proceed any further with the analysis.

Let us next assume that 24 tons of coal C can be pulverized per hour. (Had x_8 been an existing variable, this change would be a change in an LHS coefficient.) We call this new variable x_9, and it has the LHS coefficients 0.8, 1, $\frac{1}{24}$, and 1000, with $c_9 = 21$. Using the same analysis as we did previously, we obtain

$$z_9 = 0.8(6) + 1(0) + \tfrac{1}{24}(336) + 1000(0) = 18.8$$

Thus $(z_9 - c_9) = (18.8 - 21) = -2.2 < 0$. The current basis is no longer optimal. Variable x_9 is a candidate to enter the basis.

We now want to find the revised optimal tableau for this new basis that includes the variable x_9. We can do this using equations (5-8). In their original form, the constraint equations are

$$\begin{aligned}
&\tfrac{1}{2}x_1 + x_2 + x_3 + 0.8x_9 = 12\\
(5\text{-}16)\quad &x_1 + x_2 + x_4 + x_9 = 20\\
&\tfrac{1}{16}x_1 + \tfrac{1}{24}x_2 + x_5 + \tfrac{1}{24}x_9 = 1\\
&1200x_1 - 800x_2 - x_6 + 1000x_9 = 0
\end{aligned}$$

If we transfer the x_9 terms to the RHS, we have the equations in the same form as they appear in equations (5-14), with $\Delta_1 = -0.8x_9$, $\Delta_2 = -x_9$, $\Delta_3 = (-\tfrac{1}{24})x_9$, and $\Delta_4 = 1000x_9$. (These give the changes in the resources available for the original variables if x_9 units of coal C are burned.) The RHS terms of (5-14) give the RHS's of the canonical form equations. Thus, in our case, the RHS's of the canonical form equations are

$$\begin{aligned}
(5\text{-}17)\quad 6 + \tfrac{3}{2}\Delta_1 - 12\Delta_3 &= 6 + (\tfrac{3}{2})(-0.8x_9) - 12(-\tfrac{1}{24}x_9) = 6 - 0.7x_9\\
2 - \tfrac{1}{2}\Delta_1 + \Delta_2 - 12\Delta_3 &= 2 - (\tfrac{1}{2})(-0.8x_9) - x_9 - 12(-\tfrac{1}{24}x_9) = 2 - 0.1x_9\\
9600 - 2400\Delta_1 + 38400\Delta_3 - \Delta_4 &= 9600 - 2400(-0.8x_9) + 38400(-\tfrac{1}{24}x_9) - (-1000)x_9\\
&= 9600 + 1320x_9\\
12 - \Delta_1 + 24\Delta_3 &= 12 - (-0.8x_9) + 24(-\tfrac{1}{24}x_9) = 12 - 0.2x_9
\end{aligned}$$

Combining equations (5-8) with the RHS's in (5-16), we get the following canonical form equations (with the x_9 transferred to the LHS):

$$\begin{aligned}
&x_2 + \tfrac{3}{2}x_3 - 12x_5 + 0.7x_9 = 6\\
(5\text{-}18)\quad &-\tfrac{1}{2}x_3 + x_4 - 12x_5 + 0.1x_9 = 2\\
&-2400x_3 + 38400x_5 + x_6 - x_7 - 1320\ x_9 = 9600\\
&x_1 - x_3 + 24x_5 + 0.2x_9 = 12
\end{aligned}$$

From equations (5-18) and the value of $(z_9 - c_9) = -2.2$, we form the new simplex tableau for the current basis (x_2, x_4, x_6, x_1), but with x_9 included as a nonbasic variable. Table 5-8 gives this tableau and the new optimal tableau, with x_9 replacing x_2 in the basis.

Now let us consider another issue. For what range of values of the pulverizer coefficient in variable x_9 does the current basis of Table 5-1 remain optimal? The requirement is that $(z_9 - c_9) \geqslant 0$. Let α denote the pulverizer coefficient. Then, by the principle discussed earlier,

$$z_9 = 0.8(6) + 1(0) + \alpha(336) + 1000(0) = 4.8 + 336\alpha$$

and

$$(z_9 - c_9) = 4.8 + 336\alpha - 21 = 336\alpha - 16.2$$

As long as $336\alpha \geqslant 16.2$, or as long as $\alpha \geqslant 16.2/336$ (or about 0.048), $(z_9 - c_9) \geqslant 0$. Interpreted another way, Table 5-1 gives the optimal solution as long as no more than $1/\alpha = 20.74$ tons of coal C can be pulverized per hour.

Table 5-8. *Inserting the new variable x_9*

	c_j			24	20	0	0	0	0	0	21
	c_j	Basis	Solution	x_1	x_2	x_3	x_4	x_5	x_6	x_7	x_9
←	20	x_2	6	0	1	$\frac{3}{2}$	0	-12	0	0	$\frac{7}{10}$
	0	x_4	2	0	0	$-\frac{1}{2}$	1	-12	0	0	$\frac{1}{10}$
	0	x_6	9600	0	0	-2400	0	38400	1	-1	-1320
	24	x_1	12	1	0	-1	0	24	0	0	$\frac{2}{10}$
		$z_j - c_j$	408	0	0	6	0	336	0	0	$-\frac{22}{10}$
	21	x_9	$\frac{60}{7}$	0	$\frac{10}{7}$	$\frac{15}{7}$	0	$\frac{-120}{7}$	0	0	1
	0	x_4	$\frac{8}{7}$	0	$\frac{-1}{7}$	$\frac{-5}{7}$	0	$\frac{-72}{7}$	0	0	0
	0	x_6	$\frac{146400}{7}$	0	$\frac{13200}{7}$	$\frac{3000}{7}$	0	$\frac{110400}{7}$	1	-1	0
	24	x_1	$\frac{72}{7}$	1	$\frac{-2}{7}$	$\frac{-10}{7}$	0	$\frac{192}{7}$	0	0	0
		$z_j - c_j$	$426\frac{6}{7}$	0	$\frac{22}{7}$	$\frac{75}{7}$	0	$\frac{2088}{7}$	0	0	0

5-8 COMPUTER CODES AND POSTOPTIMAL ANALYSIS

Most commercially available linear programming computer codes provide, as a routine procedure, a large portion of the sensitivity analysis that can be determined from the optimal simplex tableau. The computer codes give

- optimal dual variables or shadow prices,
- individual ranges on RHS parameters for which the corresponding dual variables remain unchanged,
- variable to leave and variable to enter the basis for each RHS change beyond these ranges,
- $(z_j - c_j)$ values for nonbasic variables,
- individual ranges on c_j for basic variables,
- variable to enter for changes beyond these ranges on each c_j.

They may also allow the user to specify a series of different right-hand sides and/or objective functions which are solved in sequence, usually using the previous optimal solution as the new initial solution. As a rule, this reduces the additional computations required. Some computer codes can perform parametric programming with respect to both the objective function and the RHS.

Most computer codes also allow the solution to be saved on disc or magnetic tape and provide *restart* procedures, at which point new variables or constraints can be added and old variables or constraints can be deleted.

EXERCISES

5.1 (a) Verify that c_2 in the power generating problem must lie in the range $16 \leq c_2 \leq 48$ for the final tableau in Table 5-1 to give the optimal solution.
(b) Verify that b_1, the RHS parameter of the smoke constraint, must lie in the range $8 \leq b_1 \leq 16$ for the basis (x_2, x_4, x_6, x_1) to give the optimal basic feasible solution.
(c) From Figure 5-3, find the optimal solution when $b_3 = \frac{1}{2}$.
(d) A device is marketed to reduce the sulfur oxide content of the gases by 10 percent. How much extra steam can be generated?
(e) A newly available coal (very hard, and low in pollutants) is contemplated. It has a smoke emission rate of $\frac{1}{3}$ kg/ton. The pulverizer can handle 12 tons of it per hour. The new coal has a sulfur content of 1500 PPM. Like all other coals, it uses loader capacity. It produces 30,000 lb of steam/ton. Should it be used?

5.2 For the problem in exercise 4.3(b) and the tableau in exercise 4.8:
(a) What is the optimal solution if the RHS is changed to $b_1 = 15$ and $b_2 = 5$? Find the change in the objective function using the values of the dual variables.
(b) For what value of c_1 is the original optimal solution still optimal?
(c) Consider a new variable x_6, with $a_{16} = -1$, $a_{26} = 3$ and $c_6 = 2$. If the introduction of the new variable could improve the solution, find the new optimal tableau.

5.3 A cabinet maker has recently taken over an enterprise making luxury mahogany desks. The only constraints he has are on the capacity of the plant (in machine hours) and on the availability of mahogany, which is delivered weekly by a regular supplier. The table summarizes the data for each week for four possible types of desks.

Desk Type	1	2	3	4	Availability
Machine	1	3	4	3	1000 hours
Mahogany (m^2)	4	2	6	8	2500 m^2
Profit/desk ($)	20	20	50	40	

The cabinet maker sets the problem up as a linear program to maximize profit. The number (in hundreds) of type j desks to be produced is x_j.

$$\text{maximize } z = 2x_1 + 2x_2 + 5x_3 + 4x_4 \qquad \text{(profit in \$1000)}$$

$$\text{subject to} \qquad x_1 + 3x_2 + 4x_3 + 3x_4 \leq 10 \qquad \text{(plant capacity in 100 hours)}$$

$$4x_1 + 2x_2 + 6x_3 + 8x_4 \leq 25 \qquad \text{(mahogany in 100 m}^2\text{)}$$

$$x_j \geq 0, \quad j = 1, \ldots, 4$$

The optimal tableau is as shown. Starting at this optimal solution, consider the following questions separately.
(a) Perform parametric programming of the profit values of desk type 3, $0 \leq \theta \leq \infty$.
(b) A major customer insists that 100 desks of type 2 be delivered each week for 4 weeks. What is the optimal production for each of those weeks, and what is the weekly profit?

(c) A shipping delay forces the regular supplier to reduce weekly mahogany supplies to 2000 m². What is now the optimal production schedule and profit? However, another source is willing to supply her with up to 1000 m² at \$6/m² instead of the normal prices she pays of \$4/m². How much should she buy at this price? Why?
(d) The cabinet maker is considering another type of desk that uses 4 hours of machine time and only 2 m² of mahogany. It would yield a profit of \$36 per desk. Should she produce it?

	c_j		2	2	5	4	0	0
c_j	Basis	Solution	x_1	x_2	x_3	x_4	x_5	x_6
2	x_1	4	1	−1	0	1.4	−0.6	0.4
5	x_3	1.5	0	1	1	0.4	0.4	−0.1
	$z_j - c_j$	15.5	0	1	0	0.8	0.8	0.3

5.4 A firm can produce four products in its factory. It takes only one day to produce a unit of each product, but production is limited by floor space in the factory and the amount of labor available. The relevant data are given in the table.

Product	1	2	3	4	Availability
Floor area, m²/unit	10	30	80	40	900 m²
Labor/unit	2	1	1	3	80 workers
Variable cost/unit	20	30	45	58	
Sales revenue/unit	30	50	85	90	

The following linear program is formulated, where x_j is the daily production of product j:

$$\text{maximize } z = x_1 + 2x_2 + 4x_3 + 3.2x_4 \quad \text{(profit in units of \$10)}$$

$$\text{subject to} \quad x_1 + 3x_2 + 8x_3 + 4x_4 \leq 90 \quad \text{(factory space in units of 10 m}^2\text{)}$$

$$2x_1 + x_2 + x_3 + 3x_4 \leq 80 \quad \text{(labor)}$$

$$x_j \geq 0, \quad \text{for all } j$$

The optimal tableau is as shown.

	c_j		1	2	4	3.2	0	0
c_j	Basis	Solution	x_1	x_2	x_3	x_4	x_5	x_6
1	x_1	10	1	-1	-4	0	$-\frac{3}{5}$	$\frac{4}{5}$
3.2	x_4	20	0	1	3	1	$\frac{2}{5}$	$-\frac{1}{5}$
	$z_j - c_j$	74	0	$\frac{1}{5}$	$\frac{8}{5}$	0	$\frac{17}{25}$	$\frac{4}{25}$

(a) A raw material used in products 1 and 3 is very unstable in price. At the moment, it costs \$100 a ton. Product 1 uses $\frac{1}{10}$ of a ton, and product 3 uses $\frac{1}{5}$ of a ton. The cost of the raw material is included in the variable costs shown above. What is the price range of this raw material for which the present solution is still optimal?

(b) What are the optimal values of the dual variables of this problem? Interpret these variables. What is the range of RHS values in which these variables' values hold?

(c) The firm can increase its effective floor space to 1000 m^2 by renting a new conveyor and stacking system. The machine costs \$50 a day to rent and operate. Should it be rented? If so, what is the new production schedule?

5.5 A farmer has just bought an unstocked farm of 1040 acres, all in pasture. He has a working capital of \$10,400 to spend on stocking the farm. He can buy breeding ewes, wethers, or beef breeding cattle. The current market price, his estimate of annual profit per animal, and the number of acres required per animal are given in the table.

	Market Price per Animal	Acres per Animal	Annual Profit per Animal
Ewes	\$ 7.00	1.0	\$12.00
Wethers	\$10.00	0.5	\$ 7.00
Cattle	\$100.00	3.0	\$40.00

He uses a linear programming model to determine how he should stock his farm if he is to maximize profit in the first year. The initial tableau and final tableau of the computations are shown. Respectively, x_4 and x_5 are variables representing unused land and capital.

	c_j		12	7	40	0	0
c_j	Basis	Solution	x_1	x_2	x_3	x_4	x_5
Initial Tableau							
0	x_4	1040	1.0	0.5	3.0	1	0
0	x_5	10,400	7.0	10.0	100.0	0	1
	$z_j - c_j$	0	−12	−7	−40	0	0
Final Tableau							
12	x_1	800	1	7	−3.077	1.538	−0.077
7	x_2	480	0	1	12.154	−1.077	0.154
	$z_j - c_j$	12,960	0	0	8.154	10.923	0.154

(a) If the portion of the profit from ewes and wethers due to the sale of wool is $4.00 in each case, by what percentage can the assumed price of wool drop before cattle should be stocked?

(b) The farmer can borrow up to $7800 at 10 percent interest to use either as further working capital or to purchase more land. An additional 104 acres of farm land is for sale, and the cost of buying this land and getting it ready for use is $50 per acre. What action should the farmer take? What will his optimal stocking policy be now?

(c) Another possible way of increasing the productivity of the farm is through the application of more fertilizer. Fertilizer costing $6 per acre will increase the carrying capacity of the land for ewes, wethers, and cattle to 0.6, 0.33, and 2.0 acres per animal, respectively. Assuming that not all the farm needs to be fertilized and assuming that animals can be separated on these different portions of the farm, how many acres (if any) should be fertilized? What will the optimal stocking policy be now? (The $6/acre fertilizer cost must be paid from working capital.)

5.6 Consider the linear program

$$
\begin{aligned}
\text{maximize } z &= 3x_1 + 2x_2 + 2x_3 \\
\text{subject to} \quad & x_1 + x_2 + x_3 \leq 10 \\
& 2x_1 + x_2 + 2x_3 \leq 15 \\
& 2x_1 + 3x_2 + x_3 \leq 20 \\
& x_1, x_2, x_3 \geq 0
\end{aligned}
$$

The initial and optimal tableaux are shown.

c_j			3	2	2	0	0	0
c_j	Basis	Solution	x_1	x_2	x_3	x_4	x_5	x_6
0	x_4	10	1	1	1	1	0	0
0	x_5	15	2	1	2	0	1	0
0	x_6	20	2	3	1	0	0	1
	$z_j - c_j$	0	-3	-2	-2	0	0	0
0	x_4	$\frac{5}{4}$	0	0	$\frac{1}{4}$	1	$-\frac{1}{4}$	$-\frac{1}{4}$
3	x_1	$\frac{25}{4}$	1	0	$\frac{5}{4}$	0	$\frac{3}{4}$	$-\frac{1}{4}$
2	x_2	$\frac{5}{2}$	0	1	$-\frac{1}{2}$	0	$-\frac{1}{2}$	$\frac{1}{2}$
	$z_j - c_j$	$\frac{95}{4}$	0	0	$\frac{3}{4}$	0	$\frac{5}{4}$	$\frac{1}{4}$

(a) What are the optimal values of x_1, x_2, x_3, and z? Which constraints are binding at the optimal solution?

(b) For what range of values of c_1 does this optimum hold? Derive the optimal tableau for $c_1 = 2$.

(c) Find the optimal solution if the RHS parameters b_2 and b_3 are changed to 16 and 24, respectively.

(d) What is the value of the dual variable of the second constraint? What does it mean? For what range of values of b_2 does it hold?

5.7 A publisher has 4500 spare man–machine hours available in the printing department and 4000 spare man–machine hours available in the binding department. Four books eligible for reprinting require the following time in each department per book produced.

Book	1	2	3	4
Printing dept. (hr)	0.1	0.3	0.8	0.4
Binding dept. (hr)	0.2	0.1	0.1	0.3

The profit on each book is as follows: book 1, \$1; book 2, \$1; book 3, \$4; book 4, \$3. Let x_j be production of book j measured in thousands. We get

$$\begin{array}{lrl} \text{maximize } z = & x_1 + x_2 + 4x_3 + 3x_4 & \text{(profit in \$1000's)} \\ \text{subject to} & x_1 + 3x_2 + 8x_3 + 4x_4 \leq 45 & \text{(printing dept. in 100's hr)} \\ & 2x_1 + x_2 + x_3 + 3x_4 \leq 40 & \text{(binding dept. in 100's hr)} \\ & x_j \geq 0, & \text{for all } j \end{array}$$

The optimal tableau is shown. Consider each of the following eventualities separately.

c_j			1	1	4	3	0	0
c_j	Basis	Solution	x_1	x_2	x_3	x_4	x_5	x_6
1	x_1	5	1	-1	-4	0	$-\frac{3}{5}$	$\frac{4}{5}$
3	x_4	10	0	1	3	1	$\frac{2}{5}$	$-\frac{1}{5}$
	$z_j - c_j$	35	0	1	1	0	$\frac{3}{5}$	$\frac{1}{5}$

(a) The marketing department considers the solution to be unreasonable. They think that at most 5000 copies of book 4 could be sold at that price. In order to sell 10,000 copies, the price would need to fall by $2 per copy. Analyze the implications of these observations, and find the most profitable solution in light of them. (Do *not* answer by resolving the system with an additional constraint.)

(b) The manager is disappointed that book 2 is not suggested for reprinting. She wants to know what would be the effect on the production of books 1 and 4 and on the profit if 2000 copies of book 2 were produced.

(c) As an alternative approach to getting book 2 published, the manager suggests that it be bound by another firm which would charge $0.5 a copy more than it would cost the publishers to bind it themselves. Would this make book 2 a profitable proposition? If so, what is the new production schedule?

(d) Another approach to publishing book 2 is to change its price. Perform parametric programming of c_2. Vary c_2 in the range from 0 to ∞. Assuming that it costs $6 a copy to produce book 2, give an overall production schedule for the various selling prices of that book.

5.8 A firm blends five different special-purpose cleaning fluids, code-named 401, 402, 403, 404, 405. Two basic ingredients are used in manufacture, both of which are in scarce supply (see table).

Fluid	401	402	403	404	405	Availability/wk
Ingredient 1 (liters)	0.1	0.3	0.2	0.6	0.9	240
Ingredient 2 (liters)	0.2	0.1	0.1	0.2	0.1	90
Profit ($/liter)	1	3	2.25	6.25	8	

These cleaners are exclusive to this firm, and the market is limited. It is estimated that 2000 liters of 401, or 1000 liters of 402, or 1000 liters of 403, or 400 liters of 404, or 250 liters of 405 (or any proportional combination) would satisfy the market each week. The problem is to be solved by linear programming with profits being maximized. By using the simplex method, we reach the following tableau. The units are 100 liters (production activities and market constraint), 10 liters (input constraints), and 100 dollars. x_6 is the slack variable for ingredient 1, x_7 is the slack variable for ingredient 2, and x_8 is the slack variable for the market.

	c_j		1	3	$2\frac{1}{4}$	$6\frac{1}{4}$	8	0	0	0
c_j	Basis	Solution	x_1	x_2	x_3	x_4	x_5	x_6	x_7	x_8
3	x_2	2	3	1	0	0	−5	1	2	−2
$2\frac{1}{4}$	x_3	3	5	0	1	0	−6	−1	3	0
$6\frac{1}{4}$	x_4	2	−3	0	0	1	6	0	−2	1
	$z_j - c_j$	$\frac{101}{4}$	$\frac{1}{2}$	0	0	0	1	$\frac{3}{4}$	$\frac{1}{4}$	$\frac{1}{4}$

Starting at this solution, the firm wishes to consider the effect of a number of alterations.

(a) Another cleaning liquid using 0.8 liter of ingredient 1 and 0.1 liter of ingredient 3 (not in scarce supply) could be made. This cleaner belongs to a different market with unlimited demand, and gives $7.00 profit per liter. What will be the optimal production scheme with this alternative available?

(b) Another supplier suggests that she could obtain more of either ingredient 1 or ingredient 2 or both, up to an aggregate limit of 15 liters per week. The cost would be $7 per liter for ingredient 1 and $1 per liter for ingredient 2. Should any more be obtained? How much? What will the new solution be?

(c) What is the price range of cleaning fluid 402 that will ensure that the present solution is optimal? What is your reaction to the result?

5.9 Find the dual simplex tableaux for the parametric programming of the RHS given in Section 5-6.

REFERENCES

Most of the references to Chapters 3 and 4 cover sensitivity analysis. In particular, G. Hadley gives a complete but terse exposition in Sections 11-2 through 11-6, and L. W. Swanson presents a more readable but less complete analysis in Chapter 5.

CHAPTER SIX

Transportation and Assignment Problems

A number of important operations research problems can be viewed as *networks* of *nodes* connected by *links*. For example, if we want to find the shortest road distance between two points in a city, we can represent the major crossroads as nodes and the road connection between crossroads as the link. Another example deals with sending messages between points A and B through a network of transmission centers. Each center represents a node. They are connected by transmission links with limited transmission capacity. What is the maximum volume of messages that can be sent from A to B? Although each of these networks is derived from a meaningful problem, in general a network is a totally abstract mathematical concept. Chapters 6 through 9 study such networks. We will see how we may exploit their special structure to efficiently solve certain classes of operations research problems.

This chapter concentrates on the *transportation* (or *distribution*) *problem* and one of its special variants—the *assignment problem*. A commodity is available at a number of *sources* and is required at a number of *destinations* where it is needed for distribution to local customers. Sources and destinations are the nodes, while the flow of goods between sources and destinations is represented by the links of the network. With each link we associate a *transportation cost*. We want to find the least-cost transportation schedule from sources to destinations—a problem that can be solved by linear programming. We will show, however, that the special network structure leads to simplifications in the simplex method that result in a computationally much more efficient algorithm.

6-1 FORMULATING THE TRANSPORTATION PROBLEM

Although the transportation problem gets its name from a particular application, it should be viewed simply as a problem with a specific mathematical structure. A great variety of seemingly unrelated problems also exhibit this particular mathematical structure.

Let us now consider a classical transportation problem. A New Zealand carpet manufacturer produces the same type of carpet in two factories. The carpet is sold through five regional distribution warehouses. The corresponding network is depicted in Figure 6-1. Each factory has a given *availability* of carpet. This can be viewed either as actual goods ready for shipment or as available production capacity. Each warehouse has given *demands* for the goods. The numbers attached to the links between factories and warehouses represent the lowest cost of transporting one unit of the commodity (one roll of carpet) from a given factory to a given warehouse. The problem is to determine a transportation schedule, from the two factories to the five warehouses, that has the lowest possible transportation cost. The solution, though, must meet the demand at each warehouse and must not ship away from any factory more than is available.

Table 6-1 reproduces the costs of transporting one unit of the commodity from factory Fi to warehouse W$_j$. We assume that the total transportation cost from a factory to a warehouse is directly proportional to the quantity shipped. This is the usual linearity assumption of linear programming.

The decision variables of the problem are the quantities of the commodity shipped from each factory to each warehouse. Let x_{ij} be the quantity shipped from factory Fi to warehouse Wj. We shall first formulate this problem as a linear program.

Figure 6-1. *Graph of transportation problem.*

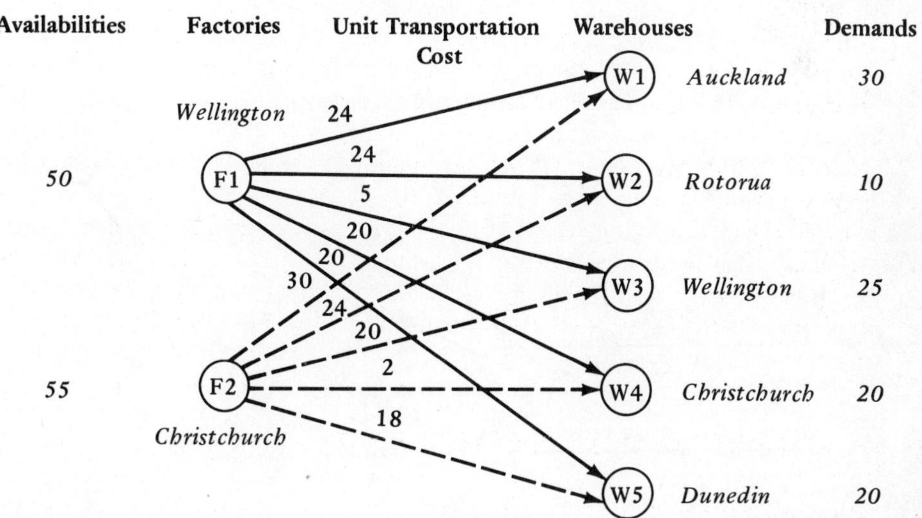

Table 6-1. *Unit transportation costs in dollars*

	Warehouses				
Factories	W1	W2	W3	W4	W5
F1	24	24	5	20	20
F2	30	24	20	2	18

Objective function:

The objective is to minimize total transportation costs. From Table 6-1 we obtain the function

$$\text{minimize } z = 24x_{11} + 24x_{12} + 5x_{13} + 20x_{14} + 20\,x_{15} + 30\,x_{21} + 24x_{22} + 20x_{23} + 2x_{24} + 18x_{25}$$

Constraints:

The supply situation at factory F1 (or the flow out of node F1) is shown in Figure 6-2. The total amount shipped from factory F1 to all the warehouses must be no more than the amount available at the factory:

(6-2) $$x_{11} + x_{12} + x_{13} + x_{14} + x_{15} \leq 50 \quad \text{(availability constraint)}$$

Similarly, for factory F2,

(6-3) $$x_{21} + x_{22} + x_{23} + x_{24} + x_{25} \leq 55$$

Figure 6-2. *Availability at factory F1.*

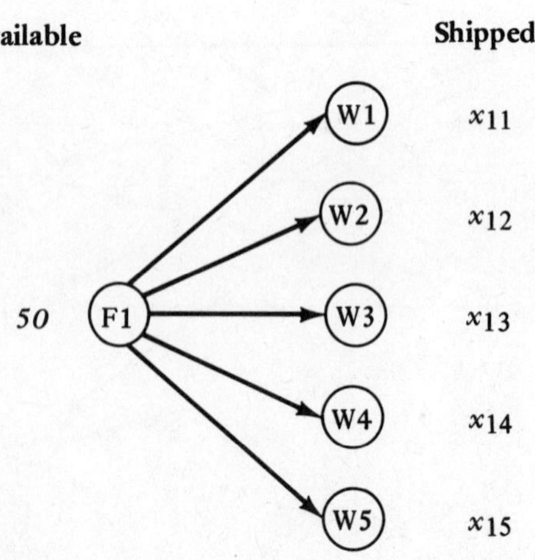

The demand situation at warehouse W1 is depicted in Figure 6-3. The total amount shipped to warehouse W1 from all the factories (or the flow into W1) must be no less than the amount required at the warehouse:

$$x_{11} + x_{21} \geqslant 30 \qquad \text{(demand constraint)} \tag{6-4}$$

Similarly, for the other warehouses,

$$\begin{aligned} x_{12} + x_{22} &\geqslant 10 \\ x_{13} + x_{23} &\geqslant 25 \\ x_{14} + x_{24} &\geqslant 20 \\ x_{15} + x_{25} &\geqslant 20 \end{aligned} \tag{6-5}$$

Finally we have the usual nonnegativity conditions:

$$x_{ij} \geqslant 0, \qquad \text{for all } i \text{ and } j \tag{6-6}$$

Equations (6-1) through (6-6) show the linear programming formulation of the transportation problem.

In Table 6-2 we show the linear program in detached coefficient form (without slack variables). We notice that all the LHS coefficients are unity and that they have a special horizontal and diagonal structure. Each activity has only two nonzero coefficients, one in the row associated with its factory and one in the row associated with its warehouse.

Table 6-2. *Transportation problem in detached coefficient form*

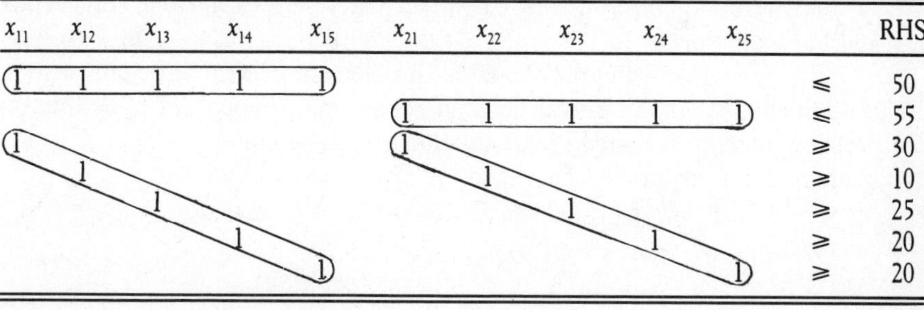

x_{11}	x_{12}	x_{13}	x_{14}	x_{15}	x_{21}	x_{22}	x_{23}	x_{24}	x_{25}		RHS
1	1	1	1	1						$\leqslant$	50
					1	1	1	1	1	$\leqslant$	55
1					1					$\geqslant$	30
	1					1				$\geqslant$	10
		1					1			$\geqslant$	25
			1					1		$\geqslant$	20
				1					1	$\geqslant$	20

Figure 6-3. *Requirements at warehouse W1.*

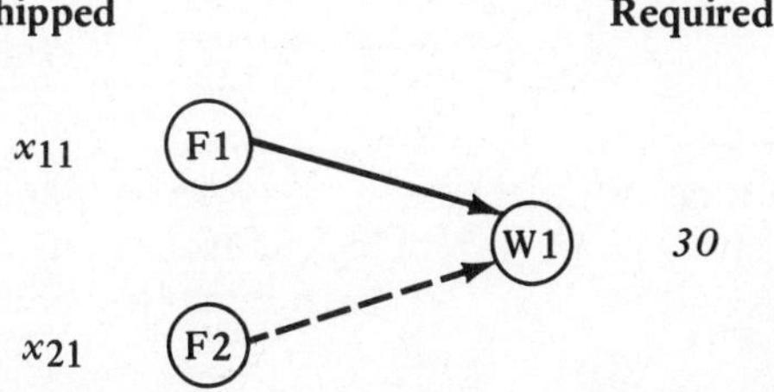

6-2 TRANSPORTATION PROBLEM IN GENERAL TERMS

Until now we have talked about factories and warehouses. Since the importance of the structure is mathematical, an identical analysis holds for *sources* and *destinations* of quite different sorts. If a particular problem can be thought of as the allocation of something from sources to destinations (in any sense of the words), then it is probably a transportation problem. For instance, the sources might be production capacity per period; the destinations, sales requirements per period; and the problem, the allocation of production capacity over time. A sure way to identify a transportation problem is to look at the structure of the associated linear program in detached coefficient form.

Often a transportation problem has an imbalance between the total amount available at the sources and the total demanded by the destinations. There exists a feasible solution to the transportation problem only if the amount available at the sources is at least as much as the amount required by the destinations. However, in order to use the special solution technique to be discussed, the amount available at the sources *must equal* the amount required by the destinations, and equality must hold for all the availability and demand constraints. When the availability is greater than requirements, we add a dummy warehouse or a destination whose demand for the commodity is equal to the difference between the quantity available from the sources and the quantity required by the real destinations. Transportation costs to the dummy destination are zero from all sources. This restores the assumption that total availability equals total demand. Units shipped from a source to a dummy destination are interpreted as slack capacity at that source. (Exercise 6.2 requires the use of dummy warehouses.) When requirements are greater than availability, we introduce a dummy source. However, in this case, a more appropriate optimization criterion is usually the maximization of the difference between total revenues and total costs of production and transportation.

Let us write out the transportation problem in general terms for m sources and n destinations, assuming total demand equals total supply. Let c_{ij} be the unit transportation cost from source i to destination j, a_i the quantity available at source i, and b_j the quantity required at destination j. Then the problem is to

$$\text{minimize } z = \sum_{i=1}^{m} \sum_{j=1}^{n} c_{ij}x_{ij}$$

$$\text{subject to} \quad \sum_{j=1}^{n} x_{ij} = a_i, \quad i = 1, \ldots, m \qquad \text{(availability constraints)}$$

$$\text{(6-7)} \qquad \sum_{i=1}^{m} x_{ij} = b_j, \quad j = 1, \ldots, n \qquad \text{(demand constraints)}$$

$$x_{ij} \geq 0, \quad \text{for all } i \text{ and } j$$

There are m times n variables and $m + n$ constraints. Since, by assumption, $\Sigma_i a_i = \Sigma_j b_j$, one of the constraints of (6-7) is redundant. Therefore, a basis for this linear program has only $(m + n - 1)$ basic variables. Although the optimal solution to problem (6-7) could be found by the simplex method, there are computationally more efficient methods that exploit the special structure of the transportation problem. We will discuss one such method—*the stepping-stone algorithm*—which is a streamlined version of the simplex method.

In the next section, we will show how any feasible solution (and in particular a basic feasible solution) to the transportation problem can be displayed efficiently in a tableau similar to Table 6-1. We will also demonstrate a simple way of finding an initial basic feasible solution. Section 6-4 studies the network structure corresponding to a change from one basic feasible solution to an adjacent one, while Section 6-5 formalizes the insight gained and develops the stepping-stone algorithm.

6-3 THE TRANSPORTATION TABLEAU AND AN INITIAL BASIC FEASIBLE SOLUTION

With each combination of source i and destination j, we have associated a variable x_{ij}, denoting the amount shipped from source i to destination j. The values of the x_{ij}'s can thus be displayed as the cells in a tableau where the rows refer to sources and the columns refer to destinations. Table 6-3 shows the tableau for our example. For convenience, we add an additional column displaying the amount available a_i at each source, and an additional row giving the requirements b_j at each destination. The availability constraints can be generated simply by adding the x_{ij}'s in each row and setting the sum equal to the corresponding a_i value. The demand constraints are found by summing the x_{ij}'s in each column and equating the sum to the corresponding b_j value.

Table 6-3. *Transportation tableau*

	Destinations					
Factories	W1	W2	W3	W4	W5	Availability
F1	x_{11}	x_{12}	x_{13}	x_{14}	x_{15}	a_1
F2	x_{21}	x_{22}	x_{23}	x_{24}	x_{25}	a_2
Requirements	b_1	b_2	b_3	b_4	b_5	

Any set of x_{ij} values that satisfies all availability and all demand constraints is a feasible solution. As we have seen, a feasible solution is also a basic solution if no more than $(m + n - 1)$ variables are positive.

How do we find an initial basic feasible solution from which to start the iterations of the stepping-stone algorithm? One of the simplest ways is called the *northwest corner rule*. We start at the top left-hand cell, the northwest corner, and proceed down and to the right, in that order of preference, allocating as much as possible to each cell until the b_j requirement is satisfied but no a_i availability is violated. Starting at cell $i = 1$, $j = 1$, we find that the most that cell can take is minimum $(b_1, a_1) =$ minimum $(30, 50) = 30$. The first column is now satisfied, leaving $(a_1 - b_1) = (50 - 30)$ still to be allocated from F1. We now proceed to the second column. Here $x_{12} =$ minimum $(b_2, a_1 - b_1) =$ minimum $(10, 50 - 30) = 10$, leaving $(a_1 - b_1 - b_2) = (50 - 40) = 10$ still to be allocated from F1. The third column gives $x_{13} =$ minimum $(25, 50 - 40) = 10$. The availability at F1 is now exhausted, so we proceed down column 3 to row 2: $x_{23} =$ minimum $(25 - 10, 55) = 15$; $x_{24} =$ minimum $(20, 55 - 15) = 20$; and $x_{25} = 20$. All other x_{ij}'s are nonbasic and, thus, set equal to zero. Their cells are left blank. The resulting basis is shown in Table 6-4.

Table 6-4. *Initial basis by northwest corner rule*

	W1	W2	W3	W4	W5	a_i
F1	30	10	10			50
F2			15	20	20	55
b_j	30	10	25	20	20	

The method used guarantees that the initial solution is feasible. The basic variables are x_{11}, x_{12}, x_{13}, x_{23}, x_{24}, and x_{25}. As required, there are $(m + n - 1)$, or 6, basic variables.

Other more sophisticated and efficient methods for finding an initial basic feasible solution take into account the values of the cost coefficients, and so tend to give a better initial solution than the northwest corner rule. A method called column minimization is introduced in Section 6-8.

6-4 NETWORK FLOWS ASSOCIATED WITH A BASIS CHANGE

The key to the transportation technique is the way the transportation network responds to a unit reallocation in the shipping schedule. Figure 6-4 depicts the network associated with the initial basic feasible solution found by the northwest corner rule in Table 6-4. The basic variables are represented by the solid lines and the nonbasic variables by the broken lines. The sum of the flows from each source exactly matches the availability, while the sum of the flows into each destination exactly matches the demand. Let us now decide to ship one unit along a link not used in this solution—for instance, from F2 to W2. The reason for exploring such reallocations is to test if

Figure 6-4. *A feasible transportation schedule.*

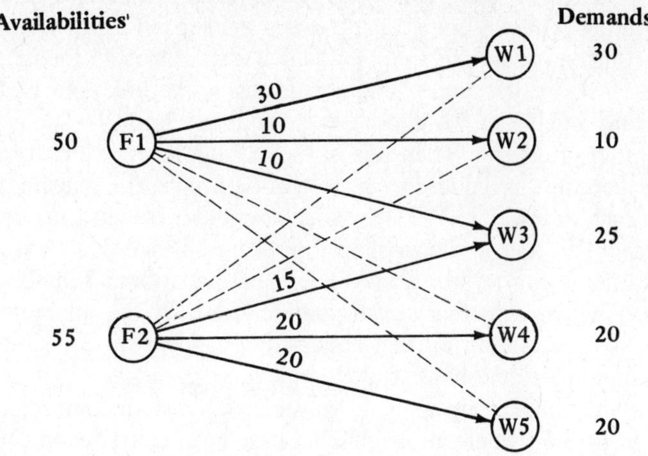

they yield any cost savings. In order to maintain feasibility, we must adjust some of the existing flows. There is only one choice: decrease the flow from F1 to W2 by one unit, increase the flow from F1 to W3 by one unit, and finally decrease the flow from F2 to W3 by one unit. The new solution is shown in Figure 6-5. It again exactly balances availabilities at all sources and demands at all destinations. A crucial result

Figure 6-5. *Adjusted transportation flows.*

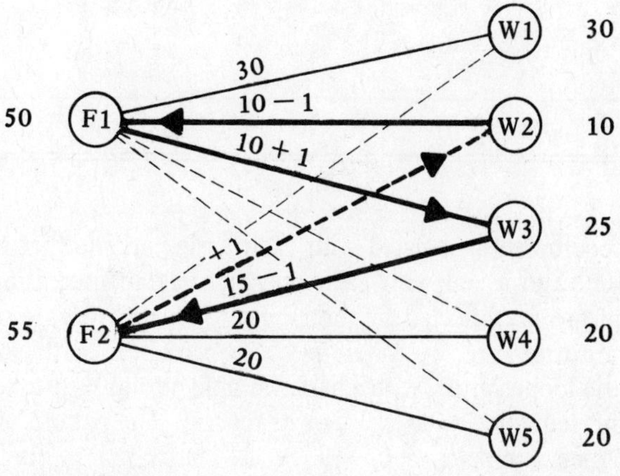

now emerges. The set of existing links that are adjusted, together with the new link, forms a loop in the network. This is depicted in Figure 6-5 by the solid and the broken heavy lines. The adjustment pattern is characterized by an alternating sequence of subtracting and adding one unit to the flows in the loop. A similar adjustment pattern results for the reallocation of additional units to the link from F2 to W1.

How much can we allocate to a nonbasic link? To maintain feasibility, the reallocation must stop when one of the existing flows, which is decreasing through this reallocation, is reduced to zero. In our example, the maximum amount that can be allocated from F2 to W2 is the smaller of the two decreasing flows from F1 to W2 and F2 to W3, i.e., the flow of 10 units from F1 to W2.

Not only can we find the value of a particular basic solution using the network structure; we will show that we can also infer from it all the other information contained in the simplex tableau for that basic solution. Consider the simplex tableau corresponding to the same basis (x_{11}, x_{12}, x_{13}, x_{23}, x_{24}, x_{25}), as shown in Table 6-5. (This tableau was obtained by applying the simplex transformation rules to expressions (6-1) through (6-6), where all inequalities have been converted to equalities—the usual form of the balanced transportation problem.) We do not show how this table was derived because we are only interested in using its structure. Note that the tableau elements for the LHS coefficients are either +1, −1, or 0. Compare the coefficients in the x_{22} column with the loop of heavy arrows in Figure 6-5. This loop depicts the change in flows associated with x_{22} entering the basis. In the simplex tableau, there

Table 6-5. *Simplex tableau for basis (x_{11}, x_{12}, x_{13}, x_{23}, x_{24}, x_{25})*

	c_{ij}		24	24	5	20	20	30	24	20	2	18
c_{ij}	Basis	Solution	x_{11}	x_{12}	x_{13}	x_{14}	x_{15}	x_{21}	x_{22}	x_{23}	x_{24}	x_{25}
24	x_{11}	30	1	0	0	0	0	1	0	0	0	0
24	x_{12}	10	0	1	0	0	0	0	1	0	0	0
5	x_{13}	10	0	0	1	1	1	−1	−1	0	0	0
20	x_{23}	15	0	0	0	−1	−1	1	1	1	0	0
2	x_{24}	20	0	0	0	1	0	0	0	0	1	0
18	x_{25}	20	0	0	0	0	1	0	0	0	0	1
	$z_{ij} - c_{ij}$	1710	0	0	0	−33	−17	9	15	0	0	0

is a +1 coefficient associated with each basic variable that has a decreasing flow in the network and a −1 with each one that has an increasing flow. Those with a 0 coefficient are not affected by the change of basis (i.e., are not in the loop of heavy arrows). Furthermore, consider the basic variables in the order implied by a pass through the loop, starting with a basic variable next to x_{22} (the variables being increased) i.e., in the sequence x_{12}, x_{13}, x_{3}, or its reverse. The pattern of tableau coefficients for this sequence alternates +1, −1, + 1. Verify that a similar pattern holds for all columns of nonbasic variables. Hence, we can infer the simplex tableau entries for the LHS coefficients directly from the network.

Consider now the $(z_{ij} - c_{ij})$ values. From Chapter 3 you recall that the z_j's can be obtained by multiplying each coefficient in column j with the c_j value of the basic variable associated with that row and summing these products. Applying this rule to x_{22}, we get

$$z_{22} = (0)c_{11} + (1)c_{12} + (-1)c_{13} + (1)c_{23} + (0)c_{24} + (0)c_{25} = c_{12} - c_{13} + c_{23}$$

Hence,

$$(z_{22} - c_{22}) = c_{12} - c_{13} + c_{23} - c_{22} = 24 - 5 + 20 - 24 = 15$$

In terms of the network representation, this corresponds to adding and subtracting c_{ij}'s around the loop, starting with the arrow next in line after x_{22}. This has an intuitively appealing interpretation. As we introduce one unit from F2 to W2, we save \$24 in not sending one unit from F1 to W2, incur a cost of \$5 for an extra unit from F1 to W3, save \$20 in moving one unit less from F2 to W3, and incur the cost of the unit going from F2 to W2. Thus, $(z_{22} - c_{22})$ is the net savings in cost for each unit of x_{22}. If $(z_{22} - c_{22})$ is positive, then x_{22} should enter the basis.

So we see that all the entries of the simplex tableau for a given basis can be inferred from the corresponding network representation. We can thus do away with the regular simplex tableau. Rather than use a diagrammatic representation like Figure 6-5, we go to a more efficient tableau structure. In fact, the representation of Table 6-3, along with some additional information, will do well. In each cell of that tableau, we store the corresponding c_{ij} value in the top left-hand corner box. The values of the basic variables are inserted in a circle in the center of the cell. The $(z_{ij} - c_{ij})$ values for the nonbasic variables are displayed in a box at the bottom left-hand corner of the cell. Table 6-6 gives the full tableau for the initial solution of Table 6-4.

We can also display in the transportation tableau the loop structure of the network representation for each possible basis change. In Table 6-6 we show the loop for x_{22} and the +1 and −1 coefficients associated with each basic variable involved in the loop. The loops can be found as follows.

Table 6-6. *First transportation tableau*

	W1	W2	W3	W4	W5	a_i
F1	24 (30)	24 +1 (10) →	5 −1 (10) ↓	20 −33	20 −17	50
F2	30 9	24 X ↑	20 +1 (15) → X; 15	2 (20)	18 (20)	55
b_j	30	10	25	20	20	Total cost 1710

Step 1 Locate the nearest cell with a circle (denoting a basic variable) in the same column as the nonbasic variable being considered. Go to Step 2.

Step 2 If the original nonbasic variable is in the same row as the basic variable located in the previous step (Step 1 or 3), find it and go to Step 4. Otherwise, find the nearest circled cell in the row and go to Step 3. If there is no such cell, return to the previous step (Step 1 or 3), find the next nearest circled cell at that step, and return to Step 2.

Step 3 Locate the nearest circled cell in the column of the cell found in Step 2 and go to Step 2. If no such cell exists, return to Step 2, find the next nearest circled cell, and return to Step 3.

Step 4 Draw lines between the adjacent cells in the loop. Cells reached by Steps 1 or 3 get a + 1 coefficient assigned to them; those reached by Step 2 get a − 1 coefficient.

If ties for the "nearest" cell occur, the choice is arbitrary. With the +1 and −1 coefficients so generated, the $(z_{ij} - c_{ij})$'s can be evaluated. Verify the values for all other nonbasic variables.

The next section formalizes these findings and develops the stepping-stone algorithm.

6-5 THE STEPPING-STONE ALGORITHM

Starting with the basic feasible solution recorded in Table 6-6, we evaluate the $(z_{ij} - c_{ij})$ values for all cells corresponding to nonbasic variables. Then we look for the cell that gives the greatest net saving per unit.

CRITERION 1: VARIABLE TO ENTER THE BASIS

The variable x_{qr} to enter the basis is the nonbasic variable with the maximum value of $(z_{ij} - c_{ij})$ for all $(z_{ij} - c_{ij}) > 0$.

By analogy to the simplex method, if no $(z_{ij} - c_{ij}) > 0$ exists, the optimal solution has been found.

OPTIMALITY CRITERION

The solution associated with a given basis is optimal if all $(z_{ij} - c_{ij}) \leq 0$.

In Section 6-4 we showed that the maximum value of the variable entering the basis is the minimum of the values of those flows that decrease as a result. This flow gives the variable leaving the basis. (Verify that the same conclusion is reached from the simplex tableau in Table 6-5.) For x_{22} entering the basis, x_{22} = minimum (x_{12}, x_{23}) = minimum (10, 15) = 10. Thus, x_{12} leaves the basis.

CRITERION 2: VARIABLE TO LEAVE THE BASIS

The variable x_{st} to leave the basis is the one with the smallest x_{ij} value for all x_{ij} with +1 coefficients in the loop for the variable to enter the basis.

The network representation for a basis change studied in the previous section provides us also with the transformation rules to determine the values of the new basic variables. A basic variable with a +1 coefficient decreases by an amount x_{st}, while a variable with a − 1 coefficient increases by x_{st}. Basic variables not in the loop do not change. (Verify that the simplex tableau transformation rules result in the same adjustments when applied to Table 6-5.)

NEW BASIC FEASIBLE SOLUTION

(6-8)
(1) $x_{qr} = x_{st}$
(2) $x_{ij} = x_{ij} - x_{st}$ for all x_{ij} with +1 coefficients in the x_{st} loop
(3) $x_{ij} = x_{ij} + x_{st}$ for all x_{ij} with −1 coefficients in the x_{st} loop
(4) $x_{ij} = x_{ij}$ for all x_{ij} with 0 coefficients for the x_{st} loop

If there is a tie among variables to satisfy criterion 2, any of the tied variables may be chosen to leave the basis. However, at the next tableau all the other variables in the tie will be basic at value zero, or degenerate. We shall have more to say about this in Section 6-6.

Now that we have developed all of the criteria of the stepping-stone algorithm and applied them to Table 6-6, we can write the next solution down (as in Table 6-7) and apply the algorithm again. We first compute the $(z_{ij} - c_{ij})$ values. Criterion 1 chooses x_{21} to enter the basis—it is the only nonbasic variable with a positive $(z_{ij} - c_{ij})$ value. In the loop for x_{21}, the basic variables with +1 coefficients—those which decrease in value—are x_{11} and x_{23}. The minimum $(x_{11}, x_{23}) = x_{23} = 5$. Thus, x_{23} leaves the basis. The new solution is displayed in the second tableau of Table 6-7. Having found the $(z_{ij} - c_{ij})$ values for this tableau, we discover that all $(z_{ij} - c_{ij}) < 0$. The last solution is the optimal solution, with a cost of 1515. The optimal schedule is

Fl to W1	25 units	F2 to W1	5 units
Fl to W3	25 units	F2 to W2	10 units
		F2 to W4	20 units
		F2 to W5	20 units

You may have noticed that all the variables have integer values in all the solutions. An important feature of the transportation problem is that all solutions are in integers provided the initial demand and availability parameters are in integers. We can see that this is so because, first, the northwest corner rule will give an initial integer solution for integer a_i's and b_j's. Further, the stepping-stone rules for finding the new basic feasible solution merely add and subtract the values of the variables. Hence, every solution after the first is also an integer solution. We shall see in Chaptpr18 that in normal linear programming problems, an integer solution cannosually be achieved without considerable effort.

Until recently, most computer codes for solving transportation problems did not use the stepping-stone algorithm. The codes were based on a minimal cost flow network algorithm, called the out-of-kilter algorithm, developed by D. Fulkerson. (See L. Ford and D. Fulkerson, *Flows in Networks*, Princeton University Press, 1962.)

Table 6-7. *Second and third transportation tableaux*

	W1	W2	W3	W4	W5	a_i
F1	24 (30) +1	24 −15	5 (20) −1	20 −33	20 −17	50
F2	30 X 9	24 (10)	20 (5) +1	2 (20)	18 (20)	55
b_j	30	10	25	20	20	Total cost 1560
F1	24 (25)	24 −6	5 (25)	20 −24	20 −8	50
F2	30 (5)	24 (10)	20 −9	2 (20)	18 (20)	55
b_j	30	10	25	20	20	Minimum cost 1515

However, recent work by Glover et al. and also some work by Bradley *et al.* have shown that it is possible to devise very efficient versions of the stepping-stone algorithm.

6-6 DEGENERACY

Degeneracy is a frequent occurrence in the transportation problem. During the search for an initial basic feasible solution, degeneracy occurs when the allocation to a given cell satisfies both the unfilled requirement of the column and the remaining availability of a row, except for the very last cell. Unless one appropriate cell is given a zero value and made basic, the resulting set of variables will not form a basis. Not many sets of $(m + n - 1)$ variables will form a basis. There must be at least one basic variable in every row and one in every column, and it must not be possible to form loops consisting only of basic variables. The simplest way of choosing the degenerate variable while finding an initial basic solution is to leave open either the row or the column with an amount of zero still to be allocated from it. This ensures that some cell in an appropriate position is rendered basic with zero value. This case is illustrated in Table 6-8, where we have slightly altered the previous problem.

In Table 6-8, when the allocation is made to x_{12}, both row 1 and column 2 are satisfied. We leave row 1 open, with 0 to be assigned. Thus, x_{13} = minimum (0, 15) = 0. (We could have left column 2 open, in which case x_{22} would equal zero, with x_{22} basic. The choice is arbitrary.)

As is true for the simplex method, degeneracy may cause the stepping-stone algorithm to go from iteration to iteration without any improvement of the objective function. Occasionally, degeneracy may cause cycling among the same set of basic feasible solutions. To prevent cycling, we could allocate to each degenerate cell (if there is more than one) an infinitesimal amount, e_k, with magnitude $e_1 > e_2 > e_3, \ldots$. With this convention, we can again apply the stepping-stone algorithm in the usual manner. Once the optimal solution has been found, the values of all degenerate cells are set equal to zero. In practice, it is not usual to perturb the solution in this way.

Table 6-8. *Initial basis with degeneracy*

	W1	W2	W3	W4	W5	a_i
F1	30	20	0			50
F2			15	20	20	55
b_j	30	20	15	20	20	

6-7 DUALITY AND THE *uv* METHOD

The dual of a transportation problem has a particularly interesting structure that is useful for deriving a quick method of finding the $(z_{ij} - c_{ij})$ values of the primal transportation problems. The method is known as the *uv method* (or MODI method).

Let us derive the dual of our transportation problem using Table 6-2, but with equality constraints. First, we define a dual variable for each constraint of the primal. In the primal, there is an availability constraint for each factory, F*i*, and a demand constraint for each warehouse, W*j*. We will find it useful to distinguish between these two types of constraints. So, we define u_i to be the dual variable associated with the availability constraint of F*i*, and v_j to be the dual variable associated with the demand constraint of W*j*. Table 6-9 shows, in detached coefficient form, the result of applying the duality relations of Sections 4-1 and 4-2. All u_i and v_j are unrestricted in sign.

Table 6-9. *Dual transportation problem in detached coefficient form*

Primal Variable	Dual Variable								
	u_1	u_2	v_1	v_2	v_3	v_4	v_5		RHS
x_{11}	1		1					$\leq$	24
x_{12}	1			1				$\leq$	24
x_{13}	1				1			$\leq$	5
x_{14}	1					1		$\leq$	20
x_{15}	1						1	$\leq$	20
x_{21}		1	1					$\leq$	30
x_{22}		1		1				$\leq$	24
x_{23}		1			1			$\leq$	20
x_{24}		1				1		$\leq$	2
x_{25}		1					1	$\leq$	18
Objective Function	50	55	30	10	25	20	20	maximize	

We can see that each dual constraint contains exactly two variables—the ones for the source and the destination of the associated primal activity. For example, the dual constraint associated with x_{23} is $u_2 + v_3 \leq 20$.

This structure permits us to effectively use the simplex multipliers (developed in Section 4-5) for finding all of the $(z_{ij} - c_{ij})$ values. You will recall that we first solve the dual for the simplex multipliers by applying the complementary slackness theorem. For example, for the basic solution of Table 6-6, the complementary slackness conditions give us the following set of equations:

$$
\begin{aligned}
u_1 \quad + v_1 \quad\quad\quad\quad\quad\quad &= 24 \\
u_1 \quad\quad\quad + v_2 \quad\quad\quad\quad &= 24 \\
u_1 \quad\quad\quad\quad\quad + v_3 \quad\quad &= 5 \\
u_2 \quad\quad\quad\quad + v_3 \quad\quad &= 20 \\
u_2 \quad\quad\quad\quad\quad\quad + v_4 &= 2 \\
u_2 \quad\quad\quad\quad\quad\quad\quad + v_5 &= 18
\end{aligned}
\tag{6-9}
$$

Note that all u_i and v_j are present in this set of equations because a basis must have a variable in every row and column of the tableau. Also, there are seven variables $(m + n)$, but only six equations $(m + n - 1)$ because of the redundancy noted in Section 6-2. We can solve equations (6-9) recursively as soon as one of the variables has been given an arbitrary value. Let us follow the usual tradition of setting u_1 equal to zero. We immediately obtain $v_1 = 24$, $v_2 = 24$, and $v_3 = 5$. From $v_3 = 5$, we obtain $u_2 = 15$; then $v_4 = -13$ and $v_5 = 3$.

It is now easy to write the $(z_{ij} - c_{ij})$ values for the nonbasic variables. For example, z_{22} is the value of the left-hand side of the dual constraint associated with x_{22} (i.e., $z_{22} = u_2 + v_2 = 15 + 24$), and c_{22} is the right-hand side of that constraint (i.e., $c_{22} = 24$). So,

$$(z_{22} - c_{22}) = u_2 + v_2 - c_{22} = 15 + 24 - 24 = 15$$

In general, we have

SIMPLEX MULTIPLIERS FOR THE TRANSPORTATION PROBLEM

(6-10) $$z_{ij} - c_{ij} = u_i + v_j - c_{ij}$$

These calculations can be performed much more compactly by incorporating the u_i and v_j values into the tableau format. Table 6-10 repeats Table 6-6 using the *uv* method. It is unnecessary to write out the dual constraints, since the relationships are so simple. We start by entering $u_1 = 0$ into the u_i column, and calculate the appropriate v_j values from basic variables in the first row, using $u_i + v_j = c_{ij}$ for these variables. Starting from the left, the first basic variable in the first row is x_{11}, so $v_1 = c_{11} - u_1 = 24 - 0 = 24$. The next is x_{12}, so $v_2 = c_{12} - u_1 = 24 - 0 = 24$; and then x_{13}—giving $v_3 = c_{13} - u_1 = 5$. We now use the columns of the v_j values, which we have just determined to calculate further u_i values. There are no further basic variables in column 1 and column 2, so no additional u_i values can be found by using them. In column 3, however, x_{23} is basic, so we have $u_2 = c_{23} - v_3 = 20 - 5 = 15$. We do not know any more v_j values, so we now look at the rows for the u_i values we have just calculated—in our case, row 2. The procedure we used for row 1 is repeated for row 2, and so on, until all u_i and v_j have been calculated.

To find the $(z_{ij} - c_{ij})$ values of the nonbasic variables, we use the equations (6-10).

Returning to the question of duality, we find that the simplex multipliers become the optimal dual solution at the optimal primal tableau. The perceptive reader may be uneasy because the values are relative and not absolute. With a little more thought, we realize that not one of the a_i or b_j values can be changed on its own (since $\Sigma a_i = \Sigma b_j$), but always must be accompanied by a change in at least one of the other RHS parameters. It is not hard to show that the net effect of the two (or more) changes is absolute. You are asked to consider this sort of postoptimal analysis in exercise 6.3.

Table 6-10. *First transportation tableau—uv method*

	W1	W2	W3	W4	W5	a_i	u_i
F1	24 (30)	24 (10)	5 (10)	20 −33	20 −17	50	0
F2	30 9	24 15	20 (15)	2 (10)	18 (20)	55	15
b_j	30	10	25	20	20	1710	
v_j	24	24	5	−13	3		

6-8 ALLOCATION OVER TIME—A REGULAR TIME/OVERTIME PROBLEM

A manufacturer has orders for one of its products for the next four months as follows:

Month	1	2	3	4
Units ordered	5000	8000	12000	7000

Each month the manufacturer can produce 6000 units in regular time and 3000 units in overtime. The unit cost of production is \$10 in regular time and \$15 in overtime. Inventory costs from one month to the next are \$2 per unit. The manufacturer wishes to schedule production in regular time and overtime to meet the demand, minimizing total cost. No back ordering is permitted.

Let us formulate this problem as a linear program. We define

- r_{ij} to be regular time production in month i to meet demand in month j, and
- q_{ij} to be overtime production in month i to meet demand in month j.

In both cases the variables are defined only for $j \geqslant i$.

The cost of producton is

$$\sum_{i=1}^{4} \sum_{j=i}^{4} (10r_{ij} + 15q_{ij})$$

The inventory cost is

$$\sum_{i=1}^{4} \sum_{j=i}^{4} [2(j - i)(r_{ij} + q_{ij})]$$

So, the objective function is

$$\text{minimize } z = \sum_{i=1}^{4} \sum_{j=i}^{4} [(10 + 2(j - i))r_{ij} + (15 + 2(j - i))q_{ij}]$$

There are three sets of contraints: production capacity regular time, production capacity overtime, and demand requirements—one constraint of each type for each month.

Production capacity regular time month i is

$$\sum_{j=i}^{4} r_{ij} \leqslant 6000$$

Production capacity overtime month i is

$$\sum_{j=i}^{4} q_{ij} \leqslant 3000$$

Demand requirements month j is

$$\sum_{i=1}^{j} (r_{ij} + q_{ij}) \geqslant D_j$$

where D_j is the number of units ordered for month j.

The problem almost has the transportation structure; only the absence of variables r_{ij} and q_{ij} for $j < i$ precludes it. If we could introduce these variables, but at the same time make sure that they would never appear in the optimal solution, then we could make the transportation structure complete without violating the original problem. This can be achieved easily by arbitrarily assigning to these variables extremely large objective function coefficients, say $+\infty$.

Using this trick, we can now cast the problem into the format of the transportation tableau, as shown in Table 6-11. Our sources are regular-time capacity and overtime capacity in each of the months—the source of the production. Our destinations are orders to be filled in each of the months—the destination of the production. We also include a dummy destination called "slack," which has a "demand" equal to the excess production capacity over the four-month period, i.e., 36000 − 32000 = 4000. We assume that the slack capacity is costless. In this problem our allocation is not over space, as in the previous problem, but over time. The inadmissible activities (those with $+\infty$) are represented by crossed out cells in Table 6-11. A feasible solution exists only if the accumulated production capacity is at least as great as the accumulated demand at each month.

For this problem we find the initial basic feasible solution by a rule called *column minimization*. Starting in column 1, the cells to be allocated are chosen not by the downward-and-to-the-right rule as in the northwest corner rule, but by ascending order of cost value. First, the cell with the lowest cost in column 1, i.e., x_{11} (since $c_{11} = 10$), is filled as much as possible: minimum (6000, 5000) = 5000. If the column is not satisfied, the next lowest cost is chosen, and the procedure is repeated until the column is fully allocated. The same procedure is followed for column 2, i.e., min-

Table 6-11. *Regular time/overtime transportation tableau*

	Demand					
Production	Month 1	Month 2	Month 3	Month 4	Slack	a_i
Regular time Month 1	10 5000	12 1000	14 0	16 −6	0 −5	6000
Overtime Month 1	15 0	17 0	19 1000	21 −6	0 2000	3000
Regular time Month 2	×	10 6000	12 0	14 −6	0 −7	6000
Overtime Month 2	×	15 1000	17 2000	19 −6	0 −2	3000
Regular time Month 3	×	×	10 6000	12 −6	0 −9	6000
Overtime Month 3	×	×	15 3000	17 −6	0 −4	3000
Regular time Month 4	×	×	×	10 6000	0 −5	6000
Overtime Month 4	×	×	×	15 1000	0 2000	3000
b_j	5000	8000	12000	7000	4000	

imum (c_{i2}, all i) $= c_{32} = 10$. So, $x_{32} =$ minimum (6000, 8000) $= 6000$. The column is not satisfied. The next lowest c_{i2} is $c_{12} = 12$, so

$$x_{12} = \text{minimum}\,(6000 - 5000,\ 8000 - 6000) = 1000$$

Still column 2 is not satisfied. The next lowest c_{i2} is $c_{42} = 15$, so

$$x_{42} = \text{minimum}\,(3000,\ 1000) = 1000$$

When column 2 is finished, we start column 3, and so on. In column 3, neither x_{13}

nor x_{33} can be allocated anything because rows 1 and 3 are already completely used.

We have described the column minimization method because when it is used on a simple regular time/overtime problem like this, it always gives the optimal solution immediately—as we see from the $(z_{ij} - c_{ij})$ values in Table 6-11. The minimum cost schedule is achieved by producing at full regular-time capacity every month, and full overtime capacity in months 2 and 3, but only 1000 units in overtime in months 1 and 4.

The regular time/overtime problem with back ordering involving a late delivery penalty is considered in exercise 6.9.

*6-9 THE TRANSSHIPMENT PROBLEM

A company has two factories, two warehouses, and three stores. Each month the company ships its production to the two warehouses, where goods are redistributed to the three stores. Figure 6-6 gives the configuration with factory capacities, store requirements, and the unit shipping costs. Initially, we assume that the warehouses have unlimited capacity. We wish to minimize distribution costs.

We can solve this as a simple 2 × 3 transportation problem by using the fundamental principle for deriving the c_{ij} values—they are the *least costs* from the sources to destinations. By inspection we can verify that the least cost from F1 to S1 is

Figure 6-6. *Two-stage transportation problem.*

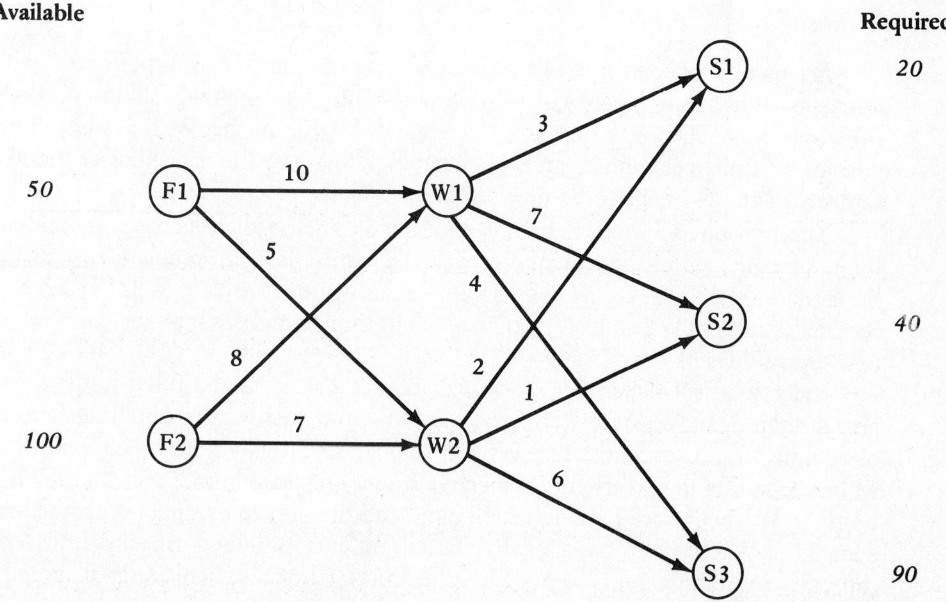

minimum (10 + 3, 5 + 2) = 7, i.e., from F1 to W2 to S1. Hence, we obtain Table 6-12.

Table 6-12. *Least costs from factories to stores*

	S1	S2	S3
F1	7 via W2	6 via W2	11 via W2
F2	9 via W2	8 via W2	12 via W1

The optimal tableau is shown in Table 6-13.

Table 6-13. *Optimal two-stage tableau*

	S1	S2	S3	a_i
F1	[7] 20	[6] 30	[11] [−1]	50
F2	[9] [0]	[8] 10	[12] 90	100
b_j	20	40	90	

Let us now alter this problem. First, we assume that W1 is rather small, with a maximum handling capacity of 50 units per month. The optimal solution in Table 6-13 with $x_{23} = 90$ is no longer feasible. Second, we assume that W2 has some direct sales of 30 units per month, and we accordingly increase the capacities of the two sources. Figure 6-7 depicts the new situation.

The previous solution method cannot handle intermediate nodes with capacity limits or demands of their own. We want to reformulate the problem so that the sources are F1, F2, W1, and W2, while the destinations are W1, W2, S1, S2, and S3. Nodes such as W1 and W2, which are both sources and destinations, are referred to as *transshipment nodes*.

Transshipment nodes have both availabilities and demands. What values do we give to their a_i and b_j parameters? The most W1 may receive is its handling capacity of 50 units. If the warehouse receives less, some of its capacity remains unused. Also, we must assume that every unit it receives is sent on. If we introduce a dummy link from the W1 node back to itself (which represents the unused capacity), then the total demand of W1 can be viewed as what it sends on plus its unused capacity, or its total capacity. So in this case, $b_j = 50$. Since the dummy link represents unused capacity,

Figure 6-7. *Revised two-stage transportation problem.*

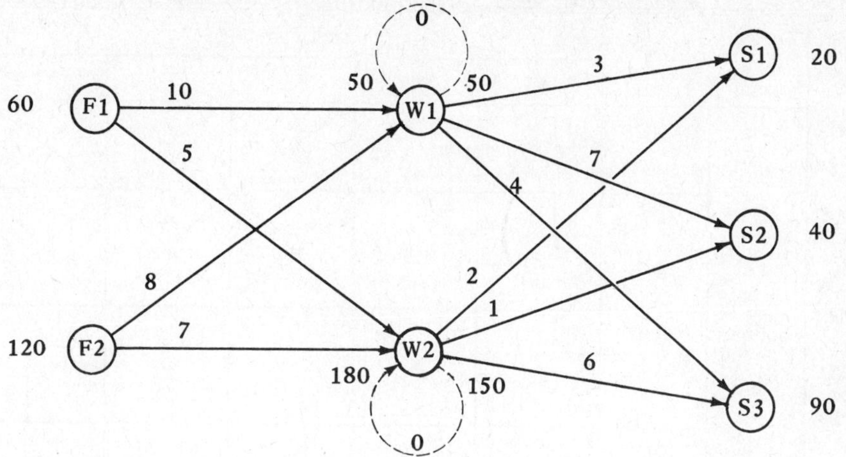

its unit cost is obviously zero. We depict the dummy link with a broken-line arrow in Figure 6-7. The availability at W1 is again restricted by its handling capacity, hence its $a_i = 50$ also.

W2 has no upper handling capacity. However, we can arbitrarily introduce a handling capacity. All we have to ensure is that this capacity is sufficiently large so as to never be restrictive on the optimal solution. Setting the handling capacity equal to the total supply of 180 units is one way of guaranteeing this. Hence its $b_j = 180$. The dummy link to itself has zero cost and represents unused capacity. However, at most 150 units can leave W2, because W2 has a true destination demand of 30 units. Thus. its a_i value is only 150.

With these tricks we can now construct the transportation tableau shown in Table 6-14 for the revised problem. Each inadmissible cell involving shipments from factories directly to stores or from one warehouse to the other is shown as a crossed cell, equivalent to an infinitely large cost.

The feasible solution shown in Table 6-14 sends 50 units from F1 through W1 to S1 and S2; 10 units from F1, and 120 units from F2 through W2 to W2 (itself), S2, and S3. The 50 units in the W2/W2 cell constitute the amount of capacity at W2 that is unused. (Find the optimal solution.)

This last example involves most of the concepts of the *transshipment problem*, which is a transportation problem that allows a shipment from source to destination through other sources and destinations.

6-10 THE ASSIGNMENT PROBLEM

Consider the problem of assigning M candidates to N jobs, such as M young lawyers to N different legal cases, or M mechanics to N repair jobs (in both instances involving

Table 6-14. *Revised two-stage transportation*

		Destinations					
		W1	W2	S1	S2	S3	a_i
Sources	F1	[10] 50	[5] 10	X	X	X	60
	F2	[8] [4]	[7] 120	X	X	X	120
	W1	[0] [11]	X	[3] 20	[7] 30	[4] [8]	50
	W2	X	[0] 50	[2] [−5]	[1] 10	[6] 90	150
	b_j	50	180	20	40	90	

roughly equal amounts of work). Let c_{ij} denote the suitability of the ith candidate to handle the jth job. The problem consists of assigning the candidates to the various jobs so as to achieve a maximum overall suitability. Problems of this sort are known as *assignment problems*. As was true for the transportation problem, several problems quite different in nature exhibit the same mathematical structure.

A transport manager of a small manufacturing firm is reviewing the existing composition of the firm's fleet of trucks and delivery vehicles. Some section supervisors have been complaining about the inappropriate size of the vehicles assigned to them, while another supervisor who currently has no vehicle would like to have one assigned. Funds are tight, so there is no possibility of getting additional or different vehicles in the foreseeable future. The next best alternative, therefore, is to see whether a reassignment of vehicles will be beneficial to the firm as a whole in terms of reducing overall transport costs. After considerable investigation, the firm's cost analyst produces Table 6-15, which shows the annual cost (in thousands of dollars) of assigning vehicle $i = 1, 2, 3$ to section $j =$ A, B, C, D. Since there are three vehicles and four sections, one of the sections will have to go without, unless vehicles are shared. The cost of having no vehicle is also shown in Table 6-15 as row 4. The manager would like to find the vehicle assignment that minimizes the firm's total cost.

Viewing each vehicle i as a source with availability $a_i = 1$ and viewing each section j as a destination with demand $b_j = 1$, you will immediately recognize that this is a transportation problem with the special property that all RHS parameters are equal to 1. Therefore, the optimal solution to an assignment problem has the same feature as solutions to the transportation problem, namely that all decision variables

Table 6-15. *Annual transport cost ($1000's)*

Assigned to Section	A	B	C	D
Vehicle 1	6	4	1	5
Vehicle 2	10	6	3	8
Vehicle 3	7	6	4	5
(None) 4	9	10	3	8

are integers—in this case either 0 or 1. Each vehicle is thus assigned to one and only one section and is not shared. In our example, this is fortunate, since for operational reasons the sharing of vehicles is inconvenient.

6-11 THE HUNGARIAN METHOD

The best-known solution technique for the assignment problem is the *Hungarian method.* It can be derived from the special structure of the dual of the assignment problem and the following theorem proved by Hungarian mathematician König in 1916 (hence the name of the method):

> If the elements of a matrix are divided into two classes by property R, then the minimum number of lines drawn through rows or columns needed to cover all elements with property R is equal to the maximum number of elements with the property R where no two such elements appear in the same row or column.

Using the same notation as for the dual to the transportation problem in Section 6-7, the dual of the assignment problem can be stated as follows:

$$\text{maximize } z = \sum_i u_i + \sum_j v_j$$

(6-11)
$$\text{subject to} \quad u_i + v_j \leqslant c_{ij}, \quad \text{for all } i, j$$

$$u_i, v_j \text{ unrestricted in sign}$$

Each u_i is associated with a "candidate" (or "row") constraint and each v_j with a "job" (or "column") constraint. These variables are unrestricted in sign because the primal constraints are equalities. By the complementary slackness theorems (DR6 of Chapter 4), the following relations will hold at the optimal solution to the primal problem:

(6-12)
$$u_i + v_j = c_{ij}, \quad \text{for all } x_{ij} = 1$$

(6-13)
$$u_i + v_j \leqslant c_{ij}, \quad \text{for all } x_{ij} = 0$$

In the search for the optimal u_i and v_j values, the algorithm uses the property:

MATRIX REDUCTION PROPERTY

Given a cost matrix $\{c_{ij}\}$, if we replace each element c_{ij} by the reduced-cost element

$$\hat{c}_{ij} = c_{ij} - u_i - v_j \tag{6-14}$$

where u_i and v_j are arbitrary constants, this will have no effect on the optimal assignment.

This result can be established by showing that the $(z_{ij} - c_{ij})$ values do not change under a transformation such as expression (6-14). We leave it to you to use the logic of Section 6-7 to prove this property. However, some thought should convince you that it is true. Consider a given row. If each element in row i is replaced by $(c_{ij} - u_i)$, the relative costs remain unchanged. Since an assignment must be made in that row, the optimal assignment will not change except that its total cost will be reduced by u_i.

The Hungarian method uses the matrix reduction property to reduce the original cost matrix until the elements associated with the optimal assignment are all zero and all other elements are nonnegative. Thus u_i and v_j are created that satisfy expressions (6-12) and (6-13).

At each iteration the Hungarian method reduces the matrix so that there is at least one zero in every row and column. König's theorem is used to test whether we have found the optimal solution. The set with the property R is the set of zero elements in the reduced-cost matrix. The minimum number of lines using this theorem determines the maximum number of rows that can be assigned to columns using the zero elements. If the minimum number of lines needed to cover all zeros is equal to $M = N$, then an optimal (not necessarily unique) assignment has been found. König's theorem establishes that the assignment exists. The assignment is optimal because all other elements of the reduced-cost matrix are nonnegative. If this reduced-cost matrix does not yield an optimal assignment, we use a scheme to create new zero elements not covered by the existing lines at the expense of only those existing zero elements covered by both a row and a column line. Thus, the new reduced-cost matrix will require more lines to cover all the zeros.

At the optimal solution, the sum of the constants subtracted from a particular row or column gives the corresponding optimal u_i or v_j value. A reduced-cost matrix that requires $M = N$ lines to cover the zeros cannot be further reduced by subtracting constants without violating expressions (6-13). This fact confirms the optimality of the solution. The cost is equal to

$$Z = \sum_i u_i + \sum_j v_j \tag{6-15}$$

The algorithm is as follows.

HUNGARIAN METHOD FOR THE ASSIGNMENT PROBLEM

Step 1 In each row, subtract the smallest cost from all elements in the row, i.e., for row i find

$$c_{ij}^{(0)} = c_{ij} - \underset{j}{\text{minimum}}\, c_{ij}, \qquad \text{for all } i$$

Step 2 In each column of the new matrix $\{c_{ij}^{(0)}\}$, subtract the smallest cost from all elements in the column, i.e., for column j find

$$c_{ij}^{(1)} = c_{ij}^{(0)} - \underset{i}{\text{minimum}}\, c_{ij}^{(0)}, \qquad \text{for all } j$$

Set $k = 1$.

Step 3 Find the minimum number n of lines through rows and columns needed to cover all zero reduced-cost elements in matrix $\{c_{ij}^{(k)}\}$. If $n = N = M$, *stop*—an optimal assignment can be found using only zero reduced-cost elements. Otherwise, increase k to $k + 1$.

Step 4 Find the smallest uncrossed element h_k in matrix $\{c_{ij}^{(k)}\}$; subtract h_k from all uncrossed rows and add it to all elements of crossed columns. Return to step 3.

We now demonstrate this algorithm on the problem in Table 6-15.

Iteration 1:

Step 1 Original matrix

6	4	1	5	−1	smallest row elements (shown negative to indicate operation); sum = 11
10	6	3	8	−3	
7	6	4	5	−4	
9	10	3	8	−3	

Step 2 New matrix

5	3	0	4	
7	3	0	5	
3	2	0	1	
6	7	0	5	smallest column elements; sum = 11 + 6 = 17
−3	−2	0	−1	

Step 3 New matrix

2	1	0	3	$n = 2 < 4 = N$; hence, no optimal assignment can be found yet
4	1	0	4	
0	0	0	0	
3	5	0	4	

(Row 3 and column 3 are crossed out.)

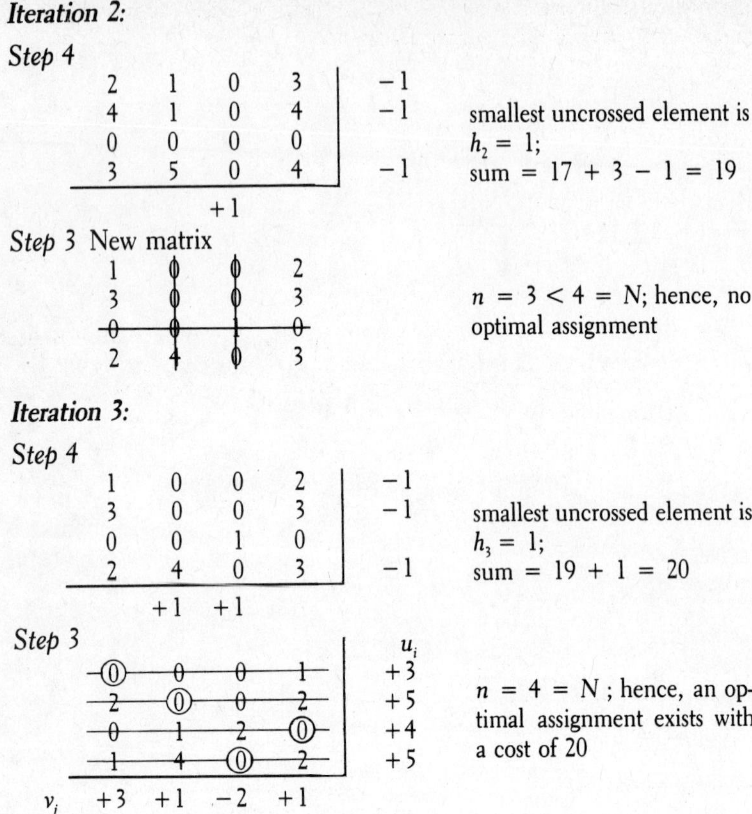

Iteration 2:

Step 4

2	1	0	3	−1
4	1	0	4	−1
0	0	0	0	
3	5	0	4	−1
		+1		

smallest uncrossed element is $h_2 = 1$; sum = 17 + 3 − 1 = 19

Step 3 New matrix

1	0	0	2
3	0	0	3
0	0	1	0
2	4	0	3

$n = 3 < 4 = N$; hence, no optimal assignment

Iteration 3:

Step 4

1	0	0	2	−1
3	0	0	3	−1
0	0	1	0	
2	4	0	3	−1
	+1	+1		

smallest uncrossed element is $h_3 = 1$; sum = 19 + 1 = 20

Step 3

					u_i
	(0)	0	0	1	+3
	2	(0)	0	2	+5
	0	1	2	(0)	+4
	1	4	(0)	2	+5
v_j	+3	+1	−2	+1	

$n = 4 = N$; hence, an optimal assignment exists with a cost of 20

The optimal assignment is as follows: vehicle 1 to section A, vehicle 2 to section B, vehicle 3 to section D, and no vehicle to section C. The associated u_i and v_j values are shown at the margins of the last matrix. Verify that relations in expressions (6-12) through (6-15) are satisfied.

In the above example, the number of candidates equals the number of jobs. If more candidates are available than jobs, we introduce dummy jobs with a zero suitability score. If there are fewer candidates than jobs, additional dummy candidates are introduced having identical rows of suitability scores, such as the cost of not executing the job. Finally, if the problem is to maximize the sum of suitability scores, we can again obtain the standard problem by simply subtracting each c_{ij} from the maximum c_{ij} in the table and then minimizing the sum of the resulting scores.

EXERCISES

6.1 A manufacturer has three factories, one each in cities A, B, and C, and four warehouses located in cities 1, 2, 3, and 4. The table gives the monthly production capacities of the factories, the monthly requirements at the warehouses, and the per unit transportation costs. Solve this transportation problem.

Factories	Warehouses 1	2	3	4	Availability
A	2	3	6	2	5000
B	4	6	1	7	10000
C	9	8	3	9	15000
Demand	4000	10,000	8000	8000	

6.2 Solve problem 6.1 with the amount available at factory A changed to 10,000.

6.3 Consider the transportation tableau.

Factories	Warehouses 1	2	3	4	Dummy	a_i
1	[4]	[1] 100	[4]	[2] 150	[0] 50	300
2	[1] 200	[4]	[5]	[1]	[0]	200
3	[2] 0	[2]	[6] 175	[1]	[0] 25	200
b_j	200	100	175	150	75	

(a) Find the optimal solution.
(b) Write schedules for the production manager and the distribution manager.
(c) *Find the new optimum for $c_{34} = 3$. Do *not* start from scratch.
(d) *Using the optimal dual variables, find the change in minimum cost if warehouse 4 requires 50 additional units.

6.4 Three factories are operated by the Link Manufacturing Company of Hamilton, New Zealand. Currently, the products manufactured are shipped to three different warehouses. The locations and the capacities of these warehouses are as follows: Auckland 1200 units, Wellington 800 units, and Christchurch 1000 units. The capacity of each factory, together with the freight cost per unit from each factory to each warehouse, is given in the table.

Factory	Capacity	Freight Cost to	Cost/Unit
1 (Hamilton)	400 units	Auckland	\$5
		Wellington	\$6
		Christchurch	\$7
2 (Gisborne)	800 units	Auckland	\$4
		Wellington	\$7
		Christchurch	\$7
3 (Nelson)	1400 units	Auckland	\$8
		Wellington	\$6
		Christchurch	\$6

(a) Formulate this problem as a transportation problem.
(b) Give an initial feasible solution using the northwest corner rule.
(c) Starting with the solution of (b), iterate to an optimal solution using the stepping-stone algorithm.
(d) State the optimal *simplex tableau* corresponding to your solution of (c). (Note: This should be done directly, without any computations.)
(e) What happens to the optimal solution of (c) if we add \$$k$ to each unit cost in the first column of the transportation tableau?
(f) Find *all* alternative optimal basic solutions in the optimal tableau of part (c). Do these solutions really represent alternative optimal shipping routes?

6.5 A nationwide retailing organization, Bargains Inc., is running a special line of shirts. Three suppliers have bid for the job, the first offering to supply up to 200,000 shirts at \$3 each; the second up to 150,000 at \$3.50 each; and the third, 150,000 at \$3.20 each. The company has five warehouses that service the retailing stores. These warehouses estimate requirements of 40,000, 70,000, 60,000, 100,000, and 50,000 shirts, respectively. Bargains Inc. will pay freight from the suppliers to their own warehouses. Freight costs (in \$100's) per 1000 shirts are given in the table. The company wants to know how many shirts to buy from each supplier and the shipping schedule from suppliers to warehouses. The objective is to minimize total cost.

From Supplier	To Warehouse 1	2	3	4	5
1	4	2	7	2	1.5
2	3	6	1	2.5	3
3	3.5	3	4	1.5	1

6.6 Set up the following network as a transportation problem showing transshipment through all nodes. The amount available at each node is indicated. A negative value indicates a requirement at that node. The following table indicates the cost per unit of shipping between the nodes.

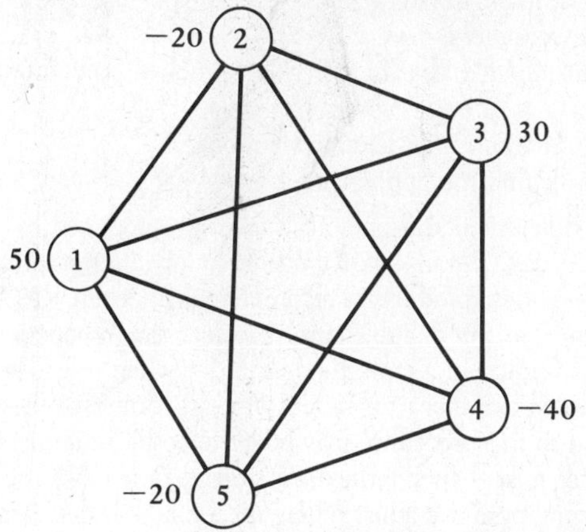

Shipping Costs in $100's

1	2	3	4	5	Nodes
–	2	3	5	1	1
	–	2	4	3	2
		–	1	2	3
			–	6	4
				–	5

6.7 A manufacturer can normally product 450 units of product X in a month. But with special arrangements, at a cost of $1.50 for each additional unit, the capacity can be increased to 600 units a month. Demands for the next four months are 200, 800, 600, and 400 units, respectively. The company stores and distributes its product from its warehouse some distance away. Transport from the factory to the warehouse presents a problem because the manufacturer has only one suitable truck that can deliver up to 300 units a month at a cost of $2 per unit. An identical vehicle is available for hire for any portion of the month. However, costs are $2.50 per unit when this truck is used. Inventory cost is $1.00 per unit per month, and inventory on hand at the beginning of month 1 is 100 units. Formulate this problem as a transportation problem to minimize cost. Construct the initial tableau.

6.8 A medical research center is planning to conduct an important 5-day experiment. The experiment uses a large number of a special type of container which must be thoroughly cleaned after each day's use. Since the cleaning process is intricate and costly, an industrial cleaner has contracted to do it. To have a container ready for the next day, the cleaning charge is $3 per container. A slower process taking a day longer costs $2 per container. The price of a new container is $10, and these containers are available on demand. They do not need cleaning. The research center estimates that it needs 3000, 2500, 4000, 2000, and 2500 containers for days 1 through 5, respectively. Each day approximately 10 percent of these containers will be broken. The medical research center wishes to minimize the cost of purchasing and cleaning the containers. Set up the problem as a transportation problem. Perform the first iteration.

6.9 Solve the regular time/overtime problem of Section 6-8 with the following extension. Back ordering (i.e., postponement of delivery) is permitted for two months. The cost of back ordering (administration and loss of goodwill) for one month is $1 per unit, and for two months is $5 per unit. Does the column minimization method produce the optimal solution at the initial basic feasible solution?

6.10 The officials of a young farmers club need catering staff for a 2-day anniversary function. They need the equivalent of 8 workdays on Saturday and 6 on Sunday. They approach two catering outfits: "Homestyle" (A), and "Country Club" (B). A can spare a total of 5 workdays for the weekend given its present workload, and B can supply 12 workdays. A would charge $80/workday on Saturday and $160 on Sunday. B would charge $75 on Saturday, but $140 on Sunday. How many workdays should the club officials contract for from each catering outfit on each of the two days?

(a) Show that this problem can be formulated as a transportation problem by defining the unit cost array.

(b) Using the northwest corner rule, find an initial feasible solution.

(c) Using the stepping-stone algorithm, find the optimal solution. What is its cost?

*6.11 Purair Petrochemicals produces 10 different liquid chemicals. All are produced by a batch process that takes at most one day. Purair has 6 bulk tanks of different sizes available for intermediate storage of 6 of these products. The problem is to decide which of the 10 products should be assigned to the 6 bulk tanks. The current production system is as follows: If a product is not stored in a tank, then each day when orders are received, a batch is produced for direct shipment to the customer(s). Some of these batches obviously may be small, and so this procedure may be quite costly in terms of production set-up costs. If a product is kept in intermediate storage in a tank, then customer orders are satisfied by drawing from the tank. Whenever the tank is depleted, a new batch is produced to fill it. Demand and cost data are as shown. There are 250 working days per year. Each dollar invested in stocks for one year incurs a holding cost penalty of 24 percent. Total annual cost per product covers: (a) average total annual batch set-up costs to satisfy customer demands for products not kept in tanks; and (b) sum of average total annual batch set-up costs to replenish for products kept in tanks. The 6 tanks have the following capacities: 60, 150, 150, 150, 300, and 400 barrels.

Product	1	2	3	4	5	6	7	8	9	10
Value/barrel ($)	20	8	12	15	9	15	10	16	18	25
Annual demand in barrels	800	1600	5000	4000	1200	3600	2000	6000	500	1000
Number of days/year with positive demand	100	120	200	80	150	240	60	160	125	40
Set-up cost/batch ($)	12	20	16	40	8	15	20	10	6	24

(a) Formulate this problem as a transportation problem. What aspect represents the sources, what aspect represents the destinations, and what are the availabilities and the demands? What are the unit costs? Find the unit cost matrix. (Hint: See Section 1-11 for some help in finding the unit costs.)

(b) Find an initial feasible solution using the northwest corner rule, and then compute the optimal assignments of tanks to products.

6.12 The table gives a firm's production capacity and orders for a special product. Costs are $15/unit on regular time, $20/unit on overtime, and $1/unit/month for inventory. Set up the first transportation tableau. Is it optimal? If not, give the next tableau.

Month	Production Capacities	Orders
March	Regular time 3000, overtime 1000	—
April	Regular time 3000, overtime 1000	5000
May	Regular time 2000, overtime 1000	2000
June	Regular time 2000, overtime 1000	6000

6.13 For the problem in Exercise 6.12, assume that the warehouse facilities are limited so that at most 3000 units can be inventoried (i.e, held over to a subsequent month) at any time.

(a) Express this situation diagrammatically as a *transshipment problem*.
(b) Set up the first transshipment tableau.
(c) If the first tableau is not optimal, find the second.

6.14 A carpet manufacturer has 2 factories, A and B, which have monthly outputs of 2000 and 3000 carpets, respectively. The carpets are made in 2 colors—red and blue. There is no additional time or cost involved in switching from production of one color to the other. Orders are as follows for deliveries in the next 3 months:

Month	1	2	3
Red	1000	3000	5000
Blue	1000	4000	2000

Inventory on hand includes 3000 red and 0 blue carpets. Inventory required at the end of three months is 1000 red and 1000 blue. At factory A, the marginal cost of production of red is constant at \$10; the marginal cost of production of blue is \$8 (month 1), \$9 (month 2), and \$10 (month 3). At factory B, the marginal cost of production is \$12 for red and \$10 for blue in all months. It costs \$1 per carpet held from one month to the next. As warehouse space is only available at factory A, there is a handling cost of \$1 per unit produced at factory B inventoried at factory A. What is the least-cost production schedule for each factory in each month?

6.15 A manufacturer of complex electronic equipment has just received a sizable contract and plans to subcontract part of the job. He has solicited bids for 6 subcontracts from 4 firms. Each job is sufficiently large that any one firm can take on only 1 job. The table below shows the bids and the cost estimates (in \$1000's) for doing the jobs internally. Note that no more than 2 jobs can be performed internally.

Job	1	2	3	4	5	6
Firm 1	48	72	36	52	50	65
2	44	67	41	53	48	64
3	46	69	40	55	45	68
4	43	73	37	51	44	62
Internal	50	65	35	50	46	63

(a) How do you complete this table so that the problem can be solved by the Hungarian method?

(b) Solve the problem by the Hungarian method, minimizing total costs.

6.16 The chief detective of the city's investigation bureau is assigned 5 new cases. At present she has 6 detectives who have not been assigned to investigations yet. The cases require different amounts of experience, and the detectives available have different suitabilities. The chief is able to assign the suitability indices shown on a scale from 0 to 10. Assign the detectives to jobs so as to maximize the total suitability score.

	Job	1	2	3	4	5
Detective	A	6	8	2	4	0
	B	7	9	1	3	5
	C	0	0	6	5	4
	D	0	2	4	5	6
	E	3	5	5	6	6
	F	4	4	5	7	5

6.17 An engineering company has the problem of assigning the day's jobs to various machines. Most machines can do most of the jobs, but with differing efficiencies. Also to be considered is the set-up cost of each machine for each job; this varies according to what the machine was previously set up to do and the job to which it is now assigned. With the data detailed in the table, the company wishes to minimize the total cost of today's work. (The tasks that the machines were previously set up to do are implicit in the table of set-up costs.) Find the optimal job assignment.

Cost of each job on each machine in $100's

	Job	1	2	3	4	5	6
Machine	1	8	4	10	2	1	6
	2	6	6	12	4	3	5
	3	2	4	8	1	1	4
	4	10	8	15	6	2	3
	5	5	7	20	4	4	1
	6	8	2	10	4	2	4

Set-up cost of each machine for each job in 100's

	Job	1	2	3	4	5	6
Machine	1	1.0	0.5	1.5	0.8	0	0.1
	2	1.0	0.8	1.0	0.5	0.1	0.2
	3	0	1.0	2.5	1.5	1.0	0.5
	4	1.5	1.5	0	2.0	1.0	1.0
	5	2.0	1.0	1.0	1.0	0.5	0.5
	6	0.5	0.8	0	0.4	0.5	1.0

REFERENCES

Bradley, G. H., G. G. Brown, and G. W. Graves, "Design and Implementation of Large-Scale Primal Transshipment Algorithms," *Management Science*, Vol. 24, Sept. 1977. Description of what is probably currently the most efficient network code, called GNET. GNET is available from its authors.

Daellenbach, H. D., and E. Bell. *A User's Guide to Linear Programming*. Englewood Cliffs, N.J.: Prentice-Hall, 1970.

Glover, F., D. Karney, D. Klingman, and A. Napier. "A Computation Study on Start Procedures, Basis Change Criteria, and Solution Algorithms for Transportation Problems," *Management Science*, Vol. 20, Jan. 1974. This is a comparative study of different techniques for solving the transportation problem.

Hadley, G. *Linear Programming*. Reading, Mass.: Addison-Wesley, 1962.

Sprinivasan, V. "A Transshipment Model for Cash Management Decision," *Management Science*, Vol. 20, June 1974. This article presents an interesting and efficient use of the transportation problem to cash management.

CHAPTER SEVEN

Network Flow Problems

The transportation problem of the preceding chapter can be viewed as a special case of a network flow problem. This chapter will look at another network flow problem. A commodity, available at a given node called a source, is required at another node called a sink. It can be routed from the source node to the sink node via a number of possible paths consisting of a sequence of links. Several paths may share the same link. Each link may have an upper carrying, or flow, capacity. We would like to find the maximum total flow through the network from the source to the sink—hence the name *maximum flow problem*.

This problem can be formulated as a linear program. However, as was the case for the transportation problem, the particular network structure of a maximum flow problem can be exploited to develop a much more efficient solution method called either the *labeling technique* or the *Ford-Fulkerson maximum flow algorithm* (in honor of its inventors).

7-1 THE MAXIMUM FLOW PROBLEM

A diagram such as the one in Figure 7-1 is called a *graph*. It consists of a series of points called *nodes* (also referred to as *vertices*) joined by *links* (also referred to as *lines*, *arcs*, *edges*, or *branches*). If we associate each link with a distance, a cost, or a capacity, we call the graph a *network*. The networks of particular interest to us now are those that have a flow of goods, information, or signals through the links.

Let us introduce some definitions and notations that we will need as we go along:

- a *link* (or line) joining nodes i and j is written (i, j). With each link we associate a flow from i to j, or both;
- a link is *directed* if the flow is limited to a given direction. A directed link from i to j is written $(i \rightarrow j)$. When a link (i, j) can have a flow in either direction, it can be thought of as the two directed links $(i \rightarrow j)$ and $(j \rightarrow i)$;

Figure 7-1. *Example of a network.*

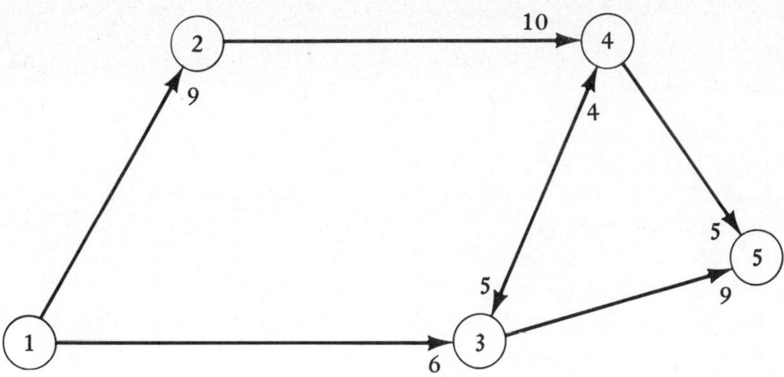

- a *source* is a node such that all links connected to it are directed away from it;
- a *sink* is a node such that all the links connected to it are directed toward it;
- a *path* between two nodes i and j is a set of connected links (i, p), (p, q), . . ., (t, u), (u, j) such that any node is passed through only once.

In the network in Figure 7-1, an arrow on a link indicates the direction of possible flow, and the number beside the arrow gives the capacity limit of that flow. The nodes are numbered with 1 as the source and 5 as the sink. A path through this network may be represented as: (1→2), (2→4), (4→5).

The network in Figure 7-1 could represent the following problem. An oil company has pipelines across a country from its unloading port (node 1) to its refinery (node 5). There are three pumping stations along the pipelines (nodes 2, 3, and 4). Between nodes 3 and 4 the flow can go in either direction at different capacities. The numbers attached to each link in Figure 7-1 are the capacities for each section of the pipeline in units of 1000 barrels per hour. The company wants to know the maximum amount of oil it can pump hourly through the links from the unloading port to the refinery.

We will first consider formulating the maximum flow problem in general terms. The decision variables are the amount of flow through each section of the pipeline network, or each link. Let x_{ij} be the flow through link $(i \rightarrow j)$, with node $i = 1$ denoting the source and $j = N$ denoting the sink. If d_{ij} is the capacity limit in $(i \rightarrow j)$, then

(7-1) $$0 \leq x_{ij} \leq d_{ij}$$

We assume that no flow is lost within the network. This is called the assumption of a *conservation of flow*. So for all nodes other than the source and sink, the flow into node i [$= \Sigma_k x_{ki}$ for all k connected to i by a link $(k \rightarrow i)$] must equal the flow out of node i [$= \Sigma_r x_{ir}$ for all r connected to i by a link $(i \rightarrow r)$]:

(7-2) $$\sum_k x_{ki} = \sum_r x_{ir}, \qquad i = 2, \ldots, N - 1$$

The objective is to maximize the flow from source to sink. But this is the same as maximizing the total flow out of the source (or into the sink), i.e.,

$$\text{(7-3)} \qquad \text{maximize } z = \sum_{s} x_{1s} \qquad \left(\text{or} \sum_{q} x_{qN}\right)$$

Expressions (7-1), (7-2), and (7-3) represent a linear program. The problem associated with Figure 7-1 in linear programming form has 7 decision variables, 3 constraints, and 7 upper-bound restrictions. The problem can be solved by the simplex method, but the labeling technique is a much more efficient solution technique for this type of problem. Although based on an iterative algorithm, the approach has no analogy with the simplex method.

The above example is a one-source/one-sink problem. There is no difficulty in handling multiple sources and multiple sinks. A more complex problem can be converted into a simple problem by linking all sources back to a *super-source* and linking all sinks forward to a *super-sink*. The flow from the super-source to each source gives the total flow from that source, and the flow from each sink to the supersink gives the total flow into that sink.

We will assume that all links can have a flow in either direction. If a flow exists in both directions, the actual flow is the difference of the two opposing flows, or the net flow $(x_{ij} - x_{ji})$. A flow direction that is not permitted is given a capacity limit of zero.

Let us now consider the network with a flow going through it. We define the *excess capacity* g_{ij} from i to j of link $(i \rightarrow j)$ as the difference between the capacity limit d_{ij} and the actual net flow $(x_{ij} - x_{ji})$ in that direction:

$$\text{(7-4)} \qquad g_{ij} = d_{ij} - x_{ij} + x_{ji}, \qquad \text{for all } i \text{ and } j$$

The excess capacity is the greatest feasible increase in x_{ij} in the link $(i \rightarrow j)$. Using the idea that a positive excess capacity in a link means that more flow can go through that link, we obtain the following result for the whole network.

CRITERION 1: INCREASING THE FLOW IN A NETWORK

Given a flow through the network, the total flow can be increased if there exists a path from source to sink with a positive excess capacity in every link in the path.

Let us assume a flow of zero in the network of Figure 7-2, i.e., $x_{ij} = 0$ for all i and j. Consider the path $(1 \rightarrow 2)$, $(2 \rightarrow 4)$, $(4 \rightarrow 5)$, with excess capacities $g_{12} = 9$, $g_{24} = 10$, and $g_{45} = 5$, respectively. It is thus possible to increase the flow through the network. By what amount can the flow be increased? The largest amount by which the flow can be increased using a path cannot exceed the smallest excess capacity of any link on that path. In our example, this is the minimum $(9, 10, 5) = 5$.

A simple extension of the idea of criterion 1 gives us a criterion to identify the optimality of a flow.

> CRITERION 2: OPTIMALITY OF FLOW IN A NETWORK
>
> If no path exists from source to sink with positive excess capacities in every link, then the solution is optimal.

7-2 THE LABELING TECHNIQUE

The purpose of the labeling technique is to find at each iteration a path from source to sink with a positive excess capacity in every link of the path. The iterations continue until no such path exists.

Consider a path from the source to some node j. We will define the *excess capacity of the path* as the minimum of the excess capacities of the links in the path. Also, we will call a path from the source to node j a *feasible path* if it has a positive excess capacity.

The operations of the labeling technique have two purposes. The first is to keep track of a feasible path (if one exists) from the source to each node of the network, until a feasible path is found from the source to the sink. The second purpose is to record the excess capacity of the feasible path to each node. Not all feasible paths are considered at each iteration—it is sufficient to keep track of one such path to each node in the network.

Figure 7-2. *First iteration of labeling technique.*

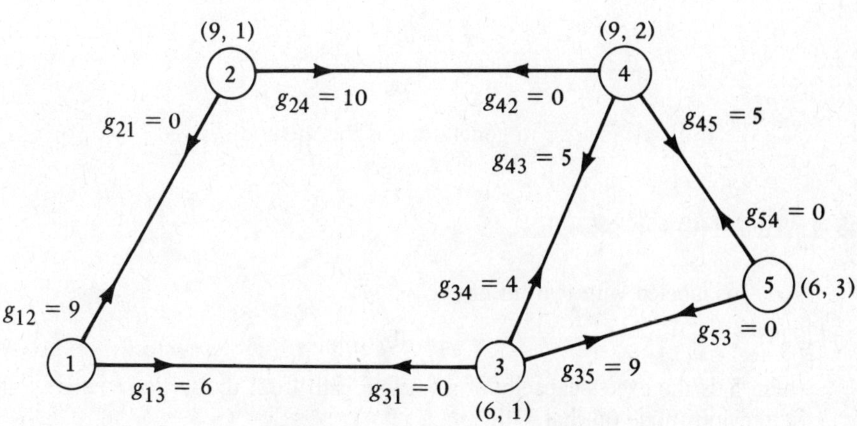

Consider Figure 7-2, which is the network of Figure 7-1 with an initial flow of zero. A feasible path exists from the source (node 1) to node 2. This path has an excess capacity of 9. So at node 2 we store two numbers: the excess capacity of the feasible path up to that point (9), and the previous node in the path (1). These are the labels at node 2. In terms of notation, the excess capacity of the path to node j is δ_j and the previous node in the path is γ_j. Node 2 is thus labeled $(\delta_2, \gamma_2) = (9, 1)$. We continue by attempting to label all nodes j where there are links $(1 \rightarrow j)$. We do not label a node if $g_{1j} = 0$, since a feasible path does not exist even though the link exists. Thus, node 3 is labeled $(\delta_3, \gamma_3) = (6, 1)$.

To proceed in extending the feasible paths, we take one of the labeled nodes and try to label the unlabeled nodes away from it, using the same principles. The convention is to take the nodes in numerical order. Thus, starting at node 2, there is a link to node 4 with positive excess capacity. Hence, there is a feasible path to node 4 via node 2. This path has an excess capacity of either the excess capacity of the path up to node 2 ($\delta_2 = 9$) or the excess capacity of the link $(2 \rightarrow 4)$ ($g_{24} = 10$), whichever is smaller. So $\delta_4 =$ minimum $(\delta_2 = 9, g_{24} = 10) = 9$, and the previous node is $\gamma_4 = 2$. No more nodes can be labeled from node 2, so we take the next lowest numbered node that has been labeled (i.e., node 3), and label from it.

From node 3, node 4 cannot be labeled, even though $g_{34} > 0$, because node 4 has already been labeled from node 2. We can, however, label node 5 (the sink) from node 3. Its excess capacity is $\delta_5 =$ minimum $(\delta_3 = 6, g_{35} = 9) = 6$, and hence $\gamma_5 = 3$.

Having labeled the sink, we need label no further. We have found a feasible path from source to sink, with an excess capacity of $\delta_5 = 6$. We use the γ_i's to trace the feasible path. At node 5, we come from node $\gamma_5 = 3$. At node 3, we come from node $\gamma_3 = 1$. The path is thus $(1 \rightarrow 3)$, $(3 \rightarrow 5)$. Now we can update the flow solution. The new flows are $\hat{x}_{13} = x_{13} + \delta_5 = 0 + 6$, and $\hat{x}_{35} = x_{35} + \delta_5 = 0 + 6$. Note that the technique is designed to give the incremental increase in flow along a feasible path. All links not on the feasible path have no change in their flow. The total flow in the network increases to $\hat{z} = z + \delta_5 = 0 + 6 = 6$. So the flows in the updated solution are

$$x_{12} = 0 \qquad x_{24} = 0 \qquad x_{35} = 6 \qquad x_{45} = 0$$

$$x_{13} = 6 \qquad x_{34} = 0 \qquad x_{43} = 0$$

We will now express in general terms the method derived.

7-3 LABELING OF NODES

Node j is labeled with two numbers:

(7-5) $$(\delta_j, \gamma_j)$$

where δ_j is the excess capacity of a feasible path from the source to node j and γ_j is the previous node on that path.

Figure 7-3. *Flow chart of labeling technique.*

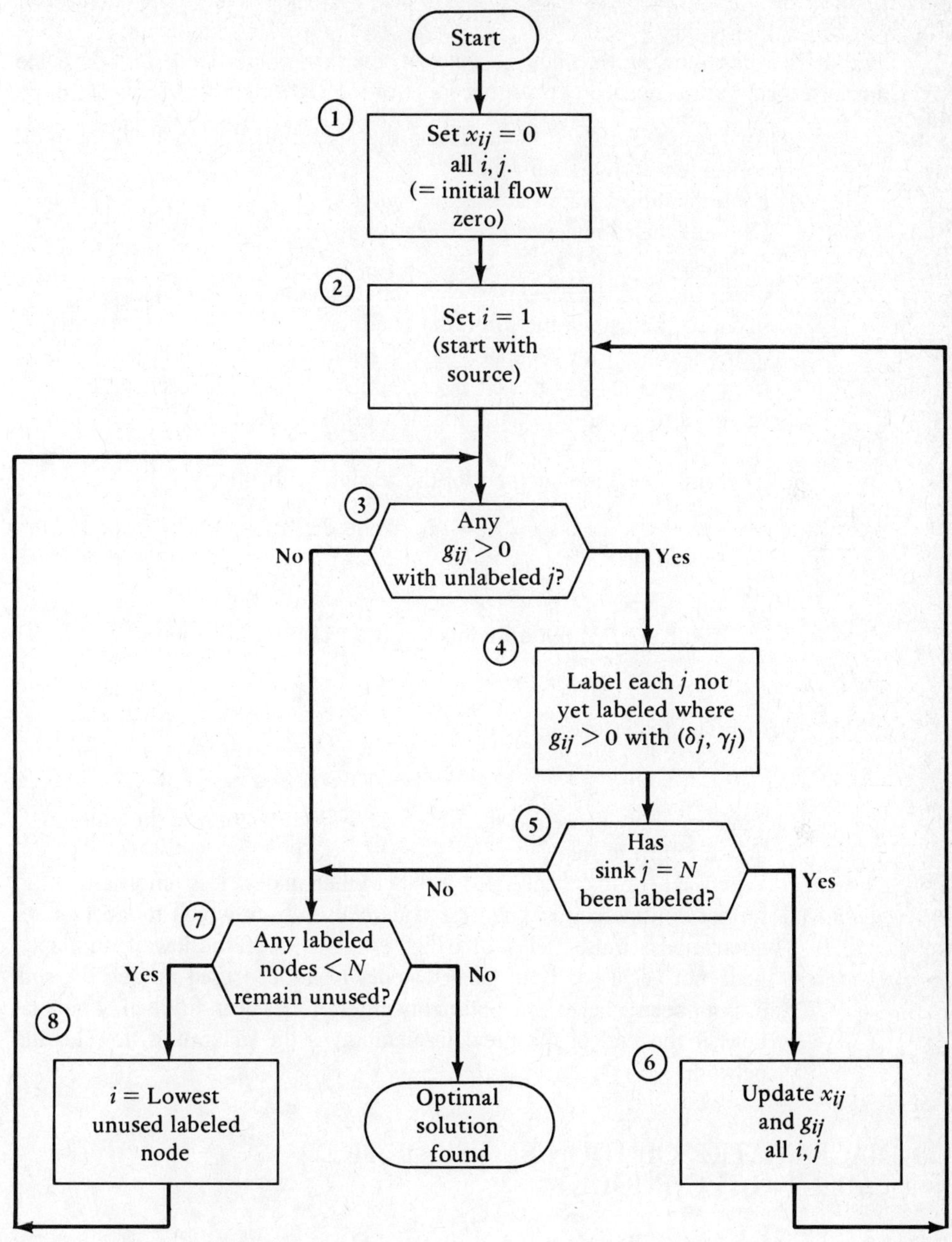

If node i immediately precedes j on the feasible path, then $\gamma_j = i$, and δ_j will be given by

(7-6) $$\delta_j = \text{minimum}\ (\delta_i, g_{ij})$$

The logic of the labeling technique is given in the flow chart of Figure 7-3. Some further explanation is needed concerning some of the eight steps involved.

Step 1 Any flow will suffice for initiating the algorithm. Often it will be most convenient to use a zero flow.

Step 2 Each iteration always starts at the source.

Step 4 Only unlabeled nodes can be labeled at this step. Previously labeled nodes are ignored.

Step 6 Once the sink has been labeled, one iteration is complete except for updating the data of the solution. The increase in flow is δ_N, the capacity of the feasible path generated. The feasible path is found by tracing back from $\gamma_N = k$ to $\gamma_k = r$, $\gamma_r = p$, etc., until the source is reached. The new values of the solution $\hat{x}_{ij}$ and the new excess capacities $\hat{g}_{ij}$ are given by:

(i) If link $(i \rightarrow j)$ is a member of the feasible path, then

(7-7) $$\hat{x}_{ij} = x_{ij} + \delta_N \qquad \hat{x}_j = x_{ji}$$
$$\hat{g}_{ij} = g_{ij} - \delta_N \qquad \hat{g}_{ji} = g_{ji} + \delta_N$$

(ii) If link $(i \rightarrow j)$ is not a member of the feasible path, then

(7-8) $$\hat{x}_{ij} = x_{ij} \qquad \hat{g}_{ij} = g_{ij}$$

(iii) The total flow in the network is

(7-9) $$\hat{z} = z + \delta_N$$

This new flow is used as the flow for the next iteration of the procedure. So we return to step 2.

Steps 7 and 8 When a node has been used to label other nodes, it is eliminated from further consideration. The next node chosen from which to label subsequent nodes must itself be labeled, and it is to be the lowest numbered node not yet used. If all labeled nodes have been used up and the sink has not been labeled, the optimality criterion has been fulfilled. The total flow at the end of the previous iteration is the maximum flow for the network.

7-4 DIAGRAMATIC SOLUTION BY USE OF THE LABELING TECHNIQUE

We now continue the solution of the pipeline problem. In the previous section, we reached step 6 and updated the x_{ij}'s. Before we can start the second iteration, we also need to update the excess capacities of all links, g_{ij}. By expression (7-7) we get $\hat{g}_{13} = 6 - 6 = 0$, $\hat{g}_{31} = 0 + 6 = 6$, etc., while by expression (7-8), $\hat{g}_{12} = 9$, $\hat{g}_{21} = 0$, etc. Figure 7-4 gives the whole set of new excess capacities.

Figure 7-4. *Second iteration.*

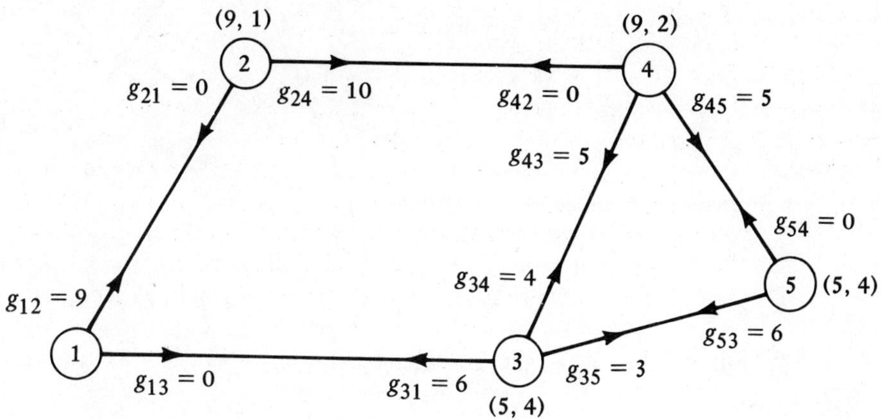

We perform the search directly on Figure 7-4 to find a new feasible path at the second iteration. Verify the steps below.

Step 2 — $i = 1$
Step 3 — node $j = 2$ with $g_{12} = 9$ unlabeled
node $j = 3$ with $g_{13} = 0$ unlabeled
Step 4 — $(\delta_2, \gamma_2) = (9, 1)$
Steps 5, 7, 8 — $i = 2$
Step 3 — node $j = 4$ with $g_{24} = 10$ unlabeled
Step 4 — $(\delta_4, \gamma_4) = (9, 2)$, using expression (7-6)
Steps 5, 7, 8 — $i = 4$
Step 3 — node $j = 3$ with $g_{43} = 5$ unlabeled
node $j = 5$ with $g_{45} = 5$ unlabeled
Step 4 — $(\delta_5, \gamma_5) = (5, 4)$, using expression (7-6)
Step 5 — sink labeled
Step 6 — The increase in the flow is $\delta_5 = 5$, and the feasible path is (1→2), (2→4), (4→5). From expressions (7-7), (7-8), and (7-9), we obtain:

$\hat{x}_{12} = 0 + \delta_5 = 5 \quad \hat{x}_{24} = 0 + \delta_5 = 5 \quad \hat{x}_{35} = 6$
$\hat{x}_{43} = 0 \quad \hat{x}_{13} = 6 \quad \hat{x}_{34} = 0$
$\hat{x}_{42} = 0 \quad \hat{x}_{45} = 0 + \delta_5 = 5 \quad \hat{z} = 6 + \delta_5 = 11$

The updated excess capacities are given in Figure 7-5.

Figure 7-5. *Third iteration.*

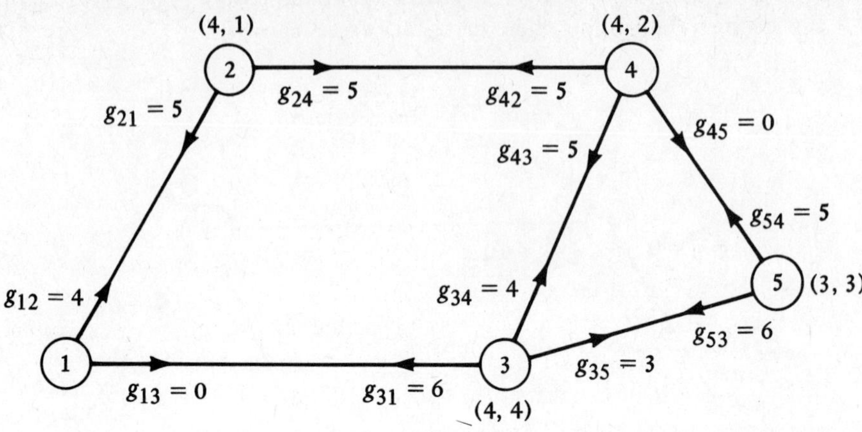

The third iteration yields the feasible path (1→2), (2→4), (4→3), (3→5), with $\delta_5 = 3$. By (7-7), (7-8), and (7-9), the new flows are

$$\hat{x}_{12} = 8 \quad \hat{x}_{24} = 8 \quad \hat{x}_{35} = 9 \quad \hat{x}_{45} = 5$$
$$x_{13} = 6 \quad \hat{x}_{34} = 0 \quad \hat{x}_{43} = 3 \quad \hat{z} = 11 + \delta_5 = 14$$

At the fourth iteration, we see from Figure 7-6 that we can label nodes 2, 3, and 4, but not the sink. So another feasible path through this network does not exist. The above solution is thus the optimal flow.

We have calculated the flows at each iteration to help us see the progression toward the optimum. However, this is not necessary. It is possible to calculate the

Figure 7-6. *Final iteration.*

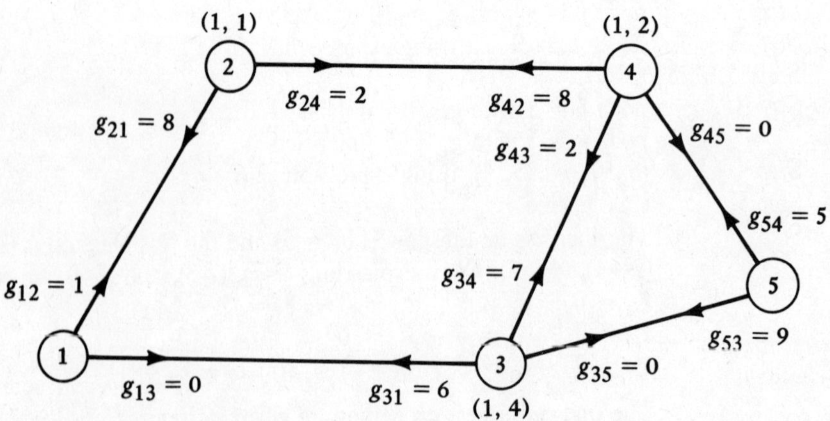

optimal net flows in each link directly from the original capacity limits (the d_{ij} values) and from the final excess capacities (the g_{ij} values). Using equation (7-4), we can write the value of the net flows as

$$(x_{ij} - x_{ji}) = d_{ij} - g_{ij}, \qquad \text{for all } i \text{ and } j$$

7-5 THE MAX FLOW/MIN CUT THEOREM

We can establish that this solution is optimal by use of the *Max Flow/Min Cut theorem*. A *cut* in a network is defined as a collection of directed links such that every directed path from source to sink contains at least one link in the cut. The *capacity value* of a cut is the sum of the capacities of the links in the cut. The *minimum cut* is the cut with the smallest capacity value.

MAX FLOW/MIN CUT THEOREM

The maximum flow in a network equals the capacity value of the minimum cut.

This theorem is conceptually reasonable. Since the flow in every path from source to sink must go through one of the links in the minimum cut, the maximum flow can be no more than the capacity value of the minimum cut. Conversely, if the flow were less than the capacity value of the minimum cut, it could be increased until it reached that value.

In the pipeline problem, the minimum cut is the pair of links (3→5) and (4→5). All paths from source to sink contain one or the other of these two links. The capacity value of the cut is $d_{35} + d_{45} = 9 + 5 = 14$, and so the maximum flow is 14.

7-6 AN APPLICATION OF THE MAXIMUM FLOW PROBLEM

A number of uses have been found for the maximum flow idea in addition to the pipeline type of problem we introduced in Section 7-1. It has been used in transport studies to maximize the traffic through a transport network such as a railroad or a highway system. These studies usually include a time dimension, so a node is defined as a physical position (e.g., railway station, highway interchange) at a particular time. The links between the nodes then represent a traffic flow over space and time.

For example, a traffic engineer is studying the road links between two cities at morning peak traffic, 7:00 A.M. to 9:00 A.M. During that period, workers travel from the satellite city 1 to city 3. Two routes exist, one direct and one through an interchange at city 2. Figure 7-7 gives the physical network. The traffic engineer wishes to find the maximum flow from city 1 to city 3 over this peak period.

Figure 7-7. *Highway network from city 1 to city 3.*

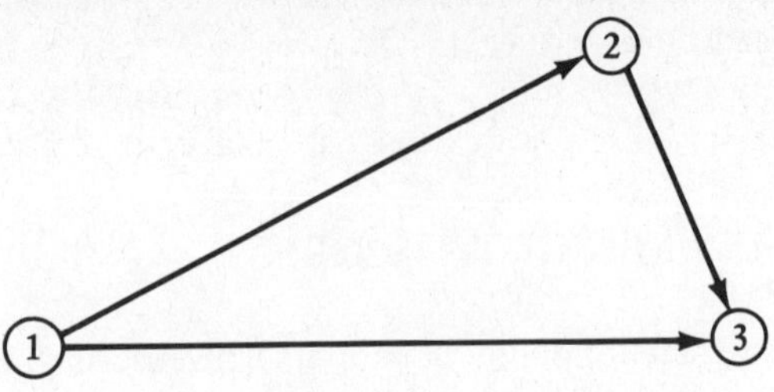

Data are available for maximum traffic capacity over a 30-minute interval for each link. City 1 to city 2 has 2000 units of capacity; city 1 to city 3 has 5000 units of capacity; and city 2 to city 3 has 3000 units of capacity. The average trip times are as follows: city 1 to city 2 requires 60 minutes; city 1 to city 3 requires 60 minutes; and city 2 to city 3 requires 30 minutes. Vehicles that cannot enter a link because its capacity is used up will queue. For simplicity it is assumed that any number of vehicles can queue at city 1 or city 2.

Figure 7-8 shows a network, with traffic flow graphed in 30-minute periods. Node O is a super-source, and node D is a super-sink. Each of the other nodes is designated ij, where i is the city and j is the time. Each link represents either a trip from one city to another or a 30-minute wait at a city. We define only those links that enable a worker to leave city 1 no earlier than 7:00 A.M. and arrive at city 3 no later than

Figure 7-8. *Time/space network for highway flow.*

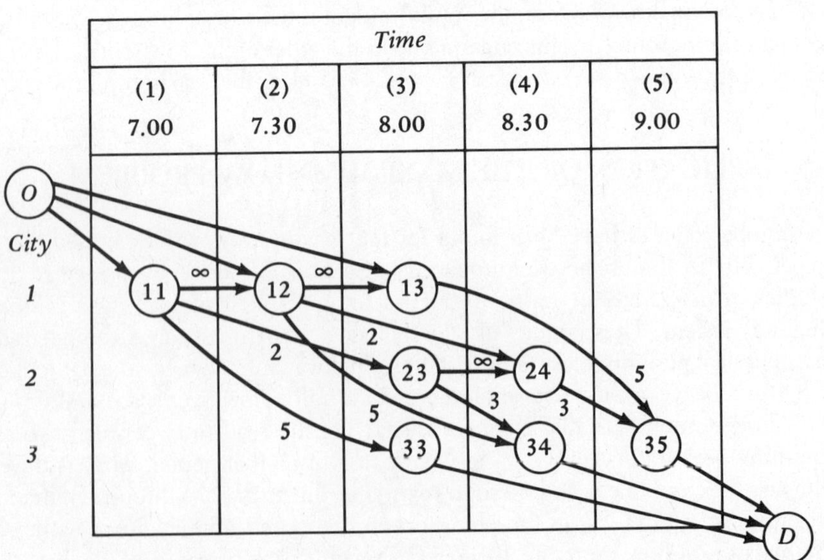

9:00 A.M. The flow into D is the maximum possible flow into city 3 within the time restriction. The capacities on the links are given in thousands of units per 30 minutes.

Further applications of maximum flow in a network include calls being routed in a telephone network, cargo flows in a particular transport node or in a complex of nodes, and flows in electrical circuits.

*7-7 EXTENSIONS TO MAXIMUM FLOW AND TRANSPORTATION PROBLEMS

The network flow problem can be extended to include a cost per unit flow in each link. The *minimum cost flow* problem entails finding the system of flows that will

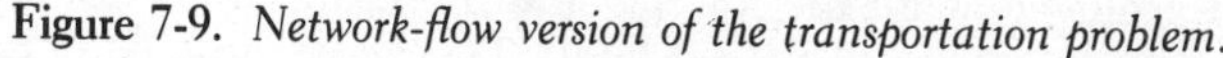

Figure 7-9. *Network-flow version of the transportation problem.*

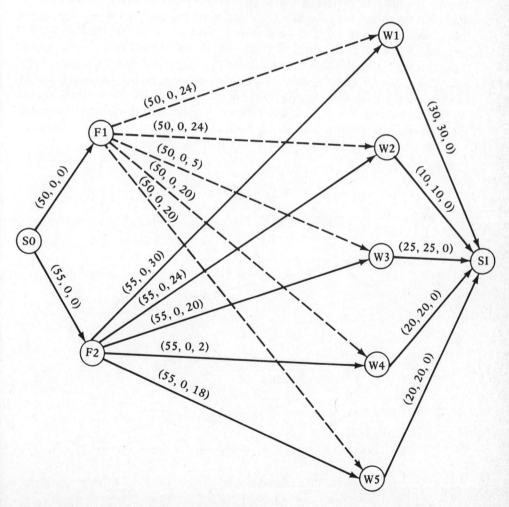

send a certain flow from source to sink. A generalization of this problem places upper and lower bounds on the flows in each link, and finds the minimum-cost feasible flow. The solution method that solves this general problem is known as the *out-of-kilter algorithm*, which is an extension of the labeling technique of this chapter.

We can formulate the transportation problem of Chapter 6 as a minimum-cost flow problem with upper and lower bounds on the links. Figure 7-9 shows the transportation problem of Figure 6-1 as a minimum-cost flow problem.

The sources are linked back to a super-source (SO), and the sinks are linked forward to a super-sink (SI). The vector (U, L, c) associated with each link gives the upper bound, lower bound, and unit cost, respectively, for that link. The links from Fi to Wj have as their upper bound the maximum amount available at Fi; their lower bound is zero; and the costs are the unit transport costs on this route. All this information comes from Figure 6-1. The links from SO to Fi have as their upper bound the amount available at Fi; the lower bound is zero to allow for all destinations to require less than the sources have available. This link has no cost. The link from Wj to SI has upper and lower bounds equal to the amount required at Wi. The upper bound could be given a higher value if more than the minimum required was acceptable. Again the cost for the link is zero. It is the upper and lower bounds on the links that force a feasible flow through the system when we minimize cost.

The particular advantage of this formulation is that it allows genuine capacity bounds on the links. For example, there may be an upper limit on the number of units that can be sent from a particular source to a particular destination. The upper limit will then become the U value for that link. A transportation problem with such capacity limits is called a *capacitated transportation problem*.

EXERCISES

7.1 Using the labeling technique, find the maximum flow in the following network.

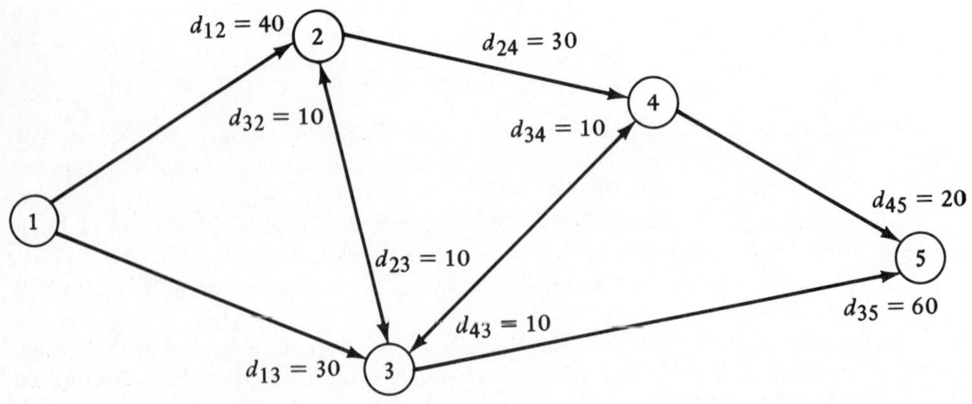

7.2 Draw the network with the following capacity limits, and find the maximum flow from node 1 to nodes 6 and 7 in the network: $d_{12} = 40$, $d_{13} = 30$, $d_{14} = 40$, $d_{23} = 20$,

$d_{25} = 25$, $d_{32} = 20$, $d_{34} = 10$, $d_{35} = 20$, $d_{36} = 25$, $d_{37} = 15$, $d_{43} = 15$, $d_{46} = 30$, $d_{57} = 30$.

7.3. Beginning at Figure 7-6, find the maximum flow for each of the following changes, considered separately.
(a) d_{35} increases from 9 to 11.
(b) d_{13} increases from 6 to 8, and d_{45} increases from 5 to 9.
(c) A new link from 1 to 4 is opened, with a capacity limit $d_{14} = 6$, and d_{45} increases from 5 to 9.

7.4. Draw the network with the following capacity limits: $d_{12} = 25$, $d_{13} = 30$, $d_{23} = 8$, $d_{24} = 15$, $d_{25} = 16$, $d_{26} = 8$, $d_{32} = 10$, $d_{34} = 10$, $d_{35} = 6$, $d_{46} = 25$. Assuming the following initial flow, find the optimal flow through each link and the overall optimal flow: $x_{12} = 25$, $x_{13} = 10$, $x_{23} = 6$, $x_{24} = 8$, $x_{25} = 3$, $x_{26} = 8$, $x_{34} = 10$, $x_{35} = 6$, $x_{46} = 18$, and $z = 35$.

7-5. Draw the network with the following capacity limits: $d_{12} = 4$, $d_{15} = 2$, $d_{16} = 2$, $d_{23} = 2$, $d_{26} = 3$, $d_{34} = 3$, $d_{36} = 3$, $d_{47} = 4$, $d_{53} = 4$, $d_{67} = 5$. Using the labeling method, find the maximum flow from source (1) to sink (7) starting with the following flow: $x_{12} = x_{23} = x_{34} = x_{47} = 2$.

7.6 The following are the excess capacities of a network at its optimal flow: $g_{12} = 0$, $g_{21} = 10$, $g_{13} = 0$, $g_{31} = 20$, $g_{23} = 0$, $g_{32} = 15$, $g_{24} = 10$, $g_{42} = 10$, $g_{34} = 5$, $g_{43} = 20$, $g_{35} = 0$, $g_{53} = 15$, $g_{45} = 10$, $g_{54} = 15$.
(a) What is the optimal flow?
(b) If the capacity limit d_{13} is raised from 20 to 25, what is the new optimal flow?

7.7 The following are the nonzero capacity limits and optimal excess capacities of a network: $d_{12} = 20$, $d_{13} = 20$, $d_{14} = 10$, $d_{23} = 10$, $d_{25} = 10$, $d_{26} = 15$, $d_{32} = 10$, $d_{34} = 15$, $d_{35} = 10$, $d_{43} = 5$, $d_{45} = 15$, $d_{52} = 5$, $d_{56} = 30$; $g_{13} = 5$, $g_{21} = 20$, $g_{23} = 15$, $g_{31} = 15$, $g_{32} = 5$, $g_{34} = 15$, $g_{41} = 10$, $g_{43} = 5$, $g_{45} = 5$, $g_{52} = 15$, $g_{53} = 10$, $g_{54} = 10$, $g_{62} = 15$, $g_{65} = 5$.
(a) Write down the optimal flow in each link, indicating the direction of that flow. What is the total flow?
(b) Write down the minimum cut.
(c) If d_{26} is increased from 15 to 25, derive the new optimal tableau.

REFERENCES

Bennington, G. E. "An Efficient Minimal Cost Flow Algorithm," *Management Science*, Vol. 19, May 1973. A superior technique to the out-of-kilter algorithm for the minimum cost flow problem.

Bradley, G. H., G. G. Brown, and G. W. Graves, "Design and Implementation of Large-Scale Primal Transshipment Algorithms," *Management Science*, Vol. 24, Sept. 1977. A description of GNET, currently one of the most efficient network codes. GNET is available from its authors.

Elmaghraby, Salah E. "The Theory of Networks and Management Science: Part I," *Management Science*, Vol. 17, Sept. 1970. An expository treatment of two network models (shortest path and flow networks) with examples.

Hu, T. C. *Integer Programming and Network Flows*. Reading, Mass.: Addison-Wesley, 1969. A thorough and advanced text. Part II gives a complete treatment of network flows commencing with the maximal flow problem.

Kaufmann, A. *Graphs, Dynamic Programming and Finite Games.* New York: Academic Press, 1967. Section 6B of Chapter I describes the maximal flow problem applied to a traffic system, and 6E outlines an actual study made on the railroad between Paris and Lyons.

Minieka, E. *Optimization Algorithms for Networks and Graphs.* New York: Dekker, 1978. Oriented to a first course on the subject, with intuitive interpretations of algorithms.

Noble, K. J., and R. B. Potts. "Network Flow Model of the Australia-Europe Container Service," in G. F. Newell, ed., *Traffic Flow and Transportation.* New York: American Elsevier, 1972. This study builds on a time/space traffic flow network of container movements between Australia and Europe.

Plane, D. R., and C. McMillan, Jr. *Discrete Optimization.* Englewood Cliffs, N.J.: Prentice-Hall, 1971. Chapter 6 develops, at a level suitable for the average reader, network optimization techniques.

CHAPTER EIGHT

Project Planning and Scheduling Techniques

Research and development projects usually consist of a number of interrelated tasks or activities. Certain tasks can be executed simultaneously. Some tasks can only be started after other tasks have been completed, i.e., precedence relationships exist between the various tasks. Each task takes a given time to complete, and tasks may require scarce resources, such as manpower or funds. We may be interested in finding the earliest time that the project can be completed with the resources available. Other planning and scheduling problems such as construction projects, periodic overhaul or maintenance of large installations, most capital expenditure projects, or the introduction of new products or procedures all require a coordinated plan that involves sequencing of interrelated ordered tasks and deployment of limited resources.

In the late 1950s, a number of closely related approaches based on network analysis were developed to deal with such problems. This chapter gives a brief survey of the two best known techniques, the *critical path method* (or *CPM*) and the *program evaluation and review technique* (or *PERT*). Both have proven themselves not only as tools for planning but also as tools for controlling the execution of the plans.

Section 8-5 requires some elementary knowledge of random variables and their probability distributions, as reviewed in Chapter 10, Sections 10-4 and 10-6.

8-1 NETWORK EVENT REPRESENTATION

Let us digress to the abbreviated case study discussed in Section 1-9 of Chapter 1. The problem there deals with an inventory control project. After a two-week orientation period, the operations researcher begins working out a detailed project proposal for an integrated inventory control and demand forecasting system. Figure 8-1 lists all tasks and the order in which they have to be undertaken to complete the project. For instance, task C (formulate a mathematical model for the proposed inventory control system, or ICS) can only start when task A (detailed analysis of environment for proposed ICS) has been completed. Task H (formulate forecasting model) can only start after detailed analyses of the environment for the proposed inventory control system and of the demand data sources (tasks A and G) have been completed. Similarly, the computation of the control limits for the products stored in inventory (task Q) can start only if both the input forms for the ICS program have been filled in (task N) and the demand forecasting base file, from which the ICS program obtains demand forecasts, has been created (task P). Table 8-1 lists the precedence relations and the durations of the tasks.

Table 8-1. *Tasks for inventory control project*

Tasks	Precedence	Duration (wk)
A	—	3
B	A	12
C	A	4
D	C	10
E	C	2
F	D, E	3
G	—	2
H	A, G	4
I	G	3
J	H	16
K	H	2
L	J, K	2
M	F, L	2
N	B, M	2
O	I, M	1
P	O	2
Q	N, P	3

Assume that we can draw on sufficient resources to have any number of tasks executed simultaneously. If the project is given the go-ahead, what is the earliest project completion date? This is one of the questions we would like to answer.

For small problems, the answer can easily be found by enumerating all possible sequences of tasks. In our example, there are 14 different sequences. The project is only completed when the sequence with the longest time has been completed.

The critical path method (CPM) efficiently finds the longest time sequence. In Figure 8-1, we use blocks (or nodes) to represent each activity. The arrows between the nodes indicate the precedence relations. Although this flow chart could be used directly to perform the computations of CPM, there are certain advantages in reversing

Figure 8-1. *Flow of tasks for an inventory control project.*

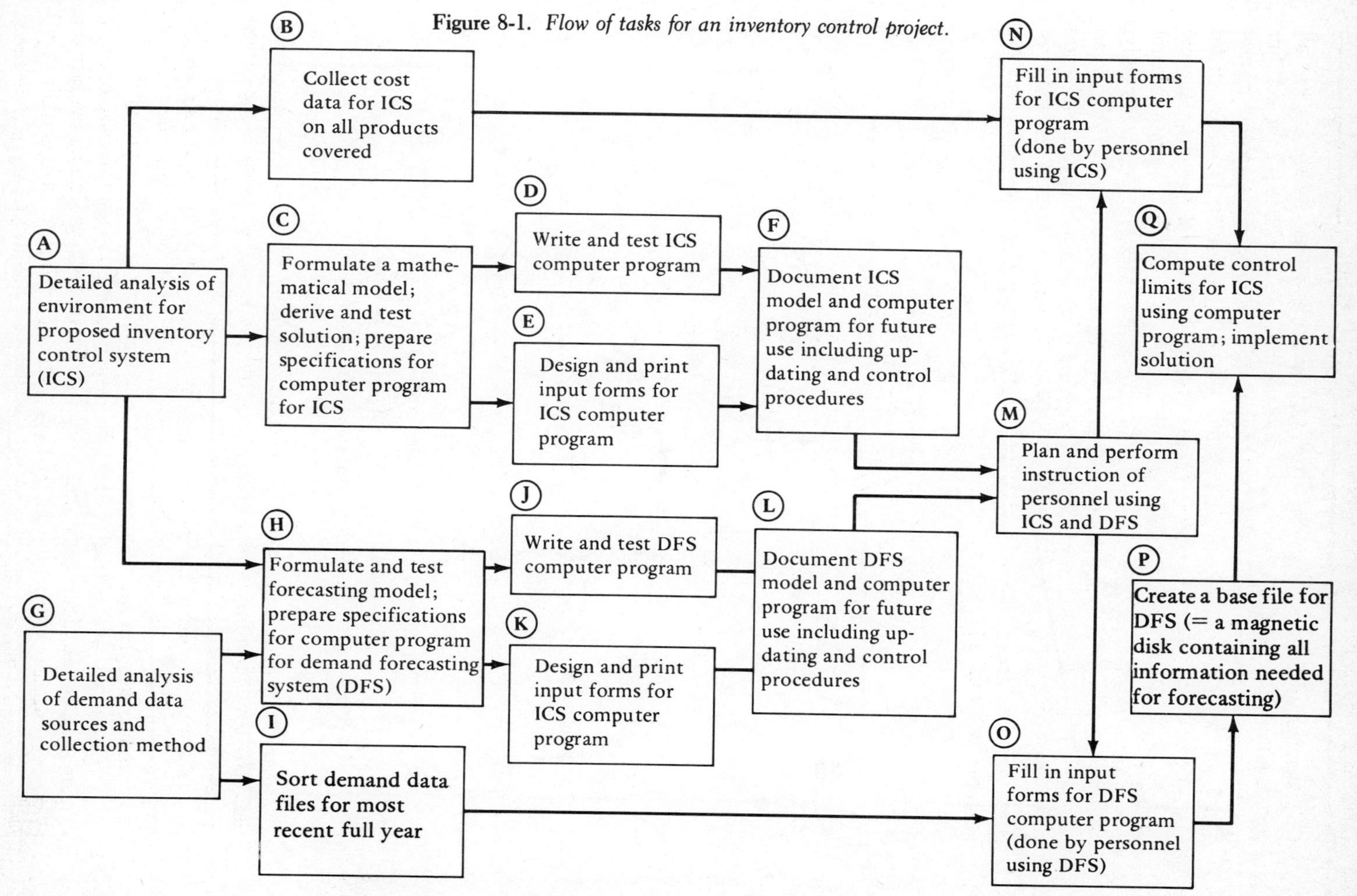

Figure 8-2. *Network diagram for an inventory control project.*

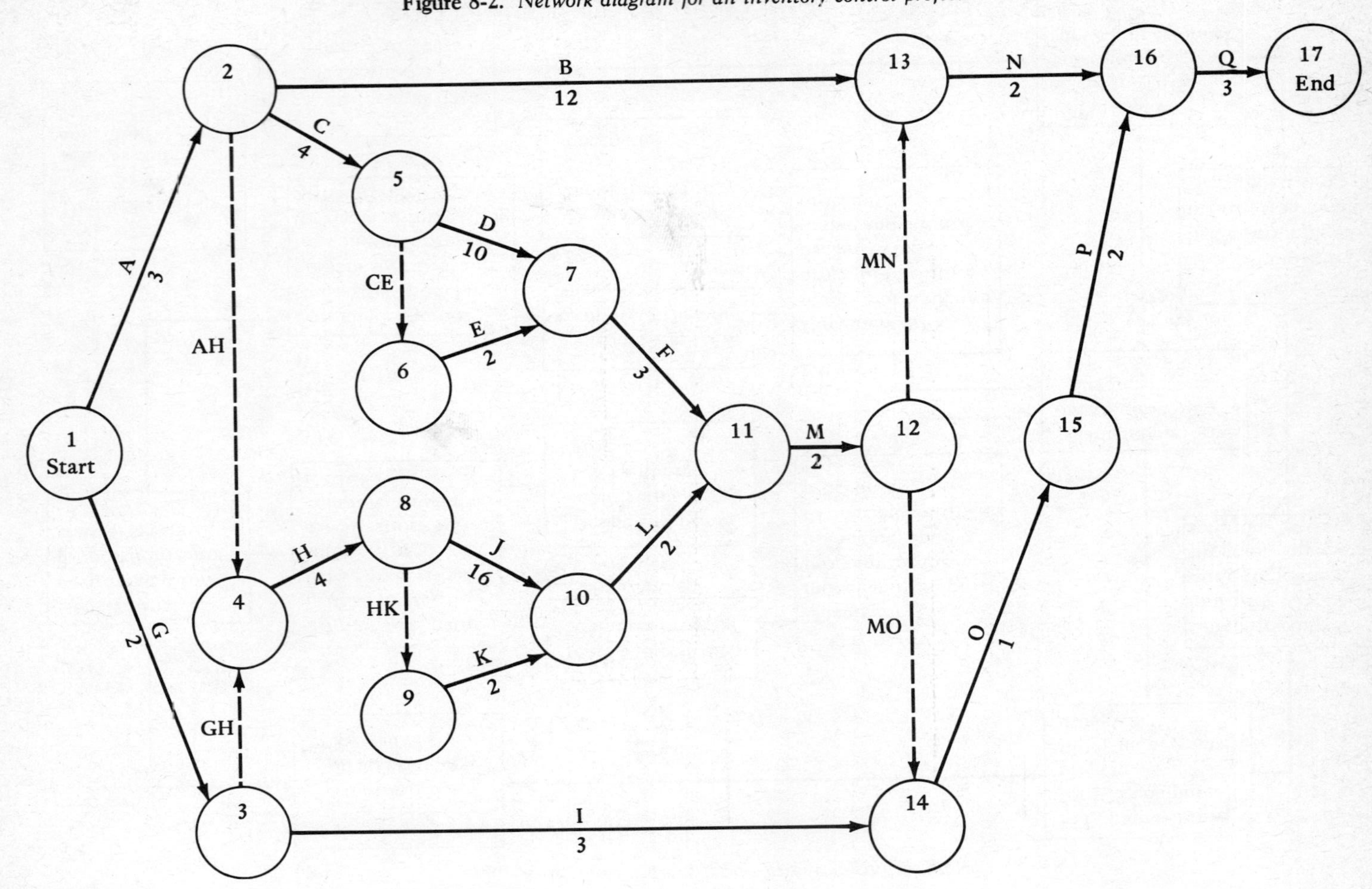

this convention and drawing a network in which directed lines or links represent tasks and nodes indicate the precedence relationships. With each link we associate a number that represents the duration of the task. Since each link starts at a node and ends at a node, nodes also represent the event of starting or completing a task. Therefore, nodes are often referred to as *events*.

Figure 8-2 depicts the network associated with the tasks listed in Table 8-1. The nodes are numbered consecutively in such a manner that each link always leads from a lower order node to a higher order node. Node 1 represents the start of the project. The number under each link is the duration of the corresponding task. The length of the link is usually not drawn in proportion to the duration of the tasks.

In this representation each task is uniquely defined by the two nodes where the corresponding link starts and ends. For instance, task A can be denoted by (1, 2). The duration of task A is denoted by t_{12}. In general, a task is identified by nodes (i, j), and its duration is denoted by t_{ij}. If the problem is solved on a computer, this is a convenient way to specify tasks and task durations.

Our network shows several links as broken lines. They are introduced to avoid ambiguities in the network logic or to allow proper representation of precedence relations. Consider, for instance, the sequence of tasks, C, D, E, and F as shown in Figure 8-1. Tasks D and E both follow C, and F requires both D and E to be completed. This ordering could be represented as shown in Figure 8-3. Tasks D and E both start and end at the same nodes. If tasks are referred to by the starting and ending nodes, then both would be denoted by (5, 7). To avoid this, we introduce a *dummy task* with a zero duration that leads to a new node. In Figure 8-2, the dummy task gives rise to link CE (connecting tasks C and E), which leads from node 5 to node 6. Task E is then started from this new node 6. Each task is again uniquely defined by two node numbers. The same reasoning leads to the introduction of dummy task HK. The dummy task could precede task D rather than task E, or it could follow rather than precede either task D or task E. (However, whenever possible the dummy task should precede a task that gives rise to it; otherwise, the computations of free float, described in Section 8-3, are less straightforward.)

A somewhat different situation gives rise to the remaining four dummy tasks. For instance, the dummy tasks AH and GH are required because task H has both A and G as predecessors, whereas tasks B and C depend only on task A but not on task G,

Figure 8-3. *An ambiguous representation of tasks.*

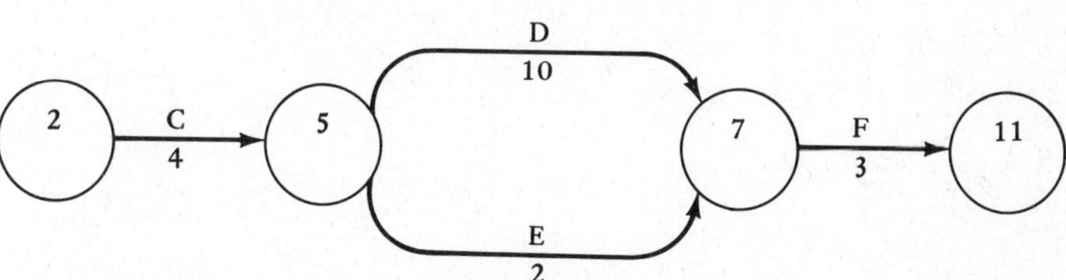

and task I requires only task G but not task A. The dependence of task H on tasks A and G is indicated by the dummy tasks AH and GH. Explain why dummy tasks MN and MO are needed.

In terms of this network, the earliest project completion date is equivalent to the longest path through the network.

8-2 EARLIEST PROJECT COMPLETION TIME

Assume that we are able to determine that the *earliest finish times* for tasks N and P are the end of week 29 and the end of week 30, respectively. Thus, the *earliest time* at which all tasks prior to node 16 are finished is the end of week 30—the latest of the two earliest finish times. Only at that time can task Q be started. The *earliest start time* of a task is therefore defined to be equal to the earliest time of the node where the task starts, i.e., the latest of the earliest finish times of all preceding tasks. In our case, this is the end of week 30. The duration of task Q is 3; hence we find that its earliest finish time is the end of week 33. Task Q being the last task to be performed, the end of week 33 is also the earliest completion time of the entire project.

In fact, we do not yet know the earliest finish times of tasks N and P. They could be determined if we knew the earliest times of nodes 13 and 15. These in turn could be found if we had the earliest finish times of the preceding tasks, etc. This gives us the idea for an algorithm. We begin at the starting node and systematically evaluate the earliest times for each node until we reach the final node.

For this evaluation, it is convenient to divide each node circle into three parts, as shown in Figure 8-4. Initially we are only interested in the ET_j portion. Here we insert the earliest time (ET) that node j can be reached. At least that many periods (weeks in our case) must elapse after the beginning of the project before any task following node j can be started. The earliest time thus refers to the end of period ET_j.

Figure 8-4. *Use of node circles in computations.*

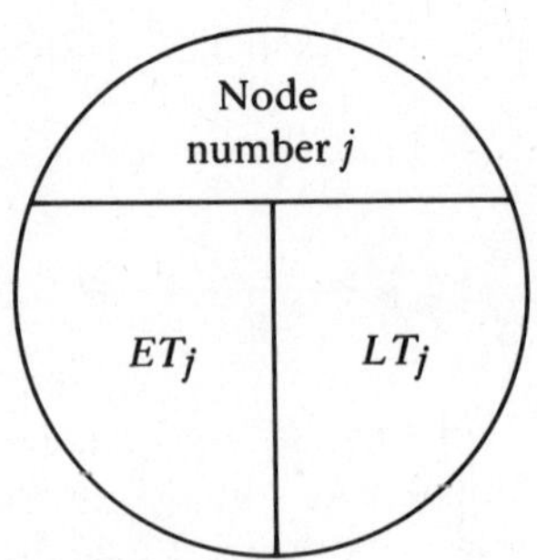

EARLIEST TIME (ET_j) OF NODE j

ET_j is equal to the latest of the earliest finish times for all tasks preceding node j, i.e.,

(8-1) $$ET_j = \text{maximum } (EF_{i_k,j}, \text{ for all } i_k)$$

where (i_k, j) is a task ending at node j and $EF_{i_k}j$ is the earliest finish time of task (i_k, j).

EARLIEST FINISH TIME OF TASK (i, j)

Let t_ij be the duration of task (i, j). Then the earliest finish time of task (i, j) is

(8-2) $$EF_{ij} = ET_i + t_{ij}$$

The complete evaluation for our project is shown in Figure 8-5. If the nodes have been properly numbered, i.e., no higher numbered node leads to a lower numbered node, then the nodes can be evaluated in numerical order. The evaluation uses the following simple algorithm.

ALGORITHM FOR EVALUATING EARLIEST PROJECT COMPLETION TIME

1. Set $ET_1 = 0$.
2. Go to next higher numbered node. Evaluate earliest finish times of all tasks that end at that node. Find the earliest time for that node using expression (8-1).
3. If any nodes have not been evaluated, return to step 2; otherwise, stop.

You should now test your understanding of this algorithm. Using Figure 8-2, work out the earliest times of all nodes, and verify the results with the solution shown in Figure 8-5.

It is usually convenient to have only one terminal node. If the original problem has more than one terminal node, simply introduce dummy tasks leading to a single terminal node. Then the earliest time of the last node evaluated gives the earliest project completion time.

Figure 8-5. *Evaluation of critical path.*

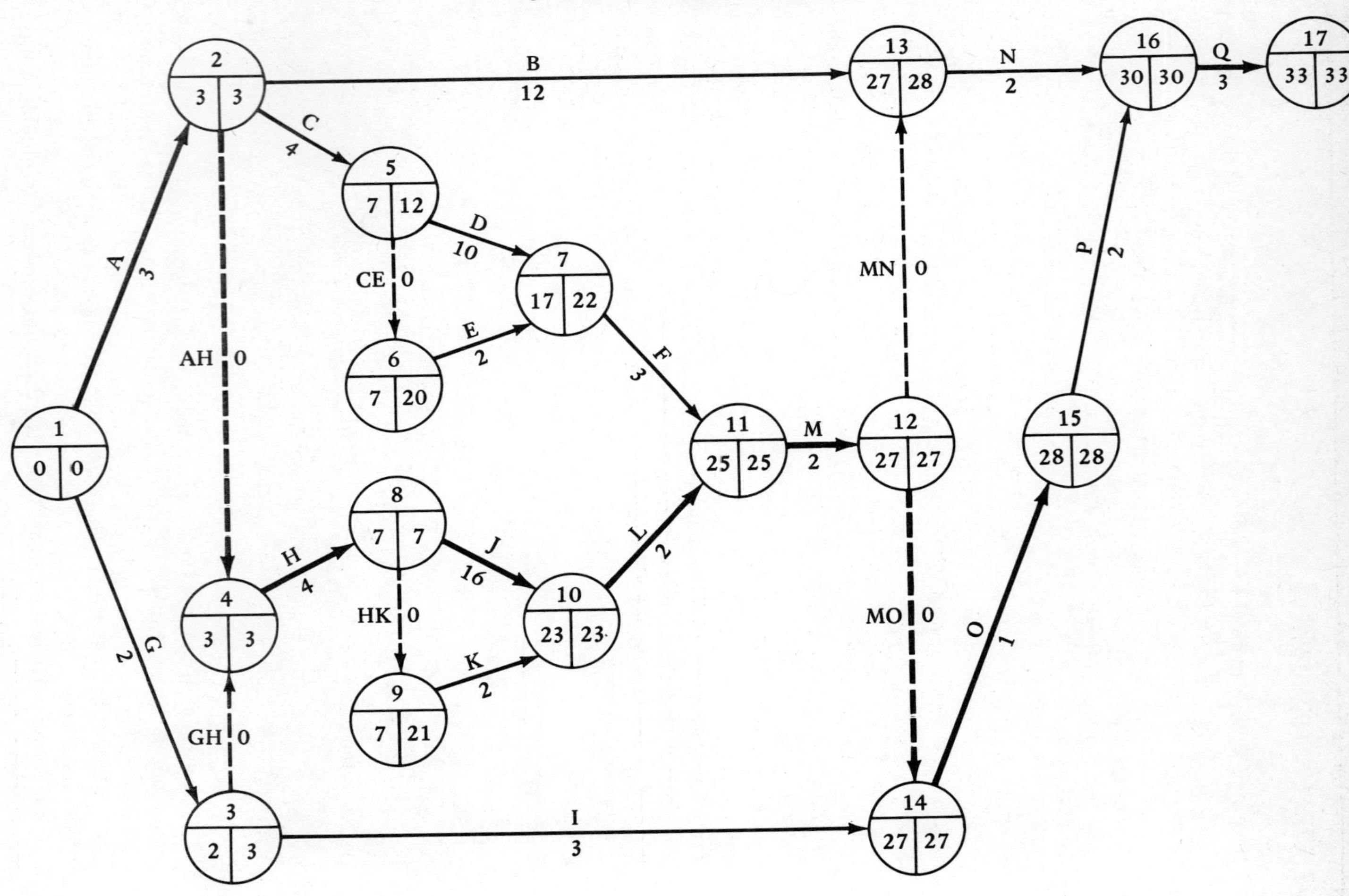

8-3 THE CRITICAL PATH

We now have a method for finding the earliest project completion time. Our next problem is to find which path of tasks has the longest completion time. Any delay in these tasks will delay the earliest project completion time. Thus, the tasks on this path are the critical ones, and this path is referred to as a *critical path* of the network. There may be several paths that have the same longest completion time. Each such path is a critical path.

How can we identify a critical path? Consider node 13 in Figure 8-5. The earliest time all tasks preceding it can be finished is $ET_{13} = 27$. (Remember that it denotes the end of a period.) This is also the earliest start time for task N. However, since task N takes only 2 weeks and the earliest time of node 16 is $ET_{16} = 30$, task N can be delayed by at least one week without delaying the completion time of the entire project. The *latest start time* for task N is the end of week 28. If any tasks preceding task N are delayed such that the start time for tasks from node 13 is later than the end of week 28, the project completion time is also delayed. In other words, the *latest time* (*LT*) all tasks preceding node 13 can be finished without delaying the whole project is the end of week 28.

On the other hand, task P can be started at the earliest by the end of week 28—the earliest time of node 15. Given that task P takes 2 weeks to complete and the earliest time of node 16 is 30, the latest start time of task P is also the end of week 28. There is no leeway. Unless all tasks preceding node 15 are finished by this time, the project completion will be delayed. In other words, the latest start time of task P is the same as the earliest time of node 15. This property holds for all tasks on a critical path.

CRITICAL TASKS AND CRITICAL PATHS

A task for which the latest start time is equal to the earliest time of its starting node is a critical task. Each path from the start node to the end node of the network that consists of critical tasks only is a critical path.

Thus, we have a simple way to identify the critical tasks of a network and all critical paths.

To determine the latest times of all nodes, we use an algorithm similar to the one we used to find the earliest times.

LATEST TIME (LT_i) OF NODE i

LT_i is equal to the earliest of the latest start times for all tasks following node i, i.e.,

(8-3) $$LT_i = \text{minimum } (LS_{i,jk}, \text{ for all } j_k)$$

where (i, j_k) is a task starting at node i and $LS_{i,jk}$ is the latest start time of task (i, j_k).

LATEST START TIME OF TASK (i, j)

The latest start time of task (i, j) is

(8-4) $$LS_{ij} = LT_j - t_{ij}$$

ALGORITHM FOR FINDING LATEST TIMES

1. Set $LT_I = ET_I$, where I is the terminal node.
2. Go to the first lower numbered node. Evaluate latest start times of all tasks that begin at that node. Find the latest time for that node using expression (8-3).
3. If the starting node has been evaluated, stop; otherwise, return to step 2.

These computations are also shown in Figure 8-5 in the right-hand-side portion of the node circles (labeled LT_j in Figure 8-4). Verify the results!

We can now identify the critical path by the nodes with $ET_i = LT_j - t_{ij}$:

nodes	1 → 2	→	4 →	8 →	10 →	11 →	12	→	14 →	15 → 16 →	17
tasks	A	dummy	H	J	L	M		dummy	O	P	Q

This path is identified by the heavy solid and broken lines in Figure 8-5.

Any task not on the critical path can be delayed, within limits. If we consider each task by itself (neglecting any interactions with preceding or subsequent tasks), then the difference between the earliest time of the node from which the task starts and its latest start time is the largest amount by which the task can be delayed without affecting the earliest completion time of the project. This difference is called the *total slack*, or *total float* (*TF*), of the task. Thus, critical tasks have zero total float.

TOTAL FLOAT OF TASK (i, j)

(8-5) $$TF_{ij} = LS_{ij} - ET_i = LT_j - ET_i - t_{ij}$$

For example, the noncritical task B = (2, 13) has

$$TF_{2,13} = LS_{2,13} - ET_2 = (28 - 12) - 3 = 13$$

If task B is delayed by more than 13 weeks, then the earliest completion time of the entire project will be delayed.

Delaying one task may, however, affect the amount by which subsequent tasks can be delayed, since the float along a segment of the network is shared by all the tasks along that segment. For example, tasks C, D, and F all share the same float of 5. The largest amount by which a task may be delayed without affecting the earliest start time of all subsequent tasks is called *free slack*, or *free float* (*FF*). Free float is the amount of float available when all other tasks take place at their earliest times. For instance, the noncritical task B may be delayed by up to 12 weeks without affecting task N. Its free float is thus 12. On the other hand, the noncritical task G cannot be delayed at all without delaying any of the subsequent tasks. Free float can never exceed total float. Along any segment of the network where all tasks have the same total float, only the last task has a positive free float. For example, of tasks C, D, and F, which have the same total float of 5, only F has a free float, and its free float is 5.

FREE FLOAT OF TASK (i, j)

(8-6) $$FF_{ij} = ET_j - EF_{ij} = ET_j - ET_i - t_{ij}$$

Again, for task B = (2, 13),

$$FF_{2,13} = ET_{13} - EF_{2,13} = 27 - (3 + 12) = 12$$

Both free float and total float are useful for planning decisions. The planner has some choice as to when to start tasks with float. This may allow the planner to schedule such tasks in a manner that reduces the amount of manpower needed. For instance, tasks E and K are similar in nature and thus require the same professional training. Both could be started after week 7. Since both have float, they can be scheduled in such a manner that the same person can do both tasks consecutively.

8-4 ACTUAL PROJECT PLANNING AND CONTROL THROUGH CPM

The computations for finding the critical path and the total and free floats are so simple that projects with up to a few hundred tasks can still be worked by hand. Any self-contained segments of the network that have only a beginning and an ending node in common with other parts can be analyzed separately. If only the final results of this analysis are inserted into the total project structure, the whole segment can be regarded as a single task. Using this trick, a complex network can be broken into a number of smaller networks, each of which is analyzed for its critical paths.

Larger projects are best analyzed by computer, and most computer manufacturers provide computer programs to analyze critical path networks. These programs can handle projects with several thousand tasks and automatically keep track of the amount of various resources required during the project. Some programs allow the input to be in the form of Figure 8-1; tasks are attached to nodes rather than to links, eliminating the translation process. The program may contain a calendar covering up to 25 years, which includes all official holidays. All start and finish dates are assigned by the program to their projected calendar dates. The program may also allow special work and shift patterns to be specified.

The practical use of CPM is twofold. It is a tool for detailed planning and scheduling of projects made up of a large number of interconnected tasks. However, it is also a highly useful aid in continuously measuring the actual progress of the project according to the plan. This control allows management to predict delays or to pinpoint situations that could lead to delays—often well ahead of their actual occurrence. Corrective action can thus be taken early enough to counteract some of the consequences of late project completion. Furthermore, by using the current progress status as the starting point, management can work out the new projected critical path and the earliest completion time in light of the latest information.

Continuous control is more effectively achieved if we redraw the CPM network as a *schedule graph*. On this graph, the horizontal projection of all links is drawn to a time scale representing task duration. We also have to fix the starting dates for noncritical tasks. Figure 8-6 shows a possible schedule graph for our example. Actual task times are drawn as solid lines, and float times are shown as dotted lines. Tasks that require the same professional training are scheduled, as far as possible, in such a manner that the same person can perform them. For example, task H (formulate forecasting model) is followed by task C (formulate inventory control model). The former is on the critical path; the latter has considerable float.

As the project progresses, we continuously monitor the actual execution by marking the progress of each task on the schedule graph. When we observe or predict any irregularities, such as late starts or excessive task durations, we can immediately determine whether they will cause a delay in project completion.

For large projects, this control is best done directly by computer. Some CPM computer programs are specifically designed for control purposes—the current status of a project is kept on a random access disk file. Progress on task completions, any new estimates of task durations for tasks not yet started or completed, or other changes

Figure 8-6. *Schedule graph of a CPM network.*

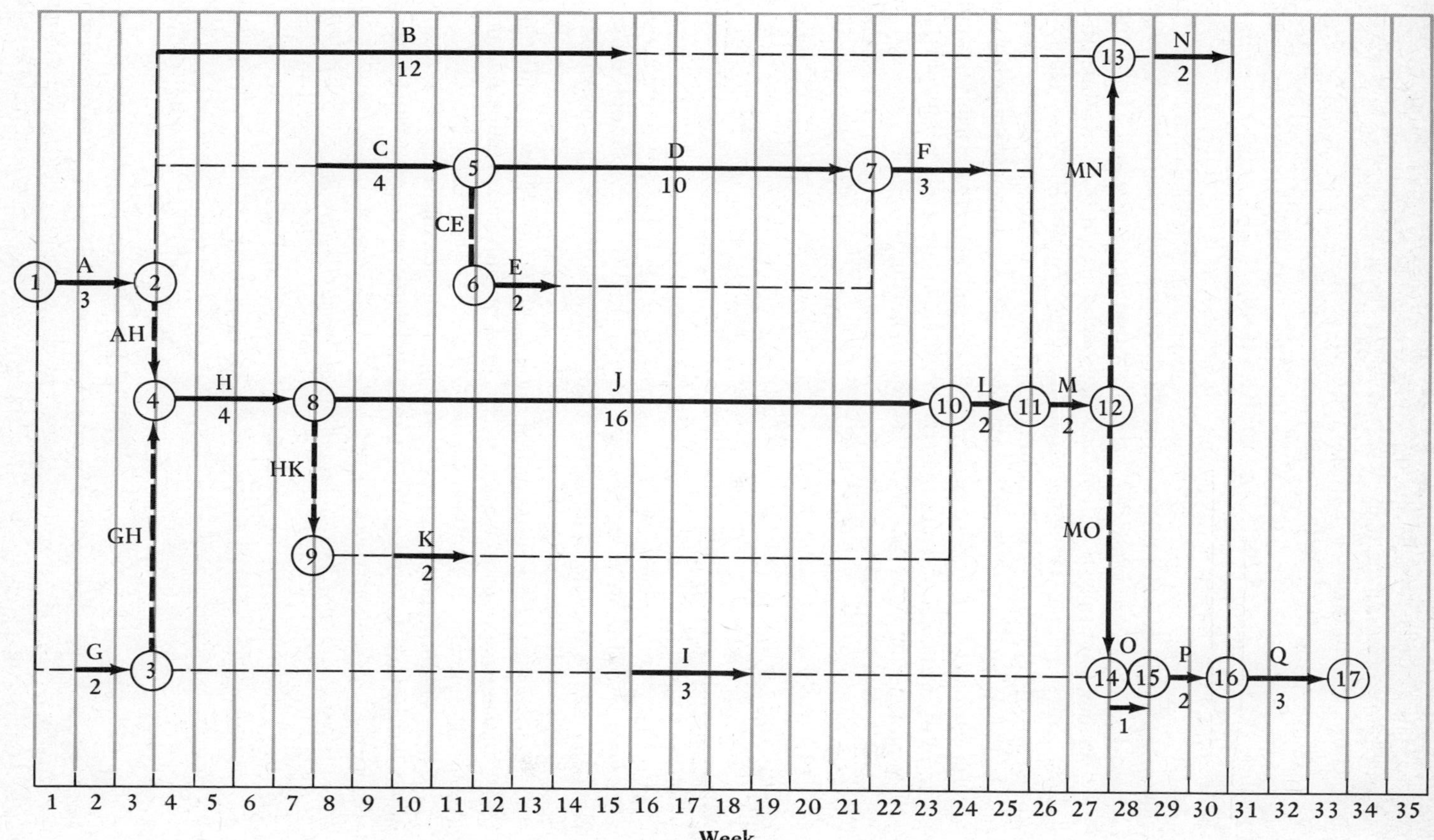

in the project can be fed into the computer at any time. The program can also be instructed to provide a new status report, to flag present and predicted delays in task completions, and to update the critical path and float times.

8-5 PROGRAM EVALUATION AND REVIEW TECHNIQUE—PERT

Although PERT was developed concurrently with and independently of CPM, it can be viewed as an extension of CPM that deals with uncertainties in the task durations. PERT attempts not only to determine the expected length of the critical path, but also to obtain some measure of the variability of the earliest project completion time. We say *attempt* because PERT does not fully succeed in this objective.

In PERT, task durations are assumed to be independent random variables, each with expected value t_{ij} and variance σ^2_{ij}. Thus, any path through the network represents a sum of independent random variables. In particular, the length of the critical path as determined by CPM is such a random variable with

(8-7) $$\text{expected value } \mu = \sum_{\substack{\text{all } (i,\, j) \text{ on} \\ \text{critical path}}} t_{ij}$$

and

(8-8) $$\text{variance } \sigma^2 = \sum_{\substack{\text{all } (i,\, j) \text{ on} \\ \text{critical path}}} \sigma^2_{ij}$$

Expression (8-8) follows from the fact that the variance of the sum of independent random variables is equal to the sum of the variances of the random variables. (See Section 10-4 of Chapter 10.)

Traditionally, PERT assumes that the individual tasks follow a particular form of the *beta distribution*, which lends itself to an intuitively appealing interpretation for the task duration, as shown in Figure 8-7.

The operations researcher may be hard pressed to determine the actual distribution of task durations. On the other hand, management may be less reluctant to summarize

Figure 8-7. *Beta distribution and task duration.*

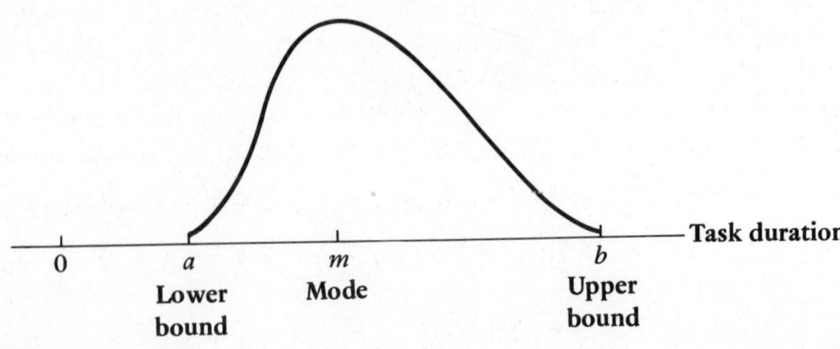

the distributions by the minimum, maximum, and most likely duration times. Using the transformation shown in Section 10-6 for the beta distribution, the three estimates yield the following values for the expected task duration and its variance:

$$t_{ij} = \tfrac{1}{3}[2m + \tfrac{1}{2}(a + b)] \qquad (8\text{-}9)$$

$$\sigma_{ij}^2 = [\tfrac{1}{6}(b - a)]^2$$

Consider a simple example. The heavy-duty diesel motor of the emergency power generating plant of a factory needs an extensive overhaul job. At the same time, the concrete base, which is cracked, also has to be replaced. Management plans to have this job performed during the annual vacation of the factory when the factory closes for 15 working days. Management would like to know whether the overhaul can be completed in this time. Table 8-2 lists the various tasks.

Table 8-2. *Diesel motor overhaul (all times shown in days)*

Task	Precedence	Mode m	Minimum a	Maximum b	t_{ij}	σ_{ij}^2
A. Dismantle motor	—	2	2	2	2	0
B. Overhaul motor	A	7	6	14	8	$\frac{16}{9}$
C. Rebuild motor base and cure	A	9	8	10	9	$\frac{1}{9}$
D. Test and adjust motor	B	2.5	2	6	3	$\frac{4}{9}$
E. Mount motor on base	C, D	2	2	2	2	0

The t_{ij} and σ_{ij}^2 values are found using expressions (8-9). Note that if the minimum and the maximum times are equal, there is no variability in the task duration, and hence the variance is zero. This is the case for tasks A and E. For task B, we obtain

$$t_{ij} = \tfrac{1}{3}[2m + \tfrac{1}{2}(a + b)] = \tfrac{1}{3}[2(7) + \tfrac{1}{2}(6 + 14)] = \tfrac{24}{3} = 8$$

$$\sigma_{ij}^2 = [\tfrac{1}{6}(b - a)]^2 = [\tfrac{1}{6}(14 - 6)]^2 = (\tfrac{4}{3})^2 = \tfrac{16}{9}$$

The t_{ij} values so computed are now used as input in finding the critical path in the same manner as for CPM. Since the t_{ij} values are estimates of expected values, the duration of the critical path is also an estimate of an expected value. For our simple problem, the critical path can be found by inspection. The path consists of tasks A, B, D, E. By expressions (8-7) and (8-8), we find the following statistics for the expected length of the critical path and its variance, or standard deviation:

$$\text{Expected length of critical path} = 2 + 8 + 3 + 2 = 15 \text{ days}$$

$$\text{Variance of duration} = 0 + \tfrac{16}{9} + \tfrac{4}{9} + 0 = \tfrac{20}{9}$$

$$\text{Standard deviation} = \sqrt{\tfrac{20}{9}} = 1.49 \text{ days}$$

Thus, the expected length of the critical path is just equal to the closing period.

The length of any path in the network and, in particular, the length of the critical path is the sum of random variables. It may be useful to know its probability distribution. From probability theory we know that no matter what the form of the individual probability distributions, the probability distribution of a sum of independent random variables is approximately normal for a sufficiently large number of variables. If the individual distributions are not highly skewed and none of the tasks dominates the length, this property holds approximately for as few as $n = 10$ tasks. (If the individual distributions are close to normal, it holds for even smaller numbers.) Therefore, we can use the normal distribution to make probability statements about the duration of any path.

For demonstration purposes, let us assume that for our problem the normal distribution is a sufficiently good approximation. We can then state that with probability 0.9099 the duration of the critical path does not exceed 17 days, and that with probability 0.9778 the duration does not exceed 18 days, as shown in Figure 8-8. Since the expected earliest project completion time is equal to the length of the critical path, it is easy to fall into the trap of concluding that the probability of an earliest project completion time of no more than 17 days is 0.9099. This would be a fallacy! Let us see why.

Although noncritical tasks will not affect the *expected* earliest project completion time, they may affect its variability. Tasks with a small amount of slack but large variability may have a significant probability that the length of the paths on which they lie turns out to be longer than the critical path. PERT simply ignores these effects and, therefore, tends to underestimate the variability of the earliest project completion time. Unfortunately, no analytic methods exist to deal with this problem. *Simulation* is the only way to derive the empirical distribution of the earliest project completion time. (Refer to Chapter 16 on simulation.)

In our example, a probability statement about the length of the critical path is practically equivalent to a statement about the earliest project completion time. The reason for this is the small variance of the only noncritical task—task C.

Figure 8-8. *Probability of length of critical path.*

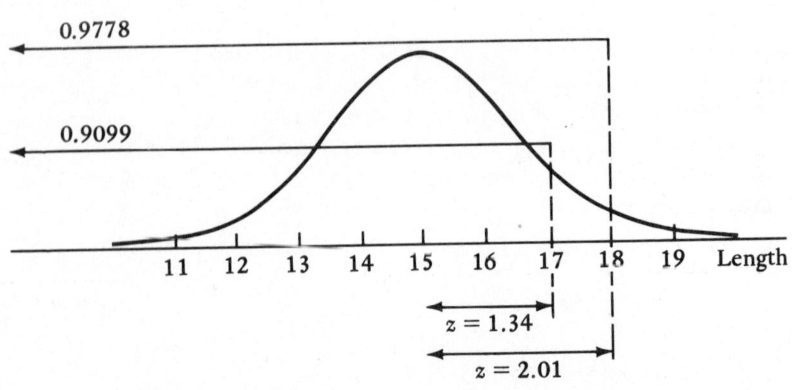

Since the variability of the earliest project completion time depends on the variability of all tasks on the critical path, as well as of tasks on "near" or "close-to-critical" paths, any action that can reduce the variance of these tasks reduces the variability of the earliest project completion time and therefore increases the probability of meeting project target dates.

8-6 THE CRITICAL PATH METHOD COST MODEL

The cost of completing a project can usually be divided into the costs directly related to the individual tasks, such as manpower and equipment applied to the task, and the costs related to the duration of the project as a whole, such as managerial services and other overhead items. Most tasks can be expedited if more resources are applied to them. Figure 8-9 illustrates such relationships. In simplest form, they are linear.

Direct costs are lowest for a task duration at a normal level, b_{ij}. Any slow-down beyond this level does not produce further cost savings. The duration cannot be cut below the *crash* level, a_{ij}. If costs are linear, they can be expressed as $(c_{ij} - t_{ij}v_{ij})$, where c_{ij} is the intercept for $t_{ij} = 0$ and v_{ij} represents the increase in direct costs for a unit reduction in the task duration. Our objective is to find a schedule of task durations that minimizes total direct and indirect costs.

For small problems, the following heuristic reasoning will usually find the optimal schedule. We start out with an initial schedule using normal duration times for all tasks, which yields, in some sense, the maximum length critical path. We now attempt to stepwise reduce the total project duration by expediting one or more of the critical tasks. As critical tasks are shortened, the float of parallel noncritical tasks decreases and ultimately vanishes. They also become critical. Therefore, further decreases in the earliest project completion time may entail reducing several critical tasks on parallel critical paths simultaneously. Any critical task or combination of parallel critical tasks

Figure 8-9. *Costs associated with a project.*

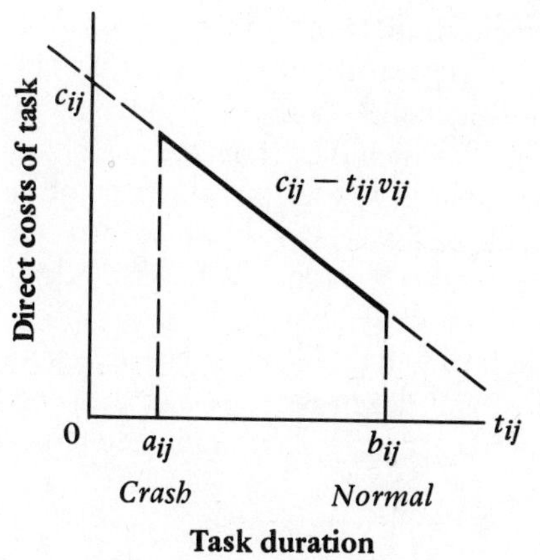

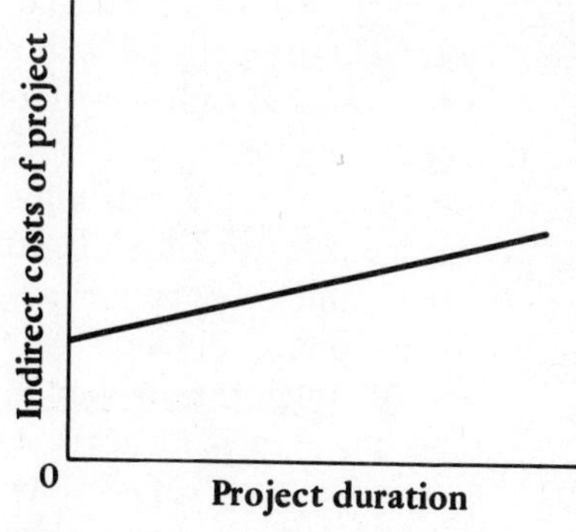

is a candidate for being expedited when the combined rate of increase of direct costs as measured by their v_{ij} components is less than the rate of savings on indirect costs. At each stepwise reduction or iteration, the critical task or combination of critical tasks with the smallest total rate of increase of direct costs is chosen as the candidate for expediting. At least one candidate task is shortened to its crash level, a_{ij}, in each iteration unless a noncritical task becomes critical on a parallel path prior to reaching this level. For small projects, these computations are best done on a schedule graph.

Consider the data shown in Table 8-3. Indirect project costs are $500 per week. Part (*a*) of Figure 8-10 shows the schedule graph of the critical path for normal task durations, $t_{ij} = b_{ij}$. Its length is 11 weeks. The total cost is given by the sum of the direct costs, $c_{ij} - t_{ij}v_{ij}$, over all tasks and the indirect project costs. The indirect costs amount to $500 multiplied by the length of the critical path, or $5500. The direct cost for task A is 3200 − 8(300) = $800. Verify that direct costs for the remaining tasks are $600, $1000, and $100. The total for normal task duration is thus $8000.

Table 8-3. *CPM cost project*

Task	Precedence	Normal Time b_{ij}	Crash Time a_{ij}	Direct Costs c_{ij}	v_{ij}
A	—	8 weeks	4 weeks	3200	300
B	—	4	3	1000	100
C	B	2	1	1800	400
D	A, C	3	2	700	200

We now find the task on the critical path with the lowest rate of increase of direct costs v_{ij}. This is task D, with v_{ij} = $200. Since this is less than the weekly rate of indirect project costs, task D is expedited, in this case to its crash time of $a_{ij} = 2$. Direct costs go up by $200, and indirect costs go down by $500. The new critical path has a length of 10 weeks and a total cost of $7700. This is shown in part (*b*) of Figure 8-10. At the second iteration, task A is expedited by 2 weeks. At that point, the total float for tasks B and C has been reduced to zero, and they become critical tasks. The new critical path of length 8 is shown in part (*c*). We now study tasks on parallel critical paths for simultaneous time reductions. Tasks A and B have a rate of increase of direct costs of $300 + $100, or $400, which is less than the rate of indirect project costs. The maximum reduction possible is 1 week, at which point task B reaches its crash time. The new critical path of 8 weeks is shown in part (*d*). No further time reduction can be made now without increasing total costs. Why? The optimal project duration is thus 8 weeks at a cost of $7200.

Although this method is fairly effective for small problems, it becomes cumbersome for even moderate-size problems of several dozen tasks, and at that point an optimal solution can no longer be guaranteed. Linear programming is one possible means to solve some problems.

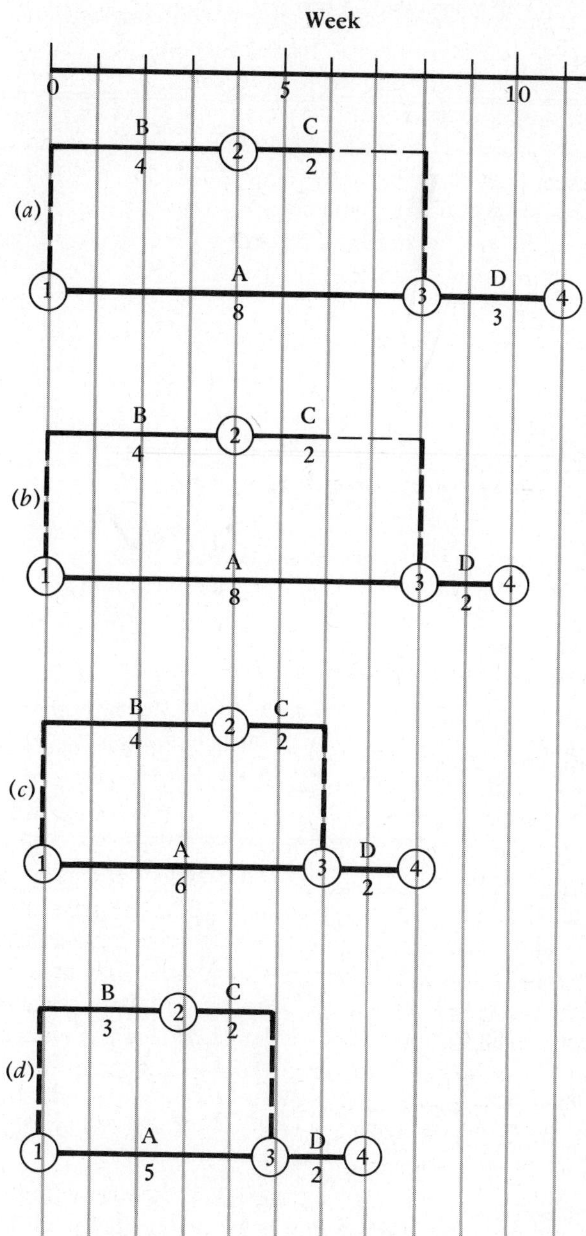

Figure 8-10. *Iterations of CPM cost model.*

Critical path for normal times:
Total cost \$8000
Task D has lowest $v_{ij} = 200 \leqslant 500$ and is a candidate for expediting.

First iteration:
Task D reduced to $a_{ij} = 2$; new total cost \$7700
Task A now has lowest $v_{ij} = 300 \leqslant 500$ and is a candidate for expediting.

Second iteration:
Task A reduced to $t_{ij} = 6$; B and C now become critical.
New total cost \$7300
Tasks A and B together have sum of v_{ij} of $300 + 100 \leqslant 500$ and are candidates for expediting.

Third iteration:
Task B reduced to $a_{ij} = 3$, task A reduced to $t_{ij} = 5$.
New total cost \$7200
No combinations of tasks on critical paths have rates of direct costs totalling less than 500. Minimum cost schedule reached.

EXERCISES

8.1 The maintenance job described in the table has to be performed periodically on the heat exchangers in a refinery. All durations are in hours.

Task	Precedence	Duration (hr)
A Dismantle pipe connections	—	14
B Dismantle header, closure, and floating head front	A	22
C Remove tube bundle	B	10
D Clean bolts	B	16
E Clean header and floating head front	B	12
F Clean tube bundle	C	10
G Clean shell	C	6
H Replace tube bundle	F, G	8
I Prepare shell pressure test	D, E, H	24
J Prepare tube pressure test and reassemble	I	16

(a) Draw a CPM network. Introduce dummy tasks as needed.
(b) Find the earliest and latest times for each node. Identify the critical path. What is its length?
(c) Find the total float and the free float for each task.
(d) Draw a schedule graph.

8.2 The brain trust of Creative Toys has just come up with the idea for a new plastic toy. Can it be ready for Christmas sales? It is July now. Working from past experience, the assistant manager breaks the project into the tasks listed in the table.

	Task	Precedence	Duration (wk)
A	Initial market survey	—	1
B	Detailed design of toys and dies	A	3
C	Cost and demand analysis	B	2
D	Manufacture of dies	B	2
E	Procurement of materials for toy	B	4
F	Trial manufacture	D	1
G	Planning of sales promotion	C, F	4
H	Retooling of injection molding machines	F	2
I	Training of labor	F	1
J	Production run	C, E, H, I	8
K	Distribution to wholesalers	G, J	2
L	Distribution to retailers	K	2
M	Advertising campaign "watch for"	G	4
N	Advertising campaign "hard sell"	L, M	2

(a) Draw a CPM network. Introduce dummy tasks as needed.
(b) Find the earliest and latest times for each node. Identify the critical path. What is its length? If it is now July 10, when is the project completion date?
(c) Find the total float and the free float for each task.
(d) Draw a schedule graph.

8.3 A firm has developed a new product and wants its prerelease marketing campaign to be started on August 20. The individual tasks are as listed in the table.

	Task	Precedence	Duration (wk)
A	Preparing and approval of project plan and budget	—	1
B	Training of servicepeople	A	8
C	Training of salespeople	A	4
D	Sales promotion to distributors	C	4
E	TV and radio advertising brief	A	4
F	TV and radio contract negotiating with agent	E	1
G	TV film making	F	8
H	Radio script taping and approval	F	4
I	Approval of TV film from management	G	3
J	Press and household advertising brief	A	2
K	Advertising contract negotiations	J	1
L	Advertising illustrations and text making	K	4
M	Printing of above	L	4
N	Distribution of product to distributors	D	2
O	Distribution of product to retailers	N	4
P	Press conference	B, O, I, H, M	0

(a) Draw a CPM network, and determine the critical path. When will the press conference be held, at the earliest?
(b) Determine the amount of total float and free float for each task.

8.4 A toy factory is making kites. The activities have to be performed in the precedence order given in the table.

	Task	Precedence	Duration (min)
A	Cut plastic to shape of kite	—	5
B	Make wooden frame	—	15
C	Punch holes and attach rivets	A	5
D	Paste on picture transfers	A	2
E	Put string through holes in plastic so plastic is attached to frame	C, B	3
F	Attach tail to kite	C, B	2
G	Stick warning message ("Do not fly near power lines") across kite	D, E	1
H	Fold kite up for dispatch	F, G	1

(a) Draw a CPM network.
(b) Find the critical path. What is its length?
(c) Draw a schedule graph.

8.5 A catering service has accepted a contract for a three-course dinner for 100 people. The manager wants to know at what time the kitchen staff must be called for duty. The minutes required for the various tasks and the immediately preceding tasks are as shown in the table.

	Task	Precedence	Duration (min)
A	Prepare chicken for roasting	—	10
B	Prepare pastry for apple pudding	—	15
C	Prepare potatoes, carrots, and marrows	—	30
D	Wrap cutlery in paper napkins	—	15
E	Put chicken in oven to roast	A	50
F	Open tins of apples and put on pastry	B	5
G	Make meringue topping for pudding	B	15
H	Prepare vegetables and put in steamers	C	25
I	Put pudding in oven to cook	F, G	5
J	Make thickening for gravy	A	5
K	Remove vegetables from steamers and put in bain-marie	H	5
L	Heat milk in one steamer for custard	I, K	10
M	Remove pudding from oven and place in warmer	I	5
N	Make custard and place in jugs	L	10
O	Remove roast from oven and make gravy	E, J	10
P	Make soup in steamer using vegetable water	K	20
Q	Set tables	D	20
R	Attend to dinner guests	M, N, O, P, Q	120
S	Wash plates, cutlery, pots, and pans	R	60
T	Clean tables	R	10

(a) Draw a CPM network.
(b) Find the earliest and latest times for each node. Identify the critical path. What is its length?
(c) Find the total float and the free float for each task.
(d) Draw a schedule graph for tasks A through R. What is the minimum number of people who must work in the kitchen to prepare the meal in the minimum time?

8.6 Consider the manufacture of a machine that consists of three subassemblies and is produced on order. Each subassembly is processed and assembled individually, and then the whole product is assembled. The various tasks have the precedence relations and task durations shown in the table.

	Task	Precedence	Duration (days)
A	Produce subassembly X	—	3
B	Produce subassembly Y	A	3
C	Produce subassembly Z	—	1
D	Assemble X	A	4
E	Assemble Z	C, D	2
F	Assemble Y	B, D	1
G	Finish assembly	D, E, F	2

(a) What is the minimum delivery lead time needed to complete 1 unit of the machine? Which tasks are critical? What are the amounts of total and free float for each task?

(b) The production engineer hopes to cut the delivery lead time by 2 days by rearranging subassemblies of tasks C and D. This would reduce the duration of task D from 4 to 2 days, but would increase the duration of task C by 3 days. Since the latter has sufficient float, increasing its duration will not interfere. Is the engineer correct? Why or why not?

8.7 Listed in the table are the activities and sequencing requirements necessary for the completion of a research report.

Activity	Description	Precedence	Duration (wk)
A	Literature search	—	6
B	Formulation of hypothesis	—	5
C	Preliminary feasibility study	B	2
D	Formal proposal	C	2
E	Field analysis	A, D	2
F	Progress report	D	1
G	Formal research	A, D	6
H	Data collection	E	5
I	Data analysis	G, H	6
J	Conclusions	I	2
K	Rough draft	G	4
L	Final copy	J, K	3
M	Preparation of oral presentation	L	1

(a) Draw a CPM network for this project.

(b) Find the critical path. What is its length?

(c) Find the total float and the free float for each task.

(d) Draw a schedule graph.

(e) Tasks A, B, C, D, F, G, J, K, L, and M require similar professional training; so do tasks E, H, and I. Redraw the schedule graph so that only two people are needed to perform the project.

8.8 Cosmetics, Inc. has decided to market a revolutionary new product for the consumer market. The problems of how to plan and control the various phases of this project—sales promotion, the training of salespeople, pricing, packaging, advertising, and manufacturing—are obvious to the management of this firm. They have asked you to guide them through this difficult venture using CPM, since time is of the essence. The first firm to market this type of product will reap substantial profits and will enhance its image by marketing such a revolutionary product. A list of the tasks, with the expected time duration for each, is given in the table in terms of weeks.

	Task	Precedence	Time (wk)
Manufacturing Activities			
A	Study equipment requirements	none	$\frac{1}{2}$
B	Select supplier of equipment	A	$\frac{1}{2}$
C	Study manufacturing procedures	B	2
D	Study quality control procedures	C	2
E	Study purchasing and inventory rules	B	2
F	Receive and install equipment	B	7
G	Place order for raw materials	E	1
H	Manufacture from raw materials for test and first production runs	G	3
I	Receive containers and packaging supplies	P	$\frac{1}{2}$
J	Have personnel available for first production run	F	0
K	Run manufacturing test	D, J, H, I, T	2
L	Run first production	K	6
Marketing Activities			
M	Price product	B, S	1
N	Do artwork for advertising	M	3
O	Send out advertising material and packaging orders to suppliers	N	$\frac{1}{2}$
P	Produce advertising and packaging materials	O	4
Q	Hold sales meeting	K, S	$\frac{1}{2}$
R	Training salespeople	Q	1
Accounting Activities			
S	Determine cost of the new product	B	1
T	Determine cost of the new product inventory	S	2

(a) Draw a CPM network for the problem.
(b) Identify the critical path, and determine its length.
(c) What happens to the critical path if activity S takes 2 weeks instead of 1 week?

8.9 Consider the construction project for a boiler house, described in the table.

	Task	Precedence	Duration (days)
A	Construct floor slabs	—	8
B	Erect boiler house frame	A	21
C	Construct chimney base	A	3
D	Erect precast chimney	C	6
E	Construct boiler bases	A	6
F	Position boilers	E	2
G	Construct pump bases	A	4
H	Construct oil tank piers	A	3
I	Position oil tanks	H	1
J	Construct oil line trenches	A	5
K	Position pumps	G	1
L	Install roof decking	B, D, F	8
M	Erect structures for chimney flue and vent	D	3
N	Erect flue headers	D, F	3
O	Brick out and fit burners	D, F	6
P	Fit boiler mountings and controls	F	2
Q	Install oil lines	F, I, J	10
R	Install water pipe system	F, K, L	25
S	Test pipe system	R	2
T	Install plant wiring	M, O, P, Q, S	20
U	Commission boiler house	N, T	1

(a) Draw a CPM network. Find the critical path. What is its length?

(b) The suppliers require the following delivery lead times: boilers, 90 days; burners, 105 days; oil tank, 60 days; pumps, 72 days. If construction is planned to begin (task A) on July 12, at what date do these various units have to be ordered at the latest so as not to cause any delay in the completion of the project?

(c) Find the amounts of total float and free float for each activity.

(d) The following jobs require the same skills:

(1) Concreting skills: A, C, D, E, G, H, J

(2) Carpentry skills: B, L

(3) Technical installations: F, I, K, Q, R, S

(4) Masonry skills: D, M, N, O

(5) Electrical wiring: P, T

Plan a schedule graph such that tasks requring similar skills have minimum overlap without causing any delay in project completion time.

8.10 A promoter is organizing a sports meeting. The task sequence and the most likely minimum and maximum durations of the tasks in days are as shown in the table.

	Task	Precedence	Mode	Minimum	Maximum
A	Prepare draft program	—	7	3	11
B	Send to sports organizations and wait for comments	A	21	14	28
C	Obtain promoters	A	14	11	17
D	Prepare and sign documents for stadium hire	A, C	2	2	2
E	Redraft program and request entries	B	$3\frac{1}{2}$	2	8
F	Enlist officials	D, E	14	10	21
G	Arrange accommodations for touring teams	E	4	3	5
H	Prepare detailed program	E, F	$4\frac{1}{2}$	4	8
I	Make last-minute arrangements	G, H	2	1	4

(a) Find the expected task durations and their variances.
(b) Draw a network, and find the critical path. What is the expected length of the critical path, and what is its variance?
(c) What is the probability that the length of the critical path does not exceed 56 days = 8 weeks?

8.11 A passenger–freight vessel is nearing the Golden Gate to berth in San Francisco. The activities listed in the table have to be performed before it can sail for Acapulco. All times are in hours.

	Activity	Precedence	Mode	Minimum	Maximum
A	Get towed to berth	—	2	$1\frac{1}{4}$	$2\frac{3}{4}$
B	Disembark passengers	A	1	$\frac{1}{2}$	2
C	Unload cargo	A	4	3	8
D	Carry out safety inspection	B, C	$1\frac{1}{2}$	1	$2\frac{1}{2}$
E	Refuel ship	D	3	3	4
F	Load cargo	C	5	4	10
G	Board passengers	E, F	2	1	4
H	Order tug	E, F	3	$2\frac{1}{2}$	$3\frac{1}{2}$
I	Leave port	G, H	$2\frac{1}{2}$	2	$3\frac{1}{2}$

(a) For this PERT network, find the expected task durations and the variances of each task duration.
(b) Draw a network, and find the critical path. What is the expected length of the critical path, and what is its variance?
(c) What is the probability that the length of the critical path does not exceed 12 hours? 17 hours?

8.12 A sociologist plans a questionnaire survey consisting of the tasks described in the table. All times shown in days.

	Task	Precedence	Mode	Minimum	Maximum
A	Designing questionnaire	—	5	4	6
B	Sampling design	—	12	8	16
C	Testing questionnaire and refinements	A	5	4	12
D	Recruiting interviewers	B	3	1	5
E	Training interviewers	D, A	2	2	2
F	Allocating areas	B	5	4	6
G	Conducting interviews	C, E, F	14	10	18
H	Evaluating results	G	20	18	34

(a) For this PERT network, find the expected task durations, t_{ij}, and the variances of task durations, σ_{ij}^2.

(b) Draw a network for this project, and find the critical path. What is the expected length of the critical path and its variance?

(c) What is the probability that the length of the critical path does not exceed 60 days?

8.13 A publisher has just signed a contract for the publication of a book. What is the earliest date that the book can be ready for distribution? The tasks in the table are involved, with time estimates given in weeks.

	Task	Precedence	Mode	Minimum	Maximum
A	Appraisal of book by reviewers	—	8	4	10
B	Initial pricing of book	—	2	2	2
C	Assessment of marketability	A, B	2	1	3
D	Revisions by author	A	6	4	12
E	Editing of final draft	C, D	4	3	5
F	Typesetting of text	E	3	3	3
G	Plates for artwork	E	4	3	5
H	Designing and printing of jacket	C, D	6	4	9
I	Printing and binding of book	F, G	8	6	16
J	Inspection and final assembly	I, H	1	1	1

(a) For this PERT network, find the expected task durations, t_{ij}, and the variances of task durations, σ_{ij}^2.

(b) Draw a network, and find the critical path. What is the expected length of the critical path, and what is its variance?

(c) What is the probability that the length of the critical path does not exceed 32 weeks? 36 weeks?

8.14 Holiday Prefabs Inc. assembles prefabricated vacation houses in its factory and transports them to the site, where they are attached to foundations. Each transaction covers the tasks listed in the table. Indirect project labor costs amount to \$100 per day.

	Task	Precedence	Time (days)		Direct Labor Costs	
			Normal	Crash	Normal	Crash
A	Inspection of site, preparation of plans	—	3	2	\$180	\$230
B	Leveling of foundation site, building of foundations	A	4	2	\$240	\$360
C	Construction of wall panels, floors, and roof, and assembly	A	5	2	\$800	\$950
D	Transportation to site and positioning on foundations	C	1	1	\$200	\$200
E	Attaching prefab to foundations, and final installations	B, D	4	2	\$220	\$350

(a) From the cost figures for normal and crash durations, determine the coefficients of the equations of $(c_{ij} - t_{ij}v_{ij})$ for each task.
(b) Find the critical path for normal task duration and the total labor cost associated with the project.
(c) Using the method described in Section 8-6, determine the least-cost schedule and the associated project duration.
(d) What is the total project cost for a minimum project completion time?

8.15 Consider the pipeline laying project described in the table, where the tasks for the various sections are overlapping. All costs are in thousands of dollars.

	Task	Precedence	Duration (days)		Direct Costs (\$)	
			Normal	Crash	c_{ij}	v_{ij}
A	Install pump 1	—	12	10	48	2
B	Dig trench section 1	—	4	3	15	3
C	Lay pipe section 1	A, B	6	3	48	4
D	Fill trench section 1	C	2	1	4	1
E	Dig trench section 2	B	6	4	21	3
F	Lay pipe section 2	C, E	8	5	64	4
G	Fill trench section 2	D, F	3	2	6	1
H	Install transmission pump	—	14	10	48	2
I	Dig trench section 3	E, H	4	3	15	3
J	Lay pipe section 3	F, H, I	6	3	48	4
K	Fill trench section 3	G, J	2	1	4	1
L	Dig trench section 4	I	4	3	15	3
M	Lay pipe section 4	J, L	6	3	48	4
N	Fill trench section 4	K, M	2	1	4	1
O	Connect pipe to terminal	M	3	2	12	2

(a) Determine the critical path for normal task duration, and draw a schedule graph. Allow all tasks to start at their earliest start times.

(b) The indirect costs amount to $6000 per week. Use the scheme explained in Section 8-6 to find the least-cost schedule. What is the total cost reduction achieved, and what is the decrease in project completion time? (Hint: The costs for sections 1, 3, and 4 are exactly the same; therefore, any time reductions can be made on all three sections in one iteration.)

8.16 The Sweetpeas Farmers' Cooperative is preparing for the coming season's bumper crop of peas. Unless the crop is processed within 4 weeks, part of it will have to be used as animal feed. In fact, fixed costs and product losses amount to $800/day during harvesting and processing of peas, but are only $250 during the remaining periods. Preparation and processing of the crop consists of the activities enumerated in the table.

	Task	Precedence	Duration (days) Normal	Crash	Direct Costs ($) c_{ij}	v_{ij}
A	Inspect pea plots, estimate crop size, arrange options, order cans and bags	—	12	8	1800	50
B	Prepare machinery for harvesting and processing	—	10	7	3000	80
C	Order cans (delivery lead time)	A	14	12	1500	100
D	Order plastic bags (delivery lead time)	A	21	16	1320	60
E	Hire picking and processing staff	A	10	6	3200	200
F	Harvest first batch of peas	B, E	2	2	2000	0
G	Harvest balance of peas	F	21	14	30,000	600
H	Process first batch of peas	F, C	3	3	3000	0
I	Process balance of peas* into cans and frozen goods	D, H	28	21	40,000	400
J	Arrange contracts for sale of canned and frozen peas	A	60	50	9000	50
K	Service, clean, and repair harvesting machinery	G	14	10	4000	80
L	Clean, service, and repair processing machinery	I	10	8	3000	100
M	Compile cost and revenue data, prepare profit statement for season	J, K, L	20	14	3400	70

*Harvesting and processing can occur simultaneously with a minimum lag of 2 days.

(a) Find the critical path for normal task duration, and draw a schedule graph allowing all tasks to be started at their earliest time. If the harvest (task F) is to start on July 15, on what day does the earliest task have to be started?

(b) Use the scheme explained in Section 8-6 to find the lowest cost of reducing the total time for harvesting and processing peas to 28 days. Any task that is part of harvesting and processing or that overlaps with it is eligible for reduction if feasible.

(c) Find the minimum-cost completion time for the entire project.

8.17 The Primalscream Counseling Institute is preparing a revolutionary therapy workshop. Being a cost-conscious leader, the manager of the institute has recourse to CPM (does not stand for consciousness-promoting method). The tasks are as shown in the table. Indirect costs amount to $500/week.

			Duration (wk)		Direct Costs ($)	
		Precedence	Normal	Crash	c_{ij}	v_{ij}
A	Workshop research	—	12	9	4200	200
B	Potential customer groups canvassed	—	7	5	3000	400
C	Workshop design	A	10	7	2600	200
D	Preparation of advertising brochure	A	4	3	1000	100
E	Preparation of workshop material, training of course leaders	C	11	6	3400	300
F	Mailing of workshop advertising	B, D	8	6	1400	100
G	Processing of applications	F	7	5	1000	100
H	Therapy workshop	E, G	3	2	1300	400

(a) Determine the critical path for normal task duration, and draw a schedule graph allowing all tasks to start at their earliest start time.

(b) Use the scheme explained in Section 8-6 to find the least-cost schedule. What is the total cost reduction achieved, and what is the decrease in project completion time?

REFERENCES

Burman, P. J. *Precedence Networks for Project Planning and Control*. London: McGraw-Hill, 1972. A voluminous 350-page text that covers most aspects of CPM from bar charting, project budgeting, use of computers, project control, to implementation with real-life type examples.

Elmaghraby, Salah E. "The Theory of Networks and Management Science: Part II," *Management Science*, Vol. 17, Oct. 1970. An expository treatment of activity networks, reviewing CPM, PERT, and some generalizations, where activities may not necessarily be executed, i.e., may be probabilistic: generalized activity networks (or GAN) and graphical evaluation and review technique (or GERT).

Horowitz, J. *Critical Path Scheduling*. New York: Ronald Press, 1967. A detailed and complete development of CPM and PERT and extensions at an elementary level.

Kaufmann, A., and G. Desbazeille. *The Critical Path Method*. New York: Gordon and Breach, 1969. As is the case for all of Kaufmann's books, this short text is concise, to the point, and well organized. More than a third is devoted to advanced approaches for cost minimization. Although it is at a higher level mathematically than most CPM texts, it is very practical, with excellent realistic examples.

Kelley, J. "Critical-Path Planning and Scheduling: Mathematical Basis," *Operations Research*, Vol. 9, May–June 1961. Critical path least-cost linear programming model that takes advantage of the problem's special structure to derive a solution algorithm more efficient than the simplex method.

Siemens, Nicolai, "A Simple CPM Time-Cost Tradeoff Algorithm," *Management Science*, Vol. 17, Feb. 1971. A simple algorithm ideally suited for hand computations is explained with an example.

Thornley, Gail, *Critical Path Analysis in Practice*. London: Tavistock, 1968 (paperback). This short text contains a collection of excellent papers on various aspects of project control including implementation, communication, and training.

Van Slyke, R. M. "Monte Carlo Methods and the PERT Problem," *Operations Research*, Vol. 11, Sept.–Oct., 1963. Uses simulation to determine a critical index (equal to probability) that a task is on the critical path.

Weist, Jerome D., and Ferdinand K. Levy. *A Management Guide to PERT/CPM*. Englewood Cliffs, N.J.: Prentice-Hall, 1969 (paperback). A thorough discussion at an elementary level of PERT, CPM, and various extensions.

CHAPTER NINE

Deterministic Dynamic Programming

In contrast to linear programming, *dynamic programming* is not a mathematical model with which we can associate an algorithm that can be programmed once and for all to solve all problems satisfying the assumptions of the model. Rather, dynamic programming is a *computational method*. It allows us to break up a complex problem into a sequence of easier subproblems by means of a *recursive relation*, which can be evaluated by *stages*. If you have never encountered this type of reasoning, you may find the mathematical notation somewhat strange, even confusing, and many of the basic concepts difficult to grasp. For this reason, learning about dynamic programming can be slow. It is only by studying a number of typical examples of different types that you will become accustomed to viewing a problem in terms of a recursive solution technique rather than a mathematical model. This is what we propose to do in this chapter. Here we deal only with deterministic problems; Chapter 14 studies stochastic problems.

9-1 A SOMEWHAT DISGUISED ROUTING PROBLEM

An electric power supply company considers upgrading one of its power transmission lines that serves a number of communities. A preliminary analysis indicates that four transformer stations will be able to economically supply all communities involved. However, each transformer station could be placed at a number of alternative sites. A detailed survey of the area also suggests alternative possible routes over which the transmission line could be taken. Figure 9-1 shows the network of possible transformer sites, represented by circles, and the alternative routes of the transmission line, depicted

Figure 9-1. A *routing problem.*

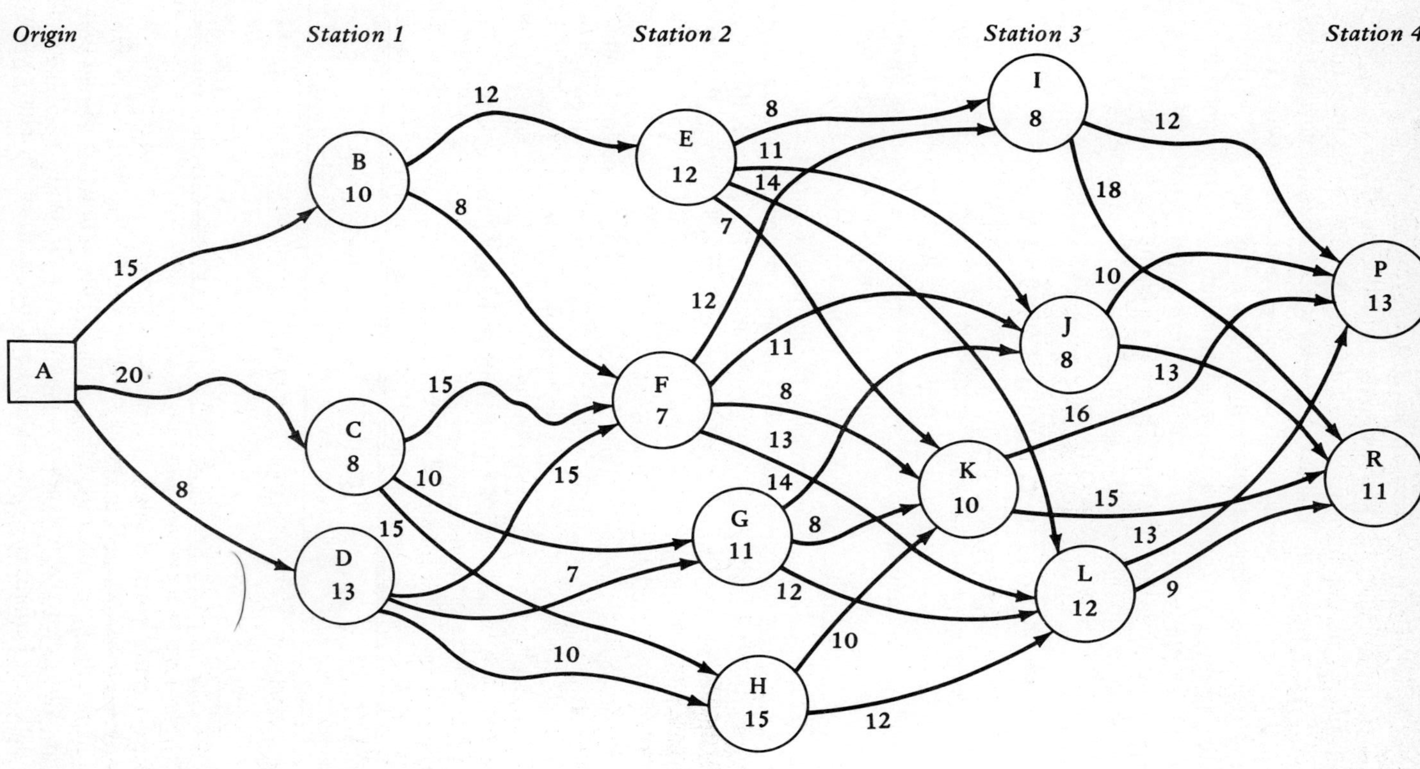

by links between circles. The number attached to each link gives the construction cost of each section of the transmission line, and the number in each circle is the cost ($100,000) of the transformer station and the additions to the feeder lines required for that site. Which route and set of transformer sites has the lowest total cost? For this simple example, it would be an easy matter to find the cheapest route by *enumerating* all possible combinations of links. Check that there are 52 different routes. For larger problems, complete enumeration requires an exorbitant number of computations. Dynamic programming reduces this computational effort through a streamlined partial enumeration scheme. Dynamic programming systematically discards any combination of links that can be identified as worse than some other combination.

9-2 SOLUTION OF ROUTING PROBLEM BY STAGES

The construction of the transmission line can be viewed as a *multi-stage process* in which each of the four stages involves the choice of a transformer site and the transmission line section to connect it with the preceding transformer (or the origin, in the case of the first section). Similarly, if we are to restrict our attention to only a subproblem—for example, the continuation of the transmission line from site B—the problem again can be viewed as a multi-stage process with a structure analogous to that of the original problem. Each stage involves the choice of a transformation site and the associated transmission line section. In this instance, only three stages remain to be completed. The same observation can be made not only for all other sites of the first transformer station, but also for the second and third transformer station, except that fewer stages are left to be completed.

This suggests an efficient line of attack for finding the optimal route. Let us say that by some means we are able to find that the minimum cost of completing the line to the best site for station 4 from each of the three alternative sites for station 1 is 67 for site B, 72 for site C, and 75 for site D. (The transformer cost for station 1 is already included.) It is now a simple matter to find the minimum cost from the origin A. From A we have the following choices:

Route	Cost of Line Section	Minimum Cost of Completing Line	Total Cost
From A to B	15	67	82
From A to C	20	72	92
From A to D	8	75	83

The lowest cost is achieved by running the section from A to B and then continuing on the best route from there. Thus, we could find the optimal route from the origin A to station 4 if we knew the optimal route to station 4 from each of the sites for station 1. Unfortunately, we do not have this information. However, we observed earlier that the problem of completing the line from each site for station 1 is also a multi-stage process. Hence, we could use the same trick as before if we knew the minimum cost of completing the line from each of the sites for station 2, and so on.

These "ifs" provide us with the basic idea underlying dynamic programming. Starting with only one stage to be completed, we find the minimum cost of completing the line for each site of station 3. Then, working backward stage by stage, we evaluate the minimum cost of completing the line from each site of the preceding station until we have reached the origin A and found the overall minimum-cost solution. For each site, we ask the hypothetical question: "If we were to complete the line from this site with n stages left to go, what would be the best site to go to?" At each node we thus carry forward only the minimal-cost combination from that node on, eliminating all other combinations from further consideration. It is this feature that so drastically reduces the number of enumerations. Note, though, that we have to answer the hypothetical question separately from each site at each stage, as we do not know at this moment in our evaluation which sites will be on the optimal route for the whole problem.

Figure 9-2 shows the evaluation for the entire network. Note that we number the stages backward, starting at the end (i.e., in reverse order of the stations), so that the stage number gives the number of stages left to be completed. We start out by recording the cost of each of the two possible sites for station 4, which is at the end of the line. These costs are inserted in the square boxes above the circles depicting sites P and R. We now evaluate the best decision for each site of station 3 (i.e., at stage 1, or with one stage left to be completed). What is the best decision for site I?

Choice	Cost of Station at Site I	Cost of Line Section	Cost at Last Site	Total
Route I to P	8	12	13	33
Route I to R	8	18	11	37

The best decision at site I is a line to site P, at a cost of 33. These computations are shown in the box attached to circle I. The best site to go to next is indicated by the letter P at the top right-hand corner of the box. We now proceed to evaluate each of the other three sites at that stage. Verify the computations in Figure 9-2 for all sites of station 3 (stage 1).

By now, knowing the optimal route from each site at stage 1, we can go back another step and find the best decision for each site at stage 2, or with two stages left to be completed, as shown in Figure 9-2. Proceeding in this manner, stage by stage, we finally evaluate the minimum cost for the origin A. Verify the calculations.

The optimal route from the origin A can be found easily by back-tracking the sequence of best decisions, given the best decision at site A. The optimal route leads us from site A to site B (as indicated by the letter B shown above the box attached to circle A), from site B to site F, from site F to site J, and on to site P at a total cost of 82. There is no solution that has a lower cost. Although such is not the case here, a problem may have two or more alternative optimal routes having the same minimum cost.

Figure 9-2. *Evaluation of a routing problem.*

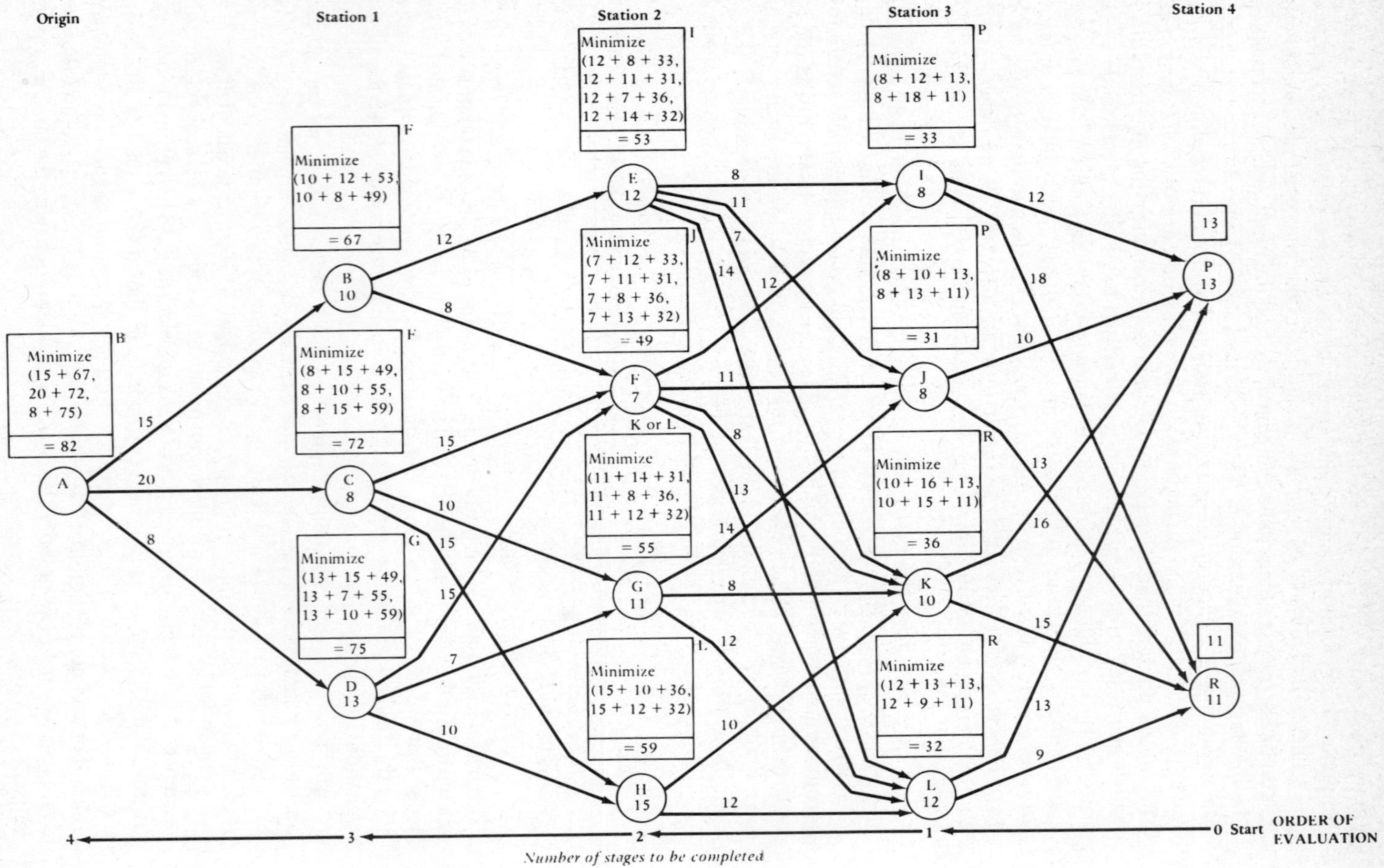

Origin | Station 1 | Station 2 | Station 3 | Station 4

A: Minimize (15 + 67, 20 + 72, 8 + 75) = 82 — B

B 10: Minimize (10 + 12 + 53, 10 + 8 + 49) = 67 — F

C 8: Minimize (8 + 15 + 49, 8 + 10 + 55, 8 + 15 + 59) = 72 — F

D 13: Minimize (13 + 15 + 49, 13 + 7 + 55, 13 + 10 + 59) = 75 — G

E 12: Minimize (12 + 8 + 33, 12 + 11 + 31, 12 + 7 + 36, 12 + 14 + 32) = 53 — I

F 7: Minimize (7 + 12 + 33, 7 + 11 + 31, 7 + 8 + 36, 7 + 13 + 32) = 49 — J

G 11: Minimize (11 + 14 + 31, 11 + 8 + 36, 11 + 12 + 32) = 55 — K or L

H 15: Minimize (15 + 10 + 36, 15 + 12 + 32) = 59 — L

I 8: Minimize (8 + 12 + 13, 8 + 18 + 11) = 33 — P

J 8: Minimize (8 + 10 + 13, 8 + 13 + 11) = 31 — P

K 10: Minimize (10 + 16 + 13, 10 + 15 + 11) = 36 — R

L 12: Minimize (12 + 13 + 13, 12 + 9 + 11) = 32 — R

P 13: 13

R 11: 11

4 ← 3 ← 2 ← 1 ← 0 Start — ORDER OF EVALUATION

Number of stages to be completed

The approach used to solve this problem contains most basic aspects of dynamic programming and the structurally related theory of *optimal control*, which will not be studied in this text. Solving problems by these two techniques consists of taking a particular process in stages from a given initial position to a desired ending position, passing through a sequence of alternative intermediate positions.

These positions—the alternative transformer sites, in our example—are referred to as *states*. The attributes of each state, or the *state description*, must contain all information relevant for future decisions about the process from that state on. The state description can be viewed as reflecting the cumulative effect of all decisions that can be made prior to reaching that state. In our example, the only piece of information relevant to deciding how to continue the route is the current site position. Many problems require us to specify several distinct elements of the process for a complete state description.

For every state at each stage, a decision has to be made. Any sequence of decisions that leads the process from the initial state to the desired state is called a *policy* in dynamic programming and a *trajectory* in optimal control theory. The objective is to find the *optimal policy*.

Note that in our example we started at the states where we wanted to end, i.e., sites P and R, rather than at the beginning, the origin A. Then we worked backward, stage by stage, until we reached the beginning. This particular formulation is called the *backward solution*. For each state at stage n, we found the optimal immediate decision for leaving that state, given n stages left to go. We also could have solved the problem by working forward, resulting in the *forward solution*. We then reword the crucial question to be answered at each state as, "If we were to reach state i after completing n stages, which would be the best state to come from?" Note: This implies that the state description now reflects all relevant aspects of the position in which the process ends after completing n stages, rather than those aspects of the position in which it starts, with n stages remaining. It is then convenient to number the stages in chronological order, starting from the beginning position rather than the ending position. It is clear that the optimal route (or routes, if alternative optima exist) will be the same for the forward and backward solutions.

We now suggest that you stop reading and solve this problem anew, using a forward solution approach. Draw the network on a sheet of paper, renumbering the stages. Use 0 for node A, 1 for nodes B, C, and D, etc. Once you have evaluated the optimal policy for both end nodes, (P and R), the overall optimal policy for the problem can be determined by taking the best of the two policies.

9-3 REVIEW AND IMPLICATIONS OF COMPUTATIONAL PROCESS

We shall now look at this problem in more general terms, using the backward solution. Let i_n be the state of the process with n stages remaining. A route from the initial state to the final state consists of a sequence of decisions. Each decision involves defining a link between two states at consecutive stages. A policy can thus be described by a sequence of pairs of states $(i_n, i_{n-1}), (i_{n-1}, i_{n-2}), \ldots, (i_1, i_0)$. With each link (k, j), we associate a cost t_{kj}, the cost of the *one-step transition* from state k to state j. In our example, this includes the cost of the transformer station at state (site) k plus the cost of the transmission line from state k to state j. For an N-stage process, the cost of each feasible policy is the sum of N variables,

$$\sum_{n=1}^{N} t_{i_n, i_{n-1}} \tag{9-1}$$

where consecutive pairs of states are properly linked together. We wish to find the optimal policy. In our example, this is the least-cost policy. In terms of expression (9-1), this is a minimization problem involving N variables—one variable for each stage of the process.

DECOMPOSITION OF PROBLEM

Dynamic programming decomposes an N-variable problem sequentially into N stages, where each stage involves optimization over one variable only.

Consider the truncated problem of being in state s with $n < N$ stages left to go. We have seen that this new problem has the same structure as the original problem. With this new problem we can associate an *optimal subpolicy*. Let $f_n(s)$ be the cost of this optimal subpolicy. We wish to stress that $f_n(s)$ is already the result of a minimization operation, not merely the cost of an arbitrary subpolicy. This optimal subpolicy depends on both the number of stages left to go (as indicated by the subscript n) and the state the process is in at that point (as indicated by the argument). We refer to s as the *state variable*. In our example, for $s = P$ and $s = R$ and $n = 0$ stages left to go, $f_0(P) = 13$ and $f_0(R) = 11$. From this we can determine $f_1(s)$. For instance, for $s = I$:

$$f_1(I) = \underset{i_0 = P,R}{\text{minimum}} \, [t_{I,i_0} + f_0(i_0)] = \text{minimum}\,[20 + 13, 26 + 11] = 33$$

In general,

$$f_1(s) = \underset{i_0}{\text{minimum}} \, [t_{s,i_0} + f_0(i_0)], \qquad \text{for all } s \tag{9-2}$$

Using the $f_1(s)$ evaluated in this fashion, we then proceed to find $f_2(s)$, etc., by the same principle. The generalization of expression (9-2) for stage n yields the following expression.

RECURSIVE RELATIONS OF DYNAMIC PROGRAMMING

$$(9\text{-}3) \qquad f_n(s) = \underset{i_{n-1}}{\text{minimum}} \, [t_{s,i_{n-1}} + f_{n-1}(i_{n-1})], \qquad \text{for all } s, \text{ all } n \geq 1$$

where $f_0(i_0) = c_{i_0}$ (= given constants).

At each stage, this recursive relation has to be evaluated for all values of the state variable. The recursive relations are based on the following principle, coined by the inventor of dynamic programming, United States mathematician Richard Bellman.

PRINCIPLE OF OPTIMALITY OF DYNAMIC PROGRAMMING

An optimal policy has the property that whatever state the process is in at a given stage and whatever the decision taken from that state, the remaining decisions must constitute an optimal subpolicy for the state resulting from this decision.

Or, an optimal policy must have the property that regardless of how the process entered into a given state, the remaining decisions must constitute an optimal subpolicy.

Or, the optimal policy can be formed only from optimal subpolicies.

The proof of this principle is found by contradiction. If the remaining decisions are not an optimal subpolicy, then the whole policy (of which the remaining decisions are a part) cannot be optimal. The principle of optimality contains the necessary condition which a problem must satisfy for it to be decomposable by dynamic programming.

INDEPENDENCE OF PRECEDING DECISIONS

The measure of effectiveness of a given subpolicy from any state depends only on the state the process is in and the number of stages remaining, but not on how the process entered that state.

The current state at any stage has to be a sufficient summary of all aspects of the current condition of the process that are relevant for future decisions or for the future performance of the process. The optimal subpolicy is then independent of the decisions made prior to reaching this state. In terms of the backward solution, this property implies that to find the optimal subpolicy from the current state, we only have to worry about decisions to be taken at the current and subsequent stages and can ignore decisions taken at all stages prior to reaching the current state. This allows us to effectively separate "past" and "future" decisions at each stage. However, this is not the same as asserting that the decisions taken at each stage are independent of all other stages. Clearly, the best decision in the current state depends on the best decisions at subsequent stages. On the other hand, if the best current decision also depended on decisions of preceding stages, the N-variable problem could not be decomposed into N one-variable problems unless the effect of these prior decisions could be summarized uniquely in the state description.

Note that these properties imply only that the overall measure of effectiveness to be optimized can be decomposed into n stages. Beyond this, there are no assumptions or restrictions on the particular mathematical form taken by the measure of effectiveness or by the state and decision variables. The functional relationships may be linear or nonlinear, and the variable may assume any real value or may be restricted to discrete values only. Dynamic programming always finds the overall optimum. Hand in hand with this, however, goes the fact that dynamic programming is not a mathematical model like linear programming, with which we can associate a computational algorithm and which can be programmed once and for all to solve all problems satisfying the assumptions of the model. Rather, dynamic programming is a computational method for solving certain problems that have a particular structure. So each problem usually requires its own tailor-made computer program that solves the problem by using this computational method.

Although dynamic programming solves problems in a sequential manner, not every multi-stage decision problem can be formulated by dynamic programming, nor is dynamic programming restricted to *a priori* multi-stage decision problems. In fact, many problems that do not involve a sequence of decisions can, by some trick, be converted to multi-stage decision problems. Hence, dynamic programming seldom reduces to rote, but leaves ample room for ingenuity and imagination. Thus, as a tool, dynamic programming is rather deceptive. A problem may look simple once it has been formulated, but prior to formulation it often looks forbidding.

9-4 A RENTAL DECISION PROBLEM

Problems that involve decisions to be made at specific points in time are natural multi-stage processes, and hence they are usually ideal for dynamic-programming formulations. Consider the following rental equipment problem.

A highway construction firm rents certain of its specialized earth-moving equipment from a leasing company as needed during the various phases of a construction job. Equipment has to be rented for full weeks, and it can only be obtained at the beginning of a week and released at the end of a week. Assume that the beginning of a week coincides with the end of the preceding week. The rental cost per week is \$200. Each time a unit is rented, there is a preparation and transport charge of \$120 by the leasing company. Each time a unit is returned to the leasing company, there is a servicing, cleaning, and transport charge of \$150. No units will be required after 6 weeks. Therefore, all units are released at the beginning of week 7. The number of units required during any time period of 1 week cannot be predicted exactly, since the requirement depends on a variety of factors, such as the weather and soil conditions. If, during any week, the construction firm has fewer units on hand than the number required, (i.e., the company is short), it has to farm out the excess work to a local contractor at a cost of \$400 per unit short per week or any part of a week. Table 9-1 shows the average number short for various possible numbers of units rented during each week of the planning horizon. Fractions denote units required for less than a full week. This information implies that in no week will more than 4 units be required, since no work is farmed out if 4 units are rented. Given that the firm has 3 units on hand initially, what is the rental policy that minimizes the total cost incurred over the entire 6 weeks?

Table 9-1. *Rental equipment problem: average number short*

Number of Units Rented/During Week n	Average Number Short $R_n(z_n)$					
z_n	$n = 1$	$n = 2$	$n = 3$	$n = 4$	$n = 5$	$n = 6$
0	1.2	2.0	0.2	0.5	2.2	2.0
1	0.4	1.0	0	0	1.2	1.0
2	0	0.3	0	0	0.4	0.2
3	0	0	0	0	0.1	0
4	0	0	0	0	0	0

What comprises a rental policy? It can be defined either in terms of the number of rental units on hand during each week or in terms of the change in the number of rental units on hand from week to week. Let us assume that the decision as to whether to increase or decrease the number of rental units on hand during a particular week is made at the beginning of that week. Thus, we define the decision variable

- $x_n > 0$ as the number of additional units hired at the beginning of week n, and
- $x_n < 0$ as the number of units released at the beginning of week n.

At the beginnning of week n, prior to any change, we start out with y_n rental units. So the number of units on hand during week n (and consequently at the end of the week) is

(9-4)
$$z_n = y_n + x_n$$

Since y_n is the number of units carried forward to period n from period $n - 1$, it follows that $y_n = z_{n-1}$. Eliminating y_n in equation (9-4) we have

(9-5)
$$z_n = z_{n-1} + x_n$$

with $z_0 = y_1 = 3$, as stated earlier.

The cost of a rental decision during period n consists of

$$\begin{bmatrix}\text{Cost in}\\ \text{period}\end{bmatrix} = \begin{bmatrix}\text{Cost of hiring}\\ \text{or releasing units}\end{bmatrix} + \begin{bmatrix}\text{Rental}\\ \text{cost}\end{bmatrix} + \begin{bmatrix}\text{Cost of}\\ \text{being short}\end{bmatrix}$$

(9-6) $$C_n(x_n, z_n) = \begin{bmatrix} 120x_n & \text{for } x_n \geq 0 \\ -150x_n & \text{for } x_n < 0 \end{bmatrix} + 200z_n + 400R_n(z_n)$$

(Do you understand why the coefficient of x_n in the bottom part of the first term of expression (9-6) has to be negative?)

Expressions (9-5) and (9-6) hold for each of the first 6 periods. At the beginning of period 7, all units are returned. Hence, $x_7 = -z_6$, implying $z_7 = 0$, and (9-6) simplifies to

(9-7) $$C_7(x_7 = -z_6, z_7 = 0) = 150z_6$$

The total cost over all 7 periods is given as the sum

(9-8) $$\sum_{n=1}^{7} C_n(x_n, z_n)$$

We wish to determine values for x_n, $n = 1,2, \ldots, 7$, so as to minimize (9-8).

9-5 DYNAMIC PROGRAMMING FORMULATION OF THE RENTAL PROBLEM

Let us solve this problem using a forward formulation. The first task is to determine

1. What aspects of the problem represent the stages?
2. What are the decision variables at each stage?
3. What aspects uniquely define the state variable?
4. How is the new state defined in terms of the current state and the decision taken at that state—or the *state transformation function?*

Since a decision must be made at the beginning of each of 7 periods, the periods become the stages, $n = 1,2, \ldots, 7$. For a forward formulation, we number the stages in the chronological sequence of the periods. We have already seen that the change in the number of units rented, x_n, is the decision variable at each stage (period). The choice of the state variable is often the most difficult part of a formulation. For inventory-type problems that involve carrying stocks of goods over time, the number of units on hand usually gives a complete description of the state of the process. It summarizes in one number all of the past history and is all that must be known to continue the process into the future. The number of rental units is a type of stocks. For a forward formulation, the state description refers to the position in which the process ends up after the decision is made at stage n. Hence, the ending stock level—in our case, the number of rental units on hand at the end of a period, z_n—is the correct choice of state variable. Since the number of units on hand cannot be negative, and since more than 4 units are never needed in any period, $z_n = 0, 1, 2, 3,$ or 4, for $n = 1, \ldots, 6$. The *initial state* is given as $z_0 = 3$ and the desired *final state* as $z_7 = 0$. Given z_n, the value of the state variable at the preceding stage (z_{n-1}) is uniquely defined for each value of the decision variable. By equation (9-5), the state transformation function is thus

(9-9) $$z_{n-1} = z_n - x_n, \qquad n = 1, \ldots, 7$$

Note that any dynamic programming problem with discrete outcomes can be represented as a network, as in Figure 9-2. We suggest that you now take a break and draw the network associated with this problem. The nodes are given by the values of z_n, while the links represent the values of x_n.

Now we are ready to formulate the recursive relation of dynamic programming. It states that the optimum cost to reach state z_n after n transitions is given by the minimum, over all feasible values of the decision variable x_n, of the sum of the immediate cost in period n and the cost of the optimal policy for state z_{n-1} resulting from z_n and the choice of x_n. If we let

(9-10) $$f_0(z_0) = 0, \qquad \text{for all } z_0 \text{ (we only need } z_0 = 3)$$

then

(9-11) $$f_n(z_n) = \underset{x_n \leq z_n}{\text{minimum}} \, [C_n(x_n, z_n) + f_{n-1}(\underbrace{z_n - x_n}_{z_{n-1}})], \qquad \text{for all } z_n, \text{ all } n \geq 1$$

9-6 EVALUATION OF RECURSIVE RELATION FOR RENTAL PROBLEM

To evaluate the recursive relation, we need two tables at each stage n. The first one, referred to here as table 1, contains the $f_{n-1}(z_{n-1})$ values determined at the preceding stage. The second, referred to here as table 2, is used to find $f_n(z_n)$ using the recursive relation (9-11). For $n = 1$, table 1 consists of the single number $f_0(z_0 = 3) = 0$. Determining table 2 for $f_1(z_1)$ is also trivial. Since $z_0 = 3$, it follows by equation (9-9) that x_1 can assume only one value for each value of z_1, namely $x_1 = z_1 - 3$, and (9-11) simplifies to $f_1(z_1) = C_1(x_1, z_1)$. The value of $f_1(z_1)$ must be determined for all viable values of z_1.

Often, the range of values of the state variable for which the recursive relation has to be evaluated cannot be inferred exactly from the problem. This is the case for most inventory control problems. We then make a first educated guess and subsequently alter it as necessary during the computations. For our example, however, the exact range can be inferred from the shortage data in Table 9-1. As stated earlier, $z_n = 0$, 1, 2, 3, and 4.

Table 9-2 shows the evaluation of $f_1(z_1)$ (this is table 2 for $n = 1$). Let us show how the cost for $z_1 = 0$ is obtained. $z_1 = 0$ implies that $x_1 = -3$. From Table 9-1, $R_1(z_1 = 0) = 1.2$. Hence, by expression (9-6), we have

$$C_1(-3, 0) = -150(-3) + 200(0) + 400(1.2) = 930$$

Table 9-2. *Table 2 for n = 1*

(1) z_1	(2) x_1	(3) $C_1(z_1, x_1)$	(4) $f_1(z_1)$
0	−3	930	930
1	−2	660	660
2	−1	550	550
3	0	600	600
4	+1	920	920

For $n = 2$, table 1 is formed of columns (1) and (4) of Table 9-2. It is convenient to include additional columns in table 2 for this and later stages, as is shown in Table 9-3, which displays the computations for stages 2 and 3.

Table 9-3. *Table 2 for n = 2 and 3*

n	(1) z_n	(2) x_n	(3) $C_n(z_n, x_n)$	(4) $z_{n-1} = z_n - x_n$	(5) $f_{n-1}(z_{n-1})$	(6) Total	(7) $f_n(z_n)$
2	0	−4	1400	4	920	2320	
		−3	1250	3	600	1850	
		−2	1100	2	550	1650	
		−1	950	1	660	1610	1610
		0	800	0	930	1730	
	1	−3	1050	4	920	1970	
		−2	900	3	600	1500	
		−1	750	2	550	1300	
		0	600	1	660	1260	1260
		1	720	0	930	1650	
	2	−2	820	4	920	1740	
		−1	670	3	600	1270	
		0	520	2	550	1070	1070
		1	640	1	660	1300	
		2	760	0	930	1690	
	3	−1	750	4	920	1670	
		0	600	3	600	1200	1200
		1	720	2	550	1270	
		2	840	1	660	1500	
		3	960	0	930	1890	
	4	0	800	4	920	1720	
		1	920	3	600	1520	1520
		2	1040	2	550	1590	
		3	1160	1	660	1820	
		4	1280	0	930	2210	

To illustrate some of the calculations in Table 9-3, let us outline how the value for $f_2(z_2 = 0)$ was determined. By equation (9-9), x_2 can assume values of -4, -3, -2, -1, and 0, implying values for z_1 of 4, 3, 2, 1, and 0, respectively, as shown in columns 2 and 4 of Table 9-3. For each x_2, we find $C_2(x_2, z_2)$, using expression (9-6). Next, we find in Table 9-2 (which is now table 1 for $n = 2$) the value of $f_1(z_1)$ associated with each choice of x_2 (repeated in column 5 of Table 9-3); and we find the sum of corresponding pairs of $C_2(x_2, z_2)$ and $f_1(z_1)$ (columns 3 and 5), shown in column 6. By the recursive relation (9-11), $f_2(z_2 = 1)$ is the minimum of the values in column 6, i.e., 1610—the value for $x_2 = -1$.

The same computations are done for each of the other 4 states at stage 2. Columns 1 and 7 of Table 9-3 for $n = 2$ now form table 1 for the computations at stage $n =$

n	(1) z_n	(2) x_n	(3) $C_n(z_n, x_n)$	(4) $z_{n-1} = z_n - x_n$	(5) $f_{n-1}(z_{n-1})$	(6) Total	(7) $f_n(z_n)$
3	0	−4	680	4	1520	2200	
		−3	530	3	1200	1730	
		−2	380	2	1070	1450	1450
		−1	230	1	1260	1490	
		0	80	0	1610	1690	
	1	−3	650	4	1520	2170	
		−2	500	3	1200	1700	
		−1	350	2	1070	1420	1420
		0	200	1	1260	1460	
		1	320	0	1610	1930	
	2	−2	700	4	1520	2220	
		−1	550	3	1200	1750	
		0	400	2	1070	1470	1470
		1	520	1	1260	1780	
		2	640	0	1610	2250	
	3	−1	750	4	1520	2270	
		0	600	3	1200	1800	
		1	720	2	1070	1790	1790
		2	840	1	1260	2100	
		3	960	0	1610	2570	
	4	0	800	4	1520	2320	
		1	920	3	1200	2120	
		2	1040	2	1070	2110	2110
		3	1160	1	1260	2420	
		3	1280	0	1610	2890	

3. There is never any need to explicitly write out table 1. Table 9-3 also contains the computations for $n = 3$.

As you can see, the number of computations even for a simplified problem like this one becomes enormous. For space reasons, we will not show the detailed table 2 computations for stages 4 through 6. It is imperative, though, that you construct these tables yourself. So that you may verify the correctness of your work, we summarize

Table 9-4. *$f_n(z_n)$ evaluated for all 7 stages*

Stage	z_n	$f_n(z_n)$	Optimal x_n	z_{n-1} Implied
1	0	930	−3	3
	1	660	−2	3
	→ 2	550	→ −1	3
	3	600	0	3
	4	920	1	3
2	0	1610	−1	1
	1	1260	0	1
	→ 2	1070	→ 0	→ 2
	3	1200	0	3
	4	1520	1	3
3	0	1450	−2	2
	→ 1	1420	→ −1	→ 2
	2	1470	0	2
	3	1790	1	2
	4	2110	2	2
4	0	1650	0	0
	→ 1	1620	→ 0	→ 1
	2	1870	0	2
	3	2190	1	2
	4	2510	2	2
5	0	2530	0	0
	→ 1	2300	→ 0	→ 1
	2	2300	1	1
	3	2500	2	1
	4	2780	3	1
6	0	3250	−1	1
	→ 1	2900	→ 0	→ 1
	2	2780	0	2
	3	3020	1	2
	4	3340	2	2
7	0	3050	−1	→ 1

in Table 9-4 the $f_n(z_n)$ values and the corresponding optimal x_n values for all 7 stages. Since all units are to be returned at the beginning of week 7, $z_7 = 0$ is the only value of the state variable that has to be evaluated at the last stage. The minimum cost of the optimal rental policy is seen to be $f_7(z_7 = 0) = 3050$. We can now back-track through this table to find the optimal policy. The last line in Table 9-4 indicates that the optimal $x_7 = -1$. Equation (9-9) implies that $z_6 = 1$. We now go to the panel for $n = 6$, and find the optimal decision associated with $z_6 = 1$. This is $x_6 = 0$. Again, equation (9-9) implies that $z_5 = 1$, and from the panel for $n = 5$ and $z_5 = 1$ we find the optimal $x_5 = 0$. Continuing in this fashion, as shown by the arrows in Table 9-4, we find that the optimal policy is

Week	1	2	3	4	5	6	7
Number of units rented	2	2	1	1	1	1	0
Change from previous week	−1	0	−1	0	0	0	−1

This example also could be solved using the backward solution. It goes without saying that the optimal solution would be the same.

9-7 COMPUTATIONAL ASPECTS

As was true for linear programming, few real-life dynamic programming problems are ever solved by hand. Although dynamic programming, in comparison with complete enumeration, tremendously reduces the number of evaluations, the computational effort is still very large. Therefore, the analyst usually writes a computer program to perform the computations.

Figure 9-3 shows a flow chart of the sequence of computations for the rental problem, which could serve as a basis for such a computer program. The evaluation of the recursive relation for all types of problems has basically the same nested structure of an outer loop on the stages, a middle loop on the values of the state variable, and an inner loop on the values of the decision variable. It is mainly the cost, or return function, and the determination of the state transformation function in the heavy-lined box that will change from problem to problem.

9-8 A RESOURCE ALLOCATION PROBLEM

A firm operates three factories located on the same river. All three factories discharge their industrial waste water into the river with little or no processing. As a result, the water quality of the river has suffered severely. Under pressure from government and

Figure 9-3. *Flow chart of computations.*

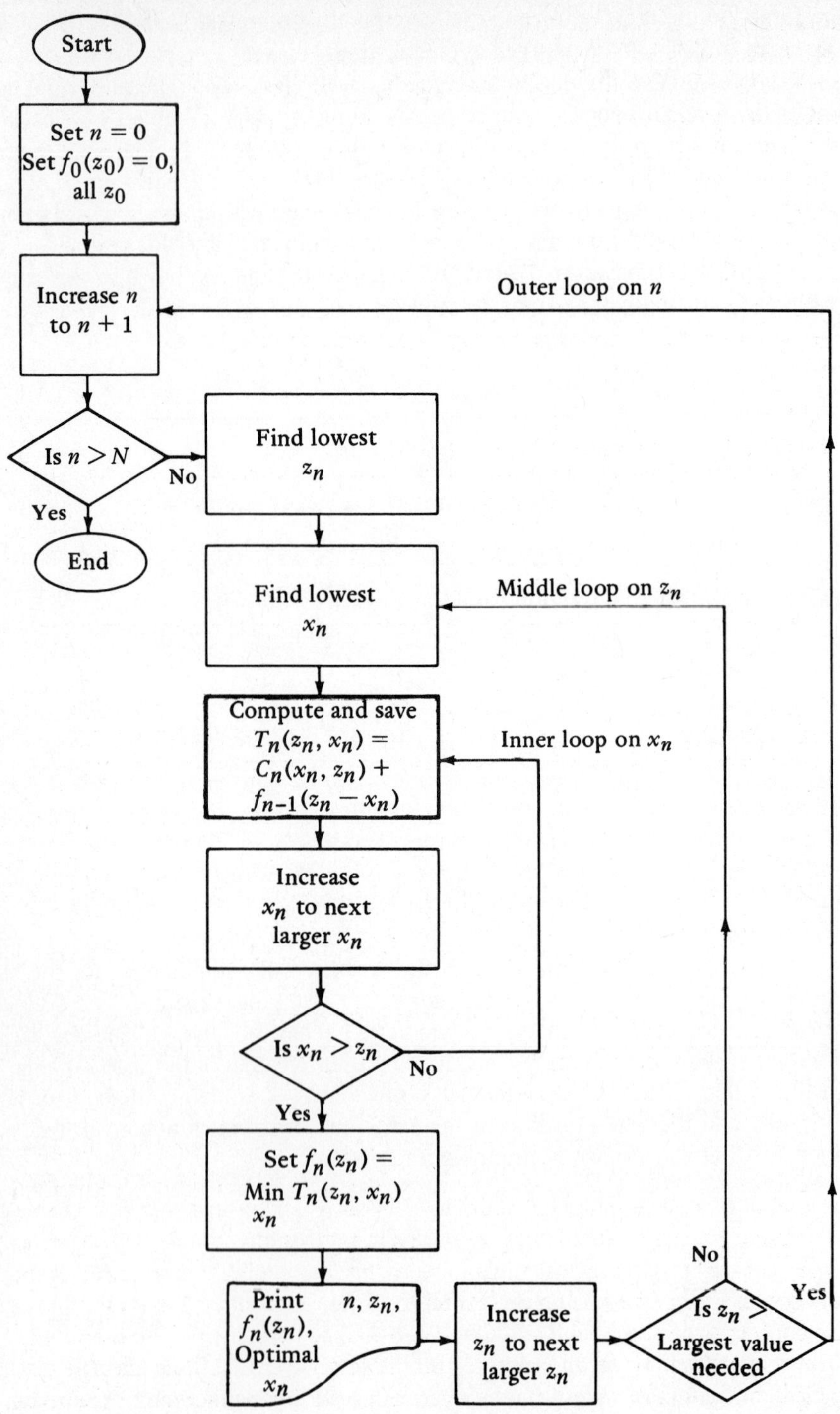

various citizens groups, the management of the three factories decides to implement a joint plan for waste water treatment, so as to upgrade the water quality of the river to a standard that would permit the river to purify itself prior to reaching a main recreational area. A water pollution expert is called in. Her analysis indicates that the total biological oxygen demand on the river water by all three factories combined should not exceed 1.6 parts per million (PPM).

Each factory can process waste water either by primary treatment only, by primary and secondary treatment, or by primary, secondary, and tertiary treatment, each method reducing the oxygen demand of the treated effluent to progressively lower levels. Table 9-5 lists the oxygen demand by each factory for the various degrees of waste water treatment and lists the cost of the installations.

Table 9-5. *Oxygen demand and installation costs*

Highest Degree of Treatment	Oxygen Demand (PPM x_{nj})			Installation Costs ($1000's)		
	Factory			Factory		
	$n = 1$	$n = 2$	$n = 3$	$n = 1$	$n = 2$	$n = 3$
$j = 0$: none	1.2	0.8	1.6	0	0	0
$j = 1$: primary	0.6	0.6	1.0	80	40	100
$j = 2$: secondary	0.2	0.4	0.6	140	80	150
$j = 3$: tertiary	0	0	0	170	140	220

Management wants to determine the degree of treatment at each factory such that the sum of the oxygen demand by all three factories does not exceed 1.6 PPM, minimizing the combined cost for all installations.

This problem, a version of allocating a scarce resource to a number of competing uses, goes under the descriptive name of the *knap-sack problem* (or the *fly-away-kit problem*). The scarce resource to be allocated is the river's capacity to support a certain amount of oxygen demand. It is to be allocated in an optimal fashion to one or several uses or activities (in our case, to the natural biological purification of partially treated effluent from each factory).

Our first task in solving this problem by dynamic programming is to identify the decision variables, the stages, the state variable, and the state transformation function. The highest degree of treatment to be used in each factory is the natural choice for the decision variable. Recall that we associate a decision variable with each stage. Hence, each factory represents a stage. Note that this problem is not really a multi-stage decision process. All three decisions have to be made at the same time. The stage concept—the uses of the resource—is introduced artificially. The amount of the scarce resource left to be allocated at each stage serves as the state variable. By the principle of optimality, the formulation implies the following type of reasoning: If there is an amount s of the resource left to be allocated to the nth, $(n - 1)$th, . . ., second, and first use (or factory, in our case), and we allocate an amount x_{nj} to the nth use, then the balance of the resource $(s - x_{nj})$ is to be allocated optimally to the remaining $n - 1$ uses. $(s - x_{nj})$ is thus the state transformation function from stage n to stage $n - 1$.

Starting with $n = 1$ (only one factory left), we find the optimal use of an amount s of the resource left. We do this for every possible value of s. Knowing the optimal use for the first factory, we next find the optimal allocation over two stages, i.e., over the second and first factories, for each value of s. Finally, we find the optimal allocation over three stages for $s = 1.6$.

We now translate this reasoning into mathematics. Let $f_n(s)$ be the minimum cost of optimally allocating an amount s of the resource to the first n factories. If c_{nj} is the cost, and x_{nj} is the oxygen demand of alternative j for factory n, then

$$f_1(s) = \underset{\substack{j \\ x_{1j} \leqslant s}}{\text{minimum}}\, c_{1j} \tag{9-12}$$

and

$$f_n(s) = \underset{\substack{j \\ x_{nj} \leqslant s}}{\text{minimum}}\, [c_{nj} + f_{n-1}(s - x_{nj})], \qquad n > 1 \tag{9-13}$$

Note that by defining $f_0(s) = 0$, for all s, we can use expression (9-13) also for $n = 1$. The condition $x_{nj} \leqslant s$ guarantees that the minimum is chosen only over those alternatives that have an oxygen demand not exceeding the amount left to be allocated. The state variable ranges over the values 0 to 1.6. Since all oxygen demands are multiples of 0.2, $f_n(s)$ has to be evaluated only for $s = 0, 0.2, 0.4, \ldots, 1.4$, and 1.6. Table 9-6 shows the computations. The evaluation for $n = 1$ is trivial. The minimum is always obtained for the lowest degree of treatment feasible for the given value of s. At stage 3, we need to evaluate $f_3(s)$ only for $s = 1.6$. However, it is interesting to perform some sensitivity analysis with respect to the maximum oxygen demand, which is the reason for computing $f_3(s)$ for all values of s.

Table 9-6. *Evaluation of the water pollution project*

(1) n	(2) s	(3) j	(4) x_{nj}	(5) c_{nj}	(6) $s-x_{nj}$	(7) $f_{n-1}(s-x_{nj})$	(8) Total	(9) $f_n(s)$
1	0	3	0	170	0	0	170	170
	→0.2	2	0.2	140	0	0	140	140
	0.4	2	0.2	140	0.2	0	140	140
	0.6	1	0.6	80	0	0	80	80
	0.8	1	0.6	80	0.2	0	80	80
	1.0	1	0.6	80	0.4	0	80	80
	1.2	0	1.2	0	0	0	0	0
	1.4	0	1.2	0	0.2	0	0	0
	1.6	0	1.2	0	0.4	0	0	0

(1) n	(2) s	(3) j	(4) x_{nj}	(5) c_{nj}	(6) $s-x_{nj}$	(7) $f_{n-1}(s-x_{nj})$	(8) Total	(9) $f_n(s)$
2	0	3	0	140	0	170	310	310
	0.2	3	0	140	0.2	140	280	280
	0.4	3	0	140	0.4	140	280	
		2	0.4	80	0	170	250	250
	0.6	3	0	140	0.6	80	220	
		2	0.4	80	0.2	140	220	
		1	0.6	40	0	170	210	210
	0.8	3	0	140	0.8	80	220	
		2	0.4	80	0.4	140	220	
		1	0.6	40	0.2	140	180	
		0	0.8	0	0	170	170	170
	→ 1.0	3	0	140	1.0	80	220	
		2	0.4	80	0.6	80	160	
		1	0.6	40	0.4	140	180	
		→ 0	0.8	0	→ 0.2	140	140	140
	1.2	3	0	140	1.2	0	140	
		2	0.4	80	0.8	80	160	
		1	0.6	40	0.6	80	120	120
		0	0.8	0	0.4	140	140	
	1.4	3	0	140	1.4	0	140	
		2	0.4	80	1.0	80	160	
		1	0.6	40	0.8	80	120	
		0	0.8	0	0.6	80	80	80
	1.6	3	0	140	1.6	0	140	
		2	0.4	80	1.2	0	80	
		1	0.6	40	1.0	80	120	80
		0	0.8	0	0.8	80	80	
3	0	3	0	220	0	310	530	530
	0.2	3	0	220	0.2	280	500	500
	0.4	3	0	220	0.4	250	470	470
	0.6	3	0	220	0.6	210	430	430
		2	0.6	150	0	310	460	
	0.8	3	0	220	0.8	170	390	390
		2	0.6	150	0.2	280	430	
	1.0	3	0	220	1.0	140	360	360
		2	0.6	150	0.4	250	400	
		1	1.0	100	0	310	410	
	1.2	3	0	220	1.2	120	340	340
		2	0.6	150	0.6	210	360	
		1	1.0	100	0.2	280	380	
	1.4	3	0	220	1.4	80	300	300
		2	0.6	150	0.8	170	320	
		1	1.0	100	0.4	250	350	
		0	1.6	0	0	310	310	
	→ 1.6	3	0	220	1.6	80	300	
		→ 2	0.6	150	→ 1.0	140	290	290
		1	1.0	100	0.6	210	310	
		0	1.6	0	0	310	310	

The optimal solution is shown by the arrows in Table 9-6. For a maximum permissible oxygen demand level of $s = 1.6$, the optimal solution calls for factory 3 to install $j = 2$, or primary and secondary waste water treatment; for factory 2 to install $j = 0$, or no treatment whatsoever; and for factory 1 to install $j = 2$, or primary and secondary treatment. The total cost is $290,000.

Figure 9-4 depicts the cost increase as the maximum permissible oxygen demand is decreased. An initial tightening of 0.2 PPM down to 1.4 PPM is relatively cheap; thereafter, the cost increases by about $30,000 per 0.2 PPM.

Figure 9-4. *Sensitivity of optimal solution to tightening of the effluent standards.*

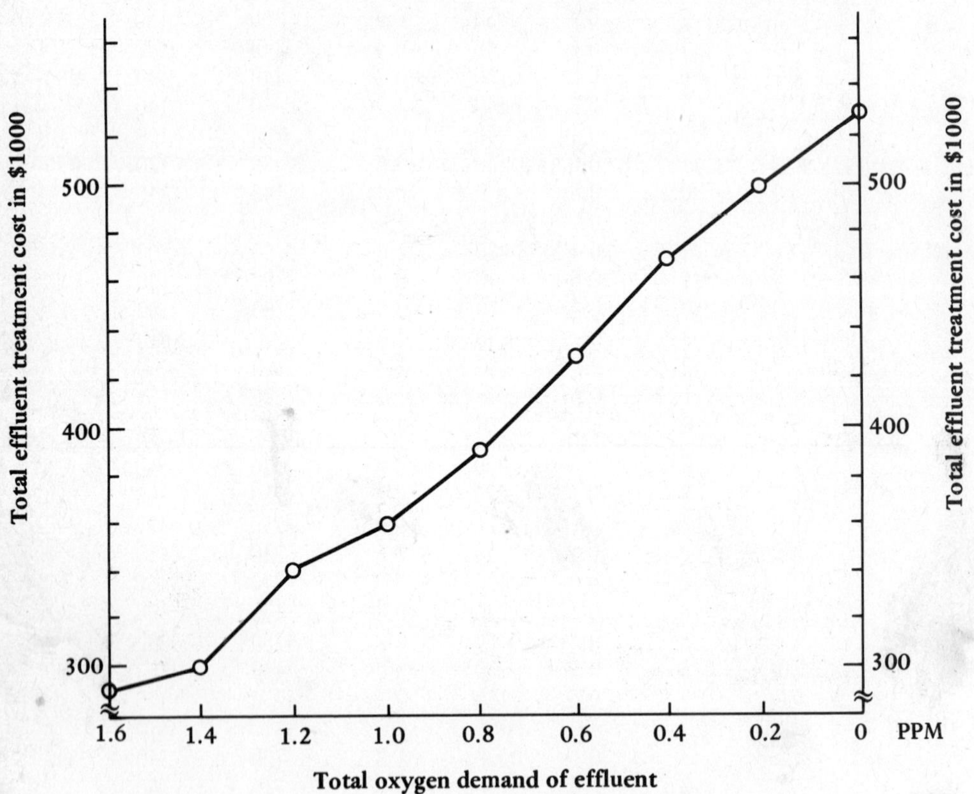

9-9 AN EQUIPMENT REPLACEMENT MODEL

As a piece of equipment, such as a machine, a truck, or an airplane, ages, its efficiency decreases, whereas operating and maintenance costs increase. Therefore, there comes a time when it becomes more economical to replace the equipment with a new, similar piece. What is the optimal time of replacement? This section deals with this question.

Pick-up trucks are subjected to a lot of beating. They age fast. Past records of a cartage contractor show the following pattern of operating and maintenance costs, opportunity costs of down-time (= lost revenue), and resale or salvage value for a given model, in dollars.

Year of operation	1	2	3	4	5	6
Operating and maintenance costs	8000	8200	9000	8400	9400	8800
Opportunity cost for down-time	1000	1100	1600	1200	2000	1600
End-of-year salvage value	14,000	12,000	11,000	8000	7000	5000

No truck was ever used for more than 6 years. The maintenance costs reflect major overhauls at the beginning of the third and fifth years. A new truck has a cost of $18,000. When should this model be replaced?

Let us initially look at this problem over an arbitrarily chosen planning horizon of 9 years. We start out with a new truck, and we will sell whatever truck we have on hand at the end of the ninth year. Starting with the second year, the owner must make a decision at the beginning of each year. The alternatives are to (1) keep the truck for at least another year, or (2) replace the truck with a new one of the same model. (Although models and prices change slightly over the years, such changes are assumed not to affect the relative operating characteristics to any major degree. The same operating data are thus assumed to be valid over the entire 9 years.)

The decision process is depicted graphically in Figure 9-5. The numbers in the circles denote the age of the truck prior to making a decision. We start out with a truck of age 0 (new). After 1 year, that truck is age 1 (1 year old). At that point, either we can keep it (top branch) and end up with a truck of age 2 at the end of year 2, or we can trade it in for a new truck (bottom branch) and have a truck of age 1 at the end of year 2, and so on. No truck is kept for more than 6 years. The numbers attached to the branches are the total net annual cost associated with the corresponding action. All branches leading to a one-year-old truck in years 2 through 9 are obtained as

$$\text{(purchase price of new truck)} - \text{(salvage value of truck replaced)}$$
$$+ \text{(sum of operating, maintenance, and down-time costs for new truck)}$$

For instance, branches leading from a 3-year-old truck to a 1-year-old truck have a cost of ($18,000 − $11,000) + ($8000 + $1000) = $16,000. The negative numbers shown at the end of the planning horizon are the cash inflows from salvage values of the truck.

The diagram immediately suggests that each year represent a stage and the age of the truck on hand at the end of a year serve as the state variable. Stage 10 represents

Figure 9-5. *Truck replacement problem—decision diagram.*

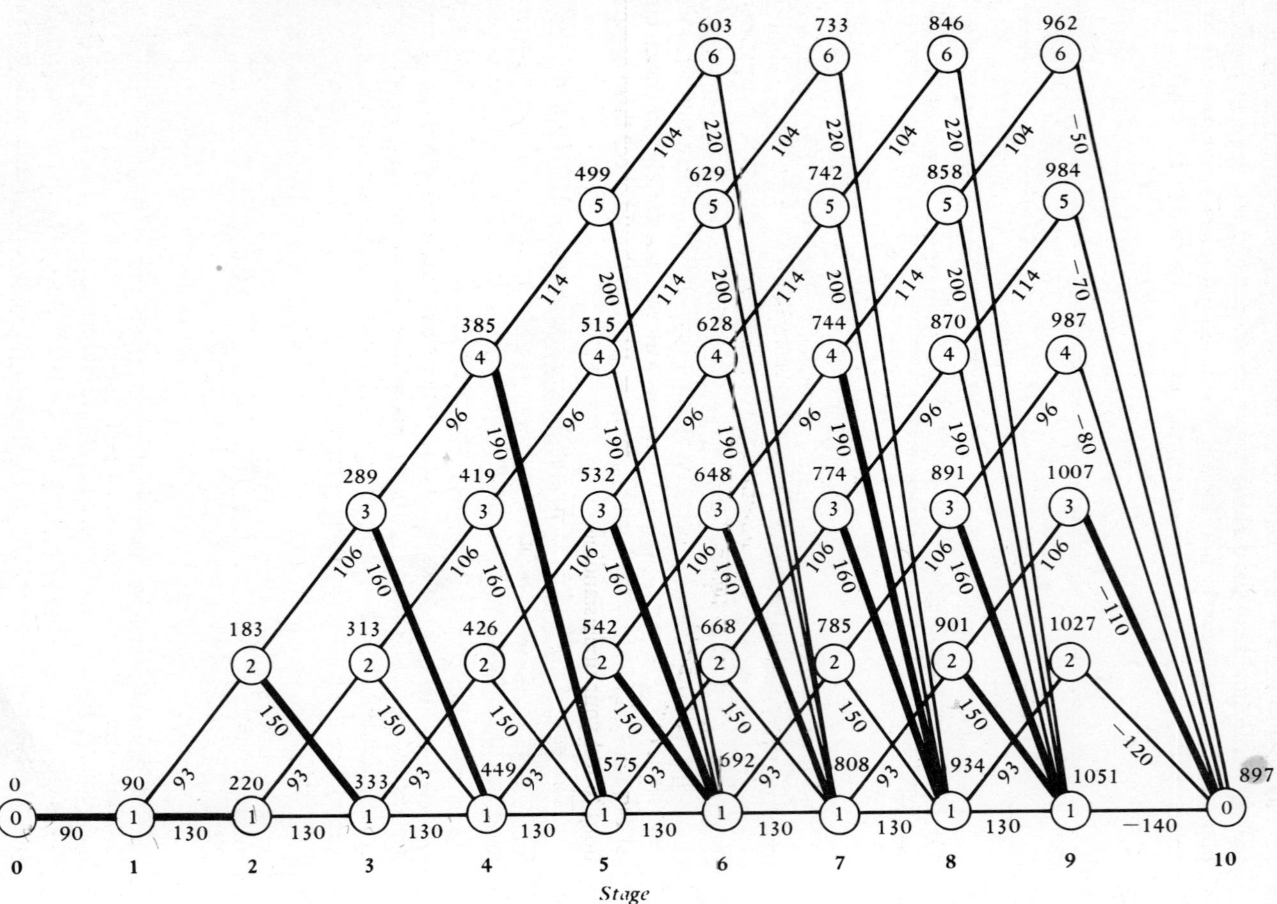

the action of selling the truck on hand at the end of year 9. The objective is to determine a policy that minimizes total costs over the planning horizon.

We shall use a forward formulation. Let $f_n(s)$ be the total minimum cost through period n if the truck on hand at the end of period n is of age s. Let c_s be the sum of all operating, maintenance, and down-time costs during a truck's sth year of operation. Let p be the purchase price of new truck, and let b_s be the salvage value of a truck of age s. Then

$$
\begin{aligned}
&f_1(1) = c_1 \\
(9\text{-}14)\qquad &f_n(s) = c_s + f_{n-1}(s-1), \qquad \text{for } s > 1 \qquad 1 < n \leq 9 \\
&f_n(1) = \underset{s}{\text{minimum}}\,[(p - b_s) + c_1 + f_{n-1}(s)], \qquad 1 < n \leq 9
\end{aligned}
$$

Finally, let f_{10} be the minimum cost, given that the truck is sold at the end of year 9:

$$
(9\text{-}15)\qquad f_{10} = \underset{s}{\text{minimum}}\,[f_9(s) - b_s]
$$

Note that only for $f_n(1)$, $n = 1, \ldots, 9$, and f_{10} does the evaluation of expressions (9-14) and (9-15) involve any minimization. All other terms of $f_n(s), s > 1$, are obtained by a simple addition of two numbers.

For a small problem like this, the diagram might as well be directly used for the evaluation of the forward solution. The number shown immediately above each circle in Figure 9-5 is $f_n(s)$ for $n \leq 9$, and f_{10} for $n = 10$. You should check these computations to test your understanding.

The heavy lines leading to the bottom row of circles (age 1) indicate the optimal action. The optimal action for stage 10 is to sell a truck of age 3. A heavy line leads from state 3 of stage 9 (end of year 9) to the end point. This implies that this truck was age 1 at stage 7 (end of year 7). The heavy line leading from state 3 of stage 6 to state 1 at stage 7 indicates that a truck replacement occurred at the end of year 6. Tracing the optimal policy back to the initial point in this manner, we see that the first truck was replaced at the end of year 3. So for a 9-year horizon the optimal policy is to replace the truck every three years.

9-10 ALTERNATIVE FORMULATION OF REPLACEMENT PROBLEM—A REGENERATION MODEL

Each time a replacement occurs, the process of aging starts anew. The owner also has to decide again how long the new truck should be kept until that truck in turn is replaced. In other words, at each replacement the process regenerates itself. The replacement is a *regeneration point*. The time between replacements is the *regeneration period*. Viewed from this angle, the replacement problem changes to one of finding the optimal sequence of regeneration periods.

Figure 9-6 shows the network of all possible regeneration periods for each year in the 9-year planning horizon. Each branch leaving a regeneration point represents

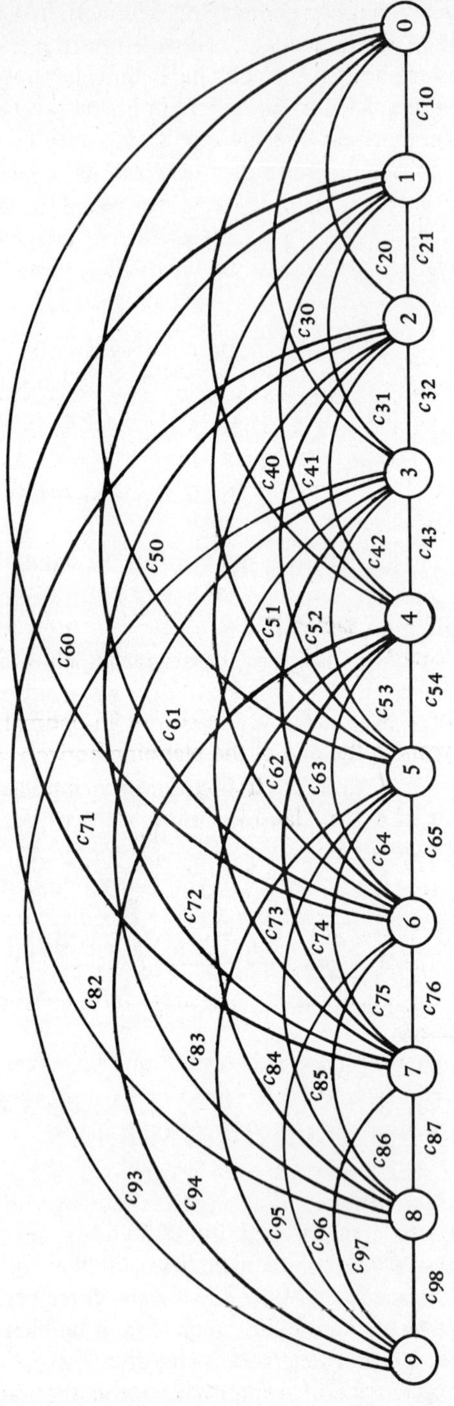

Figure 9-6. *Regeneration problem.*

one of the feasible regeneration periods. Since we wish to use a backward formulation, we have now relabeled the nodes in reverse chronological order, with n being the number of periods remaining until the end of the planning horizon.

Note how Figures 9-5 and 9-6 differ. In Figure 9-5, each year we could either keep a truck for another year or replace it. In Figure 9-6, we start with a new truck at each regeneration point. Hence there is no need to introduce a state variable for the age of the truck. In Figure 9-5, transitions are restricted to states in consecutive stages only. In Figure 9-6, we allow transitions from stage n to any stage $(n-k)$, where k denotes the length of a regeneration period. In our case, k may assume values 1, 2, . . ., 6.

Each regeneration period has a regeneration cost c_{ij}, where i and j are two consecutive regeneration points, $j < i$. c_{ij} covers the purchase price of the new truck obtained at the beginning of year i, all operating costs during years i through $(j + 1)$ (remember reverse chronological ordering), less the salvage value of a truck of age $(i - j)$. Let us also discount the cash stream. Then c_{ij} is the present value of the net cost at the beginning of year i. In the notation of Section 9-9, we find

$$c_{ij} = p + \sum_{s=1}^{i-j} \alpha^{s-1} c_s - \alpha^{i-j} b_{i-j} \tag{9-16}$$

where α^m is the discount factor over m years, $0 < \alpha \leqslant 1$. (See Section 1-13 for a review of discounting.) We assume operating costs are assessed as of the beginning of a year.

Let f_n denote the present value of the cost of an optimal regeneration policy over the remaining n years to the end of the planning horizon, starting with a new truck at the beginning of year n . From the relationships implied in Figure 9-6, we may derive the following recursive relations for this regeneration model:

$$f_n = \underset{k}{\text{minimum}}\,[c_{n,n-k} + \alpha^k f_{n-k}], \qquad \text{for } n = 1, 2, \ldots, N \tag{9-17}$$

Expression (9-17) embodies a special version of the principle of optimality. Namely, no matter what length k for the initial regeneration period is chosen at stage n, the policy over the remaining $(n - k)$ stages must constitute an optimal subpolicy of regeneration periods.

Table 9-7 shows the evaluation of expression (9-17) over all 9 stages for an annual discount factor of $\alpha = 0.9$. The row labeled $c_{n,n-k}$ shows the regeneration costs. For instance, the cost for $k = 2$ is obtained as follows:

$$c_{n,n-2} = 18{,}000 + (8000 + 1000) + 0.9(8200 + 1100) - 0.9^2(12{,}000) = 25{,}650$$

Each of the remaining 9 rows shows the total of $c_{n,n-k} + \alpha^k f_{n-k}$, for all feasible k. The numbers in parentheses give the next stage, $(n - k)$. The minimum in each row is f_n and is shown in boldface. The optimal replacement policy over an $n = 9$ year planning horizon is to keep the initial truck for $k = 6$ years and then replace it with a new one. Note that discounting tends to lengthen the optimal replacement period.

Replacement problems, like many other regeneration problems, frequently form part of an unspecified but potentially long sequence of regeneration decisions. At the

Table 9-7. *Evaluation of recursive relation for regeneration problem*

	$k = 1$	$k = 2$	$k = 3$	$k = 4$	$k = 5$	$k = 6$
$c_{n,n-k}$	14,400	25,650	35,937	45,706	54,301	61,918
$n = 1$	**14,400**(0)					
$n = 2$	27,360(1)	**25,650**(0)				
$n = 3$	37,485(2)	37,314(1)	**35,937**(0)			
$n = 4$	46,743(3)	46,427(2)	46,435(1)	**45,706**(0)		
$n = 5$	55,535(4)	54,759(3)	54,636(2)	55,153(1)	**54,301**(0)	
$n = 6$	63,271(5)	62,672(4)	62,135(3)	62,535(2)	62,804(1)	**61,918**(0)
$n = 7$	70,126(6)	69,634(5)	**69,257**(4)	69,284(3)	69,447(2)	69,571(1)
$n = 8$	76,731(7)	75,804(6)	75,522(5)	75,694(4)	**75,521**(3)	75,549(2)
$n = 9$	82,369(8)	81,748(7)	81,075(6)	81,333(5)	81,290(4)	**81,016**(3)

time of problem analysis only the initial decision will be implemented. The problem will be analyzed anew by the end of the initial regeneration period. The choice of a finite planning horizon is only an approximation for computational convenience. Hence, we want to make sure that the planning horizon chosen does not cause the initial decision to be adversely affected. In our example, it turns out that 9 years is just sufficient—8 years would be too short. Verify that the initial regeneration period of 6 years remains optimal as the planning horizon is lengthened to 10, 11, and 12 years.

What is the minimum length planning horizon needed? We shall not attempt to answer this question. Instead, we shall outline a method for finding an upper bound to this length. We established an optimal regeneration period for $N = 9$ of $k^* = 6$. This in itself does not mean much since $k = 6$ was also optimal at stage 6 but not optimal at stages 7 and 8. However, as you already verified, $k = 6$ remains optimal as we lengthen the planning horizon N to 10, 11, and 12. For $N = 12$, a $k^* = 6$ implies exactly 2 equal-length regeneration periods. We can thus assert that, were we to increase N to 18, the optimal policy over the 12-year problem would be an optimal subpolicy after the initial regeneration period of $k^* = 6$. But this is true for any N that is a multiple of 6. Hence, $k = 6$ must be the optimal policy as N goes to infinity.

This yields the following procedure to determine the initial optimal decision. Using a backward formulation, we determine the optimal regeneration period k for consecutively larger values of N. As N goes to $(N + 1)$, the optimal policy over N periods becomes the input for the $(N + 1)$-year problem. In terms of Table 9-7 this means we simply add another row. We stop as soon as we reach a value of N that is equal to $2k^*$, where k^* is the optimal initial regeneration period over the N-period planning horizon. k^* is then the optimal regeneration period at the beginning of the unbounded planning horizon.

*9-11 TWO OR MORE STATE VARIABLES

Sometimes more than one state variable is needed to provide a complete description of the state of a process. For instance, in the rental equipment problem, the firm may require equipment at more than one location. Equipment rented may be transferred from one location to another at a certain cost. Rather than have only one state variable for the total number of pieces rented, we introduce a separate state variable for each location. Similarly, the firm may rent more than one type of equipment, and costs may depend on the combination of equipment rented. Again, a separate state variable would be introduced for each type of equipment. In fact, most dynamic programming problems need more than one state variable.

There is no conceptual difficulty in having more than one state variable. However, there are severe computational limitations on the viable number of state variables. Let us look at the number of computations required to evaluate the recursive relation for more than one state variable. Assume that each state variable can take on 100 different values. Then, for two state variables there are 100^2 state combinations. This may not pose any problems other than increasing the computational time by 100-fold. For three state variables, the number of combinations at each stage is 100^3 (or 1 million), resulting in a 10,000-fold increase in computational time. For example, if a one-state variable problem takes one second of computation time on a computer, an equivalent three-state variable problem would take close to three hours. Since the number of decision variables of each stage may also increase to two or more as the number of state variables increases, the computational effort per state variable combination may increase manifold, compounding this problem even more. Furthermore, the amount of computer memory needed at each stage is now also at least two times 100^3 (if only f_n and f_{n-1} are stored). Therefore, for more than two state variables to be handled by internal memory alone, the number of states for each variable has to be drastically reduced. It is hardly ever feasible to go beyond three state variables. This explosion of the computational effort and the memory requirement has been aptly named *the curse of dimensionality of dynamic programming*. A number of special techniques and approximation procedures have been devised to overcome some aspects of dimensionality. Most are structure specific, i.e., they are only suitable if the problem has a certain mathematical form. They also will not find the global optimum unless the one-stage cost functions are U-shaped. For a more extensive discussion, see the texts listed in the references for this chapter.

*9-12 CONTINUOUS STATE VARIABLES

So far we have discussed the case where the state and decision variables assume only a finite set of discrete values. In fact, dynamic programming is admirably suited for discrete problems. If the state and decision variables may assume any real value a number of difficulties appear, and the temptation is great to make an arbitrary discrete approximation. For many applications, this is adequate. If the state variable is left real-valued, the usual approach to the problem is to evaluate the state variable for a discrete set of values only—a so-called *finite grid*.

Usually, state transitions will not necessarily be made only to values of the state variable that have been evaluated at the preceding stage. Hence, if f_{n-1} is needed for other values of the state variable, interpolation (usually linear) between the two adjacent grid points is used. Note again that no global optimum can be guaranteed then, since the global optimum may have been missed by the choice of an initial grid that was too coarse. This is, however, less a shortcoming of dynamic programming than a failure caused by an inadequate approximation.

9-13 SOME FURTHER APPLICATIONS

Dynamic programming has been used to solve a most diverse collection of problems. We will briefly highlight a few problems with deterministic state transitions.

1. *Resource allocation (knapsack-type problems)*: A limited amount of a resource—e.g., funds, space, carrying capacity, water—is available for allocation to several different projects or uses that all can be undertaken at several discrete levels of intensity. The objective is to maximize the total benefits over all project allocations. (Stage: each use type or project type; state: amount of unused resource left to be allocated over remaining uses; decision: level of intensity of each use.) The allocation of salespeople to sales regions is an example.
2. *Production scheduling over time*: A production facility with limited capacity has to be scheduled over time. The objective is to meet specified demands per period over a given planning horizon so as to minimize total production and inventory costs. (Stage: each period; state: inventory level; decision: amount to produce each period.)
3. *Assortment (or trim) problems*: A product is required for use in a number of sizes, widths, or strengths. It is produced or can be procured only in a limited number of standard sizes y_i, where $i = 1, 2, \ldots, I$. If the product is required at a size x other than one of the standard sizes y_i, then it has to be supplied from the next larger (wider, stronger) standard size, resulting in wastage. The problem is to find an assortment of $N < I$ standard sizes so as to minimize the wastage or the total cost of satisfying the given requirement combination. (Stage: one for each standard size used; state: length (or width or strength) of a standard size; decision: length (or width or strength) of the next smaller standard size used.)
4. *Multi-stage processing operations*: A product has to be processed in a prescribed sequence through a number of machines, each performing varying amounts of processing. For instance, a rolling mill consists of N independent stands, each stand reducing a strip of metal by a certain amount. The processing speed of a stand is a decreasing function of the amount of reduction. The objective is to maximize the overall processing rate of the mill. (Stage: each machine; state: amount of processing left to be done, e.g., input gauge of stand; decision: amount of processing done, e.g., output gauge of stand.) Other examples of this type occur in the management of biologically renewable resources, such as fisheries and forests. For instance, in forest management, each stand of trees can be subjected to a number of possible operations over time, such as thinning, pruning, selective logging, and clear-felling. The amount and the value of the

wood depends on the intensity and timing of these operations. The objective is to maximize the value of the forest stand. (Stage: age of trees; state: volume of wood standing; decision: intensity of operation, e.g., thinning.)

5. *Control of chemical processes:* A product has to go through a sequence of chemical reactions. The objective is to minimize the cost of the final product. (Stage: each reaction; state: composition or quality of entering material; decision: amount of catalyst or temperature, etc.)

EXERCISES

9.1 Consider the network shown in the illustration, where the numbers attached to the links are the distances between two points.

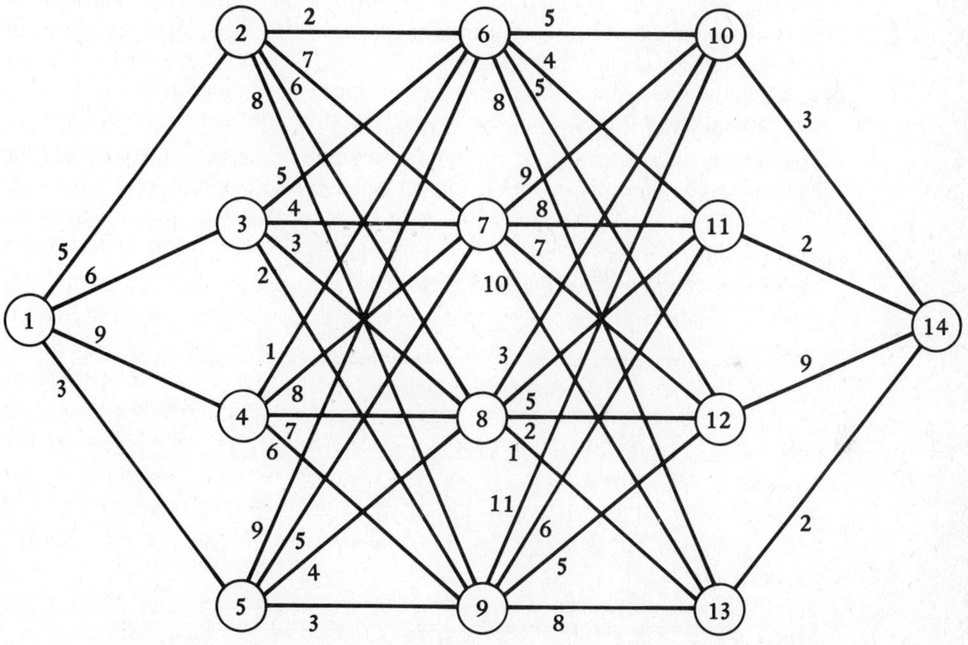

(a) Using the backward solution of dynamic programming, find the shortest path from point 1 to point 14.

(b) Using the forward solution of dynamic programming, find the shortest path from point 1 to point 14.

9.2 A firm has just developed a new product. Management figures that it has about three months before its main competitor will have a similar product on the market, and, therefore, wishes to contact as many potential customers as possible. The territory to be covered is divided into five sales areas. For each sales area, the incremental number of customers that can be contacted by the 1st, 2nd, 3rd, etc., salesperson within the three-month period is as follows.

		Sales Area 1	2	3	4	5
Number of Salespeople Assigned to the Area	1	31	36	40	28	32
	2	31	33	36	25	30
	3	30	31	32	24	29
	4	28	24	29	22	27
	5	25	20	25	12	18
	6	20	14	18	8	12
	7	12	9	10	0	6
	8	8	0	0	0	0

(a) The firm has ten salespeople trained for this promotion. Formulate the recursive relation of dynamic programming. Find the optimal assignment of salespeople to each sales area so as to maximize the number of potential customers contacted.

(b) How many additional customers could be contacted if the firm trained one additional salesperson? two additional salespeople?

(c) Is there any conceptual difference in the dynamic programming formulation between a forward and a backward solution for this problem?

9.3 A weather monitoring station is supplied once a month by air drop. The plane making the air drop has an excess weight capacity for nonessential items of W kg. Each month the weather station radios its needs for various nonessential items and assigns utility values for the first, second, . . ., kth unit of the item included in the shipment. On a particular occasion, the list is as shown in the table.

	Incremental Utility for Units					
Item	1st	2nd	3rd	4th	5th	Weight per Unit (kg)
1	12	8	4	0	0	2
2	15	5	1	0	0	3
3	6	6	5	4	2	1
4	8	5	2	1	0	1
5	20	10	0	0	0	4

The total excess weight capacity is $W = 10$ kg. Formulate the recursive relation of dynamic programming maximizing total utility, and use it to evaluate the optimal solution.

9.4 A firm is planning its advertising budget. Three different media are considered: television, glossy periodicals, and store promotions. The advertising agency comes up with the following proposals listed. The total amount of advertising funds available for the campaign is $40,000. The problem is to find the optimal combination of advertising media. This problem can be solved by dynamic programming.

Television ads:				
Number of time slots taken	1	2	3	
Total cost	$20,000	$30,000	$40,000	
Total number of potential customers reached (in 1000's)	180	280	320	
Glossy periodicals:				
Number of ad sequences	1	2	3	4
Total cost	$10,000	$20,000	$30,000	$40,000
Total number of potential customers reached (in 1000's)	120	190	250	300
Store promotions:				
Number of displays	1	2	3	4
Total cost	$10,000	$20,000	$30,000	$40,000
Total number of potential customers reached (in 1000's)	80	160	240	310

(a) What do you use as the stage, and what is the state variable? Formulate the recursive relation of dynamic programming. Clearly define in full detail all notations used.

(b) Solve the problem. Let the state variable assume only discrete values in multiples of 10,000. What is the optimal program?

9.5 A manufacturer can produce a limited number of units using his work force at regular-time wages and additional units employing labor at overtime rates. Because of variations in the cost of raw materials, unit costs over the next 6 months vary as shown in the table. Inventory-holding costs amount to $1/month. Inventories cannot exceed 3 units. We initially have 2 units on hand and do not want any inventories at the end of the 6-month cycle. Formulate the recursive relations of dynamic programming, and use them to evaluate the optimal solution. Use a backward formulation.

	Period	1	2	3	4	5	6
Regular	cost/unit	6	7	6	9	6	6
	capacity	2	5	2	4	2	7
Overtime	cost/unit	8	9	8	11	9	9
	capacity	3	2	1	1	2	3
Demand		2	6	4	5	1	10

9.6 A product is produced by a batch process. The set-up cost per batch amounts to $10. The variable production cost is $8 for the first unit produced, $6 for the second, $4 for the third, and $3 for each additional unit. The maximum production capacity per week is 6 units. The product can be stored in inventory at a cost of \$2 per week. The beginning inventory is zero, and no inventory is wanted at the end of the planning horizon.

(a) If the demand over the next 8 weeks is 2, 1, 2, 3, 0, 1, 3, and 3, formulate the recursive relation of dynamic programming, and find the optimal solution using a backward formulation, i.e., starting at the end of the planning horizon.

(b) If the demand is 1 unit per week over the next 8 weeks, formulate the recursive relation of dynamic programming using a forward formulation, and find the optimal solution.

(c) If there is also a handling cost of \$1 for each unit put into inventory, how does this change the form of the recursive relation for (a)? You do not have to solve the problem again—merely reformulate it.

9.7 The price of one of the raw materials needed in the manufacturing process of a firm is subject to fairly regular seasonal fluctuations. The prices predicted and the amounts required for the coming 6 months are

Month	1	2	3	4	5	6
Price/unit	\$11,000	\$13,000	\$18,000	\$19,000	\$19,000	\$21,000
Requirement	2	4	4	4	4	2

Material purchased in a given month can be used in the production process of the same month or stored for later use. The maximum storage capacity is 8 units. Material carried forward in inventory for one period incurs a holding cost of \$2000 per unit. Each purchase requires a trip by a specialized vehicle at a cost of \$3000 per purchase, regardless of the amount procured. Beginning inventory and ending inventory are zero. Formulate the recursive relations of dynamic programming minimizing total cost, and find the optimal purchasing and storage policy.

9.8 An electronic monitoring device consists of N components that work in series. Each must function for the device to function as a whole. Each component is subject to random failure, causing the device to fail. The reliability of the device can be improved by installing more than one unit of a component. If this component fails, one of the spare units is automatically switched into the circuit to take its place. The number of units installed for each component is restricted by the total cost of the device. Consider the simple example for $N = 4$ in the table.

Component	1	2	3	4
Probability of no failure for				
0 spare unit	0.7	0.9	0.8	0.6
1 spare unit	0.85	0.96	0.9	0.8
2 spare units	0.97	0.99	0.98	0.95
Cost/unit	\$100	\$300	\$100	\$200

Assume that 1 unit of each component has been included. If \$600 of additional funds are available for spare units, how many spare units of each component should be included in the device so as to maximize the probability that the device will not fail? Formulate the recursive relations of dynamic programming, and find the optimal solution. *Hint:* The probability that the device will not fail is equal to the product of the probabilities of each component not failing. For example, if no spare units are included for components 1, 2, and 3, and 1 spare unit is included for component 4, the probability of no failure is (0.7) (0.9) (0.8) (0.8). Let $f_n(s)$ denote the maximum probability of no failure if s dollars are allocated for spares for the first n components.

9.9 Consider the network in the illustration. The numbers attached to each branch represent the throughput capacity of that branch in the direction of the arrow. The problem is to find the single route from either point 1 or point 2 to point 9 that has the maximum capacity. The capacity of any route is given by the branch on the route that has the lowest capacity.

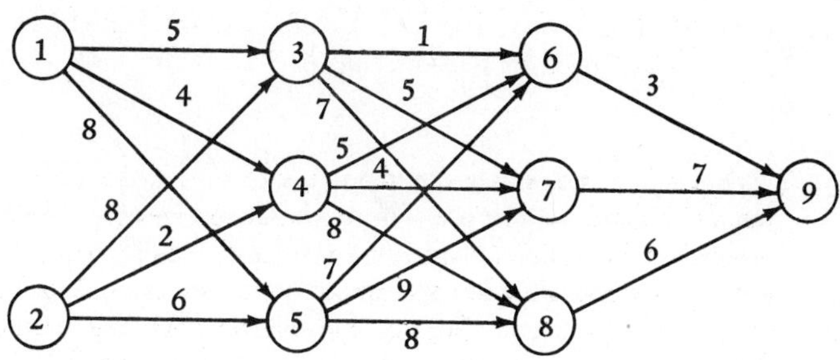

(a) Let c_{ij} denote the capacity from node i to node j. Formulate the recursive relations of dynamic programming for a backward solution, i.e., starting at node 9 and working backward. Define stage, state, and decision.

(b) Using your recursive relations, solve the problem. What nodes are on the optimal route, and what is the capacity of that route?

9.10 Consider a 4-stand rolling mill. Each stand reduces a metal strip of gauge y to gauge x, $x \leq y$. Steel is transported from stand to stand in a negligible amount of time. Refeeding the steel into the same stand would take a significant amount of time. Thus, reducing stands are operated in sequence. The throughput rate of a stand with the input gauge set at y and output gauge set at x is $t(y, x)$. The table gives $t(y, x)$ for various feasible reductions. The input gauge on the initial stand is fixed at 8. The throughput rate of the mill is equal to the lowest throughput rate of any stand used. Note that a stand can be used just to transport the strip at maximum speed (= 1) to the next stand without performing any reduction. The objective of running the mill is to maximize the total throughput rate by optimally selecting the reduction performed on each of the four stands.

y	x=1	x=2	x=3	x=4	x=5	x=6	x=7	x=8
1	1							
2	0.75	1						
3	0.68	0.81	1					
4	0.52	0.71	0.82	1				
5	0.45	0.62	0.73	0.9	1			
6	0.39	0.5	0.67	0.84	0.92	1		
7	0.34	0.47	0.58	0.78	0.82	0.94	1	
8	0.3	0.32	0.49	0.63	0.79	0.86	0.95	1

(a) Formulate the recursive relation of dynamic programming in general terms for an input gauge of size $\bar{y}$ and a final output gauge of size $\bar{x}$ with N stands.

(b) Find the optimal reduction on each of the four stands for the above data for $\bar{y}$ = 8 and $\bar{x}$ = 7, 6, 5, 4, 3, 2, 1. (Note that some solutions can be found by inspection.)

9.11 A plastic coating firm sells paper rolls laminated on one side with plastic foil. These rolls are used mainly for bag manufacture and for other wrapping material that has to be moisture-proof. The rolls are sold in 9 different widths, with annual demands as follows:

Roll width x	10	12	15	18	24	30	36	48	60	Inches
Demand	200	400	240	600	480	250	320	160	80	Rolls

The plastic foil used for laminating has to be at least as wide as the paper rolls. Plastic foil is available in 8 different widths at the following costs:

Foil width y	12	15	21	24	32	36	48	60	Inches
Cost/roll	14	17	22	24	28	30	36	42	Dollars

(a) It is inconvenient to stock more than 3 different foil widths. Which foil width sizes should be procured to minimize total costs? Formulate this problem by dynamic programming, and use the recursive relations to find the optimal solution.

(b) What is the cost reduction if the number of foil widths procured is increased to 4, 5, 6, 7, 8?
(*Hint:* Determine first a table listing the cost of using a foil width y to laminate all paper rolls of width $x \leq y$.)

9.12 As seen in Section 9-2, some types of shortest-path problems can be solved using dynamic programming. The condition is that the points must be able to be grouped into sets, such that each path from the start to the end node has to go through exactly one point in each set. The sets can then be numbered as stages. With each stage, we also associate a state variable (= a possible location at that stage). There are shortest-path problems where the points cannot be grouped into such sets. Consider for instance the problem illustrated. The numbers attached to the arrows represent the distances between two connected points. If we drop the notion of stages, then the principle of optimality can still be applied to find the shortest path for sequential problems of this sort.

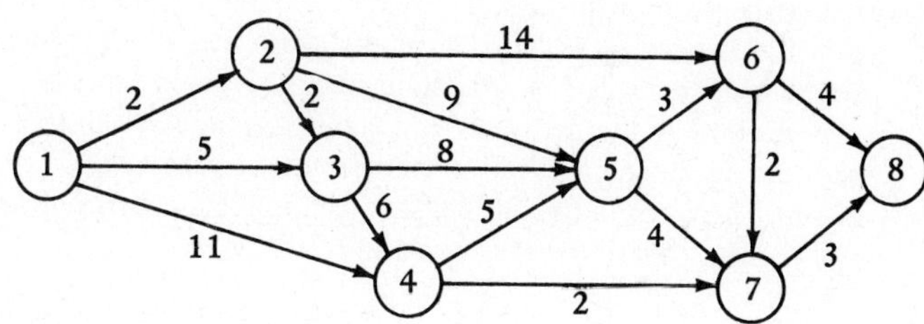

(a) Formulate a recursive expression for this problem where t_{ij} is the distance from i to j.
(b) Use the recursive expression from part (a) to find the shortest path from 1 to 8. What is the minimum distance?

9.13 A machine in a production plant is inspected annually and is either overhauled or replaced. The cost of an overhaul and the scrap value of the machine are related to its age as shown in the table. (All figures are in units of \$1000.) A machine of age 4 cannot be overhauled any more and has to be replaced. A new machine costs $c_0 = 20$. The current machine is 3 years old and could be replaced immediately if desired. The remaining life of the plant is 4 years, at the end of which time the machine in use will be scrapped.

Age (k)	1	2	3	4
Overhaul cost (c_k)	7	3	9	
Scrap value (b_k)	10	5	2	0

(a) Formulate in general terms (using letter symbols) the recursive relations of dynamic programming for a *backward* solution. Define stage, state, and decisions.
(b) Evaluate the recursive relations to find the optimal replacement policy.

9.14 Consider the tabulated costs associated with operating and maintaining a machine. The cost of a new machine is \$1200. The present machine is 3 years old. Using a 12-year planning horizon, formulate the recursive relations of dynamic programming and find the least-cost replacement policy. How is the initial decision affected by the age of the machine in year 12?

Operating year	1	2	3	4	5	6	7	8	9
Operating costs/year	200	200	210	240	280	350	450	600	800
Salvage value (end of year)	900	750	600	450	300	200	100	50	0

9.15 The Electricity Board of No-Growth County recently installed a substation serving a new housing development under construction. The present substation is of size 1. This substation will be able to serve the requirements of the area during the coming 3 years (years 1, 2, and 3) but will have to be replaced by the beginning of year 4 at the latest. One replacement choice is a substation of size 2 that would be able to meet the requirements through the end of year 6, and then would have to be replaced by a larger substation of size 3, which is large enough to meet the final requirements expected in year 8 and thereafter. A substation of size 3 could obviously also meet the smaller requirements of the first years and could be purchased instead of a size 2. The table gives the operation costs $R_i(j)$ and the purchase and installation costs $C_i(j)$ for a substation of size j in year i (all in \$10,000's). The problem consists of determining the optimal replacement pattern over the 8 years.

Year i	1	2	3	4	5	6	7	8
Initial cost if bought beginning of i								
for size 2	8	9	10	11	—	—	—	—
for size 3	10	12	14	16	16	16	16	—
Operating costs								
for size 1	3	4	6	∞	∞	∞	∞	∞
for size 2	4	5	7	9	10	11	∞	∞
for size 3	4	5	7	10	11	12	13	14

(a) Formulate this problem in general terms by dynamic programming using a forward formulation. Show the recursive relation of dynamic programming for year 1 and for years $1 < i \leq 8$.

(b) Evaluate the recursive relation in table form for years 1 through 8. What is the optimal replacement policy?

9.16 Solve exercise 9.13 as a regeneration problem.

9.17 Solve exercise 9.14 as a regeneration problem.

9.18 *Two-state-variables problem.* Consider exercise 9.3. Assume that there is not only a maximum excess weight limit but also a limit on the excess space, S. The amount of space required per unit for the five item is

Item	1	2	3	4	5
Space (cu ft)	1	2	1	2	3

Assume that for a given flight the excess space is $S = 5$ and the excess weight is $W = 6$. Formulate the recursive relations of dynamic programming, maximizing total utility, and use it to evaluate the optimal solution.

9.19 A product is manufactured by a continuous production process. Each month the production engineer has to set the rate of production. Changes in the rate of production result in a so-called smoothing cost. If x_{t-1} is the rate of production in period $t - 1$, and x_t is the rate of production in period t, then the smoothing cost is equal to $c_s(x_t - x_{t-1})^2$. Other costs involved are a cost of c_h per unit carried in inventory from one period to the next, and a variable unit production cost which depends on the rate of production as follows.

Rate of production	$x_t \leq 6$	$7 \leq x_t \leq 8$	$x_t \geq 9$
Cost per unit	c_1	c_2	c_3

The demand in period t is d_t. All demand has to be met. The beginning inventory and ending inventory are both zero. The present production rate is $\hat{x}$. The final rate can be arbitrary.

(a) Formulate this problem as a dynamic programming problem using a backward formulation. Show the recursive relations for $t = 1$, $1 < t < N$, and $t = N$.

(b) If $c_s = 4$, $c_h = 2$, $c_1 = 5$, $c_2 = 4$, $c_3 = 6$, and if the demand over a 6-month planning horizon is $d_6 = 6$, $d_5 = 8$, $d_4 = 10$, $d_3 = 7$, $d_2 = 8$, $d_1 = 6$, and $\hat{x} = 7$, what is the optimal production plan?

REFERENCES

Bellman, Richard E. *Dynamic Programming.* Princeton University, 1957. The first text in dynamic programming by the father of this most versatile tool.

———, and Stuart E. Dreyfus. *Applied Dynamic Programming.* Princeton University, 1962. A thorough discussion of numerous completely worked examples, including a number of computer program flow charts.

Dreyfus, S.E., and A. M. Law. *The Art and the Theory of Dynamic Programming.* New York: Academic Press, 1977. Thorough coverage of dynamic programming with numerous problems and fully worked out solutions.

Hadley, George. *Nonlinear and Dynamic Programming.* Reading, Mass.: Addison-Wesley, 1964. Chapters 10 and 11 have a thorough treatment of dynamic programming and computational refinements. Highly recommended as additional reading to this chapter.

Jacobson, D. N., and D. Q. Mayne. *Differential Dynamic Programming.* New York: American Elsevier, 1970. A method for overcoming the curse of dimensionality by approaching the optimal trajectory via a sequence of successive quadratic approximations.

Nemhauser, George L. *Introduction to Dynamic Programming.* New York: Wiley, 1966. Still a classical text, advanced. Unconventional notation. Excellent chapter on computational refinements.

Wagner, H. M. *Principles of Operations Research,* 2nd ed. Englewood Cliffs, N.J.: Prentice-Hall, 1975. Chapters 8, 9, and 10 discuss deterministic models, with Chapter 9 devoted entirely to inventory control.

PART TWO

Stochastic Models

CHAPTER TEN

Elements of Probability and Stochastic Processes

Many problems in operations research contain elements that we cannot control or predict. For example, in an inventory system serving a number of customers, we could probably predict the daily demand for a particular item with great accuracy if we kept records of the stock levels and the usages of each customer. Unless the inventory is very specialized, however, this will be an expensive and time-consuming process. It is not that the demand is actually unpredictable, but rather than the model of the system would be too large if we attempted to set it up exactly. Our usual response to these problems is to assume that the uncontrollable inputs are generated by some kind of probabilistic process. For example, we assume that there is a fixed chance or probability of a certain level of daily demand. In our model the actual demand is then selected by the outcome of some experiment having these probabilities. Part 2 of this text looks at models with probabilistic elements. This chapter is intended to give a rather brief review of the types of probabilistic structures that will be used.

10-1 RULES OF PROBABILITY

Any experiment whose outcome depends on chance is called a *random experiment*. Any possible outcome of a random experiment that cannot be decomposed into more basic components is called an *elementary event*. The collection of all possible elementary events of a random experiment represents the *sample space* S. For instance, rolling two dice is a random experiment with elementary events: [the number of dots on the first die is i, the number of dots on the second die is j]. Since both i and j may assume any of the integers from 1 to 6, the sample space has 6 × 6, or 36, elementary events.

Let A be any outcome or *event* of a random experiment. A consists of one or several elementary events. A is thus a subset of S.

AXIOM 1

With each random event A of S, there is associated a real number denoted as $P(A)$, called the probability of A, where $P(A) \geq 0$.

AXIOM 2

At least one of the possible elementary events has to occur, i.e., $P(S) = 1$.

AXIOM 3: ADDITION RULE

If events $A_1, A_2, \ldots, A_k$ are pairwise mutually exclusive (i.e., sets of elementary events with no elementary events in common), then the probability of their union is given by

$$P(A_1 \cup A_2 \cup \cdots \cup A_k) = \sum_{i=1}^{k} P(A_i) \tag{10-1}$$

where $A_i \cup A_j$ denotes the collection of all elementary events that are either in A_i or in A_j or in both.

Define $\bar{A}$ as the set of all elementary events of S not in A. A and $\bar{A}$ are mutually exclusive, and their union is equal to S. Hence, it follows from axioms 2 and 3 that $P(\bar{A}) = 1 - P(A)$.

In many experiments each elementary event is equally likely. For instance, each elementary event of rolling two dice is equally likely, assuming that the dice are absolutely fair. Let the event A = [the sum of the dots is 6]. Then $P(A)$ is obtained as the ratio of the number of elementary events favorable to A (of which there are 5) over the total number of elementary events, or $P(A) = 5/36$. Similarly, let the event B = [the sum of the dots is 5]. Verify that $P(B) = 4/36$. $A \cup B$ is the event [the sum of the dots is either 5 or 6]. It is the union of events A and B. Since events A and B are *mutually exclusive*, we have, by axiom 3: $P(A \cup B) = P(A) + P(B) = 9/36$.

What is the probability that the sum of the dots on the two dice is 6 and at the same time that each die has an even number of dots? If we let event A = [the sum of the dots is 6] and C = [each die shows an even number of dots], then we are asking for the probability of the joint event that both A and C occur, referred to as the intersection of A and C, of the 36 satisfy both A and C simultaneously are considered. Verify that 2 out of the 36 elementary events have both properties, hence $P(A \cap C) = 2/36$.

What is the probability that the sum of the dots on the two dice is 6 (event A), given that both dice show an even number of dots (event C)? This probability refers to the occurrence of event A, subject this time, however, to the condition that event C has occurred. Such a probability is appropriately called a *conditional probability* and is denoted by $P(A|C)$—read as probability of A given C—where C stands for the condition. Note that the condition of event C excludes all those elementary events where either one die or the other or both dice show an odd number of dots. Thus, the essence of conditional probabilities is that we define a new sample space, which is a subset of the original sample space and which contains only those elementary events that satisfy the condition C.

CONDITIONAL PROBABILITY

(10-2)
$$P(A|C) = \frac{P(A \cap C)}{P(C)}$$

or

(10-3)
$$P(A \cap C) = P(A|C)P(C)$$

For our example, expression (10-2) yields

$$P(A|C) = \frac{2/36}{9/36} = 2/9$$

Expression (10-3) tells us how to find the probability of the intersection of two dependent events.

If event A is *statistically independent* of event C, then the probability of A is not affected by whether event C has occurred or not, i.e.,

$$P(A|C) = P(A|\overline{C}) = P(A)$$

It follows that if two events A and C are independent, expression (10-3) simplifies to

(10-4)
$$P(A \cap C) = P(A)P(C) \quad \textit{(Multiplication rule)}$$

For instance, referring to one die as the first die and to the other as the second die, the event D = [the first die shows an even number of dots] and the event E =

[the second die shows an even number of dots] are clearly independent. The outcome of one does not influence the outcome of the other. Each has a probability of $\frac{1}{2}$. Hence by (10-4):

$$P(C) = P(D \cap E) = P(D)P(E) = (\tfrac{1}{2})(\tfrac{1}{2}) = \tfrac{1}{4}$$

as we have seen earlier.

The concepts of mutually exclusive events and independent events are often confused, especially since the nonmathematical meaning of "independence" has to do with the absence of any relationships or common elements, a property that we use here to characterize mutually exclusive events. In order to prove that two events are independent, we must verify that expression (10-4) holds. Absence or presence of common elements is not enough, as we can see from this example. Let F = [the number of dots shown on the die is divisible by three], and G = [the number of dots shown on the die is divisible by two]. Obviously F occurs if we roll a 3 or a 6, and G occurs if we roll a 2, 4, or a 6. So $P(F) = \frac{1}{3}$ and $P(G) = \frac{1}{2}$. Are F and G independent? Intuition might lead us to say that they are not, since the event of rolling a 6 leads to them both. But in this case intuition would be wrong, since $P(F \cap G) = \frac{1}{6} = P(F)P(G)$!

10-2 BAYES'S THEOREM

Suppose we have a number of possible hypotheses, $A_1, A_2, \ldots, A_n$, to account for a particular phenomenon, and suppose we can test these hypotheses by means of the outcome of an experiment, B. The relationship between our probabilistic beliefs about the hypotheses after the experiment (the *posterior probabilities*) and those before the experiment (the *prior probabilities*) is given by *Bayes's Theorem*. Formally, let A_1, $A_2, \ldots, A_n$ be mutually exclusive events whose union is the sample space S of an experiment. Let B be an arbitrary event of S such that $P(B) \neq 0$. Then

$$P(A_i|B) = \frac{P(A_i \cap B)}{P(B \cap S)} \qquad \text{by (10-2)}$$

But $P(B = P(S \cap B) = P(A_1 \cup A_2 \cup \cdots \cup A_n) \cap B) = P((A_1 \cap B) \cup (A_2 \cap B) \cup \cdots \cup (A_n \cap B)) = \Sigma_{j=1}^{n} P(A_j \cap B)$ by (10-1). Hence

$$P(A_i|B = \frac{P(A_i \cap B)}{\sum_{j=1}^{n} P(A_j \cap B)}$$

Using (10-3) to express $P(A_i \cap B)$ as $P(B|A_i)P(A_i)$, we get

BAYES'S THEOREM

(10-5) $$P(A_i|B) = \frac{P(B|A_i)P(A_i)}{\sum_{j=1}^{n} P(B|A_j)P(A_j)}, \qquad i = 1, 2, \ldots, n$$

In (10-5) we have expressed the posterior probability of A_i given B in terms of the prior probabilities of $A_1, A_2, \ldots, A_n$, together with the probabilities of B given A_1, B given A_2, and so on. Note as an aid to remembering (10-5) that the expression in the numerator always occurs as one of the terms in the denominator.

10-3 RANDOM VARIABLES

Often we are interested in the probabilistic behavior of some variable (usually numerically valued) associated with events, rather than in the events themselves. Let us associate with each elementary event in S a real number x. This correspondence need not be unique, i.e., several elementary events may map into the same value x. This mapping of the elementary events onto the real line is called a *random variable*, denoted by X. We usually use capital letters to denote the random variable and small letters to denote particular values of the random variable.

Example 1. Let X denote the sum of the dots on the faces up when two dice are rolled. X can assume values 2, 3, . . ., 12. Only one elementary event of the experiment maps into the number 2; however, two map into 3, three into 4, etc.

We now redefine the three axioms of probability in terms of random variables. Define $F(x) = P(X \leq x)$ as the *probability distribution function* of the random variable X. Then

AXIOM 1A

$F(x)$ is monotonic nondecreasing in x. If $a < b$, then $F(a) \leq F(b)$.

AXIOM 2A

$$F(\infty) = 1 \quad \text{and} \quad F(-\infty) = 0$$

AXIOM 3A

$$P(a < X \leq b) = F(b) - F(a)$$

This follows immediately if we let event $A = [X \leq a]$, $B = [a < X \leq b]$, and event $C = A \cup B = [X \leq b]$, and use axiom 3.

If the random variable X assumes only discrete values $x_1, x_2, \ldots$, then the probability distribution function is given by

$$P(X \leq x_k) = F(x_k) = \sum_{i=1}^{k} p(x_i), \qquad k = 1, 2, \ldots$$

where $p(x_i)$ is the probability that $X = x_i$. The function $p(x_i)$ is called the probability function. Clearly $\sum_{i=1}^{\infty} p(x_i) = 1$. Try to find the probability function for the random variable "the sum of the dots on both dice."

If the random variable X is continuous (i.e., can assume any value in a given interval) and its distribution function can be differentiated, then

$$P(X \leq a) = F(a) = \int_{-\infty}^{a} f(x)\,dx$$

where $f(x) = dF(x)/dx$ is called the ***probability density function***. $f(x)\,dx$ is the (approximate) probability that the random variable assumes a value between x and $x + dx$, provided that dx is very small. Again, $\int_{-\infty}^{\infty} f(x)\,dx = 1$. Figure 10-1 depicts some of these concepts.

Figure 10-1. *Probability distribution and density functions for a continuous random variable.*

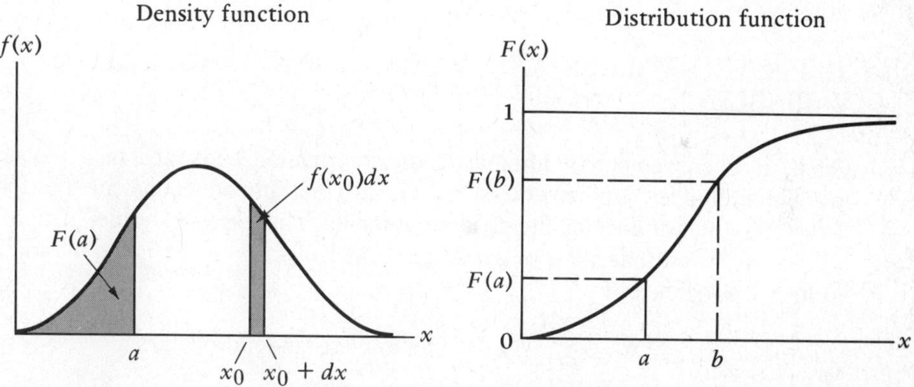

Random variables may be vector-valued. For example, $Z = (X, Y)$ is a bivariate random variable. The distribution function of Z, or the joint distribution function of X and Y, is $P(X \leq a, Y \leq b) = F(a, b)$. If X and Y are both continuous, the joint distribution function is obtained by integrating the joint density function $f(x, y)$ over both variables:

$$F(a, b) = \int_{-\infty}^{a} \int_{-\infty}^{b} f(x, y)\,dydx$$

Each of the variables X and Y can be considered as a random variable by itself. The distribution of X or of Y alone, regardless of what value the other random variable assumes, is called the *marginal distribution* of X or of Y. Its density function is defined as

$$g(x) = \int_{-\infty}^{+\infty} f(x, y)\, dy \quad \text{for X} \qquad \text{or} \qquad h(y) = \int_{-\infty}^{+\infty} f(x, y)\, dx \quad \text{for Y}$$

Any two continuous random variables X and Y are said to be independent if their joint density function can be factorized into the product of the marginal densities, i.e.,

$$f(x, y) = g(x)h(y) \tag{10-6}$$

We can determine the distribution of one of the random variables conditional on a fixed value of the other. The conditional density function of, say, X given $Y = y$ is defined as

$$g(x|y) = f(x, y)/h(y) \tag{10-7}$$

Note that there may well be a different conditional density function for each possible value of Y.

It is left to the reader to define the joint, marginal, and conditional probability functions when X and Y are discrete random variables.

10-4 EXPECTED VALUES AND VARIANCES OF RANDOM VARIABLES

Often, it is convenient to summarize the information contained in a probability distribution by a few summary measures. The two most important ones are the *expected value* and the *variance* of the random variable. The expected value, denoted by $E(X) = \mu$, is an indication of where the center of mass of the random variable is located. It is defined by

$$E(X) = \sum_{i=1}^{\infty} x_i\, p(x_i) \qquad \text{for discrete random variables} \tag{10-8}$$

and

$$E(X) = \int_{-\infty}^{\infty} x f(x)\, dx \qquad \text{for continuous random variables} \tag{10-9}$$

Thus, for a discrete random variable, E(X) is seen to be the weighted sum of all values that the random variable can assume, with the probabilities serving as weights.

The variance, denoted by $VAR(X) = \sigma^2$, is an indication of how dispersed the mass of the random variable is around its expected value μ. It is defined by

$$VAR(X) = \sum_{i=1}^{\infty} (x_i - \mu)^2 p(x_i) \qquad \text{for discrete random variables} \tag{10-10}$$

and

(10-11) $$\mathrm{VAR}(X) = \int_{-\infty}^{\infty} (x - \mu)^2 f(x)\,dx \qquad \text{for continuous random variables}$$

The square root of the variance is called the *standard deviation*, denoted by σ.

Example 2. Let X denote again the sum of the dots when rolling two dice. Then, as you can verify,

$X = x_i$	2	3	4	5	6	7	8	9	10	11	12
$p(x_i)$	1/36	2/36	3/36	4/36	5/36	6/36	5/36	4/36	3/36	2/36	1/36

and

$$E(X) = 2(1/36) + 3(2/36) + 4(3/36) + 5(4/36) + 6(5/36) + 7(6/36) + 8(5/36) + 9(4/36) + 10(3/36) + 11(2/36) + 12(1/36) = 7$$

$$\mathrm{VAR}(X) = (2-7)^2(1/36) + (3-7)^2(2/36) + (4-7)^2(3/36) + (5-7)^2(4/36) + (6-7)^2(5/36) + (7-7)^2(6/36) + (8-7)^2(5/36) + (9-7)^2(4/36) + (10-7)^2(3/36) + (11-7)^2(2/36) + (12-7)^2(1/36) = 5\tfrac{5}{6}$$

and

$$\sigma = \sqrt{5\tfrac{5}{6}} = 2.415$$

Other measures of central location are the *mode* (value of X for the highest point in the probability or probability density function) and the median (value of X that divides the function into two equal parts, i.e., the number M such that $P(X \leq M) = P(X \geq M) = \frac{1}{2}$).

PROPERTIES OF $E(X)$

1. Let $Y = cX$, c constant, then

(10-12) $$E(Y) = E(cX) = cE(X)$$

2. Let $Y = X + c$, c constant, then

(10-13) $$E(Y) = E(X + c) = E(X) + c$$

3. Let $Y = \Sigma_{j=1}^{k} X_j$, where each X_j is a random variable. Then

(10-14) $$E(Y) = E(X_1 + X_2 + \ldots + X_k) = \sum_{j=1}^{k} E(X_j)$$

Note that the third property of E(X) does not require that the random variables be independent.

PROPERTIES OF VAR(X)

1. Let $Y = cX$, c constant, then

(10-15) $$VAR(Y) = VAR(cX) = c^2 VAR(X)$$

2. Let $Y = X + c$, c constant, then

(10-16) $$VAR(Y) = VAR(X + c) = VAR(X)$$

3. If $Y = \Sigma_{j=1}^{k} X_j$, where the X_j form a set of mutually independent random variables, then

(10-17) $$VAR(Y) = VAR(X_1 + X_2 + \cdots + X_k) = \sum_{j=1}^{k} VAR(X_j)$$

Using these properties, we may rewrite VAR(X) as follows. Let $Y = (X - \mu)^2$. Then, by the definition of E(X),

$$\begin{aligned} VAR(X) = E(Y) &= E(X - \mu)^2 = E(X^2 - 2\mu X + \mu^2) \\ &= E(X^2) - E(2\mu X) + E(\mu^2) \qquad \text{by expression (10-14)} \\ &= E(X^2) - 2\mu E(X) + \mu^2 \qquad \text{by (10-12)} \end{aligned}$$

But $\mu = E(X)$, hence

(10-18) $$VAR(X) = E(X^2) - [E(X)]^2$$

This is computationally a more efficient formula for the variance than expression (10-10) or (10-11).

Example 3. (a) Let X denote the random variable for monthly sales (in units sold) for a given product. Assume that X has the following probability function:

x_i	1	2	3	4
$p(x_i)$	0.4	0.3	0.2	0.1

Verify that $E(X) = 2$ and $VAR(X) = 1$.

Each unit sold brings in a revenue of \$4.00. Let Y denote the revenue in dollars generated by this product per month; $Y = 4X$ is also a random variable. If $c = 4$, then by (10-12) $E(Y) = 4E(X) = 4(2) = 8$, and by (10-15) $VAR(Y) = 4^2\ VAR(X) = 4^2(1) = 16$.

(b) Consider now sales over 6 months. Each month's sales follows the same probability distribution as for (a). Let X_i be the random variable for sales in month i, and let Y be sales over 6 months. $Y = \Sigma_{i=1}^{6} X_i$. Then the expected sales over 6 months is

$$E(Y) = \sum_{i=1}^{6} E(X_i) = 12 \qquad \text{by (10-14)}$$

and the variance of sales over 6 months is

$$VAR(Y) = \sum_{i=1}^{6} VAR(X_i) = 6 \qquad \text{by (10-17)}$$

assuming sales in consecutive months are independent.

10-5 DISCRETE PROBABILITY DISTRIBUTIONS

Uniform Distribution

A random variable X, which takes any one of a finite number of values (say 1, 2, . . ., n) with equal probability, has a uniform distribution. Its probability function has the form

$$p(x) = \frac{1}{n}, \qquad x = 1, 2, \ldots, n \tag{10-19}$$

with

$$E(X) = \frac{n+1}{2} \tag{10-20}$$

$$VAR(X) = \frac{n^2 - 1}{12} \tag{10-21}$$

Geometric Distribution

An experiment consisting of a sequence of independent trials is called a sequence of *Bernoulli trials* if each trial has only two outcomes, such as success or failure, and the probability of success, p, is constant from trial to trial. If the random variable X is the number of trials until the first success in a sequence of Bernoulli trials, then X has a geometric distribution, with its probability function given by

(10-22) $$p(x) = p(1-p)^{x-1}, \qquad x = 1, 2, \ldots$$

with

(10-23) $$E(X) = \frac{1}{p}$$

(10-24) $$VAR(X) = \frac{1-p}{p^2}$$

Binomial Distribution

The random variable X denoting the number of successes in n Bernoulli trials has a binomial distribution, with a probability function given by

(10-25) $$p(x) = \frac{n!}{x!\,(n-x)!}\,p^x(1-p)^{n-x}, \qquad x = 0, 1, \ldots, n$$

with

(10-26) $$E(X) = np$$

(10-27) $$VAR(X) = np(1-p)$$

Binomial distributions are important for attribute sampling, where p is the probability that a particular individual in a population has that attribute.

As n gets large, binomial probabilities can be approximated by areas under a normal probability density function, with $\mu = np$ and $\sigma^2 = np(1-p)$. For $np > 5$ and $n(1-p) > 5$, the normal approximation is usually considered satisfactory. If $p \leqslant 0.01$, the Poisson distribution provides a good approximation for $n \geqslant 50$.

Poisson Distribution

A random variable has a Poisson distribution with parameter λt if its probability function is defined by

(10-28) $$p(x) = \frac{(\lambda t)^x e^{-\lambda t}}{x!}, \qquad x = 0, 1, 2, \ldots$$

with

(10-29) $$E(X) = \lambda t$$

(10-30) $$VAR(X) = \lambda t$$

Consider a sequence of events that occur over time. If the rate at which events occur per unit time, λ, is constant, then the random variable representing the number of events over a length of time t has a Poisson distribution.

The Poisson distribution is particularly suitable for depicting the random behavior of individual events that occur relatively infrequently within the time span considered, such as the demand for individual spare parts or the number of individual arrivals at a service counter. For $\lambda t > 20$, the normal distribution provides a good approximation, except at the extreme tails.

10-6 CONTINUOUS PROBABILITY DISTRIBUTIONS

Uniform (Rectangular) Distribution

A random variable X defined over the interval from a to b has a uniform probability distribution if its density function has the form

$$f(x) = \begin{cases} \dfrac{1}{b - a} & \text{for } a \leq x \leq b \\ 0 & \text{otherwise} \end{cases} \tag{10-31}$$

with

$$E(X) = \frac{a + b}{2} \tag{10-32}$$

$$VAR(X) = \frac{(b - a)^2}{12} \tag{10-33}$$

Exponential (Negative Exponential) Distribution

A random variable X defined for all nonnegative values has an exponential probability distribution if its density function has the form

$$f(x) = \begin{cases} \lambda e^{-\lambda x} & \text{for } x \geq 0 \\ 0 & \text{otherwise} \end{cases} \tag{10-34}$$

with

$$E(X) = 1/\lambda \tag{10-35}$$

$$VAR(X) = 1/\lambda^2 \tag{10-36}$$

$$F(x) = 1 - e^{-\lambda x} \tag{10-37}$$

The exponential distribution is often used to depict the random behavior of the time interval between the occurrence of two consecutive events, such as the time between two consecutive arrivals or the time to the next breakdown of a machine. This distribution has the often overlooked implication that the probability of, say, a breakdown occurring within the next 20 hours of operation does not depend on when the last breakdown occurred.

Normal Distribution

The normal distribution is the most important probability distribution. For numerous random phenomena, the value of the random variable is the cumulative result of a large number of individually small random effects. Such phenomena tend to follow a normal distribution. Furthermore, the limiting form of a number of other distributions (binomial, Poisson, gamma, chi-square) is normal. The normal distribution is completely determined by two parameters, the expected value or mean μ and the variance σ^2 of the random variable. Its density function has the form

(10-38) $$f(x) = \frac{1}{\sigma\sqrt{2\pi}}e^{-\frac{1}{2}\left(\frac{x-\mu}{\sigma}\right)^2}, \quad \text{for } -\infty \leq x \leq \infty$$

This expression cannot be integrated analytically. However, any normal random variable X with mean μ and variance σ^2 can be expressed in terms of the standardized normal random variable Z with mean 0 and variance 1 for which extensive tables exist. We use the transformation $x = \mu + z\sigma$, so $z = (x - \mu)/\sigma$. Now

(10-39) $$P(X \leq a) = P\left(Z \leq \frac{a - \mu}{\sigma}\right)$$

The Central Limit Theorem

As well as describing the limiting behavior of a number of theoretical probability distributions, the normal distribution provides an approximation for the distribution of sums of almost any kind of random variables. If $X_1, \ldots, X_n$ are n independent random variables, then, provided n is sufficiently large, $Y = X_1 + X_2 + \ldots + X_n$ will be approximately normally distributed, with $\mu = \Sigma_{i=1}^{n} \mu_{X_i}$ and $\sigma^2 = \Sigma_{i=1}^{n} \sigma_{X_i}^2$, where μ_{X_i} and $\sigma_{X_i}^2$ are the mean and the variance of the random variable X_2, respectively. That is, as n becomes large,

(10-40) $$P\left(\frac{Y - \mu}{\sigma} \leq z\right) \cong P(Z \leq z)$$

where Z is a standard normal random variable. If the individual distributions are not highly skewed and if none of the random variables dominates all others in terms of the relative size of its parameters, the normal approximation may already be satisfactory for the sum of as few as $n = 10$ random variables.

This is one version of the famous *central limit theorem*. Another version asserts that the distribution of the average value (or sample mean) $\bar{x} = \Sigma_{i=1}^{n} x^{(i)}/n$ of n independent observations $x^{(1)}, x^{(2)}, x^{(3)}, \ldots, x^{(n)}$ on an arbitrarily distributed random variable X also tends to be normally distributed as n gets large, with parameters $\mu_{\bar{x}} = \mu_X$ and $\sigma_{\bar{x}}^2 = \sigma_X^2/n$.

All the probability distributions considered up to now are distributions that result from particular kinds of probabilistic experiments. There are a number of other probability distributions that are used largely because the shapes of their density functions or the values of their parameters approximate those that have been observed for some particular process.

Log Normal Distribution

If a random variable X is such that $U = \log_e X$ is normally distributed with mean μ and variance σ^2, then X has a log normal distribution with

(10-41) $$E(X) = e^{\mu + (\sigma^2/2)}$$

(10-42) $$VAR(X) = [E(X)]^2(e^{\sigma^2} - 1)$$

Figure 10-2. *Log normal distribution.*

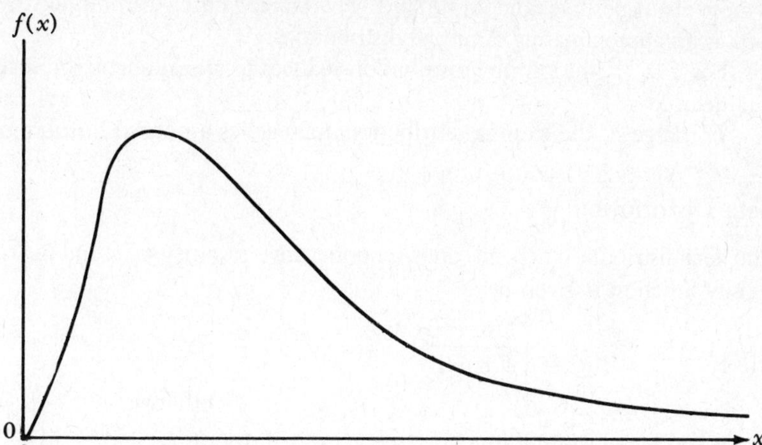

The distributions of a number of positive random variables that usually take values clustered about the mean, but may also take very high values, have been approximated by the log normal distribution. Some examples of these are the heights of annual floods on a river, the sizes of a particular species of insect, and the distribution of incomes in a certain population. From the central limit theorem, we can also see that if a random variable is the *product* of a large number of independent positive random variables, then the random variable's distribution will tend toward a log normal distribution.

Gamma Distribution

The gamma distribution depends on two nonnegative parameters, a and b. Its probability density function is given by

(10-43)
$$f(x) = \begin{cases} \dfrac{b^a}{\Gamma(a)} x^{a-1} e^{-bx} & \text{for } x > 0 \\ 0 & \text{otherwise} \end{cases}$$

where $\Gamma(a) = \int_0^\infty t^{a-1} e^{-t} dt$ is the *gamma function*. For a integer, $\Gamma(a) = (a-1)!$

(10-44)
$$E(X) = \frac{a}{b}$$

(10-45)
$$VAR(X) = \frac{a}{b^2}$$

This means that we can find a gamma distribution with the same mean and variance as those of any positive random variable. Therefore, gamma distributions are frequently used as an approximating family of distributions.

For $a = 1$, the gamma distribution reduces to an exponential distribution with parameter $\lambda = b$.

For large a, the gamma distribution approaches a normal distribution.

Beta Distribution

The beta distribution depends on two nonnegative parameters, α and β. Its probability density function is given by

$$f(x) = \begin{cases} \dfrac{\Gamma(\alpha + \beta)}{\Gamma(\alpha)\Gamma(\beta)} x^{\alpha - 1}(1 - x)^{\beta - 1} & \text{for } 0 < x < 1 \\ 0 & \text{otherwise} \end{cases} \tag{10-46}$$

where $\Gamma(s)$ is the gamma function (see gamma distribution) and

$$E(X) = \frac{\alpha}{\alpha + \beta} \tag{10-47}$$

$$VAR(X) = \frac{\alpha\beta}{(\alpha + \beta)^2(\alpha + \beta + 1)} \tag{10-48}$$

The finite range and the skewed distribution of a beta-distributed random variable have led to their common use in representing task durations in PERT models. For the models in Chapter 8, we use the following transformation:

$$T = a + (b - a)X$$

with

$$E(T) = a + (b - a)\left(\frac{\alpha}{\alpha + \beta}\right)$$

$$VAR(T) = (b - a)^2 \frac{\alpha\beta}{(\alpha + \beta)^2(\alpha + \beta + 1)}$$

The mode of the distribution of T occurs at

$$m = \frac{a(\beta - 1) + b(\alpha - 1)}{(\alpha + \beta - 2)}$$

Setting $\alpha = 3 + \sqrt{2}$ and $\beta = 3 - \sqrt{2}$, the expected value and the variance of T simplify to

$$E(T) = \frac{a + b + (\alpha + \beta - 2)m}{\alpha + \beta} = \frac{a + b + 4m}{6}$$

$$VAR(T) = \left(\frac{a - b}{6}\right)^2$$

which are the expressions used in Section 8-5.

Laplace Distribution

The Laplace distribution is a symmetric exponential distribution specified by its mean μ and variance σ^2. Its probability density function is given by

(10-49) $$f(x) = \frac{1}{\sigma\sqrt{2}} e^{-\frac{\sqrt{2}}{\sigma}|x-\mu|}, \qquad \text{for all } x$$

Figure 10-3. *Laplace distribution.*

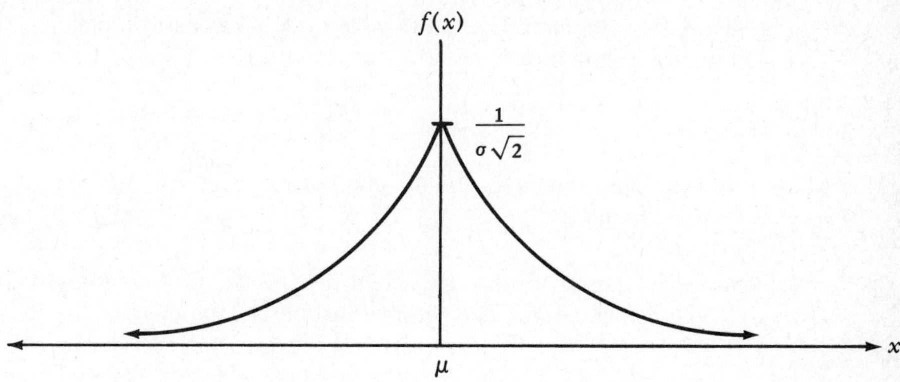

It is mainly used as a simple approximation to the demand distribution in inventory control models with $\sigma^2 = \mu$.

10-7 DISTRIBUTIONS OF FUNCTIONS OF RANDOM VARIABLES

In operations research, we quite often deal with functions of random variables, such as benefit or cost functions that involve random variables or sums of random variables.

Let $Y = g(X)$ be a single-valued function of a discrete random variable. Then

$$P(Y = y_i) = P(Y = g(x_i)) = p(x_i)$$

and

(10-50) $$E(Y) = E(g(X)) = \sum_{\text{all } i} g(x_i)\, p(x_i)$$

(10-51) $$VAR(Y) = VAR(g(X)) = \sum_{\text{all } i} [g(x_i) - E(g(X))]^2 p(x_i)$$

Example 4. Let X be the random variable for the monthly demand with probability function $p(x)$, as listed in Example 3(a). Assume that at the beginning of a given month there are 2 units left for sale. New units will only become available at the beginning of next month. If more than 2 units are demanded, some sales will be lost. What is the probability distribution of lost sales for that month? If Y denotes lost sales, then

$$Y = g(X) = \begin{cases} 0 & \text{for } X \leq 2 \quad \text{with } p(Y = 0) = p(X = 1) + p(X = 2) \\ X - 2 & \text{for } X = x > 2 \quad \text{with } p(Y = x - 2) = p(x) \end{cases}$$

The expected value of lost sales is

$$\begin{aligned} E(Y) &= 0(p(X = 1) + p(X = 2)) + (3 - 2)\,p(X = 3) + (4 - 2)\,p(X = 4) \\ &= 0(0.4 + 0.3) + 1(0.2) + 2(0.1) = 0.4 \text{ unit} \end{aligned}$$

Similarly, for continuous random variables, if X has a density function $f(x)$, then $Y = g(X)$ has the density function

$$h(y) = f(\psi(y))\left|\frac{d\psi(y)}{dy}\right| \tag{10-52}$$

where $x = \psi(y)$ is the unique inverse function of $y = g(x)$. All other properties can now be obtained from $h(y)$.

Example 5. Let $Y = a + bX$. Then the inverse function is given by $X = (Y - a)/b$ with derivative $1/b$. The density function of Y becomes

$$h(y) = f((y - a)/b)\left|\frac{1}{b}\right| \tag{10-53}$$

If X is normally distributed with mean μ and variance σ^2, for example, then

$$h(y) = \frac{1}{\sigma\sqrt{2\pi}} e^{-\frac{1}{2}\left[\frac{y - (a + b\mu)}{b\sigma}\right]^2}\left|\frac{1}{b}\right| \qquad \text{(from 10-53)}$$

which we see is also the density function of a normal random variable, with mean $E(Y) = a + b\mu$ and variance $VAR(Y) = b^2 VAR(X)$.

Next, we consider the distribution of a sum of independent random variables, often referred to as the *convolution* of their probability distributions. We shall demonstrate the concept by looking at the sum of two independent random variables. The generalization follows immediately by repeated application of the same argument.

Let X and Y be two discrete random variables with probability functions $p(x)$ and $r(y)$ for $x = 0, 1, 2, \ldots$, and $y = 0, 1, 2, \ldots$. Let $Z = X + Y$, and let $h(z)$ be the probability function. Then Z can assume values $z = 0, 1, 2, \ldots$. $Z = 0$ if both $X = 0$ and $Y = 0$. Given that X and Y are independent, the probability that they are both 0 and hence $Z = 0$ is $h(0) = p(0)r(0)$ by expression (10-2). Similarly, $Z = 1$ if $X = 0$ and $Y = 1$, or if $X = 1$ and $Y = 0$. Hence, $h(1) = p(0)r(1) + p(1)r(0)$ by expression (10-6). Using the same principle, we get

$$h(z) = \sum_{x=0}^{z} p(x)r(z - x), \qquad z = 0, 1, 2, \ldots \tag{10-54}$$

For two independent continuous random variables with density functions $f(x)$ and $r(y)$, the density function of $Z = X + Y$ is

$$h(z) = \int_{-\infty}^{\infty} f(x)r(z - x)\,dx \tag{10-55}$$

Example 6. Consider again the demand distribution in Example 3(a). What is the demand distribution over two months, assuming sales on consecutive months are independent?

Let X_1 be the demand for month 1 and X_2 for month 2, and let $Z = X_1 + X_2$. Then

$$p(Z = 2) = p(X_1 = 1)p(X_2 = 2 - 1) = (0.4)(0.4) = 0.16$$

$$\begin{aligned} p(Z = 3) &= p(X_1 = 1)p(X_2 = 3 - 1) + p(X_1 = 2)p(X_2 = 3 - 2) \\ &= (0.4)(0.3) + (0.3)(0.4) = 0.24 \end{aligned}$$

$$\begin{aligned} p(Z = 4) &= p(X_1 = 1)p(X_2 = 4 - 1) + p(X_1 = 2)p(X_2 = 4 - 3) \\ &\quad + p(X_1 = 3)p(X_2 = 4 - 3) \\ &= (0.4)(0.2) + (0.3)(0.3) + (0.2)(0.4) = 0.25 \end{aligned}$$

$$\begin{aligned} p(Z = 5) &= p(X_1 = 1)p(X_2 = 5 - 1) + p(X_1 = 2)p(X_2 = 5 - 2) \\ &\quad + p(X_1 = 3)p(X_2 = 5 - 3) + p(X_1 = 4)p(X_2 = 5 - 4) \\ &= 0.04 + 0.06 + 0.06 + 0.04 = 0.20, \text{ etc.} \end{aligned}$$

Verify that $p(Z = 6) = 0.10$, $p(Z = 7) = 0.04$, $p(Z = 8) = 0.01$ and, as required, their sum is 1.

It is not easy to find closed formulas for the convolution of probability distributions from expressions (10-54) and (10-55). Usually this will involve either probability generating functions or Laplace transformations, both of which are beyond the immediate needs of this book. However, for particular random variables there are a number of useful results that we shall quote without proof in Table 10-1. These results can all be extended to more than two random variables.

Table 10-1. *Convolutions of some probability distributions*

Distributions of X and Y	Distribution of $Z = X + Y$
X normal with parameters μ_x and σ_x^2 Y normal with parameters μ_y and σ_y^2	normal with parameters $\mu_x + \mu_y$ and $\sigma_x^2 + \sigma_y^2$
X binomial with parameters n_x and p Y binomial with parameters n_y and p	binomial with parameters $n = n_x + n_y$ and p
X Poisson with parameter λ_x Y Poisson with parameter λ_y	Poisson with parameter $\lambda_x + \lambda_y$
X and Y both exponential with parameter λ	gamma with $a = 2$ and $b = \lambda$ (also known as an Erlang-2 distribution)

10-8 STOCHASTIC PROCESSES

In many applications of probability models, we are actually concerned with a sequence of random variables. Suppose we consider the replacement of lightbulbs in a building, for example. We could look either at the sequence of times between replacements, or at the random variables giving the numbers of bulbs replaced up to time t. Because of its probabilistic behavior, any such sequence of random variables is called a stochastic process. (The name comes from a Greek word that can, perhaps significantly, be translated as "proceeding by guesswork"!) To order the sequence of random variables, we require an index set, which almost always refers in some way to time. We may consider this index set to be continuous, so that we talk about the random variable occurring at time t, say $X(t)$. Or we may consider the index set to be discrete, so that we talk of the nth random variable from a sequence $\ldots X_{n-1}, X_n, X_{n+1}, \ldots$. In either case, we presume that, at a particular time, X is a random variable that takes values governed by some probability distribution. For example, $\{X_n\}$, the sequence of times between the nth and $(n + 1)$th bulb replacement $(n = 0, 1, 2, \ldots)$ is a continuous-valued stochastic process with a discrete index set; while $[N(t), t \geq 0]$—the number of bulbs replaced by time t—is a discrete-valued process with a continuous index set. Notice that since each stochastic process is concerned with the behavior of particular random variables, it is often possible to define several different stochastic processes on a given physical process.

The stochastic models of physical processes considered in operations research commonly have to involve many simplifying assumptions, to the point that the models often appear quite unrealistic. There are two reasons for this. Consider a discrete time stochastic process $\{X_n\}$, $n = 0, 1, 2, \ldots$. In general, the future behavior of the process will (at least to some extent) depend on its entire past history. So, strictly speaking, we should consider conditional probability distributions for X_{n+1}, say, $P(X_{n+1} \leq x | X_n = a, X_{n-1} = b, X_{n-2} = c, \ldots)$, that depend on all the values of the process in the past. Such conditional distributions are usually far too complex mathematically to be of any practical use. The second reason is the difficulty such dependence will cause when we come to estimate the probability distribution of X_{n+1}. Normally, we would base this estimate on the frequencies of similar types of events in the past history of the process. However, each possible past history of $\{X_n\}$ may generate a different conditional distribution for X_{n+1}, none of which (except the one that actually occurred) we have ever seen! In order to get enough values to estimate the distribution of X_{n+1}, we must assume that the dependence of X_n on its past values is very limited. If the stochastic process is discrete-valued, we usually assume that X_n depends at most on the value of X_{n-1}. Such a process is called a *Markov chain*. If the process takes continuous values, even this may be too much, so we usually assume that X_n is independent of all past values. With the additional assumption that all the X_n's have the same distribution, we call this process a *renewal process*.

10-9 POISSON PROCESSES

An important subclass of renewal processes in which the random variables have an even stronger independence property is the subclass where X_n has a negative exponential distribution. We shall make extensive use of such *Poisson processes* in Chapter 15 when we look at some waiting-line models. Consider a sequence of events in time. These events could be the arrival of customers at a service facility or the receipt of calls at a telephone exchange. X_n is the time between the $(n-1)$th and nth event, and N_t is the total number of events that have occurred by time t. We will formally define the process in terms of the distribution of N_t. $\{X_n\}$, $n = 0, 1, 2, \ldots$, is said to be a *Poisson process* if N_t has a Poisson distribution for any value of t. That is,

$$(10\text{-}56) \qquad P(N_t = n) = e^{-\lambda t}\frac{(\lambda t)^n}{n!}, \qquad n = 0, 1, 2, \ldots$$

λ is called the rate of the process.

Expression (10-56) implies, in fact, that the distribution of the times between events must be negative exponential. Assume that we start observing the process immediately after an event, which we will say occurred at time 0. The probability that we will have had no events by time t is given by the first term of expression (10-56):

$$(10\text{-}57) \qquad P(\text{no event in } (0, t)) = e^{-\lambda t}\frac{(\lambda t)^0}{0!} = e^{-\lambda t}$$

But

$$(10\text{-}58) \qquad \begin{aligned} P(\text{no event in } (0, t)) &= P(\text{next event occurs after } t) \\ &= P(\text{time between two successive events exceeds } t) \end{aligned}$$

since we assumed we had an event at time 0.

Now the distribution function of the time between two successive events, X_n, is

$$P(X_n \leq t) = P(\text{time between two successive events does not exceed } t)$$

So from expression (10-58) we see that

$$P(\text{no event in } (0, t)) + P(X_n \leq t) = 1$$

$$P(X_n \leq t) = 1 - P(\text{no event in } (0, t)) = 1 - e^{-\lambda t} \qquad \text{by (10-57)}$$

The probability density function of X_n is

$$(10\text{-}59) \qquad \frac{d}{dt}P(X_n \leq t) = \lambda e^{-\lambda t}$$

As we claimed, this is a negative exponential distribution.

There is a further property of a Poisson process that makes it very useful for modeling. This is the *lack of memory property*. In other words, at any instant of time the future behavior of the process does not depend on what happened in the past. Let us find the conditional probability that the first event occurs in the interval $(t, t + h)$, given that no events occurred up to time t. This is

$$\frac{P(\text{first event in } (t, t+h) \text{ and no event in } (0, t))}{P(\text{no event in } (0, t))} \qquad \text{by (10-2)}$$

$$= \frac{\int_t^{t+h} \lambda e^{-\lambda x}\, dx}{e^{-\lambda t}} \qquad \text{by (10-57)}$$

$$= \frac{1 - e^{-\lambda(t+h)} - (1 - e^{-\lambda t})}{e^{-\lambda t}} = 1 - e^{-\lambda h}$$

This is again a negative exponential distribution, depending only on the length h of the interval and independent of the time t since the last event.

PROPERTY OF STATIONARITY AND LACK OF MEMORY

In a Poisson process, events are completely independent of one another or of the state of the system, and the probability of an event occurring in any interval of time h does not depend on the starting point of the interval or on the specific history of events preceding it, but depends only on the length h of the interval.

So in addition to the renewal process property that we need not consider the times of events before the last event, we now have the stronger property that, in predicting the future, we need not consider the time since the last event. Among continuous-valued renewal processes, this latter property is unique to the Poisson process. Another interpretation of this property is that the Poisson process is the only process for which the instantaneous rate at which events occur is a constant, λ. Consider again a very short time interval of length h. What is the probability of exactly one event in $(0, h)$? By the second term of expression (10-56) we obtain

$$P(\text{exactly one event in } h) = \lambda h e^{-\lambda h}$$

For a very small h, $e^{-\lambda h}$ is very close to 1 ($= e^0$). Hence, for a very small h, we get the approximation

$$P(\text{exactly one event in } h) \cong \lambda h \tag{10-60}$$

From expression (10-56), it also follows that for a very small value of h, the probability of observing more than one event in h is almost zero, since these terms contain higher order powers of h that are negligible when h is very small. We can safely assume that when h is sufficiently small, no more than one event can occur. Only the terms for no event and for one event are thus significant, and

$$\begin{aligned} P(\text{no event in } h) &\cong 1 - P(\text{exactly one event in } h) \\ &\cong 1 - \lambda h, \qquad \text{for a very small value of } h \end{aligned} \tag{10-61}$$

Expressions (10-60) and (10-61) can, in fact, be used to define a Poisson process. We shall use this definition extensively in Chapter 15.

EXERCISES

10.1 Consider an urn that contains five balls numbered 0, 1, 2, 3, and 4. Balls numbered 0 and 3 are black; the other three balls are white.

(a) You draw a ball at random from the urn and record its number. It is then replaced, and a second ball is drawn at random from the urn and its number recorded. Define the sample space for this experiment.

(b) What is the probability of event A_i = [the sum of the numbers is i], for i = 6, 7, and 8? What is the probability of event B = [the sum is at least 6]? event C = [the sum is no more than 5]?

(c) What is P (the sum is at least 6 and at least one ball is black)?

(d) What is the conditional probability that the sum is at least 6, given that at least one ball drawn is black? First use the definition (10-2) and then verify the result directly from the reduced sample space.

(e) What is the probability that at least one ball is black, given that the sum is at least 6?

(f) Consider the drawing of each ball as a separate experiment. Let event A = [first ball is black] and event B = [second ball is black]. Are A and B independent events? If so, find P(C), where $C = A \cap B$, using the multiplication rule.

(g) Two balls are drawn consecutively without replacement. Find the probability that both balls are black.

10.2 The firm XYZ considers submitting a bid as a subcontractor for a large computer system. It is known that three major computer manufacturers, A, B, and C, compete for the main contract. Firm XYZ has previously been subcontractor for A and B. The president of XYZ estimates that A has a 15 percent chance and B a 30 percent chance of getting the contract. If A gets the contract, XYZ has an 80 percent chance of being the subcontractor, whereas if B gets the contract, XYZ's chance is only 50 percent. It is only profitable for XYZ to prepare a bid if its chances of being chosen as subcontractor are at least 25 percent.

(a) Should XYZ prepare a bid? Why?

(b) Find the conditional probability that XYZ is chosen as subcontractor, given that it is known that either A or B has been given the contract.

(c) Find the conditional probability that A got the main contract, given that XYZ is the subcontractor.

10.3 Suppose that 5 percent of all men and 0.25 percent of all women are colorblind. A person is chosen at random from a population consisting of equal numbers of men and women and is found to be colorblind. What is the posterior probability that the person is male?

10.4 A binomial model has been proposed to measure the effect of a series of three insertions of a newspaper advertisement. The events A, B, and C are presumed to be independent, where

A = [individual does not see the first insertion]
B = [individual does not see the second insertion]
C = [individual does not see the third insertion]

and any individual has the same chance of seeing a particular insertion. Under these assumptions:

(a) Calculate the probability that an individual does not see any of the insertions.

(b) Find a suitable binomial model for calculating the mean and the variance of the number of persons in a large population of size N who have been exposed to the advertisement (i.e., have seen at least one of the insertions).

10.5 The random variables (X, Y) have a joint probability function

$$p(x, y) = C(\tfrac{1}{2})^{x+y}, \quad x = 0, 1, 2 \ldots, \quad y = 0, 1, 2, \ldots$$

(a) Find the value of C.
(b) Find the marginal distribution of X.
(c) Find the conditional distribution of X, given Y = 1.
(d) Are X and Y independent? Give a reason for your answer.

Note that the sum of the series $\sum_{k=1}^{\infty} kx^{k-1}$ is $1/(1 - x)^2$.

10.6 Consider a random variable that assumes the value 1 with probability p and assumes the value 0 with probability $(1 - p)$ (known as a *Bernoulli variable*). Find the expected value and the variance and standard deviation of this variable. (Note that a binomial variable is given as the sum of n Bernoulli variables.)
(a) Verify expressions (10-26) and (10-27) using the properties of E(X) and VAR(X) for the sum of independent variables.
(b) Show, from expression (10-54), that the sum of a Bernoulli variable and a binomial random variable with parameters n and p is also binomial.

10.7 A product has the following probability density function for its daily sales: $f(x) = 0.1 - 0.005x$ for $0 \leq x \leq 20$ and $f(x) = 0$ elsewhere (a triangular distribution).
(a) Find $P(X \leq 10)$, $P(X > 10)$.
(b) Find E(X) and VAR(X).
Note: Integration is required.

10.8 The monthly demand for a given spare part has a normal distribution. Chances are 50 percent that the demand is at most 200, and for approximately 9 out of 10 months sales lie between 140 and 260 units.
(a) Determine the two parameters of the corresponding normal distribution.
(b) What is the probability that monthly sales exceed 280?

10.9 Consider the following weekly demand distribution:

x	0	1	2	3	4	5	6	7	8
$p(x)$	0.10	0.20	0.25	0.20	0.12	0.06	0.04	0.02	0.01

The stock on hand at the beginning of a given week is 4.
(a) Find the probability distribution for the amount short.
(b) If each unit sold brings in a profit of $2.50, find the expected value of profits lost through shortages.

10.10 Consider the probability distribution of exercise 10.9. Assuming that sales in consecutive weeks are independent, find the probability distribution of sales over a 2-week period.

10.11 Consider the distribution given in exercise 10.7. Assume that stocks on hand at the beginning of the day amount to 15.
(a) Determine the probability density function of lost sales.
(b) If each unit brings in a profit of \$3, what is the expected value of the daily profits lost through shortages?

10.12 Find the approximate probability distribution for sales over 30 days for the distribution defined in exercise 10.7. Assume that each day has the same distribution and that sales between days are independent.

10.13 Prove that the geometrically distributed random variable X has a lack of memory property similar to that of a Poisson process. That is, if s and t are two positive integers, then $P(X > s + t|X > t) = P(X > s)$. Can you explain from expression (10-60) why this is not surprising?

10.14 The times in minutes at which events occur in a sample from a Poisson process are as follows: 1, 6.3, 8, 9.2, 15, 16.1, 19, 19.2, 19.8, 20.
(a) What would you estimate to be the rate of the process?
(b) What is the mean number of events that will occur in any 5-minute period?
(c) Roughly, does this sample appear to you to actually come from a Poisson process? Why or why not?
(d) If no event has occurred in the last 4 minutes, what is the mean time until the next event?

REFERENCES

Burington, R. S., and D. C. May. *Handbook of Probability and Statistics with Tables*. Sandusky, Ohio: Handbook Publishers, 1953. A reference book of this sort with tables of the binomial, Poisson, normal, and exponential distributions is part of every operations researcher's library.

Hogg, R. V., and A. T. Craig. *Introduction to Mathematical Statistics*. New York: Macmillan, 1970. An advanced but not impossibly difficult book. Very reliable, and certainly good enough to quote from.

Mosteller, F., R. E. K. Rourke, and G. B. Thomas. *Probability with Statistical Applications*. Reading, Mass.: Addison-Wesley, 1969. A good introductory text for a thorough review.

Snedecor, George W., and William G. Cochran. *Statistical Methods*. Ames, Iowa: Iowa State University, 1967. An excellent text for the practitioner or for those who have to use statistical tools without wanting to learn all the mathematical bases and proofs. Very thorough coverage of most tools with lots of good examples and useful pointers. Highly recommended as a reference text.

There are a number of texts that cover the application of statistical methods to management. For example:

Mendenhall, W., and J. Reinmuth. *Statistics for Management and Economics*. Belmont, Ca.: Duxbury, 1978.

Stochastic processes and their applications to O.R. models are studied in:

Karlin, S. A *First Course in Stochastic Processes*. New York: Academic Press, 1969.
Parzen, E. *Stochastic Processes*. San Francisco: Holden-Day, 1962.

A modern approach, requiring some mathematical sophistication, is given in:

Cinlar, Erhan. *Introduction to Stochastic Processes*. Englewood Cliffs, N.J.: Prentice-Hall, 1975.

CHAPTER ELEVEN

Bayesian Decision Analysis

As we saw in Chapter 1, most decision problems involve some elements of uncertainty. This uncertainty may arise from a lack of information about the environment in which the problem is set or about the effects of any action we may take. The converse of this statement is also true. Almost all probability models are set up as an aid to some decision-making process. In *decision analysis,* the trend has been to incorporate probability models into the actual formulation of the decision problem. Provided we have an easily quantified decision criterion and are prepared to assign probability distributions to the elements of uncertainty, complex decision problems can be solved using the ideas of conditional probability and Bayes's Theorem, discussed in Section 10-1 and 10-2 of Chapter 10.

The title "decision analysis" has been used to cover a range of methods, from the most precise mathematical techniques to highly subjective, intuitive procedures for which no formal foundation is available. The papers in the two special journal issues listed in the references at the end of this chapter indicate the variety of approaches possible. Here we can cover only a small set of what might be termed the conventional techniques for decision problems.

11-1 SETTING UP A DECISION PROBLEM

Consider this example. The Air Pollution Control Agency has given a pulp milling firm two years to reduce its emissions of air pollutants. As research contractor to the Association of Pulp Mills, the firm has already started some preliminary research (financed by association members) on an air pollution control device. This device, if successfully developed, promises to reduce the emission of chemicals and particles to a point below the maximum levels set by the control agency when the mills are operated at below 90 percent of full capacity. The research plans prepared by the director of research indicate that it will take another 18 months to determine whether or not such a device can be developed, with most of the crucial tests occurring toward the end of this period. If the research is successful, the devices could easily be installed in all of the firm's pulp mills within the remaining 6 months before the deadline set by the control agency. However, the director of research cannot guarantee that the device will be developed successfully. In fact, she estimates that chances of success are about 60 percent. If the results of the tests at the end of the 18-month period are negative, she plans to abandon the project.

In view of the state of the research project and the deadline to clean up, the firm has essentially two available alternatives. It can start the necessary steps to convert the operations of all its pulp mills to a new process that has a substantially lower emission of pollution-contributing chemicals and solid particles. This conversion would take about 2 years and would therefore have to be started immediately. The new process would permit the firm to meet the standards imposed when operating its mills at 80 percent of full capacity without the pollution control device, and at full capacity with the device. The other alternative is to take a wait-and-see attitude in which the firm would wait for the results of the research project. If the research was successful, the devices could be installed within the 2-year limit. However, if the research was a failure, then the firm would have to undertake a crash effort to convert all facilities to the new process as fast as possible. Until then, the mills could operate at only 40 percent of full capacity.

These alternatives have the following consequences on the net present value of earnings of the company over a 10-year planning horizon: If conversion to the new process is undertaken right now, earnings of the firm would amount to \$24,000,000 if the device becomes available in time, and \$11,000,000 if the device cannot be developed. If the wait-and-see alternative is chosen, the firm would have earnings of \$32,000,000 if the device becomes available in time (despite the reduction in the maximum level of operations), but it would incur a loss of about \$2,000,000 if the device does not materialize. What course of action should the firm choose?

The firm has two *actions* available to it:

A_1 = Wait 18 months to see if the pollution control device is successful
A_2 = Start conversion to the new process immediately

The amount the firm will earn under each action depends on whether or not the pollution control device is developed successfully. Since the firm cannot control this, we will refer to the outcomes of the research as *states of nature*, or *events*. We label them

- E_1: device is developed successfully,
- E_2: device is not developed successfully.

Using the research director's estimate of the chances of success, we can put a probability distribution on these events: $P(E_1) = 0.6$ and $P(E_2) = 0.4$. Since we know what the earnings of the firm will be if either action is taken, we can represent the set of possible outcomes as a payoff table (see Table 11-1).

Table 11-1. *Payoff table for the pulp mill ($1,000,000's)*

	Event E_1	Event E_2
Action A_1	32	−2
Action A_2	24	11

There are a number of decision criteria that the firm can use in deciding which action to take. Which one they select depends very much on their objective. Suppose the firm wishes to take the action that offers the highest possible payoff regardless of which event may occur, called the *maximax criterion*. From Table 11-1, the highest possible payoff of $32,000,000 occurs if the firm takes action A_1 and event E_1 occurs. On the other hand, they may prefer to protect themselves against serious financial losses and use a more conservative criterion, such as the *maximin criterion*. In that case they would determine for each action the lowest possible payoff that can occur, and then select the action that maximizes the lowest possible payoff. From Table 11-1, the lowest possible payoff for action A_1 is −$2,000,000, while for action A_2 it is $11,000,000. Hence, the maximin criterion leads to the choice of action A_2.

11-2 EXPECTED MONETARY VALUE DECISION CRITERIA

Note that neither of the decision criteria considered so far has taken into account the probability that each event will occur. In fact, if we are very confident that the device will be developed successfully, we will want to select action A_1, since this action now offers us a very high chance of earning $8,000,000 ($32,000,000 − $24,000,000) more than would the selection of action A_2. On the other hand, if we are sure that event E_2 will occur, the profit of $11,000,000 produced by action A_2 is clearly preferable to the loss of $2,000,000 resulting from action A_1. What we have done in these two cases is to attach weights to the two events and to select in each case the action that gave us the highest weighted average payoff, or *expected monetary value (EMV)*. It seems natural to use the probabilities of the events as the weights and, therefore, to use as our decision variable the expected values of the payoffs under each action. Using the research director's probability distribution, the *EMV* of action A_1, for example, is $EMV(A_1) = 32(0.6) + (-2)(0.4) = \$18{,}400{,}000$.

EXPECTED MONETARY VALUE DECISION CRITERION

The best action is the one with the highest expected monetary value.

Table 11-2 shows the *EMV* for each action. Thus, under the *EMV* criterion, we select action A_2.

Table 11-2. *The EMV's for the pulp mill ($1,000,000's)*

	Event E_1	Event E_2	EMV(A_i)
Action A_1	32	−2	18.4
Action A_2	24	11	18.8
Probability	0.6	0.4	

An alternative approach to expected monetary value decision criteria is based on the concept of *opportunity loss*, or *regret*. For each action-event pair, the opportunity loss is defined to be the difference between what the payoff could have been if we had chosen the optimal action for that event and what the payoff actually was. Formally, we can derive an *opportunity loss table* from a payoff table as follows:

1. For each event, identify the best possible payoff value.
2. For each action, subtract the actual payoff from this best possible value. These are the opportunity losses.

For instance, let us assume that E_1 occurs. Then the best possible payoff of $32,000,000 occurs if action A_1 is taken. So if the firm actually takes action A_1 and event E_1 occurs, no opportunity loss is incurred. If action A_2 is taken and event E_1 occurs, the opportunity loss is ($32,000,000 − $24,000,000) = $8,000,000. The complete opportunity loss table is given in Table 11-3.

Table 11-3. *The opportunity loss table for pulp mill*

	Event E_1	Event E_2	EOL(A_i)
Action A_1	0	13	5.2
Action A_2	8	0	4.8
Probability	0.6	0.4	

EXPECTED OPPORTUNITY LOSS DECISION CRITERION

The best action is the one with the lowest expected opportunity loss (*EOL*).

Thus the *EOL*'s for the two actions the firm can take are $EOL(A_1) = 0(0.6) + 13(0.4) =$ $5,200,000 and $EOL(A_2) = 8(0.6) + 0(0.4) =$ $4,800,000. Under the *EOL* criterion, we again select action A_2. It is not just a coincidence that the *EMV* and the *EOL* decision criteria both lead to the selection of action A_2. Note that the size of the difference between the two expected monetary values ($18,800,000 −

$18,400,000 = $400,000) is exactly the same as the size of the difference between the expected opportunity losses ($4,800,000 − $5,200,000 = −$400,000), so that the margin by which we choose action A_2 is the same in either case. In fact, the *EMV* and the *EOL* decision criteria will always lead to the selection of the same action, and by the same margin.

Let us suppose that we can determine for sure whether or not the pollution control device would be developed successfully prior to making our decision. If we know that the device will be developed, obviously we choose action A_1 and wait for the device to be completed. This will lead to earnings of $32,000,000. If the device cannot be produced, we should start conversion to the new process immediately for a payoff of $11,000,000. Thus, under *perfect information* our payoff table simplifies to Table 11-4. Before we are told whether the device will be developed successfully, the research director's estimates, or *prior probabilities*, are our best guide as to what the outcome of the research project will be. Using these estimates, we can calculate the *expected payoff under perfect information (EPPI)* as *EPPI* = 32(0.6) + 11(0.4) = $23,600,000. Comparing Table 11-2 and Table 11-3, we see that for each event (i.e., column), the payoffs and the opportunity losses corresponding to each action always sum to a constant: 32 for the first column and 11 for the second. This is simply a consequence of the definition of opportunity loss. As a result, the *EOL* and the *EMV* of any action will also always add to a constant. In fact, they add exactly to the expected payoff under perfect information.

Table 11-4. *The payoff table under perfect information*

	Event E_1	Event E_2	*EPPI*
Payoff	32	11	23.6
Probability	0.6	0.4	

11-3 THE EXPECTED VALUE OF PERFECT INFORMATION

There is another way to look at opportunity loss, and that is in terms of the *value of information*. We have seen that if we had perfect information about the outcome of the research program prior to making a decision, we could, on the average, expect to earn $23,600,000. At least that would be the average earnings if a large number of identical firms were faced with this decision. Without this information, the average earnings would be $18,800,000. The increase in earnings of $4,800,000 is the average value to the firm of receiving this information. Note that this is exactly equal to the *EOL* of the optimal decision.

We also can determine the *expected value of perfect information (EVPI)* directly from the opportunity loss table. If, after obtaining the perfect information, the firm knows that event E_1 will occur, then this information is worth $8,000,000 to them. Information that E_2 will occur has no value, since A_2 is still the optimal action. Thus, prior to receiving that information, we have $EVPI = 8(0.6) + 0(0.4) = \$4,800,000$. To summarize, we have the following relationships.

RELATIONSHIPS BETWEEN THE EXPECTED VALUES

(11-1) $EPPI = EMV(A_i) + EOL(A_i)$, for any action A_i

(11-2) $EPPI = EMV(A^*) + EOL(A^*)$, where A^* is the optimal action

(11-3) $EVPI = EPPI - EMV(A^*)$

(11-4) $EVPI = EOL(A^*)$ by expression (11-2)

Usually, perfect information is not available. We have to settle for imperfect information obtained by sampling or experimentation. We will consider the value of this information in Section 11-5. Knowledge of the value of perfect information gives us a guide as to whether such experimentation will be worthwhile in the first place.

11-4 DECISION TREES

So far we have only considered the effects of a single action and a single set of events. Because of this, the outcomes of the decision problem could conveniently be represented in the form of a payoff table. Many decision problems, however, involve a sequence of actions and events. For these problems, a tree diagram, or *decision tree*, is a very useful way of representing the situation. A decision tree is simply a chronological record—starting at the initial action or event—of all possible sequences of actions and events leading to the final outcomes. Under the EMV decision criterion, we shall see that a simple process of "rolling back" the tree, commencing at the final outcomes (as we did in dynamic programming evaluations in Chapter 9), eventually determines the optimal decision strategy.

In Figure 11-1, the payoff table given in Table 11-2 has been redrawn as a decision tree. From node 1 there are four paths leading to the final outcomes. Node 1 is a *decision node*, denoted by a square. At this point, we must choose one of the two paths (actions), A_1 or A_2. Nodes 2 and 3, however, are *chance nodes*, denoted by circles, from which the paths are determined by chance. For each chance node, we can determine the expected payoff over the branches at that node. For instance, at node 2 our expected payoff is \$18,400,000, while at node 3 it is \$18,800,000. Under the EMV criterion, we will choose the path leading to node 3, or action A_2. Since action A_1 is not optimal, that path has been blocked off. Thus the procedure for rolling back the decision tree is as follows: Starting from the final outcomes, we work our way backward through the tree, retaining at each chance node the expected payoff at that node, and retaining at each decision node the action with the highest EMV at that node.

Figure 11-1. *The payoff table represented as a decision tree.*

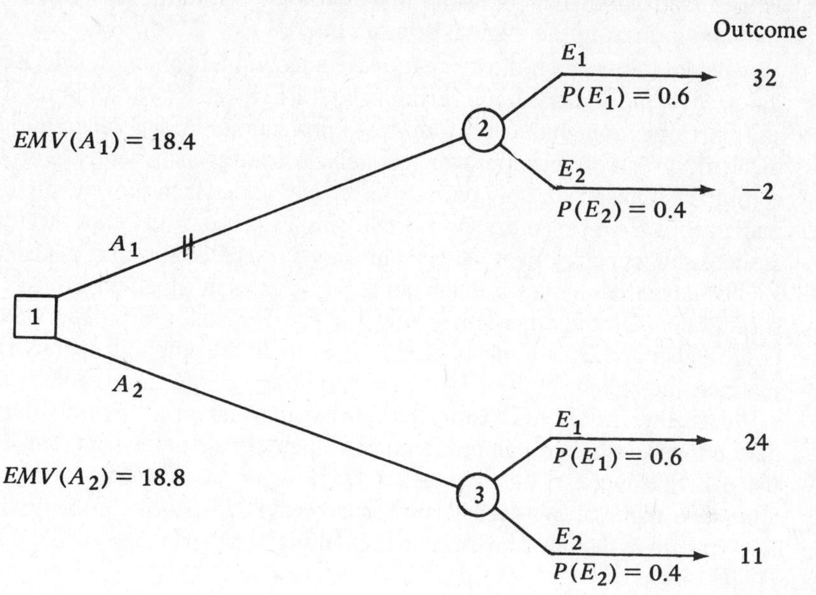

11-5 EXPERIMENTATION FOR DECISION MAKING

While we have been busy looking at trees, there has been a further development back at the pulp mill. The research director has suggested that the firm engage the services of I.E.R.—short for Industrial Ecology Research—to carry out a feasibility study of the proposed pollution control device. This would involve building a highly simplified, small-scale version of the proposed device, and then performing certain crude tests with the unit which would provide some indication as to the technical and economic feasibility of the approach used. Since this study could not be very extensive because of the time pressure to produce a report, the appraisal of the device by I.E.R. would only be tentative. The research consultants would simply report either that the appraisal was positive (which means the development of the device is likely to be successful) or that the appraisal was negative (which means the development is likely to be unsuccessful). I.E.R. has served as a consultant to the pulp industry on several occasions, and their appraisals have been fairly accurate. There is a chance, though, that their appraisal may be incorrect—a fact that is openly admitted by I.E.R. The cost of obtaining an appraisal amounts to $500,000. Should the firm hire I.E.R.'s services or not?

We can now expand the decision tree of Figure 11-1 to include this additional option. This is done in Figure 11-2. The initial decision is now whether or not to hire I.E.R. If no appraisal is obtained, the remainder of the branches are identical to the original decision tree of Figure 11-1. Hiring I.E.R. leads to chance node 2 with either a positive or a negative appraisal; the decision nodes 4 and 5 again have the same form as in the original decision tree.

Before the research director can make a recommendation for a decision strategy, she needs some additional information about I.E.R.'s track record in making appraisals. Checking through the pulp industry's information file, she finds a number of cases involving proposed inventions or technological advances where I.E.R. served as a consultant. Obviously, only projects ultimately undertaken provide any useful information on I.E.R.'s record. The file contains 15 projects that either were brought to a successful conclusion or, after vain efforts, were finally abandoned as failures. I.E.R.'s appraisal was positive in 7 out of the 10 cases in which the projects terminated successfully. On the other hand, only 1 of the 5 abandoned projects had received a positive appraisal. Assuming that I.E.R. goes about the pulp mill appraisal in a similar manner, the records of the 10 successful and the 5 unsuccessful projects give a guide as to whether I.E.R. will correctly indicate the outcome. If the pollution control device is successfully developed (event E_1), the estimate of the conditional probability that I.E.R.'s appraisal was positive (P) is $P(P|E_1) = \frac{7}{10}$. The estimated probability of a negative appraisal (N) given eventual success is $P(N|E_1) = \frac{3}{10}$. Similarly, if the device is eventually a failure, the estimated conditional probabilities are $P(P|E_2) = \frac{1}{5}$ and $P(N|E_2) = \frac{4}{5}$.

Now if the firm does decide to hire I.E.R., they will know the result of the appraisal before deciding which pollution control program to adopt, and the additional information contained in the appraisal will obviously change the research director's estimate of the chances of success. She will need to revise her *prior probability* of success, $P(E_1) = 0.6$, to produce a set of *posterior probabilities*, $P(E_1|P)$ and $P(E_1|N)$, conditioned on the result of the appraisal. These are the probabilities needed to evaluate those paths in the expanded decision tree that follow from the decision to hire I.E.R. The revision can be carried out by Bayes's Theorem. (See Section 10-2 of Chapter 10.)

$$P(E_1|P) = \frac{P(P \cap E_1)}{P(P)} = \frac{P(P|E_1)P(E_1)}{P(P|E_1)P(E_1) + P(P|E_2)P(E_2)}$$

$$= \frac{(0.7)(0.6)}{(0.7)(0.6) + (0.2)(0.4)} = 0.84$$

Similarly,

$$P(E_1|N) = \frac{P(N|E_1)P(E_1)}{P(N|E_1)P(E_1) + P(N|E_2)P(E_2)}$$

$$= \frac{(0.3)(0.6)}{(0.3)(0.6) + (0.8)(0.4)} = 0.36$$

Since E_1 and E_2 are mutually exclusive events, the remaining posterior probabilities are $P(E_2|P) = 1 - 0.84 = 0.16$ and $P(E_2|N) = 1 - 0.36 = 0.64$. The research director's estimate of the probability that the appraisal is positive is $P(P) = P(P|E_1)P(E_1) + P(P|E_2)P(E_2) = 0.5$. These probabilities have been attached to the appropriate branches of the tree in Figure 11-2.

Figure 11-2. *The complete decision tree for the pulp firm.*

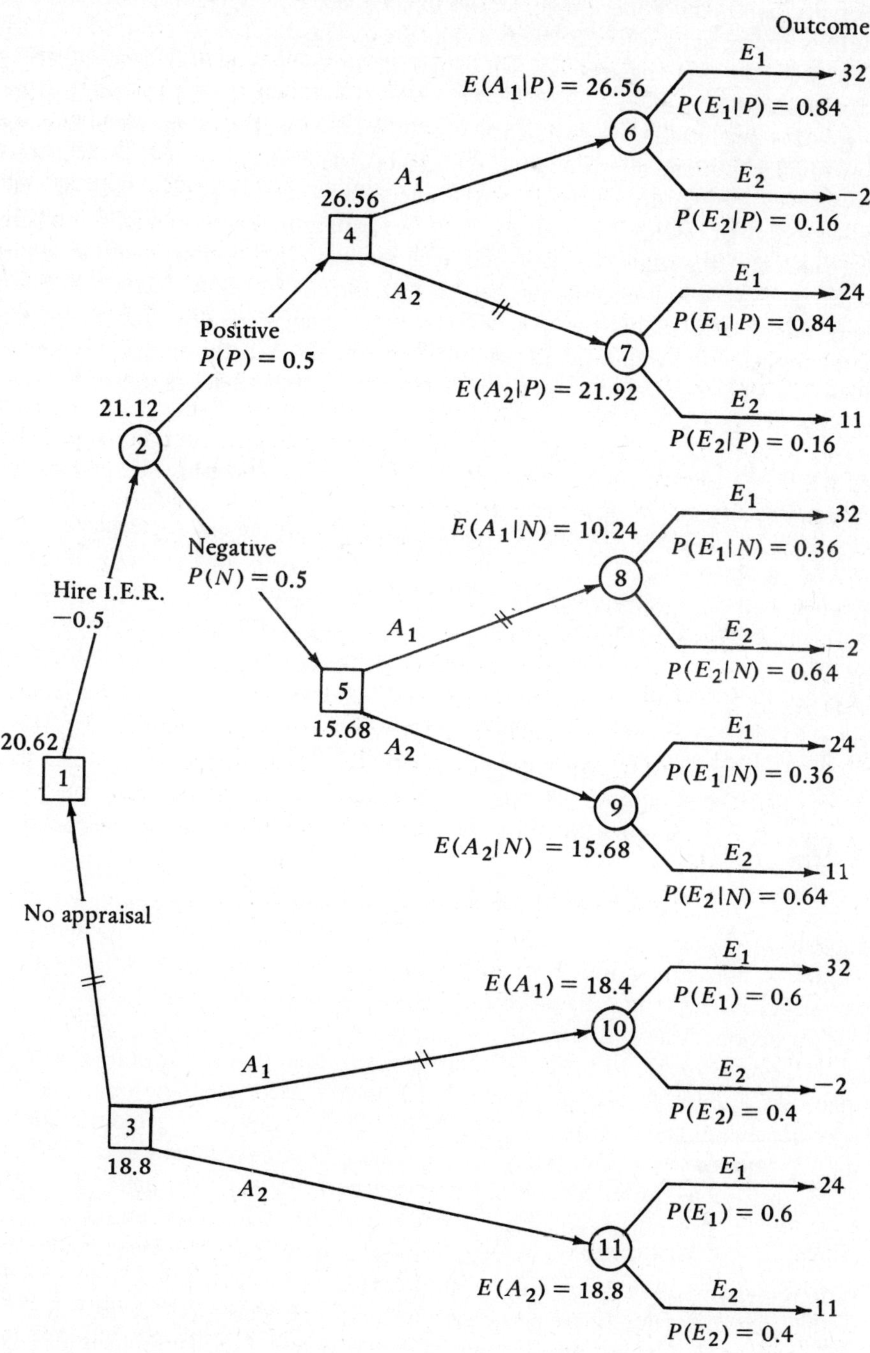

The tree now can be rolled back, retaining the *EMV* of the optimal action at each decision node. For example, let us suppose that I.E.R.'s appraisal is positive and we then choose action A_1. This leads us to node 6. The *conditional expected monetary value* of action A_1, given a positive appraisal, $E(A_1|P)$, is $32(0.84) - 2(0.16) =$ \$26,560,000. Since this exceeds $E(A_2|P) =$ \$21,920,000, $E(A_1|P)$ is the expected payoff that goes back to node 4, and the path from node 4 to node 7 is blocked off. In a similar fashion, the paths from node 5 to node 8 and from node 3 to node 10 are blocked off. Finally, since the *EMV* after deducting I.E.R.'s fee (\$20,620,000) still exceeds that *EMV* without an appraisal, the path from node 1 to node 3 is blocked off. Since only the paths to node 6 and node 9 remain, the optimal decision strategy under the *EMV* decision criterion can be read directly from the decision tree. The pulp milling firm should hire I.E.R. If their appraisal is negative, the firm should start conversion to the new process immediately. If, however, the appraisal is positive, the firm should risk waiting to see if the pollution control device is successful.

11-6 THE EXPECTED VALUE OF SAMPLE INFORMATION

The difference between the expected payoff if I.E.R. is hired and the expected payoff without an appraisal is (\$21,120,000 − \$18,800,000) = \$2,320,000. This is the *expected value of sample information (EVSI)* for this problem. Imperfect information is usually obtained by experiment, as in this case, or by sampling. The *EVSI* tells us something about the "worthwhileness" of this sampling. Since the *EVSI* considerably exceeds I.E.R.'s fee, it is clear that even under the limitations of the expected monetary value decision criterion, the appraisal is worthwhile. Note that \$2,320,000 < \$4,800,000. As we might expect, the *EVSI* cannot exceed the *EVPI*.

11-7 UTILITY FUNCTIONS

The expected monetary value decision criterion usually works well where the decision must be taken repeatedly and the risks are not very large. Under these conditions, we should be able to continue operating even if we make the wrong decision at some stage; and in the long run, the average return should tend toward the *EMV* of the chosen action. Many people, however, are averse to risk, especially when the risk could be catastrophic to them. So their decisions tend to avoid actions that involve high risks. In Section 1-14 of Chapter 1, we noted that the decision to buy insurance is obviously not based on maximizing *EMV*. Conservative management at the pulp milling firm may well place much more emphasis on the potential loss of \$2,000,000 if the pollution control device is not developed than on the potential profit of \$32,000,000 that may result if the device is installed. The *EMV* criterion provides us with a means of scaling monetary values to incorporate the probabilities of the various outcomes. We may wish to expand this scaling to also include some assessment of the subjective value of the particular outcomes to the decision maker. Since these values are to be used in situations involving risk, we use a similar (but simplified) risk model—a *reference lottery*—to determine them.

Let us consider a decision problem in which the best possible outcome is a return 15of \$6000 and the worst possible outcome is a loss of \$4000. Since \$6000 is the most desirable outcome, we assign it a *utility* of 1, or $U(\$6000) = 1$. Similarly, the loss of \$4000 is assigned a utility of zero, or $U(-\$4000) = 0$. Notice that since we intend to scale all the monetary values, these utility values can be assigned arbitrarily. We could take $U(\$6000) = 0$, $U(-\$4000) = -1$, or $U(\$6000) = 100$, $U(-\$4000) = 0$. To determine the utility of intermediate monetary values, we define the reference lottery for this problem as either

- accept a fixed amount of \$C, or
- take part in a lottery, denoted as $L(p)$, where the probability of winning \$6000 is p and the probability of losing \$4000 is $(1 - p)$.

The expected value of the lottery is $E[L(p)] = (\$6000)(p) + (-\$4000)(1 - p)$. If \$C is very much less than $E[L(p)]$, most decision makers will prefer the lottery over the certainty of receiving \$C. As we increase \$C, however, we reach a point where the certain payoff starts to become more attractive to the decision maker. At the point where the switch occurs the decision maker is indifferent between receiving \$C for certain or participating in the lottery $L(p)$. This value of \$C is the decision maker's *certainty equivalent* of the lottery. At this point, we should be able to equate the *expected utility* of the lottery to the decision maker with his or her utility value for the certain payoff. Let us suppose that careful questioning reveals that the decision maker finds the lottery with $p = 0.5$ and a certain payoff of \$0 to be equally attractive. Then

$$U(\$0) = [U(\$6000)](0.5) + [U(-\$4000)](0.5) = (1)(0.5) + (0)(0.5) = 0.5$$

Thus, the utility of \$0 is 0.5.

To determine more utility values, we could change the probability of the lottery, p. Many people, however, find it difficult to assess the value of lotteries in which the outcomes are not equally likely. The following five-point assessment procedure is usually preferable.

THE FIVE-POINT ASSESSMENT PROCEDURE

1. Find the value of the best possible outcome, x_1, and the worst possible outcome, x_0. Set $U(x_0) = 0$ and $U(x_1) = 1$.
2. Determine the decision maker's certainty equivalent, $x_{0.5}$, for a lottery with $p = 0.5$, between x_0 and x_1. Then $U(x_{0.5}) = [U(x_0)](0.5) + [U(x_1)](0.5) = 0.5$.
3. Find certainty equivalents, $x_{0.25}$ using a lottery $L(0.5)$ involving outcomes x_0 and $x_{0.5}$, and $x_{0.75}$ using $L(0.5)$ involving outcomes $x_{0.5}$ and x_1. Then $U(x_{0.25}) = 0.25$ and $U(x_{0.75}) = 0.75$.

A utility function now can be fitted through the five points $(x_0, 0)$, $(x_{0.25}, 0.25)$, $(x_{0.5}, 0.5)$, $(x_{0.75}, 0.75)$, $(x_1, 1.0)$, either by hand or, if a particular functional form for the utility function can be specified, by using statistical curve-fitting methods. For the above example, our decision maker eventually admits to having certainty equivalents of −$2100 for a lottery with $p = 0.5$ between − $4000 and $0, and $2500 for a lottery between $0 and $6000. This utility function is sketched in Figure 11-3.

In the decision tree procedure, we rolled back the tree by replacing each event node by the expected payoff at that node. Thus, we implicitly assumed that the decision maker was indifferent between receiving the expected payoff and taking part in the lottery represented by that node. With utility numbers, we now know exact certainty equivalents for similar kinds of lotteries, also calculated as expected values. We should be able to improve our expected value decision criterion (in the sense of more closely representing the decision maker's preferences) if we select the action that has the maximum *expected utility* rather than the one that has the maximum expected monetary value.

Figure 11-3. *Three utility functions.*

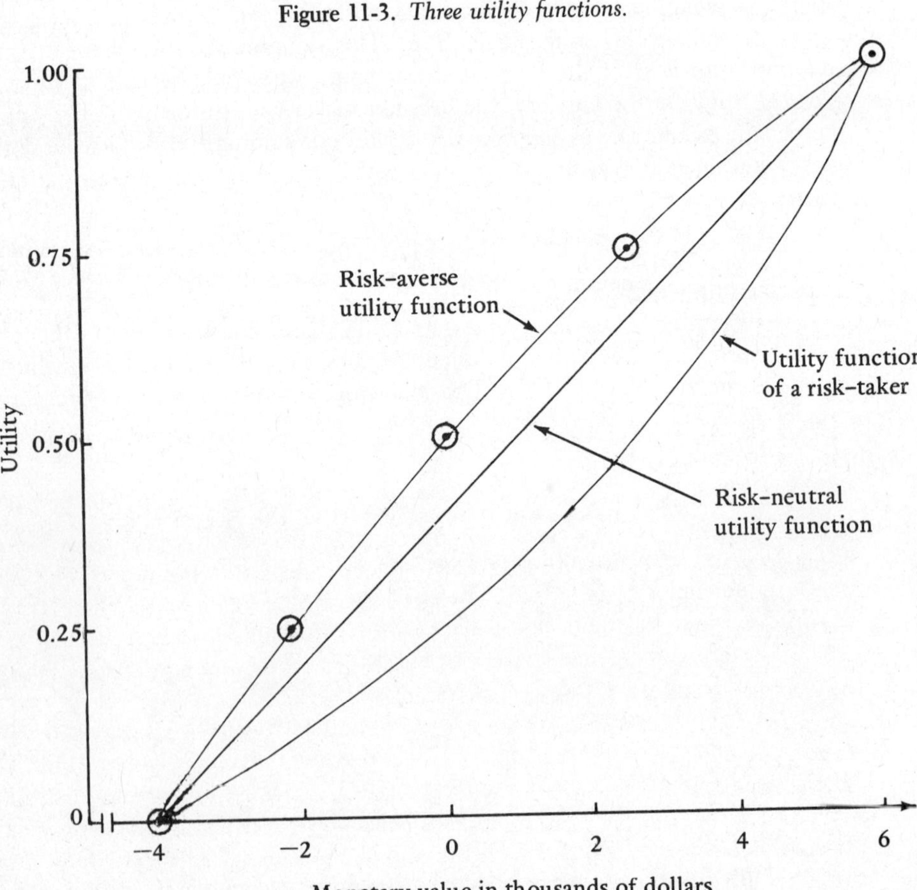

After extensive consideration, the management of the pulp milling firm has come up with the following utility values: $U(-\$2,000,000) = 0$, $U(\$11,000,000) = 0.5$, $U(\$24,000,000) = 0.9$, and $U(\$32,000,000) = 1$. Without the I.E.R. appraisal, the expected utility of action A_1 is $1(0.6) + 0(0.4) = 0.6$, and that of A_2 is $0.9(0.6) + 0.5(0.4) = 0.74$. Again, the optimal action is to start conversion to the new process immediately.

Up to now we have presumed that our decision makers were *risk-averse*. Given a choice between accepting the expected value of a lottery and taking part in the lottery, these decision makers will always prefer the certainty of the expected value over the risk of the lottery. Equivalently, we can say that the utility of the expected value of the lottery must be greater than the expected utility of the lottery. What does this mean in terms of utility functions? For two possible outcomes x and x' and a lottery $L(p)$ between them, we must have

$$U[xp + x'(1 - p)] > pU(x) + (1 - p)U(x')$$

This implies, of course, that the utility function must be *concave*. (You can find a discussion of concave and convex functions in Chapter 19.) If the decision maker is *risk-prone*, or a *risk taker*, on the other hand, he or she will prefer the lottery to the expected value of the lottery. It is left to the reader to show that this implies a convex utility function. Finally, we may encounter a *risk-neutral* decision maker, who has a straight-line utility function such as that shown in Figure 11-3. Since this is simply a linear transformation of the monetary values, the *EMV* and expected utility decisions will be identical.

It is important to note that utility functions can also be constructed for problems in which the outcomes are not expressed in monetary terms. Provided the decision maker is prepared to take part in the reference lottery, this procedure will produce utility functions for any numerically scaled set of outcomes.

11-8 DECISION MAKING WITH CONTINUOUS PRIOR DISTRIBUTIONS

A month has gone by since the pulp milling firm hired I.E.R. Because the consultants' appraisal was positive, the firm decided to wait and see if the pollution control device will be successful. Research on the device has been proceeding well—so well, in fact, that the research director is now completely sure that the device can be developed. The question is whether it will be done in time. The work so far has revealed a number of technical problems with the construction of the device and with the formulation and large-scale manufacture of the chemical catalysts required. These problems still have to be solved. Using the Program Evaluation and Review Technique—PERT—studied in Section 8-5 of Chapter 8, the research director now estimates the critical path for the development program to have a mean length of 29 months and a standard deviation of 2 months. If the development program is going to take too long, it may be better, considering the anticipated life of the mills, to abandon the pollution device and convert to the new process immediately (action A_2). If this is done, the cost of the pollution control program will amount to \$22,000,000 over the life of the mills. On the other hand, if the firm adheres to the development program (action A_1), the pollution control costs will increase by \$2,000,000 for every extra 3 months that the program takes. The director decides that, over the region of interest, the total cost can be reasonably approximated by a linear function of the form $(2 + \frac{2}{3}X)$ (expressed in millions of dollars), where X is the program length. What should the firm do now? From Figure 11-4 we can see that if the development time exceeds 30 months, immediate abandonment of the pollution control device is preferable. We will see that because the cost functions in this problem are linear, we can use the *mean* development time as a certainty equivalent in an EMV decision.

Figure 11-4. *Break-even analysis for the pulp mill.*

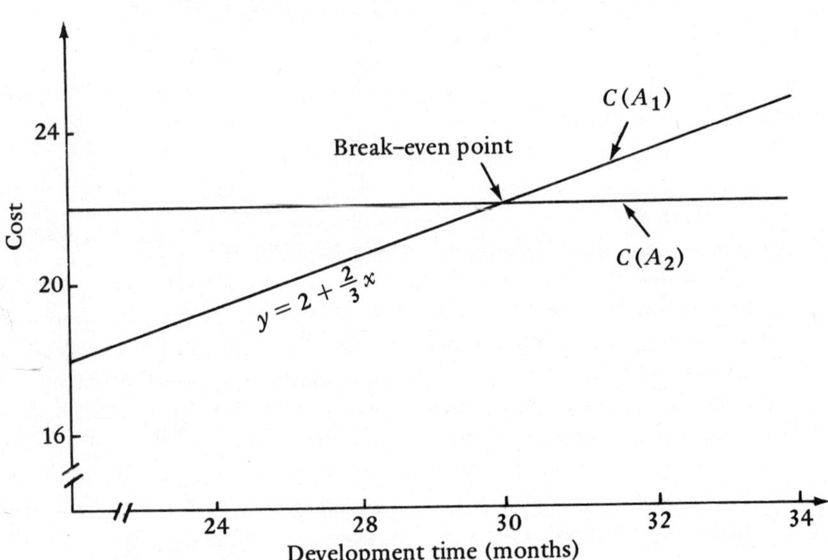

Let us consider a general decision problem in which the possible events are given by values of a continuous-valued random variable, X. We have two actions, A_1 and A_2, with linear cost or loss functions of the form

$$C(A_1) = m_1X + d_1 \qquad C(A_2) = m_2X + d_2 \tag{11-5}$$

We assume that $0 \leq m_2 < m_1$ and $0 \leq d_1 < d_2$. The *break-even point* is the value of X, denoted as x^*, at which $C(A_1) = C(A_2)$. Hence,

$$m_1x^* + d_1 = m_2x^* + d_2 \qquad \text{or} \qquad x^* = \frac{d_2 - d_1}{m_1 - m_2} \tag{11-6}$$

Under the EMV decision criterion, we prefer action A_1 if the expected cost of A_1,

$E[C(A_1)]$, is less than the expected cost of A_2, $E[C(A_2)]$. Now if $E[C(A_1)] < E[C(A_2)]$, then $E(m_1X + d_1) < E(m_2X + d_2)$ from expression (11-5); and so $m_1E(X) + d_1 < m_2E(X) + d_2$ from expression (10-13) of Chapter 10. Solving for $E(X)$, we get

$$E(X) < \frac{d_2 - d_1}{m_1 - m_2} = x^*, \qquad \text{from expression (11-6)} \tag{11-7}$$

In other words, we prefer action A_1 if the *mean value* of X, $E(X)$, is less than the break-even point. Similarly, we can show that A_2 is preferable if $E(X)$ is greater than x^*. In general, then, provided the cost functions are linear, *the action with the lower cost at the mean of the prior distribution* is the optimal action under the *EMV* criterion.

The cost functions for the pulp milling firm are

$$C(A_1) = 2 + \tfrac{2}{3}X$$

$$C(A_2) = 22$$

so that

$$x^* = \frac{22 - 2}{\frac{2}{3} - 0} = 30 \text{ months}$$

Since $E(X) = 29$ months is less than x^*, we prefer action A_1.

Note that we did not have to make any assumptions about the form of the distribution of X. Linear cost functions, however, are a necessary assumption for the use of the mean as a certainty equivalent. If any of the cost functions are not linear, the density function (and hence the expected cost of the action) must be calculated from the probability density function of X, using the method outlined in Section 10-7 of Chapter 10. An alternative approach, in this case, would be to assume that only a finite number of discrete events could occur, and to approximate the event distribution by a discrete distribution. The expected cost of each action can then be calculated as in Section 11-2.

11-9 *EVPI* FOR A NORMAL PRIOR DISTRIBUTION

Even when the cost functions are all linear, the *value of information* in a decision problem with a continuous prior distribution will depend on the exact form of the distribution. Because of this, the use of a discrete approximation to the prior distribution may be a computationally much simpler method of determining the *EVPI* than the integral expression (11-8), that we consider below. In one case, however—when the prior distribution is considered to be normal—the *EVPI* can be found directly from tables of the *unit normal loss integral.*

In Section 11-3 we showed that the *EVPI* was exactly the expected opportunity loss of the optimal action. Let us find the opportunity losses for the pulp milling firm if it takes action A_1. If the development program takes less than 30 months, the opportunity loss will be zero, since A_1 is indeed the best possible action. From the break-even point on, the opportunity loss is the difference between the cost of action A_1 and the cost of action A_2. In Figure 11-5 we have plotted the opportunity loss of action A_1 against the length of the development program. Superimposed on the figure is the probability density function, $f(x)$, for the program length. From expression (11-5) we have

$$\begin{aligned} \mathrm{EOL}(A_1) &= \int_{x=x^*}^{\infty} (C(A_1) - C(A_2))f(x)\,dx \\ &= (m_1 - m_2)\int_{x=x^*}^{\infty} xf(x)\,dx + (d_1 - d_2)\int_{x=x^*}^{\infty} f(x)\,dx \end{aligned} \tag{11-8}$$

If we substitute for $(d_1 - d_2)$ from expression (11-6), we get

$$\mathrm{EVPI} = \mathrm{EOL}(A_1) = (m_1 - m_2)\left[\int_{x=x^*}^{\infty} xf(x)\,dx - x^*\int_{x=x^*}^{\infty} f(x)\,dx\right] \tag{11-9}$$

The expression in square brackets in expression (11-9) can be evaluated analytically only for certain prior distributions. Often we can assume, however, that because of the *central limit theorem* (see Section 10-6 of Chapter 10) the prior distribution is approximately normal, with mean $E(X) = \mu$ and variance σ^2. It turns out that after some calculus operations have been performed, (11-9) can be expressed as

$$\mathrm{EVPI} = (m_1 - m_2)\sigma N(z^*) \tag{11-10}$$

where $z^* = (x^* - \mu)/\sigma$ and $N(z^*)$ is the value of the *unit normal loss integral at* z^*. (Values of $N(z)$ are listed in the Appendix.)

Figure 11-5. *The opportunity loss for* A_1 *and the prior density function.*

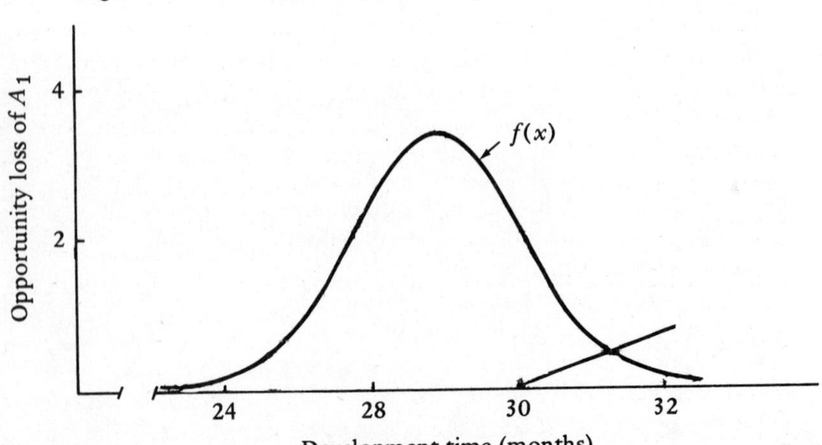

Note that the *EVPI* increases with the standard deviation of the prior distribution in expression (11-10). The greater the uncertainty (i.e., the standard deviation), the more valuable the perfect information becomes.

I.E.R. has approached the firm again. With their greater experience of PERT/CPM, the consultants claim that they should be able to determine the development time exactly. How much, on the average, is this information worth? Assuming the critical path length is normally distributed with a mean $\mu = 29$ months and a standard deviation $\sigma = 2$ months, we get $z^* = \frac{1}{2}$. From Table 2 of Appendix B, $N(\frac{1}{2}) = 0.1978$. Therefore, the *EVPI* is $(\frac{2}{3})(2)(0.1978) = \$263{,}733$. The firm should not pay more than this amount to find out exactly how long the program will take.

As an example of the discrete approximation method, we can also calculate the *EVPI* by assuming that the program takes an integral number of months and using areas under the normal distribution as approximate probabilities.

Month	30	31	32	33	34	35	36	37
Opportunity loss	0	$\frac{1}{3}$	1	$1\frac{2}{3}$	$2\frac{1}{3}$	3	$3\frac{2}{3}$	$4\frac{1}{3}$
Probability	0.191	0.150	0.092	0.044	0.016	0.004	0.001	0

For example, the area under the normal distribution between months 33 and 34 is approximately 0.016, and we have taken the opportunity loss at the middle of month 33 ($2\frac{1}{3}$ million dollars) to represent the average opportunity loss over the month. For the discrete approximation, the *EVPI* is $(\frac{1}{3})(0.150) + (1)(0.092) + \ldots = \$264{,}666$. This is close enough to the exact value for most purposes.

11-10 REVISION OF CONTINUOUS PRIOR DISTRIBUTIONS

The concept of the revision of prior probabilities to include information gained by experimentation or by sampling, which we considered in Section 11-5, can be extended to the case of continuous prior distributions. The effect of such information is to produce a *posterior* event distribution, possibly with a different mean and with a reduced variance reflecting the reduction of uncertainty brought about by the additional information. Provided we can model the uncertainty in the information by means of a probability distribution, Bayes's Theorem can be used to find the posterior event distribution, conditional on the value of the new information. Algebraically, if $f(x)$ is the probability density function of the prior distribution, and if $h(y|x)$ is the conditional density of the sample or experimental results, then, as in Section 11-5, we require the posterior distribution, $g(x|y)$. From expression (10-7) of Chapter 10, this can be expressed as

$$g(x|y) = f(x)\,h(y|x) \Big/ \int_{-\infty}^{\infty} f(x)\,h(y|x)\,dx \qquad (11\text{-}11)$$

When both the prior distribution, $f(x)$, and the sampling distribution, $h(y|x)$, are normal, it can be shown from expression (11-11) that the posterior distribution is also normal with mean and variance as follows:

$$\mu_2 = \frac{\sigma_1^2\mu_0 + \sigma_0^2\mu_1}{\sigma_1^2 + \sigma_0^2} \tag{11-12}$$

$$\sigma_2^2 = \left(\frac{\sigma_1^2}{\sigma_0^2 + \sigma_1^2}\right)\sigma_0^2 \tag{11-13}$$

μ_0 and σ_0^2 are the parameters of $f(x)$, and μ_1 and σ_1^2 are the parameters of $h(y|x)$. The proof of this is rather long, so we shall omit it.

The most obvious example of this type of revision is where the sample information has been obtained by means of a random survey on a population with normal prior distribution.

A small manufacturing company has a new seasonal novelty item that it would like to add to its product line. The fixed cost of setting up full-scale production of the item is estimated to be \$8000, with a variable cost of \$5 per unit produced. The company believes that it can sell the item for \$7.50 through each of its 80 retail outlets. Total sales of similar items in past years have averaged 3300 units (μ_0), with a standard deviation of 200 units (σ_0). Should the company go ahead with production or not? The two cost functions for cost of production and for revenue are $C_1 =$ \$8000 + (\$5)X and $C_2 =$ (\$7.5)X. Since the break-even point (equal to sale of 3200 units) is less than the mean of the prior distribution, the answer seems to be to go ahead. However, the company finds the situation a little too close for comfort. It decides to conduct a small survey of 10 of the retail outlets. The survey shows a mean anticipated demand of 38 units per outlet and a standard deviation of 4 units. Hence, the estimates from the sample survey of the mean and the standard deviation over all 80 outlets are $\mu_1 = 80(38) = 3040$ and $\sigma_1^2 = 80(4^2) = 1280$. The mean of the posterior distribution is

$$\mu_2 = \frac{(1280)(3300) + (40000)(3040)}{(1280 + 40000)} = 3048 \qquad \text{from (11-12)}$$

and its variance is

$$\sigma_2^2 = \left(\frac{1280}{40000 + 1280}\right)(40000) = 1240.3 \qquad \text{from (11-13)}$$

Since the posterior mean is considerably less than the break-even point, obviously the company would be unwise to introduce the product.

This example illustrates the effect of the revision formulas (11-12) and (11-13). We have said that to some extent the variances of the prior and the sampling distributions measure the degree of uncertainty about the information that they contain. In fact, the reciprocal of the variance is sometimes called the *information content* of the distribution. We can see that the mean of the posterior distribution is a weighted average of μ_0 and μ_1, with weights that depend upon the relative sizes of the variances. Because the sample information in the example appears to have a much lower degree of uncertainty, the mean of the posterior distribution comes out much closer to μ_1 than to μ_0. Similarly, the high quality of the sample information causes a considerable reduction in the variance of the posterior distribution.

On sales of X units, the net return to the company is $[(7.5 − 5)X − 8000]. The expected net return, based on the posterior distribution with $E(X) = \mu_2$, would be

$$E(2.5X - 8000) = 2.5E(X) - 8000 = -\$380$$

if the company decided to market the item. (Notice again that when the cost functions are linear, calculation of the expected return requires only the mean of the event distribution.) Yet the *EVPI*, calculated from the prior distribution, is $\$(2.5)(200)N(\frac{1}{2}) = \$98.90$. On the basis of this, the company could have decided—perfectly reasonably—that the sampling exercise was not likely to produce any useful improvement, and so they could have gone ahead with the item for an expected net loss of $380. Because the prior distribution turned out to be poor, the *EVPI* obviously was not a good guide to the actual value of sampling. We must remember that the *EVPI*, the *EMV*, and the *EOL* are *expected values* based on the prior distribution. They can only tell us when the prior distribution is reasonably accurate what the long-run expectations will be. An unreliable prior distribution will give an unreliable *EVPI*.

11-11 CONCLUDING REMARKS

In this chapter we have had space to lay out only the very bare bones of decision making under conditions of uncertainty. In the last twenty years, decision analysis has become a very important part of operations research methodology. A great deal has been learned about formal models for decision processes. Something much more difficult, however, that we have not considered is the subjective aspect of decision making.

Traditionally, we define probabilities in terms of the long-run relative frequencies of events. In the determination of *EMV*'s, however, we considered events that may occur once at most, if at all. Regardless of how much we may prefer the traditional definition, the numbers used in the *EMV* calculations usually will have to be derived from at least one individual's intuitive beliefs about the future course of events. The determination of such *subjective* probability distributions poses special problems. A good discussion of methods for solving these problems can be found in Chapter 12 of the book by Holloway listed in the references.

The simple—but extremely powerful—device of utility functions, considered in Section 11-7, allows us to scale outcomes in an almost unlimited fashion to reflect the decision maker's preferences. Unfortunately, the assessment of such utility functions is not an easy task. The attitudes that individuals exhibit toward risk are often extremely complex. Chapter 5 of Schlaifer, 1969 (see references) sets out some of the problems and gives some of the mathematical theory behind various types of utility functions that can be used.

The process of revision of prior probabilities, which we considered in Sections 11-5 and 11-10, should also be extended to include any kind of available information in the posterior distribution. How precisely this process is carried out depends on the intuition and the experience of each individual decision maker. Chapter 10 of Raiffa discusses some related philosophical issues.

EXERCISES

11.1 An oil company is considering an offshore drilling venture. A preliminary geological survey indicates that the rock formations off the coast are generally favorable to oil and gas deposits. From past information on similar rock formations, the exploration department comes up with the following estimates, where L denotes large deposits and S denotes small deposits: $P(L) = 0.1$, $P(S) = 0.9$. The firm has two actions available: to start explorations or not to explore. Explorations will cost \$800,000. If large oil deposits are found, the company expects to make a profit of \$15,800,000, less the exploration costs. If small deposits are discovered, the project will have to be abandoned as unprofitable for production.

(a) Set up a payoff table for the problem, and find the action with the maximum expected payoff.

(b) Assume that the firm can somehow procure perfect information about the rock formations at a cost of \$980,000. Should the firm obtain perfect information at this cost?

11.2 A firm sells a certain electronic control instrument. Part of the manufacturing process for these instruments involves an alignment of the instrument's reading device under simulated operation conditions. The instruments are then shipped to the customers' plants for installation. Unfortunately, the reading device sometimes gets out of alignment during transport. In fact, past experience shows that this happens in about 10 percent of all shipments. The firm has three possible actions that it can take. It can go ahead and install the instrument as it is unloaded from the trucks. If the instrument is still aligned, everything is fine, and the transaction is completed. However, if the instrument is out of alignment, the cost of correcting things after installation amounts to \$10,000. The second action is always to send out during installation an engineer who will make another alignment of the instrument, regardless of its actual condition. This operation has a cost of \$800. The third action that the firm can take is to make a simple field check of the equipment prior to installation at a cost of \$200. Then, if the instrument is found to be properly adjusted, it can be installed as is. If it is found to be out of adjustment, the engineer can be called in (at an additional cost of \$800) to make an adjustment during installation.

(a) Set up a payoff table, and find the action with the lowest expected costs.

(b) What is the *EVPI*?

11.3 A recording company is approached by a new rock band to make an album. On the basis of a preliminary audition, management feels that such an album has only a 40 percent chance of being a success. However, the company would hate to make a wrong decision and reject the taping of an album on an erroneous basis. A success for such an album means a profit of \$50,000, and a failure results in a loss of \$40,000.

(a) What is the prior *EVPI*?

(b) Management decides to do additional analysis. In particular, they decide to let a consumer test panel rate the group. Past experience for other groups who were reviewed by such panels provides the following information as to the reliability of the ratings:

	Album Successful	Album Not Successful
Panel rated group favorably	6	1
Panel rated group unfavorably	2	3

Based on this past experience, what is the *EVSI*?

(c) The test panel for this group rates the group favorably. Should the firm now proceed with taping the album or should it decline?

11.4 Consider exercise 11.1. The same firm decides to obtain some additional information. They wonder whether they should hire a well-known mining expert for \$100,000 to perform a preliminary quick-and-dirty oil sniffing survey. The expert would report the survey results using one of the following statements: statement N, no large oil deposits likely; statement Y, large oil deposits likely; statement X, oil sniff inconclusive. The expert's surveys are obviously not always correct. Looking over his past performance, we get the following table. The table entries indicate the percentage of cases in which his report was N, Y, or X, given that subsequent explorations turned up *L* or *S*:

		Prediction		
		N	Y	X
Actual results	*L*	20%	60%	20%
	S	80%	10%	10%

(a) Determine the probabilities of the prediction, *P*(N), *P*(Y), *P*(X).

(b) Determine the posterior probabilities if the prediction is (i) N, (ii) Y, (iii) X.

(c) Set up a decision tree to decide if the firm should start exploration.

11.5 Consider exercise 11.2. However, assume this time that the simple field check is not entirely foolproof. In fact, if the device is still properly adjusted after unloading, the chances are 1 out of 20 that the field check will show (erroneously) that the instrument is out of adjustment. On the other hand, if the instrument is out of adjustment after the transport, chances are 1 out of 10 that the field check will show (erroneously) that the instrument is properly adjusted.

(a) Find the posterior probabilities of the instrument being properly adjusted and of its being out of adjustment, given the results of the field check.

(b) Set up a decision tree for the problem to find the action that minimizes the expected cost of installing the instrument.

11.6 A large chemical company maintains an in-service program to update the technical skills of its middle managers. In the past, the company has sent all qualified personnel to a four-week course that costs the company \$1000 per student. An alternative scheme is being contemplated. The company proposes sending all students to a very intensive five-day screening program that costs \$200 per student. Those who pass will be sent to an advanced course at a cost of \$600 per student. Those who fail will be enrolled in the regular \$1000-per-student course. Based on the caliber of people now in middle management positions, the initial estimate of the proportion of students who will fail the screening course is given by the following distribution:

Proportion failing	0.3	0.4	0.5	0.6
Probability	0.2	0.5	0.2	0.1

Because of the uncertainty and subjectivity involved in the estimate of the distribution above, the company also decides to send a random sample of 6 middle managers through the two-day screening program. Of the 6 students, 2 pass the course.

(a) Find cost functions for the actions the company can take, and determine the break-even point in terms of the proportion of students who fail.

(b) Based on the prior distribution, which scheme should the company adopt?

(c) *(Requires binomial probabilities)* Taking the sample information into account, revise the prior distribution of the proportion failing. What should the company do now?

11.7 The recording company considered in exercise 11.3 has had a string of failures recently and cannot afford another. They have a certainty equivalent of $0 for a lottery with $p = 0.5$ between a profit of $50,000 and a loss of $40,000. Using the maximum expected utility criterion and the posterior distribution, determine whether or not they should make the album.

11.8 The management of the pulp milling firm considered in Sections 11-1 and 11-5 has shown itself to be uniformly risk-averse.

(a) Accurately sketch the graph of its utility function, using the utility values $U(-\$2{,}500{,}000) = 0$, $U(\$11{,}000{,}000) = 0.5$, $U(\$24{,}000{,}000) = 0.9$, and $U(\$32{,}000{,}000) = 1$.

(b) Redraw the complete decision tree given in Figure 11-2 so that the outcomes are now in terms of utility values. The extra utility values required can be read from the graph.

(c) Now, using the expected utility decision criterion, reevaluate the pulp milling firm's decision strategy.

11.9 *(Exercise 11.6 continued)* Suppose that instead of 2 out of a random sample of 6 middle managers, the chemical company had found that 10 out of a random sample of 30 middle managers passed the course.

(a) Explain qualitatively what you would expect the posterior distribution to look like, and what you would now expect the decision to be.

(b) If you are unsure of your answer to (a), carry out the revision of the prior distribution, using either binomial tables or the normal approximation to the binomial distribution, to determine the conditional probabilities of the sample result.

11.10 *(Exercise 11.9 continued)* Assume that the prior distribution of the portion failing the screening program was actually considered to be normally distributed, with the same mean and variance as the discrete distribution in exercise 11.6. Use the normal revision formulas in expressions (11-12) and (11-13) to determine the parameters of an approximate normal posterior distribution, and calculate the approximate *EVPI*.

11.11 Let us assume that the prior distribution of the research director in Section 11-8 for the length of the development program was actually a uniform distribution, with a mean of 31 months and a standard deviation of 2 months.

(a) Should the pulp milling firm continue the development program?

(b) If the firm still continues the development program, find the expected cost of the pollution control program.

(c) Calculate the *EVPI* directly from expression (11-9).

(d) Compare the answer to (c) with the *EVPI* based on a normal prior distribution with the same parameters.

11.12 *(Requires calculus)* The cost of production for the small manufacturing firm considered in Section 11-10 turns out not to be linear after all. The firm only has enough materials on hand to make 3400 units. If sales exceed 3400 units, the company will have to buy fresh materials that will cost $1 more per unit.

(a) Draw the new cost function.

(b) Calculate the expected cost. Since the cost function is no longer linear, this must be done directly. However, with a little thought it can be done from normal loss tables. Note that $N(z) = \int_z^\infty (x - z)f(x)\,dx$, where $f(x)$ is the standard normal density function.

(c) Compare the expected cost with the expected return, using the manufacturer's prior distribution. Should the firm produce the item?

REFERENCES

Holloway, Charles A. *Decision Making Under Uncertainty*. Englewood Cliffs, N.J.: Prentice-Hall, 1979. This book concentrates on the types of models that can be used for decision systems. Chapters 12, 16, 17, and 18 in particular cover the subjective aspects of the assessment of probability distributions and risk that we have not considered. Easy to read and mathematically undemanding.

Keeney, Ralph L., and Howard Raiffa. *Decisions with Multiple Objectives*. New York: Wiley, 1976. Chapter 4 has a good treatment of utility functions. Although the applications considered in Chapters 7 and 8 involve multiple objectives (which we will consider in Chapter 22), they are still worth reading at this point.

Raiffa, Howard. *Decision Analysis*. Reading, Mass.: Addison-Wesley, 1968. A very lucid introduction to problems of choice under uncertainty, written in a delightfully conversational style. Chapters 0 to 4 especially recommended as additional reading.

Schlaifer, Robert. *Analysis of Decisions Under Uncertainty*. New York: McGraw-Hill, 1969. Essentially a course in decision analysis rather than a reference text. Expansive discussion of a number of examples.

———. *Computer Programs for Elementary Decision Analysis*. Boston: Division of Research, Graduate School of Business Administration, Harvard University, 1971. This is the manual for a set of computer programs for fitting utility and probability functions to typical sets of data, and for performing the calculations of Bayesian revision. As well as illustrating the application of these programs, the book also gives the details of the mathematical theory and numerical methods for many of them.

Winkler, Robert L. *Introduction to Bayesian Inference and Decision*. New York: Holt, Rinehart, and Winston, 1972. The Bayesian approach of including any available sample or cost information to reduce uncertainty can be applied to almost all statistical problems. Chapters 4, 5, and 6 consider the revision of prior distributions, decision theory, and the value of information.

These two special journal issues on decision analysis contain a number of specific applications and discussion papers.

IEEE Transactions on Systems Science and Cybernetics SSC-4, 1968. R. A. Howard, ed.

Operations Research, Vol. 28, January–February 1980. Craig W. Kirkwood, ed.

CHAPTER TWELVE

Inventory Control

For many organizations, both private and public, inventories are a major investment. Some military organizations stock over 600,000 different parts and items. Large department stores deal in up to 150,000 items. Medium-sized manufacturing outfits may stock thousands of individual components or subassemblies needed as input into their own products, in addition to spare parts for discontinued models and supplies and spare parts for their own manufacturing equipment.

Inventories occur in all forms and for the most diverse purposes. We usually think of inventories as goods for sale, raw materials for production, partially finished goods held for later production stages, supplies and spare parts. But livestock held for fattening, cash in the till or in bank accounts, marketable securities, water in reservoirs, blood in bloodbanks, and personnel who need special training all have similar characteristics. They are all held to meet some future demands, either from external customers or from internal users; and they are controllable within limits, with some costs increasing and other costs decreasing as the inventory increases.

The fundamental questions in inventory control are *when* to order and *how much* to order. In other words, when should the inventory for a given item be replenished and by how much? This chapter looks at methods and models useful in answering these two questions under a variety of premises. As you study the models, it is important to keep firmly in mind that the potential annual savings per item is usually small—often only a few dollars. Therefore, sophisticated models may yield smaller net savings than simple ones because of higher operating costs. What renders inventory control successful is the pooling of thousands of individually small savings on a large number of items. For this reason, we will take a pragmatic approach and discuss only those models that have found widespread use in practice.

Before discussing techniques, we need to study the nature of inventories and inventory systems and the relevant components of their environments. To put you into the right frame of mind and to refresh some terminology, we suggest that you read the case study in Section 1-9 again.

12-1 STRUCTURE OF INVENTORY SYSTEMS

Inventory control systems fall into two broad categories: distribution merchandising systems and manufacturing systems. In a distribution system, the same product is stocked at various echelons along the path between where it is "produced"—interpreted in its widest sense—and where it is "consumed." As depicted in Figure 12-1, the product passes from the manufacturer, to the wholesaler, to the retailer, and finally to the ultimate consumer. Each echelon and even each outfit on the same echelon may be an independent legal entity—a separate decision maker—or some or all levels may be controlled by the same organization, as in the lubricating oil case study.

The best inventory policy for each storage point depends on the policy followed at other echelons. Serious distortions in stocking patterns and delayed reaction to changes in usage at the consumer level may occur if these interactions are ignored. In particular, both manufacturers and wholesalers may wish to let their inventory replenishment system be driven by the final demand at the retail level, rather than by direct response to the ordering pattern of the next lower level.

Manufacturing processes exhibit another type of multilevel inventory structure. Starting with raw materials and supplies, the process may result in inventories of

Figure 12-1. *Multi-echelon inventory structure in distribution systems.*

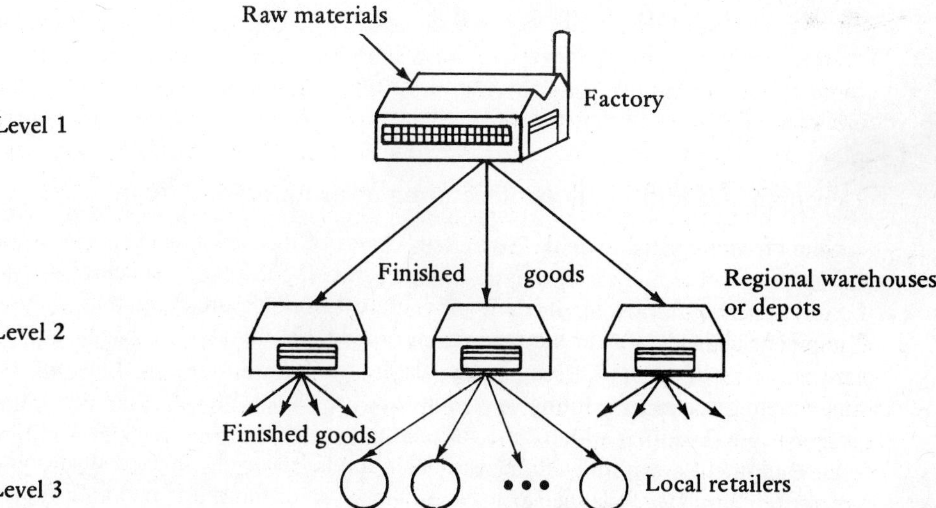

components, subassemblies, and partially finished goods at several intermediate levels, before reaching the final finished goods stage. This is depicted in Figure 12-2. The need for inventories at intermediate levels will largely depend on the degree of coordination in production at consecutive levels. Again, the best policy cannot be determined independently.

Figure 12-2. *Multi-level inventory structure for manufacturing.*

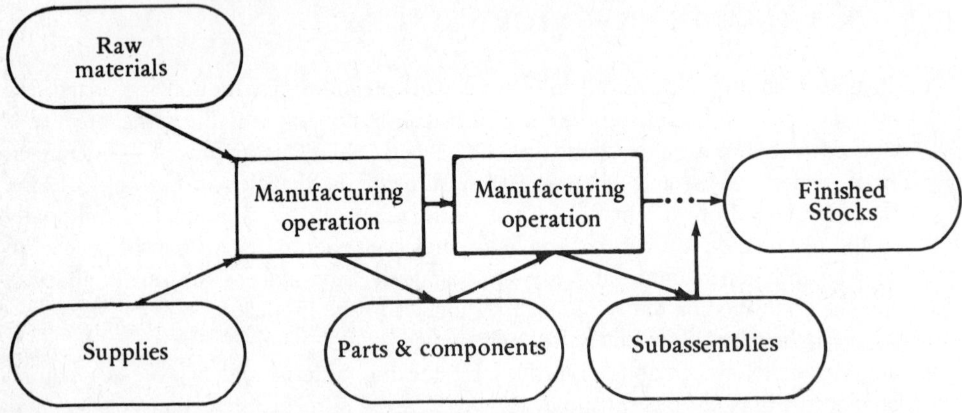

In the relevant literature, most inventory models that find "optimal" policies restrict themselves to single-stage inventory replenishments. So far, the complexity of multistage systems has precluded practical optimization over several levels. Heuristic rules are used to coordinate "good" policies. Any benefits gained are more the result of tighter control and coordination, rather than optimization. Discussion of control policies for multistage systems is beyond the scope of this text.

12-2 FUNCTIONS OF INVENTORIES

In order to properly understand the reasons for keeping inventories, it is useful to study briefly the functions that inventories serve.

Decoupling of multilevel manufacturing or distribution systems

Inventories are created to achieve a certain degree of independence between consecutive stages in the manufacturing process or between consecutive echelons in distribution systems. As a rule, modern production technology requires that whenever equipment changes over to the production of a different product, it has to be *set up* for the new product. These setups may take from a few minutes (for changing labels and resetting scales in a filling operation) to several days or weeks (for rearranging assembly lines), during which time no production occurs. Hence, in order to keep such equipment downtime within reasonable limits, relatively large production runs are made. Similarly, in order to make efficient use of transport, handling, and inspection facilities, the amounts of goods transferred between successive stages in a

Figure 12-3. *Cycle inventory behavior over time.*

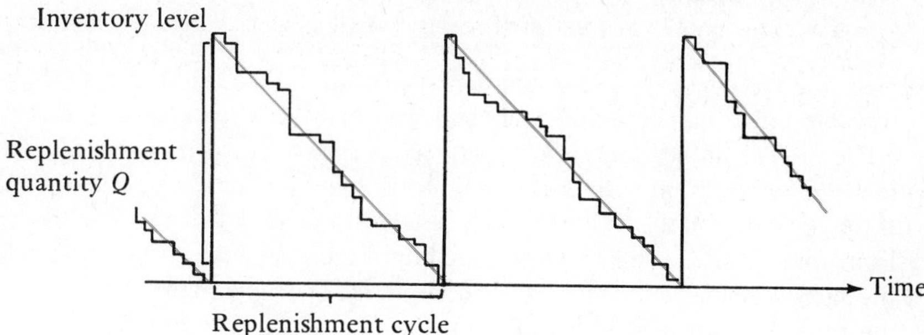

distribution system must also be in sufficiently large batches. In all cases, the batch sizes may be far in excess of immediate demand, resulting in so-called *cycle inventories.*

Figure 12-3 depicts the behavior pattern over time of cycle inventories. After each replenishment, inventories rise sharply and then are gradually depleted as individual customer demands are satisfied, resulting in a typical saw-tooth pattern.

If demand occurs in individual units or in small amounts relative to the replenishment quantity Q, the inventory depletion over time can be approximated by a constant rate R equal to the average demand per period (e.g., per month or per year). This is depicted by the gray lines in Figure 12-3. The time between replenishments—the *replenishment cycle*—is equal to $1/R$ periods (e.g., years), while the average cycle inventory during each replenishment cycle is equal to half the replenishment size, or $\frac{1}{2}Q$.

Anticipation of demand or smoothing of production

Demand and supply of products may be seasonally out of phase, as is the case for many agricultural products; or demand may be subject to large seasonal fluctuations, while production capacity remains constant (except for costly overtime). In either case, if demand is to be satisfied, it may be necessary to accumulate stocks in response to supply or in anticipation of peak demands, thereby creating *anticipation inventories.* Stocks held or purchased in anticipation of price increases also fall into this class.

Goods-in-process or goods-in-transit

Goods passing through the production process—such as goods on the assembly line or temporarily waiting between processing stations, or goods en route from one echelon to another in a distribution system—give rise to *pipeline inventories,* in a narrow sense. The size of such inventories depends to some extent on the processing time for manufactured goods and on the in-transit time in distribution systems.

Protection against uncertainty in demand and uncertainty in replenishment lead times

If *replenishment lead times*—the elapsed time between placing a replenishment and receiving the goods in stock—and demands during these lead times are both known with certainty, then cycle inventory replenishments can be timed such that the goods arrive in stock at the exact time that the last unit is withdrawn. The critical inventory level, or *reorder point*, that triggers a replenishment is equal to the lead-time demand. If the replenishment is placed earlier, some units in stock will never be used; if placed later, some customer may go unsatisfied until the new stock arrives. (Note that if the inventory is not reviewed after each stock transaction, the lead time should also include the time between reviews because replenishments are only initiated at those *review points* and not in between. In fact, for some models the time between reviews becomes a decision variable. On the other hand, the portion of the delivery time offered to customers that is in excess of the actual time required for the delivery can be subtracted from the replenishment lead time, such as in the lubricating oil case study. We always assume that the lead time includes these adjustments.)

For many products, the demand is subject to some degree of uncertainty. Similarly, replenishment lead times may fluctuate unpredictably. In that case, demand during the lead time can no longer be predicted exactly, and it becomes impossible to time replenishments such that idle stock or stock shortages do not occur. Stock shortages are usually more costly than idle stock. Hence, it may be desirable to carry some additional inventory—a *safety stock*—as protection against some (but not necessarily all) shortages. This safety stock is maintained by initiating a replenishment when the inventory level is still larger than the average demand during the lead time; i.e., the reorder point covers the average lead-time demand plus the safety stock.

Thus, the control policy is to initiate a replenishment of size Q, whenever the *inventory position* falls below the reorder point r. The inventory position is defined as the stock on hand plus any outstanding replenishments. For a *transaction reporting system* the inventory position is updated after each stock transaction, while for a *periodic review system* it is updated at each review point. Figure 12-4 shows the actual and the approximated average inventory patterns. The horizontal band under the cycle stock pattern represents the safety stock. Note that the cycles now vary in length.

This chapter studies some of the most basic control models for cycle inventories and safety stocks. Policies for anticipation inventories under certainty can be determined by linear programming or by transportation-type models—the subjects of Chapters 2 and 6. For short production processes, pipeline inventories are often small, and therefore little or no attempt is made to control them. For lengthy production processes, their control should be integrated into the cycle inventory policy.

12-3 COSTS ASSOCIATED WITH INVENTORY DECISIONS

The next two sections will analyze the components that affect inventory control decisions. At this point, it may be useful to briefly review Section 1-7, which discusses the conditions of relevance for environmental parameters.

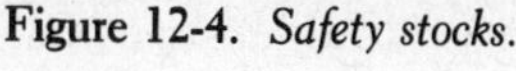

Figure 12-4. *Safety stocks.*

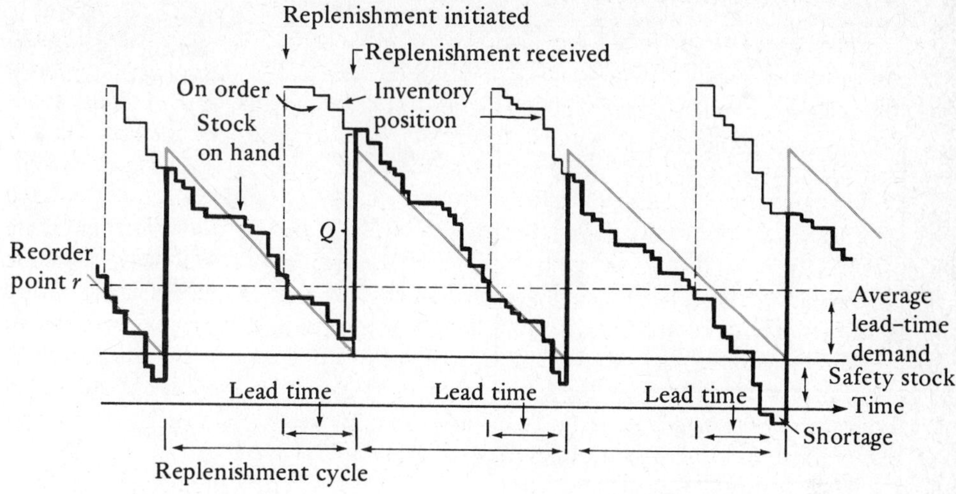

Most inventory decisions are based on the assumed overall organizational goal of profit maximization or cost minimization. Exceptions to this would be so-called *hospital stocks*. These are items, such as hospital equipment, for which full supplies are vital. Shortages may have serious consequences to which it may be difficult to attach a dollar figure. Vital spare parts also fall into this category.

What costs are relevant for inventory control?

Unit cost of product (V)

Inventories represent an investment of funds. In most instances, the value of this investment can be measured by historical costs. In a distribution system, the product unit cost covers primarily the purchase cost, but may also cover transportation, receiving, inspection, and handling costs that vary with the size of the replenishment. For manufactured goods, product unit cost includes costs of raw materials and supplies, variable production costs such as labor and machine costs, plus variable inspection and handling costs. (Note that in a world of steady inflation, historical costs may considerably undervalue the inventory investment. In such cases, *replacement costs* may be more relevant for decision making.)

The product unit cost may vary as a function of the replenishment quantity, i.e., $V = f(Q)$. This may be due to economies (or diseconomies) of scale—the production process becomes more efficient (or requires expensive overtime) as output increases—or may simply reflect the pricing policy of the supplier who offers *quantity discounts*. If a supplier offers quantity discounts, the unit price decreases in steps—so-called *price breaks*—as the quantity purchased increases, as shown in part (a) of Figure 12-5. The discount may apply to all units purchased or to only those units purchased in excess of a price break. In the first instance, the total purchase cost consists of discontinuous

Figure 12-5. *Quantity discounts.*

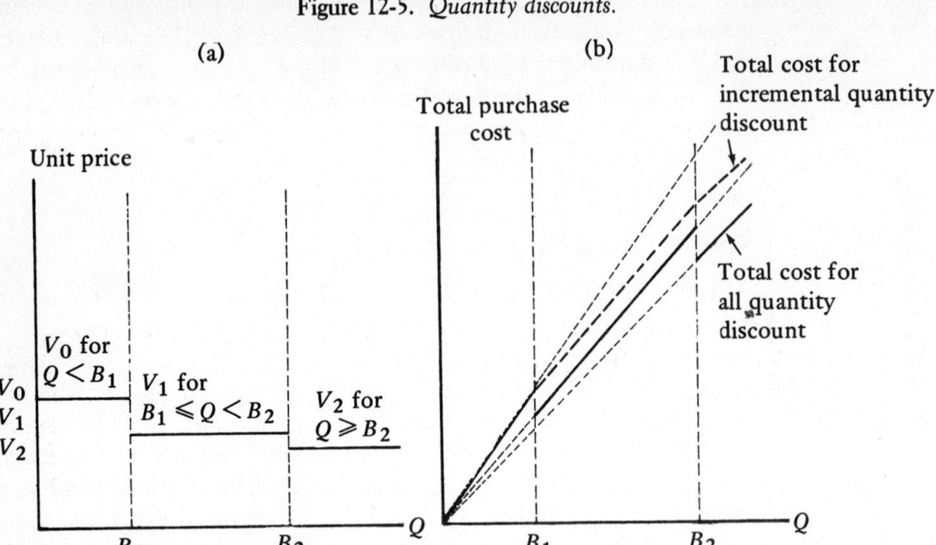

linear segments with progressively smaller slopes, as shown by the solid line in part (b) of Figure 12-5. In the second case, the total purchase price is a continuous piecewise linear function, as depicted by the broken line in part (b).

Inventory holding or carrying costs (c_1)

Funds invested in inventories are not available to earn a return in some other investment opportunity. Hence, inventories should be penalized by a cost equal to the return that could have been obtained on the best alternative investment opportunity foregone. Although in theory this concept sounds fine, in practice it is not operational because the best alternative investment opportunity foregone changes almost continuously. The opportunity cost is therefore measured either as the desired rate of return for investments of comparable risk—usually a policy decision by top management—or as the average cost of capital of the organization. For governmental or public agencies and institutions, this cost may be equal to the cost of loan capital.

Other charges that may be relevant to carrying inventories include storage space costs, insurance costs, pilferage and breakage costs, and taxes assessed on average inventories. Each of these costs is relevant only if it varies in proportion to the size of the inventory. For instance, if the organization owns its warehouse and has no alternative use for unused storage space, this cost is not relevant to inventory decisions. On the other hand, an organization might not carry enough insurance to cover the entire inventory. It thus implicitly carries self-insurance on the other portion. The cost of self-insurance is then a relevant charge.

In general, total inventory holding and carrying costs vary proportionately with the size of inventories. For a given product, these costs are a constant dollar penalty per unit stocked. However, since most costs (except for storage space) tend to vary in proportion to the value of inventories, inventory holding costs are traditionally expressed as a fraction c_1 per dollar invested per year (i.e., \$/\$/year). The per unit cost is thus c_1V.

Replenishment set-up or order costs (c_2)

Whenever a replenishment is initiated, certain fixed costs are incurred that do not depend on the size of the replenishment. These fixed changes include: production set-up or change-over costs; any clerical costs for processing a replenishment; and costs for transporting, receiving, and inspecting the goods (if the costs do not vary with the replenishment quantity). The set-up cost in manufacturing processes should cover not just direct labor costs of the people involved in the machine setup (including fringe benefits dependent on wages, excluding most overhead costs), but also the opportunity cost of the *learning effect* experienced at the beginning of a new production run, when the production rate has not reached the full rated capacity or when scrap and reject rates are still higher than normal.

Stockout or shortage costs (c_3)

The nature of shortage costs depends to some extent on what happens when a shortage occurs. In the *backorder case*, sales are not lost. Either customers are willing to wait until the goods are supplied at a later date, or they do not even know that a shortage has occurred. In the first case, the shortage cost is largely intangible and difficult to assess in monetary terms. It represents the potential decrease in sales that may result from the bad image conveyed and the loss of goodwill. Furthermore, the longer it takes to make up any shortages, the larger will be the goodwill lost. Hence, such shortage costs may need to be expressed as functions of the time short. If shortages do not cause a delay in delivery, the shortage cost consists of the increased expenses of expediting a regular production run or of making a special run. This usually means tearing down existing production runs and rescheduling them later. Occasionally, it may be possible to obtain the goods needed from another supply point, at extra transport or acquisition costs. Therefore, depending on the circumstances, the shortage costs may be (1) fixed per shortage, independent of the amount short, or (2) a function (usually assumed to be linear) of either the amount short or the amount and time short.

In the *lost-sales case*, customers are not willing to wait for a late delivery. The sales in question are lost. The shortage cost consists partly of the immediate profit foregone, and partly of the intangible effect of the loss of goodwill. This opportunity cost is usually assumed to be linear in the amount short.

In real systems, both cases may occur for the same product. Some sales are lost outright, and an ever-increasing part of the back-ordered demand is canceled as the shortage period increases.

Costs of operating the inventory control system

The costs of operating the inventory control system will depend to a large extent on the complexity of the model used, but they do not enter into the cost function of the optimal inventory policy. For alternative models, estimates of these costs should be contrasted to projected savings as early as possible in the analysis. Only then will it be possible to evaluate which model yields the best control policy in terms of the difference between projected savings and projected operating costs.

Most computer manufacturers have developed integrated inventory control and forecasting packages, which can be purchased. Before developing its own system, an organization should carefully study whether one of these packages will do the trick. Not only does adoption of such a package considerably speed up implementation, but it also gives assurance of continued maintenance and updating of the system. Careful study of this chapter will enable you to make an informed judgment about such packages.

12-4 DEMAND

The purpose of holding inventories is to satisfy demands in the not-too-distant future for the items stocked. (Items that have no demand—so-called *dead stocks*—or items that are very slow moving (except for "hospital" stocks) should be disposed of by some means, either by reducing the price sufficiently to create a demand, or by stripping the stock of any useful components, or by selling the stock as scrap.) Hence, it is important to forecast demand over a planning horizon of sufficient length to allow proper stock control. The planning horizon used has to cover at least one complete replenishment cycle, including the replenishment lead time. For fast-moving items, this may be a few days or weeks; for slower-moving but active items, the forecast may have to be extended to a year or more. Demand forecasting is thus an integral part of any inventory control system.

For some products (particularly supplies and components stocked by the firm for internal use in a manufacturing process), the demand over the required planning horizon can be determined accurately from the production schedules. However, for products sold to external customers, the demand will in most instances fluctuate randomly over time and may also be seasonal. If the product is sold in lots of ones, twos, or threes, to a large number of customers, and if its use is not subject to climatic variations, the demand may only exhibit small fluctuations around a fairly constant rate over time. In such instances, it is usually adequate to approximate the demand by a constant rate. The approximate control model may then be deterministic.

Demand fluctuations tend to be substantial if a product's use is affected by climatic conditions, or if the number of customers is relatively small, or if customer demands are not in individual units but are in lots of widely varying sizes. Unfortunately, lumpiness of customer orders and the presence of serial correlation usually make it very difficult and costly to model the random process(es) generating such demands. Serial correlation is particularly serious if there are, among the users, a few regular customers with very large orders. (Why?) Furthermore, unless the product is extremely important as a source of revenue, the additional benefits captured by sophisticated forecasting and control models rarely justify the increased costs incurred and the need for more highly trained people to operate such systems. It is because of this generally unfavorable cost-benefit balance that, in practice, demand distributions are approximated by a *normal*, *Poisson*, or *Laplace* probability distribution. The normal distribution is particularly suitable for relatively long lead times, while the Poisson distribution is often a good approximation for slow-moving items with single-unit demands such as spare parts.

Except for products newly introduced into the market, demand from external customers is usually forecasted on the basis of past data. What data are available for this purpose? Most firms keep accurate records only on actual usage or sales, the point of sale being the delivery. Sales may differ from actual demand in terms of volume and pattern. Requests that could not be met are usually recorded incompletely or not at all. Sales may thus underestimate demand, particularly for larger orders. When stocks are low, some firms may ration the remaining stock to many customers. When the goods arrive, back-ordered demands are likely to be shipped all at once. These problems are serious only if stockouts occur frequently. In such cases, it may be necessary to institute procedures for recording actual demands rather than sales—at least for the more important revenue-producing items. The introduction of tighter inventory control should reduce the incidence of stockouts, and consequently sales become a better (though never perfect) data base for demand. There always remains, though, the question of how valid past records are for predicting future demand in an often turbulent environment, with rapidly changing tastes and technology.

12-5 A SIMPLE DEMAND-FORECASTING METHOD

The characteristics of an inventory control system impose extra requirements on the methods that can be used to forecast demand. As well as being accurate and responsive to changes in demand, the method must allow the forecasts to be updated frequently and quickly. The large number of items in many inventory systems means that the updating method must be numerically simple, and it must be based on two or three numbers, which are all we can afford to record for each item.

One such approach is based on the notion of *exponential smoothing*. Consider a series of monthly demands for a particular item, such as those given in column 2 of Table 12-1. At month n, we form a new *smoothed estimate* S_n of the demand by taking a weighted average of that month's demand X_n and the smoothed estimate calculated in the previous month:

$$S_n = \alpha X_n + (1 - \alpha)S_{n-1} \tag{12-1}$$

α is a number between 0 and 1 and is called the *smoothing constant*.

Formula (12-1) implies that the smoothed estimate is a linear combination of all the past demands, with coefficients that decrease geometrically with the age of the observations. If we substitute in (12-1) for S_{n-1}, then for $S_{n-2}, S_{n-3}, \ldots$, we get

$$S_n = \alpha X_n + \alpha(1 - \alpha)X_{n-1} + \alpha(1 - \alpha)^2 X_{n-2} + \ldots \tag{12-2}$$

We hope that the effect on our forecasts of using a small value for α will be to remove or reduce the effects of random fluctuations in past demands. Note that if α is large, however, the most recent months are given more weight and thus have a stronger influence on the smoothed estimate. Hence, if demand changes fast, the average will also adjust more quickly. In practice, it has been found that a smoothing constant of 0.05 to 0.3 is most satisfactory. For our data and a choice of $\alpha = 0.1$, we get the smoothed estimates shown in column 3 of Table 12-1.

Table 12-1. *Demand forecasting by double exponential smoothing*

1	2	3	4	5	6	7	8	9	10	11
Month	Demand	Smoothed Estimate	Doubly Smoothed Estimate	Intercept	Slope	Forecast	Error	Smoothed Error	Mean Absolute Deviation	Track
n	X_n	S_n	$S_n^{(2)}$	a	b	F_n	E_n	$\lvert SMER_n \rvert$	MAD_n	$TRACK_n$
		175.6	175.6					3.55	20.00	
1	169	174.9	175.6	174.3	−0.07	175.6	+6.6	3.85	18.66	.21
2	180	175.4	175.5	175.4	−0.01	174.3	−5.7	2.89	17.37	.17
3	135	171.4	175.1	167.7	−0.41	175.4	+40.4	6.64	19.67	.34
4	213	175.6	175.2	176.0	+0.04	167.3	−45.7	1.41	22.27	.06
5	181	176.1	175.3	177.0	+0.09	176.0	−4.9	0.77	20.54	.03
6	148	173.3	175.1	171.5	−0.19	177.1	+29.1	3.60	21.39	.17
7	204	176.4	175.2	177.5	+0.13	171.3	−32.7	0.03	22.52	.00
8	228	181.5	175.8	187.2	+0.63	177.7	−50.3	5.05	25.30	.20
9	225	185.9	176.8	194.9	+1.00	187.9	−37.1	8.27	26.48	.31
10	198	187.1	177.9	196.3	+1.03	195.9	−2.1	7.65	24.04	.32
11	200	188.4	178.9	197.9	+1.05	197.3	−2.7	7.15	21.90	.33
12	187	188.2	179.8	196.6	+0.93	198.9	+11.9	5.24	20.90	.25
13	162					197.6	+35.6	1.16	22.37	.05

Assume that we start with an initial smoothed estimate of 175.6. This estimate could have been carried forward from previous calculations using exponential smoothing, or it could simply be the average monthly demand during the last year. Given that the demand in month 1 is 169, the new smoothed estimate for month 1 is $0.1(169) + 0.9(175.6) = 174.9$. Similarly, the new smoothed estimate for month 2 is $0.1(180) + 0.9(174.9) = 175.4$. Note that only two pieces of data are needed to update the estimate.

If there is no steady change, or *trend*, in the data, then the new smoothed estimate computed after observing the demand for month n can be used as the forecast for the demand in month $n + 1$ and later. If the demand is steadily increasing or decreasing, however, the smoothed estimated—being a convex combination of past demands—will lag behind the demand experienced in the most recent months.

We can fit a linear trend model of the form $X_k = a + bk$ by *double smoothing.* The smoothed estimates, S_n, are smoothed again, using an exponential formula like (12-1), to produce *doubly smoothed estimates,* $S_n^{(2)}$.

(12-3) $$S_n^{(2)} = \alpha S_n + (1 - \alpha)S_{n-1}^{(2)}$$

If the assumption of a linear trend model is correct, it can be shown that estimators with good statistical properties for a and b are

(12-4) $$a_n = 2S_n - S_n^{(2)} \qquad b_n = \frac{\alpha}{1 - \alpha}(S_n - S_n^{(2)})$$

The computations for (12-4) are shown in columns 5 and 6 of Table 12-1. For instance, the current estimates of the level a_1 and the slope b_1 in month 1 are

$$a_1 = 2(174.9) - 175.6 = 174.3 \qquad b_1 = 0.1(174.9 - 175.6)/0.9 = -0.07$$

The *demand forecast* in month $n + k$, F_{n+k}, is given by

(12-5) $$F_{n+k} = a_n + b_n k$$

The forecast for the next month ($k = 1$) is shown in column 7 of Table 12-1.

To start forecasting we need initial estimates of the smoothed and the doubly smoothed estimates. If estimates of a and b from old data on this or a similar item are available, they can be used in (12-4) to solve for S_0 and $S_0^{(2)}$. If no old data are available, we can start forecasting by initially setting the smoothing constant α equal to 1, so that no initial values are required. We then decrease α gradually to the desired level, say over the next six months. One method of choosing the smoothing constant is to simulate the forecasting process with existing data and to choose the value of α that gives the "best" forecasts. A measure of this is the ratio of the *smoothed error* $SMER_n$ to the *mean absolute deviation* MAD_n. We take the *forecasting error* in month n, E_n, to be the difference between the forecast and the observed demand in month n. The smoothed error is produced by smoothing these errors with an exponential smoothing formula like (12-1), while the mean absolute deviation is produced by smoothing the absolute values of the errors:

(12-6) $$\left.\begin{aligned} E_n &= F_n - X_n \\ SMER_n &= \alpha E_n + (1 - \alpha)SMER_{n-1} \\ MAD_n &= \alpha|E_n| + (1 - \alpha)MAD_{n-1} \\ TRACK_n &= SMER_n/MAD_n \end{aligned}\right\} \text{Columns 8–11 of Table 12-1}$$

When the forecasting system is behaving well, positive and negative errors will tend to cancel out in $SMER_n$, and hence $TRACK_n$ will be small. As soon as the system goes out of control, errors will have consistently large negative or large positive values, and TRACK_n will become near to $+1$ or -1. In an automatic forecasting system, TRACK can be used to monitor the system's performance. If $|\text{TRACK}|$ becomes too large, say consistently greater than 0.3, it is probable either that the demand pattern has suddenly changed or that the forecasts are not responding fast enough to recent values of demand. Corrective action may have to be taken at that time. A completely automatic response is to use the current value of $|\text{TRACK}|$ as the smoothing constant in equations (12-1), (12-3), and (12-4). As the forecasts start to consistently under- or overestimate demand, $|\text{TRACK}|$ will rise so that the forecasts depend more on current demand. When the forecasts are back "on track," $|\text{TRACK}|$ will fall to allow greater smoothing of random fluctuations in demand.

12-6 OVERVIEW OF MODELS DISCUSSED

The models discussed in the following sections fall into three groups:

- stationary models with deterministic demands (Sections 12-7 and 12-8),
- stationary models with stochastic demands (Sections 12-9 through 12-12), and
- dynamic models with deterministic demands (Sections 12-14 and 12-15).

Section 12-13 discusses some guidelines as to which stationary model to use under various operating conditions.

Most stationary demand models result in cost expressions that can be solved by the classical optimization techniques of differential calculus. These techniques are discussed in the advanced part of the text (Chapter 19) and assume a working knowledge of the most basic rules of differentiation and simple integration. If you possess this background, you may find it helpful to study parts of Chapter 19, as referred to over the next few sections, along with this chapter.

12-7 ECONOMIC ORDER QUANTITY MODELS

In Chapter 1, Section 1-11, you were introduced to the most basic inventory control model—namely, the *economic order quantity model* (also given various other names, such as *EOQ model*, *economic batch size model*, *Wilson lot size*, *square root formula*, etc.). Let us briefly review that model again.

The EOQ model deals only with the replenishment of cycle inventories. Demand is assumed to occur at a constant rate R over time. As depicted in Figure 12-3, whenever stocks are depleted to zero, a batch of size Q instantly replenishes stocks to the level Q. No shortages can occur. The total cost over a given planning horizon is equal to the sum of inventory holding costs, replenishment set-up or order costs, and the product cost. Let the planning horizon be one year. Hence, R refers to the annual demand, VR is the annual product cost, and the holding cost is assessed on the average inventory investment, $V(\frac{1}{2}Q)$. The number of replenishments per year is R/Q. The total annual cost $T(Q)$ is therefore

$$T(Q) = \underbrace{\tfrac{1}{2}c_1VQ}_{\substack{\text{inventory}\\ \text{holding cost}}} + \underbrace{c_2R/Q}_{\substack{\text{replenishment}\\ \text{set-up cost}}} + \underbrace{VR}_{\substack{\text{product}\\ \text{cost}}} \tag{12-7}$$

The term VR is a constant. It is not affected by changes in Q and can therefore be dropped from expression (12-7). Figure 12-6 shows the remaining two components of (12-7) and their sum for the set of parameters listed in the box adjacent to the graph.

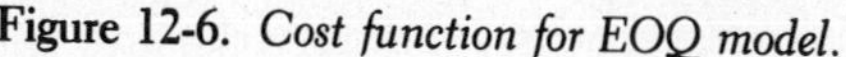

Figure 12-6. *Cost function for EOQ model.*

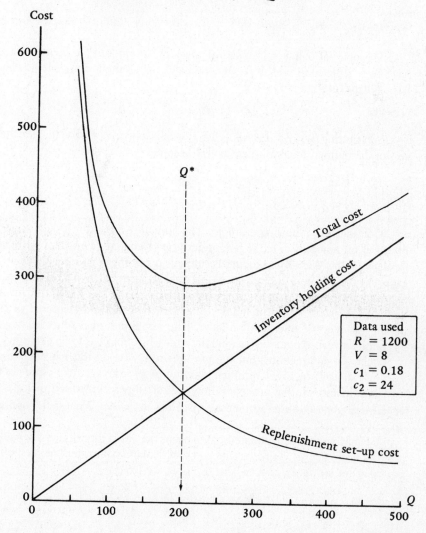

The value of Q that minimizes the total cost (12-7) can be determined by the use of elementary calculus (refer to Section 19-1). Alternatively, we note from Figure 12-6 that the minimum cost occurs at the point where the annual holding costs are equal to the annual replenishment set-up costs, i.e., where

$$c_1VQ/2 = c_2R/Q \quad (12\text{-}8)$$

This is a property of the EOQ model. Rearranging terms and solving for Q yields the well-known

EOQ FORMULA

$$Q^* = \sqrt{2Rc_2/c_1V} \quad (12\text{-}9)$$

The optimal policy is to replenish stock by an amount Q whenever inventories have been depleted to zero. If R is the annual demand, then each replenishment cycle has a length (in years) of

$$L = Q^*/R = \sqrt{2c_2/c_1VR} \quad (12\text{-}10)$$

Substituting Q^* into expression (12-7) and simplifying, we find that the theoretical cost of the optimal replenishment policy becomes

$$\begin{aligned} T(Q^*) &= \tfrac{1}{2}c_1V\sqrt{2Rc_2/c_1V} + c_2R/\sqrt{2Rc_2/c_1V} = 2\sqrt{c_1VRc_2/2} \\ &= \sqrt{2c_1VRc_2} \end{aligned} \quad (12\text{-}11)$$

Consider the following example. The annual demand for a special-purpose lubrication oil amounts to 1200 gallons per year. Demand occurs at a fairly even rate throughout the year. The product is stocked in cartons containing 24 quart cans (6 gallons). The value of the oil, including package material, is \$8 per gallon. The oil is mixed and filled in batches. Each setup for a mixing and filling run involves one hour of labor cost at \$8 (including fringe benefits). Solvents required to clean the mixing vat after use have a value of \$5. The first gallon of product feeding through the lines between the mixing vat and the filling machine has to be discarded because of possible contamination from the previous run. The oil lost has a value of about \$7. Clerical costs of a replenishment amount to \$4. Management estimates that any inventory investment has an opportunity cost of 18 percent, which includes the cost of self-insurance. Unused warehouse space has no value. What is the optimal order quantity?

Given that the demand rate is fairly even, the EOQ model seems suitable. From the data given above, verify that the cost and demand parameters are as shown in the box adjacent to Figure 12-6. Then, by (12-9) we have

$$Q^* = \sqrt{2(1200)24/0.18(8)} = 200 \text{ gallons}$$

The optimal policy is therefore to replenish inventory in batches of 200 gallons. The time between replenishments is $L^* = 200/1200$ years, or 2 months. From (12-11) we find that the theoretical total annual cost (without the product cost) is

$$T(200) = \sqrt{2(0.18)8(1200)24} = \$288$$

Note that 200 gallons is not a multiple of 6 gallons. Hence, the actual replenishment quantity may need to be rounded up to 204 gallons (plus one gallon discarded) or rounded down to 198 gallons (plus one gallon discarded). Verify that in either case the theoretical annual cost difference is less than 6 cents. In fact, even a deviation of 40 gallons will increase costs by 2.5 percent at most. The cost function is thus very flat around the optimum. From these observations we conclude that the potential savings of using this model are very small, unless the previous policy was highly inefficient.

How sensitive is the theoretical minimum cost to changes or errors in the input parameters? Consider errors in the demand. When the EOQ model is implemented, the value of R used is based on the forecast of the expected demand for the coming year. Let $\hat{R}$ denote this forecast. Being a forecast, $\hat{R}$ might differ from the true but unknown demand R. By how much would the theoretical incurred costs be off if the forecast were in error by a factor of k, i.e., if $\hat{R} = kR$? Using $\hat{R} = kR$ in formula (12-9), we get an "optimal" order quantity of

$$\hat{Q} = \sqrt{2\hat{R}c_2/c_1V} = \sqrt{2kRc_2/c_1V} = Q^*\sqrt{k} \tag{12-12}$$

The true annual cost of $\hat{Q}$, given that the true demand is R, is

$$\begin{aligned} T(\hat{Q}) &= \tfrac{1}{2}c_1V\hat{Q} + c_2R/\hat{Q} = \tfrac{1}{2}c_1VQ^*\sqrt{k} + c_2R/Q^*\sqrt{k} \\ &= \sqrt{c_1VRc_2/2}\,(\sqrt{k} + 1/\sqrt{k}) \end{aligned}$$

Multiplying by $2\sqrt{k}/2\sqrt{k}$ and then simplifying, we get

$$T(\hat{Q}) = \sqrt{2c_1VRc_2}(k + 1)/2\sqrt{k} = T(Q^*)(k + 1)/2\sqrt{k} \tag{12-13}$$

Thus, the answer to our question is that the true theoretical cost will be off by a factor of $(k + 1)/2\sqrt{k}$. This result depends only on the relative error and not on the actual values of R and $\hat{R}$. $(k + 1)/2\sqrt{k} = 1$ if $k = 1$, and its value will be larger than 1 for all values of $k \neq 1$, as is to be expected. Figure 12-7 shows $(k + 1)/2\sqrt{k}$ as a function of k.

Say that the forecast overestimated the true demand by 44 percent, i.e., $k = 1.44$. Then

$$\hat{Q} = Q^*\sqrt{k} = 1.2Q^*$$

and

$$(k + 1)/2\sqrt{k} = (1.44 + 1)/2\sqrt{1.44} = 1.0167$$

Figure 12-7. *Error factor of EOQ model.*

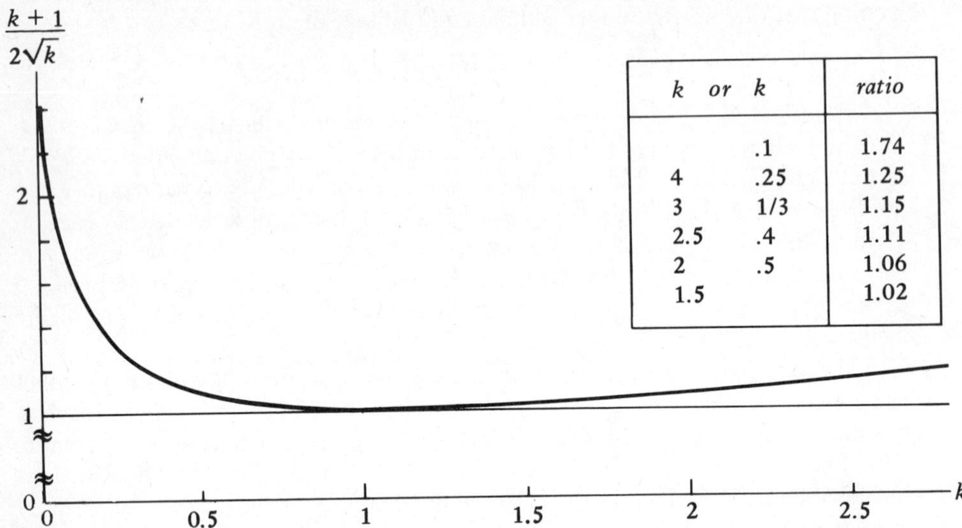

k or k		ratio
	.1	1.74
4	.25	1.25
3	1/3	1.15
2.5	.4	1.11
2	.5	1.06
1.5		1.02

The theoretical cost using $\hat{Q}$ will be only 1.67 percent larger than the minimum cost using Q^*. On the other hand, underestimating the demand by 44 percent (i.e., $k = 0.56$, resulting in $\hat{Q} = \sqrt{0.56}Q^* = 0.75Q^*$) causes the theoretical cost to be larger by 4.23 percent. Overestimation is thus less costly than underestimation. From this analysis we may infer that the EOQ model is not very sensitive to fairly large errors in the demand forecast and therefore does not require a high forecasting accuracy.

The previous model assumes that the entire replenishment arrives in stock as one lot. In a manufacturing process, it may take several days or even weeks to complete a production run. The goods may thus be added to inventory in small quantities (e.g., daily lots) until the production run has been completed. During this time, withdrawals from stock for sale and internal usage will continue. Figure 12-8 shows the approximated inventory behavior over time.

During the interval over which production occurs, inventories increase at a daily rate of $b - a$, where b is the daily production rate and $a = R/250$ is the daily demand rate based on 250 working days per year. Once production has been completed, inventories are depleted at a daily rate a. Obviously $b > a$. (Why?) For a replenishment of size Q, production takes Q/b days. During this time, a quantity $a(Q/b)$ is sold. Therefore, the maximum inventory level reached at the completion of the production run is not Q, but

$$Q - a(Q/b) = Q(1 - a/b) \tag{12-14}$$

The average inventory is half of (12-14). With this small change, the total relevant

Figure 12-8. *Finite replenishment rate model.*

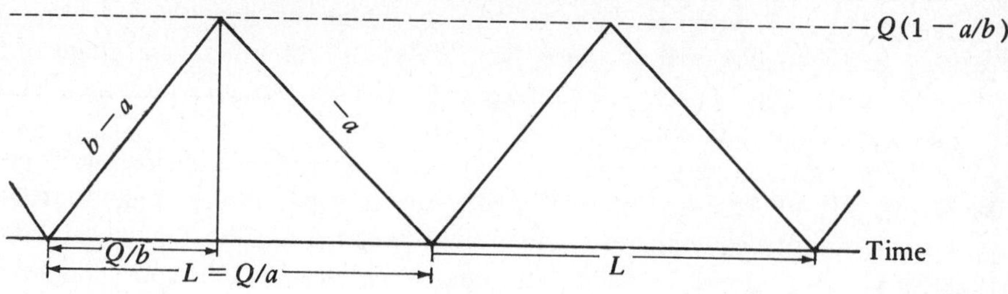

annual cost of replenishing inventory periodically by an amount Q (excluding product costs) is

(12-15) $$T(Q) = \tfrac{1}{2}c_1VQ(1 - a/b) + c_2R/Q$$

By the same analysis as we used for the simple EOQ model, the optimal replenishment batch is now

(12-16) $$Q^* = \sqrt{2c_2R/c_1V(1 - a/b)}$$

Another extension to the basic EOQ model that has been reported on at length in the literature involves planning for systematic shortages to occur at the end of each replenishment cycle. Although it is conceivable that a firm might get away with this practice for a limited time, customers are bound to react negatively, affecting sales. If the users are internal to the organization, they will carry larger safety stock. In either case, the potential long-term losses are likely to outweigh any long-term benefits. That extension of the EOQ model is thus mainly an exercise in academic trivia.

12-8 ECONOMIC ORDER QUANTITY MODEL FOR QUANTITY DISCOUNTS

In the cost function for the EOQ model—expression (12-7)—the product cost shows up as a constant and therefore can be ignored. If a supplier offers quantity discounts, this is no longer true. Assume that quantity discounts apply to all units purchased in a batch. Then the total purchase cost is a discontinuous function of linear segments, as shown by the solid line in Figure 12-5, part (b). All other cost parameters remain the same as for the basic EOQ model. For the two-price-break case shown in Figure 12-5, the total annual cost expression is

(12-17) $$T(Q) = c_2(R/Q) + \begin{Bmatrix} c_1V_0(Q/2) + V_0R & \text{for } Q < B_1 \\ c_1V_1(Q/2) + V_1R & \text{for } B_1 \leq Q < B_2 \\ c_1V_2(Q/2) + V_2R & \text{for } Q \geq B_2 \end{Bmatrix}$$

This is depicted in Figure 12-9 for the parameters shown in the box adjacent to that figure. For each purchase price, the base for the annual set-up and holding costs is given by the total annual purchase cost, RV_i. Hence the general cost shape of Figure 12-6 repeats itself on each purchase cost base. The segment for which each set is valid is shown by the solid lines.

For a given purchase price, the optimal value of Q is therefore again given by formula (12-9). However, this value of Q may not fall into the proper range for its price V_i and consequently may not be valid. For instance, the optimal value of Q for price V_0 (denoted by Q_0^*) falls into its proper range, whereas the corresponding values Q_1^* and Q_2^* for the prices V_1 and V_2, respectively, fall outside of their proper ranges. Furthermore, from the graph of the total annual cost, it follows that the minimum cost may also occur at a price break B_i. This is in fact the case for our example. The shape of the total cost curve suggests the following procedure for finding the optimal value Q^* for I price breaks ($I + 1$ prices).

ALGORITHM FOR OPTIMAL REPLENISHMENT SIZE UNDER PRICE BREAKS

Step 1 Using (12-9), compute Q_i^* for each V_i, $i = 0, \ldots, I$.
If $B_i \leq Q_i^* < B_{i+1}$, save Q_i^*; otherwise, discard it.

Step 2 Find the highest value of $i = \hat{\imath}$ for which Q_i^* was saved. If $\hat{\imath} = I$, set $Q^* = Q_I^*$ and stop. If $\hat{\imath} < I$,
(a) compute $T(Q_i^*)$, and
(b) compute $T(B_i)$ for all $i > \hat{\imath}$.

Step 3 From the values of $T(Q)$ computed in (a) and (b) of Step 2, find the lowest value. The optimal Q^* is then equal to the corresponding Q.

Applying this procedure to the problem represented in Figure 12-9, we get

Step 1 $i = 0$: $Q_0^* = 333$. Q is inside its range and hence is saved.
$i = 1$: $Q_1^* = 354$. Q is outside its range and hence is discarded.
$i = 2$: $Q_2^* = 358$. Q is outside its range and hence is discarded.

Step 2 $\hat{\imath} = 0$, and
(a) $T(Q_0^* = 333) = \$22{,}320$
(b) $T(B_1 = 500) = \$19{,}920$, $T(B_2 = 1200) = \$19{,}943$.

Step 3 $T(B_1 = 500)$ is the minimum cost; hence $Q^* = 500$.

12-9 SINGLE-CYCLE STOCHASTIC INVENTORY CONTROL MODELS

The model discussed in this section is the simplest inventory control model for stochastic demands. It answers the question "What is the optimal beginning inventory

Figure 12-9. *Total annual costs for quantity discount model.*

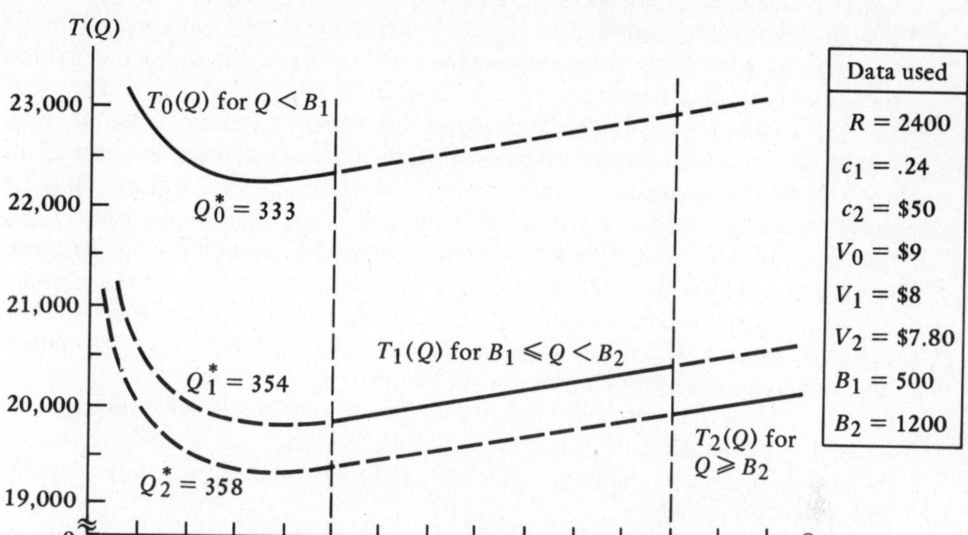

to meet a random demand during a single period?" All stocks are sold or used during the period, or else they are disposed of at the end of the period at a loss, say, as scrap or as special below-cost bargains. A rather wide variety of real-world problems fit this model. There are repetitive decisions such as the newsboy problem (how many copies of a newspaper to stock) and the Christmas tree problem (how many Christmas trees to stock). As a matter of fact, the model is often referred to as the *newsboy* or *Christmas tree problem*. There are also many production or stocking decisions about perishable goods such as hot meals in a cafeteria. There are nonrepetitive decisions, such as the number of spare parts to order when buying special-purpose equipment and the size of production runs for fad items with a limited season.

Mt. McKinley Airlines operates five 8-seater Skylark airplanes for its scenic flights from Anchorage, Alaska. These planes will be replaced by newer models within two years. Skylark has just notified Mt. McKinley Airlines that it will make a final production run of ring gears for planes of this type and has asked the airline to place an order for that spare part. Given the unusual flying conditions under which the airplanes are operated by Mt. McKinley Airlines, these ring gears are subject to random wear. Over the past eight years, an average of 2 gears had to be replaced annualy. Skylark quotes a price of \$900 per ring gear ordered now, whereas any subsequent orders will require special setups at a cost of \$1600 per gear, with a delivery lead time of at least 2 weeks. Any gears left in stock at the end of the two years will have only a scrap value of \$100. The loss in net revenues when a plane is grounded for lack of replacement gears amounts to \$1200 per week. How many gears should the airline order?

In Section 19-2 we solve such a problem by formulating a function for the expected total cost. In *this* section, however, we will apply *marginal analysis* to find the optimal replenishment size.

There are two types of costs involved in such a problem: the cost of ordering too many units and thus having units left over—referred to as the *overage cost*, c_o—and the cost of not ordering enough units and being short—referred to as the *underage cost*, c_u. For our example, the overage cost is the difference between the price of the gears for the regular production run now and the scrap value two years from now, or ($900 − $100) = $800 per unit. (Holding costs could possibly be added.) The underage cost is the sum of the special set-up cost and the 2-week loss in net revenues, or ($1600 + $2400) = $4000 per unit.

In marginal analysis, we consider increasing our replenishment quantity one unit at a time, starting with a base of zero. For each additional unit, the probability of incurring the overage cost increases, while the probability of saving the underage cost decreases. Hence, for each additional unit, the expected incremental overage cost incurred increases while the expected incremental underage cost saved decreases. We reason that as long as the former is smaller than the latter, it pays to increase the replenishment quantity.

Let x denote the random variable for the number of units required (or demanded), and let $P(x < k)$ denote the probability that fewer than k units are needed, or that the kth unit is not needed. Then the expected incremental overage cost incurred for adding the kth unit is $c_oP(x < k)$, while the expected incremental underage cost saved is $c_uP(x \geqslant k)$. It pays to increase the order quantity as long as

$$c_oP(x < k) < c_uP(x \geqslant k) \tag{12-18}$$

We stop as soon as

$$c_oP(x < k + 1) \geqslant c_uP(x \geqslant k + 1) \tag{12-19}$$

Substituting $P(x \geqslant k) = 1 - P(x < k)$ in (12-18) and (12-19), rearranging terms, and combining both relationships, we derive the following conditions for the optimal value of $k = k^*$.

CONDITIONS FOR OPTIMAL BEGINNING STOCK (OR REORDER LEVEL)

$$P(x < k^*) < \frac{c_u}{c_o + c_u} \leqslant P(x < k^* + 1) = P(x \leqslant k^*) \tag{12-20}$$

If (12-20) is satisfied as an equality, then both k^* and $k^* + 1$ are optimal.

For products with infrequent, individual, random demands or usages (such as spare parts), the Poisson distribution is often a good approximation for the demand probability distribution (see Section 10-5). This distribution is defined by a single parameter, λt, where λ is the average rate per period and t is the number of periods. For our example, $\lambda = 2$ and $t = 2$; hence, $\lambda t = 4$. The first few terms of the corresponding Poisson distribution are as follows.

k	0	1	2	3	4	5	6	7	8	9	10
$p(k)$	0.018	0.073	0.147	0.195	0.196	0.156	0.104	0.060	0.030	0.013	0.008
$p(x < k)$	0	0.018	0.091	0.238	0.433	0.629	0.785	0.889	0.949	0.979	0.992

The ratio of costs in expression (12-20) is $4000/(800 + 4000) = 0.8333$. This falls between the values $k = 6$ and $k + 1 = 7$. Hence, if no parts are currently in stock, the optimal replenishment is $k^* = 6$. It is 2 larger than the average demand over the two-year period. The safety stock is thus 2. (Verify that, in fact, the expected incremental overage cost becomes larger than the expected incremental underage cost for $k = 7$.)

This model can easily be generalized to continuous random variables. The "increments" (equal to 1 in the previous example) can then be made arbitrarily small. Hence, it will always be possible to satisfy expressions (12-18) and (12-19) as equalities. Let $F(S)$ denote the probability distribution function for the random variable x with density function $f(x)$, i.e., $F(S) = P(x \leq S) = \int_0^S f(x)\,dx$. Then, the optimal replenishment quantity S^* is obtained from

$$F(S^*) = \frac{c_u}{c_o + c_u} \qquad \text{(12-21)}$$

(This is the formula derived in Section 19-2.)

For goods ordered for resale—such as fashion garments—profit maximization is the relevant criterion, rather than cost minimization. This has no effect, though, on the validity of the conditions (12-20) and (12-21). We simply redefine the overage and underage costs. The overage cost is the loss incurred in disposing of the goods at the end of the season, while the underage cost is the profit foregone on lost sales opportunities.

12-10 SAFETY STOCKS FOR THE LOST-SALES CASE

The EOQ model is often used as an approximation to find optimal replenishment quantities even where demand is not strictly deterministic but in fact exhibits a reasonably small degree of randomness. If the replenishment lead time is positive, some safety stock may be needed. The situation we face is the one shown in Figure 12-4, except that shortages result in lost sales. Let Q again be determined by the EOQ model. How much safety stock should be carried? Or, equivalently, since the safety stock is a function of the reorder point r, what is the optimal value of r?

If we initially restrict our analysis to a single replenishment cycle, finding the optimal reorder point is almost identical to finding the optimal replenishment quantity in the single-cycle model of the previous section. In both cases, we want to find the optimal amount of stock to have on hand at the beginning of a specified time interval, which now covers only the replenishment lead time. The difference is that now any goods left unsold at the end of the lead time will be carried forward to the next cycle. This simply means that the overage cost includes only the cost of holding a unit in stock over a replenishment cycle of length L, i.e., $c_o = c_1VL$. The underage cost is still given by the shortage cost on lost sales, i.e., $c_u = c_3$. Hence, the optimal reorder point, r^*, can be derived from conditions (12-20) or (12-21).

In each cycle, this process repeats itself, unchanged. Thus, r^* is the optimal reorder point for each cycle. By tradition, overage and underage costs are expressed on an annual basis. This is easily achieved by multiplying each cost by the average number of cycles per year, namely $1/L$, or R/Q. Hence, $c_o = c_1V$, and $c_u = c_3R/Q$. This will not affect the value of the ratio in (12-20) or (12-21). With this change, we get the following procedure for finding a nearly optimal inventory replenishment policy for the lost-sales case under demand uncertainty and assuming demand is continuous.

"OPTIMAL" Q AND r FOR APPROXIMATE TWO-PHASE MODEL (LOST-SALES CASE)

Step 1 Find Q^* using expression (12-9) or (12-16), whichever applies, and evaluate R/Q^*.

Step 2 Find r^* from condition

$$F(r^*) = \frac{c_3(R/Q^*)}{c_1V + c_3(R/Q^*)} = \int_0^{r^*} f(x)\,dx \tag{12-22}$$

where $f(x)$ is the probability density function for the lead-time demand.

For discrete demands, conditions (12-20) with $r^* = k^*$ are substituted for (12-22). (The backorder case is briefly discussed at the end of Section 12-11. Expression (12-29) should be used in place of condition (12-22).)

Continuing our first example in Section 12-7, assume that the weekly demand is normally distributed with mean $\mu = 1200/52 \cong 23$ and standard deviation $\sigma = 6$. The lead time is 4 weeks. The unit shortage cost is estimated at $c_3 = \$4.80$. All other parameters remain unchanged.

Step 1 By (12-9), $Q^* = 200$, and $R/Q^* = 1200/200 = 6$.

Step 2 By the properties of the normal distribution for independent random variables, the lead-time distribution is also normally distributed, with mean $4\mu = 92$ and standard deviation $\sigma\sqrt{4} = 6\sqrt{4} = 12$. The ratio of condition (12-22) is

$$\frac{(4.8)6}{(0.18)8 + (4.8)6} = 0.9524$$

From the tables of the normal distribution (Table 1 in Appendix B), we find that $P(\textit{lead-time demand} \leq r^*) = F(r^*) = 0.9524$ corresponds to a z-value of approximately 1.67. Hence $r^* = 92 + 1.67(12) = 112.04$, or about 112.

The nearly optimal policy is thus to initiate a replenishment of size 200 whenever the inventory level, including any replenishments outstanding, has been reduced to 112 or below.

In this approach, we made a number of simplifications. First, we ignored the fact that some demand may be lost, and hence the number of cycles per year is less than R/Q. Note, though that if the amount of shortages is small, the effect on r due to the slightly smaller R/Q ratio may be negligible. In this model, shortages will in fact be small if shortage costs are significantly larger than holding costs. Second, we assumed that the lead time is constant. (For variable lead times, $f(x)$ must be found as the marginal demand distribution from the joint probability distribution of the demand and the lead time, as shown in Section 10-3.) Finally, we considered only the effect of Q on the reorder point r, but not any possible effects of r on Q.

The effect of Q on r works via the ratio R/Q in (12-22). As Q increases, this ratio decreases, and hence r decreases somewhat. However, if c_3 is very large, it may be advantageous to reduce the number of times shortages may occur. This can be achieved by increasing Q and thereby reducing R/Q. It is this feedback loop that is ignored in the above approximation. This point will be taken up in the next section.

12-11 THE (Q, r) MODEL

We shall now explicitly recognize the major mutual interactions between Q and r. The objective is to minimize the sum of the inventory holding costs, the replenishment set-up costs, and the shortage costs. The inventory holding costs are assessed on the average inventory level. This consists of the average cycle inventory, $Q/2$, plus the average safety stock. The latter is approximated by the average inventory level at the end of the replenishment lead time. The safety stock is thus equal to r less the expected lead-time demand met from stocks. Let the demand during the lead time be denoted by the continuous random variable x, subject to the probability density function $f(x)$. Then for the lost-sales case, the ending inventory just prior to the arrival of the replenishment is

$$I(r, x) = \begin{cases} r - x & \text{for } x \leq r \\ 0 & \text{for } x > r \end{cases}$$

The expected safety stock is therefore

$$\int_0^\infty I(r, x) f(x)\, dx = \int_0^r (r - x) f(x)\, dx \tag{12-23}$$

The shortage cost is assessed on the average amount short. At the end of each cycle, the amount short is

$$J(r, x) = \begin{cases} 0 & \text{for } x \leq r \\ x - r & \text{for } x > r \end{cases}$$

The expected amount short in each cycle is therefore

$$\int_0^\infty J(r, x)f(x)\,dx = \int_r^\infty (x - r)f(x)\,dx \tag{12-24}$$

The expected annual amount short is obtained by multiplying (12-24) by the number of cycles per year. Assuming again that the expected annual amount short is very small in comparison to the total demand, the number of cycles can be approximated by R/Q. We now have all components. The (approximate) expected total annual cost is

$$\begin{aligned} T(Q, r) = {} & c_1V\left\{\tfrac{1}{2}Q + \int_0^r (r - x)f(x)\,dx\right\} && \text{(expected holding costs)} \\ & + c_2(R/Q) && \text{(expected replenishment set-up cost)} \\ & + c_3(R/Q)\int_r^\infty (x - r)f(x)\,dx && \text{(expected shortage cost)} \end{aligned} \tag{12-25}$$

The optimal values of Q and r can be found by using the methods of differential calculus, as shown in Section 19-5. This yields the following conditions: condition (12-26) for Q^* in terms of r^*, and condition (12-27) for the value of the distribution function of x at r^* in terms of Q^*.

$$Q^* = \sqrt{\left\{2R\left(c_2 + c_3\int_{r^*}^\infty (x - r^*)f(x)\,dx\right)\right\}\Big/ c_1V} \tag{12-26}$$

$$F(r^*) = \frac{c_3(R/Q^*)}{c_1V + c_3(R/Q^*)} \tag{12-27}$$

An interesting result emerges. Note that expression (12-27) is identical to expression (12-22). But expression (12-26) will, as expected, yield a slightly larger value for Q^* than the simple EOQ formula (12-9).

To find the optimal values of Q^* and r^*, we use an algorithm for successive approximations.

ALGORITHM FOR (Q, r) MODEL

Step 0 Set $k = 0$ and $Q_0 = \sqrt{2Rc_2/c_1V}$.

Step 1 Determine r_k from expression (12-27) using Q_k. If $k = 0$, go to step 3. Otherwise:

Step 2 If both $|Q_k - Q_{k-1}| \leq \epsilon$ and $|r_k - r_{k-1}| \leq \epsilon$, set $Q^* = Q_k$ and $r^* = r_k$ and *stop*. Otherwise:

Step 3 Increase k to $k + 1$. Find Q_k from expression (12-26) using r_{k-1}. Return to step 1.

ϵ is chosen arbitrarily small. In most cases $\frac{1}{2} \leqslant \epsilon \leqslant 1$ suffices. This algorithm usually converges in two or three iterations.

Let us apply this algorithm to the example in the previous section. For a normally distributed random variable, expression (12-24)—needed in (12-26)—can be expressed in terms of the *standard normal loss function* N(Z) (Table 2 of Appendix B), i.e.,

$$\int_r^\infty (x - r)f(x)\,dx = \sigma N\left(\frac{r - \mu}{\sigma}\right) \tag{12-28}$$

We set $\epsilon = 0.5$.

Iteration 1:

Step 0 $Q_0 = 200$ from Section 12-7.
Step 1 $r_0 = 112.04$ from Section 12-10.
Step 3 $N\left(\frac{r_0 - \mu}{\sigma}\right) = N\left(\frac{112.04 - 92}{12}\right) = N(1.67) = 0.01967$, and

$$Q_1 = \sqrt{\frac{2(1200)[24 + (4.8)12(0.01967)]}{0.18(8)}} = 204.67.$$

Iteration 2:

Step 1 $F(r_1) = \frac{4.8(1200/204.67)}{0.18(8) + 4.8(1200/204.67)} = 0.9513$ implies $z = 1.66$ and $r_1 = 92 + 1.66(12) = 111.92$.
Step 2 $|Q_1 - Q_0| = |200 - 204.67| = 4.67 > 0.5$.
Step 3 $N(1.66) = 0.02015$, and $Q_2 = 204.78$.

Iteration 3:

Step 1 $F(r_2) = 0.9513$ implies $r_2 = 111.92$.
Step 2 $|Q_2 - Q_1| = 0.11 < 0.5$, and $|r_2 - r_1| = 0 < 0.5$.
Hence $Q^* = 204.78$ and $r^* = 111.92$.

The policy is to replenish inventory by $Q^* \cong 205$ whenever inventories (including replenishments on order) fall to $r^* \cong 112$ or less. The policy for the (Q, r) model is thus only marginally different from the one in the preceding section. In fact, the theoretical cost difference is less than 8 cents, or less than 0.03 percent. Similar results hold in most cases. No wonder this and other sophisitcated models are put aside in favor of the simple approximate two-phase model in the previous section.

Needless to say, the (Q, r) model can also be formulated for the backorder case. Since the inventory at the end of the lead time may now also be negative, the average inventory is slightly smaller. Expression (12-23) becomes $\int_0^\infty (r - x)f(x)\,dx$. With this change Q^* is again given by expression (12-26), but r^* is now determined from

$$F(r^*) = \frac{c_3(R/Q^*) - c_1 V}{c_3(R/Q^*)} \tag{12-29}$$

which will always yield a slightly lower reorder point than expression (12-27).

12-12 (s, S) POLICIES

In the preceding section, we selected a commonly used, albeit arbitrary, inventory policy. It was defined by two decision variables, Q and r, for which we determined "optimal" values. However, the policy chosen may not be the best one for the cost structure used so far, namely that of a fixed cost per replenishment, with holding costs linear in the average inventory level and shortage costs linear in the amount short. Does there exist a policy that is optimal for that cost structure?

Indeed, there does. It is called an (s, S) policy. The reorder point is s, and the *order-up-to-level*, or the *reorder level* is S. If i is the inventory level and q the replenishment quantity, the replenishment rules for an (s, S) policy are as follows:

- if $i < s$, set $q = S - i$,
- if $i \geq s$, set $q = 0$.

As long as the inventory level i is between s and S, inclusive, no replenishment is initiated. Once the inventory level i falls below the reorder point s, the inventory position is brought up to S. The formal proof that the optimal (s, S) policy has a cost that is no larger than the cost of any other policy is rather involved. We shall give only an intuitive graphical demonstration for the single-period case.

Consider Figure 12-10. The U-shaped curve represents the sum of the expected inventory holding and inventory shortage cost $K(i)$ over the period, expressed as a function of the beginning inventory level i. It has its minimum value of $K(S)$ at S. Hence, we would never wish to have more than S units on hand at the beginning of a period. For $i < S$, $K(i)$ increases as i decreases. If i decreases sufficiently, the difference $K(i) - K(S)$ will exceed the fixed set-up cost c_2 of replenishing inventory. So, it will become advantageous to incur the cost c_2 and replenish inventories by an amount q. The total cost is then $c_2 + K(i + q)$. Since c_2 is a constant, it is clear that $c_2 + K(i + q)$ assumes its minimum when $i + q = S$. Hence, the optimal replenishment would raise the inventory to the level S. Let $i = s$ denote the point where $K(s) = c_2 + K(S)$. Then it follows that the optimal replenishment policy has the form

- if $i < s$, $K(i) > c_2 + K(S)$: replenish stocks up to S;
- if $i \geq s$, $K(i) \leq c_2 + K(S)$: do not replenish.

Note that if all sales transactions are in individual units only and if inventory is reviewed after each transaction (*transaction reporting*), then $s = r$ and $S = s + Q$, and the (s, S) and (Q, r) policies are identical. However, if transactions are lumpy or if the inventory is reviewed at discrete points in time, then the (s, S) model results in replenishment quantities $S - i$, which may be different for each replenishment. This is often considered one of the policy's major drawbacks, since it may lead to errors in requisitions or in production specifications.

Unfortunately, the computational effort involved in deriving the optimal (s, S) pair is prohibitive. In practice, approximations to the (s, S) values are used, such as $s = r^*$ from expression (12-22) and $S = s + Q^*$ from the EOQ formula (12-9). For the example of Section 12-10, this approximation rounded to the nearest integer yields

Figure 12-10. *Cost structure for the (s, S) policy.*

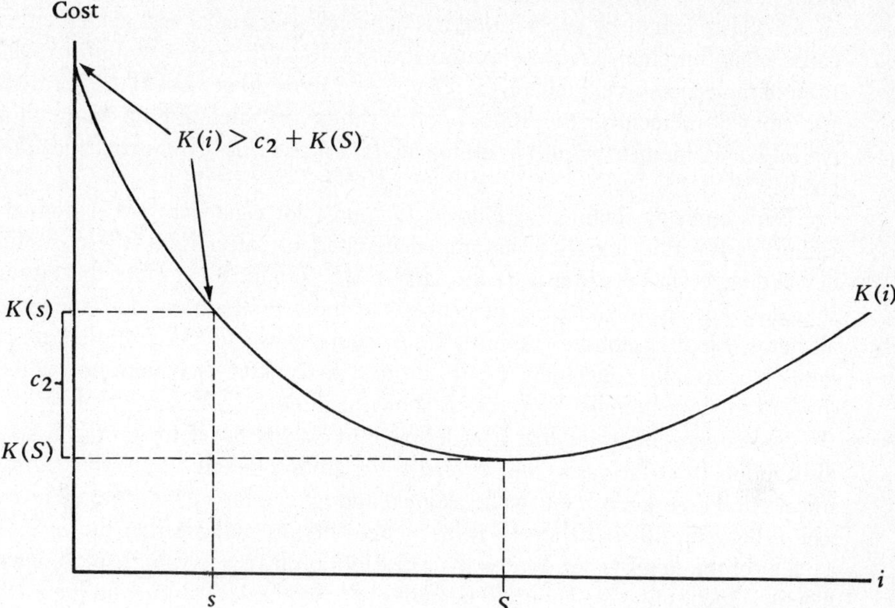

$s = 112$ and $S = 112 + 200 = 312$, while the optimal (s, S) pair is (112, 317). The theoretical cost difference is about 8 cents, or less than 0.03 percent. Sources for more accurate approximations are listed in the references to this chapter. In Chapter 14, the optimal (s, S) policy for a discrete-variable case is computed.

12-13 PRACTICAL STOCK CONTROL—WHICH MODEL TO USE?

As pointed out earlier, the potential savings that can be achieved by the use of mathematical inventory control models are relatively small on an individual item basis, while the cost of such control models (including demand forecasting) may be relatively high for a (Q, r) or (s, S) type model. For slow-moving or low-value items, the net benefits of a sophisticated inventory control model may, in fact, be negative. On the other hand, for expensive or high-volume items, management may not consider the control offered by a computerized system to be tight enough. Furthermore, any item that is still in the fast-growth phase of its life cycle or that has reached the stage of rapid decline in its demand needs a type of tight control that is usually beyond a mechanical system. Therefore, it is important to identify the suitable level and the type of control for each item stocked. This can best be achieved by classifying goods along some appropriate criterion.

A classification by *usage-value* has achieved widespread acceptance largely because of its simplicity. A close examination of actual inventory systems reveals that most of these systems exhibit a typical regularity: about 20 percent of the items account for about 80 percent of the annual dollar volume of sales. Figure 12-11 illustrates typical curves for *distributions by annual dollar usage-value* of industrial and consumer goods.

This curve is obtained as follows. Compute for each item i the product V_iR_i, where V_i is value and R_i is its annual demand or sales. Rank these products in descending order. Starting with the largest V_iR_i product, compute the cumulative subtotals, and express them as percentages of the overall annual dollar volume over all items. Finally, plot these cumulative percentages as a function of the rank of each item. It is usually convenient to also express the rank of each item as a percentage mark of the total number of items, as shown in Figure 12-11.

Experience indicates that it is desirable to classify the items on the basis of the distribution by usage-value into at least three groups, referred to as the *A-B-C classification*. The exact percentage breakdown appropriate for a given firm will vary anywhere between 10-30-60 and 5-10-85. These figures indicate that the first 5 to 10 percent of the items (as ranked by their distribution by usage-value) are designated as A items, accounting for about 50 percent of the total sales volume; the next 10 to 30 percent of the ranked items (accounting for about 40 percent of the total sales volume) are designated as B items; while the remaining 60 to 85 percent of all items (accounting for the remaining 10 percent of the total sales volume) form the C class of items. High-profit items, regardless of their ranking, may be included in the A group.

The degree of control exercised over each item is tailored according to its A-B-C classification. Class A items should receive the highest degree of individual attention. Tight control is justified by the special position of Class A items in terms of the overall operation of the organization. Since they cover no more than 10 percent of all items, the cost of the extra effort involved in tight control is kept within strict limits. Here are some accepted guidelines:

1. Demand is forecasted for each item individually. Forecasts obtained from a computerized system are reviewed regularly and adjusted manually in the light of information directly obtained from the sales force or from the users. Probability distributions of daily demand for large physical volume items are either based on the empirically observed distribution over the most recent six or twelve months or approximated by normal distributions. The demand distribution for high-value/low-physical-volume items is approximated by a Poisson or a Laplace distribution.
2. Considerable efforts are made to keep tight control over replenishment lead times. For instance, for goods produced internally, progress over the manufacturing stages is monitored, and corrective action is taken if necessary. For goods procured externally, firm commitments are obtained from suppliers. If

Figure 12-11. *Distribution of dollar usage-value.*

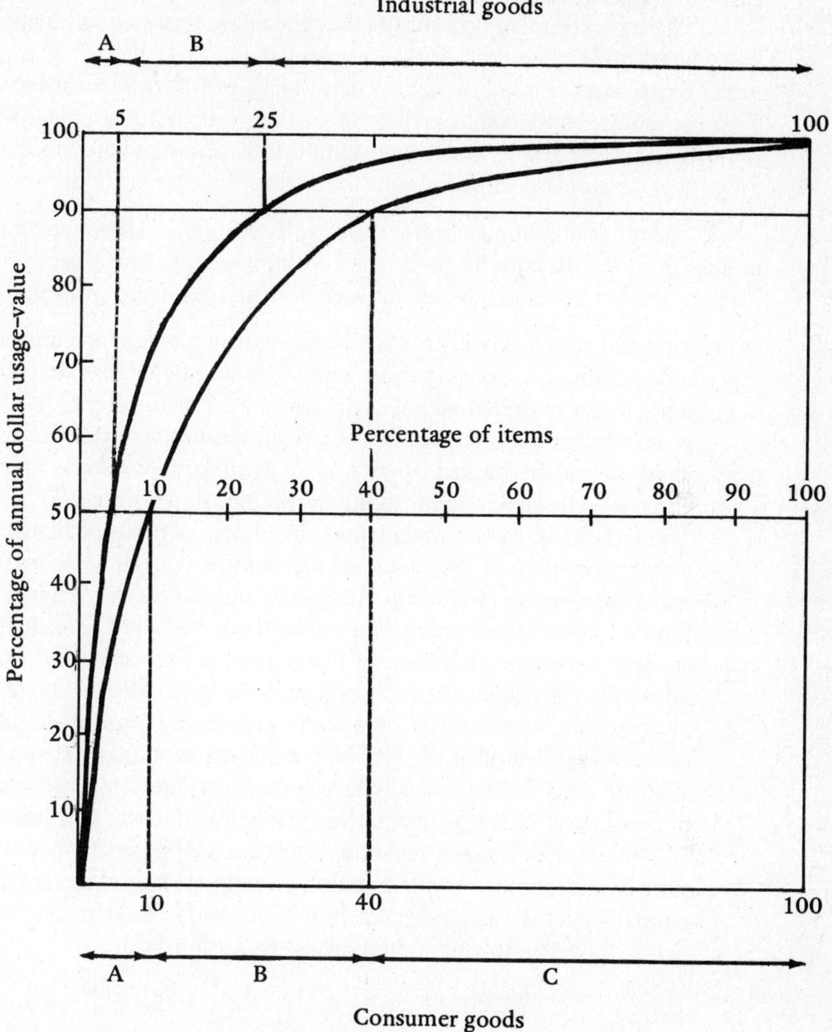

such steps are not possible, lead-time distributions are determined from past experience.

3. Cost factors needed as input into mathematical models are determined individually for each item and are updated whenever significant changes occur (see Section 1-20).

4. Transaction reporting (or at least daily updating of inventory records) is used to trigger replenishments, based on a (Q, r) or an approximate (s, S) model. The replenishment decisions of the models are reviewed routinely before being acted upon.
5. Since stock control is tight, safety stocks can be kept relatively small, thus providing considerable savings in inventory investments. Any shortages will usually give rise to direct intervention to expedite production or supply. Unavoidable delays will be communicated to the customers or users.

At the other end of the control scale are the C items. These represent the largest number of items. Because of their relative unimportance, the objective of inventory management here is to obtain adequate control inexpensively. Hence:

1. Demand forecasts are, in most instances, simple extrapolations of last year's usage. The only exceptions are new items and items that have experienced a rapid drop-off in demand over the last year. For the latter, it is important to guard against overstocking so as to avoid accumulation of dead stocks. Such items should be flagged as soon as a significant slowdown in movement is observed. No demand probability distributions are estimated.
2. Shortages may have consequences as serious as those of higher usage-value items. For instance, stockouts of inexpensive trim or washers for machines may cause serious production disruptions and unnecessary build-up of partially finished stock. Hence, fairly large safety stocks are kept to ensure that shortages are very small. For fast-moving items, rather than determine minimum-cost safety stock levels on the basis of actual shortage costs, firms set safety stocks by specifying a so-called *service level*. This level is expressed either in terms of the average number of years N without stockouts (say, on the average, one stockout every $N = 5$ years, which for a particular item i is equivalent to one stockout every $N(R_i/Q_i)$ replenishments) or else in terms of the average fraction of demand met between replenishments (say, 99 percent). Given an assumed (conservative) probability distribution for usage of item i during a (conservative) estimate for the replenishment lead time, each of these statements yields a reorder point by solving the following expression for r_i.

$$P(\text{demand for item } i \leq r_i) = \beta = \text{service level} \tag{12-30}$$

where

$$\beta = \begin{cases} 1 - (Q_i/NR_i) \\ \text{or (fraction of demand satisfied)} \end{cases}$$

For a particular Laplace distribution, which is defined by a single parameter μ_i, that represents both the mean and the variance of the demand for item i during the lead time, the reorder point is $r_i = \mu_i + k\sigma_i = \mu_i + k\sqrt{\mu_i}$. By the properties for the Laplace distribution shown in Section 10-6 of Chapter 10, expression (12-30) becomes

$$P(x_i \leq r_i) = P(x_i \leq \mu_i + k\sqrt{\mu_i}) = \beta = 1 - \tfrac{1}{2}e^{-k\sqrt{2}} \qquad \text{for } k \geq 0 \tag{12-31}$$

Solving (12-31) for k, we get

$$k = (1/\sqrt{2})\log_e\left[\frac{1}{2(1-\beta)}\right]$$

If $\beta = 1 - (Q_i/NR_i)$, (12-32) simplifies to $k = (1/\sqrt{2})\log_e(NR_i/2Q_i)$. In practice, N is likely to be the same for all C items or restricted to a few values for individual subgroups. Two-way tables for K as a function of R_i and Q_i can be constructed easily for the various values of N.

3. C items are often group-controlled. The items are classified into subgroups with similar cost characteristics. For each group, average values of the product value V and the replenishment set-up cost c_2 are determined. The EOQ formula (12-9) is then simplified to

(12-33) $$Q_i = \sqrt{R_i}\sqrt{2c_2/Vc_1} \qquad \text{for each item } i$$

   where the term $\sqrt{2c_2/Vc_1}$ is the same for all items in the subgroup.

4. Often no individual stock records are maintained. Adequate control is achieved by using a physical *two-bin system*. The second bin contains a quantity equal to the reorder point r_i for item i. Stock withdrawals are always made from the first bin as long as any units remain in it. Emptying the first bin automatically triggers an inventory replenishment. The second bin may in fact be sealed by a tag in the form of a replenishment order card, completely filled in except for the date. When the second bin is opened, this card is then used to initiate the replenishment. When the replenishment arrives, bin 2 is filled first with the new stock, and the balance (plus any old stock carried forward) is then put into bin 1. If a physical two-bin system is impractical, C items may be reviewed only once a month, at which time a decision is made as to whether or not to place a replenishment. In this case, the lead time has to be increased accordingly.
5. For slow-moving items, the replenishment rules are even more streamlined. Replenishment quantities may be set equal to either 6, 12, or 18 months of average demand, based on the annual usage-value of each item—the lower the usage-value, the longer the average interval between replenishments. Good break points are set on a sampling basis and reviewed about once a year.
6. Slow-moving C items are always potential candidates to be dropped from the product lines. For a discussion of the relevant issues for abandonment decisions, we refer you to the excellent text by Peterson and Silver, listed in the references.

The control of B items follows lines similar to the control of A items, except that management and control by exception replaces the continuous individual attention given to A items. As a rule, B items are controlled individually by computerized forecasting and replenishment models. Transaction reporting may be replaced by periodic but frequent automatic review—say daily or weekly. The normal, Poisson, or Laplace distributions are used as approximations for the lead-time demand, depending on whether the item is fast-moving or slow-moving. A shortage cost model such as the one in Section 12-10 may be used for fixing reorder levels. For the lower usage-value B items, a service-level approach may be used instead. Cost parameters are updated at least once a year.

12-14 THE DYNAMIC ECONOMIC ORDER QUANTITY MODEL

So far, we have assumed that the demand, although possibly a random variable, remained stable over a sufficient length of time—several months for fast-moving items, a year or more for slow-moving items. It is clear that the static EOQ formula will not give the optimal replenishment policy if demand is seasonal or is subject to predictable variations resulting from planned changes in production that uses these items as input. The optimal replenishment quantities will then also vary over time.

The best-known deterministic model for dealing with demand that varies over time is the *dynamic economic order quantity model*, developed by T. M. Whitin and H. M. Wagner in 1958. Although the formal model is based on a dynamic programming formulation (see Chapter 9), the resulting solution method can be developed without recourse to dynamic programming. As for the static EOQ model, the total cost is given by the sum of replenishment set-up costs and inventory holding costs. The set-up costs are fixed regardless of the replenishment size, and the holding costs are linear in the inventory level and are usually assessed on the amount of inventory i_n carried forward from period n to period $n + 1$. No shortages are allowed. The demand is known with certainty, but it varies over time. Let d_n denote the demand in period $n = 1, 2, \ldots, N$, where N is the planning horizon. Let q_n be the replenishment (e.g., a production run) during period n. Any replenishment in period n is available to meet the demand for the same and for later periods. Let c_2 denote, as usual, the fixed set-up cost, while c_h denotes the holding cost per unit per period. The periods are assumed to be sufficiently short so that no more than one replenishment will ever occur in the same period. With these assumptions, the inventory behavior over time is described by the following equation:

$$\begin{bmatrix}\text{ending inventory}\\ \text{in period } n\end{bmatrix} = \begin{bmatrix}\text{beginning inventory}\\ \text{in period } n\end{bmatrix} + \begin{bmatrix}\text{replenishment}\\ \text{in period } n\end{bmatrix} - \begin{bmatrix}\text{demand in}\\ \text{period } n\end{bmatrix}$$

or

$$i_n = i_{n-1} + q_n - d_n$$

Since all demand has to be met, $q_n \geqslant \text{maximum}\,(0, d_n - i_{n-1})$. The cost in period n is

$$C_n(i_n, q_n) = \begin{Bmatrix} c_2 & \text{if } q_n > 0 \\ 0 & \text{if } q_n = 0 \end{Bmatrix} + c_h i_n \tag{12-35}$$

The total cost over the entire planning horizon is found by summing (12-35) over all N periods:

$$T_N = \sum_{n=1}^{N} C_n(i_n, q_n)$$

subject to (12-34). We may assume without loss of generality that both i_0 and i_N are zero. If $i_0 > 0$, then we chronologically allocate all goods available at the start of the planning horizon to the demand for the first few periods, and adjust the d_n values accordingly (i.e., set them equal to zero or to the unsatisfied balance). Similarly, if i_N is fixed at a positive level, that amount is simply added to d_N.

The objective is to find a replenishment sequence that minimizes T_N. This is a problem of finding the optimal values of N variables. Fortunately, the search of the optimal sequence of q_n's can be simplified by taking advantage of the following two properties:

1. Consider two consecutive periods, $n - 1$ and n. Assume that it is optimal to replenish stocks in period n, i.e., $q_n^* > 0$. Then clearly no stocks should be carried forward from period $n - 1$ to period n, since any demand satisfied from stocks carried forward can also be met by increasing the replenishment in period n (q_n) by the amount of such stocks. This increase in q_n would not add any costs in period n, but would reduce holding costs in previous periods on the units not carried forward to period n.

   Conversely, assume now that it is optimal not to replenish stocks in period n, i.e., $q_n^* = 0$. Then demand has to be met from stock carried forward to period n. Hence, the amount carried forward to period n (i_{n-1}) has to be at least equal to d_n, given that all demand must be met. These two observations lead to the following property.

   PROPERTY 1 OF DYNAMIC EOQ MODEL: OPTIMAL REPLENISHMENT QUANTITY

   The optimal replenishment quantity in any period always covers the demand over an integral number of periods, i.e.,

   $$q_n = 0, \text{ or } d_n, \text{ or } d_n + d_{n+1}, \text{ or } d_n + d_{n+1} + d_{n+2}, \text{ etc.}$$

   From this property, we can also conclude that if demand for period $j > n$ is satisfied from the replenishment in period n, then the demands for all periods from n to $j - 1$ will also be satisfied by the same replenishment; otherwise, we would violate property 1. Furthermore, there will be a strict limit on how far into the future the demand will be covered by the replenishment in period n. Eventually, the cost of carrying inventory from period n to some period j in the future will exceed the set-up cost c_2 for a new replenishment in period j to meet the demand for that period. Thus, property 1 and the form of the cost structure will restrict drastically the number of values for q_n that need to be evaluated at each period.
2. Consider now a subinterval covering the first m periods of the planning horizon. The second property is as follows.

PROPERTY 2 OF DYNAMIC EOQ MODEL: SEPARATION OF PLANNING HORIZON

If, for a subinterval covering the first m periods, the lowest m-period cost is achieved by a replenishment in period $n \leq m$, then it will never be optimal to satisfy the demand for a later period $j > m$ by a replenishment prior to period n.

Naturally, the demand for periods beyond m could and will often also be met by a replenishment in a period later than n. We give only an informal proof of this property. When evaluating the best decision for period m, we determined (by assumption) that it is less costly to replenish stocks in period n to meet the demand for periods $n, n + 1, \ldots, m$, rather than to replenish in an earlier period, say $n - 1$. Adding the demand for a later period—say $m + 1$—will increase holding costs for a replenishment in period $n - 1$ even more than for a replenishment in period n. Hence, it can never be optimal. Property 2 allows us to separate the planning horizon for computational purposes into independent subintervals.

Using these two properties, we can derive an algorithm for finding the optimal sequence of replenishments. The algorithm proceeds by considering longer and longer subintervals. So we start with an interval of only the first period. Next we solve the problem for the first two periods, etc., until finally we have solved the problem for the entire interval of N periods. When evaluating a subinterval, we always work on the assumption that the ending inventory in that subinterval is zero. Once period N has been evaluated, the optimal replenishment policy can be found by backtracking through the computations.

DYNAMIC EOQ MODEL ALGORITHM

Step 1 Set $Q_1 = d_1$, $T_0 = 0$, and $T_1 = c_2$. Let $n = 1$, and now set $m = 2$.

Step 2 Determine period $n \leq k \leq m$ that has

$$\underset{n \leq k \leq m}{\text{minimum}} \, [K_m(q_k) + T_{k-1}] = T_m \tag{12-36}$$

where $K_m(q_k)$ is the cost of a replenishment in period k to meet the demand for periods $k, k + 1, \ldots, m$, on the assumption that $i_m = 0$.

Step 3 If $k > n$, set $n = k$; otherwise, leave n as before.

Step 4 If $m = N$, *stop*. Trace the optimal replenishment policy. Otherwise, increase m to $m + 1$ and *return to step 2*.

(Note: If you have already covered the material in Chapter 9, you will recognize expression (12-36) in step 2 as relating to a regeneration problem.)

It is step 3 that separates the planning horizon into subintervals. The computations are best performed by using a format as for the 12-period example solved in Table 12-2. The demand for each period is listed in the second header row. We assume a beginning and an ending inventory of zero. The set-up cost c_2 is \$250, while the unit holding cost c_h for each period is \$1. The first few iterations are as follows.

Step 1 $q_1 = d_1 = 170$; $T_1 = c_2 = 250$. The value for T_1 is entered into Table 12-2 in column $m = 1$ and row $k = 1$. The row for $k = 1$ refers to a replenishment in period 1. We set $n = 1$ and enter it in the column labeled n in row $k = 1$. Finally, we set $m = 2$.

Step 2 m is now equal to 2. Step 2 determines whether it is cheaper to replenish in period 1 ($k = 1$) to meet the demand in periods $m = 1$ and 2, or to replenish again in period 2 ($k = 2$) to meet the demand in period $m = 2$. Hence, expression (12-36) becomes

$$\text{minimum}\begin{bmatrix} k = 1; c_2 + c_h d_2 + T_0 = 250 + 80 + 0 \\ k = 2: c_2 + T_1 \qquad = 250 + 250 \end{bmatrix} = 330$$

The minimum is obtained for $k = 1$. Considering the first two periods only, it is cheapest to replenish in period 1 only. Column $m = 2$ shows the two costs in the rows for $k = 1$ and $k = 2$, respectively. The starred entry denotes the lowest cost in this column.

Step 3 $k = n = 1$, so we proceed to step 4.

Step 4 m is increased to 3 and we return to step 2.

Table 12-2. *Dynamic EOQ model: example*

		$m = 1$	2	3	4	5	6	7	8	9	10	11	12
n	k	$d_m = 170$	80	120	40	100	200	150	30	60	90	90	70
1	1	250*	330*	570*	690								
	2		500	620	700								
3	3			580	620*	820*	1420						
	4				820	920	1320						
	5					870	1070						
6	6						1070*	1220*	1280*	1460*	1820		
	7							1320	1350	1470	1740		
	8								1470	1530	1710		
9	9									1530	1620*	1800*	
10	10										1710	1800*	1940*
11	11											1870	1940*
	12												2050

Step 2 Rather than use expression (12-36), we can take a shortcut by using the entries in column 2 to find the sum of $K_m(q_k) + T_{k-1}$ directly. If we replenish in period $k = 1$, then we add to entry 330 (= the cost to the end of period 2, the entry in column $m = 2$ and row $k = 1$) the holding cost of $2c_1d_3 = 2(120)$ incurred for carrying 120 units from period 1 to period 3 (2 periods). This gives the entry in column $m = 3$ and row $k = 1$. Similarly, if we replenish in period $k = 2$, we add to the entry 500 in column $m = 2$ and row $k = 2$ the cost of holding 120 units from period 2 to period 3. This gives 620, the entry in column $m = 3$ and row $k = 2$. Finally, the entry in row $k = 3$ implies a new replenishment in period 3 at a cost of 250, to be added to the lowest cost through period $k - 1 = 2$, given by the starred entry 330. Hence, that total is 580. The lowest cost is still achieved for $k = 1$, which is shown starred.

Steps 3 *and* 4 There is no change in n, and m is increased to 4.

Verify the computations for step 2 shown in column $m = 4$. The minimum is now achieved for $k = 3$. So considering the first 4 periods only, the best decision for period 4 is to replenish in period 3. As we now reach step 3, we find that $k = 3 > n = 1$, and we can set $n = 3$. The consequence of this is that for $m = 5$ we do not have to consider the possibility of replenishing in any period earlier than period 3; i.e., we only explore the costs for $k = 3$, 4, or 5. This follows from property 2. The planning horizon now has been separated into two subintervals: one covering periods 1 and 2 and another covering periods 3 through 12. This is indicated in Table 12-2 by the horizontal line under row $k = 2$. For practice, you should complete the computations for the remaining periods. Note that another planning horizon separation occurs in period 6, where we have the special case $k = m$. A separation occurs again in period $m = 10$, where n increases to 9, and so forth. Note also that for periods 11 and 12 we get alternative optimal decisions.

Once $m = 12$ has been evaluated, we can trace the optimal sequence of decision back through the table. For period 12, the minimum cost occurs for a replenishment either in period $k = 11$ or in period $k = 10$, the two starred entries in column $m = 12$. If we pursue the option of $k = 11$, this implies a production of $q_{11} = (d_{11} + d_{12}) = (90 + 70)$. We now have the subinterval over the first 10 periods left. For period 10, the minimum cost occurs for a replenishment in period $k = 9$. This implies $q_9 = (60 + 90)$ and leaves a reduced subinterval of the first 8 periods. For period 8, the minimum cost occurs for $k = 6$ with $q_6 = (200 + 150 + 30)$, leaving the first 5 periods. For period 5, the minimum cost occurs for period 3 with $q_3 = (120 + 40 + 100)$. Finally we have an initial replenishment in period 1 of $q_1 = (170 + 80)$. Summarizing, we get the following replenishment sequence:

Period	1	3	6	9	11
Demand for period	1, 2	3, 4, 5	6, 7, 8	9, 10	11, 12
Amount	250	260	380	150	160

Verify that the alternative option for $k = 10$ has replenishments in periods 10, 6, 3, and 1. In either case, the total cost is \$1940.

In practice, demand forecasts for the distant future will be relatively unreliable. The separation of the planning horizon into independent subintervals can thus be used to advantage to truncate the computations. Since we are really only interested in the *optimal initial decision*, there is no need to continue the computations once a separation point has been found. A new optimization is performed when the inventory level has been depleted to the lead-time demand. This reduces the computational effort substantially. In our example, we would have stopped the computations after evaluating period 4.

Unfortunately, the dynamic EOQ model has not found any widespread acceptance in practice. This is probably because of its somewhat greater computational effort. Also, the more complex reasoning behind the derivation of its algorithm in comparison with several simple approximate replenishment rules—such as the *Silver-Meal heuristic*, discussed in the next section—has discouraged the use of the dynamic EOQ model.

(For comparison, using the same cost and demand parameters, the EOQ formula for $R = 1200$ and $c_1V = 12$ yields $Q = 224$. This requires about 6 replacements. If we simulate the use of the EOQ policy for the 12 months and charge holding costs only on goods carried forward to a new period rather than on the average inventory, we find that the total annual cost incurred exceeds \$2500.)

12-15 THE SILVER-MEAL HEURISTIC FOR VARIABLE DEMAND PATTERNS

In contrast to the dynamic EOQ model, the *Silver-Meal heuristic* does not guarantee an optimal policy. However, extensive tests have indicated that in most instances the overall cost difference is less than 1 percent. In fact, the heuristic often gives the optimal initial decision. Its attraction lies in the intuitively simple reasoning of its derivation and in the relatively small computational effort—although in many cases the effort is not significantly less than for the truncated dynamic EOQ model.

The basic idea of the Silver-Meal heuristic is to minimize the average cost per period for each replenishment. As in the dynamic EOQ model, a replenishment covers the demand for an integral number of consecutive periods. For a replenishment that covers n periods, the total cost is the sum of set-up and holding costs:

$$K(n) = c_2 + c_hd_2 + 2c_hd_3 + 3c_hd_4 + \cdots + (n - 1)c_hd_n \tag{12-37}$$

The average cost per period is

$$A(n) = K(n)/n \tag{12-38}$$

The Silver-Meal heuristic assumes that $A(n)$ first decreases and then increases for increasing values of n, i.e., is U-shaped. The heuristic computes $A(n)$ for increasing values of n until for the first time

$$A(n + 1) > A(n) \tag{12-39}$$

The associated value of $n = n^*$ for which this condition occurs is the number of periods that the replenishment should cover. The replenishment to arrive at the beginning of period 1 is equal to

$$q_1 = \sum_{n=1}^{n^*} d_n \tag{12-40}$$

Table 12-3. *Example for Silver-Meal heuristic*

m	d_m	Number of Periods n	Incremental Cost	$K(n)$	$A(n)$	Periods Covered	q_m
1	170	1	250	250	250	1, 2	$q_1 = 250$
2	80	2	80	330	165		
3	120	3	240	570	190		
3	120	1	250	250	250	3, 4	$q_3 = 160$
4	40	2	40	290	145		
5	100	3	200	490	163.3		
5	100	1	250	250	250	5, 6	$q_5 = 300$
6	200	2	200	450	225		
7	150	3	300	750	250		
7	150	1	250	250	250	7, 8, 9	$q_7 = 240$
8	30	2	30	280	240		
9	60	3	120	400	133.3		
10	90	4	270	670	167.5		
10	90	1	250	250	250	10, 11, 12	$q_{10} = 250$
11	90	2	90	340	170		
12	70	3	140	480	160		
.							
.							
.							

Table 12-3 contains the computations for the Silver-Meal heuristic for the example used in the previous section. For each m considered, the incremental cost is equal to c_2 if it is the first period in a replenishment cycle, and $(n - 1)c_h d_m$ if it is the nth period in a replenishment cycle. So that we can compare the Silver-Meal heuristic with the dynamic EOQ model, the computations are executed over all 12 periods. Hence, every time the condition (12-39) is satisfied—as indicated by the horizontal line—a new replenishment cycle starts, and we repeat the period $n^* + 1$ in which the condition occurred. (Note that we stop in period 12 before (12-39) is satisfied. However, for any $d_{12} > 160/3$, a new replenishment cycle would begin with period 13.) The total cost over all 12 periods is \$1950, or \$10 higher than for the dynamic EOQ model—a small difference indeed.

In practice, one would obviously stop computations in period 3, when condition (12-39) is satisfied for the first time. A new set of computations is initiated when the inventory position is reduced to the (known) lead-time demand.

As simple as the Silver-Meal heuristic is, its application is only justified if the demand variations are sufficiently large.

12-16 SOME FURTHER CONSIDERATIONS

The text by R. Peterson and E. A. Silver (listed in the bibliography), which we highly recommend as a reference book on inventory control, contains almost 800 pages. This chapter, therefore, can only scrape the surface of the important topic of inventory control. There are many aspects that we have not touched upon, such as the optimal time between reviews for periodic review systems, group discounts rather than individual quantity discounts, joint replenishments for products sharing part of the set-up costs, stocking versus not stocking an item, approaches to perishable goods or to items with a limited *shelf life*, and control policies for multi-echelon merchandising and manufacturing systems (including the important topic of *material requirement planning*).

Chapters 9, 14, and 19 of this text contain additional inventory control models. Section 19-7 shows how constraints on certain resources, such as funds or warehouse space, applied to all items or to groups of items, can be handled by so-called *Langrange multipliers*. This concept is similar to the shadow prices in linear programming. The Langrange multiplier models seem to be of limited practical usefulness, though. Not only are they computationally demanding, but they also assume that the scarce resource is infinitely divisible, which may not be the case. For instance, warehouse space may be allocated in discrete pallet areas only. This condition cannot be handled by Lagrange multipliers, while a marginal analysis that computes the incremental cost of successively reducing the warehouse space allocated to each product by a full pallet area can easily be applied.

EXERCISES

12.1 Sales for a given product over the last six months have shown the following trend:

Month	−6	−5	−4	−3	−2	−1
Sales	520	550	540	565	590	600

Management would like to use exponential smoothing to forecast the demand.

(a) Starting with an initial estimate for the average demand of 500 units, a slope of 10, and a smoothing constant of 0.2, update the parameters using the six months' data given. Find a forecast for the demand in months 1, 2, and 3.

(b) The demand over the next six months turns out as follows:

Month	1	2	3	4	5	6
Demand	580	610	620	660	640	680

Continue updating this system, and find the forecast for months 7, 8, and 9.

12.2 Consider again the first six months' data shown in exercise 12.1. No initial estimates are provided.

(a) From these data, find an initial intercept and a slope, and then apply them to the entire twelve months' data. Use a smoothing constant of 0.1.

(b) Get started on the first six months' data in the following manner. Give the first month's sales a weight of 1 (i.e., this is the initial estimate for the average); the second month's sales a weight of 0.5; the third, 0.3; the fourth, 0.2; and then continue with a weight of 0.1. Use the exponential smoothing formulas to update both the average and the trend. Continue with the second six months' data. Which method performs better when there is a trend in the data?

12.3 For the EOQ model discussed in Section 12-7, find the optimal value of Q and the minimum annual cost for $c_1 = 0.24$, $c_2 = 200$, $V = 20$, and $R = 3600$. What is the length of each replenishment cycle?

12.4 A public utility has a large capital expansion program over the next few years, with demands for funds fairly constant at 4.8 million dollars per year. The treasurer plans to raise the funds by floating several bond issues at equally spaced intervals over the life of the program. She expects that the bond market for her company's bonds will be stable at an interest cost of 12 percent per year. Each issue will cost the company $200,000 in fixed issuing costs plus 0.5 percent on the size of each issue. What is the optimal size of each bond issue and the optimal time between issues?

12.5 A liquid is mixed in heated mixing vessels and then filled into cans on an automatic filling machine. Preparing a mixing batch requires 2 hours of an operator's time, including the time needed to clean the vessel between batches. The cost of the cleaning solvent used is $8.00 per batch. The cost of the ingredient mixed is $1.80 per gallon. The cost of the power consumed for the mixing operation is $0.40 per batch. During the actual mixing operation, which takes 2 hours, no operator attendance is needed. At the end of the mixing, $\frac{1}{4}$ gallon of product is tested chemically. The test takes 30 minutes of a laboratory technician's time. About 10 percent of all batches fail the test the first time. A failed batch is upgraded, involving an average of 24 minutes of an operator's time. An upgraded batch is retested. Reports show that no batch has failed the test more than once during the last 5 years. The liquid is then pumped to the filling machine. The first 2 gallons of product have to be discarded for possible contamination from the previous product filled. Preparation of a filling run takes 48 minutes. The product is filled at a rate of 2500 gallons/hour. Two machine operators are in attendance during both the setup and the filling time. Power costs are negligible. Labor costs, including fringe benefits of 25 percent, amount to $12.50/hour. Company overhead is spread over all operations at a rate of 20 percent on direct labor costs. The cost of the cans is $0.19 per gallon filled. The annual demand for the product is 40,000 gallons. The opportunity cost on capital invested is 24 percent. Insurance, inventory taxes, and other indirect costs amount to another 2 percent on the value of the product in stock. Evaluate the various cost parameters needed for the EOQ model, and find the optimal replenishment policy, its cost, and the length of the replenishment cycle.

12.6 A manufacturer assembles pumps from parts purchased from subcontractors. For a particular type of pump, it takes one technician 8 hours to set up the assembly line. Certain of the parts are picked up from the subcontractors the day before a new production run starts. This requires a 2-hour trip by a truck and a driver; a truck with a driver is costed at \$30 per hour. Four people are involved in the actual assembly, and they can produce 12 pumps per day. The value of the finished pumps is \$108. The hourly cost of the technician is \$12, while the people on the assembly line get \$8. Both rates include 20 percent fringe benefits. Direct overhead amounts to 10 percent of labor cost; company overhead is allocated at 15 percent of labor cost. The opportunity cost on capital invested is 18 percent. No other holding costs are incurred. The annual demand for that particular pump is 800. There are 250 working days per year. What is the optimal replenishment policy and its annual cost? How many runs are made per year?

12.7 Assume that the set-up cost for the EOQ model is erroneously estimated to be $\hat{c}_2$ rather than c_2.

(a) Find an expression that shows by how much the actual incurred cost deviates from the minimum cost associated with the true value of the set-up cost, c_2.

(b) For the data used in the example in Section 12-7 and a value of $\hat{c}_2 = 32$, what is the deviation in percentage and in dollar value?

12.8 A manufacturer procures n different products from the same supplier. This manufacturer periodically replenishes all n products at the same time, and sends a truck to the supplier to take delivery for all products at a cost of c_2 dollars per trip. Other ordering costs are negligible. The capacity of the truck used is such that no more than one trip has to be made for the entire order. The value of product i is V_i, and the holding cost per dollar invested per year is c_1. The annual demand for product i is R_i, and it occurs at a constant rate.

(a) Find a general expression for the total annual holding and ordering cost, and show that this cost can be expressed as a function of one decision variable only. (Hint: The proportion of the total annual requirement ordered for each replenishment is the same for all products.)

(b) Find the value of the decision variable that minimizes total annual costs, and express each Q_i in terms of the optimal value of the decision variable.

(c) For $n = 3$ products, with $c_1 = 0.2$, $c_2 = 120$, $V_1 = 10$, $V_2 = 6$, $V_3 = 20$, $R_1 = 600$, $R_2 = 240$, $R_3 = 1500$, find the optimal order quantities and the total annual cost. How many times is inventory replenished per year?

12.9 For the model in Section 12-8, find the optimal Q and the annual cost for the following data: $c_1 = 0.16$, $c_2 = 40$; $R = 800$; and the price breaks of $V_0 = 10$ for $Q < 160$, $V_1 = 9.80$ for $160 \leq Q < 240$, and $V_2 = 9.75$ for $Q \geq 240$.

12.10 (*Advanced*) Consider the example in Section 12-8. Assume now that the quantity discounts do not apply to the total amount Q purchased at one time, but only to incremental amounts; i.e., the purchase cost is

- $C(Q = V_0 Q$ for $Q < B_1$,
- $C(Q) = V_0 B_1 + V_1(Q - B_1)$ for $B_1 \leq Q < B_2$,
- $C(Q) = V_0 B_1 + V_1(B_2 - B_1) + V_2(Q - B_2)$ for $Q \geq B_2$.

All other aspects remain unchanged.

(a) Find the new total annual cost as a function of Q. Sketch it graphically.

(b) Find a procedure to determine the optimal value of Q in general terms.
(c) Apply this procedure to determine the optimal Q for the data given in the example.

12.11 A product is mixed in batches. There are 3 mixers available, each with different capacities and different costs. The annual demand amounts to 12,000 gallons, and the inventory holding cost per dollar invested per year is $0.20.

Mixer	1	2	3
Minimum batch	200 gal	800 gal	2400 gal
Maximum batch	1000 gal	3000 gal	6000 gal
Set-up costs	$36	$48	$64 per batch
Variable cost of product	$1.20	$1.19	$1.18

(a) Find the total annual cost as a function of the batch size Q. Note the similarity with the quantity discount model.
(b) Find the optimal batch size and the minimum annual cost.

12.12 A supermarket is offered cases of Kiwi fruit—the latest import from New Zealand. Each case costs $12.00 and is packed into 30 punnets, which are sold for $1 each. Past experience indicates that the store would be able to sell the fruit within one week, according to the following distribution:

Number of cases	1	2	3	4	5	6	7
Probability	0.10	0.15	0.20	0.25	0.15	0.10	0.05

Fruit not sold by the end of the week is sold on special for $0.25/punnet. How many cases should the supermarket buy?

12.13 PG&E is considering placing an order for a set of *two* generators from an overseas supplier. It is customary also to place orders for certain of the more expensive spare parts at the same time the main order is submitted. Past experience indicates that the breakdown probabilities for a particular spare part over the lifetime of *one* generator are 0.7, 0.2, and 0.1 for 0, 1, and 2 breakdowns, respectively. Spare parts ordered with the generators cost $2000, whereas spare parts ordered individually later on are estimated to cost $10,000, since they have to be produced by a special production setup. Furthermore, if a breakdown occurs and no spare parts are available for immediate replacement, there is an additional shortage cost of $8000. Unused parts have no value at the end of the generators' productive life. How many spare parts should PG&E order now?

12.14 A caterer is preparing a fruit punch for a company ball. The cost of the punch ingredients amount to $2.50 per quart. Any punch not consumed will have to be thrown away at the end of the evening. Each glass of punch is sold for $1. There are 6 glasses to the quart. The catering manager estimates that chances are 3 out of 4 that sales will be between 200 and 300 glasses. How much of the punch should be prepared? (Assume sales are normally distributed.)

12.15 The weekly demand for a slow-moving part has a Poisson distribution with mean 2. The part has to be procured from overseas, so the replenishment lead time is 12 weeks. The part has a cost of \$8/unit. Fixed replenishment costs amount to \$20. Annual holding costs are 25 percent of the value invested in stock. It is estimated that shortages will result in an immediate loss of profit of about \$5 and an intangible opportunity cost of \$15 for loss of goodwill. Using a two-phase model, find the optimal replenishment policy. (Note that for a lead time of 12 weeks, the normal distribution serves as a good approximation for the actual demand distribution.)

12.16 Redo exercise 12.15 for a lead time of only 1 week, using the Poisson distribution with a mean of 2 shown below:

x	0	1	2	3	4	5	6	7 or more
$p(x)$	0.135	0.271	0.271	0.181	0.090	0.036	0.012	0.004

12.17 Demand for a given product emanates from two different sources: wholesale and retail. Wholesale demand has to be satisfied within 5 days after receipt of an order from the customer, whereas retail demand has to be satisfied instantly, or else is lost. The fixed set-up cost to produce a batch of size Q is $c_2 = \$400$. Inventory holding cost amounts to $c_h = \$20$ per unit stored for one year. Holding costs are assessed on the average inventory. Any retail sales lost means foregoing a profit of $c_3 = \$50$ per unit lost. Daily wholesale demand is normally distributed with mean $\mu_1 = 24$ and standard deviation $\sigma_1 = 4$, while daily retail sales are normal with mean $\mu_2 = 8$ and standard deviation $\sigma_2 = 2$. The current policy is to produce a batch of size Q whenever inventory falls below a level r. The replenishment lead time is only 4 days. There are $N = 360$ days per year. Use a two-phase model to find the optimal replenishment policy. Why is the two-phase model a very good approximation in this instance?

12.18 Use the (Q, r) model of Section 12-11 to find the optimal replenishment policy for the data given in exercise 12.15.

12.19 Use the (Q, r) model of Section 12-11 to find the optimal replishment policy for the data given in exercise 12.16.

12.20 For a service level of no more than 1 stockout every 2 years, find the optimal replenishment quantity and the associated reorder point for the data shown in exercise 12.15.

12.21 For a service level of 99 percent, find the corresponding replenishment policy for the data given in exercise 12.16.

12.22 Redo exercise 12.21 using a Laplace distribution instead of a Poisson distribution.

12.23 The requirements for a given product are as follows:

Month	1	2	3	4	5	6	7	8	9	10	11	12
Demand	50	10	20	60	90	10	5	10	70	100	120	40

It costs \$2 to hold one unit in stock for one month. The cost of a production setup is \$300. Find the optimal replenishment policy using the dynamic EOQ model.

12.24 The requirements in lots of 100 for a component used in various assemblies over the coming 16 weeks are as follows:

Week	1	2	3	4	5	6	7	8	9	10	11	12	13	14	15	16
Amount	12	18	25	10	2	2	2	16	20	2	2	4	10	25	25	1

The fixed cost of a replenishment run, regardless of size, is $280. The cost of carrying lots of 100 units in stock for one year is $130. Use the dynamic EOQ model to find the optimal replenishment policy.

12.25 Redo exercise 12.23 using the Silver-Meal heuristic.

12.26 Redo exercise 12.24 using the Silver-Meal heuristic.

REFERENCES

Brown, R. G. *Statistical Forecasting for Inventory Control.* New York: McGraw-Hill, 1959. An elementary discussion of exponential smoothing, including its adaptation to seasonal demand patterns.

Ehrhardt, Richard. "The Power Approximation for Computing (s, S) Inventory Policies," *Management Science,* Vol. 25, August 1979, pp. 777–86. Simple analytic approximation for computing optimal (s, S) control parameters for the case of backlogged demand.

Hadley, G., and T. M. Whitin. *Analysis for Inventory Systems.* Englewood Cliffs, N.J.: Prentice-Hall, 1963. The treatment is at an advanced level. Very clear exposition with many fully discussed examples. Contains two appendixes listing properties of both the normal and the Poisson distribution useful for solving expressions involving these distributions. Strong in theory.

Makridakis, S., and S. C. Wheelwright. *Forecasting Methods and Applications.* New York: Wiley, 1978. A bewildering array of forecasting methods are available. This text surveys most of them—including adaptive filtering, the somewhat controversial alternative of these authors to the Box-Jenkins method.

Orlicky, J. *Material Requirement Planning.* New York.: McGraw-Hill, 1975. A thorough introduction to this important topic from a practitioner's point of view.

Peterson, R., and E. A. Silver. *Decision Systems for Inventory Management and Production Planning.* New York: Wiley, 1979. Currently the most up-to-date and complete reference text on practical inventory control. Anybody interested in what "works" rather than in theory should study this 800-page text.

Scarf, Herbert E. "The Optimality of (s, S) Policies in the Dynamic Inventory Problem." In K. J. Arrow, S. Karlin, and H. E. Scarf, Eds., *Studies in Applied Probability and Management Science.* Stanford: Stanford University Press, 1962. This is the original work showing the conditions under which such a policy is optimal.

CHAPTER THIRTEEN

Markov Chains

A finite-state stochastic process in which the future probabilistic behavior of the process depends only on the present state is called a Markov chain. In this chapter, we find that the long-run behavior of a Markov chain—unlike that of most stochastic processes—can quite easily be studied. For this reason, Markov chains are often used as approximations of quite complex physical processes, even when it is clear that their behavior may depend on more than just the present state, or that they really cannot be represented as being in one of a finite number of states.

This chapter assumes that you are familiar with the concepts of matrices, vectors, and systems of linear equations. If you have any doubts about these topics, we suggest you review Sections A-6, A-7, and A-8 of Appendix A. Basic probability concepts are reviewed in Sections 10-1 and 10-2 of Chapter 10, while Section 10-8 discusses stochastic processes.

13-1 TRANSITION MATRIX

A regional water board plans to build a reservoir for flood control and irrigation purposes on one of the rivers under its jurisdiction. The proposed maximum capacity of the reservoir is 4 million cubic meters or, for short, 4 units of water. Before proceeding with the construction, the board wishes to have some idea about the reservoir's long-run effectiveness.

The weekly flow of the river can be approximated by the following discrete probability distribution:

Weekly water flow in units of one million cubic meters	2	3	4	5
Probability	0.3	0.4	0.2	0.1

The board considers acceptance of water contracts for irrigation using 2 units of water per week. Furthermore, to maintain minimum water quality standards downstream of the reservoir, at least 1 unit of water per week will have to be released over the spillway. So, the total weekly target release is 3 units. If the reservoir level plus the water inflow is less than that, any shortages are at the expense of irrigation. If the reservoir is full, any further inflow is immediately released over the spillway. The reservoir level cannot be reduced below 1 unit of water.

The two most basic concepts of the behavior of such a system are the *state* of the system and the *state transitions* that the system may undergo. The state of a system represents all those aspects that completely describe the "position" of the system at any instant of time and that are relevant for the future behavior of the system. In physical systems, the *state space* can often be specified in terms of the values of one or several variables, referred to as *state variables*. Note the analogy to dynamic programming. For the reservoir problem, the variable that completely defines the state of the system is the reservoir level at the beginning (or end) of a week. If s denotes this variable, then the state space covers all real numbers between 1 and 4 units of water, inclusive. In view of the fairly crude form of the weekly water inflow data, we shall approximate the state space by the discrete values $s = 1, 2, 3$, and 4. In fact, in this chapter we will discuss only processes with a finite discrete state space.

As time passes, the system may move from a given state to another state, i.e., it may undergo a *transition* from one state to another. Say we observe our reservoir at the beginning of each week. Then, from one week to the next, depending on the water inflow (a random variable) and the water releases (a controllable variable), the reservoir level may rise, fall, or remain the same. Figure 13-1 depicts states and possible transitions in the form of a *transition diagram* for this example. Each circle denotes a state, and the arrows represent possible transitions. Note that for completeness no change in the water level is depicted as a transition back to the same state. For instance, if the reservoir is in state 1 (i.e., contains 1 unit of water) at the beginning of a week, the water inflow during the week is 5 units of water, and the total outflow to satisfy the target release is 3, then the reservoir will move to state 3 (i.e., it will contain 3 units of water) by the end of the week (= beginning of next week). If the water inflow is 4, the system will move to state 2. If the water inflow is 3, the reservoir will remain in state 1. However, the reservoir will also remain in state 1 if the water

Figure 13-1. *Transition diagram for reservoir system.*

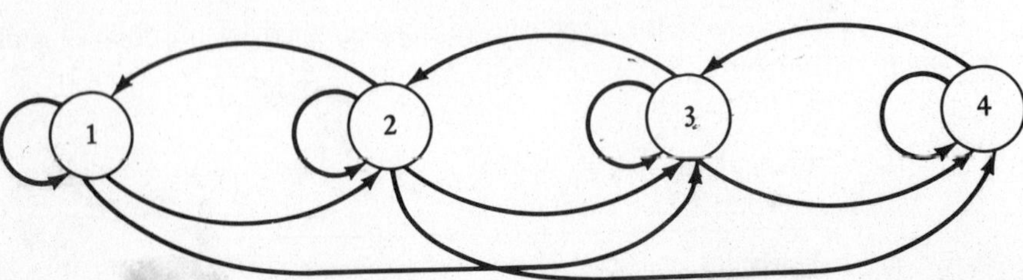

inflow is only 2, and, consequently, the target release cannot be satisfied completely. You should verify the meaning of all other arrows. Again, we shall restrict our discussion in this chapter to processes in which transition occurs at discrete points in time. In our example, this means that, strictly speaking, the inflow and the outflow occur simultaneously at an instant of time either at the beginning or at the end of each week. However, this results in the same end-of-week reservoir levels as if inflows and outflows occurred at constant rates throughout the week. Chapter 15 looks at processes in which a transition can occur at any instant of time.

With each possible transition from state $s = i$ to state $s = j$, we associate a probability, p_{ij}, called a *one-step transition probability*. If no transition can occur from state i to state j, $p_{ij} = 0$. On the other hand, if the system, when it is in state i, can move only to state j at the next transition, $p_{ij} = 1$. With this convention, transition probabilities can be defined from each state i to each state j. For a system with r states, the p_{ij} values can be arranged as an $(r \times r)$ matrix, called a *transition matrix*:

$$\mathbf{P} = \begin{bmatrix} p_{11} & p_{12} & \cdots & p_{1r} \\ \cdot & \cdot & & \cdot \\ \cdot & \cdot & & \cdot \\ \cdot & \cdot & & \cdot \\ p_{r1} & p_{r2} & \cdots & p_{rr} \end{bmatrix} \tag{13-1}$$

Each row represents the *one-step transition probability distribution* over all states. From this it follows immediately that the row sums of $\mathbf{P}$ are equal to 1:

$$\sum_j p_{ij} = 1, \qquad \text{all } i \tag{13-2}$$

Any matrix with elements $0 \leqslant p_{ij} \leqslant 1$, whose row sums are 1, is called a *stochastic matrix*.

For our reservoir system, the one-step transition probabilities can be determined from the probability distribution of the weekly water inflows and the target release. For instance, the one-step transition probabilities for state 1 (= row 1) are obtained as follows. (Referring back to Figure 13-1 will be helpful at this point.)

Water Inflow	Probability	Water Outflow	New State j	p_{ij}
5	0.1	3	3	$p_{13} = 0.1$
4	0.2	3	2	$p_{12} = 0.2$
3	0.4	3	1	$p_{11} = 0.7$
2	0.3	2	1	

From state 1, no transition is possible to state 4, and the sum $p_{11} + p_{12} + p_{13} + p_{14} = 1$ as required. By the same reasoning, we obtain the other elements in $\mathbf{P}$.

$$\text{(13-3)} \qquad \mathbf{P} = \begin{bmatrix} 0.7 & 0.2 & 0.1 & 0 \\ 0.3 & 0.4 & 0.2 & 0.1 \\ 0 & 0.3 & 0.4 & 0.3 \\ 0 & 0 & 0.3 & 0.7 \end{bmatrix} \begin{matrix} \text{(row 1)} \\ \text{(row 2)} \\ \text{(row 3)} \\ \text{(row 4)} \end{matrix}$$
$$\text{(col. 1)} \quad \text{(col. 2)} \quad \text{(col. 3)} \quad \text{(col. 4)}$$

If we observe the system in state i at the beginning of any week, then the ith row of the transition matrix **P** represents the probability distribution over the states at the beginning of the next week. The same transition matrix completely describes the probabilistic behavior of the system for all future one-step transitions. The probabilistic behavior of such a system over time is called a *Markov chain with stationary transition probabilities*—stationary because **P** remains constant over time.

Note that the future (probabilistic) behavior of this system depends only on the current state of the system and not on how it entered this state. Knowledge of the past history of the process does not alter the probability of any future transition. This lack of memory is known as the *Markovian assumption.*

> MARKOVIAN ASSUMPTION
>
> Given the transition matrix **P**, knowledge of the current state occupied by the process is sufficient to completely describe the future probabilistic behavior of the process.

Again, note the analogy to dynamic programming.

13-2 *n*-STEP TRANSITION PROBABILITIES

Suppose the system is in state 2 (i.e., the reservoir has 2 units of water) at the beginning of a week, and we would like to know the probability of finding the system in each of the 4 states after 16 weeks, or 16 transitions. We call these the *state probabilities after 16 transitions.*

Let $p_{ij}^{(n)}$ denote the probability of finding the system in state j after n transitions, given that the initial state is i. (Note that n is not a power.) The term $p_{ij}^{(n)}$ is called an *n-step transition probability.* Clearly, by definition, $p_{ij}^{(1)} = p_{ij}$, the one-step transition probability. In 2 transitions, the process can move from state i to state k in the first transition, and then on to state j in the second transition. The probability of this is $p_{ik}^{(1)}p_{kj}$. Since state k can be any one of r states, there are r mutually exclusive ways of doing this. Hence, $p_{ij}^{(2)}$ is equal to the sum of their probabilities:

$$\text{(13-4)} \qquad p_{ij}^{(2)} = \sum_k p_{ik}^{(1)} p_{kj}, \qquad i, j = 1, \ldots, r$$

Repeated use of the same reasoning allows us to build up the n-step transition probabilities, $p_{ij}^{(n)}$, for $n = 3, 4, \ldots$, as follows:

$$p_{ij}^{(n)} = \sum_k p_{ik}^{(n-1)} p_{kj}, \qquad i, j = 1, \ldots, r \tag{13-5}$$

Let us look at expression (13-4) more carefully. The values of the $p_{ik}^{(1)}$ $(= p_{ik})$, for all k, are the elements of row i in the transition matrix **P**. Similarly, the p_{kj} values are the elements of column j in **P**. Thus, each $p_{ij}^{(2)}$ is the result of multiplying the vector of transition probabilities given by row i in **P** by the vector of transition probabilities given by column j in **P**. Hence, the $p_{ij}^{(2)}$ values are the elements of a stochastic matrix that is obtained by multiplying the transition matrix by itself. In other words, the matrix of the two-step transition probabilities is simply equal to $\mathbf{PP} = \mathbf{P}^2$. By analogy from expression (13-5) we find that the matrix of the three-step transition probabilities with elements $p_{ij}^{(3)}$ is given by $\mathbf{P}^2\mathbf{P} = \mathbf{P}^3$. In general, the matrix of the n-step transition probabilities, $p_{ij}^{(n)}$, is equal to

$$\mathbf{P}^{n-1}\mathbf{P} = \mathbf{P}^n \tag{13-6}$$

Each row i of $\mathbf{P}^n$ represents the *state probability distribution* after n transitions, given that the process starts out in state i.

Applying this to the reservoir problem, we get

$$\mathbf{P}^2 = \mathbf{PP} = \begin{bmatrix} 0.7 & 0.2 & 0.1 & 0 \\ 0.3 & 0.4 & 0.2 & 0.1 \\ 0 & 0.3 & 0.4 & 0.3 \\ 0 & 0 & 0.3 & 0.7 \end{bmatrix} \begin{bmatrix} 0.7 & 0.2 & 0.1 & 0 \\ 0.3 & 0.4 & 0.2 & 0.1 \\ 0 & 0.3 & 0.4 & 0.3 \\ 0 & 0 & 0.3 & 0.7 \end{bmatrix}$$

$$= \begin{bmatrix} 0.55 & 0.25 & 0.15 & 0.05 \\ 0.33 & 0.28 & 0.22 & 0.17 \\ 0.09 & 0.24 & 0.31 & 0.36 \\ 0 & 0.09 & 0.33 & 0.58 \end{bmatrix}$$

$$\mathbf{P}^4 = \mathbf{P}^3\mathbf{P} = \mathbf{P}^2\mathbf{P}^2 = \begin{bmatrix} 0.399 & 0.248 & 0.200 & 0.153 \\ 0.294 & 0.229 & 0.235 & 0.242 \\ 0.157 & 0.196 & 0.281 & 0.366 \\ 0.059 & 0.157 & 0.314 & 0.470 \end{bmatrix}$$

$$\mathbf{P}^{16} = \mathbf{P}^4\mathbf{P}^4\mathbf{P}^4\mathbf{P}^4 = \begin{bmatrix} 0.210 & 0.203 & 0.263 & 0.324 \\ 0.205 & 0.201 & 0.265 & 0.329 \\ 0.198 & 0.200 & 0.267 & 0.335 \\ 0.193 & 0.198 & 0.269 & 0.340 \end{bmatrix}$$

If the process starts out in state 2 as assumed, then the state probability distribution after 16 weeks is given by row 2 of $\mathbf{P}^{16}$. So the probability is 0.205 of finding the process in state $s = 1$ after 16 weeks, 0.201 for $s = 2$, 0.265 for $s = 3$, and 0.329 for $s = 4$, given that we begin in state 2.

13-3 CLASSIFICATION OF FINITE MARKOV CHAINS

Before we study the long-run behavior of finite Markov chains, it is helpful to classify them according to the general structure of the transition matrix.

State j is said to be *accessible* from state i if it is possible to go from state i to state j in a sufficiently large number of transitions. Mathematically, this means that $p_{ij}^{(n)} > 0$ for some n. Two states i and j are said to *communicate* if j is accessible from i and if i is accessible from j, i.e., it is possible to go from state i to j and back to i after a sufficiently large number of transitions. Communication is a class property. If state i communicates with j and with k, then j also communicates with k. Thus, all states that communicate with i also communicate among themselves. Let us clarify these concepts with a few examples.

$$\mathbf{P}_1 = \begin{array}{c} \\ 1 \\ 2 \\ 3 \\ 4 \end{array} \begin{array}{c} \begin{array}{cccc} 1 & 2 & 3 & 4 \end{array} \\ \begin{bmatrix} \frac{1}{2} & \frac{1}{2} & 0 & 0 \\ \frac{1}{3} & \frac{2}{3} & 0 & 0 \\ \frac{1}{4} & \frac{1}{4} & \frac{1}{6} & \frac{1}{3} \\ 0 & 0 & \frac{1}{4} & \frac{3}{4} \end{bmatrix} \end{array} \qquad \mathbf{P}_2 = \begin{array}{c} \\ 1 \\ 2 \\ 3 \\ 4 \end{array} \begin{array}{c} \begin{array}{cccc} 1 & 2 & 3 & 4 \end{array} \\ \begin{bmatrix} 1 & 0 & 0 & 0 \\ 0 & 1 & 0 & 0 \\ \frac{1}{2} & 0 & \frac{1}{6} & \frac{1}{3} \\ 0 & \frac{1}{3} & \frac{1}{2} & \frac{1}{6} \end{bmatrix} \end{array}$$

$$\mathbf{P}_3 = \begin{array}{c} \\ 1 \\ 2 \\ 3 \end{array} \begin{array}{c} \begin{array}{ccc} 1 & 2 & 3 \end{array} \\ \begin{bmatrix} 0.2 & 0.5 & 0.3 \\ 0.1 & 0.2 & 0.7 \\ 0.6 & 0.3 & 0.1 \end{bmatrix} \end{array} \qquad \mathbf{P}_4 = \begin{array}{c} \\ 1 \\ 2 \\ 3 \\ 4 \end{array} \begin{array}{c} \begin{array}{cccc} 1 & 2 & 3 & 4 \end{array} \\ \begin{bmatrix} 0 & 0 & 0.7 & 0.3 \\ 0 & 0 & 0.4 & 0.6 \\ 0.2 & 0.8 & 0 & 0 \\ 0.6 & 0.4 & 0 & 0 \end{bmatrix} \end{array}$$

In the process of matrix $\mathbf{P}_1$, states 1 and 2 are both accessible from states 3 and 4, but not vice versa. States 1 and 2 can be reached from state 3 in one transition, whereas from state 4 they can only be reached in $n = 2$ transitions. States 1 and 2 communicate with each other, and so do states 3 and 4. Each set forms a class of communicating states. Note, however, that once the process has made a transition to either state 1 or state 2, it cannot return to state 3 or 4. The process has been absorbed in the set of states 1 and 2. Such a set of states is called an *ergodic set*, and the states that belong to it are called *ergodic states*; states 3 and 4 are called *transient states*. No matter where the process starts out, it will sooner or later end up in the ergodic set. If we are only interested in the long-run behavior of the chain, we can forget about the transient states. In fact, higher powers of $\mathbf{P}_1$ will still have zeros in the upper right-hand portion, whereas the probabilities in the lower right-hand portion will get smaller and smaller.

It is possible for a process to have more than one ergodic set of states. For a chain of this sort, it may be interesting to know the probability with which the process is absorbed in each of the ergodic sets, given that it starts out in a transient state.

In $\mathbf{P}_2$, the process will be absorbed, sooner or later, in either state 1 or state 2 and then will never leave that state again. This can be seen from the one-step transition probabilities p_{11} and p_{22}, which are both equal to 1, with all other p_{1j} and p_{2j} zero. A state that has this property is called an *absorbing state*.

In $\mathbf{P}_3$, all states communicate and form a single ergodic set. Such a chain is called *irreducible*. The states in $\mathbf{P}_4$ also communicate with one another, and thus also form a single ergodic set. However, note that if the process is in state 1 or 2, it will always move to either state 3 or state 4; similarly, if it is in state 3 or 4, it will move back to state 1 or 2. Thus, if the process starts out in state 1 or 2, after every odd number of transitions it will be in state 3 or 4, and after every even number of transitions it will be back in state 1 or 2. Such a chain is called *cyclic*. The states in $\mathbf{P}_4$ can be divided into two cyclic sets, namely (1, 2) and (3, 4). The process can only return to either set after $d = 2$ transitions. The number, d, of transitions needed for returning is known as the *period*. Note that the period is equal to the number of cyclic sets. The long-run behavior of such a chain will remain cyclic.

A chain that is not cyclic is called *aperiodic*. A Markov chain that is irreducible and aperiodic is called *regular*. Which of the four transition matrices belongs to a regular chain?

13-4 LIMITING STATE PROBABILITIES

Consider again in the three matrices $\mathbf{P}^2$, $\mathbf{P}^4$, and $\mathbf{P}^{16}$ in Section 13-2; in particular, compare the columns. The differences in the elements of a given column become smaller as n increases. In other words, all elements of a given column tend toward a common limit as n increases. Since this is true for each column, it follows that all rows tend to the same limiting row vector. Does this imply that the state probability distribution approaches a common limiting distribution as n increases, irrespective of the initial state in which the process started? The answer is yes for all *regular* Markov chains. This is not the case for cyclic chains, or for chains with transient states or several ergodic sets (although each of these may be analyzed individually as a regular chain).

THEOREM: LIMITING BEHAVIOR OF REGULAR MARKOV CHAINS

If $\mathbf{P}$ is the transition matrix of a regular Markov chain, then $\mathbf{P}^n$ approaches a unique limiting matrix Π with all rows equal to $\boldsymbol{\pi} = [\pi_1, \pi_2, \ldots, \pi_r]$ as n tends to infinity.

The common row vector $\boldsymbol{\pi}$ represents the limiting state probability distribution or the steady-state probability distribution that the process approaches regardless of the initial state.

How do we find these limiting state probabilities? From the preceding theorem it follows that for n arbitrarily large,

$$p_{ij}^{(n)} = p_{ij}^{(n+1)} = \pi_j, \qquad \text{for all } j$$

Using this result in expression (13-5), we obtain

(13-7) $$\pi_j = \sum_k \pi_k p_{kj}, \qquad \text{for all } j$$

Expressed in matrix notation, (13-7) is equivalent to

(13-8) $$\boldsymbol{\pi} = \boldsymbol{\pi}\mathbf{P}$$

The limiting state probabilities are thus the solution of the system of linear equations, such that the row sum of $\boldsymbol{\pi}$ is 1, i.e.,

(13-9) $$\sum_j \pi_j = 1$$

With condition (13-9), we have $r + 1$ linear equations in r unknowns. To solve for the unknowns, we may discard any one of the r linear equations obtained from (13-8), but never (13-9).

Let us now find the limiting state probabilities for the reservoir problem. The five equations are

(13-10)
$$\begin{aligned}
\pi_1 &= 0.7\pi_1 + 0.3\pi_2 \\
\pi_2 &= 0.2\pi_1 + 0.4\pi_2 + 0.3\pi_3 \\
\pi_3 &= 0.1\pi_1 + 0.2\pi_2 + 0.4\pi_3 + 0.3\pi_4 \\
\pi_4 &= 0.1\pi_2 + 0.3\pi_3 + 0.7\pi_4 \\
1 &= \pi_1 + \pi_2 + \pi_3 + \pi_4
\end{aligned}$$

Discarding any one of the first four equations and solving the remaining ones, we obtain

$$\pi_1 = \frac{1}{5} \qquad \pi_2 = \frac{1}{5} \qquad \pi_3 = \frac{4}{15} \qquad \pi_4 = \frac{1}{3}$$

In many applications of finite Markov chains, the limiting state probabilities are the only quantities of interest.

*13-5 MATRIX METHOD FOR COMPUTING LIMITING STATE PROBABILITY VECTOR

For chains with large numbers of states, we can transform (13-8) and (13-9) into a matrix expression that can be solved by a numerical method. If we take the transpose of both sides of (13-8) (we denote the transpose of vector $\mathbf{x}$ by $\mathbf{x}'$), it becomes

(13-11) $$\boldsymbol{\pi}' = \mathbf{P}'\boldsymbol{\pi}'$$

Note that the transpose of the product of two matrices is the product, in reversed order, of their transposes. (13-11) can be rearranged as

$$(\mathbf{P}' - \mathbf{I})\boldsymbol{\pi}' = 0$$

where 0 is a column vector of zeros.

To incorporate (13-9), we replace the last row of $(\mathbf{P}' - \mathbf{I})$ by a row of ones to give a matrix we shall call **A**, and we replace the last element of the column vector **0** by a one.

We now have a system of linear equations of the form

$$\mathbf{Ax} = \mathbf{b}$$

where $\mathbf{b} = [0, 0, \ldots, 0, 1]'$ and where the column vector **x** is the transpose of the required steady state probability distribution. We can solve for **x** by a method such as that of Gaussian elimination, given in Section A-8 of Appendix A.

For the reservoir problem, you should check that

$$\mathbf{A} = \begin{bmatrix} -0.3 & 0.3 & 0 & 0 \\ 0.2 & -0.6 & 0.3 & 0 \\ 0.1 & 0.2 & -0.6 & 0.3 \\ 1 & 1 & 1 & 1 \end{bmatrix} \qquad \mathbf{b} = \begin{bmatrix} 0 \\ 0 \\ 0 \\ 1 \end{bmatrix}$$

13-6 INTERPRETATION OF LIMITING STATE PROBABILITIES

What do limiting state probabilities mean?

> INTERPRETATION OF LIMITING STATE PROBABILITIES
>
> Limiting state probabilities represent the probabilities of finding the system in each state at the beginning (or end) of a transition, after a sufficiently large number of transitions have occurred for the memory of the initial state to be more or less lost.

There is a second, even more useful, interpretation. Instead of predicting the state of the process at a random point in time in the more distant future, we look at the process over a large number of transitions in the future. Define a dichotomous random variable that assumes the value 1 if the process occupies state i (or makes a transition to state i), and otherwise assumes the value 0. In the steady state, these two values are assumed with probabilities π_i and $1 - \pi_i$, respectively. We would like to know the expected value of this random variable over k transitions, once the process is approximately in steady state. For one transition, this is $1\pi_i + 0(1 - \pi_i) = \pi_i$; summing over k transitions, we obtain

$$\sum_{n=1}^{k} \pi_i = k\pi_i \tag{13-12}$$

The fraction of transitions that the process occupies state i is

$$\frac{k\pi_i}{k} = \pi_i \tag{13-13}$$

FREQUENCY INTERPRETATION OF LIMITING STATE PROBABILITIES

The limiting state probabilities represent the fraction of transitions that the process occupies each state in the long run or makes a transition to each state in the long run.

In the reservoir problem, we therefore expect that in the long run the reservoir will start, or end, with a level of

1	2	3	4	units of water
20%	20%	$26\frac{2}{3}$%	$33\frac{1}{3}$%	of all weeks

Often, in practice, the number of transitions needed for these approximations to be useful is not very large, particularly if the transition matrix is relatively well balanced, i.e., the matrix does not contain large concentrations of zeros in the lower left-hand and upper right-hand corners. Also, the larger the number of states and/or the smaller the tendency of the process to move significantly away from the current state, the larger the number of transitions needed to approach a steady-state situation.

Yet another interpretation is in terms of the mean number of transitions between leaving state i and returning to state i for the first time, or the *mean recurrence time* m_{ii}. If the process enters state i on a fraction π_i of transitions, then we can see that, on the average, there should be about $1/\pi_i$ transitions between each such entry.

MEAN RECURRENCE TIME INTERPRETATION OF LIMITING STATE PROBABILITIES

The limiting state probability π_i equals $1/m_{ii}$, where m_{ii} is the recurrence time for state i.

*13-7 TRANSIENT BEHAVIOR OF FINITE MARKOV CHAINS

Frequently, we want to know how long it will take for the Markov chain to reach a particular state for the first time, given that it started in some other state. Such *first-passage time probabilities* can be determined iteratively from the n-step transition probabilities. Let $f_{ij}^{(n)}$ be the probability that the process first enters state j at the nth step, given that the initial state is i. Of course,

$$f_{ij}^{(1)} = p_{ij}$$

If the process is in state j at the nth step, either this is the first time it has entered this state or else it first entered state j at some previous transition (say the kth transition) and has returned to state j after further $n - k$ transitions. Adding up the probabilities of all the possible paths, we get

$$p_{ij}^{(n)} = f_{ij}^{(n)} + \sum_{k=1}^{n-1} f_{ij}^{(k)} p_{jj}^{(n-k)}$$

or

$$f_{ij}^{(n)} = p_{ij}^{(n)} - \sum_{k=1}^{n-1} f_{ij}^{(k)} p_{jj}^{(n-k)}, \qquad \text{for } n = 2, 3, 4, \ldots \tag{13-14}$$

Thus, we can calculate $f_{ij}^{(2)}$, then $f_{ij}^{(3)}$, and so on iteratively.

If only the mean time until the first entry to a particular state is desired, it can be found directly. First, consider a regular Markov chain. For convenience, we relabel the states so that the particular state of interest is state r. Let n_{ij} be the expected number of visits the process makes to state j before its first visit to state r. Then n_{ij} must satisfy the equations

$$n_{ij} = \delta_{ij} + \sum_{k=1}^{r-1} p_{ik} n_{kj}, \qquad i, j = 1, \ldots, r - 1 \tag{13-15}$$

where $\delta_{ij} = 1$ if $i = j$, and 0 otherwise. If we write the transition matrix $\mathbf{P}$ in the form

$$\mathbf{P} = \begin{bmatrix} \mathbf{Q} & \mathbf{r} \\ \mathbf{s} & p_{rr} \end{bmatrix}$$

where $\mathbf{r}$ is a column vector and $\mathbf{s}$ is a row vector, then the system of $r - 1$ sets (each of $r - 1$ equations in $r - 1$ unknowns, represented by (13-15)) can be written in matrix notation as

$$\mathbf{N} = \mathbf{I} + \mathbf{Q}\mathbf{N} \qquad \text{or} \qquad (\mathbf{I} - \mathbf{Q})\mathbf{N} = \mathbf{I} \tag{13-16}$$

Since each column of $\mathbf{N}$ appears in only one set of equations, (13-16) can be solved by $r - 1$ applications of the Gauss-Jordan method. The total mean time to the first entry to state r from state i, m_{ir}, is given by the sum of the elements of the ith row of N. If we multiply (13-16) on the right by the sum vector, $[1, 1, \ldots, 1]'$, we can see that these mean times can be found directly by solving the system of equations

$$(\mathbf{I} - \mathbf{Q})\mathbf{m} = \mathbf{1} \tag{13-17}$$

where $m = (m_{1r}, m_{2r}, \ldots, m_{r-1,r})'$. Note that (13-16) and (13-17) also can be used to calculate mean times to absorption in state r, if state r is the only absorbing state in the chain. These formulas can be applied to chains with more than one absorbing state by forming a new chain in which all the absorbing states are lumped together.

For example, the mean times to absorption in state 3 for a Markov chain whose transition matrix is

$$\mathbf{P} = \begin{array}{c} \\ 1 \\ 2 \\ 3 \end{array}\!\!\begin{array}{c} \begin{array}{ccc} 1 & 2 & 3 \end{array} \\ \begin{bmatrix} \frac{1}{2} & \frac{1}{4} & \frac{1}{4} \\ \frac{1}{3} & \frac{1}{3} & \frac{1}{3} \\ 0 & 0 & 1 \end{bmatrix} \end{array} \qquad \text{and hence} \quad \mathbf{Q} = \begin{bmatrix} \frac{1}{2} & \frac{1}{4} \\ \frac{1}{3} & \frac{1}{3} \end{bmatrix}$$

are found by solving the system of equations

$$\begin{bmatrix} 1 - \frac{1}{2} & -\frac{1}{4} \\ -\frac{1}{3} & 1 - \frac{1}{3} \end{bmatrix} \begin{bmatrix} m_{13} \\ m_{23} \end{bmatrix} = \begin{bmatrix} 1 \\ 1 \end{bmatrix} \qquad \text{(from 13-17)}$$

You can verify that $m_{13} = 11/3$ and $m_{23} = 10/3$.

13-8 FITTING A MARKOV CHAIN MODEL

Once we have decided that a Markov chain is an appropriate model for a particular process, there are two questions that have to be answered. These are

1. What are the states of the Markov chain?
2. What are the transition probabilities for these states?

If we are lucky, the process will have only a few discrete physical states, which can be used directly. However, this is often not the case. To produce a manageable model whose transition probabilities we can reasonably estimate, we must keep the number of states fairly small. The addition of one new state to an m-state chain involves the estimation of $2m + 1$ additional transition probabilities. States that are rarely visited often can be lumped together into one state without too much loss of accuracy. The Markovian assumption, however, requires that the state space be large enough so that the present state of the process contains all the information that is of value in predicting the future behavior of the process. Let us consider transitions from state i to state j at time n. If the estimates of p_{ij} are found to differ significantly, say for two different subclasses of values of the state occupied at time $n - 1$, it will probably be necessary to split state i into two substates reflecting these subclasses. Such an incremental lumping and splitting process, although statistically crude, is the way many chains are fitted in practice. We expand or contract the state space until we reach an acceptable trade-off between manageability and detail.

Once we have decided that the process does appear to behave as a Markov chain and the states have been determined, estimating the transition probabilities is relatively easy. After n transitions, let $N_{ij}(n)$ be the number of transitions from state i to state j that have occurred. $N_i(n)$ is the number of times the process left state i. Then an estimator with good statistical properties for p_{ij} is given by $N_{ij}(n)/N_i(n)$.

Markov chain models tend to be very specific to the problem being considered. For some problems, setting up the chain is all that is required. In others, we require the steady state distribution or the time-dependent behavior of the chain. In the remainder of this chapter, we will look at three problems that illustrate a few of the kinds of analysis that can be carried out.

13-9 A SHARE-OF-THE-MARKET MODEL

Over the last few months, a firm has experienced a decreasing share of the market, attributed largely to the entry of a newcomer into the field. Last year the firm managed to capture about 40 percent of the total market. Before deciding on the best counterstrategy, management would like to have some indication of how this trend is likely to affect its share of the market over time. Maybe the decline is only temporary, and the firm's sales will recover without active intervention.

This situation can be studied by a *brand-share* or *brand-switching model.* The purchasing pattern of a typical customer for this product can be viewed as a Markov chain. Suppose interviewers are stationed at a number of randomly selected supermarkets that carry all the competitive brands of this product. Each customer who buys one of the brands is asked for the name of the brand previously purchased. Let us say that 400 such observations are made. What we have done is to sample randomly from the Markov chains of 400 customers. Provided that this sampling has been done fairly, however, the results can be used as estimates of the average customer transition probabilities. We get the following pattern for two consecutive purchases, where brand A is our firm's brand and brand X represents the products of all competitors combined.

	Present Purchase		
Previous Purchase	Brand A	Brand X	Total
Brand A	117	108	225
Brand X	35	140	175

We can now set up a two-state Markov chain model for the average customer, where state 1 denotes "customer buys brand A" and state 2 denotes "customer buys brand X."

The method of the previous section can be used to estimate the transition probabilities. Of the 225 customers who were in state 1 previously, 117 (or 52 percent) stayed in state 1, whereas 108 customers (or 48 percent) moved to state 2. Similarly, of those who were in state 2, 20 percent moved to state 1 and 80 percent stayed in state 2. Our estimate of the transition matrix associated with this process is

$$\hat{\mathbf{P}} = \begin{bmatrix} 0.52 & 0.48 \\ 0.20 & 0.80 \end{bmatrix}$$

The state probabilities after n transitions can be used to predict the firm's share of the market, since the fraction of customers who buy brand A is exactly the same as the probability that a randomly selected customer turns out to be a brand A purchaser. We can use last year's split in the market share between brand A and its competitors as the initial state distribution. Denoting the initial state distribution by the vector $\boldsymbol{\pi}^{(0)} = [\pi_1^{(0)}, \pi_2^{(0)}]$, then for a 40 percent share of the market for brand A we have

$$\boldsymbol{\pi}^{(0)} = [0.4, 0.6]$$

You recall that each row i of $\mathbf{P}^n$ represents the state probability distribution if the process starts out in state i. With $\boldsymbol{\pi}^{(0)}$ as the initial state distribution, the state probabilities after n transitions are given by

$$\boldsymbol{\pi}^{(n)} = \boldsymbol{\pi}^{(0)}\mathbf{P}^n \tag{13-18}$$

For our problem, $\boldsymbol{\pi}^{(n)}$ behaves as follows:

$n =$	0	1	2	3	4	5	6	7
$\pi_1^{(n)}$	0.4	0.328	0.305	0.2976	0.2952	0.2945	0.2942	0.2942
$\pi_2^{(n)}$	0.6	0.672	0.695	0.7024	0.7048	0.7055	0.7058	0.7058

Thus, the firm's share of the market will ultimately decline to 29 percent if no counteraction is undertaken to reverse the trend.

A more sophisticated study of individual customer purchase patterns finds that the brand of product purchased next can be shown to depend significantly on the types of the last two purchases. If we judge that we have to model this effect, it will be necessary to double the size of the state space. Consider the following sequence of purchases: AAXAXXXAAXAAAA. The first two purchases are a set of two consecutive purchases of brand A, denoted by AA. The next set is formed by dropping the first purchase and adding the third—the customer switches to the sequence AX. The third set consists of the third and fourth purchases, the sequence XA. This is followed by AX, XX, etc. Viewing each possible sequence of two consecutive purchases as a state, we get the four states AA, AX, XA, and XX. Notice that in this model the steady-state probabilities for states AX and XA will always be equal. These probabilities represent the rate of switching from one brand to the other. Unless these rates cancel each other, the process cannot be in steady state. The form of the transition matrix for the more sophisticated model will be

$$\begin{array}{c} \\ \text{AA} \\ \text{AX} \\ \text{XA} \\ \text{XX} \end{array} \begin{array}{c} \begin{array}{cccc} \text{AA} & \text{AX} & \text{XA} & \text{XX} \end{array} \\ \begin{bmatrix} 1-u & u & 0 & 0 \\ 0 & 0 & 1-v & v \\ w & 1-w & 0 & 0 \\ 0 & 0 & y & 1-y \end{bmatrix} \end{array}$$

The limiting share of the market for brand A can be found by adding the steady-state probabilities for states AA and XA. Both have A as the second purchase.

13-10 MARKOV CHAINS WITH REWARDS

Let us continue with our analysis of the reservoir problem. We are interested in finding the net benefit that could be gained by operating the reservoir as outlined—namely, having a target release of 3 units, 1 of which is used to maintain minimum downstream water quality and the remainder for irrigation. The weekly return from 2 units of water for irrigation in terms of additional agricultural output is \$5000, with a loss of \$3000 if the irrigation target of 2 units is missed, i.e., if only 1 unit is available. The reservoir would also be available for recreational purposes for the residents of the area. Assuming that the transportation cost of getting to the reservoir is a measure of its recreational value, the regional water board figures that, given the attendance rates projected, the reservoir would be able to generate the following dollar equivalents for recreational value.

Reservoir level in units at the beginning of a week	1	2	3	4
Weekly recreational benefits in dollars	0	1000	6000	2000

Finally, if the downstream water flow exceeds 2 units per week, flood risks are incurred, with expected damages of \$5000.

With each state and each possible water flow, we can associate the weekly benefits and costs shown in Table 13-1 in units of \$1000. These costs are used to find the expected value of the weekly net benefits for each state, as the sum of the total net benefits for a given water inflow times the probability of that water inflow. For instance, for state 1 it is equal to $(-3)(0.3) + (5)(0.7) = 2.6$ thousand dollars.

Table 13-1. *Weekly benefits and costs of reservoir operating policy in \$1000's*

	Water Flow						
State	Amount	Probability	Irrigation Benefits	Recreational Benefits	Flood Damages	Total Net Benefits	Expected Net Benefits
1	2	0.3	−3	0	0	−3	2.6
	3 or more	0.7	5	0	0	5	
2	all levels		5	1	0	6	6.0
3	all levels		5	6	0	11	11.0
4	4 or less	0.9	5	2	0	7	6.5
	5	0.1	5	2	−5	2	

Let us denote the expected weekly net benefits associated with state i by c_i. Given the long-run average fraction of transitions that the process is in each state (starts out in each state)—the limiting state probabilities π_i—the long-run average benefits or returns, g, are given by

(13-19) $$g = \sum_i c_i \pi_i$$

The π_i serve as weights.

For the proposed reservoir operating policy, the long-run average net benefits per week are

$$g = \tfrac{1}{5}(2.6) + \tfrac{1}{5}(6.0) + \tfrac{4}{15}(11.0) + \tfrac{1}{3}(6.5) = \$6820$$

In downstream areas, this policy has a risk of flooding that is equal to the product of the probability of being in state 4 and experiencing a water inflow of 5, or (1/3) (0.1) = 1/30. In view of this danger, the water board wishes to consider the alternative policy of increasing the minimum water release over the spillway to 2 units whenever the reservoir level at the beginning of a week is at its maximum of 4. No change in policy would occur for the other 3 states. This would tend to keep the reservoir level away from its maximum and, hence, reduce the risk of flooding. Check that under this alternative policy the transition matrix becomes

$$\mathbf{P} = \begin{bmatrix} 0.7 & 0.2 & 0.1 & 0 \\ 0.3 & 0.4 & 0.2 & 0.1 \\ 0 & 0.3 & 0.4 & 0.3 \\ 0 & 0.3 & 0.4 & 0.3 \end{bmatrix}$$

Only the last row changes. The limiting state probabilities for this alternative policy are

$$\pi_1 = 0.3 \qquad \pi_2 = 0.3 \qquad \pi_3 = 0.25 \qquad \pi_4 = 0.15$$

The risk of flooding is reduced to (0.15) (0.1) = 0.015, less than half of the first policy. The net benefits and costs associated with each state are exactly the same as shown in Table 13-1. Therefore, the long-run average benefits per week become

$$g = 0.3\,(2.6) + 0.3\,(6.0) + 0.25\,(11.0) + 0.15\,(6.5) = \$6305$$

or \$515 less than under the first policy. Apparently the gain obtained by reducing the risk of flooding is more than offset by smaller benefits from irrigation and recreation.

If the maximum reservoir level is allowed to become a decision variable, the same analysis could be made for different maximum reservoir levels, such as 3, 5, and 6, and the one with the highest expected total benefits would be recommended as the best choice.

13-11 A FAILURE MODEL

A control device contains N parallel circuits, all of which have to function for the device as a whole to operate properly. Each circuit is subject to random failure. The failure rate increases with the age of the circuit units. Past records of 122 units give the following *survival function:*

Number of weeks used	0	1	2	3	4	5	6	7
Number of units surviving	122	122	116	109	98	78	39	0
Fraction of surviving units failing during following week	0	0.05	0.06	0.10	0.20	0.50	1.0	

Any circuit unit that fails is replaced by the beginning of the following week. No unit survives to age 7 weeks. For this reason, all 6-week-old units are replaced automatically. The failure and replacement pattern of each circuit, considered individually over time, can be modeled as a Markov chain. Each week represents a transition. The age (in weeks) of the circuit unit is the state of the process. The states are thus 0, 1, 2, 3, 4, and 5. A unit of age 6 is replaced and becomes a unit of age 0. The transition probabilities can be determined from the survival function. For instance, all new units survive to age 1, so $p_{01} = 1$ and $p_{0j} = 0$, for all $j \neq 1$. A fraction of 0.05 of 1-week-old units will fail during the second week of use. Failure means that the unit is replaced at the beginning of the next period, and the process moves to state 0. Hence $p_{10} = 0.05$. Any 1-week-old unit that does not fail survives to age 2. Hence $p_{12} = 1 - p_{10} = 0.95$, and the transition probabilities to all other states are 0, i.e., $p_{1j} = 0$, $j \neq 0, 2$. Continuing in this manner, we obtain the transition matrix shown. Since no unit is used for more than 6 weeks (even those that survive to age 6), p_{50} equals one.

$$\text{(13-20)} \qquad \mathbf{P} = \begin{array}{c} \text{Age} \\ 0 \\ 1 \\ 2 \\ 3 \\ 4 \\ 5 \end{array} \begin{array}{c} \begin{array}{cccccc} 0 & 1 & 2 & 3 & 4 & 5 \end{array} \\ \begin{bmatrix} 0 & 1 & 0 & 0 & 0 & 0 \\ 0.05 & 0 & 0.95 & 0 & 0 & 0 \\ 0.06 & 0 & 0 & 0.94 & 0 & 0 \\ 0.10 & 0 & 0 & 0 & 0.9 & 0 \\ 0.20 & 0 & 0 & 0 & 0 & 0.8 \\ 1 & 0 & 0 & 0 & 0 & 0 \end{bmatrix} \end{array}$$

We may wish to find the answer to a number of questions about the operating characteristics of this process. How often, on the average, does the device fail? What is the average rate of replacement of units? If each failure costs \$8 and each circuit unit replaced costs \$6 when replaced individually, would a policy of forced individual replacement at an earlier age (say after 4 or even 3 weeks) lower the average weekly cost? Let us now answer these questions.

What is the percentage of weeks, in the long run, that the device fails? This is the same as the probability that the device fails in any week. This probability is equal to (1 − probability that the device works). The device works only if all circuits work. Since each circuit is independent, the probability that the device works is the product of the probabilities that each circuit works. For instance, if there are $N = 3$ circuits (one of age 0, one of age 1, and one of age 3), then $P(\text{device works}) = (1)(0.95)(0.9)$.

However, what we want is not the probability for a certain age combination of the circuit units, but the long-run probability, once the process has approached sufficiently close to the steady state. At that point, the age of each circuit unit is known only in terms of probability. Thus, before we can find the long-run probability that the device works, we need to know the long-run age distribution of the circuits.

Let us first consider one circuit unit only. The long-run age distribution of an individual unit is given by the steady-state probabilities of the Markov process associated with its failure and replacement pattern. For the transition matrix (13-20), we find the following steady-state probabilities:

$$\pi_0 = 0.189 \quad \pi_1 = 0.189 \quad \pi_2 = 0.180 \quad \pi_3 = 0.169 \quad \pi_4 = 0.152 \quad \pi_5 = 0.121$$

By the mean recurrence time interpretation of π_0, the average life of each circuit unit is $1/\pi_0 = 5.29$ weeks. Each π_i represents the probability that at the beginning of a week the circuit unit is of age i. For each age, we know the probability of failure during the following week of use. Let us denote these by b_i. Then the probability that an individual unit fails is

$$\begin{aligned} P(\text{unit fails}) &= \sum_i P(\text{unit is of age } i)\, P(\text{unit fails} \mid \text{age } i) \\ &= \sum_i \pi_i b_i \end{aligned} \tag{13-21}$$

Using the data of our example, we obtain

$$\begin{aligned} P(\text{unit fails}) = {} & (0.189)(0) + (0.189)(0.05) + (0.180)(0.06) \\ & + (0.169)(0.1) + (0.152)(0.2) + (0.121)(0.5) = 0.128 \end{aligned}$$

The probability that the circuit works is $1 - P(\text{unit fails}) = 0.872$.

In the steady state, each circuit unit has the same probability of failure. Hence, for three circuit units, the probability that the device fails is

$$\begin{aligned} P(\text{device fails}) &= 1 - P(\text{device works}) \\ &= 1 - [1 - P(\text{unit fails})]^3 \\ &= 1 - (0.872)^3 = 0.337 \end{aligned} \tag{13-22}$$

Thus we conclude that, on the average, the device fails in 33.7 percent of all weeks.

Let us next find the long-run average rate of replacement of units, remembering that the average long-run behavior of each circuit unit is the same. Each time the process moves to state 0, the circuit unit is replaced, regardless of whether it failed or not. Using a version of the long-run frequency interpretation of the steady-state probabilities, π can be taken as the fraction of units replaced, on the average, each week. If there are N units, then π units are replaced, on the average, each week. For $N = 3$, this is $(0.189)(3) = 0.567$ unit.

What is the average cost per week of the present policy? This cost is the sum of the expected cost of failure of the device plus the expected cost of the number of units replaced per week:

Total average cost per week

$$\begin{aligned} &= \text{expected cost of failure} + \text{expected cost of units replaced} \\ &= (\text{cost of failure})\ P(\text{device fails}) \\ &\quad + (\text{cost of units replaced})\ (\text{expected number of units replaced}) \\ &= \$8\ (0.337) + \$6\ (0.567) = \$6.10 \end{aligned}$$

To answer the last question, we perform this analysis for each alternative policy of forced replacement of individual units. For a forced replacement after 4 weeks of use, we drop state 5 and adjust the transition probabilities for state 4 accordingly:

$$\mathbf{P} = \begin{array}{c} \text{Age} \\ 0 \\ 1 \\ 2 \\ 3 \\ 4 \end{array} \begin{array}{c} \begin{array}{ccccc} 0 & 1 & 2 & 3 & 4 \end{array} \\ \begin{bmatrix} 0 & 1 & 0 & 0 & 0 \\ 0.05 & 0 & 0.95 & 0 & 0 \\ 0.06 & 0 & 0 & 0.94 & 0 \\ 0.10 & 0 & 0 & 0 & 0.9 \\ 1 & 0 & 0 & 0 & 0 \end{bmatrix} \end{array}$$

The steady-state probabilities are $\boldsymbol{\pi} = [0.215, 0.215, 0.205, 0.192, 0.173]$. (Note that these probabilities can be found by dividing the original steady-state probabilities by $(1 - \pi_5)$. Why is this?) By expression (13-21), the probability that a circuit unit fails is 0.077, and by expression (13-22) the probability that the device fails is 0.214. The average number of units replaced is 0.645. The long-run average cost can then be found as follows:

$$\$8\ (0.214) + \$6\ (0.645) = \$5.58$$

The analogous computations for forced replacement of individual units after 3 weeks yield a long-run average cost per week of \$5.85. Therefore, forced replacement of individual units after 4 weeks is the optimal policy.

*13-12 A GROUP REPLACEMENT MODEL—ANALYSIS OF THE TRANSIENT BEHAVIOR

In group replacement, all units are replaced at specific regular time intervals, regardless of their age; between group replacements, individual units are replaced as they fail. Such a scheme becomes attractive if it costs less to replace units in groups than individually. Assume that for the problem we discussed in Section 13-11, it costs $c_1 = \$3$ per unit for group replacements, and $c_2 = \$6$ for individual replacements.

Each time a group replacement occurs, all units start out in state 0 (new). Then we allow the process to go over n transitions, at which point all units are again replaced and the process starts back in state 0 for each unit. Thus, the process for each unit is periodically interrupted and brought back to the beginning. It never reaches a steady state. So we are only interested in the *transient behavior* of the process.

For this analysis, we do not provide for individual forced replacements of units, but we let each unit potentially go to the end of its productive life, which in this case is age 6; thus we add state 6 to the transition matrix (13-20). **P** is now

$$\mathbf{P} = \begin{array}{c} \text{Age} \\ 0 \\ 1 \\ 2 \\ 3 \\ 4 \\ 5 \\ 6 \end{array} \begin{array}{c} \begin{array}{ccccccc} 0 & 1 & 2 & 3 & 4 & 5 & 6 \end{array} \\ \begin{bmatrix} 0 & 1 & 0 & 0 & 0 & 0 & 0 \\ 0.05 & 0 & 0.95 & 0 & 0 & 0 & 0 \\ 0.06 & 0 & 0 & 0.94 & 0 & 0 & 0 \\ 0.1 & 0 & 0 & 0 & 0.9 & 0 & 0 \\ 0.2 & 0 & 0 & 0 & 0 & 0.8 & 0 \\ 0.5 & 0 & 0 & 0 & 0 & 0 & 0.5 \\ 1 & 0 & 0 & 0 & 0 & 0 & 0 \end{bmatrix} \end{array} \tag{13-23}$$

Let us start out by finding the total expected cost over n transitions (n weeks), if a group replacement occurs every n transitions. This cost is made up of the initial cost of starting with a complement of N new units, the cost of replacing the units that fail prior to the next group replacement, and the cost of the device failing.

The cost of the initial group replacement is c_1N. For the second term, we need the expected number of individual replacements at failure between group replacements. Units failing just prior to a scheduled group replacement will not be replaced individually. In the previous section, we interpreted the steady-state probability for state 0 as the fraction of units that are replaced each week. Here, we use the state probability for state 0 for the same purpose. We can interpret this probability as the average fraction of units that failed in the preceding week. To find the expected fraction of units that fail over the $n - 1$ weeks between group replacements, we need to sum the state probabilities for state 0 over all $n - 1$ transitions, starting with new units in week 1. Table 13-2 lists the state probabilities for $n = 1, 2, 3, 4,$ and 5 week replacement periods. Strictly, the nth row of Table 13-2 should be calculated using an n by n transition matrix in the formula $\boldsymbol{\pi}^{(n)} = \boldsymbol{\pi}^{(0)}\mathbf{P}^n$. However, because of the form of **P**, all the rows of Table 13-2 can be found from $\boldsymbol{\pi}^{(n)} = \boldsymbol{\pi}^{(n-1)}\mathbf{P}$, where **P** is given by (13-23) and $\boldsymbol{\pi}^{(0)} = [1,0,0,0,0,0,0]$. The $\pi_0^{(n)}$ column of Table 13-2 gives the expected fraction of units that fail in weeks 1, 2, 3, 4, and 5 after group replacement, and the final column of the table gives the accumulated expected fraction through week n. The expected number of units that fail, where there are N units in total, for an interval of n weeks between group replacements is

$$N \sum_{k=1}^{n-1} \pi_0^{(k)}$$

Table 13-2. *State probabilities for individual replacement at failure*

n	$\pi_0^{(n)}$	$\pi_1^{(n)}$	$\pi_2^{(n)}$	$\pi_3^{(n)}$	$\pi_4^{(n)}$	$\pi_5^{(n)}$	$\sum_{k=1}^{n} \pi_0^{(k)}$
1	0	1	0	0	0	0	0
2	0.05	0	0.95	0	0	0	0.05
3	0.057	0.05	0	0.893	0	0	0.107
4	0.0918	0.057	0.0475	0	0.8037	0	0.1988
5	0.1664	0.0918	0.0542	0.0446	0	0.6430	0.3652

For $N = 3$, we get the following expected number of individual replacements at failure, and the associated cost for group replacements every $n = 2, 3, 4$, and 5 weeks:

Group replacement interval, n	2	3	4	5
Fraction replaced at failure through week $n - 1$	0	0.05	0.107	0.1988
Total expected number replaced individually	0	0.15	0.321	0.5964
Expected cost of individual replacements at $6.00/unit	$0	$0.90	$1.93	$3.58

The failure probability for the device is now different from week to week. Let us consider first the probability of failure of an individual unit in the kth week. This is given by $\pi_0^{(k)}$, so by (13-22) we get

Week n	1	2	3	4	5
P (unit fails) $= \pi_0^{(n)}$	0	0.05	0.057	0.0918	0.1664
P (device fails) $= 1 - (1 - \pi_0^{(n)})^n$	0	0.1426	0.1614	0.2509	0.4207
Expected cost of failure at $8/failure	$0	$1.14	$1.29	$2.01	$3.37

We now have all the ingredients needed to find the optimal lengh of the group replacement interval n. Table 13-3 contains the computations.

Table 13-3. *Cost computations for group replacements*

$n =$	2	3	4	5
Cost of initial group replacement	$9.00	$9.00	$9.00	$9.00
Cost of individual replacements at failure	0	0.90	1.93	3.58
Cost of failure $k = 2$	1.14	1.14	1.14	1.14
$k = 3$		1.29	1.29	1.29
$k = 4$			2.01	2.01
$k = 5$				3.37
Total costs for n weeks	$10.14	$12.33	$15.37	$20.39
Average cost per week	$5.07	$4.11	$3.84	$4.08

Thus, the lowest average cost per week is obtained for group replacements every 4 weeks. This is lower than the best forced individual replacement policy and therefore is the optimal replacement policy.

EXERCISES

13.1 A delicate precision instrument has a component that is subject to random failure. In fact, if the instrument is operating properly at a given moment in time, then with probability 0.1 it will fail within the next 10-minute period. If the component fails, it can be replaced by a new one—an operation that also takes 10 minutes. The present supplier of replacement components does not guarantee that all replacement components are in proper working condition. The present quality standards are such that about 1 percent of the components supplied are defective. However, this can be discovered only after the defective component has been installed. If the component is defective, the instrument has to go through a new replacement operation. Assume that when a failure occurs, it always occurs at the end of a 10-minute period.

(a) Find the transition matrix associated with this process.

(b) Given that it was working properly initially, what is the probability that the instrument is not in proper working condition after 30 minutes? after 60 minutes?

(c) Find the steady-state probabilities. For what fraction of time is the instrument being repaired?

(d) Assume that each replacement component has a cost of 30 cents, and that the opportunity cost in terms of lost profit during the time the instrument is not working is \$10.80 per hour. What is the average cost per 10-minute period?

13.2 A local craft shop selling wall carpets to tourists can produce one carpet per day. The craftsman never produces a carpet that is identical to any that are still in the shop unsold. For this reason, the choice of carpets increases with the number of unsold carpets, and the selection also increases the chances of selling carpets. Past experience shows that if only one carpet is on hand, chances are 1 out of 3 that the carpet will be sold. If two carpets are available, chances are $\frac{1}{2}$ that at least one is sold, and $\frac{1}{4}$ that both are sold. For three carpets, chances are $\frac{2}{3}$ that at least one is sold, $\frac{1}{3}$ that at least two are sold, and $\frac{1}{5}$ that all three are sold. If at the beginning of the day three carpets remain unsold, the craftsman takes a day off; i.e., he does not make a carpet that day, but just tries to sell.

(a) Define the states of this process, and find the associated transition probabilities.

(b) What is the average fraction of evenings that he will have only the carpet produced during that day on hand and none other? What is the fraction of days that he takes a day off from production?

(c) What is the average inventory level of carpets at the end of a day?

(d) If each carpet brings in \$40 net, what is the average daily net profit?

13.3 The market for a product is shared by 4 brands. The table gives the present share-of-the-market distribution and the percentage of people who switch from each brand to the other brands for consecutive purchases.

		To Brand				Market Share
		1	2	3	4	
From Brand	1	60	8	20	12	40%
	2	15	40	25	20	20%
	3	25	16	50	9	30%
	4	28	12	20	40	10%

(a) If, on the average, 1 purchase is made every 2 months, predict the distribution of the share of the market after 6 months.
(b) What is the long-run average share of the market for each brand if present purchasing patterns are not altered?

13.4 A machine shop operates two identical machines, which are supervised by one operator. Each machine requires the operator's attention at random points in time. The probability that the machine requires service in a period of 5 minutes is $p = 0.4$. The operator is able to service a machine in 5 minutes. Let us approximate this situation by assuming that a machine requires service always at the beginning of a 5-minute period.
(a) Construct a transition diagram for this problem, and find the transition matrix associated with it.
(b) If both machines are operating properly at 8 A.M., find the state probabilities after 5 minutes, 10 minutes, and 40 minutes.
(c) Find the steady-state probabilities for this process. What is the long-run probability that the operator is idle for a 5-minute period? For what fraction of 5-minute periods is the operator busy? What is the long-run average number of machines that require service within any 5-minute period?
(d) Assume that the opportunity cost in terms of lost production, if a machine is down or being serviced for a 5-minute period, is \$5. What is the long-run average opportunity cost for an 8-hour shift (96 5-minute periods)?

13.5 Markov chains are frequently used as models of disease processes. A nonfatal tropical disease takes three weeks to run its course. The chance of a healthy individual contracting the disease in any week is 0.1. Two drugs are available to shorten the length of the disease. The first drug can be used only during week 1, and it cures 50 percent of the patients immediately. The second drug must be used in week 2, when the cure rate is also 50 percent.
(a) What fraction of the population is infected at any time if no drugs are available?
(b) If both drugs are used when appropriate, what fraction of the infected population will have the length of the disease reduced by drugs?
(c) The cost of the drug program per week for each individual in the entire population is \$5. If the cost of each week of work lost through the disease is assessed at \$50, will the program pay for itself?

13.6 Some electronic components are found to have a negative exponentially distributed lifetime, with a mean of 10 hours. Components are inspected every 10 hours, at which time those that have failed since the last inspection are replaced. Any component that reaches 30 hours is replaced whether or not it has failed. (Consult Section 10-9.)
(a) Explain why the replacement process can be modeled as a Markov chain, and find the transition matrix for the state of the component in a particular site.
(b) Write down the failure distribution for the components.
(c) If the forced replacement takes place at 40 hours instead of at 30 hours, the number of components replaced at each inspection clearly will be reduced. Calculate what the percentage reduction will be. Note that this can be done without finding the actual number of replacements.

13.7 An independent taxi operator works in the area of San Francisco and Oakland. In San Francisco, chances are 3 out of 5 that the next rider wants to make a trip within San Francisco, and 2 out of 5 that the rider wants to go to Oakland. In Oakland, 1 out of 4 riders want to go to San Francisco, and 3 out of 4 want a trip within Oakland.

(a) Find the transition matrix associated with this process. What aspect of the problem represents the states, and what aspect is a transition?
(b) If the driver starts out in San Francisco, what is the probability of finding her in San Francisco after 4 trips? in Oakland after 4 trips?
(c) What is the long-run average fraction of calls that have the taxi go from

- San Francisco to San Francisco,
- San Francisco to Oakland,
- Oakland to Oakland,
- Oakland to San Francisco?

(d) If a trip within San Francisco produces, on the average, an intake of \$7, a trip from San Francisco to Oakland \$8, a trip within Oakland \$3, and a trip from Oakland to San Francisco \$6, what is the long-run average intake per call?
(e) The present method of attracting customers is to cruise until someone hails the taxi. The driver experiments with a different approach—namely, always returning to the main bus terminal in each city after a call. She finds that with this approach, 50 percent of all calls involve trips from San Francisco to Oakland and 40 percent of all calls in Oakland involve trips to San Francisco. What is her optimal policy, given that she is willing to allow any combination of the two approaches in each city?

13.8 The operational efficiency of a machine producing parts tends to deteriorate randomly from a condition of (1) properly adjusted to (2) slightly out of adjustment, and from that condition to (3) completely out of adjustment. The condition of the machine can be ascertained only at the end of each one-hour period, on the basis of the number of defective parts produced during the preceding hour. If the machine was properly adjusted in the preceding hour, the rate of defective parts is 1 percent; if it was slightly out of adjustment, the rate is 5 percent; and if it was completely out of adjustment, the rate is 20 percent. Past experience indicates that if the machine is found to be properly adjusted at the end of a one-hour period, the probability is 0.1 that at the end of the next one-hour period it is found to be slightly out of adjustment. If it is slightly out of adjustment, the probability that the machine is found to be completely out of adjustment by the end of the next hour is 0.25. Once completely out of adjustment, it will remain in that condition. Each hour, 100 parts are produced by the machine. At the beginning of any hour, the machine can be properly adjusted by an operation that takes 12 minutes and thus reduces the output of the machine during the coming hour by 20 percent. Defective parts have to be reworked on a different machine at a cost of \$2.50 per part. Each part produced brings in a net revenue (gross revenue less cost of material) of \$2.
(a) Find the transition matrix for this process, if the machine is adjusted whenever it is found that the rate of defective parts produced during the preceding hour is 20 percent.
(b) Find the steady-state probabilities for this mode of operation, and determine the long-run average total number of parts and the long-run average number of defective parts produced per hour. What is the long-run average gross profit per hour (net revenue less cost of reworking defective parts)?
(c) Find the optimal policy for adjusting the machine.

13.9 Past records indicate that the survival function for lightbulbs of traffic lights has the following pattern:

Age, n, of bulbs in months	0	1	2	3	4	5
Number surviving to age n	1000	950	874	769	615	0

(a) If each lightbulb is replaced after failure, find the transition matrix associated with this process. Assume that a replacement during the month is equivalent to a replacement at the end of the month.

(b) Determine the steady-state probabilities. What is the long-run average length of time that a bulb is used prior to being replaced? If an intersection has 40 bulbs, how many bulbs fail on the average per month? If an individual replacement has a cost of \$2, what is the long-run average cost per month?

13.10 Consider the survival function of exercise 13.9.

(a) Assume now that all bulbs—regardless of age—are replaced every 3 months and that individual bulbs are replaced at failure, including those that fail during the month prior to a scheduled group replacement. On the basis of the transition matrix for the failure pattern of an individual bulb, determine the number of bulbs that are replaced at failure between group replacements. Note that failures in the month just prior to a group replacement are replaced also at failure. If group replacements cost \$0.20 per bulb plus a \$5.00 fixed cost per intersection, find the average cost per month for this policy.

(b) Find the least-cost group replacement policy. Is its average monthly cost lower than that of a policy of individual replacements at failure only?

13.11 Past records of a department store indicate that 20 percent of all new charge account customers become delinquent in the following month. Of all charge accounts delinquent for 1 month, 50 percent become fully paid during the next month, 30 percent remain delinquent by 1 month, and 20 percent become delinquent for 2 months' purchases. Of the 2-month delinquent group, 10 percent become fully paid, 20 percent pay partially and become delinquent by 1 month, 30 percent remain delinquent by 2 months, and 40 percent become delinquent by 3 months. Any charge account that is delinquent for 3 months is canceled.

(a) Find the transition matrix for this process. What type of Markov chain is it?

(b) During a given month, 100 new charge accounts are opened. What percentage of those accounts will have their charge account canceled after 4 months? after 6 months?

(c) What is the mean time before a new charge account is canceled?

13.12 An investor bought shares of a certain speculative stock at \$38, and has given orders to a broker to sell the stock as soon as its price rises to \$40 or above or falls to \$37 or below. From observations about this stock over the last few weeks, the investor estimates that the probability of a price rise of \$1 is 0.5 and that the probability of a price decline of \$1 is 0.2 for each day.

(a) Find the transition matrix for this process. Which states are transient states, and which are absorbing?

(b) What is the probability that the broker sells the stock within 4 days? What is the expected net gain, or loss, per share when the broker sells within these 4 days if the selling conditions are met or at the current price at the end of the fourth day?

(c) What is the mean time before the broker sells the stock?

13.13 For the lightbulbs considered in exercise 13.9, use equation (13-14) to find the probability that a particular bulb is first replaced (a) after exactly 2 months and (b) after exactly 3 months. You can check your answers directly from the survival function.

REFERENCES

Billingsley, P. "Statistical Methods in Markov Chains," *Annals of Mathematical Statistics*, Vol. 32, 1961, pp. 12–40. There are a large number of possible statistical hypotheses that test the fit of a Markov chain. This survey paper gives a number of the test statistics for these hypotheses.

Howard, Ronald A. *Dynamic Programming and Markov Processes*. Cambridge, Mass.: MIT Press, 1960. Chapters 1 and 2 discuss Markov processes. Later chapters are relevant to Chapter 14 of this text. Easy reading. All future operations researchers should look at this book.

———. *Dynamic Probabilistic Systems. Vol. 1: Markov Models. Vol. 2: Semimarkov and Decision Processes*. New York: J. Wiley, 1971. An ambitious but not necessarily difficult text. Should be part of any reference library.

Kemeny, John G., Arthur Schleifer, J. Laurie Snell, and Gerald L. Thompson. *Finite Mathematics with Business Applications*. Englewood Cliffs, N.J.: Prentice-Hall, 1962. Markov processes are discussed on pages 193–197 and 274–294 at a level similar to that of this chapter. The discussion of absorbing Markov chains is more extensive. Recommended as first reading on this subject.

Kemeny, John G., and J. Laurie Snell. *Finite Markov Chains*. Princeton: Van Nostrand, 1960 (out of print). Thorough development of Markov chains, both regular and absorbing, using matrix algebra only. Contains a number of interesting examples. This is a highly readable text.

See also the books on stochastic processes listed in the references to Chapter 10.

The following articles give some interesting applications:

Barker, Tansu. "Target Market Selection Using Markov Chains," *New Zealand Operational Research*, Vol. 9, July 1981.

Bessent, E. W., and A. M. Bessent. "Student Flow in a University Department," *Interfaces*, Vol. 10, April 1980.

Cyert, R. M., H. J. Davidson, and G. L. Thompson. "Estimation of the Allowance for Doubtful Accounts by Markov Chains," *Management Science*, Vol. 8, April 1962.

Kemeny, John G., and J. Laurie Snell. *Mathematical Models in the Social Sciences*. Waltham, Mass.: Blaisdell, 1962. Chapter 5 discusses an application in sociology. Appendix C gives a short summary of the essentials of Markov chains.

Meliha, Dileep. "Markov Processes and Credit Collection Policy," *Decision Sciences*, Vol. 3, April 1972.

Meredith, Jack. "A Markovian Analysis of a Geriatric Ward," *Management Science*, Vol. 19, February 1973.

CHAPTER FOURTEEN

Stochastic Dynamic Programming and Markovian Decision Processes

This chapter again picks up the theme of dynamic programming. This time, however, we allow random phenomena to enter the picture. We shall first generalize the recursive relation of dynamic programming to cater to state transformations that are subject to probability distributions dependent upon the decision taken.

The focus of attention changes somewhat in the second part of the chapter. With the exception of Markov chains, the decision models discussed so far all have covered either a single period or a finite planning horizon of several periods. The distant future was ignored. This approach implicitly assumes that current decisions are independent of future events and of decisions beyond the planning horizon. Undoubtedly, this assumption applies to some one-shot or limited-time decision problems. However, much more decision making has to be viewed as an integral part of a never-ending sequence of actions, in which current decisions leave some imprint on the future and future decisions may influence what is the best course of action now. We will thus look at a class of sequential decision models in which the unboundedness of the planning horizon is explicitly incorporated into the analysis. In particular, we will study how an extension of dynamic programming can be used to solve decision problems whose probabilistic behavior can be described by Markov chains.

14-1 DYNAMIC PROGRAMMING WITH STOCHASTIC STATE SPACE

Consider the network in Figure 14-1. The problem consists of getting from state 1 to state 8 or 9 at the lowest cost. As in the routing problem in Section 9-1, the states can be partitioned into four sets. Each route from state 1 to state 8 or 9 has to go through one state at each of the four sets labeled 0, 1, 2, and 3. In each state of sets 1, 2, and 3, one of two possible actions can be taken—action A or action B, each leading to a new state with a certain probability. We can thus look at this problem again as a sequential decision process with three stages. In contrast to the analysis of deterministic sequential decision problems in Chapter 9 (where the new state resulting from a decision is known with certainty), in this problem the new state resulting from a decision is known only in terms of probability. The new state variable is therefore a *random variable*. For instance, if we take decision A at state 5 (at a cost of 5), then with probability 0.3 we will go to state 8, and with probability 0.7 we will go to state 9. In other words, the random variable for the new state assumes either the value 8 or the value 9. If we reach state 8, a cost of 2 is incurred, whereas if we reach state 9, a cost of 10 is incurred. The cost associated with the new state is therefore also a random variable. For this reason, the criterion for optimization usually applied is *minimization of the expected cost* (or *maximization of the expected return*).

To solve this problem, we start again at the end and, working backward, evaluate each state at each stage until we reach the known starting position. For each state and each action, we compute the expected cost over all states that can be reached for this action, in a procedure similar to that used for the evaluation of decision trees in Chapter 11. The expected costs are the numbers shown above the small circles denoting the action in Figure 14-1. Adding the immediate cost for a given action to the corresponding expected cost over all future states, we obtain the total cost associated with each action. The action with the minimum total cost is the optimal action at each state. The minimum expected cost and the corresponding action are shown in the rectangles above each of the large circles denoting the states. For instance, given that the costs in states 8 and 9 are 2 and 10, respectively, the expected cost from state 5 to the end is

$$5 + (0.3)2 + (0.7)10 = 12.6 \qquad \text{for action A}$$

$$8 + (0.6)2 + (0.4)10 = 13.2 \qquad \text{for action B}$$

Action A has the lower expected cost, so it is the optimal action u at state 5, denoted as $u^*(5) = \text{A}$. Verify the other computations.

The recursive relation is now

$$\text{(14-1)} \quad f_n(i_n) = \underset{\text{all } u \in I_n}{\text{minimum}} \left[t_{u,i_n} + \sum_{i_{n-1}} p_{i_n,i_{n-1}}(u) f_{n-1}(i_{n-1}) \right], \qquad \text{for all } i_n, \text{ all } n \geq 1$$

where $f_0(i_0) = c_{i0}$, for all i_0; c_{i0} is given; t_{u,i_n} denotes the cost of taking action u in state i_n; $p_{i_n,i_{n-1}}(u)$ is the probability of going from state i_n to state i_{n-1} if action u is taken in state i_n; and I_n is the set of all possible actions in state i_n.

Figure 14-1. *Probabilistic routing problem.*

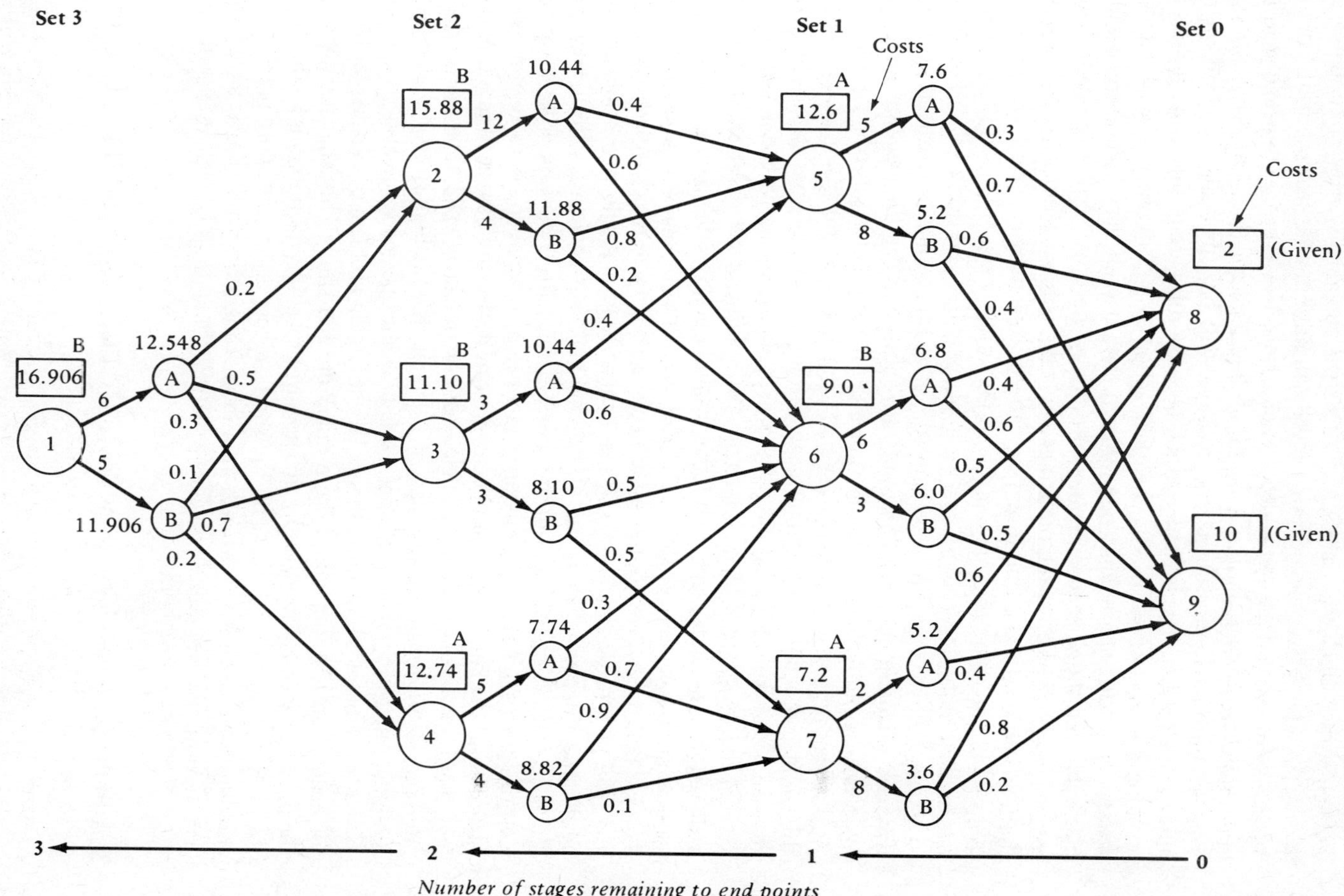

What is the meaning and form of an optimal solution to a dynamic programming problem with a stochastic state space? Once the supposedly known (chronological) starting point has been evaluated, we know the minimum expected cost. Furthermore, we also know the optimal initial decision or action. However, in contrast to a deterministic dynamic programming problem, for the stochastic state space we cannot tell with certainty what the subsequent decisions will be, since these depend on the outcome of random events. The optimal decision rules are of the form "if the state resulting from a decision is . . ., then take action . . . ." In other words, we have a *strategy of conditional actions*, one for each state at each stage; hence our notation $u^*(i_n)$ showing the dependence on state i_n. Only the initial decision can be implemented. For instance, in the present example the optimal action at state 1 is action B. This decision is the only one that can be implemented. Only when we have observed the outcome of a random event (i.e., when we know which state at stage 2 has resulted from this decision) can we implement the next decision at stage 2.

One further point has to be stressed. As was true for decision trees, **stochastic dynamic programming problems can only be solved by the backward solution.** Why? This is immediately clear if we consider the chronological sequence of events. At the beginning of a period (or transition), the process is in a given known state. At this point, an action is taken that leads to one of several future states—each state reached with a known probability. We cannot choose which particular state we will reach. The backward solution maintains this chronological sequence of a decision followed by a random event. In a forward solution, we would ask ourselves what the best path is to reach a given state; i.e., the state reached by a random event is arbitrarily fixed, which is a contradiction. This difficulty is not present in deterministic problems.

The presence of randomness in a sequential decision problem does not necessarily result in a stochastic state space. If the randomness is contained within each stage, the state space remains deterministic. For instance, this is the case if the single-stage cost or return is a function involving random elements that do not carry over into the state transformation. In most instances, we can deal with this type of randomness by computing expected values of the single-stage cost or return t_{u,i_n}. The recursive relations are then identical to those of Chapter 9. Hence, the methods of that chapter apply. Only the interpretation of f_n changes; it is now an expected value also.

(As a footnote, remember the rental equipment problem of Chapter 9. The cost of being short is a function of the number of units short. The latter usually cannot be predicted accurately. All we might know are probability distributions for the number of units needed in each week. So the shortage cost, as for inventory problems, is a random variable which is a function of the number of units on hand, for which we can determine expected values. This is, in fact, how the $R_n(z_n)$ values were found.)

14-2 A FOREST STAND MANAGEMENT PROGRAM WITH PROBABILISTIC TREE GROWTH

Ten years ago, the Green County Council had ten acres of county land planted with radiata pines. At year 6, about half of the trees were thinned and sold as Christmas trees. The trees are now 10 years old, and the council would like to determine the best management program. A stand management program is a timetable for thinning the forest and pruning the trees. Properly done, such operations can considerably increase the value of the remaining trees at clear-felling age, and at the same time these operations may provide some income prior to clear-felling. The best program is the one that maximizes the present value of the net revenues over the life of the stand. Let us see how dynamic programming is currently used to help develop such stand management programs. To allow hand computations, though, we will simplify the problem to thinning only.

The forest industry has developed growth tables for commercial tree species as a function of stand density, soil quality, etc. From these tables, we can extract the growth information applicable to the council's forest. Since the area is prone to repeated drought conditions, the growth is probabilistic, but otherwise fairly uniform. Table 14-1 summarizes the growth in terms of volume (e.g., in cubic meters) over each 6-year interval during the fast growth rate of this species. For instance, if at age 10 the stand has a volume of 200, then at age 16 the probability distribution of the stand volume is given by the column headed "200." Subtracting 200 from each entry in the column gives the increase in volume.

Table 14-1. *Growth table for 6-year intervals from age 10 to age 28*

	Volume at Beginning of Interval After Thinning										
Probability	100	150	200	250	300	350	400	450	500	550	600
0.4	200	300	350	400	450	500	550	600	650	700	750
0.4	300	400	450	500	550	600	650	700	750	800	850
0.2	350	450	500	550	600	650	700	750	800	850	900

The council's forester has been advised that at most 3 thinnings should be contemplated, to occur at ages 10, 16, and 22. The forest will be clear-felled at age 28, and the trees will be used for pulp production. For a stand volume of 350 or more, at least 20 percent should be thinned at each thinning age. Never more than 50 percent of the trees should be taken out in any thinning. To reduce the computational effort, we will assume that a thinning will always be in integral multiples of 50 units, or zero (unless restricted otherwise).

There is, at this point in time, little information available about the net price that thinned or clear-felled wood will fetch in 6, 12, or 18 years. Under such conditions, we usually assume that the price relationships between the goods and services involved will be the same as those now. Thus, we can use the current prices and current inflation-free rate of return as input into our calculations. Currently, each thinning or clear-felling operation incurs a fixed cost of \$400. The net revenues per unit of pulp wood are given in Table 14-2. The desired inflation-free rate of return is 4 percent. The annual discount factor is thus $\alpha = 1/1.04$. Over a 6-year interval, the discount factor is α^6, or approximately 0.8. (See Section 1-13 for a short review of discounting.)

Table 14-2. *Net revenues from thinning and clearfelling*

	Age of Trees			
Volume Taken	10	16	22	28
Less than 150	\$9	\$12	\$15	\$20
150 to 299	\$10	\$14	\$18	\$24
300 or more	\$10.5	\$15	\$20	\$26

We now have all information needed to formulate the problem by dynamic programming. The stages are given by the 3 thinning ages:

Age	10	16	22	28
Stage n	3	2	1	0

The growth over each 6-year interval depends on the volume at the beginning of the interval after all thinning has been done. We will use the volume v_n as the state variable. The amount of thinning, x_n, is our decision variable. Given the volume v_n at the beginning of a 6-year interval, prior to thinning, and given the volume of thinning x_n, the state transformation is a random variable as a function of $v_n - x_n$, i.e.,

(14-2) $$v_{n-1} = g_i(v_n - x_n) \text{ with probability } p_i, \qquad \text{for } i = 1,2,3$$

These are the entries in Table 14-1. The initial state v_3 is given as 200 units.

We would like to find the thinning strategy, starting at age 10, that will maximize the present value of all revenues generated over the remaining 18 years from clearfelling. Let $f_n(v_n)$ denote the present value of the optimal strategy over the remaining n stages for an incoming stand volume of v_n. Then

(14-3) $$f_n(v_n) = \underset{x_n \in X}{\text{maximum}} \left[\begin{Bmatrix} 0, & \text{for } x_n = 0 \\ -400 + R_n(x_n), & \text{for } x_n > 0 \end{Bmatrix} + 0.8 \sum_i p_i f_{n-1}[g_i(v_n - x_n)] \right], \qquad \text{for } n = 1,2,3$$

where $f_0(v_0)$ and $R_n(x_n)$ are obtained from the cost information shown earlier and where X represents the set of feasible thinnings.

Table 14-3 shows the evaluation of expression (14-3). The top portion for $n = 0$ lists the revenue less the fixed cost for clear-felling at age 28. For instance, for a final volume of $v_0 = 300$ units, Table 14-2 gives a net revenue per unit of 26; hence, $f_0(300) = -400 + (300)\,26 = \$7400$. In this example, the range of values for each

Table 14-3. *Solution of forest stand management problem*

n	v_0	$f_0(v_0)$	v_0	$f_0(v_0)$	v_0	$f_0(v_0)$
0	200	4400	450	11,300	700	17,800
	250	5600	500	12,600	750	19,100
	300	7400	550	13,900	800	20,400
	350	8700	600	15,200	850	21,700
	400	10,000	650	16,500		

n	(1) v_n	(2) x_n	(3) $R_n(x_n)$	(4) $\alpha \sum_i p_i f_{n-1}[g_i(v_n - x_n)]$	(5) Total	(6) $f_n(v_n)$
1	200	**0**	0	8416	8416	8416
		50	350	7376	7726	
		100	1100	5168	6268	
	250	**0**	0	9456	9456	9456
		50	350	8416	8766	
		100	1100	7376	8476	
	300	**0**	0	10,496	10,496	10,496
		50	350	9456	9806	
		100	1100	8416	9516	
		150	2300	7376	9676	
	350	100	1100	9456	10,556	
		150	2300	8416	10,716	10,716
	400	100	1100	10,496	11,596	
		150	2300	9456	11,756	11,756
		200	3200	8416	11,616	
	450	100	1100	11,536	12,636	
		150	2300	10,496	12,796	12,796
		200	3200	9456	12,656	
	500	100	1100	12,576	13,676	
		150	2300	11,536	13,836	13,836
		200	3200	10,496	13,696	
		250	4100	9456	13,556	
	550	**150**	2300	12,576	14,876	14,876
		200	3200	11,536	14,736	
		250	4100	10,496	14,596	

n	(1) v_n	(2) x_n	(3) $R_n(x_n)$	(4) $\alpha \sum_i p_i f_{n-1}[g_i(v_n - x_n)]$	(5) Total	(6) $f_n(v_n)$
	600	150	2300	13,616	15,916	
		200	3200	12,576	15,776	
		250	4100	11,536	15,636	
		300	5600	10,496	16,096	16,096
	650	150	2300	14,656	16,956	
		200	3200	13,616	16,816	
		250	4100	12,576	16,676	
		300	5600	11,536	17,136	17,136
	700	150	2300	15,696	17,996	
		200	3200	14,656	17,856	
		250	4100	13,616	17,716	
		300	5600	12,576	18,176	18,176
		350	6600	11,536	18,136	
2	200	**0**	0	9737.60	9737.60	9737.60
		50	200	9168.00	9368.00	
		100	800	7766.40	8566.40	
	250	**0**	0	10,569.60	10,569.60	10,569.60
		50	200	9737.60	9937.60	
		100	800	9168.00	9968.00	
	300	**0**	0	11,430.40	11,430.40	11,430.40
		50	200	10,569.60	10,769.60	
		100	800	9737.60	10,537.60	
		150	1700	9168.00	10,868.00	
	350	100	800	10,569.60	11,369.60	
		150	1700	9737.60	11,437.60	11,437.60
	400	100	800	11,430.40	12,230.40	
		150	1700	10,569.60	12,269.60	12,269.60
		200	2400	9737.60	12,137.60	
	450	100	800	12,320.00	13,120.00	
		150	1700	11,430.40	13,130.40	13,130.40
		200	2400	10,569.60	12,969.60	
	500	100	800	13,152.00	13,952.00	
		150	1700	12,320.00	14,020.00	14,020.00
		200	2400	11,430.40	13,830.00	
		250	3100	10,569.60	13,669.60	
3	200	**0**	0	10,104.96	10,104.96	10,104.96
		50	50	9684.86	9734.86	
		100	500	8603.78	9103.78	

state variable v_n, for $n = 1,2,3$, can easily be determined from the set of feasible thinnings for each v_n, given that we start out with $v_3 = 200$. Let us demonstrate how $f_1(350)$ was determined. By the thinning restrictions $0.2v_1 \leq x_1 \leq 0.5v_1$, x_1 can only assume the values 100 and 150. $R_1(100) = -400 + (100)15 = \$1100$, while $R_1(150) = -400 + (150)18 = \$2300$. For $x_1 = 100$, $v_1 - x_1 = 250$, so by Table 14-1, $g(250)$ can assume values 400, 500, and 550, with probabilities 0.4, 0.4, and 0.2, respectively. Thus the entry in column 4 is

$$0.8 \sum_i p_i f_0[g_i(250)] = 0.8[0.4(10{,}000) + 0.4(12{,}600) + 0.2(13{,}900)] = \$9456$$

Similarly, for $x_1 = 150$, the entry in column 4 is \$8416. Adding entries in columns 3 and 4 in each row, we get the entries in column 5. Since the entry for $x_1 = 150$ is the larger one, $f_1(350) = \$10{,}716$; the corresponding optimal decision $x_1^*(v_1)$ is $x_1^*(350) = 150$ (shown in boldface). For $n = 3$, only $v_3 = 200$ has to be evaluated. From this we see that the maximum expected present value is \$10,104.96, and the initial optimal decision $x_3^*(200)$ is to do no thinning at age 10. This is the only decision that can be implemented at this stage. Before we can implement a decision for the next stage, we first have to await the random growth that will occur between years 10 and 16.

14-3 OPTIMIZATION OVER AN UNBOUNDED PLANNING HORIZON

When dealing with decision problems that have no well-defined terminal point but go on indefinitely over the foreseeable future, we have several options.

1. We may consider a finite planning horizon, and select terminal conditions that the system has to satisfy (for deterministic problems) or penalize deviations from desired terminal conditions (for stochastic problems). For instance, in an inventory model, the terminal condition consists of the inventory level desired at the end of the planning horizon. This approach is particularly suitable for problems subject to seasonal cycles in which the carry-over from one cycle to the next is small.
2. We may choose a planning horizon long enough so that the optimal current decisions are not affected by reasonable changes in events and decisions toward the end of the planning horizon. The exact length required is best determined by sensitivity analysis. The period may only cover a few months if we are dealing with routine decisions, but may cover 10 to 20 years for strategic decisions, such as those dealing with capital investments. Since information about the future behavior of the system becomes less and less reliable as we project into the more distant future, this approach has considerable appeal. Only the current optimal decision would ever be implemented. The problem would be reoptimized for each later decision, at which time better information about the more distant future would probably be available. For each optimization, the planning horizon has the same form constant length as shown in Figure 14-2.
3. We may build a model for an *unbounded planning horizon*.

Figure 14-2. *Rolling planning horizon of constant length.*

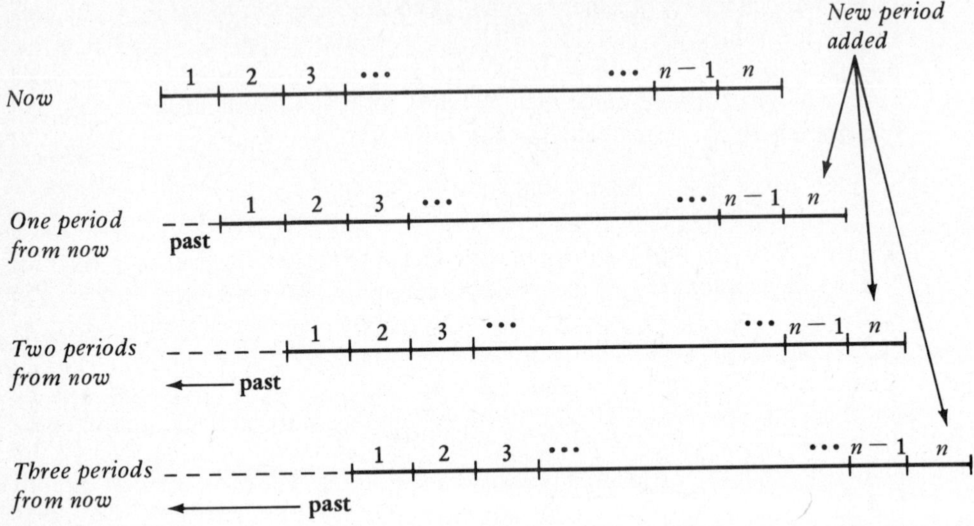

Once we let the planning horizon become unbounded, we have to introduce restrictive assumptions about the behavior of the system studied.

> **ASSUMPTION OF STATIONARITY**
>
> We assume that the environment in which the decisions have to be made and the actions available to the decision maker remain stationary over time.

For instance, for an inventory control problem, this implies that either the demand (in the deterministic case) or the demand probability distribution (in the stochastic case) is identical in each period, and that all costs associated with a given decision and the set of possible decisions available in each period remain the same. This is analogous to the assumption of stationarity already encountered for Markov chains in Chapter 13. Note that in a narrow sense this assumption excludes seasonal variations even if they are identical from year to year. Admittedly, few real-life processes remain stationary for any extended length of time. Nevertheless, this assumption may be a suitable approximation to reality for many problems, such as routine day-to-day decisions in a slowly changing environment, or long-term, recurrent strategic decisions. In the first instance, the potential increase in benefits of a nonstationary analysis usually will not justify the higher cost of data collection. This is the case for most inventory problems covering hundreds or thousands of products, each generating only small savings. In the second instance, uncertainty about events and alternative courses of action in the more distant future and the fact that they have a small impact on the present (because of discounting of future benefits and costs) may justify the assumption of stationarity and may result in better current decisions than those obtained by ignoring the distant and uncertain future altogether. We shall see this shortly.

As our focus shifts from a finite to an infinite planning horizon, the optimization criteria of the finite case have to be altered or adapted appropriately. Since the sum of a stream of finite returns or costs per period may become infinitely large as the number of periods considered goes to infinity, we may look at either

- the *present value* of a infinite stream of returns or costs, or
- the *average return* or *average cost* per period.

In the finite period case, the optimal policy or strategy depends on both the state occupied by the system and the number of periods (or stages) remaining. For an unbounded planning horizon, the number of periods remaining stays the same from period to period. Therefore, the optimal policy no longer is dependent on the number of periods remaining, but becomes uniquely a function of the state of the system.

STATIONARY POLICIES

A stationary policy has the property that whenever the process returns to a given state, the same decision is taken; i.e., the decision taken in each period depends only on that current state of the system.

14-4 FUNCTIONAL EQUATIONS

Consider the following dynamic inventory problem. The stock level of a given product is reviewed at the beginning of each week, and a decision is made as to whether or not to schedule a production run. Goods from a production run will be available for sale in the same period. Total costs are made up of the cost of holding goods in inventory, the fixed and variable production costs, and the opportunity cost on sales lost because of insufficient stocks. The demand during each period is a random variable with known probability distribution. The problem is to find an optimal inventory and production policy so as to minimize the present value of the total expected costs over a finite planning horizon of N periods.

We first introduce some symbols. The periods are numbered consecutively from end to beginning. The last period in the planning horizon is period 1, and the first period is period N. Let

z_n denote the beginning inventory with n periods left to go to the end of the planning horizon;

x_n denote the amount produced in the nth-to-last period, $x_n \epsilon X_n$, where X_n is the set of all feasible production levels;

d_n denote the demand in the nth-to-last period, subject to a known probability distribution with terms $p_n(d_n)$;

c_h denote the holding cost per period per unit carried forward from the preceding period;

c_s denote the shortage cost per unit short;

$k_n(x_n)$ denote the production cost to produce x_n units in period n, $k_n(0) = 0$, $k_n(x_n) \geqslant a$ for $x_n > 0$, where a represents the fixed cost;

α denote the discount factor per period.

The cost $C_n(z_n, x_n)$ in the nth-to-last period, given a beginning inventory of z_n and a production of x_n, is equal to the sum of production cost, inventory holding cost, and expected shortage cost:

$$C_n(z_n, x_n) = k_n(x_n) + \begin{bmatrix} z_n c_h, & \text{for } z_n > 0 \\ 0, & \text{for } z_n \leqslant 0 \end{bmatrix} + c_s \sum_{d_n > z_n + x_n} (d_n - z_n - x_n)\, p_n(d_n) \tag{14-4}$$

where $d_n - z_n - x_n$ is the amount of lost sales with probability $p_n(d_n)$. Note that for simplicity holding costs are assessed on the beginning inventory. This has no effect on the optimal policy, but reduces the computational effort somewhat. Inventories in two consecutive periods are related by

$$z_{n-1} = \begin{cases} z_n + x_n - d_n, & \text{for } d_n < (z_n + x_n) \\ 0, & \text{otherwise} \end{cases}$$

The expected total cost is given by the present value of the $C_n(z_n, x_n)$ terms summed over all N periods. For the dynamic programming formulation, let the periods denote the stages. The state of the process is given by the beginning inventory level z_n. Then by the principle of optimality, the present value of the minimum expected total cost $f_n(z_n)$ of starting with an inventory level of size z_n and n periods left to go the end of the planning horizon is given by the following recursive relations:

$$f_n(z_n) = \underset{x_n \epsilon X_n}{\text{minimum}} \left[C_n(z_n, x_n) + d\sum_{d_n} f_{n-1}(z_n + x_n - d_n)\, p_n(d_n) \right], \text{ all } z_n,\ n \geqslant 1 \tag{14-5}$$

where $f_0(z_0) = C_0(z_0)$, for all z_0, is given. For instance, $C_0(z_0)$ could reflect the cost of ending up with an inventory of z_0 at the end of the planning horizon. This cost might include a penalty for deviating from a given target ending inventory of z.

Suppose that the planning horizon becomes unbounded. Then by the assumption of stationarity,

$$\begin{aligned} C_n(z_n, x_n) &= C(z, x) \\ p_n(d_n) &= p(d) \\ X_n &= X, \qquad \text{for all } n \end{aligned} \tag{14-6}$$

After each period, the decision maker again faces an unbounded planning horizon. The number of stages left to go therefore remains infinitely large, and the subscript n on f and z may be dropped also. Substituting the terms (14-6) into (14-5), the recursive relation for the minimum discounted expected cost over all future periods becomes

$$(14\text{-}7) \qquad f(z) = \underset{x \epsilon X}{\text{minimum}} \left[C(z, x) + \alpha \sum_{d} f(z + x - d)\, p(d) \right], \qquad \text{for all } z$$

Expression (14-7) is the present value of the minimum cost over all future periods starting in state z. It is equal to the minimum, over all possible decisions, of two cost terms. The first term is the cost in the current period. The second is the present value, one period from now, of the expected present value of the minimum cost over all future periods, discounted for one period.

Note that the same value of the state variable z may appear in f on both sides of the equal sign. A relation of the form (14-7) is called a *functional* or *extremal equation*. The set of functional equations (14-7) states what optimization condition f has to satisfy for all values of the state variable z.

It is also immediately clear that the conventional approach of dynamic programming for finding the optimal policy—namely, to evaluate the recursive relation stage by stage, starting with the last stage in the planning horizon—cannot be used any longer. There is no last period in the planning horizon. The two best-known computational procedures for finding the optimal strategy go under the names *approximation in function space* and *approximation in policy space*. We shall study only the latter. But before doing this, let us first look at the probabilistic structure of expression (14-7).

14-5 MARKOVIAN DECISION PROCESSES

Suppose the demand distribution for a given product to be controlled by the inventory model in the preceding section is as follows:

Weekly demand, d	0	1	2	3	4 or more
Probability, $p(d)$	0.4	0.3	0.2	0.1	0

Recall that any demand not met in a period is lost. Let us arbitrarily decide that the maximum inventory level cannot exceed 5. Therefore, the state variable in (14-7) that stands for the beginning inventory (carried forward from the preceding week) can assume value 0, 1, 2, 3, 4, or 5. A stationary inventory policy or strategy consists of a replenishment decision—a value of x— for each value of the state variable. Given that the maximum inventory cannot exceed 5, we have the choice of decisions in each state, as shown.

State z	Choices for x
0	0,1,2,3,4,5
1	0,1,2,3,4
2	0,1,2,3
3	0,1,2
4	0,1
5	0

For instance, (4, 3, 0, 0, 0, 0) would be a possible policy. It says that whenever the state of the system (beginning inventory) is 0 or 1, the state is instantaneously increased to 4, whereas no change (no replenishment) is made if the state of the system is 2 or more. (In Section 12-12, this was called an (s, S) policy.)

During the week, a random demand d occurs with probability $p(d)$. It affects the inventory level carried forward to the next period. In the terminology for Markov chains, we say that, given the decision x, the state of the system undergoes a transition from state i to state $j = i + x - d$ with probability $p_{ij}(x) = p(d)$. The transition probabilities, $p_{ij}(x)$, are seen to be a function of both the probability distribution of the demand and the particular decision chosen in state i. For any given strategy (i.e., a decision for each state), the probabilistic behavior of the system is that of a Markov chain.

With each state i and each decision x, we also associate a one-period cost $c_i(x)$. Table 14-4 lists the transition probabilities and the associated cost for each state and each decision. The former are based on $p(d)$, and the latter are based on the assumption that (a) the unit holding cost per period is $c_h = \$1$; (b) the production cost is $k_n(x) = \$3$ for $x > 0$ and 0 otherwise; and (c) the unit shortage cost is $c_s = \$20$. For instance, the first row in Table 14-4 refers to a beginning inventory of $i = 0$ and a production of $x = 0$. In this case, no goods are available to meet the demand, and the entire demand is lost. The inventory level at the beginning of the next period is $j = 0$, with probability $p_{00}(0) = 1$ and all other transition probabilities equal to 0. No costs are incurred for carrying goods in inventory [column (a) is 0] and for replenishing inventory [column (b) is 0]. Shortage costs are found as the expected value of the amount short times the shortage cost per unit:

$$E(\text{shortage cost}) = \$20\left[\sum_{d>i+x}(d-i-x)p(d)\right]$$
$$= \$20\,[(1-0)0.3 + (2-0)\,0.2 + (3-0)0.1] = \$20$$

The total cost $c_0(0) = 0 + 0 + 20 = \$20$. Consider another row, e.g., row 8, with a beginning inventory of $i = 1$ and a production of $x = 1$. If demand is $d = 0$, then the new inventory is $j = i + x - 0$, or $j = 2$. This demand occurs with probability 0.4, so $p_{12}(1) = 0.4$. If demand is $d = 1$, then $j = i + x - 1$ or $j = 1$ with probability 0.3, so $p_{11}(1) = 0.3$. If demand is $d = 2$ or $d = 3$, then the new inventory is $j = 0$. These demands occur with probabilities 0.2 and 0.1, so $p_{10}(1) = 0.2 + 0.1 = 0.3$.

Table 14-4. *Transition probabilities and costs for inventory control problem*

Row	State i	Decision x	Transition Probabilities, $p_{ij}(x)$ $j=0$	$j=1$	$j=2$	$j=3$	$j=4$	$j=5$	Costs (a)	(b)	(c)	Total $c_i(x)$
1	0	0	1	0	0	0	0	0	0	0	20	20
2		1	0.6	0.4	0	0	0	0	0	3	8	11
3		2	0.3	0.3	0.4	0	0	0	0	3	2	5
4		3	0.1	0.2	0.3	0.4	0	0	0	3	0	3
5		4	0	0.1	0.2	0.3	0.4	0	0	3	0	3
6		5	0	0	0.1	0.2	0.3	0.4	0	3	0	3
7	1	0	0.6	0.4	0	0	0	0	1	0	8	9
8		1	0.3	0.3	0.4	0	0	0	1	3	2	6
9		2	0.1	0.2	0.3	0.4	0	0	1	3	0	4
10		3	0	0.1	0.2	0.3	0.4	0	1	3	0	4
11		4	0	0	0.1	0.2	0.3	0.4	1	3	0	4
12	2	0	0.3	0.3	0.4	0	0	0	2	0	2	4
13		1	0.1	0.2	0.3	0.4	0	0	2	3	0	5
14		2	0	0.1	0.2	0.3	0.4	0	2	3	0	5
15		3	0	0	0.1	0.2	0.3	0.4	2	3	0	5
16	3	0	0.1	0.2	0.3	0.4	0	0	3	0	0	3
17		1	0	0.1	0.2	0.3	0.4	0	3	3	0	6
18		2	0	0	0.1	0.2	0.3	0.4	3	3	0	6
19	4	0	0	0.1	0.2	0.3	0.4	0	4	0	0	4
20		1	0	0	0.1	0.2	0.3	0.4	4	3	0	7
21	5	0	0	0	0.1	0.2	0.3	0.4	5	0	0	5

All other transition probabilities are again 0. One unit is carried forward to the current period at a cost of \$1— column (a). Inventory is replenished at a cost of \$3— column (b). Finally, shortage costs are incurred when demand exceeds $i + x = 2$. Hence column (c) is \$20(3 − 2) (0.1) = \$2. The total cost $c_1(1)$ amounts to \$(1 + 3 + 2) = \$6. To test your understanding, verify some of the other rows!

For the policy (4, 3, 0, 0, 0, 0), the corresponding transition matrix **P** and the vector of one-period costs (c_i) is constructed from Table 14-4 by taking, for each i, the row of transition probabilities associated with the decision x taken in state i. So we take rows 5, 10, 12, 16, 19, and 21.

$$(14\text{-}8) \quad \mathbf{P} = \begin{bmatrix} 0 & 0.1 & 0.2 & 0.3 & 0.4 & 0 \\ 0 & 0.1 & 0.2 & 0.3 & 0.4 & 0 \\ 0.3 & 0.3 & 0.4 & 0 & 0 & 0 \\ 0.1 & 0.2 & 0.3 & 0.4 & 0 & 0 \\ 0 & 0.1 & 0.2 & 0.3 & 0.4 & 0 \\ 0 & 0 & 0.1 & 0.2 & 0.3 & 0.4 \end{bmatrix} \quad \text{and} \quad \begin{bmatrix} c_0(4) \\ c_1(3) \\ c_2(0) \\ c_3(0) \\ c_4(0) \\ c_5(0) \end{bmatrix} = \begin{bmatrix} 3 \\ 4 \\ 4 \\ 3 \\ 4 \\ 5 \end{bmatrix}$$

State 5 is a transient state, whereas the remaining states form an ergodic subset. Since each policy generates a transition matrix and a vector of costs, selecting the optimal policy is equivalent to finding the optimal combination of transition probability rows and their related costs. This can be seen by rewriting expression (14-7) in terms of our new notation as

$$f_i = \underset{x \in X}{\text{minimum}} \left[c_i(x) + \alpha \sum_j p_{ij}(x) f_j \right], \qquad \text{for all } i \tag{14-9}$$

where f_i stands for the present value of the cost of following an optimal policy over all future periods, starting the process in state i. Such a problem is known as a *Markovian decision process.*

In this example, x is a numerical variable. There are many applications in which the set of actions cannot be expressed numerically. For instance, in a maintenance problem, the decisions may be "do nothing," "inspect and replace only if needed," and "replace without inspection." If each possible action is numbered from 1 to M_i, where M_i is the number of possible actions in state i, then x stands for this number. However, the numerical value x has no significance in itself.

14-6 APPROXIMATION IN POLICY SPACE WITH DISCOUNTING

How can the optimal values of x and the minimum f_i be determined for all i? The boot strap operation which follows does the trick.

STEP 1: INITIAL POLICY

Guess an initial policy labeled by the superscript $k = 0$ by choosing for each state i a decision $x = x_i^{(0)}$.

For instance, we could decide to use in each state that decision x which minimizes the one-period cost $c_i(x)$.

Having decided on the policy k, we associate with each decision $x_i^{(k)}$ the transition probabilities $p_{ij}(x_i^{(k)})$ and the one-period cost $c_i(x_i^{(k)})$. With these we can find $f_i^{(k)}$,the discounted cost using policy k over all future periods, starting in state i, for all i. This is our next step. (For the first time through, $k = 0$.)

STEP 2: POLICY EVALUATION ROUTINE

Determine the values of $f_i^{(k)}$ that are the solution of the system of linear equations

$$f_i^{(k)} = c_i(x_i^{(k)}) + \alpha \sum_j p_{ij}(x_i^{(k)}) f_j^{(k)}, \text{ for all } i \tag{14-10}$$

Equations (14-10) arise from the following reasoning: If the process starts out in state i using policy k, it first incurs the cost associated with this policy in state i $[= c_i(x_i^{(k)})]$ and then moves to state j by the beginning of the next period. One period from now, the present value of the cost from state j over all future periods is $f_j^{(k)}$. This cost is weighted by the probability of going from state i to state j using policy k. The sum of all these terms is then discounted by one period.

The term $f_j^{(k)}$ should not be confused with f_j of expression (14-9). Except at the last iteration, when we have found the optimal policy, $f_j^{(k)}$ is not the minimum cost, but simply the present value of the cost associated with the (arbitrary) policy k.

Step 2 implies that we commit ourselves to using policy k for all future periods and want to know the cost of starting it in each state. We now have some second thoughts. We decide to postpone the use of this policy by one period and at the same time try to find a better policy for the current period.

STEP 3: POLICY IMPROVEMENT ROUTINE

Determine a new policy $k + 1$ by finding for each i the decision $x_i^{(k+1)}$ that will

(14-11) $$\underset{x}{\text{minimize}}\left[c_i(x) + \alpha \sum_j p_{ij}(x)\, f_j^{(k)}\right]$$

Expression (14-11) arises from a reasoning similar to that behind (14-10).

If the minimum is obtained for several decisions, the choice for $x_i^{(k+1)}$ is arbitrary, except if $x_i^{(k)}$ is one of them, in which case $x_i^{(k+1)} = x_i^{(k)}$. This avoids cycling of the iterative scheme.

Now we examine the new policy $k + 1$. If $x_i^{(k+1)} = x_i^{(k)}$ for all states, then we have a policy that satisfies expression (14-9) with $f_i = f_i^{(k)} = f_i^{(k+1)}$, which is what we were looking for. On the other hand, if policy $k + 1$ differs from policy k in at least one state, we reason that if policy $k + 1$ is better for the first period, surely it is also better for all subsequent periods! Fortunately, it can be shown that this is so. Since the trick worked this time, we go back to step 2 for a new iteration of this algorithm.

STEP 4: STOPPING RULE

If $x_i^{(k+1)} = x_i^{(k)}$, for all i, the optimal policy has been found, and the $f_i^{(k+1)}$ are the minimum expected discounted costs of starting in state i. If the new policy $k + 1$ differs from the previous one in at least one state, increase the count k by one and go back to step 2.

The better the initial choice in step 1, the faster the algorithm finds the optimal solution. Often, technical knowledge about the system modeled may indicate what is a good initial policy.

For a maximization problem the only change needed is to substitute "maximize" for "minimize" in expression (14-11).

If the number of possible decisions in each state i is finite, then the number of possible combinations of decisions or the number of possible different policies is also finite. In step 2, expression (14-10) results in a unique solution for the $f_i^{(k)}$ values for each policy. By step 3, each new policy is at least as good as the preceding one; and by step 4, no policy can repeat itself without terminating the algorithm. Therefore, this method will converge to the optimal solution in a finite number of iterations.

This advantage has to be paid for, however, by a large amount of computation. If there are r different states, then step 2 involves solving a system of r linear equations in r unknowns. For practically all real-life problems, this job has to be done by computers. However, in contrast to n-stage dynamic programming problems, this algorithm can be programmed for computers as a *general-purpose code* for a standard input format that can solve all Markovian decision processes.

14-7 SOLUTION OF INVENTORY CONTROL PROBLEM FOR DISCOUNTING

To apply this algorithm, it is always helpful to first set up a table listing the transition probabilities and the expected costs for each action in each state, as we did in Table 14-4. Let us use a discount factor of $\alpha = 0.99$ per week (this corresponds to an annual interest rate of about 60 percent).

First iteration:

Step 1 Initial policy $= (x_0^{(0)} = 4, x_1^{(0)} = 3, x_2^{(0)} = 0, x_3^{(0)} = 0, x_4^{(0)} = 0, x_5^{(0)} = 0)$ with transition probabilities and costs as shown in the transition matrix and the cost vector (14-8).

Step 2 Solve the following set of linear equations:

$$f_0^{(0)} = 3 + 0.99(0.1f_1^{(0)} + 0.2f_2^{(0)} + 0.3f_3^{(0)} + 0.4f_4^{(0)})$$
$$f_1^{(0)} = 4 + 0.99(0.1f_1^{(0)} + 0.2f_2^{(0)} + 0.3f_3^{(0)} + 0.4f_4^{(0)})$$
$$f_2^{(0)} = 4 + 0.99(0.3f_0^{(0)} + 0.3f_1^{(0)} + 0.4f_2^{(0)})$$
$$f_3^{(0)} = 3 + 0.99(0.1f_0^{(0)} + 0.2f_1^{(0)} + 0.3f_2^{(0)} + 0.4f_3^{(0)})$$
$$f_4^{(0)} = 4 + 0.99(0.1f_1^{(0)} + 0.2f_2^{(0)} + 0.3f_3^{(0)} + 0.4f_4^{(0)})$$
$$f_5^{(0)} = 5 + 0.99(0.1f_2^{(0)} + 0.2f_3^{(0)} + 0.3f_4^{(0)} + 0.4f_5^{(0)})$$

The solution is

$$f_0^{(0)} = 364.6, f_1^{(0)} = 365.6, f_2^{(0)} = 365.7, f_3^{(0)} = 364.3, f_4^{(0)} = 365.6, f_5^{(0)} = 367.4$$

Step 3 Find a new action for each state using expression (14-11). This is shown in Table 14-5.

Table 14-5. *Policy improvement routine for iteration 1*

State i	Action x	$c_i(x) + \alpha \sum_j p_{ij}(x) f_j^{(0)}$		Minimum for x
0	0	20 + 0.99 [(1)364.6]	= 380.9	
	1	11 + 0.99 [(0.6)364.6 + (0.4)365.6]	= 372.3	
	2	5 + 0.99 [(0.3)364.6 + (0.3)365.6 + (0.4)365.7]	= 366.6	
	3	3 + 0.99 [(0.1)364.6 + (0.2)365.6 + (0.3)365.7 + (0.4)364.3]	= 364.3	$x = 3$
	4	3 + 0.99 [(0.1)365.6 + (0.2)365.7 + (0.3)364.3 + (0.4)365.6]	= 364.6	
	5	3 + 0.99 [(0.1)365.7 + (0.2)364.3 + (0.3)365.6 + (0.4)367.4]	= 365.4	
1	0	9 + 0.99 [(0.6)364.6 + (0.4)365.6]	= 370.3	
	1	6 + 0.99 [(0.3)364.6 + (0.3)365.6 + (0.4)365.7]	= 367.6	
	2	4 + 0.99 [(0.1)364.6 + (0.2)365.6 + (0.3)365.7 + (0.4)364.3]	= 365.3	$x = 2$
	3	4 + 0.99 [(0.1)365.6 + (0.2)365.7 + (0.3)364.3 + (0.4)365.6]	= 365.6	
	4	4 + 0.99 [(0.1)365.7 + (0.2)364.3 + (0.3)365.6 + (0.4)367.4]	= 366.4	
2	0	4 + 0.99 [(0.3)364.6 + (0.3)365.6 + (0.4)365.7]	= 365.7	$x = 0$
	1	5 + 0.99 [(0.1)364.6 + (0.2)365.6 + (0.3)365.7 + (0.4)364.3]	= 366.3	
	2	5 + 0.99 [(0.1)365.6 + (0.2)365.7 + (0.3)364.3 + (0.4)365.6]	= 366.6	
	3	5 + 0.99 [(0.1)365.7 + (0.2)364.3 + (0.3)365.6 + (0.4)367.4]	= 367.4	
3	0	3 + 0.99 [(0.1)364.6 + (0.2)365.6 + (0.3)365.7 + (0.4)364.3]	= 364.3	$x = 0$
	1	6 + 0.99 [(0.1)365.6 + (0.2)365.7 + (0.3)364.3 + (0.4)365.6]	= 367.6	
	2	6 + 0.99 [(0.1)365.7 + (0.2)364.3 + (0.3)365.6 + (0.4)367.4]	= 368.4	
4	0	4 + 0.99 [(0.1)365.6 + (0.2)365.7 + (0.3)364.3 + (0.4)365.6]	= 365.6	$x = 0$
	1	7 + 0.99 [(0.1)365.7 + (0.2)364.3 + (0.3)365.6 + (0.4)367.4]	= 369.4	
5	0	5 + 0.99 [(0.1)365.7 + (0.2)364.3 + (0.3)365.6 + (0.4)367.4]	= 367.4	$x = 0$

Step 4 From the last column of Table 14-5, we find the new policy

$$(x_0^{(1)} = 3, x_1^{(1)} = 2, x_2^{(1)} = 0, x_3^{(1)} = 0, x_4^{(1)} = 0, x_5^{(1)} = 0)$$

Going back to Table 14-4, we find the new transition probabilities and costs associated with this policy;

$$\begin{bmatrix} 0.1 & 0.2 & 0.3 & 0.4 & 0 & 0 \\ 0.1 & 0.2 & 0.3 & 0.4 & 0 & 0 \\ 0.3 & 0.3 & 0.4 & 0 & 0 & 0 \\ 0.1 & 0.2 & 0.3 & 0.4 & 0 & 0 \\ 0 & 0.1 & 0.2 & 0.3 & 0.4 & 0 \\ 0 & 0 & 0.1 & 0.2 & 0.3 & 0.4 \end{bmatrix} \quad \text{and} \quad \begin{bmatrix} 3 \\ 4 \\ 4 \\ 3 \\ 4 \\ 5 \end{bmatrix} \tag{14-12}$$

This policy is different from the previous one, so we go through another iteration. Note that now both states 4 and 5 are transient states.

Second iteration:

Step 2 Solve the following set of linear equations:

$$\begin{aligned}
f_0^{(1)} &= 3 + 0.99(0.1f_0^{(1)} + 0.2f_1^{(1)} + 0.3f_2^{(1)} + 0.4f_3^{(1)}) \\
f_1^{(1)} &= 4 + 0.99(0.1f_0^{(1)} + 0.2f_1^{(1)} + 0.3f_2^{(1)} + 0.4f_3^{(1)}) \\
f_2^{(1)} &= 4 + 0.99(0.3f_0^{(1)} + 0.3f_1^{(1)} + 0.4f_2^{(1)}) \\
f_3^{(1)} &= 3 + 0.99(0.1f_0^{(1)} + 0.2f_1^{(1)} + 0.3f_2^{(1)} + 0.4f_3^{(1)}) \\
f_4^{(1)} &= 4 + 0.99(0.1f_1^{(1)} + 0.2f_2^{(1)} + 0.3f_3^{(1)} + 0.4f_4^{(1)}) \\
f_5^{(1)} &= 5 + 0.99(0.1f_2^{(1)} + 0.2f_3^{(1)} + 0.3f_4^{(1)} + 0.4f_5^{(1)})
\end{aligned}$$

The solution is

$$f_0^{(1)} = 356.0, f_1^{(1)} = 357.0, f_2^{(1)} = 357.2, f_3^{(1)} = 356.0, f_4^{(1)} = 357.3, f_5^{(1)} = 359.2$$

Step 3 Find a new action for each state using expression (14-11), as shown in Table 14-6.

Table 14-6. *Policy improvement routine for iteration 2*

State i	Action x	$c_i(x) + \alpha \sum_j p_{ij}(x) f_j^{(1)}$		Minimum for x
0	0	20 + 0.99 [(1)356.0]	= 372.5	
	1	11 + 0.99 [(0.6)356.0 + (0.4)357.0]	= 363.8	
	2	5 + 0.99 [(0.3)356.0 + (0.3)357.0 + (0.4)357.2]	= 358.2	
	3	3 + 0.99 [(0.1)356.0 + (0.2)357.0 + (0.3)357.2 + (0.4)356.0]	= 356.0	$x = 3$
	4	3 + 0.99 [(0.1)357.0 + (0.2)357.2 + (0.3)356.0 + (0.4)357.3]	= 356.3	
	5	3 + 0.99 [(0.1)357.2 + (0.2)356.0 + (0.3)357.3 + (0.4)359.2]	= 357.2	
1	0	9 + 0.99 [(0.6)356.0 + (0.4)357.0]	= 361.8	
	1	6 + 0.99 [(0.3)356.0 + (0.3)357.0 + (0.4)357.2]	= 359.2	
	2	4 + 0.99 [(0.1)356.0 + (0.2)357.0 + (0.3)357.2 + (0.4)356.0]	= 357.0	$x = 2$
	3	4 + 0.99 [(0.1)357.0 + (0.2)357.2 + (0.3)356.0 + (0.4)357.3]	= 357.3	
	4	4 + 0.99 [(0.1)357.2 + (0.2)356.0 + (0.3)357.3 + (0.4)359.2]	= 358.2	
2	0	4 + 0.99 [(0.3)356.0 + (0.3)357.0 + (0.4)357.2]	= 357.2	$x = 0$
	1	5 + 0.99 [(0.1)356.0 + (0.2)357.0 + (0.3)357.2 + (0.4)356.0]	= 358.0	
	2	5 + 0.99 [(0.1)357.0 + (0.2)357.2 + (0.3)356.0 + (0.4)357.3]	= 358.3	
	3	5 + 0.99 [(0.1)357.2 + (0.2)356.0 + (0.3)357.3 + (0.4)359.2]	= 359.2	
3	0	3 + 0.99 [(0.1)356.0 + (0.2)357.0 + (0.3)357.2 + (0.4)356.0]	= 356.0	$x = 0$
	1	6 + 0.99 [(0.1)357.0 + (0.2)357.2 + (0.3)356.0 + (0.4)357.3]	= 357.3	
	2	6 + 0.99 [(0.1)357.2 + (0.2)356.0 + (0.3)357.3 + (0.4)359.2]	= 360.2	
4	0	4 + 0.99 [(0.1)357.0 + (0.2)357.2 + (0.3)356.0 + (0.4)357.3]	= 357.3	$x = 0$
	1	7 + 0.99 [(0.1)357.2 + (0.2)356.0 + (0.3)357.3 + (0.4)359.2]	= 361.2	
5	0	5 + 0.99 [(0.1)357.2 + (0.2)356.0 + (0.3)357.3 + (0.4)359.2]	= 359.2	$x = 0$

Step 4 The new policy implied by Table 14-6 is

$$(x_0^{(2)} = 3, x_1^{(2)} = 2, x_2^{(2)} = 0, x_3^{(2)} = 0, x_4^{(2)} = 0, x_5^{(2)} = 0)$$

It is the same as the policy at the end of the preceding iteration and therefore is the optimal policy. The minimum discounted costs are those found in step 3 of this iteration, i.e., $f_0 = 356.0$, $f_1 = 357.0$, $f_2 = 357.2$, $f_3 = 356.0$, $f_4 = 357.3$, and $f_5 = 359.2$.

The algorithm converges on the optimal solution in two iterations. The policy found says: Replenish inventory to a level of 3 whenever it has been reduced to 1 or less, and do nothing otherwise—an (s, S) policy as the initial policy. It can be shown that for inventory control problems with fixed inventory replenishment costs, linear holding costs, and constant per unit shortage cost—as is the case here—the optimal policy always has the form of an (s, S) policy.

How does the optimal policy change as a function of the discount rate α? Sensitivity analysis, with respect to the discount rate, often provides useful insight to the decision maker. In this particular case, the present policy remains optimal for all α, $0 \leq \alpha \leq 1$.

14-8 AVERAGE GAIN PER PERIOD

For routine day-to-day or month-to-month decisions, the appropriate discount factor per period may be close to 1. Then, the discounted gain over all future periods tends to become extremely large. Furthermore, the discounting procedure implies a long-term behavioral pattern, whereas the stationary assumptions may have been introduced as a convenient approximation of the short-term or intermediate-term behavior of the system. Thus, we may not be interested in the discounted gain over all future periods, but only in the average gain per (short) period or the total gain for a limited interval of perhaps one year, where the effect of discounting may be negligible. Maximizing average gain (or minimizing average cost) then becomes the more appropriate criterion to use.

As we have seen in Section 13-10, with each Markov chain containing only one ergodic subset of states, we can associate the unique long-run average benefit (or cost) per period given by expression (13-19), i.e.,

$$g = \sum_i c_i \pi_i$$

Here, c_i is the one-period benefit (or cost) of starting the process in state i, and the π_i are the steady-state probabilities associated with the transition matrix **P**. In this chapter, we study systems that can be governed by any one of a number of alternative policies, each defining its own Markov chain and resulting in a unique long-run average benefit (or cost) per period.

Suppose we operate the inventory system discussed in Section 14-5 under a given (arbitrary) policy for n periods. Let $v_i(n)$ be the undiscounted expected cost of this policy over n periods, given that the process starts out in state i (i.e., with an initial inventory of i). These costs satisfy the following recursive relation:

$$(14\text{-}13) \qquad v_i(n) = c_i(x) + \sum_j p_{ij}(x) v_j(n-1), \qquad \text{for all } i,\ n = 1, 2, \ldots$$

The reasoning used to obtain expression (14-13) is analogous to that used for expression (14-10). If the process starts out in state i, it first incurs the cost $c_i(x)$ associated with using a given policy, and then moves to state j with probability $p_{ij}(x)$. The cost over the remaining $n - 1$ periods onward from state j is $v_j(n - 1)$. Again, we take the expected value over all possible states j.

As we have seen, in the steady state, the long-run average cost per period is g and is independent of the initial state i. Thus, in the steady state, the average long-run cost over n periods is ng. On the other hand, for n finite, the cost over n periods,

$v_i(n)$, depends on the initial state i. Let n now be sufficiently large, and consider the difference between these two terms, denoted by v_i:

(14-14) $$v_i = v_i(n) - ng$$

For n sufficiently large, v_i represents the *transient effect* of the initial state on the cost of the process. The difference of the transient effects for two different initial states, $v_i - v_j$, can be given the following economic interpretation. By (14-14), $v_i(n) = ng + v_i$; and we have for n sufficiently large

(14-15) $$v_i(n) - v_j(n) = [ng + v_i] - [ng + v_j] = v_i - v_j$$

$v_i - v_j$ represents the difference in the total cost of starting the process in state i rather than state j. This is the amount that a rational person should be willing to pay (if $v_i < v_j$) or receive (if $v_i > v_j$) for being able to start the process in state i rather than in state j.

The v_i values turn out to be useful quantities in our search for the optimal policy. But first, let us see how we can determine their values. Substituting $ng + v_i$ for $v_i(n)$ in (14-13), we obtain

(14-16) $$\begin{aligned} ng + v_i &= c_i(x) + \sum_j p_{ij}(x)[(n-1)g + v_j] \\ &= c_i(x) + (n-1)g\sum_j p_{ij}(x) + \sum_j p_{ij}(x)v_j \end{aligned}$$

But $\sum_j p_{ij}(x) = 1$, and so (14-16) becomes

$$ng + v_i = c_i(x) + (n-1)g + \sum_j p_{ij}(x)v_j$$

Canceling equal terms on both sides, we finally derive

(14-17) $$g + v_i = c_i(x) + \sum_j p_{ij}(x)v_j, \qquad \text{for all } i$$

The term n conveniently drops from (14-16). For n sufficiently large, the v_i are independent of n. Thus, g and the v_i are the solution to a system of r linear equations in $r + 1$ variables, where r is the number of states. These equations will not have a unique solution. We need to set the value of one variable in order to solve for the other r variables uniquely. It is easily shown that if $(v_1, v_2, \ldots, v_r, g)$ is a solution to (14-17), so is $[(v_1 + b), (v_2 + b), \ldots, (v_r + b), g]$ for any scalar b. Clearly, the differences $v_i - v_j$ will then remain undisturbed for any b. So we might set b equal to any one of the v_i values, say v_0, and solve for the remaining v_i in terms of v_0; i.e., the solution values are $\hat{v}_i = v_i - v_0$, for all i. Therefore, we shall refer to them as *relative values*. Note that this approach implies that we simply set $\hat{v}_0 = 0$ to get a solution to the relative values. We shall now drop the separate notation, $\hat{v}_i$, and simply use v_i for the relative values.

Let us find the long-run average cost and the relative values for the policy (4, 3, 0, 0, 0, 0) used earlier with the transition matrix **P** and the one-period costs $c_i(x)$

given by expression (14-8). By expression (14-17), they are the solution to the following system of six equations in seven unknowns:

$$
\begin{aligned}
g + v_0 &= 3 + 0v_0 + 0.1v_1 + 0.2v_2 + 0.3v_3 + 0.4v_4 + 0v_5\\
g + v_1 &= 4 + 0v_0 + 0.1v_1 + 0.2v_2 + 0.3v_3 + 0.4v_4 + 0v_5\\
g + v_2 &= 4 + 0.3v_0 + 0.3v_1 + 0.4v_2 + 0v_3 + 0v_4 + 0v_5\\
g + v_3 &= 3 + 0.1v_0 + 0.2v_1 + 0.3v_2 + 0.4v_3 + 0v_4 + 0v_5\\
g + v_4 &= 4 + 0v_0 + 0.1v_1 + 0.2v_2 + 0.3v_3 + 0.4v_4 + 0v_5\\
g + v_5 &= 5 + 0v_0 + 0v_1 + 0.1v_2 + 0.2v_3 + 0.3v_4 + 0.4v_5
\end{aligned}
\tag{14-18}
$$

Setting $v_0 = 0$, we obtain

$$g = 3.652, \quad v_0 = 0.0, \; v_1 = 1.0, \; v_2 = 1.08, \; v_3 = -0.213, \; v_4 = 1.0, \; v_5 = 2.856$$

14-9 APPROXIMATION IN POLICY SPACE FOR AVERAGE COST PER PERIOD

To determine the optimal policy that minimizes the average cost per period, we shall again use a bootstrap operation analogous to the one developed for discounting.

STEP 1: INITIAL POLICY

Guess an initial policy (labeled by the superscript $k = 0$) by choosing for each state i a decision $x = x_i^{(0)}$.

STEP 2: POLICY EVALUATION ROUTINE

Determine for policy k the expected cost g and the relative values v_i, for all i, that are the solution to the system of linear equations

$$g^{(k)} + v_i^{(k)} = c_i(x_i^{(k)}) + \sum_j p_{ij}(x_i^{(k)})v_j^{(k)}, \qquad \text{for all } i \tag{14-19}$$

by setting one of the relative values, v_i, equal to zero.

At this time we again decide to determine a new policy, $k + 1$, for the first period, followed by policy k in all periods thereafter. To derive the appropriate expressions for this optimization, we will again revert to an n-period case first. If we were to determine the optimal policy in the first period, given that we would use policy k in the remaining $n - 1$ periods, we would find for each state i the action x that would

$$\underset{x}{\text{minimize}} \left[c_i(x) + \sum_j p_{ij}(x)v_j(n - 1) \right] \tag{14-20}$$

where $v_j(n - 1)$ is the cost for policy k over the remaining $n - 1$ periods. For n sufficiently large, we may now again approximate (14-20) by substituting $(n - 1)g^{(k)} + v_j^{(k)}$ for $v_j(n - 1)$:

(14-21) $$\text{minimize } c_i(x) + \sum_j p_{ij}(x)[(n - 1)g^{(k)} + v_j^{(k)}]$$

But, $\Sigma_j\, p_{ij}(x)(n - 1)g^{(k)}$ is a constant and does not affect the minimization. We are left with $c_i(x) + \Sigma_j\, p_{ij}(x)v_j^{(k)}$. As for the policy evaluation routine, the resulting expression is independent of n. We now see that the relative values v_i hold the key to the policy improvement routine.

STEP 3: POLICY IMPROVEMENT ROUTINE

Determine a new policy $k + 1$ by finding for each i the decision $x_i^{(k+1)} = x$ that will

(14-22) $$\text{minimize } c_i(x) + \sum_j p_{ij}(x)v_j^{(k)}$$

If $x_i^{(k)}$ is one of several for which the minimum in (14-22) is obtained, $x_i^{(k+1)} = x_i^{(k)}$ is retained as the best decision in state i to avoid cycling.

STEP 4: STOPPING RULE

If $x_i^{(k+1)} = x_i^{(k)}$, for all i, the optimal policy has been found, and $g^{(k)}$ is the minimum average cost per period. If the new policy $k + 1$ differs from the previous one in at least one state, increase the count k by one and go back to step 2.

Each new policy produced by the policy improvement routine has an average cost per period that is at most as high as for the previous policy. As for $\alpha < 1$, this algorithm converges to the optimal policy in a finite number of iterations.

For a maximization problem, we substitute *maximize* for *minimize* in (14-22).

14-10 SOLUTION FOR AVERAGE GAIN PER PERIOD

Table 14-4 contains all information needed for the algorithm in Section 14-9.

First iteration:

Step 1 Initial policy $= (x_0^{(0)} = 4,\ x_1^{(0)} = 3,\ x_2^{(0)} = 0,\ x_3^{(0)} = 0,\ x_4^{(0)} = 0,\ x_5^{(0)} = 0)$, with transition probabilities and costs as shown by expressions (14-8).

Step 2 Solve the set of linear equations (14-18) whose solution is $g^{(0)} = 3.652$, $v_0^{(0)} = 0$, $v_1^{(0)} = 1.0$, $v_2^{(0)} = 1.08$, $v_3^{(0)} = -0.213$, $v_4^{(0)} = 1.0$, $v_5^{(0)} = 2.856$.

Step 3 Find a new action for each state using (14-22). The computations are shown in Table 14-7.

Table 14-7. *Policy improvement routine for iteration 1*

State i	Action x	$c_i(x) + \sum_j p_{ij}(x)v_j^{(0)}$					Minimum for x
0	0	20 + (1)0				= 20	
	1	11 + (0.6)0	+ (0.4) 1			= 11.4	
	2	5 + (0.3)0	+ (0.3) 1	+ (0.4) 1.08		= 5.732	
	3	3 + (0.1)0	+ (0.2) 1	+ (0.3) 1.08	+ (0.4)(−0.213)	= 3.439	$x = 3$
	4	3 + (0.1)1	+ (0.2) 1.08	+ (0.3)(−0.213)	+ (0.4) 1	= 3.652	
	5	3 + (0.1)1.08	+ (0.2)(−0.213)	+ (0.3) 1	+ (0.4) 2.856	= 4.508	
1	0	9 + (0.6)0	+ (0.4) 1			= 9.4	
	1	6 + (0.3)0	+ (0.3) 1	+ (0.4) 1.08		= 6.732	
	2	4 + (0.1)0	+ (0.2) 1	+ (0.3) 1.08	+ (0.4)(−0.213)	= 4.439	$x = 2$
	3	4 + (0.1)1	+ (0.2) 1.08	+ (0.3)(−0.213)	+ (0.4) 1	= 4.652	
	4	4 + (0.1)1.08	+ (0.2)(−0.213)	+ (0.3) 1	+ (0.4) 2.856	= 5.508	
2	0	4 + (0.3)0	+ (0.3) 1	+ (0.4) 1.08		= 4.732	$x = 0$
	1	5 + (0.1)0	+ (0.2) 1	+ (0.3) 1.08	+ (0.4)(−0.213)	= 5.439	
	2	5 + (0.1)1	+ (0.2) 1.08	+ (0.3)(−0.213)	+ (0.4) 1	= 5.652	
	3	5 + (0.1)1.08	+ (0.2)(−0.213)	+ (0.3) 1	+ (0.4) 2.856	= 6.508	
3	0	3 + (0.1)0	+ (0.2) 1	+ (0.3) 1.08	+ (0.4)(−0.213)	= 3.439	$x = 0$
	1	6 + (0.1)1	+ (0.2) 1.08	+ (0.3)(−0.213)	+ (0.4) 1	= 6.652	
	2	6 + (0.1)1.08	+ (0.2)(−0.213)	+ (0.3) 1	+ (0.4) 2.856	= 7.508	
4	0	4 + (0.1)1	+ (0.2) 1.08	+ (0.3)(−0.213)	+ (0.4) 1	= 4.652	$x = 0$
	1	7 + (0.1)1.08	+ (0.2)(−0.213)	+ (0.3) 1	+ (0.4) 2.856	= 8.508	
5	0	5 + (0.1)1.08	+ (0.2)(−0.213)	+ (0.3) 1	+ (0.4) 2.856	= 6.508	$x = 0$

Step 4 The new policy from Table 14-7 is ($x_0^{(1)} = 3$, $x_1^{(1)} = 2$, $x_2^{(1)} = 0$, $x_3^{(1)} = 0$, $x_4^{(1)} = 0$, $x_5^{(1)} = 0$). This policy is different from the initial policy, and hence we go through another iteration. The transition matrix and costs for the new policy are given by expressions (14-12) in Section 14-7.

Second iteration:

Step 2 Solve the set of simultaneous equations obtained from (14-19). (For convenience, superscripts are deleted.)

$$g + v_0 = 3 + 0.1v_0 + 0.2v_1 + 0.3v_2 + 0.4v_3$$
$$g + v_1 = 4 + 0.1v_0 + 0.2v_1 + 0.3v_2 + 0.4v_3$$
$$g + v_2 = 4 + 0.3v_0 + 0.3v_1 + 0.4v_2$$
$$g + v_3 = 3 + 0.1v_0 + 0.2v_1 + 0.3v_2 + 0.4v_3$$
$$g + v_4 = 4 + 0.1v_1 + 0.2v_2 + 0.3v_3 + 0.4v_4$$
$$g + v_5 = 5 + 0.1v_2 + 0.2v_3 + 0.3v_4 + 0.4v_5$$

Setting $v_0 = 0$, the solution is

$$g^{(1)} = 3.567,\ v_0^{(1)} = 0,\ v_1^{(1)} = 1,\ v_2^{(1)} = 1.222,\ v_3^{(1)} = 0,\ v_4^{(1)} = 1.296,\ v_5^{(1)} = 3.241$$

Step 3 Find a new action for each state using (14-22), as shown in Table 14-8.

Table 14-8. *Policy improvement routine for iteration 2*

State i	Action x	$c_i(x) + \alpha \sum_j p_{ij}(x) f_j^{(1)}$					Minimum for x
0	0	20 + (1)0				= 20	
	1	11 + (0.6)0	+ (0.4)1			= 11.4	
	2	5 + (0.3)0	+ (0.3)1	+ (0.4)1.222		= 5.789	
	3	3 + (0.1)0	+ (0.2)1	+ (0.3)1.222	+ (0.4)0	= 3.567	$x = 3$
	4	3 + (0.1)1	+ (0.2)1.222	+ (0.3)0	+ (0.4)1.296	= 3.863	
	5	3 + (0.1)1.222	+ (0.2)0	+ (0.3)1.296	+ (0.4)3.241	= 4.807	
1	0	9 + (0.6)0	+ (0.4)1			= 9.4	
	1	6 + (0.3)0	+ (0.3)1	+ (0.4)1.222		= 6.789	
	2	4 + (0.1)0	+ (0.2)1	+ (0.3)1.222	+ (0.4)0	= 4.567	$x = 2$
	3	4 + (0.1)1	+ (0.2)1.222	+ (0.3)0	+ (0.4)1.296	= 4.863	
	4	4 + (0.1)1.222	+ (0.2)0	+ (0.3)1.296	+ (0.4)3.241	= 5.807	
2	0	4 + (0.3)0	+ (0.3)1	+ (0.4)1.222		= 4.789	$x = 0$
	1	5 + (0.1)0	+ (0.2)1	+ (0.3)1.222	+ (0.4)0	= 5.567	
	2	5 + (0.1)1	+ (0.2)1.222	+ (0.3)0	+ (0.4)1.296	= 5.863	
	3	5 + (0.1)1.222	+ (0.2)0	+ (0.3)1.296	+ (0.4)3.241	= 6.807	
3	0	3 + (0.1)0	+ (0.2)1	+ (0.3)1.222	+ (0.4)0	= 3.567	$x = 0$
	1	6 + (0.1)1	+ (0.2)1.222	+ (0.3)0	+ (0.4)1.296	= 6.863	
	2	6 + (0.1)1.222	+ (0.2)0	+ (0.3)1.296	+ (0.4)3.241	= 7.807	
4	0	4 + (0.1)1	+ (0.2)1.222	+ (0.3)0	+ (0.4)1.296	= 4.863	$x = 0$
	1	7 + (0.1)1.222	+ (0.2)0	+ (0.3)1.296	+ (0.4)3.241	= 8.807	
5	0	5 + (0.1)1.222	+ (0.2)0	+ (0.3)1.296	+ (0.4)3.241	= 6.807	$x = 0$

Step 4 The new policy from Table 14-8 is the same as after iteration 1, and is thus optimal. The minimum average cost per period is $g = 3.567$.

The optimal policy turns out to have the same (s, S) form as for $\alpha < 1$.

*14-11 LINEAR PROGRAMMING FORMULATION OF MARKOVIAN DECISION PROCESSES

Numerical solutions to Markovian decision processes for the present-value or the average-cost per-period formulation can be obtained by linear programming. Consider expression (14-9) again:

$$f_i = \underset{x \in X}{\text{minimum}} \left[c_i(x) + \alpha \sum_j p_{ij}(x) f_j \right]$$

The term f_i being the minimum discounted expected cost, it must be true that

$$(14\text{-}23) \qquad f_i \leq c_i(x) + \alpha \sum_j p_{ij}(x) f_j, \qquad \text{for all } x \in X,\ i = 1, 2, \ldots, r$$

For each i there is at least one x for which strict equality holds in (14-23). Rearranging (14-23), we obtain

$$(14\text{-}24) \qquad f_i - \alpha \sum_j p_{ij}(x) f_j \leq c_i(x), \qquad \text{for all } x \in X,\ i = 1, 2, \ldots, r$$

In the dynamic programming formulation, the f_i are constants. We now allow them to become variables. Let y_i be the variable denoting the expected discounted cost over all future periods, starting in state i. Then (14-24) becomes

$$(14\text{-}25) \qquad y_i - \alpha \sum_j p_{ij}(x) y_j \leq c_i(x), \qquad \text{for all } x \in X,\ i = 1, 2, \ldots, r$$

where, for each i, equality holds for at least one value of x. There are $\Sigma_i M_i$ constraints in r variables, where M_i is the number of possible actions in state i. Note that in this formulation nothing is known about the sign of the y_i values. Hence, they are unrestricted in sign.

For linear programming, we need an objective function. It can be shown that the f_i values of (14-9) are equal to the optimal y_i values obtained by using the following objective function:

$$(14\text{-}26) \qquad \text{maximize} \sum_i q_i y_i$$

where $q_i > 0$, for all i. For instance, we could set all $q_i = 1$. Alternatively, by selecting the values of q_i such that $\Sigma_i q_i = 1$, each q_i can be interpreted as the probability of starting the process in state i.

To identify the optimal policy, all we have to do is to observe those constraints that are satisfied as an equality for each state i. The x associated with this constraint is the optimal action for that state i.

In this formulation, the number of constraints, $\Sigma_i M_i$, is usually very much larger than the number of variables. Since the computational effort required to solve a linear program is much more sensitive to the number of constraints than to the number of variables, it seems natural to solve the dual of (14-25) and (14-26). The dual has only r constraints in $\Sigma_i M_i$ variables. We leave it to you to formulate the dual.

Table 14-9 shows the structure of the primal problem in detached coefficient form and its optimal solution for $\alpha = 0.99$. Obviously, the optimal values of the variables y_i, $i = 0, 1, 2, 3, 4, 5$, coincide with the optimal f_i values obtained in Section 14-7.

Table 14-9. *Primal problem of linear program for Markovian decision process in detached coefficient form*

State	x	y_0	y_1	y_2	y_3	y_4	y_5	$c_i(x)$	Constraint Status	Optimal Decision
0	0	$1 - \alpha$						≤ 20	Slack	
	1	$1 - 0.6\alpha$	-0.4α					≤ 11	Slack	
	2	$1 - 0.3\alpha$	-0.3α	-0.4α				≤ 5	Slack	
	3	$1 - 0.1\alpha$	-0.2α	-0.3α	-0.4α			≤ 3	Binding	$x = 3$
	4		-0.1α	-0.2α	-0.3α	-0.4α		≤ 3	Slack	
	5			-0.1α	-0.2α	-0.3α	-0.4α	≤ 3	Slack	
1	0	-0.6α	$1 - 0.4\alpha$					≤ 9	Slack	
	1	-0.3α	$1 - 0.3\alpha$	-0.4α				≤ 6	Slack	
	2	-0.1α	$1 - 0.2\alpha$	-0.3α	-0.4α			≤ 4	Binding	$x = 2$
	3		$1 - 0.1\alpha$	-0.2α	-0.3α	-0.4α		≤ 4	Slack	
	4			-0.1α	-0.2α	-0.3α	-0.4α	≤ 4	Slack	
2	0	-0.3α	-0.3α	$1 - 0.4\alpha$				≤ 4	Binding	$x = 0$
	1	-0.1α	-0.2α	$1 - 0.3\alpha$	-0.4α			≤ 5	Slack	
	2		-0.1α	$1 - 0.2\alpha$	-0.3α	-0.4α		≤ 5	Slack	
	3			$1 - 0.1\alpha$	-0.2α	-0.3α	-0.4α	≤ 5	Slack	
3	0	-0.1α	-0.2α	-0.3α	$1 - 0.4\alpha$			≤ 3	Binding	$x = 0$
	1		-0.1α	-0.2α	$1 - 0.3\alpha$	-0.4α		≤ 6	Slack	
	2			-0.1α	$1 - 0.2\alpha$	-0.3α	-0.4α	≤ 6	Slack	
4	0		-0.1α	-0.2α	-0.3α	$1 - 0.4\alpha$		≤ 4	Binding	$x = 0$
	1			-0.1α	-0.2α	$1 - 0.3\alpha$	-0.4α	≤ 7	Slack	
5	0			-0.1α	-0.2α	-0.3α	$1 - 0.4\alpha$	≤ 5	Binding	$x = 0$
Maximize		1	1	1	1	1	1			
Optimal solution for $\alpha = 0.99$		356.0	357.0	357.2	356.0	357.3	359.2			

EXERCISES

14.1 Using the stochastic inventory control model formulated in Section 14-4, find the optimal production policy over a 6-month planning horizon for the following data: $c_h = \$1$, $c_s = \$4$, $k_n(x_n) = \$4$, $x_n > 0$, for all n (i.e., the production cost consists only of a set-up cost that is constant), and $p_n(d_n)$ as shown. Because of storage restrictions, no more than 6 units can be kept in inventory from one period to the next. The beginning inventory is 2.

$n =$	6	5	4	3	2	1
$d_n = 0$	0.5	0.2	0.4	0.5	0.2	0.2
$d_n = 1$	0.3	0.3	0.2	0.5	0.3	0.3
$d_n = 2$	0.2	0.4	0.2	0	0.3	0.3
$d_n = 3$	0	0.1	0.2	0	0.2	0.2

14.2 A stockbroker speculating on the forward market has signed an agreement to deliver a certain stock at a price of \$49 per share on Friday. She does not hold any of this stock on Monday, but will have to buy it prior to the due date. The present price is \$48. The price per share changes randomly from day to day. Her subjective estimates of the probability distribution of price changes are as shown. The broker would like to buy the shares at the lowest possible price. Once she has made her purchase, she will hold the shares until Friday evening when she makes the delivery. She would like to find the optimal purchasing strategy, given that the last price change observed was a decrease. Formulate the recursive relations of dynamic programming so as to maximize her expected gain or to minimize her expected loss. *Hint:* Let the state variable be given by a combination of current price and price change on the preceding day; e.g., $z_n = (49, +1)$ denotes a current price of \$49 and a price change the preceding day of $+1$.

Change of price from day $n+1$ to n	-1	0	$+1$
Probability if price decreased from day n to $n-1$	0.4	0.4	0.2
Probability otherwise	0.3	0.35	0.35

14.3 A machine is subject to random failure. If a failure occurs, the machine has to be replaced with a new one by the beginning of the following year. The operating efficiency of the machine also decreases with time. Consider the data given. If a failure occurs, an additional cost of \$200 is incurred. A new machine costs \$800. Solve this problem by dynamic programming for an 8-year planning horizon. Formulate the recursive relations in general terms first. The current machine on hand has had one year of use. Whatever machine is on hand at the end of the planning horizon is sold, provided it has not failed.

Year of operation	1	2	3	4	5	6
Probability of failure	0	0.1	0.2	0.3	0.4	0.5
Operating costs	\$100	\$110	\$140	\$170	\$210	\$260
Salvage value if machine is sold prior to failure	\$600	\$500	\$350	\$200	\$100	\$50

14.4 Using the stochastic inventory model formulated in Section 14-4, find the optimal policy over a 10-week planning horizon for the given demand distribution for each week.

Weekly demand d	0	1	2
$p(d)$	0.7	0.2	0.1

The following cost factors are also given: c_h = \$0.2/unit/week; c_s = \$1.0; $k_n(x_n)$ = \$3 for $x_n > 0$ and \$0 for $x_n = 0$, for all n. Observing the optimal value of x_n for large

n, would you expect x_n to change any further as n is increased beyond 10? (In other words, has the solution become stable?)

*14.5 A product is subject to the following demand distribution:

Daily demand x	0	1	2	3	4	5
$p(x)$	0.50	0.30	0.10	0.05	0.03	0.02

The product can be produced the same day a customer orders it. The production setup cost is $c_1 = \$4$ per setup, regardless of the size of the production run. Cost of keeping a unit in inventory for one day amounts to $c_2 = \$0.10$. Each time the product is handled, a handling cost of $c_3 = \$0.50$ per unit is incurred. Customer demand can be satisfied either from inventory (the product is then handled twice) or by a special production run directly from the production floor (the product is then handled only once). Consider the following inventory/production policy: If demand x on a given day is equal to $P(i)$ or larger, given that the inventory level at the beginning of the day is i, then the demand is satisfied by a special production run, and the inventory remains at i. If $x < P(i)$, the demand is met from inventory if possible. Whenever inventory is insufficient to satisfy the demand—$x > i$, but $x < P(i)$—then a production run is scheduled to replenish inventories to the level $S(i)$. The production run is thus equal to $S(i) - i + x$. $S(i) - i$ is added to inventory, and x is shipped directly from the production floor.

(a) Formulate the recursive relations of dynamic programming. Note that only one state variable, but two decision variables are needed.

(b) Solve the problem for a 10-day planning horizon. The optimal S will be less than 6, and the optimal $P(i)$ will be less than or equal to $S(i) + 1$, for all i. What is the optimal policy with 10 days left to the end of the planning horizon?

14.6 Each month the management of a small chain of service stations has to make a decision as to the promotion campaign for the coming month. If sales in the current month are high, three possible actions are available. (1) Management can decide to continue the current promotion for next month; then, with probability 0.4, sales in the next month will be high and will generate a net revenue of \$8000, and with probability 0.6, sales will be low and will generate a net revenue of \$4000. The costs incurred for continuing the present promotion amount to \$1000. (2) Management can offer a new free gift; then, with probability 0.8, sales in the month will be high and will generate a net revenue of \$7000, and with probability 0.2, sales will be low and will generate a net revenue of \$3000. The cost of this action is \$2500. (3) Management can undertake no promotion; then, with probability 0.25, sales will be high with a revenue of \$10,000, and with probability 0.75, sales will be low with a revenue of \$5000. No costs are incurred then. If sales in the current month are low, two possible actions are available. (1) Management can decide to offer a new gift; then, with probability 0.5, sales will be high with a revenue of \$6000, and with probability 0.5, sales will be low with a revenue of \$2000. The cost of this action is \$2500. (2) Management can decide to copy the main competitor's promotional campaign; then, with probability 0.4, sales will be high with a revenue of \$7000, and with probability 0.6, sales will be low with a revenue of \$3000. The cost of this action is \$1000.

(a) Construct a table similar to Table 14-4 showing columns for the current state, the decision, the transition probabilities, and the expected gross profit of the action (difference between expected net revenue and costs).

(b) For an initial policy of continuing the current promotion if sales are high and offering a new free gift if sales are low, find the present value of gross profits for each state for a discount factor of $\alpha = 0.9$.

(c) Use the four-step algorithm for approximation in policy space to find the optimal policy for a discount factor of 0.9. Note that this is a maximization problem!

(d) Determine the sensitivity of the optimal policy to $0 \leq \alpha < 1$.

14.7 An automobile manufacturer makes a decision once each year about whether to introduce a new model and, if so, what kind of stylistic changes to make. Developing a new model has a cost of 10 million dollars, whereas making minor changes in the current model has a cost of 2 million dollars. The manufacturer always has the option of not making any changes at all. Expected net revenues (= sales proceeds less variable production costs) for next year depend on whether the current model is achieving high sales or low sales, as follows:

Action	Current Sales	P(Sales Next Year)		Net Revenue Next Year	
		P(high)	P(low)	High Sales	Low Sales
New model	high	0.8	0.2	16	6
	low	0.5	0.5	16	6
Minor changes	high	0.5	0.5	12	0
	low	0.4	0.6	12	0
No changes	high	0.5	0.5	10	0
	low	0.1	0.9	10	0

(a) Construct a table similar to Table 14-4. This table should contain all information needed to use the algorithm of approximation in policy space.

(b) Starting with a policy of no changes, regardless of the level of current sales, find the optimal policy maximizing profits, using a discount factor of $\alpha = 0.75$.

14.8 A machine goes through several stages of deterioration that can be classified as 0 (properly adjusted), 1, 2, and 3 (inoperative). The state of the machine can be inferred with certainty from the number of defectives produced during the preceding day. At the beginning of each day, a decision has to be made as to whether or not the machine should be adjusted. If the machine is not adjusted, then the probability that its state of deterioration will progress to the next higher one is as follows:

State i as of end of day	0	1	2
Probability of state $i + 1$ as of end of next day	0.1	0.2	0.3

Once in state 3, the machine will remain there. If the machine is adjusted at the beginning of the day, its pattern of deterioration is the same as if it were in state 0. Total operating costs, including losses on defective parts, are as shown.

State as of end of next day	0	1	2	3
Operating cost next day in dollars	10	12	15	30

The cost of an adjustment (including loss of production) is \$8.

(a) Construct a table similar to Table 14-4, containing all information needed for the algorithm for approximation in policy space.

(b) Use the algorithm for approximation in policy space to find the optimal policy for a discount factor 0.99.

14.9 Consider a simplified car replacement problem. Toystar, the latest cheap import to hit the domestic market, has a fairly limited useful life (as the manufacturer admits), but it is also the cheapest car on the market. The manufacturer surprisingly supplied us with the operation statistics shown. A broken down car is only replaced by the beginning of next year and has no salvage value. A new Toystar costs \$4000. At the beginning of each year, a decision has to be made whether to replace the car with a new one or keep it for another year.

(a) Construct a table similar to Table 14-4 of the text. Make sure that it contains all information needed to apply the algorithm for approximation in policy space.

(b) For a discount factor of 0.8, determine the optimal policy that minimizes the discounted cost over all future periods.

Age of car at beginning of year	0	1	2	3
P(breakdown beyond repair during next year of operation)	0.1	0.2	0.4	1
Salvage value of car in operating condition (\$)	—	3000	1000	0
Operating cost during next year (\$)	1000	2000	2000	3000

14.10 Consider the water reservoir example in Sections 13-1 and 13-10. This can be viewed as a Markovian decision process, where for each state the size of the target release represents the decision variable. Indicate why the algorithm for approximation in policy space may result in an optimal policy that is nonoptimal for practical or technical reasons.

14.11 A reservoir is used to generate electric power for a small factory with a constant power demand equivalent to 4 units of water. The decision variables are the target releases to be scheduled for each reservoir level. If the target release cannot be met or is less than 4 units of water, power has to be purchased from a public utility at a cost of \$5000 for the first unit and \$6000 for the second unit of water. If more water is available than is needed, excess power can be sold on a firm basis at a price of \$3000 per unit of water. Use the water inflow pattern of the example in Section 13-1. The reservoir has a maximum capacity of 4 and can be emptied completely. Construct a table similar to Table 14-4 that contains all information needed to apply the algorithm for approximation in policy space. The objective is to minimize (costs—revenues). You do not have to solve the problem.

14.12 The emergency treatment station at a hospital has the policy of having two surgeons on duty at all times. Studying the records of the station, the chief medical officer notices that at times one surgeon would be able to handle all emergency calls, whereas at other times the number of emergencies is more than the two surgeons can cope with. Therefore, he wants to investigate this problem to determine an optimal staffing policy for the station. Some practical experimentation with the number of surgeons on duty yields the following information as to the probabilistic behavior of the system: $p(i, j \mid s)$ = the probability of finding j cases to be treated at the end of a one-hour period, if i cases were waiting for treatment at the beginning of the period and s surgeons were on duty for $i; j = 0, 1, \ldots, K$, and $s = 1, 2, \ldots, S < K$. Calling a surgeon on duty has a fixed cost of a dollars and an hourly cost of c dollars. The intangible cost of having a patient waiting for treatment at the end of each one-hour period is assessed at amount b. Construct, in general terms, a table similar to Table 14-4 that (given numbers for K, S, $p(i, j \mid s)$, a, c, and b) could be completed to contain all information needed to use the algorithm for approximation in policy space. Indicate why such a model may not sufficiently represent the true situation.

14.13 Consider exercise 14.6.

(a) For the policy listed under (b) of exercise 14.6, find the average return per period and the relative values. Assume that sales in the current period are low. How much would it be worth to management to start out from a position of high current sales?

(b) Using the algorithm for approximation in policy space for the average return per period, find the optimal policy.

14.14 Consider the taxi problem in exercise 13.7 of Chapter 13. Find the optimal policy using the algorithm for approximation in policy space, maximizing average return per trip. Initial policy: Cruise in both cities.

14.15 Find the optimal policy that minimizes average cost per day for the machine adjustment problem in exercise 14.8.

14.16 Find the optimal policy for exercise 14.7 that maximizes the average return per period.

14.17 Find the optimal replacement policy for exercise 14.9 that minimizes the average cost per period.

14.18 A machine producing high precision parts can be in any of three states of adjustment: state 1, fraction of rejects produced is 0.1; state 2, fraction of rejects produced is 0.2; state 3, fraction of rejects produced is 0.4. A reject causes a loss of 10 cents a piece. The machine produces 1000 parts a day. At the end of any given day, the state of adjustment of the machine can be readily identified. Adjustments are made during the night, so that no production time is lost. Adjustments can be made either by a hired technician or by the head operator of the machine. Adjustment times and cost per hour are as follows:

State of Machine	Hired Technician	Head Operator
1	0.5 hour	0.5 hour
2	1 hour	1.5 hours
3	2 hours	3 hours
Cost per hour	20 dollars	10 dollars

If no adjustment is performed on the machine, then the following transition probabilities hold:

To state	1	2	3
From state 1: no adjustment	0.7	0.2	0.1
2: no adjustment	0	0.8	0.2
3: no adjustment	0	0	1
From any state: Hired technician	0.9	0.1	0
Head operator	0.8	0.2	0

(a) Set up a table that contains all information needed to solve this problem using the policy evaluation and improvement routines.
(b) Find the optimal policy minimizing average cost per day.

14.19 Consider exercise 14.4. Assume that the maximum inventory is restricted to 3 units. Construct a table similar to Table 14-4, containing all information needed to apply the algorithm for approximation in policy space. Find the optimal solution for the average cost per period criterion.

14.20 Consider exercise 14.5. Construct a table containing all information needed to apply the algorithm for approximation in policy space. Assume that the maximum inventory will not exceed 3 units. Find the optimal policy for the average cost per period criterion.

14.21 Formulate the linear program associated with exercise 14.9.

14.22 Formulate the linear program associated with exercise 14.8. If you have access to a computer, solve the linear program and interpret the optimal solution.

14.23 Formulate the linear program associated with exercise 14.7. Note that this is a maximization problem. Therefore, expressions (14-23) through (14-26) have to be adjusted accordingly.

REFERENCES

Most texts on dynamic programming deal with the stochastic state space and Markovian decision processes. Also see the references to Chapter 9.

de Ghellinck, Guy T., and Gary D. Eppen. "Linear Programming Solutions for Separable Markovian Decision Problems," *Management Science*, Vol. 15, Jan. 1967. This important paper shows that if the transition probabilities depend only on the decision taken in state i and not on state i itself, and if $c_i(x)$ can be separated into two parts (one depending on the state only and one depending on the decision only), then the problem can be solved by a streamlined linear program that is considerably smaller than the normal linear programming formulation of the problem.

Hadley, George. *Nonlinear and Dynamic Programming.* Reading, Mass.: Addison-Wesley, 1964. Chapter 11 has several excellent sections at an advanced level which develop the theoretical basis of Markovian decision processes, including proofs.

Howard, Ronald A. *Dynamic Probabilistic Systems. Volume II: Semimarkov and Decision Processes.* New York: Wiley, 1971. Advanced treatment of Markovian decision processes, discrete and continuous. Cannot be properly studied without Volume I. (See References to Chapter 13.)

———. *Dynamic Programming and Markov Processes.* Cambridge, Mass.: M.I.T. Press, 1960. This 130-page book is delightful reading on this subject, at a very leisurely pace.

Norman, J.M., and D.J. White. "A Method for Approximate Solutions to Stochastic Dynamic Problems Using Expectations," *Operations Research,* Vol. 16, March–April 1968. Describes and illustrates a technique for obtaining approximate solutions to Markovian decision processes. The technique substitutes the return of the expected state only in place of the expected value over all future states. It uses no policy evaluation routine. See also the followup article by E. Porteus, "An Adjustment to the Norman-White Approach to Approximating Dynamic Programs," *Operations Research,* Vol. 27, Nov.–Dec. 1979, pp. 1203–1207.

Wagner, Harvey M. "On the Optimality of Pure Strategies," *Management Science,* Vol. 6, April 1960. Proof that the optimal strategy of a Markovian decision problem will always involve taking a single decision in each state, rather than using a mixed strategy (as in game theory), in which randomization over several strategies may be optimal.

———. *Principles of Operations Research,* 2nd ed. Englewood Cliffs, N.J.: Prentice-Hall, 1975. Chapters 11 and 12 deal with the principles of decision making over an unbounded planning horizon for deterministic problems (using discounting) and discuss the two solution methods "approximation in function space" and "approximation in policy space."

Examples of applications of Markovian decision processes are

Derman, Cyrus. "Optimal Replacement and Maintenance under Markovian Deterioration with Probability Bounds on Failure," *Management Science,* Vol. 9, Jan. 1963.

Eppen, Gary D., and Eugene F. Fama. "Solutions for Cash Balance and Simple Dynamic Portfolio Problems," *Journal of Business,* Vol. 41, Jan. 1968.

Liebman, Leon H. "A Markov Decision Model for Selecting Optimal Credit Control Policies," *Management Science,* Vol. 18, June 1972.

CHAPTER FIFTEEN

Introduction to Waiting Lines

Waiting lines or *queues* are everyday occurrences familiar to all of us. We experience them in our daily lives in one form or another—waiting at a bus stop or elevator, queueing at the cafeteria or ticket office, waiting in shops or at a gasoline station. Queues also occur extensively within an economic, industrial, or social context, sharing the common features of people or objects arriving at a service facility requiring some service and the ensuing delays when the service facility is occupied.

Although the number of potential uses of waiting line or queueing theory is very large, two major types of situations give rise to successful economic applications. The first deals with the case where an organization controls a sufficiently large number of similar or identical service facilities, such as gasoline pumps, bank tellers, machine operators or repair crews (for looms and knitting machines in a textile factory, machine tools in a machine shop, copying machines in a geograpical area), or telephone exchanges. In fact, the first applications of queueing theory dealt with the operation of telephone exchanges. Although queueing theory may offer only small economic incentives for each facility by itself, the pooling of large numbers of individually small gains makes such applications economically worthwhile. The second type of application deals with the planning and design of single facilities involving large capital investments, such as the purchase and operation of port facilities or a computer installation. In particular, the design of communication and computer systems is an area where extensive use is made of queueing theory. Here the objects are messages or pieces of information.

In contrast to most other operations research tools, waiting line models have no general pattern of optimization. Waiting line theory is concerned mainly with determining, for a given service facility, certain crucial characteristics of a proposed mode of operation, such as average waiting times, average queue length, and average idle time of the facility. These operating characteristics serve as input into the decision-making process about the facility studied—a process that often reduces to the economic evaluation of a small number of possible facilities and operating modes, with the "best" solution found by enumeration.

Most real-life applications of waiting line theory are highly complex. Many defy any formal analytic treatment—simulation is the only approach with any hope of capturing their essential features. In other cases, the tools of waiting line theory only serve as a first approximation to provide some quantitative information about the behavior of the more complex situation. Even so, the level of mathematics required to analyze such problems goes well beyond the scope of this text. The models discussed here are, therefore, a far cry from the complexities encountered in reality and are only intended to give some qualitative insights into waiting line phenomena.

We presume that aspects of the waiting line models, such as the times between arrivals and the length of service required, are not fixed but instead are drawn from particular probability distributions. Thus, we will make a lot of use of the material in Chapter 10 on probability, expected values, and stochastic processes. In particular, the negative exponential distribution is used in most theoretical models for which the operating characteristics have been determined. Even for theoretical models that can be described quite simply, the derivation of formulas for these characteristics is often very complex, if, in fact, formulas have been determined at all. For this reason, certain results will have to be stated without proof, whereas others are derived by heuristic reasoning. Before proceeding, you should review the relevant material in Chapter 10, especially Section 10-9 on Poisson processes.

15-1 GENERAL STRUCTURE OF WAITING LINES

The physical structure of waiting lines consists of three components:

- one or several *sources of arrivals*,
- *queues*, and
- a *service facility* consisting of one or several parts.

Table 15-1. *Examples of waiting line phenomena*

Source of Arrivals	Nature of Service Requested	Service Facility
population of customers	sales transaction	shop attendant(s)
aircraft	landing or takeoff	runway(s)
ships at sea	unloading or loading	port dock(s)
telephones	telephone connection	telephone exchange
cars	crossing	ferry
machines on shop floor	repairs	operators or mechanics
mechanics on shop floor	tools or parts	attendants at tool crib
inventory withdrawals	inventory replenishment	supplier

Figure 15-1. *Waiting line structure.*

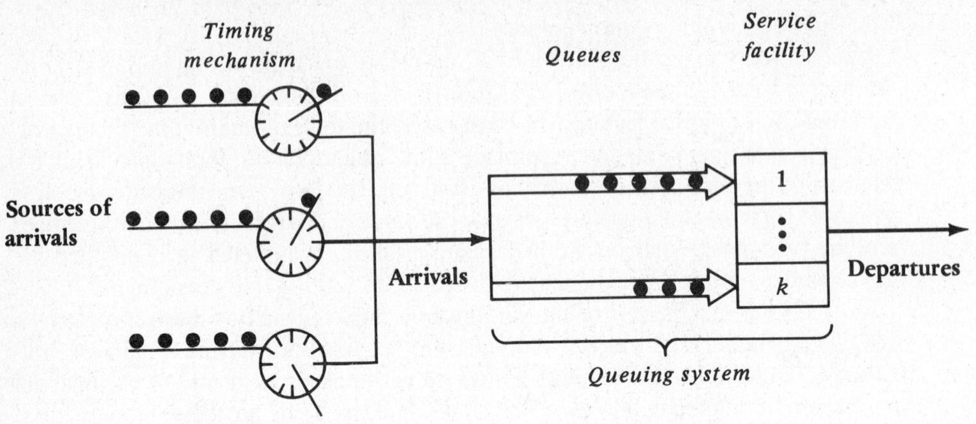

The queues and service facility together are referred to as the *system*. Table 15-1 lists a few typical examples.

Arrivals may originate from one or several sources or pools of potential customers, referred to as the *calling populations*. We assume that each source has a well-defined arrival pattern over time. It may be helpful to visualize that each source is equipped (figuratively speaking) with an *arrival timing mechanism*, which releases units with a known pattern of *interarrival times*—the times between two consecutive arrivals. Arrivals may be uniformly spaced over time (i.e., the interarrival times are constant) or randomly spaced over time with a known *interarrival time probability distribution*.

A calling population may be inexhaustible, in the sense that the number of potential customers in the source is assumed to be always very much larger than the number of units in the system, or a calling population may be sufficiently limited in size that the arrival pattern varies as a function of that size. The number of telephones serviced by a telephone exchange is an example of an inexhaustible source (under most conditions), whereas the number of machines on a factory floor is an example of a limited source. In the first instance, the call rate will hardly be affected by the number of telephones busy at any given moment in time, so we may be able to assume the interarrival times form a *renewal process*. In the second case, however, every machine that requires the attention of an operator, i.e., enters the queueing system, may significantly reduce the rate of arrivals, and every machine that has been serviced, i.e., departs from the system, may again significantly increase the rate of arrivals. If the number of units being served or waiting for service tends to be a relatively small fraction of the total calling population, an unlimited source model may be a satisfactory approximation.

The service facility may consist of one or several *stations* or *channels*. They may operate either *in parallel*, in which case an arrival has to go through one channel only before being discharged from the system, or they may operate *in series*, in which case an arrival has to go through several channels in sequence before being discharged.

The service times at each channel may be constant or random with a known *service time distribution*.

There may be no queue, one queue, or several queues. Queues do not have to be physical in nature, as the queue in front of a bank teller, but may consist of geographically separated units awaiting service, such as equipment operated at different locations that requires some service. The manner in which units are taken from the queue is called the *queue discipline*. It may, for example, be on a first-come-first-served basis, random, or subject to *service priorities*, as for instance in an emergency clinic. We shall only look at the first scheme. It may also be possible to switch queues, and the choice of which queue to join may be open to an arrival. Furthermore, the maximum queue length may be unlimited or finite. In the latter case, units arriving when the queue is full immediately depart, i.e., are lost to the system. Finally, potential arrivals may *balk* if the queue length becomes excessive and decide not to join, or arrivals may join the queue and subsequently *renege*, i.e., become impatient and leave before being served. In either case, they are lost to the system. The variety of possible waiting line configurations seems almost unlimited.

The waiting line problems of interest to us are those that have either random interarrival times or random service times, or both. In this case, queues of random lengths will occur. If no units are waiting most of the time, then the service facility will tend to be idle for a large portion of the time. If there are costs associated with idle service channels, then this is undesirable. On the other hand, if the service facility is busy and queues exist most of the time, arrivals will frequently have to wait prior to service. If the waiting times are long, this may again result in tangible or intangible costs, such as lost production time (mechanics waiting for parts or tools, machines down), deterioration of certain attributes of arrivals (cement trucks or banana boats waiting to be unloaded, patients waiting for surgery), or loss of goodwill (customers becoming impatient). The problem in waiting line models is to determine a system such that the sum of all costs associated with operating the system is minimized.

The controllable aspects of queueing systems are

- arrival rate (e.g., by choosing quality of parts that may fail or require service);
- number of service facilities;
- service times, both in terms of average length and service time variations;
- maximum queue length (e.g., by providing a certain number of spaces, say, in a parking lot); and
- priority rules and queue discipline.

15-2 ARRIVAL TIME DISTRIBUTION

We shall consider models where arrivals and services occur only in single or individual units, rather than in groups of several units (called *bulk arrivals* or *bulk service*).

The simplest waiting line models assume that the number of arrivals occurring within any interval of time, t, follows a *Poisson distribution* with parameter λt, where

λt is the average number of arrivals in the interval of time t. (Recall that for the Poisson distribution, λt is also equal to the variance.) If n denotes the number of arrivals in the interval t, then the probability functon $p(n)$ is given by

$$p(n) = \frac{(\lambda t)^n}{n!}e^{-\lambda t}, \qquad n = 0, 1, 2, \ldots \tag{15-1}$$

This arrival process is called *Poisson input*. λ represents the *arrival rate.* A Poisson input implies certain behavioristic assumptions that may look somewhat unrealistic, but the process still models many practical situations surprisingly well.

The lack of memory property of the Poisson process means that we are assuming not only that interarrival times are independent of one another or the state of the system, but also that the probability of an arrival in an interval of time h does not depend on the starting point of the interval or on the history of arrivals preceding it, but only on the length of the interval.

From expression (10-60) and (10-61) in Chapter 10, it follows that for h very small,

$$\begin{aligned} &P\,(\text{exactly one arrival in } h) \cong \lambda h \\ &P\,(\text{no arrival in } h) \qquad\quad\; \cong 1 - \lambda h \end{aligned} \tag{15-2}$$

As we saw in Chapter 10, expression (15-1) also implies that the probability density function of the time between arrivals is

$$a(t) = \lambda e^{-\lambda t}, \qquad t \geqslant 0$$

i.e., a *negative exponential distribution* with parameter λ. The mean interarrival time and the standard deviation of the interarrival times are both $1/\lambda$.

To verify that the Poisson input is a satisfactory representation of a particular real-life arrival process, we would gather data on a large number of interarrival times, or on the number of arrivals in a large number of equal time intervals, and compare one or the other of the empirical distributions observed with the corresponding theoretical distribution, usually by performing a *goodness of fit test.*

Let us demonstrate the second approach with the following example. A firm operates a 10-ton crane truck on a job contracting basis. Arrivals into the system are given by job requests. Data are gathered over a 100-day period and are compiled into a frequency table as shown in the first two columns of Table 15-2. Does the daily number of job requests or arrivals have a Poisson distribution?

We want to test the null hypothesis that the distribution is Poisson with a mean of λ. To test this, we first determine an estimate of the daily arrival rate, which turns out to be 1.4 job requests per day. This is used as the value of λ in the Poisson probability function (15-1), and the theoretical frequencies of this distribution—usually obtained from tables—are compared with the observed frequencies using a *chi-square goodness of fit test.* The computations leading up to this test are shown in the last three columns of Table 15-2.

The observed chi-square value corresponds to a level of significance of about 0.2. This means that the hypothesis of a Poisson distribution is not rejected for all smaller

Table 15-2. *Chi-square test for arrival process*

Arrivals in an 8-hour Day	Observed Frequencies F_i	Theoretical Frequencies f_i	$(F_i - f_i)^2/f_i$
$i = 0$	28	24.7	0.44
1	35	34.5	0.01
2	20	24.1	0.70
3	8	11.3	0.96
4	6	4.0	
5	2 } 9	1.1 } 5.4	2.40
6	0	0.2	
7	1	0.1	
	100	100	4.51

Number of classes = 5
Number of degrees of freedom = number of classes − number of estimated parameters − 1 = 5 − 1 − 1 = 3
$P(\text{chi-square} > 4.51) > 0.2$

Note that small classes with a frequency of less than 5 should be lumped together to give frequencies for all classes of at least 5. This reduces the effective number of classes available to 5.

levels of significance. This strongly suggests that we can safely approximate the arrival process by a Poisson input.

We could assume that the arrival process forms a renewal process other than a Poisson process. Analysis of waiting line problems then becomes much more difficult, however. We shall postpone further discussion of this possibility to Section 15-13.

15-3 SERVICE TIME DISTRIBUTIONS

Most simple waiting line models also assume that service times have a *negative exponential distribution* with parameter μ, i.e.,

$$s(t) = \mu e^{-\mu t}, \qquad t \geqslant 0$$

Hence, for h very small,

$$P(\text{one service completion in } h) \cong \mu h$$

(15-3)

$$P(\text{no service completion in } h) \cong 1 - \mu h$$

The property of lack of memory has some revealing consequences. If a unit arrives at the service facility (when the queue is empty) and finds the service facility busy, the probability that this unit has to wait a length of time of at least h is independent ot how long the current service has been in progress. In fact, the residual service time distribution is also negative exponential with parameter μ.

What is the expected waiting time for a unit that joins the queue and finds n units ahead of it ($n - 1$ in the queue and 1 unit in the service facility)? Since each unit takes, on the average, a length of time $1/\mu$, the total expected time needed to process n units is n/μ, and by independence of the service times, the standard deviation is $\sqrt{n}/\mu$. Since the total waiting time is equal to the sum of n random variables, all with identical negative exponential distributions, its probability distribution is given by the *convolution* of n negative exponential distributions, and hence has a *gamma distribution* with parameters (n, μ), i.e.,

$$f(t) = \frac{\mu^n t^{n-1} e^{-\mu t}}{(n-1)!}, \qquad t \geq 0 \tag{15-4}$$

We shall again postpone further discussion of service time distributions other than the negative exponential to Section 15-13.

15-4 QUEUEING MODEL NOMENCLATURE

The literature of queueing theory tends to use a standardized terminology, consisting of four symbols separated by vertical bars to describe the most basic types of models:

$$I|F|S|N$$

where I designates the input process, F the service time distribution, S the number of service channels in parallel, and N the number of customers allowed in the system.

The standard symbols are

M = negative exponential time distribution (*M* stands for *Markovian*)
D = deterministic or constant times
E_n = Erlang distribution of order n (see Section 15-13)
GI = general independent interarrival time distribution
G = general service time distribution

For instance, a waiting line model that has Poisson input, constant service times, and 1 service channel is denoted by $M|D|1|\infty$. When N is infinite, the three-symbol notation $M|D|1$ is often used.

15-5 THE MOST BASIC WAITING LINE MODEL, $M|M|1$

Mathematically speaking, the simplest waiting line model assumes that arrivals join a queue that is unlimited in size, wait in line until their turn for service comes on a first-come-first-served basis, and then enter a service facility consisting of a single channel.

The input process is assumed to be Poisson, i.e., interarrival times have a negative exponential distribution with parameter λ, and the service channel has service times that also follow a negative exponential distribution with parameter μ.

As was the case with Markov chains, in waiting line models we are often interested only in the long-run operating characteristics of such systems, i.e., when the system is in *statistical equilibrium* or in *steady state*. The time interval needed to approach the steady state sufficiently closely—the so-called *transient* behavior of the process—is ignored. However, it should be realized that many systems never reach a steady state. This is the case for processes that are periodically interrupted (e.g., daily) before they approach a steady state and then are restarted, usually with empty queues, such as a bank teller service, or systems whose input distribution does not remain stationary but changes over time, such as the traffic flow at a toll bridge during various times of the day. In such cases, we study the transient behavior of the system. However, this requires a level of mathematics far beyond the scope of this text.

At any moment in time, the state of this waiting line process is completely described by the number of units in the system. For an $M|M|1$ process, this is the number of units in the queue plus the number in the service channel—the latter is either 0 or 1. Thus, the state of the process can assume values 0 (service facility idle, no units in queue), 1 (service facility busy, no units in the queue), 2, 3, . . ., n units (service facility busy, $n - 1$ units in the queue).

In contrast to the type of processes discussed in Chapter 13, in queueing systems a transition from one state to another can occur at any moment in time and not only at specified evenly spaced points in time. However, the process will nevertheless approach a steady state that is independent of its starting position or state.

Let these steady-state probabilities be denoted by P_n, $n = 0, 1, 2, \ldots$, where the subscript refers to the number of units in the system. As we have seen, for a Poisson input and a negative exponential service time, the probabilities that an arrival occurs or a service is completed in an interval of length h do not depend on the history of the system before the start of the interval. Hence, the probability of a transition from a given state to another state in the interval h does not depend on how long the system occupied that state. All the information needed to describe the system's future behavior is contained in that state specification. For this reason, queues such as $M|M|1$ are sometimes called *Markovian*. For such systems, if we look at the process in the steady state at two randomly chosen moments in time, separated by a short interval of time h, then it must be true that the probabilities of finding the process in the various states remain unchanged—by the very definition of the steady state. But this requires that, for each state, the probability of being in that state and leaving it during h exactly balances the probability of being in other states and entering that state during h.

15-6 THE BALANCE EQUATION METHOD

Recall from Section 10-9 that for a sufficiently small interval of length h, no more than 1 arrival and no more than 1 service completion can occur. Similarly, the probability of observing an arrival and a service completion in the same interval, given by $\mu\lambda h^2$, is approximately zero for h very small, since it also involves a higher order term of h. This leaves only the 4 compound events associated with each state for $n > 1$, shown in Table 15-3.

Table 15-3. *Events of state transitions*

Events	Probability
(1) There are n units in the system	P_n
and 1 arrival occurs in h	λh
(2) There are n units in the system	P_n
and 1 service is completed in h	μh
(3) There are $n - 1$ units in the system	P_{n-1}
and 1 arrival occurs in h	λh
(4) There are $n + 1$ units in the system	P_{n+1}
and 1 service is completed in h	μh

For $n = 0$, only events 1 and 4 are possible. Figure 15-2 shows a transition diagram for these events.

In terms of the events shown in Table 15-3, we have for $n \geqslant 1$

$$P\begin{pmatrix}\text{being in state } n \text{ and}\\ \text{leaving it}\end{pmatrix} = P\begin{pmatrix}\text{being in state } n-1 \text{ or } n+1\\ \text{and entering state } n\end{pmatrix}$$

$$P(\text{event } 1) + P(\text{event } 2) = P(\text{event } 3) + P(\text{event } 4)$$

This yields the following equation known as a *steady state balance equation*:

$$P_n\lambda h + P_n\mu h = P_{n-1}\,\lambda h + P_{n+1}\mu h \tag{15-5}$$

In terms of Figure 15-2, the left-hand side of (15-5) is obtained by adding the products of the probabilities of state n and the probabilities on the arrows leaving state n, whereas the right-hand side is the sum of the products of the probabilities of the states where arrows entering state n originate and the probabilities on these arrows.

For $n = 0$, we equate the probabilities of event 1 and event 4 of Table 15-3:

$$P_0\lambda h = P_1\mu h \tag{15-6}$$

Consider now the first few terms of (15-5):

$$\begin{aligned} P_1\lambda h + P_1\mu h &= P_0\lambda h + P_2\mu h \\ P_2\lambda h + P_2\mu h &= P_1\lambda h + P_3\mu h \\ P_3\lambda h + P_3\mu h &= P_2\lambda h + P_4\mu h \\ &\cdot \\ &\cdot \\ &\cdot \end{aligned} \tag{15-7}$$

Figure 15-2. *Transition diagram for M|M|1.*

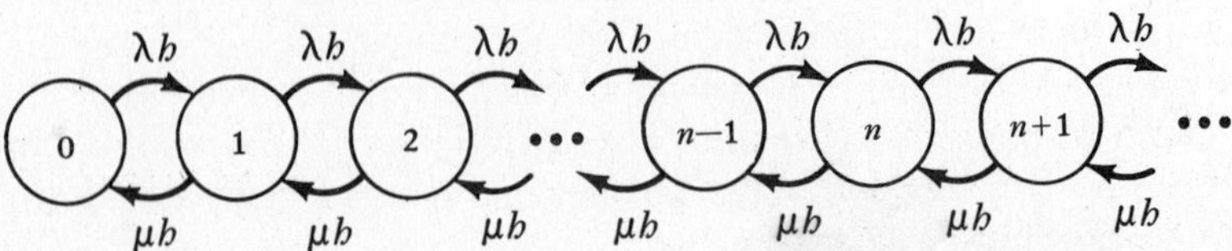

Using (15-6), we can substitute $P_1\mu h$ for $P_0\lambda h$ in the first equation of (15-7):

$$P_1\lambda h + P_1\mu h = P_1\mu h + P_2\mu h$$

Canceling equal terms and dividing through by h, we get

$$P_1\lambda = P_2\mu$$

This result can now be substituted into the second equation of (15-7). Continuing in this fashion, we get

$$P_2\lambda = P_3\mu$$
$$P_3\lambda = P_4\mu$$
$$\vdots$$

Starting with (15-6), it thus follows that $P_1 = (\lambda/\mu)P_0$, $P_2 = (\lambda/\mu)P_1 = (\lambda/\mu)^2P_0$, $P_3 = (\lambda/\mu)P_2 = (\lambda/\mu)^3P_0$, and so on. In general,

(15-8) $$P_n = (\lambda/\mu)^n P_0, \qquad n \geq 1$$

Using the information that $\Sigma_n P_n = 1$ or $\Sigma_{n=0}^{\infty}(\lambda/\mu)^n P_0 = 1$, and that $\Sigma_{n=0}^{\infty}(\lambda/\mu)^n = 1/(1 - \lambda/\mu)$ for $0 < \lambda/\mu < 1$, we find

$$P_0 = \frac{1}{\sum_{n=0}^{\infty}(\lambda/\mu)^n} = 1\Big/\left(\frac{1}{1 - \lambda/\mu}\right)$$

or

(15-9) $$P_0 = 1 - \frac{\lambda}{\mu}$$

and (15-8) simplifies to

(15-10) $$P_n = \left(\frac{\lambda}{\mu}\right)^n \left(1 - \frac{\lambda}{\mu}\right), \qquad \text{all } n \geq 0 \qquad (\textit{geometric distribution})$$

The term λ/μ is known as the *utilization factor* or *traffic intensity*. It is also equal to the probability that the service channel is busy. Because the arrival process is Poisson, (15-10) is also the distribution of the number of units that an arriving customer will find in the system in steady state. Hence, λ/μ is also the probability that an arrival will have to wait. You should note, however, that this equality of the arriving customer's and the steady-state distribution does not usually hold for non-Poisson arrivals.

From the derivation of expression (15-9), we see that the arrival rate λ has to be smaller than the service rate μ. This is intuitively obvious. If the arrival rate is equal to or larger than the service rate, the queue tends to become longer and longer. The process never reaches a statistical equilibrium, and the above analysis does not apply.

Given the steady-state distribution, we can derive a number of important system operating characteristics that may be needed as inputs into the measures of effectiveness of the system.

1. The average number of units in the system (including the one in service), denoted by L:

$$L = \sum_{n=1}^{\infty} nP_n = \sum_{n=1}^{\infty} n\left(\frac{\lambda}{\mu}\right)^n\left(1 - \frac{\lambda}{\mu}\right) = \left(1 - \frac{\lambda}{\mu}\right)\frac{\lambda}{\mu}\sum_{n=1}^{\infty} n\left(\frac{\lambda}{\mu}\right)^{n-1} = \frac{\lambda/\mu}{1 - \lambda/\mu} \tag{15-11}$$

(since $\Sigma_{n=1}^{\infty} n(\lambda/\mu)^{n-1}$ is the derivative of $\Sigma_{n=1}^{\infty}(\lambda/\mu)^n = (\lambda/\mu)/[1 - \lambda/\mu]$).

2. The average number of units waiting in the queue, denoted by L_q:

$$\begin{aligned} L_q = \sum_{n=1}^{\infty} (n-1) P_n &= \underbrace{\sum_{n=1}^{\infty} nP_n}_{} - \underbrace{\sum_{n=1}^{\infty} P_n}_{} \\ &= \quad L \quad -(1 - P_0) = \frac{(\lambda/\mu)^2}{1 - \lambda/\mu} \end{aligned} \tag{15-12}$$

3. The *average time the system is idle* and *average busy time* of the service facility. An alternative interpretation for the steady state probabilities is that they represent the average fraction of time that the system is in each state. Hence, $P_0 = 1 - \lambda/\mu$ is the average fraction of time that no unit is in the system or the average idle time, and $P(\text{system is busy}) = 1 - P_0 = \lambda/\mu$ is the average fraction of time that there is at least 1 unit in the system or the average busy time of the facility.

4. The average time spent in the system by an arrival, denoted by W. This is the sum of the expected waiting time, W_q, and the expected service time. So

$$W = W_q + \frac{1}{\mu} \tag{15-13}$$

Little's formula gives a very useful relationship between L and W that holds for a wide class of arrival and service processes, as well as Poisson input and exponential service times. Consider an arrival that is just leaving the system after service. On the average, it has spent a time W in the system. Left behind in the system are an average of L customers, who arrived at intervals which averaged $1/\lambda$. But in steady state, these two average times must be equal; so $W = L(1/\lambda)$, or

LITTLE'S FORMULA

$$L = \lambda W \tag{15-14}$$

Note that this relationship also holds for multiserver queues. (Why?) Since $L = L_q + (\lambda/\mu)$ and $W = W_q + (1/\mu)$, we also have

$$L_q = \lambda W_q \tag{15-15}$$

(15-15) can be obtained directly by an argument such as the one used for (15-14), if we consider an arrival who is just about to enter service.

Substituting (15-11) into (15-14) and solving for W, we obtain

(15-16) $$W = \frac{1}{\mu - \lambda}$$

(15-17) $$W_q = W - \frac{1}{\mu} = \frac{\lambda}{\mu(\mu - \lambda)}$$

The operating characteristics of queueing systems tend to be highly sensitive to changes in the utilization factor and rise steeply as this factor approaches 1, as can be seen from Table 15-4. It is important that both λ and μ be estimated with a sufficiently high degree of accuracy.

Table 15-4. *Sensitivity of operating characteristics to utilization factor for M|M|1 models*

λ/μ*	0.2	0.4	0.5	0.6	0.7	0.8	0.9	0.95	0.98	0.99
L	0.25	0.667	1.0	1.5	2.333	4.0	9.0	19.0	49.0	99.0
W	1.25	1.667	2.0	2.5	3.333	5.0	10.0	20.0	50.0	100.0

*Assuming μ = 1, λ is the rate of arrival per average service time, and W is in units of average service time.

15-7 EXAMPLES OF *M*|*M*|1

Let us return to the firm operating a 10-ton crane truck on a job contracting basis. We shall use 1 day as our basic time unit. From the data of Table 15-2, we conclude that the input process is Poisson, with a mean arrival rate of $\lambda = 1.4$ per day. The average service time amounts to 4 hours or $\frac{1}{2}$ of an 8-hour day, and we assume that the service time distribution is approximately negative exponential with a mean service rate of $\mu = 2$ per day. The M|M|1 model applies, and we obtain the following operating characteristics:

$$\text{Utilization factor} = P(\text{crane busy}) = \frac{\lambda}{\mu} = 1.4/2 = 0.7$$

$$\text{Average idle time} = P_0 = 1 - \frac{\lambda}{\mu} = 0.3 \text{ or } 30\% \text{ of the time}$$

$$L = \frac{\lambda/\mu}{1 - \lambda/\mu} = \frac{0.7}{1 - 0.7} = 2.33 \text{ jobs in the system}$$

$$L_q = \frac{(\lambda/\mu)^2}{1 - \lambda/\mu} = \frac{0.7^2}{1 - 0.7} = 1.63 \text{ jobs waiting}$$

$$W = \frac{1}{\mu - \lambda} = \frac{1}{2 - 1.4} = 1.67 \text{ days in the system}$$

$$W_q = \frac{\lambda}{\mu}\left(\frac{1}{\mu - \lambda}\right) = 0.7(1.67) = 1.17 \text{ days waiting time}$$

P(more than job waiting for service) = P(more than 2 jobs in the system)

$$= P(n \geq 3) = 1 - P_0 - P_1 - P_2 = 1 - 0.3 - (0.7)0.3 - (0.7)^2 0.3 = 0.343$$

Therefore, about one-third of the time, the crane is more than 1 job behind.

Assume now that customers with job requests do not wait if there is already another job request ahead of them waiting for service. Hence, the maximum number of units in the system will never be more than 2. This particular type of balking is equivalent to the case where the maximum queue length is limited to a finite number. In the *finite queue* case, expressions (15-10) and (15-9) have to be adjusted accordingly. Now, $\Sigma_n P_n = 1$ only covers the terms for $n = 0$, 1, and 2, i.e.,

$$\sum_{n=0}^{2} \left(\frac{\lambda}{\mu}\right)^n P_0 = 1$$

Since $\sum_{n=0}^{k} (\lambda/\mu)^n = 1 - (\lambda/\mu)^{k+1}/[1-(\lambda/\mu)]$, this yields

$$P_0 = \frac{1}{\sum_{n=0}^{2} (\lambda/\mu)^n} = \frac{1 - (\lambda/\mu)}{1 - (\lambda/\mu)^3} = 0.457$$

Note that here we do not need $\lambda < \mu$ any longer.

From the result of this expression, we note that if customers balk when there is already another job waiting, the average idle time of the crane increases from 30 percent to almost 46 percent. Furthermore, a certain fraction of jobs will be lost. Customers balk if the system is in state 2. The fraction of time the system is in state 2 is

$$P_2 = \left(\frac{\lambda}{\mu}\right)^2 P_0 = 0.7^2(0.457) = 0.224$$

This is also the fraction of jobs lost. On the average, almost 1 out of 4 job requests will be lost.

In general, if the length of the queue is limited to $N - 1$ places, then

$$P_n = \begin{cases} \dfrac{1 - (\lambda/\mu)}{1 - (\lambda/\mu)^{N+1}} \left(\dfrac{\lambda}{\mu}\right)^n & \text{for } \lambda \neq \mu \\[2ex] \dfrac{1}{N + 1} & \text{for } \lambda = \mu \end{cases} \qquad 0 \leq n \leq N$$

The average number of jobs in the system, as well as the average number of jobs waiting, can be computed from the definition of expected values:

$$L = \sum_{n=1}^{N} nP_n \quad \text{and} \quad L_q = \sum_{n=1}^{N} (n - 1)P_n$$

To find W, we use the same reasoning as for expression (15-14), except that arrivals can join the queue only when there are fewer than N jobs in the system. Thus, the average arrival rate is $\lambda(1 - P_N)$. Hence, $L = W\lambda(1 - P_N)$, and

$$W = \frac{L}{\lambda(1 - P_N)}$$

Verify that for our example $L = 0.76$, $L_q = 0.22$, and $W = 0.65$. All are substantially lower than the corresponding result for the unlimited queue case.

Limiting the queue length or having arrivals balk or renege has the following consequences: average idle time increases, average queue length and average waiting time decrease, and a portion of the customers will be lost. It is usually possible to assign costs and benefits to each of these effects. If the queue length is a controllable variable, then the optimal queue length can be determined.

15-8 MULTIPLE CHANNEL MODELS, *M|M|S*

Assume now that the service facility consists of S channels operating in parallel, each having an exponentially distributed service time with mean $1/\mu$. The arrival process is Poisson with rate λ. Arrivals join a single queue and enter the first available service channel on a first-come-first-served basis.

As long as the number of units in the system, n, is less than S, an arrival immediately enters an idle service channel. Since each channel services units at a rate μ, the average service rate is $n\mu$. A queue starts building up only when the number of units in the system exceeds S. At that point, all service channels are busy, and the average service rate attains its maximum $S\mu$. If the queue length is unlimited, such a system can reach a steady state only if the arrival rate is less than the maximum service rate, i.e., $\lambda < S\mu$. For a finite queue length, where customers bypass the system once the queue is full, this restriction is not needed.

Since this is a Markovian system, we can again find the steady-state probabilities by the balance equation method. Figure 15-3 allows us to derive the following equations:

$$\lambda P_0 = \mu P_1$$
$$(\lambda + \mu) P_1 = \lambda P_0 + 2\mu P_2, \text{ etc.}$$

or, in general,

$$(\lambda + n\mu) P_n = \lambda P_{n-1} + (n+1)\mu P_{n+1}, \qquad 0 < n \leq S-1 \tag{15-18}$$
$$(\lambda + S\mu) P_n = \lambda P_{n-1} + S\mu P_{n+1}, \qquad n \geq S$$

Figure 15-3. *Transition diagram for M|M|S.*

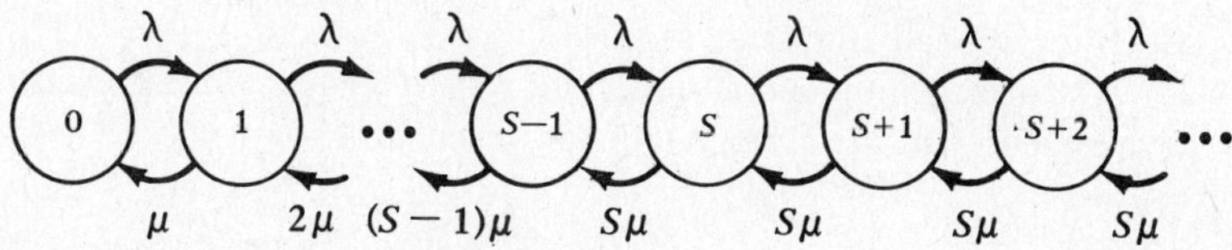

Again, as you will find with most simple balance equation models, we can cancel out terms in (15-18) to give

$$P_n = \begin{cases} \dfrac{(\lambda/\mu)^n}{n!} P_0 & \text{for } n < S \\[2ex] \dfrac{(\lambda/\mu)^n}{S!S^{n-S}} P_0 & \text{for } n \geqslant S \end{cases}$$

Using the property that $\Sigma_{n=0}^{\infty} P_n = 1$, we must have

$$P_0\left(1 + \sum_{n=1}^{S-1} \frac{(\lambda/\mu)^n}{n!} + \frac{(\lambda/\mu)^S}{S!} \sum_{n=0}^{\infty} (\lambda/S\mu)^n\right) = 1$$

or

(15-19) $$P_0 = \frac{1}{\left[\sum_{n=0}^{S-1} (\lambda/\mu)^n/n!\right] + \left[(\lambda/\mu)^S/S!(1 - \lambda/S\mu)\right]}$$

All service channels are busy when $n \geqslant S$. Using the results of (15-19), we find that the average fraction of time all service channels are busy or the probability that an arrival will have to wait is

(15-20) $$P(n \geqslant S) = \sum_{n=S}^{\infty} P_n = \frac{(\lambda/\mu)^S}{S!(1 - \lambda/S\mu)} P_0$$

and the average number of service channels busy is

(15-21) $$E(\text{channels busy}) = \sum_{n=1}^{S-1} nP_n + S \sum_{n=S}^{\infty} P_n = \frac{\lambda}{\mu}$$

It is independent of S.

The average number of units waiting in the queue is

(15-22) $$L_q = \sum_{n=S+1}^{\infty} (n-S)P_n = P(n \geqslant S)\left(\frac{\lambda/\mu}{S-\lambda/\mu}\right) = \frac{(\lambda/\mu)^{S+1}}{SS![1 - (\lambda/S\mu)]^2} P_0$$

Note that (15-22) can be expressed in terms of (15-20) as

(15-23) $$L_q = \frac{\lambda/S\mu}{(1 - \lambda/S\mu)} P(n \geqslant S)$$

which is essentially the same as (15-12).

The average number of units in the system is equal to the average number waiting in the queue plus the average number in service:

(15-24) $$L = L_q + \frac{\lambda}{\mu}$$

To find the average time in the system, W, and the average waiting time in the queue, W_q, we use the same reasoning as for the single channel model, i.e., $\lambda W = L$. From expression (15-24) we obtain

$$W = \frac{L}{\lambda} = \frac{L_q}{\lambda} + \frac{1}{\mu} = W_q + \frac{1}{\mu} \tag{15-25}$$

The last part of expression (15-25) follows from the fact that the average service time per unit is $1/\mu$.

15-9 A CASE STUDY OF AN *M|M|S* SYSTEM

In large factories, most tools for use by mechanics on the factory floor are stored in one or several tool cribs. How many clerks should attend the counter of such a tool crib? This is a classic application of a multiple-channel queueing system. The service facility consists of the counter of the tool crib where one or several clerks attend to mechanics requesting tools. The clerks represent service channels, working independently and in parallel. The mechanics on the factory floor form the source of arrivals. Although their number is finite, it is sufficiently large that the fraction of mechanics waiting for service or being served represents a negligible portion of the total population. If their number were relatively small, such that the arrival rate would vary as a function of the number of mechanics at the tool crib, the model of the preceding section would not be suitable.

In the particular study on which this example is based (G. Brigham, "On a Congestion Problem in an Aircraft Factory," *Operations Research*, Nov. 1955), a sample of service times was measured with a stopwatch by an observer stationed at the counter. An electrical device was used to record arrival times of mechanics at the counter. The average time between arrivals was found to be 35 seconds, corresponding to an arrival rate of $\lambda = 60/35 = 1.71$ per minute. The average service time amounted to 50 seconds, yielding a service rate of $\mu = 1.2$ per minute. The interarrival time and service time distributions found on this basis were compared to the corresponding negative exponential distributions by means of a chi-square goodness of fit test, and the associated null hypotheses were accepted.

Assuming an unlimited queue length, we need at least 2 clerks for the steady state analysis of the preceding section to apply. (Why?) For $S = 2$, we find the following operating statistics:

$$P_0 = \frac{1}{\sum_{n=0}^{1} (1.71/1.2)^n/n! + ((1.71/1.2)^2/2!(1 - 1.71/2(1.2)))} = 0.167$$

[by expression (15-19)]

i.e., the fraction of time both clerks are idle is 1/6.

$$P(\text{both clerks busy}) = P(n \geq 2) = \frac{(1.71/1.2)^2}{2!(1 - 1.71/2(1.2))} 0.167 = 0.595$$

[by expression (15-20)]

i.e., the fraction of time both clerks are busy is 59.5 percent. The average number of clerks busy or the average number of mechanics being serviced is

$$E(\text{channels busy}) = 1.71/1.2 = 1.43 \text{ [by expression (15-21)]}$$

The average number of mechanics being serviced or waiting for service is

$$L = 0.595\left(\frac{1.71/1.2}{2 - 1.71/1.2}\right) + \left(\frac{1.71}{1.2}\right) = 2.92 \text{ [by expressions (15-22) and (15-24)]}$$

from which we find the average time in the system as

$$W = \frac{L}{\lambda} = \frac{2.92}{1.71} = 1.70 \text{ minutes or 102 seconds [by expression (15-25)]}$$

On the average, a mechanic requesting a tool will wait in the queue

$$W_q = W - \frac{1}{\mu} = 102 - 50 = 52 \text{ seconds}$$

For a working day of 7½ hours or 450 minutes, on the average 450λ mechanics request tools at the counter. Hence the average total waiting time in the queue by all arrivals is

$$(\text{number of arrivals})\ (52) = ((1.71)\ (450))\ 52 = 770(52) \text{ seconds} = 11.12 \text{ hours/day}$$

whereas the total service time amounts to (number of arrivals) times ($1/\mu$) seconds, or 770(50)/3600 = 10.69 hours/day. If two clerks are at the counter, working a total of 15 hours per day, the total idle time is 15 − 10.69 = 4.31 hours.

Verify some of the operating characteristics for S = 3 and S = 4 clerks, summarized in Table 15-5.

For each additional server, the idle time increases by 7.5 hours. On the other hand, the number of mechanics in the system and their waiting time both decrease. Idle time of the servers and waiting time for the mechanics are both costly to the firm.

Table 15-5. *Operating characteristics for S = 2, 3, and 4 servers*

Operating Characteristic	S = 2	S = 3	S = 4
P_0	0.167	0.229	0.239
P(all clerks busy)	0.595	0.210	0.064
L	2.92	1.615	1.460
W_q	52 sec	6.67 sec	1.23 sec
Daily waiting time	11.12 hr	1.43 hr	0.26 hr
Daily clerk time	15.0 hr	22.5 hr	30.0 hr
Daily service time	10.69 hr	10.69 hr	10.69 hr
Daily idle time	4.31 hr	11.81 hr	19.31 hr
Daily cost of clerk time at $8/hr	$120.00	$180.00	$240.00
Daily cost of waiting time at $16/hr	$177.92	$ 22.88	$ 4.16
Total daily cost	$297.92	$202.88	$244.16

The cost of the servers is monotonically increasing, and the cost of waiting time is monotonically decreasing, as the number of servers increases. Their total will therefore have a unique minimum for some number (or adjacent numbers) of servers.

Assume that the hourly rate including fringe benefits is \$8 for clerks and \$16 for mechanics. Then the total expected cost is lowest for $S = 3$ clerks.

15-10 THE EFFECTS OF POOLING

One benefit of the study of theoretical models of queues is that, even though the models we can handle are rather limited, they may indicate some general principles that hold true in most situations. One of these is the reduction in average waiting times that can be achieved by pooling, i.e., combining a number of independent service facilities, each of which provides the same type of service, into one central location.

Consider this example. Two departments in a hospital each have a one-person diagnostic lab attached to them, providing a large but similar range of tests. At each lab, requests for tests arrive as a Poisson process with rate λ. Although a particular type of test always takes about the same time, the wide range of tests means that a negative exponential distribution for test times is reasonably acceptable. Building alterations have given an opportunity to combine the two labs into one which would handle the tests for both departments. We have been asked to comment on the benefits of this move. Obviously one major consideration is the waiting time before a test can be started. Will combining the two labs change this, and if so, by how much?

As we have set them up, each of the labs can be modeled as an $M|M|1$ queue, with arrival rate λ. If the two labs are combined, requests for tests will arrive at a rate 2λ. Since the separate arrival processes were independent, this process will also be Poisson. So we can model the pooled lab as an $M|M|2$ queue with arrival rate 2λ. In Table 15-6, we compare the average delay for a test at either of the labs with the case when the facilities are pooled. We assume that $1/\mu = 1$ hour.

Table 15-6. W_q *for the separate and combined labs*

λ/μ	Unpooled: $M\|M\|1$ (arrival rate λ)	Pooled: $M\|M\|2$ (arrival rate 2λ)
0.1	0.11	0.01
0.2	0.25	0.04
0.4	0.67	0.19
0.8	4.00	1.78
0.9	9.00	4.26

Clearly the combined lab will provide much better service. Whether or not this improvement will be enough to persuade the two department heads to relinquish control of their own labs is, of course, another question!

Usually you will find that pooling of similar service facilities considerably reduces average delay, regardless of the type of interarrival and service distributions. Although we must often take into account factors such as location, travel time for customers, and customer preferences, any one of which can upset this inequality, the general rule is that big facilities are more efficient than little ones.

15-11 OTHER MARKOVIAN MODELS

For any Markovian queueing system, we can use the balance equation method to write down the steady-state queue length equations. Although we must always presume that service times and interarrival times follow negative exponential distributions, we can allow the parameters of these distributions to depend on the number of customers in the system. For example, we might assume that servers provide a faster rate of service when they see more customers in the queue, either by increasing their own rate or by calling in extra servers, or that the arrival rate of customers depends on the number of customers in the queue. Let us consider a system whose transition diagram is given in Figure 15-4. Here both the arrival and service rates are state dependent.

The balance equations are

$$
\begin{aligned}
\lambda_0 P_0 &= \mu_1 P_1 \\
(\lambda_1 + \mu_1)P_1 &= \mu_2 P_2 + \lambda_0 P_0 \\
&\ \vdots \\
(\lambda_{N-1} + \mu_{N-1})P_{N-1} &= \mu_N P_N + \lambda_{N-2} P_{N-2} \\
\mu_N P_N &= \lambda_{N-1} P_{N-1}
\end{aligned}
\tag{15-26}
$$

We can cancel out terms in (15-26) and solve the equations. The general solution is

$$
P_n = \frac{\lambda_{n-1}\lambda_{n-2} \cdots \lambda_0}{\mu_n \mu_{n-1} \cdots \mu_1} P_0, \qquad 1 < n \leq N \tag{15-27}
$$

There are two special cases of the system depicted in Figure 15-4 which are worth mentioning. One of these is the class of models in which the pool of potential customers is finite, sometimes referred to as *machine repair problems*. So far, the

Figure 15-4. *A state-dependent service and arrival rate model.*

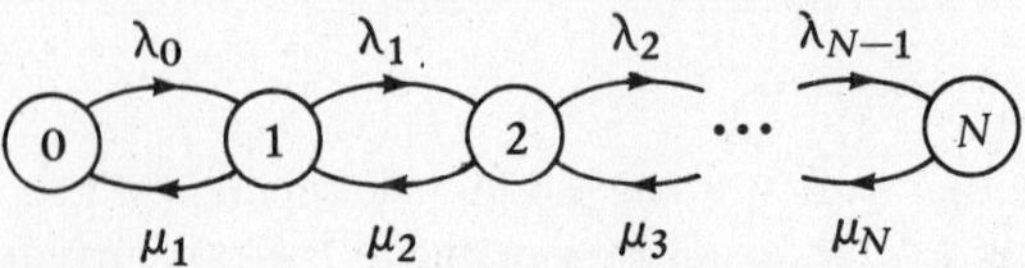

calling population has been assumed to be infinitely large, so that the input process did not depend on the number of units in the system. For many industrial applications, the calling population is so small that this assumption is no longer reasonable. For instance, it may consist of a limited number of machines on a factory floor, each of which may break down. A breakdown represents an arrival, while a repair completion represents a departure. Once a machine has been repaired, it reenters the pool of potential arrivals. Therefore, each arrival decreases the rate of arrivals, and each departure increases the rate of arrivals.

Let us assume that an operator is in charge of 4 identical machines. On the basis of the first few hours of operation for a new production run (after the operator has become thoroughly familiar with the process), the production engineer estimates that, on the average, each machine halts and requires the operator's attention about 6 times per hour, and that the operator takes, on the average, 2 minutes to service a machine. Both the interarrival and service time patterns seem to follow approximately negative exponential distributions. Can one operator properly handle 4 machines, or is the total machine down time excessively large?

Expressing the arrival rates and service rates for each machine on an hourly basis, we obtain $\lambda = 6$, $\mu = 60/2 = 30$. The state of the system refers to the number of machines requiring attention, so that, in terms of the general model in Figure 15-4, we have $N = 4$, $\lambda_0 = 4\lambda$, $\lambda_1 = 3\lambda$, $\lambda_2 = 2\lambda$, $\lambda_3 = \lambda$, and $\mu_1 = \mu_2 = \mu_3 = \mu_4 = \mu$.

From (15-27), we can find the following steady-state results:

$$P_n = \frac{4!}{(4-n)!}\left(\frac{\lambda}{\mu}\right)^n P_0, \qquad \text{for } n = 1, 2, 3, 4$$

so that

$$P_0 = \frac{1}{1 + \frac{4!}{3!}\left(\frac{\lambda}{\mu}\right) + \frac{4!}{2!}\left(\frac{\lambda}{\mu}\right)^2 + \frac{4!}{1!}\left(\frac{\lambda}{\mu}\right)^3 + \frac{4!}{0!}\left(\frac{\lambda}{\mu}\right)^4}$$

Since $\lambda/\mu = 0.2$, $P_0 = 0.398$. The operator is thus idle about 40 percent of the time, waiting for machines to require service. From this result, we can find P_n, the fraction of time that n machines require service:

$$P_1 = \frac{4!}{3!}0.2\,(0.398) = 0.319 \qquad P_2 = 0.191 \qquad P_3 = 0.077 \qquad P_4 = 0.015$$

The average number of machines being serviced or waiting for service is

$$L = \sum_{n=1}^{N} nP_n = 0.990$$

We note that the average arrival rate per hour is not λ, but

$$\text{(15-28)} \qquad \sum_{n=0}^{N} \lambda(N-n)P_n = \lambda\left(N - \sum_{n=1}^{N} nP_n\right) = \lambda(N-L)$$

By analogy with the infinite calling population case, $L = \lambda(N - L)W$. Hence, the average downtime per machine per service request is

$$W = \frac{L}{\lambda(N - L)} = \frac{0.99}{6(4 - 0.99)} = 0.0548 \text{ hours}$$

or about 3.3 minutes per service request. During 1 hour of operation, the average number of arrivals is 6(4 − 0.99) = 18.06 [by expression (15-28)]. Hence, the total downtime per hour for all 4 machines taken together is 18.06 (0.0548) = 0.99 hours or 59.4 minutes. Of this time, $18.06W_q = 18.06[0.0548 - (1/30)] = 0.388$ hour, or 23.3 minutes, is spent waiting for service. So, on the average, a fraction (0.388/4) = 0.097, or 9.7 percent, of the productive capacity of all machines is lost as downtime waiting for the operator.

Another special case of the system in Figure 15-4 has considerable application in the design of telephone systems. Consider this situation. Incoming calls (customers) arrive as a Poisson process at a telephone exchange that has a total of S lines (servers) available. The distribution of the length of calls is approximately negative exponential, with mean $1/\mu$.

If calls are permitted to wait (*blocked calls delayed*), an M|M|S model is appropriate, so by (15-21) the expected number of lines in use is λ/μ, the average number of calls waiting is given by (15-22), and the probability that a call will have to wait is given by (15-20). In this context, (15-20) is known as the *Erlang*-C formula, after the Danish mathematician who first published this work in 1917.

What if calls that do not find a line available are cleared from the system (*blocked calls cleared*)? Only as many calls as we have lines (S) are permitted in the system, so an appropriate model is M|M|S|S. In terms of Figure 15-4, we have N = S, $\lambda_{n-1} = \lambda$, $\mu_n = n\mu$, for $n = 0, 1, 2, \ldots, S$. So from (15-27)

$$P_n = \frac{(\lambda/\mu)^n}{n!} P_0, \qquad \text{for } n \leq S$$

Since this depends only on the ratio λ/μ, $a = \lambda/\mu$ is often called the *offered load* and is expressed in units called *erlangs*. Thus

$$P_n = \frac{a^n}{n!} \Big/ \sum_{k=0}^{S} \frac{a^k}{k!}, \qquad \text{for } n \leq S$$

The fraction of calls which will be cleared is given by the well-known *Erlang-B formula*, sometimes written as $B(S, a)$. Any call that arrives when all S lines are busy will be cleared. The fraction of time when this is so, and hence the fraction of calls lost, is

$$\text{(15-29)} \qquad B(S, a) = P_S = \frac{a^S}{S!} \Big/ \sum_{k=0}^{S} \frac{a^k}{k!}$$

Surprisingly, (15-29) can be shown to hold for any call length distribution.

What about more general Markovian systems? Provided the system has a finite number of states, there is always the possibility of solving the balance equations numerically. As an example of this, note that if we replace the first equation in (15-26) with the equation $\sum_{n=0}^{N} P_n = 1$, the entire system of equations can be written in matrix form as

$$\begin{bmatrix} 1 & 1 & 1 & & \cdots & & 1 \\ -\lambda_0 & (\lambda_1 + \mu_1) & -\mu_2 & & & & \\ & -\lambda_1 & (\lambda_2 + \mu_2) & -\mu_3 & & & \\ & & \ddots & \ddots & \ddots & & \\ & & & -\lambda_{N-2} & (\lambda_{N-1} + \mu_{N-1}) & -\mu_N & \\ & & & & -\lambda_{N-1} & \mu_N & \end{bmatrix} \begin{bmatrix} P_0 \\ P_1 \\ \cdot \\ \cdot \\ \cdot \\ P_N \end{bmatrix} = \begin{bmatrix} 1 \\ 0 \\ 0 \\ \cdot \\ \cdot \\ 0 \end{bmatrix}$$

We could now apply the technique of Gaussian elimination (see Appendix A) to find the solution to this system. What if the number of states is infinite? Probably the best thing to do is to consider an approximate model on which you have imposed a finite but very large waiting space. Provided the original system does tend to some steady-state distribution, the differences between its state probabilities and those of the finite approximation should be very small.

15-12 QUEUEING TABLES AND GRAPHS

The computations of operating characteristics are often extremely time-consuming. Since they all depend on a small number of parameters, λ, μ, S, and N, a number of extensive tables and graphs have been published for the most commonly used operating characteristics. These are some of the important ones:

Hillier, F. S., and O. S. Yu. *Queueing Tables and Graphs*. Amsterdam: Elsevier/North-Holland, 1979.

Peck, L. G., and R. N. Hazelwood. *Finite Queueing Tables*. New York: Wiley, 1958. Lists P_n for $M|M|S$ queues with finite calling population.

Bowman, E. H., and R. B. Fetter, Ed. *Analysis of Industrial Operations*. Homewood, Ill.: Irwin, 1959.
(1) Graphs of μW_q versus λ/μ for $M|M|S$ queues.
(2) Graphs of optimum number of machines assigned to a service crew as a function of machine down cost and labor cost.

Bhat, U. N. "Two Measures of Describing Queue Behavior," *Operations Research*, March–April 1972.
Most queueing systems are periodically interrupted and then started anew, usually with empty queues. In order to determine whether a steady-state analysis can adequately describe the behavior of the system during the major portion of its operation, one should know how fast the system approaches the steady state. Bhat gives extensive tables that show the transient behavior of the system as a function of the number of arrivals.

15-13 NONEXPONENTIAL ARRIVAL AND SERVICE DISTRIBUTIONS

We have seen that Poisson arrivals and negative exponential service time distributions give rise to relatively simple balance equations for the steady-state probabilities. For other distributions, where the probability of a transition depends on the length of time that the system occupies a given state, the expressions become much more complicated. Yet there are many real-life situations where both the interarrival time and the service time distributions are appreciably different from the exponential.

Although considerable progress has been made in describing the probabilistic behavior of waiting line systems with arbitrary distributions, relatively simple expressions for the operating characteristics have been derived only for M|G|1 systems.

For Poisson input and arbitrary service time distribution, with mean s and variance σ_s^2, we find for infinite calling populations

$$P_0 = 1 - \lambda s$$

Although the probabilities of the other states are not geometrically distributed, there is a formula for the mean number of customers in the queue.

THE POLLACZEK–KHINCHIN FORMULA

(15-30) $$L_q = \frac{\lambda^2\sigma_s^2 + (\lambda s)^2}{2(1 - \lambda s)}, \qquad \text{provided } \lambda s < 1$$

The other operating characteristics can be found from

$$L = L_q + \lambda s \qquad L = \lambda W \qquad W_q = W - s$$

The Pollaczek–Khinchin formula suggests another basic principle that holds for most systems. Note that for a fixed average service time s, queue length and waiting times increase as the variance of the service time increases. Thus, the performance of the system can be improved by reducing the variance of the service time. If the variance of the service time can be reduced to zero, i.e., an M|D|1 system, then service times become a constant and the operating characteristics are minimized, with

$$L_q = \frac{(\lambda s)^2}{2(1 - \lambda s)}$$

Note that this is half as large as for the equivalent M|M|1 system.

Although there is no result like (15-30) for arbitrary input processes, there are a number of bounds on the operating characteristics available. If the service time distribution has mean s and variance σ_s^2, and if the interarrival distribution has mean a and variance σ_a^2, then for any GI|G|1 queue

(15-31) $$W_q \leq \frac{\sigma_a^2 + \sigma_s^2}{2(a - s)}, \qquad \text{for } a > s$$ *(Kingman's bound)*

Bounds on the other characteristics follow from $L_q = W_q/a$ and $W = W_q + s$.

Expression (15-31) suggests the important principle that for most queues the mean delay can also be reduced by reducing the variance of the interarrival time distribution.

One method that allows us to approximate other distributions while retaining the balance equation solution is the *method of stages*, in which we approximate distributions by compound systems of negative exponentially distributed stages. For example, suppose we require a service distribution with mean $1/\mu$ and variance $1/k\mu^2$. This can be produced by assuming that the distribution consists of k exponential stages, each with mean $1/k\mu$, i.e., an *Erlang-k distribution*.

The state of the system now represents the number of service stages that must be completed in order to service all the customers in the system. Thus, state $nk + j$ means that there are $n + 1$ customers in the system and that the customer in service has completed $k - j + 1$ service stages. Each stage of service completed decreases the state variable by one, whereas the arrival of a customer increases the state variable by k.

Suppose the service time consists of three exponentially distributed stages. Transitions from one state to another are again independent of the length of time a given state has been occupied. The steady-state balance equations can be obtained from Figure 15-5 in the usual manner. Of course, the resulting state probabilities, P_0, P_1, P_2, . . ., will refer to the number of service stages required. The probability distribution of the number of customers can easily be obtained from them. The probability of 1 customer in the system is $P_1 + P_2 + P_3$, the probability of 2 customers in the system is $P_4 + P_5 + P_6$, and so on. Formulas have been derived for the queue length distributions for $M|E_k|1$ and $E_k|M|1$ queues, but more complex stage models will usually have to be solved by the numerical method, which we outlined in Section 15-11. Further details of the method of stages can be found in Chapter 4 of Kleinrock, Volume 1, listed in the references.

Figure 15-5. *Transition diagram for an* $M|E_3|1$ *queue.*

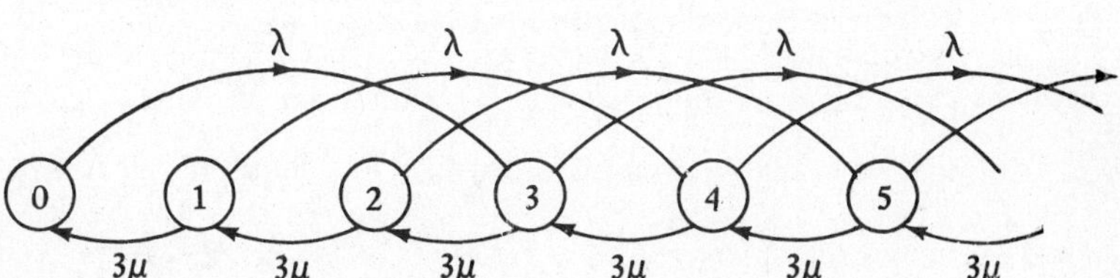

*15-14 MARKOVIAN NETWORKS

Many of the queueing situations we would like to model actually involve a network of nodes around which customers travel, rather than a single service facility. The output of one of these nodes may form part or all of the input to the next node. If we consider a model of a large computer system, for example, jobs (requests for service) are entered from a number of terminals and stored on disk until they can be handled by the central processor. Each job may receive a fixed amount of processing and then be returned to the disk unit or some output device such as a lineprinter. Jobs may generate requests for data to be read from magnetic tape, or for other programs to be loaded into the central processor.

Volume 2 of Kleinrock (listed in the references) looks at a number of probabilistic models that have been used to study specific parts of this problem. There are, however, very few models that are available for studying the behavior of a queueing network as a whole. The difficulty is that the stream of customers leaving a particular service facility usually cannot be represented as a simple stochastic process. As a result, when this stream arrives at the next service facility, we find that we have no formulas available to determine its queueing behavior. The output from this node will be yet more complicated, and so forth.

There is, however, a class of Markovian queueing networks for which steady-state queue length distributions can be found relatively easily. We have a network of service facilities for which

(15-32)
1. All external input streams are Poisson.
2. Service time distributions at each node are exponential.
3. On leaving a node, there is a fixed probability that a customer will travel to another particular node.
4. There is unlimited waiting space at each node.

Such a system is an example of a *Jackson network*.

In the example drawn in Figure 15-6, external traffic arrives at each of nodes (1) and (2) as Poisson streams with rates γ_1 and γ_2, respectively. On leaving (1), a customer goes to node (3) with probability p or to (2) with probability $(1 - p) = q$. Node (3) receives all the output from (2). A fraction r of the customers who leave node (3) go to (2). A fraction $s = 1 - r$ leave the network entirely. The service rates at node (i) is μ_i, $i = 1,2,3$.

Let us calculate the rate, λ_i, at which arrivals occur at each of the nodes. Obviously $\lambda_1 = \gamma_1$, since the only input to node (1) is the external Poisson process. Now

$$[\text{input rate to } (2)] = q[\text{output rate from } (1)] + r[\text{output rate from } (3)] + \gamma_2$$

Figure 15-6. A *simple Jackson network.*

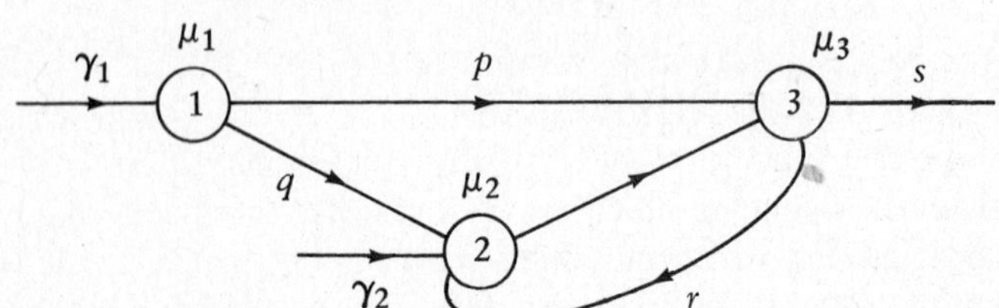

and

$$[\text{input rate to (3)}] = p\,[\text{output rate from (1)}] + [\text{output rate from (2)}]$$

So, in steady state,

$$\lambda_1 = \gamma_1 \quad \lambda_2 = q\lambda_1 + r\lambda_3 + \gamma_2 \quad \lambda_3 = p\lambda_1 + \lambda_2$$

These are called *traffic equations.*

In general, if we have a system of N nodes and if r_{ij} is the probability that a customer goes to node j on leaving node i and $1 - \Sigma_{j=1}^{N} r_{ij}$ is the probability that he or she instead leaves the network permanently, the rates of flow into each node, $\lambda_1, \ldots, \lambda_N$, satisfy

$$\text{(15-33)} \qquad \lambda_i = \gamma_i + \sum_{j=1}^{N} \lambda_j r_{ji} \qquad \text{or} \qquad \boldsymbol{\lambda} = \boldsymbol{\gamma} + \boldsymbol{\lambda}\mathbf{R}$$

where $\boldsymbol{\lambda} = (\lambda_1, \ldots, \lambda_N)$, $\boldsymbol{\gamma} = (\gamma_1, \ldots, \gamma_N)$, and $\mathbf{R} = \begin{bmatrix} r_{11} & \cdots & r_{1N} \\ & & \vdots \\ r_{N1} & \cdots & r_{NN} \end{bmatrix}$.

In our example, $\boldsymbol{\gamma} = (\gamma_1, \gamma_2, 0)$ and $\mathbf{R} = \begin{bmatrix} 0 & q & p \\ 0 & 0 & 1 \\ 0 & r & 0 \end{bmatrix}$. We can again solve this system of linear equations by a technique such as Gaussian elimination (see Appendix A).

So far, we have only used the concept of *conservation of flow* in the network. It turns out, however, that we can write down the joint steady-state queue length distribution. Let $P(k_1, k_2, \ldots, k_N)$ be the probability that the number of customers at node i is k_i, $i = 1, \ldots, N$. Then:

Theorem. For any network satisfying the conditions (15-32),

$$\text{(15-34)} \quad P(k_1, k_2, \ldots, k_N) = \left(1 - \frac{\lambda_1}{\mu_1}\right)\left(\frac{\lambda_1}{\mu_1}\right)^{k_1}\left(1 - \frac{\lambda_2}{\mu_2}\right)\left(\frac{\lambda_2}{\mu_2}\right)^{k_2} \cdots \left(1 - \frac{\lambda_N}{\mu_N}\right)\left(\frac{\lambda_N}{\mu_N}\right)^{k_N}$$

provided $\lambda_1/\mu_1, \lambda_2/\mu_2, \ldots, \lambda_N/\mu_N < 1$.

The general proof of this result requires rather complex notation, so we will omit it. You can easily check that it appears correct by writing down the balance equations for a simple network and verifying that the appropriate form of (15-34) is a solution for them.

Note that (15-34) can be written as

$$P(k_1, k_2, \ldots, k_N) = P_1(k_1)P_2(k_2) \cdots P_N(k_N)$$

where $P_i(k_i)$ is the queue length probability distribution of an M|M|1 queue with arrival rate λ_i and service rate μ_i. We thus see that in steady state, the queue lengths are independent. However, it is not true that each node is an M|M|1 queue, as internal flows in the network may not be Poisson. Thus, the steps required to determine the joint queue length distribution for a network satisfying the conditions (15-32) are

1. Set up the *routing matrix* **R**.
2. Solve the *traffic equations* $\lambda = \gamma + \lambda\mathbf{R}$.
3. Check that $\lambda_i < \mu_i$, $i = 1, \ldots, N$.

Then the joint steady-state queue length distribution is given by (15-34).

In our example, provided $\gamma_1 < \mu_1$, $(\gamma_1(1 - ps) + \gamma_2)/s < \mu_2$, $(\gamma_1 + \gamma_2)/s < \mu_3$,

$$P(k_1, k_2, k_3) =$$

$$\left(1 - \frac{\gamma_1}{\mu_1}\right)\left(\frac{\gamma_1}{\mu_1}\right)^{k_1}\left(1 - \frac{\gamma_1(1 - ps) + \gamma_2}{s\mu_2}\right)\left(\frac{\gamma_1(1 - ps) + \gamma_2}{s\mu_2}\right)^{k_2}\left(1 - \frac{\gamma_1 + \gamma_2}{s\mu_3}\right)\left(\frac{\gamma_1 + \gamma_2}{s\mu_3}\right)^{k_3}$$

If the network has no external input or output streams and if it contains a finite number of K customers, then the rate at which customers arrive at a node will depend on the service rates of the nodes that feed it and the routing matrix. In this case, for any possible state $(k_1, k_2, \ldots, k_N)$, $(k_1 + k_2 + \cdots + k_N = K)$,

$$P(k_1, k_2, \ldots, k_N) = C\,(x_1)^{k_1}(x_2)^{k_2}\cdots(x_N)^{k_N} \tag{15-35}$$

where $x_1, x_2, \ldots, x_N$ are the solutions of the traffic equations,

$$\mu_i x_i = \sum_{j=1}^{N} \mu_j x_j r_{ji}, \qquad \text{for } i = 1, \ldots, N \tag{15-36}$$

and where C is a normalizing constant such that the sum of the probabilities over all possible states is 1. Note that the system of equations (15-36) is not well determined. One of the x_i's must be given some arbitrary value to solve the system.

Conditions (15-32) can be weakened slightly and yet still lead to an easily calculated joint queue length distribution. The possibilities include multiple servers at some nodes, state-dependent service rates, and state-dependent external arrival rates. Details of some of these can be found in Kleinrock.

Although the class of queueing networks for which solutions are known is rather limited, it may well be worth trying what you feel is the "nearest" Jackson network model. The only alternative to an approximate analytic approach, namely simulation of large (more than 10-node) networks, can be very expensive, especially if some of the distributions involved are not exponential. Experience indicates that it is often far too expensive to run the simulation long enough to find joint distributions such as that of (15-34). Often, all that can be produced at reasonable cost is an average queue length at each node. Manipulating the parameters of an appropriate Jackson network model may give as much information with less effort, with greater speed, and at far lower cost.

EXERCISES

15.1 A coal mine operates its own barge loading port, which consists of one berth with automatic railroad unloading facilities.

(a) Past records of barge arrivals over a 200-day interval show the following:

Number of arrivals per day	0	1	2	3	4	5	6
Number of days	18	61	60	37	16	4	4

For what levels of significance would you accept the hypothesis that the input pattern is Poisson? Do you conclude that the Poisson approximation is good enough? What is the average arrival rate per day?

(b) Past records of berth occupancy times for barges show the following cumulative frequencies.

Fraction of working day	0.1	0.2	0.3	0.4	0.5	0.6	0.7	0.8	0.9	1.0
Number of shorter occupancy times	24	42	53	63	75	85	90	94	98	100

The average berth occupancy time is about one-third of a working day. For what levels of significance would you accept the hypothesis that the occupancy times are approximately exponentially distributed with mean 1/3? What is your conclusion? *Hint*: To determine the theoretical frequencies for the negative exponential distribution with parameter $\mu = 1/3$, use the property that $P(a \leqslant t < b) = e^{-\mu a} - e^{-\mu b}$. The value of e^{-t} can be obtained from tables of the exponential function.

15.2 Consider exercise 15.1 again. Assuming that the average daily arrival rate is 2, and that occupancy times can be taken as the service times for loading barges with a mean time of one-third day:

(a) Determine the steady state probabilities for this queueing system.
(b) What fraction of time is the berth empty? busy?
(c) What is the average number of barges waiting to be loaded?
(d) What is the average waiting time per barge arrival?

15.3 The mine management of exercise 15.1 considers installing new rail unloading facilities that would accelerate the barge loading process. Two types of facilities are considered: one with an average barge loading time of 0.25 working day and a daily operating cost of \$800, and the other with an average loading time of 0.2 working day and a daily operating cost of \$1000. The present system has a daily operating cost of \$700, and the cost of barge waiting and servicing time is \$500 per day. Determine the operating characteristics required to compute operating costs for each of the three systems (the present one and the two new alternatives). Which installation has the lowest total daily cost?

15.4 A car wash at a busy shopping center finds the following arrival frequencies of cars requesting service per hour. Test if the arrival pattern is Poisson.

No. of arrivals	0	1	2	3	4	5	6	7	8	9	10	11	12	13	14	15	16
Frequency	1	3	5	14	20	41	68	73	77	65	52	29	20	18	6	5	3

15.5 The car wash has only a single lane, and the next car cannot go into the wash until the car in front is completely finished. Because of various types of service requests, service times vary substantially. Although extremely short service times do not occur, the assumption of negative exponentially distributed service times seems adequate. On the average, 10 cars can be served per hour, while the car arrival pattern follows the data of problem 15.4. Define a suitable queueing model and find

(a) P(car wash idle) and average number of hours car wash is idle in a 10-hour day.
(b) Average number of cars waiting to be washed.
(c) Total average waiting time of all customers arriving in a 10-hour day.

15.6 Assume now that the car wash has a capacity of only 6 cars, including the car being washed. Cars arriving when the system is full are lost. Reformulate the model and find

(a) P(car wash idle) and number of hours in a 10-hour day car wash idle.
(b) Average number of cars lost in a 10-hour day.
(c) Average number of cars in the system.
(d) The probability of finding more than 2 cars in the system.
(e) The net profit per 10-hour day, if each car brings in an average revenue of $5, the fixed cost of operating the facility is $10/hour, and the variable cost when the facility is washing a car is $16/hour.

15.7 A downtown car service station has facilities for a maximum of 4 cars being serviced or waiting for service on its premises. Past experience indicates that no potential customers join the queue once these 4 places are filled. The arrival rate of customers is 24 per hour during off-peak hours, and the input process is approximately Poisson. The service times are exponential with a mean of 3 minutes.

(a) Find the steady-state probabilities for this system.
(b) What is the average idle time of the attendant?
(c) What is the fraction of customers lost? If the average profit per customer is $0.80, what is the lost profit per hour? What is the average waiting time of an arrival?

15.8 An office has two inward telephone lines. One erlang of Poisson traffic attempts to use the lines, and the mean length of a call has been found to be 3 minutes.

(a) If blocked calls are delayed and call lengths are exponential, what is the probability that neither of the lines are busy?
(b) If blocked calls are cleared, what fraction of calls will be lost, and what is the probability that neither of the lines is busy? How would your answer change if we found that the standard deviation of call length were 2 minutes?

15.9 A small repair shop has been found to have the following characteristics. The shop does not accept any new work when there are 3 jobs in the shop. Of the 2 workers in the shop, one takes an average of half a day for each repair, and the other takes an average of a third of a day. The same worker who started a job will finish it, and the faster worker gets called on first. Requests for service arrive at a rate of 4 per day. All distributions are negative exponential.

(a) Draw a transition diagram and write down the balance equations for the state of the system (you will need at least five states).
(b) Express the balance equations in a suitable matrix form of the type $\mathbf{Ax} = \mathbf{b}$ that could be solved by Gaussian elimination.

15.10 Consider the example in Section 15-11. Determine the average number of machines down, the average downtime per service call, the total average downtime per hour for all machines with 3, 4, and 5 machines supervised by one operator. If the firm operates 60 machines of this type, if each operator has a cost per hour of \$6, and if the lost profit per hour of downtime per machine is \$20, what is the optimal number of machines supervised by each operator?

15.11 Barges arrive at a river dam lock system at an average rate of 4 per hour. Each lock deals with traffic in only one direction to reduce the danger of collisions. The arrival pattern is approximately Poisson. The time to enter a barge into the lock, raise the barge, vacate the lock, and lower the water level in the lock is approximately normally distributed, with a mean of 10 minutes and a standard deviation of 3 minutes.

(a) Find the average fraction of time the lock is busy.
(b) Find the average number of barges waiting to be raised and the average waiting time per service request.
(c) If, by redesigning the water valve system, we can reduce the standard deviation of service times to 1 minute, by how much will this reduce average waiting time per service request?
(d) If the standard deviation of the arrival time were 1 minute, how would this tend to change your answer to (b)?

15.12 Consider the service station problem in exercise 15.7. Assume now that customers balk (i.e., refuse to join the queue) in the following manner: All customers join if fewer than 2 cars are in the service station. If 2 cars are in the service station, only 75 percent of potential customers decide to join. If 3 cars are in the service station, only 50 percent join, and if 4 cars are in the station, no additional customers join. Arrival and service distributions are otherwise unchanged.

(a) Construct a transition diagram for this system and attach transition rates to each arrow.
(b) Derive the state balance equations on the basis of this diagram. Find the steady-state probabilities.
(c) What is the average idle time of the attendant? What is the average number of customers lost?
(d) What is the average number of customers waiting for service? What is the average waiting time per customer?

15.13 An operator supervises 2 identical machines. Each has an arrival rate of λ per hour, with negative exponential interarrival times. Service times follow an Erlang distribution with $k = 2$ phases and a mean service time of $1/\mu$.

(a) Construct a transition diagram for this system and attach transition rates to each arrow.
(b) Derive the state balance equations on the basis of this diagram for $\lambda = 1$ and $\mu = 2$. Find the steady-state probabilities.
(c) What is the average idle time of the operator? What is the busy time?
(d) What is the average number of machines down (= being serviced or waiting for service)? What is the average arrival rate? What is the average downtime per service request? What is the average total downtime per hour for both machines?

15.14 Consider again problem 15.5. A more careful study shows that the service time is approximately normally distributed with a mean of 6 minutes and a standard deviation of 2 minutes. Answer questions (a), (b), and (c) under this new condition. What effect will this new condition have on the length of an average idle period?

15.15 A firm finds that it is running 2 separate service facilities, each operated by a single repairperson. Requests for work arrive at a rate of 3 per hour at one facility and at 2.5 per hour at the other. The mean service time at both places is 15 minutes. No new work is accepted after 4 P.M. Friday, and any work remaining then has to be done on overtime rates at an additional cost of $10 per hour per person. Assuming exponential distributions and steady state.

(a) Calculate the expected additional overtime cost each week.

(b) The firm calculates that it will incur an extra cost of $10 per week for traveling if the 2 facilities are pooled. Considering any overtime reduction that may occur, should the firm pool the facilities?

15.16 A simple queueing network consists of 3 nodes. External Poisson streams arrive at nodes I and II with parameters γ_1 and γ_2, respectively. A fraction p of the customers leaving I join the queue at II, while $q = (1 - p)$ go to III. A fraction r of the customers leaving II go to I, while $s = (1 - r)$ go to III. The service time at node i is negative exponential with mean $1/\mu_i$, and there is a single server at each node.

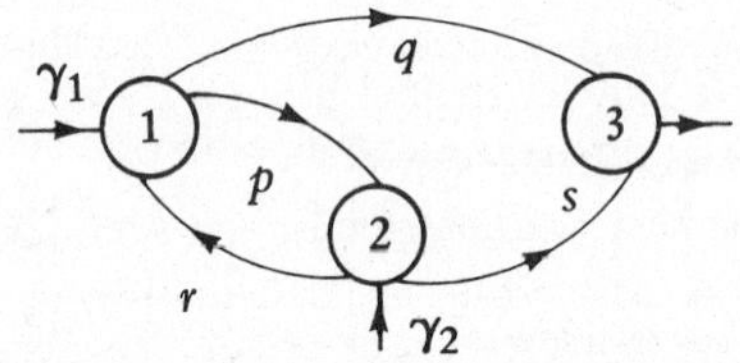

(a) Set up the traffic equations for the network and solve them so as to find the steady-state queue length distributions. What extra conditions on the network do we need?

(b) Write down an expression for the average number of customers in the system in steady state.

15.17 Consider a three-node network around which customers must travel cyclically. The service time at node i is negative exponentially distributed with mean $1/\mu_i$, $i = 1,2,3$. If there is only one customer in the system, set up balance equations to calculate the fraction of time he or she spends at each node, and solve them. Check that your answer agrees with that given by the use of (15-35).

REFERENCES

The journal *Operations Research* has from the start devoted a substantial portion of its space to queueing problems. The reader is also referred to Chapter 16 on Simulation.

Bhat, U. N. "Sixty Years of Queueing Theory," *Management Science*, Vol. 15, Feb. 1969. Reviews the major strides taken by queueing theory. Refutes the accusation that the systems solvable mathematically are of little practical use, includes an extensive bibliography.

Cooper, Robert B. *Introduction to Queueing Theory*, 2nd ed, New York: Elsevier/North-Holland, 1981. An intermediate level text with emphasis on telephone traffic models. It contains many results not found elsewhere.

Edie, Leslie C. "Traffic Delays at Toll Booths," *Operations Research*, Vol. 2, May 1954 (reprinted in C. W. Churchman et al., *Introduction to O. R.*, Chapter 15. New York: Wiley, 1957). A complete study of the Port of New York Authority toll booth operations.

Gross, D., and Harris, C. M. *Fundamentals of Queueing Theory*. New York: Wiley, 1974. A good general reference for most models. Especially good on statistical inference and design for queues.

Howard, Ronald A. *Dynamic Programming and Markov Processes*. Cambridge, Mass.: MIT Press, 1960. Chapter 8 deals with continuous-time Markovian decision processes and shows how the techniques discussed in Chapter 14 of this text can be adapted to such problems that cover some queueing systems.

Kleinrock, Leonard. *Queueing Systems* (2 vols.). New York: Wiley, 1975. The most interesting present applications of queueing theory are in the areas of computers and communications systems. Volume 1 covers all of the standard queueing models, while Volume II considers their application to problems in communications networks. Both are highly recommended.

Krell, Bruce E., and Maria Armino. "Queueing Theory Applied to Data Processing Networks," *Interfaces*, Vol. 12, Aug. 1982. Jackson networks used to model a private computer communications network.

Lee, A. M. *Applied Queueing Theory*. New York: Macmillan, 1966. Contains some interesting case histories that apply queueing theory to practical problems.

Maaloe, Erik. "Approximation Formulae for Estimation of Waiting-Time in Multiple Channel Queueing System," *Management Science*, Vol. 19, Feb. 1973. Shows how the waiting time in a multiple channel system with Erlang service time distribution can be approximated as a fraction of the corresponding single channel system.

McKeown, Patrick G. "An Application of Queueing Analysis to the New York State Child Abuse and Maltreatment Register Telephone Reporting System," *Interfaces*, Vol. 9, May 1979. A neat application of the Erlang-B formula.

Newell, G. F. *Applications of Queueing Theory*. London: Chapman and Hall, 1971. The author takes a novel approach to queueing based on graphical methods of representation, deterministic fluid approximations, and diffusion approximations.

Prabhu, N. U. *Queues and Inventories*. Wiley: New York, 1965. Classical treatment of queues using transforms. A very complete text, but intended for the advanced student, fairly demanding mathematically.

Siegel, Stan, and Paul Torelli. "The Value of Queueing Theory: A Case Study," *Interfaces*, Vol. 9, Nov. 1979. An application of Jackson networks to a naval command and control system.

CHAPTER SIXTEEN

Simulation

To simulate is to duplicate the dynamic behavior of some aspect of a system, real or proposed, by substituting the properties of another system for the essential properties of the system simulated. In operations research, we usually build a descriptive mathematical model to represent the properties of the system simulated. This descriptive mathematical model is then used to trace step by step how the system responds to various inputs provided to the model. Simulations are thus *input–output models*. This means that simulations are "run," rather than "solved."

Through simulation, the operations researcher has at his or her disposal a laboratory technique for observation and experimentation, which has long been part of the scientific methods in the physical, medical, and biological sciences. On a computer, the viability of proposed policies for operating a system can be explored and compared with relative ease. Practical evaluations would take years to accomplish by real-life observations and would be very costly. Simulation often provides the only practical vehicle for experimentation with real or proposed systems.

The basic concepts involved in simulation may look deceptively simple. However, putting them into practice to obtain valid and reliable results is far from simple. Performing simulations is extremely time-consuming. Therefore, for all practical purposes, simulations are always performed on computers.

Nowhere in applied operations research does the systems approach appear as naturally as in simulation. Much of the discussion in Chapter 1 on systems and model building within a systems framework is therefore directly applicable to this chapter. Before embarking into this chapter, you may want to review the relevant sections of Chapter 1, in particular Sections 1-5 and 1-6. When we discuss validation of simulation studies in Section 16-7, it may also be helpful to refer to the sections on testing and sensitivity analysis, Sections 1-17 and 1-18.

In one short chapter, we cannot do justice to a subject as vast as simulation. All we can do is to introduce the basic aspects and demonstrate them with some simple examples. For a detailed treatment, we refer you to the references listed at the end of this chapter, particularly the excellent text by Shannon (1975).

16-1 SIMULATION OF AN INVENTORY SYSTEM

The basic principles of simulation will be explored initially by simulating the performance of a proposed inventory control model. As discussed in Chapter 1, such a simulation may be part of testing the theoretical model as to its suitability before proceeding to its implementation. In order to provide some appreciation of the realism possible in simulation in contrast to the simplifications and approximations needed for any theoretical model, we will use the (Q, r) inventory control model presented in Chapter 12, Section 12-11.

A wholesale distributor proposes to use that model for all major products stocked. This model has the following policy: Whenever the inventory position (= inventory on hand plus any replenishments outstanding) falls to or below a reorder point r, a replenishment of size Q is placed. Before implementing this model, the wholesaler would like to ascertain how well it performs in practice. Simulation is the tool for such a test! How do we go about this task?

We select a random sample of an appropriate size from the population of all products to be controlled by the (Q, r) model. For each product i in the sample, we assemble all input data needed. These are then used to compute the optimal control parameters Q_i and r_i. Next, we construct a simulation model for the inventory behavior over time. Once we are satisfied that the simulation model properly reflects the system's dynamic behavior, we simulate the operation of the inventory for each product in the random sample, based on its control parameters Q_i and r_i. This will allow us to collect performance statistics on average annual costs, on the fraction of lost sales, and on other characteristics of interest. Finally, we extrapolate these statistics to obtain estimates of the system's performance for the population of all products to be controlled by the (Q, r) model.

Let us now go through these steps for a particular product in the sample. From past records of customer orders, the daily demand is seen to be a random variable with the following empirical distribution:

Demand	0	1	2	3	4	5	6	7	8	9	10	11	12	13
Frequency	0.26	0.14	0.12	0.10	0.08	0.07	0.06	0.05	0.04	0.03	0.02	0.01	0.01	0.01

The daily demand distribution is extremely skewed, having an average of 3.2 units per day and a standard deviation of 3.2. Similarly, past records indicate that the replenishment lead time averages about 10 working days, but, in fact, is a random variable with the following approximate frequency distribution:

Lead time	7	8	9	10	11	12	13	14
Frequency	0.07	0.12	0.18	0.25	0.20	0.10	0.05	0.03

These data could be used to derive the lead-time demand distribution, $f(x)$, required in the (Q, r) model. However, in order to reduce both the cost of data collection and the cost of computations, the wholesaler decides to approximate the lead-time demand distribution in the model by a normal distribution, based on the average lead time of 10 days. Assuming that demands on consecutive days are independent, this gives a lead-time demand distribution with a mean of $10(3.2) = 32$ and a standard deviation of $3.2(\sqrt{10}) = 10$. (See Section 10-7 of Chapter 10.) Although it is true that for a lead time that is sufficiently long the lead-time demand distribution will be approximately normal, no matter what the shape of the daily demand distribution, for highly skewed distributions a lead time of 10 days results in a rather crude approximation, particularly at the tails of the distribution.

From the daily demand distribution we can also estimate the average annual demand R. For 250 working days per year, R is $250(3.2) = 800$. Other data needed are as follows. The value of the product is \$10 per unit, the annual inventory holding cost per dollar invested is \$0.20, the inventory replenishment cost is \$4.50 per replenishment, and the shortage cost is \$1.50 per unit short. With these simplifications, the (Q, r) model yields the following optimal control parameters: $Q^* = 60$ and $r^* = 48$, with a theoretical total expected annual cost of \$157.20.

The next step in our task is to build a simulation model of the inventory system. We are interested in its cost performance over time. Since costs of an inventory system depend on the amount of stocks on hand, the number of replenishments, and the amount of shortages, it is these aspects that we want to observe over time. The model should thus describe in detail how the inventory on hand for a given product changes each day in response to incoming customer orders and to shipments received from suppliers and what conditions trigger the placement of an inventory replenishment. This system description will consist of simple material balance equations that keep track of the amount of stock on hand over time and the amount of goods on order from suppliers over time. Conditions that trigger certain actions are expressed in the form of "if . . ., then . . ." statements. We also have to supply the model with a sequence of customer orders over time as well as a sequence of replenishment lead times. Alternatively, we could build into the model mechanisms that generate these sequences from some other source of data.

This model could take the form of a detailed flow chart. We have done this in Figure 16-1 for our example. To construct this flow chart, we may have to split what in the real world looks like a single operation or a single decision point into a number of more detailed intermediate steps, which, in the simulation, are followed in a rigid sequence. The reverse may also happen—a sequence of real-life operations may be combined into a single step. Similarly, we may have to introduce steps that have no real counterparts.

In our case, the daily control procedure starts with the processing of inventory replenishments received on that day (usually received in the morning) and the processing of incoming customer orders for the day. The updated inventory file, listing all stock levels and outstanding replenishments, is then reviewed. If the stock level i plus the outstanding replenishments y for a product have been reduced by sales to the reorder point r, or below, a replenishment of size Q is scheduled. Translating this sequence of steps into the diagram of Figure 16-1, we arbitrarily assume that replen-

Figure 16-1. *Flow diagram of inventory system.*

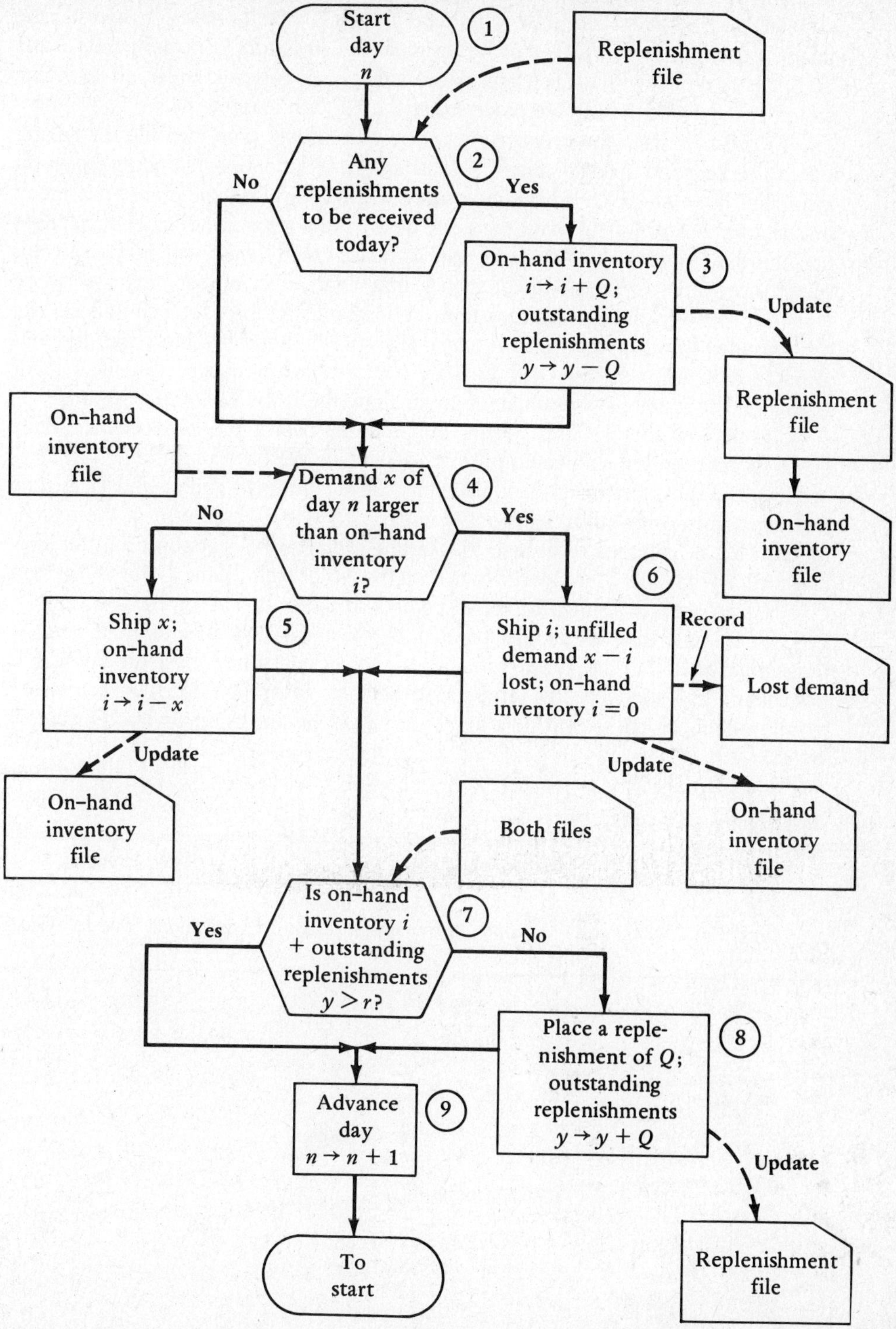

ishments received are added to the inventory prior to the processing of incoming customer orders (points 2 and 3). These are processed next (points 4, 5, and 6), and finally a decision as to whether or not to replenish inventory is made (points 7 and 8). Since we do not wish to keep track of each individual customer order, all incoming customer orders for the day are processed at the same time (point 4).

In order to trace the events in detail over *simulated time*, two files or records have to be kept and updated: an *on-hand inventory file* and an *outstanding replenishment file*. If we are given a beginning on-hand inventory balance of size i, a file of outstanding replenishments with their due dates, and a sequence of daily demands—one number for each day—then we can simulate exactly what will happen in this system over time. On the basis of such a flow chart, a computer program can be written to perform the actual simulation. Performance statistics for a simulation run are compiled from the information recorded in the on-hand inventory file, the outstanding replenishment file, and auxiliary files specifically created to collect status reports on the system. An example of an auxiliary file is the file of lost demand.

Let us now simulate this system. Suppose that over a 100-day sequence, daily demands are those shown in column 3 of Table 16-1. We have a beginning inventory of $i = 60$ (as shown in the on-hand inventory file of columns 1 and 4), and we assume that there are no replenishments outstanding, i.e., $y = 0$ (as shown in the replenishment file of columns 6 through 9). Starting on day $n = 1$ at point 1 in the flow diagram of Figure 16-1, we leave point 2 via the No branch. Since $x = 3$ is less than $i = 60$, we proceed from point 4 via point 5 to point 7. The on-hand inventory, $i = 57$, is larger than the reorder point, $r = 48$, and we advance to 9. At point 9, the *simulated time* is advanced by one day, and we start a new cycle for day $n = 2$ from point 1. Verify that this same path repeats itself through day $n = 6$. On day $n = 7$, we branch out from point 7 to point 8, since the sum of the on-hand inventory

Table 16-1. *Simulation of inventory system*

						Replenishments			
Period	Beginning On-Hand Inventory 1	Receipts 2	Demand 3	Ending On-Hand Inventory 4	Demand Lost 5	Placed 6	Lead Time 7	Date Due In 8	On Order 9
Start	—			60		—	—	—	0
1	60		3	57					
2	57		0	57					
3	57		0	57					
4	57		1	56					
5	56		6	50					
6	50		1	49					
7	49		2	47		60	8	15	60
8	47		5	42					60
9	42		0	42					60
10	42		4	38					60
11	38		5	33					60
12	33		4	29					60

Period	Beginning On-Hand Inventory 1	Receipts 2	Demand 3	Ending On-Hand Inventory 4	Demand Lost 5	Replenishments Placed 6	Lead Time 7	Date Due In 8	On Order 9
13	29		4	25					60
14	25		10	15					60
15	15	60	3	72					0
16	72		0	72					
17	72		5	67					
18	67		1	66					
19	66		10	56					
20	56		0	56					
21	56		0	56					
22	56		2	54					
23	54		6	48		60	11	34	60
24	48		6	42					60
25	42		3	39					60
26	39		1	38					60
27	38		3	35					60
28	35		0	35					60
29	35		2	33					60
30	33		2	31					60
31	31		1	30					60
32	30		0	30					60
33	30		0	30					60
34	30	60	2	88					0
35	88		2	86					
36	86		4	82					
37	82		3	79					
38	79		8	71					
39	71		4	67					
40	67		0	67					
41	67		7	60					
42	60		0	60					
43	60		4	56					
44	56		0	56					
45	56		3	53					
46	53		0	53					
47	53		9	44		60	10	57	60
48	44		12	32					60
49	32		6	26					60
50	26		6	20					60
51	20		6	14					60
52	14		2	12					60
53	12		5	7					60
54	7		0	7					60
55	7		6	1					60
56	1		0	1					60
57	1	60	0	61					0

Table 16-1. *Simulation of inventory system (continued)*

Period	Beginning On-Hand Inventory 1	Receipts 2	Demand 3	Ending On-Hand Inventory 4	Demand Lost 5	Replenishments: Placed 6	Lead Time 7	Date Due In 8	On Order 9
58	61		11	50					
59	50		0	50					
60	50		2	48		60	8	68	60
61	48		1	47					60
62	47		1	46					60
63	46		3	43					60
64	43		0	43					60
65	43		0	43					60
66	43		0	43					60
67	43		1	42					60
68	42	60	0	102					0
69	102		7	95					
70	95		0	95					
71	95		1	94					
72	94		1	93					
73	93		6	87					
74	87		4	83					
75	83		2	81					
76	81		8	73					
77	73		2	71					
78	71		5	66					
79	66		0	66					
80	66		3	63					
81	63		5	58					
82	58		5	53					
83	53		5	48		60	11	94	60
84	48		8	40					60
85	40		11	29					60
86	29		7	22					60
87	22		2	20					60
88	20		6	14					60
89	14		5	9					60
90	9		1	8					60
91	8		0	8					60
92	8		3	5					60
93	5		11	0	6				60
94	0	60	8	52					0
95	52		2	50					
96	50		0	50					
97	50		0	50					
98	50		5	45		60	8	106	60
99	45		0	45					60
100	45		10	35					60

plus the outstanding replenishments (= 47) is less than the reorder point, $r = 48$. Therefore, a replenishment of size $Q = 60$ is placed on day 7 (point 8). Let us assume that this replenishment will be received on the morning of day 15 and is available to satisfy demand on that day. Skipping to day $n = 15$, the process takes the Yes branch from point 2 and the on-hand inventory available is updated from 15 to 75. After sales of 3 are deducted for that day, the ending on-hand inventory is shown as 72. You should trace this process through for some additional days. Observe what happens on day 93.

The cost of this particular simulation run is obtained as follows:

Ordering cost: 6 replenishments at \$4.50	\$27.00
Shortage cost: 6 units short at \$1.50	\$9.00
Holding cost: Average daily ending inventory 47.55 costed for 100 out of 250 working days per year at an annual rate of (0.2)(\$10.00)	\$38.04
	\$74.04
Extrapolated to an annual basis (of 250 working days)	\$185.10

The extrapolated annual cost of this simulation differs substantially from the theoretical cost. Let us emphasize that this does not mean that something went wrong in the simulation. It is only one trial, and even a short one. The exact results obtained for this 100-day simulation run are unique to the particular sequence of daily demands and replenishment lead times used. Had we used a different set of demands, we would have found a different set of results. But, if the simulation properly reflects the real-world processes, and if the input data are representative of the real world, then these results are also representative of the type of answers usually experienced in the real world. However, to be able to draw a valid conclusion, we usually need many more runs covering a sufficient length of time.

Let us now look more formally into the structure of simulation models.

16-2 STRUCTURE OF SIMULATION MODELS

A simulation model describes the *dynamic behavior* of a system over time. In the terminology of simulation, a system is composed of *entities*—components or things whose behavior is traced through the system. Entities may belong to various types or *classes*, such as people, machines, goods, or documents in the system. They may be abstract, such as pieces of information or signals. Entities have identifying *attributes*, such as their size or their service needs, that characterize their behavior in the system. The entities of a given class will usually have the same set of attributes—but their attribute values will not necessarily be identical—and will tend to follow similar behavior patterns over time. Entities sharing some temporary attributes or some purpose at given stages in the simulation may belong to sets or *files*, which may also have attributes, such as capacity. For instance, a queue of people waiting at a service counter represents a file. There may only be room for at most N people in front of the counter.

As simulated time advances, new entities may be created and existing entities canceled; entities may change their file membership, leave a file, enter a file. Entities may engage in *activities*, either singly or jointly with other entities. During the course of the activity, entities jointly engaged in it are *bound* to one another. For instance, a machine operator (entity 1) may set up a machine (entity 2) for a new job. During the setup (activity), the two entities are bound together. They cannot engage individually in other activities at the same time. Once the machine has been set up, the operator and machine entities separate again. In simulation, activities are defined by their starting time and their finishing time. Activities may change the attributes of entities. Similarly, when entities change file membership, some of their attributes may change. At any given point in time, the system simulated has a given configuration, defined by the ongoing activities of entities, the file membership of entities, and entity and file attributes. This is the *state* of the system. Any change in the state of the system is an *event*. The sequence of events occurring represents the dynamic behavior of the system.

The components of a simulation model are therefore

1. Entities and their attributes;
2. Files of entities and their attributes;
3. Activities of entities;
4. Events or changes in the state of the system.

To fix ideas, consider the simulation of 2 car ferries between 2 ferry terminals A and B, as shown in Figure 16-2. Cars represent one class of entities, their length and weight being some of their attributes. The 2 ferries form another class of entities, with deck space and traveling speed as their attributes. The 2 docks represent files; they contain entities (cars) sharing a purpose (namely, the intent to cross by ferry) and all having the temporary attributes of waiting. The docks have attributes, such as the parking space. Arriving at one terminal and leaving from another are activities. Ferries and cars engage jointly in the activity of crossing from A to B and vice versa. During this activity, the ferry and the cars it carries are bound together. The state of the system is described by the number of cars waiting at each dock for a crossing; the status of each ferry, i.e., whether it is loading or unloading at a given dock and the number of cars currently on the ferry, or whether it is crossing and the direction of crossing and the number of cars it carries; and the events already scheduled to occur. The dynamic phenomena of the system are given by the arrival pattern of cars at each dock; how cars proceed from the dock to the ferry and vice versa; and the operating

Figure 16-2. *Car ferry system.*

Dock at A

Cars depart

Cars arrive

Ferry 2

Ferry 1

Dock at B

Cars arrive

Cars depart

characteristics of the ferries, such as traveling speed, which may be a function of their load, and the berthing process. These give rise to events, such as arrivals of cars at docks, the departure and berthing of ferries, the loading and unloading of cars.

In the inventory simulation, one class of entities consists of the daily demands, their size being the only attribute of interest to us. Another class of entities is given by the replenishments, with attributes of size and lead time. We maintain two files: the on-hand inventory file and the replenishment file. The first one is in the form of a simple *counter*, since we do not keep track of individual units of products in stock. We also introduce additional counters needed to measure the system's performance. These counters are the amount of lost demand, the inventory level accumulator needed to compute the average inventory level, and the replenishment counter (none of which are shown explicitly in the flow diagram of Figure 16-1). The events are the occurrence of the daily demand and the placing and the receipt of replenishments.

Events may be imposed on the simulation from outside, i.e., they are specified as input into the model by the analyst. The timetable of the ferries or the daily demands in the inventory simulation are possible examples. Such events are referred to as *exogenous events*. Alternatively, events may be created by the simulation model itself without explicit outside intervention. They are called *endogenous events*. They are a consequence either of an exogenous event or of another endogenous event. The start of unloading a ferry is a consequence of its berthing, the berthing is a consequence of its departure on the opposite terminal, and so on. The placing of an inventory replenishment is a consequence of a daily demand depleting stocks below the reorder point.

If all events, including the creation of new entities and their attributes, are either exogenous inputs into the simulation or deterministic consequences of other events, then the simulation is *deterministic*. For instance, if the sequence of daily demands and lead times to be used in the inventory simulation are both actually experienced inputs taken from the accounting records of the firm, and hence the two types of endogenous events of placing a replenishment and receiving a replenishment are deterministic consequences, then the simulation is deterministic. There are a number of important applications where deterministic simulations are a useful tool of analysis. Simulations of the output mix of a refinery, as a function of the input characteristics of the crude oils and the instrument settings of the various processing units in the refinery, are deterministic. Many corporate financial planning models translate forecasts by product by period into production schedules, purchasing schedules for raw materials, inventory positions, variable and fixed production costs, and, ultimately, both detailed cash flows by period and profit-and-loss statements. These models are deterministic simulations. The effects of uncertain aspects in the system are explored by considering various deterministic scenarios for possible demand forecasts and other random factors. Another example is the simulation of rail operations. For instance, traffic flow in a given network of railroad lines is simulated for various fixed departure timetables of trains at terminal points or important transfer stations in the network. In a deterministic simulation, the same set of exogenous inputs will always result in exactly the same sequence of endogenous events and hence the same simulation outputs.

A larger portion of simulations deal with systems that are subject to random phenomena. If these are modeled in the simulation, we have a *stochastic simulation* or *Monte Carlo simulation*. A stochastic simulation model has certain features that allow endogenous events to be generated internally by randomization devices. The randomness may be in terms of the timing of events (including the creation of new entities), in terms of initial attribute values of these entities or changes in attributes at later stages in the simulation, or in terms of both. For instance, rather than specify a sequence of demands and lead times, we use as input the probability distribution of daily demands and the probability distribution of lead times, and generate random demands and random lead times during the simulation. Similarly, the arrival times and characteristics of the cars may be generated internally in a simulation of a ferry system, using probability distributions derived from past actual observations of car arrivals. The randomization in a stochastic simulation is achieved with the help of *pseudorandom numbers*. Different sequences of random numbers will generate different sequences of endogenous events for the same set of probability distributions and exogenous events. Hence, the simulation output will also differ from simulation to simulation.

16-3 RANDOM NUMBERS AND OTHER VARIATES

What are random numbers? They are lists of the digits from 0 to 9 that appear to be drawn as completely independent random samples from a uniformly distributed random variable that can assume integer values 0 through 9. Table 16-2 is a short list of 5-digit random numbers.

The most popular methods used to generate random numbers are the *additive* and *multiplicative congruential methods*. The multiplicative congruential method finds the nth random number r_n, consisting of k digits, from the $(n - 1)$th random number r_{n-1} by using the recurrence relation:

$$r_n \equiv pr_{n-1} \text{ (modulo } m) \tag{16-1}$$

where p and m are positive integers, $p < m$, $m - 1$ is a k-digit number, and modulo m means that r_n is the remainder when pr_{n-1} is divided by m. Therefore, r_n and pr_{n-1} differ by an integer multiple of m. The first random number r_0, or the *seed*, is specified as an input. This method will generate a sequence of k-digit random numbers with *period* $h < m$ at which point the number r_0 occurs again, and hence the sequence repeats itself.

Table 16-2. *Uniform pseudorandom numbers*

59210	33177	29451	67204	65736	86395	57187	13396	01194	28069
79603	75509	41442	90224	50486	65290	65118	62067	04552	19342
98778	18247	75067	91908	97245	01432	36600	71223	29188	51333
27816	54589	46761	16070	73746	48897	84507	97626	25579	78945
00107	21323	95397	91528	89117	16541	61308	91074	83879	03065

Consider an example. Suppose $p = 37$, $m = 100$, and $r_0 = 53$. Since $m - 1$ is a 2-digit number, this will yield 2-digit random numbers:

$$r_1 = pr_0(\text{modulo } m) = (37)(53)(\text{modulo } 100) = 1961\,(\text{modulo } 100) = 61$$
$$r_2 = (37)(61)(\text{modulo } 100) = 2257\,(\text{modulo } 100) = 57$$
$$r_3 = (37)(57)(\text{modulo } 100) = 2109\,(\text{modulo } 100) = 09$$

and the sequence continues as (33, 21, 77, 49, 13, 81, 97, 89, . . .). You may wish to verify that the period is 20. Note that the low order digit is far from random, repeating the sequence 3, 1, 7, 9. Therefore, great care has to be taken in the input parameters used. There are certain principles that help in the proper choice of r_0 and p for any given value of m, so as to maximize the period h.

Clearly, the methods commonly used to generate random numbers are not random processes, since the sequence of numbers generated is completely determined by the input data used for the method—hence the term *pseudorandom numbers.*

It is convenient to express these uniform random numbers in the form of a fraction between 0 and 1 with a desired degree of precision of k-digits. This is achieved by dividing r_n by m, i.e., $u_n = r_n/m$ is a *uniformly distributed random decimal fraction* between 0 and 1 with at most k significant digits after the decimal point.

Most computer systems provide *random number generator* subroutines in their software packages that will generate uniform random decimal fractions between 0 and 1. Thus, you will hardly ever have to write a computer subroutine to do this.

On the basis of these uniform random decimal fractions, we can generate *random variates* (observations from a statistical population) for any probability distribution. This can be seen from Figure 16-3, which shows the cumulative distribution function of some random variable. With each value of the random variable on the x axis, we associate a value of the cumulative distribution function on the y axis. The cumulative distribution function is a transformation of the values of the random variable onto the interval [0, 1]. In fact, it can be regarded as the transformation of the random variable to a uniformly distributed random variable on the [0, 1] interval. By taking the *inverse transformation,* we can therefore generate random variates for any desired probability distribution. For example, for the distribution depicted in Figure 16-3, the fraction 0.7548 produces the value x_0 of the random variable.

This inverse transformation can sometimes be done analytically, such as for the *uniform, triangular,* or *negative exponential distribution.* For instance, for the negative exponential distribution with density function $f(x) = \lambda e^{-\lambda x}$, $x \geqslant 0$, the cumulative distribution function is

$$F(x_0) = \int_0^{x_0} \lambda e^{-\lambda x}\,dx = 1 - e^{-\lambda x_0} \tag{16-2}$$

from which we obtain the inverse transform

$$x_0 = \frac{-\log_e(1 - F(x_0))}{\lambda} \tag{16-3}$$

where $\log_e$ is the natural logarithm. Hence, if u_n is a uniform random decimal fraction

Figure 16-3. *Use of uniform random decimal fractions to generate variates from any arbitrary distribution.*

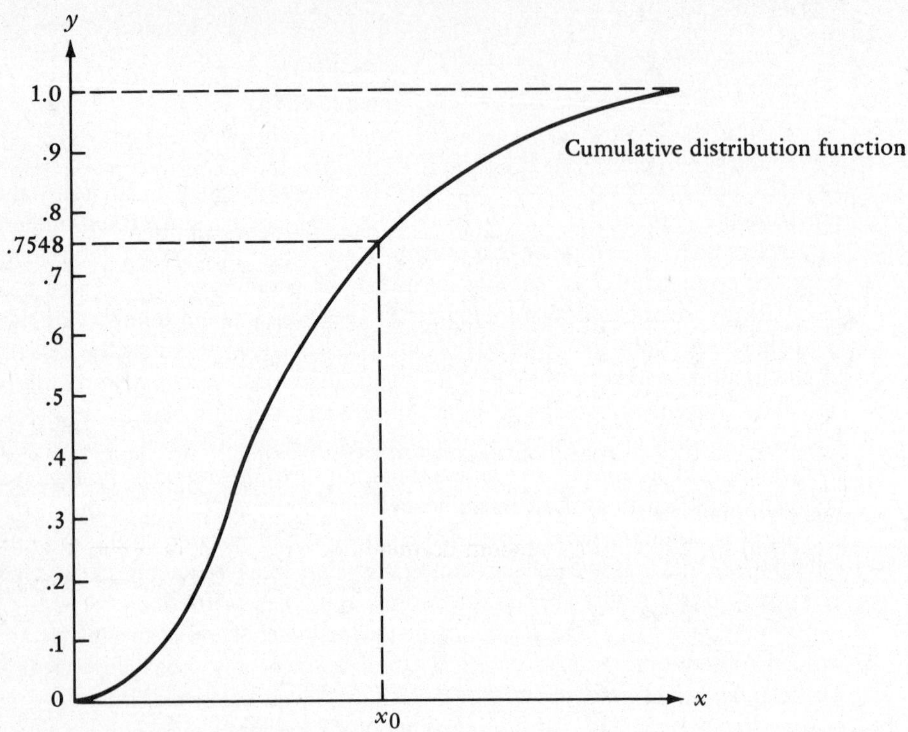

between 0 and 1, then the exponential variate associated with u_n is

$$x_n = \frac{-\log_e(1 - u_n)}{\lambda} \tag{16-4}$$

Random variates from *Erlang distributions* of order k or *gamma distributions* with parameter $a = k$ integer (Section 10-6) can be obtained as the sum of k exponential variates. Random variates from a normal distribution can be generated by taking advantage of the *central limit theorem* (see Section 10-6), which states that for large samples the sample mean $\bar{x}$ is approximately normally distributed, regardless of the distribution from which the observations were obtained. Thus, to generate a *normal random variate* or *deviate,* we simply compute the average of a number of uniform random decimal fractions, usually 12. Since a uniformly distributed random variable over the range [0, 1] has a mean of $\frac{1}{2}$ and a variance of $\frac{1}{12}$, the sum of 12 such variables has a mean of $12(\frac{1}{2}) = 6$ and a variance of $12(\frac{1}{12}) = 1$. Hence, we obtain the random variate z from a standard normal distribution $N(0, 1)$ as

$$z = \sum_{n=1}^{12} u_n - 6 \tag{16-5}$$

This is the approach used by some computer subroutines that generate approximate normal random variates from N(0, 1). The value of z generated by (16-5) can then be used to obtain a normal random variate with mean μ and standard deviation σ by

$$x = \mu + z\sigma \tag{16-6}$$

If no algebraic expressions exist or if we are dealing with discrete variables, it is always possible to use a *tabular method.* Let $x - 1$ and x be two consecutive values of a discrete random variable X, and let $F(x - 1) = P(X \leqslant x - 1)$ and $F(x) = P(X \leqslant x)$ be the corresponding values of the cumulative distribution function. Given a uniform random decimal fraction u, $0 \leqslant u < 1$, the associated random variate is found as that value x such that $F(x - 1) \leqslant u < F(x)$. Thus, with each value of x we associate a range of uniform random decimal fractions of size $P(X = x)$. If $F(x)$ is specified with up to k significant digits after the decimal point, we use uniform random decimal fractions with k significant digits. The range of u for each x is $[F(x - 1), F(x) - 10^{-k}]$, where for $x = 0$, $F(x - 1) = 0$ (specified as k zeros). Consider the daily demand distribution listed in Section 16-1. Table 16-3 lists the correspondence between the values x and the ranges of 2-digit uniform random decimal fractions. Now, refer to the table of pseudorandom numbers, Table 16-2. The first 2 digits of the table yield a random decimal fraction $u_1 = 0.59$. From Table 16-3, we see that the corresponding variate has a value of $x_1 = 3$. The second set of 2 digits in Table 16-2 yields $u_2 = 0.21$, with which we associate a value of $x_2 = 0$. Continuing in this fashion, we find

$n =$	3	4	5	6	7
u_n	0.03	0.31	0.77	0.29	0.45
x_n	0	1	6	1	2

Table 16-3. *Tabular method of inverse transformation*

Daily Demand, x	Relative Frequency	Cumulative Frequency, $F(x)$	Associated Range of Values for u
0	0.26	0.26	0.00 to 0.25
1	0.14	0.40	0.26 0.39
2	0.12	0.52	0.40 0.51
3	0.10	0.62	0.52 0.61
4	0.08	0.70	0.62 0.69
5	0.07	0.77	0.70 0.76
6	0.06	0.83	0.77 0.82
7	0.05	0.88	0.83 0.87
8	0.04	0.92	0.88 0.91
9	0.03	0.95	0.92 0.94
10	0.02	0.97	0.95 0.96
11	0.01	0.98	0.97
12	0.01	0.99	0.98
13	0.01	1.00	0.99

These are the demands for the first seven periods shown in Table 16-1. The eighth 2-digit set is used to generate a lead-time variate of 8 from the lead-time distribution. The next 16 sets are again used to generate daily demand variates, etc. Check your understanding of the tabular method by verifying the demands and lead times shown.

For a continuous random variable with a finite range, we select a suitable grid of values covering its range: $x_0, x_1, x_2, \ldots, x_n, \ldots, x_N$. For each grid point x_n, we find $F(x_n)$. The range of uniform random decimal fractions associated with the interval $[x_{n-1} < x \leq x_n]$ is $[F(x_{n-1}), F(x_n) - 10^{-k}]$ for k-digit random numbers. The exact value of x associated with a given value of u is found by interpolation (usually linear) between x_{n-1} and x_n, as

$$x = x_{n-1} + (x_n - x_{n-1})\frac{u - F(x_{n-1}) - 10^{-k}}{F(x_n) - F(x_{n-1})} \tag{16-7}$$

(For a fine grid size, we may wish to approximate x simply by the midpoint of each interval.)

For random variables with an infinite range, tails are truncated at a point where the probability of the random variable falling outside the finite range becomes smaller than 10^{-k}. (This approximation is also used for discrete random variables.)

For hand simulations, we may need to gencrate normally distributed random variates. There exist tables for standardized random normal variates (see the text by Shannon, listed in the references). Alternatively, we can apply the tabular method, using the standard normal distribution (Table 1 of Appendix B) and expression (16-6). Since most tables of the standard normal distribution only show $P(0 \leq Z \leq z)$, we replace u by

$$u' = \begin{cases} u - 0.5, & \text{for } u \geq 0.5 \quad \text{with } z \geq 0 \\ 0.5 - u & \text{for } u \leq 0.05 \quad \text{with } z \leq 0 \end{cases} \tag{16-8}$$

16-4 STOCHASTIC SIMULATION BY COMPUTER

For a deterministic simulation of the inventory system, where daily demands and lead times are exogenous events and are specified in detail as input data to the simulation, the flow diagram of Figure 16-1 is all we need to trace the course of events. In a stochastic simulation, daily demands and lead times are endogenous events generated from their probability distributions. Prior to the creation of each endogenous event, a value of a random variate is determined. This operation consists of three steps:

1. Using the uniform random number seed, r_{n-1}, from the preceding computation, generate a new r_n.
2. Convert r_n into a uniform random decimal fraction, u_n.
3. Transform u_n into a random variate for the distribution specified (as input).

Steps one and two are usually combined into one subroutine as part of most computer systems' software packages. Figure 16-4 is a flow diagram of these three

Figure 16-4. *Flow diagram for generating a random variate.*

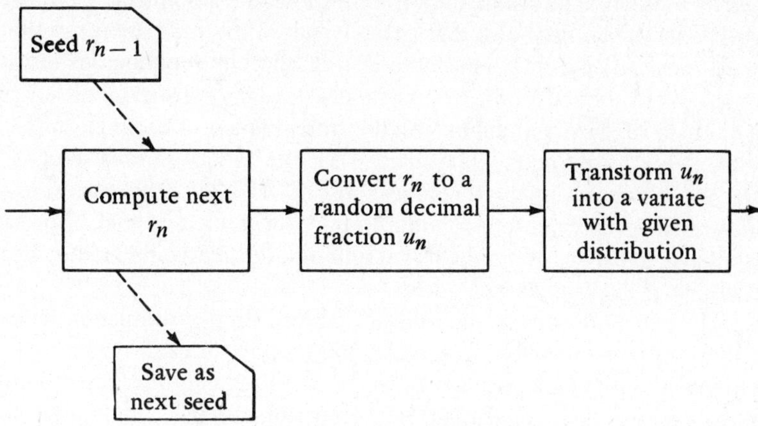

steps, where the uniform random number, r_n, becomes the seed for the $(n + 1)$th random number generated.

This portion is added to the flow diagram in Figure 16-1 just prior to box 4 to generate a daily demand and just following box 8 to generate a lead time (which is also recorded in the replenishment file for later use). This expanded flow diagram of the events for day n serves as the basis for writing a computer program.

Table 16-1 is actually a modified computer printout of an inventory simulation program, written in FORTRAN, and listed in the excellent text by R.C. Meier et al. As we saw in Section 16-1, the results of this simulation over 100 working days extrapolated to an annual basis of 250 working days yield a cost of $185.10. The same problem simulated over 1000 days yields the following summary statistics.

Total demand	3124 units	Demand satisfied	99.2%
Average inventory	47.23 units	Total cost	$646.40
Number of replenishments	52	Average annual cost	$161.60

This differs from the theoretical expected annual cost of $157.20 by only $4.40, a small difference considering the approximations made in the theoretical model. Without simulation, this fact could not have been established.

The outcome of stochastic simulations depends on a large number of randomly generated events. Hence, a priori, such simulation results are random variables and each simulation run represents one observation on this random variable. For instance, different sequences of random numbers yield the following average annual costs (all based on simulation runs over 1000 working days):

154.70 154.80 161.00 161.60 162.10 163.20 165.90 167.00
Mean = 161.30 Standard deviation = 4.50

On the basis of these 8 observations, we obtain an estimate of the average annual costs of \$161.30. The standard error of this estimate amounts to $\$4.50/\sqrt{8} = \$1.60$ ($= \sigma/\sqrt{n}$). It can be shown that as the length of the simulation run (the number of periods covered) becomes large, the distribution of simulation results approaches a normal distribution. Hence, we may apply standard statistical tools for small sample methods to analyze simulation results. For instance, the sample of 8 observations yields a 99 percent confidence interval for the average annual cost of \$155.70 to \$166.90, which covers the theoretical cost of \$157.20. If the two were substantially different, the analyst should attempt to discover the reason and, if necessary, adjust the model. Analysis of simulation results should always include a measure of the variability of the estimates obtained.

The standard error of the statistics derived from a simulation tends to become smaller as the run length (in our case, the number of days) is increased. Therefore, the reliability of simulation results can be increased either by lengthening individual simulation runs or by increasing the number of runs (i.e., the sample size). In both instances, the marginal increase in reliability gained drops off rapidly as these two parameters are increased. A simulation project should always include at least a minimal amount of sensitivity analysis with respect to the best length of the simulation runs.

16-5 EXAMPLE USING EVENT INCREMENTATION

In the inventory example, simulated time was advanced by equal time increments of one working day. All events are considered in the same predetermined sequence each day of the simulation. Each day may have one or all of three types of events considered in this sequence: receipt of replenishments, execution of customer orders, and placement of replenishments. All events are assumed to occur at a given point in time during the period. Replenishments are received at the beginning of each day, customer orders are executed by the end of the day, and replenishments are placed at the end of a day. This method of keeping simulated time is referred to as *fixed time incrementation*. It is suitable if some events occur in most periods or if the exact time at which an event occurs within each period does not significantly affect the performance of the operations simulated.

There are many dynamic phenomena where the exact time at which the various events occur is a crucial element of an operation's performance. This is the case for waiting line problems, or for problems where most periods have no events. Rather than advance simulated time by a constant (often small) time increment, we can advance simulated time, after processing each event, to the scheduled time of the next most imminent event in the simulation. This type of keeping time is called *event-step incrementation* or *variable time incrementation*.

Consider the following simple assembly line problem. A product is to be assembled on a two-station assembly line, with task A performed at the first station followed by task B at the second station. Each task completes about half of the assembly job, and each consists of a series of individual steps or operations. After completing task A, the operator at station 1 places the partially assembled product on a gravity conveyor belt on which it rolls to station 2. Once the operator there has completed the assembly, the finished product is placed on a cart which is periodically taken away to the stock location. The engineer in charge of methods and procedures establishes the following standard times.

	Average Time	Standard Deviation	Probability Distribution
Task A	35 seconds	6 seconds	normal
Task B	38 seconds	5 seconds	normal
Conveyor belt time	6 seconds	zero	constant

We wish to simulate the performance of this assembly line using event-step incrementation. How do we go about this? The first task is to identify those components of the system needed to measure its performance.

Entities are given by assemblies in process. We wish to keep track of each one individually as it passes through the system. These entities are created at the first station. They leave the system once they have passed through the second station. Their attributes are the times taken for each task. Each entity engages consecutively in three activities: *task* A, *transport* from station 1 to the end of the conveyor belt, and *task* B. There is one file, namely the units that have accumulated at the end of the conveyor belt, waiting for task B, called the *in-process file*. Each activity results in two events: the start of the activity and the end of the activity.

For a simulation using fixed time incrementation, like the inventory simulation, we created a flow chart that processed all events that could happen during each time period (in our case, a day) in a prescribed fixed sequence. Each time the simulation had checked out all possible events and reached the bottom of the flow chart, simulated time was advanced by one period and the simulation returned to the first event at the beginning of the flow chart, until a specified number of periods had been simulated. For simulations using event-step incrementation, it is more convenient to use a multipath cyclic structure. At each cycle, the simulation goes through the following three phases. *Phase* A discovers the next most imminent event to occur in the simulation. Ties may be broken according to some suitable rules of priority. In *phase* B, the simulation completes or starts any activities arising unconditionally from the event just identified. In *phase* C, the simulation checks whether or not certain conditions are satisfied that allow any other activities to be started or completed. In practice, this search can be restricted to those activities that follow conditionally from the events processed in the preceding B phase. The simulation then returns to a new phase A. Phase A is facilitated by the introduction of a new type of master file—the *file of scheduled events*—which is a complete listing of all events scheduled but not yet executed at a given point in simulated time. Our example has six possible events, the start and end of each activity. However, some events are always a direct consequence of some other events. For instance, the start of activities "task A" and "transport" on the conveyor belt both follow unconditionally from the event "task A completed."

They are thus both part of the B phase for this event, and therefore do not need to be shown explicitly in the file of scheduled events. Similarly, the start of activity "task B" can only occur if either station 2 is idle and an entity ends the activity "transport" or activity "task B" ends and an entity is waiting at the end of the conveyor belt, i.e., the "in-process" file is not empty. These two conditions are discovered in the C phases following the two events "end of conveyor belt reached" and "task B completed." Hence, only the three events referring to the end of activities will ever appear in the file of scheduled events.

For each of these events, a separate event path is created, as shown in the flow diagram of Figure 16-5. Boxes 1 and 2 refer to the A phase, where the next most imminent event is removed from the file of scheduled events. Box 3 is the switch that directs each cycle of the simulation to the event path corresponding to the last event identified in the A phase. Boxes 4, 5, and 6 are the B phase for event "task A completed." This event path has no C phase. Box 7 is the B phase for the event "task B completed," while box 8 and its "Yes" and "No" branches represent the C phase. Identify the B phase and C phase for the event path starting at Box 11.

Note how along each path, new events are scheduled to occur at some time in the future and are entered into the file of scheduled events.

Suppose that the simulation has been in progress for some time and that simulated time is at t = 817 seconds after the start of the simulation. Twenty-two entities have already been completely assembled. The state of the system at time t = 817 is as follows:

- Entity 24 has been in station 1 (task A) for 31 seconds, with 13 seconds of activity left to go.
- Entity 23 has just started task B at station 2, with 30 seconds of activity left to go.
- The conveyor belt is empty.

The file of scheduled events corresponding to this state of the system at t = 817 is as follows:

Event Time	Entity	Event Type
830	24	completion of task A
847	23	completion of task B

We have just left block 14 at the bottom of the event path, starting at block 11 in the flow chart. We will now start a new cycle with phase A. At block 1 we search the file of scheduled events for the first event scheduled to occur at or after simulated time t = 817 seconds. This is entity 24, completing task A at time 830. This event is removed from the file. The current simulated time is updated to t = 830 at block 2. This completes phase A. We now proceed to phase B. The switch at block 3 directs us to block 4. Entity 24 leaves station 1 and enters the conveyor belt (block 5). Since the time taken to roll to the end of the conveyor belt is 6 seconds, entity 24 will reach

Figure 16-5. *Flow chart for event-step incrementation.*

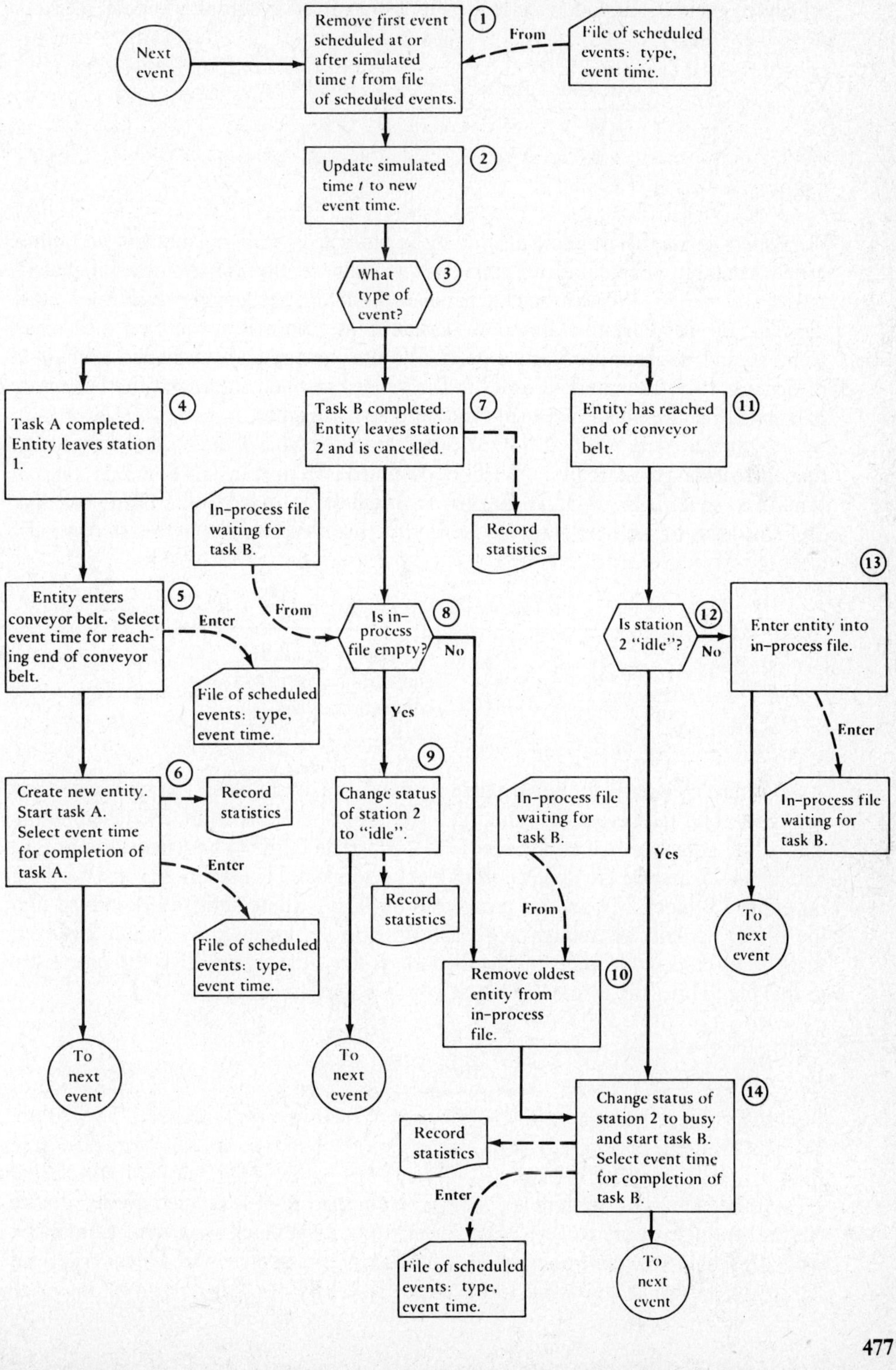

Next event

(1) Remove first event scheduled at or after simulated time t from file of scheduled events.

From: File of scheduled events: type, event time.

(2) Update simulated time t to new event time.

(3) What type of event?

(4) Task A completed. Entity leaves station 1.

(5) Entity enters conveyor belt. Select event time for reaching end of conveyor belt.

Enter: File of scheduled events: type, event time.

(6) Create new entity. Start task A. Select event time for completion of task A.

Record statistics

Enter: File of scheduled events: type, event time.

To next event

(7) Task B completed. Entity leaves station 2 and is cancelled.

Record statistics

In-process file waiting for task B.

From

(8) Is in-process file empty?

Yes

(9) Change status of station 2 to "idle".

Record statistics

To next event

No

In-process file waiting for task B.

From

(10) Remove oldest entity from in-process file.

(11) Entity has reached end of conveyor belt.

(12) Is station 2 "idle"?

No

(13) Enter entity into in-process file.

Enter

In-process file waiting for task B.

To next event

Yes

(14) Change status of station 2 to busy and start task B. Select event time for completion of task B.

Record statistics

Enter

File of scheduled events: type, event time.

To next event

the end of the conveyor belt at time 836, and we enter a new event into the file of scheduled events. The following is the file of scheduled events at $t = 830$ (first).

Event Time	Entity	Event Type
847	23	completion of task B
836	24	end of conveyor belt reached

There is another B phase activity to be processed—station 1 has not yet started a new assembly. Therefore, we create a new entity (entity 25) at block 6 that starts task A at $t = 830$. We now need to generate a time for the length of task A for entity 25. This means generating a random deviate from a normal distribution with mean $\mu = 36$ and standard deviation $\sigma = 6$. We use the approach suggested at the end of Section 16-3, rounding all times to the nearest second. Starting at the beginning of Table 16-2, we obtain a 4-digit random decimal fraction $u = 0.5921$. By (16-8), we substitute $u' = u - 0.5 = 0.0921$. Verify from the table of the normal distribution that this yields a z-value of $z = +0.23$ (rounded). Hence, by (16-6) we get a task A time of $x = \mu + z\sigma = 35 + 0.23(6) = 36.38$ or, rounded to the nearest second, 36. This leads to the next entry in the file of scheduled events at $t = 830$ (second).

Event Time	Entity	Event Type
847	23	completion of task B
836	24	end of conveyor belt reached
866	25	completion of task A

We are now ready for a new phase A, so we go back to block 1 at simulated time $t = 830$. The next event (in time) removed from the file is entity 24, reaching the end of the conveyor belt at 836 seconds. We update current simulated time to $t = 836$ (block 2), and we are directed from block 3 to block 11. Station 2 is busy working on entity 23 (block 12), and we proceed to block 13, where entity 24 is entered into the file of partially assembled products waiting to be processed by station 2. Given that the in-process file was empty just prior to this time, entity 24 is the only entry in this file. Thus, the in-process file at $t = 836$ appears as

End of Belt Time	Entity
836	24

At the next pass, we remove entity 23 from the file of scheduled events, update current simulated time to $t = 847$, cancel entity 23 at block 7, proceed from block 8 to 10, where we remove entity 24 from the in-process file, start a new task B on

Table 16-4. *Simulation using event-step incrementation*

			File of Scheduled Events				In-Process File		Station Status	
t	Entity	Event	Event Time	Entity	Event Type	√	Entity	In/Out	1	2
817			830	24	Task A completed	√			busy	busy
			847	23	Task B completed	√			↓	↓
830	24	Task A completed								
	24	Start conveyor	836	24	End conveyor	√				
	25	Start task A	866	25	Task A completed	√				
836	24	End conveyor					24	in		
847	23	Task B completed								
	23	Canceled								
	24	Start task B	876	24	Task B completed	√	24	out		
866	25	Task A completed								
	25	Start conveyor	872	25	End conveyor	√				
	26	Start task A	905	26	Task A completed	√				
872	25	End conveyor					25	in		
876	24	Task B completed								
	24	Canceled								
	25	Start task B	913	25	Task B completed		25	out		
905	. . .	. . .								

entity 24, and enter a new event time for completion of task B on entity 24 into the file of scheduled events. Verify the results for some additional events, as shown in Table 16-4.

This process is repeated until the simulated time has reached the time set for the end of the simulation run. The statistics collected at strategic points during the simulation, such as at the start or completion of an operation and when entities are created or canceled, are then summarized and analyzed.

In a computer program, blocks 1 to 3 form the main program, and each sequence of blocks starting at 4, 7, and 11 forms one or more subroutines.

*16-6 ACTIVITY CYCLE DIAGRAMS

Activity or *entity cycle diagrams* are simple, yet effective, representations of the structure of a simulation model and the dynamic behavior of the entities in it. They facilitate a clearer understanding of the interactions between the various entities in the system, provide an excellent vehicle for communication with the client of a simulation project, and can be used as a basis for a computer program.

Consider again the assembly line problem of the preceding section. Here we identified one class of entities—namely, assemblies. Each "assembly" entity is created by station 1 at the beginning of activity "task A." At the end of this activity, the entity is discharged onto the conveyor belt, i.e., it immediately engages in a new activity, "transport." After completing that activity, it may wait in a queue (the "in-process" file). As soon as station 2 becomes available, the assembly entity that has been in the queue longest engages together with station 2 in the activity "task B." At the end of that activity, the entity disappears—in technical terms, it is canceled. Instead of assuming that a new assembly entity is created at the beginning of "task A" and is canceled at the end of "task B," we could equally well assume that there exists an infinitely large pool of such entities waiting out in the "world" to enter station 1 and that after being discharged from station 2, these entities return again to that pool. Hence, each ASSEMBLY entity starts in the WORLD pool and passes through a cycle of activities and queues to finally rejoin the WORLD. This is depicted in Figure 16-6. Such a loop is called an activity cycle. Note that a rectangle denotes an activity, a circle denotes a queue, and two circles joined (a large infinity sign) denotes an infinitely large pool of entities.

For activities TASK A and TASK B, we need the presence of both an ASSEMBLY and either station 1 or station 2. It is helpful to view each of these also as an entity. The situation is different for the activity TRANSPORT. Since several ASSEMBLIES may occupy the conveyor belt simultaneously, this activity simply has the character of retaining each ASSEMBLY for a given length of time before it can proceed to the IN-PROCESS queue. Hence, no entity class is needed for the conveyor belt.

So we now have an entity class STATION 1, which contains only one entity. It also has its own activity cycle. This cycle happens to be very simple: After completion of TASK A, this entity immediately returns to start a new TASK A, as shown in part (a) of Figure 16-7.

Figure 16-6. *Activity cycle for assembly entities.*

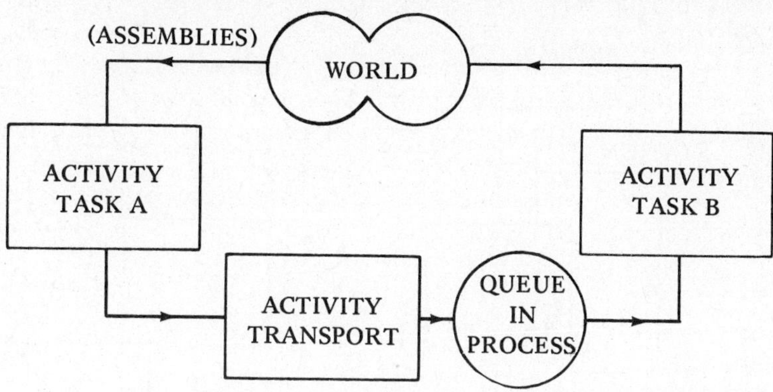

The entity class STATION 2 also has only one member. It can only engage in activity TASK B if there is an assembly entity waiting in the queue IN-PROCESS. Hence, entity STATION 2 may sometimes be idle. Its activity cycle therefore includes the queue IDLE, as shown in part (b) of Figure 16-7.

Figure 16-7. *Activity cycles for station 1 and 2.*

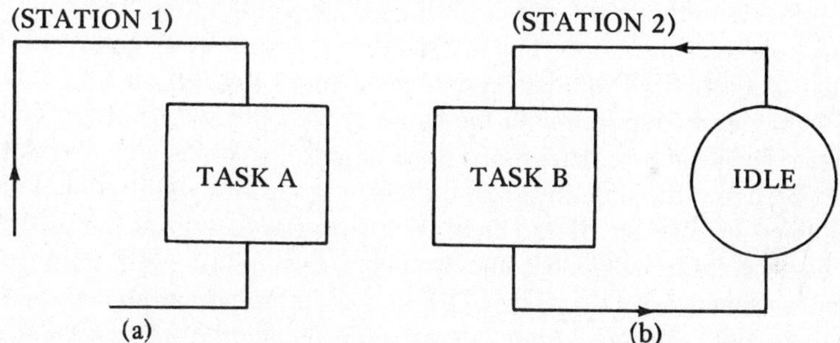

We can now join these individual activity cycles together. This is done in Figure 16-8. It is convenient to differentiate the activity cycles for different entity classes by different colored lines. The complete diagram immediately reveals the interrelationships among various entity classes. We see that the entity ASSEMBLY leaves the WORLD and is bound with entity STATION 1 for activity TASK A. After TASK A, it engages in activity TRANSPORT, after which it enters queue IN-PROCESS where it may have to wait for entity STATION 2 to become available, whereupon it is bound with that entity in activity TASK B and finally returns to the WORLD. Since there is only one entity STATION 1, no two assemblies can be engaged in TASK A at the same time. The same is true for TASK B.

This diagram could be used as a basis for a hand simulation, using the three-phase approach presented in the previous section. Its main usefulness is, however, as a display device for communication purposes.

Figure 16-8. *Activity cycle diagram for assembly line problem.*

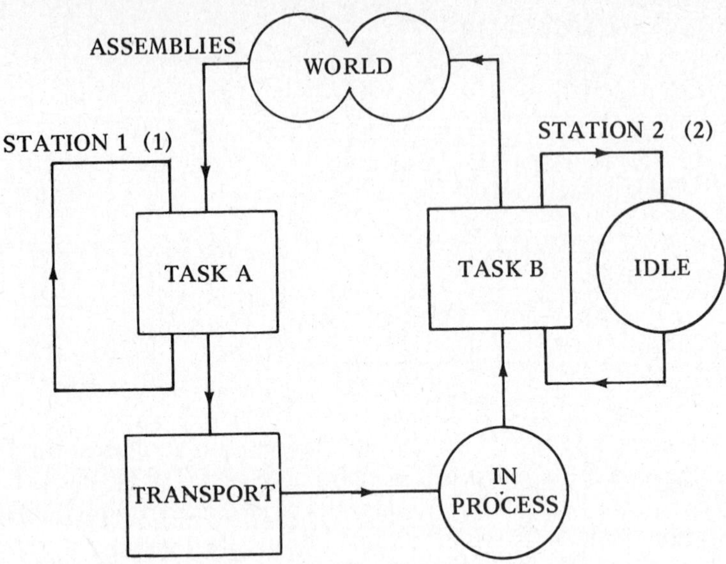

To demonstrate the power of this device, consider the somewhat more complicated example for the operation of a small port, depicted in Figure 16-9. The WORLD is the source of SHIP entities. They arrive at the port at random times. This is achieved by letting each ship join with the single entity INPUT for activity COMES, which takes a length of time determined by some specified probability distribution. To enter the port basin, the ship must pass through a single lock. If the entity LOCK is already occupied by another SHIP, then the arrival has to wait at the queue OUTSIDE. When the entity LOCK becomes available, it joins any SHIP waiting in OUTSIDE for the activity ENTER. The SHIP is now in the port basin. A ship on a domestic journey, not requiring customs clearance, will enter the queue BASIN, and if a TUG and a DOCK (both separate entities) are available, it will BERTH (an activity jointly engaged by SHIP, TUG, and DOCK). Once at the dock, the TUG becomes FREE again (a queue), while the SHIP engages in activity UNLOAD AND LOAD. The SHIP can leave the dock unaided. It may again have to wait in a queue INSIDE for the LOCK to become available, at which point it LEAVES (an activity jointly engaged in with LOCK) and returns to the WORLD. A ship on an international journey has to go through customs clearance. Hence, after ENTER it WAITS for CUSTOMS officers to BOARD. If a TUG and a DOCK are available, the SHIP proceeds to BERTH-ALSO, releasing the TUG. Clearance may take longer than that, so the SHIP and CUSTOMS officers engage in the activity CLEAR, after which they separate. CUSTOMS officers become IDLE, while the SHIP now joins the other ship path to UNLOAD AND LOAD. Note the form of the activity cycle for TUG and DOCK. The number in brackets behind the entity name indicates how many entities of that class there are.

Figure 16-9. *Activity cycle diagram for a port operation (courtesy S. Mathewson, Imperial College of Science and Technology, London).*

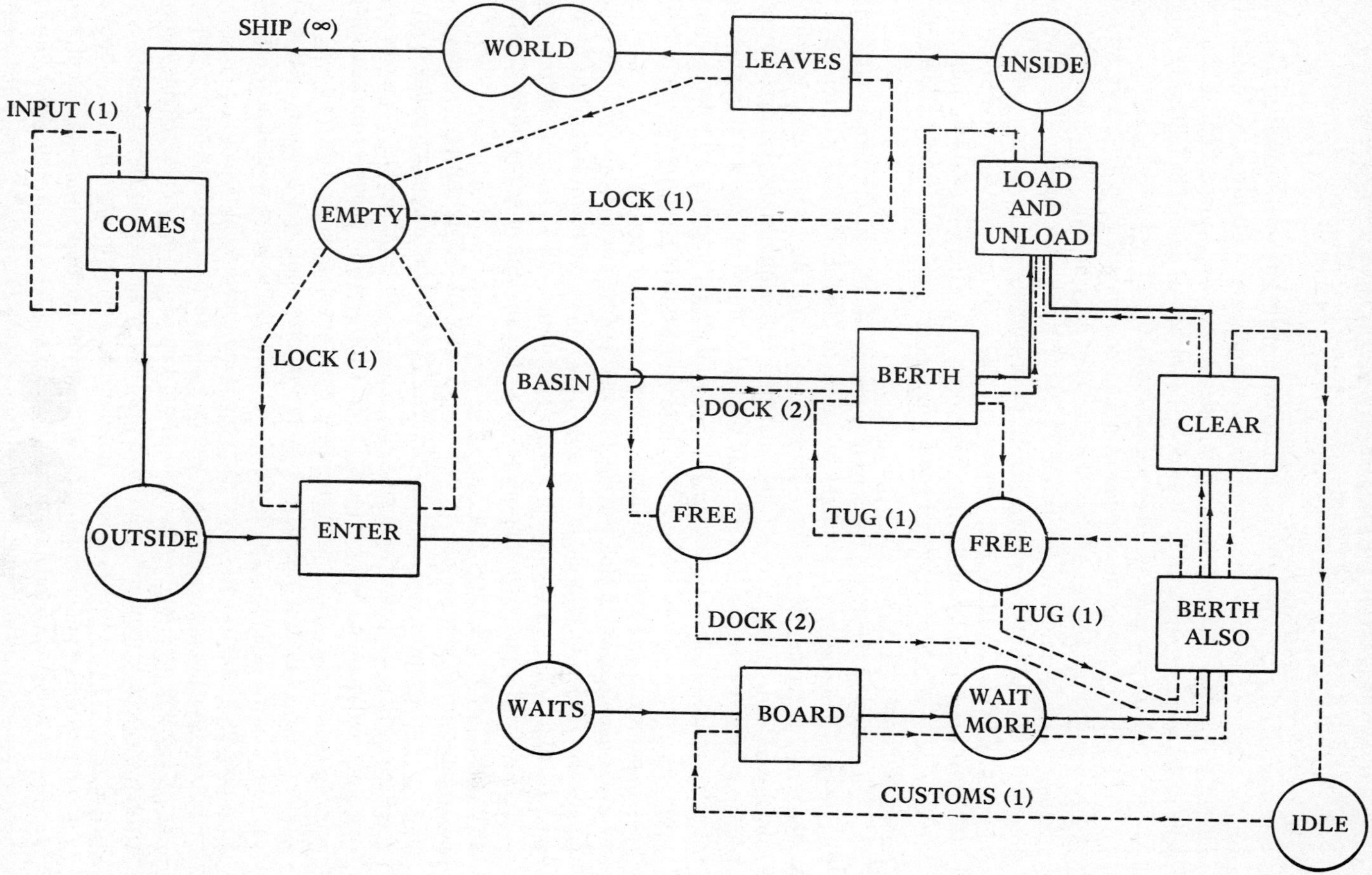

16-7 TACTICAL CONSIDERATION AND VALIDATION OF STOCHASTIC SIMULATION

When simulating dynamic phenomena we are usually interested mainly in their long-run or average behavior after the process has reached a steady state. For Markov processes (Chapter 13), we saw that this steady state was independent of the initial state of the process and could be approached as closely as desired by letting the process go over a sufficiently large number of transitions.

The same ideas can be applied in stochastic simulation, provided the structure of the system simulated is such that it approaches a steady state. For instance, for the inventory system simulated in Section 16-1, the steady state implies that if we were to observe the state of the system repeatedly at random points in time, after a large number of days we would expect to have observed each inventory position in the range [48, 108] about equally often. In other words, as the length of the simulation run increases, the effects of the initial conditions under which the simulation was started are washed out.

The speed at which this happens may also be affected by the choice of the initial conditions. Therefore, care should be taken to choose initial conditions that are representative for the steady state. Starting a system at an empty state, i.e., with no initial workload, empty queues, etc., may be a rather unfortunate choice, except for dynamic phenomena, where the empty state is a natural occurrence at the beginning of every period, such as waiting line situations that go through a daily cycle. For our inventory system, any initial inventory level between the maximum inventory and the reorder point is a representative initial choice.

A convenient way to remove any bias in the simulation results due to the initial conditions chosen is to exclude the initial portion of each simulation run from the analysis and begin accumulating operating statistics only after this initial period. Alternatively, the ending conditions of each run can be used as the initial conditions of the next run.

Many simulation projects involve comparison of several different modes of operation. For example, we want to compare the present inventory policy with the proposed policy, and determine the difference in average annual costs and other operating statistics. In such instances, it is advantageous to use the same sequence of random events, e.g., the same sequence of daily demands and production lead times. Although corresponding runs are no longer independent, this approach reduces the variability of the differences observed. It is a common practice in statistical inference. Corresponding runs are all started with the same initial conditions.

As we saw in Section 16-4, the outcome of a stochastic simulation run represents one observation on a random variable. If we wish to get sufficiently reliable estimates (in terms of small standard errors), we need either simulation runs covering a long period of simulated time or a large number of smaller simulation runs. There exist a number of techniques to improve the *efficiency of estimators* from simulation, known as *variance reducing techniques*. Although even a cursory discussion of this topic goes beyond the scope of this text, let us at least attempt to impart some of the flavor of one of them referred to as the *antithetic variate method*.

Suppose that the simulation involves generating daily demands from a given probability distribution. Rather than generating a total of n independently generated demands, we generate two sequences of $n/2$ demands that exhibit a high negative correlation. This can easily be achieved by using, for the first sequence, the actual random decimal fractions, u_n, generated; and for the second sequence, $(1 - u_n)$, which are also random decimal fractions. Clearly, whenever u_n produces a demand value above the mean, $(1 - u_n)$ produces a value below the mean and vice versa. As a consequence, the average demand over both sequences tends to be closer to the expected value of the demand than that of a single sequence of n independently generated demands, thus reducing the variability of the simulation results.

Most of these variance reducing techniques were developed for simulations in the physical sciences. The complexity of systems encountered in operations research problems renders their use much more difficult. The improvements gained may often not justify the additional modeling and programming costs incurred. Improvements in reliability of similar magnitude may sometimes be achieved more cheaply by increasing either the length of each simulation run or the number of runs.

As we have seen, simulation models usually comprise a number of separate parts (or subroutines) representing the various subsystems of the process simulated. Each of these should be tested separately. However, once these parts have been put together as one interacting package, the model as a whole has to be tested. This validation consists of two steps.

We first determine whether the logical connections between the various parts are correct. This is best done by running the whole simulation model over a number of events, suitably chosen to test the various paths through the simulation logic. The events chosen should include exceptional and extreme circumstances. For a computer simulation, intermediate status reports are printed out at various crucial points in the simulation, such as all decision forks along each path. These status reports are then carefully checked against the results obtained by duplicating the simulation by hand. (Once the internal logic has been checked, these intermediate status report printouts are eliminated from the program.)

The second step is to test whether the model as a whole can properly reproduce the real-world process. This validation is considerably more difficult. If the simulation describes an existing real-life process, it can presumably be tested against past data and its performance compared to the results actually experienced. Many simulation models, however, describe hypothetical or planned future systems for which no past performance data are available. In such instances, the operations researcher has no alternative but to carefully perform the first step of the validation process and then make a value judgment about the reasonableness of the results obtained. The operations researcher will constantly be on the watch for possible anomalies or counterintuitive and unusual results, and attempt to find reasonable or satisfactory explanations for any discrepancies until he or she has gained a sufficient degree of confidence in the correctness of the model as a whole.

16-8 SIMULATION COMPUTER LANGUAGES

Simulation and computers go hand in hand. Practically all simulations are executed with the aid of high-speed electronic computers. It is for this reason that we deliberately represented the logic of simulation processes by computer language–type flow charts. Simulation studies have given rise to a number of specially designed general purpose simulation packages and simulation languages that ease and speed up the writing of simulation computer programs. No matter whether you translate these flow charts into a computer program yourself or have it done by an experienced computer programmer, it is essential that you be familiar with the basic *world view* and essential properties, advantages, and drawbacks of these simulation languages. All we can do here, though, is to give some pointers.

It goes without saying that the conventional computer languages, such as FORTRAN, BASIC, ALGOL, PASCAL, COBOL, and others, may often be the most convenient or the only languages available. They are flexible, there is no additional learning cost, and no special (and often costly) processing system is needed. Execution time is usually faster than for simulation languages. On the other hand, simulation languages provide a number of facilities that are used in all simulations, such as random variate generators for many theoretical probability distributions and any desired empirical distribution, automatic updating of files of entities, automatic collection of various statistics, routines to read in inputs, routines to print out status reports and summary statistics, and the crucial timing routine to update simulated time. These parts usually constitute the major portion of the programming effort. With simulation packages and languages, all that requires programming is the actual logic of the simulation process itself. The remaining parts are done for you.

One of the easiest, though by no means the least powerful, simulation packages is the *General Purpose Systems Simulator* (GPSS), developed and maintained by IBM for most of its advanced computer systems. Little or no computer programming knowledge is required for GPSS. The first step is to construct a flow chart of the simulation process using the block types and symbols provided by GPSS. Each block type asks for the execution of a given operation, action, or process. The names chosen for the block types are descriptive of the operations. For instance, the block called GENERATE creates entities (called *transactions* in GPSS) spaced according to a specified interarrival time. ENTER allows an entity to occupy space (for example, in a service facility). The block QUEUE holds an entity until it can proceed to the next block. ADVANCE represents an operation that takes a (random) time. PICK sends an entity to one of a number of blocks with specified probability, and so on. Certain blocks perform the function of accumulating operating statistics. Once the complete block diagram has been drawn, a separate card is punched for each block. These, together with control cards and data cards, such as empirical probability distributions, form the input deck. Simulated time is advanced by event-step incrementation—the time unit used by GPSS is implied by the input data. By the very choice of block types, the world view implied by GPSS seems to be particularly efficient at simulating waiting line problems.

On the other extreme of the scale is SIMSCRIPT, a proper programming language with great flexibility and generality. Although the programming statements resemble English in sentence structure, familiarity with FORTRAN and its logic is essential. In SIMSCRIPT, the simulation process is defined in terms of events, entities, sets of entities, and attributes of entities *and* of sets. Entities may be permanent, such as the ferries in the ferry system example, or temporary, such as the cars wanting to use the ferry, created at one point and erased or destroyed at another. Sets are files where entities can be stored. Sets may belong to entities; for instance, the load of cars transported by the ferries belongs to a given entity—namely, the ferry. SIMSCRIPT provides facilities for searching these sets and for removing entities with certain attributes from them. For each event type that changes the status of the system, a separate event routine is written. Thus, SIMSCRIPT is an event-oriented language. SIMSCRIPT provides its own event-step incrementation timing routine.

There are a number of other simulation languages with similar features. One of the most recent ones, SLAM (see Pritsker, 1979), is also based on FORTRAN. SIMULA, based on ALGOL, is included in the software packages of advanced Burroughs computer systems.

Between these two extremes are a number of simulation packages consisting of collections of subroutines that can be used in conjunction with a programming language, such as FORTRAN or ALGOL. These subroutine facilitate file handling, file search to remove entities with specified attributes, generation of random variates from specified distributions, scheduling of future events, updating of simulated time, as well as collection of statistics. Examples of such packages are GASP, SIMON, and SPURT.

More recently, a number of interactive computer simulation systems have been developed, such as APL GPSS by IBM, NPGS by Heidorn (both based on the GPSS system), CAPS/ECSL by A. T. Clementson of the University of Birmingham, and DRAFT by S. Mathewson from the Imperial College of Science and Technology, London. The last two use a representation of the problem by means of activity cycle diagrams. These systems allow the user to input the problem structure and run data interactively on a computer console in a question-and-answer format. Illegal configurations are flagged for possible alterations. The computer version of the model, input data, and output statistics can be saved on disk and updated for future use. Such systems can reduce weeks or even months of programming effort to a few sessions on a computer console.

DYNAMO is one of the few simulation languages that are capable of simulating continuous processes. This language is best known in conjunction with J. W. Forrester's *Industrial Dynamics* (MIT Press, 1961). Events are not considered individually, as for all discrete simulation languages, but in the aggregate. In industrial dynamics, the basic components of a system are *levels of variables* (or *stocks*) and *rates of flow* (or *rates of change of levels*). Levels may represent stocks of resources, inventories, numbers of people, amounts of information, levels of feeling, levels of activities. Any activity, movement of material or of information, or any decision function in the system that affects level variables gives rise to rates of flow.

DYNAMO is best suited for dynamic systems that involve *feedback loops*. A production-inventory-sales system, where the rate of production varies inversely with the inventory level, is an example of a feedback loop. The interrelationships among various level variables and rates of flow are expressed mathematically in the form of difference equations representing time lags of various lengths. Given initial starting conditions, DYNAMO obtains, for each time period, numerical solutions to each difference equation in the sequential order specified by the user. Thus, simulated time is incremented by a constant amount at each iteration. DYNAMO includes facilities for the more common types of functional relations, such as exponential, logarithmic, trigonometric, as well as user-specified step and ramp functions. The language has a close resemblance to FORTRAN. One of the special features of DYNAMO is the option to produce plots of the values of the various variables over simulated time.

DYNAMO has been particularly successful in simulating systems covering the economy or an industry of a region or country. It was used to simulate the various scenarios for the world's economic, social, and ecological development reported in *Limits to Growth* (D. H. Meadows and associates, London, Potomac Associates, 1972).

An excellent summary of most major simulation languages, including some guidelines for selecting the most appropriate one for the problem at hand, is given in Chapter 3 of Shannon.

16-9 CONCLUDING REMARKS

Nowhere in applied operations research does the concept of system come forth as naturally as in simulation. Whereas for mathematical optimization tools the complexities of the real world leave the operations researcher little choice but to make abstractions, approximations, and simplifications in the models, no such limitations need to hamper a simulation model. The mathematical complexities of simulation seldom go beyond simple numeric computations or logical operations. Hence much more detail and more interactions among the various parts of a system can be taken into account. As a result, simulation models may be fairly true representations of the real world. This is one of the great attractions of simulation over mathematical optimization techniques.

But hand in hand with this advantage go two potentially crippling handicaps. Simulation is not an a priori optimizing tool, but rather a tool of analysis, often used for evaluating the performance of decisions derived by other means. Each simulation run just traces through the effects of decision rules that are specified in full detail as part of the input. Attempts at optimization have to be made by a slow process of trial and error. All we can usually strive for is "good" decision rules rather than optimal ones, and even this may be fairly costly in terms of computer time.

In order to be successful, simulation models have to incorporate a large amount of detail. As a consequence, the effort that goes into building a simulation model is usually much larger than for comparable optimization models. Thus, simulation projects turn out to be rather expensive projects.

The uses for simulation are almost unlimited. Some of the better known applications cover such diverse fields as:

- waiting lines—evaluation of alternative proposed facilities or evaluation of alternative modes of operations of existing facilities.
- job shop scheduling—evaluation of alternative dispatch rules and forecasting of workloads at each machine center. Workload forecasts may be used to initiate corrective action to eliminate potential bottlenecks.
- operation of process plants—the entire operation of a process plant, such as a refinery, is simulated, unit by unit, to determine output composition as a function of input mix and instrument setting (deterministic).

- company-wide planning models and budget simulations—using the conventional accounting structure, balance sheets, income statements, and cash budgets are projected over time (deterministic).
- evaluation of PERT networks to determine more representative completion time distributions.
- evaluation of complex facility location and distribution systems.
- transport systems operation, such as ocean or river shipping, railroad systems, and airline scheduling.
- simulation of economic sectors of a region or a whole economy to explore various industrial and economic development policies.
- simulation of energy use and production systems on a national or international level.
- operational gaming. Simulation that allows human intervention is a valuable training tool for all sorts of skills. Business games, mock-up jet airliner cockpits, and simulated space flights are some of the more glamorous applications.

With minor exceptions, such as operational gaming, simulation is best used as a means of last resort only—when all else fails. Mathematical tools are, as a rule, much more efficient for evaluating and optimizing a system's performance. Only if mathematical optimization techniques cannot adequately reproduce the complexities of a real system should the operations researcher take refuge in simulation. The apparent simplicity of simulation is deceptive and may lead the unsuspecting analyst into a quagmire that may prove expensive if not disastrous. Before a simulation project is embarked upon, the objectives of the analysis and the likely outcomes should be clearly spelled out and rough cost estimates obtained. Properly used, simulation can be an effective tool in the hands of an experienced operations researcher.

EXERCISES

16.1 (*Deterministic*) Use the flow diagram in Figure 16-1 to simulate the performance of an inventory control system, using the same cost parameters as in Section 16-1, for the sequence of daily demands listed below and a sequence of lead times of 11, 8, 10, 13, 7, 9, 14, 10, 9, 11, 10. The beginning inventory is 54, and no replenishments are outstanding. Compute the average inventory level and the total cost over the 100-day run. Only days with a positive demand are listed.

Day	1	3	4	5	7	9	10	14	15	18	20	21	22	23	24	25	27	28	30	
Demand	1	4	8	2	1	6	3	7	4	2	5	1	3	2	1	1	11	12	4	
Day	31	32	36	37	39	40	42	43	46	47	48	50	51	52	54	55	56	58	59	60
Demand	3	4	1	12	1	1	6	2	4	5	9	4	11	12	8	12	3	1	6	2
Day	62	64	65	67	68	69	71	74	75	76	78	79	80	81	83	84	85	87	89	90
Demand	2	3	10	4	1	11	6	2	5	3	13	1	1	8	2	10	1	3	8	6
Day	91	92	93	95	96	97	98	99	100											
Demand	5	4	2	11	3	7	6	8	1											

16.2 Consider the following container port operation. The port has two berths. Each berth has one container crane. Each crane can only work one ship at a time. Ships arrive at the port and wait for a tug to pilot them to a berth if one is free. There is only one tug. Once a ship has docked, it will be unloaded by a crane. The containers are lifted off the ship and placed directly onto flatdeck railwagons, of which there is an unlimited supply. Once all containers have been removed, the ship is loaded with new containers, also brought to the dock by rail. The number of containers to be unloaded and loaded varies from ship to ship. Loaded ships clear their berth with the help of the tug. Identify the components of this system in terms of entities, files, attributes of entities and files, activities, and their associated events.

16.3 (*Deterministic*) A soft drink manufacturer forecasts the following demand pattern over the coming 12-month period (in 1000 gallons):

Month	1	2	3	4	5	6	7	8	9	10	11	12
Demand	2500	1800	2000	2800	3500	4800	5600	6000	4500	3200	1200	3600

The manufacturing facilities can be operated with one or two shifts, with or without overtime. The following are the maximum output capacities and associated costs:

	One Shift		Two Shifts	
Production Setup	No Overtime	With Overtime	No Overtime	With Overtime
Maximum output	2000	2500	4000	5000
Costs ($1000's)	120	165	200	280

Goods produced in each period can be used to satisfy the demand in that period or any subsequent periods. Any goods carried forward to later periods incur a storage cost of $100 per 1000 gallons stored per month. An increase in the number of shifts results in a "hiring and training" cost of $18,000, while a decrease from two to one shifts costs the firm $20,000 in severance pay. At the beginning of the planning horizon there are no goods in stock, and in the preceding period the firm was operating with only one shift. Overtime cost is proportional to amount used.

(a) Simulate this operation, assuming that the plant is always operated at the maximum regular capacity for each production setup. Two shifts are used from periods 5 through 10 only, and overtime is used as necessary. What is the cost of this schedule?

(b) By trial and error, determine what you consider is the optimal production schedule and its cost through simulation. Regular production may be at less than full capacity, but at full capacity cost.

16.4 (*Deterministic*) Consider the operation of a single-track railway line, connecting stations A to B, B to C, C to D, D to E. No more than one train can be on the track between adjacent stations. A new train may enter a track segment only when the previous train has cleared it. Trains may cross only at stations C and D; station B does not have sufficient siding for two trains. Hence, no train may enter the track from C to B if there is already a train traveling from A to B. However, a second train may enter the track from A to B if there is already a train traveling from B to C. The same rules hold also in the opposite direction. The sidings at each station are not considered part of the track between adjacent stations. No more than 3 trains can be in each of station C and D simultaneously. The travel and switching times in minutes for regular and express trains are as follows:

	Travel Times								Switching Times		
	A-B	B-C	C-D	D-E	E-D	D-C	C-B	B-A	B	C	D
Regular	20	12	30	16	24	28	14	18	10	30	20
Express	15	8	15	12	16	24	10	14	0	5	5

The timetable provides the following departure times: at A in the direction of E, regular at 8:00, express at 10:00, regular at 10:20; at E in the direction of A, express at 9:10, regular at 9:30, regular at 11:00. Simulate this operation using event incrementation for the 4-hour period from 8 A.M. to 12 A.M. At 8 A.M., there is one regular train at station D ready to depart toward A.

16.5 Using the short list of random numbers in Table 16-2, generate 10 random variates for the following frequency distribution.

Value x	0	1	2	3	4	5	6	7	8
Frequency	0.156	0.234	0.208	0.161	0.095	0.064	0.036	0.028	0.018

16.6 Starting in row 2 of the list of random numbers in Table 16-2, generate for each distribution 10 random variates from 3-digit random numbers for
(a) A uniform distribution with limts $b = 8$, $a = 3$.
(b) A negative exponential distribution with parameter $\lambda = 10$.
(c) A normal distribution with mean $\mu = 100$ and standard deviation $\sigma = 20$.

16.7 Using the demand distribution and lead-time distribution listed in Section 16-1, simulate the behavior of the inventory system depicted in Figure 16-1 over a 40-day period for the same cost parameter and starting inventory. To obtain random numbers, read Table 16-2 backward, starting with the last digit (which gives 56030 978 . . .). Find the average inventory and the total cost over this period.

16.8 PERT network: Consider the PERT problem discussed in Section 8-5 of Chapter 8. Rather than using the beta distribution, assume that the duration of each task follows a normal distribution with parameters as shown in Table 8-2. Simulate the project completion time using stochastic simulation. To determine random deviates accurate to 1/10 of a day, use 2-digit random numbers in Table 16-2, starting at the beginning of the table. Simulate 12 separate project completion times, and determine the average and standard deviation of the project completion time and compare it with the theoretical results found in Section 8-5.

16.9 A firm wishes to investigate the profitability of an expansion project. Consumer tests on samples of the project made at a small test plant have given favorable results. From these tests and other market surveys, it is estimated that the potential sales of the product should range between 40 to 100 in about 9 out of 10 quarters within 3 years of its introduction. One of the alternatives considered involves the construction of a plant with a capacity of 100 tons per quarter at a cost of $400,000. Such a plant would be in operation within 1 year of the decision to go ahead with the expansion project. Since the product can only be stored for very short periods, production would follow actual sales very closely. Hence, any potential sales above 100 tons per quarter would be lost. The fixed production cost per quarter is estimated at $30,000, while the variable production costs per ton of products produced are highly nonlinear, as follows:

$$\begin{aligned} \text{for } 0 \leqslant 1 \leqslant\ & 50, \$(100 - q) \text{ per ton} \\ 50 \leqslant q \leqslant\ & 80, \$50 \text{ per ton} \\ 80 \leqslant q \leqslant\ & 100, \$0.625q \text{ per ton} \end{aligned}$$

Sales predictions are as follows:

Operating Year	Sales Range	Sales Price/Ton
1	20 to 60 tons per quarter	$880
2	30 to 90 tons per quarter	$890
From 3 on	40 to 100 tons per quarter	$900

All ranges are quoted with odds of 9 out of 10, and actual sales are assumed to be approximately normally distributed. (Note that sales cannot be negative.) Management would like to determine by simulation the distribution of the cumulative net cash flow over the first 5 years of operating the plant (after its construction). Round sales figures to nearest ton.

(a) Using 3-digit random numbers and starting in row 1 of Table 16-2, simulate the cash flow quarter by quarter over a 5-year period. What is the net cash flow?

(b) (*Large amount of work*) Redo the simulation for another 9 runs, continuing in Table 16-2 where you left off in (a). Once you reach the end of Table 16-2, just wrap around to the start again. Find the average net cash flow and the standard deviation of the net cash flow.

(c) (*Requires access to computers*) Write a computer program to perform this simulation. Make 100 runs, each over a 10-year period, discounting the quarterly cash flows at a rate of 3 percent per quarter. Construct a frequency histogram of the net discounted cash flows containing about 10 class intervals. (If you need a refresher on discounting, read Section 1-13 of Chapter 1.) What conclusion do you reach about the profitability of the project, assuming that 10 years is the productive life of the plant?

16.10 Using the flow chart of Figure 16-5, simulate the two-station assembly line for the following sequence of time durations of 20 assemblies and a conveyor belt time of 6 seconds.

Assembly	1	2	3	4	5	6	7	8	9	10
Time										
task A	33	38	40	42	36	32	30	35	33	37
task B	36	35	33	38	40	44	40	41	37	39

Assembly	11	12	13	14	15	16	17	18	19	20
Time										
task A	35	34	30	37	31	32	40	42	35	38
task B	44	42	37	40	41	36	38	35	38	40

Both stations are empty at the start, and the operator at station 1 is just ready to start task A for the first assembly. What is the elapsed time to complete all assemblies on both stations? What is the largest number of assemblies waiting on the conveyor belt at any given time? What is the total idle time of the operator at station 2?

16.11 (a) Using the flow chart of Figure 16-5, simulate the two-station assembly line for a time interval of 10 minutes, starting out with empty stations with the operator at station 1 ready to begin task A on the first assembly. Generate task duration times (rounded to the nearest full second) using the task-time probability distribution given in Section 16-5. Use 2-digit random numbers to generate the random variates required, and start at the beginning of Table 16-2. Determine the number of assemblies completed, the maximum number of assemblies waiting on the conveyor belt, and the total idle time of the operator at station 2.

(b) The assembly operations can be regrouped in such a way that the average time for task A is increased to 36 seconds and the average time for task B decreases to 37 seconds, without affecting the standard deviations of the tasks. Redo (a) for this change in data, and compare the two modes of operations. Which one gives a more even work flow?

16.12 Canal A is connected to the lower level Canal B by a lock. Boats enter from Canal A into the lock, the gates are closed, the water level is lowered to the level of Canal B, the gates toward Canal B are opened, and the boats leave, at which point any boats in Canal B wanting to be raised to Canal A enter the lock, the gates are closed, the water level is raised to the level of Canal A, the gates are opened, the boats leave, and so on. The lock has a capacity of 4 boats only. It takes 4 minutes to lower or raise the water level. Only 1 boat may enter the lock at a time, and a boat takes 1 minute to be moored. However, all boats leave the lock one after the other. The time needed for all boats to leave the lock is 2 minutes (regardless of the number of boats). Boats arrive at the lock in Canal A at a rate of 12 per hour, and in Canal B at a rate of 15 per hour. Arrivals in both canals follow a Poisson distribution. The current mode of operation during the busy hours, for which the above arrival rates hold, is to fill or empty the lock whenever 4 boats have been moored inside the lock. At 11 A.M., the system is in the following state: The lock gates are open to traffic from Canal A. Three boats are already moored in the lock, and the next arrival from A is scheduled to arrive at the lock at 11:02. Five boats are currently waiting in Canal B to go through the lock to A. The next boat arrival is scheduled at 11:04. Simulate this system until 11:30.

Keep enough detail to determine the number of boats passing through the lock in each direction, the average time boats spend at the lock between arrival and departure in each direction, and the number of times the lock has been raised and lowered. Use the following sequence of 2-digit random numbers to generate the arrivals: 56 03 09 78 38 47 01 98 03 16 14 56 17 11 98 82 51 97 93 04.

16.13 (*Deterministic*) Consider a queueing system that has two service facilities in sequence with an unlimited queue in front of the first facility, but no queue between the two facilities.

(a) Identify the phase A, B, and C events. Develop a flow chart similar to Figure 16-5.

(b) Use this flow chart to simulate the processing of the following sequence of arrivals:

Arrival	1	2	3	4	5
Arrival time	01	02	05	12	14
Service time on facility 1	2	5	3	6	4
Service time on facility 2	4	4	1	8	3

16.14 A job shop has three work centers: X, Y, Z. Each job has to go through some or all centers in a prescribed unique sequence. A work center can only work on one job at a time. The next job can enter a work center immediately after the previous job has been processed. The current state of the system is as follows:

Jobs currently in the system:	1	2	3	4	5	6	7	8	9	10
Sequence of centers left to be entered	Z	Z	X	XY	XYZ	XZ	YXZ	Y	YZ	Y

Work center X is currently processing job 1; the scheduled release time from the center is at simulated time 124 minutes. Work center Y is currently processing job 2 with a scheduled release time at 180 minutes. Jobs are processed by each center on a first-come basis. The current priority at center X is job 1, 3, 4, 5, 6, and at center Y, 2, 7, 8, 9, 10. Note that center Z is currently idle. Processing times in minutes at each work center are normally distributed as follows:

Work center	X	Y	Z	
Mean	120	200	180	minutes
Standard deviation	40	40	60	minutes

New jobs enter the system at the beginning of each day, at which time they are added to the file of jobs waiting for processing at each center. Current simulated time is t = 100 minutes.

(a) Identify the phase A, B, and C events and draw a flow chart similar to Figure 16-5.

(b) Simulate the system with the data given until simulated time t = 480 minutes. Use the short list of random numbers given in Table 16-2, starting at the beginning. Use 4-digit random digits and round results to the nearest positive minute.

16.15 (*Deterministic, lengthy*) A job shop has three work centers, A, B, and C. Each job has to go through some or all centers in a given sequence. A work center can only work on one job at a time. A job only vacates a work center when all operations to be done at that center have been completed. The present work load in terms of partially completed jobs and jobs on the order list, is as shown in the table. In the last column, the letters identify the work center, the numbers following it identify the processing times. The work must be done in the sequence of work center shown. Simulate the processing of these jobs, using the following rules for determining priority of jobs waiting at work center.

(a) The first to arrive at the work center is the first processed.

(b) At each station, take first the job ready for processing with the least amount of slack, where slack is determined as

(due date) − (total processing time left on job) − (simulated time)

Draw a flow diagram first. For each rule, find the earliest time that job 20 is completed, find the average lateness of jobs, the total idle time on each center, and compare the two rules in terms of these characteristics.

Job	Date Received	Date Due	Sequence Work Center–Processing Time
1	01	05	C-2
2	01	04	B-1, C-1
3	01	06	A-2, C-2
4	03	10	A-2, C-2
5	03	10	A-2, C-2
6	04	20	B-2, A-6, B-3
7	06	20	A-1, C-3, B-5
8	06	10	B-2
9	08	16	B-4
10	10	24	C-2
11	10	20	C-2, A-2
12	12	26	B-2, A-3, C-4
13	15	30	A-2, C-4, A-1
14	15	36	B-4
15	18	30	A-5, C-2
16	20	36	B-2, C-6
17	20	40	B-4, A-6
18	24	32	C-2
19	24	40	B-5, A-1, C-4
20	25	38	A-4, B-4

16.16 Draw two activity cycle diagrams for the problem in exercise 16.2, one for the movement of ships and one for the unlooading and loading operations. The latter contains the detail for the load and unload activity of the former.

16.17 Draw an activity cycle diagram for the problem in exercise 16.13. Introduce additional activities and a queue for blocking phase.

16.18 Draw an activity cycle diagram for the problem in exercise 16.12. Let each successive mooring be a separate activity and switch arrivals to appropriate one.

16.19 Air-Couriers Inc. operates a 24-hour parcel pick-up service for air freight delivery to East Coast cities. Customers make pick-up requests by phone to a dispatcher, who fills in a pick-up order and then assigns the request to the first available driver. After completing a pickup, the driver fills in a pick-up report, which he or she files with the dispatcher, and then waits for a new assignment. A dispatcher will interrupt assigning a job to a driver to take customer phone calls and only continues with the job assignment after having prepared the pick-up order. There are two dispatchers who alternate taking customer calls, except when a call comes in while a dispatcher is still engaged with the previous call taken. The number of incoming phone lines is sufficiently large so that no customer ever gets a busy signal. All pick-up orders are available to both dispatchers for assignment to drivers. Past records for a particular office show that

- The average rate of pick-up requests is 24 per hour and follows a Poisson process.
- The time required to receive a pick-up request and fill in the pick-up order is normal with mean 120 seconds and standard deviation 20.
- The time to make a job assignment is a constant 60 seconds.
- The time to make a pickup and file the pick-up report is normal with mean 1500 seconds and standard deviation 400.
- The number of drivers is 16.

(a) Identify entity classes, files, and activities, and list all entities jointly engaged in each activity. Identify the phase A, B, and C events.

(b) Assume that at 11 A.M. the system is in the following state: (1) no pending requests; (2) dispatcher 1 idle; (3) dispatcher 2 processing a pick-up request with 80 seconds to go; (4) next pick-up request to be received at 100 seconds after 11 A.M.; (5) drivers 1, 2, 3, and 4 idle; (6) busy drivers and pick-up completion times (including filing a pick-up report) in seconds after 11 A.M. are as follows: 5—240, 6—1250, 7—680, 8—560, 9—1650, 10—960, 11—180, 12—1140, 13—1370, 14—510, 15—870, 16—1410. Simulate this system for 1 hour. Use 4-digit random numbers starting in line 1 of Table 16-2. If you reach the end of the list, use the table in reverse order. Round all times to the nearest 10 seconds. Collect statistics on the total idle time of dispatchers and drivers and on the total time pick-up orders wait in the office until assignment to a driver. Generate all activity times at the start of each activity only.

REFERENCES

Fishman, G. S. *Principles of Discrete Event Simulation.* New York: Wiley, 1978. Strong emphasis on statistical aspects. Many lengthy exercises. Recommended for practitioners.

Forrester, Jay W. *Industrial Dynamics.* Cambridge, Mass.: MIT Press, 1969. This classic text on this important simulation tool has obtained new prominence through its use to predict the future development of this globe as a result of population pressures, incidence of pollution, and scarcity of natural resources. See also *Urban Dynamics* (Cambridge, Mass.: MIT Press, 1969); and *World Dynamics* (Cambridge, Mass.: Wright-Allen Press, 1972), both by the same author.

Hammersley, J. M., and D. C. Handscomb. *Monte Carlo Methods.* New York: Wiley, 1964. The classic text on variance or error reducing techniques, such as importance sampling, control variates, regression, and antithetic-variate methods and conditional Monte Carlo. An advanced text.

Markowitz, H. M. "Simulating with SIMSCRIPT," *Management Science,* Vol. 12, June 1966. A general description of the basic features of SIMSCRIPT, showing copies of coding input sheets and a sample program.

Mattessich, Richard. *Simulation of the Firm Through a Budget Computer Program.* Homewood, Ill.: Irwin, 1964. Deterministic simulation of a firm's financial position over time.

Meier, Robert C., William T. Newell, and Harold L. Pazer. *Simulation in Business and Economics.* Englewood Cliffs, N.J.: Prentice-Hall, 1969. An easy, introductory text. Contains a listing of the inventory simulation program used in this chapter. The text has a whole chapter on computer simulation languages, and one on industrial dynamics.

Mihram, G. Arthur. *Simulation—Statistical Foundations and Methodology.* New York: Academic Press, 1972. An advanced text covering the statistical basis of simulation.

Mize, Joe H., and J. Grady Cox. *Essentials of Simulation.* Englewood Cliffs, N.J.: Prentice-Hall, 1968. A text on fundamentals of simulation, such as the basic concepts of probability, sampling of multi-variable random events, and estimation for simulation. Assumes knowledge of FORTRAN programming. Contains simple FORTRAN computer programs for examples discussed.

Naylor, Thomas H., Joseph L. Balintfy, Donan S. Burdick, and Kong Chu. *Computer Simulation Techniques.* New York: Wiley, 1966. A classic text on simulation at an intermediate level.

Pritsker, A. A. B., and C. D. Pegden. *Introduction to Simulation and SLAM.* New York: Halsted Press (Wiley), 1979. Detailed description of an advanced FORTRAN-based simulation language, SLAM, which the authors claim is easy to apply. Good selection of illustrative examples.

Pugh, A. L. *DYNAMO II User's Manual.* Cambridge, Mass.: MIT Press, 1970. Shows how to use the simulation language DYNAMO.

Shannon, R. E. *Systems Simulation: The Art and Science.* Englewood Cliffs, N.J.: Prentice-Hall, 1975. Highly recommended. Excellent on methodology. Complete review of simulation languages available at the time. Includes six detailed case studies.

PART THREE

Advanced Techniques

CHAPTER SEVENTEEN

Extensions to Linear Programming

Chapter 3 developed the rudiments of the simplex method. We will now explore some of the refinements that extend its usefulness and increase its efficiency. We have already discussed one extension in Chapter 4—the dual simplex method. Our first topic in this chapter is how to deal with bounded variables more efficiently. Next, we develop the *revised simplex method*. Its compact form is particularly suitable for computer implementation. Finally, we show how certain nonlinear problems can be approximated by piecewise linear systems and solved by *separable programming*.

We will use the power generating problem of Chapter 2 for the first two topics. It may be helpful to briefly review the mathematical summary of that problem in Section 2-7.

17-1 LOWER-BOUNDED VARIABLES

The simplex method uses an implicit lower bound of zero on all variables. This is achieved by having all nonbasic variables with a value zero and all basic variables nonnegative. The nonnegativity of basic variables is maintained by the rules for the vector to leave the basis. When we have a variable x_j with a lower bound L_j, we could introduce a constraint $x_j \geqslant L_j$. We can avoid this by defining a new variable y_j that represents the amount by which x_j exceeds its lower bound L_j; i.e.,

$$y_j = x_j - L_j, \qquad y_j \geqslant 0 \tag{17-1}$$

y_j is substituted for x_j in all constraints and in the objective function. This changes the RHS of all constraints from b_i to $b_i - a_{ij}L_j$ and gives the objective function an initial value of $z_0 = c_jL_j$.

Most commercial computer codes for linear programming automatically do these variable transformations and unscramble them again before displaying the optimal solution.

17-2 UPPER-BOUNDED VARIABLES

Consider problem (3-1), but with the additional constraints that the mining capacity for coal A is limited to $U_1 = 15$ tons and the capacity for coal B is limited to $U_2 = 10$ tons per hour. The new problem is now

$$\text{(17-2)} \qquad \begin{aligned} \text{maximize} \quad & z = 24x_1 + 20x_2 \\ \text{subject to} \quad & 0.5x_1 + x_2 \leq 12 \\ & \tfrac{1}{16}x_1 + \tfrac{1}{24}x_2 \leq 1 \\ & 0 \leq x_1 \leq 15 \\ & 0 \leq x_2 \leq 10 \end{aligned}$$

The last two constraints are the upper bounds on x_1 and x_2. We would like to solve this problem by the simplex method without explicitly including these two upper bounds. Unfortunately, a simple transformation of the variables is not enough. Some changes to the simplex method rules are needed also.

Let us define the variables

$$\text{(17-3)} \qquad x_1' = 15 - x_1, \qquad \text{where } 0 \leq x_1' \leq 15$$

$$\text{(17-4)} \qquad x_2' = 10 - x_2, \qquad \text{where } 0 \leq x_2' \leq 10$$

If x_j is at its lower bound, then x_j' is at its upper bound, and vice versa. Note also that the LHS coefficients of x_j' are the negative of the LHS coefficients of x_j. The upper-bounding routine takes advantage of these two properties to eliminate the upper-bound constraints on the variables. It uses x_j as a nonbasic variable when $x_j = 0$, and uses x_j' as a nonbasic variable when x_j is at its upper bound. When the value of the variable lies between these limits, either x_j or x_j' may be basic.

Table 17-1 shows the initial simplex tableau for problem (17-2) without the upper-bound constraints (see Table 3-1). It implies that all variables are at their lower bound. By simplex criterion 1, x_1 enters the basis. Simplex criterion 2 determines both the variable to leave the basis and the value of the new basic variable. Here the ratio minimum is assumed for $x_1 = 16$. However, we observe that this violates its upper-bound restriction. So we set x_1 to its upper bound of $U_1 = 15$. But now the simplex transformation rules do not drive x_5 to zero. A value of $x_1 = 15$ implies current basic variables of

$$\text{(17-5)} \qquad x_3 = 12 - (0.5)(15) = 4.5 \qquad x_5 = 1 - (\tfrac{1}{16})(15) = \tfrac{1}{16}$$

Table 17-1. *First tableau with upper bounding*

	c_j		24	20	0	0	Ratio
c_j	Basis	Solution	x_1	x_2	x_3	x_5	x_i/γ_i
0	x_3	12	0.5	1	1	0	24
0	x_5	1	$\frac{1}{16}$	$\frac{1}{24}$	0	1	16
	$z_j - c_j$	0	−24	−20	0	0	
			↑				

Transforming Table 17-1 to correspond to this solution would result in a tableau that is not in canonical form. By substituting the x_1 column by x_1', with all coefficients reversed in sign, we can generate a new tableau in canonical form that corresponds to the solution (17-5), with $x_1 = 15$ implicitly. Since $x_1' = 15 - x_1$, we get $x_1' = 0$. Hence, x_1' has the usual property of a nonbasic variable. Making this substitution, we get the second simplex tableau, as shown in Table 17-2. The value of z is $24x_1 = 24(15) = 360$.

Table 17-2. *Second tableau with upper bounding*

	c_j		−24	20	0	0	Ratio
c_j	Basis	Solution	x_1'	x_2	x_3	x_5	x_i/γ_i
0	x_3	4.5	−0.5	1	1	0	4.5
0	x_5	$\frac{1}{16}$	$-\frac{1}{16}$	$\frac{1}{24}$	0	1	1.5
	$z_j - c_j$	360	24	−20	0	0	
				↑			

At the next iteration, x_2 is the variable selected to enter the basis. The minimum ratio value is assumed for $x_2 = 1.5$. Since this is below $U_2 = 10$, x_2 enters the basis at that value, with x_5 leaving it. The third tableau is shown in Table 17-3.

At the third iteration, x_1' is chosen to enter the basis. This means that x_1' will increase from 0 (or, equivalently, x_1 will decrease from 15). As x_1' increases, there are three ways that the solution must be kept feasible, each creating a limit on the value of x_1':

1. $x_3 \geq 0$; this is assured by simplex criterion 2 for the variable leaving the basis.
2. $x_1' \leq U_1 = 15$.
3. $x_2 \leq U_2 = 10$, since a negative γ_i value increases the value of x_i (see Section 3-5).

Let us look at the effect of setting $x_1' = \theta$. Using the equations in canonical form implied by Table 17-3, $x_3 = 3 - \theta$ and $x_2 = 1.5 + 1.5\theta$. For feasibility, we

Table 17-3. *Third tableau with upper bounding*

	c_j		-24	20	0	0	Ratio
c_j	Basis	Solution	x_1'	x_2	x_3	x_5	x_i/γ_i
0	x_3	3	1	0	1	-24	3
20	x_2	1.5	-1.5	1	0	24	—
	$z_j - c_j$	390	-6 ↑	0	0	480	

require $x_3 = 3 - \theta \geq 0$, or $\theta \geqslant 3$, and $x_2 = (1.5 + 1.5\theta) \leq 10$, or $\theta \leq (10 - 1.5)/1.5 = 17/3$. Therefore, x_1 cannot exceed the minimum ratio of simplex criterion 2, its own bound U_1, or the θ value implied by the upper bound on x_2. We get the following criterion, expressed in general terms.

UPPER BOUNDING CRITERION:
VALUE OF NONBASIC VARIABLE THAT IS BEING INCREASED

(17-6) $$x_j = \theta = \text{minimum}\,[\beta, U_j, \delta]$$

where $$\beta = \text{minimum}\left[\frac{\text{value of basic variable } x_i}{\text{corresponding } \gamma_i}\right], \text{ for all } \gamma_i > 0$$

U_j = upper bound of variable entering the basis

$$\delta = \text{minimum}\left[\frac{\text{(basis value–upper bound) of variable } x_i}{\text{corresponding } \gamma_i}\right], \text{ for all } \gamma_i < 0$$

Applying this criterion to our example, we have $x_1' = \text{minimum}\,[3, 15, \frac{17}{3}] = 3$. Hence, $x_3 = 0$ is the first boundary condition met when x_1' is increased to 3. Thus, x_1' replaces x_3 in the basis. This leads to Table 17-4, which is optimal.

Table 17-4. *Optimal tableau with upper bounding*

	c_j		-24	20	0	0
c_j	Basis	Solution	x_1'	x_2	x_3	x_5
-24	x_1'	3	1	0	1	-24
20	x_2	6	0	1	1.5	-12
	$z_j - c_j$	408	0	0	6	336

When we read the solution of Table 17-4, we must remember that $x_1 = 15 - x_1'$ $= 15 - 3 = 12$. Using this result, we see that Table 17-4 is substantially the same as the final tableau in Table 3-2.

For completeness, we need to clarify the action to be taken from the criterion for the value of the nonbasic variable that is being increased. If the minimum of (17-6) is

1. β, replace the current basic variable by the nonbasic variable being increased, as in the normal simplex method.
2. U_j, replace the nonbasic variable being increased, $x_j(x_j')$, by $x_j'(x_j)$. The corresponding column of the tableau must be multiplied by -1. The updated values of the variables are

$$\hat{x}_i = x_i - U_j\gamma_i, \quad \text{for all basic variables}$$
$$\hat{x}_j = U_j \,(\text{or } x_j' = U_j) \tag{17-7}$$

where γ_i is the coefficient in row x_i and column x_j.

3. δ, set the basic variable to its upper bound; i.e., replace $x_k(x_k')$ by x_k' (x_k). The corresponding column is multiplied by -1. The nonbasic variable being increased (x_j) enters the basis in place of $x_k(x_k')$. The new values of the variables are

$$\hat{x}_k = U_k \,(\text{or } \hat{x}_k' = U_k)$$
$$\hat{x}_i = x_i - \delta\gamma_i, \quad \text{for the current basic variables other than } x_k(x_k') \tag{17-8}$$
$$\hat{x}_j = \delta$$

with γ_i defined as for (17-7).

In cases (2) and (3), the objective function value is updated to

$$\hat{z} = \sum_{p=1}^{n} c_p\hat{x}_p$$

*17-3 REVISED SIMPLEX METHOD

Large linear programming problems contain huge amounts of data, and they require tens of thousands of calculations at each iteration. Using the full simplex tableau method, we find many of the data are irrelevant at any given iteration. In particular, the only nonbasic variable of interest at an iteration is the one that is to enter the basis. Similarly, a problem with many columns and few rows requires much updating of nonbasic columns, which may not be needed until many iterations later, if ever. The revised simplex method substantially reduces avoidable data storage and computational effort. The underlying simplex logic remains the same.

The principles underlying the revised simplex method are more easily explained and more readily understood if we use matrix algebra. If you are not at ease with matrix algebra, you may wish to skip this section. At this point, it may also be advisable to briefly study Section A-9 of Appendix A, which presents the essentials of linear programming in matrix form.

We can write a linear program as

$$\begin{aligned} &\text{maximize} && z = \mathbf{cx} \\ &\text{subject to} && \sum_{j=1}^{n} \mathbf{a}_j x_j = \mathbf{b}, \qquad \text{all } x_j \geq 0 \\ &\text{or} && \mathbf{Ax} = \mathbf{b}, \qquad \text{all } \mathbf{x} \geq 0 \end{aligned}$$

Thus at a particular basic solution, we have a matrix **B** in which each column represents a vector of the coefficients of a basic variable (or *basic vector*). The corresponding vector of basic variables is denoted as $\mathbf{x}_B$. Since all nonbasic variables are zero, the basic solution is

$$\mathbf{Bx}_B = \sum_i \mathbf{a}_i x_i = \mathbf{b} \tag{17-9}$$

where $\mathbf{a}_i$'s are basic vectors.

The coefficients of x_j in canonical form (call them vector $\mathbf{y}_j$) are the coefficients of $\mathbf{a}_j$ expressed as a linear combination of the set of basic vectors. (The correct usage of the term "basis" is the set of basic vectors.) Thus,

$$\mathbf{a}_j = \mathbf{By}_j = \sum_i = y_{ij}\mathbf{a}_i \tag{17-10}$$

where the $\mathbf{a}_i$'s are basic vectors.

The entries in the full simplex tableau are the vector $\mathbf{x}_B$ in the "Solution" column, the vectors $\mathbf{y}_j$ for each nonbasic vector in the x_j columns, an identity matrix for the basic vectors, and the $(z_j - c_j)$ values. Let us perform a matrix inverse manipulation on both (17-9) and (17-10). (The inverse of **B** exists by the definition of a basis; the basic vectors are linearly independent.)

$$\mathbf{x}_B = \mathbf{B}^{-1}\mathbf{b} \qquad \text{and} \qquad \mathbf{y}_j = \mathbf{B}^{-1}\mathbf{a}_j \tag{17-11}$$

b and the $\mathbf{a}_j$'s are the RHS and LHS vectors of the original linear program. Thus, if we know $\mathbf{B}^{-1}$ at each iteration, we need not store $\mathbf{x}_B$ or the $\mathbf{y}_j$'s. Similarly, if $\mathbf{c}_B$ are the objective function coefficients of the basic variables, we recall from the way we define z_j in Section 3-4 that $z_j = \mathbf{c}_B\mathbf{y}_j$, or, using equation (17-11),

$$z_j = \mathbf{c}_B(\mathbf{B}^{-1}\mathbf{a}_j) = (\mathbf{c}_B\mathbf{B}^{-1})\mathbf{a}_j \tag{17-12}$$

Again, $\mathbf{c}_B$ and $\mathbf{a}_j$ are original data, so z_j can be calculated using $\mathbf{B}^{-1}$. Hence, all information needed at each iteration is contained in the original data and the basis inverse. However, for convenience, we also store $\mathbf{x}_B$ and $\mathbf{c}_B\mathbf{B}^{-1}$. Since $\mathbf{B}^{-1}$ usually has many fewer columns than the full simplex tableau, fewer computations are needed to update $\mathbf{B}^{-1}$ at each iteration. The revised simplex method efficiently exploits these features.

The $\mathbf{B}^{-1}$ matrix is already a part of the full simplex tableau. It is the set of columns in the tablcau that corresponds to the initial basis of the first tableau—i.e., the positive slack variables and the artificial variables. (There would be a problem with the order of the columns of $\mathbf{B}^{-1}$ if the original basic vectors were not in normal order for an identity matrix. However, we could simply reshuffle the columns to correspond with the proper order.) Hence, the $\mathbf{B}^{-1}$ matrix was updated and carried along in the full simplex tableau. So in the revised simplex method, it can be updated using the same simplex transformation rules.

Let us now illustrate the revised simplex method using the reduced power generating problem—problem (3-1). For later reference, it is useful to show this problem in detached coefficient form, including the slack variables x_3 and x_5, as in Table 17-5.

Table 17-5. *Reduced power generating problem in detached coefficient form*

	x_1	x_2	x_3	x_5	RHS
Smoke	0.5	1	1	0	12
Pulverizer	$\frac{1}{16}$	$\frac{1}{24}$	0	1	1
Obj. function	24	20	0	0	maximize

The initial basis is

$$\mathbf{B} = (\mathbf{a}_3, \mathbf{a}_5) = \begin{bmatrix} 1 & 0 \\ 0 & 1 \end{bmatrix}$$

so

$$\mathbf{B}^{-1} = \begin{bmatrix} 1 & 0 \\ 0 & 1 \end{bmatrix}$$

This allows us to compute the following information from the original data in Table 17-5.

$$\mathbf{x}_B = \begin{bmatrix} x_3 \\ x_5 \end{bmatrix} = \mathbf{B}^{-1}\mathbf{b} = \begin{bmatrix} 1 & 0 \\ 0 & 1 \end{bmatrix}\begin{bmatrix} 12 \\ 1 \end{bmatrix} = \begin{bmatrix} 12 \\ 1 \end{bmatrix}$$

$$\mathbf{c}_B\mathbf{B}^{-1} = (0, 0)\begin{bmatrix} 1 & 0 \\ 0 & 1 \end{bmatrix} = (0, 0)$$

$$z = \mathbf{c}_B\mathbf{x}_B = (0, 0)\begin{bmatrix} 12 \\ 1 \end{bmatrix} = 0$$

We store these data in the tableau shown in Table 17-6. In addition, we have a spare column in which to put the $\mathbf{y}_j$ of the variable to enter the basis, which we have yet to determine.

Let us now use equation (17-12) to find the $(z_j - c_j)$'s. We apply this equation to each of the nonbasic variables, using the original information in Table 17-5:

$$z_1 = (0, 0)\begin{bmatrix} 0.5 \\ \frac{1}{16} \end{bmatrix} = 0, \qquad \text{so } (z_1 - c_1) = -24$$

$$z_2 = (0, 0)\begin{bmatrix} 1 \\ \frac{1}{24} \end{bmatrix} = 0, \qquad \text{so } (z_2 - c_2) = -20$$

Table 17-6. *Initial revised simplex tableau*

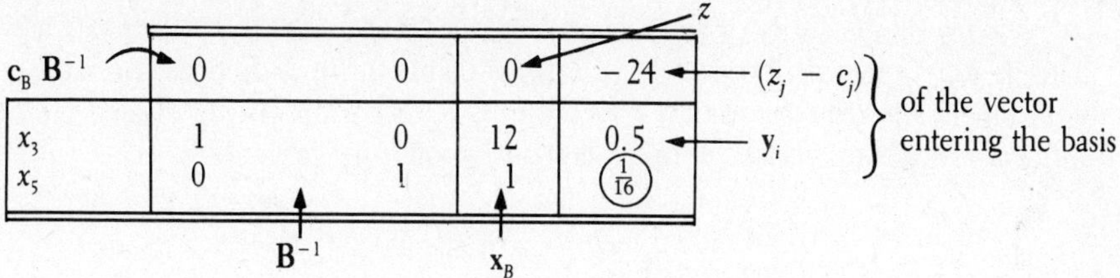

$\mathbf{c}_B\mathbf{B}^{-1}$	0	0	0	−24
x_3	1	0	12	0.5
x_5	0	1	1	$\frac{1}{16}$ (circled)

We now use simplex criterion 1, i.e., minimum $[(z_j - c_j) < 0]$. This gives us x_1 to enter the basis. To determine the variable to leave the basis and to update the tableau, we require $\mathbf{y}_1$. We find this by equation (17-11), using the original data in Table 17-5:

$$\mathbf{y}_1 = \mathbf{B}^{-1}\mathbf{a}_1 = \begin{bmatrix} 1 & 0 \\ 0 & 1 \end{bmatrix}\begin{bmatrix} 0.5 \\ \frac{1}{16} \end{bmatrix} = \begin{bmatrix} 0.5 \\ \frac{1}{16} \end{bmatrix}$$

The rule for the variable to leave the basis is found from the last two columns of Table 17-6. For each positive element in the $\mathbf{y}_j$ vector, we find the minimum $(x_{Bi}/\mathbf{y}_{ij})$ ratio. In this case, we see it is the minimum $(12/0.5,\ 1/\frac{1}{16})$, or 16. Thus x_5 leaves the basis. You should check that these calculations are equivalent to those of the first simplex iteration in Section 3-6. Using the regular simplex transformation rules, with $\frac{1}{16}$ as the pivot element (circled), we get the new revised simplex tableau of Table 17-7. The $\mathbf{y}_j$ column and $(z_j - c_j)$ square are left blank until the new variable to enter has been determined.

Table 17-7. *Second revised simplex tableau*

	0	384	384	−4
x_3	1	−8	4	$\frac{2}{3}$ (circled)
x_1	0	16	16	$\frac{2}{3}$

Updated at iteration 1 — Determined at iteration 2

At the second iteration, we find the $(z_j - c_j)$ values by equation (17-12) and the original data:

$$(z_2 - c_2) = (0,\ 384)\begin{bmatrix} 1 \\ \frac{1}{24} \end{bmatrix} - 20 = -4 \qquad (z_5 - c_5) = (0,\ 384)\begin{bmatrix} 0 \\ 1 \end{bmatrix} - 0 = 384$$

The variable to enter is thus x_2. We insert $(z_2 - c_2)$ into the empty top right-hand square of Table 17-7, and calculate $\mathbf{y}_2$ for this basis, using equation (17-11):

$$\mathbf{y}_2 = \mathbf{B}^{-1}\mathbf{a}_2 = \begin{bmatrix} 1 & -8 \\ 0 & 16 \end{bmatrix} \begin{bmatrix} 1 \\ \frac{1}{24} \end{bmatrix} = \begin{bmatrix} \frac{2}{3} \\ \frac{2}{3} \end{bmatrix}$$

This is now entered into the $\mathbf{y}_j$ column in Table 17-7. When the variable-to-leave criterion is applied, we find x_3 leaves the basis. Pivoting on the circled element ($\frac{2}{3}$), we derive the third revised simplex tableau, shown in Table 17-8.

Table 17-8. *Third revised simplex tableau (optimal)*

	6	336	408
x_2	$\frac{3}{2}$	-12	6
x_1	-1	24	12

The new $(z_j - c_j)$ are

$$(z_3 - c_3) = (6, 336)\begin{bmatrix} 1 \\ 0 \end{bmatrix} - 0 = 6 \qquad (z_5 - c_5) = (6, 336)\begin{bmatrix} 0 \\ 1 \end{bmatrix} - 0 = 336$$

Since all $(z_j - c_j) \geqslant 0$, this tableau is optimal.

The revised simplex method has another important aspect besides the advantages of less storage and often less computations. When the solution is performed by computer, there is always the problem of the precision of the computed data. At each iteration, the rounding and truncation errors are compounded. After many iterations, the table elements may be significantly in error. This affects the $(z_j - c_j)$ values and the ratio for the variable to leave. As a consequence, the wrong variable could be chosen to enter or to leave the basis. We can keep these errors within reasonable bounds by finding the basis inverse $\mathbf{B}^{-1}$ from scratch at any particular iteration. There are trade-offs to be considered in doing this. A matrix inversion is a lengthy process and is prone to computer errors also. Normally in a commercial computer code, a reinversion is performed every so many iterations—e.g., every 50 iterations. It is also standard practice to reinvert when the optimality criterion is satisfied. Special procedures for storing and updating $\mathbf{B}$ or $\mathbf{B}^{-1}$ that take into account the sparsity of the matrices (the proportion of nonzero elements) help to reduce errors, speed up reinversions, and also further reduce storage needs.

17-4 SEPARABLE PROGRAMMING

Consider a problem with a nonlinear objective function and nonlinear constraints of the following form: Find values $x_1, x_2, \ldots, x_n$ that

$$\begin{aligned} &\text{maximize } \sum_{j=1}^{n} f_j(x_j) \\ (17\text{-}13) \qquad &\text{subject to } \sum_{j=1}^{n} g_{ij}(x_j) \leqslant b_i, \qquad \text{for } i = 1, \ldots, m \\ &x_j \geqslant 0 \qquad j = 1, \ldots, n \end{aligned}$$

This is called a *separable programming problem* because the objective function and the constraints are all *separable functions.* A function h in the variables x_1, $x_2, \ldots, x_n$ is separable if it can be expressed as the sum of n functions in one variable each:

$$h(x_1, x_2, \ldots, x_n) = h_1(x_1) + h_2(x_2) + \cdots + h_n(x_n)$$

The function $h(x_1, x_2) = x_1^2 - x_2^3 + x_1 + x_2$ is separable since $h(x_1, x_2) = h_1(x_1) + h_2(x_2)$, with $h_1(x_1) = x_1^2 + x_1$ and $h_2(x_2) = x_2 - x_2^3$. But $h(x_1, x_2) = x_1^2 - x_2^3 + x_1x_2$ is not a separable function. However, we can make this function separable by a suitable transformation of variables: Let $y = (x_1 + x_2)$, so $y^2 = x_1^2 + x_2^2 + 2x_1x_2$. Then the term $x_1x_2 = \frac{1}{2}(y^2 - x_1^2 - x_2^2)$, and $h(x_1, x_2)$ can be replaced by the system:

$$H(x_1, x_2, y) = \tfrac{1}{2}x_1^2 - x_2^3 - \tfrac{1}{2}x_2^2 + \tfrac{1}{2}y^2$$

$$\text{subject to } y - x_1 - x_2 = 0$$

Many nonseparable functions can be transformed into a separable system. You should consult more advanced texts for further examples.

To solve problem (17-13) by the simplex method, we first have to approximate each nonlinear function by a suitable linearization. The resulting set of linear objective function and linear constraints is referred to as the *approximating problem*. It is this problem that is solved by a suitably modified version of the simplex method.

Consider the following problem: A cabinet maker is asked by a jeweller to build two display boxes, with lids made from a special shatterproof and breakproof transparent material. Only 8 square feet of the material is in stock at present, and no more can be procured within the time available to build the boxes. Figure 17-1 shows the dimensions of the two boxes. For box 1, the length has to be 1 foot, whereas the width and height are to be of equal but unspecified size x_1. For box 2, the height has to be 1 foot, whereas the width and length are to be of equal but unspecified size x_2. The dimensions x_1 and x_2 are to be chosen so as to satisfy the material constraint on the lids of the two boxes. The lid of box 1 requires (length) (width) $= 1x_1$ square feet

Figure 17-1. *Display box manufacturing problem.*

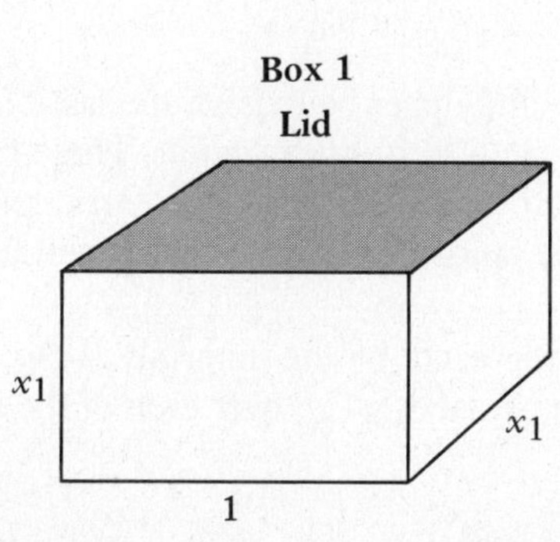

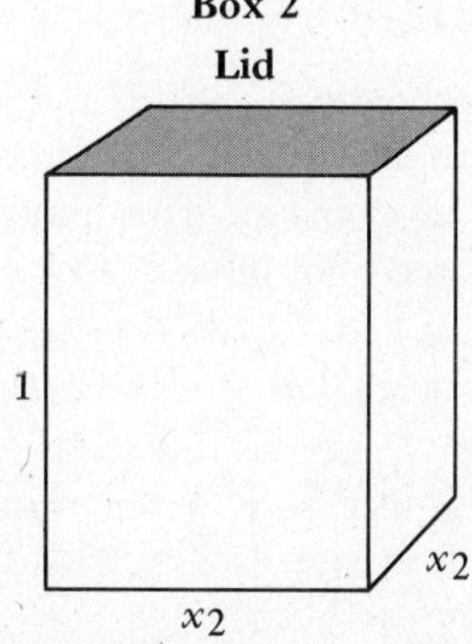

of the material, and the lid of box 2 requires (length) (width) $= x_2x_2 = x_2^2$ square feet of the material. The sum of these cannot exceed the amount available, i.e.,

$$x_1 + x_2^2 \leq 8$$

The cost for material and labor is \$0.5 per square foot of the outside of each box. For box 1, four of the sides are equal to $1x_1$ square feet, and two sides are equal to x_1^2. The total outside area is thus $2x_1^2 + 4x_1$. Similarly, for box 2, four of the sides are equal to $1x_2$ square feet, and two sides are equal to x_2^2, summing to $2x_2^2 + 4x_2$. The charge to the customer is proportional to the sum of the three dimensions of the boxes, i.e., width + length + height (\$2 per foot for box 1, and \$2.5 per foot for box 2).

The profit for each box is

$$\text{box 1:} \quad 2(x_1 + x_1 + 1) - 0.5(2x_1^2 + 4x_1) = 2x_1 - x_1^2 + 2$$

$$\text{box 2:} \quad 2.5(x_2 + x_2 + 1) - 0.5(2x_2^2 + 4x_2) = 3x_2 - x_2^2 + 2.5$$

Total profits for both boxes are

$$2x_1 - x_1^2 + 3x_2 - x_2^2 + 4.5$$

The objective is to determine the dimensions x_1 and x_2 so as to maximize profits, subject to the constraint on the material available. Thus, we get the following nonlinear programming problem, where the constant has been dropped from the objective function:

$$\begin{aligned} &\text{maximize } z = f(x_1, x_2) = 2x_1 + 3x_2 - x_1^2 - x_2^2 \\ \text{(17-14)} \quad &\text{subject to } g_1(x_1, x_2) = x_1 + x_2^2 \leq 8 \\ &\qquad x_1, x_2 \geq 0 \end{aligned}$$

These functions are separable as follows:

$$\text{(17-15)} \qquad f(x_1, x_2) = f_1(x_1) + f_2(x_2)$$

where $f_1(x_1) = 2x_1 - x_1^2$ and $f_2(x_2) = 3x_2 - x_2^2$, and

$$\text{(17-16)} \qquad g_1(x_1, x_2) = g_{11}(x_1) + g_{12}(x_2)$$

where $g_{11}(x_1) = x_1$ and $g_{12}(x_2) = x_2^2$.

Our first task is to estimate some lower and upper bounds on the feasible values of x_1 and x_2. This limits the computations involved in linearization. These estimates need not be very accurate, but should be on the conservative side. An examination of $g_1(x_1, x_2) \leq 8$ shows that x_1 will lie in the range $0 \leq x_1 \leq 8$, and x_2 will lie in the range $0 \leq x_2 \leq 3$.

Let us linearize $f_1(x_1)$ and $g_{11}(x_1)$ over each of the intervals $0 \leq x_1 \leq 2$, $2 \leq x_1 \leq 4$, $4 \leq x_1 \leq 6$, $6 \leq x_1 \leq 8$, and $f_2(x_2)$ and $g_{12}(x_2)$ over each of the intervals $0 \leq x_2 \leq 1$, $1 \leq x_2 \leq 2$, $2 \leq x_2 \leq 3$.

We define p_j to be the number of intervals for variable x_j, so $p_1 = 4$ and $p_2 = 3$. The points dividing each of the variables into intervals are called *grid points.* So, for example, the grid points for x_1 are 0, 2, 4, 6, 8. Let us define x_{k1} to be the grid point at the right-hand end of the kth interval for x_1. Similarly, let x_{k2} be the grid point at the right-hand end of the kth interval for x_2. These are shown in columns 1 and 5 of Table 17-9. The length of the kth interval is $(x_{k1} - x_{(k-1)1}) = \Delta x_{k1}$ for x_1, and $\Delta x_{k2} = (x_{k2} - x_{(k-1)2})$ for x_2, shown in columns 2 and 6 of Table 17-9. Selecting a good set of grid points for each variable is largely a matter of experience and the analyst's understanding of the nature of the nonlinearities.

Table 17-9. *Data for linearization of problem (17-14)*

(1)	(2)	(3)	(4)	(5)	(6)	(7)	(8)
$x_{01} = 0$		$f_{01} = 0$	$g_{011} = 0$	$x_{02} = 0$		$f_{02} = 0$	$g_{012} = 0$
$x_{11} = 2$	$\Delta x_{11} = 2$	$f_{11} = 0$	$g_{111} = 2$	$x_{12} = 1$	$\Delta x_{12} = 1$	$f_{12} = 2$	$g_{112} = 1$
$x_{21} = 4$	$\Delta x_{21} = 2$	$f_{21} = -8$	$g_{211} = 4$	$x_{22} = 2$	$\Delta x_{22} = 1$	$f_{22} = 2$	$g_{212} = 4$
$x_{31} = 6$	$\Delta x_{31} = 2$	$f_{31} = -24$	$g_{311} = 6$	$x_{32} = 3$	$\Delta x_{32} = 1$	$f_{32} = 0$	$g_{312} = 9$
$x_{41} = 8$	$\Delta x_{41} = 2$	$f_{41} = -48$	$g_{411} = 8$				

Looking at function $f_1(x_1)$, let us define $f_{k1} = f_1(x_{k1})$ as the value of f_1 at the grid point x_{k1}. For $f_2(x_2)$, $f_{k2} = f_2(x_{k2})$. These are shown in columns 3 and 7 of Table 17-9. Similarly, we define $g_{k11} = g_{11}(x_{k1})$ and $g_{k12} = g_{12}(x_{k2})$, as shown in columns 4 and 8.

We call the functions of linear segments the *approximating functions.* To distinguish between the original and the approximating function, we shall denote the approximating function of f_j by $\hat{f}_j$. Figures 17-2 and 17-3 show the original functions and the approximating functions. We now express the original nonlinear programming problem in terms of the approximating functions as follows:

$$\begin{aligned} &\text{maximize } \sum_{j=1}^{2} \hat{f}_j(x_j) \\ (17\text{-}17)\qquad &\text{subject to } \sum_{j=1}^{2} \hat{g}_{1j}(x_j) \leq 8 \\ &x_j \geq 0, \qquad j = 1, 2 \end{aligned}$$

This is the *approximating problem* that we will manipulate into a form that can be solved by a version of the simplex method.

17-5 THE λ-FORMULATION OF THE APPROXIMATING PROBLEM

We will now look at the problem of formulating the approximating problem explicitly. To do this, we will view the values of a variable in the approximating problem in terms of proportions of the grid points of the variable. Let us consider a value of x_1

Figure 17-2. *Linearization of $f_1(x_1)$ and $g_{11}(x_1)$.*

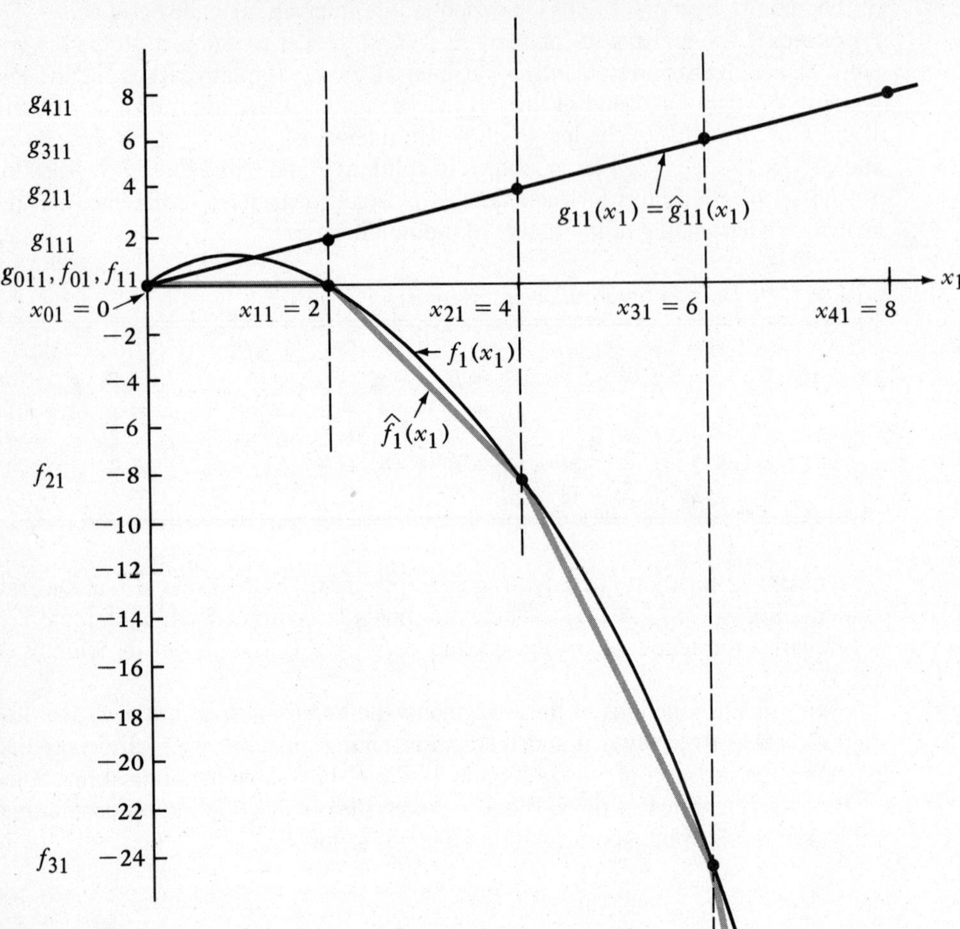

that lies in the kth interval; i.e., $x_{(k-1)1} \leq x_1 \leq x_{k1}$. Since x_1 lies on the line segment between $x_{(k-1)1}$ and x_{k1}, it can be expressed as

(17-18) $$x_1 = \lambda x_{(k-1)1} + (1 - \lambda)x_{k1}$$

where $0 \leq \lambda \leq 1$. The terms λ and $(1 - \lambda)$ give the proportions (or weights) of the grid points defining the kth interval. So, for example, if $x_1 = 5$ (it lies in the third interval), then $x_1 = \frac{1}{2}x_{21} + \frac{1}{2}x_{31}$ [i.e., $5 = \frac{1}{2}(4) + \frac{1}{2}(6)$].

More generally, $x_1 = 5$ can be expressed in terms of all the grid points of x_1, by giving a zero weight to all those grid points other than x_{21} and x_{31}:

$$x_1 = 5 = 0x_{01} + 0x_{11} + \tfrac{1}{2}x_{21} + \tfrac{1}{2}x_{31} + 0x_{41}$$

Since a given interval is defined by only two grid points, at most two grid points

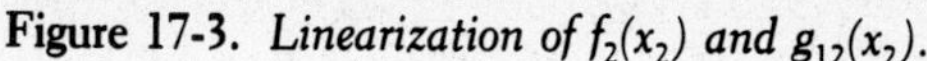

Figure 17-3. *Linearization of $f_2(x_2)$ and $g_{12}(x_2)$.*

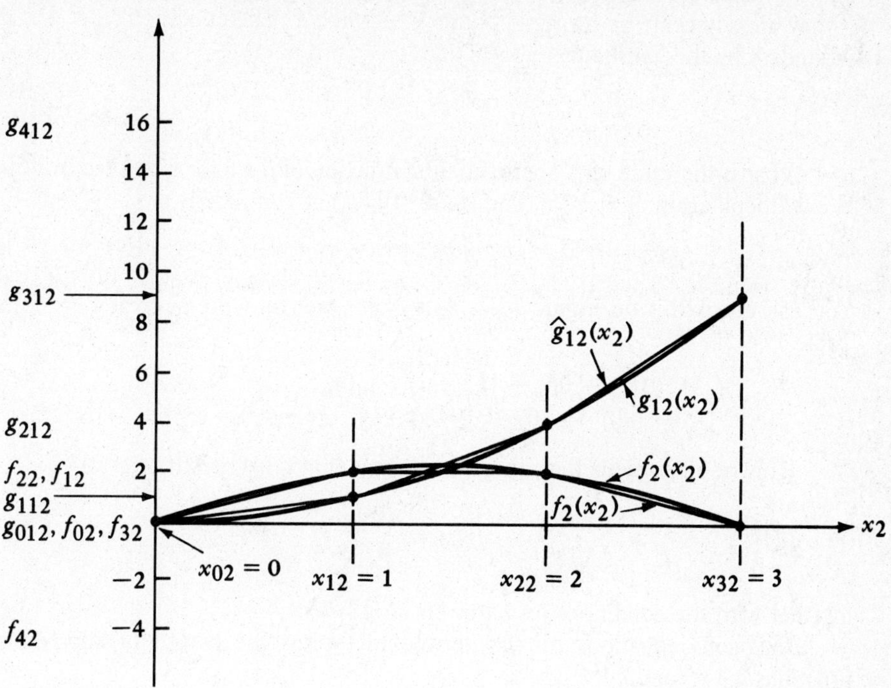

can have positive (and nonzero) weights, and those two will always be adjacent. If x_1 has the exact value of the grid point, there will be only one nonzero weight. For example, $x_1 = 2 = 0x_{01} + 1x_{11} + 0x_{21} + 0x_{31} + 0x_{41}$.

We will now generalize this result. Let λ_{uj} be the weight given to the uth grid point of x_j, $(u = 0, \ldots, p_j)$. Each λ_{uj} must satisfy $0 \leqslant \lambda_{uj} \leqslant 1$; and, since the weights represent proportions of the end points of an interval, we have $\Sigma_{u=0}^{p_j} \lambda_{uj} = 1$, provided that no more than two weights can be nonzero and they must be adjacent. Then by analogy to (17-18), if x_j is in the kth interval,

$$x_j = \lambda_{(k-1)j}x_{(k-1)j} + \lambda_{kj}x_{kj} \tag{17-19}$$

with

$$0 \leqslant \lambda_{(k-1)j} \leqslant 1$$

$$0 \leqslant \lambda_{kj} \leqslant 1$$

and

$$\lambda_{(k-1)j} + \lambda_{kj} = 1$$

By including all the other grid points and giving them zero weights, we obtain

$$x_j = \sum_{u=0}^{p_j} \lambda_{uj}x_{uj} \qquad \text{with} \qquad \sum_{u=0}^{p_j} \lambda_{uj} = 1, \qquad \lambda_{uj} \geqslant 0 \tag{17-20}$$

and the usual proviso that for each j, at most two λ_{uj} can be positive and then only if they are adjacent, i.e., for grid points $k - 1$ and k. The condition $\lambda_{uj} \leq 1$ is made redundant by the constraint

$$\Sigma_u \lambda_{uj} = 1$$

What is the value of $\hat{f}_j$ [approximating function of $f_j(x_j)$] for x_j defined by (17-20)? We will look again at $x_1 = 5$. The value of $\hat{f}_1(x_1)$ at $x_1 = 5$ is

$$\hat{f}_1(x_1) = \hat{f}_1(5) = \tfrac{1}{2}f_{21} + \tfrac{1}{2}f_{31} = \tfrac{1}{2}(-8) + \tfrac{1}{2}(-24) = -16$$

You can check this on Figure 17-2. As with x_1, we can write $\hat{f}_1(x_1)$ at $x_1 = 5$, using Table 17-9, as

$$\begin{aligned} f_1(5) &= 0f_{01} + 0f_{11} + \tfrac{1}{2}\hat{f}_{21} + \tfrac{1}{2}\hat{f}_{31} + 0f_{41} \\ &= 0(0) + 0(0) + \tfrac{1}{2}(-8) + \tfrac{1}{2}(-24) + 0(-48) = -16 \end{aligned}$$

This result suggests that, in general terms, for x_j in the kth interval,

$$\hat{f}_j(x_j) = \sum_{u=0}^{p_j} \lambda_{uj} f_{uj} \tag{17-21}$$

together with the conditions on λ_{uj} given in (17-20).

Analogous equations can be derived to express the constraint approximating functions $\hat{g}_{11}(x_1)$ and $\hat{g}_{12}(x_2)$:

$$\hat{g}_{1j}(x_j) = \sum_{u=0}^{p_j} \lambda_{uj} g_{u1j} \tag{17-22}$$

with the conditions on λ_{uj} given in (17-20).

In expressions (17-20), (17-21), and (17-22), we have derived the *λ-formulation of the approximating problem* (17-17). It is summarized as follows:

$$\begin{aligned} &\text{maximize } \sum_{j=1}^{2} \left(\sum_{u=0}^{p_j} \lambda_{uj} f_{uj} \right) \\ &\text{subject to } \sum_{j=1}^{2} \left(\sum_{u=0}^{p_j} \lambda_{uj} g_{u1j} \right) \leq 8 \\ &\sum_{\theta=0}^{p_j} \lambda_{uj} = 1, \quad j = 1, 2 \\ &\lambda_{uj} \geq 0, \quad \text{all } u \text{ and } j \end{aligned} \tag{17-23}$$

with the condition that at most two λ_{uj} can be nonzero for each j, and then only if they are adjacent.

The data in Table 17-9 enable us to write (17-23) in full:

(17-24)

$$\begin{aligned} \text{maximize } & 0\lambda_{01} + 0\lambda_{11} - 8\lambda_{21} - 24\lambda_{31} - 48\lambda_{41} + 0\lambda_{02} + 2\lambda_{12} + 2\lambda_{22} + 0\lambda_{32} \\ \text{subject to } & 0\lambda_{01} + 2\lambda_{11} + 4\lambda_{21} + 6\lambda_{31} + 8\lambda_{41} + 0\lambda_{02} + 1\lambda_{12} + 4\lambda_{22} + 9\lambda_{32} \leq 8 \\ & \lambda_{01} + \lambda_{11} + \lambda_{21} + \lambda_{31} + \lambda_{41} = 1 \\ & \lambda_{02} + \lambda_{12} + \lambda_{22} + \lambda_{32} = 1 \\ & \lambda_{uj} \geq 0, \qquad \text{all } u \text{ and } j \end{aligned}$$

with the special condition that at most two λ_{uj} can be nonzero for each j, and then only if they are adjacent.

Problem (17-24) is a linear programming problem with the λ_{uj} as variables. The only snag is the special condition on the variables. However, by superimposing special housekeeping rules on the simplex method that restrict entry of variables into the basis, we can solve the λ-formulation by that powerful algorithm. The major disadvantage of separable programming is that it may expand considerably the number of variables and constraints in the original nonlinear program. In our case, problem (17-14) had two variables (x_1 and x_2) and one constraint, while problem (17-24) has nine variables and three constraints. The last two constraints are in a form that can be handled by a generalized upper-bounding technique incorporated in most advanced linear programming computer codes.

17-6 ANALYSIS OF THE SOLUTION OF THE λ-FORMULATION

When we solve problem (17-24), we obtain four alternative optimal basic solutions, shown in Table 17-10.

The values of the x_j variables can be found from these solutions by equation (17-20) and Table 17-9. Solution 1 is $x_1 = 0$, $x_2 = 1$; solution 2 is $x_1 = 0$, $x_2 = 2$; solution 3 is $x_1 = 2$, $x_2 = 1$; and solution 4 is $x_1 = 2$, $x_2 = 2$. In every case, $\hat{f}_1(x_1) = 0$ and $\hat{f}_2(x_2) = 2$, so the objective function value of the approximating problem is 2. These are not the only optimal solutions; every convex combination of them is also optimal to the approximating problem.

In terms of the original problem (17-14), we can show that the four solutions in Table 17-10 also give $z = 2$. However, these solutions are not optimal. The optimal solution to (17-14) is $x_1 = 1$, $x_2 = \frac{3}{2}$, and $z = 3\frac{1}{4}$.

Thus, we face a difficulty with separable programming. There is no reason, in general, to believe that the optimum of the approximating problem is the optimum—or even a good approximation of the optimum—for the original problem. The accuracy depends on how the variables were segmented. Usually, finer intervals give greater accuracy, but they also lead to a larger approximating problem. Some computer codes avoid this problem to some extent by making the intervals smaller as the algorithm nears the optimal solution.

Table 17-10. *Optimal solutions to problem (17-24)*

	Solution 1	Solution 2	Solution 3	Solution 4
λ_{01}	1	1	0	0
λ_{11}	0	0	1	1
λ_{21}	0	0	0	0
λ_{31}	0	0	0	0
λ_{41}	0	0	0	0
λ_{02}	0	0	0	0
λ_{12}	1	0	1	0
λ_{22}	0	1	0	1
λ_{32}	0	0	0	0

Separable programming solves certain types of nonlinear problems. As we shall see in Chapters 19, 20, and particularly 21, all nonlinear programming techniques share one weakness—namely, they cannot guarantee to find the *overall* (or *global*) *optimum*, unless the objective function and the feasible region satisfy certain properties. For separable programming with an objective function to be maximized, the objective function has to exhibit decreasing or constant returns to scale. For constraints referring to resource use, incremental amounts of each variable must require increasing or constant resource use. This is the case for our example. Hence, the solution found is the global optimum. Section 21-3 states these conditions rigorously.

In fact, if a separable programming problem satisfies the properties for a global optimum, then it can be linearized as demonstrated and we can solve it directly by the simplex method without imposing restrictions on the variables to enter the basis.

EXERCISES

17.1 Reformulate exercise 2.2, with the constraint on vitamin X as a lower bound on the appropriate decision variable.

17.2 Reformulate the media selection problem of Section 2-14, given by expressions (2-19) through (2-23), replacing (2-22) and (2-23) by upper bounds on the variables. Solve using the upper-bounded simplex method.

17.3 Reformulate exercise 2.4 with upper-bounded variables, and solve using the upper-bounded simplex method.

17.4 Solve the problem in exercise 3.10(a), with an upper bound on x_1 of 2. Use the big M method.

17.5 Solve this problem using the upper-bounding algorithm:

$$\begin{aligned} \text{maximize } z &= 4x_1 + 5x_2 + \tfrac{5}{2}x_3 \\ \text{subject to} \quad & 2x_1 + 3x_2 + x_3 \leq 9 \\ & 2x_1 + 1x_2 + 2x_3 \leq 9 \end{aligned}$$

$$1 \leq x_1 \leq 4 \qquad 0 \leq x_2 \leq 1 \qquad x_3 \geq 0$$

Find also the alternative optimal basic solution.

17.6 Consider exercise 3.6. Use the revised simplex method to solve:
(a) The problem of part (a).
(b) The problem of part (b).

17.7 Consider exercise 3.10. Use the revised simplex method for the big M formulation to solve:
(a) The problem of part (a).
(b) The problem of part (b).

17.8 Consider the problem

$$\begin{aligned} &\text{maximize } f(x) = -2x_1^2 - (x_2 - 3)^2 \\ &\text{subject to} \quad 2x_1 + x_2 \leq 4 \\ &\qquad x_1, x_2 \geq 0 \end{aligned}$$

Set up the approximating problem using the λ-formulation of separable programming. Use the grid points

$$x_1 = (0, \tfrac{1}{4}, \tfrac{1}{2}, 1, 2) \qquad x_2 = (0, \tfrac{1}{2}, \tfrac{3}{2}, 2, 3, 4)$$

17.9 Set up the following as a separable programming problem:

$$\begin{aligned} &\text{maximize } z = (x_1 - 3)(x_1 - 15)^2 - (x_2 - 4)(x_2 - 8) \\ &\text{subject to} \quad x_1^2 + x_2^2 \leq 25 \\ &\qquad x_1 + 2x_2 \geq 2 \\ &\qquad x_1, x_2 \geq 0 \end{aligned}$$

17.10 Set up the following problem as a separable programming problem using the λ-formulation:

$$\begin{aligned} &\text{maximize } f(x) = 16x_1 + 20x_2 - 4x_1x_2 - x_1^2 - x_2^2 \\ &\text{subject to} \quad x_1^2 + 4x_2^2 \leq 16 \\ &\qquad a_1x_1 + a_2x_2 \geq 3 \\ &\qquad x_1, x_2 \geq 0 \end{aligned}$$

where $\begin{Bmatrix} a_1 = 1, a_2 = 1, & \text{if } x_1 \geq 2, x_2 \leq 1 \\ a_1 = \frac{3}{4}, a_2 = \frac{3}{2}, & \text{if } x_1 < 2, x_2 > 1 \end{Bmatrix}$.

Justify briefly your choice of grid points.

17.11 Set up the following problem as a separable programming problem using the λ-formulation:

$$\begin{aligned} &\text{maximize } f(x) = 6x - 4x^2 + x^3 \\ &\text{subject to } x^2 - 6x \leq 5, \qquad x \geq 0 \end{aligned}$$

REFERENCES

General

Dantzig, G. *Linear Programming and Extensions*. Princeton, N.J.: Princeton University Press, 1963. An authoritative but difficult text. Somewhat out-of-date.

Garvin, W. W. *Introduction to Linear Programming.* New York: McGraw-Hill, 1960.
An old text, but well written. It is particularly useful because it uses no matrix algebra. Chapters 11 and 13 deal with upper bounding and the revised simplex method, respectively.

Hadley, G. *Linear Programming.* Reading, Mass.: Addison-Wesley, 1962.
This text covers, in matrix form, bounded variables in Chapter 11 and the revised simplex method in Chapter 7.

Separable Programming

Beale, E. M. L. "Numerical Methods." In J. Abadie (ed.), *Nonlinear Programming.* Amsterdam: North-Holland, 1967. Sections V and VI contain an interesting introduction to the theory and practical use of the λ-formulation—well worth reading.

Beale, E. M. L., P. J. Coen, and A. D. J. Flowerdew. "Separable Programming Applied to an Ore-Purchasing Problem," *Applied Statistics*, Vol. 14, 1965.

Hadley, G. *Nonlinear and Dynamic Programming*, Reading, Mass.: Addison-Wesley, 1964. Chapter 4 gives a good exposition of separable programming. The λ-formulation is also included, along with comprehensive proofs and applications.

MacMillan, C. *Mathematical Programming*, 2nd ed. New York: Wiley, 1975. The text gives a tableau-by-tableau solution of the λ-formulation in Chapter 6. Also of particular interest is the FORTRAN program for the λ-formulation in Appendix E, with a worked example on pages 207-216. The average student should have little trouble following the exposition.

CHAPTER EIGHTEEN

Integer Programming

In linear programming, we assume that all variables are continuous. If the variables measure quantities (such as time, liquids, or funds), this is an accurate representation. If the variables refer to discrete commodities (machines, people) and the solution gives the variables large values, rounding to the nearest integer may be close to optimal. However, if the optimal value is small, rounding it to the nearest integer may be far from optimal.

Techniques for solving linear programs with integer restrictions on some or all variables are called *integer programming techniques*. Before we deal with these, let us go through a few examples of how integer programming arises.

18-1 A SIMPLE INTEGER PROBLEM

A university has received a grant of $2.5 million for purchasing new computer equipment. It is impossible for the university to supplement this sum from any other source. Feasibility studies indicate that only two machines are suitable. The setup of the university is such that any number of either type of machine or any combination of them would be quite acceptable. Benchmark tests have enabled the university to evaluate the load capacity in units of "average jobs" per hour for the two types of machines.

Computer	Cost ($ million)	Capacity (per hr)
1	1.4	28 jobs
2	0.6	11 jobs

The university wishes to maximize its potential job capacity. Clearly, the machines can be purchased only in whole units.

Let x_1 be the number of type 1 computers, and let x_2 be the number of type 2 computers. The job capacity per hour (in average jobs) is $28x_1 + 11x_2$. This is to be maximized. Hence, the objective is

$$\text{maximize } z = 28x_1 + 11x_2$$

subject to the finance constraint, nonnegativity conditions, and integrality constraints

$$\begin{aligned} &14x_1 + 6x_2 \leq 25 \quad \text{(units \$100,000)} && \text{(finance constraint)} \\ (18\text{-}1) \qquad &x_1, x_2 \geq 0 && \text{(nonnegativity conditions)} \\ &x_1, x_2 \quad \text{integers} && \text{(integrality)} \end{aligned}$$

Although problem (18-1) has the structure of an ordinary linear programming problem, it must be solved by integer programming because of the small solution values of the variables. We will discuss the actual solution to this problem later.

The structure of integer programming allows some interesting twists in the formulations, such as the introduction of *zero-one variables*, i.e., variables restricted to the values 0 and 1. These can be ordinary decision variables, as in the *assembly line balancing* problem, or "dummy" variables especially introduced to permit logical statements to be formulated as linear constraints, as in the *fixed charge* problem.

18-2 ASSEMBLY-LINE BALANCING PROBLEM

An assembly line consisting of a collection of work stations has to perform a series of jobs in order to assemble a product. At each work station, one or more of the jobs may be performed. Normally, there are some restrictions on the order in which jobs may be done; these are called ***precedence relations***. There is also a limit on the time a product can stay at any particular work station. Consider an example of a product with 5 jobs. The decision involved allocating each job to a work station so that the number of work stations is minimized. Table 18-1 gives the jobs, any precedence relations that exist, and the time needed to complete each job.

Job i is either done at station j or not done at station j. This is an either/or situation that fits in well with 0–1 variables.

$$\text{Let } x_{ij} = \begin{cases} 1 & \text{if } i \text{ is done at station } j \\ 0 & \text{if } i \text{ is not done at station } j \end{cases}$$

Table 18-1. *Data for assembly-line balancing*

Job i	Time p_i (min)	Precedence
1	6	—
2	5	—
3	7	—
4	6	3
5	5	2, 4

Let us assume that there are 4 stations (this is certainly an upper limit). Suppose the maximum time at each work station is 12 minutes. So we obtain the following time constraint on each solution:

(18-2) $$\sum_{i=1}^{5} p_i x_{ij} \leq 12, \qquad j = 1, \ldots, 4$$

(i.e., the time taken for jobs assigned to station j must be less than 12 minutes). Equations (18-2) expand to

(18-3)
$$\begin{aligned}
6x_{11} + 5x_{21} + 7x_{31} + 6x_{41} + 5x_{51} &\leq 12 \\
6x_{12} + 5x_{22} + 7x_{32} + 6x_{42} + 5x_{52} &\leq 12 \\
6x_{13} + 5x_{23} + 7x_{33} + 6x_{43} + 5x_{53} &\leq 12 \\
6x_{14} + 5x_{24} + 7x_{34} + 6x_{44} + 5x_{54} &\leq 12
\end{aligned}$$

Next, we must handle precedence relations between jobs. By saying that job 3 must be done before job 4, we mean that job 3 must be performed either at the same station as job 4 or at a prior station. Job i has been done at or before station k if $\sum_{j=1}^{k} x_{ij} = 1$, and has not been done if $\sum_{j=1}^{k} x_{ij} = 0$. At station k, if $\sum_{j=1}^{k} x_{4j} \leq \sum_{j=1}^{k} x_{3j}$, then job 4 cannot be done unless job 3 has been done because $\sum_{j=1}^{k} x_{4j} = 1$ only if $\sum_{j=1}^{k} x_{3j} = 1$. For the precedence relations to be satisfied, this must hold at all stations. So we obtain

(18-4) $$\sum_{j=1}^{k} x_{4j} \leq \sum_{j=1}^{k} x_{3j}, \qquad k = 1, \ldots, 4$$

If neither job is done by station k, expression (18-4) holds trivially (i.e., $0 \leq 0$), and it also holds if both jobs have been done (i.e., $1 \leq 1$).

The precedence relations for job 5 are

(18-5) $$\left.\begin{aligned}
\sum_{j=1}^{k} x_{5j} &\leq \sum_{j=1}^{k} x_{2j} \\
\sum_{j=1}^{k} x_{5j} &\leq \sum_{j=1}^{k} x_{4j}
\end{aligned}\right\} \qquad k = 1, \ldots, 4$$

It is also necessary to ensure that each job is done once and only once:

(18-6) $$\sum_{j=1}^{4} x_{ij} = 1, \qquad i = 1, \ldots, 5$$

The objective is to find the minimum number of stations to set up. This is achieved by allocating a lower "cost" to job i done at station 1 than for job i done at station 2, etc. By minimizing these costs, we force the jobs to the earliest possible work stations. The costs are arbitrary. We will give a cost of j to x_{ij} (= job i done at station j). Thus we obtain

(18-7) $$\text{minimize } z = \sum_{i=1}^{5} x_{i1} + 2\sum_{i=1}^{5} x_{i2} + 3\sum_{i=1}^{5} x_{i3} + 4\sum_{i=1}^{5} x_{i4}$$

The collection of equations (18-3) through (18-7), together with the nonnegativity and integrality conditions on the variables

$$x_{ij} \geq 0 \text{ and integer-valued for all } i \text{ and } j \tag{18-8}$$

make up the integer program for this problem. We do not need to put an upper limit of 1 on each x_{ij}; equation (18-6) does that implicitly.

18-3 THE FIXED-CHARGE PROBLEM

A firm can produce 5 products on a production line that goes through 3 different departments. Product j requires a_{ij} man-hours in department i. Department i has M_i man-hours per month available. A unit of product j makes a gross profit of $\$c_j$ (i.e., selling price less variable cost = $\$c_j$). However, it costs $\$F_j$ to set up the production line for producing a run of product j. The firm wants to schedule monthly production so as to maximize profits.

Where a fixed cost is incurred if, and only if, some variable is positive, an ordinary linear programming formulation does not work. In linear programming, we assume that all costs are variable costs (i.e., proportional to the magnitude of the variable), whereas here there is both a fixed cost and a variable cost.

Let x_j be the size of the production run of product j. The profit from producing x_j is

$$P_j = \begin{Bmatrix} c_j x_j - F_j & \text{for} \quad x_j > 0 \\ 0 & \text{for} \quad x_j = 0 \end{Bmatrix}, \qquad j = 1, \ldots, 5 \tag{18-9}$$

We define variables

$$\delta_j = \begin{Bmatrix} 1 & \text{for} \quad x_j > 0 \\ 0 & \text{for} \quad x_j = 0 \end{Bmatrix}, \qquad j = 1, \ldots, 5 \tag{18-10}$$

Using (18-10), expressions (18-9) can be written

$$P_j = (c_j x_j - F_j \delta_j) \qquad j = 1, \ldots, 5 \tag{18-11}$$

Since the objective is to maximize profits, it follows directly from (18-11) that the objective function is

$$\text{maximize } z = \sum_{j=1}^{5} (c_j x_j - F_j \delta_j) \tag{18-12}$$

The man-hour production constraints are

$$\sum_{j=1}^{5} a_{ij} x_j \leq M_i, \qquad i = 1,2,3 \tag{18-13}$$

Equations (18-10) must be written in linear constraint form in order to fit the constraints into the integer programming structure. We do this by finding an upper limit on x_j—say U_j—which we know to be above any possible value of x_j. Then using (18-10), we form the constraints

(18-14) $$x_j \leq U_j\delta_j, \qquad j = 1, \ldots, 5$$

(18-15) $$\left.\begin{array}{r} x_j \geq 0 \\ 0 \leq \delta_j \leq 1 \quad \text{and integer-valued} \end{array}\right\}, \qquad j = 1, \ldots, 5$$

Equations (18-12) through (18-15) are the integer programming formulation. Together they ensure that $\delta_j = 0$ only when $x_j \leq 0$ and $x_j \geq 0$ simultaneously (i.e., $x_j = 0$). The δ_j variables are referred to as *dummy variables* or *logical variables*. They are merely an aid to formulating the problem and are not decision variables.

18-4 FURTHER APPLICATIONS

Integer programming has been used to solve a variety of problems. The following is a list of some further applications.

1. *Capital budgeting problem:* allocating limited funds to various investment projects to maximize the discounted net return.
2. *Covering problem:* given a set of elements and various feasible groupings of these elements, assigning each element to a group so that all elements are covered. An example is the loading and arranging of items in delivery trucks in such a way that all items are delivered at minimum cost.
3. *Location problems:* choosing between various alternative sites for the location of a factory, warehouse, or store to minimize transport cost, to maximize revenue, etc.
4. *Knapsack problem:* choosing between items to pack into a limited space, to get as much "value" into the space as possible. There are a host of problems that fit this structure; some are seemingly quite different.
5. *Matching problem:* selecting items to match from different groups so that as many matching sets as possible are formed, e.g., selecting gears, bearings, and shafts from batches of each of them, to form matching sets that conform to certain precision tolerances.
6. *Sequencing problems:* sequencing a number of jobs on a machine to minimize the set-up cost or the time taken. (The enumeration of all possibilities, heuristic approaches, or dynamic programming—where applicable—are often better than integer programming.)
7. *Traveling salesman problem:* choosing an optimal route (e.g., minimum cost or distance) for a traveling salesman. (Heuristic methods are usually more tractable.)
8. *Scheduling problems:* determining schedules and timetables for vehicles, machines, school classes, etc. (Again, heuristic approaches are often better for large problems.)

18-5 INTRODUCTION TO SOLVING INTEGER PROGRAMMING PROBLEMS

Consider again problem (18-1):

$$\begin{aligned}\text{maximize } z = \; & 28x_1 + 11x_2 \\ \text{subject to} \quad & 14x_1 + 6x_2 \leq 25 \\ & x_1, x_2 \geq 0\end{aligned}$$

The integer programming solution is

$$x_1 = 0 \qquad x_2 = 4 \qquad z = 44$$

The linear programming solution is

$$x_1 = 25/14 \qquad x_2 = 0 \qquad z = 50$$

These solutions appear in graph form in Figure 18-1.

Let us try rounding the linear programming solution to the nearest integer solution: i.e., $x_1 = 2$, $x_2 = 0$, $z = 56$. This yields a solution that is not feasible. Trying the nearest feasible integer solution, we obtain $x_1 = 1$, $x_2 = 0$, $z = 28$. This time,

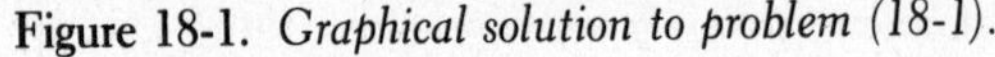

Figure 18-1. *Graphical solution to problem (18-1).*

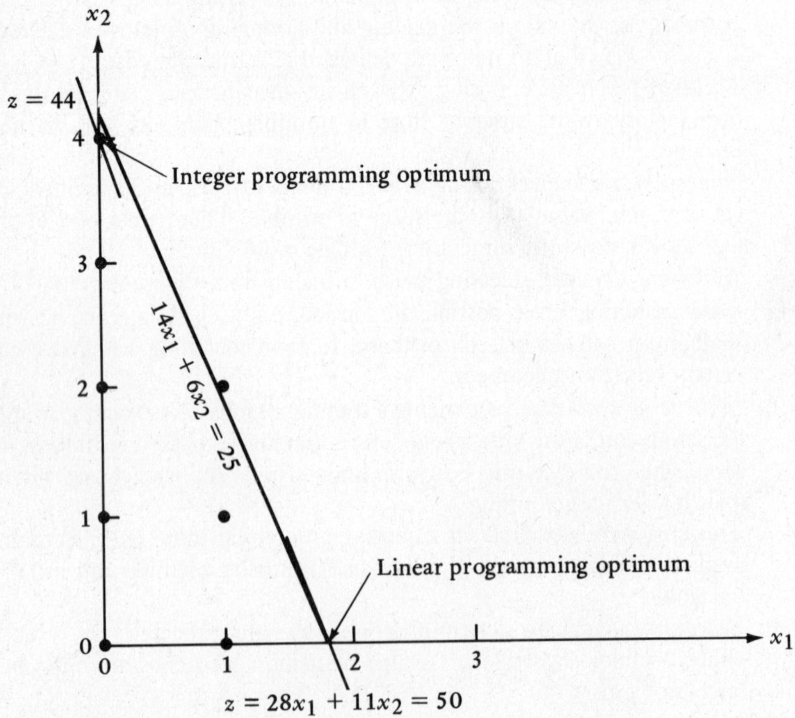

however, the solution is well below the optimal integer solution. This case demonstrates that seeking the integer programming optimum by rounding the linear programming optimum (even in simple examples) may be unreliable. As the integer programming problem gets larger, such a naive technique is quite useless. We need techniques that systematically work to the optimal integer solution.

18-6 GENERAL STRUCTURE OF INTEGER PROGRAMMING TECHNIQUES

Several techniques using different concepts are employed to solve integer programming problems. It is possible to summarize their basic approaches and their variations under three principles: *separation*, *relaxation*, and *fathoming*.

Consider the problem

$$
\begin{aligned}
&\text{maximize } z = \sum_j c_j x_j \\
&\text{subject to} \quad \sum_j a_{ij} x_j \leqslant b_i, \qquad i = 1, \ldots, m \\
&\qquad\qquad\qquad x_j \geqslant 0, \qquad \text{all } j \\
&\qquad\qquad\qquad x_j \text{ integer-valued for some of the } j
\end{aligned}
\tag{18-16}
$$

We have not assumed that all the variables take integer values. We call a problem a *mixed-integer problem* when it has both integer and continuous variables. A problem where variables all have integer restrictions is called an *all-integer problem*.

Let P be a maximization problem involving integer restriction, either a mixed-integer problem or an all-integer problem. Let $F(P)$ be the set of feasible solutions to the problem P, i.e., the set of solutions that satisfies the inequalities and the integer restrictions.

It is sometimes convenient to solve a problem through a series of smaller subproblems of the original. A valid separation of the problem into subproblems should satisfy the following principle.

PRINCIPLE OF SEPARATION

P is separated into the subproblems, or descendants, $P_1, P_2, \ldots, P_q$ if:

S1. Every feasible solution to P is a feasible solution of one and only one of the descendants.

S2. Every feasible solution of every descendant is a feasible solution to P.

Separation can occur in a number of ways. The following example illustrates the most useful form of separation for our purposes.

Consider problem (18-1) again as problem P:

$$(P)\qquad \begin{aligned} \text{maximize } z &= 28x_1 + 11x_2 \\ \text{subject to } \quad 14x_1 + 6x_2 &\leq 25 \\ x_1, x_2 &\geq 0 \quad \text{and integer-valued} \end{aligned}$$

This can be separated into the two descendants:

$$(P_1)\qquad \begin{aligned} \text{maximize } z_1 &= 28x_1 + 11\,x_2 \\ \text{subject to } \quad 14x_1 + 6\,x_2 &\leq 25 \\ x_2 &\leq 2 \\ x_1, x_2 &\geq 0 \quad \text{and integer-valued} \end{aligned}$$

and

$$(P_2)\qquad \begin{aligned} \text{maximize } z_2 &= 28x_1 + 11x_2 \\ \text{subject to } \quad 14x_1 + 6x_2 &\leq 25 \\ x_2 &\geq 3 \\ x_1, x_2 &\geq 0 \quad \text{and integer-valued} \end{aligned}$$

We have separated P around the interval $2 < x_2 < 3$.

P_1 is the feasible region of P for $x_2 \leq 2$, and P_2 is the feasible region of P for $x_2 \geq 3$. Since the region $2 < x_2 < 3$ contains no integer values, it can be excluded from consideration.

We can show that P, P_1, and P_2 satisfy S1 and S2. S1 is satisfied because every integer solution of P belongs to exactly one of P_1 and P_2. S2 is satisfied because there are no integer solutions to P_1 and P_2 that are not solutions of P.

Of course, there is nothing special about the interval $2 < x_2 < 3$. Any other interval that excludes no integer solutions (such as $0 < x_1 < 1$, or $4 < x_2 < 5$) will do just as well.

The problem P is relaxed by removing or weakening some of its constraints or restrictions. We call a relaxation of P the problem P_R. The most common use of relaxation in integer programming is to drop the integrality requirement, although other forms of relaxation are also used.

Relaxation requires that the following conditions be satisfied.

PRINCIPLE OF RELAXATION

When a problem P is relaxed to a problem P_R, every feasible solution to the problem P must be a feasible solution to the problem P_R. This leads to three results:

R1. If there is no feasible solution to P_R, there is no feasible solution to P.
R2. The maximum value of P_R is no less than the maximum value of P.
R3. If an optimal solution of P_R is a feasible solution of P, it is an optimal solution of P.

Finally, we have fathomed a problem when the problem needs no further analysis in the quest for the integer programming solution. The principle of fathoming gives three different ways in which a problem is fathomed. The importance of the second case will become clear in the next section.

PRINCIPLE OF FATHOMING

We say a problem P is fathomed when any of the following three conditions are satisfied:

$F1$. P has no feasible solution.
$F2$. P has no solution that has an objective function value better than some predetermined value z^*.
$F3$. An analysis of P reveals the optimal solution.

The integer programming techniques for solving expression (18-16) vary. Nearly all relax the original problem by removing the integer restriction; some fathom it without separating it into descendants, and others fathom totally through the descendants. We will study how integer programming uses these principles by looking at two entirely different solution techniques: the first is a simple version of *branch and bound algorithms*, and the second is *Gomory's cutting plane algorithm*. For ease of exposition, we will always deal with a maximizing problem.

18-7 A BRANCH AND BOUND ALGORITHM

A branch and bound algorithm solves the integer programming problem by a combination of relaxation and separation. Fathoming is done through the descendants of the original integer programming problem. The original integer program and its descendants that are generated by the branch and bound procedure are relaxed to linear programs for solution. If a particular descendant is not fathomed when its linear programming solution is found, it is separated (or *branched*) into two new descendants. If it is fathomed at the linear programming solution, then that branch is terminated. We have not fathomed the original problem until we have fathomed all of the descendants. The optimal solution to the original integer programming problem is the greatest of the optimal solutions of the descendant problems.

The collection of unfathomed problems is called the *reserve* or *candidate list*. Each time a problem is chosen for fathoming from the reserve, we start a new iteration of the branch and bound algorithm, and the problem chosen is referred to as the *candidate problem*, or CP. At the first iteration, the reserve contains only the original integer programming problem, which is thus the initial candidate problem.

Let us assume that at each iteration of the algorithm we know that the objective function value of the optimal solution to the integer programming problem is at least as great as some specified value. This value is a lower bound on the optimal integer programming solution. If, while solving a candidate problem, we find a feasible integer

Figure 18-2. *Branch and bound algorithm flow chart.*

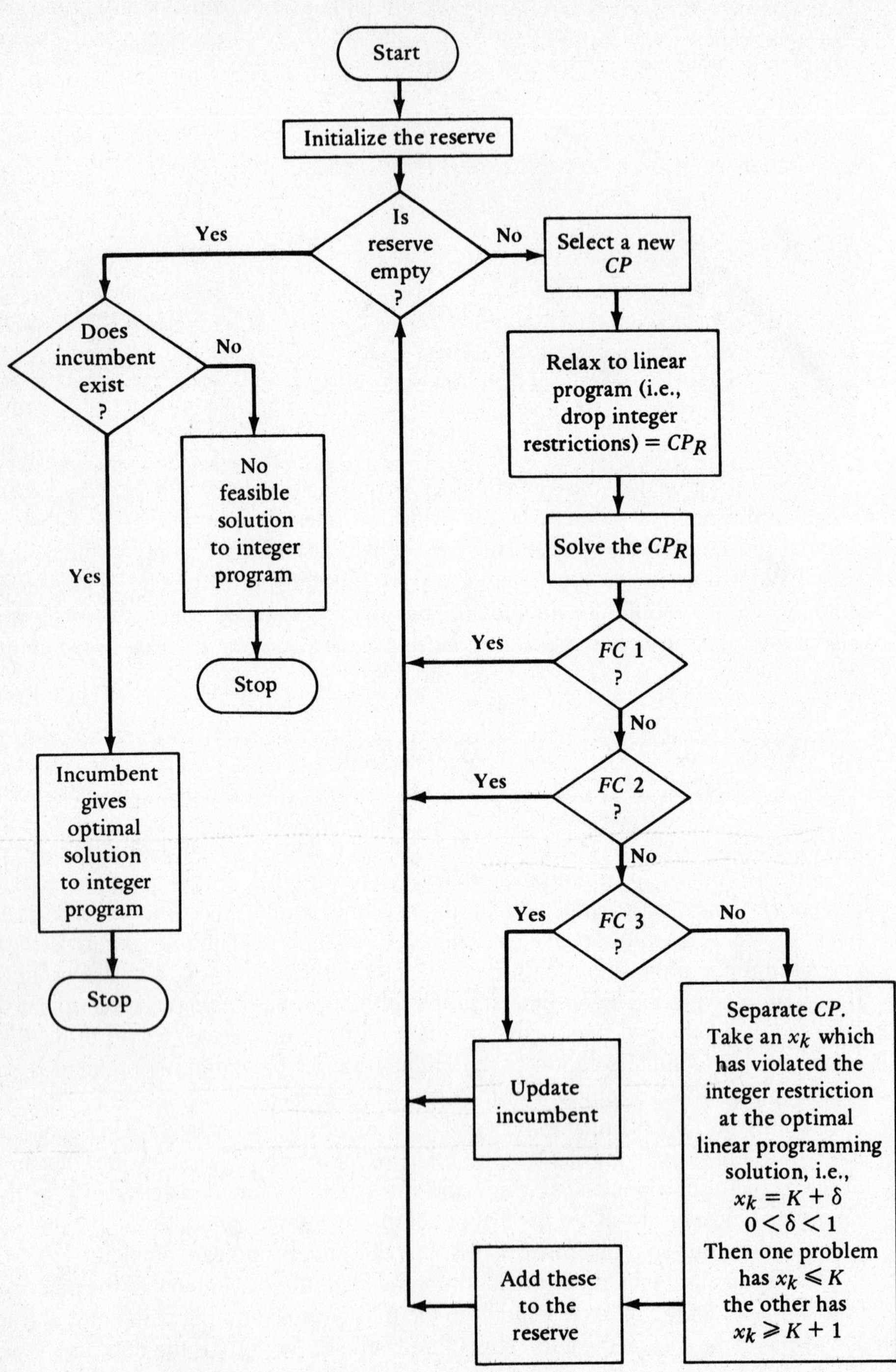

solution with an objective function value higher than the previously greatest known lower bound, then we can update the greatest known lower bound to this new value. The integer programming solution that supplies this new greatest known lower bound is called the *incumbent*. Conversely, if the optimal objective function value of the candidate problem solved at an iteration is less than that of the incumbent, this candidate problem can be discarded from further consideration—it has been fathomed. Let CP_R be the problem created by relaxing the integer restrictions on CP.

BRANCH AND BOUND FATHOMING

If CP_R is a relaxation of CP, then CP is fathomed when:

*FC*1. The analysis of CP_R reveals that CP has no feasible solution. (See *R*1.)
*FC*2. The analysis of CP_R reveals that CP has no feasible solution better than the incumbent. (See *R*2.)
*FC*3. The analysis of CP_R reveals the optimal solution to CP. (See *R*3.)

The branch and bound algorithm is summarized in the flow chart of Figure 18-2.

18-8 EXAMPLE OF BRANCH AND BOUND ALGORITHM

Let us solve problem (18-1) by the branch and bound algorithm. Figure 18-3 shows the progression of candidate problems as they are created and solved. Each rectangle represents the solution to a problem. A branch is created when separation generates new descendent problems, and a branch is terminated when the fathoming criteria are satisfied by a problem. The order in which the problems have been extracted and solved from the reserve is given by the problem numbers in Figure 18-3.

Implicit in Figure 18-3 is a rule for the order of entering descendant problems into the reserve, and also a rule for choosing the candidate problem from the reserve. When two new descendants are created, the problem with $x_k \leq K$ is first entered at the top of the candidate list. Then the problem with $x_k \geq K + 1$ is entered ahead of it. Candidates are chosen from the top downward. This means that the latter problem is always solved prior to the former. In terms of Figure 18-3, the right-hand branch just created is always chosen first (this means that there are never any right-hand branches in the reserve); then the left-hand branches are chosen, starting from the last one created.

For our problem, when the reserve is empty, all the branches have been terminated; and the incumbent has the solution $z = 44$, $x_1 = 0$, $x_2 = 4$. This is the optimal solution.

Figure 18-4 depicts graphically the sequence of problems created by the branch and bound algorithm. The solution of problem i is shown as *SOLN*(i).

Figure 18-3. *Solution to problem (18-1) by branch and bound.*

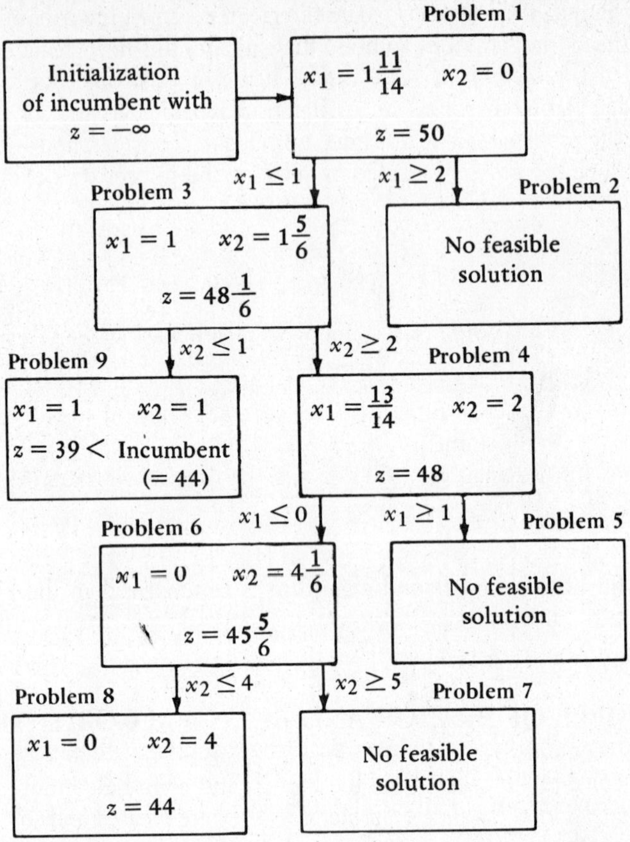

Initialization of incumbent with $z = -\infty$

Problem 1: $x_1 = 1\frac{11}{14}$, $x_2 = 0$, $z = 50$

$x_1 \leq 1$ → Problem 3; $x_1 \geq 2$ → Problem 2

Problem 2: No feasible solution

Problem 3: $x_1 = 1$, $x_2 = 1\frac{5}{6}$, $z = 48\frac{1}{6}$

$x_2 \leq 1$ → Problem 9; $x_2 \geq 2$ → Problem 4

Problem 9: $x_1 = 1$, $x_2 = 1$, $z = 39 <$ Incumbent $(= 44)$

Problem 4: $x_1 = \frac{13}{14}$, $x_2 = 2$, $z = 48$

$x_1 \leq 0$ → Problem 6; $x_1 \geq 1$ → Problem 5

Problem 5: No feasible solution

Problem 6: $x_1 = 0$, $x_2 = 4\frac{1}{6}$, $z = 45\frac{5}{6}$

$x_2 \leq 4$ → Problem 8; $x_2 \geq 5$ → Problem 7

Problem 8: $x_1 = 0$, $x_2 = 4$, $z = 44$

Problem 7: No feasible solution

More sophisticated branch and bound algorithms carefully choose the variable around which to separate and the candidate problem to be solved at each iteration. These choices can have a significant influence on the number of descendants created and the order in which they are solved. These conditions, in turn, influence the way each branch is terminated and, thus, the time the algorithm takes to reach the optimal solution.

Some algorithms take special account of 0–1 variables. An all 0–1 problem can usually be solved more quickly by specialized branch and bound algorithms that specifically take advantage of the 0–1 property.

*18-9 CUTTING-PLANE TECHNIQUE

The branch and bound technique does not persist in the fathoming of a particular problem. If it cannot fathom the problem, it separates it into descendants.

The technique we come to now is at the opposite extreme. It never separates, but always persists in fathoming a problem until the solution is found. As with branch and bound, the initial step is to relax the integer programming problem to a linear program by removing the integer restrictions. The relaxed problem is then solved. If

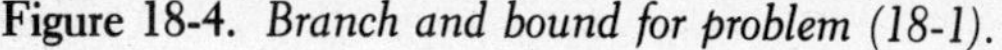

Figure 18-4. *Branch and bound for problem (18-1).*

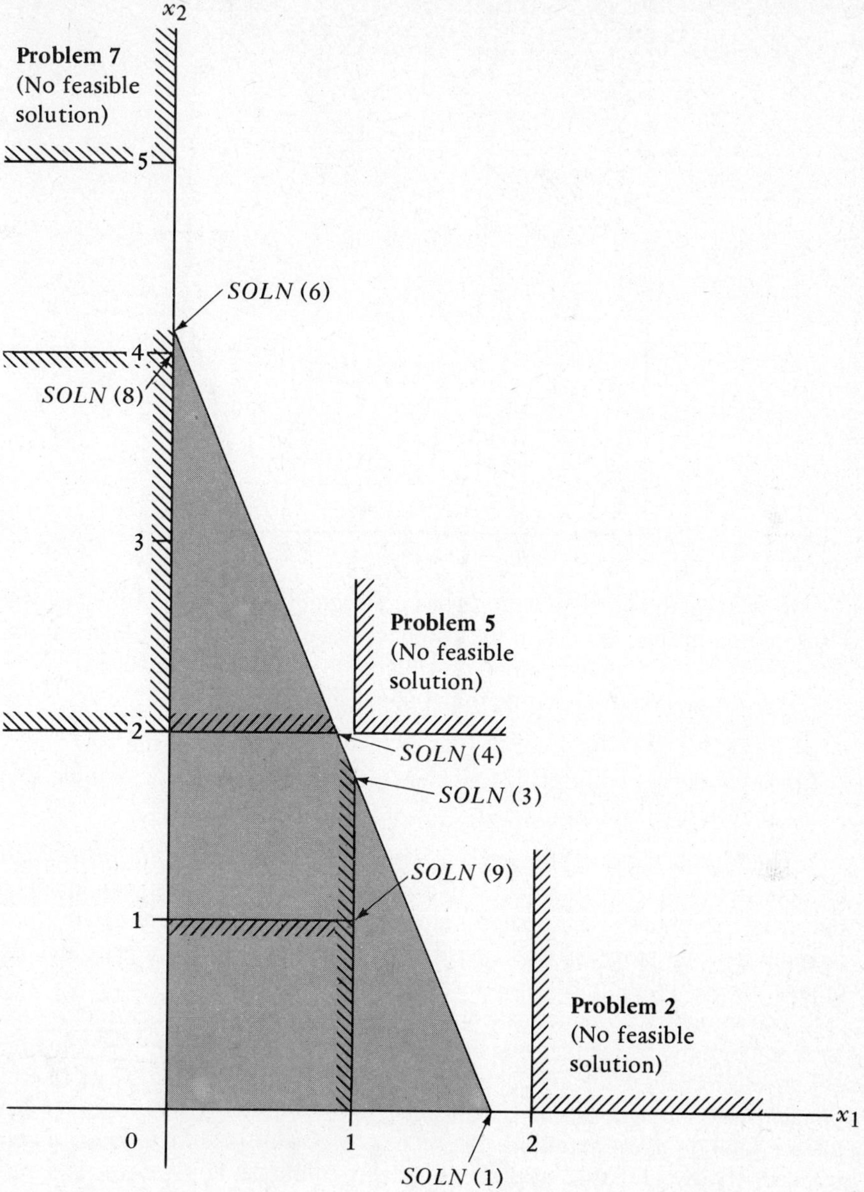

this does not fathom the integer programming problem, then the relaxation is modified; it is in fact tightened by the addition of a new constraint. The integer restrictions are never formally reimposed, but they are embodied in new constraints added to the continuous problem. The principle behind this technique is illustrated in Figure 18-5.

Figure 18-5. *Convex hull of the feasible solution to problem (18-1).*

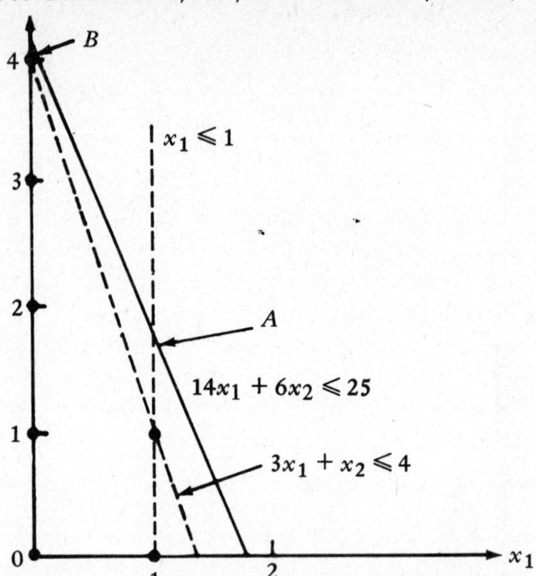

If we solve the problem with dashed constraint lines instead of the one with the black constraint line, we obtain the optimal integer solution as the optimal solution of an ordinary linear programming problem (with continuous variables).

We can see some interesting things about this new problem:

(i) Every integer solution of the old problem is a solution of the new one.
(ii) Every corner point of this problem (and hence every basic feasible solution) is an integer solution.

The feasible region of the new problem is the *convex hull of the integer solutions* of problem (18-1). It is the smallest linear programming feasible region to contain all the integer solutions. For solution purposes, it is not necessary to obtain the linear program that has property (ii); it is sufficient to obtain a linear program that has the optimal integer solution as its optimal continuous solution.

The solution techniques called *cutting-plane techniques* add constraints that cut away some of the feasible region, but never cut away a feasible integer solution. The objective is to start at the optimal linear programming solution and create a new linear program with a smaller feasible region. If the new linear program does not have an integer solution as its optimum, the process is continued until a linear program is reached whose optimal solution is an integer solution. This process is a series of relaxations of the integer programming problems, each relaxation being more restrictive than the previous one. By principle R3, the integer solution obtained by this technique is optimal to the integer program.

R. E. Gomory ("An Algorithm for Integer Solutions to Linear Programming," *Princeton-IBM Mathematics Research Project, Technical Report* No. 1, Nov. 1958) is responsible for a type of cut that guarantees that the process will terminate, in theory, at the optimal solution in a finite number of stages. To illustrate Gomory's reasoning for the all-integer problem, we will derive the cut equations for the relaxation of problem (18-1) where x_3 is the slack variable in the finance constraint, i.e., for

$$\text{(18-17)}\qquad \begin{aligned} \text{maximize } z &= 28x_1 + 11x_2 + 0x_3 \\ \text{subject to}\quad & 14x_1 + 6x_2 + x_3 \doteq 25 \\ & x_1, x_2, x_3 \geqslant 0 \end{aligned}$$

The optimal linear programming solution is $x_1 = 25/14$. So x_1 is the basic variable, with x_2 and x_3 nonbasic. We reason that, if the optimal linear programming solution is not integer, then at least one of the nonbasic variables at the optimal linear programming solution must become a positive integer at the optimal integer programming solution. Let us consider the change in the basic solution if some of the nonbasic variables are allowed to assume positive values. In other words, what is the new value of x_1, if at least one of x_2 and x_3 is allowed to assume a positive integer value? The constraint in canonical form at the optimal basis is

$$x_1 + \tfrac{6}{14}x_2 + \tfrac{1}{14}x_3 = \tfrac{25}{14}$$

or

$$\text{(18-18)}\qquad x_1 = \tfrac{25}{14} + \tfrac{6}{14}(-x_2) + \tfrac{1}{14}(-x_3)$$

Let us separate each coefficient and parameter on the right-hand side of (18-18) into its integer and its positive fractional parts. For instance, a coefficient of 2.7 is separated into +2 and +0.7, whereas −2.7 is separated into −3 and +0.3. Thus (18-18) becomes

$$x_1 = (1 + \tfrac{11}{14}) + (0 + \tfrac{6}{14})(-x_2) + (0 + \tfrac{1}{14})(-x_3)$$

or

$$\text{(18-19)}\qquad x_1 = (1 - 0x_2 - 0x_3) + (\tfrac{11}{14} - \tfrac{6}{14}x_2 - \tfrac{1}{14}x_3)$$

Now, we want to derive from (18-19) a condition that must be met by all solutions (x_1, x_2, x_3) that are integer. Whenever x_2 and x_3 are integer, the first bracket on the right-hand side of (18-19) is an integer since, by construction, the parameters and coefficients in it are integer. We are left with the term

$$\text{(18-20)}\qquad (\tfrac{11}{14} - \tfrac{6}{14}x_2 - \tfrac{1}{14}x_3)$$

which must also be integer for x_1 to be integer. It is the integrality of (18-20) that determines the Gomory cut. For (18-20) to be integer, it cannot be positive, since the only positive term $\tfrac{11}{14}$ is by definition fractional—i.e., less than one.

So (x_1, x_2, x_3) can be integer only if

$$\tfrac{11}{14} - \tfrac{6}{14}x_2 - \tfrac{1}{14}x_3 \leqslant 0$$

or

$$\text{(18-21)}\qquad -\tfrac{6}{14}x_2 - \tfrac{1}{14}x_3 + x_4 = -\tfrac{11}{14}$$

This is the first Gomory cut with x_4 as its slack variable. Using the constraint of problem (18-17) to substitute for x_3 in (18-21), we see that this constraint is equivalent to $x_1 \leqslant 1$.

The whole reasoning holds for any feasible integer solution. Thus, no integer solutions are excluded by the cut. On the other hand, the old linear programming optimum is not satisfied by the cut. From (18-21), we see that the left-hand side is always zero at the old linear programming optimum (since the nonbasic variables are zero), whereas the right-hand side is by definition always a negative fraction. In fact, the cut always excludes the fractional part of the variable around which it was constructed—in this case, x_1.

Note carefully that the coefficients on the left-hand side of (18-18) are the coefficients of $(-x_j)$ for each nonbasic variable x_j. Had there been more than one constraint in (18-17), there would be an expression like (18-21) for each noninteger basic variable. Gomory's procedure takes only one of the noninteger basic variables at the optimal linear programming solution and derives a cut constraint. The choice is arbitrary. In this case, x_1 is the only eligible variable.

With the new constraint included, the canonical form for the basic solution (x_1, x_4) is

$$\begin{aligned} x_1 + \tfrac{6}{14}x_2 + \tfrac{1}{14}x_3 &= \tfrac{25}{14} \\ -\tfrac{6}{14}x_2 - \tfrac{1}{14}x_3 + x_4 &= -\tfrac{11}{14} \end{aligned}$$

Table 18-2. *Dual simplex tableaux for Gomory cuts*

	c_j		28	11	0	0	0	
c_j	Basis	Solution	x_1	x_2	x_3	x_4	x_5	
28	x_1	$\frac{25}{14}$	1	$\frac{6}{14}$	$\frac{1}{14}$	0		
0	x_4	$-\frac{11}{14}$	0	$\left(-\frac{6}{14}\right)$	$-\frac{1}{14}$	1		1st Gomory cut
	$z_j - c_j$	50	0	1	2	0		
28	x_1	1	1	0	0	1	0	
11	x_2	$\frac{11}{6}$	0	1	$\frac{1}{6}$	$-\frac{14}{6}$	0	
0	x_5	$-\frac{5}{6}$	0	0	$-\frac{1}{6}$	$\left(-\frac{4}{6}\right)$	1	2nd Gomory cut
	$z_j - c_j$	$\frac{289}{6}$	0	0	$\frac{11}{6}$	$\frac{14}{6}$	0	
28	x_1	$-\frac{1}{4}$	1	0	$\left(-\frac{1}{4}\right)$	0	$\frac{3}{2}$	
11	x_2	$\frac{19}{4}$	0	1	$\frac{3}{4}$	0	$-\frac{7}{2}$	
0	x_4	$\frac{5}{4}$	0	0	$\frac{1}{4}$	1	$-\frac{3}{2}$	
	$z_j - c_j$	$\frac{181}{4}$	0	0	$\frac{5}{4}$	0	$\frac{7}{2}$	
0	x_3	1	−4	0	1	0	−6	
11	x_2	4	3	1	0	0	1	
0	x_4	1	1	0	0	1	0	
	$z_j - c_j$	44	5	0	0	0	11	

Table 18-2 shows the dual simplex tableau for this problem and the new optimal linear programming solution $x_1 = 1$, $x_2 = \frac{11}{6}$. (The second Gomory cut in the second tableau is added later.) This is point A in Figure 18-5. This solution is not all integer; hence we introduce another Gomory cut. We take a noninteger basic variable (in this case, $x_2 = \frac{11}{6}$); taking the positive fractional part of each coefficient in the x_2 row, we generate the second Gomory cut:

$$\frac{5}{6} - \frac{1}{6}x_3 - \frac{4}{6}x_4 \leq 0 \tag{18-22}$$

Using the equations $x_3 = 25 - 14x_1 - 6x_2$ and $x_4 = 1 - x_1$, expression (18-22) becomes $3x_1 + x_2 \leq 4$. With (18-22) added, the new linear program is solved by the dual simplex method in Table 18-2. The solution in the last tableau is $x_1 = 0$, $x_2 = 4$, $x_3 = 1$, and $x_4 = 1$. This solution is integer and thus optimal.

The linear program with both cuts added is, in fact, the convex hull of the integer solutions; the optimal solution is point B in Figure 18-5.

18-10 GENERAL COMMENTS

The branch and bound algorithm and the cutting-plane technique represent extremes of the separation-relaxation-fathoming principles. Many techniques fall somewhere in between.

Figure 18-6 is the flow chart for the general procedure. Particular techniques omit certain stages, or treat certain stages in different ways.

For example, the branch and bound algorithm described earlier never persists in fathoming the same candidate problem (i.e., never pursues the Yes branch at the question "Persist?"), whereas the cutting-plane procedure always persists.

18-11 A PLANT UPGRADING PROBLEM

A manufacturer of electrical wire is reviewing its machinery. Some of the present machines are nearly worn out or obsolete, so that running costs are becoming unacceptably high. At the same time, a shift in technology has caused an expansion in demand for the type of wire this manufacturer produces. The present plant cannot meet the demand projected for the near future. Figure 18-7 demonstrates the product flow and the types of machines now installed. Covered wire can be made by either of two different processes. The first process produces the copper wire of the desired diameter on one machine and covers it on a separate machine. The second process uses a single machine to produce the wire and to cover it. While the second process eferable because it involves less handling and less wastage, there is a demand for ıcovered wire—hence, some wire-reducing facilities for bare wire are essential.

Figure 18-6. *Flow chart for general integer programming techniques.*

Start
Stop
Yes
Initialize candidate list
Is list empty ?
No
Select a candidate problem
Relax
Solve
Yes
F 1 ?
No
Yes
F 2 ?
No
Modify relaxation
Update incumbent if necessary
Yes
F 3 ?
No
Separate
No
Persist ?
Yes

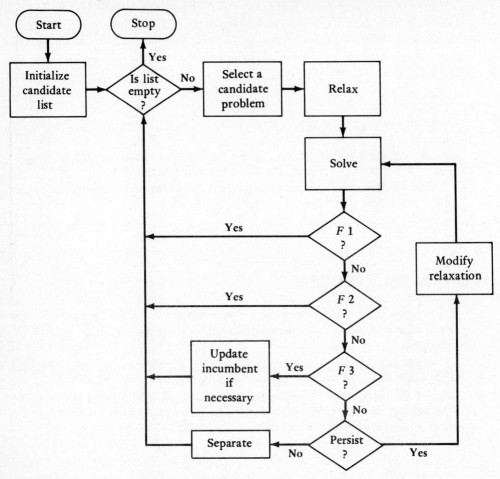

Figure 18-7. *Existing plant and product flow.*

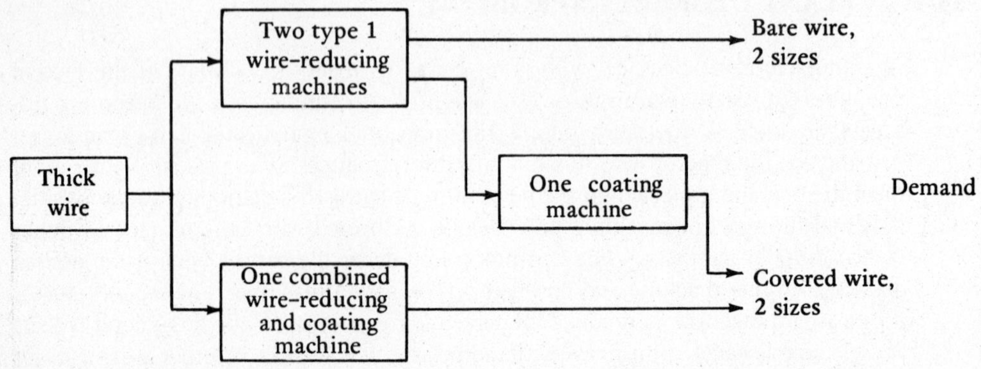

Table 18-3. *Machine options and data*

	Wire-Reducing Machines		Coating Machines		Combined Machines
	Existing Type 1	New Type 2	Existing	Upgrade Existing	New
Machine option	1	2	3	4	5
Capital cost ($1000's)	0	200	0	100	500
Running cost per hour ($)	5	7	8	8	12
per annum ($1000's)	30	50	80	100	140
Rate of production					
Wire size 1 (meters/hours)	1000	1500	1200	1600	1600
Wire size 2 (meters/hours)	800	1400	1000	1300	1200
Waste percent of product	2%	2%	3%	3%	3%
Cost of waste ($ per 1000m)	30	30	50	50	50

The manufacturer has various options, including retaining and modifying some existing machines and purchasing new machines. Table 18-3 outlines these options, along with the cost and the production data for each of the alternatives. More than one machine may be purchased for options 2 and 5. None of the new or old machines have any resale value.

What the production engineer must do is present a recommended configuration of the plant to meet the projected demand. She has a number of qualitative considerations in the decision. For example, she sees a need to bring in as many new machines as management will permit—although there will be uncertainty about the capital budget until management has carefully studied the "best" alternatives. The engineer also wishes to have the plant as compatible as possible, for both ease of maintenance and for availability of spare parts. To help with her decision, she wants to know the lowest capital-cost configuration and the lowest running-cost configuration. These will be used as benchmarks for other configurations that more closely fit her qualitative criteria.

Any configuration of machines recommended has to be capable of meeting the projected annual demand for the final products. Therefore, a decision has to involve not only what configuration of machines to get, but also which product to produce on what machine. Hence, we have variables for the number of each type of machine and variables for the amount of each wire size produced on each machine. Let M_i be the number of machines of option i, and let x_{ij} be the proportion of annual machine time on machines of option i to produce wire size j ($i = 1, \ldots, 5$ and $j = 1, 2$).

Note that x_{ij} may be larger than 1, since more than one machine of option i may be needed to produce wire of size j. If we assume a 6000-hour year, then the machines of option i spend $6000x_{ij}$ hours per year producing wire size j.

The first objective function we consider is to minimize the capital cost of the machines:

(18-23) $$\text{minimize } 0M_1 + 200M_2 + 0M_3 + 100M_4 + 500M_5 \qquad \text{(CAPCST)}$$

The second objective function looks at total running costs. Each machine has a running cost of a form similar to the fixed charge problem. For example, machines of option 1 have a running cost for a 6000-hour year, made up as three parts: a fixed running cost of \$30,000M_1; a variable running cost of (\$5)(6000)($x_{11} + x_{12}$) = \$30,000($x_{11} + x_{12}$); and the cost of waste. The cost of waste for wire 1 is (\$30)(0.02)(6000)x_{11} = \$3600x_{11}, and the cost of waste for wire 2 is (\$30)(0.02)(0.8)(6000)x_{12} = 2880x_{12}. This gives a total running cost in \$1000's of $30M_1 + 33.6x_{11} + 32.88x_{12}$. Similar calculations for the other machines yield a running cost objective function of

(18-24) $$\begin{aligned} \text{minimize } & 30M_1 + 33.6\,x_{11} + 32.88x_{12} + 50M_2 + 47.4x_{21} + 47.04x_{22} \\ & + 80M_3 + 58.8x_{31} + 57x_{32} + 100M_4 + 62.4x_{41} \\ & + 59.7x_{42} + 140M_5 + 86.4x_{51} + 82.8x_{52} \qquad \text{(RUNCST)} \end{aligned}$$

Production is constrained to meet projected sales demand, which is given in Table 18-4. The total demand for bare wire of size 1 consists of the actual sales demand for bare wire plus the wire to be coated using machines of option 3 and 4; i.e.,

$$3000 + (1200x_{31} + 1600x_{41})\frac{6000}{1000} = 3000 + 7200x_{31} + 9600x_{41} \text{ kilometers}$$

Table 18-4. *Projected sales demand (in kilometers, 1 kilometer = 1000 meters)*

Bare Wire		Covered Wire	
Size 1	Size 2	Size 1	Size 2
3000	2000	14,000	10,000

This demand has to be met by output from machines of options 1 and 2. This output is equal to (6000/1000)($1000x_{11} + 1500x_{21}$). Because of waste of 2 percent on these machines, only 98 percent of this output is available. Hence,

$$0.98(6000/1000)(1000x_{11} + 1500x_{21}) \geq 3000 + 7200x_{31} + 9600x_{41}$$

Expressed in the usual constraint form, the production constraint for bare wire of size 1 is

(18-25) $$5880x_{11} + 8820x_{21} - 7200x_{31} - 9600x_{41} \geq 3000 \qquad \text{(BARE1)}$$

Verify that for bare wire of size 2 the production constraint is

(18-26) $$4704x_{12} + 8232x_{22} - 6000x_{32} - 7800x_{42} \geq 2000$$ (BARE2)

while for covered wire of sizes 1 and 2 we get

(18-27) $$6984x_{31} + 9312x_{41} + 9312x_{51} \geq 14000$$ (COVRD1)

(18-28) $$5820x_{32} + 7566x_{42} + 6984x_{52} \geq 10000$$ (COVRD2)

Next, we have to make certain that the number of machines available for each option provides a production capacity that covers the production needs. The number of machines must be an integer (but not necessarily 0–1). Hence the number of machines of type i must be at least as large as the sum of the proportions of time that that type machine is required for the production of all wire sizes:

$$M_i \geq x_{i1} + x_{i2}, \qquad i = 1, \ldots, 5$$

or

(18-29) $$x_{i1} + x_{i2} - M_i \leq 0, \qquad i = 1, \ldots, 5$$ (MATCHi)

Finally, we must consider the restrictions of the machine options. Only two machines of option 1 are available, so

(18-30) $$M_1 \leq 2$$ (REST1)

Options 3 and 4 are mutually exclusive and only one machine exists, so

(18-31) $$M_3 + M_4 \leq 1$$ (REST34)

We require, of course, that all variables be nonnegative and the M_i's be integer-valued.

18-12 SOLUTION TO THE PLANT UPGRADING PROBLEM

The plant upgrading problem of the previous section was solved separately for each objective function, using Burrough's TEMPO mathematical programming system. The problem has 11 constraints and 15 nonslack variables, of which 5 are integer variables. For the CAPCST function, 12 nodes were considered, and 2 integer solutions were found before the algorithm terminated. The algorithm took longer to solve for the RUNCST function. Here, it searched 21 nodes, and also found 2 integer solutions before it terminated.

The branch and bound algorithm has the unfortunate feature that the solution of similar problems may take substantially different amounts of computational effort. Thus, it is very difficult to predict the time it will take to solve a problem. In a real version of the plant upgrading problem that the authors solved, the algorithm did not terminate in a "reasonable" time. This is fairly common in integer programming. In such cases, the incumbent solution is taken to be optimal. In fact, even if this is not true, it will probably be close enough. Most good branch and bound algorithms allow the user to alter the way the nodes are selected. An experienced user can thus increase the probability that the optimal node is found early in the branch and bound sequence.

From Table 18-5 we see that the capital-cost solution has a 10.4 percent higher running cost than the running-cost solution, while the running-cost solution has a 15.4 percent higher capital cost than the capital-cost solution. The machine configurations of the two solutions are also substantially different. The capital-cost solution requires the purchase of 1 wire-reducing machine and 2 combined machines. Under the running-cost solution, we dispose of 1 of the existing wire-reducing machines and the coating machine, and we purchase 3 combined machines.

In Figures 18-8 and 18-9, we have the production flow implied by the solution of Table 18-5. Here we notice that the running-cost solution is simpler to schedule, has less waste, is more modern, and uses fewer types of machines. However, the capital-cost solution has more room for expansion without incurring extra capital cost.

Table 18-5. *Optimal solutions in computer output form*

	Capital-Cost Solution			Running-Cost Solution		
Name	Status	Activity	Input Cost	Status	Activity	Input Cost
M1	IV	2.000	—	IV	1.000	30.00
M2	IV	1.000	200.00	IV	—	50.00
M3	IV	—	—	IV	—	80.00
M4	IV	1.000	100.00	IV	—	100.00
M5	IV	2.000	500.00	IV	3.000	140.00
X11	LL	—	—	BS	0.510	33.60
X12	BS	2.000	—	BS	0.425	32.88
X21	BS	0.340	—	LL	—	47.40
X22	BS	0.048	—	BS	—	47.04
X31	LL	—	—	LL	—	58.80
X32	BS	—	—	LL	—	57.00
X41	LL	—	—	LL	—	62.40
X42	BS	1.000	—	LL	—	59.70
X51	BS	1.651	—	BS	1.503	86.40
X52	BS	0.348	—	BS	1.432	82.80
CAPCST		1300.000			1500.000	
RUNCST		805.368			729.576	

Note: BS denotes *basic variable*, LL denotes *variable at lower limit*, and IV denotes *integer variable*.

18-13 SENSITIVITY ANALYSIS

In Chapter 5 we discovered the wealth of information the optimal simplex tableau provides for sensitivity analysis. Since integer programming is so akin to linear programming, you may ask: What can we say about the sensitivity of the solution in the integer programming situation? The short answer is that we can say very little of practical value. The reason is simply that integer programming involves discrete jumps from solution to solution, rather than a continuous change.

If we have used branch and bound as our solution technique (as the case usually will be), we can say almost nothing analytically about sensitivity analysis. The best

Figure 18-8. *Product flow for capital cost solution.*

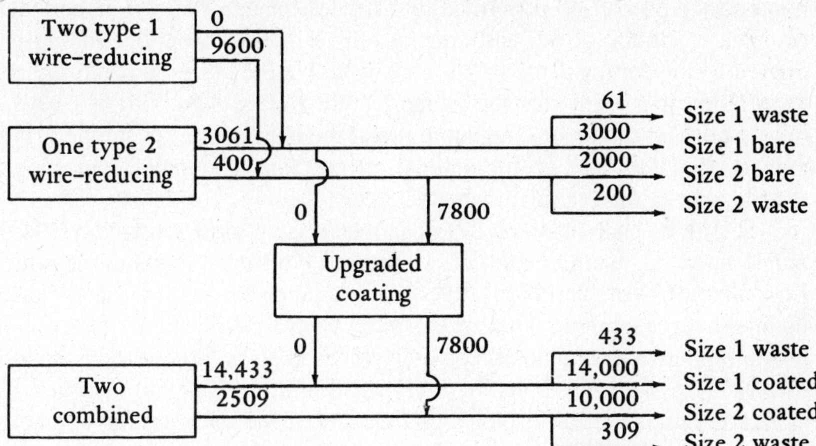

Slack capacity: 2327 hours on type 2 wire-reducing machine
888 hours on combined machine

we can do is to ask the branch and bound algorithm to find the *K* best solutions to the problem. (See H. Wagner, *Principles of Operations Research*, 2nd ed., Prentice-Hall, New York, 1975, pp. 498–499 for a discussion.) By applying changes of parameters and coefficients to these solutions, we can gain useful but not necessarily conclusive information. There seems to be no easy way of finding the new optimum when the constraint set is relaxed. The only option is to rerun the branch and bound algorithm using the old integer programming optimum as the new incumbent. When a constraint is tightened, it may be necessary to repeat the whole procedure from scratch.

Figure 18-9. *Product flow for running cost solution.*

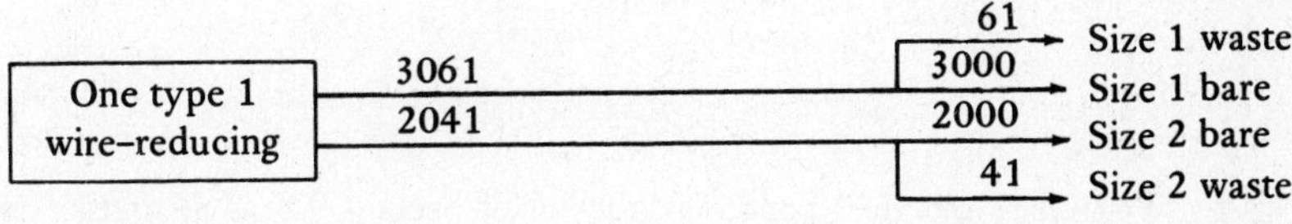

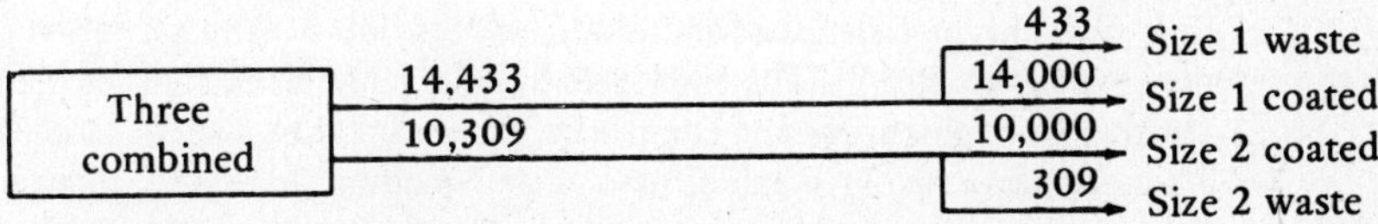

Slack capacity: 388 hours on type 1 wire-reducing machine
388 hours on combined machines

If Gomory's cutting-plane algorithm is being used, ranging of the objective function coefficients can be performed to a limited extent. We can be confident of the complete accuracy of the cost-ranging only if the linear programming constraints derived by the cutting plane are the convex hull of the integer programming problem. Remember, it is likely that the Gomory cutting-plane algorithm will have cut away only enough of the feasible region to reveal the optimal integer solution. If this is so, any cost-ranging based on the optimal integer programming tableau underestimates the true cost ranges. (Explain why this is so.)

Sensitivity analysis of the RHS parameters is no more satisfactory. An important article by R. E. Gomory and W. J. Baumol ("Integer Programming and Pricing," *Econometrica*, Vol. 28, 1960) developed a scheme for finding shadow prices at the optimal integer solution. These prices result from a modification of the optimal linear programming dual variables by correcting for each of the Gomory cuts. Unfortunately, the scheme is far from foolproof, and the prices are not easy to interpret. If we relax a slack constraint in linear programming, there is no effect on the optimal solution. This is not necessarily true in integer programming, where a constraint may be slack only because of the integer condition on the variable. In linear programming, any change in the solution as the RHS parameter changes is continuous; in integer programming, there is no change in the solution until a superior integer solution becomes feasible. Then, the change is a discrete jump.

Using either technique, we can state bounds on the changes in objective function value for a change in an RHS parameter. These bounds come from the optimal linear programming tableau. We can determine with ease the change in the linear programming optimal objective function value for a change in the RHS, and we know that the integer programming optimum can have no better value than the linear programming optimum. So the difference between the new linear programming value and the old integer programming value of the objective function is an upper bound on the change in the integer programming value for a relaxation of the RHS, and a lower bound on the change in the integer programming value for a tightening of the RHS that renders the old integer programming optimum infeasible.

EXERCISES

18.1 Formulate the river pollution problem of Section 9-8 as an integer programming problem.

18.2 A firm has a job to perform that involves 4 job-steps. The table below gives the number of days each job-step takes, the number of workers required each day for each job-step, and any precedence relationships between job-steps (e.g., job-step 1 must be done before job-step 3). The employees work in gangs for each job-step; therefore, the stated labor requirements and completion times cannot be altered, *except that* job-step 2 can be performed by either a fast or a slow method. Job-step 2(a) gives the data for the fast method, and 2(b) gives the data for the slow method. It is not possible to mix the two methods.

Job-Step	Predecessor	Completion Time	Labor
1	—	5	5
2(a)	—	5	4
2(b)	—	6	3
3	1	2	7
4	3	5	2

Once started, a job-step must be completed without a break. The firm wishes to minimize the time taken to complete the whole job, with the restriction that only 10 workers are available for the first 10 days, and 8 workers are available after that. Formulate the problem as an integer programming problem.

18.3 Show how the following shaded region can be formulated in an integer programming problem.

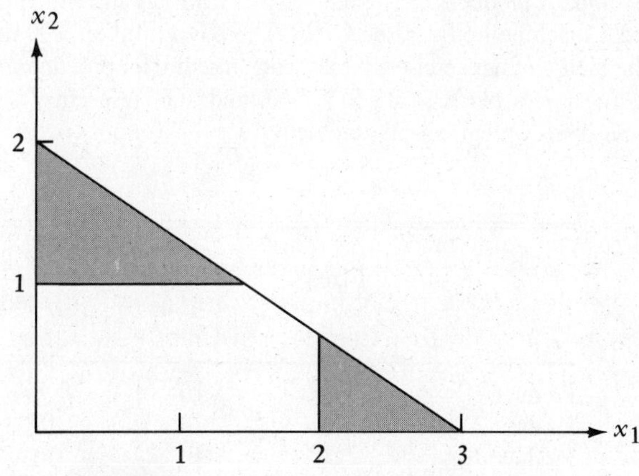

18.4 Formulate the following as a constraint set for an integer program.

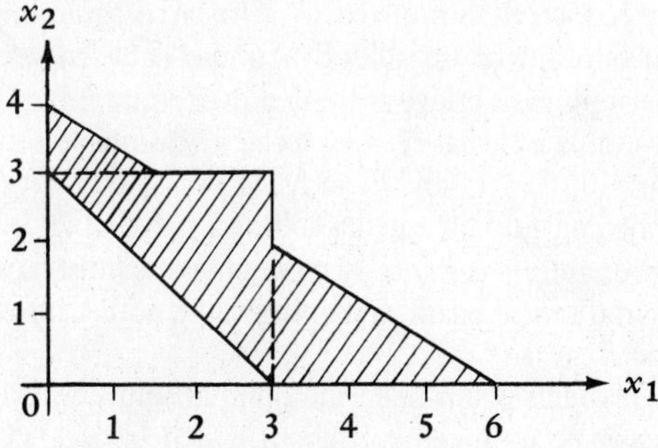

18.5 Show how each of the following situations can be formulated as part of an integer programming problem.

(a) In blending one of its products, a blending company uses 10 different ingredients. For certain reasons, the mixture can contain no more than 5 of the ingredients at once. x_j is the quantity of ingredient j. The x_j's are continuous variables.

(b) The same blending company has 3 different mixing vessels; the mixing of the product is to be done in only *one* of them. Vessel 1 mixes 2000 liters a day, vessel 2 mixes 3000 liters, and vessel 3 mixes 2500 liters. It costs \$500, \$800, and \$600 per day, respectively, to use vessels 1–3. Show the relevant parts of the constraint set and objective function.

(c) In a formulation, only *one* of the following sets of equations can hold at a time:

$$\sum_{j=1}^{n} a_{ij}x_j \leq b_i, \qquad i = k_1, \ldots, k_2$$

$$\sum_{j=1}^{n} a_{ij}x_j \leq b_i, \qquad i = k_3, \ldots, k_4$$

18.6 A company produces three products that require 1 machine-hour, 1.5 machine-hours, and 2 machine-hours, respectively. There is a limit of 2000 machine-hours per week. The table in this exercise gives the cost structure for production runs of various lengths. Selling prices per unit are \$15, \$40, and \$60, respectively. Formulate the problem as an integer programming problem.

	Fixed Set-up Cost (\$)	Variable Cost (\$ per unit)		
		1–100 Units	101–500 Units	Over 500 Units
Product 1	100	10	8	5
Product 2	50	20	18	15
Product 3	200	40	30	20

18.7 State highway planners are trying to determine the optimal locations of bridges to cross a lake. They have limited their choices to five possible locations: 1, 2, 3, 4, and 5. The problem has been formulated as a linear programming problem to maximize transportation values, with variables B_i bounded between zero and one. In other words, if $B_i = 1$, that implies a bridge is located over route i; $B_i = 0$ implies no bridge. The planners first evaluated what seemed to be a reasonable solution, and obtained $B_1 = 0$, $B_2 = 1$, $B_3 = 0$, $B_4 = 0$, and $B_5 = 1$, with value 600. Next, they solved the problem as a linear program, and obtained a solution value of 700, with $B_1 = 0.3$, $B_2 = 0.9$, $B_3 = 0$, $B_4 = 0$, and $B_5 = 0.7$. Since the planners must have an integer solution, they fixed $B_2 = 0$ and solved again, obtaining value 550, with $B_1 = 0.8$, $B_2 = 0$, $B_3 = 0$, $B_4 = 0.3$, and $B_5 = 1$.

(a) Have the planners determined the optimal solution yet? Why or why not?

(b) Can you make any statements about which bridges are certain to be established and which are certain not to be established?

18.8 A company is preparing its 5-year plan for a period commencing a year from now. Part of the plan involves investment in the expansion of facilities. Four projects present themselves as viable. The company wishes to know which of the projects to implement in the 5-year period, and when to start each of them. The object is to maximize discounted net return from these projects for the 5-year period and the 3 years following. For the 5 years, the company is budgeting the following amounts each year from existing operations: year 1, \$200,000; year 2, \$100,000; year 3, \$250,000; year 4, \$100,000; and year 5, \$200,000. Any amount unused in a period is accumulated for later periods. In addition to this, a quarter of the positive net return from any of these projects (once implemented) is available to finance other projects. The table in this exercise shows the expected net returns for the years after each of the projects is *commenced*. Any implemented project that requires funds after the 5-year planning period must get the funds from amounts accumulated from the budget of the 5-year planning period and from funds created by other projects. By their nature, projects 2 and 3 cannot both be implemented, since project 3 is a larger-scale version of project 2. Formulate the problem as an integer programming problem. Use a discount rate of 0.9.

	Year 1	Year 2	Year 3	Year 4 Onward
Project 1	−100,000	0	100,000	200,000
Project 2	−50,000	−150,000	20,000	100,000
Project 3	−300,000	−100,000	100,000	400,000
Project 4	−400,000	100,000	200,000	400,000

18.9 The ABC Furniture Store has to make 5 deliveries to customers in rural areas in an afternoon. The weights of the deliveries are as follows: customer 1, 50 kg; customer, 2, 150 kg; customer 3, 250 kg; customer 4, 500 kg; and customer 5, 1000 kg. The company's 4 vans vary in carrying capacity as follows: van A, 250 kg; van B, 750 kg; van C, 1250 kg; and van D, 1250 kg. If van A is used, it costs \$100 per run regardless of the load. Similarly, van B costs \$150, and vans C and D each cost \$200 per run. Due to the distance, customers 3 and 4 cannot both receive deliveries from the same van.

(a) Formulate the problem of allocating deliveries to each of the vans as a minimum-cost integer program.

(b) Change the formulation if no more than 2 deliveries per van can be made.

(This is an example of the covering problem.)

18.10 Solve problem (18-1) in the text using the opposite order for entering candidate problems to that used in Section 18-8; i.e., place the newly created descendant with $x_k \geq K + 1$ on top first, then $x_k \leq K$ on top of that, and again choose the candidate problem from the top.

18.11 Solve the problem

$$\begin{aligned} \text{maximize } z = 10x_1 + 3x_2 \\ \text{subject to } \quad 5x_1 + 2x_2 \leq 17 \\ x_1, x_2 \geq 0 \text{ and integer-valued} \end{aligned}$$

(a) By the branch and bound algorithm.
(b) By Gomory's cutting-plane algorithm.

18.12 Using the branch and bound algorithm, find the optimum to problem (18-1) of the text when the grant is increased to \$3.3 million. The optimum to problem (18-1) can be used as the initial incumbent. Choose the $x_k \geq K + 1$ problem first.

18.13 Repeat exercise 18.12, choosing the candidate problem, $x_k \leq K$, first.

18.14 Solve the problem in exercise 18.12 using Gomory's cutting-plane algorithm.

18.15 Solve by the branch and bound algorithm (using a graph, or otherwise):

$$\text{maximize } z = 4x_1 + 4x_2$$

$$\text{subject to} \quad x_1 + 2x_2 \leq 6$$

$$8x_1 + 3x_2 \leq 24$$

$$18x_1 + 14x_2 \leq 63$$

$$x_1, x_2 \geq 0 \text{ and integer-valued}$$

18.16 Solve the problem of exercise 18.15 assuming that only x_1 is to be integer.

18.17 Solve the following problem by the branch and bound algorithm. Use a graph to find the solution to the descendant problems.

$$\text{maximize } z = 8x_1 + 4x_2$$

$$\text{subject to} \quad x_1 + 4x_2 \leq 19$$

$$12x_1 + 5x_2 \leq 45$$

$$5x_1 + x_2 \leq 16$$

$$x_1, x_2 \geq 0 \text{ and integer-valued}$$

Construct a graph of the form of Figure 18-4, and a tree of the form of Figure 18-3.

18.18 The optimal simplex tableau to the problem in exercise 18.15 is as shown. Create a Gomory cut for each of the variables. (Note: We can assume that x_4, x_5, and x_6 are restricted to being integers also. Why?) Show on a graph the original problem and each of the cuts, and show the new optimum with each cut added. Which of the cuts would normally be chosen? Perform the dual simplex method on this cut.

	c_j		4	4	0	0	0
c_j	Basis	Solution	x_1	x_2	x_3	x_4	x_5
4	x_2	$\frac{45}{22}$	0	1	$\frac{9}{11}$	0	$-\frac{1}{22}$
0	x_4	$\frac{57}{22}$	0	0	$\frac{29}{11}$	1	$-\frac{13}{22}$
4	x_1	$\frac{21}{11}$	1	0	$-\frac{7}{11}$	0	$\frac{1}{11}$
	$z_j - c_j$	$\frac{174}{11}$	0	0	$\frac{8}{11}$	0	$\frac{2}{11}$

18.19 Solve by the branch and bound algorithm:

$$\begin{aligned} \text{maximize } z = \ & 4x_1 + 4x_2 \\ \text{subject to} \quad & 3x_1 + 5x_2 \leq 15 \\ & 8x_1 + 3x_2 \leq 24 \\ & 18x_1 + 14x_2 \geq 63 \\ & x_1, x_2 \geq 0 \text{ and integer-valued} \end{aligned}$$

18.20 The optimal simplex tableau for the problem in exercise 18.19 is as shown. Write out the Gomory cut for each variable. Show these constraints on a graph of the problem. Perform the dual simplex method on the cut for x_2.

	c_j		4	4	0	0	0
c_j	Basis	Solution	x_1	x_2	x_3	x_4	x_5
0	x_5	2.226	0	0	1.871	1.548	1
4	x_1	2.419	1	0	−0.097	0.161	0
4	x_2	1.548	0	1	0.258	−0.097	0
	$z_j - c_j$	15.871	0	0	0.645	0.258	0

REFERENCES

More extensive coverage, at a level similar to that of this chapter, can be found in the following texts:

Plane, D. R., and C. McMillan. *Discrete Optimization*. Englewood Cliffs, N.J.: Prentice-Hall, 1971. Chapter 2 gives a good series of applications of 0–1 integer programming, Chapter 5 gives further general examples, and Chapter 7 gives a case study. Implicit enumeration techniques for the 0–1 problem are in Chapter 3, and branch and bound and the cutting-plane algorithm are in Chapter 4. In addition, there are computer codes for implicit enumeration of 0–1 problems and a cutting-plane algorithm. This book is a good place to start a more detailed study of integer programming without complicated mathematics.

van de Panne, C. *Linear Programming and Related Techniques*. Amsterdam: North-Holland, 1971. Of particular interest in this text is the material of Chapters 15 and 16, which expounds more extensively on the basic principles of branch and bound methods.

More advanced texts on integer programming include:

Garfinkel, R. S., and G. L. Nemhauser. *Integer Programming*. New York: Wiley, 1972. This is a very comprehensive text on integer programming. It covers a wide range of techniques, skimping neither on the theory nor or worked examples. This somewhat difficult book is suitable only for competent students.

Greenberg, N. *Integer Programming* New York: Academic Press, 1971. A text for intermediate and advanced students. The theory is tempered with good applications and examples.

Hadley, G. *Non-linear and Dynamic Progamming.* Reading, Mass.: Addison-Wesley, 1964. For those well equipped mathematically, Chapter 8 has a good series of formulated integer programming problems and a complete treatment of the Gomory cutting-plane theory, for both the all-integer and the mixed-integer cases.

There are two excellent journal articles that survey integer programming. Both are pitched at a fairly advanced level.

Balinski, M. L. "Integer Programming: Methods, Uses, Computation," *Management Science*, Vol. 12, Nov. 1965. Despite its age, this article is still a very important reference in integer programming literature. A thorough reading of the article requires good mathematics and some knowledge of integer programming. However, pages 274–275 give a valuable resumé of the success (or otherwise) of integer programming applications. There is a comprehensive list of references up to 1965.

Geoffrion, A. M., and R. E. Marsten. "Integer Programming Algorithms—A Survey," *Management Science*, Vol. 18, May 1972. An excellent survey of integer techniques. The approach used in this article greatly influenced our own treatment in this chapter.

CHAPTER NINETEEN

Classical Optimization Methods with Applications to Inventory Control

Many problems in operations research, particularly in inventory control, involve nonlinear functions in only a few decision variables, where the classical methods of continuous and discrete calculus may be powerful enough for finding the optimal solution. In this chapter, we review the classical approach for finding extreme values of differentiable functions in one or several variables. All examples used deal with inventory control models of various degrees of sophistication. Chapters 20 and 21 will explore more recent and more powerful methods for solving nonlinear optimization problems subject to constraints.

We assume that you are familiar with the basic concepts and operations of differential calculus—in particular, differentiation and partial derivatives of simple polynomials. Some of the models presented involve probabilistic elements. The essential concepts of probability used are reviewed in Sections 10-1, and 10-3 to 10-7 of Chapter 10. If you have not already studied Chapter 12 on inventory control, you may wish to briefly review the economic order quantity model in Section 12-7. Wherever possible, we shall use the same notation for cost parameters as in that chapter. In fact, this chapter is best studied in conjunction with the stationary inventory models in Sections 12-7 to 12-11.

19-1 OPTIMIZATION OF DIFFERENTIABLE FUNCTIONS OF ONE VARIABLE

Let f be a function in the variable x defined over the interval $a \leq x \leq b$, (denoted as $[a, b]$), with first and second order derivatives, and let $f(x)$ be the value of the function evaluated at the point x. Suppose f assumes an *extreme value*—a *maximum* or a *minimum*—at the point x_0 in the interval $[a, b]$. Let x be any other points in $[a, b]$.

LOCAL MAXIMUM

The function f has a local or relative maximum at x_0, if and only if

$$f(x) \leqslant f(x_0) \tag{19-1}$$

for all x in some neighborhood of x_0 in the interval $[a, b]$ (i.e., there exists a $\varepsilon > 0$ so that the inequality holds for all x in $[a, b]$ and for $0 < |x - x_0| < \varepsilon$).

GLOBAL MAXIMUM

The function f has a global or absolute maximum at x_0 if (19-1) holds for all x in the interval $[a, b]$.

If expression (19-1) holds with strict inequality, i.e., $f(x) < f(x_0)$, then x_0 is a *strict maximum*. For a minimum of f, the inequality in expression (19-1) is reversed, i.e.,

$$f(x) \geqslant f(x_0)$$

The function f in Figure 19-1 has local maxima at x_0, x_3, and a, with x_3 being the global maximum; x_1, x_2, and b are local minima, with x_2 being the global minimum. Maxima correspond to the hilltops. The global maximum is the highest hilltop in the range considered. All other hilltops are local maxima. Minima correspond to the valley floors. The global minimum is the lowest of all the valley floors, whereas all other valley floors represent local minima in the range considered.

Consider again the definition of a maximum in expression (19-1) in conjunction with Figure 19-1. As we move from left to right toward the hilltop at x_0, we are going uphill. In geometric terms, the slope of the hillside looking toward x_0 is positive for points to the left of x_0. If we proceed to the right past the hilltop at x_0, we are going downhill, i.e., the slope is now negative for points to the right of x_0. As we go past x_0, the slope has to change from positive to negative. At the hilltop itself the slope is horizontal or zero. In mathematical terms, the slope of a function f is given by its first derivative, denoted by $df(x)/dx = f'(x)$. Therefore, at x_0 the derivative must be zero. Any point at which $f'(x) = 0$ is called a *stationary point*. Analogous reasoning shows that if the function f assumes a local or a global minimum at a point x_0, its derivative is also equal to zero at x_0.

Figure 19-1. *Stationary points.*

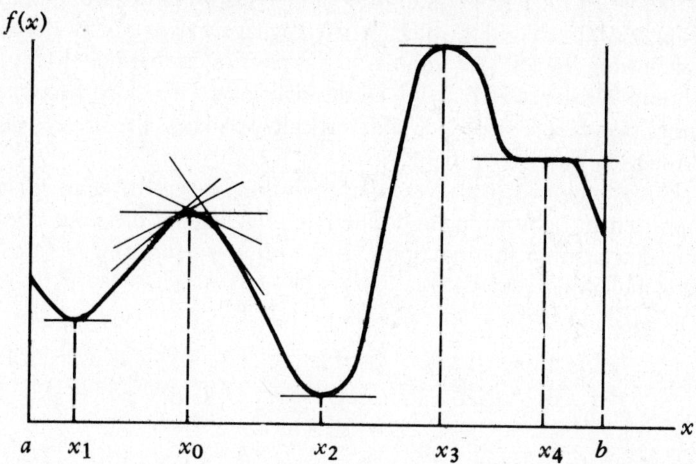

NECESSARY CONDITION FOR AN EXTREME VALUE OF f

A necessary condition for the function f to have an extreme value (a maximum or a minimum) at an interior point x_0 of the interval $[a, b]$ is that x_0 be a stationary point, i.e.,

$$f'(x) = 0 \quad \text{at } x_0 \tag{19-2}$$

Unfortunately, the function also has a stationary point at x_4, which is an *inflection point* of f. A stationary point is therefore not a *sufficient condition* for an extreme value of f. The sufficient condition for a stationary point to yield an extreme value of f can be obtained by examining the Taylor expansion of f around x_0 for h small:

$$f(x_0 + h) = f(x_0) + hf'(x_0) + \frac{h^2}{2}f''(x_0) + R_2 \tag{19-3}$$

where $f'(x_0)$ is the first derivative evaluated by x_0, $f''(x_0)$ is the second derivative evaluated at x_0, and, for h small, the remainder term R_2 is less, in absolute value, than the term containing $f''(x_0)$.

At the stationary point x_0, the term containing $f'(x)$ is zero, and h^2 is positive for all values of h, negative or positive. Hence, $f(x_0 + h)$ will be less than $f(x_0)$ if $f''(x_0) < 0$ and larger than $f(x_0)$ if $f''(x_0) > 0$.

Let us view this in terms of our previous picture in Figure 19-1 of approaching the hilltop from the left of x_0 and going past it—assuming the hilltop is, mathematically speaking, "well behaved" (which in lay language means round and smooth). As we approach from the left, the slope, which is positive on that side, becomes less and less steep until it reaches zero at x_0. To the right of x_0, the slope becomes negative and becomes steeper and steeper. Mathematically speaking, the slope is decreasing as we go through x_0 from left to right.

This situation is just reversed at the valley floor—the slope is increasing as we go from left to right through x_0. The rate of change of the slope corresponds to the second derivative of the function f. If the slope is decreasing, $f''(x) < 0$, and if the slope is increasing, $f''(x) > 0$.

SUFFICIENT CONDITION FOR AN EXTREME VALUE OF f

If x_0 is a stationary point, the function f has a maximum at x_0 if $f''(x_0) < 0$, and it has a minimum at x_0 if $f''(x_0) > 0$.

If $f''(x_0) = 0$, we find the first of the higher order derivatives of f which is nonzero at x_0. If the order of this derivative is odd, f has an inflection point at x_0. If the order of this derivative is even, this derivative is substituted for $f''(x_0)$ in the sufficient condition above.

You will have noticed that neither the necessary nor the sufficient conditions allow us to determine whether a stationary point yields a local or a global extreme value of the function f. This has to be determined by evaluating the function at all relevant stationary points as well as at the end points a and b of the interval on x.

The following section will apply these conditions to determine the optimal production quantity for a one-period inventory model with a random demand.

19-2 A CONSTANT-CYCLE INVENTORY REPLENISHMENT MODEL WITH RANDOM DEMAND

A meat processing firm prepares a batch of spicy sausages every Wednesday for sale by butchers and supermarkets prior to the weekend. The sausages are sold by weight. Any sausages not sold by the weekend are sold to a petfood manufacturer on Monday. The petfood manufacturer accepts any amount of old sausages. The gross profit (i.e., wholesale price less manufacturing costs) is c_u dollars per kilogram of fresh sausages sold. The gross loss per kg on sales to the petfood manufacturer (i.e., manufacturing cost less proceeds) amounts to c_o dollars. The weekly demand for spicy sausages is a random variable with a probability density function $h(x)$, $x \geqslant 0$. The objective is to determine the size of the weekly batch, denoted by S, which maximizes the expected total net profit (i.e., gross profit less losses).

The net profit depends on the demand—a continuous random variable. Hence, the net profit π is a function of a continuous random variable and is, therefore, a random variable itself. The form of the net profit depends on whether sales are larger or smaller than S. If the weekly demand x exceeds S, the entire batch is sold fresh at a net profit of $c_u S$, or

$$\pi(x) = c_u S, \qquad \text{for all } x \geqslant S$$

If the weekly demand is less than S, an amount x is sold fresh at a gross profit of $c_u x$, and an amount $(S - x)$ is sold old at a loss of $c_o(S - x)$, or

$$\pi(x) = c_u x - c_o(S - x), \qquad \text{for all } x < S$$

The expected value of the function π of the continuous random variable x is equal to $\int_0^{+\infty} \pi(x)h(x)\,dx$. Hence, for any given value of S, the expected net profit is

$$T(S) = \int_0^S [c_u x - c_o(S - x)]h(x)\,dx + \int_S^\infty c_u\,Sh(x)\,dx \tag{19-4}$$

To find the value of S for which expression (19-4) attains a maximum, we need $T'(S) = 0$. For this operation we have recourse to the following formula for differentiating an integral whose limits of integration are functions. Let

$$F(y) = \int_{g(y)}^{k(y)} f(x, y)\,dx$$

Then

$$\frac{d}{dy}F(y) = \int_{g(y)}^{k(y)} \frac{\partial f(x, y)}{\partial y}\,dx + f(k(y), y)\frac{dk(y)}{dy} - f(g(y), y)\frac{dg(y)}{dy} \tag{19-5}$$

We apply expression (19-5) separately for each of the two integrals in expression (19-4). For the first integral, let $y = S$, $x = x$; then $k(y) = S$, $g(y) = 0$, $f(x, y) = [c_u x - c_o(S - x)]h(x)$, and $dF(y)/dy$ becomes

$$\int_0^S [-c_o]h(x)\,dx + [c_u S - c_o(S - S)]h(S)\,dS/dS - [c_u(0) - c_o(S - 0)]h(0)\,d0/dS \tag{19-6}$$

The last term of (19-6) is zero, since $d0/dS = 0$. Canceling all zero terms, we get

$$-c_o\int_0^S h(x)\,dx + c_u Sh(S) \tag{19-7}$$

Verify that the derivative of the second integral is

$$c_u\int_S^\infty h(x)\,dx - c_u Sh(S) \tag{19-8}$$

Adding expressions (19-7) and (19-8) yields

$$T'(S) = -c_o\int_0^S h(x)\,dx + c_u\int_S^\infty h(x)\,dx \tag{19-9}$$

Setting expression (19-9) equal to zero, we see that the optimal batch size S^* has to satisfy

$$c_u \int_{S^*}^{\infty} h(x)\,dx = c_o \int_0^{S^*} h(x)\,dx \tag{19-10}$$

$\int_{S^*}^{\infty} h(x)\,dx$ is the probability that demand exceeds S^* or that the marginal unit produced is sold. Hence, the left-hand side of (19-10) is the expected profit from selling the marginal unit produced by regular sales, and the right-hand side represents the expected loss from selling the marginal unit produced to the pet food manufacturer. At the optimum, these two must be equal. This is precisely the basic principle in economics that the optimal output equates marginal revenue and marginal cost—the reasoning we applied in Section 12-9 for this type problem.

Using the property that

$$\int_0^{S} h(x)\,dx + \int_S^{\infty} h(x)\,dx = 1$$

and rearranging (19-10), we obtain again condition (12-21) of Section 12-9:

$$\int_0^{S^*} h(x)\,dx = \frac{c_u}{c_o + c_u} \tag{19-11}$$

At the optimum, the probability that the weekly demand is at most S^* is equal to the ratio of gross profit over gross profit plus loss per unit.

Let $c_u = \$0.50$, $c_o = \$0.10$, and let the weekly demand be normally distributed with a mean of 800 and a standard deviation of 100. Then

$$\frac{c_u}{c_u + c_o} = \frac{0.50}{0.50 + 0.10} = 0.833$$

and from Table 1 of the normal distribution in Appendix B we find that

$$P(\text{weekly demand} \leq S^*) = 0.833$$

implies $S^* = 800 + 0.97(100) = 897$. The optimum weekly batch is thus almost 900 kg.

To determine whether or not this solution represents a maximum, we verify that the sufficient conditions for a maximum, i.e., $T''(S) < 0$, are satisfied. From (19-9) we obtain the second derivative as

$$T''(S) = -(c_u + c_o)h(S)$$

In this case, there is no need to evaluate $T''(S)$ at S^*. Since $h(S) > 0$ for all values of S for a normal probability density function, and c_u and c_o are both positive, $T''(S)$ is negative for all S. Hence, condition (19-11) yields the optimum S^*, which maximizes (19-4).

19-3 CONVEX AND CONCAVE FUNCTIONS IN ONE VARIABLE

The function f of the variable x is *convex* if the straight line between any two arbitrary points on its graphs falls on or above the graph of the function, as depicted in Figure

Figure 19-2. *Convex functions.*

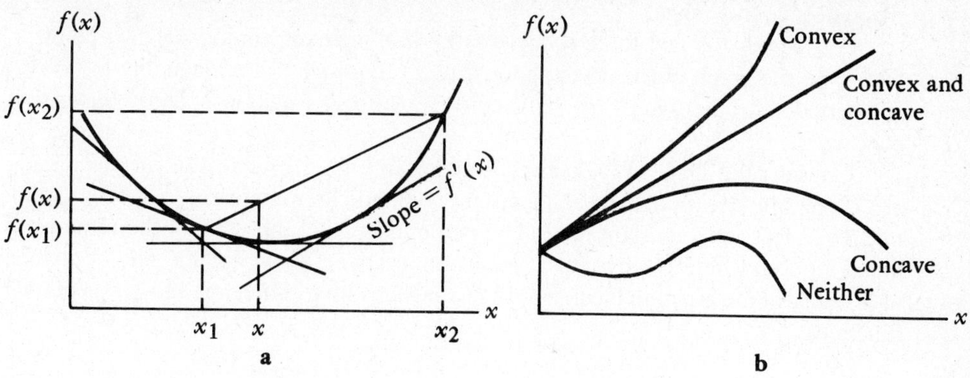

19-2(a). The function is *strictly convex* if the straight line between any two points is always above the graph of the function.

Consider the line segment between the values of the function f on its graph for any two points, x_1 and x_2. The value of this line segment at the point x, $x_1 \leq x \leq x_2$, is given by a linear combination of $f(x_1)$ and $f(x_2)$. Let the proportion of the interval $[x_1, x_2]$ from x_1 to x be λ. Then

$$\lambda = \frac{x - x_1}{x_2 - x_1} \qquad \text{or} \qquad x = (1 - \lambda)x_1 + \lambda x_2$$

with $0 \leq \lambda \leq 1$, by definition. The value of the line segment at x is

$$f(x_1) + \lambda[f(x_2) - f(x_1)] = (1 - \lambda) f(x_1) + \lambda f(x_2)$$

For a convex function, the value at the point x of the line segment joining any two points x_1 and x_2 on the graph of f will never be less than $f(x)$. We will use this property as our mathematical definition of convexity.

CONVEX FUNCTIONS

A function f is convex if and only if for all pairs (x_1, x_2) of x, and for all λ, $0 \leq \lambda \leq 1$,

(19-12) $$f((1 - \lambda)x_1 + \lambda x_2) \leq (1 - \lambda)f(x_1) + \lambda f(x_2)$$

For instance, $f(x) = x^2$ is convex, but $f(x) = R/x$ is not convex for all values of x. However, if $f(x) = R/x$ is only defined for nonnegative values of x for a particular problem, then it is also convex. Suppose $f(x)$ represents the number of production batches, as a function of the size x of the production batches, needed to meet an annual demand of size R. Clearly, x cannot be negative. Therefore, it may often be useful to say that a function is convex between two points x_1 and x_2, disregarding its shape outside this range.

A function f is said to be *concave* if the line segment joining any two points x_1 and x_2 on the graph of f is never above $f(x)$. f is concave if the inequality in (19-12) is reversed—in other words, if $-f$ is convex. A linear function is both convex and concave.

Consider the shape of the convex function in Figure 19-2(a). It is first decreasing at a decreasing rate (or at most at a constant rate), and then increasing at an increasing rate (or at least at a constant rate). The rate of change of the slope of the function is therefore everywhere positive (or at least nonnegative). However, the rate of change of the slope of the function is equal to its second derivative. Therefore, for differentiable functions

(19-13) $$\text{if} \quad f''(x) \geq 0, \qquad \text{for all } x, f \text{ is convex}$$

By analogous reasoning we find that

(19-14) $$\text{if} \quad f''(x) \leq 0, \qquad \text{for all } x, f \text{ is concave}$$

Note the strong analogy between these two properties and the sufficient conditions for an extremum of f.

In economic terms, if f is a cost function, then expression (19-13) corresponds to the case of *increasing marginal cost*, and if f is a profit function, then expression (19-14) implies *decreasing marginal return*.

The graphical representation of convex and concave functions reveals that these functions can have one stationary point at most, if one exists. The implications of this property in terms of finding the global optimum of a function are evident.

GLOBAL OPTIMA

	Convex Functions	Concave Functions
(i) Global Minimum	At a stationary point if one exists; otherwise, at one of the end points.	At one of the end points.
(ii) Global Maximum	At one of the end points.	At a stationary point, if one exists; otherwise, at one of the end points.

The sum of convex (concave) functions is also convex (concave), i.e., if f_1, f_2, . . ., f_n are convex (concave) functions in x, then the function defined by

(19-15) $$f(x) = \sum_i a_i f_i(x), \qquad \text{for all} \quad a_i \geq 0$$

is also convex (concave). This is a very useful property, since it allows us to determine whether a function consisting of the sum of several parts is convex or concave by considering each part separately.

Let us now apply these concepts to the sausage example in Section 19-2. The total expected net profit to be maximized is

$$T(S) = \int_0^S [c_u x - c_o(S - x)]\, h(x)\, dx + \int_S^\infty c_u S h(x)\, dx \tag{19-16}$$

with a stationary point defined by (19-10). Does this stationary point yield a global maximum? To answer this question we determine whether the function T is concave in S. Since we are dealing with a differentiable function, we use expression (19-14). To demonstrate the use of the property summarized by expression (19-15), let us separate T into the two parts, multiplied by nonnegative constants c_u and c_o:

$$T_1(S) = \int_0^S xh(x)\, dx + \int_S^\infty Sh(x)\, dx \tag{19-17}$$

and

$$T_2(S) = \int_0^S -(S - x)\, h(x)\, dx \tag{19-18}$$

Then, since $h(x) \geqslant 0$ for all probability distributions, we find from (19-17)

$$T_1''(S) = -h(S) \leqslant 0, \qquad \text{for all} \quad S \geqslant 0 \tag{19-19}$$

and from (19-18)

$$T_2''(S) = -h(S) \leqslant 0, \qquad \text{for all} \quad S \geqslant 0 \tag{19-20}$$

Therefore, each part of T is concave, and for c_u, $c_o \geqslant 0$, their sum is also concave. S^* obtained from expression (19-11) is the global maximum.

19-4 DIFFERENTIABLE FUNCTIONS OF TWO VARIABLES

Optimization of functions of two decision variables warrants separate discussion not only because there are many practical applications, but also because the principles of classical optimization for several decision variables can best be demonstrated in terms of the two-variable case. Let f be a function in the variables x and y defined over some region R. The function f has a maximum at (x_0, y_0) if

$$f(x_0, y_0) \geqslant f(x, y), \qquad \text{for all } x, y \text{ in some neighborhood of } (x_0, y_0) \tag{19-21}$$

This maximum will be a global maximum if expression (19-21) holds for all values of (x, y) in R. It is a local maximum if (19-21) holds for all values around a neighborhood of (x_0, y_0). Geometrically, a maximum corresponds to a hilltop—this time viewed in three dimensions. For a minimum, the inequality in (19-21) is reversed.

As in the one-variable case, the necessary condition for f to have an extreme value at (x_0, y_0) is that (x_0, y_0) be a stationary point, unless the maximum occurs on the boundary of R.

NECESSARY CONDITION FOR
AN EXTREME VALUE OF f

A necessary condition for the function f in x and y to assume an extreme value at (x_0, y_0) in the interior of R is that

(19-22) $$f_x = 0 \quad \text{and} \quad f_y = 0 \quad \text{at } (x_0, y_0)$$

where $f_x = \partial f/\partial x$ and $f_y = \partial f/\partial y$

From the Taylor expansion of f around (x_0, y_0), we obtain the sufficient conditions for a maximum or a minimum.

SUFFICIENT CONDITIONS FOR
AN EXTREME VALUE OF f

The stationary point (x_0, y_0) of the function f evaluated at (x_0, y_0) is a maximum if

(19-23) $$f_{xx} < 0 \quad \text{and} \quad f_{xx}f_{yy} - (f_{xy})^2 > 0$$

It is a minimum if

(19-24) $$f_{xx} > 0 \quad \text{and} \quad f_{xx}f_{yy} - (f_{xy})^2 > 0$$

It is neither if

(19-25) $$f_{xx}f_{yy} - (f_{xy})^2 < 0$$

where f_{xx}, f_{yy}, and f_{xy} are the second order partial derivatives of f.

For functions in $n > 2$ variables, the necessary conditions require that the partials of f with respect to each variable be equated to zero, and the sufficient conditions generalize to the evaluation of the $(n \times n)$ Hesian matrix at the stationary point considered. For further details see the text by Teichroew, pp. 547–548, listed among the references to this chapter.

19-5 A TWO-VARIABLE EXAMPLE: THE (Q, r) INVENTORY MODEL

In Section 12-11 we developed the total cost function for the (Q, r) model for the lost-sales case [expression (12-25)], where Q is the replenishment quantity and r the reorder point:

(19-26) $$T(Q,r) = c_1V\left[\tfrac{1}{2}Q + \int_0^r (r - x)f(x)\,dx\right] + \frac{R}{Q}\left[c_2 + c_3\int_r^\infty (x - r)f(x)\,dx\right]$$

From the necessary conditions (19-22), the minimum of expression (19-26) is found by setting the partials of $T(Q,r)$ equal to zero:

$$\partial T/\partial Q = \tfrac{1}{2}c_1V - \frac{R}{Q^2}\left[c_2 + c_3\int_r^{\infty}(x - r)f(x)\,dx\right] = 0 \tag{19-27}$$

$$\partial T/\partial r = c_1V\int_0^r f(x)\,dx - \frac{R}{Q}c_3\int_r^{\infty} f(x)\,dx = 0 \tag{19-28}$$

where we used formula (19-5) to obtain (19-28). Solving (19-27) for Q and (19-28) for r, we get expressions (12-26) and (12-27); namely, Q^* as a function of r^*, and the value of the distribution function at r^* as a function of Q^*:

$$Q^* = \left[2R(c_2 + c_3\int_{r^*}^{\infty}(x - r^*)f(x)\,dx)/c_1V\right]^{1/2} = G(r) \tag{19-29}$$

$$F(r^*) = c_3\frac{R}{Q^*}\Big/\left[c_1V + c_3\frac{R}{Q^*}\right] = H(Q) \tag{19-30}$$

No further simplication is possible. How can we find the optimal values of Q and r from these expressions? Figure 19-3 depicts the shape of the two functions $G(r)$ and $H(Q)$. Verify that as $r \to \infty$, $G(r) \to [2Rc_2/c_1V]^{1/2}$, while for $r = 0$, $G(r) = [2R(c_2 + c_3\mu)/c_1V]^{1/2} = \hat{Q}$, where μ is the expected lead-time demand. Similarly, as $Q \to 0$, $H(Q) \to 1$, which implies that $r \to \infty$; while for $Q \to \infty$, $H(Q) \to 0$, implying that $r \to 0$. The two functions thus intersect each other. Expressions (19-29) and (19-30) represent the point of intersection. The optimal values of Q and r can thus be approximated to any degree of accuracy desired by successive substitutions. One such approach is the algorithm for the (Q, r) model presented in Section 12-11. The dashed line depicts the progress of these successive approximations.

Figure 19-3. *Successive approximations for (Q, r) model.*

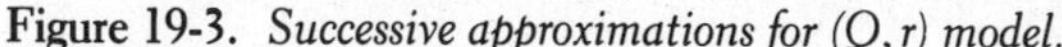

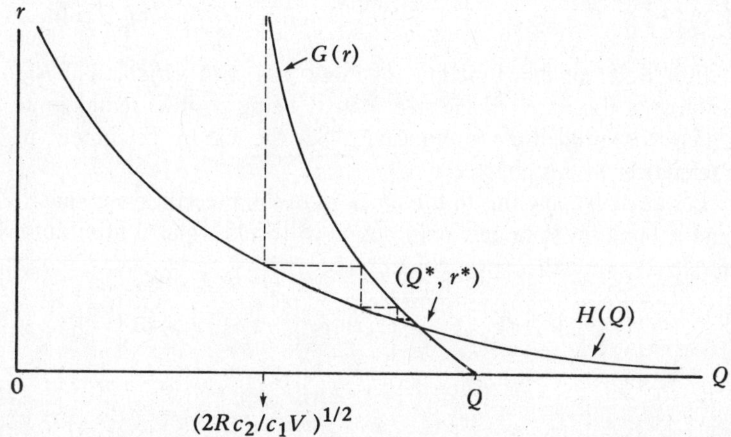

This simple example demonstrates how the necessary conditions for stationary points of functions in more than one variable may easily result in expressions too complex to be solved by analytic methods. It is for such reasons that methods of classical optimization are often impractical from a computational point of view. Unfortunately, the tremendous advances in more powerful methods have so far not produced any general method for finding the global optimum of any arbitrary function in several variables. Some methods work better for some type of mathematical structures, some better for others, as we shall see in Chapters 20 and 21.

19-6 CONVEX AND CONCAVE FUNCTIONS OF SEVERAL VARIABLES

A cereal bowl represents a typical example of a convex function in two variables. The definition of convexity for functions in two or more variables is a generalization of expression (19-12).

CONVEX FUNCTIONS IN SEVERAL VARIABLES

A function f of the variables $x, y, \ldots,$ and z is convex if and only if for any two points $(x_1, y_1, \ldots, z_1)$ and $(x_2, y_2, \ldots, z_2)$ and all λ, $0 \leq \lambda \leq 1$,

$$(19\text{-}31)\quad f((1-\lambda)x_1 + \lambda x_2, (1-\lambda)y_1 + \lambda y_2, \ldots, (1-\lambda)z_1 + \lambda z_2) \leq (1-\lambda)f(x_1, y_1, \ldots, z_1) + \lambda f(x_2, y_2, \ldots, z_2)$$

For differentiable functions of two variables, expression (19-31) is equivalent to

$$(19\text{-}32)\qquad f_{xx} \geq 0, \qquad f_{yy} \geq 0, \qquad \text{and} \qquad f_{xx}f_{yy} - (f_{xy})^2 \geq 0$$

For concave functions, the inequality in (19-31) is reversed, and (19-32) becomes

$$(19\text{-}33)\qquad f_{xx} \leq 0, \qquad f_{yy} \leq 0, \qquad \text{and} \qquad f_{xx}f_{yy} - (f_{xy})^2 \geq 0$$

[For differentiable functions of more than two variables, (19-32) and (19-33) generalize to the $(n \times n)$ Hessian matrix, being positive semidefinite for convexity and negative semidefinite for concavity. See the text by Teichroew, p. 547, listed in the references to this chapter.]

Let us now apply this to the problem in the preceding section. If T is convex in Q and r, then any stationary point found will yield a global minimum. From expressions (19-27) and (19-28) we obtain

$$T_{QQ} = \frac{2R}{Q^3}\left[c_2 + c_3 \int_r^{\infty} (x - r)f(x)\,dx\right]$$

$$T_{rr} = f(r)[c_1V + (R/Q)c_3]$$

$$T_{Qr} = (R/Q^2)c_3 \int_r^{\infty} f(x)\, dx$$

Although T_{QQ} and T_{rr} are nonnegative for $Q \geqslant 0$ and $r \geqslant 0$, we cannot show that $T_{QQ}\,T_{rr} - (T_{Qr})^2 \geqslant 0$ for all probability distributions. Hence, we cannot conclude that T is convex in Q and r.

19-7 CONSTRAINED OPTIMIZATION AND LAGRANGE MULTIPLIERS

So far items stocked in inventory were always optimized individually. This approach is only permissible as long as there are no interactions among the items, such as limited production facilities, limited warehouse space, or necessity for joint ordering of groups of items. If such restrictions are present, then interdependent items will have to be considered jointly. Some of these restrictions can be handled with the approach discussed next.

Consider the case where items compete for a limited amount of funds for inventory investments. The average inventory investment for all n items stocked is not to exceed an amount F. F could be a function of the firm's total short-term funds available and/or a fraction of total yearly purchases. The latter would have the effect of forcing the overall inventory turnover to be at least equal to a certain size. If Q_i is the inventory replenishment quantity, and if V_i is the cost in the warehouse per unit of item i, then it must be true that the average inventory investment, $V_iQ_i/2$, summed over all n items, cannot exceed F, i.e.,

$$\tfrac{1}{2}\sum_{i=1}^{n} V_iQ_i \leqslant F \tag{19-34}$$

Let R_i denote the annual demand for item i. Let c_1 denote the annual holding cost per dollar invested in inventory and c_{2i} the fixed cost incurred whenever item i is ordered. By analogy with the EOQ model of expression (12-7) in Section 12-7, the total annual cost for all n items is

$$T(Q_1, Q_2, \ldots, Q_n) = \sum_{i=1}^{n}\left[\frac{R_i}{Q_i}c_{2i} + \frac{Q_i}{2}c_1V_i\right] \tag{19-35}$$

The objective is to find optimal order quantities, $Q_1^*, Q_2^*, \ldots, Q_n^*$, that minimize expression (19-35) subject to the investment constraint (19-34).

Generalizing the principles of Section (19-4) to the n-variable case, the unconstrained optimum is obtained by setting all first order partial derivatives of (19-35) equal to zero and solving the equations obtained for the n variables:

$$\partial T/\partial Q_i = -R_ic_{2i}/Q_i^2 + c_1V_i/2 = 0, \qquad i = 1, 2, \ldots, n \tag{19-36}$$

The unconstrained optimal Q_i^* have the familiar EOQ form:

$$Q_i^* = \sqrt{2R_ic_{2i}/c_1V_i}, \qquad i = 1, 2, \ldots, n \tag{19-37}$$

We now require that the solutions to expression (19-37) also satisfy constraint (19-34). How should we approach this constrained optimization problem? We do not know a priori whether or not the constraint is binding at the optimal solution. The first step is therefore to find out whether or not this is the case.

CONSTRAINED OPTIMIZATION: STEP 1

Find the optimal values for the decision variables, ignoring the constraint. If they satisfy the constraint, the constraint is not active and the optimal solution to the constrained problem is the same as the optimal solution to the unconstrained problem. If the constraint is violated, go to step 2.

If the original constraint is in the form of an equation from the outset, rather than an inequality, step 1 can be skipped.

CONSTRAINED OPTIMIZATION: STEP 2

The constraint is binding and will hold as an equality at the optimal solution. Hence, solve the problem with the constraint in the form of an equality.

To motivate the solution method for minimizing a function subject to an equality constraint, we revert to a two-variable case. We want to minimize the function f in x and y, subject to the equality constraint $g(x, y) = b$. In Figure 19-4 we show *contour lines* for the objective function. Eash line traces all combinations of x and y that yield the same value of f. The curve for $g(x, y) = b$ shows all combinations of x and y that satisfy the constraint as an equality. The optimal solution to the constrained problem occurs at the point (x_0, y_0), where a contour line just touches $g(x, y) = b$. This is the lowest value f can assume while still satisfying the constraint. At (x_0, y_0), the slopes of f and g coincide.

The change in f for marginal changes in x and y is given by the total differential

$$df = f_x\,dx + f_y\,dy$$

Along a contour line, $df = 0$. So we find that

$$dy/dx = -f_x/f_y$$

By the same reasoning we also find that

$$dy/dx = -g_x/g_y$$

At the point (x_0, y_0) these two slopes are equal, i.e.,

$$f_x/f_y = g_x/g_y$$

Figure 19-4. *Constrained minimization of $f(x, y)$ subject to $g(x, y) = b$.*

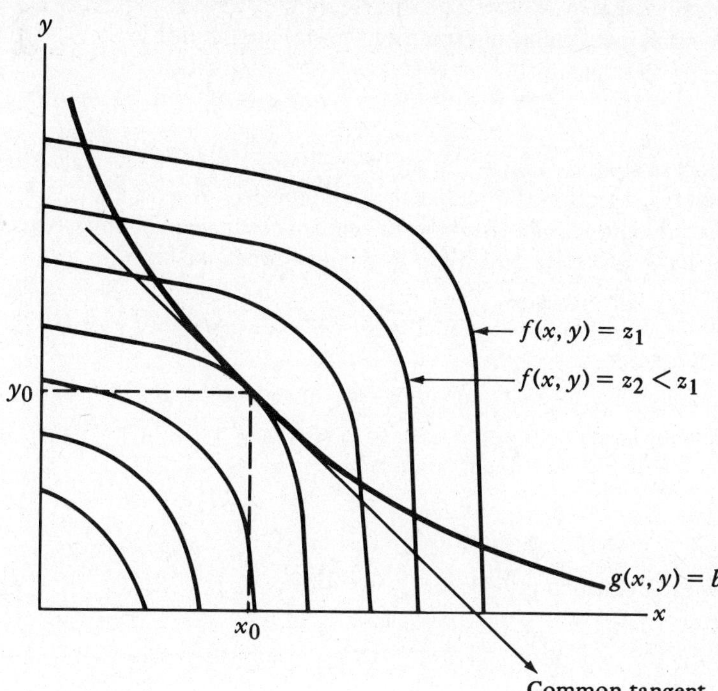

or, rearranging terms,

(19-38) $$f_x/g_x = f_y/g_y$$

Let the common ratio of expression (19-38) be equal to λ. Hence the optimal values of x and y satisfy the following two equations:

(19-39) $$f_x - \lambda g_x = 0 \qquad f_y - \lambda g_y = 0$$

as well as the constraint $g(x, y) = b$. Letting λ become a variable, we can now take advantage of this property and use it to find the optimal constrained values for x and y and the new variable λ by solving the three simultaneous equations:

(19-40) $$f_x - \lambda g_x = 0 \qquad f_y - \lambda g_y = 0 \qquad g(x, y) = b$$

It turns out that exactly the same set of equations can be generated by considering the unconstrained minimization of the following augmented objective function:

(19-41) $$L(x, y, \lambda) = \underbrace{f(x, y)}_{\substack{\text{original}\\ \text{function}}} + \lambda\underbrace{(b - g(x, y))}_{\text{constraint}}$$

known as the *Lagrangian function.* λ is called a *Lagrange multiplier.* The Lagrangian function for one constraint has one variable more than the original function—the price we must pay for being able to apply methods of classical optimization to such problems.

The stationary points of expression (19-41) are defined by

$$(19\text{-}42)\quad \partial L/\partial x = f_x - \lambda g_x = 0 \quad \partial L/\partial y = f_y - \lambda g_y = 0 \quad \partial L/\partial \lambda = b - g(x, y) = 0$$

which is exactly the same as the set of equations (19-40). (The reader is referred to more advanced texts for the sufficient conditions.)

We are now equipped to perform step 2 of constrained optimization. Combining (19-35) and (19-34), we obtain the Lagrangian function:

$$(19\text{-}43)\quad L(Q_1, Q_2, \ldots, Q_n, \lambda) = \sum_{i=1}^{n} [c_{2i}R_i/Q_i + \tfrac{1}{2}Q_ic_1V_i] + \lambda\left[F - \tfrac{1}{2}\sum_{i=1}^{n} V_iQ_i\right]$$

and the following necessary conditions for an optimum:

$$(19\text{-}44)\quad \partial L/\partial Q_i = -R_ic_{2i}/Q_i^2 + \tfrac{1}{2}c_1V_i - \tfrac{1}{2}\lambda V_i = 0, \qquad i = 1, 2, \ldots, n$$

$$(19\text{-}45)\qquad \partial L/\partial \lambda = F - \tfrac{1}{2}\sum_{i=1}^{n} V_iQ_i = 0$$

Solving each equation (19-44) for Q_i, we obtain

$$(19\text{-}46)\qquad Q_i^* = \sqrt{\frac{2R_ic_{2i}}{V_i(c_1 - \lambda^*)}}, \qquad i = 1, 2, \ldots, n$$

where λ^* is the value of λ, such that the Q_i^* of (19-46) satisfy (19-45). Viewing (19-46) as functions of λ, and substituting them into (19-34), we see that

$$(19\text{-}47)\qquad F - \tfrac{1}{2}\sum_{i=1}^{n} V_i[2R_ic_{2i}/V_i(c_1 - \lambda)]^{1/2}$$

is a monotonic decreasing function of λ. Hence there is a unique value $\lambda < 0$, such that expressions (19-44) are satisfied. We can thus find the constrained optimal solution by setting (19-47) equal to zero and solving for $\lambda = \lambda^*$. This in turn allows us to find all Q_i^* from (19-46).

Table 19-1 gives the data for an example involving $n = 3$ items. The holding cost per dollar invested per year is $c_1 = 0.2$, and the average investment should not exceed $28,000.

Table 19-1. *Data for constrained example*

Item	1	2	3
R_i	2000	8000	4000
V_i	$200	$100	$40
c_{2i}	$150	$200	$100

Step 1 The unconstrained optimal order quantities are

$$Q_1^* = \sqrt{2(2000)(150)/(0.2)200} = 122.5, \text{ or about } 122$$

$$Q_2^* = \sqrt{2(8000)(200)/(0.2)100} = 400.0$$

$$Q_3^* = \sqrt{2(4000)(100)/(0.2)40} = 316.2, \text{ or about } 316$$

The average investment required amounts to

$$\tfrac{1}{2}[122(200) + 400(100) + 316(40)] = \$38{,}520$$

Since this violates the upper limit of \$28,000, we go to step 2.

Step 2 From (19-47) we find that the optimal λ^* is the solution to

$$\frac{1}{2}\left[200\left(\frac{2(2000)(150)}{200(0.2-\lambda^*)}\right)^{1/2} + 100\left(\frac{2(8000)(200)}{100(0.2-\lambda^*)}\right)^{1/2} + 40\left(\frac{2(4000)(100)}{40(0.2-\lambda^*)}\right)^{1/2}\right] = 28{,}000$$

which yields $\lambda^* = -0.1795$. Inserting this result into expression (19-46), we obtain the constrained optimal order quantities as

$$Q_1^* = \sqrt{2(2000)(150)/200(0.2 + 0.1795)} = 88.91, \text{ or about } 89$$

$$Q_2^* = \sqrt{2(8000)(200)/100(0.2 + 0.1795)} = 290.38, \text{ or about } 290$$

$$Q_3^* = \sqrt{2(4000)(100)/40(0.2 + 0.1795)} = 229.57, \text{ or about } 230$$

Verify that these values exactly use up the entire \$28,000 available. The total annual cost of the constrained optimum is \$24,491, versus \$15,430 for the unconstrained optimum. Therefore, the limit imposed on the average inventory investment costs the firm \$9061 per year in the form of higher inventory operating costs.

In this example, the Lagrange multiplier could be determined analytically. There are many problems where the optimal value of λ has to be found by a search method. A systematic approach, easily programmed for computers, is to select two initial values for λ, λ_0 and λ_1, such that the constraint holds as a $<$ inequality for λ_0, and as a $>$ inequality for λ_1. The next guess for λ is $\lambda_2 = \frac{1}{2}(\lambda_0 + \lambda_1)$. If λ_2 forces the constraint to hold as $>$, $\lambda_3 = \frac{1}{2}(\lambda_0 + \lambda_2)$; otherwise, $\lambda_3 = \frac{1}{2}(\lambda_2 + \lambda_1)$. In this fashion the optimal λ can be approximated as closely as desired. More sophisticated search procedures will be discussed in Chapter 20.

In theory this method can be extended to several constraints. The Lagrangian function would include one Lagrange multiplier for each constraint. Since it is not known a priori which constraints are binding at the optimal solution, all possible combinations of binding and slack constraints have to be evaluated. For two constraints that means solving up to four problems: the unconstrained problem, two problems with one constraint only, and a fourth with both constraints binding. For k constraints, up to 2^k problems have to be evaluated. Adding to this the disadvantage of the increased number of variables, the method of Lagrange multipliers is hardly a practical solution method for problems with more than two constraints.

19-8 INTERPRETATION OF LAGRANGE MULTIPLIERS

Assume now that the amount of funds is not limited, but that there is an additional inventory investment cost of α dollars for every dollar invested per year, assessed on the average inventory investment. Added to the total annual cost in (19-35), this gives

$$T(Q_1, Q_2, \ldots, Q_n) = \sum_{i=1}^{n} \left[\frac{R_i}{Q_i} c_{2i} + \frac{Q_i}{2}(c_1 V_i + V_i \alpha) \right] \tag{19-48}$$

The optimal order quantities are now

$$Q_i^* = \sqrt{\frac{2R_i c_{2i}}{V_i(c_1 + \alpha)}}, \qquad \text{for all } i \tag{19-49}$$

Comparing (19-49) with expression (19-46) obtained from the Lagrangian function, we see that if we set $\alpha = -\lambda^*$, the two formulas result in exactly the same optimal order quantities. The Lagrange multiplier is thus a penalty on a resource use.

> **INTERPRETATION OF OPTIMAL LAGRANGE MULTIPLIERS**
>
> The optimal value of the Lagrange multiplier represents the marginal value or shadow price of the scarce resource.

λ^* is a function of the amount of the scarce resource b. It will change as b changes. Figure 19-5 depicts how $-\lambda$ behaves as a function of the amount of funds

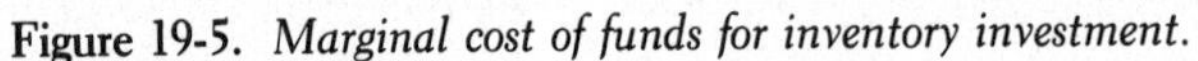

Figure 19-5. *Marginal cost of funds for inventory investment.*

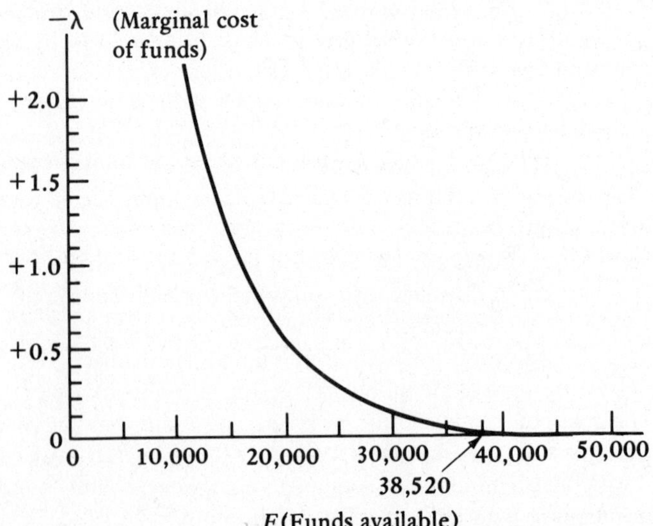

available for inventory investment. When funds reach a value of \$38,520, the constraint just ceases to be binding, and the optimal $\lambda = 0$ from there on. (Why?)

EXERCISES

19.1 Consider the EOQ model developed in Section 12-7, expression (12-7). Find the necessary and sufficient conditions for that model, and verify the square-root formula.

19.2 A product is produced by a process consisting of several operations that have to be performed on the batch as a whole. At the end of the production process, all units produced are added to finished inventories all at the same time as one batch. The total length of time to produce a batch of size B is as follows: $v + wB$. The holding cost per dollar invested per year is c_1, and the average value of the in-process inventory is V_2 dollars per unit, while finished goods have a value of V_1 dollars per unit. The production set-up cost is c_2 dollars per setup. Demand is evenly distributed over the whole year and amounts to R units per year.

(a) Find an expression for the total annual relevant cost, consisting of set-up costs and holding costs on finished goods and goods in process. It may help to draw a graph depicting how stocks for both goods in process and finished goods behave over time.

(b) What is the optimal value of B?

(c) For $V_1 = 12$, $V_2 = 10$, $c_1 = 0.24$, $c_2 = 120$, $R = 2400$, $v = 30$ days, $w = 0.2$ days, $N = 360$ days per year, find the optimal value of B.

(d) Is the total cost expression convex?

19.3 Consider the following waiting line problem. Ships arrive at a port at a rate of λ ships per day. Unloading and loading of ships can be done at a rate of μ ships per day. Then (as shown in Chapter 15), the average time a ship is in port waiting and being unloaded is $1/(\mu - \lambda)$ days. The cost for unloading a ship is μc_1 at the rate μ. The cost of a ship in port is c_2 dollars per day.

(a) Find an expression for the total cost per ship unloaded as a function of μ and λ.

(b) Find an expression for the optimal rate μ^* of unloading ships so as to minimize total cost per ship.

(c) Let $\lambda = 8$, $c_1 = \$2000$, $c_2 = 8000$. Find the optimal μ, and verify if the sufficient conditions are satisfied.

(d) Show whether or not the total cost function is convex or concave.

19.4 A machine produces parts at a constant rate of 360 units per hour. The rate of defectives produced depends on the length of time t between adjustments of the machine as follows: $144t$, where $t = 1$ is one hour. Defective parts have to be reworked on a different machine at a cost of \$2 per unit. Whenever an adjustment is made, the output of the machine is temporarily stopped. The opportunity cost of the lost production amounts to \$32. The objective is to determine the length of time between successive adjustments so as to minimize the total cost.

(a) Find an expression for the total cost as a function of the time between successive adjustments.

(b) Find the optimal length of time between successive adjustments, the check whether the sufficient conditions are satisfied.

(c) Determine whether the cost function is convex or concave.

19.5 For the model discussed in Section 19-2, find the optimal value of S for the following data: $c_1 = \$3$, $c_2 = \$7$, $h(x) = 0.02 - 0.0002x$ for $x \leq 100$ and 0 for $x > 100$ (i.e., a triangular distribution). Verify that the sufficient conditions are satisfied at the optimum.

19.6 A manufacturer of seasonal fashion clothing would like to determine the size of the production run for a given item which is subject to a random demand. Only one run will be made for the entire season. Any goods not sold by the end of the season are essentially worthless, and therefore the production cost k_1 incurred is not recovered. If the demand exceeds the production run, then the manufacturer suffers an opportunity cost for lost sales of k_2 dollars per unit short. The probability density function of the demand is $h(r)$, where r denotes demand.

(a) Find a general expression for the sum of expected lost production cost and expected opportunity costs on lost sales if a run of size Q is made at the beginning of the season.

(b) Find an expression to determine the optimal value of Q that minimizes the total expected costs. Compare the expression derived with condition (19-11) obtained for maximizing profits. Verify that the sufficient conditions are satisfied for all positive cost factors. Find the optimal value of Q for $k_1 = \$9.50$, $k_2 = \$30$, and $h(r)$ normal with mean 400 and standard deviation 80.

*19.7 A product is replenished once at the beginning of each month. Monthly demand x is random with a probability density function $h(x)$. If demand exceeds stocks, a shortage cost is incurred which is proportional both to the amount short and the length of time short. The shortage cost per unit short per month is c_2. Holding costs are assessed on the average inventory on hand at the end of the month, and amount to c_1 per unit per month. We want to find the optimal beginning inventory level each month that minimizes the sum of the expected holding and expected shortage costs.

(a) Let S be the beginning inventory level. Find an expression for the expected monthly cost as a function of S. To properly assess shortage costs, it may help to draw a diagram for the possible inventory behaviors over the one-month period.

(b) Find the necessary and sufficient conditions for a minimum.

(c) Determine whether the cost function is convex.

19.8 Find the (approximate) total expected annual cost for the (Q, r) model in Section 19-5 for the backorder case (i.e., sales are not lost, but filled after receipt of a replenishment). Find expressions to determine the optimal values of Q and r. Construct the graph corresponding to Figure 19-3. Find the optimal values of Q and r for the cost and demand parameters used in Section 12-11.

19.9 A subcontractor has to supply a given part at a rate of 20 units per day. One day's supply is brought to the customer every morning. The subcontractor produces these parts in batches of Q units at a rate of 50 units per day. It costs him \$7.50 to hold one unit in stock for one month. The contract provides for a late delivery penalty of \$2 per part per day late. Each time a production batch is started, there is a production set-up cost of \$4000. The objective is to find the optimal batch size Q^* and the optimal amount Z^* of late deliveries each replenishment cycle. Assume a month has 20 working days.

(a) Find an expression for the sum of annual production set-up costs, inventory holding costs, and late delivery penalties as a function of Q and Z.

(b) Determine the optimal values of Q and Z, and check whether the sufficient conditions for a minimum are satisfied.

(c) Determine whether the total cost function is convex or concave.

19.10 Consider the one-period (s, S) model discussed in Section 12-12. Let the holding cost for each unit left in stock at the end of the period be $c_1 = \$2$; let the shortage cost per unit short be $c_3 = \$8$; let the fixed set-up cost be $c_2 = \$24$; and let the demand distribution be negative exponential with a mean demand per period of 10.

(a) Find $K(i)$, and determine the value $i = S$ for which $K(i)$ is a minimum.

(b) Determine s.

(c) If $i = 6$, what is the optimal q?

*19.11 Lube Oil Inc. can meet daily customer demands either from stock or by scheduling a special production run. The latter option is chosen when the total demand on that day is sufficiently large, i.e., larger than a cutoff point Z. Inventories are replenished by an amount Q whenever stocks are reduced to zero. The daily demand is a random variable with density function $f(x)$. Each production run for inventory replenishment or for direct shipment to customers incurs a set-up cost of c_2 dollars. Holding costs amount to c_1 per dollar invested per year. Products added to inventory incur a handling cost of c_4 dollars per unit. There are $N = 250$ working days per year. The product value is V per unit.

(a) Find an expression for the total expected annual cost of this operating policy, covering inventory holding, production setup for both inventory replenishments and direct shipments to customers, and stock handling costs.

(b) Find expressions for the optimal values of Q and Z. How would you solve them?

(c) For $c_1 = 0.2$, $V = \$20$, $c_2 = \$10$, $c_4 = \$0.20$, and $f(x) = \lambda e^{-\lambda x}$ with $\lambda = 0.1$ (negative exponential with mean 10), use the results of (b) to find the optimal values of Q and Z to full integer values.

(d) Show that the total cost expression is not convex for all types of demand distributions.

19.12 For the problem discussed in Section 19-7, find the optimal order quantities Q_i and the unconstrained and constrained minimum cost for the following data: $c_1 = 0.24$, average inventory investment limit \$30,000, and $R_1 = 8000$, $R_2 = 6000$, $V_1 = \$120$, $V_2 = \$200$, $c_{21} = \$80$, $c_{22} = \$50$.

19.13 A firm stocks different items in the same warehouse. Item i requires a_i square feet of warehouse space per unit. The total warehouse space available is A square feet. All N items are replenished independently in batches of size Q_i. Holding costs assessed on the average inventory level amount to c_1 dollars per dollar invested per year. The value of item i is V_i dollars per unit. The fixed ordering costs is c_{2i} per batch ordered for item i, and the annual demand for item i is R_i.

(a) Find an expression for the annual total inventory holding and ordering costs for all N items. If each item is allotted a space in the warehouse required to store Q_i, what is the total amount of warehouse space needed?

(b) Given that the warehouse space available is A, form the Lagrangian function and determine expressions to find the optimal order quantities Q_i^*.

(c) Use $A = 2000$ sq ft, $c_1 = 0.2$, and the following data to find the optimal Q^* and the minimum cost. What is the cost of the warehouse restriction?

$i =$	1	2	3
R_i	12,000	5,000	2,000
V_i	\$20	\$40	\$50
c_{2i}	\$160	\$200	\$100
a_i in sq. ft.	1	2	4

19.14 A firm produces N products on the same machine. Total productive capacity of the machine is 250 days per year. Each product is produced in batches of size Q_i. For every batch of product i produced, the set-up time amounts to a_i days. The product is produced at a rate b_i per day. Let R_i be the annual demand, V_i the product value per unit, c_1 the holding cost per dollar invested per year, and c_{2i} the fixed set-up cost per batch for product i.

(a) Find a general expression for the total annual cost and express the constraints on the production capacity mathematically.

(b) Find expressions that, given data, would allow you to determine the optimal constrained batch sizes Q_i.

(c) Using common sense, discuss why this model is only a suitable approximation if the number of products N is relatively large, and why it could not be implemented if N were small—say, 2, 3, or 4.

19.15 Machine I produces a certain item at a uniform rate of 960 for a 480-minute day, machine II at a uniform rate of 1440 per day. The item has a market value of $2 each and can be sold immediately after manufacture. Adjustment of the machines are critical, and the number of defective parts produced is dependent on the number of adjustments made per day. Past experience shows that the number of defective parts produced by machine I is 256/N, where N is the number of adjustments made on machine I; similarly, for machine II it is 125/M, where M is the number of adjustments made on machine II. Each part produced has a material cost of $0.80, regardless of whether the part is salable or defective. Defective parts cannot be sold. Each adjustment has a cost of $4 for machine I and $6 for machine II. Each adjustment takes 10 minutes, during which time no production occurs. A fractional number of adjustments per day simply means that the days are not necessarily started with an adjustment, but that an adjustment is made after 960/N or 1440/M parts produced. However, because of manpower restrictions no more than 6 adjustments can be made daily. The firm wishes to maximize daily profits. How should it operate the two machines?

REFERENCES

Hadley, G. *Elementary Calculus*. San Francisco: Holden-Day, 1968. An elementary treatment of calculus.

Sasieni, M. W., A. Yaspan, and L. Friedman. *Operations Research: Methods and Problems*. New York: Wiley, 1959. Chapter 2 shows a number of inventory examples solved by classical methods of continuous and discrete calculus.

Teichroew, Daniel. *An Introduction to Management Science: Deterministic Models*. New York: Wiley, 1964. One of the few texts that contains an adequate treatment of classical optimization at an introductory level. Numerous worked examples. Good treatment of Lagrange multiplier approach.

CHAPTER TWENTY

Unconstrained Nonlinear Programming Methods

Nonlinear programming techniques are mathematically advanced and conceptually difficult. They require some fluency in differential calculus and linear algebra. They also contain design features to handle complexities, such as nonlinear objective functions that do not have a unique minimum and feasible regions that have nonlinear boundaries or that are nonconvex. No general "best" technique has yet been identified, although some avenues have emerged as more promising than others. Rather, the field abounds with many different techniques to cope with particular mathematical structures. All modern techniques use a numerical algorithm to find the "optimal" solution. Often, these algorithms have a structure similar to that of the simplex method.

It is not possible for us to present even the promising techniques in detail because of their mathematical sophistication. We have chosen to introduce some of the basic concepts and building blocks underlying most of the modern algorithms and demonstrate them by simple versions of the techniques. Whether an algorithm proves to be efficient ultimately depends on the computer time needed to reach an accurate solution. This is not simply a matter of the number of iterations needed, but also of the ease of data handling and the computational effort at each iteration—crucial aspects that we shall not be able to discuss.

This chapter is the first of two dealing with this topic. We begin with the optimization of one-dimensional (or univariate) functions. Such an algorithm is an integral part of most nonlinear techniques. Sections 20-4 to 20-8 look at three multivariate unconstrained nonlinear techniques that form the basis of the constrained nonlinear programming algorithms covered in the next chapter. In Section 20-5, we outline the framework on which most nonlinear algorithms are built.

20-1 UNIVARIATE OPTIMIZATION METHODS

Let x be the decision variable and $f(x)$ the objective function of the problem. *Univariate* (or *one-variable* or *one-dimensional*) optimization methods solve the problem

$$\underset{x}{\text{maximize}} \text{ (or } \underset{x}{\text{minimize}}\text{) } f(x) \tag{20-1}$$

We will assume that $f(x)$ is *unimodal*, i.e., has only one turning point. The techniques can be used on other functions but in that case may converge to a local optimum.

For demonstration purposes, consider the following simple example. A machine produces parts at a constant rate of 120 per hour. Each part produces a net revenue (sales price less material cost) of \$6. The rate of defective parts produced per hour is proportional to the length of time x between machine adjustments, i.e., $27x$, where $x = 1$ is one hour. Defective parts have to be reworked on a different machine at a cost of \$4 per part. Whenever an adjustment is made, the machine is temporarily stopped for one minute, the time needed to produce 2 parts. The profit per hour is equal to the number of parts produced times the net revenue per part less the cost of reworking defective parts: $f(x) = (120 - 2/x)6 - (27x)4 = 720 - (12/x) - 108x$. The objective is to determine the length of time between adjustments so as to maximize profit. Let us assume that at least one adjustment has to be made per hour, hence the decision variable x is restricted to the interval $[0, 1]$. We can now state the optimization problem as

$$\underset{0 \leq x \leq 1}{\text{maximize}} \; f(x) = 720 - (12/x) - 108x \tag{20-2}$$

At $x = 0$, $f(x) = -\infty$, and at $x = 1$, $f(x) = 600$. Although this problem is simple enough to solve by calculus, we will use it to illustrate univariate methods. You should verify that the optimal adjustment interval is $x^* = \sqrt{12/108} = 1/3$. The maximum profit per hour is $f(x^*) = \$648$.

Univariate methods fall into two major groups—*interval elimination methods* and *function approximation methods*. The basic idea behind interval elimination methods is to reduce the solution space that contains the optimal value of x to smaller and smaller intervals. For our example, the original solution space is the interval $[0, 1]$. At each iteration, some part of the current interval will be identified as not containing the optimum. That part is eliminated and the search continues over the reduced interval. As a rule, an interval elimination method does not pinpoint the optimum exactly; it provides an "acceptably small" interval in which the optimum lies. The function values at the end points of the interval (and in some cases a point within it) give estimates of the value of the optimum. There is a tradeoff in accuracy and computation time which depends on the acceptable size of the final interval. Methods such as *block search*, *Fibonacci search*, and *golden section search* are interval elimination methods. Fibonacci search is the most efficient, but it requires that the number of iterations be specified in advance. Golden section, which we consider in the next section, is a version of Fibonacci which allows the size of the final interval to be specified instead.

Function approximation methods iterate to the optimal value of x by approximating the function at each iteration by a function of a simple form, e.g., a quadratic or a cubic. The optimum of the *approximating function* is found analytically. These methods then use information about the true function at the optimum of the approximating function to update the approximation. By repeating the procedure the methods will converge on an optimum to the original function. Methods of this type vary according to the type of data they require and the type of approximation they make. *Powell's quadratic interpolation algorithm*, for example, uses the function value at three values of the variable to find a quadratic approximation. *Newton's method*, introduced in Section 20-3, uses the first and second derivatives at a single point to generate a quadratic approximation.

In the choice of a univariate search method, the nature of the function (e.g., whether or not it is differentiable or unimodal) and the relative size of the initial and final interval are important considerations. It is not surprising that many general-purpose methods are hybrid techniques designed to overcome the weaknesses—slowness or even lack of convergence—of each of the pure techniques.

20-2 GOLDEN SECTION SEARCH METHOD

As we shall see shortly, the key to the golden section search is in the number τ that satisfies $\tau^2 = \tau + 1$. This number is equal to $\frac{1}{2}(1 + \sqrt{5}) = 1.6180339. . . .$ We use τ because it generates a highly efficient interval elimination procedure.

Let the end points of the interval at the start of iteration k be $a^{(k)}$ and $b^{(k)}$. The golden section method finds two new points, $x_1^{(k)}$ and $x_2^{(k)}$, which exhibit the relationships shown in Figure 20-1. Mathematically, these relationships allow us to express $x_1^{(k)}$ in the form

$$(b^{(k)} - a^{(k)}) = \tau^2 L = \tau^2(x_1^{(k)} - a^{(k)})$$

or

$$x_1^{(k)} = a^{(k)} + \frac{1}{\tau^2}(b^{(k)} - a^{(k)}) \tag{20-3}$$

By symmetry,

$$x_2^{(k)} = b^{(k)} - (x_1^{(k)} - a^{(k)})$$

We now use these points to eliminate the part of the interval from $a^{(k)}$ to $b^{(k)}$, which cannot contain the optimal value of x. Only the remaining portion is retained for the next iteration. If $f(x_1^{(k)}) > f(x_2^{(k)})$, then, assuming that f is unimodal, the optimal

Figure 20-1. *Golden section search.*

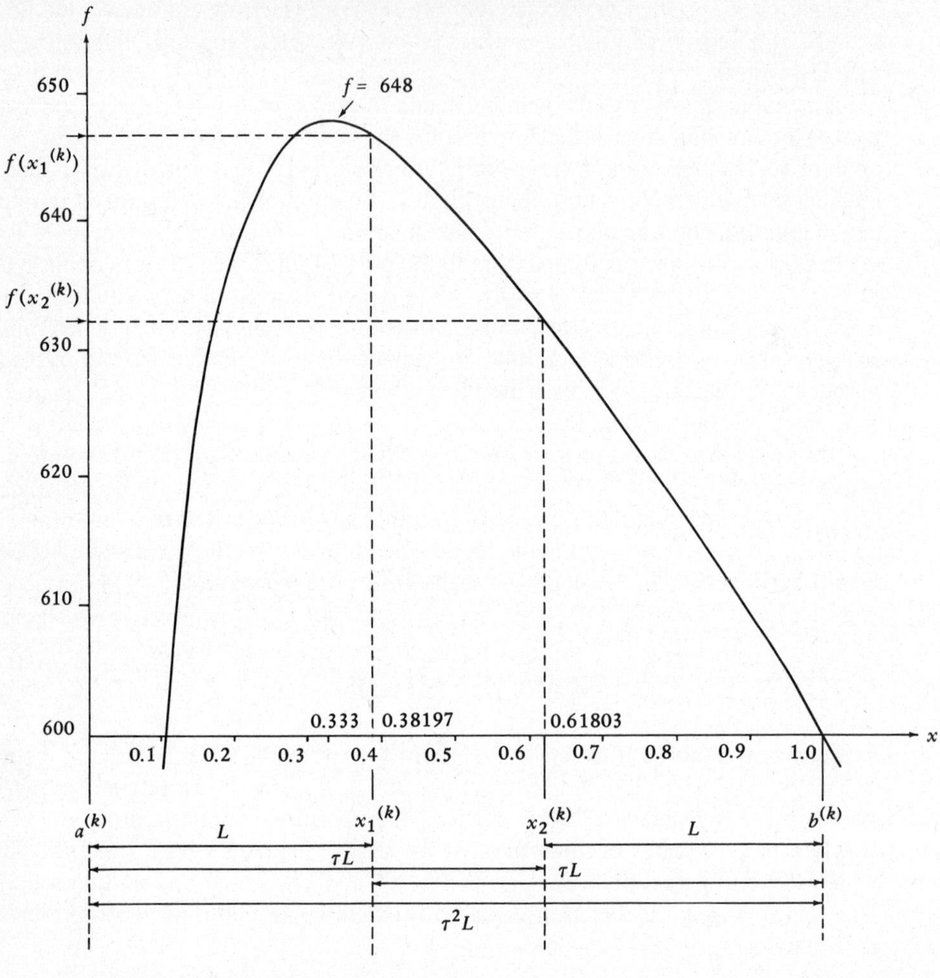

value of x must be smaller than $x_2^{(k)}$, so the interval $[x_2^{(k)}, b^{(k)}]$ is eliminated from further consideration. Similarly, if $f(x_1^{(k)}) < f(x_2^{(k)})$, we eliminate $[a^{(k)}, x_1^{(k)}]$. The new interval becomes the starting point for the next iteration. The algorithm stops when the interval becomes arbitrarily small, i.e., $(b^{(k)} - a^{(k)}) < \varepsilon$. The point in the last iteration with the best function value is then used as an approximation to the maximum. By choosing ε sufficiently small, we can obtain a high degree of accuracy.

It turns out that we do not have to use equation (20-3) beyond the first iteration. From Figure 20-1 you can see that if $x_1^{(k)}$ is the point with the largest function value, it will become $x_2^{(k+1)}$ at iteration $k + 1$. This follows because the distance $(x_1^{(k)} - a^{(k)})$ is in the same proportion to $(x_2^{(k)} - a^{(k)})$ as the distance $(x_2^{(k)} - a^{(k)})$ is to $(b^{(k)} - a^{(k)})$. Similarly, if $x_1^{(k)}$ replaces $a^{(k)}$ as the new end point, then $x_1^{(k+1)}$ equals $x_2^{(k)}$.

GOLDEN SECTION ALGORITHM

For the problem maximize $f(x)$:

Step 1 Let $a^{(1)}$ and $b^{(1)}$ be the end points of the initial interval. Compute

$$x_1^{(1)} = a^{(1)} + (b^{(1)} - a^{(1)})/(1.6180339)^2$$
$$x_2^{(1)} = b^{(1)} - (x_1^{(1)} - a^{(1)})$$

Set $k = 2$.

Step 2 (1) If $f(x_1^{(k-1)}) > f(x_2^{(k-1)})$, then

$$a^{(k} = a^{(k-1)} \quad \text{and} \quad b^{(k)} = x_2^{(k-1)}$$

$$x_1^{(k)} = a^{(k)} + (x_2^{(k-1)} - x_1^{(k-1)}) \quad \text{and} \quad x_2^{(k)} = x_1^{(k-1)}$$

(2) If $f(x_1^{(k-1)}) < f(x_2^{(k-1)})$, then

$$a^{(k)} = x_1^{(k-1)} \quad \text{and} \quad b^{(k)} = b^{(k-1)}$$

$$x_1^{(k)} = x_2^{(k-1)} \quad \text{and} \quad x_2^{(k)} = b^{(k)} - (x_2^{(k-1)} - x_1^{(k-1)})$$

Step 3 *Stop* when $(b^{(k)} - a^{(k)}) < \varepsilon$, arbitrarily small, and let the optimal x^* be equal to the point $a^{(k)}, b^{(k)}, x_1^{(k)}, x_2^{(k)}$ with the maximum function value. Otherwise, let k go to $k + 1$ and return to step 2.

Let us now apply this algorithm to problem (20-2), starting with an interval of $[a^{(1)} = 0, b^{(1)} = 1]$ and $\varepsilon = 0.01$.

Iteration 1:

Step 1 $x_1^{(1)} = 0 + (1 - 0)/(1.6180339)^2 = 0.382$
$x_2^{(1)} = 1 - (0.382 - 0) = 0.618$
$k = 2$

Iteration 2:

Step 2 $f(x_1^{(1)}) = f(0.382) = 720 - (12/0.382) - 108(0.382) = 647.33$
$f(x_2^{(1)}) = f(0.618) = 720 - (12/0.618) - 108(0.618) = 633.84$

Since $f(x_1^{(1)}) > f(x_2^{(1)})$,
$a^{(2)} = 0$ and $b^{(2)} = 0.618$
$x_1^{(2)} = 0 + (0.618 - 0.382) = 0.236$ and $x_2^{(2)} = 0.382$

Step 3 $b^{(2)} - a^{(2)} = 0.618 - 0 > \varepsilon = 0.01$

Hence, $k = 3$; return to step 2.

The algorithm continues as shown in Table 20-1, until the remaining interval is less than 0.01. At iteration 11, the maximum function value is obtained at $x_1^{(11)} = 0.334368$, where the profit is $f(x_1^{(11)}) = \$647.9997$, as compared to the true optimum profit of \$648.00. You should note that rounding errors may be compounded by this algorithm. It is important either to keep sufficient significant digits or to restart with a step 1 computation on the remaining interval every so many iterations.

Table 20-1. *Golden section method*

k	$a^{(k)}$	$b^{(k)}$	$b^{(k)} - a^{(k)}$	$x_1^{(k)}$	$x_2^{(k)}$	$f(x_1^{(k)})$	$f(x_2^{(k)})^2$
1	0	1	1	0.381966	0.618034	647.3313	633.8359
2	0	0.618034	0.618034	0.236068	0.381966	643.6718	647.3313
3	0.236068	0.618034	0.381966	0.381966	0.472136	647.3313	643.5929
4	0.236068	0.472136	0.236068	0.326238	0.381966	647.9833	647.3313
5	0.236068	0.381966	0.145898	0.291796	0.326238	647.3614	647.9833
6	0.291796	0.381966	0.090170	0.326238	0.347524	647.9833	647.9374
7	0.291796	0.347524	0.055728	0.313082	0.326238	647.8585	647.9833
8	0.313082	0.347524	0.034442	0.326238	0.334368	647.9833	647.9997
9	0.326238	0.347524	0.021286	0.334368	0.339394	647.9997	647.9883
10	0.326238	0.339394	0.013156	0.331264	0.334368	647.9986	647.9997
11	0.331264	0.339394	0.008130	0.334368	0.336290	647.9997	647.9972

20-3 NEWTON'S METHOD (UNIVARIATE)

Newton's method (or the *Newton-Raphson method*, as it is sometimes called) requires the objective function $f(x)$ to have an unconstrained maximum in the range we are considering and to have both first and second derivatives. We have chosen to study Newton's method in depth because it is easily extended to the multivariate case and, in one form or another, becomes a central part of many nonlinear programming algorithms. Newton's method is often viewed as a way of finding the roots of a function. However, we wish to interpret it as a series of quadratic approximations of f. Consider the first three terms of a Taylor's series expansion of the function f at point $x^{(k)}$ at iteration k.

$$F(x) = f(x^{(k)}) + f'(x^{(k)})(x - x^{(k)}) + \tfrac{1}{2}f''(x^{(k)})(x - x^{(k)})^2 \tag{20-4}$$

The function $F(x)$ is a quadratic approximation to $f(x)$ and has the same first and second derivatives at $x^{(k)}$. We can maximize $F(x)$ directly. If we are close to the maximum of $f(x)$, the curve of $F(x)$ will approximate the curve of the true function at the maximum. Hence by maximizing the approximating function $F(x)$, we approximately maximize $f(x)$. Figure 20-2 illustrates this. The maximum of (20-4) occurs

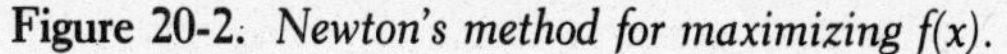

Figure 20-2. *Newton's method for maximizing f(x).*

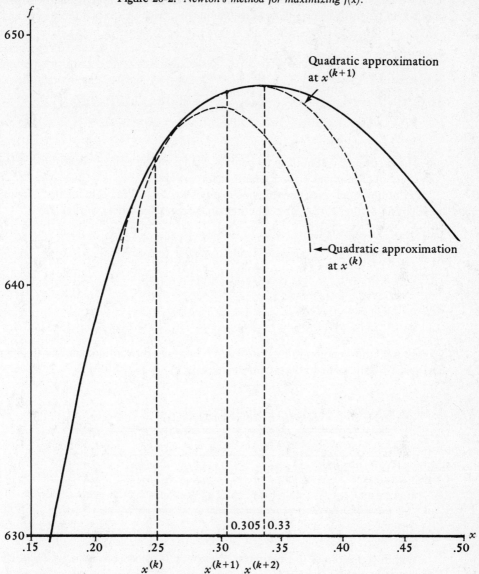

where

$$F'(\hat{x}) = f'(x^{(k)}) + f''(x^{(k)})(\hat{x} - x^{(k)}) = 0$$

or at

(20-5) $$\hat{x} = x^{(k)} - [f'(x^{(k)})/f''(x^{(k)})]$$

At each iteration k, the optimum $\hat{x}$ of the quadratic approximation becomes the point we use to construct the next quadratic approximation. Thus, we set $x^{(k+1)} = \hat{x}$ in (20-5) to obtain Newton's iterative equation.

NEWTON'S ITERATIVE EQUATION

(20-6) $$x^{(k+1)} = x^{(k)} - [f'(x^{(k)})/f''(x^{(k)})]$$

The procedure is terminated when the change in the estimated optimum is less than some small number ε, i.e., when $|x^{(k+1)} - x^{(k)}| < \varepsilon$.

Let us now apply Newton's method to problem (20-2). We begin the first iteration by arbitrarily setting $x = 0.250$. The first and second derivatives of $f(x)$ are

(20-7) $$f'(x) = (12/x^2) - 108 \qquad f''(x) = -24/x^3$$

At $x^{(1)} = 0.25$, $f'(x^{(1)}) = 84$ and $f''(x^{(1)}) = -1536$. So

$$F(x) = 576 + 468x - 768x^2$$

and

$$x^{(2)} = x^{(1)} - f'(x^{(1)})/f''(x^{(1)}) = 0.25 - (84)/(-1536) = 0.305$$

We illustrate this iteration in Figure 20-2. $x^{(2)}$ becomes the starting point for iteration 2. Table 20-2 shows that at the third iteration $|x^{(k+1)} - x^{(k)}| < 0.01$.

Table 20-2. *Newton's method for problem (20-2)*

k	$x^{(k)}$	$f'(x^{(k)})$	$f''(x^{(k)})$	$x^{(k+1)}$	$f(x^{(k+1)})$
1	0.25	84.00	−1536.00	0.305	647.72
2	0.305	21.00	−845.89	0.330	647.996
3	0.330	2.19	−667.84	0.333	648.00

Within a region of the optimum, Newton's method converges very quickly. Unfortunately it does not always converge. It may diverge or wander without converging if the function is badly behaved, or it may find the minimum rather than the maximum. By using a few iterations of an interval elimination algorithm, such as golden section, before applying Newton's method, we can usually prevent the method from misbehaving.

Another weakness of Newton's method is that it requires knowledge of the second derivative of the function. Second derivatives may not always exist or may be computationally expensive to evaluate, as in the multivariate case discussed in the next section. *Quasi-Newton methods* overcome these difficulties by estimating the values of second derivatives. These are then modified on the basis of the information we gain about the first derivatives at each additional point.

20-4 MULTIVARIATE UNCONSTRAINED OPTIMIZATION: AN EXAMPLE PROBLEM

In the remaining sections of this chapter, we will formalize and extend the ideas used in the one-variable optimization techniques to the multi-variable or multivariate case. For this purpose we will use the following simple example. A manufacturer makes three products. The sales volume of each product is dependent on its price, and in one case, product 3, sales volume is also dependent on the price of another product. The marketing division estimates the following relationship between monthly sales volume x_j (thousands of units) and unit price p_j for each product:

(20-8) $$x_1 = 10 - p_1$$

(20-9) $$x_2 = 16 - p_2$$

(20-10) $$x_3 = 6 - \tfrac{1}{2}p_3 + \tfrac{1}{4}p_2$$

The variable costs for the three products are \$6, \$7, and \$10 per unit, respectively. The manufacturer wishes to find the monthly sales schedule that will maximize profits. Total profit for each product is equal to total revenue minus total variable cost for the product. For product 1, total revenue is $R_1 = p_1x_1$. From (20-8), $p_1 = 10 - x_1$, so $R_1 = p_1x_1 = 10x_1 - x_1^2$. Total variable cost for product 1 is $V_1 = 6x_1$. So the total profit for product 1 is

$$\pi_1 = R_1 - V_1 = 10x_1 - x_1^2 - 6x_1 = 4x_1 - x_1^2$$

Verify from (20-9) that for product 2 the total revenue amounts to $R_2 = p_2x_2 = 16x_2 - x_2^2$, and the total variable cost $V_2 = 7x_2$, with the difference of

$$\pi_2 = R_2 - V_2 = 16x_2 - x_2^2 - 7x_2 = 9x_2 - x_2^2$$

Product 3 presents a new problem, since x_3 depends on p_2 as well as p_3. Total revenue is $R_3 = p_3x_3 = 2(6 - x_3 + \tfrac{1}{4}p_2)x_3$. Using $p_2 = 16 - x_2$ from expressions (20-9), we obtain

$$R_3 = 2(6 - x_3 + \tfrac{1}{4}(16 - x_2))x_3 = 20x_3 - 2x_3^2 - \tfrac{1}{2}x_2x_3$$

Variable cost is $V_3 = 10x_3$. Hence, total profit for product 3 is

$$\pi_3 = R_3 - V_3 = 20x_3 - 2x_3^2 - \tfrac{1}{2}x_2x_3 - 10x_3 = 10x_3 - 2x_3^2 - \tfrac{1}{2}x_2x_3$$

Summing π_1, π_2, and π_3, we obtain the total profit function:

(20-11) $$f(\mathbf{x}) = f(x_1, x_2, x_3) = 4x_1 - x_1^2 + 9x_2 - x_2^2 + 10x_3 - 2x_3^2 - \tfrac{1}{2}x_2x_3$$

We want to find values for x_1, x_2, and x_3 that maximize expression (20-11). Before studying specific techniques, let us look at the general structure of mathematical programming algorithms.

20-5 GENERAL STRUCTURE OF NONLINEAR PROGRAMMING ALGORITHMS

For several of the solution techniques developed in earlier chapters, we have, without stating so explicitly, used a variation of the following general algorithmic structure.

GENERAL STRUCTURE OF NONLINEAR PROGRAMMING ALGORITHMS

Step 1 Initiate the algorithm at a solution, denoted by

$$\mathbf{x}^{(1)} = (x_1^{(1)}, x_2^{(1)}, \ldots, x_n^{(1)})$$

Step 2 Find a *direction of movement* away from the current solution which improves the value of the objective function

$$f(\mathbf{x}) = f(x_1, x_2, \ldots, x_n)$$

Step 3 Determine how far to move away from the current solution in the direction of improvement of the objective function, or, in other words, find a *step size.*

Step 4 Repeat steps 2 and 3 using always the last solution found in 3 until no further direction of improvement of the objective function can be found or until the improvement in the objective function is less than a specified amount. The last solution found is then used as the optimal solution $\mathbf{x}^* = (x_1, x_2, \ldots, x_n)$.

Most techniques that follow this structure differ in their way of handling steps 2 and 3.

The direction of movement from a solution is given by a direction vector $\mathbf{d}$. An example of such a direction vector is depicted graphically in Figure 20-3. The direction vector, $\mathbf{d} = [d_1, d_2]$ (in two-dimensional space), is the vector that allows us to generate all points along a ray emanating from the current solution, $\mathbf{x} = (x_1, x_2)$, in the desired direction. This ray is defined in terms of the direction vector $\mathbf{d}$ and scalar θ as the set $\hat{\mathbf{x}} = (\hat{x}_1, \hat{x}_2)$ such that

$$\hat{\mathbf{x}} = \mathbf{x} + \theta\mathbf{d}, \qquad \text{for all } 0 < \theta < \infty \tag{20-12}$$

In Figure 20-3, $(\mathbf{x} + \theta\mathbf{d})$ is the line from $\mathbf{x}$ in the direction $\mathbf{d}$. The iterative equation of an algorithm at iteration k with step size $\theta^{(k)}$ is thus

$$\mathbf{x}^{(k+1)} = \mathbf{x}^{(k)} + \theta^{(k)}\mathbf{d}^{(k)} \tag{20-13}$$

Figure 20-3. *Direction vector.*

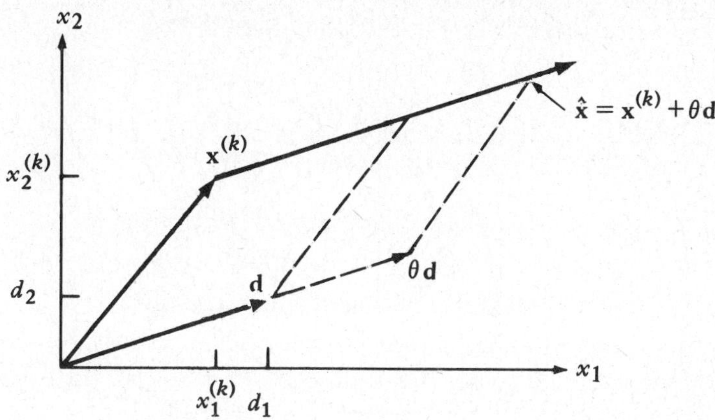

Let us illustrate how this structure applies to Newton's method equation (20-6) where $\hat{\mathbf{x}} = \hat{x}$. This equation finds the new solution $\hat{x} = x^{(k+1)} = x^{(k)} - (f'(x^{(k)})/f''(x^{(k)})$. $x^{(k)}$ represents the current solution x at iteration k. The direction is given by $-f'(x^{(k)})/f''(x^{(k)})$, while the step size is $\theta^{(k)} = 1$. In Newton's method, the direction of movement and the step size are both determined by equation (20-6). In the methods studied next, these two operations will normally be separated. Starting at the point $\mathbf{x}^{(k)}$, we will first find the direction vector $\mathbf{d}^{(k)}$, and then determine the step size $\theta^{(k)}$ to find the new solution $\mathbf{x}^{(k+1)}$.

20-6 GRADIENT METHODS FOR UNCONSTRAINED OPTIMIZATION

Gradient methods choose the *gradient vector* at a solution $\mathbf{x}$ as the direction of movement at step 2 of our general algorithmic structure. The gradient vector $\mathbf{g} = (g_1, g_2, \ldots, g_n)$ at a point $\mathbf{x}$ is the vector whose components (directional numbers) are the first partial derivatives of f evaluated at the point $\mathbf{x}$, i.e.,

$$\mathbf{g} = (\partial f/\partial x_1, \partial f/\partial x_2, \ldots, \partial f/\partial x_n) \qquad \text{evaluated at } \mathbf{x}$$

The gradient vector gives the greatest rate of increase in the value of the objective in the immediate vicinity of a point. It is, therefore, the locally best direction of movement. Geometrically, the gradient vector is the vector at right angles to the tangent plane at $\mathbf{x}$, as shown in Figure 20-4 for point $\mathbf{x}^{(1)}$. This technique is also called the *method of steepest ascent*. A "best" choice for the step size in the gradient direction is to move to the point that gives the largest value of the objective function in that direction.

Figure 20-4 graphically depicts the progression toward the optimal solution along gradient vectors starting from an arbitrary point $\mathbf{x}^{(1)}$. This technique finds a solution

Figure 20-4.

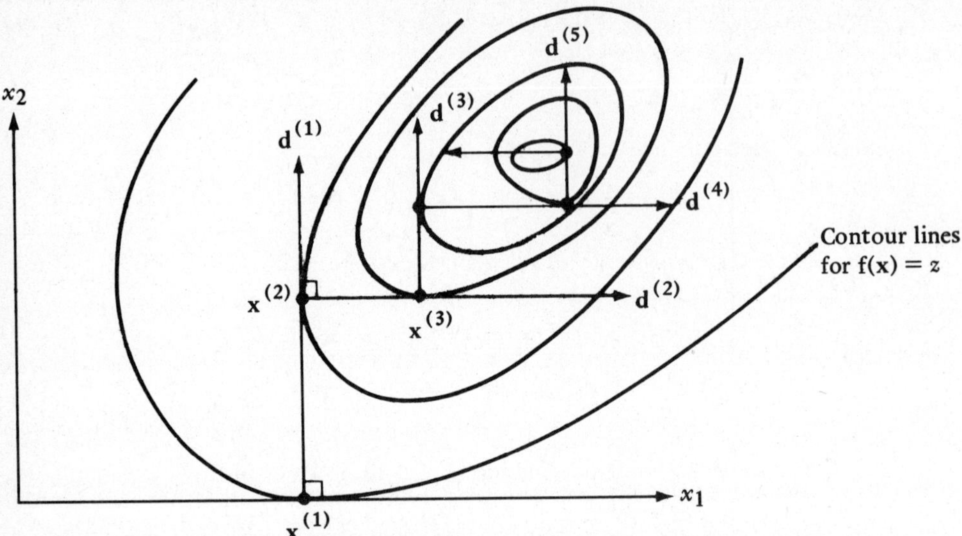

that is arbitrarily close to the optimal solution (or a local optimum if several optima exist) in a finite number of moves.

Let us now apply these ideas to the problem formulated in Section 20-4, namely

$$\text{maximize } f(\mathbf{x}) = 4x_1 - x_1^2 + 9x_2 - x_2^2 + 10x_3 - 2x_3^2 - \tfrac{1}{2}x_2x_3$$

The first partial derivatives of $f(\mathbf{x})$ are

(20-14) $\partial f/\partial x_1 = 4 - 2x_1 \qquad \partial f/\partial x_2 = 9 - 2x_2 - \tfrac{1}{2}x_3 \qquad \partial f/\partial x_3 = 10 - 4x_3 - \tfrac{1}{2}x_2$

Assume an initial point of $\mathbf{x}^{(1)} = (1, 2, 2)$. Substituting these values for the variables into the three partials of (20-14), we find the gradient vector at $\mathbf{x}^{(1)}$:

(20-15)
$$\partial f/\partial x_1 = 4 - 2(1) = 2 \qquad \partial f/\partial x_2 = 9 - 2(2) - \tfrac{1}{2}(2) = 4$$
$$\partial f/\partial x_3 = 10 - 4(2) - \tfrac{1}{2}(2) = 1$$

Hence,

(20-16)
$$\mathbf{g}^{(1)} = (2, 4, 1)$$

The next problem is to find a step size in the direction of the gradient vector at $\mathbf{x}^{(1)}$. If we choose the largest improvement of the objective function in the direction of the gradient vector as our criterion, then we want to find a step size θ that yields the point $\mathbf{x}^{(2)}$ defined by

(20-17)
$$f(\mathbf{x}^{(2)}) = \underset{0 \leq \theta < \infty}{\text{maximum}}\, f(\mathbf{x}^{(1)} + \theta \mathbf{g}^{(1)})$$

where $(\mathbf{x}^{(1)} + \theta\mathbf{g}^{(1)}, 0 \leq \theta < \infty)$ is the line from $\mathbf{x}^{(1)}$ in the direction of $\mathbf{g}^{(1)}$. Expression

(20-17) can be solved either by using classical methods of calculus, if that is computationally viable, or by using a univariate search technique on θ. Our example is simple enough for the use of calculus. Since $\mathbf{x}^{(1)} = (1, 2, 2)$ and $\mathbf{g}^{(1)} = (2, 4, 1)$, the line $\mathbf{x}^{(1)} + \theta\mathbf{g}^{(1)}$, $0 \leq \theta < \infty$, is given by

$$(1 + 2\theta, 2 + 4\theta, 2 + \theta), \qquad 0 \leq \theta < \infty \tag{20-18}$$

and (20-17) becomes

$$f(\mathbf{x}^{(2)}) = \underset{0 \leq \theta < \infty}{\text{maximum}}\, f(1 + 2\theta, 2 + 4\theta, 2 + \theta)$$

Using the functional relationship (20-11) with $x_1 = 1 + 2\theta$, $x_2 = 2 + 4\theta$, and $x_3 = 2 + \theta$, this is equivalent to

$$\begin{aligned}\underset{0 \leq \theta < \infty}{\text{maximize}}\, & 4(1 + 2\theta) - (1 + 2\theta)^2 + 9(2 + 4\theta) - (2 + 4\theta)^2 \\ & + 10(2 + \theta) - 2(2 + \theta)^2 - \tfrac{1}{2}(2 + 4\theta)(2 + \theta) \\ & = \underset{0 \leq \theta < \infty}{\text{maximize}}\,(27 + 21\theta - 24\theta^2)\end{aligned}$$

The maximum occurs when $(21 - 48\theta) = 0$, i.e., $\theta = 7/16$. By (20-18), with $\theta = 7/16$, we find that $\mathbf{x}^{(2)} = (1, 2, 2) + 7/16(2, 4, 1) = (30/16, 15/4, 39/16)$.

These steps are now repeated starting with the new solution $\mathbf{x}^{(2)}$. Theoretically we would terminate the algorithm when a solution $\mathbf{x}^{(k)}$ has been reached for which $\partial f/\partial x_j = 0$, for all j. In practice the algorithm is made to terminate when the difference between consecutive solutions $\mathbf{x}^{(k+1)}$ and $\mathbf{x}^{(k)}$ is arbitrarily small. This can be done either in absolute terms, e.g., as $|x_j^{(k+1)} - x_j^{(k)}| < \varepsilon$, for all j, or in relative terms, e.g., as $|x_j^{(k+1)} - x_j^{(k)}| < \beta|x_j^{(k+1)}|$, for all j. This procedure will find a solution that is arbitrarily close to the optimum, assuming that the technique does converge. If you are interested in learning more about convergence and the rate of convergence, we suggest you consult a text such as D. C. Luenberger, listed in the references.

Let us now express this method in the form of an algorithm.

METHOD OF STEEPEST ASCENT

Step 1 Select an initial solution $\mathbf{x}^{(1)} = (x_1^{(1)}, x_2^{(1)}, \ldots, x_n^{(1)})$. Set $k = 1$.

Step 2 Evaluate the gradient vector $\mathbf{g}^{(k)} = (\partial f/\partial x_1, \ldots, \partial f/\partial x_n)$ at point $\mathbf{x}^{(k)}$.

Step 3 Find the step size $\theta^{(k)}$ as the solution to $\underset{\theta \geq 0}{\text{maximize}}\, f(\mathbf{x}^{(k)} + \theta\mathbf{g}^{(k)})$.

Step 4 Find a new solution $\mathbf{x}^{(k+1)} = \mathbf{x}^{(k)} + \theta^{(k)}\mathbf{g}^{(k)}$. If $|x_j^{(k+1)} - x_j^{(k)}| < \varepsilon$, arbitrarily small, all j, set $\mathbf{x}^* = \mathbf{x}^{(k+1)}$ and $f(\mathbf{x}^*) = f(\mathbf{x}^{(k+1)})$ and *stop*. Otherwise, return to step 2 with $k \rightarrow k + 1$.

Using this algorithm, verify the results over the first few iterations for the above example, as shown in Table 20-3. We used $\varepsilon = 0.05$ to terminate the algorithm. $\mathbf{x}^{(5)} = (1.9967, 3.9849, 2.0003)$ is used as the "optimal" solution with a function value of $f(\mathbf{x}^{(5)}) = 31.9989$. The true optimum is (2, 4, 2) with a function value of 32.

Table 20-3. *The method of steepest ascent for problem (20-11)*

k	$\mathbf{x}^{(k)}$	$\mathbf{g}^{(k)}$	θ	$\mathbf{x}^{(k+1)}$	$f(\mathbf{x}^{(k+1)})$
1	1 2 2	2 4 1	0.4375	1.8750 3.7500 2.4375	31.5938
2	1.8750 3.7500 2.4375	0.2500 0.2813 −1.6250	0.2678	1.9420 3.8253 2.0023	31.9663
3	1.9420 3.8253 2.0023	0.1161 0.3482 0.0781	0.4386	1.9929 3.9781 2.0366	31.9972
4	1.9929 3.9781 2.0366	0.0143 0.0256 −0.1353	0.2681	1.9967 3.9849 2.0003	31.9989

20-7 NEWTON'S METHOD (MULTIVARIATE)

We saw in Section 20-3 that Newton's method for the univariate problem is a quadratic approximation to the function. At each successive point a new approximation is made, and the point $\hat{\mathbf{x}}$, at which the optimum of that approximation occurs, becomes the next solution in the algorithm. Precisely the same logic is true in the multivariate case. Figure 20-5 illustrates this procedure geometrically. The true function is represented by the continuous contour lines. At the initial solution $\mathbf{x}^{(1)}$, the quadratic approximation is shown by the dotted contours. The point $\hat{x}$ at which the optimum of the approximating function occurs becomes the next solution $\mathbf{x}^{(2)}$; this solution is used for a new quadratic approximating function which assumes its optimum at $\mathbf{x}^{(3)}$; and so on.

The convergence rate of Newton's method when $\mathbf{x}^{(k)}$ is still a considerable distance from the optimal solution may often be rather slow. It is possible to speed up convergence by introducing an additional computational step. Instead of using the quadratic approximating function to determine the next solution $\mathbf{x}^{(k+1)}$, we could use that solution only to define a direction vector, and then search the true function in that direction to determine the best step size by using a univariate search method. This is shown in Figure 20-5 by the extension of the direction vector to $\bar{\mathbf{x}}$. It is, though, not possible to state with confidence that the reduction in the number of iterations achieved will justify the extra computational effort. As a compromise, the search for the "best" step size could be limited to one or two iterations of the univariate search method. We shall not pursue this modification any further.

Figure 20-5. *Newton's method.*

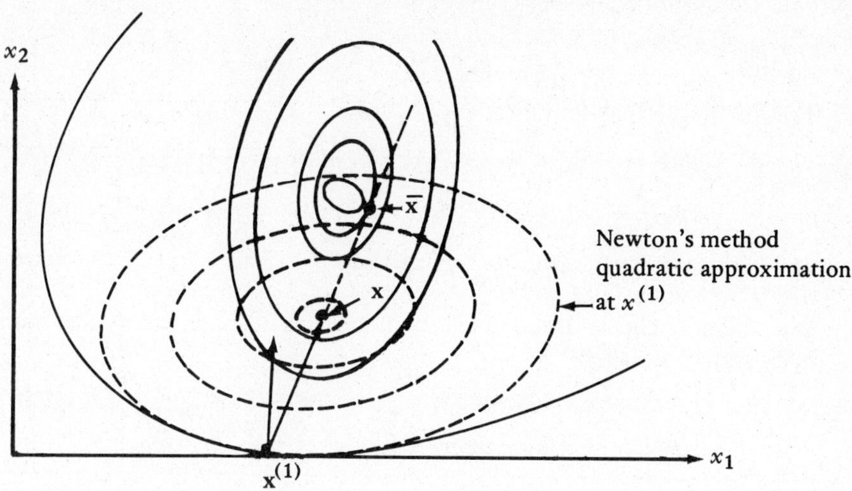

At iteration k, the initial terms of the multivariate version of Taylor's expansion of the solution $\mathbf{x}^{(k)}$ are used as the quadratic approximating function:

$$F(\mathbf{x}) = f(\mathbf{x}^{(k)}) + \sum_{j=1}^{n} (x_j - x_j^{(k)}) \frac{\partial f}{\partial x_j} + \tfrac{1}{2} \sum_{j=1}^{n} \sum_{i=1}^{n} (x_j - x_j^{(k)})(x_i - x_i^{(k)}) \frac{\partial^2 f}{\partial x_j \partial x_i} \tag{20-19}$$

where $\partial f/\partial x_j$ and $\partial f/\partial x_i \partial x_j$ are evaluated at $\mathbf{x}^{(k)}$. The optimum $\hat{\mathbf{x}}$ of equation (20-19) is obtained from the following conditions:

NEWTON'S METHOD EQUATIONS

$$\frac{\partial F}{\partial x_j} = \frac{\partial f}{\partial x_j} + \sum_{i=1}^{n} (\hat{x}_i - x_i^{(k)}) \frac{\partial^2 f}{\partial x_j \partial x_i} = 0, \qquad \text{for } j = 1, \ldots, n \tag{20-20}$$

If the function to be optimized is quadratic, then Newton's method is simply the solution of that function using the necessary conditions for an optimum of classical calculus, as discussed in Chapter 19. This is so because the approximation function (20-19) to a quadratic is the quadratic itself. If the function f is not quadratic, although nearly so, then Newton's method should also converge very quickly to an optimum. It turns out that most functions near an unconstrained optimum are approximately quadratic. Therefore, Newton's method converges very quickly as we get near the optimal value of $\mathbf{x}$.

We will now demonstrate the use of Newton's method on a nonquadratic function. Consider the problem of maximizing

$$f(\mathbf{x}) = -x_1^2 + 4x_1 - 2x_2^2 + 2x_2 - (x_1x_2)^{3/2} \tag{20-21}$$

The first and second derivatives are

$$\partial f/\partial x_1 = -2x_1 + 4 - \tfrac{3}{2}x_1^{1/2}x_2^{3/2} \qquad \partial f/\partial x_2 = -4x_2 + 2 - \tfrac{3}{2}x_1^{3/2}x_2^{1/2}$$

$$\partial^2 f/\partial x_1^2 = -2 - \tfrac{3}{4}(x_1^{-1/2}x_2^{3/2}) \qquad \partial^2 f/\partial x_2^2 = -4 - \tfrac{3}{4}(x_1^{3/2}x_2^{-1/2})$$

$$\partial^2 f/\partial x_1\partial x_2 = \partial^2 f/\partial x_2\partial x_1 = -\tfrac{9}{4}x_1^{1/2}x_2^{1/2}$$

We arbitrarily choose as the initial solution $\mathbf{x}^{(1)} = (2, 0.5)$. Verify that the approximating function (20-19) is

$$F(\mathbf{x}) = 3.75 + (x_1 - 2)(-0.75) + (x_2 - 0.5)(-3) + \tfrac{1}{2}[(x_1 - 2)^2(-2.1875) + 2(x_1 - 2)(x_2 - 0.5)(-2.25) + (x_2 - 0.5)^2(-7)]$$

or

$$F(\mathbf{x}) = -0.75 + 4.75x_1 + 5x_2 - 1.0938x_1^2 - 3.5x_2^2 - 2.25x_1x_2$$

By conditions (20-20), we get

$$\partial F/\partial x_1 = 4.75 - 2.1875x_1 - 2.25x_2 = 0$$
$$\partial F/\partial x_2 = 5 - 2.25x_1 - 7x_2 = 0$$

Their solution is $x_1 = 2.1463$, $x_2 = 0.0244$. Thus $\mathbf{x}^{(2)} = (2.1463, 0.0244)$. Three further iterations are given in Table 20-4. With a tolerance of $\varepsilon = 0.01$, the method terminates after 4 iterations at the solution $\mathbf{x} = (1.9505, 0.1307)$. The small values of the first derivatives confirm that this solution is nearly optimal, since the first derivatives are zero at optimality.

We can get further insight into Newton's method by rearranging expressions (20-20) as follows:

Table 20-4. *Newton's method for problem (20-21)*

Iteration k	$\mathbf{x}^{(k)}$	$f(\mathbf{x}^{(k)})$	$\partial f/\partial x_j$	$\partial^2 f/\partial x_j^2$	$\partial^2 f/\partial x_1\partial x_2$	$\mathbf{x}^{(k+1)}$
1	2 0.5	3.75	−0.75 −3	−2.1875 −7	−2.25	2.1463 0.0244
2	2.1463 0.0244	4.0142	−0.3011 1.2017	− 2.0020 −19.1009	−0.5148	1.9786 0.1985
3	1.9786 0.1985	4.0716	−0.1438 −0.6538	− 2.0471 − 8.6854	−1.4100	1.9579 0.1266
4	1.9579 0.1266	4.0960	−0.0103 0.0318	− 2.0241 − 9.7756	−1.1200	1.9505 0.1307

(20-22) $$-\sum_{i=1}^{n}(\hat{x}_i - x_i^{(k)})\frac{\partial^2 f}{\partial x_j \partial x_i} = \frac{\partial f}{\partial x_j}, \qquad \text{for } j = 1, \ldots, n$$

which are of the form

(20-23) $$\sum_{i=1}^{n} a_{ij}(\hat{x}_i - x_i^{(k)}) = \partial f/\partial x_j, \qquad \text{for } j = 1, \ldots, n$$

For Newton's method, $a_{ij} = -(\partial^2 f/\partial x_i \partial x_j)$. Equations (20-23) find a solution $\hat{\mathbf{x}}$ that by equation (20-13) implies a direction vector $\mathbf{d}^{k)} = (\hat{\mathbf{x}} - \mathbf{x}^{(k)})$ and $\theta = 1$. It is of particular importance that this direction vector is a linear transformation of the gradient vector—the right-hand side of equations (20-23) shows the $\partial f/\partial x_j$ values.

The direction vector in the steepest ascent method is also of this form. Using $\mathbf{x}^{(k+1)} = \mathbf{x}^{(k)} + \theta^{(k)}\mathbf{g}^{(k)}$, we can show that this is equivalent to (20-23) with $a_{ij} = 0$, $i \neq j$, and with $a_{jj} = 1/\theta^{(k)}$.

The effect of the system of equations (20-23) is to swivel the gradient vector around when $a_{ij} \neq 0$ and to change its length when $a_{jj} \neq 1$. The realization that Newton's method performs such a transformation has led to other methods that transform the gradient vector differently and overcome some of the weaknesses of Newton's method. Among these are the *conjugate direction methods,* which select the new direction vector by means of the concept of conjugate directions for a quadratic function. These methods can be applied to nonquadratic functions. (Versions of conjugate direction methods also exist that avoid the explicit evaluation of derivatives. See the text by R. C. Brent (1973), listed in the references.) The major strengths of conjugate direction methods are their small data needs and their computational efficiency.

A major weakness of Newton's method is that it requires all first and second derivatives at each iteration. The second derivatives, in particular, may not exist or else may be computationally expensive to determine. The quasi-Newton methods, discussed in the next section, attempt to remedy this problem. They also fall in the structure of equations (20-23).

20-8 QUASI-NEWTON METHODS

Perhaps the most sophisticated nonlinear unconstrained techniques are the *quasi:Newton* or *variable metric methods.* They sidestep the need to compute, at each iteration, the values of second order partial derivatives. This sidestepping is achieved by approximating their values on the basis of the first derivatives. These approximations are updated at each iteration. It is the updating procedure that distinguishes the various methods.

In most cases, the initial estimate of the second derivatives is arbitrary except for the requirement that it define a direction that improves the objective value of the solution. Often the first iteration is identical to the first iteration of the steepest ascent method. This implicitly assumes that $\partial^2 f/\partial x_j^2 = 1$ and $\partial^2 f/\partial x_j \partial x_i = 0$. The updating procedures then produce at each iteration increasingly more accurate estimates of the second derivatives. For a quadratic objective function in n variables, the true second derivatives are found after n iterations. Hence at the final step, the optimum is reached by a simple pure Newton method iteration. For nonquadratic functions, more than n iterations may be needed.

Another important feature of most quasi-Newton methods is that they ensure that for a maximizing problem the direction of search is always an ascent direction. This feature overcomes the method's inherent problems of converging to a turning point (other than a maximum) or failing to converge altogether.

The details of the quasi-Newton methods are well beyond the scope and mathematics of this text. For our purposes, it is sufficient to outline the general ideas underlying such methods.

Many of the most successful nonlinear programming methods have a quasi-Newton algorithm at their core. Unfortunately, for large problems the data requirement of quasi-Newton methods becomes a serious handicap. The smaller data needs of conjugate direction methods render them more attractive.

EXERCISES

20.1 Using the initial point $x^{(1)} = 0.5$ and a stopping criterion of $\varepsilon = 0.01$, find the optimal solution to each of the following functions by golden section search.
(a) Maximize $f(x) = -5x^2 + 6x + 5$ in the interval $0 \leq x \leq 1$.
(b) Maximize $f(x) = -2x^4 + 2x + 1$ in the interval $0 \leq x \leq 2$.
(c) Maximize $f(x) = 4x^3 - 7x^2 + 14x + 6$ in the interval $0 \leq x \leq 1$.
(d) Minimize $f(x) = 2x^2 - x^{3/2} + 1$ in the interval $0 \leq x \leq 1$.
(e) Maximize $f(x) = 4x^3 - 7x^2 - 4x + 6$ in the interval $0 \leq x \leq 2$.
(f) Minimize $f(x) = e^x - x$ in the interval $0 \leq x \leq 1$.

20.2 Solve the problems in exercise 20.1 using Newton's method. Ignore the interval restrictions.

20.3 Perform two iterations of the method of steepest ascent for each of the following problems. Illustrate the progress of the method.
(a) Maximize $f(\mathbf{x}) = 7x_1 - 2x_1^2 + x_1x_2 - x_2^2 + x_1\, x_2$. Commence at $\mathbf{x}^{(1)} = (1, 0)$. The optimum is (2, 1).
(b) Maximize $f(\mathbf{x}) = -x_1^3 + 9x_1^2 - 5x_2^2 + 20x_2$. Commence at $\mathbf{x}^{(1)} = (1, 1)$.
(c) Repeat (b) commencing at $\mathbf{x}^{(1)} = (-1, 1)$.
(d) Maximize $f(\mathbf{x}) = -x_1^4 + 8x_1^3 - 10x_1^2 - x_2^2 + 2x_2$. Commence at $\mathbf{x}^{(1)} = (0, 0)$. The local optima are at (0, 1) and (5, 1). The global optimum is (5, 1).

20.4 Find the first two iterations of the method of steepest ascent for the following functions, starting at (0, 0) in each case.
(a) Maximize $f(\mathbf{x}) = 16x_1 + 20x_2 - 4x_1x_2 - x_1^2 - x_2^2$.
(b) Maximize $f(\mathbf{x}) = -2x_1^2 - (3 - x_2)^2$.
(c) Maximize $f(\mathbf{x}) = 6x_1 + 8x_2 - x_1^2 - x_2^2$.
(d) Maximize $f(\mathbf{x}) = -(1 - 2x_1)^2 - (2 - 3x_2)^2 - x_1x_2$.

20.5 Use Newton's method to solve the problems of exercise 20.3 with the same starting points.

20.6 Solve exercise 20.3 using the modification to Newton's method in which a line search is performed at each iteration. Thus $\mathbf{x}^{(k+1)} = \mathbf{x}^{(k)} + \theta^{(k)}(\hat{\mathbf{x}} - \mathbf{x}^{(k)})$, where $\hat{\mathbf{x}}$ is the optimum of the quadratic approximation at the kth iteration.

REFERENCES

Box, M. J., D. Davies, and W. H. Swann. *Nonlinear Optimization Techniques*. Imperial Chemical Industries. Monograph No. 5, 1969. An excellent, easy-to-read exposition of nonlinear optimization. Chapters 2 and 3 on univariate search are suitable for all readers of this text. Chapter 4 on multivariate methods uses matrix algebra but is very clear for readers with a background in matrices.

Brent, R. P. *Algorithms for Minimization without Derivatives*. Englewood Cliffs, N.J.: Prentice-Hall, 1973. A research book that includes in Chapter 7 conjugate direction methods that do not require the gradient vector. The book also includes a computer program for Brent's own algorithm for solving multivariate functions using conjugate directions. This algorithm has within it a routine for univariate search using quadratic interpolation.

Fletcher, R. *Practical Methods of Optimization, Vol. 1, Unconstrained Optimization*. New York: Wiley, 1980. For unconstrained optimization this is probably the most complete treatment available. Recommended for advanced study and competent mathematicians only.

Luenberger, D. G. *Linear and Nonlinear Programming*. Reading, Mass.: Addison-Wesley, 1973. Detailed discussion of convergence properties. One of the best advanced texts available, although now a little dated.

CHAPTER TWENTY-ONE

Constrained Nonlinear Programming

We now come to constrained nonlinear programming. The decision variables $\mathbf{x} = (x_1, x_2, \ldots, x_n)$ have to satisfy m constraints of the form $g_i(\mathbf{x}) \leq b_i$. The general form of a nonlinear programming problem can be written as: Find values $\mathbf{x} = (x_1, x_2, \ldots, x_n)$ so as to

$$\begin{aligned} &\text{maximize} \quad f(\mathbf{x}) = f(x_1, x_2, \ldots, x_n) \\ &\text{subject to} \quad g_i(\mathbf{x}) \leq b_i, \qquad i = 1, \ldots, m \\ &\qquad\qquad\quad \mathbf{x} \geq 0 \end{aligned} \tag{21-1}$$

As for unconstrained nonlinear programming, there is yet no single technique that has proved itself generally superior for most nonlinear constrained optimization problems. In this chapter, we will study simple versions of some currently used techniques, each suitable for solving a specific form of problem (21-1). We will again skip over the refinements that render these techniques computationally efficient.

We start out by generalizing the Lagrangian conditions of Chapter 19 to form the famous *Kuhn-Tucker conditions*. We use these in Section 21-4 to develop a technique for the *quadratic programming problem*. That problem assumes that $f(\mathbf{x})$ is a quadratic and concave function, that the constraints $g_i(\mathbf{x})$ are linear, and that the variables are restricted to being nonnegative. In Sections 21-5 and 21-6, we develop the *reduced gradient method*, which handles both linear and nonlinear constraints. For problems with linear constraints, it is currently one of the most powerful techniques available. In Sections 21-7 and 21-8, we adopt a quite different solution strategy. Rather than solve the original problem, we deal with an equivalent unconstrained problem. Terms are added to the objective function that penalize any solution that is not feasible—hence their name *penalty methods*. It is this idea of penalty functions that has led to some of the modern nonlinear programming techniques, such as the *augmented Lagrangian method* touched upon in Section 21-9.

21-1 AN EXAMPLE OF A NONLINEAR PROGRAMMING PROBLEM

Let us impose some restrictions on the unconstrained problem of Section 20-4. Production is limited by available machine time and manpower. Each month 1000 machine-hours and 2000 man-hours are available. Product 1 uses 0.4 machine-hour and 0.2 man-hour per unit, product 2 uses 0.2 machine-hour and 0.4 man-hour per unit, and product 3 uses 0.1 hour of each per unit.

The new problem is to maximize the profits, as given by expression (20-11), subject to the constraints on monthly machine time and man-hours:

$$\begin{aligned}
&\text{maximize} && f(x_1, x_2, x_3) = 4x_1 - x_1^2 + 9x_2 - x_2^2 + 10x_3 - 2x_3^2 - \tfrac{1}{2}x_2x_3 \\
&\text{subject to} && 4x_1 + 2x_2 + x_3 \leqslant 10 \text{ (machine time)} \\
& && 2x_1 + 4x_2 + x_3 \leqslant 20 \text{ (man-hours)} \\
& && x_1 \geqslant 0,\ x_2 \geqslant 0,\ x_3 \geqslant 0 \text{ (nonnegativity conditions)}
\end{aligned} \tag{21-2}$$

We shall use this problem to illustrate the techniques discussed in the following sections.

21-2 THE KUHN-TUCKER CONDITIONS

The Lagrangian conditions in Section 19-7 are necessary conditions for an optimum of a function, subject to equality constraints and the variables unrestricted in sign. Generalized to inequality constraints and nonnegative variables, they are known as the *Kuhn-Tucker conditions*, after their founders H. W. Kuhn and A. W. Tucker ("Nonlinear Programming," *Proceedings Second Berkeley Symposium on Mathematical Statistics and Probability*, University of California Press, Berkeley, Cal., 1951).

Consider again the general nonlinear programming problem (21-1). So that the $\mathbf{x} \geqslant 0$ constraints are seen as just another set of constraints, we will rewrite $x_j \geqslant 0$ as

$$g_{m+j}(\mathbf{x}) = -x_j \leqslant 0 = b_{m+j}, \qquad j = 1, \ldots, n \tag{21-3}$$

Problem (21-1) then becomes

$$\begin{aligned}
&\text{maximize} && f(\mathbf{x}) \\
&\text{subject to} && g_i(\mathbf{x}) \leqslant b_i, \qquad i = 1, \ldots, m + n
\end{aligned} \tag{21-4}$$

Expanding the ideas of Section 19-7, we can write the Lagrangian function for problem (21-4) as

$$L(\mathbf{x}, \lambda) = f(\mathbf{x}) + \sum_{i=1}^{m+n} \lambda_i [b_i - g_i(\mathbf{x})] \tag{21-5}$$

where there is an $\lambda_i[b_i - g_i(\mathbf{x})]$ term for each constraint. For example, problem (21-2) written in the form of (21-4) is

$$\begin{aligned} \text{maximize} \quad & f(\mathbf{x}) = 4x_1 - x_1^2 + 9x_2 - x_2^2 + 10x_3 - 2x_3^2 - \tfrac{1}{2}x_2x_3 \\ \text{subject to} \quad & g_1(\mathbf{x}) = 4x_1 + 2x_2 + x_3 \leq 10 = b_1 \\ & g_2(\mathbf{x}) = 2x_1 + 4x_2 + x_3 \leq 20 = b_2 \\ & g_3(\mathbf{x}) = -x_1 \leq 0 = b_3 \\ & g_4(\mathbf{x}) = -x_2 \leq 0 = b_4 \\ & g_5(\mathbf{x}) = -x_3 \leq 0 = b_5 \end{aligned} \tag{21-6}$$

The Lagrangian function for problem (21-6) is

$$\begin{aligned} L(\mathbf{x}, \lambda) = {} & 4x_1 - x_1^2 + 9x_2 - x_2^2 + 10x_3 - 2x_3^2 - \tfrac{1}{2}x_2x_3 \\ & + \lambda_1(10 - 4x_1 - 2x_2 - x_3) + \lambda_2(20 - 2x_1 - 4x_2 - x_3) \\ & + \lambda_3(x_1) + \lambda_4(x_2) + \lambda_5(x_3) \end{aligned} \tag{21-7}$$

So far we have not considered the effect of the inequalities on the constraints. To do this, let us initially ignore all but the first constraint of problem (21-6). Now the Lagrangian function is

$$L(\mathbf{x}, \lambda_1) = 4x_1 - x_1^2 + 9x_2 - x_2^2 + 10x_3 - 2x_3^2 - \tfrac{1}{2}x_2x_3 + \lambda_1(10 - 4x_1 - 2x_2 - x_3)$$

If the constraint is slack at a maximum, the necessary conditions for a stationary point are those of the unconstrained case; namely,

$$\begin{aligned} & \partial f/\partial x_1 = 4 - 2x_1 = 0 \qquad \partial f/\partial x_2 = 9 - 2x_2 - \tfrac{1}{2}x_3 = 0 \\ & \partial f/\partial x_3 = 10 - 4x_3 - \tfrac{1}{2}x_2 = 0 \qquad g_1(\mathbf{x}) = 4x_1 + 2x_2 + x_3 < 10 \end{aligned} \tag{21-8}$$

If the constraint is binding at the maximum, the necessary conditions are those for the Lagrangian problem with an equality constraint:

$$\begin{aligned} & \partial L/\partial x_1 = 4 - 2x_1 - 4\lambda_1 = 0 \qquad \partial L/\partial x_2 = 9 - 2x_2 - \tfrac{1}{2}x_3 - 2\lambda_1 = 0 \\ & \partial L/\partial x_3 = 10 - \tfrac{1}{2}x_2 - 4x_3 - \lambda_1 = 0 \qquad \partial L/\partial \lambda_1 = 10 - 4x_1 - 2x_2 - x_3 = 0 \end{aligned} \tag{21-9}$$

Since a priori we do not know which case applies, we need necessary conditions that cover both cases. In Section 19-7, we defined λ as the marginal change of f with respect to b. For a maximization problem subject to an inequality constraint of the form $g_1(\mathbf{x}) \leq b_1$, a marginal increase in b_1 enlarges the feasible region. If the constraint is binding, the maximal value of f increases or, at worst, is unchanged, and if the constraint is slack, f remains unchanged. In the first instance, $g_1(\mathbf{x}) = b_1$ and $\lambda_1 \geq 0$; in the second instance, $g_1(\mathbf{x}) < b_1$ and $\lambda_1 = 0$. These conditions can be combined to $\lambda_1[b_1 - g_1(\mathbf{x})] = 0$ and $\lambda_1 \geq 0$, or

(21-10) $$\lambda_1(10 - 4x_1 - 2x_2 - x_3) = 0, \qquad \lambda_1 \geq 0$$

At the maximum, L must have a stationary point with respect to $\mathbf{x}$, i.e., $\partial L/\partial x_j = 0$, as we have in the first three equations of (21-9). Furthermore, the stationary point must be feasible, i.e., $b_1 - g_1(\mathbf{x}) \geq 0$, or

(21-11) $$10 - 4x_1 - 2x_2 - x_3 \geq 0$$

The five expressions—the first three of (21-9), plus (21-10), and (21-11)—combine to give us the Kuhn-Tucker conditions:

(21-12)
$$\begin{aligned}
\partial L/\partial x_1 &= \partial f/\partial x_1 - \lambda_1(\partial g_1/\partial x_1) = 4 - 2x_1 - 4\lambda_1 = 0 \\
\partial L/\partial x_2 &= \partial f/\partial x_2 - \lambda_1(\partial g_1/\partial x_2) = 9 - 2x_2 - \tfrac{1}{2}x_3 - 2\lambda_1 = 0 \\
\partial L/\partial x_3 &= \partial f/\partial x_3 - \lambda_1(\partial g_1/\partial x_3) = 10 - \tfrac{1}{2}x_2 - 4x_3 - \lambda_1 = 0 \\
\partial L/\partial \lambda_1 &= b_1 - g_1(\mathbf{x}) = 10 - 4x_1 - 2x_2 - x_3 \geq 0 \\
\lambda_1(\partial L/\partial \lambda_1) &= \lambda_1[b_1 - g_1(\mathbf{x})] = \lambda_1(10 - 4x_1 - 2x_2 - x_3) = 0, \qquad \lambda_1 \geq 0
\end{aligned}$$

Using exactly the same principles, we can expand (21-12) to deal with the whole of problem (21-6). From the Lagrangian function (21-7), the Kuhn Tucker conditions are

(21-13)
$$\begin{aligned}
\partial L/\partial x_1 &= 4 - 2x_1 - 4\lambda_1 - 2\lambda_2 + \lambda_3 = 0 \\
\partial L/\partial x_2 &= 9 - 2x_2 - \tfrac{1}{2}x_3 - 2\lambda_1 - 4\lambda_2 + \lambda_4 = 0 \\
\partial L/\partial x_3 &= 10 - \tfrac{1}{2}x_2 - 4x_3 - \lambda_1 - \lambda_2 + \lambda_5 = 0 \\
\partial L/\partial \lambda_1 &= 10 - 4x_1 - 2x_2 - x_3 \geq 0 \\
\partial L/\partial \lambda_2 &= 20 - 2x_1 - 4x_2 - x_3 \geq 0 \\
\partial L/\partial \lambda_3 &= x_1 > 0 \qquad \partial L/\partial \lambda_4 = x_2 \geq 0 \\
\partial L/\partial \lambda_5 &= x_3 \geq 0 \\
\lambda_1(\partial L/\partial \lambda_1) &= \lambda_1(10 - 4x_1 - 2x_2 - x_3) = 0 \\
\lambda_2(\partial L/\partial \lambda_2) &= \lambda_2(20 - 2x_1 - 4x_2 - x_3) = 0 \\
\lambda_3(\partial L/\partial \lambda_3) &= \lambda_3 x_1 = 0 \qquad \lambda_4(\partial L/\partial \lambda_4) = \lambda_4 x_2 = 0 \\
\lambda_5(\partial L/\partial \lambda_5) &= \lambda_5 x_3 = 0 \qquad \lambda_1, \ldots, \lambda_5 \geq 0
\end{aligned}$$

We can modify (21-13) to eliminate the need to write the nonnegativity conditions explicitly as constraints. For example, from the first equation of (21-13), $-\lambda_3 = 4 - 2x_1 - 4\lambda_1 - 2\lambda_2$. Hence $\lambda_3 \geq 0$, $\lambda_3 x_1 = 0$, together with the first equation of (21-13) can be replaced by the two conditions

$$(21\text{-}14)\qquad \begin{aligned} \partial \mathrm{L}/\partial x_1 &= 4 - 2x_1 - 4\lambda_1 - 2\lambda_2 \leq 0 \\ x_1(\partial \mathrm{L}/\partial x_1) &= x_1(4 - 2x_1 - 4\lambda_1 - 2\lambda_2) = 0 \end{aligned}$$

where $\hat{L}$ is the Lagrangian function (21-7) without the last three terms.

Thus we have the following Kuhn-Tucker conditions.

KUHN-TUCKER NECESSARY CONDITIONS FOR OPTIMUM TO CONSTRAINED MAXIMIZATION PROBLEM

For the constrained maximization problem (21-1) and the Lagrangian function

$$L(\mathbf{x},\lambda) = f(\mathbf{x}) + \sum_{i=1}^{m} \lambda_i[b_i - g_i(\mathbf{x})]$$

the necessary conditions for an optimum are

$$(21\text{-}15)\qquad \left.\begin{aligned} \partial \mathrm{L}/\partial x_j = \partial f/\partial x_j - \sum_{i=1}^{m} \lambda_i(\partial g_i/\partial x_j) \leq 0 \\ x_j(\partial \mathrm{L}/\partial x_j) = 0 \qquad\qquad x_j \geq 0 \end{aligned}\right\} j = 1, \ldots, n$$

$$\left.\begin{aligned} \partial \mathrm{L}/\partial \lambda_i = [b_i - g_i(\mathbf{x})] \geq 0 \\ \lambda_i(\partial \mathrm{L}/\partial \lambda_i) = 0 \qquad \lambda_i \geq 0 \end{aligned}\right\} i = 1, \ldots, m$$

(There is a further condition known as the *constraint qualifications* which must be satisfied before the Kuhn-Tucker conditions hold. For a discussion of this see W. I. Zangwell, *Non-linear Programming*, Prentice-Hall, Englewood Cliffs, N.J., 1969, pages 39–40.)

The astute reader may have noticed not only the similarity between the definition of λ and the dual variables of linear programming in Chapter 4, but also the similarity between the second and fifth set of equations in (21-15) and complementary slackness in Chapter 4.

In the derivation of the Kuhn-Tucker conditions above, we dealt with a standard maximization problem subject to a ($\leq$) constraint. For the standard minimization problem subject to a ($\geq$) constraint, the direction of the inequalities of the first and fourth conditions in (21-15) is reversed. If we deviate from either of these two standard forms, there will be other changes. For example, for a maximization problem subject to a ($\geq$) constraint, in addition to the reversal of the direction of the fourth condition in (21-15), the sign of the corresponding Lagrangian multiplier is also reversed. What are the changes to (21-15) when the constraint is an equality?

The Kuhn-Tucker conditions for problem (21-2) can be written as a set of linear equations with simple nonlinear restrictions on the variables. We leave it to you to verify that (21-16) are the Kuhn-Tucker conditions. (x_4 and x_5 are the slack variables of the g_1 and g_2 constraints, respectively, and the v_j are the slack variables of the $\partial \mathrm{L}/\partial x_j$ constraints.)

$$
\begin{array}{llllr}
 & 2x_1 & + 4\lambda_1 + 2\lambda_2 - v_1 & & = 4 \\
 & 2x_2 + (\tfrac{1}{2})x_3 & + 2\lambda_1 + 4\lambda_2 & - v_2 & = 9 \\
 & (\tfrac{1}{2})x_2 + 4x_3 & + \lambda_1 + \lambda_2 & - v_3 & = 10 \\
(21\text{-}16) & 4x_1 + 2x_2 + x_3 + x_4 & & & = 10 \\
 & 2x_1 + 4x_2 + x_3 + x_5 & & & = 20 \\
 & \multicolumn{4}{l}{x_j \geqslant 0, \quad \text{all } j; \quad v_j \geqslant 0, \quad j = 1,2,3; \quad \lambda_i \geqslant 0, \quad i = 1,2} \\
 & \multicolumn{4}{l}{x_1 v_1 = 0 \quad x_2 v_2 = 0 \quad x_3 v_3 = 0 \quad \lambda_1 x_4 = 0 \quad \lambda_2 x_5 = 0}
\end{array}
$$

21-3 SUFFICIENT CONDITIONS FOR MAXIMUM TO CONSTRAINED PROBLEM

The Kuhn-Tucker conditions are necessary conditions for an optimum. To guarantee that these conditions give the global optimum, we need to develop some sufficient conditions that ensure that the problem has a unique point at which the Kuhn-Tucker conditions hold, and that this point is a maximum.

First, we need an objective function that has a single stationary point that is a maximum. From Figure 19-2(b) we see that this will occur if the function is concave. So, the first part of our sufficient conditions is to require that f be a concave function.

This is not enough. We must also place conditions on the feasible region. For instance, Figure 21-1(a) illustrates the case where a concave objective function does not yield a unique optimum. Point $\mathbf{x}^{(A)}$ is the global maximum and $\mathbf{x}^{(B)}$ is a local maximum. The local maximum exists because not all the points on the line segment between $\mathbf{x}^{(A)}$ and $\mathbf{x}^{(B)}$ are feasible solutions. We can establish fairly easily from the definition of a concave function that if all the points on this line segment are feasible, then $\mathbf{x}^{(B)}$ cannot be a local optimum. If we let $\hat{\mathbf{x}}$ be any point on the line segment between $\mathbf{x}^{(A)}$ and $\mathbf{x}^{(B)}$, then, by definition, $\hat{\mathbf{x}} = (1 - \lambda)\mathbf{x}^{(A)} + \lambda\mathbf{x}^{(B)}$, $0 \leqslant \lambda \leqslant 1$. Also, from expression (19-31), we can show that if the objective function is concave,

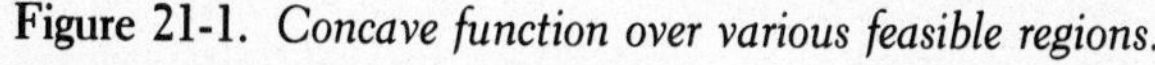
Figure 21-1. *Concave function over various feasible regions.*

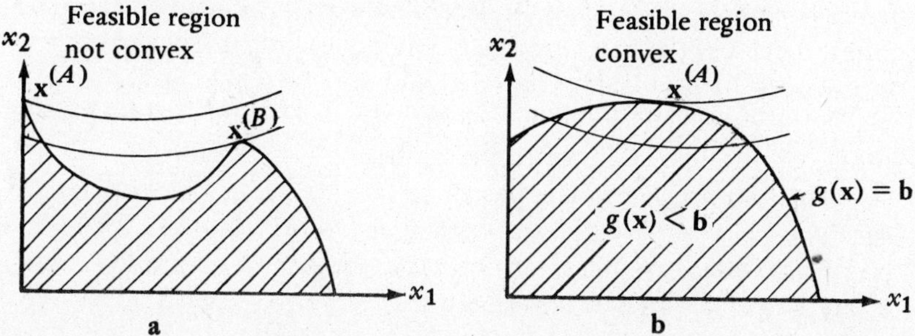

$f(\hat{\mathbf{x}}) \geq (1 - \lambda)f(\mathbf{x}^{(A)}) + \lambda f(\mathbf{x}^{(B)})$. But we know that $f(\mathbf{x}^{(A)}) \geq f(\mathbf{x}^{(B)})$, because $\mathbf{x}^{(A)}$ is the global maximum. So,

$$(1 - \lambda)f(\mathbf{x}^{(A)}) + \lambda f(\mathbf{x}^{(B)}) \geq f(\mathbf{x}^{B})$$

hence, $f(\hat{\mathbf{x}}) \geq f(\mathbf{x}^{(B)})$. The importance of this result is that if, for all λ, $\hat{\mathbf{x}}$ is a feasible solution to the constraints, there is no neighborhood around $\mathbf{x}^{(B)}$ where $f(\mathbf{x}) \leq f(\mathbf{x}^{(B)})$ for all feasible $\mathbf{x}$, i.e., $\mathbf{x}^{(B)}$ is not a local maximum. So if we extend the feasible region to include the line segment between $\mathbf{x}^{(A)}$ and $\mathbf{x}^{(B)}$, the local optimum disappears. To ensure that the constraint set does not create local optima, we require that any point on the line segment between any pair of feasible points also be feasible. This is the case in Figure 21-1(b). A set with this property is called a *convex set* (not to be confused with a convex function).

CONVEX SET

A set is a convex set if, for any two members of the set $\mathbf{x}^{(1)}$ and $\mathbf{x}^{(2)}$, any point on the line segment between them (i.e., $\mathbf{x} = (1 - \lambda)\mathbf{x}^{(1)} + \lambda\mathbf{x}^{(2)}$, for any λ, $0 \leq \lambda \leq 1$) is also a member of the set.

What can we say about the constraint functions that will ensure that the feasible region is a convex set? Figure 21-1(b) shows that if the constraint function g is a convex function, then $g(\mathbf{x}) \leq b$ describes a convex set. Similarly, if g is a concave function, then $g(\mathbf{x}) \geq b$ describes a convex set. If $g(\mathbf{x}) = b$, the feasible region is a convex set if and only if g is a linear function. Verify this for yourself. Where there is more than one constraint, the feasible region is a convex set if each constraint describes a convex set. (The intersection of convex sets is a convex set.) So the feasible region of $g(\mathbf{x}) \leq b$ and $\mathbf{x} \geq 0$ is a convex set if g is a convex function. (Since a linear function is both a concave function and a convex function, the nonnegativity conditions on the variables yield convex sets.)

We can now state sufficient conditions for the Kuhn-Tucker conditions to give a global optimum.

SUFFICIENT CONDITIONS FOR GLOBAL OPTIMUM TO CONSTRAINED MAXIMIZATION PROBLEM

The Kuhn-Tucker conditions to the constrained maximization problem:

$$\begin{aligned} &\text{maximize} && f(\mathbf{x}) \\ &\text{subject to} && g_i(\mathbf{x}) \leq b_i, \quad \mathbf{x} \geq 0 \end{aligned}$$

are also sufficient conditions for a global optimum if f is a concave function and the g_i's are convex functions.

It is reasonably straightforward to develop sufficiency conditions for a general constrained maximization problem.

A weak form of these conditions states that if the function is concave in the region of a solution that satisfies the Kuhn-Tucker conditions, then the point is a local maximum. For practical purposes, concavity of a function is usually expressed in terms of the second partial derivatives.

21-4 QUADRATIC PROGRAMMING

Quadratic programming looks at the problem of solving a quadratic objective function subject to linear constraints. Depending on the technique used, restrictions on the nature of the quadratic function are sometimes imposed. We will consider an algorithm suggested by P. Wolfe. This algorithm is restricted to the case of maximizing a concave function.

Equations (21-16) are the Kuhn-Tucker conditions for problem (21-2), which is a quadratic programming problem. These conditions form a set of linear equations, except for a nonlinear restriction on the variables. Since the quadratic function is concave, the Kuhn-Tucker conditions are both necessary and sufficient. So the solution to equations (21-16) will be optimal.

In solving (21-16) all we seek is a feasible solution. It is a system of linear simultaneous equations without an objective function; so we can use the simplex method purely to find this feasible solution. Since a feasible solution cannot generally be found by inspection, we introduce artificial variables and use the two-phase method. We can tell there is a feasible solution to (21-16) provided there is a feasible solution to the constraints of the original quadratic program. It is convenient to first seek a feasible solution to the original constraints (given by the fourth and fifth equations of (21-16)), and then, starting with that solution, use the two-phase method on the whole system (21-16). Thus, if there is no feasible solution to the constraint set, there is no need to solve the Kuhn-Tucker equations.

A natural initial basis to choose for the original constraints is (x_4, x_5), so $x_4 = 10$ and $x_5 = 20$. We now add artificial variables (u_1, u_2, u_3) to the first three equations of (21-16). The resulting linear program to be solved is shown in Table 21-1. The initial basic solution for the full problem is

$$u_1 = 4 \qquad u_2 = 9 \qquad u_3 = 10 \qquad x_4 = 10 \qquad x_5 = 20$$

At this basic solution, we have the initial tableau shown in Table 21-2.

Table 21-1. *Linear program for solving quadratic program*

$$\begin{array}{llllllll}
\text{maximize } \omega = & & & & & -u_1 - u_2 - u_3 & & \\
\text{subject to} & & & & & & & \\
2x_1 & + 4\lambda_1 + 2\lambda_2 - v_1 & & & & + u_1 & & = 4 \\
\quad 2x_2 + \tfrac{1}{2}x_3 & + 2\lambda_1 + 4\lambda_2 & - v_2 & & & & + u_2 & = 9 \\
\quad + \tfrac{1}{2}x_2 + 4x_3 & + \lambda_1 + \lambda_2 & & - v_3 & & & + u_3 & = 10 \\
4x_1 + 2x_2 + x_3 + x_4 & & & & & & & = 10 \\
2x_1 + 4x_2 + x_3 & + x_5 & & & & & & = 20 \\
x_j \geqslant 0, \; j = 1, \ldots, 5; & v_j, u_j \geqslant 0, \; j = 1, 2, 3; & & \lambda_i \geqslant 0, \; i = 1, 2 & & & & \\
\text{with restrictions } x_j v_j = 0, & j = 1, 2, 3; & x_4\lambda_1 = 0; & x_5\lambda_2 = 0 & & & &
\end{array}$$

Table 21-2. *Simplex tableaux for quadratic program*

Initial tableau

c_j	Basis	Solution	x_1	x_2	x_3	x_4	x_5	λ_1	λ_2	v_1	v_2	v_3	u_1	u_2	u_3
	c_j		0	0	0	0	0	0	0	0	0	0	−1	−1	−1
−1	u_1	4	2	0	0	0	0	4	2	−1	0	0	1	0	0
−1	u_2	9	0	2	0.5	0	0	2	4	0	−1	0	0	1	0
−1	u_3	10	0	0.5	4	0	0	1	1	0	0	−1	0	0	1
0	x_4	10	4	2	1	1	0	0	0	0	0	0	0	0	0
0	x_5	20	2	4	1	0	1	0	0	0	0	0	0	0	0
	$z_j - c_j$	−23	−2	−2.5	−4.5	0	0	−7	−7	1	1	1	0	0	0

Tableau 2

c_j	Basis	Solution	x_1	x_2	x_3	x_4	x_5	λ_1	λ_2	v_1	v_2	v_3	u_1	u_2	u_3
−1	u_1	4	2	0	0	0	0	4	2	−1	0	0	1	0	0
−1	u_2	7.75	0	1.9375	0	0	0	1.875	3.875	0	−1	0.125	0	1	−0.125
0	x_3	2.5	0	0.125	1	0	0	0.25	0.25	0	0	−0.25	0	0	0.25
0	x_4	7.5	4	1.875	0	1	0	−0.25	−0.25	0	0	0.25	0	0	−0.25
0	x_5	17.5	2	3.875	0	0	1	−0.25	−0.25	0	0	0.25	0	0	−0.25
	$z_j - c_j$	−11.75	−2	−1.9375	0	0	0	−5.875	−5.875	1	1	−0.125	0	0	1.125

Tableau 5: Optimal Tableau (tableaux 3 and 4 not shown)

c_j	Basis	Solution	x_1	x_2	x_3	x_4	x_5	λ_1	λ_2	v_1	v_2	v_3	u_1	u_2	u_3
0	λ_1	0.79487	0	0	0	−0.0993	0	1	0.795	−0.1987	−0.0962	−0.0128	0.1987	0.0962	0.0128
0	x_2	3.23077	0	1	0	0.0962	0	0	1.2308	0.1923	−0.4231	0.0769	−0.1923	0.4231	−0.0769
0	x_3	1.89744	0	0	1	0.0128	0	0	−0.1026	0.0256	0.0769	−0.2564	−0.0256	−0.0769	0.2564
0	x_1	0.41026	1	0	0	0.1987	0	0	−0.5897	−0.1026	0.1923	0.0256	0.1026	−0.1923	−0.0256
0	x_5	4.35897	0	0	0	−0.795	1	0	−3.6411	−0.5897	1.2308	−0.1026	0.5897	−1.2308	0.1026
	$z_j - c_j$	0	0	0	0	0	0	0	0	0	0	0	1	1	1

Applying the simplex method criterion for the variable to enter the basis gives either λ_1 or λ_2. However, to enter either of these into the basis would violate the restrictions, $x_4\lambda_1 = 0$ and $x_5\lambda_2 = 0$. So neither of them is permitted to enter. The next best vector is x_3 which is allowed to enter the basis. Vector u_3 leaves the basis. The second tableau of Table 21-2 gives the solution after the first iteration. The optimal solution is reached after four iterations. It is shown in tableau 5 as

$$x_1 = 0.4103 \qquad x_2 = 3.2308 \qquad x_3 = 1.8974 \qquad x_5 = 4.3590 \qquad \lambda_1 = 0.795$$

$$x_4 = \lambda_2 = v_1 = v_2 = v_3 = u_1 = u_2 = u_3 = 0 \qquad \omega = 0$$

The optimal value of the original objective function to (21-2) is $z = 28.82054$. The values of λ_1 and λ_2 are, of course, the imputed values of constraints 1 and 2, respectively.

Wolfe's algorithm is suitable for solving any quadratic program with a concave objective function and a linear constraint set. (However, to guarantee the convergence of the algorithm to a finite maximum, the objective function must be *strictly concave.* See the text by D. G. Luenberger listed in the references, pp. 114–115.)

This general quadratic program can be written

$$\text{maximize} \quad z = \sum_{j=1}^{n}\left(c_j x_j + \sum_{k=1}^{n} d_{kj} x_k x_j\right)$$

$$\text{subject to} \quad \sum_{j=1}^{n} a_{ij} x_j = b_i, \qquad i = 1, \ldots, m$$

$$x_j \geqslant 0, \qquad j = 1, \ldots, n$$

We can apply the Kuhn-Tucker conditions in the same manner as we did for problem (21-2): There exist $\lambda_1, \ldots, \lambda_m$ unrestricted in sign, such that

$$c_j + 2\sum_{k=1}^{n} d_{kj} x_k - \sum_{i=1}^{m} a_{ij}\lambda_i = -v_j \leqslant 0, \qquad j = 1, \ldots, n$$

$$(21\text{-}17) \qquad b_i - \sum_{j=1}^{n} a_{ij} x_j = 0, \qquad i = 1, \ldots, m$$

$$x_j \geqslant 0 \qquad x_j v_j = 0, \qquad j = 1, \ldots, n$$

There are several other quadratic programming algorithms. The references at the end of this chapter give sources for some of the better known ones. Among those, *Beale's algorithm* is particularly important because of its computational strength. In addition, Beale's algorithm can be applied to a nonconcave objective function. When this is the case, we cannot be sure that the solution obtained is the global optimum; it could be a local optimum or even a saddle point.

There are two areas of application for quadratic programming that are of some interest. Quadratic programming is used in multiple regression where there are inequality constraints on some of the coefficients. This is particularly useful in econometric models where simultaneous equation systems are being estimated. The objective function of the quadratic program is the minimization of the squared deviations from the mean used in least squares estimates. The quadratic programming constraints are any linear constraints that exist on the coefficients. Thus, the quadratic programming optimum is the set of constrained least squares estimates of the coefficients.

A second area of application is in goal programming (see Section 2-14 for a simple example). In goal programming, the objective may be to minimize the weighted sum of deviations from target levels for one or several partially or completely conflicting objectives. Rather than penalize deviations linearly, one approach suggested in the literature is to have the penalty proportional to the square of the deviations. This leads to a quadratic programming problem.

21-5 THE REDUCED GRADIENT METHOD

The reduced gradient method is another technique designed by P. Wolfe, this time to solve the problem

$$\text{maximize} \quad z = f(x_1, \ldots, x_n)$$

$$\text{(21-18)} \qquad \text{subject to} \quad \sum_{j=1}^{n} a_{ij}x_j = b_i, \qquad i = 1, \ldots, m$$

$$x_j \geq 0, \qquad j = 1, \ldots, n$$

where $f(x_1, \ldots, x_n)$ is a differentiable function. When f is concave, any optimum to (21-18) is a global optimum. However, the reduced gradient method can be used to solve (21-18) for any differentiable f, provided a local optimum is an acceptable solution.

This method is a generalization of the simplex method. At each iteration, it linearizes the true objective function. However, while it uses the ideas of basic variables and nonbasic variables, it does not restrict itself to basic solutions because the optimum to (21-18) need not be a basic solution. In the simplex method, we choose only one nonbasic variable to change and drive it to its largest feasible value. In contrast, the reduced gradient method generally alters a number of nonbasic variables simultaneously in some chosen search direction. The simplex type tableau is used to store the relationships between nonbasic and basic variables and also to maintain the feasibility of the solution. Like most nonlinear techniques, the reduced gradient method proceeds in the direction of search as long as the true objective function is increasing and the solution remains feasible. A line search is conducted to find the maximum value of the function in that direction. The direction of search is a *projection* of an unconstrained search direction onto the constraints. We will use the steepest ascent direction—the gradient vector—whose linearization is the tangent line. However, there is no reason why a different unconstrained direction vector could not be used. Sophisticated versions of the reduced gradient method use directions defined by such techniques as quasi-Newton methods. The method of projecting the unconstrained direction onto the constraints is based on the simplex method relationships between basic and nonbasic variables.

Let us go back to problem (21-2). Adding slack variables, we obtain

$$\text{(21-19)}\quad \begin{aligned} &\text{maximize} \quad z = f(x) = 4x_1 - x_1^2 + 9x_2 - x_2^2 + 10x_3 - 2x_3^2 - \tfrac{1}{2}x_2x_3 \\ &\text{subject to} \qquad 4x_1 + 2x_2 + x_3 + x_4 \qquad = 10 \\ &\qquad\qquad\qquad 2x_1 + 4x_2 + x_3 \qquad + x_5 = 20 \\ &\qquad\qquad\qquad x_1, x_2, x_3, x_4, x_5 \geq 0 \end{aligned}$$

Any basic solution to (21-19) is sufficient to initiate the reduced gradient method. In this case, the obvious basic solution is $x_4 = 10$, $x_5 = 20$ with x_1, x_2, x_3 equal to zero. We now substitute a linearization for the actual objective function, using its tangent at this solution. Thus, the c_j values are given by $c_j = \partial f/\partial x_j$ evaluated at $\mathbf{x}^{(1)}$. The first derivatives are

$$\text{(21-20)}\quad \partial f/\partial x_1 = 4 - 2x_1 \qquad \partial f/\partial x_2 = 9 - 2x_2 - \tfrac{1}{2}x_3 \qquad \partial f/\partial x_3 = 10 - 4x_3 - \tfrac{1}{2}x_2$$

Evaluating these at $\mathbf{x}^{(1)}$, we obtain the tangent plane

$$\text{(21-21)}\quad \bar{z} = 4x_1 + 9x_2 + 10x_3 + 0x_4 + 0x_5$$

Table 21-3 gives the first tableau with the basis (x_4, x_5), the solution $\mathbf{x}^{(1)} = (0, 0, 0, 10, 20)$, and the objective function (21-21). The $(z_j - c_j)$ values are calculated as they were in Chapter 3. For example $(z_1 - c_1) = (0)(4) + (0)(2) - 4 = -4$.

Table 21-3. *First reduced gradient method tableau*

(1)	$\mathbf{x}^{(1)}$	$z = 0$	0	0	0	10	20
$\frac{\partial f}{\partial x_j}(\mathbf{x}^{(1)}) = c_j$			4	9	10	0	0
c_j	Basis	Solution	x_1	x_2	x_3	x_4	x_5
0	x_4	10	4	2	1	1	0
0	x_5	20	2	4	1	0	1
	$z_j - c_j$		-4	-9	-10	0	0

In the reduced gradient method, we alter all nonbasic variables that have negative $(z_j - c_j)$. These variables are changed simultaneously in the proportions given by the $[-(z_j - c_j)]$ values. The basic variables are altered by applying the simplex method rules. This will assure that the new solution satisfies the constraints. Let $\mathbf{x}_B^{(k)}$ and $\mathbf{x}_R^{(k)}$ denote the vectors of basic and nonbasic variables at iteration k. We will denote the direction of movements of nonbasic variables by $\mathbf{r}_R^{(k)}$, the *reduced gradient vector*. It is an ascent direction because $(z_j - c_j) < 0$ gives an increase in the objective function.

Using equation (20-13), we have for the nonbasic variables

$$\mathbf{x}_R^{(k+1)} = \mathbf{x}_R^{(k)} + \theta^{(k)}\mathbf{r}_R^{(k)} \tag{21-22}$$

At the first iteration, $\mathbf{r}_R^{(1)} = -(z_1 - c_1, z_2 - c_2, z_3 - c_3) = (4, 9, 10)$ for the vector of nonbasic variables $\mathbf{x}_R^{(1)} = (x_1, x_2, x_3)$.

Next, we find the impact on the basic variables of a movement θ in the direction $\mathbf{r}_R^{(1)}$. From the equations in canonical form in Table 21-3, we observe that

$$x_4 = 10 - 4x_1 - 2x_2 - x_3 \qquad x_5 = 20 - 2x_1 - 4x_2 - x_3 \tag{21-23}$$

We now increase the nonbasic variables to $(\mathbf{x}_R^{(1)} + \theta\mathbf{r}_R^{(1)})$, or $x_1 = (0 + 4\theta)$, $x_2 = (0 + 9\theta)$, and $x_3 = (0 + 10\theta)$. Putting these values into (21-23) gives us the change in the basic variables:

$$\begin{aligned} x_4 &= 10 - 4(0 + 4\theta) - 2(0 + 9\theta) - (0 + 10\theta) = 10 - 44\theta \\ x_5 &= 20 - 2(0 + 4\theta) - 4(0 + 9\theta) - (0 + 10\theta) = 20 - 54\theta \end{aligned} \tag{21-24}$$

Taking (21-22) and (21-24) together, we get the direction of movement $\mathbf{r}^{(1)}$ from $\mathbf{x}^{(1)}$ for both basic and nonbasic variables. It is $\mathbf{r}^{(1)} = (4, 9, 10, -44, -54)$. For $\mathbf{x} = \mathbf{x}^{(1)} + \theta\mathbf{r}^{(1)}$ to be a feasible solution in the direction $\mathbf{r}^{(1)}$, we require that

$$\begin{aligned} &x_1 = 4\theta \geqslant 0 \qquad x_2 = 9\theta \geqslant 0 \qquad x_3 = 10\theta \geqslant 0 \\ &x_4 = 10 - 44\theta \geqslant 0 \qquad x_5 = 20 - 54\theta \geqslant 0 \end{aligned} \tag{21-25}$$

Verify that these conditions reduce to $0 \leqslant \theta \leqslant 0.22727$. If we denote the maximum feasible distance in the direction $\mathbf{r}^{(1)}$ by ε, then at the first iteration $\varepsilon = 0.22727$.

For a nonlinear objective function, the solution at the maximum feasible distance might not be the best solution in that direction. So we conduct a line search in the direction $\mathbf{r}^{(1)}$ up to $\theta = \varepsilon$, i.e., we find $\theta^{(1)}$ to $\underset{0 \leqslant \theta \leqslant \varepsilon}{\text{maximize}}\, f(\mathbf{x}^{(1)} + \theta\mathbf{r}^{(1)})$, and the new solution becomes $\mathbf{x}^{(2)} = \mathbf{x}^{(1)} + \theta^{(1)}\mathbf{r}^{(1)}$. Applied to our example, we have

$$\begin{aligned} &\text{maximize}\, f(\mathbf{x}^{(1)} + \theta\mathbf{r}^{(1)}) = \\ &\quad 4(4\theta) - (4\theta)^2 + 9(9\theta) \quad (9\theta)^2 + 10(10\theta) - 2(10\theta)^2 - \tfrac{1}{2}(9\theta)(10\theta) = 197\theta - 342\theta^2 \end{aligned}$$

This yields $\theta = 0.28801$, which is larger than $\varepsilon = 0.22727$, so $\theta^{(1)} = \varepsilon = 0.22727$. Hence,

$$\begin{aligned} \mathbf{x}^{(2)} &= (0, 0, 0, 10, 20) + 0.22727(4, 9, 10, -44, -54) \\ &= (0.9091, 2.0454, 2.2727, 0, 7.7274) \end{aligned}$$

and $f(\mathbf{x}^{(2)}) = 27.1073$ is the corresponding objective function value.

Since more than two variables in $\mathbf{x}^{(2)}$ are nonzero, this is not a basic solution. For the purpose of the simplex structure, we choose m (in our case, two) of the nonzero variables to be basic. These are normally the m variables with the largest solution values. In our case, we choose $x_5 = 7.7274$ and $x_3 = 2.2727$. All other variables are "nonbasic." However, we divide the nonbasic variables into two sets: the nonzero variables, called *superbasic*, denoted by $\mathbf{x}_S^{(k)}$, and the zero variables, simply referred to as *nonbasic*, denoted by $\mathbf{x}_N^{(k)}$. In our case, x_1 and x_2 are the superbasic variables, while x_4 is nonbasic. The first tableau of Table 21-4 gives the next tableau with x_3 replacing x_4. Since only one variable is changed in the basis, the usual simplex transformation rules can be used. The $\mathbf{c}_j$ values are the gradient coefficients at $\mathbf{x}^{(2)}$.

Table 21-4. *Additional reduced gradient tableaux*

(2)	$\mathbf{x}^{(2)}$	27.1073	0.9091	2.0454	2.2727	0	7.7274
$\frac{\partial f}{\partial x_j}(\mathbf{x}^{(2)}) = c_j$			2.1818	3.7729	−0.1135	0	0
c_j	Basis	Solution	x_1	x_2	x_3	x_4	x_5
−0.1135	x_3	2.2727	4	2	1	1	0
0	x_5	7.7274	−2	2	0	−1	1
	$z_j - c_j$		−2.6358	−4	0	−0.1135	0

Final Tableau

(6)	$\mathbf{x}^{(6)}$	28.8204	0.4105	3.2304	1.8971	0	4.3602
c_j			3.1790	1.5096	0.7964	0	0
1.59065	x_2	3.2304	2	1	0.5	0.5	0
0	x_5	4.3602	−6	0	−1	−2	1
	$z_j - c_j$		0.0023	0	−0.0011	0.7954	0
(7)	$\mathbf{x}^{(7)}$	28.8205	0.4102	3.2309	1.8972	0	4.3584

For the second iteration, we refine the concept of the reduced gradient. The vector $\mathbf{x}_R^{(k)}$ is now the vector of superbasic and nonbasic variables. Thus, the reduced gradient vector is defined as $\mathbf{r}_R^{(k)} = (r_{R1}, r_{R2}, \ldots)$, where

$$(21\text{-}26) \qquad r_{Rj} = \begin{cases} -(z_j - c_j) & \text{for } x_j \in \mathbf{x}_S \\ -(z_j - c_j) & \text{for } x_j \in \mathbf{x}_N \text{ and } (z_j - c_j) < 0 \\ 0 & \text{for } x_j \in \mathbf{x}_N \text{ and } (z_j - c_j) \geq 0 \end{cases}$$

We define $\mathbf{r}_R^{(k)}$ this way because it permits us to increase or decrease the superbasic variables. Since these are positive, by definition, a decrease is permissible. However, only an increase in the nonbasic variables is permitted since they are at their lower bound. Again $\mathbf{r}_R^{(k)}$ is an ascent direction because for every superbasic or nonbasic variable, the direction of change improves the objective function.

For the second iteration of our problem, we start with $\mathbf{r}_R^{(1)} = (2.6358, 4, 0.1135)$ for $\mathbf{x}_R^{(2)} = (x_1, x_2, x_5)$. The new solution to the basic variables at a distance θ in the direction $\mathbf{r}_R^{(2)}$ is then

$$x_3 = 2.2727 - 4(2.6358\theta) - 2(4\theta) - 1(0.1135\theta) = 2.2727 - 18.6567\theta$$

$$x_5 = 7.7274 - (-2)(2.6358\theta) - 2(4\theta) - (-1)(0.1135\theta) = 7.7274 - 2.6149\theta$$

So the new direction vector is $\mathbf{r}^{(2)} = (2.6358, 4, -18.6567, 0.1135, -2.6149)$ and $\varepsilon = \text{minimum } [x_i/(-r_i)]$ for $r_i < 0$. For this iteration, $\varepsilon = \text{minimum } (2.2727/18.6567, 7.7274/2.6149) = 0.1218$. We must now perform a line search for $0 \leq \theta \leq 0.1218$, i.e., find $\theta^{(2)}$ that $\underset{0\leq\theta\leq\varepsilon}{\text{maximizes}}\ f(\mathbf{x}^{(2)} + \theta\mathbf{r}^{(2)})$. This occurs at $\theta = 0.01684$. Since $0.01684 < \epsilon$, the value of $\theta^{(2)} = 0.01684$. The new solution is

$$\mathbf{x}^{(3)} = \mathbf{x}^{(2)} + \theta^{(2)}\mathbf{r}^{(2)} = (0.9535, 2.1128, 1.9585, 0.0019, 7.6834)$$

with $f(\mathbf{x}^{(3)}) = 27.3007$. Continuing this process, we get

$$\mathbf{r}^{(3)} = (-5.4974, 12.3376, -0.788, -1.8976, -37.5678)$$

with $\varepsilon = 0.001$, $\theta = 0.0963$, and $\theta^{(3)} = 0.001$.

$$\mathbf{x}^{(4)} = (0.948, 2.1251, 1.9577, 0, 7.6458) \qquad f(\mathbf{x}^{(4)}) = 27.3348$$

$$\mathbf{r}^{(4)} = (-5.438, 11.2654, -0.7788, 0, -33.4068)$$

with $\varepsilon = 0.17433$, $\theta = 0.0984$, and $\theta^{(4)} = 0.0984$.

$$\mathbf{x}^{(5)} = (0.4128, 3.2339, 1.881, 0, 4.3578) \qquad f(\mathbf{x}^{(5)}) = 28.82$$

$$\mathbf{r}^{(5)} = (-0.009, -0.0137, 0.0633, 0, 0.0093)$$

with $\varepsilon = 45.87$, $\theta = 0.2549$, and $\theta^{(5)} = 0.2549$.

These lead to the final tableau in Table 21-4, which uses

$$\mathbf{r}^{(6)} = (-0.0023, 0.00406, 0.00108, 0, -0.01488)$$

with $\varepsilon = 178.48$, $\theta = 0.1226$, and $\theta^{(6)} = 0.1226$.

We terminate the iterations when some stopping rule tolerance is satisfied. Two possible criteria are $|x_j^{(k)} - x_j^{(k-1)}| < \gamma_1$ or $|r_j| < \gamma_2$, all j, where γ_1 or γ_2 is chosen arbitrarily small. The reduced gradient method would terminate at $\mathbf{x}^{(7)}$ for either $\gamma_1 = 0.01$ or $\gamma_2 = 0.01$. In fact, we know that the true optimum is $\mathbf{x}^* = (0.4102, 3.2308, 1.8974, 0, 4.3590)$ and $z^* = 28.8205$. So solution $\mathbf{x}^{(7)}$ is very close to optimal.

As in the ordinary simplex method, we have some information for sensitivity analysis. In particular, $(z_4 - c_4)$ gives the imputed value of the first constraint, and $(z_5 - c_5)$ gives the imputed value of the second constraint. Since the objective function is nonlinear, these must be strictly interpreted as marginal values.

The reduced gradient method has been generalized by Abadie and Carpentier (1970, see references) to deal with nonlinear constraints—called the *generalized reduced gradient method* or GRG.

Sophisticated and highly efficient computer codes have been developed for the reduced gradient method (e.g., MINOS by B. A. Murtagh and M. A. Saunders, "Large-Scale Linearly Constrained Optimization," *Mathematical Programming*, Vol. 14, 1978, pp. 41–72).

21-6 REDUCED GRADIENT METHOD CRITERIA

Let us now state, in general terms, the reduced gradient method criteria developed in the example. Let $\mathbf{x}^{(k)}$ be the solution on which the kth tableau is based.

RGM CRITERION 1: THE $z_j - c_j$ VALUES

$$c_j = \partial f(\mathbf{x}^{(k)})/\partial x_j$$

z_j is found using the usual simplex method rule.

RGM CRITERION 2: THE REDUCED GRADIENT VECTOR

Let $\mathbf{x}_S^{(k)}$ be the superbasic variables (nonbasic variables with positive value), $\mathbf{x}_N^{(k)}$ be the nonbasic variables (with zeio value), and $\mathbf{x}_R^{(k)}$ be the variables in either $\mathbf{x}_S^{(k)}$ or $\mathbf{x}_N^{(k)}$. The reduced gradient vector $\mathbf{r}_R^{(k)}$ is defined as

$$r_{Rj}^{(k)} = \begin{cases} -(z_j - c_j) & \text{for } x_j \in \mathbf{x}_S \\ -(z_j - c_j) & \text{for } x_j \in \mathbf{x}_N \quad \text{and} \quad (z_j - c_j) < 0 \\ 0 & \text{otherwise} \end{cases}$$

RGM CRITERION 3: DIRECTION VECTOR $\mathbf{r}^{(k)}$

Let $\mathbf{x}_B^{(k)}$ be the basic variables, $\mathbf{x}_R^{(k)}$ be as defined in Criterion 2, and γ_{js} be the tableau element in the x_j row and x_s column. The direction vector $\mathbf{r}^{(k)}$ has elements defined by

$$r_j = \begin{cases} r_{Rj} & \text{for } x_j \in \mathbf{x}_R^{(k)} \\ -\sum_{s \in I} \gamma_{js} r_{Rs} & \text{for } x_j \in \mathbf{x}_B^{(k)} \end{cases}$$

where I is the set of indices for all superbasic and nonbasic variables.

RGM CRITERION 4: MAXIMUM FEASIBLE DISTANCE

The maximum feasible distance is

$$\varepsilon = \underset{j}{\text{minimum}}\,[x_j/(-r_j)], \qquad \text{for } r_j < 0$$

RGM CRITERION 5: FINDING $\mathbf{x}^{(k+1)}$

The solution $\mathbf{x}^{(k+1)}$, on which the next tableau is based, is found from $\mathbf{x}^{(k)}$ by $\mathbf{x}^{(k+1)} = \mathbf{x}^{(k)} + \theta^{(k)}\mathbf{r}^{(k)}$, where $\theta^{(k)}$ solves $\underset{0 \leq \theta \leq \varepsilon}{\text{maximize}} \, [f(\mathbf{x}^{(k)} + \theta\mathbf{r}^{(k)})]$.

RGM CRITERION 6: NEW BASIS

The basis for tableau $(k + 1)$ is chosen by taking the m largest components of $\mathbf{x}^{(k+1)}$ as the basic variables, where the basis is of dimension m.

RGM CRITERION 7: TERMINATION OF THE ALGORITHM

The algorithm terminates when [maximum $|r_j|$] $< \gamma$, where $\gamma > 0$, but very small.

21-7 PENALTY METHODS

In this section and the next, we introduce an approach to nonlinear programming quite different from the reduced gradient method. Two similar approaches, *penalty methods* and *barrier methods* (also called *sequential unconstrained maximization techniques*, or SUMT), provide a means of reformulating a constrained nonlinear programming problem as an unconstrained problem. The resulting unconstrained problem is solved sequentially by an ordinary unconstrained technique, such as a gradient method.

Penalty methods take the objective function and add to it a *penalty function*—a function that penalizes solutions that do not belong to the feasible region. Barrier methods add a *barrier function* that creates a barrier against movement from feasible points to infeasible points by making points near the boundary of the feasible region carry a heavy penalty.

The details of the two methods are basically similar. We will discuss only penalty methods.

Consider the following simple one-variable problem of the form (21-4):

$$\begin{aligned} &\text{maximize} && f(x) = 10x - x^2 \\ &\text{subject to} && g_1(x) = 2x \leq 4 = b_1 \\ & && g_2(x) = -x \leq 0 = b_2 \end{aligned} \tag{21-27}$$

We want to replace the constraint $2x \leq 4$ by a term in the objective function that penalizes any value of x that violates this constraint and thus turn (21-27) into

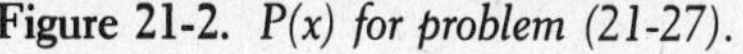

Figure 21-2. *P(x) for problem (21-27).*

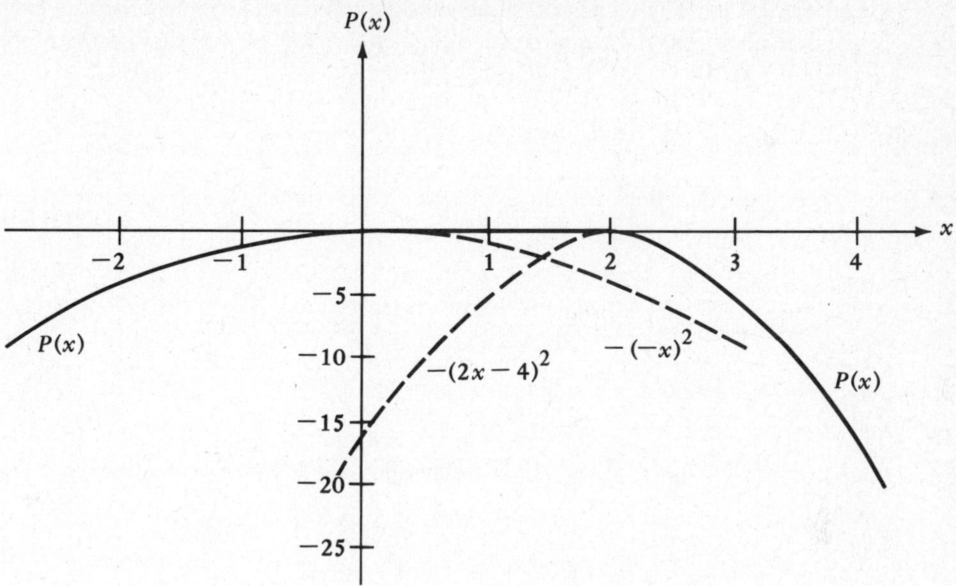

an unconstrained problem. We need a function of the general form

$$P_1(x)\begin{cases} = 0 & \text{if } 2x \leq 4 \qquad (\text{i.e., } g_1(x) \leq b_1) \\ < 0 & \text{if } 2x > 4 \qquad (\text{i.e., } g_1(x) \nleq b_1) \end{cases}$$

A possible specific form for this function is

$$P_1(x) = -(\text{maximum } [0, 2x - 4])^2$$

Similarly, for $-x \leq 0$ (i.e., $g_2(x) \leq b_2$), we derive the function

$$P_2(x) = -(\text{maximum } [0, -x])^2$$

Adding these to the objective function, we obtain

$$\text{maximize } C(x) = f(x) + P_1(x) + P_2(x)$$

or

(21-28) $$\text{maximize } C(x) = f(x) + P(x)$$

where $P(x) = -\sum_{i=1}^{2} (\text{maximum } [0, (g_i(x) - b_i)])^2$. P is the penalty function. The construction of this function for problem (21-27) is shown in Figure 21-2.

Any x that violates the constraints of (21-27) is penalized in problem (21-28). However, problem (21-28) is not exactly equivalent to (21-27) because it does not place infinite penalty on infeasible points. In many cases this penalty is insufficient to stop an infeasible point from being optimal to (21-28). In fact, from Figure 21-2, we see that the penalty function of (21-28) gives very little penalty to a large range of infeasible points. Clearly, the penalty should be as severe as possible to make the unconstrained problem closely approximate the constrained problem. Rather than define a totally different form of penalty function, we can control the severity of the penalty by a parameter λ and change (21-28) to

$$\text{maximize } C(x, \lambda) = f(x) + \frac{1}{\lambda} P(x) \tag{21-29}$$

As λ decreases, the effect of P on C increases proportionately, and infeasible points become less desirable. In general:

PENALTY FUNCTION

A penalty function is a function such that

$$P(\mathbf{x}) \begin{cases} = 0 & \text{if } \mathbf{x} \text{ is a feasible solution} \\ < 0 & \text{if } \mathbf{x} \text{ is an infeasible solution} \end{cases}$$

i.e.,

$$P(\mathbf{x}) \begin{cases} = 0 & \text{if } g_i(\mathbf{x}) \leq b_i \quad \text{for all } i = 1, 2, \ldots, m + n \\ < 0 & \text{otherwise} \end{cases} \tag{21-30}$$

As we have seen, a possible and very convenient form of P is

$$P(\mathbf{x}) = - \sum_{i=1}^{m+n} (\text{maximum } [0, (g_i(\mathbf{x}) - b_i)])^2 \tag{21-31}$$

Figure 21-3. $(1/\lambda^{(k)})P(x)$ *for problem (21-27).*

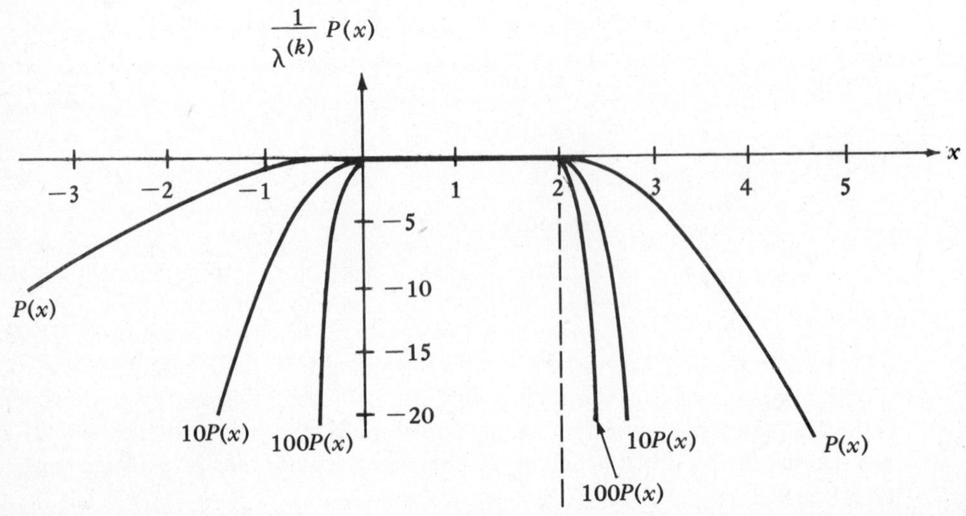

Verify that this form satisfies condition (21-30).

Sometimes it is possible to solve expressions like (21-29) analytically and give the solution $\mathbf{x}$ that results as $\lambda \to 0$. More usually the problem is solved by using a sequence of $\lambda^{(k)}$, i.e., $\lambda^{(1)}, \lambda^{(2)}, \lambda^{(3)}, \ldots, \lambda^{(k)}, \ldots$, where $\lambda^{(k+1)} < \lambda^{(k)}$ and $\lim_{k\to\infty}\lambda^{(k)} = 0$. This gives us the sequence of problems of the form

$$\text{(21-32)} \qquad \underset{\mathbf{x}}{\text{maximize}}\ C(\mathbf{x}, \lambda^{(k)}) = f(\mathbf{x}) + \frac{1}{\lambda^{(k)}} P(\mathbf{x})$$

and the resultant sequence of solutions $\mathbf{x}^{(1)}, \mathbf{x}^{(2)}, \ldots, \mathbf{x}^{(k)}, \ldots$.

To illustrate this idea, we used the sequence

$$\lambda^{(1)} = 1,\ \lambda^{(2)} = 0.1,\ \lambda^{(3)} = 0.01,\ \lambda^{(4)} = 0.001, \ldots$$

on problem (21-27). The sequence of $(1/\lambda^{(k)})P(x)$ functions is shown in Figure 21-3, and the $C(x, \lambda^{(k)})$ functions are shown in Figure 21-4. The point $x^{(0)}$ in Figure 21-4 is the solution to maximize $f(x)$. Clearly, the sequence $x^{(1)}, x^{(2)}, x^{(3)}, \ldots$ is

Figure 21-4. $C(x, \lambda^{(k)}) = f(x) + (1/\lambda^{(k)})P(x)$ *for problem (21-27).*

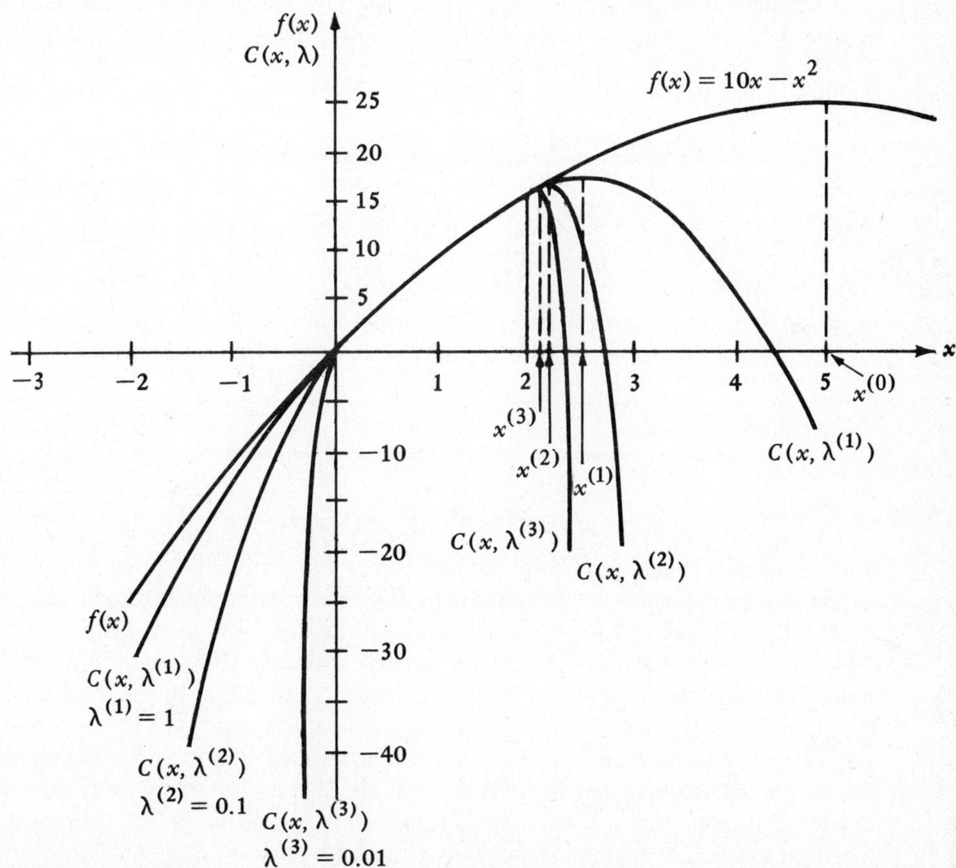

converging to the optimum $x^* = 2$. When the optimum is on the boundary of the feasible region, the nature of the penalty methods gives convergence from *outside* the feasible region, because, as the penalty becomes more severe, the optimal solutions to (21-32) get closer to feasibility.

21-8 PENALTY METHODS APPLIED TO PROBLEM (21-2)

Let us now set up and solve problem (21-2) by penalty methods, using equations (21-6). Applying the form of the penalty function defined in (21-31), we reduce this problem to the unconstrained approximating problem

$$\begin{aligned}
\underset{\mathbf{x}}{\text{maximize}} \quad C(\mathbf{x}, \lambda) = {} & (4x_1 - x_1^2 + 9x_2 - x_2^2 + 10x_3 - 2x_3^2 - \tfrac{1}{2}x_2 x_3) \\
& + \frac{1}{\lambda}[- (\text{maximum}\,[0, (4x_1 + 2x_2 + x_3 - 10)])^2 \\
& -(\text{maximum}\,[0, (2x_1 + 4x_2 + x_3 - 20)])^2 \\
& - (\text{maximum}\,[0, - x_1])^2 - (\text{maximum}\,[0, - x_2])^2 \\
& - (\text{maximum}\,[0, - x_3])^2]
\end{aligned} \tag{21-33}$$

To find the solution to (21-33) for a small λ, we again use a sequence of $\lambda^{(k)}$ values. Table 21-5 shows how the solution converges as $\lambda^{(k)}$ is decreased successively.

Table 21-5. *Sequence of solutions of problem (21-33)—Penalty methods*

$\lambda^{(k)}$	$x_1^{(k)}$	$x_2^{(k)}$	$x_3^{(k)}$	$C(\mathbf{x}, \lambda^{(k)})$
1	0.4856	3.2671	1.9021	28.9710
0.1	0.4179	3.2349	1.8981	28.8362
0.01	0.4111	3.2309	1.8977	28.8221
0.001	0.4103	3.2308	1.8974	28.8206
0.0001	0.4103	3.2308	1.8974	28.8205
0.00001	0.4102	3.2308	1.8975	28.8205
True optimum	0.4102	3.2308	1.8975	28.8205

When the problem is solved using a sequence of $\lambda^{(k)}$ the search for $\mathbf{x}^{(k+1)}$ is initiated at $\mathbf{x}^{(k)}$, since that should be fairly close, particularly when k is large. Such a procedure reduces considerably the time required at each iteration to find the new optimal point. Table 21-5 indicates that the optimum has been reached for $\lambda^{(k)} = 0.00001$.

Clearly, we could have started immediately with a small λ, say $\lambda = 0.00001$, instead of using the sequence of $\lambda^{(k)}$ shown. However, functions of the form (21-32) tend to become ill-behaved or awkwardly shaped for λ very small, and hence converge very slowly, unless a good initial solution can be guessed. For example, the optimal solution for the sequence of six λ-values in Table 21-5 was found by fewer than 300 iterations in total. Using $\lambda = 0.00001$ directly, the search procedure converged to the same solution in approximately 8000 iterations.

21-9 ADVANCED NONLINEAR PROGRAMMING

Current general nonlinear programming follows three lines of attack. The first is the direct methods approach, which seeks to solve the problem itself by techniques such as the reduced gradient method. There has been a recent leap forward in the application of direct methods to problems with nonlinear constraints. It involves using the Lagrangian function in place of the objective function. When we solve the Lagrangian over the constraint set, using a method such as the generalized reduced gradient method, we include information on the curvature of the constraints in the objective function. This has led to considerable improvement in computational efficiency.

The second approach involves penalty methods. In particular, the *augmented Lagrangian method* solves the Lagrangian function with an additional quadratic penalty. This has proved to be considerably superior to simple penalty methods. It eliminates the awkward shape that the function has near the optimum when a simple penalty is applied.

We have not introduced at all the basics of the third approach. These methods approximate one problem with another problem that has a ready solution technique, e.g., an approximation by a quadratic programming problem. At each iteration, the solution to the approximating problem is used to define a better approximating problem until the solutions of the approximating problems converge. *Recursive quadratic programming* is the most modern and efficient of these methods.

At their most sophisticated levels, these three approaches seem to be coming together. Perhaps a technique will be invented that combines aspects of all three approaches.

EXERCISES

21.1 The production possibilities of a firm are described by the following inequalities in which x_i denotes the output of product i:

$$x_1 + x_2 \leq 80 \qquad 2x_1 + x_2 \leq 120 \qquad x_1 + 3x_2 \leq 200$$

The demand equations are

$$x_1 = 100 - 2p_1 \quad \text{and} \quad x_2 = 300 - 3p_2$$

where p_i = price of good i. Average variable costs per unit are \$5 for good 1 and \$10 for good 2. Formulate this problem.

21.2 A manufacturing company has planned two new products to take up the slack in their production program. They have to decide the selling price, monthly production, and monthly promotional expenses for both of the products. The market analysts predict the following relationships among monthly sales, price, and promotional expenditure.

$$x_1 = 10 - 4p_1 + 2c_1, \qquad x_2 = 15 - \tfrac{1}{2}p_1 - 3p_2 + c_2$$

where x_j is monthly sales in thousands of units for product j, p_j is selling price per unit in dollars for product j, and c_j is monthly promotional expenses in thousands of dollars for product j.

Only \$7,000 a month is available to spend on promotion. Other expenses are \$3, and \$5 per unit, respectively. Product 1 uses 0.2 hour of production capacity per unit, and product 2 uses 0.3 hour per unit. Production capacity is limited to 1000 hours per month.

Set up this problem to find the values of the variables that give maximum total profit per month.

21.3 Using Wolfe's quadratic programming algorithm, find the first two iterations for the problems

(a) maximize $f(\mathbf{x}) = 7x_1 - 2x_1^2 + x_1x_2 - x_2^2$
subject to $x_1 + x_2 \leq 2 \quad 2x_1 + 4x_2 \leq 6 \quad x_1, x_2 \geq 0$

(b) maximize $f(\mathbf{x}) = 7x_1 - 2x_1^2 + x_1x_2 - x_2^2$
subject to $x_1 \leq 1 \quad x_1 + x_2 \geq 1 \quad x_1, x_2 \geq 0$

21.4 Find the first two iterations of Wolfe's quadratic programming algorithm for exercise 21.1.

21.5 Apply the Kuhn-Tucker conditions to the following problems, and set out the first tableau of Wolfe's algorithm. Perform the first iteration.

(a) maximize $f(\mathbf{x}) = 16x_1 + 20x_2 - 4x_1x_2 - x_1^2 - x_2^2$
subject to $x_1 + x_2 \geq 2 \quad 3x_1 + 5x_2 \leq 15, \quad x_1, x_2 \geq 0$

(b) maximize $f(\mathbf{x}) = 3x_1 + 4x_2 - x_1^2 - x_2^2$
subject to $8x_1 + 4x_2 \leq 16 \quad 3x_1 + 5x_2 \leq 15 \quad x_1, x_2 \geq 0$

21.6 Find the first three tableaux of the reduced gradient method for the following problem. Start with the solution $\mathbf{x}^{(1)} = (0, 3)$.

maximize $f(\mathbf{x}) = -x_1^2 - 2x_2^2$
subject to $4x_1 + x_2 \leq 6 \quad x_1 + x_2 = 3 \quad x_1, x_2 \geq 0$

21.7 Find the first five tableaux of the reduced gradient method for the problems in exercise 21.5. Start with $\mathbf{x}^{(1)} = (2, 0)$.

21.8 Find the first two reduced gradient method tableaux for the problem in exercise 21.1.

21.9 Set up the following problem for solution by penalty methods:
(a) Exercise 21.3(a).
(b) Exercise 21.3(b).

21.10 Set up the following problem by penalty methods:

minimize $5x_1^2 - 10x_1 - 10x_2\log_{10}x_2$
subject to $x_1^2 + 2x_2^2 \leq 4, \quad x_1, x_2 \geq 0$

(Assume $0 \log_{10} 0 = 0$.)

REFERENCES

General Nonlinear Programming

Abadie, J. "Advances in Nonlinear Programming." In *Operational Research '78*. Amsterdam: North-Holland, 1979.

Fletcher, R. *Practical Methods of Optimization, Vol. 2, Constrained Optimization.* New York: Wiley, 1981. For the reader with a thorough training in mathematics who wishes to work in nonlinear programmng at an advanced level, this book is highly recommended. It is difficult but one of the most complete and up-to-date books available.

Luenberger, D. *Introduction to Linear and Nonlinear Programming.* Reading, Mass.: Addison-Wesley, 1973. A readable, though slightly out-of-date, treatment for students with better than average mathematics. In our opinion, this is still one of the best texts available at this level. Chapters 10–13 deal with constrained nonlinear programming.

Quadratic Programming

Beale, E. M. L., "Numerical Methods." In J. Abadie, Ed., *Nonlinear Programming.* Amsterdam: North-Holland, 1967. Beale introduces his own quadratic programming technique in Sections II, III, and IV, although much of III and IV is fairly advanced. This quadratic programming technique does not require the objective function to be concave (maximizing problem).

Gradient Method and Reduced Gradient Method

Abadie, J., Ed. *Integer and Nonlinear Programming.* Amsterdam: North-Holland 1970. Of particular relevance are Chapters 1, 2, 3, 6, 8 and Appendices I, II, and III. They cover the theory and computational experience of the generalized reduced gradient (GRG) method. This is advanced reading.

Wolfe, P. "Methods of Nonlinear Programming." In J. Abadie, Ed., *Nonlinear Programming.* Amsterdam: North-Holland, 1967. In this paper, Wolfe summarizes most of the gradient techniques, constrained and unconstrained. The treatment is concise and readable. Pages 121–123 present the reduced gradient method.

Penalty and Barrier Methods

Fiacco, A. V., and G. P. McCormick. *Nonlinear Programming: Sequential Unconstrained Minimization Techniques.* New York: Wiley, 1968. This text is a synthesis of the work done on penalty and barrier methods. It is a complete treatment providing the necessary convergence proofs and discussion of finer computational features. This book is recommended for detailed study of penalty and barrier methods by a mathematically competent reader.

Other Topics in Nonlinear Programming

Geoffrion, A. M. "Elements of Large-Scale Mathematical Programming, Parts I and II," *Management Science,* Vol. 16, July 1970. A two-part survey and unification of techniques for dealing with large-scale problems in mathematical programming—linear and nonlinear. These are important survey articles.

Warren, A. D., and L. S. Lasdon. "The Status of Nonlinear Programming Software," *Operations Research,* Vol. 27, May–June 1979. A survey article on available software. It gives a summary of the packages and the methods they use, as well as some assessment of the relative merits of different methods. References to most modern programs are available from this article.

Applications of Nonlinear Programming

Beale, E. M. L., Ed. *Applications of Mathematical Programming Techniques*. London: English University Press, 1970. Applications that result in nonlinear programming problems are described on pages 100–121, 413–420, and 423–451.

Bracken, J., and G. P. McCormick. *Selected Applications of Nonlinear Programming*. New York: Wiley, 1968. Nine case study applications of nonlinear programming are presented in this book. They were all solved using penalty and barrier methods. This is valuable reading.

Ladson, L. S., and A. D. Waren. "Survey of Nonlinear Programming Applications," *Operations Research*, Vol. 28, Sept.-Oct. 1980. Considers nonlinear models, algorithms, and software in a number of problem areas. A comprehensive bibliography is included.

CHAPTER TWENTY-TWO

Multiple-Objective Decision Making

In today's complex organizational environment, a decision maker is often faced with different and conflicting objectives. Rarely will the same decision alternative simultaneously optimize all of them. Therefore, the "best" decision must be a compromise. What is considered "best" may be influenced by intangible factors, by personal attitudes and values of the decision maker. Some of these factors may not lend themselves to being expressed adequately in mathematical form. Although we shall continue to refer to some solutions as "optimal" in the sense of representing a maximum or a minimum to the objective function chosen, we also need to remind ourselves that this solution is a compromise between conflicting and often only partially modeled objectives. For these reasons, the major value of multiple-objective decision making techniques is in helping the decision maker to explore the solution space. This exploration will enable the decision maker to gain valuable insight into how the various objectives affect one another and how different emphasis given to the objectives affects the "optimal" solution.

In Chapter 1, we briefly discussed some ways of dealing with multiple objectives (Section 1-12). The most commonly used method is to convert all but one of the objectives into surrogate constraints. This approach is suitable if one objective can be clearly identified as more important, while the remaining objectives have the character of targets to be achieved. Sensitivity analysis is used to explore the effects of tightening and loosening the targets. This chapter studies a number of formal approaches that explicitly recognize the multiple-objective structure of the problem. But first, let us briefly sketch two actual problems where such techniques have been applied with some degree of success.

22-1 SOME ACTUAL MULTIPLE-OBJECTIVE DECISION PROBLEMS

Multiple land use

The Federal Land Policy and Management Act, passed by the 94th U.S. Congress in 1976, gives the following mandate to the Bureau of Land Management (BLM) for the management of the approximately 473 million acres of federally owned land under its jurisdiction:

- that the management be on the basis of multiple use and sustained yield;
- that the lands be managed in a manner that will
  (a) protect the quality of scientific, scenic, historical, ecological, environmental, air and atmospheric, water resource, and archaeological values;
  (b) where appropriate, preserve and protect certain public lands in their natural condition;
  (c) provide food and habitat for fish, wildlife, and domestic animals;
  (d) provide for outdoor recreation and human occupancy and use.

Many of these objectives are in direct conflict with one another. For some tracts of land, the BLM will be under fire from different pressure groups to have their vested interests prevail. These groups include farm lobbies who want more grazing land, mining companies who want prospecting rights, and conservation groups who want to keep some areas in their natural state. How does the BLM resolve these conflicts?

Assume that a BLM district officer has to develop a multiple-use land program for an area which at present is used largely for grazing. There are also coal deposits of economic significance. The area's recreational value is mainly for big game hunting and four-wheel-drive vehicle use. Roughly, the BLM's current procedure consists of first compiling a detailed inventory of the area's topography, soils, vegetation, and other physical features and a description of existing use for each tract in the area. This is followed by an assessment of the unlimited potential of each tract for each possible use, without regard to any other uses. Independently of this, a socioeconomic profile is compiled that provides relevant information on attitudes of current and prospective users of the area, on special interest groups, and on economic factors relating to the importance of natural resources. Armed with these two basic documents, the area manager has to develop a compromise solution that reflects both the best intrinsic use of the various tracts and the relevant socioeconomic factors. This is a very difficult task of integration and resolution of conflicting objectives.

A pilot study by F. K. Martinson at the University of Colorado implemented by the BLM in 1977 on a trial basis demonstrates the feasibility of using a *multiple-objective linear programming* approach to help the area manager with his or her decisions. We shall pick up this problem again in Section 22-5.

Mexico City airport development

In 1971, the Ministry of Public Works of Mexico (MPW) was asked by the Mexican presidential office to make recommendations for the future development of airport facilities for Mexico City. Growth in the volume of air traffic, combined with difficult operating conditions at the existing airport at Texcoco, lent considerable urgency to providing a development strategy over the next thirty years. The Texcoco airport is sandwiched between the remains of Lake Texcoco to the east and the sprawling Mexico City metropolis to the west. Upgrading Texcoco on the former lakebed or by displacement of the population would make construction very expensive. The ensuing overcrowding would further aggravate the problem of noise, the danger of landing or takeoff accidents with potentially numerous casualties, and the disruption of air services because of the frequent need for leveling and resurfacing of the runways situated on the soft former lakebed. The advantage of upgrading Texcoco was proximity to the city. The alternative site at Zumpango, in an undeveloped rural area 25 miles to the north of the city, did not suffer from any of the problems of Texcoco, but would increase travel times to and from the city.

Based on a consensus of the directors of the MPW, a partial list of objectives included

- minimizing total construction, maintenance, and operating costs;
- minimizing access time to the airport;
- maximizing the operating safety;
- minimizing the effect of air traffic noise pollution;
- minimizing social disruption to the population;
- raising the air traffic capacity of the airport.

There were many uncertainties associated with any decision. One such uncertainty was the future growth of air traffic.

How should the MPW go about developing a strategy that is "best" in terms of social, economic, and political criteria? To help in this analysis, two American experts in modern decision analysis, Professor R. de Neufville and Dr. K. L. Keeney (1976), were called in. Together with the senior staff of the MPW, they applied decision analysis based on *multiattribute utility functions*. Sections 22-7 to 22-9 summarize this approach for a simple two-attribute decision problem.

22-2 AN OVERVIEW OF MULTIPLE-OBJECTIVE DECISION TECHNIQUES

Before studying this section, we ask you to review, in Section 1-11, the distinction made between objectives and the attributes associated with an alternative course of action.

In the late sixties and through the seventies, there occurred a virtual explosion of different approaches to deal with multiple-objective decision problems. These approaches can be grouped roughly into *weighting methods*, *sequential elimination methods*, and *interactive solution methods* (for different classifications, see MacCrimmon in Cochrane and Zeleny, 1973, or Starr and Zeleny, 1977).

Weighting methods are undoubtedly the most widely applied techniques. They assume that the decision maker is able to define tradeoff relations between attributes. This allows aggregation of the attribute values associated with an alternative into a single number or index which reflects the alternative's overall desirability. The alternatives can then be ranked in terms of this desirability index. You have already encountered one such technique in Section 2-14, namely *weighted-sum goal programming*, which can be solved as a regular linear program. Decision analysis using multiattribute utility functions—an extension of the approach discussed in Section 11-7—is also a weighting method and is studied is Sections 22-7 to 22-10.

In contrast to weighting methods, sequential elimination methods do not allow tradeoffs between attributes or objectives. Some methods rank objectives in terms of their priority. Optimization begins by considering the highest priority objective first. Ties are broken by sequentially comparing lower priority objectives in descending order of priority. *Preemptive goal programming* is one such approach and is discussed in Section 22-3.

Other sequential elimination methods are based on the idea of *solution dominance*. Let r_{ik} denote the performance of alternative i in terms of objective (or attribute) k, $i = 1, 2, \ldots, I$ and $k = 1, 2, \ldots, K$. The vector $\mathbf{r}_i = (r_{i1}, r_{i2}, \ldots, r_{iK})$ measures the achievement levels of alternative i over all K objectives. Assume for simplicity that we want to maximize all objectives. Then dominance is defined as follows.

DOMINANCE OF MULTIPLE-OBJECTIVE SOLUTIONS

An alternative i is dominated if there exists at least one other alternative, e, such that

$$r_{ik} \leq r_{ek} \text{ for all } k \qquad \text{and} \qquad r_{ik} < r_{ek} \text{ for at least one } k \tag{22-1}$$

A dominated alternative is thus inferior to some other alternative for at least one objective and no better for all other objectives. An alternative that is not dominated by any other alternative is called *nondominated* or *efficient*.

Figure 22-1 demonstrates the concept of dominance for the two-objective maximization case. Each axis measures the performance toward one objective. The performance vector $\mathbf{r}_i = (r_{i1}, r_{i2})$ can be depicted as a point in this performance space. All alternatives denoted by empty circles are dominated by at least one alternative shown by a solid circle. Note that nondominated alternatives form the northeast boundary in the performance space. This boundary or the set of nondominated alternatives is called the *efficient frontier*.

Efficient solution methods find all or a specified subset of solutions on the efficient frontier. The actual choice of which alternative course of action to take is then left up to the intuitive judgment of the decision maker—no easy task in most cases. Section 22-6 looks at efficient solutions in a linear programming framework.

Interactive solution methods are designed to find the decision maker's most preferred solution through a dialogue, usually by means of an interactive computer program. The dialogue begins by presenting the decision maker with a feasible solution to the problem. Next, he or she is asked to provide tradeoff information for small

Figure 22-1. *Efficient solutions and efficient frontier.*

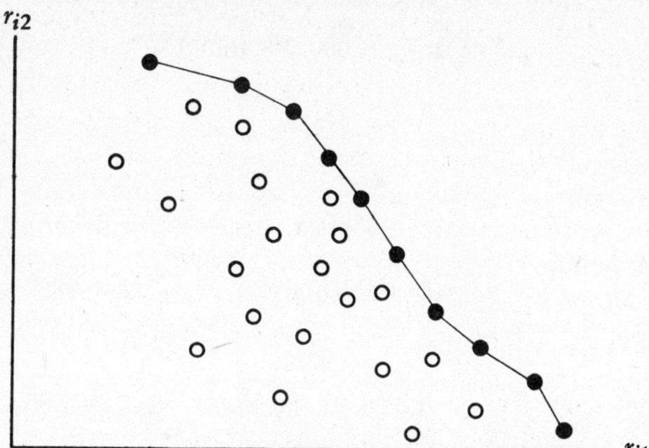

local deviations from this initial solution. These tradeoffs are the input in an algorithm—usually a mathematical program—to find a new and better feasible solution. This new solution is again submitted to the decision maker to solicit new tradeoffs. The process stops when the decision maker no longer wishes to revise the tradeoff relations. At this point (assuming the functions are well behaved), the preferred solution has been located. The papers by Geoffrion (1972) and Zionts (1976) listed in the references present examples of this approach.

As will become obvious over the following sections, this grouping (as well as other classifications) is by no means exhaustive, nor are the groups truly mutually exclusive. For instance, several efficient solution methods use a sequence of weights on the objective functions to find all efficient solutions, thus combining concepts of the first two groups.

22-3 THE SIMPLEX METHOD FOR PREEMPTIVE GOAL PROGRAMMING

In this section, we show how the simplex method can be adapted to find optimal solutions to preemptive goal programming problems. We shall use the media mix problem of Section 2-14. Please read it again now.

The problem involves three goals. Let our objectives be to minimize the following deviation from each goal target:

(22-2) $$\text{minimize } z^{(1)} = s_1^- + s_1^+ \qquad \text{(goal 1 deviations)}$$

(22-3) $$\text{minimize } z^{(2)} = s_2^- + s_2^+ \qquad \text{(goal 2 deviations)}$$

(22-4) $$\text{minimize } z^{(3)} = 2s_2^- + s_3^+ \qquad \text{(goal 3 deviations)}$$

where s_i^- denotes underachievement and s_i^+ denotes overachievement of goal i. We view an underachievement of goal 3 as being twice as undesirable as an overachievement. These objectives are subject to the following constraints:

$$3000x_1 + 2000x_2 \leqslant 16000 \qquad \text{(budget)}$$

$$x_1 \leqslant 4 \qquad \text{(insertions in X)}$$

$$x_2 \leqslant 5 \qquad \text{(insertion in Y)}$$

(22-5)
$$0.04x_1 + 0.06x_2 + s_1^- - s_1^+ = 0.32 \qquad \text{(goal 1)}$$

$$0.072x_1 + 0.036x_2 + s_2^- - s_2^+ = 0.288 \qquad \text{(goal 2)}$$

$$x_1 - 2x_2 + s_3^- - s_3^+ = 0 \qquad \text{(goal 3)}$$

$$x_j \geqslant 0, \quad \text{for all } j; \qquad s_i^-, s_i^+ \geqslant 0, \quad \text{for all } i$$

In preemptive programming, each goal is assigned a priority level k, denoted by P_k, $k = 1, 2, 3, \ldots$. The lower the value of k, the higher the priority assigned. Several goals may have the same priority level. A goal with a higher priority level is always given absolute preference over all goals with lower priority levels. We shall assign the highest priority P_1 to goal 1 (desired reach on primary group), the next priority P_2 to goal 2 (desired reach on secondary group), and the lowest priority P_3 to goal 3 (number of insertions in X and Y). This priority structure is usually expressed mathematically by the following short-hand notation:

(22-6)
$$\text{minimize } P_1(s_1^- + s_1^+) + P_2(s_2^- + s_2^+) + P_3(2s_3^- + s_3^+)$$

which replaces the individual objective functions (22-2) to (22-4). P_k denotes the priority weight, $P_1 >>> P_2 >>> P_3$. The weights P_k are not given any specific numerical values, and hence do not imply any tradeoffs between goals. They only indicate the priority level of each goal. On the other hand, any weights assigned to individual goals within the same priority level reflect tradeoff relations, as in the weighted-sum goal programming approach. To solve such a problem, we have each priority level give rise to a separate objective function. In our example, expressions (22-2) to (22-4) correspond to the three individual priority level objective functions. We first find the optimal solution for the highest priority level, ignoring any lower priority level objective functions. If there are any alternative optimal solutions, these become the feasible region for the next highest priority level. We continue in this fashion until either all individual priority level objective functions have been optimized or a unique optimal solution has been found for some priority level. At that point, no further improvements on lower priority level goals can be achieved.

Let us now apply this procedure to the media mix problem. Using the simplex method for maximizing the objective function in Chapter 3, we first find the optimal solution to objective function (22-2). Note that we maximize the negative of (22-2), as shown in tableau 1 of Table 22-1. The superscripts on the $(z_j - c_j)^{(k)}$ rows identify the priority level solved at that iteration. The optimal solution is reached in three iterations, as shown in tableau 3 (tableau 2 is not shown). The solution occurs at point E in Figure 2-14 of Chapter 2.

Table 22-1. *Simplex tableaux for preemptive goal programming—The media mix problem*

				Priority Levels					$-P_1$	$-P_1$	$-P_2$	$-P_2$	$-2P_3$	$-P_3$	
	c_j	Basis	Solution	x_1	x_2	x_3	x_4	x_5	s_1^-	s_1^+	s_2^-	s_2^+	s_3^-	s_3^+	Ratio
1	0	x_3	16,000	3000	2000	1									9
	0	x_4	4	1	0		1								∞
	0	x_5	5	0	(1)			1							5
	−1	s_1^-	0.32	0.04	0.06				1	−1					5.3333
	0	s_2^-	0.288	0.072	0.036						1	−1			8
	0	s_3^-	0	1	−2								1	−1	0
	$(z_j - c_j)^{(1)}$		−0.32	−0.04	−0.06 ↑	0	0	0	0	2					
3	0	x_3	4500	0	0	1		2500	−75,000	75,000					2.6
	0	x_4	3.5	0	0		1	1.5	−25	25					2.3333
	0	x_2	5	0	1			1	0	0					5
	0	x_1	0.5	1	0			−1.5	25	−25					—
	−1	s_2^-	0.072	0	0			(0.072)	−1.8	1.8	1	−1			1
	0	s_3^-	9.5	0	0			3.5	−25	25			1	−1	2.5714
	$(z_j - c_j)^{(1)}$		0	0	0	0	0	0	1	1	0	0	0	0	
	$(z_j - c_j)^{(2)}$		−0.072	0	0	0	0	−0.072 ↑			0	2	0	0	
4	0	x_3	2000	0	0	1		0							
	0	x_4	2	0	0		1	0							
	0	x_2	4	0	1			0							
	0	x_1	2	1	0			0							
	0	x_5	1	0	0			1			13.889	−13.889			
	−2	s_3^-	6	0	0			0			−48.61	48.61	1	−1	
	$(z_j - c_j)^{(2)}$		0	0	0	0	0	0			1	1	0	0	
	$(z_j - c_j)^{(3)}$		−12	0	0	0	0	0					0	3	

Remember that any nonbasic variables with $(z_j - c_j) = 0$ indicate the existence of alternative optimal solutions. x_1, x_2, x_5, s_2^+, and s_3^+ have zero $(z_j - c_j)^{(1)}$ values. Hence, alternative optimal solutions exist. They are given by the heavy line from E to H in Figure 2-14. This is the set of feasible solutions to all lower priority level objective functions. We now proceed to optimize the second-level objective function (22-3).

In order to remain within the reduced feasible region, we only retain the current basic variables and those nonbasic variables with zero $(z_j - c_j)$ values for objective function 22-2.

SIMPLEX CRITERION FOR ELIMINATION OF VARIABLES IN PREEMPTIVE GOAL PROGRAMMING

If $(z_j - c_j)^{(k)} > 0$ for any variable x_j at an optimal solution to priority k goals, that variable is excluded from entering any basis for priority ℓ goals where $\ell > k$.

Applying this rule for $\ell > 1$, we block off the columns for s_1^- and s_1^+ in tableau 4 of Table 22-1. The $(z_j - c_j)^{(1)}$ row is now no longer needed. We now add to tableau 3 a new row with the $(z_j - c_j)^{(2)}$ values for the permissible variables in objective function (22-3). The $(z_j - c_j)^{(2)}$ values, evaluated at the solution of tableau 3, are obtained by the rules of postoptimal analysis (see Section 5-1). For example,

$$(z_5 - c_5)^{(2)} = $$
$$2500(0) + 1.5(0) + 1(0) + (-1.5)(0) + 0.072(-1) + 3.5(0) - 0 = -0.072$$

The objective function value of $z^{(2)}$ at this basic solution is -0.072. From the $(z_j - c_j)^{(2)}$ row, we see that the solution of tableau 3 is not optimal. At iteration 4, the optimal solution for (22-3) is reached. It corresponds to point G in Figure 2-14. Of the three remaining nonbasic variables, s_3^- has a $(z_j - c_j)^{(2)}$ value of zero, indicating alternative optima for the first and second priority level goals. The columns for s_2^- and s_2^+ are now also blocked off.

Next we introduce the third priority level objective function (22-4). The $(z_j - c_j)^{(3)}$ row for the further reduced set of permissible variables is added to tableau 4. All $(z_j - c_j)^{(3)}$ are nonnegative. Hence, the solution of tableau 4 is optimal. Furthermore, no alternative optima exist anymore. The final optimal solution is $x_1 = 2$, $x_2 = 4$, and $s_3^- = 6$.

Note that preemptive goal programming relies heavily on the existence of alternative optimal solutions to achieve any of the lower priority goals. Fortunately, the presence of the goal constraints containing the deviational variables seems to favor this.

22-4 MINSUM AND MINMAX MULTIPLE-OBJECTIVE LINEAR PROGRAMMING

Let us now look at the media mix problem of Section 2-14 in its original form of maximizing the reach of each population group. (For simplicity, we drop the third goal.) Mathematically, the problem can be stated as

$$\text{(22-7)}\quad \begin{aligned} &\text{maximize} && 0.04x_1 + 0.06x_2 && \text{(goal 1)} \\ &\text{maximize} && 0.072x_1 + 0.036x_2 && \text{(goal 2)} \end{aligned}$$

$$\text{(22-8)}\quad \begin{aligned} &\text{subject to} && x_1 \leqslant 4 && \text{(number of insertions in X)} \\ & && x_2 \leqslant 5 && \text{(number of insertions in Y)} \\ & && 3000x_1 + 2000x_2 \leqslant 16{,}000 && \text{(budget)} \\ & && x_1, x_2 \geqslant 0 \end{aligned}$$

Except by some rather fortunate coincidence, the maxima of the two objective functions will not be obtained for the same values of the decision variables. As shown in Figure 22-2, the maximum of goal 1 is 0.38 and occurs at point E, while the maximum of goal 2 is 0.36 and occurs at point A. (Note that these maxima are in fact larger by 0.48 and 0.412, respectively—the constants we dropped when we formulated the original objective function in Section 2-14.) No feasible solution will exceed these maxima, and they cannot be achieved for both goals simultaneously. In fact, these maxima could be viewed as the "ideal" solution or as desirable targets to aim for.

Any feasible solution will have to be a compromise. The difference s_k between each target and the actually achieved goal level represents the amount of underachievement for goal k. No overachievement is possible. As for goal programming, each objective function of (22-7) can be expressed as a target constraint:

$$\text{(22-9)}\quad \begin{aligned} 0.04x_1 + 0.06x_2 + s_1 &= 0.38 && \text{(goal 1)} \\ 0.072x_1 + 0.036x_2 + s_2 &= 0.36 && \text{(goal 2)} \end{aligned}$$

The optimizing criterion is to minimize some suitable metric for the distance from the ideal solution.

Each deviational variable is expressed in the same units as the corresponding goal. The units of measurement may thus be different from goal to goal. Most decision makers would have difficulties in specifying tradeoffs between goals measured in different units. They would find it easier to consider tradeoffs in terms of percentage deviations from the targets. This is readily accomplished by redefining each deviational variable as the fractional deviation v_k from its target T_k:

$$\text{(22-10)}\quad v_k = s_k/T_k \quad \text{or} \quad s_k = T_k v_k$$

Figure 22-2. *Media selection problem.*

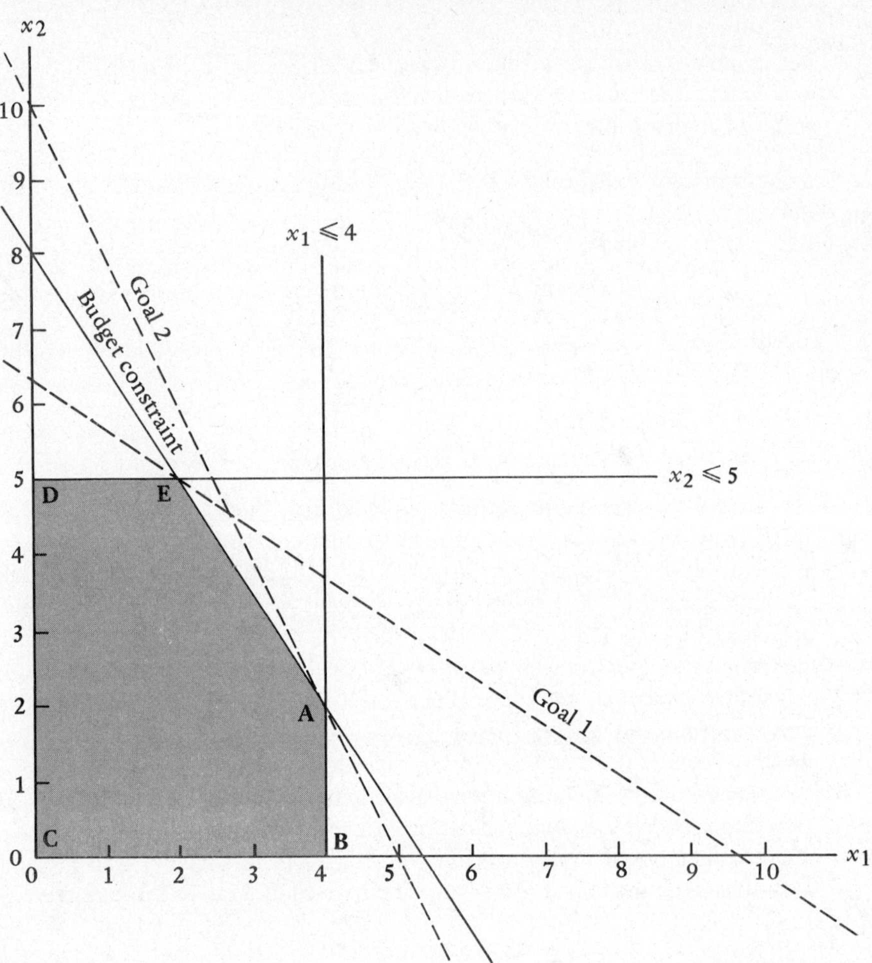

$(1 - v_k)$ (100 percent) represents the percentage goal achievement. With this change of variables, expressions (22-9) can now be rewritten as

(22-11)

$$0.04x_1 + 0.06x_2 + 0.38v_1 = 0.38 \quad \text{(goal 1)}$$

$$0.072x_1 + 0.036x_2 + 0.36v_2 = 0.36 \quad \text{(goal 2)}$$

Note that this formulation is based on the assumption that all targets are positive but finite, i.e., $0 < T_k < \infty$, for all k. Although this is usually a reasonable assumption, it may happen that some T_k value is zero. In such a case, a different normalizing constant has to be used.

The most general form of matrix is the *Euclidean distance:*

$$\left[\sum_{k=1}^{K} (w_k v_k)^p\right]^{1/p} \tag{22-12}$$

where w_k is the weight or penalty given to deviations from goal k. The criterion is to minimize this distance metric. Except for $p = 1$ and $p = \infty$, this is a nonlinear programming problem. For $p = 1$, (22-12) simplifies to the weighted sum of fractional deviations from the targets. This is the *MINSUM formulation.* For our example, setting $p = 1$ yields the following linear program:

$$\begin{aligned}
&\text{minimize } w_1v_1 + w_2v_2 \\
&\text{subject to} \qquad x_1 \leq 4 \\
&\qquad x_2 \leq 5 \\
&\qquad 3000x_1 + 2000x_2 \leq 16{,}000 \\
&\qquad 0.04x_1 + 0.06x_2 + 0.38v_1 = 0.38 \qquad \text{(goal 1)} \\
&\qquad 0.072x_1 + 0.036x_2 + 0.36v_2 = 0.36 \qquad \text{(goal 2)} \\
&\qquad x_1, x_2, v_1, v_2 \geq 0
\end{aligned} \tag{22-13}$$

The optimal solution will occur at an extreme point of the feasible region to the original constraints (22-8). On the basis of Figure 22-2, verify that Table 22-2 summarizes the response of the optimal solution to various weight combinations (w_1, w_2). (*Hint:* The ratio 3000/2000 is equal to the negative of the budget constraint slope.)

Table 22-2. *Optimal solutions to MINSUM formulations of the media mix problem*

Weight	Optimal Value of x_1	x_2	v_1	v_2	Achievement of Goal 1	Goal 2	Point in Figure 22-2
$w_1 \geq (3000/2000)w_2$	2	5	0	0.1	100%	90%	E
$w_1 \leq (3000/2000)w_2$	4	2	0.2632	0	73.68%	100%	A

Note that a potentially minor change in weights may cause the optimal solution to change quite abruptly by jumping to an adjacent extreme point of the feasible region. This feature holds for all MINSUM formulations. It goes contrary to what intuition would indicate. A decision maker would expect the optimal solution to respond gradually to repeated small changes in the weight structure.

We can overcome this shortcoming by letting p in (22-12) become infinitely large, i.e., $p \to \infty$. The largest deviation will now dominate all other deviations. Hence, we can find the optimal solution associated with minimizing (22-12) by minimizing the maximum weighted deviation of any goal achievement from the ideal solution. The problem is then transformed into the following linear program:

$$\begin{aligned}
&\text{minimize } v \\
&\text{subject to } x_1 \leq 4 \\
&\qquad x_2 \leq 5 \\
&3000x_1 + 2000x_2 \leq 16000 \qquad (22\text{-}14)\\
&0.04x_1 + 0.06x_2 + (0.38/w_1)v \geq 0.38 \qquad \text{(goal 1)}\\
&0.072x_1 + 0.036x_2 + (0.36/w_2)v \geq 0.36 \qquad \text{(goal 2)}\\
&x_1, x_2, v \geq 0
\end{aligned}$$

This is the MINMAX formulation. Note that we replaced the individual deviation variables with a single deviation variable v, which measures the largest fractional deviation of any goal achievement from the ideal. This explains why the equality constraints for the goals in (22-11) had to be converted to $\geq$ constraints.

At the optimal solution, at least one of the goal constraints is satisfied as a strict equality, while all remaining goal constraints may have slack. The goal constraint for which equality holds is the one with the largest deviation from its target. We wish to minimize this maximum deviation, hence the name MINMAX.

In order to allow deviations from the target to be weighted differently, we also incorporate the weights directly into the goal constraints. The deviational variable is thereby redefined as the largest weighted fractional deviation, which differs from the unweighted fractional deviation by a factor equal to the corresponding weight.

Table 22-3. *Optimal solutions to MINMAX formulation of the media mix problem*

Weight		Optimal Value of			Achievement of	
w_1	w_2	x_1	x_2	v	Goal 1	Goal 2
1	0	2	5	0.1	100%	90%
10	1	2.073	4.890	0.0963	99.04%	90.37%
1	1	2.551	4.174	0.0725	92.75%	92.75%
1	10	3.583	2.625	0.2083	79.17%	97.92%
0	1	4	2	0.2632	73.68%	100%

Table 22-3 shows the optimal solution for a number of relative weight assignments on the two goals. Note now that the optimal solution, except in the degenerate case where one of the weights is set to zero, does not occur at an extreme point of the feasible region to the original constraints (22-8), but occurs somewhere on the boundary between extreme points. The higher a given weight assigned to a goal, the closer the percentage achievement level is to its maximum. This is a general feature of MINMAX formulations. As a result, the optimal solution responds gradually and smoothly to changes in the weights. The MINMAX formulation also tends to give a more equitable distribution to the percentage goal achievements than the MINSUM formulation.

The major attraction of both the MINSUM and the MINMAX formulations comes from their simplicity and the fact that the original multiple-objective problem is converted into a conventional linear program. The optimal solution can thus be found by the simplex method. Furthermore, the problem can be subjected to the powerful machinery of postoptimal analysis available for linear programming.

The next section shows how the MINMAX approach can be used to analyze the multiple-use land management problem outlined earlier.

22-5 AN APPLICATION TO MULTIPLE-USE LAND MANAGEMENT

Consider again the land use management problem outlined in Section 22-1. We will now show how multiple-objective linear programming based on a MINMAX formulation can be used to help the area manager perform the difficult task of reconciling conflicting objectives. To cut the problem down to text book size, consider a small area consisting of two tracts. Tract A covers 1200 acres; tract B, 5400 acres. The boundaries of each tract were chosen in such a manner that the land contained in each is homogeneous in terms of its potential uses. In our case, the potential uses are (numbered 1 to 5) as follows:

Tract A	Tract B
Sheep grazing (1)	Sheep grazing (1)
Open cast coal mining (2)	Wildlife management (3)
Wildlife management (3)	Watershed management (4)
Watershed management (4)	Four-wheel-drive vehicle use (5)

Some of these uses are compatible, others not. It is obvious that the same acre cannot be used in the same time interval for sheep grazing and coal mining, but sheep grazing and wildlife management may be pursued side by side. The BLM considers sound watershed management policies as an integral part of both grazing and mining, so as to reduce the impact of these activities on sedimentation in adjoining rivers. This implies that our activity watershed management as defined earlier assumes the absence of grazing or mining. In other words, these three uses are also mutually and collectively incompatible. Finally, open cast mining and wildlife management are also considered incompatible uses.

Land is allocated to a given use with a view to procuring certain desirable outputs or limiting certain undesirable consequences. Maximizing desirable outputs and minimizing undesirable ones are the objectives of the land use plan. Land used for sheep grazing produces as primary output animal feed, measured in stocking rates (say, animals fattened per year). Open cast coal mining produces coal, measured in tons.

Wildlife management enhances the habitat for big game, hunted for recreation. How could we measure a qualitative output that may mean different things to different users? We could use a surrogate measure, such as the number of recreation person-days that an area may attract. This would be difficult to estimate and also depend highly on the exact location of each acre. Instead, it may be more useful to measure recreation along an arbitrary relative scale, ranging from -5 to $+5$, where $+5$ indicates the largest positive or most desirable impact that can be achieved, -5 the largest negative or most undesirable impact, and 0 a neutral or no impact. Experience indicates that decision makers are quite capable of making such subjective value judgments and that this approach is effective in capturing the relative importance of intangible outputs of this sort. This is the approach used for the output of wildlife management. Watershed management reduces sedimentation in the catchment rivers and lakes. If the areas are highly homogeneous as to sediment yield, it may be possible to express this yield in terms of tons of sediment increase or decrease per year, as compared to the status quo. Alternatively, the effect on sediment yield could again be expressed along a relative scale from -5 to $+5$, similar to the effect of recreation, with $+5$ representing the most positive impact (largest reduction in sediment yield). Finally, four-wheel-drive vehicle use is also a recreational activity. Assuming that it is commensurable with recreation from hunting, the recreational output of both uses is best expressed along the same relative scale.

Each land use also implies inputs or outputs of funds. Grazing produces rental income, mining produces royalties, wildlife management produces hunting fees offset by rangers' salaries, four-wheel-drive vehicle use requires funds for bridge and river ford construction and maintenance, etc., and watershed management requires construction funds for river course alterations and afforestation.

There are secondary or indirect outputs for some land uses. For instance, mining not only produces coal, but also destroys the scenic value of the area and hence has a negative impact on recreation even in adjoining tracts. This negative effect reduces the recreational output of the area as a whole. In fact, it might result in a total negative recreational output. This impact occurs whether or not a tract is promoted for recreation. On the other hand, the negative effect of grazing on the recreational output of wildlife management and, similarly, the negative effect of wildlife management on the output of grazing will occur only if these uses exist together on the same acre. Hence, our formulation will have to reflect this.

Table 22-4 lists the primary and secondary outputs per acre for each basic land use. We assume they are identical for both tracts. For instance, one acre of land will allow three sheep to be fattened per year (= primary output), while reducing the recreational output by 1 (= secondary output of grazing) and generating rental income of \$300 over the planning horizon. Expressing all outputs on a per acre basis implies constant returns to scale. Although the outputs from grazing and mining may be approximately linear, linearity is unlikely to hold true over the entire range of acreage allocated for wildlife management, four-wheel-drive vehicle use, and watershed management. Allocations up to some threshold may result in a zero output. Above that level, the output may initially increase more than proportionately, settling ultimately to some constant rate (increasing marginal returns followed by constant marginal

Table 22-4. *Primary and secondary outputs of each land use per acre*

Output	Grazing	Mining	Wildlife Management	Watershed Management	Four-Wheel-Drive Vehicle
Animal-years	3	0	−0.5	0	0
Coal (1000 tons)	0	4	0	0	0
Recreation impact	−1	−5	2	0	3
Sediment impact	−1	−3	1	5	−3
Present value of funds ($1000)	0.3	1	0.02	−0.05	−0.04

returns). Furthermore, the various areas allocated to each use need to be largely contiguous for the desired effects to occur. It is thus important that once the optimal solution has been found, the validity of the output coefficients be verified. If necessary, coefficients should be adjusted appropriately, and the problem resolved.

We are now ready to formulate the problem mathematically. The acreages in each tract allocated to the four uses are our decision variables. However, to properly account for the mutual reduction in output if grazing and wildlife management occur jointly on the same acre, we introduce a combined use "grazing-cum-wildlife management." These three uses thus become mutually exclusive in addition to the incompatibility restrictions discussed earlier.

Consider first tract A. The incompatibility restriction for grazing (variable AGRAZE), grazing-cum-wildlife management (AGRWLD), coal mining (AMINE), and watershed management (AWATER) forbids the allocation of the same acre to all four uses. However, each use can be pursued on a separate part of tract A. Hence, the sum of the acreages allocated to them cannot exceed the available acreage:

$$\text{(TRACTA1)} \quad \text{AGRAZE} + \text{AGRWLD} + \text{AMINE} + \text{AWATER} \leq 1200$$

Similarly, grazing, mining, and wildlife management (AWILD) are incompatible:

$$\text{(TRACTA2)} \quad \text{AGRAZE} + \text{AGRWLD} + \text{AMINE} + \text{AWILD} \leq 1200$$

For tract B, the incompatibility occurs between grazing (BGRAZE and BGRWLD) and watershed management (BWATER):

$$\text{(TRACTB1)} \quad \text{BGRAZE} + \text{BGRWLD} + \text{BWATER} \leq 5400$$

and between grazing and wildlife management (BWILD):

$$\text{(TRACTB2)} \quad \text{BGRAZE} + \text{BGRWLD} + \text{BWILD} \leq 5400$$

All uses are also individually restricted by the upper limit of the acreage in each tract. There is, though, no need to insert upper bounds for those variables that already appear in the above incompatibility constraints. This leaves only the upper bound on four-wheel-drive vehicle use:

$$\text{(TRACTB3)} \quad \text{B4 WHEEL} \leq 5400$$

The objectives of the land use plan are to maximize grazing output, maximize coal recovered, maximize recreational value, maximize sediment reduction, and maximize funds generated. Each row in Table 22-4 contains the numerical data needed to formulate one of these five objective functions. Consider grazing. Each acre of tract A or tract B allocated to grazing allows 3 animals to be fattened per year, while the same acre allocated jointly to wildlife management reduces this output by 0.5. Hence, the grazing objective function is

(OBJGRAZE) maximize 3 AGRAZE + (3 − 0.5) AGRWLD
+ 3 BGRAZE + (3 − 0.5) BGRWLD

Similarly, for the other four objective functions,

(OBJCOAL) maximize 4 AMINE
(OBJRECR) maximize (2 − 1) AGRWLD − 5 AMINE + 2 AWILD
+ (2 − 1) BGRWLD + 2 BWILD + 3 B4WHEEL
(OBJSEDMT) maximize −1 AGRAZE + (1 − 1) AGRWLD − 3 AMINE
+ 1 AWILD + 5 AWATER − 1 BGRAZE
+ (1 − 1) BGRWLD + 1 BWILD
+ 5 BWATER − 3 B4WHEEL
(OBJFUNDS) maximize 0.3 AGRAZE + (0.3 + 0.02) AGRWLD + 1 AMINE
+ 0.02 AWILD − 0.05 AWATER + 0.3 BGRAZE
+ (0.3 + 0.02) BGRWLD + 0.02 BWILD
− 0.05 BWATER − 0.04 B4WHEEL

Restricting all decision variables to nonnegative values completes the formulation of the problem as a multiple-objective linear program.

For the MINMAX formulation, we have to find first the target value for each objective. Solving the five single-objective linear programs (the optimal solutions can actually be found by inspection for this simple example), we get

Objective	OBJGRAZE	OBJCOAL	OBJRECR	OBJSEDMT	OBJFUNDS
Target value	19,800	4800	29,400	39,600	2928

The individual objective optima are used to generate the target constraints:

(MAXGRAZE) 3 AGRAZE + 2.5 AGRWLD + 3 BGRAZE + 2.5 BGRWLD
+ $(19800/w_1)v \geq 19800$
(MAXCOAL) 4 AMINE + $(4800/w_2)\ v \geq 4800$
(MAXRECR) AGRWLD − 5 AMINE + 2 AWILD + BRGWLD
+ 2 BWILD + 3 B4WHEEL + $(29400/w_3)v \geq 29400$
(MAXSEDMT) −AGRAZE − 3 AMINE + AWILD + 5 AWATER
− BGRAZE + BWILD + 5 BWATER − 3 B4WHEEL
+ $(39600/w_4)v \geq 39600$
(MAXFUNDS) 0.3 AGRAZE + 0.32 AGRWLD + AMINE + 0.02 AWILD
− 0.05 AWATER + 0.3 BGRAZE + 0.32 BGRWLD
+ 0.02 BWILD − 0.05 BWATER − 0.04 B4WHEEL
+ $(2928/w_5)v \geq 2928$

where w_k are the weights assigned to each objective. The objective function of the MINMAX problem is the minimization of the maximum deviation, given by

(OBJMINMAX) minimize v

subject to the cross-compatibility and target constraints. Table 22-5 summarizes the optimal solution for various weight structures on the five objectives.

Table 22-5. *Land-use solution for various objective weights*

Case	Objective	Weight	Percent Achievement	Land Use	Tract A	Tract B
1	animal years	1	36.8	sheep grazing	0	2911 (2911)
	coal (1000 tons)	1	36.8	coal mining	441	—
	recreation	1	36.8	wildlife mgt	759	5400 (2911)
	sediment	1	36.8	watershed mgt	759	2489
	funds ($1000)	1	41.9	four-wheel-drive	—	1202
2	animal years	10	89.6	sheep grazing	510	5400
	coal (1000 tons)	1	0	coal mining	0	—
	recreation	1	4.7	wildlife mgt	690	0
	sediment	1	−4.5	watershed mgt	690	0
	funds ($1000)	1	59.9	four-wheel-drive	—	0
3	animal years	1	27.3	sheep grazing	0	1799
	coal (1000 tons)	10	92.7	coal mining	1113	—
	recreation	1	27.3	wildlife mgt	87	3601
	sediment	1	27.3	watershed mgt	87	3601
	funds ($1000)	1	49.8	four-wheel-drive	—	2067
4	animal years	1	19.6	sheep grazing	0	1549 (1549)
	coal (1000 tons)	1	12.3	coal mining	147	—
	recreation	10	91.2	wildlife mgt	1053	5400 (1549)
	sediment	1	12.3	watershed mgt	0	3319
	funds ($1000)	1	12.3	four-wheel-drive	—	5400
5	animal years	1	3.9	sheep grazing	0	260
	coal (1000 tons)	1	18.4	coal mining	221	—
	recreation	1	37.9	wildlife mgt	979	5140
	sediment	10	90.4	watershed mgt	979	5140
	funds ($1000)	1	3.9	four-wheel-drive	—	0
6	animal years	1	58.0	sheep grazing	0	4596 (4596)
	coal (1000 tons)	1	100.0	coal mining	1200	—
	recreation	1	2.1	wildlife mgt	0	5400 (4596)
	sediment	1	2.1	watershed mgt	0	804
	funds ($1000)	10	90.2	four-wheel-drive	—	135
7	animal years	1	14.9	sheep grazing	894 (894)	287 (287)
	coal (1000 tons)	1	25.5	coal mining	306	—
	recreation	2	57.5	wildlife mgt	894 (894)	5400 (287)
	sediment	2	57.5	watershed mgt	0	5113
	funds ($1000)	1	14.9	four-wheel-drive	—	2337

An equal weight structure gives a well-balanced percentage achievement for all objectives, whereas emphasis on one objective only may have quite serious effects on the achievement of other objectives. For instance, emphasis on grazing even produces a negative result on sedimentation. Surprisingly, emphasis on coal mining, given the size of tract A, still produces a fair balance among the various objectives. Experimentation with various weight structures will allow the planning officer to explore which sacrifices in the achievement of some objectives produces good compromise solutions.

22-6 EFFICIENT SOLUTION METHODS AND INTERACTIVE APPROACHES

Without externalizing the decision maker's tradeoff relations between various goals, the best an operations researcher can do is to present the decision maker with all efficient solutions to the problem. It is then up to the decision maker to select, on an intuitive basis, the most preferred from among all efficient solutions. Consider the general form of a multiple-objective linear programming problem:

$$\text{(22-15)} \qquad \begin{aligned} \text{maximize } z_1 &= \sum_j c_{1j}x_j \\ \text{maximize } z_2 &= \sum_j c_{2j}x_j \\ &\vdots \\ \text{maximize } z_K &= \sum_j c_{Kj}x_j \end{aligned}$$

subject to

$$\text{(22-16)} \qquad \sum_j a_{ij}x_j \; (\leqslant, =, \text{ or } \geqslant) \; b_i, \qquad i = 1, 2, \ldots, m$$

$$x_j \geqslant 0, \qquad \text{for all } j$$

From the geometry of linear programming, it follows that efficient solutions can lie only on the boundary of the feasible region, either at an extreme point, along an edge between two adjacent extreme points, or on a face between several adjacent extreme points. The number of efficient solutions is thus infinitely large. However, it also follows that any efficient solution not corresponding to an extreme point can be expressed as a linear combination of efficient solutions at two or more adjacent extreme points. (See Ecker, 1980, for complete specifications.) Therefore, in order to identify all efficient solutions of a multiple objective linear program, all we need is to find all *efficient extreme point solutions.*

Consider again the media mix problem, as given by expressions (22-7) and (22-8). Table 22-6 lists the objective function values of all basic feasible solutions as shown in Figure 22-3. Solutions for points B, C, and D are all dominated by solutions at

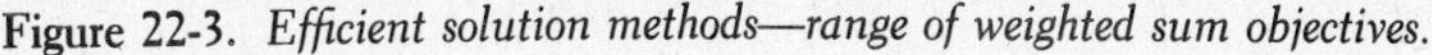

Figure 22-3. *Efficient solution methods—range of weighted sum objectives.*

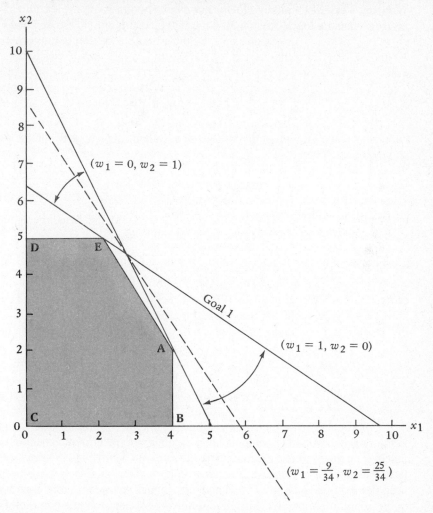

point A, point E, or both. Points A and E yield efficient extreme point solutions, and so do all points along the edge from A to E.

Table 22-6. *Performance levels for all basic feasible solutions of the media mix problem*

Solution Point	Goal 1	Goal 2	Dominated by
A	0.28	0.36	—
B	0.16	0.288	A, E
C	0	0	A, E
D	0.3	0.18	E
E	0.38	0.324	—

The set of all efficient extreme point solutions is a subset of all basic feasible solutions. Therefore, finding all efficient extreme point solutions is computationally almost as demanding as finding all basic feasible solutions. It can be shown that if $\mathbf{x}^* = (x_1^*, x_2^*, \ldots, x_n^*)$ represents an efficient extreme point solution to problem (22-15) and (22-16), then there exists a set of positive weights $\mathbf{w}^* = (w_1^*, w_2^*, \ldots, w_K^*)$, with

$$\sum_{k=1}^{K} w_k^* = 1 \qquad \text{and} \qquad w_k^* > 0, \qquad \text{for all } k \tag{22-17}$$

such that $\mathbf{x}$ is the solution of the following equivalent single-objective linear programming problem:

$$\text{maximize } z = \sum_{k=1}^{K} w_k^* \sum_{j=1}^{n} c_{kj} x_j \tag{22-18}$$

subject to (22-16) and (22-17). This property serves as the basis for a number of algorithms to find all efficient extreme point solutions.

Geometrically, expression (22-18) represents a *hyperplane* (n-dimensional plane) touching the boundary of the feasible region. As the weights change, it is tilted into a new position (its *n-dimensional slope* changes). If it is tilted sufficiently, another extreme point becomes optimal. If it is rotated through all feasible weight combinations, it will go sequentially through all efficient extreme points. Figure 22-3 depicts this property for the media mix problem. For $[w_1 = 1, w_2 = 0]$ the weighted-sum objective function $w_1 \Sigma c_{1j} x_j + w_2 \Sigma c_{2j} x_j$ coincides with the goal 1 line. As w_1 decreases and w_2 increases, the weighted-sum objective function tilts forward, until at $[w_1 = 0, w_2 = 1]$ it coincides with the goal 2 line. Any weight structure of $(w_1 \leq 9/34, w_2 = 1 - w_1)$ generates the efficient extreme point solution at point A, while $(w_1 \geq 9/34, w_2 = 1 - w_1)$ yields the point E solution.

Unfortunately, finding all efficient extreme point solutions of real-life problems is still largely beyond the computational capability of the current generation of computers. The only possible exceptions are the so-called *bicriterion problems*—i.e., problems with only two objective functions—for which several special algorithms have been devised (see Cohon, 1979). There are, though, two even more basic objections to this solution philosophy. First, the number of efficient extreme point solutions that exist for even a small problem is usually very large. Second, the "preferred" solution may in fact be an efficient nonbasic solution. Few decision makers will thus be able to identify the most preferred efficient extreme point or the set of efficient extreme points that contain the preferred solution.

There is, therefore, the need either to present the decision maker only with a sufficiently small subset of all efficient extreme points—generated so as to include the decision maker's most preferred solution(s)—or to search for the most preferred solution(s) interactively.

One such approach is *Steuer's interval criterion weight method* (Steuer, 1976). From property (22-17) it follows that a decision maker's preferred solution implies a given weight structure $\hat{w}$. (Assume for simplicity that the preferred solution is an extreme point solution.) If the decision maker were able to specify this weight structure, the preferred solution could be found by solving problem (21-18). Steuer takes the premise that, although the decision maker cannot specify the exact weight structure, he or she will at least be capable of specifying for each objective k an interval, (l_k, h_k), which most likely contains the true weight $\hat{w}_k$. If these intervals are sufficiently small, this will reduce the number of efficient extreme points to be found to a small fraction of the total. Steuer adapts this method for interactive use (1977). He starts out by presenting the decision maker with a small sample of efficient extreme points, evenly distributed over the solution space corresponding to the intervals on the weights and specified as initial input. The decision maker is then asked to indicate which of the efficient extreme points is the most attractive one. Steuer uses this response to shift and contract the weight intervals, which are then used to generate a new sample of evenly spaced efficient extreme points. This interactive process continues until the decision maker signals that the most preferred solution has been found or asks that all efficient extreme points associated with the most recent set of weight intervals be generated. (For several other interactive methods, see the references at the end of this chapter.)

22-7 DECISION ANALYSIS UNDER UNCERTAINTY WITH MULTIATTRIBUTE OUTCOMES

In Sections 1-14 and 11-7, we studied how utility functions can be used to measure the true worth of a course of actions. In this and the next three sections, we will explore how this approach, under certain assumptions, can be extended to analyze multiobjective decision problems under uncertainty. Before proceeding, read Sections 1-14 and 11-7 again.

To set the stage, imagine that you are the director of a sea search and rescue service. Your job is to decide how best to commit the resources available to the service. You consider yourself accountable to the sponsors of the service and to the public at large not only for the number of people rescued, but also for the cost of the service and the safety of your air search crews. You thus identify three partially conflicting objectives:

1. Maximize the number of people in distress rescued.
2. Minimize the cost of the service.
3. Maximize the safety of the search crews.

At this point, you may wish to reflect on the moral implications of tradeoffs between these objectives, particularly those involving tradeoffs between lives saved versus costs. Although such tradeoffs may be abhorrent to most people, there is no way to avoid them. Any decision made by the director as to which search strategy to follow implies them.

As now stated, the first objective is not really operational. A mission may fail to rescue the people in distress for reasons beyond the control of the service, such as the weather or actions taken by the people on the missing craft. As a consequence, it is difficult to directly attribute success or failure to the activities of the service. In situations of this sort, we usually look for a suitable *proxy measure*. Clearly, the longer a missing boat becomes overdue, the smaller are the chances of a successful rescue.

Also, the more intensive the search, the more likely it is to locate the craft quickly if it is still in the search area. The intensity of a search is controllable. The number of days a missing craft is overdue is thus a suitable proxy attribute for the first objective.

The total cost of a rescue mission serves as the attribute for the second objective. The third objective is difficult to assess. Conforming to current practice, we may assume that it is translated into operating conditions for the search aircraft, such as whether or not the weather situation permits flying, maximum flying times, and minimum rest periods between flights for the crews. In other words, the third objective takes the form of constraints, which leaves only two objectives.

The service has two aircraft available on a permanent basis. The operating costs of these amount to \$10,000 for each day of flying. A third aircraft can be hired at a day's notice at a cost of \$20,000 per day.

Committing aircraft to a rescue mission takes the form of a strategy. For instance, if no sighting by commercial aircraft occurs on the first day after a missing-boat report is received, one search aircraft may be assigned on the second day. If no sighting is made then, a second aircraft may be committed. A mission is usually abandoned officially after 5 days of unsuccessful search. Each strategy leads to one of several possible outcomes, defined by the two attributes, x_1 for the number of days the missing craft is overdue and x_2 for the cumulative cost of the search mission. We wish to measure the relative worth of each outcome $[x_1, x_2]$ in terms of a single index, its utility. The "preferred" strategy is the one that maximizes the expected utility.

22-8 MULTIATTRIBUTE UTILITY FUNCTIONS—ADDITIVE UTILITIES

We now wish to fit a utility function that reflects the director's assessment of the true worth of any strategy. What simplifying assumptions on the shape of such functions do we have to make so that a method can be applied that is no more difficult than the five-point assessment procedure discussed in Section 11-7?

The strongest reasonable simplification is to assume that the utility of a K-attribute outcome is equal to the weighted sum of K independently and individually derived single-attribute utilities. The weights reflect the decision maker's relative ranking of the various objectives. If $u_k(x_k)$ is the utility function of attribute k and w_k the weight assigned to objective k, the utility of the multiattribute outcome $[x_1, x_2, \ldots, x_K]$ is as follows.

ADDITIVE UTILITY FUNCTIONS

(22-19)
$$u(x_1, x_2, \ldots, x_K) = \sum_{k=1}^{K} w_k u_k(x_k)$$

where usually $\sum_{k=1}^{K} w_k = 1$.

Let us assume that this assumption holds for the search and rescue problem. First, we have to derive the two single-attribute utility functions. It seems fairly plausible that the director is risk averse. This fixes the general shape of the functions. Also, the larger each attribute value, the less preferred the outcome. It is thus convenient to assign the utility 0 to the most preferred and the utility -1 to the least preferred outcome. Past experience indicates that x_1 varies over the range from 0 to 20, while a range from 0 to 100 thousand covers x_2. A further three utility assessments based on indifference statements, say, using reference lotteries, usually suffice so that we can fit a curve through the five points obtained. Figure 22-4 shows, for each attribute, a typical five-point assessment and the corresponding utility function obtained by fitting a curve of the form $b(1 - e^{cx})$ through them. The curve for the first utility function is

(22-20) $$u_1(x_1) = \frac{1}{5.05}(1 - e^{0.09x_1})$$

and for the second it is

(22-21) $$u_2(x_2) = \frac{1}{0.492}(1 - e^{0.004x_2})$$

Next we need weights. If the decision maker is not able to provide the relative importance of each objective directly, the values of the weights or scaling constants can be inferred from a single indifference statement. Assume $w_1 > w_2$. Then the decision maker is asked to specify a value of x_1, so that he or she is indifferent between the following two outcomes: [x_1 at specified value, x_2 at its most preferred value] and [x_1 at its most preferred value, x_2 at its least preferred value]. Say the answer is $x_1 = 11$. Hence

$$u(x_1 = 11, x_2 = 0) = u(x_1 = 0, x_2 = 100)$$
$$w_1u_1(11) + w_2u_2(0) = w_1u_1(0) + w_2u_2(100)$$

Figure 22-4. *Fitted single-attribute utility functions based on five-point assessment procedure.*

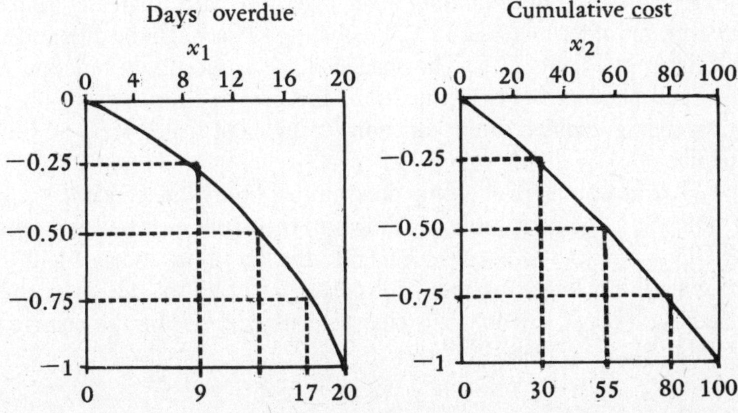

Evaluating $u_1(x_1)$ and $u_2(x_2)$ from (22-20) and (22-21), we get

$$-0.3349w_1 + 0 = 0 + (-1)w_2$$

Also,

$$w_1 + w_2 = 1$$

Solving the last two equations yields $w_1 \cong 0.75$, $w_2 \cong 0.25$. The utility function for the additive utility case is

$$(22\text{-}22) \qquad u(x_1, x_2) = \left[\frac{0.75}{5.05}\right](1 - e^{0.009x_1}) + \left[\frac{0.25}{0.492}\right](1 - e^{0.004x_2})$$

Verify that, as desired, $u(0,0) = 0$ and $u(20, 100) = -1$.

What behavioral assumptions are embodied by additive utility functions? The contribution of each attribute toward the total utility of an outcome is only a function of its own value. It is in no way affected by the values of any other attributes. Furthermore, the decision maker is willing to trade off equal amounts of weighted utilities between attributes.

22-9 MUTUAL UTILITY INDEPENDENCE

Somewhat less restrictive assumptions go under the name of *mutual utility independence*. An attribute is utility independent of all other attributes if the preference ranking of a set of values for this attribute remains constant, in relative terms, for all possible combination of values of the other attributes. Attributes are mutually utility independent if each attribute is utility independent of all other attributes. For the two-attribute case this means that, if x_1 is utility independent of x_2, the basic shape of the (conditional) utility function of x_1 remains the same for all values of x_2, only its scale may change. For instance, the difference in utility of a craft being overdue by 14 days rather than 7 may be 0.2 when the cost of the mission is 0, but 0.25 when the cost is \$70,000, or larger by 20 percent. For x_1 to be utility independent of x_2, the same scaling relationship must hold for all changes in x_1, as x_2 increases from 0 to \$70,000. However, for other increases in x_2, the scaling factor might be different. This property is depicted in Figure 22-5. The shaded shape is the utility function under mutual utility independence. For comparison, the broken lines indicate the shape of the corresponding additive utility function (though not scaled to -1). Study the graph carefully.

What functional relationship does mutual utility independence imply? Consider the outcome $[x_1^*, x_2^*]$. Its utility is shown in the graph as the sum A + B + C. A is equal to $k_1u_1(x_1^*)$; B is equal to $k_2u_2(x_2^*)$. If x_1 is utility independent of x_2, then C represents the change (increase or decrease) in utility of x_1^*, as x_2 shifts from 0 to x_2^*. Let $f_2(x_2^*)k_1u_1(x_1^*)$ denote this change, with $f_2(x_2^*)$ being the change factor. Then the utility of $[x_1^*, x_2^*]$ takes the form

Figure 22-5. *Utility function under mutual utility independence.*

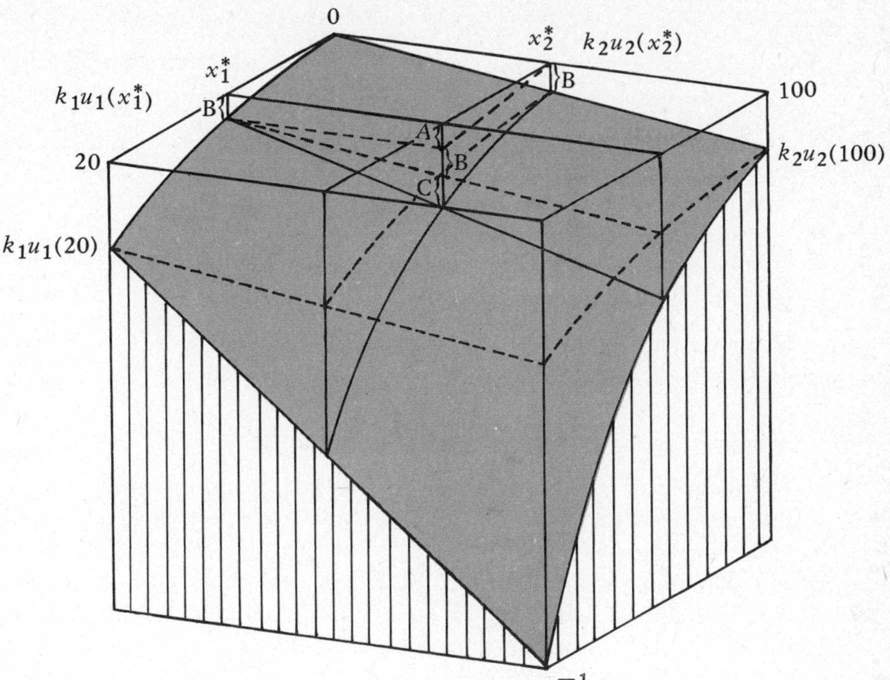

(22-23) $$u(x_1^*, x_2^*) = k_1u_1(x_1^*) + k_2u_2(x_2^*) + f_2(x_2^*)\, k_1u_1(x_1^*)$$

By an analogous reasoning, if x_2 is utility independent of x_1, then C measures also the change in utility of x_2^*, as x_1 shifts from 0 to x_1^*. Let $f_1(x_1^*)$ denote the corresponding change factor. Then

(22-24) $$u(x_1^*, x_2^*) = k_1u_1(x_1^*) + k_2u_2(x_2^*) + f_1(x_1^*)k_2u_2(x_2^*)$$

For mutual utility independence, expressions (22-23) and (22-24) must be equal. They are equal if $f_2(x_2^*)k_1u_1(x_1^*) = f_1(x_1^*)\, k_2u_2(x_2^*)$ or, rearranging terms, if

(22-25) $$f_2(x_2^*)/k_2u_2(x_2^*) = f_1(x_1^*)/k_1u_1(x_1^*) = k_3$$

Solving for $f_1(x_1^*)$ and $f_2(x_2^*)$ in (22-25), we get

(22-26) $$f_1(x_1^*) = k_3k_1u_1(x_1^*) \qquad \text{and} \qquad f_2(x_2^*) = k_3k_2u_2(x_2^*)$$

Substituting $f_1(x_1)$ into (22-24) or $f_2(x_2)$ into (22-23), we get the algebraic condition for mutual utility independence.

TWO-ATTRIBUTE UTILITY FUNCTION
UNDER MUTUAL UTILITY INDEPENDENCE

If attributes x_1 and x_2 are mutually utility independent, then their two-attribute utility function is given by

$$u(x_1, x_2) = k_1u_1(x_1) + k_2u_2(x_2) + k_1k_2k_3u_1(x_1)u_2(x_2) \tag{22-27}$$

The scaling constants, k_1, k_2, and k_3, can be inferred from two indifference statements. First, let us arbitrarily set $u(0, 0) = 0$ and $u(20, 100) = -1$. Next, we solicit the same type of indifference statement as for the additive utility case. There, we found that $[x_1 = 11, x_2 = 0]$ was indifferent to $[x_1 = 0, x_2 = 100]$. Given $u_1(11) = -0.3349$ and $u_2(100) = -1$, we get again

$$(-0.3349)k_1 = (-1)k_2 \quad \text{or} \quad k_2 = 0.3349k_1 \tag{22-28}$$

In the second indifference statement, we ask for an outcome $[x_1, x_2]$ which is indifferent to a 50–50 reference lottery involving the most preferred and the least preferred outcomes, i.e., [0, 0] and [20, 100]. We shall make this choice easier for the decision maker by fixing x_1 to its -0.5 individual utility level—namely, $x_1 = 14$. Assume the answer is $[x_1 = 14, x_2 = 70]$. From the lottery, it follows that $u(14, 70) = -0.5$. We can now evaluate (22-27) for this outcome, using (22-28):

$$u(14, 70) = k_1u_1(14) + 0.3349k_1u_2(70) + k_1(0.3349k_1)\,k_3u(14)u(70) = -0.5$$

By (22-20) and (22-21), $u_1(14) = -0.5001$ and $u_2(70) = -0.6568$. Substituting these values into $u(14, 70)$, collecting terms, and solving for k_3 in terms of k_1, we find k_3:

$$k_3 = (-0.5 + 0.7201k_1)/0.11k_1^2 \tag{22-29}$$

Finally, substituting (22-28) and (22-29) into (22-27), we find k_1 from evaluating $u(20, 100) = -1$:

$$u(20, 100) =$$
$$k_1(-1) + 0.3349k_1(-1) + k_1(0.3349k_1)\left[\frac{-0.5 + 0.7201k_1}{0.11k_1^2}\right](-1)(-1) = -1$$

Solving for k_1, we get the values of the three scaling constants:

$$k_1 = 0.609 \qquad k_2 = 0.204 \qquad k_3 = -1.502$$

The joint utility function for x_1 and x_2 under mutual utility independence is therefore

$$\begin{aligned} u(x_1, x_2) = {} & \left[\frac{0.609}{5.05}\right](1 - e^{0.09x_1}) + \left[\frac{0.204}{0.492}\right](1 - e^{0.004x_2}) \\ & - 1.502\left[\frac{0.609}{5.05}\right](1 - e^{0.09x_1})\left[\frac{0.204}{0.492}\right](1 - e^{0.004x_2}) \end{aligned} \tag{22-30}$$

As an interesting side point, note that if $k_3 = 0$, mutual utility independence reduces to a purely additive form, with the scaling constants k_1 and k_2 summing to one. Additive utility functions are thus a special case of mutual utility independence.

Life becomes extremely difficult if we abandon the assumption of mutual utility independence. For instance, if x_1 is utility independent of x_2, but not vice versa, the utility function is still defined by expression (22-23). But now the factor $f_2(x_2)$ has to be determined for all values of x_2. Ascertaining $f_2(x_2)$ empirically may be beyond the cognitive abilities of the decision maker. Most applications of multiattribute utility functions, therefore, are based on the assumptions of additivity or of mutual utility independence.

How can we verify whether attribute x_1 is mutually utility independent of attribute x_2? The procedure is surprisingly simple. Each point in the positive quadrant in Figure 22-6 represents an outcome over two attributes. Fixing x_2 at a given value x_2'—for instance, 80 thousand—we ask the decision maker to identify the value of $x_1 = x_1^*$ such that he or she is indifferent between a 50–50 reference lottery involving the worst and the best outcome for x_1 ($x_1 = 20$ and $x_1 = 0$ in our case). For our problem, we expect the answer to be $x_1^* = 14$. We then repeat this indifference assessment for a different value of $x_2 = x_2''$—say, zero. If the new value of x_1^* coincides with the previously identified one, then x_1 is utility independent of x_2. The values of x_2 should be chosen such that they fall into the normal range of experience of the decision maker, but are nevertheless sufficiently apart.

This process is repeated for x_2, with x_1 fixed first at some value x_1' and then at x_1''. If the indifference point, x_2^*, is identical for each case, then x_2 is also utility independent of x_1. (See Keeney, 1972, for an example.)

Figure 22-6. *Assessment of utility independence.*

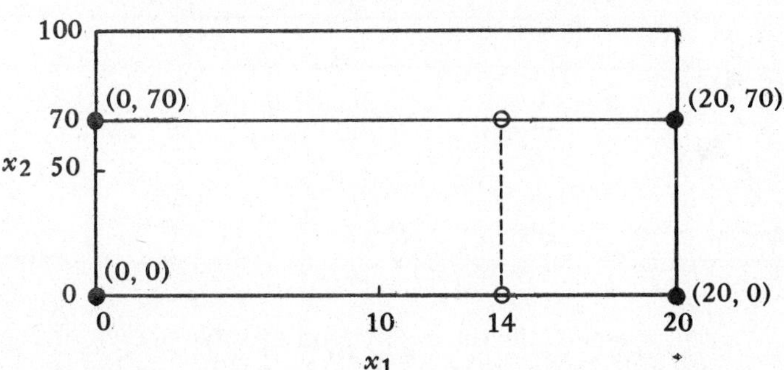

22-10 DECISION EVALUATION WITH MULTIATTRIBUTE UTILITY FUNCTIONS

We now have the necessary machinery to determine the preferred strategy for a particular impending search and rescue mission. A report has just come in that radio contact was lost five days ago with a 36-foot sloop headed toward area X. Area X had been suffering rough weather at that time. From past experience and the search pattern followed under each strategy considered, conditional probabilities of locating the missing craft by the end of search day n, provided it is in the search area, can be estimated. Table 22-7 summarizes them for five contemplated search strategies. The tapering off of the probability gains as n increases reflects the fact that the initial search is concentrated on the most likely location of the craft.

Table 22-7. *Conditional probabilities p_{in} of locating missing craft by end of day n for strategy i*

		Search Day n				
i	Strategy Description	1	2	3	4	5
1	commercial airliners only	0.10	0.16	0.2	0.23	0.25
2	1 search aircraft each day	0.30	0.50	0.64	0.75	0.80
3	1 aircraft on day 1, 2 thereafter	0.30	0.68	0.90	0.98	0.98
4	2 aircraft each day	0.50	0.80	0.95	0.99	0.99
5	2 aircraft on day 1, 3 thereafter	0.50	0.92	0.99	0.99	0.99

The preferred search strategy is the one that maximizes expected utility. Since the official search is abandoned after at most five days, the mission may fail. Let us arbitrarily assign this outcome a (dis)utility of -1, regardless of the cumulative cost of the mission. This is equivalent to setting this outcome equal to (x_1 = 20, x_2 = 100). Table 22-8 lists the cumulative costs x_2 for each strategy as a function of the number of days of search.

Table 22-8. *Cumulative search costs c_{in} (in thousand dollars) for strategy i for n days*

	Days of Search n Needed				
Strategy i	1	2	3	4	5
1	0	0	0	0	0
2	10	20	30	40	50
3	10	30	50	70	—
4	20	40	60	80	—
5	20	60	100	—	—

We can now compute the expected utility value of each strategy. Note that x_1 = 5 + n. For instance, for strategy 2 we use the following inputs, based on expression (22-30):

Days of Search n	1	2	3	4	5	Abandoned
$[x_1, x_2 \| n]$	[6, 10]	[7, 20]	[8, 30]	[9, 40]	[10, 50]	[20, 100]
$u[x_1, x_2 \| n]$	−0.1055	−0.1459	−0.1901	−0.2365	−0.3148	−1
p_{2n}	0.30	0.20	0.14	0.11	0.05	0.20

The expected utility of strategy 2 is equal to the sum of the products $u(x_1, x_2|n)p_{2n}$. Applied to all five strategies, we get the following results:

Strategy	1	2	3	4	5
Expected utility	−0.7781	−0.3283	−0.1923	−0.1823	−0.1978

Strategy 4 maximizes expected utility and hence is the preferred strategy according to this type of analysis.

In a real-life application to a search and rescue service, additional attributes, such as the number of people missing, their experience, the type of craft, and the weather conditions would be included. Utility assessments might be obtained from a panel of experts, rather than the director alone. Tables for the probabilities p_{in} for most likely search areas would be determined a priori. The actual evaluation of alternative search strategies could be made using an interactive computer program, allowing quick evaluation of many strategies.

EXERCISES

22.1 Solve the goal programming problem of exercise 2.22 with priorities defined in part (c), using the simplex method for preemptive goal programming.

22.2 Solve the following problems by the simplex method for preemptive goal programming:

$$\begin{aligned}
\text{minimize} \quad & P_1(2s_1^- + s_1^+) + P_2s_2^- + P_3s_3^- \\
\text{subject to} \quad & 4x_1 + 2x_2 + s_1^- - s_1^+ = 10 \qquad \text{(goal 1)} \\
& x_1 - x_2 + s_2^- - s_2^+ = 0 \qquad \text{(goal 2)} \\
& x_1 + s_3^- - s_3^+ = 2 \qquad \text{(goal 3)} \\
& \text{all variables} \geq 0
\end{aligned}$$

22.3 Green County wants to maximize total employment and maximize total net revenue with the following regional development proposal. Logging in forest A will provide employment for 3 persons, generate net revenue of \$12,000 and require 0.8 bulldozer and 0.6 truck per hectare logged per year. For logging in forest B, the corresponding figures are 6 persons, \$5000, 0.4 bulldozer, and 0.9 truck. The county has 4 bulldozers and 6 trucks. No more than 6 hectares can be logged per year in each forest.

(a) Formulate the problem as a multiple-objective linear program.
(b) Find the MINSUM solutions graphically for all weight combinations.
(c) Formulate the MINMAX problem. Using an LP computer code, find the optimal solution for the following weights:

w_1	1	10	1	1	0
w_2	0	1	1	10	1

22.4 Consider the investment problem of exercise 2.4, where the objective was to maximize returns. Assume now that the firm also has the objective of minimizing a measure of risk for the total investment. For simplicity, we use as a measure of risk the size of the range of the returns, which is 2% on short-term investments and 5% on long-term investments. The total risk is simply equal to the weighted sum of the individual risks. We also impose the restriction that at least half of the funds available have to be invested in long-terms funds. Reformulate this problem as a multiple objective linear program.
(a) Find the MINSUM solution graphically and determine for what values of the weights given to the two objectives the various possible solutions are optimal.
(b) Formulate the MINMAX problem. Without doing any calculations, indicate the edge(s) where the MINMAX solution is likely to be for the following weight combinations:

w_1	1	10	1	1	0
$-w_2$	0	1	1	10	1

22.5 Find all efficient solutions for
(a) The problem in exercise 22.3.
(b) The problem in exercise 22.4.

22.6 The graduate admissions committee of a prominent business school wants to streamline its admissions policy for the Ph.D. program. This policy is currently plagued by serious inconsistencies. The following factors are deemed important for admissions: the candidate's undergraduate gradepoint average, the quality of the institution where the undergraduate degree was obtained, the score in the graduate school of business admission test, and recommendations. Consider the first two attributes only. No candidate is considered if his or her gradepoint average is below 3. A consensus opinion of the committee as a whole indicates indifference between a 50–50 lottery involving a gradepoint average of 3 and 4, or a gradepoint average of 3.7 for certain; a 50–50 lottery of 3 and 3.7, or 3.5 for certain; and a 50–50 lottery of 3.7 and 4, or 3.9 for certain. Universities were ranked on a scale from 0 to 10, with 10 being the best. The committee agreed that a value of 1/10 of this scale would be a good measure for the utility attached to a degree from any institution ranked.
(a) Define individual utility functions for each of these two attributes over the range [0, 1], with 1 being the most preferred outcome. Use a utility function of the form $(x - a)^2$ for the gradepoint average.
(b) The committee also agrees that they would be indifferent between two applicants with the following scores:

- applicant A: [gradepoint average 4, university rank 0] = [4, 0], and
- applicant B: [gradepoint average 3.333, university rank 10] = [3.333, 10].

Find the two-attribute utility function associated with this statement under the assumption of additive utilities.
(c) Find the two-attribute utility function for mutual utility independence, given the statement of indifference in (b) and the following additional statement of indifference between two applicants:

- applicant A: [gradepoint average 3.7, university rank 7.5] = [3.7, 7.5], and
- applicant B: a 50–50 lottery of [3, 0], and [4, 10].

(d) There are four late applicants with the following scores: A: [3.3, 9]; B: [3.5, 6]; C: [3.9, 5]; and D: [4, 3]. Using the two-attribute utility function derived under (c), which two applicants should be accepted?

(e) Is the assumption of mutual utility independence a reasonable approximation for this problem? Why or why not?

REFERENCES

General

Cochrane, James L., and Milan Zeleny. *Multiple Criteria Decision Making.* Columbia, S.C.: University of South Carolina Press, 1973. Proceedings of 44 papers presented at a seminar, with contributions from all major names in the field, including a general review paper by K. R. McCrimmon.

Cohon, J. R. *Multiobjective Programming and Planning.* New York: Academic Press, 1978. Cohon has pioneered applications in water resource management.

Hwang, Ching-Lai, and A. S. Md. Masud. *Multiple Objective Decision Making—Methods and Applications.* Berlin: Springer, 1979. State-of-the-art survey covering over 20 different methods, their characteristics, and their applicability, including examples. Also has a brief survey of twelve areas of application and extensive bibliography.

Soland, R. M. "Multicriteria Optimization: The General Characterization of Efficient Solutions," *Decision Sciences,* Vol. 10, No. 1, 1979, pp. 26–37. Develops an elegant and simple characterization of efficient solutions and conditions for finding them. Encompasses many previously derived results as special cases. Highly recommended.

Starr, M. K., and M. Zeleny, Eds. *Multiple Criteria Decision Making.* TIMS Studies in Management Sciences, Vol. 6. Amsterdam: North-Holland, 1977. A collection of fairly mathematical papers.

Zeleny, M. *Multiple Criteria Decision Making.* New York: McGraw-Hill, 1982. An ambitious attempt to survey the entire field in 560 pages. Mathematically nondemanding.

Goal Programming

Ignizio, James. *Goal Programming and Extensions.* Lexington, Mass.: Lexington Books, 1976. Largely stressing preeemptive goal programming with extensions to integer- and simplex-based nonlinear programming. Contains FORTRAN computer codes.

Kornbluth, J. S. H. "A Survey of Goal Programming," *Omega,* April 1973, pp. 193–205. A short but authoritative review.

Lee, Sang M. *Goal Programming for Decision Analysis.* Philadelphia: Auerbach, 1972. Emphasis on preemptive goal programming with extensive discussion of applications to production, finance, marketing, and the public sector. FORTRAN computer code.

———. "Integer Goal Programming Methods," in M. K. Starr and M. Zeleny, Eds., *Multiple Criteria Decision Making.* TIMS Studies in Management Sciences, Vol. 6. Amsterdam: North-Holland, 1977.

Multiattribute Utility Analysis

Keeney, R. L. "An Illustrated Procedure for Assessing Multi-Attributed Utility Functions," *Sloan Management Review,* Fall 1972, pp. 38–50.

Keeney, R. L., and H. Raiffa. *Decisions with Multiple Objectives*. New York: Wiley, 1976. After reviewing single-attribute utility function, it develops the theory on multiattribute utility functions. Numerous detailed examples and case studies, including the Mexico City airport study. A well-written text, with easy parts and demanding parts.

Operations Research, Vol. 28, No. 1, Jan.–Feb. 1980. This special issue on decision analysis contains a number of papers dealing with multiattribute decision analysis, including an application to oil tanker safety and pollution prevention.

Multiobjective Linear and Nonlinear Programming

Cohon, J. L., et al. "Generating Multiobjective Trade-offs: An Algorithm for Bicriterion Problems," *Water Resources Research*, Vol. 15, Oct. 1979, pp. 1001–1010. An algorithm for finding all efficient solutions for a two-objective linear programming problem.

Ecker, J. G., et al. "Generating All Maximal Efficient Faces for Multiple Objective Linear Programs," *J. of Optimization Theory and Applications*, March 1980, pp. 353–80. Develops a simple procedure to identify efficient faces, based on the Ecker-Kouada algorithm reported in *Mathematical Programming*, Vol. 14, 1978, pp. 249–261.

Geoffrion, A. M., et al. "An Interactive Approach for Multicriterion Optimization, with an Application to the Operation of an Academic Department," *Management Science*, Vol. 19, Dec. 1972, pp. 357–368. Example of an interesting nonlinear programming approach.

Steuer, R. E. "Linear Multiple Objective Programming with Interval Criterion Weights," *Management Science*, Vol. 23, Nov. 1976, pp. 305–316.

Steuer, R. E. "An Interactive Multiple Objective Linear Programming Procedure." In M. K. Starr and M. Zeleny, Eds., *Mutiple Criteria Decision Making*. TIMS Studies in Management Sciences, Vol. 6. Amsterdam: North-Holland, 1977.

Zionts, S. "A Survey of Multiple Criteria Integer Programming Methods," *Annals of Discrete Mathematics*, 1979, pp. 389–398. Includes an evaluation from a user orientation.

Zionts, S., and J. Wallenius. "An Interactive Programming Method for Solving the Multiple Criteria Problem," *Management Science*, Vol. 22, Feb. 1976, pp. 652–663. Also includes an application.

CHAPTER TWENTY-THREE

Heuristic Problem Solving

The student of operations research who has mastered the techniques discussed in the previous chapters and has acquired, even if only partially, the skills of problem identification, model construction, and so on, may feel sufficiently well equipped to enter the battle of real-world problem solving. However, on entering that formidable arena, he or she will inevitably encounter many problems that cannot be solved by any of the techniques carried in the tool kit of problem-solving methods. Heuristic approaches may often be the only alternative. Heuristic problem solving is not a solution method in the sense that the simplex method of linear programming is, but rather it is a philosophy of, or strategy for, seeking out a method or methods that might produce a solution to a particular problem.

Heuristic problem solving involves inventing a set of rules that will aid in the discovery of one or more satisfactory solutions to a specific problem. The emphasis is on satisfactory—there is no guarantee of optimality. These rules are referred to as heuristics (derived from the Greek word *heuriskein* meaning to discover). In many instances, the use of heuristics may reduce the problem space sufficiently so that an analytical procedure or simulation may be applied; sometimes, the heuristics used may be, by themselves, sufficient to produce an acceptable feasible solution.

Whereas analytical procedures are based on deductive reasoning supported by mathematical proofs and known properties, heuristic methods are based on inductive inferences related to human characteristics of problem solving, such as creativity, insight, intuition, and learning. A particular heuristic is followed because it promises, intuitively or from experience, to help in the search for an acceptable solution, and if in the process a better rule is discovered, then the old one is discarded. So while heuristic problem solving involves the use of currently accepted rules, it may also involve a search for even better rules to replace them.

Why adopt a heuristic approach to solving a particular problem? We have noted that many real-world problems are not amenable to direct analytical solution by known mathematical techniques. But even where it is theoretically possible to apply such methods, if the problem is very large, the task of doing so may be impracticable. A large class of combinatorial problems (such as facility location, traveling salesman, and production scheduling problems) fall into this category.

23-1 ILL-STRUCTURED PROBLEMS

Problems for which no practicable analytic or algorithmic solution technique has been yet devised are often referred to as *ill structured*. An ill-structured problem (ISP) is a residual concept. We can only define what it is not. A problem is an ISP if it is not a well-structured problem (WSP). In operations research, a WSP possesses the following general descriptive characteristics in varying degrees:

1. Any knowledge relevant to the problem can be represented in an acceptable model.
2. An acceptable model should encompass all attainable (feasible) solutions.
3. There exist definite criteria for judging the feasibility and optimality of any solution.
4. There exists a programmable method for finding the optimal solution.
5. The solution method involves only an economically practicable amount of computation.
6. All information required by the acceptable model should be available at an economically practicable effort of data-gathering.

The boundary between ISPs and WSPs is vague and fluid. As advances in operations research methodology proceed, new and more sophisticated solution techniques in association with more powerful computers will convert ISPs to WSPs. But considering the state of the art at any given time, certain problems, such as simple linear optimization problems, can definitely be said to be well structured while certain other problems are obvious candidates for the label ill structured, such as many combinatorial problems and chess games. Many of the problems confronting operations researchers fall into neither of these clearly identified groups.

Bred in an analytical mold, operations researchers have been all too ready to treat such problems as WSPs—an assumption here, a trim there, bend a few facts, overlook a few others, and any fuzzy problem can be made to look respectable. However, models constructed using such an approach can hardly be expected to perform well. Rather than mutilate a problem until it conforms to a model for which an efficient solution technique exists, a more acceptable line of attack is to modify the solution procedure to fit the problem. It is in such situations that heuristic approaches are effective.

23-2 HEURISTICS—THE HUMAN APPROACH TO PROBLEM SOLVING

It is obvious that human problem-solving abilities, such as *perception*, *insight*, *creativity*, and *learning*, are involved at all phases of an operations research project in

Figure 23-1. *A possible heuristic solution process.*

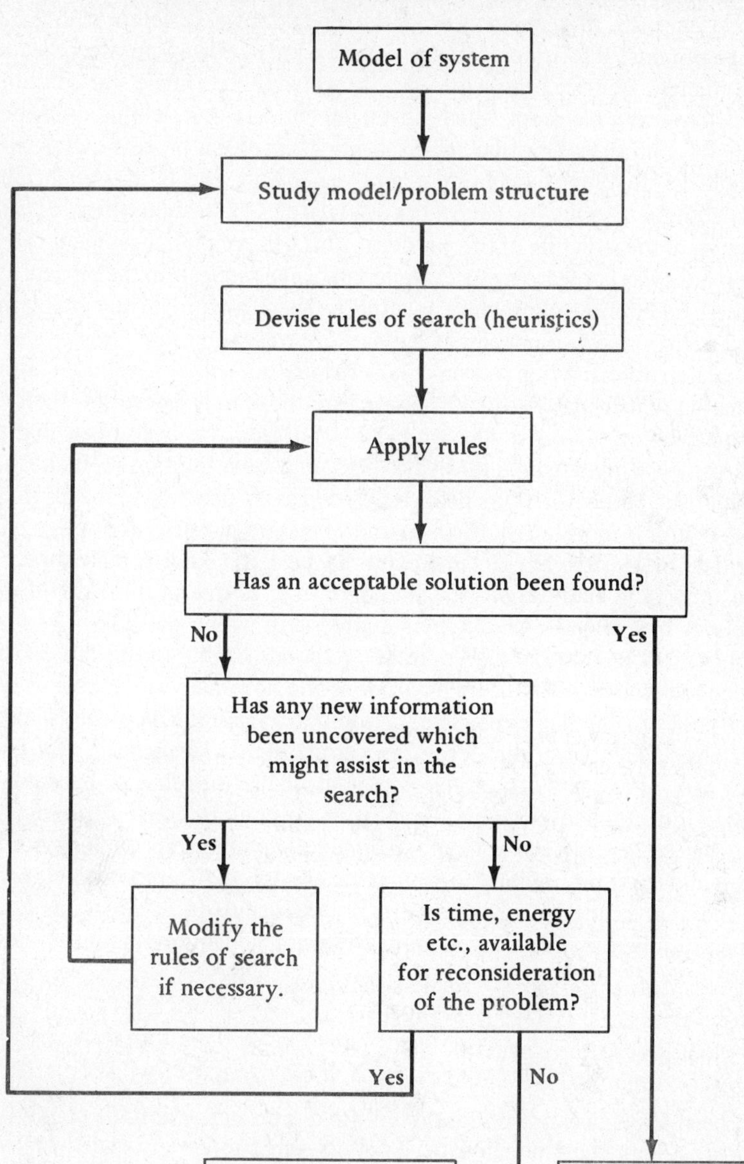

overcoming the inevitable problems that arise as such projects progress. However, our current concern is confined to phase three of the five project phases discussed in Section 1-1 of Chapter 1—namely, deriving a solution to the model.

Many operations research projects involve the application of a standard solution method. As such, the major task of the operations researcher is to construct an acceptable model that is amenable to solution by a known optimizing technique for which efficient computer programs may be available. In a sense, the solution method can be viewed as a black box which, given the correct input, will produce the required output. In contrast, a heuristic approach might involve a process such as that shown in Figure 23-1. Where are human problem-solving capabilities applicable in this process? First, in order to devise the initial rules of search, there must be some perception of the structure of the problem. This perception may come through insight (sudden discovery) or learning (accumulation of experience). In the process of applying the rules, additional information relating to the structure of the problem may be learned, which allows more efficient use of the rules or even a complete redefinition of the search rules. When a search fails to produce either a solution or additional information which may be used to restructure the search procedure, then even such a failure is useful. Given a decision to try again from the beginning, that avenue of search can be eliminated. In this way, the search for a solution method is narrowed.

Heuristic problem-solving behavior is most easily observed in the playing of games or the solving of puzzles. *Battleships* and chess are classical examples; *Mastermind* is another. In *Mastermind*, a game controller selects a color combination of marbles placed in four to six positions (depending on the degree of difficulty of the game). The player has to guess which color marble is in which position in as few trials as possible. After each guess the controller responds by informing the player of how many correct colors in their correct positions and how many correct colors not in their correct positions the player has scored, without revealing which colors and positions are involved. The player then uses this information to prepare the next guess. Most players will, after a few games, develop a detailed set of rules, or heuristics, on how to exploit the cumulative information obtained over all trials of a game. A good player will use these heuristics to gradually reduce the feasible color-position combinations to fewer and fewer possibilities. Although the correct color-position combination could be found analytically by solving a set of simultaneous linear equations formed from a certain number of trials, the human player using heuristics usually requires far fewer trials.

23-3 SATISFICING

It has been strongly implied throughout the discussion—but until now not explicitly stated—that heuristic problem-solving methods are strongly associated with satisficing, as opposed to optimizing, behavior. Heuristic methods do not normally guarantee optimal solutions. This is not necessarily a disadvantage. Many problems with ill-structured characteristics do not have optimal solutions in the strict sense. Such problems are essentially solved when one or more acceptable solutions have been identified. In fact, goal satisficing often describes human choice behavior more accurately than does goal optimizing. In business organizations, goal satisficing is likely to be most prevalent at the higher levels of management. It is there where goal conflicts, calling for tradeoffs between opposing goals, are usually most evident.

Two important features of satisficing-type problems should be noted. The first concerns the flexible nature of satisficing behavior: What is regarded as satisfactory at one point in time may become unsatisfactory when new information comes to light, and vice versa. For example, a manager may regard certain levels of profit, market share, and capital growth as satisfactory. But if it can be pointed out that all these objectives can be substantially and simultaneously increased, the previously acceptable levels may become unsatisfactory. Alternatively, if it can be adequately demonstrated that the goal levels cannot be simultaneously achieved, the manager will lower his or her aspiration level so that it becomes easier to find satisfactory solutions.

The second feature of satisficing behavior is of greater consequence. The decision maker may require that an acceptable solution possess some ill-defined set of nonquantifiable attributes—nonquantifiable at least in the sense that objective measurement is not attainable by a practicable amount of effort. For example, in a developing country, there may be a set of potential projects of which the government may be able to undertake a small subset. Some of the required attributes of the final selection might be that the chosen projects should not be unduly disruptive to cultural organization and activity, that they should result in an acceptable pattern of income distribution, and that they should be seen to contribute substantially to regional development. Rather than attempt to define explicit tradeoff relations among various attributes (which could be used to find the "optimal" solution), the decision maker chooses from several alternative solutions, each possessing the preferred characteristics in varying degrees.

23-4 HEURISTIC SOLUTION STRATEGIES

Most heuristic problem-solving procedures belong to one or a mixture of four general strategies. Let us look briefly at each in turn.

Solution-building strategies

In this approach, we attempt to construct a complete solution, one element at a time, according to a set of definite rules. The job sequencing problem in Section 23-5 is solved by a solution-building strategy, which for this problem finds the optimal solution.

Break-make strategies

Here we "break" a complex problem into a number of smaller subproblems. Each subproblem is solved individually or in some hierarchical sequence, where the output of a lower order subproblem is used as input into the next higher order problem, or vice versa, depending on the most appropriate order of solution. The solution to the whole problem is "made" by integrating the solutions to the subproblems into a consistent overall solution. Consider, for instance, the case study in Section 1-9. There the problem involves finding an optimal inventory policy for the entire operation of the lubrication oil division. It might be broken down into a number of subproblems:

determining filled stock replenishment sizes, determining filled stock reorder points, and, finally, finding empty container replenishment rules. They would be solved in sequence. The results of the subproblem for the filled stock replenishment sizes (namely, the number of replenishments per year = number of times shortages may occur) is used as input into the determination of reorder points for each product. Similarly, the size and pattern of filled stock replenishments is used as input for finding good empty container replenishment rules. Interactions in only one direction are taken into account for finding an overall solution.

Solution-modification strategies

An initial solution is modified by applying a specified sequence of heuristics aimed at improving the acceptability of the solution. The initial solution may have been built up by using a solution-building or break-make strategy, or it may have been obtained by an approximation method, such as the use of a standard optimizing technique on a simplified model of the problem. It may be that the starting solution is infeasible and the heuristic modification rules are designed to achieve feasibility and hence acceptability. The facility location solution method described in Section 23-6 is an example of this approach.

Search-learning strategies

Search-learning involves a directed search of the solution space. As new information is unearthed during the search, it is used to guide the search in new directions. The solution procedure for solving *Battleships*, chess, or *Mastermind* falls into this group of strategies because the outcome of each trial is used to guide the player in eliminating portions of the solution space and formulating trials that will provide further information needed to find the solution. The second phase of the traveling salesman solution method in Section 23-8 is also of this form.

A particular heuristic program may involve a combination of two or more of these strategies. For instance, the solution-building or the break-make strategy may provide an initial solution, which is then improved upon by a mixture of the solution-modification and search-learning strategies.

When using a solution-modification or search-learning strategy, we should carefully spell out all conditions for which the procedure should be terminated as successful or abandoned as a failure. For instance, if the procedure involves finding a feasible solution, it is terminated once such a solution has been identified, or it is abandoned if after k trials or m minutes of computer time no feasible solution has been generated. Sometimes, it may be desirable to have an interactive computer program that allows the analyst to intervene and redirect the search or terminate the procedure at will or at certain points in the search.

Many heuristic procedures incorporate optimizing methods for some of their phases. For instance, some of the subproblems created in the break-make strategy might be solved by an optimizing technique, such as linear programming. Also, simulation methods may form part of a heuristic procedure. For instance, a simulation model may be used to test the acceptability of a heuristically derived solution. Alternatively, heuristic rules may be used in conjunction with simulation to speed up the search for good solutions to complex decision problems.

Heuristic procedures, like simulation models, tend to be very problem-specific, in contrast to, say, linear programming, which can be applied to any problem that satisfies the fairly general assumptions of the model. However, the analyst should avoid devising a procedure that is parameter-specific. A procedure should not be so narrow that its effectiveness in finding acceptable solutions depends on particular or a limited range of parameter values. Should these parameters change (say, over time), the procedure becomes useless. Furthermore, the ability to test the sensitivity of the solution to changes in these parameters is lost.

23-5 PROCESSING *n* JOBS THROUGH TWO MACHINES

The following 7 jobs have to be processed through 2 machines in the same sequence—a milling machine (A) and a lathe (B)—with processing times A_i and B_i in minutes as shown:

Job	1	2	3	4	5	6	7	
A_i	30	50	60	60	20	120	70	(milling)
B_i	60	60	50	30	40	100	80	(lathing)

All jobs are due for delivery by the end of the day. Is it possible to process all jobs within the time available—namely, 480 minutes? If so, what is the best sequence of processing the jobs?

Since the total processing time on machine A is 410 minutes and on machine B is 420 minutes, a sequence may exist that allows us to meet the deadline. In a simple example of this sort, it could be found by trial and error. If we can find the minimum elapse time required to process all jobs through both machines, then we can answer both questions simultaneously. To demonstrate the type of mental processes involved in discovering heuristics, we shall now derive a solution-building strategy to find a sequence, which (as we shall not prove, though) in fact is the minimum elapsed-time sequence.

Consider first some very simple sequencing problems. Say we only look at jobs 1 and 2. The possible sequences are 1–2 and 2–1. Note that both jobs have the same time on the second machine—machine B. Figure 23-2 depicts the *Gantt chart*—a schedule graph—associated with each sequence. The total elapsed time for each sequence is given by the sum of processing and idle time of the second machine. The sequence 1–2 has the shorter total elapsed time. Observe that this sequence has $A_1 < A_2$. Consider now a second set of 2 jobs, namely jobs 3 and 4. Note that both have the same time on the first machine—machine A. Verify that the sequence 4–3 has the shorter total elapsed time. Observe that this sequence has $B_4 < B_3$. We invite

Figure 23-2. *Gantt charts for two-job/two-machine case.*

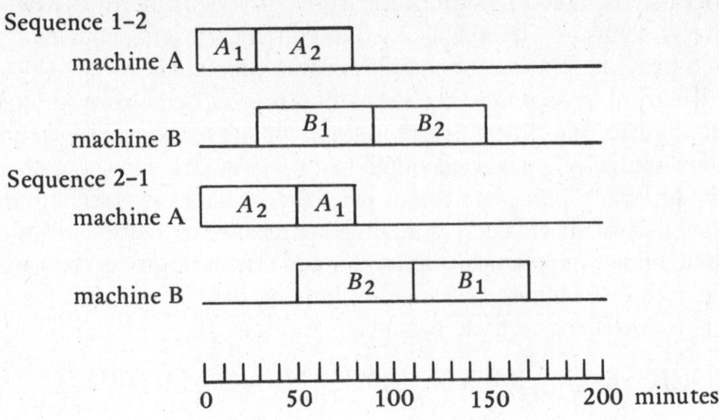

you to evaluate additional 2-job sequences, e.g., jobs 1 and 3, 4 and 5, 5 and 6, and 6 and 7. Do you discover some patterns? These observations for 2 jobs seem to suggest that if the shortest processing time occurs on machine A, the corresponding job is scheduled first, while if the shortest processing time occurs on machine B, the corresponding job is scheduled last. Although we reached these conclusions for the 2-job case only, we could use them as a basis of a heuristic program for sequencing n jobs through 2 machines.

SEQUENCING ALGORITHM FOR n JOBS ON TWO MACHINES

Step 0 Set $k = 1, j = 0$.

Step 1 Find the smallest processing time in the combined list of processing times on both machines for the remaining jobs, i.e., find $i = r$ with

$$M_r = \underset{i}{\text{minimum}}\,(A_1, A_2, \ldots, A_n, B_1, B_2, \ldots, B_n) \tag{23-1}$$

Ties are broken arbitrarily.

Step 2 If $M_r = A_r$, then schedule job r as the kth job. Increase k to $k + 1$.

If $M_r = B_r$, then schedule job r as the $(n - j)$th job. Increase j to $j + 1$.

Step 3 Remove A_r and B_r from the combined list.

Step 4 If combined list is empty, *stop*; otherwise, return to step 1.

This procedure constructs a complete solution in n iterations. It is an example of a solution-building strategy. Although we derived this procedure using heuristic problem solving, it turns out that the solution found is in fact the optimal solution, as shown by S. M. Johnson ("Optimal Two- and Three-Stage Production Schedule with Setup Times Included," *Naval Logistics Quarterly*, March 1954).

Let us now apply Johnson's algorithm to our example. The circled numbers underneath A_r or B_r indicate the sequence. Job 5 has the shortest processing time of 20. It is on machine A. Hence job 5 is scheduled first. Job 1 on machine A and job 4 on machine B have the next shortest times of 30. Hence job 1 is second, while job 4 is seventh. Verify the other results.

Job	1	2	3	4	5	6	7
A_i	30 (2)	50 (3)	60	60	20 (1)	120	70 (4)
B_i	60	60	50 (6)	30 (7)	40	100 (5)	80

The sequence of processing is thus jobs 5–1–2–7–6–3–4. Verify that the total elapsed time is 470 minutes. Machine B is idle for the initial 20 minutes and for 30 minutes after job 7, or a total of 50 minutes.

Unfortunately, extending this heuristic procedure to the m machine/n job case does not yield the minimum elapsed-time sequence any more (except for a rather trivial case discussed by Johnson). However, the basic idea of processing jobs on the first few machines in order of increasing machine times will often give "good" solutions.

23-6 DEPOT LOCATION PROBLEM

In a merchandising distribution system, goods are shipped from a factory to a number of regional warehouses or depots from which they are distributed to individual customers (e.g., to retailers or directly to households), as depicted in Figure 12-1 of Chapter 12. The costs of physical distribution have been estimated to average about 20 percent of the final product cost. These costs may be reduced somewhat if a firm locates its depots judiciously. Considerable efforts have been made to develop optimizing models for finding both the number of depots and their best location. Some use integer programming to find the best combination of depots from a preselected list of feasible sites (called the *feasible set approach*). The sheer size of such problems makes them difficult to solve. Others are based on selecting best sites in a Cartesian coordinate space. Since each depot may be sited anywhere, it is referred to as the *infinite set approach*. We will now discuss one such model, which is based on a heuristic solution-modification strategy.

To simplify matters somewhat, assume that there are only local distribution costs. The situation could, for instance, deal with siting service centers. The location of each customer j is given by the coordinates (x_j, y_j), $j = 1, 2, \ldots, n$. Each customer receives goods from one depot only—the nearest depot. The "customers" may in fact be the center of gravity of suitably chosen small local areas, such as city or town districts. Similarly, the location of each depot i is given by $(\hat{x}_i, \hat{y}_i)$, $i = 1, 2, \ldots, N$. The local distribution cost is proportional to the volume of goods w_j delivered and the straight-line distance d_{ij} from depot i to customer j, i.e., $c_j w_j d_{ij}$, where c_j is the unit-volume unit-distance cost applicable to customer j. (d_{ij} could conceivably be adjusted by a factor α to account for the fact that actual road distance will on the average be α times d_{ij}; say, $1.2\, d_{ij}$.) d_{ij} is defined as the Euclidean distance

$$d_{ij} = [(\hat{x}_i - x_j)^2 + (\hat{y}_i - y_j)^2]^{1/2} \tag{23-2}$$

The total delivery cost from all N depots is

$$T(N) = \sum_{i=1}^{N} \sum_{j=1}^{n} c_j w_j d_{ij} \delta_{ij} \tag{23-3}$$

where $\delta_{ij} = 1$ if customer j is served from depot i and 0 otherwise. If there are no throughput constraints on the depot, then for a given N the problem consists of finding N depot locations so as to minimize $T(N)$. The optimal number N of depots is usually found by enumeration or search.

To motivate the solution procedure for the N-depot case, let us first consider the case of one depot only. We shall thus drop the subscript i. We want to find location $(\hat{x}^*, \hat{y}^*)$ that minimizes

$$T = \sum_{j=1}^{n} c_j w_j d_{ij} \tag{23-4}$$

where d_{ij} is defined by (23-2). (Note that δ_{ij} is now not needed.) Since $\hat{x}$ and $\hat{y}$ can assume any real numbers, we use the methods of classical optimization (Chapter 19, Section 19-4) to find their optimum values. Taking partial derivatives of (23-4) with respect to $\hat{x}$ and $\hat{y}$ and setting them equal to zero, we get

$$\partial T/\partial \hat{x} = \sum_j c_j w_j(\hat{x} - x_j)/d_{ij} = 0 \qquad \partial T/\partial \hat{y} = \sum_j c_j w_j(\hat{y} - y_j)/d_{ij} = 0 \tag{23-5}$$

Solving for $\hat{x}$ and $\hat{y}$,

$$\hat{x}^* = \frac{\sum_j c_j w_j x_j / d_{ij}}{\sum_j c_j w_j / d_{ij}} \quad \text{and} \quad \hat{y}^* = \frac{\sum_j c_j w_j y_j / d_{ij}}{\sum_j c_j w_j / d_{ij}} \tag{23-6}$$

Expressions (23-6) cannot be evaluated for $\hat{x}^*$ and $\hat{y}^*$, since they involve the distances d_{ij}. These can only be determined if we know $\hat{x}^*$ and $\hat{y}^*$. We can apply our usual trick for such situations and find $\hat{x}^*$ and $\hat{y}^*$ by successive approximations. We start out with an initial guess of the depot location of $(\hat{x}^{(0)}, \hat{y}^{(0)})$, find the $d_{ij}^{(0)}$ distances implied by this choice, and insert them into (23-6) to obtain a new guess for the depot location $(\hat{x}^{(1)}, \hat{y}^{(1)})$. Using this new guess, we find again the associated $d_{ij}^{(1)}$ values, which in turn are inserted into (23-6) to get $(\hat{x}^{(2)}, \hat{y}^{(2)})$. This process continues until the difference in the coordinates of the depot location becomes sufficiently small. Usually, five or six iterations are sufficient. Given that T is convex in $\hat{x}$ and $\hat{y}$, this procedure will converge to the global optimum. Convergence, though, is never complete, hence the arbitrary stopping rule. Note that each iteration has the form of a solution-modification step.

Given the ease of the solution-modification procedure for the 1-depot case, why not adapt it to the N-depot case? Taking partial derivatives of $T(N)$ in (23-3) with respect to each $\hat{x}_i$ and $\hat{y}_i$, $i = 1, 2, \ldots, N$, setting them equal to zero, and solving for $\hat{x}_i$ and $\hat{y}_i$, we get

$$\text{(23-7)} \qquad x_i^* = \frac{\sum_j c_j w_j x_j \delta_{ij}/d_{ij}}{\sum_j c_j w_j \delta_{ij}/d_{ij}} \qquad y_i^* = \frac{\sum_j c_j w_j y_j \delta_{ij}/d_{ij}}{\sum_j c_j w_j \delta_{ij}/d_{ij}}, \qquad i = 1, 2, \ldots, N$$

Now, both d_{ij} and δ_{ij} are unknown. Given any set of depot locations, we need some criterion for assigning customers to depots. If the c_{ij}'s only depend on j and not on the depot location, then the most logical one is to assign customers to the nearest depot. The heuristic solution-modification algorithm is now as follows.

HEURISTIC DEPOT LOCATION ALGORITHM

Step 1 Select N initial depot locations, defined by $(\hat{x}_i^{(0)}, \hat{y}_i^{(0)})$, $i = 1, 2, \ldots, N$. Set $k = 0$.

Step 2 Assign each customer j, $j = 1, 2, \ldots, n$, to the nearest depot. Set $\partial_{ij}^{(k)} = 1$ for the corresponding combination of i and j, leaving all other $\delta_{ij}^{(k)}$ at zero. Find the corresponding $d_{ij}^{(k)}$.

Step 3 Increase k to $k + 1$.

Step 4 Find $\hat{x}_i^{(k)}$ and $\hat{y}_i^{(k)}$, $i = 1, 2, \ldots, N$, using expressions (23-7) with $d_{ij}^{(k-1)}$ and $\delta_{ij}^{(k-1)}$.

Step 5 If $|\hat{x}_i^{(k)} - \hat{x}_i^{(k-1)}| < \varepsilon$ and $|\hat{y}_i^{(k)} - \hat{y}_i^{(k-1)}| < \varepsilon$, for all i, where ε is arbitrarily small, set $\hat{x}_i^* = \hat{x}_i^{(k)}$ and $y_i^* = \hat{y}_i^{(k)}$, for all i, and *stop*; otherwise, return to step 2.

There is no guarantee that this procedure will converge to the optimal depot locations. In fact, the final depot locations found at step 5 may be different for different initial choices of $(\hat{x}_i^{(0)}, \hat{y}_i^{(0)})$. For this reason, the algorithm is usually applied to a number of different initial locations. Each final solution found is costed out, and the one with the lowest cost is selected as the "best" solution. Computer run times for this procedure are relatively small, allowing easily 100 different initial locations to be tried. Experience with this algorithm also indicates that the cost function (23-3) is fairly shallow in the region of this best solution. Hence, the decision makers may be presented with not just one, but several, of the better solutions.

Finally, to find the "best" number N of depots, the search process is repeated for different values of N, taking into account also the fixed operating costs of running the depots.

This basic model has been extended to deal with trunking costs from the factory to the depots, several factories, and nonlinear operating costs for the depots as a function of depot throughput. The interested reader is encouraged to consult the text by Eilon, Christofides, and Watson-Gandy listed in the references. The next section will demonstrate this procedure for a "practical" example.

23-7 MIDDLE EARTH WEED PROCESSING

After the War of the Rings (J. R. R. Tolkien, *The Lord of the Rings*, Allen & Unwin, 1968), when life had settled back to normal, agricultural scientists found that the legendary tobacco of Middle Earth could also be grown in other lands outside the Shire. Demand for Shireweed—as it had become known—was high and was expected to remain so, owing to the discovery that it had no injurious effects on health. In fact, it was beneficial—as evidenced by the longevity of hobbits. Somehow though, growers outside the Shire never got the knack of processing their own weed properly. After harvest, one could see long columns of pack animals carrying the leaves in big bundles to the Shire for skillful processing by the hobbits. Although the roads were fairly safe for traveling by then, the leaves suffered from the long and costly journey, resulting in an inferior product. The hobbits also began charging high prices for processing the weed, which did not contribute to neighborly harmony. The cry arose that local processing plants should be established at various places in Middle Earth, supervised by experts from the Shire. So, by Royal decree the Weed Processing Corporation (WPC) was established and was made responsible for setting up processing plants and processing the weed.

The WPC contracted researchers at the University of Middle Earth to investigate the problem of determining the number, size, and location for the proposed new weed processing plants. The terms of reference were not only that the operation should keep overall weed transport and processing costs as low as possible, but also that a view should be kept of "certain political considerations." For instance, the people of Esgaroth in Mirkwood were crying for regional development, while the inhabitants of Hobbiton in the Shire were not at all sure that they wanted a large factory in their village. "It will foul the air and pollute the stream" was the theme of many letters to the *Hobbiton Times*.

The research group (operations researchers, agricultural economists, traffic engineers—the usual type) gathered the following data:

1. The expected leaf production w_j per year for each of the 22 growing regions j (Table 23-1).

2. Transport cost per bundle per mile for each growing region c_j. These varied with the pack animals used and the traveling speed, which depended on the terrain of the region (Table 23-1).
3. The cost of operating a plant as a function of its throughput. It was found that these costs could safely be approximated by $f + vW$, where f is the fixed operating cost, v is the variable cost per bundle, and W is the plant throughput, also in bundles.
4. A detailed map of Middle Earth, showing for each region the coordinates of its center of gravity in terms of weed production (Figure 23-3), summarized in Table 23-1.

Table 23-1. *Input data for Shireweed processing plants location problem*

j	Name of Region	Production (bundles) w_j	Transport Cost (bundle/mi) c_j	Coordinates (units of 10 mi) x_j	y_j
1	Forlindon	200	0.1	4	32
2	Ered Luin	300	0.1	9	34
3	Arnor	800	0.1	20	34
4	Shire	1800	0.1	13	30
5	Harlindon	900	0.1	7	27
6	Minhiriath	700	0.1	15	24
7	Enedhwaith	500	0.1	20	24
8	Dunland	500	0.2	22	24
9	Rhudaur	400	0.2	22	28
10	Hithaiglin	1000	0.2	28	27
11	Mirkwood	300	0.3	32	28
12	Brown Lands	100	0.1	35	20
13	Wold	200	0.2	29	23
14	Rohan	900	0.1	30	19
15	Erednimrais	1200	0.1	18	15
16	Anfalas	700	0.2	21	12
17	Lebennin	800	0.2	31	11
18	Anorien	600	0.1	34	15
19	Ithilien	500	0.1	36	12
20	Gorgoroth	0	0.2	39	17
21	Nurn	100	0.2	42	13
22	South Gondor	100	0.1	34	8

After several weeks of controversy over whether to use a feasible set or infinite set approach, the latter won out when it was discovered that the last integer program to be solved on the University's MORDOR MACH III computer had aborted after 22 days. (Note that for this example the flow of goods is reversed—from the customers to the depots, rather than the other way round.) An initial trial run was made with three processing plants. Their initial sites were the centers of gravity of region 4 (Shire),

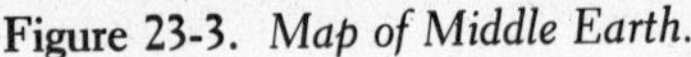

Figure 23-3. *Map of Middle Earth.*

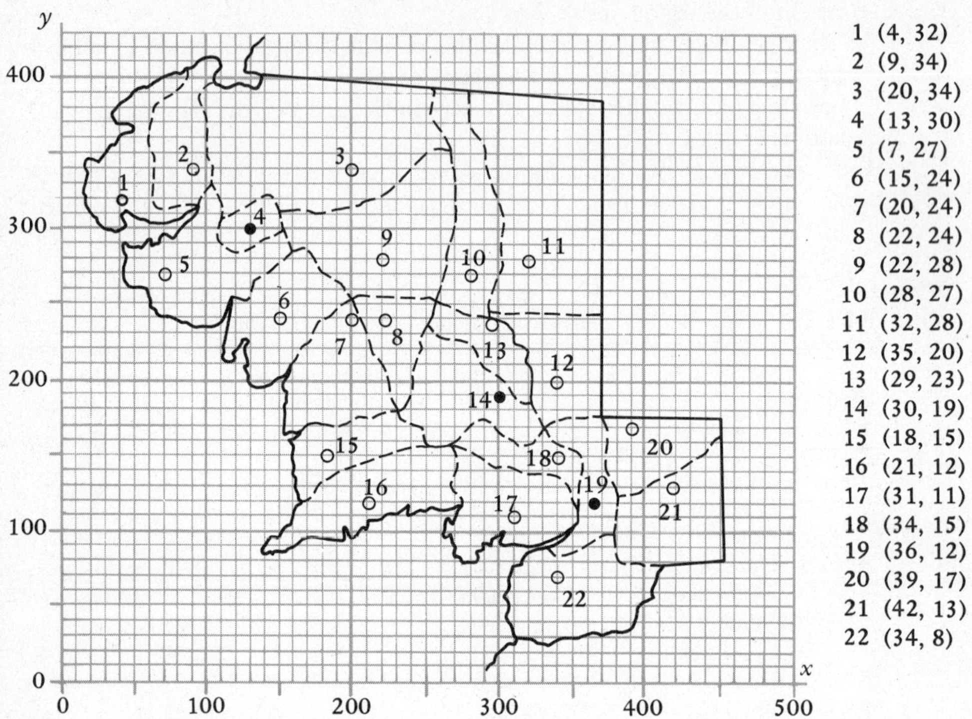

region 14 (Rohan), and region 19 (Ithilien). Allocating each region to the closest plant, we get the following initial assignments:

Plant at	Region 4	Region 14	Region 19
Assignments	1, 2, 3, 5, 6, 7, 9	8, 10, 11, 12, 13, 14, 15, 16	17, 18, 19, 20, 21, 22

(Note that the Shire was left out—the researchers realized that the hobbits preferred to process their own weed in their backyard curing holes. "It loses all flavor when processed in bulk" was a common dictum.)

Table 23-2 shows the results of the first five iterations. Let us briefly outline the first iteration. Using the initial assignment of regions to plants, expression (23-2) yields the distances $d_{ij}^{(0)}$ shown under iteration 0. At the first iteration, these distances and the corresponding $\delta_{ij}^{(0)}$ values are used in expression (23-7) to find new coordinates $(\hat{x}_i^{(1)}, \hat{y}_i^{(1)})$ for $i = 1, 2, 3$. These are shown at the bottom portion for iteration 1. From these new plant locations, we can, for each j, first compute the distances

Table 23-2 *Solution progress for Shireweed processing locations*

	Iteration 0		Iteration 1		Iteration 2		Iteration 3		Iteration 4		Iteration 5	
Regions j	Closest Depot	Distance to Depot	Closest Depot	Distance to Depot	Closest Depot	Distance to Depot	Closest Depot	Distance to Depot	Closest Depot	Distance to Depot	Closest Depot	Distance to Depot
1	1	92.20	1	111.52	1	97.40	1	90.72	1	86.86	1	84.48
2	1	56.57	1	79.02	1	69.34	1	65.59	1	63.54	1	62.32
3	1	80.62	1	78.41	1	89.62	1	95.66	1	99.07	1	101.15
5	1	67.08	1	76.67	1	61.87	1	54.60	1	50.53	1	48.06
6	1	63.25	1	43.93	1	47.83	1	51.04	1	53.43	1	55.06
7	1	92.20	2	59.40	2	53.45	2	54.38	2	56.88	2	50.08
8	2	94.34	2	40.75	2	34.01	2	34.42	2	37.11	2	39.40
9	1	92.20	2	68.41	2	59.65	2	50.74	2	49.29	2	49.65
10	2	82.46	2	53.13	2	48.56	2	37.53	2	33.02	2	30.38
11	2	92.20	2	85.69	2	84.01	2	75.57	2	71.66	2	69.10
12	2	50.99	3	80.83	3	84.93	3	90.82	3	95.50	3	97.20
13	2	41.23	2	34.20	2	37.50	2	37.85	2	37.52	2	36.62
14	2	0	2	54.00	2	62.09	2	69 69	2	71.59	2	71.83
15	2	126.49	2	105.37	2	107.95	2	118.76	2	123.39	2	125.99
16	2	114.02	2	112.41	3	114.79	3	102.56	3	99.79	3	99.89
17	3	50.99	3	21.32	3	17.25	3	7.69	3	3.51	3	1.68
18	3	36.06	3	30.36	3	34.62	3	42.74	3	47.53	3	49.00
19	3	0	3	32.76	3	35.24	3	47.56	3	50.84	3	51.15
20	3	58.31	no output									
21	3	60.83	3	92.98	3	95.86	3	108.23	3	111.65	3	111.98
22	3	44.72	3	44.26	3	41.77	3	46.31	3	45.24	3	43.90
Depot i	$\hat{x}_i^{(0)}$	$\hat{y}_i^{(0)}$	$\hat{x}_i^{(1)}$	$\hat{y}_i^{(1)}$	$\hat{x}_i^{(2)}$	$\hat{y}_i^{(2)}$	$\hat{x}_i^{(3)}$	$\hat{y}_i^{(3)}$	$\hat{x}_i^{(4)}$	$\hat{y}_i^{(4)}$	$\hat{x}_i^{(5)}$	$\hat{y}_i^{(5)}$
1	130	300	145.44	283.69	130.35	283.61	122.96	283.29	118.74	283.33	116.15	283.43
2	300	190	256.69	222.26	252.50	229.98	254.32	242.63	256.47	246.84	258.45	248.59
3	360	120	327.33	122.41	324.78	118.90	312.52	117.27	309.58	113.48	309.54	111.62
Transport cost only	111,952		96,296		94,129		90,554		89,726		89,442	

$d_{ij}^{(1)}$, all i, find the closest plant i, and then set $\delta_{ij}^{(1)} = 1$ for the corresponding i. This new assignment is shown under iteration 1, together with the corresponding distances. This process repeats itself until the coordinates of the plant locations converge. For our example, we stopped the computations when the differences in coordinates become smaller than 3. This yields the solution shown as iteration 5, with a total transport cost of 89,442 gold coins and plant throughputs of 2900, 5000, and 2300 bundles, respectively. Note how the total cost only decreases significantly at the first three iterations. The cost decrease at the fifth iteration is less than 0.4 percent. At the fifth iteration, plant 1 is located on the boundary of regions 4 and 5, plant 2 on the boundary of regions 8 and 13, and plant 3 close to the centre of gravity of region 17.

Postscript. The research team of the University of Middle Earth made 10 runs with different starting locations for N = 3, 4, and 5 plants, as well as a few special runs for which certain towns, like Hobbiton, were ruled out as possible sites, and a few other runs for which one or two sites, such as a plant in Esgaroth, were selected and kept fixed throughout the computations. The best 2 runs for each N and the more promising special runs were fully documented in the final report, which was presented to the WPC. A decision is still pending.

23-8 THE TRAVELING SALESMAN PROBLEM

A traveling salesman has to visit each of N cities. The objective is to find a tour that minimizes the distance traveled or minimizes the cost of the tour if costs are not proportional to distance. This problem has so far resisted all attempts to find a solution method that guarantees an optimum and remains efficient even for reasonably small problems. Very small problems of up to 15 cities can be solved optimally by Little's branch and bound algorithm (J. D. C. Little et al., "An Algorithm for the Traveling Salesman Problem," *Operations Research*, 1963, pp. 972–989). Integer programming can handle slightly larger problems. Realistic-size problems of 40 or more cities have to be solved approximately by heuristic methods. Some of the better known methods are the ones by S. Lin and B. W. Kernighan ("An Effective Heuristic Algorithm for the Traveling Salesman Problem," *Operations Research*, Vol. 21, No. 2, March–April 1973, pp. 498–516), and N. Christofides et al. ("Exact Algorithms for the Vehicle Routing Problem," *Math. Programming*, Vol. 20, No. 3, 1980, pp. 255–282).

We will now develop a simple set of heuristics based on the geometry of the problem. As shown by J. P. Norback and R. F. Love ("Geometric Approaches to Solving the Traveling Salesman Problem," *Management Science*, July 1977, pp. 1208–1223), these heuristics usually give surprisingly good solutions.

The method assumes that the problem can be represented in a two-dimensional space as depicted in the example of Figure 23-4. Each city i, $i = 1, 2, \ldots, N$, can be represented by the coordinates (x_i, y_i). The distance d_{ij} between any two cities is given by the Euclidean distance of expression (23-2). Alternatively, travel costs between any two cities are assumed to be proportional to the Euclidean distance. Consequently, the distances between cities can be represented by a distance matrix which is symmetrical about the diagonal, i.e., $d_{ij} = d_{ji}$, for all i, j. For the example in Figure 23-4, the distance matrix is

Figure 23-4. *Seven-city traveling salesman problem in Euclidean two-space.*

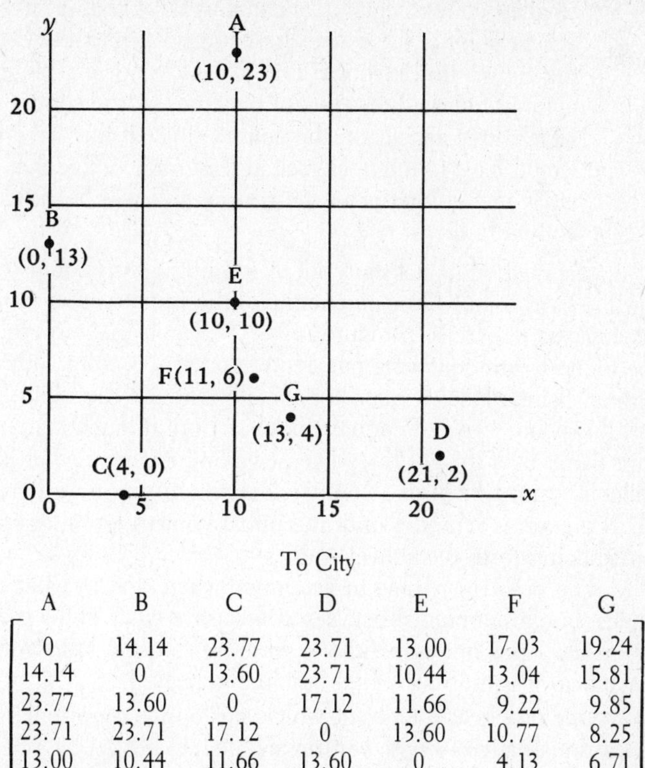

To City

		A	B	C	D	E	F	G
From City	A	0	14.14	23.77	23.71	13.00	17.03	19.24
	B	14.14	0	13.60	23.71	10.44	13.04	15.81
	C	23.77	13.60	0	17.12	11.66	9.22	9.85
	D	23.71	23.71	17.12	0	13.60	10.77	8.25
	E	13.00	10.44	11.66	13.60	0	4.13	6.71
	F	17.03	13.04	9.22	10.77	4.13	0	2.83
	G	19.24	15.81	9.85	8.25	6.71	2.83	0

For the more general form of the traveling salesman problem, distances or costs may not necessarily be symmetrical. More general solution methods are then needed.

An optimal tour in Euclidean two-space will satisfy the following two properties:

1. An optimal tour never intersects itself. That this must be so can easily be seen from Figure 23-5. The tour with the solid line intersects itself. By reversing the order of visiting cities X and Y, we obtain the tour shown by the broken line. Clearly, the latter is shorter.

Figure 23-5. *Tour -Z-Y-X-S- is longer than tour -Z-X-Y-S-.*

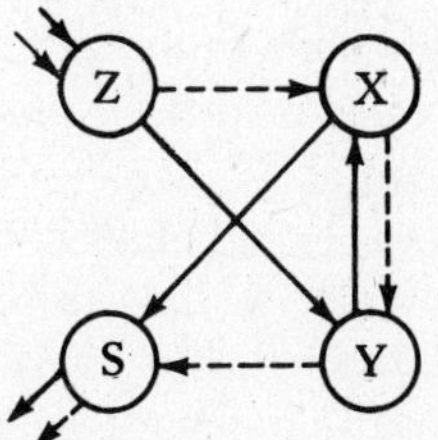

2. Consider again the problem of visiting all cities shown in Figure 23-4. The smallest convex region that contains all cities is given by the *convex hull*. Each corner point of the convex hull corresponds to a city. In Figure 23-6, part (a), the convex hull is shown as A–B–C–D–A. From property 1, it follows that an optimal tour will always visit the cities on the convex hull in the sequence in which they appear on the convex hull. If this were not true, then the tour would have to intersect itself at least once. (Note that in a complete tour, the cities in the interior of the convex hull will be visited between cities on the convex hull.)

The method in fact starts out by forming a *partial tour* containing only the cities on the convex hull. For our example, the initial partial tour is thus A–B–C–D–A, as depicted in part (a) of Figure 23-6. The points that form the convex hull can easily be found by the following procedure: Locate the point with the lowest x-coordinate (initial point). Place a ruler horizontally through this point. Keeping the ruler fixed on this point, swivel it counterclockwise until it touches a new point. Connect these two points by a straight line. The new point is now used as the swivel point, and the ruler is again turned in a counterclockwise direction until another point is touched. This process is repeated until the initial point is found again. The lines connecting these points form the convex hull.

The problem is now to determine where and in what sequence the remaining cities should be inserted between consecutive cities in the partial tour. The approach is to add cities one at a time to form new partial tours, until all cities have been included. It is thus a solution-building strategy.

One simple way to decide which city to insert next into a partial tour is as follows. Measure all angles whose vertices are at cities not yet included in the partial tour and whose sides are lines through consecutive cities on the partial tour. This is shown in part (b). The city with the largest angle is the one that is inserted next between the two corresponding consecutive cities on the partial tour. The angle C–G–D is the largest; hence city G is included into the partial tour between cities C and D. The new partial tour A–B–C–G–D–A is shown in part (c). This tour is used as the starting point for a new iteration. New angles are found for all cities not yet included, and the process is repeated until a complete tour has been generated. This process is depicted in parts (c), (d), and (e). The complete tour found is A–B–C–G–D–F–E–A. From the distance matrix (23-8), we find its total distance as 73.74. In this example, the process did not find the optimal tour A–B–C–D–G–F–E–A, depicted in part (f). Its total distance is 73.07, or 0.67 less than the tour found. The difference is less than 1 percent.

For small problems of up to 20 cities, angles may easily be estimated by eye and a tour generated quickly with equipment no more complicated than a straightedge, a pencil, and a geographical map of the problem. It is thus an effective and convenient "back of the envelope method."

Although the tour generated may not be optimal, Norback and Love report highly encouraging sample results, solving problems of up to 318 cities. For 25 smaller problems with 12 cities each, where the method could be tested against the optimal solution, almost half of the problems were solved optimally, while of the remainder only 2 were off by more than 5 percent.

Figure 23-6. *Iterations of the geometric traveling salesman method.*

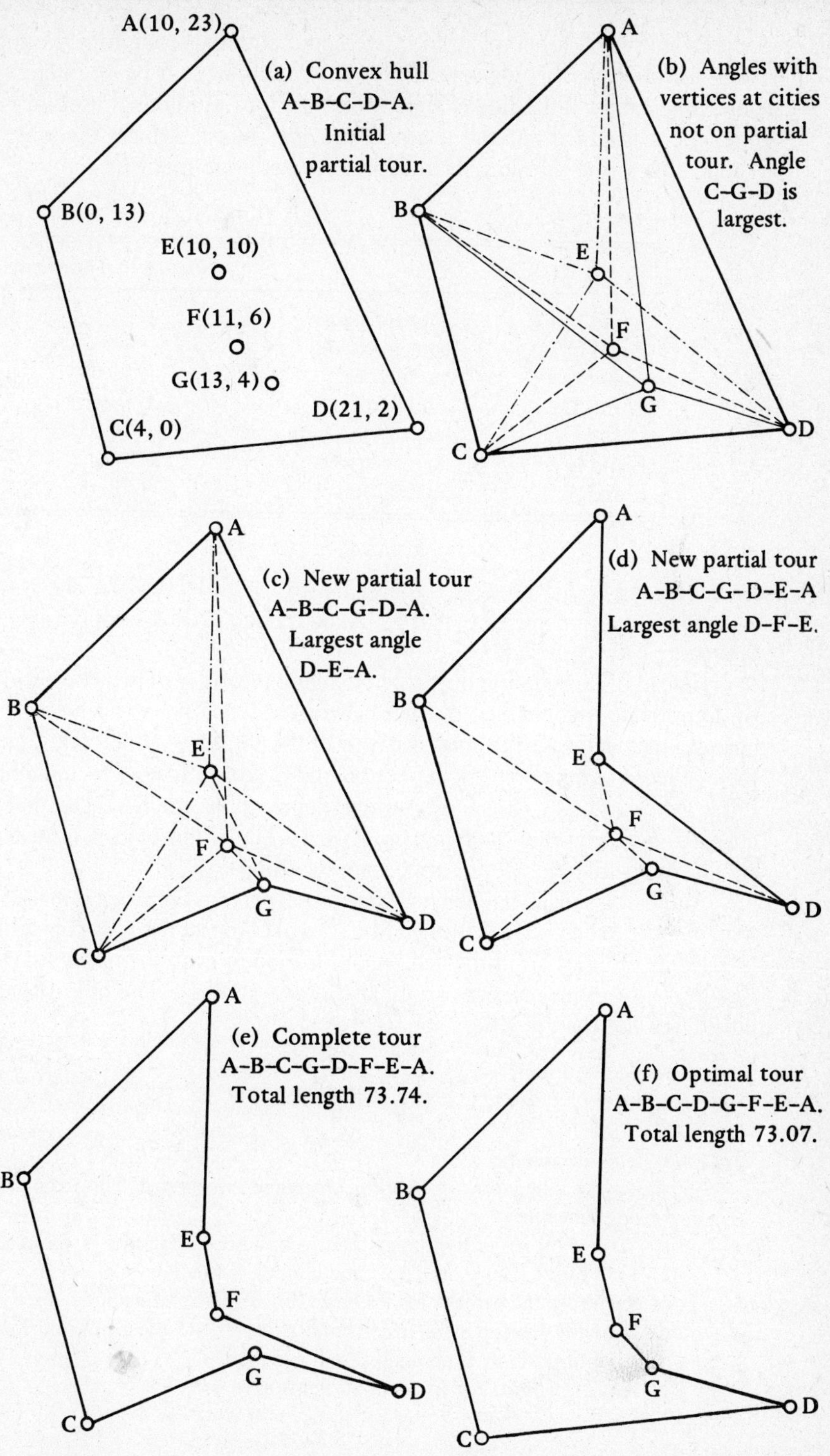
A(10, 23)
B(0, 13)
E(10, 10)
F(11, 6)
G(13, 4)
C(4, 0)
D(21, 2)
(a) Convex hull A–B–C–D–A. Initial partial tour.
(b) Angles with vertices at cities not on partial tour. Angle C–G–D is largest.
(c) New partial tour A–B–C–G–D–A. Largest angle D–E–A.
(d) New partial tour A–B–C–G–D–E–A Largest angle D–F–E.
(e) Complete tour A–B–C–G–D–F–E–A. Total length 73.74.
(f) Optimal tour A–B–C–D–G–F–E–A. Total length 73.07.

Having found a complete tour, we could attempt to improve the solution by a search-learning phase. One approach is to form a new tour by an interchange of two consecutive cities. If the interchange causes the tour to intersect itself, it is discarded. Otherwise it is costed out and retained, provided that it reduces the tour length. Let us apply this to the solution obtained by the geometric method:

Interchange		Change in Tour Length
A and B	tour intersects	
B and C	tour intersects	
C and G	no intersect	+11.08
G and D	no interesect	−0.67
D and F	no intersect	+4.05
F and E	tour intersects	
E and A	no intersect	+12.55

Interchanging G and D reduces the total tour length by 0.67 to 73.07, which in fact is the optimal tour depicted in part (f). Note, though, that it is not possible to guarantee optimality by this method.

Instead of considering only interchanging the order of two consecutive cities, we could evaluate interchanges of links between any two pairs of cities. All those interchanges that decrease the total distance of the tour are made. The resulting tour is then called *2-optimal*, i.e., it cannot be improved any further by interchanges of two links. Note, though, the large number of possible interchanges that have to be checked—the majority violating property 1. This concept can be extended to the simultaneous interchanges of more than two links.

Another approach suitable for large problems is to use a break-make strategy. The map of cities to be visited is divided into several compact natural geographical clusters, or regions, of cities. Within each region, a good or even the optimum tour is found. Finally, the various subtours are linked to one another. The task is again best done directly on the map of cities.

EXERCISES

23.1 N items of volume q_i, $i = 1, 2, \ldots, N$, have to be loaded into boxes each with capacity Q. The following heuristic procedure is suggested to find a good if not optimal packing schedule:

(a) Make a list (A) of the items in terms of descending order of volume.
(b) Take the first item on list A, and allocate it to a box.
(c) Rearrange the partially loaded boxes (list B) in ascending order of space left unused.
(d) Take the next item on list A, and allocate it to the first box in list B that will accommodate it. If none do, use a new box.
(e) Repeat steps (c) and (d) until all items have been loaded.

(f) If the number k of boxes used is equal to k_0, where

$$(1/Q)\sum_{i=1}^{N} q_i \leq k_0 < 1 + (1/Q)\sum_{i=1}^{N} q_i$$

then the loading is optimal. Stop. If $k > k_0$, go to step (g).

(g) Rearrange the partially loaded boxes in list B in ascending order of space left unused.

(h) Take the last box in list B—the one with the largest unused space. Starting with the first box in list B, check whether it is possible to reduce the unused space in that box by interchanging the last j items loaded in the last box with the last m items loaded in the other box, $j = 1, 2, 3, \ldots$ and $m = 1, 2, 3, \ldots$. Make the interchange with the largest unused space reduction. Continue these comparisons and interchanges with the second and third boxes, etc., until all boxes have been compared with the last.

(i) Remove the last box from list B, and also remove any boxes completely emptied.

(j) Stop if $k = k_0$, or if no further improvements can be made; otherwise, go to step (g).

In terms of the classification in Section 23-4, identify the various strategies used. Identify each heuristic used.

23.2 Consider the transportation algorithm of Chapter 6. In terms of the discussion of Section 23-4, identify the various strategies used in that algorithm and state each heuristic.

23.3 Consider the critical path cost model of Section 8-6. From the description given there, construct a step-by-step algorithm for the method. In terms of the discussion in Section 23-4, identify the various strategies used and list each heuristic.

23.4 In the car pool problem, the objective is to assign itineraries to a number of car drivers who may each pick up a limited number of passengers en route to a common destination. This itinerary should minimize the total distance traveled. Consider the following list of coordinates, where each point is a pickup and the distances between points are proportional to the Euclidean distance: a (−6, 0), b (−3, 10), c (−4.5, 7), d (−2, 6), e (−6, 4), f (−2.5, 2), g (0, 8), h (0, 4), i (2.5, 6), j (5, 9), k (5.5, 7.5), l (4.5, 5), m (4, 3), n (−3, −1), o (−5, −2.5), p (−1, −3), q (−4, −5), r (−5, −9), s (−5.5, − 9), t (0, −5), u (−0.5, −7), v (−1, −10), x (1, −2), y (0.5, −10), z (7, −5); destination (0, 0). No car can take more than 4 people, including the driver.

(a) Suggest a heuristic solution-building procedure aimed at minimizing total distance traveled by all cars. All cars travel to the destination (0, 0). Use the procedure to find a solution. (*Hint:* Graph the points and do it directly on the graph.)

(b) Redo (a) but allow the cars to be left at intermediate points, with the occupants merging with occupants in other cars.

23.5 Nick Dickson, a confirmed gambler, while knowing nothing about politics, enjoys betting on the outcome of elections. For the forthcoming contest, Nick had shopped around and obtained the following odds, in terms of the total payout for each \$1 bet if each candidate wins: Joe Honest \$7, Ted Algood \$10, Bob Friendly \$2, Jack Sincere \$5. "If I place my bets properly, I can't lose," thought Nick. He was able to raise \$6600 for the venture. Unfortunately, he made a mistake when placing the bets, so that when Bob Friendly won, Nick came out on the losing end. Use a heuristic procedure to determine how Nick should have placed his bets so as to ensure a gain whatever the outcome.

23.6 The air force command has received instructions to disrupt the enemy's supply lines so as to slow down their advance. Supplies are being transported along one road on which there are five major bridges. The destruction of any one of these bridges will achieve the desired effect. The amount of fuel available is 25,000 gallons. Two types of aircraft are suitable for this mission: B21.5's and F222's. There are 20 B21.5's and 15 F222's. The fuel consumption is 1 gal/mile for a B21.5 and $\frac{2}{3}$ gal/mile for an F222. Data concerning the vulnerability of each bridge to attack by each type of plane, and the distance of each bridge from the base, are given in the table below.

	Probability of Destruction		
Bridge	By a B21.5	By an F222	Distance from Base (in miles)
A	0.08	0.06	600
B	0.18	0.18	900
C	0.15	0.13	1100
D	0.28	0.23	1200
E	0.30	out of range	1500

Each plane has to carry sufficient fuel for the round trip (to target and back) plus 10 percent extra as a safety margin. For planning purposes, any bomb damage short of complete destruction is regarded as a miss because the bridge is still usable. Devise a heuristic procedure that will enable you to allocate planes to targets, so that the probability of success is maximized. In calculating the probability of success for any particular allocation, you may find the following method easiest: Suppose the allocation decided upon is for all planes to be assigned to bridge A (this allocation is not within the fuel limit). Then (probability of success) = (1 − probability of failure) = $[1 - (1 - .08)^{20}(1 - .06)^{15}] = 0.9254$.

23.7 Middle Earth is reapportioning its election districts for its high court of elders. The guiding principle of this reapportionment is one person, one vote. This means that the 22 regions should be assigned to 4 election districts such that each district has about the same population size, say within a margin of 5 percent from either side of the average. No region should be split; i.e., each should be assigned entirely to only one election district. Furthermore, to avoid gerrymandering, each district should be contiguous (i.e., it should be possible to walk from each region in a district to all other regions in the same district without leaving the district) and compact (i.e., the centers of all regions in a district should be as close together as possible). In other words, districts of a circular shape are preferred to districts with arms protruding. A suitable measure of compactness is given by the ratio of the sum of the squared distances between the region centers over the total area of the district. A list of populations, areas for each region, and distances between region centers is given in the table. Find a heuristic procedure for allocating the regions to districts, subject to the population constraint, contiguity, and achieving good compactness. Figure 23-3 in the text shows a map of Middle Earth.

			Distance to Center of Region																				
Region	Population	Area	2	3	4	5	6	7	8	9	10	11	12	13	14	15	16	17	18	19	20	21	22
1	1000	16	4	12	8	7	12	17	18	15	20	24	27	23	22	20	22	28	28	31	33	36	34
2	2000	15		8	6	7	10	15	15	12	17	21	25	20	20	19	21	26	26	29	31	33	32
3	1100	70			5	9	9	12	11	5	10	11	18	13	15	16	18	22	20	23	24	27	27
4	4100	7				4	5	10	10	7	12	16	18	14	14	13	16	20	20	25	25	27	26
5	1500	32					5	10	11	10	15	18	21	16	16	13	15	21	21	25	27	29	27
6	2600	23						5	6	7	11	16	16	12	11	8	11	16	16	20	22	24	22
7	1000	26							4	7	10	14	12	8	6	4	6	10	10	15	18	20	17
8	800	14								6	8	1	2	8	9	6	8	11	10	14	15	18	17
9	3000	40									8	11	14	9	10	11	13	15	14	17	18	21	21
10	2000	24										4	8	5	8	13	14	14	12	14	15	18	20
11	3500	65											8	7	10	16	17	15	13	14	13	17	20
12	1500	22												5	6	12	12	8	5	6	6	10	12
13	1900	11													3	9	10	9	7	10	11	14	14
14	2700	31														6	6	7	6	9	11	13	13
15	1500	16															3	9	10	13	16	18	14
16	3800	30																7	8	12	15	18	12
17	2700	31																	3	8	9	9	9
18	4500	13																		3	6	8	7
19	4000	15																			3	5	6
20	1500	18																				4	8
21	1000	28																					6
22	1500	38																					

23.8 There are n jobs $1, 2, \ldots, i, \ldots, n$ that have to be processed on either of two machines in a single pass. Each job i takes a time t_i and has associated with it a priority weighting $p_i > 0$. Higher values of p_i correspond to more urgent jobs. We have to assign each job to a machine and determine the order in which each machine processes the jobs assigned to it. At time 0 each machine starts processing its first job and upon completion immediately proceeds to the next job, and so on. Let T_i be the time in which job i is completed. Thus, if a machine processes jobs 1, 2, and 4 in that order, $T_1 = t_1$, $T_2 = T_1 + t_2$, $T_4 = T_2 + t_4$. We want to find an allocation of jobs to the two machines and a sequencing of jobs at each machine so as to minimize the weighted sum of completion times, $C = \Sigma_{i=1}^{n} p_i T_i$. Consider the following jobs:

i	1	2	3	4	5	6	7	8
t_i	4	7	2	12	7	3	5	15
p_i	9	15	4	20	10	3	4	9

(a) Develop a step-by-step heuristic solution-building procedure. (*Hint:* If there is only a single machine, then the optimal assignment of jobs is in order of nondecreasing ratios $e_i = t_i/p_i$. See D. A. Wismer, "Solution of the Flowshop-Scheduling Problem with No Intermediate Queues," *Operations Research*, Vol. 20, No. 3, May–June 1972, p. 689. Hence, to get an initial good solution, we only have to worry about assigning jobs to machines. The order of processing the jobs on a machine follows the same principle as for a single machine.)

(b) Develop a step-by-step solution-modification procedure with a view to improving the solution derived under (a). (*Hint:* Find a criterion for interchanging jobs or groups of jobs between the 2 machines, such that total weighted completion time is reduced.)

23.9 Use Johnson's sequencing algorithm to find the optimal sequence for the following jobs to be processed on two machines:

Job	1	2	3	4	5	6	7	8	9	10	11	12
A_i	5	8	11	2	4	7	12	3	9	3	6	10
B_i	5	9	4	3	7	6	9	4	5	8	9	4

What is the total processing time?

23.10 Assume now that not all jobs have the same sequence—some jobs have to go first on machine B, followed by machine A. For the data of problem 23.9, assume that jobs 8 through 12 have the order B–A. Adapt Johnson's algorithm to get a heuristic method for sequencing all 12 jobs. The objective is still to minimize total elapsed time to process all jobs.

23.11 A firm has to relocate its factory, serving six regional warehouses, located as follows:

Warehouse	1	2	3	4	5	6	
x_i-coordinate	120	160	250	220	300	180	miles
y_i-coordinate	210	40	200	100	60	280	miles
Volume of sales	40	80	50	70	30	60	units

If transport costs are linear with respect to volume and distance, find the optimal factory location.

23.12 Assume that transport costs in exercise 23.11 are a function of the warehouse location because of geographical features of the area. The costs are as follows:

Warehouse	1	2	3	4	5	6
Cost/unit/mile	1	1	1.5	2	1	1

Adapt the procedure to this situation and find the new optimal factory location.

23.13 (*Computationally heavy*) Consider the Middle Earth weed processing problem in Section 23-7. Find the optimal location if two processing plants have to be built for the first 10 regions only. (Disregard the remaining 12 regions.) Use as initial locations for the two plants the center of gravity of regions 2 and 9. Terminate iterations if the change in location for both plants is less than 5 10-mile units for all coordinates. Find the cost associated with the final solution.

23.14 Consider the following 10 cities:

City	1	2	3	4	5	6	7	8	9	10
x_i-coordinate	0	5	8	7	10	15	16	18	18	20
y_i-coordinate	0	20	12	4	15	4	18	8	15	17

(a) Use the method by Norback and Love to find a "good" tour.

(b) Apply the search-learning heuristic of interchanging consecutive cities. Can the tour be improved?

(c) Try Lin's procedure of interchanging links between 2 pairs of cities on the solution found in (a). Note that all possible interchanges of two links have to be tested, although many can be ruled out visually either as violating property 1 or as bad. Can the tour be improved?

23.15 Using the Norback and Love method, find a good tour for visiting the 22 locations in Middle Earth, whose coordinates are given in Table 23-1.

23.16 Use a break-make strategy to find a good tour for visiting all 22 locations in Middle Earth, shown in Table 23-1. Divide Middle Earth in about 4 areas. Use the Norback and Love method for each area, and then connect the subtours appropriately.

REFERENCES

Eilon, S., C. D. T. Watson-Gandy, and N. Christofides. *Distribution Management: Mathematical Modelling and Practical Analysis.* London: Griffen, 1971. Extensive coverage of facility location, particularly the infinite set approach, and vehicle scheduling. An excellent starting point in this field.

Gordon, P. J. "Heuristic Problem Solving," *Business Horizons*, Spring 1962. The author develops his discussion of heuristic problem solving around a very tricky puzzle and its method of solution. This easy-to-read article is a must for puzzle addicts.

Hinkle, Charles L., and Alfred A. Kuehn. "Heuristic Models: Mapping the Maze for Management," *California Management Review*, Fall 1967. A nontechnical introduction to the subject of heuristic problem solving with a brief survey of specific application areas. This article is reprinted in A. Rappaport, Ed., *Information for Decision Making* (Englewood Cliffs, N.J.: Prentice-Hall, 1970). It includes a substantial list of references.

Meier, R. C., W. T. Newell, and H. L. Pazer. *Simulation in Business and Economics.* Englewood Cliffs, N.J.: Prentice-Hall, 1969. Chapter 5 contains an introduction to the nature of heuristic methods, along with some detailed examples of the application of the approach. An extensive list of references up to 1968 is included.

Mercer, A., M. Cantley, and G. Rand. *Operational Distribution Research—Innovative Case Studies.* London: Taylor & Francis, 1978. Detailed analysis of ten disguised case studies in facility location, distribution management, and vehicle scheduling. Gives good insight into effective operations research.

Minieka, E. *Optimization Algorithms for Networks and Graphs.* New York: Dekker, 1978. Introductory coverage of algorithms for the Chinese postman problem, the traveling salesman problem, and location problems.

Scott, A. J. *Combinatorial Programming, Spatial Analysis and Planning.* London: Methuen and Co., 1971. Chapter 3 contains an exposition of the application of heuristic methods to combinatorial problems. Includes a comprehensive reference list.

Simon, H. A. *The New Science of Management Decisions.* New York: Harper and Brothers, 1960. This book contains a series of lectures on the impact of computer technology on managerial decision making. In lecture two, heuristic methods in relation to human problem solving activity are discussed.

______. "The Structure of Ill-Structured Problems," *Artificial Intelligence*, Winter 1973. The properties of well-structured and ill-structured problems are discussed, and the implications of these are examined by use of examples.

APPENDIX A

Introduction to Vectors and Simultaneous Equations, plus a Matrix Algebra Approach to Linear Programming

The first part of this appendix (Sections A-1 through A-8) briefly develops the concepts of vector analysis and simultaneous equations necessary for the main body of the text. In the second part of the appendix (Section A-9), linear programming is derived in terms of matrices for readers who already have a working knowledge of this type of mathematics. This latter part is not self-contained; it relies on the ideas developed in Chapters 2 and 3. Therefore, it is recommended that those chapters be read before Section A-9 is studied.

A-1 VECTORS

We are familiar with the notion of expressing a point in terms of an origin and coordinate axes. Each point in 2 dimensions (2-*space*) uniquely represents an *ordered*

Figure A-1. *Vectors in two-space.*

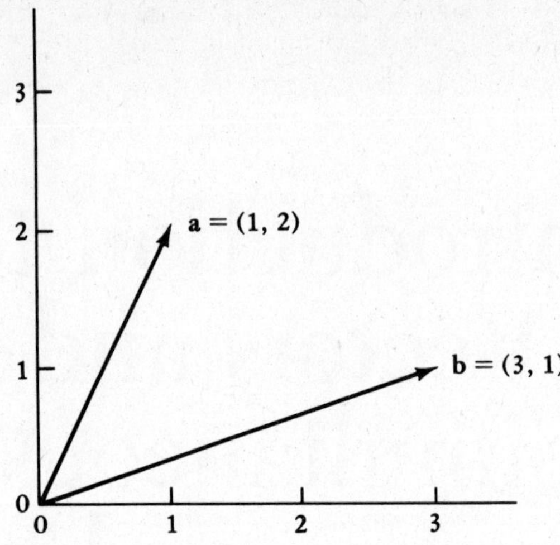

pair of real numbers. The pair is *ordered* because it matters which order the numbers are in; e.g., (0, 1) is not the same as (1, 0). Also, each point uniquely represents a line from the origin to the point. We will call this line a *vector*. The vector has *direction* (from the origin to the point) and *magnitude* (the length of the line), as illustrated in Figure A-1. Thus, in 2-space, there is a unique correspondence between vectors directed from the origin and ordered pairs of real numbers.

These concepts can be generalized to *n-space*. Every vector in n-space is uniquely represented by an ordered set of n real numbers (the *elements* of the vector). We will write the vector, in terms of its elements, as $(a_1, a_2, a_3, \ldots, a_n) = \mathbf{a}$.

Vectors are significant in that they facilitate manipulation of points and, thus, of ordered sets of real numbers. Take the two points $\mathbf{a} = (a_1, a_2, \ldots, a_n)$ and $\mathbf{b} = (b_1, b_2, \ldots, b_n)$. How do we add or multiply them? How do we find the distance between them? Geometric ideas in 2-space and 3-space can be generalized to enable algebraic analysis of points in n-space.

A-2 MANIPULATION OF VECTORS

In 2-space, the sum of two vectors—e.g., (1, 2) and (3, 1)—is given by the sum of corresponding elements $(1 + 3, 2 + 1) = (4, 3)$. This procedure is represented diagrammatically in Figure A-2 by a parallelogram.

When generalizing to n-space, it is necessary to insist that vectors can be summed only if they exist in the same space. For example, the 2-space vector (2, 1) cannot be added to the 4-space vector (1, 0, 1, 0).

Figure A-2. *Sum of vectors.*

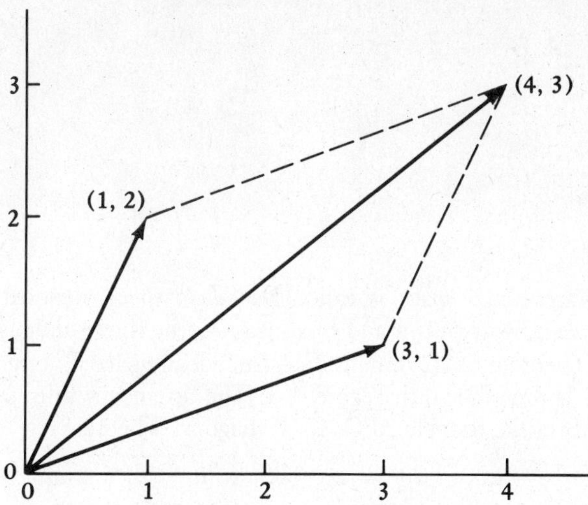

ADDITION OF VECTORS

Given two vectors in n-space, $\mathbf{a} = (a_1, a_2, \ldots, a_n)$ and $\mathbf{b} = (b_1, b_2, \ldots, b_n)$, their sum is $\mathbf{a} + \mathbf{b} = (a_1 + b_1, a_2 + b_2, \ldots, a_n + b_n)$.

Subtraction of vectors follows immediately. If $-\mathbf{b} = (-b_1, -b_2, \ldots, -b_n)$, then $\mathbf{a} - \mathbf{b} = \mathbf{a} + (-\mathbf{b}) = (a_1 - b_1, a_2 - b_2, \ldots, a_n - b_n)$.

Before we discuss multiplication of vectors, it will be necessary to distinguish between a *row vector* and a *column vector.* If the elements are written $[g_1, \ldots, g_n]$ it is a row vector; if the elements are written

$$\begin{bmatrix} g_1 \\ \cdot \\ \cdot \\ \cdot \\ g_n \end{bmatrix}$$

it is a column vector. There is no conceptual difference between them; it is purely a matter of usage. We will assume that *all vectors are column vectors unless otherwise stated* (but for convenience they will be written as row vectors). If $\mathbf{a}$ is a column vector, we can denote its row vector equivalent as $\mathbf{a}'$.

A useful multiplication of vectors is the *scalar product.* It is called the scalar product because the result of the multiplication is a *scalar* (a real number—not a vector).

SCALAR PRODUCT

If **a** and **b** are vectors in n-space, then the scalar product is

$$\mathbf{a}'\mathbf{b} = \mathbf{b}'\mathbf{a} = \sum_{j=1}^{n} a_j b_j = c$$

where c is the scalar.

An n-dimensional space is called *Euclidean space* (denoted by E^n) when the distance between two points **a** and **b** is measured by the n-dimensional extension of Pythagoras' Theorem. In 2-dimensional Euclidean space E^2, the distance between points **a** and **b** is as shown in Figure A-3. The distance γ from **a** to **b** is the length of the side AB of the triangle ABC. By Pythagoras' Theorem,

$$\gamma^2 = (b_1 - a_1)^2 + (a_2 - b_2)^2 = (a_1 - b_1)^2 + (a_2 - b_2)^2$$

and

$$\gamma = \sqrt{\left[\sum_{j=1}^{2} (a_j - b_j)^2\right]}$$

In n-space E^n, distance is defined as follows.

DISTANCE IN EUCLIDEAN SPACE E^n

The distance between $\mathbf{a} = (a_1, a_2, \ldots, a_n)$ and $\mathbf{b} = (b_1, b_2, \ldots, b_n)$ is

$$\sqrt{\left[\sum_{j=1}^{n} (a_j - b_j)^2\right]}$$

A simple extension of the idea of distance between two points gives the *length of a vector.* The length of a vector is the distance between the origin and the point identifying the vector.

LENGTH OF A VECTOR

The length of a vector $\mathbf{a} = (a_1, a_2, \ldots, a_n)$ in E^n is

$$\sqrt{\sum_{j=1}^{n} (a_j)^2}$$

Figure A-3. *Euclidean distance in* E^2.

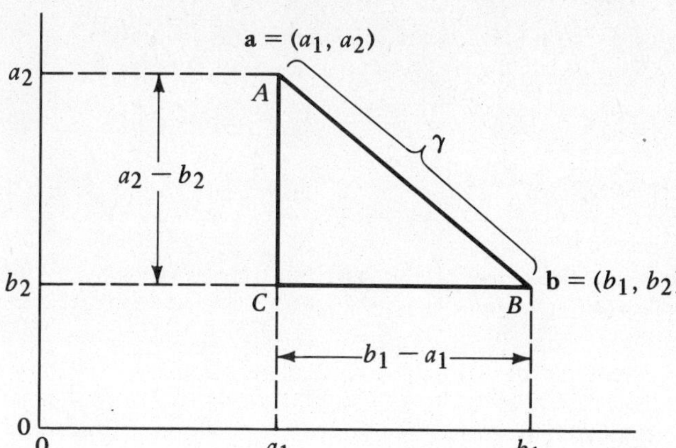

Another aspect of vectors that is of importance to us is the multiplication of a vector by a scalar.

MULTIPLICATION BY A SCALAR

If $\mathbf{a} = (a_1, \ldots, a_n)$ is a vector in E^n and λ is a scalar, then

$$\lambda\mathbf{a} = (\lambda a_1, \lambda a_2, \ldots, \lambda a_n)$$

For example, if $\mathbf{a} = (2, 1)$ and $\lambda = 3$, then $\lambda\mathbf{a} = (6, 3)$.

A-3 SPECIAL VECTORS

A number of commonly used vectors are given special names. All definitions are in Euclidean space E^n.

NULL VECTOR

The null vector is the vector whose elements are all zero:

$$\mathbf{0} = (0, 0, \ldots, 0)$$

The null vector corresponds to the origin.

SUM VECTOR

The sum vector is the vector whose elements are all unity:

$$\mathbf{1} = (1, 1, \ldots, 1)$$

UNIT VECTOR $\mathbf{e}_i$

The unit vector $\mathbf{e}_i$ is the vector with unity as its ith element and all other elements zero.

Examples of unit vectors are $\mathbf{e}_1 = (1, 0, \ldots, 0)$, $\mathbf{e}_2 = (0, 1, 0, \ldots, 0)$, etc. In 2-space, there are 2 unit vectors; in n-space, there are n unit vectors. Geometrically, these vectors lie along the axes of the space and have unit length.

A-4 REPRESENTING A VECTOR AS A LINEAR COMBINATION OF OTHER VECTORS

If we have a set of vectors in E^n, $\mathbf{a}_1, \mathbf{a}_2, \ldots, \mathbf{a}_r$, we say that $\mathbf{b}$ is expressed as a *linear combination* of these vectors if, for some scalars $\gamma_1, \gamma_2, \ldots, \gamma_r$,

(A-1) $$\mathbf{b} = \gamma_1\mathbf{a}_1 + \gamma_2\mathbf{a}_2 + \gamma_3\mathbf{a}_3 + \cdots + \gamma_r\mathbf{a}_r$$

Expression (A-1) combines the ideas of vector addition and multiplication by a scalar. We are finding proportions (the γ_i) of the vectors $\mathbf{a}_1, \ldots, \mathbf{a}_r$ that sum to $\mathbf{b}$.

In Figure A-4, we illustrate this for the case of $\mathbf{a}_1 = (2, 1)$, $\mathbf{a}_2 = (1, 3)$, and $\mathbf{b} = (8,9)$:

(A-2) $$\mathbf{b} = \gamma_1\mathbf{a}_1 + \gamma_2\mathbf{a}_2$$

or

$$\begin{bmatrix} 8 \\ 9 \end{bmatrix} = 3\begin{bmatrix} 2 \\ 1 \end{bmatrix} + 2\begin{bmatrix} 1 \\ 3 \end{bmatrix}$$

The proportions are $\gamma_1 = 3$ and $\gamma_2 = 2$; i.e., $\mathbf{b}$ is 3 times $\mathbf{a}_1$, plus 2 times $\mathbf{a}_2$.

A special case of a linear combination is where $\Sigma_i\gamma_i = 1$, with all $\gamma_i \geq 0$. For the two-vector case, this defines a vector on the straight line between the vectors (*line segment*).

For example, let $\mathbf{a}_1 = \begin{bmatrix} 12 \\ 9 \end{bmatrix}$, $\mathbf{a}_2 = \begin{bmatrix} 9 \\ 3 \end{bmatrix}$, $\gamma_1 = \frac{1}{3}$, $\gamma_2 = \frac{2}{3}$. For simplicity, let $\gamma_1 = \gamma = \frac{1}{3}$, and let $\gamma_2 = (1 - \gamma) = \frac{2}{3}$. We now look at

$$\mathbf{b} = \gamma\mathbf{a}_1 + (1 - \gamma)\mathbf{a}_2 = \frac{1}{3}\begin{bmatrix} 12 \\ 9 \end{bmatrix} + \frac{2}{3}\begin{bmatrix} 9 \\ 3 \end{bmatrix} = \begin{bmatrix} 10 \\ 5 \end{bmatrix}$$

This lies on the straight line between $\mathbf{a}_1$ and $\mathbf{a}_2$. In fact, for any $0 \leq \gamma \leq 1$, the vector $\mathbf{b} = \gamma\mathbf{a}_1 + (1 - \gamma)\mathbf{a}_2$ lies γ of the way from $\mathbf{a}_2$ to $\mathbf{a}_1$ on the line segment. Figure A-5 illustrates this.

Figure A-4. *Representing* **b** *as a linear combination of* $\mathbf{a}_1$, $\mathbf{a}_2$.

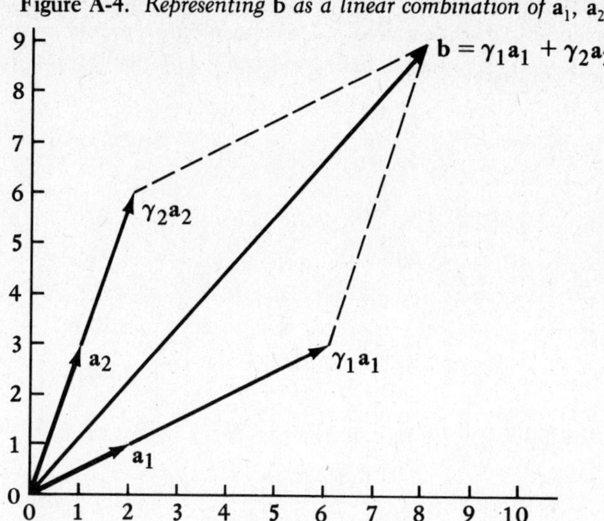

The concept provides us with a definition of the line segment between two vectors, or points.

> LINE SEGMENT BETWEEN $\mathbf{a}_1$ AND $\mathbf{a}_2$
>
> The line segment between two points $\mathbf{a}_1$ and $\mathbf{a}_2$ is the set of points
>
> $$\mathbf{b} = \gamma\mathbf{a}_1 + (1 - \gamma)\mathbf{a}_2, \qquad \text{for all } \gamma,\ 0 \leq \gamma \leq 1$$

Figure A-5. *Line segment between two vectors.*

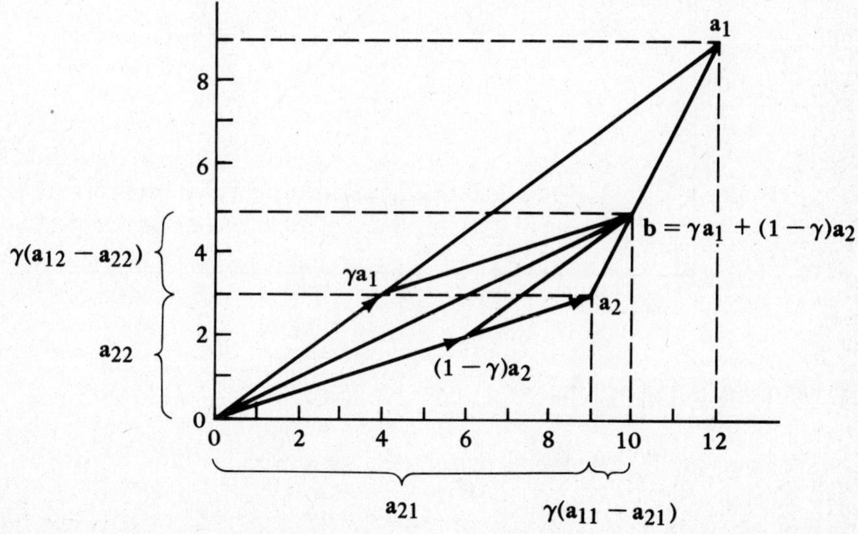

This definition can be extended to any number of points. In its more general form, this linear combination is called a *convex combination* and represents a segment of a plane. The plane segment is called the *convex hull* of the points.

> CONVEX HULL OF THE POINTS $\mathbf{a}_1, \mathbf{a}_2, \ldots, \mathbf{a}_p$ IN E^n
>
> The convex hull in E^n of p points $\mathbf{a}_1, \mathbf{a}_2, \mathbf{a}_3, \ldots, \mathbf{a}_p$ is the set of points $\mathbf{b} = \sum_{i=1}^{p} \gamma_i \mathbf{a}_i$, for all γ_i, such that $\sum_{i=1}^{p} \gamma_i = 1$ and all $\gamma_i \geq 0$.

Consider the points $\mathbf{a}_1 = \begin{bmatrix} 12 \\ 9 \end{bmatrix}, \mathbf{a}_2 = \begin{bmatrix} 9 \\ 3 \end{bmatrix}, \mathbf{a}_3 = \begin{bmatrix} 6 \\ 6 \end{bmatrix}$. the convex hull of these points is shown in Figure A-6. If $\gamma_1 = \frac{1}{3}$, $\gamma_2 = \frac{1}{3}$, $\gamma_3 = \frac{1}{3}$ (so $\sum_{i=1}^{3} \gamma_i = 1$, and all $\gamma_i \geq 0$), then

$$\mathbf{b} = \frac{1}{3}\begin{bmatrix} 12 \\ 9 \end{bmatrix} + \frac{1}{3}\begin{bmatrix} 9 \\ 3 \end{bmatrix} + \frac{1}{3}\begin{bmatrix} 6 \\ 6 \end{bmatrix} = \begin{bmatrix} 9 \\ 6 \end{bmatrix}$$

Figure A-6. *Convex hull of three points in* E^2.

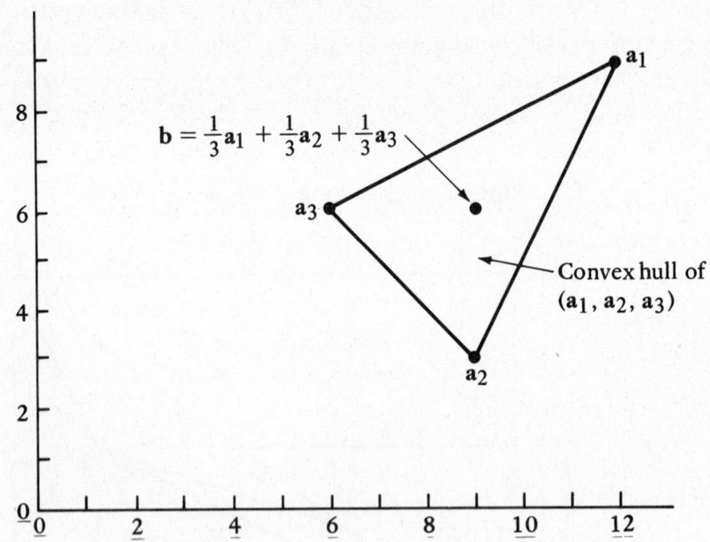

A-5 LINEAR INDEPENDENCE, SPANNING SET, AND BASIS

We now want to define some properties of sets of vectors. If, in E^n, we have a set of vectors $\mathbf{a}_1, \mathbf{a}_2, \ldots, \mathbf{a}_r$, we say that they are *linearly independent* if no one of them can be expressed as a linear combination of the remaining ones.

LINEAR INDEPENDENCE

A set of vectors $\mathbf{a}_1, \mathbf{a}_2, \ldots, \mathbf{a}_r$ is linearly independent if $\gamma_1\mathbf{a}_1 + \gamma_2\mathbf{a}_2 + \cdots + \gamma_r\mathbf{a}_r = 0$ holds only if $\gamma_1 = \gamma_2 = \cdots = \gamma_r = 0$.

A set of vectors is *linearly dependent* if it is not linearly independent.

Consider the set of vectors $\mathbf{a}_1, \mathbf{a}_2, \mathbf{a}_3, \mathbf{a}_4$ in E^2, where $\mathbf{a}_1 = (2, 1)$, $\mathbf{a}_2 = (1, 3)$, $\mathbf{a}_3 = (2, 3)$, $\mathbf{a}_4 = (4, 2)$. These are shown in Figure A-7. The set $(\mathbf{a}_1, \mathbf{a}_2)$ is linearly independent, since neither of the vectors can be expressed in terms of the other. This is clear geometrically from Figure A-7. Algebraically, only $\gamma_1 = \gamma_2 = 0$ will satisfy

$$\gamma_1 \begin{bmatrix} 2 \\ 1 \end{bmatrix} + \gamma_2 \begin{bmatrix} 1 \\ 3 \end{bmatrix} = \begin{bmatrix} 0 \\ 0 \end{bmatrix}$$

There is no finite scalar $(-\gamma_2/\gamma_1)$ such that $\begin{bmatrix} 2 \\ 1 \end{bmatrix} = (-\gamma_2/\gamma_1)\begin{bmatrix} 1 \\ 3 \end{bmatrix}$. However, the set $(\mathbf{a}_1, \mathbf{a}_2, \mathbf{a}_3)$ is not linearly independent. Geometrically, we see that $\mathbf{a}_3$ can be expressed as a linear combination of $(\mathbf{a}_1, \mathbf{a}_2)$. Algebraically, $\gamma_1\mathbf{a}_1 + \gamma_2\mathbf{a}_2 + \gamma_3\mathbf{a}_3 = 0$ is satisfied by (at least) $\gamma_1 = \frac{3}{5}$, $\gamma_2 = \frac{4}{5}$, $\gamma_3 = -1$. In fact, no set of three vectors in E^2 can be

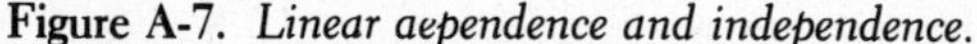

Figure A-7. *Linear aependence and independence.*

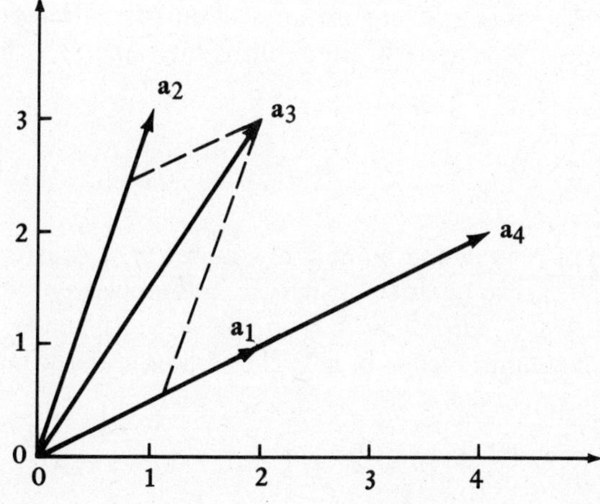

linearly independent. What about the set ($\mathbf{a}_1$, $\mathbf{a}_4$)? We can write $2\mathbf{a}_1 = \mathbf{a}_4$; so $\gamma_1 = 2$, $\gamma_4 = -1$ gives us $\gamma_1\mathbf{a}_1 + \gamma_4\mathbf{a}_4 = \mathbf{0}$. The set is linearly dependent. Is the set ($\mathbf{a}_1$) linearly independent?

The set of vectors $\mathbf{a}_1, \mathbf{a}_2, \ldots, \mathbf{a}_r$ in E^n is a *spanning set* of E^n if every vector in E^n can be expressed as a linear combination of the set. From Figure A-7 we can see that no less than two vectors are required to form a spanning set in E^2. So, for example, the set ($\mathbf{a}_1$, $\mathbf{a}_2$) is a spanning set, and so is ($\mathbf{a}_1$, $\mathbf{a}_2$, $\mathbf{a}_3$). However, the set ($\mathbf{a}_1$) is not a spanning set, and neither is ($\mathbf{a}_1$, $\mathbf{a}_4$), since many vectors in the space cannot be expressed as linear combinations of either of these sets.

A set of vectors $\mathbf{a}_1, \mathbf{a}_2, \ldots, \mathbf{a}_r$ in E^n is called a *basis* if it is both linearly independent and a spanning set in E^n. Our discussion of linear independence showed us that no set of $r > n$ vectors in E^n could be linearly independent. Similarly, no set of $r < n$ vectors in E^n could span the space. So we conclude that a basis must have exactly n vectors in E^n. Looking at Figure A-7, we see that ($\mathbf{a}_1$, $\mathbf{a}_2$) is a basis, and so is ($\mathbf{a}_3$, $\mathbf{a}_4$). How many other bases are there? Is ($\mathbf{a}_1$, $\mathbf{a}_4$) a basis? Clearly, it is not a basis because it is not linearly independent.

BASIS IN E^n

A set of vectors $\mathbf{a}_1, \mathbf{a}_2, \ldots, \mathbf{a}_r$ in E^n is a basis if it is a linearly independent spanning set of E^n. If it is a basis, then $r = n$.

A-6 MATRICES

Let us look at a few properties of matrices that will be useful in Chapters 13 and 17. There are a number of ways of understanding a matrix. We could think of it as a vector of vectors, or as a rectangular array of numbers arranged in rows and columns. Whichever way we perceive it, the result is the same. The following is an example of a matrix:

$$\mathbf{A} = \begin{bmatrix} 2 & 1 & 0 \\ 1 & 3 & 1 \end{bmatrix}$$

The number of rows m and number of columns n of $\mathbf{A}$ define the *dimensions* of $\mathbf{A}$. So $\mathbf{A}$ is a 2×3 (two by three) matrix. If the numbers of rows and columns are the same, it is a *square matrix. Let* $\mathbf{A} = (\mathbf{a}_1, \mathbf{a}_2, \ldots, \mathbf{a}_n)$ and $\mathbf{B} = (\mathbf{b}_1, \mathbf{b}_2, \ldots, \mathbf{b}_n)$ be row vectors of column vectors in E^m. The sum of $\mathbf{A}$ and $\mathbf{B}$ follows from the addition of vectors:

$$\mathbf{A} + \mathbf{B} = (\mathbf{a}_1 + \mathbf{b}_1, \mathbf{a}_2 + \mathbf{b}_2, \ldots, \mathbf{a}_n + \mathbf{b}_n)$$

Expanding this further, we get the following.

ADDITION OF MATRICES

Given two matrices

$$\mathbf{A} = \begin{bmatrix} a_{11} & a_{12} & \cdots & a_{1n} \\ a_{21} & a_{22} & \cdots & a_{2n} \\ \cdot & \cdot & & \cdot \\ \cdot & \cdot & & \cdot \\ \cdot & \cdot & & \cdot \\ a_{m1} & a_{m2} & \cdots & a_{mn} \end{bmatrix} \qquad \mathbf{B} = \begin{bmatrix} b_{11} & b_{12} & \cdots & b_{1n} \\ b_{21} & b_{22} & \cdots & b_{2n} \\ \cdot & \cdot & & \cdot \\ \cdot & \cdot & & \cdot \\ \cdot & \cdot & & \cdot \\ b_{m1} & b_{m2} & \cdots & b_{mn} \end{bmatrix}$$

their sum is

$$\mathbf{A} + \mathbf{B} = \begin{bmatrix} a_{11} + b_{11} & a_{12} + b_{12} & \cdots & a_{1n} + b_{1n} \\ a_{21} + b_{21} & a_{22} + b_{22} & \cdots & a_{2n} + b_{2n} \\ \cdot & \cdot & \cdot & \cdot \\ \cdot & \cdot & \cdot & \cdot \\ \cdot & \cdot & \cdot & \cdot \\ a_{m1} + b_{m1} & a_{m2} + b_{m2} & \cdots & a_{mn} + b_{mn} \end{bmatrix}$$

The product of matrices is also a generalization of the scalar product of vectors, though this is not as obvious as it is for addition. Let **A** be an $m \times r$ matrix, and let **B** be an $r \times n$ matrix. Consider **A** as a column vector of m row vectors in E^r, and consider **B** as a row vector of n column vectors in E^r.

$$\mathbf{A} = \begin{bmatrix} \mathbf{a}_1 \\ \mathbf{a}_2 \\ \cdot \\ \cdot \\ \cdot \\ \mathbf{a}_m \end{bmatrix}$$

$$\mathbf{B} = [\mathbf{b}_1, \mathbf{b}_2, \ldots, \mathbf{b}_n]$$

PRODUCT OF MATRICES

The product of **A** and **B** is an $m \times n$ matrix:

$$\mathbf{AB} = \begin{bmatrix} \mathbf{a}_1\mathbf{b}_1 & \mathbf{a}_1\mathbf{b}_2 & \cdots & \mathbf{a}_1\mathbf{b}_n \\ \mathbf{a}_2\mathbf{b}_1 & \mathbf{a}_2\mathbf{b}_2 & \cdots & \mathbf{a}_2\mathbf{b}_n \\ \cdot & \cdot & & \cdot \\ \cdot & \cdot & & \cdot \\ \cdot & \cdot & & \cdot \\ \mathbf{a}_m\mathbf{b}_1 & \mathbf{a}_m\mathbf{b}_2 & \cdots & \mathbf{a}_m\mathbf{b}_n \end{bmatrix}$$

where $\mathbf{a}_i\mathbf{b}_j = \Sigma_{k=1}^{r} a_{ik}b_{kj}$ is the scalar product of the ith row of **A** and the jth column of **B**.

However, note that **BA** will be defined only when $m = n$.

If **A** is a square matrix of dimension n, we can write **AA** as $\mathbf{A}^2$. Let $\mathbf{a}_i$ be the ith row, and let $\mathbf{a}_j$ be the jth column of **A**; the element of $\mathbf{A}^2$ in row i and column j is $\mathbf{a}_i\mathbf{a}_j = \sum_{k=1}^{n} a_{ik}a_{kj}$. More generally,

$$\mathbf{A}^k = \mathbf{A}\mathbf{A}^{k-1} = \underbrace{\mathbf{AAA} \cdots \mathbf{A}}_{k \text{ terms}}$$

It is often convenient for us to view a vector as a matrix with only one row or column. Thus, if $\mathbf{c} = [c_1, c_2, \ldots, c_m]$ is a row vector of m elements ($1 \times m$ matrix) and if **A** is an $m \times n$ matrix, the product **cA** is a row vector of n elements:

$$\mathbf{cA} = \left[\sum_{i=1}^{m} c_i a_{i1}, \sum_{i=1}^{m} c_i a_{i2}, \ldots, \sum_{i=1}^{m} c_i a_{in}\right]$$

For the next property, we need the concept of the *identity matrix* **I**. **I** is an $n \times n$ matrix with ones down its diagonal and all other elements equal to zero. For instance, for $n = 2$,

$$\mathbf{I} = \begin{bmatrix} 1 & 0 \\ 0 & 1 \end{bmatrix}$$

The product of any $n \times n$ matrix **A** with **I** reproduces **A**; i.e.,

$$\mathbf{AI} = \mathbf{IA} = \mathbf{A}$$

Verify this result for $\mathbf{A} = \begin{bmatrix} 2 & 1 \\ 1 & 3 \end{bmatrix}$.

THE INVERSE OF A MATRIX

If **A** is an $n \times n$ matrix for which we can find another $n \times n$ matrix **B** so that

$$\mathbf{AB} = \mathbf{BA} = \mathbf{I}$$

then **B** is called the inverse of **A**. This is written as $\mathbf{B} = \mathbf{A}^{-1}$.

Verify that $\mathbf{B} = \begin{bmatrix} 0.6 & -0.2 \\ -0.2 & 0.4 \end{bmatrix}$ is the inverse of **A** above.

A-7 LINEAR SIMULTANEOUS EQUATIONS

Let us consider the problem of finding values of the variables x_1 and x_2 that satisfy simultaneously the linear equations

$$\begin{aligned} 2x_1 + x_2 &= 8 \\ x_1 + 3x_2 &= 9 \end{aligned} \qquad \text{(A-3)}$$

Figure A-8. *Simultaneous equations.*

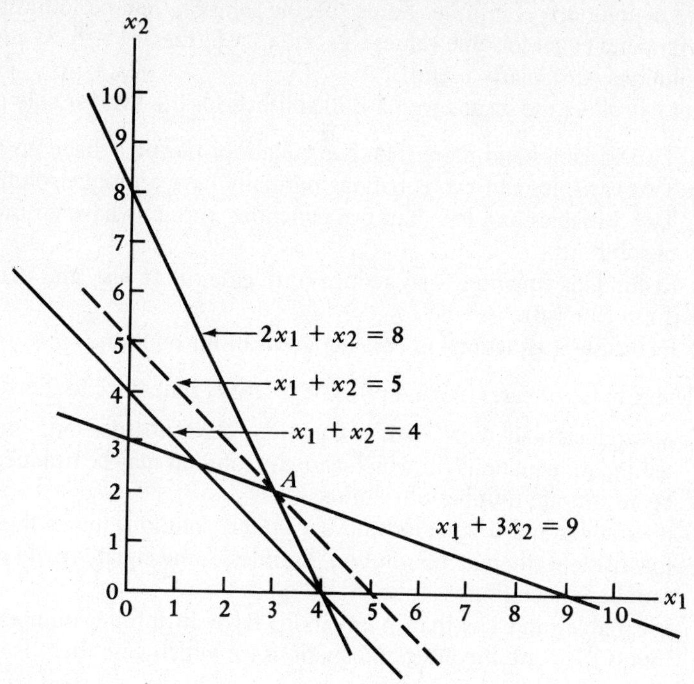

A pair of values for x_1 and x_2 satisfying (A-3) is called a *solution* to the equations. A *unique solution* exists when only one pair (x_1, x_2) will satisfy the equations, and there is *no solution* if no pair of values satisfies the equations.

We see problem (A-3) graphically in Figure A-8. The problem asks for those x_1 and x_2 that are common to both of the equation lines. In this case, the answer is a single point—point A. The solution values are $x_1 = 3$ and $x_2 = 2$.

Consider next the equations

$$\text{(A-4)} \qquad \begin{aligned} 2x_1 + x_2 &= 8 \\ x_1 + 3x_2 &= 9 \\ x_1 + x_2 &= 4 \end{aligned}$$

There is no solution to (A-4). No pair (x_1, x_2) exists that satisfies all three equations simultaneously. The equations are *inconsistent*. This is seen clearly in Figure A-8. Had the last equation been $x_1 + x_2 = 5$, point A would have provided the unique solution. In that case, any two of the three equations would have generated the solution, so one of the equations is *redundant*.

Let us change the problem again. Consider the single equation

$$\text{(A-5)} \qquad 2x_1 + x_2 = 8$$

What are the solutions to this equation? Certainly, $x_1 = 3$, $x_2 = 2$ satisfies the equation, but so does $x_1 = 4$, $x_2 = 0$; in fact, so do all points on the line $2x_1 + x_2 = 8$. The number of solutions is infinite. Some specific solutions can be found by setting one of the variables equal to some value; e.g., set $x_1 = 0$, then $x_2 = 8$. We will find some such solutions particularly useful.

Let us collect the results we have established for the two-variable case:

(i) Two variables and more than two equations normally have no solution.
(ii) Two variables and two equations normally have a unique solution.
(iii) Two variables and less than two equations normally have an infinite number of solutions.
(iv) Redundant equations may reduce (i) to case (ii) or (iii), and may reduce case (ii) to case (iii).
(v) Inconsistent equations in case (ii) result in no solution.

Provide examples of cases (iv) and (v). These results generalize to the n-variable case:

(i) n variables and more than n equations have no solution, unless there are redundant equations (in which case the solution may be unique, or there may be an infinite number of solutions).
(ii) n variables and n equations have a unique solution, unless the equations are inconsistent (there is no solution) or unless some equations are redundant (the number of solutions is infinite).
(iii) n variables and less than n equations have an infinite number of solutions, unless there are inconsistent equations (in which case there is no solution).

You may have noticed that (A-3) is the same problem as (A-2). In (A-3) we were solving for x_1 and x_2 and in (A-2) we were solving for γ_1 and γ_2, yet the answer was the same. The solution of simultaneous linear equations is synonymous with finding the linear combination of $\mathbf{b}$ in terms of $\mathbf{a}_1$ and $\mathbf{a}_2$, where $\mathbf{b}$ is the vector of the parameters on the right-hand side of the equations and $\mathbf{a}_1$ and $\mathbf{a}_2$ are the vectors of the coefficients of x_1 and x_2, respectively.

For an n-variable system with m equations, solving the simultaneous equations is the same as finding the linear combination of $\mathbf{b}$ in terms of $\mathbf{a}_1, \mathbf{a}_2, \ldots, \mathbf{a}_n$. The vectors $\mathbf{b}, \mathbf{a}_1, \mathbf{a}_2, \ldots, \mathbf{a}_n$ are vectors in E^m. When the equations have a unique solution, there is only one linear combination of $\mathbf{b}$ in terms of $\mathbf{a}_1, \mathbf{a}_2, \ldots, \mathbf{a}_n$. When the number of solutions is infinite, the number of linear combinations of $\mathbf{b}$ in terms of $\mathbf{a}_1, \mathbf{a}_2, \ldots, \mathbf{a}_n$ is infinite; and when there is no solution, there is no way of constructing the linear combination. For example, in Figure A-9,

(i) $\mathbf{b}$, in terms of $\mathbf{a}_1$ only, has no solution.
(ii) $\mathbf{b}$, in terms of $\mathbf{a}_1$ and $\mathbf{a}_2$, has a unique solution.
(iii) $\mathbf{b}$, in terms of $\mathbf{a}_1, \mathbf{a}_2, \mathbf{a}_3$, has an infinite number of solutions.

These correspond to the equation systems

(i)
$$\begin{aligned} 2x_1 &= 8 \\ x_1 &= 9 \end{aligned}$$

(ii)
$$\begin{aligned} 2x_1 + x_2 &= 8 \\ x_1 + 3x_2 &= 9 \end{aligned}$$

(iii)
$$\begin{aligned} 2x_1 + x_2 + 3x_3 &= 8 \\ x_1 + 3x_2 + 3x_3 &= 9 \end{aligned}$$

Figure A-9. *Vector representation of simultaneous equations.*

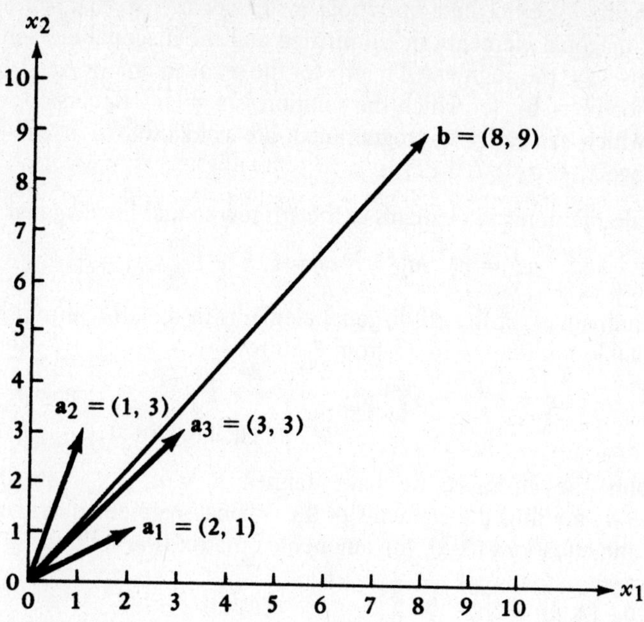

A-8 NUMERICAL SOLUTION OF SIMULTANEOUS EQUATIONS

In matrix notation, we can write a system of n equations in n variables as

$$\mathbf{Ax} = \mathbf{b} \tag{A-6}$$

where **A** is a column vector of constants and **x** is a column vector of variables. The pair of equations (A-3), for example, can be written as

$$\begin{bmatrix} 2 & 1 \\ 1 & 3 \end{bmatrix} \begin{bmatrix} x_1 \\ x_2 \end{bmatrix} = \begin{bmatrix} 8 \\ 9 \end{bmatrix}$$

Formally, the solution to (A-6) can be found if we know the inverse matrix of **A**. Using the fact that $\mathbf{A}^{-1}\mathbf{A} = \mathbf{I}$ and $\mathbf{Ix} = \mathbf{x}$, we premultiply both sides of (A-6) by $\mathbf{A}^{-1}$ and simplify:

$$\mathbf{A}^{-1}\mathbf{Ax} = \mathbf{A}^{-1}\mathbf{b} \qquad \text{or} \qquad \mathbf{x} = \mathbf{A}^{-1}\mathbf{b}$$

This is not, however, an efficient method of solving the equations. Methods based on the technique of *Gaussian elimination* require fewer operations than would be required to find the inverse of **A**. The particular method we consider is a simple version of the *Gauss-Jordan* method. The first step is to form the $n \times (n + 1)$ augmented matrix [**A**, **b**], in which the column vector **b** now forms the $(n + 1)$th column.

The operations that we are permitted to do in order to solve a system of equations such as (A-6) (i.e., addition and subtraction of equations or multiples of equations) now correspond to addition and subtraction of rows or multiples of rows of the augmented matrix. We do these operations systematically, so that, for each column of **A**, the off-diagonal elements are eliminated and the diagonal elements are scaled to one. In this way, the augmented matrix for the set of equations **Ax** = **b** is transformed into one for **Ix** = **b**′, for which the solution is **x** = **b**′. Recursion formulas for the method, which can easily be programmed, are as follows.

At stage k, $k = 1, 2, \ldots, n$:

(i) Scale the nonzero elements of the kth row so that the diagonal element is one:

$$a_{kj}^{k} = a_{kj}^{k-1}/a_{kk}^{k-1} \qquad j = k, k+1, \ldots, n+1 \tag{A-7}$$

(ii) Eliminate all of the off-diagonal elements in the kth column by subtracting a suitable multiple of row k from each row:

$$a_{ij}^{k} = a_{ij}^{k-1} - a_{ik}^{k-1}\, a_{kj}^{k}, \qquad j = k, k+1, \ldots, n+1 \tag{A-8}$$

for each row $i = 1, \ldots, n$, except row k

To simplify the formulas, we have defined $b_i = a_{i,n+1}$. Note that a_{ij}^{0}, $i, j = 1, \ldots, n+1$, are thus the elements of the original augmented matrix.

For the equations (A-3), the augmented matrix is as follows:

Stage 0 $[\mathbf{A}, \mathbf{b}] = \begin{bmatrix} 2 & 1 & 8 \\ 1 & 3 & 9 \end{bmatrix}$

Stage 1 $\begin{bmatrix} 1 & \frac{1}{2} & 4 \\ 0 & \frac{5}{2} & 5 \end{bmatrix}$ Row 1 has been scaled so that $a_{11}^{1} = 1$, then row 1 was subtracted from row 2.

Stage 2 $\begin{bmatrix} 1 & 0 & 3 \\ 0 & 1 & 2 \end{bmatrix}$ Row 2 has been scaled so that $a_{22}^{2} = 1$, then row 2 was subtracted from row 1.

This is now the augmented matrix for the system of equations $x_1 = 3$, $x_2 = 2$.

The Gauss-Jordan method can also be used to find the inverse of a square matrix **A**, should it be required. Starting from an $n \times 2n$ augmented matrix of the form [**A**, **I**] the operations that transform A to an identity matrix will also transform the original identity matrix into the inverse of **A**.

A FORTRAN subroutine for solving a system of equations by the Gauss-Jordan method is given below. The solution vector is returned as the right hand column of the augmented matrix **A**. Note that more sophisticated and robust algorithms are available, including ones which can deal better with special types of matrices. These can be found in computer packages for numerical analysis.

```
SUBROUTINE GJ(A,N)
DIMENSION A(20,21)
N1=N+1
DO 1 K=1,N
K1=K+1
DO 2 J=K1,N1
```

```
2     A(K,J)=A(K,J)/A(K,K)
      DO 1 I=1,N
      IF(I.EQ.K)GO TO 1
      DO 3 J=K1,N1
3     A(I,J)=A(I,J)-A(I,K)*A(K,J)
1     CONTINUE
      RETURN
      END
```

*A-9 LINEAR PROGRAMMING IN MATRIX NOTATION

We can write the linear program in matrix and vector notation as

$$\text{maximize } z = \mathbf{cx} \qquad \text{(A-9)}$$
$$\text{subject to } \mathbf{Ax} = \mathbf{b}, \qquad \mathbf{x} \geq 0$$

where z is a scalar, $\mathbf{x}$ is a column vector in E^n, $\mathbf{c}$ is a row vector in E^n, $\mathbf{b}$ is a column vector in E^m, and $\mathbf{A}$ is an $m \times n$ dimensional matrix.

The columns of $\mathbf{A}$ corresponding to a basic solution form a nonsingular matrix $\mathbf{B}$. There is no loss in generality in assuming that the rank of $\mathbf{A}$ is m, and thus $\mathbf{B}$ is an $m \times m$ matrix (assuming that there are no redundant constraints).

The basic solution corresponding to $\mathbf{B}$ is denoted by $\mathbf{x}_B$. If $\mathbf{R}$ is the matrix of nonbasic columns of $\mathbf{A}$ and $\mathbf{x}_R$ is the vector of nonbasic variables, then

$$\mathbf{Bx}_B + \mathbf{Rx}_R = \mathbf{b} \qquad \text{(A-10)}$$

Since $\mathbf{x}_R = 0$ (by definition),

$$\mathbf{Bx}_B = \mathbf{b} \qquad \text{(A-11)}$$

and since $\mathbf{B}$ is nonsingular,

$$\mathbf{x}_B = \mathbf{B}^{-1}\mathbf{b} \qquad \text{(A-12)}$$

where $\mathbf{B}^{-1}$ is the inverse of $\mathbf{B}$. $\mathbf{x}_B$ is a feasible solution when $\mathbf{B}^{-1}\mathbf{b} \geq 0$.

Equation (A-11) expresses $\mathbf{b}$ as a linear combination of the column vectors that form the basic matrix $\mathbf{B}$. We will define the ith column of $\mathbf{B}$ as $\mathbf{b}_i$ and the ith component of $\mathbf{x}_B$ as x_{Bi}, so (A-11) becomes

$$\mathbf{b} = \sum_{i=1}^{m} x_{Bi}\mathbf{b}_i \qquad \text{(A-13)}$$

Clearly, the x_{Bi} are the coefficients of the linear combination of $\mathbf{b}$ in terms of $\mathbf{B}$.

We will now consider expressing $\mathbf{a}_j$, any column of $\mathbf{A}$, in terms of $\mathbf{B}$. Let y_{ij} be the coefficient of the linear combination of $\mathbf{a}_j$ and $\mathbf{b}_i$, then

$$\mathbf{a}_j = \sum_{i=1}^{m} y_{ij}\mathbf{b}_i$$

Or, defining $\mathbf{y}_j$ as the column vector of the y_{ij},

(A-14) $$\mathbf{a}_j = \mathbf{B}\mathbf{y}_j$$

and

(A-15) $$\mathbf{y}_j = \mathbf{B}^{-1}\mathbf{a}_j$$

The simplex tableau corresponding to the basis $\mathbf{B}$ consists of $\mathbf{x}_B$ and the $\mathbf{y}_j$ for all the columns of $\mathbf{A}$.

The elements of $\mathbf{c}$ corresponding to the basic solution we will call $\mathbf{c}_B$. You will recall that c_j is the objective function value of $\mathbf{a}_j$, and z_j is the objective function value of $\mathbf{a}_j$ expressed in terms of the basis, i.e., of $\mathbf{B}\mathbf{y}_j$. Using logic developed in Chapter 3, we obtain

(A-16) $$z_j = \sum_{i=1}^{m} y_{ij}c_{Bi} = \mathbf{c}_B\mathbf{y}_j = \mathbf{c}_B\mathbf{B}^{-1}\mathbf{a}_j$$

When the matrix $\mathbf{A}$ contains an identity matrix $\mathbf{I}$ within it and when $\mathbf{b} \geqslant 0$, there exists an immediate initial basis—the identity matrix—that provides a basic feasible solution. When $\mathbf{A}$ does not contain an identity matrix, artificial vectors and variables are used to augment $\mathbf{A}$ until an $\mathbf{I}$ does exist.

EXERCISES

A.1 (i) Draw the vectors

$$\mathbf{a} = \begin{bmatrix} 3 \\ 1 \end{bmatrix} \quad \mathbf{b} = \begin{bmatrix} 2 \\ 4 \end{bmatrix} \quad \mathbf{c} = \begin{bmatrix} 4 \\ 3 \end{bmatrix}$$

(ii) Show graphically that $\mathbf{a} + \mathbf{b} = \begin{bmatrix} 5 \\ 5 \end{bmatrix}$.

(iii) Draw $2\mathbf{a} + \frac{1}{2}\mathbf{c}$, and verify the answer algebraically.

(iv) Find algebraically the distance between $\mathbf{a}$ and $\mathbf{c}$, and find algebraically the length of $\mathbf{b}$. Verify these on the graph.

(v) Show where the null vector, the sum vector, and the unit vectors are on the graph.

A.2 Using the vectors in exercise A.1, graphically and algebraically. express $\mathbf{b}$ as a linear combination of $\mathbf{a}$ and $\mathbf{c}$. Also express $\mathbf{a}$ as a linear combination of $\mathbf{b}$ and $\mathbf{c}$.

A.3 Using the vectors in exercise A.1, find two points on the line segment between $\mathbf{a}$ and $\mathbf{b}$.

A.4 Draw the convex hull of the points

$$\mathbf{a}_1 = \begin{bmatrix} 1 \\ 2 \end{bmatrix} \quad \mathbf{a}_2 = \begin{bmatrix} 4 \\ 1 \end{bmatrix} \quad \mathbf{a}_3 = \begin{bmatrix} 2 \\ 4 \end{bmatrix} \quad \mathbf{a}_4 = \begin{bmatrix} 6 \\ 4 \end{bmatrix}$$

(i) Find algebraically two points in this convex hull.

(ii) Position the points represented by the following values of γ_i.

(a) $\gamma_1 = 0, \gamma_2 = 0, \gamma_3 = \frac{1}{4}, \gamma_4 = \frac{3}{4}$.

(b) $\gamma_1 = \frac{1}{4}, \gamma_2 = \frac{1}{4}, \gamma_3 = \frac{1}{2}, \gamma_4 = 0$.

(iii) What are the values of γ_i that give the four corner points of the convex hull?

A.5 Consider the following vectors in E^3: $\mathbf{a}_1 = (1, 0, 0)$, $\mathbf{a}_2 = (2, 1, 1)$, $\mathbf{a}_3 = (1, 1, 1)$, $\mathbf{a}_4 = (0, 2, 0)$.

(i) Is the set $(\mathbf{a}_2, \mathbf{a}_3)$ linearly independent?

(ii) Is the set $(\mathbf{a}_1, \mathbf{a}_2, \mathbf{a}_3)$ a spanning set?

(iii) Show that the set $(\mathbf{a}_1, \mathbf{a}_3, \mathbf{a}_4)$ is a basis.

A.6 Before solving each of the following sets of simultaneous equations, indicate how many solutions you might expect them to have. How many do they in fact have? Why?

(i)
$$\begin{aligned} x_1 + x_2 &= 6 \\ 2x_1 + x_2 &= 8 \end{aligned}$$

(ii)
$$\begin{aligned} x_1 + x_2 &= 6 \\ 2x_1 + x_2 &= 10 \\ 3x_1 - 2x_2 &= 8 \end{aligned}$$

(iii)
$$\begin{aligned} x_1 + x_2 + x_3 &= 5 \\ 4x_1 + 2x_2 + x_3 &= 18 \\ 6x_1 + 4x_2 + 3x_3 &= 26 \end{aligned}$$

A.7 Solve these systems of equations by the Gauss-Jordan method.

(i)
$$\begin{aligned} x_1 + 2x_2 + 3x_3 &= 5 \\ 2x_1 + x_2 - x_3 &= 6 \\ x_1 + 3x_2 - 5x_3 &= 2 \end{aligned}$$

(ii) $\pi\mathbf{P} = \pi$, where π is a row vector whose elements sum to 1 and

$$\mathbf{P} = \begin{bmatrix} 0.6 & 0.3 & 0.1 \\ 0.2 & 0.4 & 0.4 \\ 0.2 & 0.3 & 0.5 \end{bmatrix}$$

REFERENCES

Hadley, G. *Linear Algebra*. Reading, Mass.: Addison Wesley, 1961. An excellent fairly advanced supplementary text. Sections 2-1 to 2-6 introduce vectors. Definitions of convex combination and convex hull are in Sections 6-4 and 6-5. Chapter 5 deals with linear simultaneous equations, but assumes a knowledge of matrices. For the reader who wishes to learn matrices, Sections 3-1 to 3-9, 3-21, and 4-1 to 4-3 are very good.

Kemeny, J. G., A. Schleifer, J. L. Snell, and G. L. Thompson. *Finite Mathematics with Business Applications*. Englewood Cliffs, N.J.: Prentice-Hall, 1962. Pages 229 to 261 cover vectors, matrices, and simultaneous equations. Elementary.

APPENDIX B

Tables

Table B-1. *Areas under a standard normal curve*

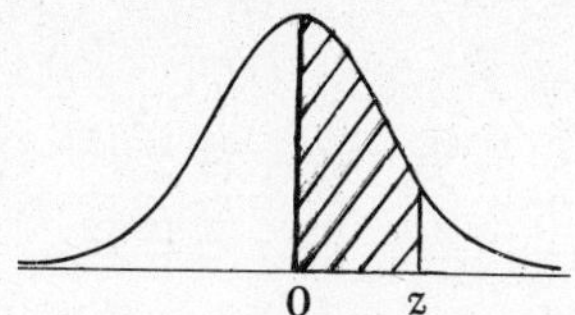

z	.00	.01	.02	.03	.04	.05	.06	.07	.08	.09
0.0	.0000	.0040	.0080	.0120	.0160	.0199	.0239	.0279	.0319	.0359
0.1	.0398	.0438	.0478	.0517	.0557	.0596	.0636	.0675	.0714	.0753
0.2	.0793	.0832	.0871	.0910	.0948	.0987	.1026	.1064	.1103	.1141
0.3	.1179	.1217	.1255	.1293	.1331	.1368	.1406	.1443	.1480	.1517
0.4	.1554	.1591	.1628	.1664	.1700	.1736	.1772	.1808	.1844	.1879
0.5	.1915	.1950	.1985	.2019	.2054	.2088	.2123	.2157	.2190	.2224
0.6	.2257	.2291	.2324	.2357	.2389	.2422	.2454	.2486	.2517	.2549
0.7	.2580	.2611	.2642	.2673	.2704	.2734	.2764	.2794	.2823	.2852
0.8	.2881	.2910	.2939	.2967	.2995	.3023	.3051	.3078	.3106	.3133
0.9	.3159	.3186	.3212	.3238	.3264	.3289	.3315	.3340	.3365	.3389
1.0	.3413	.3438	.3461	.3485	.3508	.3531	.3554	.3577	.3599	.3621
1.1	.3643	.3665	.3686	.3708	.3729	.3749	.3770	.3790	.3810	.3830
1.2	.3849	.3869	.3888	.3907	.3925	.3944	.3962	.3980	.3997	.4015
1.3	.4032	.4049	.4066	.4082	.4099	.4115	.4131	.4147	.4162	.4177
1.4	.4192	.4207	.4222	.4236	.4251	.4265	.4279	.4292	.4306	.4319
1.5	.4332	.4345	.4357	.4370	.4382	.4394	.4406	.4418	.4429	.4441
1.6	.4452	.4463	.4474	.4484	.4495	.4505	.4515	.4525	.4535	.4545
1.7	.4554	.4564	.4573	.4582	.4591	.4599	.4608	.4616	.4625	.4633
1.8	.4641	.4649	.4656	.4664	.4671	.4678	.4686	.4693	.4699	.4706
1.9	.4713	.4719	.4726	.4732	.4738	.4744	.4750	.4756	.4761	.4767
2.0	.4772	.4778	.4783	.4788	.4793	.4798	.4803	.4808	.4812	.4817
2.1	.4821	.4826	.4830	.4834	.4838	.4842	.4846	.4850	.4854	.4857
2.2	.4861	.4864	.4868	.4871	.4875	.4878	.4881	.4884	.4887	.4890
2.3	.4893	.4896	.4898	.4901	.4904	.4906	.4909	.4911	.4913	.4916
2.4	.4918	.4920	.4922	.4925	.4927	.4929	.4931	.4932	.4934	.4936
2.5	.4938	.4940	.4941	.4943	.4945	.4946	.4948	.4949	.4951	.4952
2.6	.4953	.4955	.4956	.4957	.4959	.4960	.4961	.4962	.4963	.4964
2.7	.4965	.4966	.4967	.4968	.4969	.4970	.4971	.4972	.4973	.4974
2.8	.4974	.4975	.4976	.4977	.4977	.4978	.4979	.4979	.4980	.4981
2.9	.4981	.4982	.4982	.4983	.4984	.4984	.4985	.4985	.4986	.4986
3.0	.4987	.4987	.4987	.4988	.4988	.4989	.4989	.4989	.4990	.4990

This table is abridged from Table 1 of *Statistical Tables and Formulas*, by A. Hald (New York: John Wiley & Sons, Inc., 1952). Copyright © 1952 John Wiley & Sons, Inc. Reprinted by permission of John Wiley & Sons, Inc.

Table B-2. *The unit normal loss integral,* N(*z*)

z	.00	.01	.02	.03	.04	.05	.06	.07	.08	.09
0.0	.3989	.3940	.3890	.3841	.3793	.3744	.3697	.3649	.3602	.3556
0.1	.3509	.3464	.3418	.3373	.3328	.3284	.3240	.3197	.3154	.3111
0.2	.3069	.3027	.2986	.2944	.2904	.2863	.2824	.2784	.2745	.2706
0.3	.2668	.2630	.2592	.2555	.2518	.2481	.2445	.2409	.2374	.2339
0.4	.2304	.2270	.2236	.2203	.2169	.2137	.2104	.2072	.2040	.2009
0.5	.1978	.1947	.1917	.1887	.1857	.1828	.1799	.1771	.1742	.1714
0.6	.1687	.1659	.1633	.1606	.1580	.1554	.1528	.1503	.1478	.1453
0.7	.1429	.1405	.1381	.1358	.1334	.1312	.1289	.1267	.1245	.1223
0.8	.1202	.1181	.1160	.1140	.1120	.1100	.1080	.1061	.1042	.1023
0.9	.1004	.09860	.09680	.09503	.09328	.09156	.08986	.08819	.08654	.08491
1.0	.08332	.08174	.08019	.07866	.07716	.07568	.07422	.07279	.07138	.06999
1.1	.06862	.06727	.06595	.06465	.06336	.06210	.06086	.05964	.05844	.05726
1.2	.05610	.05496	.05384	.05274	.05165	.05059	.04954	.04851	.04750	.04650
1.3	.04553	.04457	.04363	.04270	.04179	.04090	.04002	.03916	.03831	.03748
1.4	.03667	.03587	.03508	.03431	.03356	.03281	.03208	.03137	.03067	.02998
1.5	.02931	.02865	.02800	.02736	.02674	.02612	.02552	.02494	.02436	.02380
1.6	.02324	.02270	.02217	.02165	.02114	.02064	.02015	.01967	.01920	.01874
1.7	.01829	.01785	.01742	.01699	.01658	.01617	.01578	.01539	.01501	.01464
1.8	.01428	.01392	.01357	.01323	.01290	.01257	.01226	.01195	.01164	.01134
1.9	.01105	.01077	.01049	.01022	$.0^{2}9957$	$.0^{2}9698$	$.0^{2}9445$	$.0^{2}9198$	$.0^{2}8957$	$.0^{2}8721$
2.0	$.0^{2}8491$	$.0^{2}8266$	$.0^{2}8046$	$.0^{2}7832$	$.0^{2}7623$	$.0^{2}7418$	$.0^{2}7219$	$.0^{2}7024$	$.0^{2}6835$	$.0^{2}6649$
2.1	$.0^{2}6468$	$.0^{2}6292$	$.0^{2}6120$	$.0^{2}5952$	$.0^{2}5788$	$.0^{2}5628$	$.0^{2}5472$	$.0^{2}5320$	$.0^{2}5172$	$.0^{2}5028$
2.2	$.0^{2}4887$	$.0^{2}4750$	$.0^{2}4616$	$.0^{2}4486$	$.0^{2}4358$	$.0^{2}4235$	$.0^{2}4114$	$.0^{2}3996$	$.0^{2}3882$	$.0^{2}3770$
2.3	$.0^{2}3662$	$.0^{2}3556$	$.0^{2}3453$	$.0^{2}3352$	$.0^{2}3255$	$.0^{2}3159$	$.0^{2}3067$	$.0^{2}2977$	$.0^{2}2889$	$.0^{2}2804$
2.4	$.0^{2}2720$	$.0^{2}2640$	$.0^{2}2561$	$.0^{2}2484$	$.0^{2}2410$	$.0^{2}2337$	$.0^{2}2267$	$.0^{2}2199$	$.0^{2}2132$	$.0^{2}2067$

Reproduced by permission from *Introduction to Statistics for Business Decisions,* by R. Schlaifer (New York: McGraw-Hill, 1961).

APPENDIX C

Abstracts, Journals, and Case Books

OPERATIONS RESEARCH ABSTRACTS

Batchelor, James H., *Operations Research: An Annotated Bibliography*, Saint Louis University Press, Saint Louis, Vol. 1—1959, Vo. 2—1962, Vo. 3—1963, Vol. 4—1964.

A *Comprehensive Bibliography on Operations Research*, Operations Research Group, Case Institute of Technology, Publication in Operations Research Series No. 4, published by Wiley and Sons under the Sponsorship of ORSA, 1959.

International Abstracts in Operations Research, published bimonthly for IFORS by North-Holland, P.O. Box 211, Amsterdam, The Netherlands (since 1961). A must for any operations researcher.

Operations Research/Management Science, published monthly by Executive Science Institute, Inc., Whippany, N.J. 07981 (since 1961). International literature digest periodical by a commercially run service. Individual entries are more extensive than in IAOR; coverage is more restrictive.

SELECTED TECHNICAL AND PROFESSIONAL JOURNALS IN OPERATIONS RESEARCH IN ENGLISH

American Institute of Industrial Engineers Transactions (U.S.), published quarterly by A.I.I.E., 25 Technology Park, Norcross, Ga. 30092.

Computers and Operations Research, a quarterly journal published by Pergamon Press, Maxwell House, Fairview Park, Elmsford, N.Y. 10523.

Decision Sciences (U.S.), published by the American Institute for Decision Sciences, University Plaza, Atlanta, Ga. 30303.

European Journal of Operational Research, sponsored by the Association of European Operational Research Societies, published six times per year by North-Holland, P.O. Box 211, Amsterdam, The Netherlands.

INFOR (Canadian Journal of Operational Research & Information Processing) (Canada), published three times per year by University of Toronto Press, 5201 Dufferin St., Downsview, Ontario, Canada.

Interfaces (U.S.), published bimonthly by TIMS and ORSA, jointly. Dealing with practice in O.R. and management science. A most readable journal. See *Management Science* and *Operations Research* for details.

International Journal of Physical Distribution and Materials Management (U.K.), published eight times per year by MCB Publications Ltd., 200 Keighley Rd., Bradford BD9 4JQ, England.

The International Journal of Production Research (U.K.), published bimonthly by Taylor & Francis Ltd., 10–14 Macklin Street, London WC2B 5NF, England.

International Journal of Systems Science (U.K.), published monthly, by Taylor & Francis Ltd., 10–14 Macklin Street, London WC2B 5NF, England.

Journal of the Operational Research Society (formerly *Operational Research Quarterly*) (U.K.), published monthly for the Operational Research Society Ltd. by Pergamon Press, Headington Hill Hall, Oxford OX3 OBW, England.

Management Science (U.S.), published monthly, Journal of the Institute of Management Sciences (TIMS), 146 Westminster Street, Providence, R.I. 02903.

Mathematical Programming, published bimonthly by North-Holland, P.O. Box 211, Amsterdam, The Netherlands. Highly mathematical.

Mathematics of Operations Research (U.S.), a quarterly published jointly by ORSA and TIMS; subscriptions through either society. See *Management Science* and *Operations Research* for details. Highly mathematical.

Naval Research Logistics Quarterly (U.S.), published by the Office of Naval Research, Managing Editor NRLQ, Arlington, Va. 22217.

New Zealand Operational Research (N.Z.), published twice per year by the Operational Research Society of N.Z., P.O. Box 904, Wellington, New Zealand.

OMEGA (U.K.), published bimonthly by Pergamon Press, Headington Hill Hall, Oxford, OX3 0BW, England. This is an international journal of management science.

Operations Research (U.S.), published bimonthly, Journal of the Operations Research Society of America (ORSA), 428 East Preston Street, Baltimore, Md. 21202.

OPSEARCH (India), Operational Research Society of India, 7/3 Mandeville Gorden, Calcutta 700019, India.

Operations Research Letters, sponsored by ORSA, published bimonthly by North-Holland, P.O. Box 211, Amsterdam, The Netherlands.

SIAM *Journal on Algebraic and Discrete Methods* (U.S.), published quarterly by SIAM Publications, 33 South 17th Street, Philadelphia, Penn. 19103.

SIAM *Journal on Applied Mathematics* (U.S.), published eight times per year by SIAM Publications. (See above.)

Simulation, published by the Society for Computer Simulation, P.O. Box 2228, La Jolla, Ca. 92038.

Transportation Research (U.S.), published quarterly by Pergamon Press, Inc., Maxwell House, Fairview Park, Elmsford, N.Y. 10523.

Transportation Science (U.S.), published quarterly by the Operations Research Society of America, 428 East Preston Street, Baltimore, Md. 21202.

Some national O.R. society journals—such as *Operations Research Verfahren* (Germany), *Zeitschrift für Operations Research* (Germany), or the *Journal of the Operation Research Society of Japan*—regularly contain articles written in English. For a list of non-English-language journals, see *International Abstracts in Operations Research.* It goes without saying that many articles dealing with operations research problems have appeared in other journals, particularly in the fields of economics, finance, marketing research, business administration, industrial and electrical engineering, statistics, and mathematics.

CASE BOOKS IN OPERATIONS RESEARCH

Berry, W. L., C. J. Christenson, and J. S. Hammond, III. *Management Decision Sciences—Cases and Readings.* Homewood, Ill.: Irwin, 1980. A mixture of easy and more advanced cases, classified by type of analysis: cost analysis, linear programming, uncertainty, simulation, and modeling methodology. Also contains several insightful articles (reprints) entitled "Wisdom from the Experts." Read "Solving Problems" by R. Hyman and B. Anderson, and "On the Art of Modeling" by W. T. Morris.

Dyer, J. S. and R. D. Shapiro. *Management Science/Operations Research—Cases and Readings.* New York: Wiley, 1982. A mixture of brief survey lectures, reprints of applications reported in the literature, followed up by some questions; also some cases for the student to solve.

Haehling von Lanzenauer, C. *Cases in Operations Research,* London, Canada: Research and Publication Division, School of Business Administration, University of Western Ontario, 1975. Contains twenty-five comprehensive real cases in operations research, some of which originate at Harvard, Stanford, and IMEDE (Switzerland). An ideal companion book to this text. A detailed *Instructor's Manual* is available from the publishers to bona fide course instructors.

Martin, M. J. C., and R. A. Denison, Eds, *Case Exercises in Operations Research.* London: Wiley-Interscience, 1971. Contains fifteen comprehensive real cases in operations research, cost benefit analysis, and Bayesian statistical decision theory. Except for the last three, the cases are British. A detailed *Tutor's Guide* is available to instructors.

Newson, E. F. P. (Ed.). *Management Science and the Manager—A Case Book.* Englewood Cliffs, N.J.: Prentice-Hall, 1980. Paperback, with easy and intermediate cases classified by uncertainty and risk, resource allocation, simulation, model formulation, and evaluation. Solutions manual available.

Norman, J. M. and E. Ritchie. *Problem Solving Exercises in Operational Research,* Vol. 1. Lancaster, England: Lancord Ltd., University of Lancaster, 1981. A set of ten of the famous Lancaster OR cases, covering a wide spectrum of applications, including good common sense. Highly recommended. Solutions manual available.

Render, Barry, and Stair, Ralph M., Jr. *Case and Readings in Quantitative Analysis for Management.* Boston: Allyn and Bacon, 1982. Over thirty cases. Instructor's manual available.

INDEX

Page numbers in *italics* refer to exercises or references.

CASTER UNIVERSIT
RY

Lancaster University Library
64024917